Finance and Leisure

CLHBEC

Jan Whitehouse

and

Colin Tilley

Series Editor: **Peter Taylor**

PITMAN
PUBLISHING

in association with
Institute of Leisure and Amenity Management

PITMAN PUBLISHING
128 Long Acre, London WC2E 9AN

A Division of Pearson Professional Limited

© Longman Group UK Limited , 1992

A CIP catalogue record for this book can be obtained from the British Library.

ISBN 0 273 62051 7

10 9 8 7 6 5 4 3 2

Printed and bound in Great Britain by Ipswich Book Co.

The Publishers' policy is to use paper manufactured from sustainable forests.

Preface

As leisure services assume greater importance in the economic and social fabric of many societies, so the training of managers to deliver these services remains the subject of continual review and development. Reports by Yates (1984) and Gunn (1986) recognised the need for a more systematic and applied management training for the leisure industry in Britain. Training initiatives such as National Vocational Qualifications (NVQs), together with educational initiatives from bodies such as the Business and Technical Education Council (BTEC) have highlighted the vocation-specific training necessary for the leisure industry. Even at the postgraduate level there is a significant development of specialist programmes in leisure management.

Training developments necessarily require the support not only of employers but also by appropriate literature. Longman and the Institute of Leisure and Amenity Management (ILAM) have led the way in providing such literature with their Leisure Management series. Initially this was devised to support the syllabuses for the ILAM Certificate and Diploma examinations. The series now provides an important platform for the new ILAM Qualification Scheme.

The objectives of the series are to:

- introduce essential leisure management functions;
- analyse national developments which affect the leisure industry;
- illustrate good management practice by examples and case studies;
- apply management principles to specific sectors.

The principal markets for the series are actual or potential managers in the leisure industry. At the workplace it is necessary for managers not only to be aware of day-to-day tasks, but also to think strategically about problem identification and resolution, management information needs, service development and the best use of resources. Professional leisure managers will find the series of help in keeping up to date and improving their management practices. Candidates at all four levels of the new ILAM Qualification Scheme, from those new to the leisure industry to those in senior management positions, will find material relevant to their needs in the Leisure Management series. Students on leisure management courses, from BTEC courses to postgraduate programmes, will find the series a key resource.

In this particular book, one of the disciplines fundamental to good management, finance, is explored in a variety of leisure management contexts. Financial control and planning is essential to any leisure organisation, whether it is profitmaking, voluntary, or subsidised by government. Jan Whitehouse and Colin Tilley have written this much needed application of financial principles to leisure management under the assumption that *any* manager should have an understanding of the use of financial information and techniques. This is therefore a book for non-financial leisure managers. It seeks to de-mystify a discipline which has often been seen to be inaccessible for anyone but the specialist accountant. Whatever your management interests, I hope that *Finance and Leisure* is both useful and interesting for you.

Peter Taylor
Series Editor

Contents

Introduction

The leisure industry experienced what was probably unprecedented growth during the 1980s and moved from being a cinderella to a mainstream activity in a very short period of time. Leisure providers can be found within all three sectors – public, commercial and voluntary. With the notable exception of the public sector, providers in the commercial and voluntary sectors tend to operate within specific market segments. Indeed, many have become recognisable household names that immediately relate the organisation to the area of activity. Examples include Odeon and cinemas, Forte and hotels, Center Parcs and holiday villages, the Lawn Tennis Association and the Royal Shakespeare Company.

The leisure industry covers an extremely broad and diverse range of activities, including sport, the arts, hotels, pubs, marinas, bingo, restaurants to name but a very few. Within these areas, it is possible to identify different types of activities. For example, the arts encompasses, amongst others, visual arts, theatre and music. Within these exist a further set of categories such that, for example, within theatre it is possible to identify musicals, comedy and drama. In other words, the leisure sector is vastly segmented.

The single factor that is common to all sectors and segments of the industry is finance, without which there would be no leisure industry. Within this book we have attempted to provide an explanation of the relevance and application of financial principles and techniques, as opposed to the 'mechanics' of accounting. As such, we hope that it is useful to both students and managers alike and can be either studied or used as a reference to obtain insight and advice across a range of finance related areas.

Finance threads its way through many elements of the management process and the key tasks of managers. Consequently, we felt that it was important to include areas in the book such as strategic planning, pricing and management information, which are complementary and interrelated to finance.

Throughout the text, we have attempted to balance the emphasis between commercial and public sector finance. This has not always been easy. In many instances, the principles apply equally to both sectors. However, we have attempted to place greater emphasis upon the more commercial approach to financial management. This, we feel, reflects the growing needs of public sector managers who are increasingly being required to adopt a more commercial approach to service delivery and management as a result of Compulsory Competitive Tendering (CCT).

1 Accounting conventions and services

Finance is a common thread which runs through all businesses, whether in the public or private sector. In order for a manager to be able to exert financial control in a business and make both day to day and longer term planning decisions, it is necessary for relevant financial information to be provided and for the manager to be able to interpret that information. Consequently, it is necessary to have an understanding of the concepts used in the preparation of financial information, as they have a major impact on the ability to be able to understand and interpret financial information.

How is a balance sheet read and what constitutes a healthy balance sheet? How can a business, which is showing a healthy profit, go into liquidation? What are the signs of a troubled business? The purpose of this chapter is to provide an understanding of the concepts and types of accounting conventions. These can then be used in conjunction with other techniques explained throughout the book to assist the reader in answering such questions.

There are two types of accounting – financial accounting and management accounting.

Financial accounting

Financial accounting is basically concerned with the production of the statutory accounts and ensuring that legal requirements are met. In the private sector, the statutory accounts comprise the profit and loss account, the balance sheet and the flow of funds statement. The financial accounts of companies are subject to audit, which attempts to ensure that an objective and fair view of the organisation's financial situation is presented to shareholders and to those that have a right to see the accounts.

Accounts are produced in accordance with a definitive standard of financial accounting and reporting set out in the Statements of Standard Accounting Practice (SSAP). Each SSAP is numbered and deals with a specific topic. In general, each SSAP covers concepts and fundamentals relating to the specific area, definitions of terminology, how the fundamentals relate to specific businesses and the form, content and presentation of financial records, including the items that should be disclosed.

The financial accountant is bound by legislation contained in the various Companies Acts and rules surrounding the preparation of financial accounts and the disclosure of certain information. Financial accounting is mainly concerned with the external requirements of creditors, shareholders, existing and potential investors, the Inland Revenue, the Registrar of Companies and any other external requirements as well as the requirements of internal management.

There is also a statutory requirement for public sector organisations to produce annual accounts, and the requirements are laid down and revised in various Acts of Parliament.

The statutory requirements and codes of practise govern:

- the annual statements that have to be produced and their format and contents
- the external audit requirements
- the timescale for publication of the statements and their availability to the public

Under the Local Government Finance Act 1982, local authorities are required to produce Statements of Accounts which show summarised statements of income and expenditure of each statutory fund, summaries on capital expenditure, the consolidated balance sheet and the statement of sources of funds.

With the introduction of organisations set up internally to operate aspects of local authority contracts, for example refuse, maintenance and leisure facility contracts, there is a requirement for a separate annual report to be prepared for these functions, which are produced more along the lines of private sector accounts. Hence, there is a need for managers operating in these areas to understand commercial financial concepts whilst operating in a public sector environment.

Local authorities usually conform with the form of published accounts recommended by The Chartered Institute of Public Finance and Accountancy (CIPFA), and the objectives of these accounts are to inform the local taxpayers about the activities of the local authorities, to assist the local electorate and the elected representatives in making judgements about the authority and to enable comparisons to be made with other authorities.

Management accounting

Management accounting is not concerned with statutory accounts, but with the provision of information for decision-making and control purposes. Managers require information to analyse the viability of various opportunities and to test options before deciding upon the most appropriate course of action. Effective control, on the other hand, requires regular and frequent information so that actual performance can be checked and compared with original plans and budgets, thereby allowing corrective action, if required, to be taken as soon as possible.

The management accountant provides managers with information relevant to their particular business areas. This information is used internally and there is no requirement for it to be published externally. Although the management accountant will work within the same accounting concepts as the financial accountant, there are no legal or statutory constraints within which the information should be prepared or reported.

Before control and decision making techniques can be used to any degree it is essential to have some understanding of the concept of cost and costing techniques. The various different costing methods and the concept of cost including cost classification and the uses of various types of cost are discussed in chapter nine.

Accounting concepts

The main emphasis in this chapter is to explain the basic financial accounting concepts, a knowledge of which is required to understand both financial and management information. This will then pave the way to an easier understanding of management accounting techniques and management information. The accounting concepts apply to the public, private and voluntary sectors, although varying emphasis may be placed upon them through SSAPs or Codes of practice.

Monetary measurement concept

Financial accounting information relates only to those items that can be expressed in monetary terms, reducing everything in the statements to a monetary denominator. Although a common base is essential, this does provide certain difficulties in analysing and interpreting accounting statements, especially when valuing a business. For example, if a leisure centre makes a large profit in the year, it is not revealed that, for instance, the centre had longer opening hours during the year. Another area that is not translated into money terms is the strength of the management of the business, which may be extremely crucial to its success. There are instances where people are capitalised and included in the balance sheet, such as football players, as they are considered to be a major asset of the club. However, attributing value to people is not common practise.

The business entity concept

The accounts of an organisation relate to the business entity and not to the owners, managers, directors or employees of the business. The business has a legal entity of its own, with its own rights and obligations and is able to enter into contracts in its own right. As a business has a legal identity, the stewardship aspect of financial accounting becomes important in order to present a true and fair view of the financial situation of the business to interested parties. The directors of the company are entrusted with the funds, and the financial accounts indicate how effectively they have carried out their responsibility.

The going concern concept

When preparing a set of accounts it is assumed that the business will continue to exist for the foreseeable future, in its existing state, and that it is not about to be sold or restructured. This means that the assets and liabilities in the balance sheet will be valued as if the business is going to continue and will not be valued to show its break up or saleable value.

The cost valuation concept

This concept, which is closely related to the going concern concept, assumes that all entries in the accounts are based on cost and not the value or worth of the particular item. The cost of, for instance, equipment purchased for a health suite can be supported by hard facts and is not possible to dispute, unlike current value or replacement value of an asset. Cost may not be the best method to use in valuing assets, but it is simple to operate and understand. The method does produce problems when attempting to look at business valuations in mergers and acquisitions or when looking to assess the valuation of shares as it does not reflect the current value of assets.

The cost valuation concept does not mean that assets remain in the accounts at their original cost for their lifetime as the assets are normally depreciated over their useful life. It is important that depreciation is matched to the useful life of the asset and the topic of depreciation is covered in chapter four. Two other matching concepts, sales/costs of sales and accruals/prepayments, are also discussed in chapter four.

Realisation concept

The concept of realisation is that profit is only taken into consideration when it has been realised, rather than when it can be recognised. For example, if a manufacturer of sportswear is manufacturing against orders, the profit will only be realised in the accounts when the sale is realised, that is, when a sales invoice is raised. Whilst the profit can be recognised at the time the order is placed, it should not be recognised in the accounts until the sales invoice is raised.

The concept of prudence

The concept of prudence is linked closely with the concept of realisation, in that only profits which have some degree of certainty should be realised in the accounts. Provision should be made for all liabilities either on a known or best estimate basis. For example, if funds have temporarily been made available by club members to finance the purchase of additional equipment, then the liability will need to be set up in the accounts, which acknowledges that the loans have to be repaid.

The concept of materiality

Material items are items which are of a significant nature. As these may affect decisions they should be disclosed in the financial accounts. Materiality, however, is judgemental and needs to be viewed in the light of the business.

The concept of consistency

When producing financial accounts, accounting policies and bases need to be consistent from period to period otherwise the accounts will be distorted and inaccurate and comparisons will be impossible. Any change in the accounting policies should be disclosed in the notes on the accounts.

Conclusion

Financial accounting is concerned with the statutory accounts and with the requirements of persons outside the organisation as well as with the internal requirements of management. There are a number of basic concepts employed in financial accounting including money measurement, business entity, going concern, cost valuation, realisation, prudence, materiality and consistency.

Management accounting, on the other hand, is concerned with information for decision making and control purposes, which tends to be used internally and is not available for external use. Financial accounts are produced in accordance with legal requirements and standard accounting practices and although not surrounded by similar constraints, management accounts usually conform to the same accounting concepts as financial accounts. In order to understand and interpret a set of accounts, an understanding of the accounting concepts is required.

2 Accounting and auditing: services for management

In order to realise maximum benefit from accounting and auditing services within an organisation, it is important to understand the functions and objectives of managers and how general financial affairs impact on the organisation as a whole.

The main functions of management are to determine the objectives and policies of their organisation; prepare strategies and plans to attain those objectives; organise, motivate and co-ordinate the available resources to execute the plans; control the results against the original plan; measure deviations from desired results; and revise plans, where appropriate, in the light of actual results. This continuous process is required so that both the short and long term objectives of the organisation can be achieved in the most efficient and effective way, and applies equally to the public, voluntary and private sectors.

Management control is, therefore, the function that controls and monitors actual performance against planned performance, and a key factor in the process is communication of information. It is essential that policies and plans are communicated from the top to lower levels of management in order to motivate and gain commitment from within the organisation. It is equally important that information on actual results is also communicated back to managers to allow comparisons to be made with original plans. A constant flow of relevant information is crucial to the success of planning, implementing, coordinating and controlling any organisation, and financial information is a key part of the relevant information that is required.

The way in which finance relates to the objectives can be interpreted as follows:

- to achieve the target revenues and costs – the profitability problem;
- to function within available resources at all times – the liquidity problem;
- to achieve the target pattern of resources, excluding money – the asset structure problem.

If the accountant is to play a meaningful role in the control processes, then the information which is compiled, interpreted and reported upon must be regarded as an integral part of the control mechanism rather than a summary of book keeping entries. Accounting information should be kept up to date in order to adequately reflect the realities of the business. Invariably, it is necessary for the accountant to use different types of information – financial and costing – in order to provide managers with the information they need to control their operations. Information must be presented to managers frequently, in an appropriate format, and as soon as possible after the event to which the information relates. The information should be as accurate as possible, bearing in mind the purposes for which it is required.

Speed is of prime importance and a small number of relevant facts provided quickly is of more use to managers than a vast amount of detailed information provided later. If information is provided quickly, it will enable managers to be able to identify whether problems exist and to be able to take prompt action to maintain control of the organisation or modify plans. Management information and the management functions are expressed diagrammatically in figure 2.1.

Figure 2.1 The management process

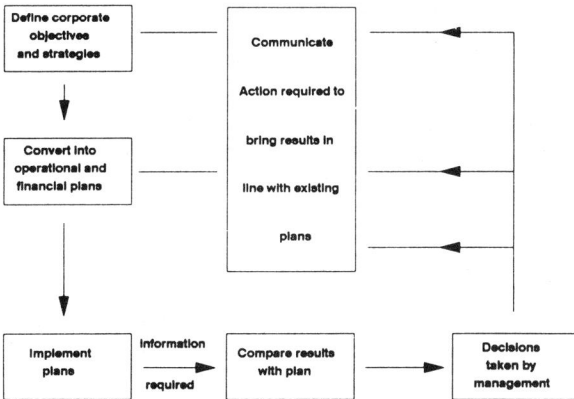

Chapter one discussed the two main types of accounting that exist – financial accounting and management accounting. The financial accounting function performs a stewardship role where published annual accounts are produced in accordance with legal requirements. These financial statements are intended for reporting to external parties and it is important to distinguish the statutory information from the supplementary information supplied to internal management.

Management accounting is, therefore, of greater use for internal purposes and has broadened the role of the accountant in an organisation. Instead of being spectators who just keep score on behalf of external interests, the accountant is now seen as a playing member of the management team. Financial information is the key to effective management and the management teams would not be able to form policy, implement and control without it.

This does not mean that the accountant usurps the place of the manager or that there is a need for the manager to learn to be an accountant in order to manage the business. However, there does need to be a mutual understanding. The accountant needs to understand the nature of the business and the professional contribution that the accountant needs to make to the management of the business. The manager needs to understand the financial environment and constraints within which the business operates as well as have an understanding of accounting concepts and the interpretation of financial information.

As the manager becomes more senior, there is a greater need to be more financially aware, more capable of using financial analysis techniques and have a greater understanding of the use of financial information and the way it can be used to highlight operational problems.

It has already been mentioned that the accountant needs to provide relevant and timely information for the purposes of control. There is also a need for the accountant to be able to prepare and use historic information in a sophisticated manner to enable management to compare current performance with past trends and previous performance.

As organisations also need to look at the future, there is also a need for the accountant to be involved in the planning process, to prepare forecasts and budgets and to assess the financial impact of future plans on the business.

The relationship between the accounting functions are set out in figure 2.2

Figure 2.2   Relationships between accounting functions

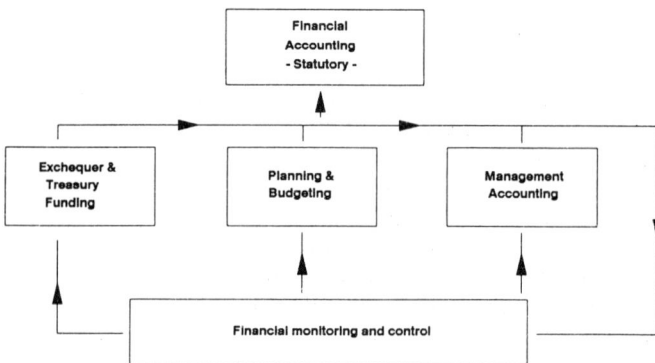

Auditing

Just as there are varying accounting functions there are also varying auditing functions, the main distinction being between external and internal auditing.

External audit

An external audit comprises the examination of the financial records and statements of a business in order to ensure that they have been correctly maintained and that accounting standards, conventions and legal requirements have been adhered to.

The auditor will be an independent third party, not employed by the organisation, and signs the accounts as providing a true and fair representation of the financial affairs of the organisation. An auditor's duties and responsibilities are defined by statute, by case law and by professional codes of conduct.

The requirement for having an external audit applies both to private and public sector organisations, except that in the case of public services the auditor is safeguarding the interests of the local tax payers, rather than the shareholders.

There is also a responsibility of the external auditors to ensure that the systems of control over income and expenditure and assets are adequate to prevent serious loss through fraud or other irregularities. If weaknesses do exist, the auditors should ensure that they have not resulted in serious loss.

There is no requirement for the auditor to prepare the accounts and this should be the responsibility of the organisation's own accountants. The auditor is only required to check the adequacy and accuracy of the accounts and supporting systems. The auditor is not required to make any comments on either the management or the running of the business, but may offer advice accordingly.

Invariaby, fraud prevention is considered to be the prime objective of auditors, but this is not the case. Statutory accounts and the presentation of information is the external auditor's primary objective, and only clerical errors or simple frauds are likely to be discovered in this way. Complex frauds are usually only uncovered by intelligent inquiry and investigations which go behind the books of accounts to the basic data from which the records have been constructed.

Although the discovery of errors or fraud may result from an auditor's report, the responsibility for their prevention rests with management and not the auditor. This can be exercised through the introduction of systems of internal checks and controls. One way in which management can exercise their responsibility is by establishing an internal audit function.

In the early 1980s the Audit Commission for England and Wales was established by statute. The audit of local authorities is the responsibility of the Audit Commission, which has control over the appointment of external auditors. Local authorities can be audited either by private sector accountancy firms or by the District Audit Service.

In a similar manner to the private sector, an external auditor of a local authority is required to certify that the Statement of Accounts 'presents fairly' in accordance with the accountancy principles.

Internal audit

Internal audit functions are usually established as an independent appraisal activity within an organisation. Originally, internal audit was concerned with the examination of financial records, but the role has developed and functions by measuring and evaluating the effectiveness of an organisation's management and operations.

It is the area of management or cost effectiveness auditing that will be of most use to service managers. The main objectives of this type of audit are to:

- analyse and assess the efficiency of the management and operational processes both in individual departments and across the organisation as a whole
- assist management in fulfilling their responsibilities by furnishing them with objective analyses, appraisal and recommendations, which are practical and will enhance the efficiency or profitability of the service under review

The roles of the internal and external auditors should be complimentary and, consequently, there will need to be a fair amount of liaison between the two, especially in respect of the more routine financial audits undertaken by the internal auditors.

The private sector is not bound by statute on the provision of internal audit but there is a statutory requirement on the Director of Finance of a local authority to maintain an 'adequate and effective internal audit' and codes of practice have been developed in order to fulfil this requirement.

The traditional financial audit will never be replaced by management audit within an organisation, but it should be considered as a foundation upon which the more comprehensive review of departmental operations can be built.

There are also differences in approach between the two types of audits. The management audit is mainly diagnostic and prognostic, being concerned with the planning and control functions of line management and staff operations. It seeks to identify under-utilisation of human, financial or operational resources. The management auditor is therefore as equally concerned with, for example, the reliability and effectiveness of, say, quality control and utilisation of space as he is with the controls over debtors.

Traditional financial audit is, however, mainly historical in nature, limits itself to matters of direct financial significance and concentrates on verifying the accuracy of accounting entries. As an example, when comparing takings on the till of a leisure centre to bankings, a financial audit is being conducted. However, an operational/management auditor may analyse the takings and raise such questions as:

- are the activities priced competitively?
- are the activities priced to make a profit or break even?
- what is the demand for the activities?
- what utilisation is being made of the respective activities?

- is there any evidence of heavier demand for activities at certain times of day which could lead to premium pricing?
- are courses effectively programmed and based on likely demand?

Internal audit divisions, to a certain extent, expand their audit activities to include non-financial management appraisals of departmental operations. But the question could be raised,

'How can finance orientated staff in general conduct a basically non-financial operational appraisal?'

Invariably, to obtain the best of both worlds, a multi-disciplinary audit team should be established which would draw on finance skills for financial, auditing, management and control expertise and non-financial skills to provide the service skills in operational processes that are being reviewed.

3 Basic financial records

The earlier chapters set out the concepts and terminology associated with financial accounting, which provides a basis for understanding accounts. This chapter sets out the main financial accounting records which will be of importance to managers and explains the various components of information. The chapter does not attempt to deal with the mechanics of accounting or how to maintain accounting records. Should the reader wish to pursue this side to any degree further, there are numerous books on accounting or book-keeping which provide the relevant material.

A balance sheet

When reviewing a business, one of the areas that will be of interest is how healthy in financial terms is the business. A balance sheet is a statement which shows the financial position at a given point in time. They are constructed at least annually as part of the year end accounting process and, possibly, more frequently depending upon the financial systems and procedures in places.

A balance sheet shows the assets of a firm, divided into fixed assets and current assets. Fixed assets are assets held by the organisation, used for the purposes of the business and not available for sale in the normal course of trading, for example a building, or equipment. Fixed assets will normally be valued at cost less depreciation, the latter being one of the subjects covered in chapter four. Current assets are assets such as debtors, stock and cash which will convert into cash in the normal course of trading. The balance sheet will also show how the assets have been financed, which could be shareholders funds, long term loans or current liabilities.

An example of a balance sheet is set out as table 3.1. The shareholders funds consist of share capital and reserves. Authorised share capital is the number and amount of shares which a company may issue, and the issued share capital is the number and amount of shares that have been issued to shareholders.

The revenue reserves are profits or surpluses which are retained within the organisation and not distributed to shareholders. These include the general reserve and the profit and loss account and are capable of distribution. Reserves can either be capital or revenue reserves and the former are not available for distribution or dividend. They may arise as a result of an asset revaluation or by issuing shares at a premium. The share premium is the amount by which the issued value of shares exceeds their nominal, par or face value.

Shareholders receive dividends out of the profits after annual charges have been met, such as loan interest, taxation, debenture interest and any fixed dividend on preference shares.

Long-term loans represent liabilities which are due twelve months or more after the balance sheet date. The providers of loan capital are paid interest, but are not entitled to a share in any profits. The interest on the loans has to be paid whether or not profits have been made. This can be a burden to an organisation in difficult times, but it does have the advantage that the interest can be offset against profits. It is usual for loans to be secured against the assets of the business.

Current liabilities are liabilities which fall due for payment in a short period of time, usually within twelve months. They also represent the part of long term loans which falls due for repayment within the year.

The difference between current assets and current liabilities is the working capital, which is available for conducting the day to day operations of the business.

The profit and loss account

The profit and loss account shows the profit or loss that has been made by an organisation in a year as a result of the ordinary activities of the business. In order to arrive at this, the account starts with the sales for the year against which is charged the annual costs associated with generating the income for the year.

Having established the net profit, the profit is then appropriated. The first appropriation is taxation, over which the directors have no control. The proposed dividend is an area where the directors determine the values, and in the example contained in table 3.2, the directors have decided to transfer £50,000 in 1990 to general reserves and pay £25,000 to the shareholders as dividends. The unappropriated profits are retained in the business and carried forward as the profit and loss account balance which appears in the balance sheet.

Companies do not have to disclose all of the details relating to their accounts in the published accounts. Read in isolation, therefore, the accounts would not be very meaningful. Consequently, there are a number of notes to the accounts, which explain the accounting policies and various items such as more detail on the turnover, operating costs, employers costs, directors emoluments and exceptional items. The notes to the accounts provide a more comprehensive breakdown of what appears in the accounts and the information that needs to be disclosed is laid down in the Companies Act 1985.

Table 3.2 shows an example of a profit and loss account. This does not conform to the requirements of published accounts as it has been produced in more detail in some areas to enable it to be of more use to the reader. Detailed notes to the accounts have not been included. However, the type of information accompanying accounts can be seen in any set of published accounts.

Source and application of funds statement

The source and application of funds statement provides a link between the balance sheet at the beginning of a period, the profit and loss account for the period and the balance sheet at the end of the period. It forms part of the audited accounts of a company and shows the funds that have entered the company, how they have been used and how any net surplus or deficiency in short and long term funds has been applied. This would tend to be used more by an accountant or financial advisor.

There are a number of ways in which a statement of source and application of funds might be prepared, but, basically, it is just a reclassification of the information contained in the profit and loss account for the period and the opening and closing balance sheets, which reflect a movement of funds. Items such as depreciation, which do not reflect a flow of funds, need to be adjusted in the statement.

The purpose of the statement is to present information in a straightforward form so that answers can be easily ascertained to questions such as:

- 'From where were funds generated – internal sources or external sources?'
- 'Why did the balance at the bank decrease even though the business made a profit?'
- 'How was the purchase of assets financed?'

Similar to the accounts, the statement is measuring historical information and, therefore, can only be used as a guide to the future. It does not take into consideration seasonal peaks or reveal how the changes were achieved. This information can only be established by producing more detailed cash flow budgets and statements. However, it does provide a useful overview when taken into consideration with the other accounts.

Table 3.1 Example of a balance sheet

Linkway Leisure Centre
Balance sheet as at 31st December 1991

	1991 £	1991 £	1990 £	1990 £
Capital employed				
Authorised and issued share capital				
600000 ordinary shares at 50p each		300000		300000
Reserves				
General reserves	110000		50000	
Profit and loss account	82500		75000	
		192500		125000
Long-term loans				
10% secured debentures		100000		
		592500		425000
Employment of capital				
Fixed assets			565000	375000
Current assets				
Stock	50000		30000	
Debtors	90000		60000	
Cash at bank and in hand	75000		60000	
	215000		150000	
Current liabilities				
Bank loan – short term	30000			
Creditors	30000		25000	
Taxation	67500		50000	
Proposed dividend	60000		25000	
	187500		100000	
Net current assets		27500		50000
		582500		425000

Table 3.2 Example of a profit and loss account

Linkway Leisure Centre
Profit and loss account for year ending 31st December 1991

	1991		1990	
	£	£	£	£
Income				
Membership	200000		150000	
Conference room hire	150000		100000	
Fees	400000		350000	
Catering/bar/catering functions	135000		110000	
		885000		710000
Direct costs		360000		320000
Gross profit		525000		390000
Administration expenses		240000		190000
Net profit before interest		285000		200000
Bank interest payable		5000		
Debenture interest payable		10000		
		270000		200000
Corporation tax		67500		50000
Net profit after tax		202500		150000
Less:				
Transfer to reserves	60000		50000	
Proposed dividend	60000		25000	
		120000		75000
Unappropriated profit		82500		75000

Further reading

Hingley W *Accounting Made Simple.* 3rd edition.
Pickles and Lafferty *Accountancy.* Pitman.
Wood F *Business Accounting* 5th edition. Pitman.

4 Matching concepts

Chapter one outlined the basic conventions upon which financial accounts are constructed, and the importance of adhering to them. One important area which is discussed further in this chapter is the matching of actual income in a given period with the actual expenses in the same period in order to determine the profit. This applies not only to statutory annual accounts but also to management accounts which are produced for internal information purposes.

When constructing the results of, say, year four of a business, it is necessary to include all income relating to that particular year and all costs relating to that income and, consequently, to that year. If the same criteria are applied in preparing year three and year five financial results, they will be comparable with year four. As results are geared around periods of time, it is important to identify in what time period the income from a particular transaction should be placed and also determine the costs associated with that period of time.

Receipts and payments are not the method used to recognise income and expenditure. A method known as accrual accounting is used, and this is based on two key conventions – the matching and the realisation conventions.

The realisation convention, as outlined in chapter one, states that revenue should only be taken into consideration when it is realised and not when it is recognised. The key is to identify when is it realised? The realisation concept holds that revenue is realised at the time the goods are sold and not when an order is placed.

The matching convention sets out that expenses incurred in earning the revenues should also be taken into account in the same time period as the revenues are taken into account.

It is important for consistency and comparative purposes that the accruals concept is used.

Depreciation

In chapter three, the classification of fixed and current assets was outlined. Further points about fixed assets are that they are not intended to be consumed or used up during the year they are purchased. Generally, they are held to further the main trading activities of a business. For example, equipment will last a number of years – however, the classification of an asset does depend upon the use which is to be made of it. A distinction also needs to be made between capital expenditure, which is basically the cost of acquiring or improving a fixed asset, and revenue expenditure, which either becomes a current asset or a revenue expense, such as repairing an asset.

As a fixed asset will provide value to a business over a number of years, it is important that a commensurate amount of use should be recognised in the same periods as the associated revenues. Therefore, the entire cost of an asset should not be written off in the period in which the asset is acquired. Instead, the asset should be converted into an expense over its life. This conversion is known as depreciation.

There are a number of ways in which depreciation can be calculated. The traditional approach is to estimate the total cost to be written off; that is, the cost of the asset less its residual value, and then to write that cost off over the estimated life of the asset by using one of the methods described below. The life of an asset is normally measured on a time basis but, in some instances, it may be measured on the basis of actual usage.

However, it may be difficult to determine accurately the life of an asset as a result of wear and tear, and obsolescence. The latter is increasing in importance due to the advancement of technology in society today.

Having decided how much needs to be written off, management then needs to decide which depreciation method to employ. The main methods of depreciation are straight-line basis and reducing balance method.

Straight-line basis

Under this method the total cost is simply spread over the number of years of expected active life giving the annual depreciation charge:

$$\frac{\text{Original cost} - \text{Residual value*}}{\text{Expected active life}} = \text{Annual depreciation charge}$$

* Residual value is the value of the asset at the end of its life.

The main advantage is that as depreciation is a fixed sum, it is easy to work out. This method is best suited, for example, to leases where there is a fixed time period. One of the main disadvantages is that it does not take usage into consideration. A variation on this method is to determine the depreciation charge per unit of use and calculate the annual depreciation charge by reference to the number of units used per annum.

$$\frac{\text{Original cost} - \text{Residual value}}{\text{Estimated total units of use}} \times \frac{\text{Units used}}{\text{per annum}} = \frac{\text{Annual}}{\text{depreciation}}_{\text{charge}}$$

Reducing balance method

Under this method, the annual depreciation charge is a fixed percentage of the 'book value' of the asset at the start of the year. The book value is the original cost of an asset less the accumulated depreciation to date. The full purchase price is never written off which takes into consideration the residual value. This method is suitable for plant, fixtures and vehicles, and the total annual costs tend to even out as there are few repairs and heavy depreciation charges in early years and heavy repairs and low depreciation in later years.

The fixed percentage which will write down the asset approximately to its residual value over the required period of time can be found by the following formula:

$$R = (1 - \sqrt[n]{r/c})^{100}$$

Where R = the desired percentage;
  n = the number of periods over which the asset is to be written off
  r = estimated residual value
  c = cost of acquisition

Depreciation fund method

This method is not commonly used. When an asset is acquired an annual amount is worked out, which, when invested outside the business, will replace the asset or pay off a large liability after a number of years. The fixed sums are usually charged against profits and are set aside for the future.

An example which compares the two main methods, the straight line and reducing balance methods, is set out in table 4.1.

Table 4.1 Comparison of straight line and reducing balance methods of depreciation

Example: Cost of equipment £10,750.
          Estimated residual value £750.
          Estimated life 5 years.

| Years | Straight Line | | Reducing Balance | |
	Opening Balance	Annual Charge	Opening Balance	Annual Charge 41.3%
	£	£	£	£
Year 1	10750	2000	10750	4440
Year 2	8750	2000	6310	2606
Year 3	6750	2000	3704	1530
Year 4	4750	2000	2174	898
Year 5	2750	2000	1276	526
Balance	750		750	
Total Depreciation		10,000		10,000

Reducing balance percentage calculation:

$$R = \left(1 - \sqrt[n]{r/c} \right) \times 100$$

$$R = \left(1 - \sqrt[5]{\frac{750}{10750}} \right) \times 100 = 41.3\%$$

In terms of deciding which method to use, the straight line basis may be more appropriate when the contribution made by the assets remains approximately constant over its life. In practice, the probable reason why it is most commonly used is that it is simple and easy to understand.

In favour of the reducing balance method, it may be argued that the revenue that the asset helps to generate reduces as the asset gets older and, therefore, higher depreciation charges should be levied in the years when the revenue is higher. In addition, as repair costs increase as an asset gets older, and in order to even out the total expense charged, higher depreciation charges should be levied in years where repair costs are low and vice versa.

On a practical note, assets in general are not written off over a period that reflects their exact life. Instead they tend to be classified and allocated into categories of, say, five, ten, and fifteen year assets, into which they best fit. Only very large or expensive assets will tend to be dealt with on an individual basis.

It is important to understand that depreciation is a method of converting an asset into expenses over the useful life of the asset. The depreciation process is not a valuation process and is not a way of ensuring that an organisation has resources available to replace assets at the appropriate time.

Cost of goods sold

Another area where the matching convention is applicable, especially in retail operations, such as the retailing of leisure goods and equipment or vending machine sales, is that when goods are sold the cost of the goods should be matched against the revenues earned.

This may sound fairly straightforward, but complications do arise when the stock is initially purchased at different cost prices. For example a sports shop in a leisure centre has made three sets of purchases of cans of tennis balls as follows:

January	6 cans at £5.50p per can
February	6 cans at £5.75p per can
March	6 cans at £5.90p per can

If in April a sale is made of three cans of tennis balls, what is the cost of the sale? In practise, it will normally be impossible to identify the source of the goods sold and be able to say that the goods come from the January stock or a combination of all three. If, say, two cans were sold from the first stock and one from the second stock, then the *actual cost* of the sale would be:

$$(2 \times £5.50p) + (1 \times £5.75p) = £16.75p$$

Actual cost is favoured when it is possible to identify the actual cost of the goods sold as it equates to the flow of goods and represents an actual cost figure. It is more suitable when dealing with goods of a high unit value and where they can be easily identified. Actual costing is accepted by the Inland Revenue but, as determining the actual cost can be difficult, other valuation methods, as set out below, tend to be applied.

First In First Out (FIFO)

If it is assumed that the oldest stock is sold first, then the cost of goods sold would be:

$3 \times £5.50p = £16.50p$

This method of valuation is known as First In, First Out (FIFO), and its main advantage is that, in certain instances, it approximates to the physical flow of stock. This would be especially the case in catering businesses. It also means that the remaining stock and, consequently, the stock appearing on a balance sheet will have a valuation closer to its current replacement cost. The FIFO concept is widely used and is acceptable for tax purposes.

Last In First Out (LIFO)

Returning to our tennis ball example, if it is assumed that the youngest stock is sold first, then the cost of goods sold would be:

$3 \times £5.90p = £17.70p$

This method of valuation is known as Last In First Out (LIFO). The most important feature with LIFO is that the cost of sales will be based on the most recent purchase prices paid for the goods, which will reflect the closest approximation to the replacement cost of the goods at the date of sale.

In the event of rising prices, the LIFO cost of sales will be greater than the FIFO cost of sales and hence the LIFO profit will be less than the FIFO profit.

Whilst LIFO gives the best approximation to the current value of the cost of goods sold that can be achieved with an historical system, it does have the disadvantage that the remaining stock, and consequently the balance sheet, will be based on older and lower prices. LIFO is not accepted by the Inland Revenue as profits are depressed which would, consequently, reduce the profits on which taxation is computed. LIFO does not tend to be widely used.

Another method is to ignore the assumed flow of goods and calculate the average costs of goods.

In this example the cost would be:

Total cost of 18 cans = £102.90p
Average cost per can = £5.72p
Cost of sales   = 3 × £5.72p
                     = £17.16p

This is known as average cost, and its main benefit is that it evens out the effect of price changes which would otherwise be directly reflected under both the FIFO and LIFO principles. It is, therefore, useful for commodities where prices fluctuate rapidly. Average cost is accepted by the Inland Revenue.

Different methods of stock valuation will create different profits for a business, but if it is consistent in its stock valuation method in the long term there will be no difference. The choice of method employed may not actually depend on the physical flow of goods in a business and, for example, the FIFO principle may be used, whereas in practise the goods that are actually sold may be those which were the most recently acquired.

5 Basic taxation

This chapter is intended to give the reader an insight into the types of taxation that will be experienced by a business. It does not attempt to deal with the computation of taxation or the technicalities of each type of tax as taxation details tend to change when the Chancellor of the Exchequer presents the Annual Budget. Further details on the respective taxes can be found in other reference books, examples of which are listed at the end of this chapter.

The profits of business are assessed for taxation quite independently of the persons who own the business, even if the business is owned by one person. However, reliefs and allowances that are available to owners may be offset against their proportion of the business taxation assessment, the profits in these instances being liable to income tax at the appropriate rate.

Corporation tax

The taxable profits of limited companies and other corporate bodies are, however, subject to corporation tax and not income tax. Where a company does not make a dividend distribution to shareholders, then all the taxable profits will be taxed at the normal rate of corporation tax appropriate for the year. if a company makes a dividend payment to shareholders, the dividend will, in fact, be a net amount after deducting income tax at the basic rate. The company will also pay to the Inland Revenue Advance Corporation Tax (ACT) on the dividend distributed, which will eventually be offset against the annual corporation tax bill of the company. The ACT is calculated as a fraction of the sum distributed, 1/3rd of the dividend when the basic rate is 25 per cent. This fraction is, and no doubt will continue to be, varied by the Government.

Irrespective of whether an organisation is subject to corporation tax (company or corporate body) or income tax (partnership or sole trader) it is inevitable that the profits shown in the accounts will need to be adjusted in order to arrive at a profit figure upon which tax is payable. This book has not attempted to cover the expenses that are allowable and disallowed or the income that is assessable and not assessable. Reference should, in these cases and for specimen computations, be made to taxation books.

It is a misconception to think that corporation tax only applies to companies. In fact, its scope is much wider. It is also applicable to unincorporated associations, which is the category into which many clubs, societies, sports leagues and governing bodies fall. These associations are generally considered to be 'companies' for taxation purposes and are, therefore, liable to corporation tax on trading, investment, letting income as well as being liable to capital gains tax. Even though, for example, these organisations exist to promote their activities rather than to make a profit, this does not confer any exemption from taxation.

The concept of 'trading' can also be unclear, but generally this includes activities undertaken with a view to making a profit, even though they may make a loss! Such activities may, for example, include the provision of a bar or the hire of club facilities, sales and sporting events. In these cases, expenses can be offset against the income to reduce the taxable profit. Tax will not normally be charged if the organisation can demonstrate that the profits will be donated to a charity, that the trading is not regular and that it is not competing with other businesses. Tax is also levied on interest received such as bank and building society interest, property rentals, stocks, and national savings.

Income from members and subscriptions are not normally taxable nor are payments made by members for facilities and services that the club provides for them. The income from members themselves to their club is used to meet the costs of the club. Consequently, the costs are not chargeable for calculating taxable profits. As the income accrues for the benefit of members, it is deemed that they cannot make a profit out of themselves. However, payments made by non-members for the use of facilities are taxable, although costs arising from earning that income are deductible.

Other non-investment income may also be taxable, such as income from sponsorship and where income from members is small in relation to total income, the majority of the activities of a club may be taxable. This may be a problem, for example, for many golf courses where a vast proportion of income may be derived from visitors fees.

Charitable status is beneficial as charitable associations are exempt from tax. However, this status is not easy to obtain and clubs may experience difficulty as their objects generally relate to the provision of one sports activity. The legal position and requirements pertaining to charities and trusts are clearly explained in detail by Michael Scott in *Law and Leisure Services Management* (chapter seven), which is also part of the Longman ILAM Series.

If an organisation is not trading there will be a limitation on the tax deductible expenses that can be claimed. Where it is partially trading any expenses must be wholly and exclusively incurred for the purpose of the trade in order for them to be tax deductible. If expenses include interest payments on a loan, then the interest may be allowed as a deductible expense depending upon the nature of the loan. It is important that all available reliefs are taken to ensure that the most beneficial tax position is established.

Most associations are also reliant on money acquired through fund raising, such as lotteries, fairs, open days and sponsorship. Potentially, this income is subject to both corporation tax and VAT.

If lottery income is raised from non-members then this is, in fact, deemed to be trading income and is subject to tax. However, the tax burden can be minimised if the lottery is structured in a certain way. Lotteries are bound by rules in local authority by-laws and also by the Lotteries and Amusement Act of 1976. If, for example, a lottery is organised by a supporter's club, or any other body external to the club, on the basis that a stated percentage of the cost of each ticket would be donated to the club for one or more of the purposes set out in the Lotteries and Amusement Act 1976, then the donated element may be excluded in computing the taxable profits of promoting the lottery. The donation is paid to the club and the tax liability of the organising body will be reduced. It may also be possible for the recipient club to avoid tax on the donation. For example, if the donation is made for a capital project, such as a new clubhouse, then it is not enhancing the annual running profits and is unlikely to be taxed by the Inland Revenue. It is important that independence can be demonstrated in that the organisation of the lottery is separate from the club's financial affairs.

Many organisations are also supported by sponsorship, where there is usually an agreement between the club and the sponsoring organisation, whereby the sponsor usually receives some form of services, such as advertising or publicity in exchange for a sponsorship payment. The recipient organisation is likely to be taxed on the sponsorship income, although expenditure directly incurred in relation of the provision of the services to the sponsor can be deducted. The sponsor will also be seeking a tax deduction for the payment and this would normally be available except where the services are in the form of entertainment facilities. In order to reduce taxation, associations may prefer sponsorship to be in kind rather than in cash.

All other activities which can be regarded as trading activities, where something is received from non members, are liable to tax. However, true donations, gifts and grants of a capital nature from statutory or non-statutory bodies are unlikely to be taxable. In addition, as assessable profits of an association are likely to be small they will probably pay corporation tax at the lower rate of 25 per cent. Also, if they do not undertake a competitive trading supply and they apply any surpluses to charities or to the club itself, then they should also be able to avoid paying corporation tax, with the exception of any interest receivable.

Value Added Tax (VAT)

VAT first came into effect for transactions made on or after the 1st April 1973 and replaced purchase tax and the Selective Employment Tax. On the 18th June 1979, a 15 per cent VAT rate was introduced for all standard rated goods and services, and this was increased to 17.5 per cent from 1st April 1991.

The system operates right through the 'chain' of buying and selling and it is, therefore, the final consumer who bears the tax on the sale price of the purchases. The VAT incurred by a business on its purchases is known as 'input tax' and that which is passed on to customers is known as 'output tax'. Some goods and services are 'exempt' from VAT, which means that a business cannot charge VAT on its sales to customers, but on the other hand it is not possible to reclaim input tax on the associated purchases.

Total exemption from VAT may also exist where the annual turnover does not exceed a certain limit. The annual registration threshold was raised to £36,600 from 11th March 1992. However, total exemption may not always be an advantage, as although the business does not charge VAT on to its customers, which will make its services cheaper to the end user, it does mean that the business cannot reclaim a credit for any input tax incurred.

VAT registration, for any association results in an additional cost to members, as they would not normally be able to recover the VAT charged on their subscriptions. The association itself would also normally end up a net VAT payer. On the other hand, a club that is not registered for VAT, whilst not having to charge VAT on its subscriptions and facilities thereby reducing the cost to the end consumer, would not be able to recover VAT on the goods and supplies it purchases. Consequently, VAT in general constitutes a cost to sport, either to the clubs and societies, or to the participants.

VAT is chargeable, for example, on subscriptions, bar and catering, activities, sponsorship income, admission charges, including charitable functions and takings from gaming machines. VAT is particularly costly to voluntary associations, but there are ways in which a potential VAT liability can be minimised. For example:

- the provision of facilities for betting and gaming are exempt based on certain conditions.
- lotteries are also an exempt activity. A lottery is a way of distributing prizes by lot or by chance, such as a raffle. If merit or skill is involved, the event is deemed to be a competition and the entry fee is standard rated. As lotteries are exempt, the partial exemption rules also apply for the recovery of input tax. These rules may be avoided if the lottery is organised outside the club.

- entry fees to competitions are normally standard rated but the fees for competitions of a sports or recreational nature are exempt if the whole of the entry fee is awarded in prizes or where the competition is organised by a non profit making body established for the purposes of sport or physical recreation.
- donations, that is a payment which secures nothing for a donor and where the payment is at the total discretion of the donor, are outside the scope of VAT. The payment can also be treated as a donation if the sole acknowledgement is just a mention as a contributor in an annual report or a programme. However, if the acknowledgement is tantamount to advertising, the payment, will be deemed to be sponsorship income rather than a donation, which is subject to VAT.
- taxable turnover may be kept below the registrations limit if a donation element is, for instance, contained within a ticket price, as donations are outside the scope of VAT.
- events could be organised outside a club and, providing the organising body is not registered for VAT, VAT will not be due on the tickets sold by the organising body.
- if a number of sports organisations share the same facilities, such as a club house, grounds and facilities, it may be advantageous for each individual sport to have a separate club with its own taxable supplies where the supplies of each are below the VAT registration limit.
- the hire of sports facilities for undertaking sport or any physical recreation attracts VAT at the standard rate unless used for a continuous period of 24 hours, when it is exempt.
- the hire of sports facilities by a school, a club, association or organisation representing affiliated clubs may also be exempt where:
  - ten individual hire periods are made, whether or not exceeding 24 hours, where the interval between each hiring is not less than one day and not more than fourteen days:
  - the hirer has exclusive use of the facility hired;
  - each hire period is in respect of the same activity carried on in the same place;
  - a formal agreement is made in advance for booking the hire period and payment is received in full.

In addition to exempt goods and services, zero rated supplies may also exist. This means that although theoretically the goods and services are taxable, the VAT rate is zero. Output VAT is, therefore, not charged on the sales of zero rated goods but input tax may be reclaimed, if appropriate.

It is important to ensure that VAT is being dealt with correctly, as failure to register or misdeclarations can result in surcharges and the collection of past liabilities which would have been due had the club been registered at the appropriate time.

Capital gains tax

Another area where businesses may be taxed is when assets, such as property, investments and land, are disposed of where a liabiity to capital gains tax may arise. It is advisable to look at the association's constitution to see who owns the assets, as sometimes trustees own them on behalf of the members and, consequently, it is the association rather than the members that make the disposal. Capital gains may also arise on, for instance, mergers of clubs where there may be a disposal of assets and also a disposal of members interests. There may be opportunities for tax planning in order to reduce the liabilities to capital gains tax, but this is beyond the scope of this book.

As well as clubs, the governing bodies and leagues also suffer taxation problems and hardships. These organisations often receive income from members and other sources and may distribute monies to members clubs within the leagues or association. As the organisations are likely to be subject to corporation tax any distributions may be deemed to be dividends, with an ACT liability being due when the distribution is made. However, this could be overcome if the constitution or rules state that the net income, after expenses, belongs to the clubs, but then the corporation tax liability would fall on the clubs.

Conclusion

UK taxation is generally unhelpful to voluntary associations, as they are treated like business entities, being viewed as trading and hence profit making organisations. Within this, no distinction is drawn between, for example, a professional football club that is seeking to make a profit and a club of amateur status where the primary concern is the development of the sport.

Sporting bodies, in particular, tend to have difficulty in obtaining charitable status and any attempts to generate income suffer from both corporation tax and VAT. It has been estimated that the Revenue receives from sport, through VAT, Corporation Tax, Income Tax and the Betting Levy, in the region of £2.4 billion per year and for every £1 that sport receives from Government it is estimated to contribute £5 in taxation. Whilst this type of revenue is not large compared with other Treasury revenue, it does have a severe impact on the associations, governing bodies and clubs upon which the taxes are levied.

UK sport does not benefit from the same support and tax benefits from the Government as experienced by other countries, where sport is regarded as a charitable activity rather than a business. In addition, the increase of the standard rate VAT from 15 per cent to 17.5 per cent dealt another blow to the leisure and tourism industries.

The changes to pools betting duty proposed by the Chancellor in the 1991/92 budget is a scheme aimed at generating funds for sports and arts. The scheme reduces the levy on pools from 40 per cent to 37.5 per cent, which would generate a tax cut of £20m. This is also subject to the pools promoters creating a foundation to donate another £40m and, therefore, a total of £60m would be donated to sports and arts. This fund is administered by The Foundation for Sports and the Arts (see also chapter fifteen).

Until corporation tax and VAT are abolished for voluntary associations, they will unfortunately have to continue to rely on donations and lotteries.

References

Scott M 1988 *Law and Leisure Services Management.* Longman

6 Interpretation of financial information

The annual accounts and financial statements of a business are used by management as a starting point to examine its overall success and underlying financial strength. Virtually all plans have a financial side to them and, in the long run, positive and effective management and control should show up through a healthy profit and loss account and balance sheet. Management should, therefore, use these statements to assess efficiency and performance and to indicate areas that may call for attention to improve results.

Chapter one set out some of the basic concepts and principles which need to be understood and form a basis for analysing and interpreting financial statements. Some figures will be more useful than others and, therefore, care needs to be exercised when selecting the information to be reviewed.

Accounting ratios

Accounting ratios tend to be the main method by which information is interpreted as they facilitate easier comparisons both within and between businesses. Comparisons between years, or between similar organisations, or comparisons with budgeted ratios tend to be more useful than absolute figures. A number of ratios need to be taken in order to assess the state of health of a business, as viewed in isolation they may lead to wrong conclusions. They also can only act as a guide as they are subject to the same weaknesses as the financial statements from which they are prepared. They do highlight areas that may require further investigations but they cannot, in themselves, form the basis for final decisions. If produced as part of an appraisal, which also includes the actual accounts, the flow of funds statement and relevant non-accounting information, they also provide a useful insight into the activities of the organisation.

If comparative ratios are used between years within a business, it may be possible to establish that its performance has improved over the years. This, however, does not put the performance into context against planned performance or with other businesses in the same industry. Consequently, a mixture of varying comparative ratios is also advisable. Comparisons between firms are also difficult, as all the information that is required for comparison may not be available from an ordinary set of accounts and the information that is available in the accounts may be subject to different accounting policies and rules.

Ratios tend to be applied to published accounts, which provide an indication of past performance. However, other than with the possible exception of the Inland Revenue, management will be more interested in the results that the organisation could potentially achieve in the future. Therefore, if the ratios are applied to the historical accounts, the manager must question to what extent the information that is being analysed will assist in forming decisions about the future. The ratios could also be applied to more current information, if available, which would result in more meaningful information, but certain changes would need to be made to some of the ratios.

This chapter explains and examines some of the key ratios applied to businesses and comments upon their use and limitations. Certain ratios are more important than others. These are known as primary ratios and are applicable to any business. In addition, there are a number of secondary ratios, which can be applied as appropriate or as circumstances dictate. This hierarchy of ratios is set out diagrammatically in figure 6.1.

Figure 6.1   Financial analysis ratio hierarchy

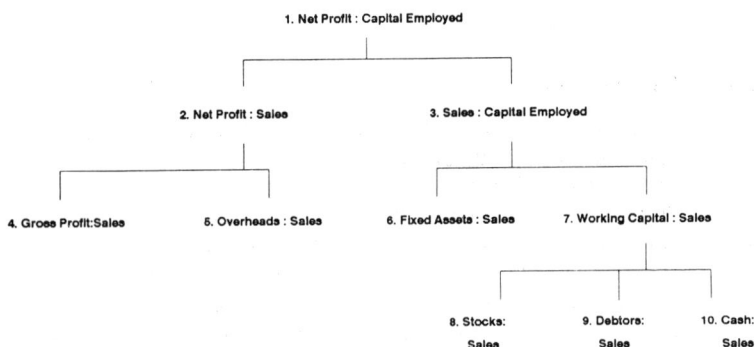

The ratios that are calculated will depend upon the purpose for which they are required. It is increasingly recognised that the readers of accounts extend beyond existing and potential shareholders and creditors, and include financing institutions, employees, government organisations, and any other interested parties. This chapter has not attempted to deal with the possible information for each class of user for decision making purposes, but has focused on two key areas that are relevant to all groups – profitability and solvency.

Tables 6.1 and 6.2 set out the profit and loss account and balance sheet relating to Linkway Leisure Centre and they are used to explain and demonstrate the ratios that are discussed in this chapter.

Table 6.1

Linkway Leisure Centre
Balance sheet as at 31st December 1991

	1991		1990	
	£	£	£	£
Capital employed				
Authorised and issued share capital				
600000 ordinary shares at 50p each		300000		300000
Reserves				
General reserves	110000		50000	
Profit and loss account	82500		75000	
		192500		125000
Long-term loans				
10% secured debentures		100000		
		592500		425000
Employment of capital				
Fixed assets		565000		375000
Current assets				
Stock	50000		30000	
Debtors	90000		60000	
Cash at hand and in hand	75000		60000	
	215000		150000	
Current liabilities				
Bank loan – short term	30000			
Creditors	30000		25000	
Taxation	67500		50000	
Proposed dividend	60000		25000	
	187500		100000	
Net current assets		27500		50000
		592500		425000

Table 6.2 Example of a profit and loss account

Linkway Leisure Centre
Profit and loss account for year ending 31st December 1991

	1991 £	1991 £	1990 £	1990 £
Income				
Membership	200000		150000	
Conference room hire	150000		100000	
Fees	400000		350000	
Catering/bar/catering functions	135000		110000	
		885000		710000
Direct costs		360000		320000
Gross profit		525000		390000
Administration expenses		240000		190000
Net profit before interest		285000		200000
Bank interest payable		5000		
Debenture interest payable		10000		
		270000		200000
Corporation tax		67500		50000
Net profit after tax		202500		150000
Less:				
Transfer to reserves	60000		50000	
Proposed dividend	60000		25000	
		120000		75000
Unappropriated profit		82500		75000

Profitability ratios

Most people looking at a set of accounts will be keen to assess how profitable a business is. The figure of profit in absolute terms tends to be meaningless unless it is compared to the resources which have been employed to generate the profit. The basic approach to measuring the profitability of an organisation is, therefore, based on the return on capital employed (ROCE):

$$\frac{\text{A measure of profit}}{\text{A measure of the resources employed}}$$

This is known as the primary ratio. There are many variations of this ratio, which leads to a lack of consistency and misuse. In order to determine which is the more appropriate ratio to use, it is necessary to consider what is the objective in calculating the company's profitability. Is it concerned with using historical information in an attempt to forecast future profitability or is it to be used in making recommendations to improve the profitability of an organisation?

There are a number of interpretations of resources or capital employed in a business:

- Gross capital employed is represented by the total funds of a company, which also equates to the total assets. Using the example set out in table 6.1, the gross capital employed of Linkways Leisure Centre Limited at 31st December 1991 was:

    £565,000 (Fixed assets) + £215,000 (Current assets) = £780,000

- Long term capital employed is the total funds employed, including long term liabilities. The long term capital employed of Linkways Leisure Centre as at 31st December 1991 was:

    £300,000 (Share capital) + £192,500 (Reserves) + £100,000 (Long-term loan) = £592,000

- Shareholders capital employed is made up of share capital plus reserves which at 31st December 1991 was:

    £300,000 (Share capital) + £192,500 (Reserves) = £492,500

Different users will have different views on which method of capital employed should be used, but, whichever is chosen, the same basis should be used for consistency from one year to the next.

As far as any manager is concerned, control over an organisation's assets has to be exercised, irrespective of the method of financing. Therefore, return on gross capital employed would be more useful as a measure of the efficiency with which managers have used the total resources available.

A further factor to be considered is that assets are normally recorded on the balance sheet on an historical cost basis. A clearer picture would emerge if all the assets were valued at their current going concern value. In this way, net profit each year measured at current value could be compared against the current value of capital employed which would provide a more realistic comparison.

Having determined a basis for calculating capital employed, the next problem is which figure to take for profit. Again, there are various opinions. One method is to take net profit before tax, which can make the measure more suitable for comparisons over time, or with other organisations. Taxation depends upon the particular circumstances of the organisation and changes in the tax rates or the implications of trading losses brought forward can obscure the ratio of net profit after tax to capital employed over a number of years.

Profit could also be stated pre- or post-interest charges. If a profit is stated before interest charges, it is possible to differentiate between the way in which an organisation uses its assets and the way in which it finances them. Using pre-interest profit is useful as it enables comparisons to be made between companies with different capital structures of the efficiency with which they use their assets. Whichever method is selected, consistency is important. It is also important to remember that gains or losses of an abnormal nature should be excluded from the net profit in order to produce a realistic ratio.

Shareholders would be interested in profit remaining in the company for dividends and expansion and, therefore, they would be interested in net profit after interest and tax.

Consistency is important and, if attempting to compare ratios with that of another company, it is essential to ensure, as best as possible, that profits have been calculated and assets have been valued on the same basis in all ratios used. The effects of inflation, the economic climate and the conditions under which the organisations have been operating should also be carefully considered.

Linkway's return on capital employed for 1990 and 1991 using gross capital employed and net profit before tax and interest is as follows:

$$\frac{\text{Profit}}{\text{Capital employed}} \quad \begin{array}{c} 1991 \\ \dfrac{285,000}{780,000} = 36.5\% \end{array} \quad \begin{array}{c} 1990 \\ \dfrac{200,000}{525,000} = 38\% \end{array}$$

Although the absolute value of profit has increased in 1991, the relative profitability in relation to capital employed has reduced from 38 per cent in 1990 to 36.5 per cent in 1991. Major changes in results could be the effect of the industry as a whole experiencing the impact of a recession and, therefore, it would be necessary to compare the ratio with that of a similar business.

Another factor to be considered, is that £190,000 (£565,000 − £375,000 = £190,000) appears to have been spent on additional leisure buildings and facilities. If the additional assets were acquired in December 1991, it would be incorrect to include this amount as capital employed for 1991. In such circumstances, it is more advisable to use average capital employed rather than the year end figure. This illustrates that the ratios can only act as a guide and cannot form the basis for final conclusions.

The next question that would probably be raised is why has the return on capital declined between the two years? This could result from a decline in the profit margins or from not utilising capital as efficiently in relation to the level of income. It is, therefore, necessary to move onto the secondary ratios of profit:sales and sales:capital employed, in order to answer such questions.

Net profit:sales ratio

The profit to sales ratio is normally expressed as a percentage rather than a ratio. The size of the net profit to sales ratio will have a direct impact on the organisation's return on capital employed, and any major changes between years or unexpectedly high or low percentages should be investigated so that corrective action and be taken as necessary.

Using table 6.2, the percentage net profit:sales for Linkway Limited in 1991 is 32 per cent and 28 per cent in 1990.

$$\frac{\text{Net profit}}{\text{Sales}} \quad \begin{array}{c} 1991 \\ \dfrac{285,000}{885,000} = 32\% \end{array} \quad \begin{array}{c} 1990 \\ \dfrac{200,000}{710,000} = 28\% \end{array}$$

In 1991, this means that for every £1 of income, 32 pence profit is made. The percentage profit on sales varies with different businesses and industries and, therefore, it is essential to compare the ratio with other similar businesses in the industry and take into consideration the economic climate. As an example, supermarkets work on relatively low profit margins, whereas furniture stores work on high profit margins.

Sales:capital employed

If profit margins decline then the return on capital employed can only be maintained by increasing efficiency without a greater proportional increase in capital employed. This ratio measures the efficiency with which the business utilises its capital in relation to its sales.

A company's rate of return on capital employed could be increased either by increasing its rate of asset turnover or by maintaining the current level of sales for a given level of assets or by a combination of both. Asset turnover is discussed later in this chapter. A high ratio is a healthy sign, for the more times capital is turned over, the greater will be the opportunities to generate profit. A low ratio, on the other hand, may indicate spare capacity.

Again, this ratio will vary according to the type of business. For example, supermarkets work on low profit margins with a high turnover, whereas furniture stores work on a higher profit margin with a lower turnover rate. In the example below the two extremes can be seen.

	Company A	Company B
Sales	£100,000	£100,000
Net profit	£ 5,000	£ 25,000
Total investment	£ 10,000	£ 50,000
Net profit:sales	5%	25%
Sales:Capital employed	10 times	2 times
Profit:Capital employed	50%	50%

Although both companies show the same profit:capital employed ratios of 50 per cent, their constituent ratios are remarkably different.

The sales:capital employed ratio for Linkway Leisure Centre from tables 6.1 and 6.2 for 1991 is 1.13 times whereas in 1990 it was 1.35 times.

$$\frac{Sales}{Capital\ employed} \quad \frac{1991}{885,000}{565,000 + 215,000} = 1.13 \quad \frac{1990}{710,000}{375,000 + 150,000} = 1.35$$

A decline in the ratio could indicate inefficiency in the use of capacity available, an increase in assets which has not been matched by an increase in sales or a reduction in sales due to, for instance, a recession in the industry. In this particular example, there has been an increase in assets between the two years based on an anticipated future demand, which so far has not materialised into additional sales. Similar comments apply to using an average capital employed figure.

It is also worth noting that the return on capital employed is the product of the sales to capital employed and net profit to sales ratios as follows:

$$\frac{\text{Net profit}}{\text{Sales}} \times \frac{\text{Sales}}{\text{Capital employed}} = \frac{\text{Net profit}}{\text{Capital employed}}$$

Using Linkway's 1991 figures, the return on capital employed is:

$$\frac{285,000}{885,000} \times \frac{885,000}{780,000} = 36.5\%$$

Having examined the key secondary ratios, it may be necessary to extract further ratios in order to answer such questions as, 'Why have profit margins declined?' or, 'Why has capital not been utilised efficiently in relation to sales?'.

Expenditure ratios

In order to answer the question on profit margins, it will probably be necessary to review the direct cost and overhead expense ratios.

Using table 6.2, the expenditure ratios have been calculated, and are set out below. Based on these ratios, there appears to be an improvement in efficiency in relation to direct costs, which has been directly converted into net profit.

	1991		1990	
		£'000		£'000
Direct costs:Sales	41%	(360/885)	45%	(320/710)
Admin. costs:Sales	27%	(240/885)	27%	(190/710)
Net profit:Sales	32%	(285/885)	28%	(200/710)
	100%		100%	

Asset turnover ratios

With regards to reviewing the effective utilisation of capital in relation to sales, it may be necessary to consider the following ratios:

- fixed asset turnover ratios
- stock turnover ratios
- debtors turnover ratios

Fixed asset turnover ratio

This ratio may reveal how efficiently the fixed assets are being utilised. If the ratio is low, this could mean that the fixed assets are not being fully employed. Using tables 6.1 and 6.2 the fixed assets ratio for Linkway Leisure Centre is:

$$\frac{\text{Sales}}{\text{Fixed assets}} = \frac{1991}{\frac{885,000}{565,000}} = 1.57 \text{ times} \quad \frac{1990}{\frac{710,000}{375,000}} = 1.89 \text{ times}$$

This indicates that each £1 invested in fixed assets produces, on average, sales of £1.57 in 1991 and £1.89 in 1990. It may also be advisable to compare the ratio for major assets where this is possible. The stock and debtors ratios are considered under the wider heading of liquidity ratios.

Liquidity solvency ratios and working capital ratios

The primary concerns of a business are to earn profits and remain solvent. As services are provided and profits are realised it may be that the profits may not be represented by cash because, if the customer was invoiced for the service, the cash will be due at a time in the future.

Therefore, a company may be successful from a profitability point of view but may be in a dangerous position if it does not have sufficient liquid assets, such as cash, and those near to cash, such as debtors, to meet its current liabilities. Liquidity is, therefore, concerned with the ability of an organisation to pay amounts owing as they become due for payment.

A profitable organisation could experience liquidity difficulties due to overtrading. This could occur when a company attempts to expand. For example, in an attempt to increase its customer base to generate more revenue, a theme park operator may decide to provide extra facilities, such as a bar, a restaurant or may purchase additional rides. In terms of cash flow, the cash outflow increases substantially as it is necessary for the organisation to pay for its purchases. However, the cash outflow occurs before any cash flows in from the increasing custom. As a result of the overtrading, the operator suffers from inadequate working capital, that is, it has insufficient current assets to cover current liabilities.

As a result of this, the organisation may slow down the rate at which it pays creditors. Credit control might also be relaxed in an attempt to encourage and increase sales. Debtors would probably increase, but the rate at which they would pay would probably decline and more bad debts may result. The downward spiral would continue and the organisation might eventually be forced into liquidation.

Liquidity and solvency ratios give some indication of the risks associated with the organisation's future cash flows and its ability to generate sufficient cash inflows to cover the cash outflows. Before discussing the ratios, it is probaby worth explaining the difference between liquidity and solvency, as both are vital to the health of an organisation.

Near cash and liquidity

Liquidity exists when quantities of cash are available, or are easily available, within a short period of time. All assets are capable of being sold at some price and within a certain period of time. Not all assets are saleable at short notice and they vary with respect to time and the effort required to sell them. For example, shares on the stock exchange have a high liquidity as they can easily be turned into cash whereas buildings have a low liquidity as they take time and effort to sell. In effect, cash and near cash represents high liquidity.

It is also possible to define near cash in terms of the cost of conversion to cash. As price risk is inherent in the valuation of liquidity, the rise and fall in its value could be used as an index of nearness to cash. Both time and value are important and it is management's tasks to achieve a balance between the two.

Cash in itself earns no return and, therefore, cash and nearness to cash can also be taken as a measure of idleness. It is, therefore, important for management to ensure that the organisation is not too liquid, as the nearer an investment is to cash the lower is its rate of return. Rates of return also tend to reflect the degree of risk involved and to earn reasonable profits, risks must be taken. There is always a conflict between profitability and safety, and management needs to decide on the appropriate balance between the two. Too much liquidity is a poor use of money as returns will be very small, but too little liquidity can lead to severe cash problems, which can result in an inability to settle debts when they become due.

Solvency

Solvency reflects a time state of liquidity. In order to be solvent an organisation should be capable of meeting debts on a due date by having funds available in the form of cash or near cash. It is not necessary to be liquid to be solvent and it is only necessary to be able to become sufficiently liquid should the need arise.

The ability to become liquid is a function of time and the state of the assets in relation to nearness of cash. If a large proportion of the assets have a long conversion time, then a problem of solvency could exist. Organisations that overtrade run the risk of insolvency. Creditors could become nervous and demand immediate payment, and if insufficient liquid funds can be generated, the organisation could be declared technically insolvent. In reality, the firm may have sufficient assets to meet the financial obligations, but insufficient time to convert the assets into cash. Legal insolvency, however, reflects a situation of permanent cash shortage irrespective of how much time is provided as creditors are in excess of the organisation's assets. The financial affairs should be managed to avoid insolvency, but the balance between idleness and overtrading is a fine one.

There are certain key ratios which can be reviewed in order to give an insight into the liquidity and solvency of an organisation.

Short-term ratios
Current ratio

This is also referred to as the working capital ratio and it gives an indication as to whether an organisation has sufficient assets, that is current assets, which can be converted into cash within a short period of time to cover those current liabilities that are due for payment either immediately or in the near future, usually over the next twelve months. This ratio is, therefore, an indication of the organisation's short-term financial strength. Creditors will want to see a sufficiently large amount of current assets to cover current liabilities. Traditionally, it is thought that current assets should cover current liabilities by at least twice, i.e. 2:1, but this will really depend upon the type of business and the requirements of individual organisations. Many reputable organisations operate with far lower ratios.

Linkway Leisure Centre – current ratio

$$\frac{\text{Current assets}}{\text{Current liabilities}} = \frac{\overset{1991}{215,000}}{187,500} = 1.15:1 \frac{\overset{1990}{150,000}}{100,000} = 1.5:1$$

Using table 6.1, the current ratio for Linkway Leisure Centre is 1.15:1 for 1991 as opposed to 1.5:1 in 1990. The decline in the current ratio from 1990 to 1991 may cause concern. Whether the ratio is satisfactory or not will depend upon the length of the time from the cash outflow until the cash inflow. It may well be that any further investments or improvements may need to be held back because of lack of funds or it could be, in some cases, that additional permanent capital may be required. It is also worthwhile looking at the components that make up the current asset figures as an organisation may have a large amount of slow moving stock and comparatively small amounts of debtors and cash. Consequently, they may still experience difficulties even though they may have a healthy current ratio.

Liquidity ratio

It is advisable not only to investigate the ability of an organisation to meet its commitments over the next twelve months but also its ability to meet its immediate commitments. Consequently, only assets which can be turned quickly into cash are included and stock is usually excluded. The liquid assets to current liabilities ratio is known as the liquidity, quick or acid test ratio. Ideally a ratio of 1:1 is required as, if it is below this and creditors pressed for payments, the organisation would have great difficulty in meeting its commitment. Using our example of the Linkway Leisure Centre, stocks do not form a large part of the current assets. In 1990, the liabilities of the Centre were covered by liquid assets whereas in 1991 the liquid assets were insufficient to cover liabilities.

Linkway Leisure Centre – liquidity ratio

$$\frac{\text{Current assets}}{\text{Current liabilities}} \quad \frac{\text{Less stock}}{} \qquad \frac{1991}{215,000 - 50,000} = 0.88:1 \quad \frac{150,000 - 30,000}{100,000} = 1.20:1$$

Stock ratios

As has already been seen, stocks do not form a large part of the financial equation in this particular example and, generally, in the leisure sector they will be of less importance than compared with the manufacturing or retail sectors. The main areas that it could apply to in the leisure industry are the food and beverage sector, and retail outlets of leisure related goods.

Excessive stocks should be avoided as, apart from incidental costs such as storage, capital will be tied up which could be otherwise profitably employed. In respect of leisurewear, stocks can become obsolete as fashions change and large amounts of stocks also run the risk of being stolen. The most appropriate measure is to identify how many times the stock has been 'turned over' and replaced during the year. If the rate of stock turnover declines this means that it is taking longer for stock to be converted into debtors or cash. The ratio is calculated as:

$$\text{Stock turnover ratio} = \frac{\text{Cost of sales}}{\text{Average of opening and closing stock}}$$

The ratio can also be divided into 365 in order to ascertain the number of days, on average, which an item of stock is held before being sold.

$$\text{Stock holding period} = \frac{365}{\text{Stock turnover ratio}}$$

This ratio would be useful to apply to major or expensive stock items as these will tend to tie up most capital.

Debtors ratio

Cash may not be available to pay creditors until customers settle their accounts. Therefore an efficient credit control system ensures that funds tied up in debtors are kept to a minimum. The debtors collection period ratio indicates the average period of credit taken by debtors in days and is expressed as follows:

$$\text{Debtors collection period} = \frac{\text{Debtors}}{\text{Credit sales}} \times 365$$

It is assumed for the Linkway Leisure Centre that membership, conference income and 50 per cent of the catering and function income were invoiced income and are, therefore, credit sales. Using tables 6.1 and 6.2, the debtors collection period would, therefore, be as follows:

1991

$$\text{Debtors collection period} = \frac{90{,}000}{200{,}000 + 150{,}000 + 67{,}500} \times 365 = 78 \text{ days}$$

$$(100\% \text{ membership}) + (100\% \text{ hire}) + (50\% \text{ bar})$$

1990

$$\frac{60{,}000}{150{,}000 + 100{,}000 + 50{,}000} \times 365 = 72 \text{ days}$$

$$(100\% \text{ membership}) + (100\% \text{ hire}) + (50\% \text{ bar})$$

The debtors collection period appears high in both years, which could indicate slack credit control or that the credit policy needs reviewing. If debtor days start to increase this also increases the risk of bad debts and reduces the rate of cash flowing into the business.

The debtors figure used in the ratio is usually the closing figure as the opening debtors figure will relate to sales from the previous year. However, if the closing debtors figure is unusually high or low then the measures will be distorted. This will also be the case with seasonal businesses such as membership fees peaking at certain times during the year, which will distort the debtors position.

Creditors payments period

This is calculated in a similar way to the debtors collection period and, therefore suffers the same problems with regard to whether the year end position reflects the position for the year as a whole. The ratio will show the average period of credit taken by an organisation, and an increase in the time taken should be an indication of cash flow problems which causes the organisation to delay the payment of its creditors. The ratio used is:

$$\frac{\text{Creditors}}{\text{Credit purchases}} \times 365 = \text{creditors payments period}$$

The debtors and creditors ratios are useful for internal purposes, but it is difficult to extract them from published accounts as, invariably, the credit sales and purchases figure are not disclosed.

Medium and long-term measures of solvency

The capital structure of an organisation depicts its long-term financial position and is the foundation upon which the short-term financial activities will be carried out. Managers, investors and shareholders will want to analyse the capital structure of a business in order to assess its longer-term financial stability and also for the purposes of financing decisions.

From where should money be obtained in order to finance expansion? Should it come from additional equity or from borrowings? What will the effect of changing capital structures have on the business? What will be the impact on returns if the capital structure is altered? There are a number of ratios that can be used to analyse the capital structure.

Investment/coverage ratios
Ordinary dividend cover

This ratio indicates how many times the profit available for ordinary dividend distribution covers the actual dividend paid. This ratio is important to the investor since it is a measure of an organisations ability to maintain dividends at their current level, it gives the investor some idea of security of future dividends, and investors can check to ensure that management are not paying out all earnings but are pursuing a prudent policy of ploughing back some part of the annual profit into the business.

Investors and would be investors may use these ratios as a basis for future investment decisions. Therefore, the ratios may have a direct effect on the demand for, and the market price of, the shares. Management should, therefore, always endeavour to maintain a careful balance between the dividends and plough back policies. If dividends are too restrictive, the market price of the shares may fall. On the other hand, distribution of dividends on too generous a scale may inhibit the ability of a company to expand without resorting to fresh capital or loans, besides depleting the current liquid resources. In practice, a dividend cover of 2–3 times is commonly found. The ratio is calculated as:

$$\frac{\text{Profits after tax and preference dividends}}{\text{Ordinary dividend}}$$

Using tables 6.1 and 6.2, the ordinary dividend cover for Linkway Leisure Limited was:

$$\begin{array}{cc} 1991 & 1990 \\ \dfrac{202,500}{60,000} = 3.38 & \dfrac{150,000}{25,000} = 6.00 \end{array}$$

This is not strictly a measure of solvency, as non payment of dividends does not give the shareholders the right to force the company into liquidation. The lower the cover, the more likely it is that a reduction in profit will lead to a reduction in the dividend.

Earnings per share

This is a widely used indicator of a company's performance and investors and potential investors are particularly interested in the total net profit attributed to the shareholders. Such an amount, compared with what the directors could have in fact paid out, gives an indication of the dividend policy of the company. The ratio is:

$$\text{Earnings per share} = \frac{\text{Profit attributable to ordinary shareholders}}{\text{Average number of ordinary shares}}$$

The earnings per share of Linkway Leisure for 1990 and 1991 is:

1991	1990
$\dfrac{202,500}{600,000} = 33.75\text{p}$	$\dfrac{150,000}{600,000} = 25\text{p}$

Using tables 6.1 and 6.2, it can be seen that the earnings per share have improved from 1990 to 1991.

When compared with the actual dividend for the years it can be seen that the shareholders actually received a dividend of 10p per share in 1991 and 4.16p in 1990, which represents quite a poor dividend policy. This means that the remaining earnings per share of 23.75p in 1991 and 20.84p in 1990 were retained in the company.

	1991	1990
Dividend per share	$\dfrac{60,000}{600,000} = 10\text{p}$	$\dfrac{25,000}{600,000} = 4.16\text{p}$

Preference dividend cover

This ratio reveals the number of times preference dividend is covered by earnings and thus indicates the preference shareholders security, in so far as income is concerned. The ratio is expressed as:

$$\frac{\text{Profit after tax}}{\text{Preference dividend}}$$

Debenture interest cover

This ratio is useful to debenture holders in order to assess the ability of a company to meet its fixed interest payments. Because debenture interest is a charge and not an appropriation of profits, it is necessary to add back the interest to net profit to determine profit before interest.

The ratio is expressed as:

$$\frac{\text{Net profit after interest} + \text{Debenture interest}}{\text{Debenture interest}}$$

An investigation of Linkway's accounts reveals that debenture interest was covered 28 times in 1991.

1991	1990
$\dfrac{270,000 + 10,000}{10,000} = 28 \text{ times}$	no debenture stock

There would, therefore, have to be an extremely large decrease in profits before the company would have difficulty in meeting its commitment to debenture holders.

Dividend yield ratio

The dividends declared are always expressed as a percentage of the nominal value of issued share capital. Therefore, Linkway had a declared dividend of 20 per cent in 1991 (£60,000/£300,000) and 8.3 per cent (£25,000/£300,000) in 1990.

The true return an investor obtains is not based on the nominal value of the share, but on the current market value. Therefore, if the asset market value of Linkway shares at the end of 1991 was £1.20p, then the shareholders would be obtaining a yield of 8.3 per cent:

$$\frac{\text{Actual dividend per share}}{\text{Market price per share}} = \frac{£60,000/600,000}{1.20} = \times 100 = 8.3\%$$

Whether this is satisfactory depends on the yield acceptable to the investor, and the potential for future capital growth. In particular, this ratio should not be considered in isolation but in the light of other investment ratios such as profits retained via earnings per share.

Price/earnings ratio

The *Financial Times* and other leading financial newspapers quote daily price/earnings ratios for companies, which is given by the expression:

$$\text{PE ratio} = \frac{\text{Share price}}{\text{Earnings per share}}$$

On the assumption that a person who buys a share is buying a proportion of earnings, the larger the PE ratio, the higher is the share valued by the market. In other words, the ratio indicates at how many times the market place values earnings. Assuming a market value of £1.20p for Linkway shares, the price/earnings would be:

$$\frac{£1.20}{33.75\text{p}} = 3.56$$

In general, firms that the market believes have better prospects have a higher price/earning ratio.

Capital structure ratios
Proprietorship ratio

This ratio shows what proportion of the total funds has been provided by the shareholders of the business and what proportion has been provided by outside parties. Potential investors and lenders are interested in this ratio because they may wish to see the owners of the business owning a large proportion of the assets. This in itself could indicate the degree of commitment by the owner(s) to their business and thereby influence the decisions by potential investors as to whether they invest or not.

The ratios for Linkway are:

$$\frac{\text{Shareholders funds}}{\begin{array}{c}\text{Total capital}\\\text{employed}\end{array}}$$

1991	1990
$\frac{300,000 + 192,500}{565,000 + 215,000} = 63\%$	$\frac{300,000 + 125,000}{375,000 + 150,000} = 81\%$

Certainly a large proportion of the funds have been provided by equity. Whether this ratio is good or bad depends upon many additional factors such as the current economic climate and taxation policy regarding dividends and fixed interest payments.

Capital gearing ratio

This ratio measures the relationship between the ordinary share capital of a company and the fixed interest capital. A company with a large proportion of fixed interest capital is said to be high geared and a company with a high proportion of ordinary share capital is said to be low geared. Where the capital structure of a company is low geared, preference shareholders and debenture holders enjoy greater security, while potential dividends payable to ordinary shareholders will not be subject to violent fluctuations with variations in profits. The opposite applies to a high geared capital structure, that is, less security for preference shareholders and debenture holders, and violent fluctuations in dividends for ordinary shareholders.

This relationship between ordinary share capital and fixed interest capital is important to an ordinary shareholder because of the effects on future earning prospects. Some use of fixed interest capital is desirable provided this capital earns a profit in excess of the fixed interest charges it creates. Any such excess profit will rebound to the ordinary shareholders who thereby enjoy a higher return than if the whole capital had been contributed by them. Capital gearing is discussed in more detail in chapter fourteen.

The capital gearing ratio is:

$$\frac{\text{Fixed interest capital}}{\text{Ordinary share capital}}$$

Using table 6.1 it can be seen that the capital gearing ratio for Linkway is:

	1991	1990
$\frac{\text{Fixed interest capital}}{\text{Ordinary share capital}}$ (i.e. debentures)	$\frac{100,000}{300,000 + 192,500} = 0.20$	completely low geared as no fixed interest capital

Public sector financial ratios

The use of ratios to assess operational performance is not a common feature in the public sector. This is possibly due, in part, to an historical reliance upon assessment against budgetary performance in terms of over or underspending against various estimate headings, combined with a basic lack of information.

The potential benefits to be gained from the use and application of performance ratios were identified by the then Audit Inspectorate (now Commission) as long ago as 1983. The principles they outlined and the range of ratios they suggested are still relevant across virtually all areas of public sector leisure provisions. The original report is now out of print, but we cover the main range of ratios in some detail in the following paragraphs, which can be divided into primary and secondary ratios.

Primary ratios

Very few areas of the public sector make a profit, consequently profitability ratios are inappropriate. However, it is important to assess the ratio of income to expenditure, which reveals to what extent the operating costs of a facility or particular service area are covered by the charges raised for use or ticket prices and so forth. This ratio is simply calculated as follows:

$$\frac{\text{Income}}{\text{Operating expenditure}} \times 100\%$$

In calculating this ratio, it is advisable not to include those profit centres that do exist such as catering and bars. These should be excluded as they tend to distort the overall performance figures and should therefore be calculated separately.

In addition to knowing the recovery rate, as shown above, another useful ratio to calculate is the subsidy level, given that most operations have a net expenditure. Again, it is important to use net operating expenditure, and the calcuation is made as follows:

$$\frac{\text{Net operating expenditure}}{\text{Number of admissions}}$$

This ratio can, again, be applied equally to leisure centres where total throughput is, in the majority of cases, a known factor, as well as to theatres, entertainment events and swimming pools.

Employee costs generally represent the highest single element of expenditure of most leisure service areas and facilities. It is, therefore, useful to express this proportion of expenditure as a ratio and monitor changes over time. It is also possible to undertake comparisons with and between similar operations. This ratio is calculated as follows:

$$\frac{\text{Employee costs}}{\text{Operating expenditure}} \times 100\%$$

Once again, catering and bar related staff should be excluded from this calculation and looked at separately.

With regard to facilities, it is possible to review the level of overheads and fixed operating costs by calculating such costs as a proportion of the area of the building, as follows:

$$\frac{\text{Other operating costs}}{\text{Number of square metres in centre}}$$

Calculated regularly, this ratio allows a check to be made on any movement in overhead costs quite quickly. It also facilitates comparisons with other similar venues.

Turning to income, as we have pointed out, catering, including vending and bar sales, tend to be areas that actually provide a contribution to net income. Accordingly, these areas should be reviewed separately in the form of gross profit or cost of sales percentages, which can also be checked against industry standards. These ratios are calculated as follows:

$$\frac{\text{Bar/catering/vending gross profit}}{\text{Bar/catering/vending revenue}} \times 100\%$$

and,

$$\frac{\text{Bar/catering/vending cost of sales}}{\text{Bar/catering/vending revenue}} \times 100\%$$

The other main income ratio to concentrate upon is average spend per head, which reflects the average amount of money customers spend during their visit and/or activity, calculated as follows:

$$\frac{\text{Income}}{\text{Number of admissions}}$$

Again, catering/bar/vending income should be calculated separately, to be of most value, as follows:

$$\frac{\text{Bar/catering/vending income}}{\text{Number of admissions}}$$

Secondary ratios

The number of ratios that can be developed is almost infinite. It is possible to calculate ratios to suit virtually every purpose or need. However, there is no virtue and little to be gained in producing ratios that perform no useful function. Consequently, managers should be selective in their use, concentrating upon a few meaningful ratios that provide key information and assessment regarding performance. Once again, a common feature of secondary ratios is to exclude profit centre income and expenditure, such as catering and bars, from the base calculations.

Looking at expenditure first, detailed analysis of various headings can be obtained from using all or a selective combination of ratios, as exemplified below:

$$\frac{\text{Energy costs}}{\text{Operating expenditure}} \times 100\%$$

$$\frac{\text{Repairs and maintenance}}{\text{Operating expenditure}} \times 100\%$$

$$\frac{\text{Establishment expenses}}{\text{Operating expenditure}} \times 100\%$$

$$\frac{\text{Marketing expenditure}}{\text{Total operating expenditure}} \times 100\%$$

$$\frac{\text{Marketing expenditure}}{\text{Number of admissions}} \times 100\%$$

$$\frac{\text{Central admin. recharge*}}{\text{Operating expenditure}} \times 100\%$$

* This is more likely to be determined in the form of a service level agreement under Compulsory Competitive Tendering (CCT), but the ratio is still a useful indicator.

Similar ratios can be calculated for income across a range of activities, such as:

$$\frac{\text{Income/bar/catering/vending}}{\text{Total income}} \times 100\%$$

$$\frac{\text{Income from special events}}{\text{Total income}} \times 100\%$$

Finally, it must be borne in mind that the main benefit of producing ratios is to undertake comparisons over a period of time in order to detect trends. Consequently, it is important to ensure that information is collected on an ongoing basis and that the ratios are expressed in constant values.

Conclusion

There are a number of ratios which exist and which can be used to gain an insight into an organisation's profitabiity, liquidity, solvency and general state of health. Ratios themselves can only act as guidelines and should not form the total basis upon which decisions are made. Ratios do have limitations, and these can be partly overcome by using them either as part of inter-firm comparisons or in a time series comparison whereby the ratios are calculated for a number of years for a company. In using time series analysis, the effect of inflation and price changes need to be taken into consideration.

Other relevant factors include the basis on which assets have been valued, accounting policies and social and economic conditions within which the organisation has been operating. Information on past performance can be used as a guide to the future if allowance is made of any known changes.

Absolute figures have limited value when measuring the success or failure of a business and it is more meaningful to compare figures by means of accounting ratios. Just like an individual, an organisation's fitness depends on healthy financial proportions rather than absolute amounts, in the same way that a person's healthy weight depends upon their height.

Certain ratios are more informative than others, but they should only be used as a guide and not the basis for final conclusions. Comparisons can be made between accounting periods to establish a trend between actual or budgeted ratios, or between similar firms. However, care should be taken to ensure that the items compared are defined in the same terms and measured by the same rules.

The ratios discussed in this chapter mainly relate to interpreting a commercial set of accounts. Although the public sector also has ratios, examples of which are given in the chapter, the leisure manager will increasingly have to be aware of the commercial type ratios as a result of the need to adopt a commercial approach and commercial accounting practices within a local government environment.

References

1 Audit Inspectorate 1983 *Development and Operation of Leisure Centres; Selected Case Studies.* HMSO

Further reading

Clarkson, Elliott *Managing Money and Finance.* Gower Press
Pickles and Lafferty *Accountancy.* Pitman
Business Accounting Wood F 5th edition. Pitman
Hingley W *Accounting Made Simple.* 3rd edition

7 Strategic and long-term financial planning

The need to plan

The leisure industry covers an extremely broad and diverse range of activities, including sport, the arts, hotels, pubs, marinas, bingo, restaurants to name but a very few. Within these areas, it is possible to identify different types of activities. For example, the arts encompasses, amongst others, visual arts, theatre and music. Within these exist a further set of categories such that, for example, within theatre it is possible to identify musicals, comedy and drama. In other words, the leisure sector is vastly segmented.

Leisure providers can be found within all three sectors – public, commercial and voluntary. With the notable exception of the public sector, providers in the commercial and voluntary sectors tend to operate within specific market segments. Indeed, many have become recognisable household names that immediately relate the organisation to the area of activity. Examples include Odeon and cinemas, Forte and hotels, Center Parcs and holiday villages, the Lawn Tennis Association and the Royal Shakespeare Company.

The concentration upon a specific area of activity within the voluntary sector is usually based around the specific interest of a group of people and their desire to organise themselves around the activity, whether at the local, regional or national level. Examples include sports clubs and amateur dramatic societies at the local level, and governing bodies of sport at the national level, where they function often as both an organisation and co-ordinating body as well as a representative pressure group for a specific sport.

Because of their voluntary nature, organisations in this sector, in the main, function from year to year with very small numbers of paid staff and precarious financial positions, with a heavy reliance upon volunteer input from members. In the majority of cases, therefore, strategic planning does not figure highly in their list of jobs to do. Things are improving in some sectors however. For example, national governing bodies of sport now have to produce rolling five year development plans, updated annually, for submission with their application for annual grant-aid from the Sports Council.

A concentration upon a specific sector or sectors of the leisure market does not generally occur by chance within the commercial sector, but most often by careful design. Thus, companies specialise in areas such as casinos, ten-pin bowling, snooker, discotheques, bingo, hotels, restaurants, pubs and marinas.

The original decision to enter a particular niche market will have been based upon specific knowledge and/or experience of the particular service or product, and a strongly held belief that an acceptable level of profit would accrue from the business activity. Companies have then developed around specific services and/or products targeted at particular age and socio-economic groups in carefully selecting geographical locations around the country.

The most successful leisure businesses have strategically positioned themselves in the market and stuck rigidly to this position. Where companies have come to grief is by diversifying into unknown areas, which results in an inordinate amount of time being taken in learning the new business to the detriment of the core activity, growing too quickly or as a result of ill-judged takeovers. There have been examples of all of these in the leisure industry during the early 1990s. An example involving all three elements was the hostile bid and subsequent takeover of Pleasurerama by the much smaller Mecca Leisure. The rapid growth and associated problems of high gearing then laid Mecca open to a successful takeover by Rank. The result was a loss of two established leisure companies. In general, however, if such businesses looked back upon the cause of the failure, it would inevitably be traced, in many instances, to a deviation from their original business strategy.

Within the public sector, leisure provision tends to be multi-service, especially at the local level where there is no chance to concentrate exclusively upon a particuar service targeted at a specific age and socio-economic grouping. Local authority leisure services departments are responsible for a wide range of provision embracing sport and recreation, arts and entertainments, parks and open spaces, children's play, public halls, catering and bars, museums and more. In many instances, leisure provision is also vested in separate library departments and the community education branch of the education service, which contains the youth and adult education services. The majority of local authorities also have an active voluntary leisure sector that makes an invaluable contribution to leisure provision overall, but which also makes demands and is reliant, to varying degrees, upon the local authority.

The public sector also functions within a political framework where decision-making ultimately rests with elected representatives and not paid professionals, and where social as well as financial objectives have to be met. However, central government has impacted significantly upon local authority leisure service provision by the imposition of capital controls, compulsory competitive tendering and community charge capping. All of these measures have conspired to become a serious drain upon available resources, both in financial and human terms. This complex framework of leisure service provision makes the need for strategic planning imperative.

The planning cycle

Planning is a dynamic process and both long and short-term planning should form an integral part of the management of any business. A long-term plan covers a period of time, usually three to five years, which will enable management to determine in which direction the business should be going, identify the opportunities and problems that may exist in the future, and assess the likely level of resources that will be required to convert the plan into action. As part of the long-term planning process, management will also be able to determine their objectives and the strategy for achieving those objectives. This type of long-term planning is often known as strategic planning.

Once the strategy has been determined, it has to be translated into operational plans for managers to implement. A manager will need to organise, co-ordinate, motivate and control resources as part of this process in order to achieve the targets set. In addition, the operational plans and results need to be controlled back to the strategic plan to ensure that the overall objectives are being achieved. This is set out diagrammatically in figure 7.1.

The final stage of the planning cycle is the translation of the appropriate parts of the long-term strategic and operational plans into the short-term planning process. This can be an annual plan and is more commonly known as an annual budget. The annual budget needs to work within the existing environment, known constraints and physical, human and financial resources that exist. The budget and budgetary control processes are the subject of Chapter eight whereas this chapter focuses on long-term planning.

It is important to clarify the division between strategic and short-term operational decisions. Strategic decisions are concerned with the *raison d'être* of an organisation. The strategy determines the purpose of the business and what it should be doing. Strategic decisions might include, for example, issues of opportunities and risks and will involve decisions on specialisation and diversification, products and service strategy, new markets, new investments, raising capital and acquiring other businesses. Such decisions often have to be made with incomplete information as they involve uncertainty and risk, and it will be necessary to assess the probability of certain events happening over a long-term horizon.

Short-term operational decisions tend to deal with matters arising over days and weeks. Whereas strategic decisions tend to be outward looking, short-term decisions tend to look inwards and are more concerned with how best to utilise available resources within existing policy. More facts are usually available to make short-term decisions, which are normally operational in nature and where the degree of uncertainty is not so great.

Figure 7.1 The manager's role in the planning process

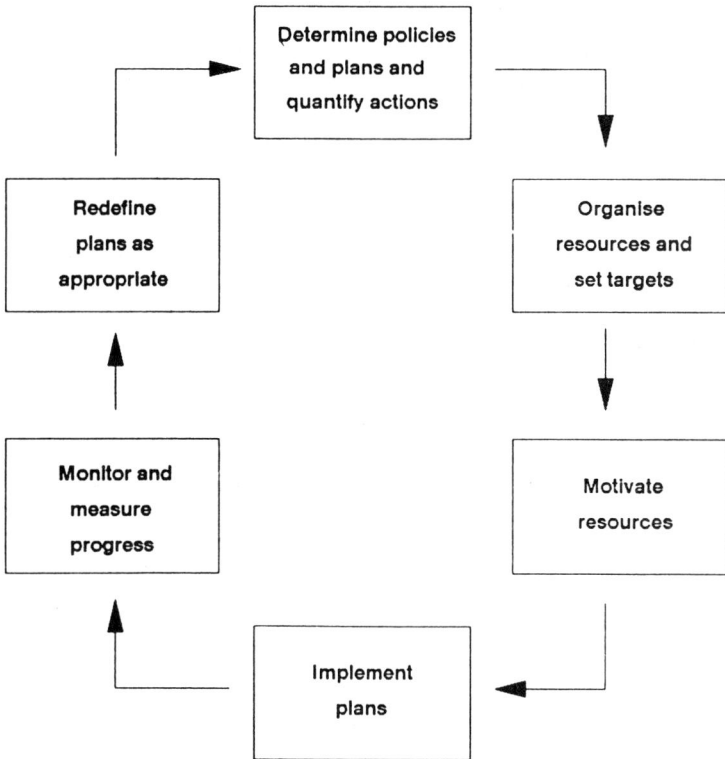

Strategic planning

As long-term financial planning is an integral part of strategic planning, it is necessary first to consider the strategic planning process. This is done in the context of a strategic plan for leisure in a local authority. However, the key components have equal applicability to the commercial and voluntary sector.

Local authorities have had to accommodate a great deal of change, with new legislation, compulsory competitive tendering, increasing demands from customers for greater choice and different types of service provision and mechanisms of service delivery. Consequently, a strategic approach to the planning, provision and development of leisure opportunities will provide guidance for the public, commercial and voluntary sectors on which are the needs of the community, what are the opportunities or improvements that need to be made, how the objectives are going to be achieved and how the respective organisations can best work together.

The strategy should be a statement of the key issues and policies which determine the appropriate course or courses of action. It should also be sufficiently flexible to enable it to evolve to accommodate new issues and changing demands. A strategy is not a technical document with detailed proposals, action plans or work programmes, but is intended to provide a framework from which the other plans and proposals evolve.

Review of existing policies and practises

At the outset of the process, it is necessary to identify current aims, policies, responsibilities and practises. It will be necessary to highlight any problems that exist, constraints or particular pressure areas. A profile of the major service areas should be established to identify the key elements of the leisure service, what is being provided, who uses it and the major strengths and weaknesses of each service area.

External influences

The next stage will be to review the impact that major external influences may have on leisure service provision in the authority. This would include any proposed legislative changes and changes in the demographic or economic profiles of the area. Where possible, the policies of other major organisations should also be reviewed where they may impact upon the authority – such as Government initiatives, national agencies, other local authorities, the National, Regional and Local Sports Councils and governing bodies.

Determine aims, objectives and issues

Having identified the current position, it is necessary to formulate the aims and objectives and identify the role that the local authority wants to adopt – direct provider or enabler.

It is necessary to establish the overall aim of the strategy, taking into consideration the results so far identified, and also the corporate and social objectives of the authority as a whole. A number of sub-aims should also be identified. The Sports Council in its publication, *District Sports & Recreation Strategies: A Guide*, put forward the following model aims for a strategy:

Aims: Foundation
        among young people, particularly primary school age, the
        acquisition of basic movement and sports skills to provide

foundation for personal development and future participation in the sport of their choice.

Participation

among all members of the community the opportunity to take part in a wide range of activities, whether for reasons of enjoyment, fitness, social contact or simply the desire to get involved in sport.

Performance

among those already participating the opportunity to improve their performance from whatever base they start; where the desire to improve is the key factor for involvement and the full realisation of improved performance is the attainment of personal excellence.

Excellence

among those with the interest and ability, the opportunity to achieve publicly recognised levels of excellence.

Having established the broad aims, it is possible to develop the objectives. These have three major benefits:

- they set out what work needs to be done;
- they establish a schedule and priority for the work; and
- they identify where everyone in the organisation fits into the scheme of things and what is expected of them.

An organisation without objectives can be likened to a rudderless ship that just drifts around in the currents, being taken in different directions at different times according to the strength of a particular influence. The result is very little forward progress and a great deal of frustration, with a poor rate of achievement. Objectives give both direction and purpose and allow resources to be channelled to achieving a desired end result at a predetermined speed.

Aims and objectives are very often confused. Whereas aims are general, long-term statements of intent, as set out above, objectives are specific, short-term statements that are action-oriented in terms of what action is to take place, when and with what anticipated outcome or results. Thus, the basic requirements of objectives are that they:

- are in writing;
- are specific;
- are realistic;
- are quantifiable and measurable;
- identify the results that are expected;
- clearly state the time limits for their achievement; and specify priorities.

Setting objectives is part of a continuing management process. Having set them, it is necessary to decide how best to implement them, which requires an action plan. Once a particular course of action has been embarked upon, it is essential to review progress regularly and decide upon any different courses of action that may be necessary. The number of objectives set will depend upon what is felt appropriate to give direction and, subsequently, allow effective control of the operation. Generally, however, four or five major objectives is a realistic norm during any one particular period of time.

The formulation of aims and objectives should then lead to questions and issues which need to be further addressed, such as:

- What opportunities exist for the local authority target groups and what are the most appropriate ways of allocating resources to increase participation?
- What opportunities and facilities need to be created to increase participation across the community?
- What improvements can be made in working with the education sector?
- What are the financial objectives associated with service provision?

Determine policy

It will then be necessary to examine the key issues and determine the policies and courses of action that can be pursued to achieve the objectives. As part of the progress of determining the policies, the authority should identify its strengths and weaknesses, identifying what resources and skills are required to carry out the policy – what are the critical resources and is the proposed strategy appropriate for the available resources?

As part of the process of determining the policy, each course of action should be appraised against selected criteria so that the most appropriate courses of action can be incorporated in the strategic plan.

The financial plan

Financial planning is a fundamental part of the strategic planning process and every decision and policy issue needs to be considered not just in the light of its current impact, but as to its longer term impact as a whole. Plans need to be translated into objectives, which also have to be formulated in financial terms, supporting information needs to be reviewed and alternative courses of action need to be evaluated. It is essential to understand the long-term financial implications of a policy in terms of profit/loss, cash flow and financing requirements.

As part of the financial planning process it is necessary to:

- Prepare background information which will serve as a prelude to planning. This will include information on past performance, demand analysis, utilisation profiles, cost-volume-profit relationships of existing services, contribution/losses of appropriate services and facilities.
- Assess the financial feasibility of proposed courses of action as part of the evaluation process. The information that is produced should be on a sufficiently reliable basis for the purposes of aiding the decision-making process.
- Consolidate the various financial plans into a master financial plan and assess the overall financial implications on the business.
- Undertake various 'what if?' scenarios to take into consideration the probability of certain factors arising.

It is also important that controls are established to help monitor the achievement in reaching the planned objectives. This phase of the process requires the integration of both long and short-term financial plans and the introduction of reporting mechanisms to management.

The strategic planning cycle is set out diagrammatically at figure 7.2.

Figure 7.2 The strategic planning process

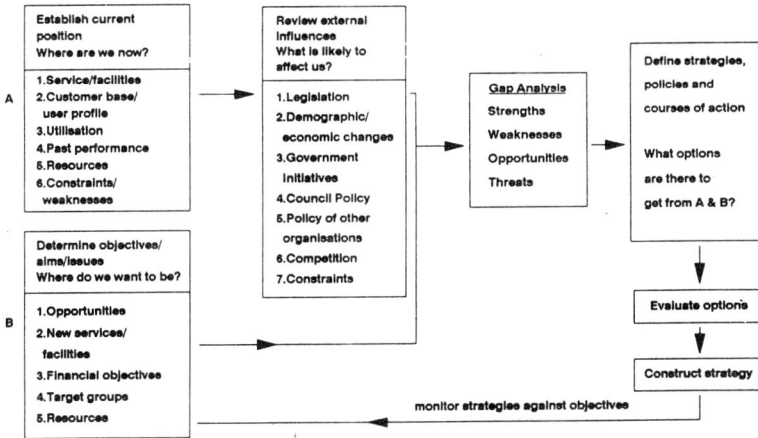

The financial evaluation of long range plans is quite copmplex, as they are invariably prepared against a background of economic uncertainty and unknown factors. Yet, if an organisation is to undertake long range planning successfully, it is important to attach financial projections to the proposals, even if they can only be regarded as broad estimates based on assumptions about the future.

Management should always be made aware of the assumptions on which the financial plans are based and the limits of their accuracy so that the appropriate degree of caution can be used when reviewing them. Long range financial plans should be flexible and dynamic, capable of being updated to meet changing needs. They should be updated:

- annually, to take into consideration progress against the annual plan;
- whenever an event of significant impact takes place which will necessitate a change in the organisation's strategy;
- every five years or so, in order for the basic objectives to be redefined and the strategy to be revised accordingly.

The need for a strategic approach to business these days is well established as organisations face new challenges and ever increasing demand for change. There are many different ways in which strategies can be developed and controlled, but finance is a thread that is common to all plans as long-term financial planning is an integral part of the strategic approach.

References

Sports Council *District Sports and Recreation Strategies: A Guide.* HMSO

8 Budgets and budgetary control

Financial planning is a fundamental part of the strategic planning process, which sets out the long-term plans and objectives of an organisation. A budget is concerned with financial planning in the short-term. Unfortunately, many managers view a budget as a time consuming exercise and, once produced, they are required to adhere to their budget until the exercise comes round again.

In reality, however, the budget is the financial action plan that reflects the objectives and activities of an organisation. It draws together all the activities and sets out in financial terms what has to be achieved over the budget period. More importantly, the budget allows managers to co-ordinate and control the activities of their organisation.

When a budgetary control system is used, budgets should be determined which set out in financial terms the responsibilities of managers in relation to the determined policy. Each responsibility area will, therefore, normally have a detailed budget so that the manager can see what resources are available for use, how they are to be used and what is the expected end result. The detailed budgets are then consolidated into the Master budget, which constitutes the overall short-term financial plan for the business.

The types of budgets that would be constructed in a commercial organisation differ from those found in the public sector. In the commercial sector, it would be more usual to commence with the preparation of a sales budget, from which the operating, manpower, administration, marketing and cash budgets would all tend to flow. As part of the annual budgeting process in the public sector, the main budgets that are produced are the revenue (income and expenditure) budgets, the capital budgets and the cash budget.

A capital budget is a statement of what the organisation intends to spend each year on various capital schemes over a number of years (traditionally over a three to five year period). Capital budgets will normally be prepared and updated as part of the annual budgetary cycle and be presented for approval at the same time as the annual revenue budget. This is logical, as it allows the aspects of both capital and revenue finances to be looked at together.

The annual budget is a statement of income and expenditure that will be attributable to an organisation during the course of a year, including the revenue consequences arising from any capital expenditure. In public sector organisations the annual revenue budget will take into consideration Government grants and subsidies and expected income from fees and charges. The annual revenue budget will be used to determine the local tax that needs to be levied in order to balance income and expenditure for the year.

Budgets which relate to a particular function of an organisation are termed functional budgets and for control purposes a budget will normally be further sub-divided into budget centres. Each budget centre is either an individual cost centre or a group of cost centres since the costs must be separately contained from the costs of other budget centres. The main issue in respect of setting up a budget centre is that one person must be responsible for controlling all its costs.

Constructing a budget

Although various budgets may be prepared, it is important that they are co-ordinated to provide an overview of the organisation. The steps that tend to be taken are:

- Prepare the assumptions on which the plans are to be produced.
- Prepare a forecast of the general economic conditions within which the organisation will be operating.
- Prepare sales/income budgets based on the projections and the capacity of the organisation.
- Prepare the appropriate annual expenditure budgets.
- Prepare a capital expenditure budget.
- Prepare a cash budget.
- Co-ordinate the individual budgets into a master budget.
- Discuss and agree the budgets with all concerned.

It is important that the budgets are prepared by the individuals that have the responsibility for their achievement in order to engender some form of ownership of and commitment to the budgets produced. It is, therefore, important that the budgeting procedure contains some form of motivation, such as performance related pay, so that achievement of the budget will be in the best interests of both the individual, or the function which the individual controls, and also in the interests of the organisation as a whole.

The construction of a budget for the respective activities of an organisation is an aid to cost control in itself as it focuses a manager's attention on the areas for which he is responsible. As the manager will invariably have to discuss the budgets with others and explain the reason for certain courses of action, it should mean that the manager will give thought to the budget to ensure that it is realistic and capable of scrutiny. This is only one part of the control process, which is discussed later in this chapter.

The type of budget that needs to be produced should also be considered – should it be, for example, a fixed budget, a flexible budget or a rolling budget.

A fixed budget is designed to remain unchanged irrespective of the level of activity achieved. A fixed budget may be suitable in circumstances where actual costs are compared with budgeted costs and where it is difficult to measure the level of activity achieved by a cost centre. For example, a marketing budget may be a fixed budget. However, the budget will only show the costs associated with the budgeted level of activity, and if the actual level of activity is different to the budgeted level the comparisons between budgets and actuals will be misleading.

A flexible budget, on the other hand, recognises the difference in behaviour between fixed, semi-variable and variable costs and their relation to the changes in the level of activity attained. If the activity level deviates from the original budgeted level then a flexible budget would allow for the variable costs achieved to be measured against the appropriate budgeted level of costs. In these circumstances, a flexible budget will enable managers to make appropriate comparisons between budgets and actual results. In order to prepare such a budget, it is necessary to divide costs into fixed, variable and semi-variable.

A rolling budget is where the short-term budget is continuously updated by replacing the budget of the latest month with the achievements. In this way, the budget reflects current conditions. Such an approach is beneficial where future costs or activity levels cannot be forecast with any degree of accuracy.

The commercial sector will tend to adopt a fixed or flexible budget that is most appropriate to their business needs. The public sector, however, tends to be more fixed in its approach, either tending to rely on historical performance to construct its budgets or just applying a percentage for inflation, to prior year figures irrespective of any changes in the level of activity.

Limitations of traditional budgeting methods

The chief executive and other members of the senior management team in every organisation are faced with conflicting demands on the use of resources. The demand to improve or maintain services often conflicts with the demand to minimise costs and keep within financial limits or meet competitive pressures. Also, the demand for growth and technological development, often requiring significant allocation of today's funds to meet tomorrow's new product, process or market, conflicts with the demand for this year's profit and cash flow. These conflicting pressures can be acute and, in many instances, the survival of the organisation has been at stake.

Decisions on the use of resources have to be made or confirmed at the time of preparing the annual budget or profit plan, but traditional budgeting systems do not provide the kinds of information needed to resolve conflicting priorities satisfactorily. Whilst most organisations put considerable effort into evaluating capital expenditure proposals, they often do not apply the same scrutiny to revenue expenditure, even though in many instances the distinction between capital and revenue expenditure is not always clear-cut and, in some situations, revenue expenditure is of greater significance to the future of the organisation.

Under traditional planning and budgeting methods, management's attention is focused primarily onto proposed changes from the previous year's level of spending, a process which is known as 'incremental' budgeting. Considerable effort may go into the development of these budgets, usually by financial managers, but the base level of spending tends to be regarded as already authorised and does not come under the same intensity of review as proposals for new expenditure.

The difficulty in reviewing current activities is aggravated further under traditional methods by the way in which budgets are presented. They do not normally provide senior management with enough information about alternative methods, nor about the consequences of reducing, or the benefits of increasing, the funds allocated into particular areas. The budgets are usually presented in the form of an accounting schedule, as a statement only of the resources required. There is often little indication of the way in which the figures have been built up, although managers may have made detailed preparatory analyses of the alternatives in reaching their budgets.

In times when the pressure to reduce costs and obtain better value for money is great, the effect of the traditional approach is to constrain any new developments or forward initiatives and often to force management into arbitrary cost reduction programmes, cutting x per cent across the board, which can be very harmful. The process by which an acceptable consolidated budget is achieved involves the recycling of departmental budgets, which in large organisations can go on for some time. The effect of this on management can be demoralising and inevitably generates defensive attitudes.

Zero base budgeting

Zero Base Budgeting is a technique which attempts to overcome the limitations of traditional budgeting and is applicable to both the public and private sector. Accordingly, the process aims to help managers at each level in the organisation to understand better the alternatives available and to simplify the task of developing an annual operating plan. The resulting plan should balance the relevant priorities of different demands on funds and carry the commitment of line managers.

Zero Base Budgeting is a planning process which involves the managers responsible for each function in making a re-assessment of their activities and documenting proposals for review by senior management. In doing this, each manager is required to:

- Establish the purposes of his activities and evaluate alternative ways of achieving them.
- Define the absolute minimum or standard level (and lowest cost) at which service could be provided, or standard to satisfy essential requirements only.
- Identify successive incremental levels of service and their costs and benefits to satisfy the more discretionary requirements of the function.

The necessity for the continued existence of the activities is questioned, alternatives are considered and eventually the optimum way of carrying out the activity is included in the budget.

The main benefits of Zero Base Budgeting compared with traditional budgeting are that it will enable senior management to:

- allocate resources better to departments and activities;
- achieve, more rationally, cost reductions after careful consideration of the consequences; and
- identify opportunities more easily to improve efficiency, both immediately and in the longer term.

An important feature of the process is that it is led by senior management and allows a high degree of involvement of managers at all levels in the organisation. It thereby enables the ideas, creative energy and commitment of the budget centre managers to be harnessed, whilst senior management gain greater insight into all activities, assign priorities and are assured that current and emerging needs are given due weight.

Many organisations produce budgets once a year for the following twelve months. Other organisations choose shorter budget periods or update their original budgets during the course of a year, and this will depend upon the stability of the market and economic conditions.

Budgetary control

Once the budgets are established, and for them to be of any further value, it is necessary to introduce a budgetary control process so that actual results are compared with budgeted results. The control process is important so that managers can review progress and react as necessary where deviations from the budget occur in an attempt to bring the performance of the activity for which they are responsible back on course.

A budget is normally broken down into monthly periods for the purposes of control and the actual results achieved each month should be compared with the budgeted results for that month and usually the same month for the previous year. When determining the appropriate control periods, consideration should be given to the nature of the business, the needs of managers, the information that is available and the cost of producing additional information for control purposes.

Budgetary control will normally be exercised over the period that has been determined, usually a month, and reports should be prepared for managers on a timely basis to enable them to compare actual performance with budget. The reports should show:

- the annual and monthly budgets;
- the actual income and expenditure for the year to date;
- the variance between actual and budget.

If the comparisons show significant variations, this will need to be highlighted, investigated and action taken accordingly. The report should be appropriate to the needs of the manager and be available five to ten days, or as soon as possible, after the month end to be of any significant value.

Figure 8.1 sets out an example of a budgetary control report for a cost centre.

Figure 8.1   Budgetary control statement

COST CENTRE : _____   MONTH : _____
MANAGER   : _____

Same month last year		Month					Year to Date			
Actual	Detail	Budget	Actual	Budget Variance		Budget	Actual	Budget Variance	
				£	%			£	%
	Income								
	Fees								
	Charges								
	Total Income								
	Expenditure								
	Salaries								
	Wages								
	Total Expenditure								
	Surplus/(Loss)								

Where possible, graphical presentation of results should also be considered. This can provide a quick and easy means of identifying problem areas and is often an easier means of recognising the extent of deviation from budget. Comparison results with prior years is also invaluable in showing trends. Invariably, managers can understand better what is happening in their areas when it is presented graphically.

Figure 8.2 shows an example of actual income compared with budget income from which it can be seen at a glance that, from month six onwards, the underachievement each month is increasing and budgeted growth is not being achieved.

Figure 8.2 Graphical presentation of actual income compared with budgeted income

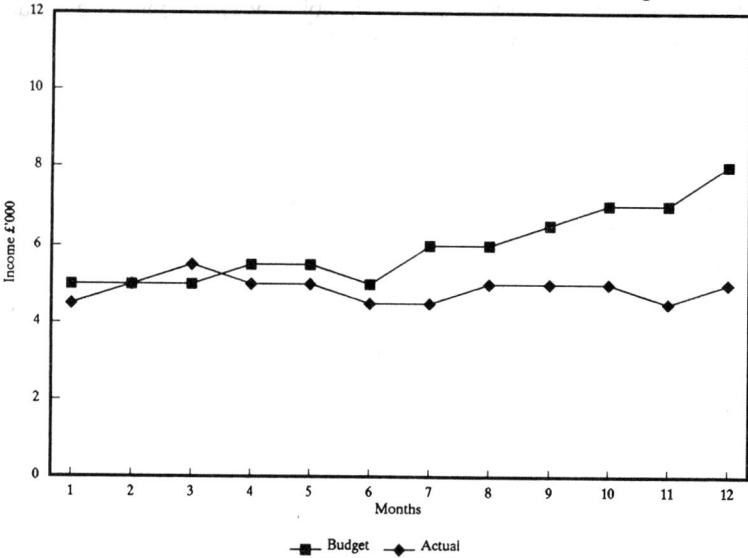

Figure 8.3 shows how comparison with previous years allows trends to be easily seen. This shows that, with the exception of month three, income for 1991 was higher than that achieved in 1990. In addition, the 1990 results did not experience the same peak and trough effect between months four and eight as was experienced in 1991.

Figure 8.3 Graphical presentation of actual income achieved showing comparisons between 1990 and 1991

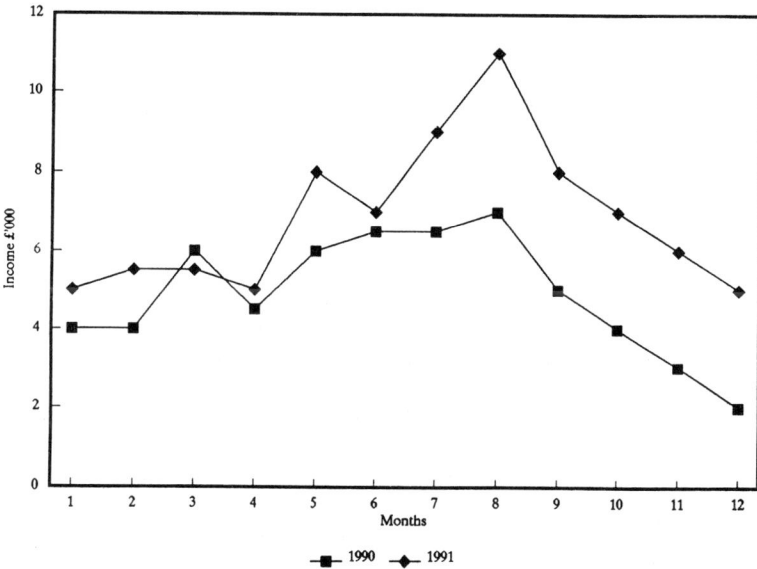

Budgetary control properly applied can be immensely valuable to those in charge of a business. It is, however, not without its dangers unless skill and intelligence are exercised both in devising the budgets and in implementing the plans to achieve them.

A leisure operation is a dynamic thing, and conditions both inside and outside the organisation constantly change. A budget should be viewed as a framework and should not be allowed to hinder the development of the operation. New opportunities must be taken where appropriate and the budget must not be used as an excuse for rejecting them. On the other hand, a continual and haphazard approach without regard to plans can deflect attention from the main objectives, and may, therefore, be dangerous. Budgetary control should ensure that new and unforeseen opportunities are directed to the level of authority capable of dealing with them. They should be neither accepted nor rejected out of hand, and the existence of budgets should assist in deciding whether they can be accommodated in the light of the overall plans for the business.

It is important to remember that organisations are controlled by people and not by financial control systems. Cost control is achieved when people take appropriate action to control costs. Budgetary control, in common with other systems of financial control, provides information which helps managers take appropriate action. An organisation will not experience the full benefits of a budgetary control system unless the managers are fully involved in establishing and operating the system and in revising the budgets whenever this becomes necessary.

Conclusion

Budgets set out the financial responsibilities of managers in relation to the requirements of the overall policy of the organisation. Actual achievement is continually compared with budgeted results, which assists management in planning, coordinating and controlling the activities of a business and provides a basis for revision to policy as necessary.

Managers should be responsible for their own budgets, including their initial preparation, in order to create ownership of the figures. Reports appropriate to the needs of managers should be produced for budgetary control purposes and, where possible, graphical presentation of results generally enhances understanding. The principles and techniques of budgeting and budgetary control apply equally to the public, private and voluntary sectors. In the public sector, with the introduction of compulsory competitive tendering, direct service organisation managers are having to work to more commercially orientated principles with greater accountability for the budgets they control.

Further reading

Rawlinson D, Tanner B *Financial Management in the 1990s.* Longman

9 The concept of cost

As part of the business process, managers need information on the cost of their facilities and products to be able to appraise past performance, determine and control future costs and to be in a position of making informed decisions. Information on costs must be relevant, accurate and as up to date as possible. The accuracy of information on costs depends directly upon the accuracy with which information is recorded.

Types of costs

There is also a need for managers to be able to understand the types of costs that they are dealing with and the impact that the various categories of costs could have upon their business. One major method of classifying costs is into fixed and variable costs. Variable costs are those which alter in direct proportion to the volume of business. For example, in catering facilities the costs of provisions will be directly proportional to the number of covers that are turned over. Fixed costs, however, are costs that do not alter with changes in business volume. For example, the rates and interest charges of a leisure centre will be constant irrespective of the number of people using the centre. Generally, leisure facilities have a higher proportion of fixed as opposed to variable costs, which is due to the high level of staffing and building related costs. Consequently, the greater the number of people using the facilities, the higher the proportion of fixed costs that are recovered.

In between these two extremes are semi-fixed and semi-variable costs, which vary as the level of activity changes, but not in direct proportion to the increase in activity. An example of a semi-fixed cost would be a coach under sub-contract who is providing coaching courses at a leisure centre. Until the course has reached maximum capacity the coach will be able to deal with increasing numbers of people.

However, once the maximum capacity of that course and coach has been reached, it will be necessary to hire a second coach to cater for the demand. This results in a 'stepped' form of relationship between cost and the volume of users.

It is important for managers to understand how costs behave in response to changes in the level of activity as this will assist them in controlling costs and making decisions on alternative courses of action. The behaviour of the costs in relation to changes in output have been set out in figure 9.1.

Figure 9.1 Relationship of costs to volume of business

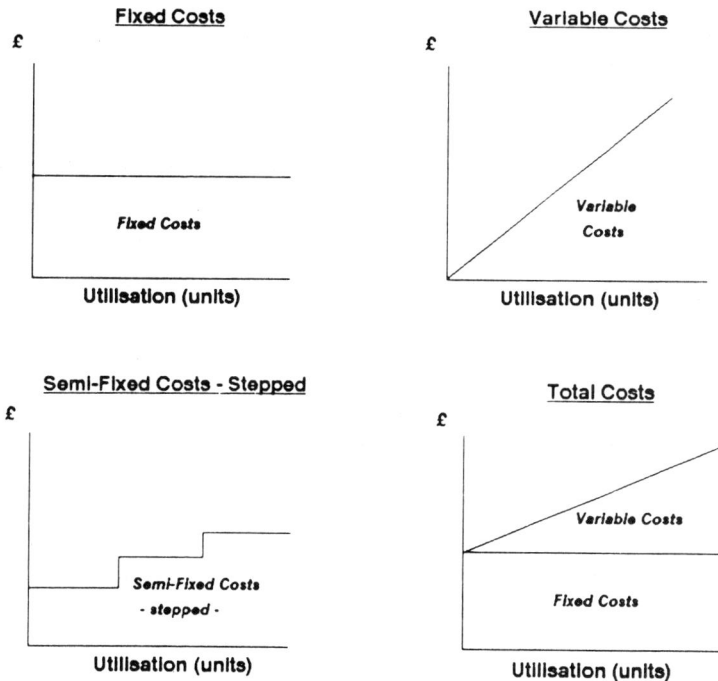

Taking the example of a restaurant in a hotel, it is possible to show how the different categories of cost vary with volume. Assuming that the restaurant has the following costs:

- Food costs — £4 per meal;
- Chef — £20,000 per annum;
- Waitresses — £3,000 per annum, each capable of dealing with 5,000 meals; and
- Building related costs — £16,000 per annum.

It is possible to undertake a cost analysis for the preparation and serving of 0, 1000, 5000, 8000, 10000 and 12000 meals, as follows:

Table 9.1 Cost analysis for the preparation of meals

Number of Meals	0	1000	5000	8000	10000	12000
Variable costs						
– food	0	4000	20000	32000	40000	48000
Semi-fixed costs						
– waitresses	3000	3000	3000	6000	6000	9000
Fixed costs						
– chef	20000	20000	20000	20000	20000	20000
– building costs	16000	16000	16000	16000	16000	16000
Total costs	39000	43000	59000	74000	82000	93000

The analysis in table 9.1 shows that food costs are totally variable and increase in direct proportion to the number of meals produced. Conversely, the building is there and has to be heated and lit, the kitchens will consume energy and the chef has to be there also to prepare and cook the meals irrespective of the number of meals produced. However, while it is essential to have waitresses to serve the prepared meals to the customers, the actual number required varies according to the number of meals being ordered and prepared. This, therefore, represents a semi-fixed cost, which steps upward according to the volume of meals needing to be served and the capacity of each waitress, which is 5,000 meals.

By undertaking this type of analysis, the restaurant manager knows precisely at which point he needs to bring in additional waitresses and how it will affect his costs and, ultimately, his profit. By aggregating these costs, he arrives at the total costs, from which he is able to determine the price of the meals in order to recover costs and achieve the required profit margin. Differing costs and their relationship to each other are shown graphically at figure 9.2.

Figure 9.2 Cost analysis for the provision of meals in a restaurant

£'000

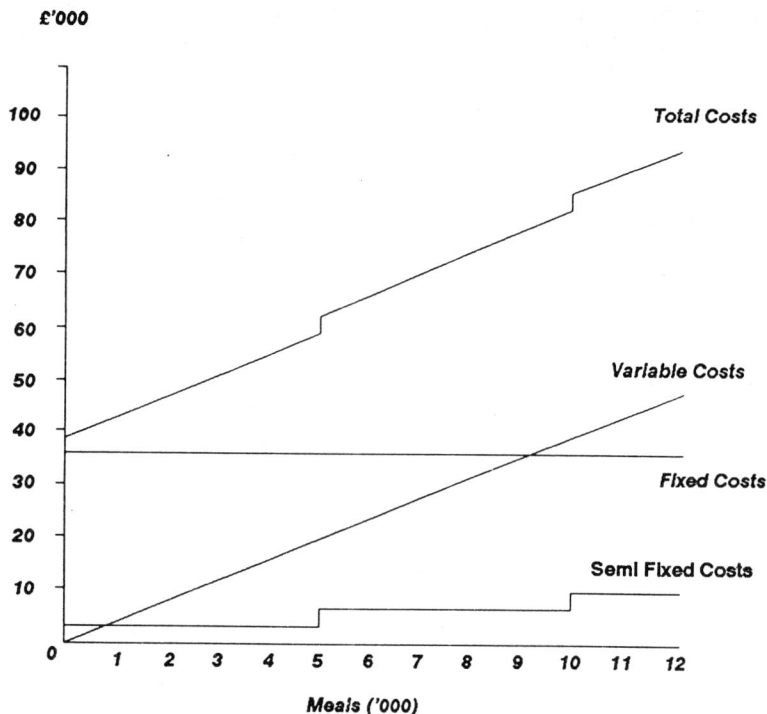

Cost centres

In order for managers to be able to effectively control their operation, it is important for them to be aware of the costs over which they have control and responsibility and then to have information which readily identifies these costs. Another method of classifying costs, which also aids control, is by cost centre, whereby a cost will be charged, where appropriate, to a cost centre to which the charge relates. For example, in a leisure complex each of the main elements, swimming pool, health suite, tennis, squash and restaurant facilities, should all be independent cost centres. The costs of each of these facilities should then be collected against the individual cost centres.

Costs which can be readily identified to a cost centre are known as direct costs. For example, the cost of swimming pool attendants, whose job is to solely man the swimming pool is a direct cost attributable to a swimming pool. If those swimming pool attendants, say, spend 75 per cent of their time manning the swimming pool and 25 per cent of their time helping out in the health suite, their costs are still direct costs but 75 per cent of them can be allocated to the swimming pool cost centre and 25 per cent to the health suite cost centre.

There are also costs that exist which cannot be related to a particular cost centre, which are known as indirect costs. These include senior management salaries, administrative costs, and costs such as heat and light. These indirect costs are, in turn, known as overheads. If it was decided to establish the total cost attributable to each cost centre, it would be necessary to clarify the proportion of overheads that relate to each cost centre. As the overheads cannot be charged and identified directly, they would need to be apportioned over the relevant cost centres in an appropriate and agreed basis. For example, rent and rates could be apportioned across the cost centres, based on the area that each facility occupies as a percentage of the whole building. Marketing costs could be apportioned in relation to turnover and electricity costs could be apportioned on the cubic capacity of the facilities.

Methods of costing

There are many methods of apportionment that can be used and there is no one method that can act as a standard by which the 'correct' cost of a facility can be established. However, the basic principles are to allocate costs, where possible, on the basis of services consumed. Where this is not possible, it is necessary to apportion costs on the basis of a factor which approximates to the amount of service consumed.

In addition to there being many different methods of apportionment, there are different schools of thought as to whether overheads should be apportioned or not. The costing convention used will really depend upon the purposes for which the cost is to be used and, unless the costs are prepared with a specific purpose in mind, they may in effect be useless and provide management with incorrect information on which to base their decisions.

Absorption or full costing

Under the absorption costing concept both variable and fixed costs are charged to cost centres in an attempt to ascertain the total cost of each of the facilities. It is important to avoid unduly complicated methods yet at the same time provide reasonable methods of allocation and apportionment, otherwise the facility costs become distorted and meaningless.

It can be argued that such a concept, apart from being complicated, may yield results which are divorced from reality. However, there are circumstances in which apportionments should be attempted, if a full cost recovery concept is the objective. These include:

- the costing and pricing of leisure service contracts;
- calculating performance bonuses for managers payable upon the profits and performance of the particular facilities or cost centres which they manage;
- calculating prices.

Even if a concept other than full cost recovery is used in determining pricing structures, it is useful to ascertain the full cost of each facility to determine, in the long run, the extent of cost recovery for each of the facilities and also the degree of cross-subsidisation. A hypothetical example of full costing is shown in table 9.2.

Table 9.2 Full costing analysis of the annual results of a leisure centre

	Swimming £	Squash £	Tennis £	Catering £	Total £
Income	400,000	120,000	250,000	100,000	870,000
Variable costs	190,000	30,000	70,000	40,000	330,000
Fixed costs	260,000	50,000	100,000	15,000	425,000
Profit	(50,000)	40,000	80,000	45,000	115,000

On the basis of table 9.2, some managers could argue that if the loss making activity, swimming, were to be no longer provided, then the overall profit would increase by £50,000. However, this is not the case because if the fixed costs cannot be reduced, they would still have to be borne by the remaining activities of the centre. The overall profit of the centre, therefore, would fall if the swimming activity were discontinued.

Marginal costing

A technique which is more useful in ascertaining the impact of changes in level of usage both on costs and profit is marginal costing. Marginal costs are variable costs which vary in direct proportion to the level of activity and would be avoided if the facility was not provided.

The difference between the selling price of an activity and its marginal costs is known as the contribution which the activity makes towards the fixed costs and the profit of a business. Only the marginal costs will be charged to the cost centre activities and the overheads are then written off in total against the sum of all the contributions made.

Marginal costing is a technique which can be used to make decisions as contained in the following example. Presenting the same figures as in table 9.2, but on a marginal cost basis, enables the contributions to be ascertained that each activity makes to the centre as a whole. A clearer picture can be seen when analysing the costs on a marginal cost basis, and this is demonstrated in table 9.3.

Table 9.3 Marginal cost analysis of the annual results of a leisure centre

	Swimming £	Squash £	Tennis £	Catering £	Total £
Income	400,000	120,000	250,000	100,000	870,000
Variable costs	190,000	30,000	70,000	40,000	330,000
Contribution	210,000	90,000	180,000	60,000	540,000
Less fixed overheads					425,000
Profit					115,000

It can be seen from the marginal cost example at table 9.3 that, in fact, swimming makes the largest contribution to fixed costs. If swimming were discontinued and the space, as is likely, could not be redeployed for other activities, the disastrous results shown in table 9.4 could be expected:

Table 9.4   Potential results with swimming activity discontinued

	Squash £	Tennis £	Catering £	Total £
Income	120,000	250,000	100,000	470,000
Variable costs	30,000	70,000	40,000	140,000
Contributions	90,000	180,000	60,000	330,000
Less fixed overheads				425,000
Profit (Loss)				(96,000)

The business has turned from a profit into a loss making situation as it has closed down the swimming activity which, although in itself appears to make a loss, actually provides the greatest contribution towards fixed costs and overheads.

The concept of cost centering down to activities is not currently widely used in the leisure industry as difficulties tend to be experienced, especially in the public sector, in ascertaining the costs and methods of apportionment. However, it is important, through a cost centre approach, to attempt to identify costs otherwise the process of decision-making and, more especially, price determination cannot be made with any degree of certainty.

In general, the vast proportion of costs associated with leisure facilities tend to be fixed costs which do not vary with the level of utilisation. Consequently, if spare capacity exists within a centre, it may be desirable to increase the utilisation so that fixed costs can be spread over a greater customer base. This could be achieved by, say, reducing prices, and is discussed further in chapter ten on Pricing decisions. The relationship between the cost categories per cost unit and the number of cost units is shown in figure 9.3.

Figure 9.3   Relationship between fixed, variable and total costs per unit of output

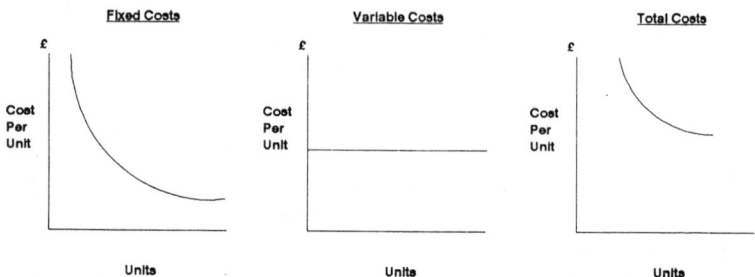

From figure 9.3, the variable cost chart shows that the variable cost per unit will be the same, irrespective of the number of units of output. However, the fixed cost per unit will decrease as the number of units of output increase.

Break even

It is important for managers to understand the relationship between cost, volume and profit as this may be essential in decision-making, especially where there may be a limiting factor or choice involved. One of the easiest methods of illustrating the relationship between volume of output, cost and profit is by a break-even chart. This shows the fixed and variable costs and sales revenues at various volumes of output. The break-even point is the level of activity at which an organisation is making neither a profit or a loss, that is, the point at which total income equals the level of cost.

The level of output above the break-even point is the margin of safety, and represents the amount by which the activity may fall before it reaches break-even point and moves into a loss making situation. Using the restaurant example contained in table 9.1, and assuming sales at an average of £10 per head, the break-even chart would be represented as set out in figure 9.4.

Figure 9.4 Break even chart for the provision of meals in a restaurant

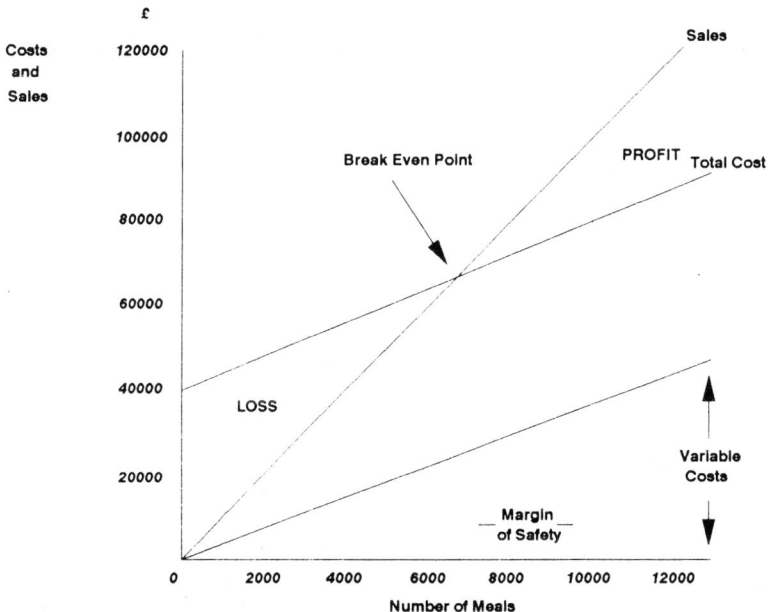

As can be seen from the chart, the break-even point arises at 6,800 meals, at which point total sales generated will be 6,800 meals × £10

= £68,000. Reading from the vertical axis, the total cost incurred at this level of activity is £68,000. Therefore, at this level of activity costs are equal to income and, consequently, the restaurant breaks even, based on a total cost concept. If the restaurant was operating at 10,000 meals, it has a margin of safety of between 10,000 and 6,800 meals, that is 3,200 meals, before the restaurant reaches break-even point and slips into a loss making situation.

It is also possible to produce the information in matrix form (table 9.5).

Table 9.5 Break even matrix

Number of meals sold '000	Fixed costs £'000	Variable costs £'000	Total cost £'000	Income at £10 per head £'000	Profit (Loss) £'000
0	39	0	39	0	(39)
1	39	4	43	10	(33)
5	39	20	59	50	(9)
8	42	32	74	80	6
10	42	40	82	100	18
12	45	48	93	120	27

The matrix shown in table 9.5 highlights that if no meals are sold there will be a loss of £39,000, which equates to the fixed costs. it can be seen that the break-even point is somewhere between 5,000 and 8,000 meals, but the matrix does not allow the exact break-even point to be identified. This can be represented as a profit/volume chart, which uses a single line to represent the three lines used in a traditional break-even chart. An example is shown in figure 9.5.

Figure 9.5 Profit/volume chart

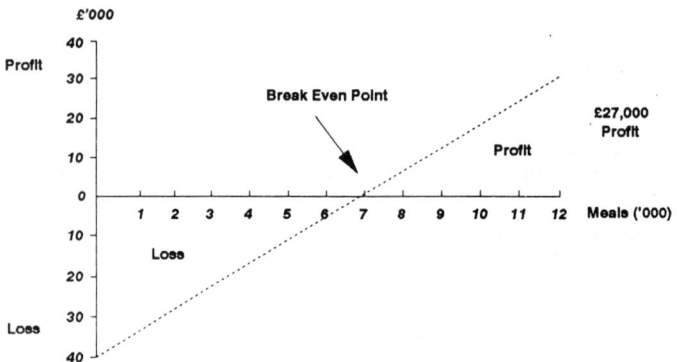

Managers generally appreciate information being presented in graphical or diagrammatic form as it is often easier and quicker to comprehend, and break-even charts are an ideal visual aid in this respect. However, they do have their limitations in view of their inflexibility as they do not take into consideration varying price levels, they assume costs are constant and that costs and income are only affected by changes in volume and no other external factors, that there are no other services or facilities offered or limiting factors which will also have an impact on any decisions made and that costs can be accurately ascertained for various levels of output.

Another important cost that should be taken into consideration in any decision making process is opportunity cost, which is the value of a benefit sacrificed in favour of an alternative course of action. For example, if a tennis tournament is staged at a club and requires all the courts, the opportunity cost would be the profits that would have been earned had the courts been used in the normal course of activity. Although opportunity costs may be difficult to measure, it is an important concept as it should make managers consider the financial implications of opportunities which have been foregone.

Organisations invariably have limiting factors, such as the number of hours a facility may be open or the availability of professional coaching hours. Marginal costing can also be used when decisions relating to profitability have to be made regarding which activity should be offered when there is a limiting factor. By calculating the contribution that each activity makes in relation to the limiting factor, the activities which should be offered can be determined. This assumes that profit is the ony criteria for determining the activity basis.

Conclusion

As part of the business process, managers need information on the cost of the facilities and services for which they are responsible for decision-making and control purposes. Costs may not necessarily be of the same type and, therefore, it is important for the various different cost concepts to be understood and applied. Variable costs alter in direct proportion to the volume of business, whereas fixed costs are not related to volume and exist even if no utilisation is made of the facilities. Costs can also be classified according to whether they are direct or indirect costs. Direct costs are those costs that can be readily identified or charged to a cost centre, whereas indirect costs cannot be related to a particular cost centre and are known as overheads.

It is important to recognise that there are different costs for different purposes and the appropriate costs and costing concepts should be used when making decisions.

The method of costing used will depend upon the intended utilisation of the cost information. Absorption costing attempts to ascertain the total cost of a facility or service whereas marginal costing ascertains the variable or marginal costs and the contribution which the activity makes towards overheads and profit. Marginal costing is more useful in terms of decision-making, especially where more than one activity exists.

Break-even analysis can be useful in determining the relationship between costs, profits and changes in volume, but, at the same time, consideration needs to be given to other factors.

Further reading

Bigg W W *Cost Accounts.* Macdonald & Evans
Management Accounting: Official Terminoogy. ICMA
Sizer J *An Insight Into Management Accounting.* Pelican

10 Pricing decisions

Pricing is probably one of the most complex areas to deal with in leisure service provision and, perhaps because of this, tends to attract the least concerted attention. And yet price plays a vital role, acting as a key and often deciding factor in the decision whether or not to purchase a product or service.

Price is the key signal between the provider of a service and the prospective purchaser as to what is required to actively complete a transaction. Few people buy anything without knowing the price beforehand and weighing it up against such factors as affordabiity, quality and what competitors are charging. If the price is too high, demand falls and a surplus of supply develops thereby driving the price down. Conversely, if the price is too low, demand exceeds supply and the price rises.

Two other important factors have to be taken into consideration. The first is that people purchase leisure services on a discretionary basis. Unlike food, clothing and somewhere to live, leisure is not vital to survival and, therefore, need not be purchased. To sell leisure requires the successful combination of a number of important factors – product, place, price and promotion, which are the main components of the marketing mix. Price is a key component, but functions in concert with the other components and not in isolation. This point is returned to later in the chapter.

The second factor to consider is that services, unlike products, are highly perishable. An unsold washing machine can be stored in a warehouse or a new car in a parking area until a buyer is found. A hotel room, squash court or theatre seat unsold for a particular night or session is lost forever after that point.

Given the important function of pricing, it should have a high profile in an organisation. But it is very unusual to find it identified as a discreet function in any organisation or the direct responsibility of any one person. In the private sector, it may be the function of the commercial director or the marketing director to co-ordinate prices amongst those divisions that have an interest. In the public sector, pricing can be more the subject of emotion than economics, with elected representatives, not managers, having the final say on the level of prices charged for leisure facilities. In either case, it is not likely to be a totally logical and cohesive process.

Pricing objectives

Price is one of the main mechanisms that is used to assist organisations achieve their objectives. It is important, therefore, that in arriving at a pricing policy and determining individual prices, due consideration is given to whether or not price reflects the objective(s) so that performance can be measured.

In the private sector, this is relatively straightforward as the main objective is financial and concerned with profit and return on investment. Pricing will reflect the need to achieve this. However, at the operational level there are likely to be separate pricing objectives relating to different products and services that reflect where an organisation is currently and where it wants to be in the short, medium and long-term. In operational terms, these objectives will take the form of pricing tactics, and these are discussed later in the chapter.

The situation in the public sector is nowhere near as simple, as both social and financial objectives have to be met. The advent of compulsory competitive tendering and the constrained financial circumstances that local authorities find themselves in currently has meant a shift of emphasis in many instances from social to financial considerations.

However, whilst there is a greater emphasis upon the adoption of a more commercial approach to leisure provision, it has tended to fall on the side of looking at cost control and/or reduction, rather than income generation potential through improved pricing and/or marketing strategies. In some ways this is not surprising as the motivation to achieve additional income is generally low. Additional income is usually accepted as being 'fortuitous' and absorbed into the general rate fund. No allowance or recognition is generally given to service managers and, consequently, the incentive is non-existent.

Particular pricing objectives are also more complex and wide ranging in the public sector. The overriding objective, albeit by implication, is generally the efficient use of resources, as reflected in the earlier comment. Price can assist this by increasing income and thereby reducing net expenditure. Consequently, service subsidy levels are increasingly under review.

But there are also pricing objectives relating to maximising opportunity to all sections of the community, with recognition of certain groups such as the elderly, unemployed and people with disabilities through special rates. Many local authorities are also increasingly concerned that priority of access to services is given to their constituent residents and are introducing differential pricing policies that require non-residents to pay more for the same leisure opportunities.

Determining price

There are two basic approaches to determining price; one is cost based and the other is demand based or 'what the market will bear'. Within these two approaches there are a number of specific methods, and these are summarised in table 10.1.

Table 10.1 Main methods used to establish price

Type of pricing method	Characteristics of pricing method
Based on the market	
Going rate pricing	Prices are set at the same level as others offering a similar service
Demand orientated pricing	Prices are set at a level that different client groups are willing to pay or what the market will bear
Based on costs	
Absorption/full cost pricing	Prices are set to cover all fixed and variable costs
Marginal/variable cost pricing	Prices are set to cover variable costs
Pricing rate of return	Prices are set to produce a required rate of return on capital employed

No one approach or method is proven or better than the other. In reality, the best way to determine price is by adopting a combination of the two main approaches, which, in some respects, represents both the science and the art of pricing. Costs are important and cannot be ignored for the reasons set out in earlier chapters. However, some costs are difficult to isolate and allocate.

But costs only represent one side of the equation. Of equal importance are factors such as the type of provision in terms of quality, quantity, its location, method of service delivery, competing services and facilities, marketing and promotion. It is also important to be aware of trends and how the business or particular service has responded over time to price and other market influences. In the remainder of this chapter we look first at how costs can influence price and then move on to the demand side of the equation to achieve a balanced picture. The chapter concludes with some suggestions regarding price tactics and the psychology of pricing.

Pricing methods based on costs or full costs

Absorption pricing

Absorption pricing tends to be used by commercial organisations where usually a unit cost, including both fixed and variable costs, plus a net profit margin is determined for a product or a facility and this is used as the basis for the charge. Under the absorption concept the volume of business is set at a predetermined level and costs and prices are based on that volume of business. The absorption costing and, consequently, pricing concept has the disadvantage that it is not easy to assess how costs are affected by changing volumes and the marginal effect of decisions on activity levels is difficult to ascertain. This is because the cost unit will contain variable costs, which vary in proportion to the change in volume and an apportionment of fixed costs, which do not vary with changes in volume. Volume is an important factor when considering price decisions. But absorption pricing ignores volume and assumes that price is totally a function of cost.

Another of the difficulties with absorption pricing is in determining the costs attributable to each activity or cost centre. Direct costs can be identified with relative ease and can be allocated on an accurate basis. For example, wages costs can be determined using timesheets and the costs of staff dedicated to a specific activity centre, such as swimming pool attendants, can be charged directly to the swimming pool cost centre.

However, complex and subjective assumptions may need to be made on how to apportion indirect costs which are not directly identifiable to an activity. For example, cleaning costs could be apportioned on an area basis, according to the area occupied by each activity. Unless the methods of apportionment are relatively sophisticated, they could lead to a profit line which could be considered to be artificial and lead to misinterpretation by managers.

An example of price determination by absorption pricing is set out in table 10.2. As can be seen, the total income requirement can be calculated and an average selling price per customer based on a standard level of usage then determined. In practise, however, there will be a number of different categories of user within each activity, for example adult, junior, senior citizens, course usage for which the organisation would want to introduce a differential pricing policy. In order to do this with any degree of accuracy, it would be necessary to further subdivide the cost centres into their respective categories and attempt to cost and price each category in turn. This becomes extremely cumbersome. Using absorption pricing as the method of apportioning indirect costs to a level lower than cost centre will be extremely arbitrary, if not inaccurate.

Table 10.2 Price determination for a leisure complex using absorption pricing

	Total costs	Swimming	Health suite	Tennis	Squash	Restaurant /bar
Direct costs						
Variable						
Wages	195000	100000	20000	30000	15000	30000
Provisions	60000	0	0	0	0	60000
Other	8000	3000	1000	2000	1000	1000
Fixed						
Salaries	420000	200000	60000	80000	40000	40000
Building costs/repairs	106000	77000	8000	8000	5000	8000
Other	153000	60000	20000	40000	18000	15000
Total direct costs	942000	440000	109000	160000	79000	154000
Indirect costs						
General Repairs/Maint.	51000	30000	5000	4000	2000	10000
Building related costs – heat, light, insurance	92000	50000	7000	25000	5000	5000
Support/admin. services	15000	7000	1000	5000	1000	1000
Financing costs	92000	35000	10000	20000	7000	20000
Other costs	44000	10000	8000	10000	6000	10000
Total indirect costs	294000	132000	31000	64000	21000	46000
Total costs	1236000	572000	140000	224000	100000	200000
Profit margin	194600	28600 (5%)	35000 (25%)	31000 (20%)	20000 (20%)	80000 (40%)
Total income required	1430600	600600	175000	255000	120000	280000
Number of user/hours		316000	50000	30000	30000	28000
Average selling price per user/hour		1.90	3.50	8.50	4.00	10.00

Rate of return pricing

Rate of return pricing works in reverse in that a predetermined rate of return on capital employed is set and prices are then established which, assuming sales targets are met, would produce the required rate of return. Again, this method is calculated using a predetermined level of activity and, therefore, suffers from the same problems as absorption pricing in that changes in demand are not reflected. It does, however, attempt to fix prices to an estimated rate of return, but there is no guarantee that the estimates will be achieved. In order to use this concept with any degree of accuracy, it would be necessary to attribute capital cost to each activity or cost centre, which may not be easy to determine, in order to determine the rate of return and, hence, prices for each activity.

This concept is more suitable to situations that may be non-competitive and, for example, where the selling price needs to be established to give the investor an acceptable return on their money.

One example might include a tennis club where the level of capital employed is £500,000 and, assuming a 20 per cent return on capital employed is required, a profit of £100,000 would need to be generated. If annual costs are £200,000, the total sales which would need to be generated in order to achieve the annual rate of return required would be £300,000. If there are an estimated 40,000 users per annum, this averages £7.50 selling price per user.

In practise, the various mixes of business would need to be considered, but under this method it would not be possible to ascertain what proportion of, say, the cost of adult tennis is being recovered compared with the cost of junior tennis or when courses are being priced to make a profit. The level of subsidisation between activities is not so discernible.

Marginal cost pricing

Setting prices based on marginal costs involves identifying the variable costs associated with an activity and adding a gross profit margin to determine the price. The price is fixed so as to maximise a contribution towards fixed costs and profit.

Contribution can be deemed to be a more accurate measure than net profit in determining the marginal effect arising from changes in the volume of an activity. It also avoids the complexities of apportioning costs and the possibility of arbitrary apportionments giving rise to artificial results. Managers will also be provided with information by which to control the costs for which they are responsible and are not burdened by apportioned costs which they cannot control.

Taking the squash activity line from the example set out in table 10.2, it is possible to see the effect upon contribution of raising or lowering prices based on a marginal cost pricing principle. The example set out in table 10.3 assumes that the courts are operating below capacity and that additional income can be generated without any increase in fixed costs.

Table 10.3 Impact of price variations on squash activity

	Assumptions		
	Estimated demand hours	Price per hour	Marginal cost per hour
Present	30,000	£4.00	£0.53
Proposed	25,000	£4.50	£0.53
	40,000	£3.50	£0.53
	45,000	£3.00	£0.53
	Results:		
Estimated demand	30,000	25,000	40,000	45,000
Selling price	£4.00	£4.50	£3.50	£3.00
Income	120,000	112,500	140,000	135,000
Less: marginal cost	15,900	13,250	21,200	23,850
Contribution	104,100	99,250	118,800	111,150

This example shows that the greatest improvement in contribution would be generated by lowering the selling price from £4.00 to £3.50. This is obviously dependent upon the market research being accurate and that the increase in estimated demand is forthcoming. It can be seen that the accuracy of demand forecasting is one of the problems associated with the marginal pricing principal.

Marginal cost pricing has the benefit that it is not constrained by a standard level of activity and the impact of varying volumes can be readily ascertained. It also deals with the future in that it takes into consideration estimated revenues and expenses and does not take into consideration any fixed costs which may be the result of historical decisions that are unchangeable.

Marginal cost pricing facilitates differential pricing and provides a more flexible approach to pricing than absorption pricing. However, the relationship between variable and fixed costs should not be overlooked and contributions should be sufficient to cover fixed costs and make a profit.

Absorption or full cost pricing tends to be more easily understood by managers than marginal pricing as the concepts of cost, gross profit and net profit are easiy understood. The breakdown of costs into fixed and variable and also direct and indirect is not a concept which is familiar to everyone and, to a certain extent, each expenditure item needs careful consideration in order to classify it. Marginal cost pricing, therefore, becomes a more difficult technique to operate.

The costing techniques used will depend upon the type of organisation and business and also on the availability of information.

Full cost pricing tends to be more easiy understood, but it is not always that easy for managers to be able to allocate and apportion all their costs to activities. Marginal cost pricing tends to be more easy to administer but it does require a manager being able to identify and determine fixed and variable costs in addition to direct and indirect costs.

In considering costs, it is important to strike the correct balance. It is difficult to develop a pricing strategy without some knowledge of costs even though in service areas it is often difficult to establish costs precisely. This is especially the case where people form the major element of cost and work across a number of activities, making allocation to specific cost centres difficult.

On the other hand, where there is a significant dependency upon costs or where they are used as the sole basis for calculating prices, there is little or no incentive to keep costs under control. Whilst this has occurred and does still occur in the private sector, the lack of cost control has been a major criticism of the public sector and the driving force behind the current Government's introduction of the concept of internal markets in a number of areas of public services. A good example within the leisure sphere has been the need to establish service level agreements between DSO's and central service departments under compulsory competitive tendering (CCT) so that they are aware of and can control this aspect of their costs.

Pricing based on the market

Having reviewed and taken into account costs, it is important to take into consideration the demand side of the equation 'or what the market will bear', which is probably one of the most hackneyed and misused terms where pricing is concerned. Setting a price with little or no knowledge of how the market functions and is likely to respond is more akin to guesswork or intuitive pricing. There are, no doubt, occasions when this plays its part, especially in instances where a new product or service is being put on to the market and there are few clues as to how the market will respond.

Demand factors are more difficult to detect and influence than costs. It is hardly surprising, therefore, that the private sector tends to concentrate more on costs. But they ignore the market, or demand, at their peril, as it is the relationship between price and sales that determines the ultimate level of profit or loss!

Going rate pricing

This is one form of pricing method loosely based around the market, and is a common feature of pricing leisure services in the public sector. Going rate pricing involves setting price by reference to the prices charged for comparative services by neighbouring authorities or other organisations. In this way, prices can be kept to the average of what is being charged elsewhere. It is also common for prices to be uplifed by the current rate of inflation, which are then checked on the going rate principle on the misconception that this represents, or takes into account, what the market will bear.

Thus, in general, the basis for setting prices in this context is largely historical. It assumes that all other elements of the demand equation are equal and do not change over time and also, perhaps of greater concern, that prices were soundly based and correctly set in the first instance. Any adjustment of price usually takes place annually and, traditionally, the uplift is based upon inflation.

Whilst such an approach is relatively quick and administratively simple, it is too insensitive and simplistic to be a reliable measure of the market when used in isolation. However, it can be of value when used as one part of the process of determining price as a check as to where a certain price level might place a leisure service in the market and the comparative level of likely acceptability by both existing and potential users. Thus, a price set too high in comparison with other providers might result in a fall off in demand as customers change their allegiance to another location. This is referred to as the price threshold, and this is returned to later in the chapter when the psychology of pricing is discussed.

Demand based pricing

Demand factors are harder to detect and influence than costs. Demand factors are external while costs are largely internal. Nevertheless, advantage can be gained from having an understanding of those market factors that relate to demand which, when brought together like pieces of a jigsaw, begin to create an overall picture.

User profile

It is important to know and understand the market in which services are being offered in terms of potential customers. Thus, a knowledge of the demographic and socio-economic profile of the area or market being served is beneficial in order to assess the existing and potential future customer base and the nature of the sectors of the market that need to be addressed.

This also assists decisions regarding market positioning of services, both intended and actual, and helps to ensure that service and pricing objectives actually reflect the real situation in the market. In this respect, it is also beneficial to develop a profile of the users of existing leisure services and facilities so that actual sales performance can be matched against the overall population and service objectives.

User trend analysis

Alongside user profiles, it is vital to know utilisation trends relating to services and facilities. This requires the collection and collation of data on a continuing basis and analysis of the trends over a number of years (usually three to five). Utilisation against capacity should also be determined by service or facility area and by day of week and hour of day if necessary to determine when peaks and troughs are occurring.

It is also useful, as part of the data collection exercise, to record the influence that external or other factors might have had upon demand. For example, the closure of all or part of a facility for a period of time should be clearly recorded. Clearly, if demand and, hence, utilisation appears to be falling external factors need to be eliminated before any decisions are taken in an attempt to rectify the situation, especially if one mechanism that is under consideration is a price change.

Elasticity of demand

Elasticity of demand is basically the response in terms of demand to a change in price. Without utilisation trend data, it is virtually impossible to assess this. It is vital for leisure service providers to know how elastic or inelastic demand is for various facilities and services in response to changes in price.

If demand is elastic, a change in price will result in an opposite change in income, that is, an increase in price will result in a drop in demand and income falls below previous levels. If demand is inelastic, an increase in price will not affect demand adversely and income increases overall. Thus, price elasticity of demand impacts directly upon the ability to change price.

If the purpose of a price rise is to increase income, prices can only be increased in those service areas for which demand is relatively inelastic. This is most likely to occur in those areas where strength of demand is such that existing supply cannot cope and additional supply cannot be readily provided. An example of this is golf whereby the majority of private clubs have waiting lists and municipal courses are under severe pressure, with queues forming early in the morning. In this instance, therefore, demand is very strong and easily outstripping supply, which cannot respond quickly, if at all, in some areas because of time, planning and resource constraints. Thus, whereas a significant price increase for public golf might result in a small drop off in demand, overall income would likely increase.

The price elasticity of demand can be largely dependent upon the availability of competing services and the price that they charge. The cinema industry has been going through a revival since the late 1980s, the result of which has been the rapid expansion of multi-screen cinemas in most major population centres. It is likely, therefore, that the price elasticity of demand for cinema seats will become elastic in the very near future as the market moves towards saturation point. At that point there is a need to carefully balance likely gains in income against potential loss of customers through price increases.

In the public sector, it is very often social objectives as opposed to price elasticity that keeps prices and subsequent price increases down. This is borne out to an extent by research and user profiling of local authority leisure centres, which revealed a predominantly middle class (BC1) domination amongst users. This would suggest that in certain areas public leisure services are likely to be price inelastic to a point consideraby beyond the current levels of prices charged. Unfortunately, very little detailed study has been done in this area to actually test price elasticity. The best way to test elasticity is by experimenting with price, which is not easy in the public sector because of the decision-making process and the advent recently of compulsory competitive tendering.

Nature and quality of provision

The pricing of facilities and services should reflect such factors as location, the range of facilities/services on offer and their quality. Leisure users are becoming increasingly more sophisticated and have higher expectations in terms of perceived value for money.

Consequently, these demand related factors need to be taken into account and reflected in the price charged.

It is in this area that knowledge of competitors and neighbouring providers, in the case of the public sector, the strength of the competition and the prices they are charging can be of benefit. But, it is important that comparative supply is put into a context of like comparison on the basis of quality and range of provision and not used in isolation as discussed in the section on going rate pricing.

Pricing tactics

A good working knowledge of the market together with an understanding of how price mechanisms work allow the vendor to adopt various pricing techniques on a tactical basis. Such techniques can be employed on a permanent or temporary basis, dependent upon the particular objectives to be met.

The particular pricing technique or tactic selected will generally depend upon the nature of the particular product being sold, the target market at which it is aimed and the market conditions that exist at the time, that is, supply in relation to demand. There are a number of price tactics available, but only those that are appropriate and more commonly used to sell leisure services are outlined here.

Differential pricing – is one of the most commonly used pricing tactics by both private and public sectors. It involves charging different prices for the same service according to varying criteria or conditions. The most common example is that of peak and off-peak pricing. Price differentials can be applied to people, time, place and product.

In the case of people, it is ability to pay that invariably necessitates a differential. In the public sector, it is common practise for swimming pool and leisure centre prices to be differentiated for such groups as senior citizens, people with disabilities and the unemployed. A more recent and growing innovation is a price differential between people who live inside and outside a particular local authority boundary.

Time-price differentials – can be used to shift or build demand for off-peak use and thereby level out fluctuations in demand. Public sector leisure centres use this tactic almost universally in pricing squash, badminton and other facility related leisure activities. In the private sector, the pricing of holidays is a common example which have significant price variations according to the time of year.

The private sector is generally more inclined to use the concept of premium pricing when peak-time usage is identified for which there is high demand. This also serves as a form of rationing. Unfortunately, the public sector tends not to respond either so readiy or so rapidly to this type of situation. Returning to our earlier golf example, given a situation of high and, therefore, relatively inelastic demand and a generally fixed, or at best slow responding, level of supply of golf courses, the market response should be to premium price. This would have the effect of maximising income, reducing queues via rationing and thereby affording some protection to the deteriorating quality of many municipal golf courses. Generally, this has not been the case.

Time-place differentials are used in pricing theatre or concert seats where the better the location in relation to the stage the higher the price that the seat commands. Another example is the sale of airline seats.

Product-price differentials occur when higher prices are charged for the same or similar facility or service in one location than elsewhere. For example, if a local authority had two swimming pools, one of which was modern, whilst the other was badly in need of refurbishment, the differing quality in the 'product' could justify a price differential even though the acitivty, swimming, was the same and not impaired or restricted.

Price could also be varied for two similar pools within the same local authority to reflect the socio-economic profile of the particular catchment areas served. This latter case would require careful consideration to ensure that price differentials that reflect social objectives do not result in resentment from customers using other similar facilities.

Discount pricing – is also common in both sectors and is generally used as a promotional device. It can be used in a similar way to a time-price differential in order to encourage off-peak sales. For example, hotel chains promote cheap weekend breaks to balance off the Monday to Thursday night business trade as well as special winter breaks. As a cautionary note, however, the travel and holiday trade are becoming increasingly aware of growing consumer sophistication in delaying purchasing decisions in anticipation of time-price differentials and discount pricing.

Another example of promotional discounting is 'happy hours' in pubs and wine bars where drinks are discounted between, for instance, 5.30pm and 6.30pm on certain quiet evenings. The intention is to attract a significant number of customers into the pub or bar during the hour of cheap drinks and then capitalise on the residual sales to the proportion that inevitably remain after the hour is ended.

Diversionary pricing – involves attracting customers by quoting a low basic price in order to give the impression of a low overall pricing structure. Thus, for example, a restaurant might promote dishes or choices of the day as house specials. Once customers are in the restaurant, they are also presented with an a la carte menu containing generally higher priced meals.

Loss – leader pricing – is closely allied to discount and diversionary pricing and is used to get customers to use facilities or services having first paid below average prices either for admission or another service. Gaming and casino operators adopt this tactic by pricing meals and drinks at a low rate with the intention of both attracting and then retaining people in the casinos for as long as possible so that whatever they gain in terms of savings in the restaurant they more than compensate for by losses at the tables and slot machines!

Discount and loss leader pricing are tactics that can also be used to penetrate markets quite rapidly with a new product or service. This generally applies to most markets where demand is elastic. However, these techniques should be used with caution and in a controlled manner over a pre-determined period. Prices that are discounted too heavily or over an extended period could lead to competitors adopting similar aggressive tactics, with a price war as a result. This inevitably leads to casualties, when only the strongest or those with the largest market share survive.

High price maintenance – is the total opposite of discount and loss leader pricing. This occurs where service providers establish a niche market that is associated with high quality and thereby is able to maintain a consistently high price. For this to happen, demand must be inelastic. This is also known as skimming when applied to the entry of a product or service into a new market. Examples would include the five star/deluxe sector of the hotel market and, more recently, golf course developments, such as Wisley, that are able to sell high priced debentures for membership of the club before the course had even been completed.

Psychology of pricing

We referred earlier in the chapter to the science and art of setting price. There is little doubt that psychological factors also play their part in pricing decisions, albeit sometimes in the form of price adjustment. People react differently and sometimes irrationally to changes in price. To anticipate this aspect of pricing, therefore, falls firmly in the category of art!

A good example of the psychological element of pricing is the widespread use of odd pricing, especially in retailing. Thus, prices are deliberately left at, say, £2.99 or £9.95p, which are just below the next price threshold, and create the illusion of a lower price than the £3 or £10 that would be charged if they had been rounded up. The degree to which such pricing actually influences purchases is a moot point, but it is never wise to round up prices just for administrative convenience. If a case can be made or some evidence exists that odd pricing is working then continue with it.

Where odd pricing might be effective is when considering the expected price threshold of a service. People tend to have some idea of the price they would expect to pay. If price is set above that threshold, they will view the service as expensive. If it is set too low, they might begin to question the quality of the service they are likely to receive.

Consequently, the initial price set for a service is vitally important as it will become the point for, and may limit, subsequent price increases.

Some leisure service areas in the public sector suffer to varying degrees from this and have become traditionally low priced. These include allotments, sports pitches and, to an extent, public swimming. Where they exist, it is difficult to ignore them because they are also high expenditure areas, but comparatively low prices have become custom and practise. A recent departure has been the small number of private sector operators who have opened waterparks and are charging admission prices that are generally twice the going public sector leisure pool rate. The impact upon the consumer in terms of expected price threshold and what is customary for them to pay for a swim could determine the success or failure of the commercial operators in attracting the volume of customers required to achieve the required rate of return.

The size of price increases can also affect customer attitudes. It is sometimes better to introduce a series of small price increases over a period of time that will be tolerated than a single major increase that is likely to meet resistance. This, of course, is relative in that a price increase of £0.25 on £0.50 is likely to meet resistance, whereas an in increase of £0.25 on £2.50 is not, even though the increase in both cases is £0.25.

We have already referred to the relationship between price and quality, and the maintenance of high prices. Price is often viewed as an indicator of quality and market research has found that people's perception of products and services vary directly with price, i.e. the higher the price, the better the quality is perceived to be. Some producers enhance the price/quality perception still further by deliberately rationing supply. This is a common feature of the quality car market.

Just as people relate price to quality, so they also relate price to value for money. A significant price increase which goes beyond people's price threshold, and for which there is also no perceived increased value for money, is likely to meet resistance. In some instances this can be countered by increased and improved promotion that focuses upon selling the benefits that might have previously been ignored or undersold. Physical improvements to facilities can also support price increases because change is apparent in terms of investment in the provision of the service. The same principle applies to the level of service and customer care that is offered. They are all tangible and can enhance the customers perception of value for money.

Conclusion

Pricing is a complex and uncertain area of activity. It is both a science and an art. There is no specific framework or process that can be adopted that allows pricing decisions to be made any less complex than they are currently. What we have outlined in this chapter are the various factors and components that need to be taken into consideration at the various stages along the way to determining price.

What is important is that managers are fully aware of these and apply them. It is also essential to have good and up to date information about how various services have and are performing in terms of their costs, the level of utilisation and the impact of previous price increases. This minimum level of financial and management information is vital, as it allows the manager to, at least, reduce the level of uncertainty in setting prices.

Prices cannot be set in isolation. They must take into account both costs and market forces and reflect the objectives of the organisation. Prices should also be reviewed regularly and systematically in order to assess performance in relation to objectives and so that adjustments can be made sooner rather than later.

It can no longer be acceptable practise to uplift prices annually on a blanket basis by a factor of inflation with, perhaps at best, some reference to what others are charging. On that basis, a mistake made by one provider can be copied and compounded by many more. Each price or price area needs to be established within an established pricing policy. Individual pricing decisions then need to take into account the outcome of sound analysis of costs, demand, general market conditions and the competition.

However, it must also be acknowledged that all markets are fickle and open to influence by fads and trends. The leisure market is possibly a more extreme example of this. Analysis will get you a fair way along the decision-making path but, at the end of the day, a good understanding and 'feel' for the market does still count for a lot. Thus, the psychology of the market place and intuition on the part of the seller will always play their part in pricing decisions. The key is to make optimum use of the science in order to minimise the potential risk in the art of pricing.

Further reading

Cowell D 1984 *The Marketing of Services.* Heinemann
Gratton C, Taylor P 1988 *Economics of Leisure Services Management.* Longman
Winkler J 1983 *Pricing For Results.* Heinemann

11 Capital investment appraisal

The decision to build any form of leisure faciity is not one to be taken lightly. Generally speaking, you get very little, if any, change from half a million pounds even for modest community provision, while specialist facilities such as swimming pools and hotels cost many millions of pounds.

Decisions regarding capital investment have a long-term impact and, therefore should be based upon a sound, rational process that examines both the feasibility and viability of a proposed project. This chapter is not concerned with the initial feasibility element of the process that concentrates upon market analysis, and forecasting demand. This is dealt with in chapter 17 and is also in another book in this series, *Economics of Leisure Services Management*, by Gratton and Taylor.

The emphasis here concentrates upon the assessment of the financial implications or viability of a leisure investment. Invariably, capital investment concerns considerable resources, which are usually limited. Therefore, it is important that capital investment opportunities are appraised and alternatives are considered before entering into any commitments.

Certainly, very few of the public sector facilities constructed over the last twenty years were subjected to such appraisal. Decisions to proceed were often based upon standards of provision that were universally applied (with no cognisance of the local situation) opportunism in terms of availability of land and/or capital finance and parochialism. In the public sector, such investment decisions were not fraught with the sort of risks confronted by the commercial sector. They were driven more by social objectives. In addition, capital allocations were such that almost every local authority was able to include a range of leisure facilities in its capital programme.

Today, capital controls have drastically reduced local authorities' ability to commit themselves to all but the most vital of facility provision. A poorly judged or wrong decision, if nothing else, deprives other

98

projects of scarce resources as well as committing the authority to servicing the debt for a facility that may well underperform.

In the commercial sector, poor investment decisions can have a detrimental effect upon an organisation's profitability, stability and even its continued existence, as some have come to realise during the current recession. Because of this, the commercial sector, generally takes a far more cautious approach. Certainly, when a project is dependent upon loan finance, full documentary evidence of a detailed investment appraisal, usually from an independent source, such as consultants, is required. Where an organisation has undertaken its own analysis and appraisal, banks will often still seek to have it independently validated before deciding whether or not to invest.

Sound investments should generate returns over a number of years. As resources become harder to obtain for both the public and commercial sectors, partnership opportunities are becoming one way of maintaining some form of momentum in leisure developments. Certainly, under CCT, the potential for capital investment in facilities by a contractor or jointly by a contractor in partnership with the client authority is being explored. In either case, investment appraisal, using the methods set out in this chapter, will feature more and more. As part of the investment appraisal, it is important to ascertain future costs and revenues for each alternatives as these form part of the equation in the appraisal process.

Appraisal methods

There are three main methods used to appraise capital investment:

- pay-back method
- rate of return
- discounted cash flow
  - net present value
  - yield method/internal rate of return

Pay-back method

This is the quickest method which can be used to assess how long it will take to recoup the original investment in a project and, consequently, how long it will take for the project to 'pay for itself'. The pay-back period is measured from the time of the initial outlay to the time that it is recovered.

Using the example in table 11.1 below, Project One has a pay-back period of only two years and six months, assuming an even cash flow, whereas Project Two has a pay-back period of three years and five months. Under the pay-back method, Project One woud be selected as it pays for itself in a shorter space of time.

Table 11.1 A simple example of the pay-back method

	Net cash flow Project 1 £	Net cash flow Project 2 £
Capital outlay	250,000	250,000
Year 1	100,000	50,000
Year 2	100,000	50,000
Year 3	100,000	100,000
Year 4	50,000	120,000
Year 5	20,000	120,000
	370,000	440,000

This method is widely used as it is simple and, if resources are limited, organisations tend to consider that the turnaround of funds is of critical importance. However, it does have limitations in that the profitability and returns over the entire life of the investment are ignored. In the above example, Project Two would generate greater receipts than Project One over its entire life but Project One would be selected purely on the pay-back method as its has the shortest pay-back period.

The pay-back method also ignores the timing of cash flow and the value attached to money over time. In the early stages of a capital project, the availability and flow of funds can be crucial. The sooner that cash flows back into the operation, the greater the liquidity and the less the risk. Furthermore, the money (that is worth more today), can be made to work for the business. Thus, for example, if £50,000 flows back into a new business earlier than expected, it can be used to finance the operation and reduce borrowings.

For instance, in the example in table 11.2 below, the pay-back period is four years for both projects, and, therefore, there would be no distinction between the projects using the pay-back method. However, cash is received far earlier on Project Three and, therefore, when taking into consideration the timing of cash flow, Project Three would prove to be a better investment, as the sooner that money is returned it can be re-used and re-invested.

Table 11.2 A simply example of the pay-back method taking account of the time value of money

	Net cash flow Project 3 £	Net cash flow Project 4 £
Capital outlay	300,000	300,000
Year 1	100,000	0
Year 2	100,000	50,000
Year 3	50,000	100,000
Year 4	50,000	150,000
Year 5	150,000	150,000
	450,000	450,000

The pay-back method, however, is easy to understand and where cash is a limiting factor, it is a useful way of undertaking an elimination process in order to identify those projects that then merit further evaluation. The pay-back method is also useful when reviewing high risk projects as, in these instances, early return on initial investment is a sound policy.

Average rate of return method

The rate of return method is concerned with the profitabiity, rather than cash flow, of a project, which is normally expressed as a percentage on the capital cost of the project. Using Projects One and Two from the previous example in table 11.1 and assuming that the average annual profit is £75,000 and £50,000 respectively, the average percentage rate of return would be:

	Project 1	Project 2
Capital outlay	£250,00	£250,00
Annual profit	£75,00	£50,00
Total net cash inflow	£370,00	£440,00
Average annual percentage rate of return	$\left(\dfrac{75,000}{250,000}\right) = 30\%$	$\left(\dfrac{50,000}{250,000}\right) = 20\%$

Using the average rate of return method, Project One would be selected as it has a higher percentage rate of return. This method assumes that profit accrues evenly over the life of the project. However, it has major disadvantages in that it does not take into consideration the cash flow of a project and the timing of receipts.

Discounted Cash Flow (DCF)

The main problem with the previous methods is that they ignore the timing of cash flow, which is a critical factor in any investment decision. Whilst the pay-back method does take into consideration cash flow, it does not take into consideration the time value of money or the impact of future returns after the pay-back period, which is necessary to obtain a full understanding of the potential of the project.

The time value of money has a significant impact in relation to investment and the value of cash flow associated with a project is dependent upon the time at which it occurs. For example, if £10,000 is invested for three years at 5 per cent, its compounded value at the end of each year would be:

	£
Investment	10,000
Year 1 value	10,500
Year 2 value	11,025
Year 3 value	11,576

Therefore, the present day value of £11,576, under these circumstances is £10,000, arrived at as follows:

The final value = amount invested $\times$ (1+ rate of interest)^n
    where n = number of years
          = 10,000 $(1 + 0.05)^3$

If interest rates are 5 per cent, then £11,576 in three years time is worth only £10,000 today, that is:

$$\text{Present value} = \frac{\text{Final value}}{(1 + \text{interest rate})^n}$$

where n = number of years

$$£10,000 = \frac{£11,576}{(1.05)^3}$$

Therefore, if an organisation is aware of the value it wishes to achieve in future years, the present day value can be found by discounting the future year figures. Discounting is really compounding in reverse and there are discount factors which can be applied for certain rates of interest in order to undertake the calculations. A discount table has been included as an appendix. As an example, the present value in ten years of £10,000 at 10 per cent, reading from the discount tables would be:

0.3855 (from table) $\times$ 10,000 = £3,855

This can be verified using the formula:

$$\text{NPV} = \frac{10,000}{(1.10)^{10}} = £3,855$$

Discounted cash flow methods take into consideration the time value of money whereby future outflows and inflows of cash are discounted back to a present value. Under this method, cash flows are assumed to occur at the end of each year whereas in practise they occur throughout the year. However, the impact on the calculations is not considered to be significant.

One of the main advantages with DCF methods is that all cash flows are converted into a common present value base and, therefore, comparisons between projects are made easier for managers.

There are basically two discounted cash flow methods:

- net present value method
- interest rate of return or yield method

Net present value method

This method discounts yearly cash flows back to their net present value based on a minimum rate of return. The difference between the present value of cash outflows and cash inflows is established. If the resulting net present value is negative, the project should not be invested in as it does not yield the required rate of return. If the net present value is positive then the profits are expected to be more valuable than the outlays and, to that extent, the project is favourable.

Using the information for Projects Five and Six in the example in table 11.3 below and the discount factors contained in the appendix, discounted cash flows can be prepared for the two projects as follows:

Table 11.3 Example of discounted cash flow using the net present value method

	Net cash flow Project 5 £	Net cash flow Project 6 £
Capital outlay	200,000	200,000
Year 1	100,000	50,000
Year 2	75,000	50,000
Year 3	50,000	80,000
Year 4	50,000	100,000
Year 5	50,000	100,000

It is assumed that the required rate of return is 10 per cent and the initial capital outlay is not discounted as it is already at present value.

Table 11.4 Discounted cash flow – Project 5

Year	Net cash flow £	Discount factor at 10%	Present value £
0	(200,000)	1.0000	(200,000)
1	100,000	0.9091	90,910
2	75,000	0.8264	61,980
3	50,000	0.7513	37,565
4	50,000	0.6830	34,150
5	50,000	0.6209	31,045
		Net present value	£55,650

Table 11.5 Discounted cash flow – Project 6

Year	Net cash flow £	Discount factor at 10%	Present value £
0	(200,000)	1.0000	(200,000)
1	50,000	0.9091	45,455
2	50,000	0.8264	41,320
3	80,000	0.7513	60,104
4	100,000	0.6830	68,300
5	100,000	0.6209	62,090
		Net present value	£77,269

The net present value of Project Five is +£55,650 and that of Project Six is +£77,269. This means that if a minimum rate of return is required then both projects would be capable of yielding the return and, therefore, both would be acceptable. Under this method, Project Six would, however, be selected as it has a greater net present value.

Internal rate of return (IRR) yield method

Under this method, the cash flow is discounted at an annual rate of compound interest, which will make the net present value of the project equal to the capital outlay. The interest rate, which has to be determined, is known as the internal rate of return (IRR) of the project. When the IRR has been found it can be compared with the rate of return on investment required by the organisation. The IRR has to be determined by a process of trial and error and by reference to compound interest tables or by computer programmes.

Taking Project Five from the previous example in table 11.4, the application of a rate of interest of 10 per cent at table 11.6 produces a positive net present value of £55,650. The 10 per cent rate is, therefore, too low as it does not reduce the net present value to zero, that is, the net present value of the project does not equal the capital outlay. The figures are re-calculated using a higher interest rate, 25 per cent (table 11.7).

Table 11.6   Discounted cash flow – Project 5 (using 10% discount factor)

Year	Net cash flow £	Discount factor at 10%	Present value £
0	(200,000)	1.0000	(200,000)
1	100,000	0.9091	90,910
2	75,000	0.8264	61,980
3	50,000	0.7513	37,565
4	50,000	0.6830	34,150
5	50,000	0.6209	31,045
		Net present value	£55,650

The application of a 25 per cent rate of interest, as set out in table 11.7, would make the project too risky in this context as it produces a negative net present value of −£9,535.

Table 11.7   Discounted cash flow – Project 5 (using 25% discount factor)

Year	Net cash flow £	Discount factor at 25%	Present value £
0	(200,000)	1.0000	(200,000)
1	100,000	0.8000	80,000
2	75,000	0.6400	48,000
3	50,000	0.5120	25,600
4	50,000	0.4096	20,480
5	50,000	0.3277	16,385
		Net present value	−£9,535

The required rate of return is, therefore, somewhere between 10 per cent and 25 per cent. This can be found by interpolation. The difference between the two rates is 15 per cent and a proportion of this difference related to the difference in the total present values is added to the lower rate as follows:

$$10 + \frac{55650}{55650 + 9535} \times (25 - 10)$$

$10 + 12.8 =$ approximately 23%

Applying a 23 per cent rate of interest would produce the following results (table 11.8):

Table 11.8 Discounted cash flow – Project 5 (using a 23% discount factor)

Year	Net cash flow £	Discount factor at 23%	Present value £
0	(200,000)	1.0000	(200,000)
1	100,000	0.8130	81,300
2	75,000	0.6610	49,575
3	50,000	0.5374	26,870
4	50,000	0.4369	21,845
5	50,000	0.3552	17,760
		Net present value	−£2,650

When applying an interest rate of 23 per cent, the net present value is not zero but is −£2,650. This, however, is accurate enough for the majority of purposes.

Applying the internal rate of return method to Project Six would produce the following results (tables 11.9 and 11.10):

Table 11.9 Discounted cash flow – Project Six

Year	Net cash flow £	Discount factor at 10%	Present value £
0	(200,000)	1.000	(200,000)
1	50,000	0.9091	45,455
2	50,000	0.8264	41,320
3	80,000	0.7513	60,104
4	100,000	0.6830	68,300
5	100,000	0.6209	62,090
		Net present value	£77,269

Table 11.10 Discounted cash flow – Project Six (using a 25% interest rate of return)

Year	Net cash flow £	Discount factor at 25%	Present value £
0	(200,000)	1.0000	(200,000)
1	50,000	0.8000	40,000
2	50,000	0.6400	32,000
3	80,000	0.5120	40,960
4	100,000	0.4096	40,960
5	100,000	0.3277	32,770
		Net present value	−£13,310

The required rate by interpolation is:

$$10 + \frac{77269}{77269 + 1331} \times 25 - 10)$$

10 + 12.8 = approximately 23%

If the required rate of return on investment is 10 per cent, both projects are acceptable as they both have an internal rate of return in excess of the required rate – coincidentally both being approximately 23 per cent in this example. Using this method, either project could be selected as they have the same internal rate of return of 23 per cent. Usually the project with the greatest internal rate of return would be selected.

Comparison of NPV and IRR methods

Net present value and internal rate of return may produce different recommendations as to which project should be selected and it is important to understand the characteristics of the methods. In the examples used in this chapter, the net present value method recommended Project Six, whereas the internal rate of return method recommended that either project could be pursued.

When looking at the discount factors, it can be seen that the higher the rate of interest used, the less valuable will cash flows be that are received in later years in the life of a project. When looking at the 10 per cent and 25 per cent discount factors it can be seen that under the 10 per cent discount factor, cash flows in year five will have a value of 62 per cent whereas under the 25 per cent discount factor, year five cash flows only have a value of 33 per cent.

Table 11.11

	10% Discount values	25% Discount values
0	1.0000	1.0000
1	0,9091	0,8000
2	0,8264	0.6400
3	0,7513	0,5120
4	0.6830	0.4096
5	0,6209	0.3277

Consequently, projects which have a greater cash flow in later years will be favoured where a lower acceptable rate of return is required.

If the net present values for various interest rates for Projects Five and Six are plotted graphically, as shown in figure 11.1, it can be seen that at the higher rates of interest, Project Five would be selected as it has a greater net present value than Project Six.

Figure 11.1 Net present values for a range of interest rates for Projects 5 and 6

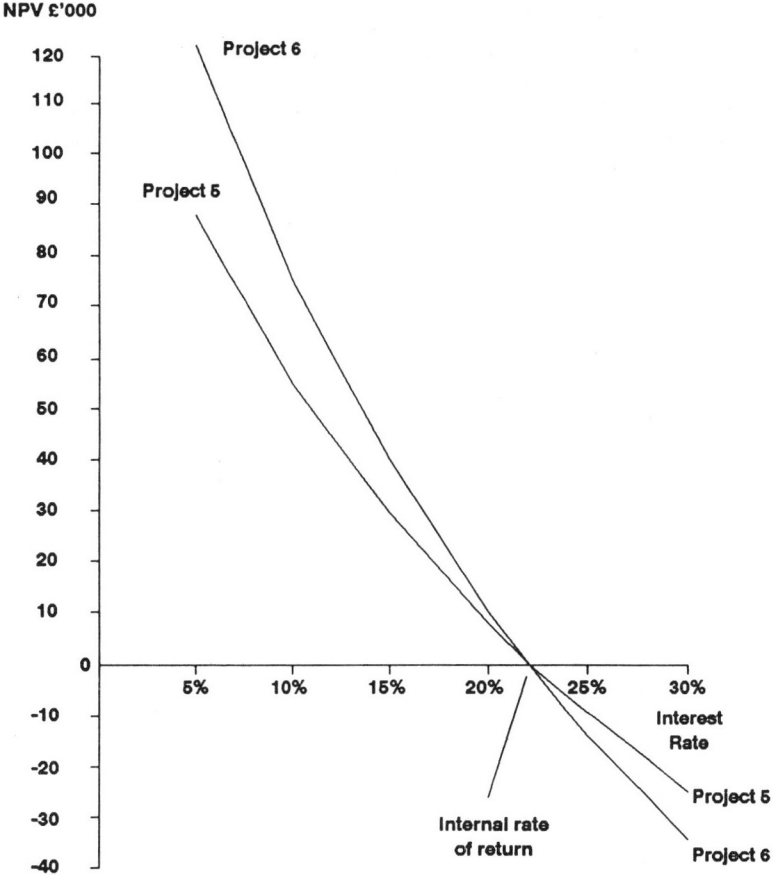

The net present value method is probably easier to understand as it is presented in absolute terms, that is value, whereas the internal rate of return method is presented as comparative percentages which can be misleading and open to misinterpretation.

Cost of capital

In order to appraise investments, it is important to be able to determine the cost of capital or the cost of raising the money to finance the project as this will affect the choice of discount rate to be used in the net present value calculations. It is important that a project can generate sufficient funds to return at least the cost of capital. Therefore, as a crude guideline, investment proposals can be discounted at the cost of capital rate to provide an initial assessment as to whether the project will generate sufficient return to cover the cost of raising finance. If the value is positive, then the project can be evaluated in further detail.

The cost of capital, however, is not solely the rate paid to the bank for funds borrowed as, invariably, there will be different forms of capital – share capital, reserves, short and long-term loan capital. There are a number of different ways of calculating the cost of capital. They are too detailed to be covered here, but if necessary, the reader can refer to books on investment appraisal and capital budgeting. One method of arriving at the cost of capital is to use a weighted average of all the various types of capital being employed. Another is to use the rate of return being made as a minimum acceptable rate for any further projects. It is important to take all appropriate factors into consideration if the discounted cash flow is to provide a meaningful indication of the potential of the investments.

Reliability of projections

Whichever method is selected to appraise the financial proposals, the results will be totally reliant upon the quality of the information upon which the projections are based. There will be certain assumptions used which may have a considerable impact upon the financial projections and success of a project, such as the demand for the product, the size of the market, the estimated market share and the potential growth.

Consequently, it is more usual to prepare more than one set of projections or undertake a series of sensitivity analyses to assess the impact of changing circumstances on the base projections. This ensures that misleading conclusions are not reached from just one set of figures. Examples of sensitivity analyses are contained in chapter sixteen. In order to assist managers in the interpretation of results, it is usual to calculate at least 'best case' and 'worse case' scenarios in addition to the base case scenarios.

Risk analyses could be undertaken instead, where probability factors are attached to various components of the proposal. For example, income or costs, and calculations could be made for the alternative options by reference to the varying probabilities. This technique is best undertaken using a computer and results can be presented graphically which profile the combination of probabilities and anticipated DCF rate of returns.

Lease or buy

One area where discounting techniques are invaluable is in assisting the decision making process as to whether to buy or lease an asset. A greater amount over time will be paid for a leased asset than if it were purchased outright. A basic example, ignoring external factors, is outlined below.

A leisure centre is considering computerising its booking and management information systems. The cost of the hardware and software is £10,000, but it can also be leased over a four year period at £3,000 per annum, payable at the beginning of the year. It is assumed that there will be a net operational saving of £3,500 per annum, that the computer will have a nil residual value and that the average cost of capital of the centre is 10 per cent. Should the computer system be purchased or leased?

The decision making process needs to be broken down into two stages – first of all to assess whether or not the investment should be made and then, secondly, on the method of financing, that is, whether to lease or fund the purchase by borrowings.

Deciding on the investment

It is necessary to establish the DCF rate of return that the investment will provide as follows:

Table 11.12

Net operational cash flow discounted at 10%			Net operational cash flow discounted at 20%		
Year	£	Discount NPV	Year	£	Discount NPV
1	3750 × 0.9091 = 3409		1	3750 × 0.8333 = 3124	
2	3750 × 0.8264 = 3099		2	3750 × 0.6944 = 2604	
3	3750 × 0.7513 = 2817		3	3760 × 0.5787 = 2179	
4	3750 × 0.6830 = 2561		4	3750 × 0.4823 = 1808	
		11886			9706
		−10000			−10000
	NPV	£+1886			−294

Using interpolation the DCF rate of return can be calculated, as follows:

$$10 + \frac{1886}{1886 - 294} \times (20 - 10) = 10 = 8.65$$
$$= 18.65\%$$

The DCF rate of return is 18.65 per cent which is favourable when compared with the organisation's average cost of capital of 10 per cent. Thus, having established that the investment is worthwhile, the method of financing can then be considered.

Deciding on the finance

By discounting the lease payments back to a present value, an assessment can be made on the cost of leasing as follows in table 11.13 assuming an outright purchase price of £10,000.

Table 11.13

Lease values discounted at 10%			Lease values discounted at 20%		
Year	£	Discount NPV	Year	£	Discount NPV
1	3000 × 1.0000 = 3000		1	3000 × 1.0100 = 3000		
2	3000 × 0.9091 = 2727		2	3000 × 0.8333 = 2500		
3	3000 × 0.8264 = 2479		3	3000 × 0.6944 = 2083		
4	3000 × 0.7513 = 2254		4	3000 × 0.5787 = 1736		
	10460			9319	
	−10000			−10000	
	NPV £+460			−681	

Interpolation:

$$10\% + \frac{460}{460 + 681} \times (20 - 10) = 10 = 4.03$$
$$= 14.03\%$$

By discounting the lease payments back, it can be seen that the centre would be paying 14 per cent per annum if the asset were leased. If a cheaper source of finance can be found to fund the outright purchase of the computer, then leasing the equipment will not be the most cost effective means of financing the investment.

There are, however, further complexities involved in decisions regarding leasing or buying, including capital allowances, taxation, grants and any further incentives that may be offered by the lessor, such as, free maintenance or installation costs. It is also important to remember that the decision to lease or buy is a financing issue and needs to be considered separately from the investment decision.

Conclusion

It is important to select the most appropriate investments for investigation and ensure that opportunities worthy of assessment are not overlooked. Capital investment appraisal is, therefore, an important part of any investment decision-making process and looks at the future potential of the investments in question. In terms of any investment, it is necessary to demonstrate that, in return for an initial capital outlay, there will be a larger amount generated from the project over a period of time. The pay-back method determines the period when the initial capital outlay will be recouped, whereas the average rate of return determines the profits that the investment will generate in relation to the capital outlay.

These are useful as crude measures but do not take into consideration the value of money over time. Discounted cash flow techniques are based on the concept of the cash and time value of money. The net present value method discounts yearly cash flows back to their net present values based on a minimum acceptable rate of return. Investments with positive net present values are favourable, those with negative values will not yield the required rate of return. The internal rate of return method discounts the yearly cash flows at an annual rate of compound interest, which will make the net present value of the project equal to the capital outlay. DCF techniques should be employed in appraising projects which involve cash flows over time and affect long-term decisions.

It is important to ensure that the base information on which the projections are prepared is sound. Sensitivity or risk analyses should also be undertaken to ensure that best and worse case scenarios have also been examined. Appraisal techniques should be used when exploring expansion, development, diversification, lease or buy decisions. Once managers are presented with appropriate financial evaluations then the decision making process can begin.

References

Gratton C, Taylor P 1988 *Economics of Leisure Services Management.* Longman

12 Information for managing

The production and use of management information is probably still one of the weakest areas in leisure organisations. Yet, information is at the very core of the management process, as set out in figure 12.1 Key information is needed at every stage in order to develop strategies, set objectives and targets, develop services, prepare budgets and bid for funds. It is virtually impossible to develop and implement the appropriate marketing strategy or monitor progress and measure performance in terms of the achievement of objectives and targets.

Figure 12.1 Relationship between the management process and information requirements

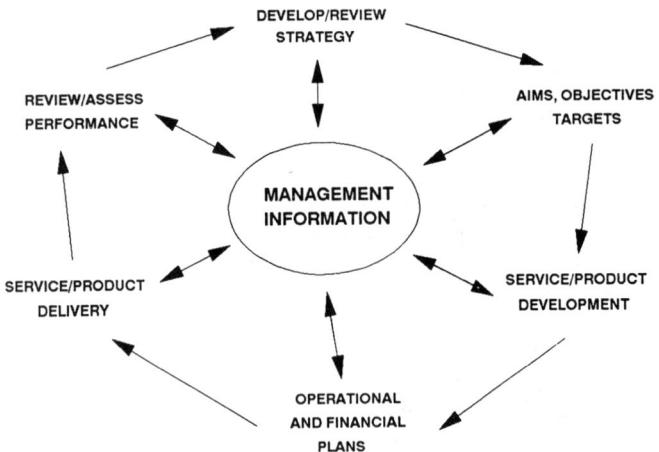

Without management information, the ability to manage effectively, if at all, becomes a real issue. Without information, the management process and, therefore, the manager becomes impotent, and decisions

tend to be taken by the 'seat of the pants'! Whilst there are times when decisions have to be taken without certain or all of the information being available, if it is done too often managers inevitably get caught out.

Management information in the right form and used correctly is a very powerful tool that can be used to make and influence decisions, challenge the status quo and effect change. At Alton Towers, for example, they discovered from analysis of throughput data that 40 per cent of all visitors came by coach. As a consequence, they began to market directly to coach operators and made sure that when coaches arrived at the park, the coach drivers were well looked after in terms of the availability and quality of on-site parking and services.

It does not necessarily follow that the success of management can be directly equated to the volume of information that is available for decision-making purposes. It is, in fact, the quality of information that is more important for effective decision-making than the quantity of information. It is also important to distinguish between data and information. Data constitutes isolated facts, which technically only become effective when they are organised or used in a way to impart knowledge. In many instances, volumes of data are provided instead of extracts of relevant, consolidated and succinct information. Being provided with a volume of data has a negative effect as it is time consuming having to sift through it to extract and then produce the information that is required in a format that is easy to assimilate and understand.

Information needs vary within an organisation and all too frequently one level of management is provided with information that has been designed for someone else. For example, senior management may be presented with detailed operational information for each of the activities. This provides them with information that is too detailed, distracting them from the more strategic issues of the business, and does not provide them with an overview of the entire operation. There is also little benefit to be gained from providing a manager with information on an activity over which he has little or no direct control, which is again time consuming and a waste of effort.

The information required by an organisation can be very specific to it. Also managers at various levels will require different types of information in order to operate, co-ordinate and control the activities for which they are responsible. An appropriate supply of information is needed at all levels. Information needs vary from senior executives to front line supervisors in the commercial sector and from members and chief officers to activity managers in the public sector.

There is no blueprint that can be produced regarding the information required by each organisation. What is needed is an appraisal of the information requirements at every level to ensure that the relevant information is prepared and supplied to managers and that relevant data is collected to produce that information.

Performance indicators

At senior management level in an organisation, the most important reports are those which summarise the financial and operational information and facilitate overall appraisal. A set of key performance indicators, both financial and non-financial, will also be required which will, at a glance, demonstrate the performance of the business. For ease and speed of reading and comparisons, these are often expressed as ratios. These are commonly used in the commercial sector, especially in the hospitality industry. Their use in the public sector is still very mixed, despite the efforts of the Audit Commission who identified their potential both in a review of leisure centre operation and as part of their work on the three 'Es' – economy, efficiency and effectiveness – in the mid 1980s.

Inherent in the concept of ratios is comparison with a standard that has been developed and adopted over time either for a specific operation or as an industry standard. A good example of the latter is the hotel industry, which has a well developed series of ratios that allow for both intra and inter-hotel comparisons between operations within the same market sectors. Thus, a hotel chain can compare performance of all its three-star hotels and identify quite quickly over and under-performance. However, comparisons can only be effective over a period of time and against historical performance.

There is no reason why performance ratios cannot be used across all sectors as, ultimately, all leisure providers have to operate within financial limits. All are concerned with economy or inputs, which is the cost of production, and efficiency, which is the relationship between inputs and outputs in producing a service at the lowest possible cost in order to achieve the objective(s) set.

We have outlined and dealt with a range of financial ratios in chapter six. These financial ratios can also be supported by operational performance ratios that add to the assessment of performance.

Occupancy is one such ratio that indicates whether a space or area is being used and is a major performance measure for the hotel industry. It can be calculated for different areas, by period (peak or off-peak) or time of day, day of week and so forth. It is simply calculated as follows:

$$\frac{\text{Number of space/area bookings made}}{\text{Total number of space/area bookings available}} \times 100\%$$

In this sense, a space or area can be a hotel room, conference/seminar room, badminton or squash court. Occupancy should also be viewed alongside utilisation, which indicates how well a space is being used, and throughput, which indicates volume of total use. Both utilisation and throughput should themselves be assessed against predetermined capacities, either maximum or optimum, so that the level of performance can be judged and variances identified.

As staff costs account for a significant proportion of total costs, it is useful to obtain some measure of effectiveness. This can be calculated as follows:

$$\frac{\text{Payroll cost of an activity/area}}{\text{Revenue generated by an acitivity/area}}$$

It was this type of information that led many local authorities to conclude that the cost of manning and collecting fees for the use of outdoor tennis courts during summer months was not cost-effective. This ratio is also widely used in the catering industry.

Another area were this type of performance ratio is useful is cleaning. One useful ratio is the calculation of the area cleaned per cleaner, which is calculated as follows:

$$\frac{\text{Area cleaned}}{\text{Number of cleaners}}$$

To this can be added a time element to the area cleaned per cleaner per hour. It should also be possible to assess the cost of cleaning by area, which is required if comparisons are required between in-house and contract cleaning operations. This is simply calculated as follows:

$$\frac{\text{Cost of cleaning}}{\text{Area cleaned}}$$

There are literally hundreds of ratios that can be used. It is important, therefore, to keep them to the minimum required to allow meaningful measurement or assessment of what is important to an operation. It is also important to read any ratios in context and not in isolation. Ratios are performance indicators, that is, they are but one source and type of information that feeds into the management process. They should be used to 'indicate' whether performance is as expected, better or worse and to spark an investigative process if it is the latter.

Ratios should not, therefore, be used in isolation or as a snapshot. They must be based upon information gathered over a period of time and used in conjunction with other management techniques or functions. For example, the last example given of operational ratios related to cleaning. Such ratios can indicate how efficiently a job is being done but not how effectively. In this instance, physical inspection is a key factor that has to take place and the results set alongside the financial and statistical information.

Another type of reporting which can either be used in addition to, or instead of, the summary and key performance indicator reports is exception reporting, whereby the attention of senior management is drawn to areas where performance is not in line with expected results and further investigation is required. Thus, for example, senior managers of an organisation running a number of leisure centres should want to see weekly income and utilisation information for each centre and monthly information on income and broad categories of expense. Comparisons of results with previous periods and with budgets will highlight areas that require further investigation. In addition, utilisation trends should be identified in order to assess whether changes in performance are in line with expected seasonal variations.

The use of more flexible visual display techniques and the graphical presentation of results enables trend information to be more easily understood and digested. Key indicators which combine financial and non-financial information will also be required, such as those outlined earlier in this chapter. If an organisation is experiencing financial liquidity problems, senior managers may also want to see daily cash balances with projections of forward cash requirements.

At the next level down in the organisation, such as managers responsible for the various activities within a leisure centre, considerably more operational information will be required. Ideally, managers will need to have information on the utilisation of the facilities in relation to time period and also to categories of user so that use can be monitored and they can respond to changing demands. It should also be possible for managers to monitor actual achievement against determined targets and data should be collected at a sufficient level of detail which then can be aggregated into information to provide answers to questions such as:

- How much use is being made of a specific facility – in total/at peak times/ at off-peak times?
- What category of user is making most use of a facility – for example, adult/junior?
- What category of user is using a specific facility, say, between 5–6pm on a Friday evening?
- Are there specific time periods which are experiencing pressure and can anything be reprogrammed to alleviate the pressure to make maximum use of the space and time?
- What type of users are contained within the customer base? Are the target markets being reached and are they using the facilities?
- Does the customer base comprise mainly of casual users or is there a hard core of frequent users? When recording that a facility has been used 10 times, does this mean that one person has used it on 10 occasions or 10 casual users on one occasion?
- How has the utilisation and the user profile changed over the past twelve months?

Such information will enable managers to monitor how successful they are in achieving their operational targets and they can provide feedback in the management process. This will enable strategies and policies to be developed and amended, as appropriate, in the light of the achieved results. Activity managers will also require detailed financial information on expenditure and income in order to monitor the actual financial performance against predetermined budgets and compare it with past performance.

The reports required by management to operate a business differ totally from the annual statutory reports, which reveal very little about the detailed operations of the business in which management is particularly interested. Consequently, a parallel but generally integrated set of management reports tend to be produced for running the business. The usefulness of the internal reports can be measured by the degree to which attention is focused on areas that need special attention. The reports should be aligned with specific activities and responsibilities and they should appear in a logical order to assist the managers concerned.

The danger, however, which must be safeguarded against is to introduce a reporting system which provides all the information that is theoretically desirable instead of the information that is really needed in practise. Consequently, if information is being received and consistently found to be of little or no practical use, scrap it and save everybody's time.

Another aspect that needs to be considered is the speed with which information should be provided and its accuracy. With external annual accounts accuracy is more important, but with internal management reports the speed with which information is made available is more important than complete accuracy. Approximate figures will probably be sufficient to provide an indication where problem areas need to be addressed. The purpose of the reports is not only to provide accurate information, but to provide it within an acceptable time period so that action can be taken by managers, as appropriate, and in good time.

Using computers for management information

Having said that all relevant data should be captured at the lowest level of detail and be capable of being aggregated into information in a number of ways, the question then arises, how should this be done? The nature, diversity and demand for information that is required these days is generally too much to be able to cope with on a manual basis, and the use of computers for the production of management information continues to increase.

Using computers to produce management information compared with manual methods brings the advantages of:

- being able to hold vast amounts and different types of data and aggregate it into different types of reports according to information needs;
- being able to produce information quickly;
- being able to produce information based on responsibility areas in complex management structures, for example, on a matrix management structure, which would be extremely difficult and time consuming to do manually;

- introducing greater efficiency in reporting;
- providing more flexibility to respond to changing needs;
- greatly assisting the planning process if modelling facilities exist to perform sensitivity analysis.

Spending on computers and systems can represent a large investment, and it is important to follow a logical process and planned systems approach to ensure that the investment is right at the end of the day. Unless the system planning is set in the context of the business, computing can become an end in itself. Consequently, the nature and structure of the organisation, as well as internal and external factors, are also important when considering the introduction and creation of any computer based system.

An initial proposal for a computer system may arise from a user department where a particular need may be recognised. A feasibility study should be undertaken in order to review the proposal for the computer system before any major commitment is entered into. The study should take into consideration what is already in existence and the various options available to achieve the desired information. The proposals should also be related to the organisation's strategy and, where one exists, the information technology strategy.

Once a decision has been made to proceed with the concept of the introduction of a computerised information system, it is then necessary to decide on which systems should be introduced. Should systems be bespoke or be tailored exactly to the organisation's requirements? Are there any computer packages available that can do the job? Should the systems stand alone or should they link with any other systems in the organisation?

To answer these questions and ultimately arrive at the most appropriate and cost effective solution requires a carefully planned approach, as set out in figure 12.2. It is first of all necessary for the person who is attempting to select the system, usually an analyst, to understand the nature, objectives, structure and activities of the business. It is necessary to identify what the requirements are from the management information system, for example, what activities should it cover? what information is required by each of the managers? over what time period and in what format is the information required?

The most productive technique for identifying the requirements is to have a thorough understanding of the business and its activities coupled with interviewing the managers involved. If left solely to management interviews this may not be so productive as, if just asked for their information requirements, managers may not be particularly helpful, as they either tend to say that they are happy with the information they already receive or that they want everything that is available. These are easier options than thinking through a process of change and identifying what is really needed. All levels of management should be involved in the process of identifying information requirements to ensure completeness and consistency.

Based on the information requirements, selected software and hardware suppliers should then normally be requested to tender to demonstrate the capabilities of their products in the light of the information needs. The products should be evaluated against selected criteria so that an eventual software and hardware solution, appropriate to the needs of the organisation, can be selected and subsequently implemented in a planned and structured manner.

Experience has shown that a structured approach to systems planning, selection and implementation produces success and results which, at the end of the day, provides managers with what they need. Approached the other way round, by introducing a system without considering what is required of it, can be a costly mistake if it is subsequently found that the system does not satisfy the information needs of managers.

The key stages involved in selecting the right computer based system are represented diagrammatically in figure 12.2.

Figure 12.2 Planned approach to introducing a computerised management information system

Result:
Objectives Achieved

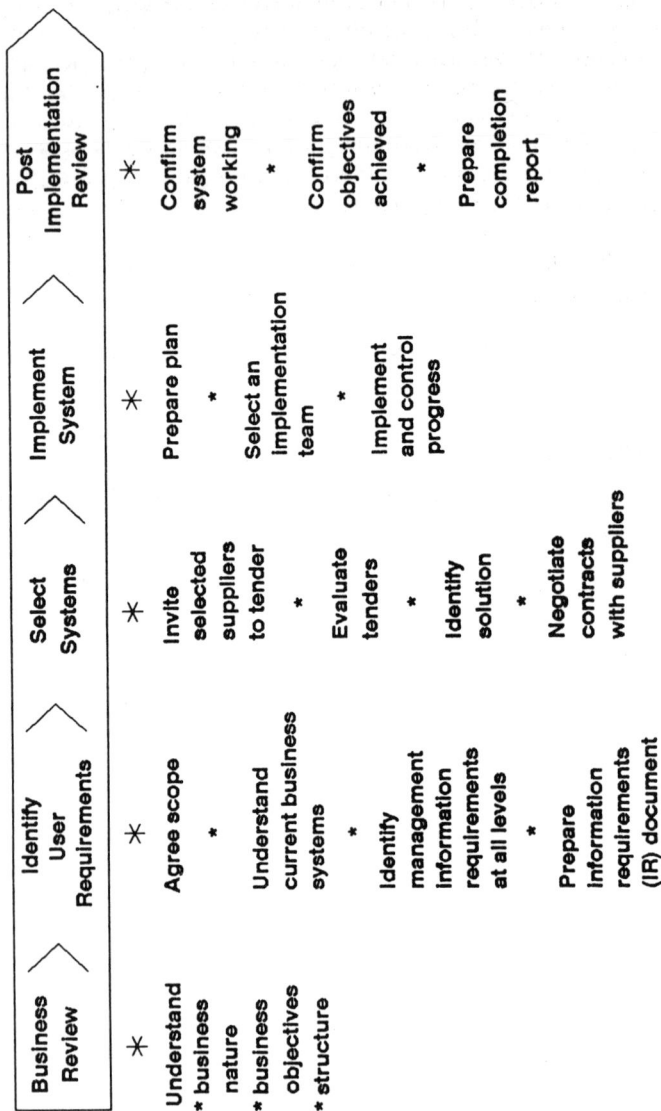

Business Review	Identify User Requirements	Select Systems	Implement System	Post Implementation Review
Understand * business nature * business objectives * structure	Agree scope * Understand current business systems * Identify management information requirements at all levels * Prepare Information requirements (IR) document	Invite selected suppliers to tender * Evaluate tenders * Identify solution * Negotiate contracts with suppliers	Prepare plan * Select an implementation team * Implement and control progress	Confirm system working * Confirm objectives achieved * Prepare completion report

Conclusion

Information is of primary importance to all levels of management in an organisation in the planning, operation and control processes although the information requirements of the various levels will differ. It is important to realise that as information is part of the management process, it is part of the process that causes change.

In most cases, the most effective way of producing management information is through the use of computer technology and as technology advances, and with the added benefit of desk top publishing, the scope for obtaining and presenting information forever increases. In designing any management information system it is necessary to understand the business and its activities and also the powers and responsibilities in an organisation.

References

1. Audit Inspectorate 1983 *Development and Operation of Leisure Centres; Selected Case Studies.* HMSO

Further reading

Cave C, Kogan M, Smith R (eds) 1990 *Output and Performance Kingsley J Measurement in Government. The State of the Art*

13 Sources and types of commercial leisure finance

This chapter discusses the types and sources of commercial finance and the confidence of the financial markets with the leisure sector. Sources and types of non-commercial finance are discussed in chapter fourteen.

The types of finance

As organisations grow they will eventually be faced with the problem that the expansion cannot be financed entirely from funds generated from internal operations. A decision needs to be made, therefore, on how to meet the funding gap and on the best type of finance to meet the organisation's requirements. Other than raising finance from internal sources, the main types of business finance are equity and borrowings. It is important to understand the differences between them and to appreciate the importance of balancing the relationship between equity and borrowings.

Equity

Equity is the owners' interest in the business and consists of the resources put in by them (shareholders) and the accumulation over the years of profits, after tax (reserves), which are retained within the business. Equity is a risk capital. It is not repaid during the course of trading and usually there is no guarantee that the shareholders will receive any payments for the use of their funds. Any payments made to shareholders are called dividends and are only usually paid if the business makes a profit. In the event of a liquidation, all of the company's liabilities and preference shares must be settled before equity is repaid. The main sources of equity arise from the founders, management, private investors, venture capitalists, the stock market and banking.

Borrowing

Borrowing is another major source of finance. Interest is usually paid to the lenders and is offset against business profits. Lenders have no voting rights or direct control over management, but invariably require security over the business assets and, occasionally, personal guarantees, which means that the owners' personal assets may be at risk in the event of the business failing. In the event of liquidation, secured loans are settled before unsecured loans and both are settled before equity is repaid.

Finance is also classified into short, medium and long-term and should be matched with the useful life of the asset for which the funding is being sought.

Short and medium-term finance

Short-term finance of up to one year is normally used to cover the trading variations in a business. For example, creditors often have to be paid before debtors have settled their invoices. The most common type of short-term borrowing is by bank overdraft, which is often secured. This will also be relevant to businesses with seasonal fluctuations. For example, theme parks and similar attractions will receive most of their visitors and therefore most of their income during the spring, summer and autumn. However, fixed costs still have to be paid during the winter when the cash flowing in will be substantially reduced. Consequently, it may be necessary to use some form of short term finance to cover this period.

Medium-term finance, covering one to five years, is normally used to purchase assets such as machinery, plant or vehicles, which have a useful life for the duration of the loan period, and also to finance general working capital, which would avoid permanent overdraft borrowing which tends to be more expensive. Common types of medium term finance which require security include bank loans, finance and operating leases, debentures, and hire purchase agreements.

Bank loan

This is the best known and most widely used source of short-term finance. It is a flexible form of finance, with interest being charged only on the amount that is used. The organisation is usually given an overdraft facility, which is a ceiling within which their financial affairs can be managed. Interest rates are linked and will be above the base lending rate. Bankers will also take into consideration the degree of risk associated with the business. Ideally, a bank overdraft should be short-term finance, being self liquidating in that it should be capable of being repaid out of trading profits. However, invariably, an overdraft facility tends to become part of the permanent capital structure of some businesses as it still remains a reasonably cost effective form of finance.

Debt factoring and invoice discounting

Debt factoring and invoice discounting is the sale of an organisation's debts to a third party (the factor), at a discount in return for prompt cash. There has been rapid growth in this type of finance over the past ten years, which tends to demonstrate a deviation from the more traditional forms of finance.

This type of finance provides working capital and improves cash flow. An organisations outstanding debts are taken as security and up to 85 per cent of the total outstanding debt can be obtained. With factoring, the debts are collectable by the commercial factor, but with invoice discounting, the debt collection remains the responsibility of the company.

This type of arrangement is more flexible than an overdraft facility and is geared to an organisation's success in terms of sales. It provides a useful source of immediate funds to an organisation, but is more expensive than an overdraft facility, with a charge of 2–3 per cent over base rate being made plus an additional service charge of 0.1–0.75 per cent of turnover. Although more costly than an overdraft, it is cheaper than venture capital finance. Venture capital finance is discussed later in this chapter.

Leasing

A lease is a contract between a lessor and a lessee for the lifetime of a specific asset. There are two kinds of lease – a finance lease, and an operating lease. A finance lease transfers all the risks and rewards of ownership of the asset to the lessee. Under an operating lease, the risks and benefits of ownership are usually the responsibility of the lessor.

There are two main costs connected with the ownership of assets. The first is a combination of wear and tear and the loss in value due to obsolescence. The second is the opportunity cost, the lost profit which could have been generated from working capital represented by these funds tied up in asset ownership. The decision to lease or buy will be influenced by the organisation's cashflow. By leasing an asset, a firm can use the funds that would have been tied up as working capital and hence increase the rate of return.

Sale and lease back is another common form of releasing funds tied up in fixed assets. The business which owns the asset sells the asset to, for instance, an insurance company and then leases the asset back at an agreed rate. In this way cash tied up in assets can be released without altering the physical use of assets.

Hire purchase

The criteria which apply to leasing also apply to the decision to buy tangible assets on hire purchase terms. The total cost of the asset plus an interest charge is spread over a period of time. In general, the net cost of hire purchase terms exceed that of leases, and they are also more expensive than overdraft facilities.

Bills of exchange

A bill of exchange allows a company a certain time to settle a debt with interest. The creditor accepts the bill and when it matures the amount outstanding plus the interest is paid to the person specified or to the bearer. The company holding the bill can sell it at least at face value or 'negotiate' it with a person or a financial institution to obtain ready cash for a 'discounted' bill. These tend to be used by large organisations to provide a source of ready cash at a cost similar to an overdraft facility.

Medium and long-term finance

Venture capital

The leisure sector tends to attract a less than favourable reputation amongst traditional financial institutions, mainly due to its unpredictable nature, generally riskier projects and because of over optimistic turnover and growth projections.

In the event of a higher risk project, it may be possible to obtain finance in the form of venture capital. Venture capital is a risk capital that forms part of a company's equity base. Venture capital is most often invested in private companies and can take the form of ordinary shares, preference shares and loans that can be converted in the future into shares. The intention is to make a good return once the shares are offered to the public. The advantages of venture capital are that an equity arrangement strengthens the balance sheet and it provides a medium to long term finance which cannot be withdrawn.

The disadvantages are that in the long run it is the most expensive form of finance (35 per cent to 40 per cent compounded per annum), the owners' equity is diluted by the issue of new shares, the company becomes answerable to external shareholders and there is also the possibility that the original shareholders may lose control. Despite its disadvantages, this type of funding is often considered by existing shareholders when they decide that it is better to own a reduced percentage of a growing business rather than 100 per cent of a business which is struggling due to the lack of an adequate equity base.

Venture capital is particularly appropriate for new or expanding businesses with above average growth prospects and where owners and managers are prepared to adopt an aggressive growth strategy in order to create value for themselves and for external shareholders. Returns are usually obtained through capital appreciation rather than dividend yield.

Venture capital is one of the areas that can provide a main source of funding for the leisure industry. This is especially the case with the banks lending capacities reduced and organisations wanting to avoid gearing up balance sheets, that is, having too much loan debt in relation to equity.

One of the factors often seen as a downside to this type of finance is the investor's exit date and exit values. Most deals are structured to give an exit after somewhere around three to five years. Estimating a company's value at exit is an inexact science and, therefore, venture capitalists tend to veer towards a conservative valuation in order to provide a margin for error. There is little point in calculating exit values unless this value can be turned into cash for the investors. The exit value is normally calculated by multiplying the projected or historical level of profits by an earnings multiple. In determining the appropriate multiple to use, the venture capitalist will take into consideration the nature of the business and growth potential, the existing earnings, the stock market view of the industry and the multiples currently being applied to comparable businesses in the sector.

If the investment is a good one, is well managed and is achieving its projections, it should be ready to follow an exit route of flotation, sale or management buy-out. Most providers will seek to establish an agreed method of realising their investment prior to committing funds.

Long-term borrowing

Long-term borrowing (in excess of five years) is used to purchase fixed assets, such as buildings and land, which have a long useful life, to provide semi-permanent working capital or to fund acquisitions of other businesses. Common types of long-term borrowings include bank loans and mortgage loans.

Share issue

If an organisation is already quoted on the Stock Exchange it can offer more shares to the public in order to raise further funds. The methods that can be adopted to do this are:

- rights issue – this gives existing shareholders the right to purchase new shares or debentures in proportion to their current holdings. These shares are usually issued at a discount on market price, thus reflecting the effect of the dilution of share capital;
- public issue – the company offers its shares to the general public along with a prospectus and all the information required by legislation. The

shares are offered at a fixed price and the public apply for the shares they require;

- offer for sale – new shares are offered to the public, usually by advertisement by a financial institution which has previously bought the shares from the company and then offers them to the public at a higher price;
- placing – the shares that are to be offered are sold privately by financial institutions. This is mainly suitable for smaller share issues.

Share Capital

There are basically two types of share capital which can be issued to raise funds for a company and they can be categorised as ordinary share capital and preference capital. There are also various classifications within the two categories.

Ordinary Share Capital

Ordinary shareholders are those with no particular rights other than the right to participate in the profits by way of dividends. There is no guaranteed fixed return and the dividend available for distribution will be totally dependent upon the profits and appropriations made by the directors. Dividends to ordinary shareholders will only be paid once all other dividends have been satisfied. In the event of liquidations all of the company's liabilities and other forms of capital are settled before ordinary share capital is repaid.

There are various classes of ordinary shares, notably A Ordinary, B Ordinary, Preferred Ordinary – which have a right to a fixed dividend after payment of dividend to the preference shareholders, and Deferred Ordinary shares, which rank for dividend after the Preferred Ordinary shares and are usually entitled to the profits then remaining. The various classifications may have different voting rights.

There may also be Deferred Founders or Management shares which have to wait for their dividend until all other classes of shareholders have participated in the profits, but they are generally entitled to the whole or a large proportion of the surplus profits after all prior claims.

Preference Share Capital

Preference shares are those which have a prior claim on any profits available for dividend and, in the case of liquidation, they have a prior claim to repayment before other shareholders. The preference shareholder will receive a fixed dividend, but under inflation conditions, the investment proposition is not so attractive. Consequently, the take-up of preference share capital has declined over the years. If the shares are not cumulative preference shares, the dividend is payable only out of profits each year and, if it is not paid, it cannot be carried forward and be received out of profits in following years.

The classes of preference shares are:

- cumulative preference shares – which entitles the holders to a fixed rate dividend and the right to have any arrears carried forward and added to the dividends of future years;
- redeemable preference shares – these are shares which can be repurchased by the company and certain reserve funds only can be used for this purpose;
- convertible preference shares – the holder has the right to convert to ordinary shares at a predetermined price and future date;
- participating preference shares – the holder is entitled to a fixed dividend and to any surplus profits after payments at a specified rate on the ordinary shares.

Debentures

As the take up of preference shares has declined, the issue of debentures has increased, which are more flexible and cheaper than preference shares. A debenture is an acknowledgement of a debt of a company, normally containing provisions as to payments of interest and the terms of repayment of the principal.

A shareholder is an 'inside' person, being a member of the company, whereas a debenture holder is an 'outside' person, merely a loan creditor. A shareholder obtains dividends on the money they have invested, whereas a debenture holder receives interest on the money lent, which is chargeable against profits, but has to be paid irrespective of whether or not there are sufficient profits. This is obviously a disadvantage to the company.

A debenture may be one of many types according to security, permanence or priority and these include:

- fixed debenture – this loan is secured on specific assets and the company may not dispose of the secured assets without obtaining the sanction of the debenture holders;
- floating debenture – this loan is secured on all of the company's assets but it does not prevent the company from dealing with the assets in the normal course of business;
- naked debenture – this is an unsecured loan and is not so popular in the current financial climate;
- convertible debenture – this loan can be converted into ordinary shares at a future date and at an agreed price. This is a popular way of providing venture capital.

In respect of permanence, debentures may be irredeemable, whereby they are only repayable in the event of liquidation. Alternatively, they may be redeemable at the end of a specified period at the company's option or by purchase on the open market. Debentures may also constitute a first or second charge on the property which is to be the security.

Debenture schemes tend to be an effective method of obtaining finance in advance and invariaby through people that are also interested in the project or potential development. For example, debenture schemes have been used to raise finance for golf club developments. Either existing or new members are offered the debentures which may then be redeemable at a later date either at the original or current value. The debenture holder will invariably be given additional privileges, for example, priority on bookings or teeing off times.

Gearing ratio

The ratio between the amount of equity capital and the fixed interest capital is known as the gearing ratio, and this affects the dividend expectations of the ordinary shareholders. A business which is highly geared has a high proportion of fixed interest capital in relation to equity capital. This means that increased profits will give the ordinary shareholder a good return on high investment, that is, better earnings per share compared to a preference shareholder who will continue to receive a fixed dividend.

If a company has only a small proportion of fixed interest capital compared to ordinary share capital, it is deemed to be low geared and any increase in profits will have little appreciable effect upon the ordinary shareholders' dividends.

There are alternative definitions of gearing which can be found in many financial accounting text books. The gearing concept is illustrated in table 13.1 using the common definition, which is the total shareholders interest compared with the total prior charge capital plus borrowings.

Table 13.1 Simple illustration of the gearing concept

Capital employed	Company A £	Company B £
Authorised and issued share capital – ordinary shares	600,000	75,000
Reserves		
Share premiums	40,000	30,000
General reserve	80,000	45,000
Profit and loss account	110,000	100,000
	830,000	260,000
Long-term loans		
12% secured debentures	200,000	770,000
	1,030,000	1,030,000
Gearing ratio	0.24 (200000/830000)	2.96 (770000/260000)
Gearing	Low	High

As can be seen, Company B is highly geared, having more fixed interest capital compared with equity capital, whereas Company A is low geared, having more equity to loan. With the same level of profits, but with different gearing ratios, the companies produce vastly different profits available for the shareholders, which can be expressed as shown in table 13.2 below.

Table 13.2 Illustrations of profitability by varying gearing ratios

	Company A	Company B
Profit	£110,000	£110,000
Less: interest on secured debentures	£24,000	£92,400
Available for distribution to ordinary shareholders	£86,000	£17,600
Number of ordinary shares	600,000	75,000
Share issue value per share	£1.00	£1.00
Profit for distribution	£86,000	£17,600
Earnings per share	£0.14p	£0.23p

The higher the gearing ratio the better the return for the ordinary shareholder. However, there is a view that, in years where low profits are made, it will not be possible to meet the interest on the fixed interest capital. Consequently, it is necessary to strike the right balance otherwise undue financial strain may be placed on the company. In addition, highly geared companies would find it difficult to increase their borrowings to fund expansion.

There is no optimum gearing ratio for all businesses and the ratio may also alter for a business during its lifetime. The main issues that need to be considered and the general guidelines used in assessing the strength of the balance sheet of a business include:

- the higher the gearing ratio, the greater the amount of interest that has to be paid in relation to earnings and the cashflow available to finance them;
- where a business is high risk, the lower the gearing ratio should be (that is, more equity relative to borrowings);
- for most organisations a gearing ratio of 1:1 indicates a sound balance sheet;
- at what point of underachievement could a business still meet its liabilities?

Sources of finance

The number of sources offering equity finance has increased, some of which may specialise in particular stages of project finance such as the start up, the development or the flotation stage whilst others may specialise in a particular sector. Some of the financial institutions may provide all types of borrowings, including equity, and, therefore, may be willing to offer a balanced package of equity and borrowings.

The principal sources of equity include venture capitalist and specialist investment institutions, equity divisions within clearing banks, merchant banks, 3I, the Stock Exchange, pension funds, insurance companies, investment trusts, issuing and accepting houses, business expansion schemes and private funding.

The types of finance which could be available are shown in table 13.3

Table 13.3 Types of finance

	Short term	Medium term	Long term
Banks	•	•	•
Venture capitalists		•	•
Debt factoring/invoice discount companies	•		
Leasing and hire purchase	•	•	
Stock exchange			•
3I's	•	•	•

Non-commercial sources of finance

Non-commercial sources of finance should also be considered, such as Government assistance, as this may fill a funding gap in respect of a particular project. There are many grants currently available, and these are discussed further in chapter fifteen.

The economy and the financial markets

The economy

The UK economy in recent years has had major concerns and seen major disasters. The leisure sector is at an historic 25 year low against the FT Index and the stream of problems and receiverships continue. Confidence in the sector is very low, with people not prepared to commit themselves to major purchase and/or repayments of any kind. The general outlook continues gloomy, with a record number of businesses going to the wall.

However, the picture may not be as clear cut as that. There are historical trends and indicators that suggest that the leisure industry may be capable of withstanding the ravages of inflation and recession better than most. The UK sports market has traditionally been quite resilient. For example, whilst the economy generally was slowing down quite considerably during 1989/90 and leisure spending generally stood still, spending on sport and recreation actually grew by 1 per cent.

It is also more indicative to view the various segments of the population to see how they are affected rather than the population as a whole. Those hardest hit by the recession are aged 25 to 44 with a mortgage and those living in the south-east are particularly hardest hit. However, those aged 16 to 24 and 55 and over may scarcely notice the recession, according to the research findings. Young employed people without heavily committed expenditure such as mortgages and associated household bills such as fuel, are still spending, as are older people, many of whom have small or no mortgages and are traditionally savers. High interest rates tend to benefit this group who receive significant returns on building society investments.

Both of these groups still have a high level of discretionary spend. There has been a view that during periods of economic hardship people tend not to give up their sport and recreation activities, especially if they are regular participants. They tend to try and find other areas in which to tighten their belts. Certainly, the indicators suggest that those who provide services and products for the younger age groups are less likely to experience a downturn in their business than others.

Predictions show, however, that during 1992 leisure sector earnings could increase by some 20.4 per cent, which is the highest growth of earnings in any of the categories on the Stock Exchange. This tends to indicate that there is significant latent leisure demand, which, once unleashed, will increase leisure spending.

The financial markets

In the past, banks have been the financial pump primers in the leisure sector, based largely on the knowledge that there was some form of security in leisure being linked to property. In the late 1980s, the principles that underpinned leisure finance were that the sector was growing fast and that it was asset rich even though cash poor. When the tide turned, the assets were not so rich. With the problems that were subsequently experienced with the collapse of leisure portfolios, the banks were keen to suppress leisure exposure and to convert loans into a more secure position. The terms of trade on lending worsened against the borrower, including the debt/equity ratio. Consequently, confidence with the leisure sector was lost amongst banking institutions, which will take a long time to regain.

The Stock Exchange

The Stock Exchange has seen leisure sector shares slide over the past two to three years, which also indicates considerable disenchantment with the leisure sector. Balance sheets have experienced extreme pressure and asset values have been decreased in order to stabilise and secure a position from which it is possible to move forward. Recapitalisation is desperately needed and if the projected growth in leisure earnings materialises and results are demonstrated, then there may be a re-emergence of an equity base back into leisure. This, however, sets a scene for a long-term recovery for an equity base as it will be necessary to demonstrate growth and profits over the next one to two years.

There has also been an increase in mergers and acquisitions activity, and this will continue to be significant as it will be a mechanism of funding and a spur to supplementary equity development. There are some dangers inherent in acquisition in that it may involve some diversification into unfamiliar areas, which was referred to in chapter seven.

The venture capital industry

The venture capital industry has also had a difficult time during the recession, experiencing significant write-off and valuation problems in the leisure sector. The problems with valuations is that there is a vast expectation gap between the vendor and the venture capital analyst. The owners perceptions are of high valuations, and to a certain extent they are locked in a time warp of the late 1980s rather than coming to terms with the more realistic and lower values of the 1990s. The venture capitalist industry has only a moderate interest in leisure and, until the expectation gap narrows, it is unlikely that it will be a major player in terms of leisure sector finance. Based on industry information, the leisure sector overall has moved down the preference list of venture capitalists, with engineering, communications and chemicals being the top preferences.

The industry is extremely liquid, but the amount of funding is still small as it perceives that good, new opportunities are scarce. Problems constantly cited by venture capitalists are the poor quality of the management of projects and inadequately capitalised schemes. There can also be endless debate on the short and long-term projections of a project and also the assessment of the net asset value. Consequently, it is difficult to fix the venture capital returns accurately.

Venture capital yields are at an all time high. In the mid 1980s returns were in the region of 25 per cent, whereas in the 1990s returns of up to 40 per cent are required, especially on new start up businesses, in view of the risk involved. When converting this back to establish sustainability and the need to balance debt, equity and cash flow, the project economics do not look very healthy for equity investors.

Traditional financing structures of debt/equity do not fit the present financial mood and there is a need for imaginative financial instruments. Areas that are seen as attractive by the venture capital industry are acquisitions and mergers, divisional spinouts or management buyouts or management buy-ins. Leisure is viewed as a cash absorber requiring capital injection and is, therefore, seen as a negative rather than positive influence. However, a venture capitalist may view favourably the situation where an organisation offers an attractive management buyout package to a certain division in order to remove the leisure subsidiary. In this way, track record, a proven product and proven management can be demonstrated.

The future

Underlying trends in the 1990s show that there is tremendous opportunity in the leisure sector. Consumer spending will increase, standards of living will be higher, the working week will be shorter and so will our working lives. Leisure time will, therefore, be increased and there will be far more discerning leisure consumers with higher disposable income, a large proportion of which could result from inherited wealth.

The recession has probably hastened the demise of the more speculative and weaker operators in the leisure market, who perceived it as an area of rapid growth and fast profit during its boom period of the late 1980s. The arrival of Euro Disney will, possibly, set new standards in facilities, entertainment, management and language capabilities. European leisure competition could, therefore, have a positive effect on the pool of competent managers, and by the mid 1990s it should be possible to dispel the 'poor management' label now widely applied to the sector by money funding initiatives.

The leisure industry is at a turning point. Growth and good results should generate a re-emergence of an equity base, but it will take a lot longer to entice banks back into the financial arena.

Further reading

National Westminster Bank plc 1992 *Finance for Growth.* Published in association with CBI Initiative 1992 Mercury Books
Allen M *The Times Guide to International Finance.* Times Books
Clarkson, Elliott *Managing Money and Finance.* Gower Press

14 Sources of non-commercial finance

Non-commercial funding is at least as important as the more traditional commercial sources and, in some instances, can actually make the difference between whether a project proceeds or not. Used either as a pump-priming or topping up device, such finance can be employed very effectively to attract investment into a specifically targeted area and/or encourage business start-ups in order to generate employment.

The most potent form of finance in this respect is grant, which enables the overall level of borrowing to be kept down, thereby reducing interest payments. Soft (low interest) loans have pretty much the same effect. It is also possible to obtain repayment 'holidays' on loans covering the first years of operation. This method of deferring the commencement of loan repayment gives a project breathing space in which to become established and avoid potential cash flow and liquidity problems during its critical early stages.

The main sources of such funding are Government, both UK and European Community (EC), and public sector agencies that are used to channel funds from government. It is often the combination of government or government agency involvement and investment that gives commercial lending institutions the confidence or 'comfort' they seek in a proposed project before deciding to invest themselves or sanction borrowing.

It is estimated that there are well over 300 different types of grant schemes covering a wide range of leisure related areas. Whilst each source will operate under its own terms and conditions of financial support, applicants for funds should expect to have to adopt the same rigorous approach as required by commercial lenders. Thus, applications will need to be supported by both financial and other information along with a business plan for the proposed project.

As there are so many potential sources of non-commercial finance, they cannot possibly all be dealt with here. Consequently, we have concentrated upon a few of the major types of grant and loan schemes

that are available. These broadly fall into the three categories of UK
Government, EC Government and UK Public Sector Agencies.

UK Government sources of finance

Before describing some of the major sources of finance, it is necessary
to mention that the UK is divided into Assisted and Non-Assisted Areas.
Assisted areas, such as the term applies, are given priority and,
therefore, attract greater levels of financial assistance from both UK
and EC Government sources. These are areas that have experienced
both general economic decline and higher than average levels of
unemployment. Assisted areas are also sub-divided further into
Development and Intermediate Areas.

Regional Selective Assistance

Regional Selective Assistance is only available in Assisted Areas, and
can take the form of either grant or exchange risk guarantees. With
regard to the latter, this essentially provides cover on exchange risks
on foreign currency loans obtained at generally favourable fixed interest
rates from organisations such as the European Coal and Steel
Community, which we describe later in this chapter.

Grants are made available through the Department of Trade and
Industry (DTI) and are aimed at the manufacturing sector. However,
some service sector areas, of which leisure is one, also qualify. Priority,
in terms of the size of grant, is given to Development as opposed to
Intermediate Areas.

Each grant is negotiable, and is based upon the fixed capital costs
of a project and the number of jobs that the project is expected to
create or safeguard. Costs eligible for inclusion in the grant application
include land acquisition, site preparation, buildings, plant and
machinery. In addition, working capital required for the project can
also be taken into account when grant levels are being fixed.

The main criteria for assessing grants are the viability of the project,
the need for assistance, that the project must be of regional or national
significance, that there is job creation or protection and that private
sector finance is also available. There is no set formula for agreeing
grants as the process functions on a top up basis whereby the amount
of grant offered is the **minimum** required to allow the project to proceed
after all other sources of funding have been accounted for.

Finally, both the level of assets and jobs have to be maintained for
an agreed period of time after the project has been completed. Disposal
of assets or a fall in the level of employment below that agreed could
result in the grant being clawed back.

Regional Enterprise Grants

These are also available from the DTI, but only in Development Areas, and are aimed at small firms with less than 25 employees. Projects must be of greater than local significance and of proven viability.

Grants cover up to 15 per cent of expenditure on fixed assets up to a maximum of £15,000. Eligible costs include land acquisition, site preparation, buildings, plant and machinery and vehicles used solely on the site.

City Grant

Available from the Department of the Environment (DoE), City Grants are aimed at urban redevelopment or renewal projects costing in excess of £200,000. Priority is given to towns and cities which submit Inner Area Programmes. Once again, there is no set formula, with the level of grant offered being that which enables the project to proceed and to be viable. In other words, it is the grant that makes the project viable.

Farm Diversification Grant Scheme

Available from the Ministry of Agriculture, Fisheries and Food (MAFF), the scheme is aimed at assisting farmers who wish to diversify into non-agricultural profit-making businesses on their farms. It covers a range of possible business activities, but the leisure related opportunities include facilities for sport and recreation, livery for horses and ponies, hire facilities for horses and ponies, craft workshops and basic tourist accommodation such as camping and bunkhouse barns.

The following types of grant are available currently under this scheme.

Feasibility study grant – covers up to 50 per cent of the cost of a feasibility study, which is required as part of the initial planning of a propject. They are subject to a maximum of £3,000 for individuals and £10,000 for groups of farmers. The feasibility study must contain a core of activities consisting of market research, business strategy, capital requirements, income and expenditure projections, labour implications, an assessment of the impact on the agricultural business, statutory requirements and recommendations.

Capital grants – generally available at a rate of 25 per cent, although this can increase to just over 30 per cent in certain cases, up to a maximum grant of £35,000. An applicant must demonstrate that the project will be viable and unable to proceed without the benefit of the grant.

Marketing grants – these are available for the first three years of a project once it commences operation, on a basis of 40 per cent in the first year, 30 per cent in the second and 20 per cent in the third and final year. These grants are intended to cover the cost of employing marketing staff as well as other associated marketing costs. Grants are subject to a maximum of £3,000 per year for individuals and £10,000 per year for groups of farmers.

Set-Aside

Also available from MAFF, this is one of the latest and, possibly, more controversial schemes, aimed primarily at reducing surplus crop production. In return for taking at least 20 per cent of land used for growing arable crops in the base year 1987/88 out of production, farmers are compensated on an annual basis for up to five years. The level of compensation is set currently at £130 per hectare for land in what is known as Less-Favoured Areas and £150 per hectare elsewhere.

As part of the scheme, farmers are allowed to use the set-aside land for certain leisure-related developments such as sporting facilities, for example, golf courses, camping and caravanning parks, tourist facilities and nature reserves. However, land set-aside cannot be used to construct permanent buildings or structures for residential use, including hotels, or for the wholesale or retail sales of goods. The exception to this rule, however, is that buildings may be erected if they form part of a business proposal eligible for a Farm Diversification Grant and covered by the leisure related activities listed there.

Others

Indirect assistance is also available from certain government departments, two of which are worth mentioning. The Department of Employment operates a scheme under which it helps both new and existing businesses to obtain medium-term (two to seven years) loan finance to a maximum of £100,000, which the Department then agrees to underwrite up to a maximum of 70 per cent. Loans can only be obtained from financial institutions that participate in the scheme. A charge is made by the Department in the form of a quarterly premium on the loan guarantees element of the loan.

The DTI operates a scheme which provides financial assistance for consultancy studies, under the Enterprise Initiative, to help businesses become more competitive in certain areas of business activity. This scheme was developed with the challenges of the single European market very much in mind. It covers business activities such as marketing, business planning, quality, design and financial and information systems.

The scheme consists of free and assisted consultancy advice. The first two days are free and consist of assessing the business operation in terms of its efficiency and potential. An area of particular need is identified and a consultancy brief is developed. The DTI then meets 50 per cent of the cost of between five and fifteen days consultancy.

In Assisted Areas the proportion of cost met rises to two-thirds.

EC Sources of Finance

European Coal and Steel Community (ECSC) loans

ECSC loans are available to both public bodies and private companies for projects that create new jobs in traditional coal and steel areas. To ensure this, the ESCS must be satisfied that the scheme will be located within approximately fifteen miles of coal and/or steel closures. In this way, new jobs should be created for ex-coal and steel workers.

Loans are available for up to 50 per cent of the fixed asset cost of a project, with a minimum capital cost of £10,000. Loans up to £4.5 million are made to small and medium sized companies through nominated agents in the UK, which includes some of the high street banks. Loans in excess of £4.5 million have to be negotiated directly with the ECSC. Security is always required.

The period of loan is usually eight years, with a four year repayment holiday. Loans generally have a fixed rate of interest on which rebates of up to 3 per cent may be available for the first five years, dependent upon the number of jobs actually created.

European Regional Development Fund (ERDF)

ERDF grants are available solely to local authorities, especially in Assisted Areas, and are aimed at urban regeneration projects that create employment. Accordingly, the main purpose of grant is for infrastructure projects, with a minimum project cost of £35,000. Applications are co-ordinated by the DoE.

Tourism related projects are particularly supported when it can be shown that at least 50 per cent of visitors will be attracted from outside of the sub-region in which the project is located, of which a significant proportion must have an overnight stay. Thus projects of local significance only are not eligible. Grants of up to 50 per cent of the eligible costs to be met by the sponsoring authority are available for projects with a total cost of up to approximately £10.5 million. Larger projects may be grant-aided at between 30 per cent and 50 per cent.

European Investment Bank (EIB) loans

The EIB is the European Community's bank for providing medium and long-term loans for public and private sector capital propjects. As such, it is both independent and non-profit making. EIB loans can only cover part of the cost of a project and, as such, complement other sources of finance. Loan guarantee is an alternative method used by the Bank to assist projects.

While there is no maximum loan, the amount lent does not usually exceed 50 per cent of the investment cost of the project. Interest rates reflect the cost of borrowing to the EIB on the money markets. Loans up to £4.5 million can be negotiated through the DTI (Industry Department). Loans in excess of that amount are negotiable direct with the EIB.

European Social Fund

The Fund is available primarily for vocational training and employment schemes aimed particularly at people under 25 years of age and the long-term unemployed. The aim of the Fund is to improve employment opportunities for people by improving their geographical and occupational mobility.

The Fund matches money given by government departments and local authorities and applications are co-ordinated by the Department of Employment. Grants are made available of between 50 per cent of the running costs of a scheme and 25 per cent of the money given by the public authority or agency.

UK public sector agencies

The Arts Council

The Council provides financial assistance for arts organisations and individuals through a multiplicity of schemes. It provides subsidies to drama, opera and dance companies, orchestras and other arts related organisations. Grants are also made to support productions, exhibitions or particular projects as well as to individuals. Assistance is also given to international initiatives in conjunction with Visiting Arts who work closely with the Arts Council to facilitate the promotion of the arts from other countries in the UK.

Grants are not directly available for building projects. However, grants may be available to contribute towards the cost of a feasibility study. The amount available will be a maximum of £6,000 or 50 per cent, whichever is less. Applications are accepted from arts organisations, local authorities and trusts. The type of schemes covered include new buildings, the adaption of existing buildings for arts use and the provision or improvement of spaces for the arts within building developments.

In England, the Arts Council is adopting a policy of delegating responsibility for the operation of an increasing proportion of its block allocation, including the provision of one-off grants, to the Regional Arts Boards. In addition, separate schemes are operated by the Scottish and Welsh Arts Councils.

British Coal Enterprise (BCE)

BCE assists business start-ups, expansion or relocation that will create new job opportunities in coal mining areas of the UK. Finance takes the form of 'soft' loans up to a maximum of £1 million repayable over five years. In addition, total loans can only equate to 25 per cent of the total funding needed, subject to creating one job for every £5,000 of loan.

Countryside Commission

The Commission awards grants to public, private and voluntary sector organisations as well as private individuals. Grant awards cover a range of activities, including land acquisition, conservation and improvement work. The overriding aim is to encourage projects that lead to the conservation and improvement of both access to and facilities in the countryside.

There is no maximum grant, but the level of grant depends upon the nature and relative priority of the project costs, although this level can be higher in certain areas, such as national parks and Areas of Outstanding Natural Beauty. The Commission also provides grant towards the costs of employing specialist conservation project and countryside advisory staff. Such staff are usually employed by local authorities or voluntary organisations.

Other grant-aiding bodies concerned with the countryside include the Forestry Commission, English Nature and the Rural Development Commission.

The Foundation for Sport and the Arts

The Foundation was established in 1991 by the Pools Promoters' Association to disburse money made available by a reduction in pools betting duty to sport and the arts in the UK. This is estimated to be worth around £20 million a year and is expected, initially, to last for four years, subject to review. In addition, the pools promoters will channel a further £40 million a year into the Foundation.

The total available money is divided on the basis of two-thirds to sports (excluding League Football and horse racing) and one-third to the arts. The overriding aim is to 'make an impact upon the population at large'. Accordingly, the Foundation is seeking to distribute grants widely across the UK for community based projects.

The initial emphasis is also upon existing facilities and activities. Thus, applications relating to the modernisation and refurbishment of existing facilities and assistance to projects and schemes already underway will find early favour.

There is currently no upper or lower limit on the cost of the projects for which applications are submitted. Applications from organisations and individuals will be accepted, although grants will not be paid directly to individual applicants, only to a parent or umbrella body on their behalf. Excellence is encouraged but, again, the early emphasis is upon the community at large. Provision for people with disabilities is one area recognised as being of special need.

The Sports Council

The Sports Council makes grants and loans available to sports organisations, clubs, local authorities, other statutory bodies and commercial organisations in order to develop and improve sport and physical recreation provision and opportunities for the public. However, while the overriding aim is common to all, each Council, covering England, Scotland and Wales, operates a different grant-aid system.

In England, grant-aid is principally available through the ten regional offices. Only national schemes, such as the Indoor Tennis Initiative, are dealt with by headquarters. Regional grants fall into two general categories; facilities (capital grant), and participation (revenue grant). Although essentially similar in nature, each region operates its own grant-aid and loan system, which reflects regional priorities. These are kept under constant review and will change as need and priorities change.

No specific level of grant is given. Each project is assessed on its merits and against current criteria. However, there is a minimum project cost of £1,500 and a minimum grant level of £750. Grants do not normally exceed one-third of the allowable cost. Interest free loans are also available to voluntary organisations repayable over five years. The minimum level of loan is £1,000.

The Tourist Boards

The Tourist Boards are responsible for making both grants and loans for tourist developments under Section Four of the Development of Tourism Act. However, the ability to grant-aid and the priorities differ between the Boards.

English Tourist Board (ETB) – the ETB's power to grant-aid tourism projects was suspended in 1989. Consequently, the role of the Board and its regions is limited to that of providing a business advisory service through a central business development team and the marketing departments in regional offices. As part of this advisory role, the Board has produced a useful development guide entitled, Funding a Tourism Business.

Scottish Tourist Board (STB) – the STB can assist with the funding of projects via capital grant, loan, revenue interest relief grant, equity participation or a combination of these. Assistance is normally subject to a maximum of 25 per cent of eligible costs, although this can increase to 50 per cent in exceptional circumstances. Total assistance from public agencies, including the STB, must not exceed 50 per cent of the capital costs of a project. Any offer of assistance in excess of £200,000 must also receive approval from the Scottish Office.

To be eligible for grant, the project must involve capital expenditure and a tangible asset must be provided. Maintenance or repair works, operating expenditure or working capital do not qualify. There must be no restriction on access and the project should provide facilities mainy for visitors as opposed to the local population. Priority is currently given to the provision and improvement of visitor attractions and recreational facilities.

A separate programme of financial assistance relating to the Highlands and Islands is operated by the Highlands and Islands Enterprise (HIE).

Welsh Tourist Board (WTB) – the WTB is able to give financial assistance in the form of grant and/or loan towards the capital cost of tourism projects that will provide or improve tourist amenities and facilities in Wales. The Board especially looks at projects in respect of their potential to create or safeguard jobs, to attract both domestic and overseas visitors and help to extend the length of the tourist season.

The Board has identified 'key' sectors comprising country house hotels, coaching hotels, activity holidays, holiday villages, major attractions of national and international significance and caravan parks. Priority is given to projects in these sectors.

In addition, the Board gives priority to projects in certain geographical area locations under its Local Enterprise and Development Initiative (LEAD). Assistance is especially targeted at the private sector under the LEAD programme.

There are two schemes in operation. The Standard Projects Scheme provides grant for projects with capital costs in excess of £13,000. Assistance does not normally exceed 25 per cent of eligible capital costs up to a maximum of £2,500. Applicants must also be existing operators who have traded for at least one season.

Note

The various funding sources and programmes outlined in this chapter were correct at the time of writing. However, both the priorities and the criteria that they adopt are likely to chance from time to time to meet changing circumstances. Consequently, it is important to contact potential sources directly and verify the up to date situation. The contact addresses and telephone numbers relating to the organisations contained in this chapter are set out in the following pages.

Sources of non-commercial finance
Contacts

Arts Council of Great Britain
14 Great Peter Street, London
SW1P 3NQ
Tel: 971-333 0010

Countryside Commission
John Dower House, Crescent Place,
Cheltenham, Gloucestershire
GL50 3RA
Tel: (0242) 521381

Department of Employment
Steel House, Tothill Street, London
SW1H 9NF
Tel: 071-273 3000

Department of the Environment
2 Marsham Street, London
SW1P 3EB
Tel: 071-276 3000

European Coal and Steel Community
Rue de la Loie 200, B-0149 Brussels,
Belgium
Tel: 010-322 2351111

European Investment bank
68 Pall Mall, London SW1Y 5ES
Tel: 071-839 3351

Forestry Commission
231 Corstophine Road, Edinburgh
EH12 7AT
Tel: 031-334 0303

Ministry of Agriculture, Fisheries and Food
Nobel House, 17 Smith Square,
London SW1P 34X
Tel: 071-238 3000

English Nature
Northminster House, Northminster
Road, Peterborough PE1 1UA
Tel: (0733) 340345

Rural Development Commission
141 Castle Street, Salisbury, Wiltshire
SP1 3TP
Tel: (0722) 336255

Foundation for Sport & The Arts
PO Box 666, Liverpool L69 7JW
Tel: 051-524 0235/6

Scottish Arts Council
12 Manor Place, Edinburgh
EH3 7DD
Tel: 031-226 6051

Scottish Sports Council
Caledonia House, South Gyle,
Edinburgh EH12 9DQ
Tel: 031-317 7200

Scottish Tourist Board
23 Ravelston Terrace, Edinburgh
EH4 3EU
Tel: 031-332 2433

The Sports Council
*16 Upper Woburn Place, London
WC1H 0QP*
Tel: 071-388 1277

Department of Trade & Industry
Kingsgate House, 66–74 Victoria
Street, London SW1E 6SJ
Tel: 071-215 5000

English Tourist Board
Thames Tower, Black's Road,
London W6 9EL
Tel: 081-846 9000

Wales Tourist Board
Brunel House, 2 Fitzalen Road,
Cardiff CF2 1UY
Tel: (0222) 499909

Welsh Arts Council
Holst House, Museum Place, Cardiff
CF1 3YX
Tel: (0222) 394711

Sports Council for Wales
National Sports Centre for Wales,
Sophia Gardens, Cardiff CF1 9SW
Tel: (0222) 397571

15 Preparing and presenting an application for finance

Although applications for finance have a common purpose in terms of raising finance, their format and content will vary considerably, and they should be structured in such a way to meet the requirements of the recipients of the plan. Applications for finance apply to all types of organisations, for example, major companies looking to finance an acquisition or merger or a voluntary club looking to finance an extension to its clubhouse.

The level of detail of the application will depend upon the existing circumstances and the type of finance required. If there is already an existing, well established business with a proven track record and assets to offer as security and only short-term finance is being sought, then it may not be necessary to produce an application in the same level of detail as would be required for longer term loans or equity finance or when the product or business does not have a proven track record.

However, it is essential that the viability of the business venture is demonstrated in a professional and well structured manner.

The format of the application

One of the main components of the application is the business plan. This plan should be organised into logical and well defined sections which will cover the business objectives, the products or services, the management team, the marketing strategy and sales plan and financial projections. The contents of these sections are covered in more detail in chapter sixteen.

Financing institutions want to know as much as possible about the project, but especially the objectives of the business, the markets in which the business will operate and the experience and expertise of the management. If a business already exists, details will need to be given about the existing business, its performance and the rationale behind the diversification or expansion and where it fits into the overall strategy. Investors tend to be cautious when considering applications for finance, especially in respect of applications for a business start-up.

It is necessary to present a comprehensive and convincing application in order to entice prospective financiers to invest in a venture. It will be necessary to emphasise the degree of thought, planning and research which has gone into the project and to demonstrate commitment to the venture. The most concrete way of demonstrating commitment to the venture is in the form of the equity put forward by the founders and senior management, as appropriate. In the case of a small venture, the equity should probably exceed the amount of borrowing being sought, although for larger projects this may not be the case.

When putting together a case it needs to be remembered that financiers will be looking at your business in different ways. Banks and other lending institutions will be looking mainly for security and the business prospects will be of secondary importance. It will be necessary to demonstrate that the project is viable and that the income will be more than sufficient to cover the interest and capital repayments.

It will also be necessary to demonstrate that there is sufficient security to cover the business in the event of it failing, and a large equity base can provide such security. Loans are usually secured against the assets of a business so that, if it fails and goes into liquidation, the assets will be sold and the proceeds will be used to finance the debt. The owners may also be asked to provide personal guarantees or offer other forms of security for the business loan if there are insufficient assets against which to secure. In these circumstances, the owners would be liable to repay the loans personally if the business collapsed.

Financiers who inject equity into a business are putting up risk capital and, therefore, they will be looking for a business with prospects and growth potential. They will be willing to take a risk and will be speculating that the future return on their investment will be sufficient to justify any risks that are taken. Consequently, small businesses may be of little interest to an equity financier as, although they may be viable, they tend not to offer sufficient expansion and growth potential. To interest an equity financier, it will be necessary to demonstrate that the business can grow and is capable of earning more than just modest profits.

Equity financiers will also not invest in a project if they lack confidence in the management of a business or if the venture has not been adequately researched or planned. The financier will be looking for a quality management team, with relevant experience, ideally with a track record in public companies. There should be balanced and complimentary skills and the team should exude commercial acumen, entrepreneurial drive and leadership.

Other reasons for equity financiers refusing applications are if the risks are too great, and, in certain instances, if the funds required are too small. Many venture capitalists, for example, have minimum size deal requirements, of for instance, not less than £500,000 or only provide funds for management buyouts. Some financiers may not wish to make a permanent investment but will provide equity for perhaps five years, at the end of which they would want to realise their shares. There is obviously a higher risk involved to potential investors with this type of financing and negotiations and agreements will be quite detailed.

The detail contained in the plan will depend upon the background of the existing business and how much information is available. If there is a sound product and an experienced management team, it is more likely that a less detailed business plan can be produced. The plan should be concise but cover all the important topics and demonstrate sufficient research into the project and a thorough understanding of the market.

Start-up business

Obtaining finance for a start-up business is extremely difficult, especially in the current financial climate where more and more businesses are having difficulty in financing their debts and are collapsing. Lack of attention to sound plans, poor research and weak management are usually the main reasons why start-up businesses fail in early stages.

Investors and lenders are very cautious when considering applications for start-up businesses and, in order to establish credibility with the financiers, it is important to present a convincing application emphasising the degree of careful planning, the experience and abilities, the markets in which the owners will operate and the business ideas.

As a start-up venture, it will also be important to demonstrate commitment to the project in the form of equity. The greater the amount of equity injected, the greater the commitment that is demonstrated and, possibly, the more receptive the institutions will be. It is, therefore, important to ensure that sufficient equity finance is raised.

Synopsis of the plan

Financing institutions receive a large number of applications each week and, in order to assist them in focusing on the main areas of the project, the key elements should be presented in a synopsis or summary. The main objective of the synopsis is to outline the opportunity and the business plan in more detail.

The synopsis should contain:

- a brief description of the business prospects, the product, the market trends and the estimated market share, including any special factors of the business which will cause it to have outstanding growth potential, and the unique selling proposition (USP) of the business;
- a brief description of the management team, their relevant experience and how they will lead the business to success;

- a summary of the financial projections;
- in respect of equity investments, how the investor will obtain a return on investment, its likely level and when the return can be expected.

The synopsis can also be used as a stand alone document which can be sent to a number of potential investors to arouse their interest. If interested in the project, the potential investors can then subsequently be sent a detailed business plan. In this way, the confidential details of the project are protected in early discussion stages.

Structuring the finance

Having said that the synopsis should contain suggestions regarding the type of finance and terms, some institutions prefer to structure the deals themselves. This should not necessarily be viewed as a disadvantage, as the investor will be aiming to structure a deal which will enable the company to grow and achieve success. Chapter thirteen sets out the types and sources of finance that are available.

When attempting to raise finance, it is likely that more than one type will be required, and, therefore, before deciding on the most appropriate types of finance, it should be necessary to:

- aim to achieve a gearing ratio which is suitable to the business, is manageable and will not stretch the business beyond its means;
- ensure the type and length of finance being suggested are suitable for the assets which are being purchased;
- prepare cash flow projections which will assess the finance required over a period of time;
- check the conditions attached to any loan offered, especially with regard to personal guarantees, to ensure they are acceptable;
- ensure that adequate financial controls will be in place and updated, timely and accurate information is available for the purposes of monitoring the performance of the business.

Equity investors, especially venture capital firms, will be seeking a percentage of equity directly proportional to risk. Consequently, a greater equity share will be sought if the management team is inexperienced, the product and the market are new or a combination of both.

Sometimes, owners are concerned about losing control of the business. Most investors invariably only take minority stakes in companies, even if they are contributing a major proportion of the funds. In the case of large transactions where institutional equity will be over 50 per cent of the share capital, the investor will often avoid taking a majority stake by syndicating a part of the investment to other institutions. The investor, however, may feel less comfortable with a minority shareholding if only one person has the controlling equity, and may prefer the majority interest to be divided.

Investors often reserve the right to appoint a director to the board in order to monitor the investment and to protect the interests of the external shareholders. Although the involvement of the investor's director is usually 'hands-off', some areas which typically require the director's consent are approval of operating budgets and capital expenditure programmes, acquisitions and disposals, changes in key management, changes in the articles of association and changes to the funding or capital structure of a business.

If control does become contentious during negotiations, it may be possible to structure a board of directors with an equal number of representatives from the management team and the investors and an independent member or chairman who holds a casting vote. The operational control would remain with the managers. Investors, by and large, do not want to actively participate in the operation of the companies and the operational control is left to the management of the company.

The capital finance structure should be kept as simple as possible, although this is not so easy in terms of venture capital funding, where part of the investment may be held as equity and part as preference shares or convertible loan. The loan carries interest which has the advantages of being tax deductible whereas dividends are not tax deductible. However, a loan has the disadvantage in that it makes the investor a creditor for that part of the investment by loan. This can tend to complicate the relationship.

Restructing finance

There are also numerous occasions when owners already have a viable leisure business, but they have inappropriate funding to support the business, which puts a financial strain on the business. Entrepreneurs in financial difficulty need to be:

- *constructive and creative* – they need to analyse their business to determine the potential for income and cash inflow generation and assess and address the needs of their bankers and equity providers. A business plan should be produced that endorses the viability of the business whilst rescheduling the debt to allow repayment and, at the same time, reducing equity returns.
- *proactive* – they need to take the initiative in order to change their banker's opinion of their business and restore and maintain good communications with both the bankers and equity lenders. It is essential to ensure that the long-term viability of the business is acknowledged by all, including the creditors. In general, creditors would rather time and freedom to pay were created rather than the company ended up in liquidation.
- *use countervailing power to negotiate a financial solution acceptable to all parties* – it is important that all parties can acknowledge the others position. This acceptance can be used to structure a refinancing package that should partially satisfy everyone. It is necessary to ensure that the restructured funding allows the entrepreneur sufficient freedom to grow their business within the revised financial covenants.

An example of the need to restructure is set out in table 15.1

Table 15.1 Company A before refinancing

	Balance Sheet				
	Liabilities £,000		Assets £,000	Profit and Loss	£,000
Equity	3000	Assets	7000	Net operating profit	700
Loan	4000			Interest	600
	7000		7000	Pre tax profit	100

In this example, the debt to equity ratio is 1.33:1 and, although the company is asset rich, there is a lack of cash to pay the interest. The interest cover is 1.16:1, that is the number of times that the profit covers interest. If interest repayment were to be required in the following quarter, the company could not meet its liabilities and is, therefore, insolvent. The finances, therefore, need to be restructured.

A potentially insolvent company will be analysed with a view to resuscitation using a revised business plan. Methods of improving cash flow and avoiding receivership need to be examined. The revised plan needs to be conservative, achievable and well argued. The banks will not take too kindly to just increasing business volume on the assumption that it will increase margin. Genuine income generation ideas will need to be explored.

An assessment of the banks requirements will need to be undertaken and the restructuring of the debt will be analysed, taking into consideration the requirements of both the bank and the business. Areas that will be discussed will include:

- better utilisation of assets such as renting out unutilised assets;
- the sale of non essential assets;
- the injection of more equity in an attempt to reduce interest charges and the repayment burden;
- the possibility of the bank converting debt to equity.

From the bank's point of view, it would be easy for them to realise their security and liquidate the business. However, in reality, when the bank originally agreed to finance the business they were agreeing to take a risk. Banks, in general, prefer a refinanced structure knowing that repayments can still be met within a reasonable time rather than forcing a business into receivership and liquidation, as asset values are destroyed by receiverships and there is no guarantee that, through this course of action, the full loan will be recovered. This is precisely the attitude adopted by the many banks involved in rescheduling and refinancing the Brent Walker Leisure empire, which actually took many months to achieve. If the new plan can 'wash its face' with repayments being met, the credit rating of the bank will not be impaired.

The views of the equity providers will also need to be considered and the following alternatives can be discussed:

- waiver or deferment of interest on preferred shares;
- conversion of preference shares to ordinary shares – by doing this fixed interest on capital will not be due;
- deferment of dividend on ordinary shares;
- extension of time to exit date;
- injection of new equity.

Equity providers are obviously seeking to maximise their return, and the counterbalance that can be used is that they will obtain a nil return if a receiver is appointed.

If a bank agrees to delaying payments, it should be possible to persuade the equity investors to postpone their exit date. If a bank is prepared to convert debt to equity, the other equity providers can be persuaded to accept the dilution. All of these possibilities will lower equity returns, but should be acceptable to equity providers if the alternative is receivership.

Referring back to the original example of Company A (table 15.1) which needed refinancing if assets are sold to the value of £500k, assuming no loss is made on the sale, assets will reduce by £500k as they are no longer owned by the company. If a loan of £500k was also originally acquired to finance the assets, then as the sales occurs, the loan of £500k will also be repaid. Consequently, the debt of £500k outstanding on the assets will also be reduced in the balance sheet. After the sale of the asset, the balance sheet would look like table 15.2.

Table 15.2 Company A after sale of asset

	Liabilities £,000		Assets £,000	Profit and loss	£,000
Equity	3000	Assets	6500	Net operating profit	700
Loan	3500			Interest	600
	6500		6500	Pre tax profit	100

The second assumption in the refinancing arrangement is that agreement has been reached to convert £2,000k from debt to equity. This conversion will have a major impact on the profit and loss account as there will be a saving in interest payments on the loan which has now been converted to equity. On the basis that 15 per cent rate of interest was being paid on the original loan of £4,000k, the new interest due will be (in £'000):

$$(£4,000 - \underset{\substack{\text{(sale of} \\ \text{asset)}}}{£500} - \underset{\substack{\text{(transfer} \\ \text{to equity)}}}{£2,000}) = £1,500 \times 15\% = £225$$

The balance sheet after total refinancing is a lot healthier.

Table 15.3 Company A after total refinancing

	Liabilities £,000		Assets £,000	Profit and loss	£,000
Equity	5000	Assets	6500	Net operating profit	700
Loan	1500			Interest	225
	6500		6500	Pre tax profit	475

The company, after refinancing, has a lower gearing ratio of 0.3:1 compared with 1.33:1 before refinancing. The burden of interest has been substantially reduced, which has improved the pre-tax profit position. The equity has been diluted, but this is preferable to the equity holders receiving no return at all.

A range of solutions to a potentially insolvent company's problem can be discussed and a particular solution partially satisfying all parties needs to be agreed. Before any corporate restructuring can take place, it is essential that a business plan exists which is supported by all concerned. Any financial covenants that are put in place should be estimated in a 'worse case' scenario, so that they cover performance at the bottom end of any new business plan. Constructive, creative and even radical action may be necessary for a business which is overburdened by debt, and good communications and rapid agreement are also essential.

Timing

Another major factor that has to be considered when structuring a deal is the timing of finance and when the facility is required. The capital cash flow budget will provide an indication to the timing of the major sources of finance and the revenue cash flow budget to the working capital requirement.

The most popular financing strategy is staged finance, which is a process of timing each stage of the financing to coincide with the achievement of measurable objectives. A staged approach represents a reduced risk to the investor and the company, because as it achieves each of its stages it increases its chance of success.

Typically, a project may go through three phases and financing can be structured at the beginning of each phase, for example:

- acquisition of land or a site on which a leisure complex is to be constructed;
- development and construction of the leisure complex;
- expansion into new facilities or building upon and expanding the market share with the existing facilities.

Staged finance may encourage more than one investor to become involved, which again reduces the risk even further to each individual investor.

The main problem with staged finance is, if unforeseen circumstances occur resulting in insufficient funds until the next stage of finance is due, the organisation may need to seek interim finance. This may not always be readily available and will usually be more expensive in the short-term.

Structuring the deal

As part of the negotiations, it will be necessary to determine how much equity the investors will receive for their investment. Basically, two factors will affect the decision – risk and investment objectives. The greater the risk, the greater the share of equity that will be required. In addition, equity investors tend to focus on long-term capital gain, and for the investment to be worthwhile, it must be possible to achieve a greater return than it could with a relatively risk free investment.

When negotiating the percentage of equity, the valuation of the business is a critical factor. Pricing is a highly subjective matter and the investor will be influenced by its assessment of the company's track record, the market, the financial projections and the financing requirements. The level of risk compared with the amount of investments will also be assessed.

Valuations are also sensitive and volatile, being influenced by both the performance of a business, and confidence in the industry. Indeed, valuations on leisure projects have declined over the past two years, mainly as a result of lack of confidence in the sector.

In the valuation process, the value should mirror the process of the market place by analysing and making an assessment of the trading potential and maintainable profit and by using multipliers which takes into consideration the risk, durability, finance and opportunity cost. Other guidelines that can be used are comparable, but problems do exist in identifying a reliable and meaningful unit of comparison.

The share pricing proposed should not be contained in the business plan and application for finance, but should be the subject of negotiations with the investors that demonstrate an interest in providing finance. It is advisable to seek professional advice before entering into pricing negotiations.

16 The business plan

'Success is simply a matter of luck. Ask any failure.'
Earl

There are many business anecdotes about people who had a simple idea that they converted into a successful business and, subsequently, became self-made millionaires. But for every such business legend, of which there are really very few, there are hundreds of others who also had a great idea (or project) that did little more than drive them into liquidation. Whilst it is undeniably helpful to have your fair share of luck in any business, this can be no substitute for sound business planning. In many ways, you create your own luck by ensuring that risk is minimised and that you are in a position to actually take advantage of the lucky breaks as and when they occur.

There is also no denying that the preparation of a business plan can be a heavy burden and for many it takes them into unchartered water. In such instances, many people often turn to professional advisors such as accountants and/or consultants to assist them with this phase.

A business plan sets out what it is you are intending to achieve, how you intend to achieve it, with what resources and over what sort of timescale. Apart from telling you at the end of the process whether or not the business proposition will be viable, the business plan also establishes the framework around which the new business venture should be established and driven forward.

A business plan should be prepared, for example, when seeking to diversify into new businesses or products, or if selling refinance or altering an existing business.

Information gathering

The business plan is an important component of the application and before commencing the application and preparing the business plan preparatory work should be undertaken. A list of the topic areas should be prepared that will be covered in the plan. This will determine the information that will need to be collected, and the work that needs to be undertaken before a business plan is prepared. This will include:

- market research information;
- information about potential competitors;
- information on potential customers and likely demand;
- profile of the organisation requesting finance;
- profile of the founder members and senior management;
- information on the product or service and the industry;
- any relevant legislation; and
- supporting financial information and comparisons with other similar businesses in the industry.

After the product and market strategies have been undertaken and all the relevant information pertaining to the project has been gathered, the task of preparing the business plan should begin. It should also be relevant at this stage to pose the following significant questions, which will highlight the thoroughness of the pre-planning stage:

- Does the project have a realistic chance of being successful?
- Has the market and potential demand been thoroughly researched and is there a need for the product in the market place?
- Does the management team have the appropriate skills and expertise required?
- Are the financial projections robust?

The aim of the business plan is to present the opportunity and demonstrate an understanding of the risks and rewards, structuring them where appropriate into packages which will be attractive to banks, equity investors and other possible funding sources. Of paramount importance, the plan should be structured in such a way to meet the requirements of the potential investors. It should also be assumed that few, if any, potential investors who actually read the business plan will know anything about the proposed activity.

The plan will need to identify the markets and the marketing strategy, the product, the financial projections and mechanisms for financial monitoring purposes, the management and the financing strategy. Each of these areas are considered in the remainder of this chapter. For the purposes of illustration, the business plan is discussed in the context of a new racquets club development that will contain squash, indoor and outdoor tennis facilities, swimming pool, gymnasium, bar, restaurant and sports shop facilities. The principles, however, have equal application for any leisure development proposal.

The project

The business plan should describe the project in detail, setting out the site to be acquired for the development, the stages of development and the facilities, products and services that will be offered. The plan should state how the project will be developed, on what basis the facilities will be provided, how the club will operate and the benefits the customers will derive from using it. Will it involve membership schemes, debenture holding, or will it be on a 'pay and play' basis?

Photographs and information about the site to be acquired should be included, and if any architects drawings on the proposed club have been prepared they should also be included. At the very least, an impression or conceptual diagram of both the exterior and interior should be included. If any new technology is being used which has a significant impact on the success of the project, such as new playing surfaces, they should, where possible, be explained in lay terms and the detailed relevant technical information included as an appendix.

The special factors and unique selling proposition (USP) of the business which will create the outstanding growth potential should also be identified and the objectives of the project clearly stated. What is the purpose of the club – is it to provide an elite playing club or is it there to attempt to increase participation at various playing levels? The objectives will be of paramount importance to the market research and marketing strategy.

It is also important to discuss the possibility of subsequent expansion and the development of other facilities or products. The plan should cover the approach to expansion and which facilities will be developed and when. This business plan is now taking the shape of a three stage project:

Stage One	– acquire the site for development
Stage Two	– construct a racquets club with squash, indoor and outdoor tennis, swimming pool, gymnasium, restaurant, bar and shop facilities
Stage Three	– acquire extra land surrounding the club for the purposes of constructing an 18 hole golf course and club house

With this particular project, stages one and two are interdependent, whereas stage three is really stand alone. A decision to go ahead or not with stage three can be made at a later date once the success of stages one and two have been ascertained. However, mentioning the potential of stage three at this stage enables financiers to have a broader indication of the potential and opportunities that may exist.

The timescale of the various stages of the project should be set out, along with any foreseen problems and plans for dealing with them. Will there be any problems with planning applications and what will be the course of action if the planning application is rejected? If special surfaces or equipment are being used, do any of them require long lead times? Are they easily obtainable or only available from one source? What are the back up arrangements if problems arise with suppliers?

If one of the objectives is to improve and achieve certain playing standards, it will be necessary to discuss the company's philosophy and approach to quality control, indicating the way in which standards will be monitored and controlled.

With certain projects, such as gaming and lotteries, there may be Government regulations that may affect the business and relevant extracts of the official documents should be included with the steps which will be taken to obtain appropriate official approval. There may also be certain environmental restrictions, such as a project involved in angling, which will require special permits and agreements and again steps should be included in order to comply with official requirements.

Marketing information

The business plan should also contain information on the markets that have been identified, as well as details of the marketing strategy since, having identified the project, it is essential to ensure it is marketable, otherwise it will be unsuccessful. Marketing encompasses more than sales, and is really the process of identifying the demand and packaging the product in such a way that it will satisfy the need. In this section of the plan it is important to convince potential investors that there is a market for the product, that the market forces are understood and that there is sufficient expertise and resource to market the product.

The market

First of all, it is necessary to describe the market for the project. An understanding of the economic background of the area in which the club will be based is important, including a socio-economic profile of the population. Is it located in a residential or business sector? What types of businesses are located nearby? What sector is the area known for – is it industrial or service based? It will also be necessary to demonstrate an understanding of the catchment area – what is the population base? Is it of sufficient size to support a club of the proposed size? How effective is the road and transport infrastructure, and does it still provide an adequate catchment area if a drive time radius of 15–20 minutes is applied?

A demographic analysis of the population will also be required and, in conjunction with the economic profile, it can be determined whether there is a large enough potential customer base to support the club. If any market surveys or market research have been undertaken in-house or by an external organisation which verifies the demand for such a project, that information or study report should also form part of the business plan.

It is also necessary to assess comprehensively the competition, giving details of the nearest clubs, their distance from the proposed project and the facilities that they offer. In particular, an assessment should be made of the strengths and weaknesses of the major competitors. An honest appraisal of the competitors will add credibility to the business plan and will demonstrate to an investor that competition has been recognised and accounted for.

The impact of the business on the market should also be assessed in terms of whether the club will actually increase the size of the market. Will a greater demand for these leisure facilities be created or will the market remain the same size and the development of the club instead have the effect of diluting the market share of competitors? If the club threatens the market share of potential primary competitors, what will they do in an attempt to retain their existing market share and what will the company's own strategy be?

There is also a need to assess the potential user profile of the area and, therefore, of the club. Does the area have a reputation of a good sporting background and what proportion of the population matches the racquet playing profile?

If there are potential major competitors, it would also be useful to obtain, if possible, some information regarding the profile of users – whether they are casual or hard core frequent users and the economic and demographic profile of such users – male/female: juniors or seniors. An assessment will also need to be made of the potential for corporate use and the likely demand that will be generated from the presence of nearby businesses.

Having looked at the specific market in which the club will operate, it will also be necessary to look at trends and the marketplace as a whole in terms of the developments of racquet sports over the next three to five years. Is it a boom industry which is likely to increase the size of the market and the demand of the sport and is it a sport which is fairly resilient to changing fads and trends?

There may also be factors common to the whole UK economy, such as the impact of a recession, which may be most important in determining the success of the project. An analysis of previous market performance and its relation to macroeconomic factors are required to produce a convincing background for the potential investors to assess any market risk. It may be possible to present a convincing analysis of the market using internal resources, but an independent market research study is indispensable, particularly for banks. Any market research should:

- research the market background as completely as possible and identify areas of uncertainty or where there is a lack of information;
- research comparable projects if possible;
- provide both historic and projected supply and demand information;
- analyse current and projected competition. The comparison of the projected performance of the project against direct competition is invaluable.

Pricing strategy

It will also be necessary to set out the basis of the pricing strategy, which should be both demand and market led as well as taking into consideration costs. Pricing strategies are described in more detail in chapter twelve. It is important to demonstrate that the pricing strategy is based on the value of the product to the customer and, in this way, potential investors will have more confidence in the pricing strategy proposed.

If the project does not allow a price to be charged that generates adequate profitability, consideration should be given to improving the product. For example, it may be necessary to improve social facilities at certain clubs before membership schemes or social member categories can be introduced.

It will also be necessary to explain in detail how the club and its facilities will be marketed in the area. Consideration will need to be given as to who will be the potential principal customers – will there be a core of people using the centre frequently or will there be a lot of casual usage? Is it likely to be mainly business or public? Are the players likely to be senior or junior? This will influence the marketing strategy. There may also be a need to advertise the club and use public and press relations in disseminating news about the new facility. Exposure on local radio may be more effective in generating custom than paid advertising.

Management and organisation structure

One of the key issues that a potential investor will be reviewing is the strength of the company and the management team. If there is already an existing company with a track record, a profile of the company including financial performance and relevant experience should be included in the plan. This should immediately provide a 'comfort factor' to a potential investor. In respect of the particular venture, they will also want to be reassured about the experience, talent, commitment and integrity of the co-founders and the proposed management team. Before financing any venture, a potential investor may wish to take up references on each key member of the team and, in particular, upon the leadership qualities of the managing director.

The organisational structure of the company should be identified in the business plan, together with details of the individuals who will fill the senior management positions and the specific responsibilities and duties of each of the people involved. There should also be a synopsis on each of the senior managers, which sets out their background, professional qualifications, previous experience and key areas and strengths that are particularly relevant to the project. There should also be a detailed curriculum vitae to support the synopsis for each person.

It is also advisable to identify any particular skills shortages and the plans for overcoming the shortages. This could take the form of a part-time executive director being appointed to the board who possesses the skills that are lacking. In the racquets club example, the organisation structure could consist of a managing director, a finance director and an operations director with a general leisure facility background, who would be responsible for the overall running of the club. This would tend to leave the restaurant and bar facilities slightly exposed, which may be of concern if they constituted a significant part of the business operation. Consequently, a part-time executive director with a catering background could be appointed to the board. This type of approach will demonstrate that the company's skills requirements have been carefully analysed.

The planned organisation and reporting structure should also be outlined as well as the composition of the board. The detailed personnel structure need not be explained, but an outline of proposed employee benefits will be of use. Details of any incentives, share options or profit sharing plans should also be included. The plan should also recognise if there is a skills shortage in the area in which the project is to be located and the plans for recruitment, relocation or training.

This section of the plan should not be underestimated as, invariably, a project will stand or fall on the strength and expertise of the management team.

Financial projections

The company seeking finance would need to supply financial accounts relating to existing businesses. In addition, if the company is taking over a 'going concern', it will be necessary to provide financial accounts relating to the existing business. Irrespective of whether the project is the acquisition and development of a going concern or the start-up of a new business, financial projections should be prepared and incorporated in the business plan.

The amount of detail that will need to be given will depend upon the size of the funding requirements and the level of risk to which the potential investor may be exposed. Irrespective of the level of detail, projections should be based on information gained from the research, on best estimates available and necessary assumptions, which should be realistic and clearly stated.

Investors will probably want to see forecasts of profit and loss, cash flow and balance sheet projections for up to five years. For the first two years, it is usual to show monthly profiles, with the remaining years being shown as quarterly profiles. For the projections to have credibility they should be prepared by a finance professional.

If there are any risks or uncertainties over aspects of the project a number of sensitivity analyses should also be produced, in addition to the base projections. These should take into consideration the financial impact of 'what if' calculations. For example, what would be the financial impact if the projected utilisation figure of the clubs were to be underachieved by 15 per cent.

Investors will always be on the defensive when reviewing leisure projects in view of the total discretionary nature of leisure spending. The turnover for leisure projects is almost always at full market risk as the customer has total freedom of choice. It is, therefore, even more important to undertake a 'worst case' sensitivity scenario – or bankbase case – for presentation to investors, which presents a conservative view of market influences on turnover. A more positive, but realistic scenario should also be prepared for equity investors, which banks would probably also like to see, but that they would not be prepared to lend against.

An example of the framework for the financial forecasts and assumptions are contained in chapter eighteen. It is extremely important that any assumptions are fully explained and, where possible, supported by research.

Income and expenditure can both be forecast, which will then enable the working capital requirement to be determined. The financial forecasts and the funding request should be linked to market expectations. It is important, in addition to providing detailed projections, to summarise the financial information and key financial ratios and to explain the financial projections in the text so that financiers do not have to interpret the projections themselves.

The financing request

In this section of the plan it is important to first demonstrate the equity that will be injected by the founders and management and also explain any other methods of finance which may be available, such as other private sources of equity, hire purchase or leasing finance. In addition, if there are any grants, loans or public sector assistance which may be available, this should be included in the plan.

It is also necessary to decide on the gearing required for the business and strike the right balance. Loan finance will be cheaper in the long run, but may be difficult to obtain and will depend upon the ability of the company to repay, initially, interest and then principal. If the company is too highly geared it could put a financial strain on the business. If maximum borrowing capacity is utilised at earlier stages, this will also reduce flexibility in the future to 'top up' any loans.

It is necessary, as part of the financing request, to state the amount, the currency and the type of finance that is being sought, for example equity or loan. It is also necessary to state why it is needed and what will be done with the money.

If the company already exists, an explanation will need to be given as to the effect that the additional funding will have on the existing capital structure. If a new company is being formed, it will be necessary to state how the funds will be capitalised, what the shareholding will be and the value of the shareholding.

It will also be necessary to indicate the timing of the finance, that is, whether staged financing is required or whether financing is required all at once. If staged finance is required, the timing of the finance and the amount required at each stage will need to be stated, which should be related to various discreet measurable stages in the business plan. Repayment suggestions should also be made, as appropriate, although this will be the subject of negotiations with the investor.

An outline should also be given of the proposed financial controls and financial management reporting arrangements. This will demonstrate that the financial and operating performance of the business will be clearly monitored, which will enable problems to be detected early so that appropriate action can be taken.

Review of financial projections

One of the areas that an investor will look at initially, before deciding whether to proceed further with the project, is the financial projections. In order to assess whether the assumptions are reasonable, several ratios will be calculated which will include key performance ratios such as operating margins, gross profit and pre-tax profit as a percentage of turnover. The profit and cash flow positions will also be reviewed to assess the ability to repay any loan interest as appropriate.

The operating margins will be compared with those of other companies in the industry, which may raise questions about the assumptions and the rationale behind the projections. It is important to have supporting information and research data to be able to justify figures if they are to be viewed with credibility.

In the case of a potential equity investor, they will wish to forecast a valuation of the business to first of all assess whether an investment will be worthwhile in terms of any capital gain that may be made and, secondly, to determine the amount of equity that the investor will need to secure to achieve its target return on investment. The investors would look at the forecast earnings at the end of a period, probably to coincide with a potential exit date, and would apply a factor to arrive at a potential valuation. The factor used would be relevant to the industry but would not be standard, as it would need to take into consideration the risk involved and an allowance to reflect that projections and forecasts are being used rather than proven historical figures. The balance sheets would also be reviewed for evidence of an understanding of fixed asset and working capital management.

In general, leisure projects require a more complicated appraisal than those of many other sectors. A business valuation is, at best, subjective and volatile and this has not been helped by the current downturn and loss of confidence in the industry. Multi-use projects may also require comparison with various sectors as there may be many businesses combined into one, as may be the case in a leisure complex which could include a number of sporting facilities, plus perhaps ten pin bowling, a cinema, restaurants, bars, space sales, advertising and ticket sales – hence the complexity. Valuation will also take into consideration any alternative use. For example, a cinema could be stripped out and the remaining shell used as a warehouse.

Investors will also be on the defensive with leisure projects due to the discretionary nature of leisure spending. Project financing of leisure facilities is ambitious as income is really short-term cash based and the life of the facilities themselves may also be relatively short. However, the business itself, with its ability to generate cash, could be justified to be an asset with a life appropriate for such financing.

Summary

It is necessary to put together a comprehensive and detailed application and business plan to potential investors. Success will depend upon how the business plan is put forward and it should be tailored to the individual requirements of the investors.

The plan and application should contain:

- a synopsis of the project which can be read as a stand alone document and precursor to the business plan. This should set out all the key information about the opportunity.
- the detailed business plan should contain:
  - an introduction and background to the venture;
  - project and product information;
  - marketing information – including market analysis and research, information on potential competitors, demand assessment, and pricing and marketing strategies;
  - management and organisation structure – to demonstrate the experience, skills and commitment of the owners and the senior management team;
- financial projections – projections should be based on best estimates available and assumptions should be realistic and clearly stated. The projections should be supported by sensitivity analyses demonstrating 'worst' and 'best' case scenarios;
- the financing strategy – this should state the reasons for seeking finance, the amount of equity or other forms of finance that will be available, the amount of finance that is being sought, what it will be used for, the terms of the finance and suggested proposals for repayments as appropriate.

A comprehensive business plan and application will enhance the organisation's credibility in the eyes of the potential investors.

Furthermore, the development of a business plan is an invaluable discipline for potential owners and managers to go through to assure themselves that their project really is as viable as they believed when the idea was originally conceived. The business plan, once developed, also becomes the blue print for the subsequent development and operation of the venture.

17 Financial forecasts

Financial forecasts are a fundamental part of the business plan and enable the business prospects and the funding requirements to be assessed. The forecasts themselves may be presented in many different formats, covering different timescales and the plan should be formatted to take into consideration the requirements of the investor. However, all forecasts should contain certain basic information, namely the base assumptions on which the forecasts have been prepared, profit and loss accounts, cash flow statements, balance sheets and a funding request statement.

The forecasts should be prepared based on realistic assumptions, which must be included in the plan. Where possible, they should be supported by facts, market research and industry comparisons. Consistency is also important and the assumptions should be provided consistently throughout the forecasts. For example, income from court fees operated on a pay and play basis will be included in the profit and loss account, exclusive of VAT. This should be included in the cash flow forecast in the same month as it is charged into the profit and loss account, and the VAT charged on the court fee should also be included in the cash flow forecast. On the other hand, income which is invoiced will be reflected in the profit and loss account but will not be reflected in the same month in the cash flow, but in a future month, which is based on assumptions made regarding the debt collection period. Some of the assumptions that will need to be stated are set out in the following paragraphs.

Price base
At the start of the plan, the price base upon which the plan will be produced should be determined. This could, for example, be on current costs and prices, whereby the price base is not adjusted from year to year to reflect inflation or, alternatively, it could be undertaken to reflect movements in yearly price levels. The method adopted will need to be

stated and it is important also to distinguish between real growth and inflation. Issues affecting pricing decisions were discussed in chapter ten.

Income
This is the most critical area, as it is income which determines the size of a business. It is necessary to explain the basis on which the income projections have been built up and it should be consistent with the market analysis. If there is more than one facility, details on income projections will need to be given for each of the facilities. For example, income projections in respect of court fees for a tennis centre will need to show the total of available court hours, the estimated percentage utilisation and the charge per hour. The calcuations themselves may become quite complex because there may also be different prices dependent upon the market segments. Income projections for a restaurant will need to take into consideration the number of covers, how many times the covers are turned over and an average spend per head.

One of the major aspects that will need specific attention, especially on leisure projects, is a seasonality factor, and the projections should reflect the change in usage patterns accordingly. The projections will gain no credibility at all if, for example, utilisation of outdoor tennis courts in the winter is predicted at the same level as summer usage, unless of course the project is located in a warmer climate.

Direct costs of operation
Explanation should be given as to the way in which the direct costs have been constructed. Instead of assuming costs to be a percentage of income, cost schedules should be created for each facility in order to build up a more accurate assessment of the cost associated with each facility.

Marketing costs
These should be based on the marketing plan and should include the costs of internal resources and also any external assistance required.

Overheads
To ascertain these costs, a detailed schedule will need to be prepared which should include the assumptions used in the calculations. Costs should include, for example, rent, rates, administrative costs, telephones and professional services.

Fixed assets
A list of all the main fixed assets, including equipment, should be made indicating when they will be obtained and the length of their useful life. The depreciation method which it is intended to use should also be specified.

Financing charges
The proposed sources of financing and assumed rates of interest should be stated.

Debtors
It will be necessary to estimate the period between the date of sale of an item and the date the monies will be received. This can be expressed as an average collection period or a turnover rate per year. This phasing will need to be reflected in the cash flow.

Creditors
The period between committing expenditure and actually paying for the goods and services will need to be estimated and reflected in the cash flow. Payment terms should be expressed as a number of days and, in order to achieve a good credit rating, it will be necessary to ensure that creditors are settled propmptly in accordance with the average creditor days for the sector.

Taxation
The impact of VAT on the cash flow will need to be taken into consideration. For example, it has been assumed that VAT payments will be made to the Customs and Excise in the month following the end of the VAT quarter.

If a company has been established, corporation tax will be chargeable on the profits and this will also have an impact on the cash flow. As tax legislation is complex and changeable, it has not been covered in this book. Advice should be sought directly from an accountant on the up to date position and the implication of such taxes. Basic taxation issues are discussed in chapter five.

Funding request
This needs to set out the level of funds required, as set out in the cash flow forecast. The length of each loan should be specified together with the terms for repayment. If staged finance is required, the total amount required should be specified and also the timing of each stage.

Any grants or government assistance should be included with an indication of when they will be received. In addition, there should be a surplus funding requirement over the projected amount – in the region of about three months working capital – to cover for any unforeseen circumstances. This should also provide sufficient finance whilst negotiations on subsequent rounds of funding are taking place.

Case study

In this case study a framework for a financial forecast has been set out, including the principle assumptions used. The framework is intended to be illustrative and, because there is no detailed activity information or marketing plan, the assumptions and level of detail is much more general than would be expected of the financial forecasts that would normally accompany a detailed business plan.

The case study is based on constructing and operating a nine indoor, nine outdoor court tennis club, which, for this purpose, has catering facilities but no additional leisure facilities.

The financial forecasts that have been prepared are:

- Funding request schedule   Table 17.1
- Forecast profit and loss accounts   Table 17.2
  - summary of years 1–4
  - monthly profiles – years 1–4   Tables 17.3–17.6
- Balance sheets
  - summary of years 1–4   Table 17.7
- Cash flow projections
  - summary years 1–4   Table 17.8
  - monthly profiles years 1–4   Tables 17.9–17.12

Detailed supporting statements have not been included.

Assumptions used in preparing the financial projections

Profit and loss account

1. Capital construction of the club will commence in January of year 1 and the club will open to customers for use from January of year 2.
2. All financial projections have been based on current costs and prices.

Court fees

3. Income from court fees has been based on the following information:

| | Utilisation | | | |
	Year 2*	Year 3	Year 4	Price
Indoor Courts				
Winter – peak	60%	80%	90%	£11.00
– off-peak	40%	60%	70%	£7.00
Summer – peak	40%	55%	60%	£11.00
– off-peak	30%	35%	40%	£7.00
Outdoor courts				
Summer – peak	20%	25%	35%	£3.00
– off-peak	10%	15%	20%	£3.00
Winter	5%	10%	10%	£3.00

- first three months utilisation has been assumed to be 40% peak and 20% off-peak

Memberships

4. The membership potential is 2250, of which 20 per cent are expected to be juniors. The membership price is £180 for adults and £60 for juniors. It is estimated that the membership take up will be:

60% – year 2
80% – year 3
90% – year 4

Membership is due at the beginning of each year.

Courses and coaching

5. A balanced coaching programme will be offered for juniors and adults. It has been assumed that there will be the folowing coaching/course hours:

Year 2 –   60 hours   (50:50 adults and juniors)
Year 3 –   80 hours
Year 4 – 100 hours

It is assumed that the courses will be 75 per cent full and that charges for courses will be £18 for adults and £13 for juniors. The courses will be run eight times per annum and each course will run for six weeks.

Catering

6. It has been assumed that customers will have an average spend of £1.00 per head and the throughput of the club will be approximately:

60,000 – Year 1
70,000 – Year 2
80,000 – Year 3

Gross profit on sales has been assumed at 45 per cent. (This would usually be the subject of a more comprehensive plan, rather than being expressed on a ratio basis.)

7. Employees costs should be constructed from a manpower schedule (not provided in this example). This should set out the staffing required in each of the years, rates of pay, bonuses and employers NIC contributions.

8. Coaching fees – this directly relates to the number of coaching hours and it is assumed that the coaches will be contracted at £10.00 per hour.

Building related costs

9. Building costs include utilities costs, business rates, cleaning, maintenance, insurance and security and these have been based on best estimates available.

Administration and general

10. Included under this heading are printing, stationery, telephone, postage, legal and audit fees and licenses. These figures have been based on best estimates available and are contained in the administration schedule (not included as part of this example).

Marketing

11. The marketing programme will commence two months prior to the opening of the centre, for which a fixed budget has been allocated. For future years the marketing budget has been based on 3 per cent of turnover.

Depreciation

12. Depreciation on furniture, fittings and equipment has been calculated on a straight line basis over the estimated useful life of the assets (five years).

The property and land are valued at cost and are not depreciated as the estimated residual value of the property is expected to be greater than the net book value.

Taxation

13. For ease of understanding, taxation considerations have not been included in

this case study. However, it is usual to state VAT, taxation and capital allowance assumptions used in the business plan.

Cash flow

Debtors

14. Due to the nature of the business, the majority of cash is received as it becomes due. In respect of membership income it is assumed that:

   70 per cent will be received at the beginning of a year
   10 per cent will be received by month two
   10 per cent will be received by month three
   10 per cent will be received by month four

Creditors

15. Creditors will be paid one month after receipt of invoice.

Other costs

16. Staffing and coaches cost will be paid in the month incurred.

Bank/interest

17. Interest will be payable and receivable quarterly.

Capital construction

18. Capital construction costs have been based on evaluated tenders, the details of which are set out in a capital expenditure schedule (not contained in the case study). The total cost of construction is estimated at £2,350,000 and furtniture, fittings and equipment at £50,000. Capital construction will commence nine months before official opening of the club.

   The land will be acquired at the beginning of year one at an all inclusive cost of £300,000.

Sources of funding and funding requests (see table 17.1)

The founders will subscribe £200,000 for paid up ordinary share capital at the start of the project. Venture capital finance is being sought for £1,000,000 at the beginning of the project, 50 per cent as shareholding and 50 per cent as a long-term loan investment to finance the acquisition and the initial stages of construction.

There will also be a capital grant available of £650,000, which will be available for drawing down in August of the start-up year.

There will be an additional venture capital requirement of £500,000 in June of year one to finance the completion of the project.

A five year loan of £180,000 will be required, which will be drawn down in October of year one. Interest will be charged at 13 per cent per annum and interest will be payable on a quarterly basis. Interest will be rolled up for the first year and payments of interest and principal will commence in October of the second year.

Overdraft facility

This will be used to fund any short-term deficits arising from trading and to allow for any unforeseen circumstances. A facility of £5,000 more than the projected monthly amounts is required. It is assumed that interest on overdrafts will be at 15 per cent per annum.

Surplus funds and short-term deposits

A working balance of £5,000 in the current account has been assumed and any surplus funds will be placed on deposit, which will earn interest at 9 per cent per annum.

Results

Key ratios

	Year 1	Year 2	Year 3	Year 4
Gross profit:Sales	–	42%	50%	51%
Net profit:Sales	–	34%	45%	48%
Current ratio	0.03	0.13	15.1	34.2
Gearing ratio	37%	34%	18%	23%
Net worth (£'000)	1839	1987	2253	2582
Return on net worth	–	7.4%	11.8%	12.7%
Return on gross capital employed	–	5.5%	9.2%	10.3%

The venture makes a loss at both gross profit and net profit level in year one, but moves into a healthy profitability situation from year two. There is a tremendous fluctuation in the current ratio and, in the early years, the venture is not able to meet its short-term liabilities, as current assets are less than current liabilities.

However, as the venture becomes established, it is more than capable of meeting its short-term liabilities. The bank will need to view this in the light that they are the major creditor in the early years, as the overdraft facility is initially being used to fund working capital. In practise, it could be that a second loan of perhaps one to two years duration may be a more appropriate way to fund the working capital, and this should be tested as one of the sensitivity analyses.

The business has a low gearing, which means that there are more shareholders funds in relation to borrowings. The venture becomes lower geared over the four years. The return that the venture makes on both net worth and gross capital employed increases substantially by the end of year four.

Key financial indicators

Potential investors invariably use financial statistics in order to evaluate the proposal and the strength of the business. The ratios should be included in the plan, therefore, in order to demonstrate to the investor that they have been considered as an integral part of the business planning process.

In respect of the profit and loss account, the gross profit as a percentage of sales should be calculated for each year. The reason for any fluctuation year on year should be explained as should any particular variances from the average ratio which would be expected for the industry sector. Key financial indicators were discussed in chapter six. The break even point should also be calculated to demonstrate the utilisation that would be required to enable overheads to be covered. The method used for calculating the break even point was set out in chapter nine.

In terms of balance sheet ratios, the key indicators will be:

Current ratio – that is, the current assets divided by the current liabiities, which will indicate the ability of the project to meet its short-term obligations as they become due.

Net current assets – that is, the current assets less current liabilities, which will give an indication of liquidity.

Gearing ratio – that is, the total borrowings, or fixed interest capital, divided by the total ordinary shareholders funds. This should preferably be expressed as a percentage. A highly geared company is financed mainly from borrowings and, assuming the project performs well, an investor may see that the project has potentially high financial rewards. However, financial institutions, such as banks, which will be seeking to lend money will normally expect to see a certain level of share capital as a demonstration of commitment and also to reduce the risk that they will not recover their loans to an acceptable amount.

Net worth – that is, the total of capital and reserves. The other statistics are meaningless when the business is generating a loss and, consequently, in order to determine the level of risk, investors and creditors will look at the net worth in order to assess the ability of the business to sustain further losses.

Return on worth – that is, the net profit divided by the average value of capital and reserves. This is a profitability ratio and is used to evaluate the potential return on investment, and also to compare the business to others in the industry sector.

Sensitivity analysis

Having prepared the basic financial projections, it is then necessary to prepare various scenarios based on changed circumstances in order to see the impact that any such changes have on the financial projections. Investors will be looking to see that relevant sensitivity analyses have been included and, as part of these analyses, a 'worst' case scenario should be prepared. Any potential investor will look very carefully at a 'worst case' scenario.

Examples of sensitivity tests could include:

- What would be the impact on the profit and loss account, the cash flow and, consequently, the funding request if the utilisation achieved was 20 per cent lower than the base case assumptions?
- What would be the impact if costs were 7 per cent higher than originally planned?
- what would be the impact if only £400,000 grant was received instead of a £650,000 grant?

For start-up businesses, and especially those where seasonality is a key issue, milestone dates will be very critical. For example, what will be the impact if construction takes longer than anticipated and the opening of the club is delayed by three months? In the case of indoor tennis, the ideal time to open is September/October to coincide with the beginning of the peak winter period of use. A three month delay, effectively, reduces the period by half when revenue generation is at its highest and required to get the project off to a good start. A delay of any longer could be potentially disastrous in terms of cash flow. This same principle applies, and can be as critical, to many leisure related projects that have peak periods or seasonal fluctuations in use, such as tourism related projects.

It will not always be necessary to provide a detailed set of financial forecasts for the sensitivity analysis, but it will be necessary to include in the results the key information from the tests, such as the revised profit and loss figures for each year and the revised cash balances and cash flow requirement. It will also be necessary to state the effect that the alternative assumptions have on profitability and the key financial ratios, and whether additional financing will be required.

Conclusion

The preparation of financial forecasts takes time and considerable thought, but if they are well prepared they will give investors all the information they need to assess the potential of the business. Once the project has received its financing and is underway, the actual progress and results achieved should be monitored against the plan in order to assess the accuracy of the projections and to ensure that any changes to the original projections do not cause a financial crisis for the project. The plans should be amended to take account of actual progress and also, as appropriate, to reflect any changing assumptions or more accurate projections.

Table 17.1 Funding request schedule

Date	Requirement	Shares	Long term loan	Medium term loan	Grant	Cash	Balances Overdraft	Deposit
Year 1								
Jan	300000	700000	500000			5000		895000
Feb	368967	700000	500000			5000		826033
Mar	563433	700000	500000			5000		631567
Apr	859233	700000	500000			5000		335767
May	1257033	700000	500000			5000	−62033	
June	1657908	1200000	500000			5000		37092
July	1957708	1200000	500000			5000	−262708	
Aug	2261083	1200000	500000		650000	5000		83917
Sept	2460550	1200000	500000		650000	5000	−115550	
Oct	2588300	1200000	500000	180000	650000	5000	−63300	
Nov	2640378	1200000	500000	180000	650000	5000	−115378	
Dec	2699930	1200000	500000	180000	650000	5000	−174930	
Year 2								
Jan	2575624	1200000	500000	180000	650000	5000	−50624	
Feb	2566070	1200000	500000	180000	650000	5000	−41070	
Mar	2550738	1200000	500000	180000	650000	5000	−25738	
Apr	2533353	1200000	500000	180000	650000	5000	−8353	
May	2531427	1200000	500000	180000	650000	5000	−6427	
June	2531433	1200000	500000	180000	650000	5000	−6433	
July	2529158	1200000	500000	180000	650000	5000	−4158	
Aug	2527216	1200000	500000	180000	650000	5000	−2216	
Sept	2527047	1200000	500000	180000	650000	5000	−2047	
Oct	2544474	1200000	500000	171000	650000	5000	−28474	
Nov	2540691	1200000	500000	171000	650000	5000	−24691	
Dec	2539255	1200000	500000	171000	650000	5000	−23255	
Year 3								
Q1	2311084	1200000	500000	162000	650000	5000		195916
Q2	2288567	1200000	500000	153000	650000	5000		209433
Q3	2285882	1200000	500000	144000	650000	5000		203118
Q4	2262371	1200000	500000	135000	650000	5000		217629
Year 4								
Q1	1999976	1200000	500000	126000	650000	5000		471024
Q2	1965853	1200000	500000	117000	650000	5000		496147
Q3	1954874	1200000	500000	108000	650000	5000		498126
Q4	1923377	1200000	500000	99000	650000	5000		520623

Table 17.2 Profit and loss account forecast

	Year 1	Year 2	Year 3	Year 4
INCOME				
Court fees	0	151441	222781	256429
Courses	0	44000	62000	76000
Membership	0	179234	238979	268851
Catering	0	60000	69900	79800
Total income	0	434675	593659	681080
EXPENDITURE				
Employees salaries	4583	73200	91200	102000
Coaching fees	0	28600	40300	49400
Catering supplies/staffing	3000	33000	38445	43890
Building related costs	4000	69000	75000	78000
Administration costs	0	33000	35150	36060
Marketing/PR	8000	13040	17810	20432
Total expenditure	19583	249840	297905	329782
Operating profit/(loss) before interest, financing, charges and depreciation	−19583	184834	295755	351297
Depreciation	0	10000	10000	10000
Loan interest	0	24588	24130	23919
Profit/(loss) before interest and taxation	−19583	150247	261624	317378
Interest received	18700	61	4810	11508
Interest on overdraft	−10242	−2274	0	0
Profit/loss before taxation	−11125	148033	266434	328886

Table 17.3 Profit and loss account forecast – Year 1

	Jan	Feb	Mar	Apr	May	Jun	Jul	Aug	Sep	Oct	Nov	Dec	Total
INCOME													
Court fees	0	0	0	0	0	0	0	0	0	0	0	0	0
Courses	0	0	0	0	0	0	0	0	0	0	0	0	0
Memberships	0	0	0	0	0	0	0	0	0	0	0	0	0
Catering	0	0	0	0	0	0	0	0	0	0	0	0	0
Total income	0	0	0	0	0	0	0	0	0	0	0	0	0
EXPENDITURE													
Employees salaries	0	0	0	0	0	0	0	0	0	1250	1250	2083	4583
Coaching fees	0	0	0	0	0	0	0	0	0	0	0	0	0
Catering suplies/staffing	0	0	0	0	0	0	0	0	0	0	0	3000	3000
Building related costs	0	0	0	0	0	0	0	0	0	0	2000	2000	4000
Administration costs	0	0	0	0	0	0	0	0	0	0	0	0	0
Marketing/PR	0	0	0	0	0	0	0	0	0	0	4000	4000	8000
Total expenditure	0	0	0	0	0	0	0	0	0	1250	7250	11083	19583
Operating profit/(loss) before interest, financing charges and depreciation	0	0	0	0	0	0	0	0	0	−1250	−7250	−11083	−19583
Depreciation	0	0	0	0	0	0	0	0	0	0	0	0	0
Loan interest	0	0	0	0	0	0	0	0	0	0	0	0	0
Profit/(loss) before interest and taxation	0	0	0	0	0	0	0	0	0	−1250	−7250	−11083	−19583
Interest received	6033	5533	4200	2200		200		533					18700
Interest on overdraft					−875		−3375		−1500	−828	−1469	−2195	−10242
Profit/loss before taxation	6033	5533	4200	2200	−875	200	−3375	533	−1500	−2078	−8719	−13278	−11125

Table 17.4   Profit and loss account forecast – Year 2

	Jan	Feb	Mar	Apr	May	Jun	Jul	Aug	Sep	Oct	Nov	Dec	Total
INCOME													
Court fees	10887	10190	11344	12004	12387	12133	12387	12451	12068	15768	15388	14415	151441
Courses	5000	5000	1000	5000	5000	1000	5000	5000	1000	5000	5000	1000	44000
Memberships	179234	0	0	0	0	0	0	0	0	0	0	0	179234
Catering	3500	3500	4000	4000	4500	4500	5000	5000	5000	7000	7000	7000	60000
Total income	198621	18690	16344	21004	21887	17633	22387	22451	18068	27786	27388	22415	434675
EXPENDITURE													
Employees salaries	6100	6100	6100	6100	6100	6100	6100	6100	6100	6100	6100	6100	73200
Coaching fees	3250	3250	650	3250	3250	650	3250	3250	650	3250	3250	650	28600
Catering supplies/staffing	1925	1925	2200	2200	2475	2475	2750	2750	2750	3850	3850	3850	33000
Building related costs	6500	6500	6500	6500	5000	5000	5000	5000	5000	6500	6500	6500	69000
Administration costs	2750	2750	2750	2750	2750	2750	2750	2750	2750	2750	2750	2750	33000
Marketing/PR	5959	561	490	630	657	529	672	674	542	834	822	672	13040
Total expenditure	26484	21086	18690	19930	20232	17504	20522	20524	17792	23284	23272	20522	249840
Operating profit/(loss) before interest, financing charges and depreciation	172138	−2395	−2346	1074	1655	129	1865	1928	276	4502	4116	1892	184834
Depreciation	833	833	833	833	833	833	833	833	833	833	833	833	10000
Loan interest	5914			6099			6226			6349			24588
Profit/(loss) before interest and taxation	165391	−3229	−3180	−5858	822	−705	−5194	1095	−557	−2680	3283	1059	150247
Interest received							11	24	25				61
Interest on overdraft	−576	−449	−252	−32	−7	−7				−321	−307	−323	−2274
Profit/loss before taxation	164815	−3678	−3432	−5890	815	−712	−5182	1119	−532	−3001	2976	736	148033

Table 17.5 Profit and loss account forecast – Year 3

	Jan	Feb	Mar	Apr	May	Jun	Jul	Aug	Sep	Oct	Nov	Dec	Total
INCOME													
Court fees	21775	20381	22688	15210	15690	15407	15690	15789	15308	22472	21883	20489	222781
Courses	7000	7000	1500	7000	7000	1500	7000	7000	1500	7000	7000	1500	62000
Memberships	238979	0	0	0	0	0	0	0	0	0	0	0	238979
Catering	7500	7500	7500	4150	4150	4150	4150	4150	4150	7500	7500	7500	69900
Total income	275253	34881	31688	26360	26840	21057	26840	26939	20958	36972	36383	29489	593659
EXPENDITURE													
Employees salaries	7600	7600	7600	7600	7600	7600	7600	7600	7600	7600	7600	7600	91200
Coaching fees	4550	4550	975	4550	4550	975	4550	4550	975	4550	4550	975	40300
Catering supplies/staffing	4125	4125	4125	2283	2283	2283	2283	2283	2283	4125	4125	4125	38445
Building related costs	7000	7000	7000	5500	5500	5500	5500	5500	5500	7000	7000	7000	75000
Administration costs	2929	2929	2929	2929	2929	2929	2929	2929	2929	2929	2929	2929	35150
Marketing/PR	8258	1046	951	791	805	632	805	808	629	1109	1091	885	17810
Total expenditure	34462	27251	23580	23652	23667	19918	23667	23670	19915	27313	27296	23514	297905
Operating profit/(loss) before interest, financing charges and depreciation	240792	7630	8108	2707	3173	1139	3173	3269	1043	9658	9087	5975	295755
Depreciation	833	833	833	833	833	833	833	833	833	833	833	833	10000
Loan interest	6189			5982			5980			5980			24130
Profit/(loss) before interest and taxation	233770	6797	7275	-4108	2340	306	-3640	2436	210	2845	8254	5141	261624
Interest received	409	409	409	417	417	417	382	382	382	395	395	395	4810
Interest on overdraft													0
Profit/loss before taxation	234179	7206	7684	-3691	2757	723	-3257	2818	592	3240	8648	5536	266434

Table 17.6 Profit and loss account forecast – Year 4

	Jan	Feb	Mar	Apr	May	Jun	Jul	Aug	Sep	Oct	Nov	Dec	Total
INCOME													
Court fees	24721	23135	25748	17850	18417	18061	18417	18522	17956	25513	24838	23252	256429
Courses	8000	8000	3000	8000	8000	3000	8000	8000	3000	8000	8000	3000	76000
Memberships	268851	0	0	0	0	0	0	0	0	0	0	0	268851
Catering	8000	8000	8000	5300	5300	5300	5300	5300	5300	8000	8000	8000	79800
Total income	309572	39135	36748	31150	31717	26361	31717	31822	26256	41513	40838	34252	681080
EXPENDITURE													
Employees salaries	8500	8500	8500	8500	8500	8500	8500	8500	8500	8500	8500	8500	102000
Coaching fees	5200	5200	1950	5200	5200	1950	5200	5200	1950	5200	5200	1950	49400
Catering supplies/staffing	4400	4400	4400	2915	2915	2915	2915	2915	2915	4400	4400	4400	43890
Building related costs	7200	7200	7200	5800	5800	5800	5800	5800	5800	7200	7200	7200	78000
Administration costs	3005	3005	3005	3005	3005	3005	3005	3005	3005	3005	3005	3005	36060
Marketing/PR	9287	1174	1102	934	952	791	952	955	788	1245	1225	1028	20432
Total expenditure	37592	29479	26157	26354	26372	22961	26372	26375	22958	29550	29530	26083	329782
Operating profit/(loss) before interest, financing charges and depreciation	271979	9656	10590	4795	5345	3400	5345	5448	3298	11963	11308	8170	351297
Depreciation	833	833	833	833	833	833	833	833	833	833	833	833	10000
Loan interest	5980			5980			5980			5980			23919
Profit/(loss) before interest and taxation	265166	8823	9757	−2018	4512	2567	−1468	4614	2465	5150	10474	7336	317378
Interest received	936	936	936	969	969	969	951	951	951	980	980	980	11508
Interest on overdraft													0
Profit/loss before taxation	266102	9758	10693	−1049	5481	3536	−517	5566	3416	6130	11454	8316	328886

Table 17.7 Balance sheet

	Year 1	Year 2	Year 3	Year 4
FIXED ASSETS				
Buildings and courts	2650000	2650000	2650000	2650000
Furniture and equipment	50000	40000	30000	20000
less depreciation				
	2700000	2690000	2680000	2670000
CURRENT ASSETS				
Debtors			394	979
Short-term deposits			217629	520623
Cash	5000	5000	5000	5000
	5000	5000	223023	526602
CURRENT LIABILITIES				
Trade creditors	11195	13837	14681	15374
Overdraft	174930	23255		
	186125	37092	14681	15374
NET CURRENT ASSETS	−181125	−32092	208342	511228
NET ASSETS	2518875	2657908	2888342	3181228
CAPITAL AND BORROWINGS				
Issued share capital	1200000	1200000	1200000	1200000
Accm. profit/loss b/fwd		−11125	136908	403342
Profit/loss for year	−11125	148033	266434	328886
Grant	650000	650000	650000	650000
Long-term loans	500000	500000	500000	500000
Medium-term loans	180000	171000	135000	99000
	2518875	2657908	2888342	3181228

Table 17.8 Cash flow

	Year 1	Year 2	Year 3	Year 4
Court fees	0	151441	222781	256429
Courses	0	44000	62000	76000
Memberships	0	179234	238979	268851
Catering	0	60000	69900	79800
Total inflow	0	434675	593659	681080
Employees salaries	4583	73200	91200	102000
Coaching fees	0	28600	40300	49400
Catering supplies/staffing	0	32150	38170	43615
Building related costs	2000	64500	74500	77800
Administration costs	0	30250	34971	35984
Marketing/PR	4000	16368	17598	20289
Total outflow	10583	245068	296738	329089
Net inflow/outflow from operations	−10583	189607	296921	351991
Capital expenditure	2700000	0	0	0
Loan repayment	0	0	0	0
Loan interest	0	24846	24130	23919
Net cash inflow/outflow	−2710583	164761	272791	328072
Opening requirement	0	−2699930	−2539255	−2262371
Interest received	18700	61	4416	10922
Interest on overdraft	−8047	−4146	−323	0
Closing cash requirement	−2699930	−2539255	−2262371	−1923377

Table 17.9 Cash flow for Year 1

	Jan	Feb	Mar	Apr	May	Jun	Jul	Aug	Sep	Oct	Nov	Dec	Total
Court fees	0	0	0	0	0	0	0	0	0	0	0	0	0
Courses	0	0	0	0	0	0	0	0	0	0	0	0	0
Memberships	0	0	0	0	0	0	0	0	0	0	0	0	0
Catering	0	0	0	0	0	0	0	0	0	0	0	0	0
Total inflow	0	0	0	0	0	0	0	0	0	0	0	0	0
Employees salaries	0	0	0	0	0	0	0	0	0	1250	1250	2083	4583
Coaching fees	0	0	0	0	0	0	0	0	0	0	0	0	0
Catering supplies/staffing	0	0	0	0	0	0	0	0	0	0	0	0	0
Building related costs	0	0	0	0	0	0	0	0	0	0	0	2000	2000
Administration costs	0	0	0	0	0	0	0	0	0	0	0	0	0
Marketing/PR	0	0	0	0	0	0	0	0	0	0	0	4000	4000
Total outflow	0	0	0	0	0	0	0	0	0	1250	1250	8083	10583
Net inflow/outflow from operations	0	0	0	0	0	0	0	0	0	-1250	-1250	-8083	-10583
Capital expenditure	300000	75000	200000	300000	400000	400000	300000	200000	125000	50000	50000	2700000	0
Loan repayment	0	0	0	0	0	0	0	0	0	0	0	0	0
Loan interest	0	0	0	0	0	0	0	0	0	0	0	0	0
Net cash inflow/outflow	-300000	-75000	-200000	-300000	-400000	-400000	-300000	-300000	-200000	-126250	-51250	-58083	-2710583
Opening requirement	0	-300000	-368967	-563433	-859233	-1257033	-1657908	-1957708	-2261083	-2460550	-2588300	-2640378	
Interest received		6033	5533	4200	2200		200		533				18700
Interest on overdraft						-875		-3375		-1500	-828	-1469	-8047
Closing cash requirement	-300000	-368967	-563433	-859233	-1257033	-1657908	-1957708	-2261083	-2460550	-2588300	-2640378	-2699930	

Table 17.10 Cash flow for Year 2

	Jan	Feb	Mar	Apr	May	Jun	Jul	Aug	Sep	Oct	Nov	Dec	Total
Court fees	10887	10190	11344	12004	12387	12133	12387	12451	12068	15786	15388	14415	151441
Courses	5000	5000	1000	5000	5000	1000	5000	5000	1000	5000	5000	1000	44000
Memberships	125464	17923	17923	17923	0	0	0	0	0	0	0	0	179234
Catering	3500	3500	4000	4000	4500	4500	5000	5000	5000	7000	7000	7000	60000
Total inflow	144851	36614	34267	38927	21887	17633	22387	22451	18068	27786	27388	22415	434675
Employees salaries	6100	6100	6100	6100	6100	6100	6100	6100	6100	6100	6100	6100	73200
Coaching fees	3250	3250	650	3250	3250	650	3250	3250	650	3250	3250	650	28600
Catering supplies/staffing	3000	1925	1925	2200	2200	2475	2475	2750	2750	2750	3850	3850	32150
Building related costs	2000	6500	6500	6500	5000	5000	5000	5000	5000	5000	6500	6500	64500
Administration costs	0	2750	2750	2750	2750	2750	2750	2750	2750	2750	2750	2750	30250
Marketing/PR	4000	5959	561	490	630	657	529	672	674	542	834	822	16368
Total outflow	18350	26484	18486	21290	19930	17632	20104	20522	17924	20392	23284	20672	245068
Net inflow/outflow from operations	126501	10130	15782	17637	1957	1	2283	1930	145	7394	4104	1743	189607
Capital expenditure													
Loan repayment													
Loan interest	0	0	0	0	0	0	0	0	0	24846	0	0	24846
Net cash inflow/outflow	126501	10130	15782	17637	1957	1	2283	1930	145	-17452	4104	1743	164761
Opening requirement	-2699930	-2575624	-2566070	-2550738	-2533353	-2531427	-2531433	-2529158	-2527216	-2527047	-2544474	-2540691	
Interest received								11	24	25			61
Interest on overdraft	-2195	-576	-449	-252	-32	-7	-7				-321	-307	-4146
Closing cash requirement	-2575624	-2566070	-2550738	-2533353	-2531427	-2531433	-2529158	-2527216	-2527047	-2544474	-2540691	-2539255	

Table 17.11 Cash flow for Year 3

	Jan	Feb	Mar	Apr	May	Jun	Jul	Aug	Sep	Oct	Nov	Dec	Total
Court fees	21775	20381	22688	15210	15690	15407	15690	15789	15308	22472	21883	20489	222781
Courses	7000	7000	1500	7000	7000	1500	7000	7000	1500	7000	7000	1500	62000
Memberships	167285	23898	23898	23898	0	0	0	0	0	0	0	0	238979
Catering	7500	7500	7500	4150	4150	4150	4150	4150	4150	7500	7500	7500	69900
Total inflow	203560	58778	55586	50257	26840	21057	26840	26939	20958	36972	36383	29489	593659
Employees salaries	7600	7600	7600	7600	7600	7600	7600	7600	7600	7600	7600	7600	91200
Coaching fees	4550	4550	975	4550	4550	975	4550	4550	975	4550	4550	975	40300
Catering supplies/staffing	3850	4125	4125	4125	2283	2283	2283	2283	2283	2283	4125	4125	38170
Building related costs	6500	7000	7000	7000	5500	5500	5500	5500	5500	5500	7000	7000	74500
Administration costs	2750	2929	2929	2929	2929	2929	2929	2929	2929	2929	2929	2929	34971
Marketing/PR	672	8258	1046	951	791	805	632	805	808	629	1109	1091	17598
Total outflow	25922	34462	23676	27155	23642	20092	23493	23667	20095	23490	27313	23721	296738
Net inflow/outflow from operations	177637	24317	31910	23103	3188	965	3347	3272	864	13481	9069	5768	292921
Capital expenditure													0
Loan repayment													
Loan interest	6189			5982			5980			5980			24130
Net cash inflow/outflow	171449	24317	31910	17121	3188	965	-2633	3272	864	7501	9069	5768	272791
Opening requirement	-2539255	-2368129	-2343403	-2311084	-2293555	-2289949	-2288567	-2290782	-2287128	-2285882	-2277998	-2268534	
Interest received		409	409	409	417	417	417	382	382	382	395	395	4416
Interest on overdraft	-323												-323
Closing cash requirement	-2368129	-2343403	-2311084	-2293555	-2289949	-2288567	-2290782	-2287128	-2285882	-2277998	-2268534	-2262371	

Table 17.12 Cash flow for Year 4

	Jan	Feb	Mar	Apr	May	Jun	Jul	Aug	Sep	Oct	Nov	Dec	Total
Court fees	24721	23135	25748	17850	18417	18061	18417	18522	17956	25513	24838	23252	256429
Courses	8000	8000	3000	8000	8000	3000	8000	8000	3000	8000	8000	3000	76000
Memberships	188196	26885	26885	26885	0	0	0	0	0	0	0	0	268851
Catering	8000	8000	8000	5300	5300	5300	5300	5300	5300	8000	8000	8000	79800
Total inflow	228916	66020	63633	58035	31717	26361	31717	31822	26256	41513	40838	34252	681080
Employees salaries	8500	8500	8500	8500	8500	8500	8500	8500	8500	8500	8500	8500	102000
Coaching fees	5200	5200	1950	5200	5200	1950	5200	5200	1950	5200	5200	1960	49400
Catering supplies/staffing	4125	4400	4400	4400	2915	2915	2915	2915	2915	2915	4400	4400	43615
Building related costs	7000	7200	7200	7200	5800	5800	5800	5800	5800	5800	7200	7200	77800
Administration costs	2929	3005	3005	3005	3005	3005	3005	3005	3005	3005	3005	3005	35984
Marketing/PR	885	9287	1174	1102	934	952	791	952	955	788	1245	1225	20289
Total outflow	28639	37592	26229	29407	26354	23122	26211	26372	23125	26208	29550	26280	329089
Net inflow/outflow from operations	200277	28428	37404	28628	5362	3240	5506	5451	3131	15306	11287	7972	351991
Capital expenditure													
Loan repayment													0
Loan interest	5980			5980			5980			5980			23919
Net cash inflow/outflow	194298	28428	37404	22648	5362	3240	-474	5451	3131	9326	11287	7972	328072
Opening requirement	-2262371	-2067679	-2038316	-1999976	-1976393	-1970062	-1965853	-1965358	-1958956	-1954874	-1944596	-1932329	
Interest received	395	936	936	936	969	969	969	951	951	951	980	980	10922
Interest on overdraft	0	0	0	0	0	0	0	0	0	0	0	0	0
Closing cash requirement	-2067679	-2038316	-1999976	-1976393	-1970062	-1965853	-1965358	-1958956	-1954874	-1944596	-1932329	-1923377	

Appendix: Discount table

n	1%	2%	3%	4%	5%	6%	7%	8%	9%	10%	11%	12%	13%	14%	15%	16%	n
1	0.9901	0.9804	0.9709	0.9615	0.9524	0.9434	0.9259	0.9174	0.9174	0.9091	0.9009	0.8929	0.8850	0.8772	0.8696	0.8621	1
2	0.9803	0.9612	0.9426	0.9246	0.9070	0.8900	0.8734	0.8573	0.8417	0.8264	0.8116	0.7972	0.7831	0.7695	0.7561	0.7432	2
3	0.9706	0.9423	0.9151	0.8890	0.8638	0.8396	0.8163	0.7938	0.7722	0.7513	0.7312	0.7118	0.6931	0.6750	0.6575	0.6407	3
4	0.9610	0.9238	0.8835	0.8548	0.8227	0.7921	0.7629	0.7350	0.7084	0.6830	0.6587	0.6355	0.6133	0.5921	0.5718	0.5523	4
5	0.9515	0.9057	0.8626	0.8219	0.7835	0.7473	0.7130	0.6806	0.6499	0.6209	0.5935	0.5674	0.5428	0.5194	0.4972	0.4761	5
6	0.9420	0.8830	0.8375	0.7903	0.7462	0.7050	0.6663	0.6302	0.5963	0.5645	0.5346	0.5066	0.4803	0.4556	0.4323	0.4104	6
7	0.9327	0.8706	0.8131	0.7599	0.7107	0.6651	0.6227	0.5835	0.5470	0.5132	0.4817	0.4523	0.4251	0.3996	0.3759	0.3538	7
8	0.9235	0.8535	0.7894	0.7307	0.6768	0.6274	0.5820	0.5403	0.5019	0.4665	0.4339	0.4039	0.3762	0.3506	0.3269	0.3050	8
9	0.9143	0.8368	0.7664	0.7026	0.6446	0.5919	0.5439	0.5002	0.4604	0.4241	0.3909	0.3606	0.3329	0.3075	0.2843	0.2630	9
10	0.9053	0.8203	0.7441	0.6756	0.6139	0.5584	0.5083	0.4632	0.4224	0.3855	0.3522	0.3220	0.2946	0.2697	0.2472	0.2267	10
11	0.8963	0.8043	0.7224	0.6496	0.5847	0.5268	0.4751	0.4289	0.3875	0.3505	0.3173	0.2875	0.2607	0.2366	0.2149	0.1954	11
12	0.8874	0.7885	0.7014	0.6246	0.5568	0.4970	0.4440	0.3971	0.3555	0.3186	0.2858	0.2567	0.2307	0.2076	0.1869	0.1685	12
13	0.8787	0.7730	0.6810	0.6006	0.5303	0.4688	0.4150	0.3677	0.3262	0.2897	0.2575	0.2292	0.2042	0.1821	0.1625	0.1452	13
14	0.8700	0.7579	0.6611	0.5775	0.5051	0.4423	0.3878	0.3405	0.2992	0.2633	0.2320	0.2046	0.1807	0.1597	0.1413	0.1242	14
15	0.8613	0.7430	0.6419	0.5553	0.4810	0.4173	0.3624	0.3152	0.2745	0.2394	0.2090	0.1827	0.1599	0.1401	0.1229	0.1079	15
16	0.8528	0.7284	0.6232	0.5339	0.4581	0.3936	0.3387	0.2919	0.2519	0.2176	0.1883	0.1631	0.1415	0.1229	0.1069	0.0920	16
17	0.8444	0.7142	0.6050	0.5134	0.4363	0.3714	0.3166	0.2703	0.2311	0.1978	0.1696	0.1456	0.1252	0.1078	0.0929	0.0802	17
18	0.8360	0.7002	0.5874	0.4936	0.4155	0.353	0.2959	0.2502	0.2120	0.1799	0.1528	0.1300	0.1108	0.0946	0.0808	0.0691	18
19	0.8277	0.6864	0.5703	0.4746	0.3957	0.3305	0.2765	0.2317	0.1945	0.1635	0.1377	0.1151	0.0981	0.0829	0.0703	0.0596	19
20	0.8195	0.6730	0.5537	0.4564	0.3769	0.3118	0.2584	0.2145	0.1784	0.1486	0.1240	0.1037	0.0868	0.0728	0.0611	0.0514	20
21	0.8114	0.6598	0.5375	0.4388	0.3589	0.2942	0.2415	0.1987	0.1637	0.1351	0.1117	0.0926	0.0768	0.0638	0.0531	0.0443	21
22	0.8034	0.6468	0.5219	0.4229	0.3418	0.2775	0.2257	0.1839	0.1502	0.1228	0.1007	0.0826	0.0680	0.0560	0.0462	0.0382	22
23	0.7954	0.6342	0.5067	0.4057	0.3256	0.2618	0.2109	0.1703	0.1378	0.1117	0.0907	0.0738	0.0601	0.0491	0.0402	0.0329	23
24	0.7876	0.6217	0.4919	0.3901	0.3101	0.2470	0.1971	0.1577	0.1264	0.1015	0.0817	0.0659	0.0532	0.0431	0.0349	0.0284	24
25	0.7798	0.6095	0.4776	0.3751	0.2953	0.2339	0.1842	0.1460	0.1160	0.0923	0.0736	0.0588	0.0471	0.0278	0.0204	0.0245	25

Appendix: Discount table (continued)

n	1%	2%	3%	4%	5%	6%	7%	8%	9%	10%	11%	12%	13%	14%	15%	16%	n
26	0.7720	0.5976	0.4637	0.3607	0.2812	0.2198	0.1722	0.1352	0.1064	0.0839	0.0663	0.0525	0.0417	0.0331	0.0264	0.0211	26
27	0.7644	0.5859	0.4502	0.3468	0.2678	0.2074	0.1609	0.1252	0.0976	0.0763	0.0597	0.0469	0.0369	0.0291	0.0230	0.0182	27
28	0.7568	0.5744	0.4371	0.3335	0.2551	0.1956	0.1504	0.1159	0.0895	0.0693	0.0538	0.0419	0.0326	0.0255	0.0200	0.0157	28
29	0.7493	0.5631	0.4243	0.3207	0.2429	0.1846	0.1406	0.1073	0.0822	0.0630	0.0485	0.0374	0.0289	0.0224	0.0174	0.0135	29
30	0.7419	0.5521	0.4120	0.3083	0.2314	0.1741	0.1314	0.0994	0.0754	0.0573	0.0437	0.0334	0.0256	0.0196	0.0151	0.0116	30
35	0.7059	0.5000	0.3554	0.2534	0.1813	0.1301	0.0937	0.0676	0.0490	0.0356	0.0259	0.0189	0.0139	0.0102	0.0075	0.0055	35
40	0.6717	0.4529	0.3066	0.2083	0.1420	0.0972	0.0668	0.0460	0.0318	0.0221	0.0154	0.0107	0.0075	0.0053	0.0037	0.0026	40
45	0.6391	0.4102	0.2644	0.1712	0.1113	0.0727	0.0476	0.0313	0.0207	0.0137	0.0091	0.0061	0.0011	0.0027	0.0019	0.0013	45
50	0.6080	0.3715	0.2281	0.1407	0.0872	0.0543	0.0339	0.0213	0.0134	0.0085	0.0054	0.0035	0.0022	0.0014	0.0009	0.0006	54

n	17%	18%	19%	20%	21%	22%	23%	24%	25%	26%	27%	28%	29%	30%	31%	32%	n
1	0.8547	0.8475	0.8403	0.8333	0.8264	0.8197	0.8130	0.8065	0.8000	0.7937	0.7874	0.7813	0.7752	0.7692	0.7634	0.7576	1
2	0.7305	0.7182	0.7062	0.6944	0.6830	0.6719	0.6610	0.6504	0.6400	0.6299	0.6200	0.6104	0.6009	0.5917	0.5827	0.5739	2
3	0.6244	0.6086	0.5934	0.5787	0.5645	0.5507	0.5374	0.5245	0.5120	0.4999	0.4882	0.4768	0.4658	0.4552	0.4485	043487	3
4	0.5337	0.5158	0.4987	0.4823	0.4665	0.4514	0.4369	0.4239	0.4096	0.3968	0.3844	0.3725	0.3611	0.3501	0.3396	0.3294	4
5	0.4561	0.4371	0.4190	0.4019	0.3855	0.3700	0.3552	0.3411	0.3277	0.3149	0.3027	0.2910	0.2799	0.2693	0.2592	0.2495	5
6	0.3898	0.3704	0.3521	0.3349	0.3186	0.3033	0.2888	0.2751	0.2621	0.2499	0.2383	0.2274	0.2170	0.2072	0.1979	0.1890	6
7	0.3332	0.3139	0.2959	0.2791	0.2633	0.2486	0.2348	0.2218	0.2097	0.1983	0.1877	0.1776	0.1682	0.1594	0.1510	0.1432	7
8	0.2848	0.2660	0.2487	0.2326	0.2176	0.2038	0.1909	0.1789	0.1678	0.1574	0.1478	0.1388	0.1304	0.1226	0.1153	0.1085	8
9	0.2434	0.2255	0.2090	0.1938	0.1799	0.1670	0.1552	0.1443	0.1342	0.1249	0.1164	0.1084	0.1011	0.0943	0.0830	0.0822	9
10	0.2080	0.1911	0.1756	0.1615	0.1486	0.1369	0.1262	0.1164	0.1074	0.0992	0.0916	0.0847	0.0784	0.0725	0.0672	0.0623	10
11	0.1778	0.1619	0.1476	0.1346	0.1228	0.1122	0.1026	0.0938	0.0859	0.0787	0.0721	0.0662	0.0607	0.0558	0.0513	0.0472	11
12	0.1520	0.1372	0.1240	0.1122	0.1015	0.0920	0.0834	0.0757	0.0687	0.0625	0.0568	0.0517	0.0471	0.0429	0.0392	0.0357	12
13	0.1299	0.1163	0.1042	0.0935	0.0839	0.0754	0.0678	0.0610	0.0550	0.0496	0.0447	0.0404	0.0365	0.0330	0.0299	0.0271	13
14	0.1110	0.0985	0.0876	0.0779	0.0693	0.0618	0.0551	0.0492	0.0440	0.0393	0.0352	0.0316	0.0283	0.0253	0.0228	0.0205	14
15	0.0949	0.0835	0.0736	0.0649	0.0573	0.0507	0.0448	0.0397	0.0352	0.0312	0.0277	0.0247	0.0219	0.0195	0.0174	0.0155	15

Appendix: Discount table (continued)

n	17%	18%	19%	20%	21%	22%	23%	24%	25%	26%	27%	28%	29%	30%	31%	32%	n
16	0.0811	0.0708	0.0618	0.0541	0.0474	0.0415	0.0364	0.0320	0.0281	0.0248	0.0218	0.0193	0.0170	0.0150	0.0133	0.0118	16
17	0.0693	0.0600	0.0520	0.0451	0.0391	0.0340	0.0296	0.0258	0.0225	0.0197	0.0172	0.0150	0.0132	0.0116	0.0101	0.0089	17
18	0.0592	0.9508	0.0437	0.0376	0.0323	0.0279	0.0241	0.0208	0.0180	0.0156	0.0135	0.0118	0.0102	0.0089	0.0077	0.0068	18
19	0.0506	0.0431	0.0367	0.0313	0.0267	0.0229	0.0196	0.0168	0.0144	0.0124	0.0107	0.0092	0.0079	0.0068	0.0059	0.0051	19
20	0.0433	0.0365	0.0308	0.0261	0.0221	0.0187	0.0159	0.0135	0.0115	0.0098	0.0084	0.0072	0.0061	0.0053	0.0045	0.0039	20
21	0.0370	0.0309	0.0259	0.0217	0.0183	0.0154	0.0129	0.0109	0.0092	0.0078	0.0066	0.0056	0.0048	0.0040	0.0034	0.0029	21
22	0.0316	0.0262	0.0218	0.0181	0.0151	0.0126	0.0105	0.0083	0.0074	0.0062	0.0052	0.0044	0.0037	0.0031	0.0026	0.0022	22
23	0.0270	0.0222	0.0183	0.0151	0.0125	0.0103	0.0086	0.0071	0.0059	0.0049	0.0041	0.0034	0.0029	0.0024	0.0020	0.0017	23
24	0.0231	0.0188	0.0154	0.0126	0.0103	0.0085	0.0070	0.0057	0.0047	0.0039	0.0032	0.0027	0.0022	0.0018	0.0015	0.0013	24
25	0.0197	0.0160	0.0129	0.0105	0.0085	0.0069	0.0057	0.0046	0.0038	0.0031	0.0025	0.0021	0.0017	0.0014	0.0012	0.0010	25
26	0.0169	0.0135	0.0109	0.0087	0.0070	0.0057	0.0046	0.0037	0.0030	0.0025	0.0020	0.0016	0.0013	0.0011	0.0009	0.0007	26
27	0.0144	0.0115	0.0091	0.0073	0.0058	0.0047	0.0037	0.0030	0.0024	0.0019	0.0016	0.0013	0.0010	0.0008	0.0007	0.0006	27
28	0.0123	0.0097	0.0077	0.0061	0.0048	0.0038	0.0030	0.0024	0.0019	0.0015	0.0012	0.0010	0.0008	0.0006	0.0005	0.0004	28
29	0.0105	0.0082	0.0064	0.0051	0.0040	0.0031	0.0025	0.0020	0.0015	0.0012	0.0010	0.0008	0.0006	0.0005	0.0004	0.0003	29
30	0.0090	0.0070	0.0054	0.0042	0.0033	0.0026	0.0020	0.0016	0.0012	0.0010	0.0008	0.0006	0.0005	0.0004	0.0003	0.0002	30
35	0.0041	0.0030	0.0023	0.0017	0.0013	0.0009	0.0007	0.0005	0.0004	0.0003	0.0002	0.0002	0.0001	0.0001	0.0001	0.0001	35
40	0.0019	0.0013	0.0010	0.0007	0.0005	0.0004	0.0002	0.0002	0.0001	0.0001	0.0001	0.0001	0.0000	0.0000	0.0000	0.0000	40
45	0.0009	0.0006	0.0004	0.0003	0.0002	0.0001	0.0001	0.0001	0.0000	0.0000	0.0000	0.0000					45
50	0.0004	0.0003	0.0002	0.0001	0.0001	0.0000	0.0000	0.0000									54

n	33%	34%	35%	36%	37%	38%	39%	40%	41%	42%	43%	44%	45%	46%	47%	48%	n
1	0.7519	0.7463	0.7407	0.7353	0.7299	0.7246	0.7194	0.7143	0.7092	0.7042	0.6993	0.6944	0.6897	0.6849	0.6802	0.6757	1
2	0.5653	0.5569	0.5487	0.5407	0.5328	0.5251	0.5176	0.5102	0.5030	0.4959	0.4890	0.4823	0.4756	0.4691	0.4628	0.4565	2
3	0.4251	0.4156	0.4064	0.3975	0.3889	0.3805	0.3724	0.3644	0.3567	0.3492	0.3420	0.3349	0.3280	0.3213	0.3148	0.3085	3
4	0.3196	0.3102	0.3011	0.2923	0.2839	0.2757	0.2679	0.2603	0.2530	0.2459	0.2391	0.2326	0.2262	0.2201	0.2142	0.2084	4
5	0.2403	0.2315	0.2230	0.2149	0.2072	0.1998	0.1927	0.1859	0.1794	0.1732	0.1672	0.1615	0.1560	0.1507	0.1457	0.1408	5

Appendix: Discount table (continued)

n	33%	34%	35%	36%	37%	38%	39%	40%	41%	42%	43%	44%	45%	46%	47%	48%	n
6	0.1807	0.1727	0.1652	0.1580	0.1512	0.1448	0.1386	0.1328	0.1273	0.1220	0.1169	0.1122	0.1076	0.1032	0.0991	0.0952	6
7	0.1358	0.1289	0.1224	0.1162	0.1104	0.1049	0.0997	0.0949	0.0903	0.0859	0.0818	0.0779	0.0742	0.0707	0.0674	0.0643	7
8	0.1021	0.0962	0.0906	0.0854	0.0806	0.0760	0.0718	0.0678	0.0640	0.0605	0.0572	0.0541	0.0512	0.0484	0.0459	0.0434	8
9	0.0768	0.0718	0.0671	0.0628	0.0588	0.0551	0.0516	0.0484	0.0454	0.0426	0.0400	0.0376	0.0353	0.0332	0.0312	0.0294	9
10	0.0577	0.9536	0.0497	0.0462	0.0429	0.0399	0.0371	0.0346	0.0322	0.0300	0.0280	0.0261	0.0243	0.0227	0.0212	0.0198	10
11	0.0434	0.0400	0.0368	0.0340	0.0313	0.0289	0.0267	0.0247	0.0223	0.0211	0.0196	0.0181	0.0168	0.0156	0.0144	0.0134	11
12	0.0326	0.0298	0.0273	0.0250	0.0229	0.0210	0.0192	0.0176	0.0162	0.0149	0.0137	0.0126	0.0116	0.0107	0.0098	0.0091	12
13	0.0245	0.0223	0.0202	0.0184	0.0167	0.0152	0.0138	0.0126	0.0115	0.0105	0.0096	0.0087	0.0080	0.0073	0.0067	0.0061	13
14	0.0185	0.0166	0.0150	0.0135	0.0122	0.0122	0.0099	0.0090	0.0081	0.0074	0.0067	0.0061	0.0055	0.0050	0.0045	0.0041	14
15	0.0139	0.0124	0.0111	0.0099	0.0089	0.0080	0.0072	0.0064	0.0058	0.0052	0.0047	0.0042	0.0038	0.0034	0.0031	0.0028	15
16	0.0104	0.0093	0.0082	0.0073	0.0065	0.0058	0.0051	0.0046	0.0041	0.0037	0.0033	0.0029	0.0026	0.0023	0.0021	0.0019	16
17	0.0078	0.0069	0.0061	0.0054	0.0047	0.0042	0.0037	0.0033	0.0029	0.0026	0.0023	0.0020	0.0018	0.0016	0.0014	0.0013	17
18	0.0059	0.0052	0.0045	0.0039	0.0035	0.0030	0.0027	0.0023	0.0021	0.0018	0.0016	0.0014	0.0012	0.0011	0.0010	0.0009	18
19	0.0044	0.0038	0.0033	0.0029	0.0025	0.0022	0.0019	0.0017	0.0015	0.0013	0.0011	0.0010	0.0009	0.0008	0.0007	0.0006	19
20	0.0033	0.0029	0.0025	0.0021	0.0018	0.0016	0.0014	0.0012	0.0010	0.0009	0.0008	0.0007	0.0006	0.0005	0.0005	0.0004	20
21	0.0025	0.0021	0.0018	0.0016	0.0013	0.0012	0.0010	0.0009	0.0007	0.0006	0.0005	0.0005	0.0004	0.0004	0.0003	0.0003	21
22	0.0019	0.0016	0.0014	0.0012	0.0010	0.0008	0.0007	0.0006	0.0005	0.0004	0.0004	0.0003	0.0003	0.0002	0.0002	0.0002	22
23	0.0014	0.0012	0.0010	0.0008	0.0007	0.0006	0.0005	0.0004	0.0004	0.0003	0.0003	0.0002	0.0002	0.0002	0.0001	0.0001	23
24	0.0011	0.0009	0.0007	0.0006	0.0005	0.0004	0.0004	0.0003	0.0003	0.0002	0.0002	0.0002	0.0001	0.0001	0.0001	0.0001	24
25	0.0008	0.0007	0.0006	0.0005	0.0004	0.0003	0.0003	0.0002	0.0002	0.0002	0.0001	0.0001	0.0001	0.0001	0.0001	0.0001	25
26	0.0006	0.0005	0.0004	0.003	0.0002	0.0002	0.0002	0.0002	0.0001	0.0001	0.0001	0.0001	0.0001	0.0001	0.0000	0.0000	26
27	0.0005	0.0004	0.0003	0.0002	0.0002	0.0002	0.0001	0.0001	0.0001	0.0001	0.0001	0.0001	0.0001	0.0000			27
28	0.0003	0.0003	0.0002	0.0002	0.0001	0.0001	0.0001	0.0001	0.0001	0.0001	0.0000	0.0000					28
29	0.003	0.0002	0.0001	0.0001	0.0001	0.0001	0.0001	0.0000	0.0000								29
30	0.0002	0.0002	0.0001	0.0001	0.0000	0.0000	0.0000	0.0000									30
35	0.0000	0.0000	0.0000	0.0000	0.0000	0.0000	0.0000	0.0000									35

Index

Busi

This

C

Management und Marketing im Sport

Betriebswirtschaftliche Grundlagen und
Anwendungen der Sportökonomie

Herausgegeben von

Prof. Dr. Gerd Nufer
Dr. André Bühler

Mit Beiträgen von

Prof. Dr. Christoph Breuer, Markus Breuer, Dr. André Bühler,
Prof. Dr. Simon Chadwick, Prof. Dr. Frank Daumann,
Prof. Dr. Helmut Digel, Dr. Marcel Fahrner, Marco Gensmüller,
Prof. Dr. Heinz-Dieter Horch, Dr. Gregor Hovemann,
Dr. Simone Jäck, Christoph Jordan, Dr. Sebastian Kaiser,
Christian Keller, Dr. Mathias Langer, Thomas Meffert,
Prof. Dr. Siegfried Nagel, Prof. Dr. Gerd Nufer, Tim Pawlowski,
Prof. Dr. Carsten Rennhak, Dr. Michael Schilhaneck,
Torsten Schlesinger, Pamela Wicker

ERICH SCHMIDT VERLAG

Bibliografische Information der Deutschen Bibliothek
Die Deutsche Bibliothek verzeichnet diese Publikation in der Deutschen
Nationalbibliografie; detaillierte bibliografische Daten sind im Internet über
dnb.ddb.de abrufbar.

Weitere Informationen zu diesem Titel finden Sie im Internet unter
ESV.info/978-3-503-11007-0

ISBN 978-3-503-11007-0

Erich Schmidt Verlag GmbH & Co., Berlin 2008
www.ESV.info

Dieses Papier erfüllt die Frankfurter Forderungen
der Deutschen Bibliothek und der Gesellschaft für das Buch
bezüglich der Alterungsbeständigkeit und entspricht
sowohl den strengen Bestimmungen der US Norm Ansi/Niso
Z 39.48-1992 als auch der ISO-Norm 9706

Druck und Bindung: Hubert & Co., Göttingen

Vorwort

Aufgrund der zunehmenden Kommerzialisierung des Sports wird betriebswirtschaftliches Wissen im Sportmanagement und Sportmarketing immer bedeutender. Viele Sportorganisationen sind heutzutage hinsichtlich ihrer Umsatzzahlen und Mitarbeiterstärken mit mittelständischen Unternehmen vergleichbar. Häufig fehlt ihnen jedoch das betriebswirtschaftliche Wissen und Verständnis, um solides und erfolgreiches Wirtschaften sicherzustellen. Das vorliegende Buch „Management und Marketing im Sport" leistet einen Beitrag, um diese Lücke zu schließen.

Der Herausgeberband wendet die grundlegenden Prinzipien wirtschaftlichen Handelns auf den Bereich des Sports an. Bei der Erläuterung der klassischen Disziplinen der Betriebswirtschaftslehre im Rahmen des Sportmanagements werden stets die Besonderheiten des Wirtschaftsmarkts Sport berücksichtigt. Das Sportmarketing bildet gegenwärtig die am weitesten ausdifferenzierte Disziplin des Sportmanagements. Präsentiert werden die aktuellsten Entwicklungen und Trends auf diesem Gebiet.

Die Autoren der einzelnen Kapitel sind renommierte Wissenschaftler aus der Sportökonomie bzw. Experten aus den jeweiligen betriebswirtschaftlichen Disziplinen, die einen sehr engen Bezug zum Thema Sport aufweisen. Der Inhalt gibt somit insgesamt den aktuellen Stand der Sportökonomie wieder.

Die Zielgruppe des Buches sind Studierende der Sportökonomie (undergraduate und graduate), die Führungspositionen in Sportbetrieben anstreben, Dozenten und Forscher der Sportwissenschaften und Betriebswirtschaftslehre mit den Schwerpunkten Sportmanagement und Sportmarketing sowie nicht zuletzt Praktiker aus den entsprechenden Bereichen in Sportorganisationen und Unternehmen. Die Autoren vermitteln in kompakter Form und gut verständlich, an vielen Stellen auch kritisch reflektierend das erforderliche betriebswirtschaftliche Know-how, um ein Sportunternehmen modern und erfolgreich zu führen.

Der Band geht von einer interdisziplinären Managementorientierung aus und stellt das gesamte Spektrum des Sportmanagements und Sportmarketing in systematischer Form vor. Ziel ist dabei ein „doppelter Brückenschlag": einerseits zwischen Sport und Wirtschaft, andererseits von der Theorie zur Praxis.

Es handelt sich um ein Werk, das es in vergleichbarer Form im deutschsprachigen Raum bislang nicht gab. Didaktisch ist das Buch insbesondere aufgrund der einheitlichen Struktur aller Beiträge und der integrierten Fallstudien sehr benutzerfreundlich aufbereitet. Der Leser erhält eine theoretisch fundierte und dennoch praxisnahe, umfassende Darstellung zum Sportmanagement und Sportmarketing auf anspruchsvollem Niveau, die besonderen Wert auf Verständlichkeit und Nachvollziehbarkeit der Ausführungen legt. Studierenden wird anhand der integrierten Kontrollfragen zusätzlich die Möglichkeit der selbständigen Übung und Leistungskontrolle angeboten.

Unser herzlicher Dank gilt den Autoren der einzelnen Kapitel, die sich mit ihrer Mitarbeit an diesem Band parallel zu ihrem Tagesgeschäft erfolgreich einer zusätzlichen Herausforderung gestellt haben – und dies in einem knapp bemessenen Zeitrahmen, der den Herausgebern eine zügige Umsetzung des Projekts ermöglichte. Die Zusammenarbeit funktionierte vorbildlich, es war für uns ein großes Vergnügen, mit diesen Persönlichkeiten zusammenzuarbeiten.

Gerd Nufer: Besonders bedanken möchte ich mich bei meiner Frau Karin für ihr Verständnis, dass ich womöglich zu häufig meine Freizeit mit der Forschung und nicht immer in angemessenem Umfang mit meiner Familie verbringe. Widmen möchte ich dieses Buch meiner einjährigen Tochter Gabriela Carina.

André Bühler: Dieses Buch möchte ich meinen Eltern sowie Bilal und ganz besonders Nadja widmen. Weil sie mich immer mal wieder daran erinnern, was im Leben wirklich zählt.

Am Ende des Buches befinden sich die Kontaktdaten der Herausgeber und Autoren. Insbesondere die Herausgeber freuen sich über Anregungen und Rückmeldungen. Wir wünschen dem interessierten Leser viel Spaß bei der Lektüre und viel Erfolg beim Umsetzen der gewonnenen Erkenntnisse.

Reutlingen und Heidelberg, im März 2008

Gerd Nufer & André Bühler

Inhaltsverzeichnis

Teil I:
Betriebswirtschaftslehre und Sport – ein Überblick

Teil II:
Sportmanagement –
die Anwendung klassischer Disziplinen der Betriebswirtschaftslehre im Sport

Teil III:
Sportmarketing –
aktuelle Entwicklungen und Trends

Teil I:

Betriebswirtschaftslehre und Sport –
ein Überblick

Kapitel 1: Sportmanagement und Sportmarketing: Einführung und Perspektive

Gerd Nufer   André Bühler

Lernziele

Nach der Durchsicht dieses Kapitels sollte der Leser in der Lage sein,

- den Begriff Sportökonomie kritisch zu reflektieren.
- den Sportmarkt systematisch zu untergliedern.
- die Besonderheiten des Sports aus wirtschaftlicher Sicht zu erörtern.
- die gewählte Struktur des Buches sowie die Besonderheiten des vorliegenden Bandes nachvollziehen zu können.

Überblick über das Kapitel

In diesem einführenden Kapitel werden zunächst die Motive der Herausgeber für die Entstehung des vorliegenden Bandes „Management und Marketing im Sport" dargelegt. Die Entwicklung der Sportökonomie wird skizziert sowie deren inhärente Probleme thematisiert. Der Sammelband versucht, die grundlegenden betriebswirtschaftlichen Disziplinen auf den Bereich des Sports anzuwenden. Dabei müssen stets die Besonderheiten des Sports berücksichtigt werden. Dies gelingt am besten auf der Basis einer einheitlichen Perspektive, die in allen nachfolgenden Kapiteln eingehalten wird. Beide Voraussetzungen hierfür, sowohl eine Systematik des Sportmarktes und die daraus abgeleitete Perspektive als auch die Besonderheiten des Sports aus wirtschaftlicher Sicht, werden in diesem Kapitel sukzessive erarbeitet. Ferner wird dem Leser die zu Grunde liegende Struktur des Bandes vorgestellt sowie nützliche Hinweise für die Lektüre des Buches gegeben.

1.1 Warum ein Buch „Management und Marketing im Sport"?

Der Sport ist im Laufe des 20. und 21. Jahrhunderts zu einem weltweit bedeutenden Wirtschaftsfaktor geworden. Aufgrund der zunehmenden Kommerzialisierung des Sports wird betriebswirtschaftliches Wissen im Sportbereich immer wichtiger. Viele Sportorganisationen sind heutzutage aufgrund ihrer Umsatzzahlen und Mitarbeiterstärke mit mittelständischen Unternehmen vergleichbar, werden jedoch häufig immer noch ehrenamtlich und vergleichsweise eher unprofessionell geführt. Vielen Sportbetrieben fehlt das notwendige betriebswirtschaftliche Wissen und Verständnis, um solides Wirtschaften sicherzustellen.

Dieses Defizit kann grundsätzlich begründet werden: Die Sportwissenschaft auf der einen Seite war lange Zeit durch eine nicht zu verleugnende *„Ökonomieferne"* geprägt (Heinemann, 1995, S. 18). Diese hat ihre Ursache darin, dass die Absolventen sportwissenschaftlicher Studiengänge überwiegend Lehrer wurden und ökonomische Kenntnisse wurden für diesen Beruf für nicht erforderlich erachtet. Seitens der Wirtschaftswissenschaften wurde Sportökonomie dagegen lange Zeit vielfach eher als *„Hobby"* denn als ernstzunehmendes Betätigungsfeld gesehen. In diesem Zusammenhang wurde oftmals der Fehler begangen, zwar gesichertes wirtschaftliches Wissen auf den Sport zu übertragen, dies jedoch, ohne dessen Besonderheiten zu kennen oder gar in adäquater Form zu berücksichtigen.

Das vorliegende Buch versucht einen Beitrag zu leisten, dieses Defizit zu beseitigen und die bestehende Lücke zu schließen, indem die grundlegenden betriebswirtschaftlichen Disziplinen auf den Bereich des Sports angewandt werden. Dabei werden nicht nur die Prinzipien wirtschaftlichen Handelns erläutert, sondern stets die Besonderheiten des Wirtschaftsmarkts Sport berücksichtigt, sowie durchgängig der Bogen vom Allgemeinen zum Besonderen geschlagen. Die Autoren der einzelnen Kapitel sind renommierte Wissenschaftler aus der Sportökonomie und/oder Experten aus den jeweiligen betriebswirtschaftlichen Disziplinen, die einen engen Bezug zum Thema Sport aufweisen.

Dieser theoretisch fundierte, aber deutlich praxisorientierte Band soll Mitgliedern von Sportorganisationen das erforderliche betriebswirtschaftliche Know-how vermitteln, um ihr Sportunternehmen modern und erfolgreich führen zu können. Zielgruppe des Buches sind somit Studierende der Sportökonomie (undergraduate und graduate), die zukünftig Führungspositionen in Sportbetrieben bekleiden werden, Dozenten und Forscher der Sportwissenschaften und Betriebswirtschaftslehre mit den Schwerpunkten Sportmanagement und Sportmarketing sowie Praktiker aus den entsprechenden Bereichen in Sportorganisationen und Unternehmen.

1.2 Aktueller Stand der Sportökonomie

Die Ökonomie des Sports ist eine vergleichsweise junge Disziplin. Insbesondere bei einer länderübergreifenden Betrachtung werden beachtliche Unterschiede im Entwicklungsstand deutlich (vgl. hierzu insbesondere die Fallstudien in den folgenden Kapiteln). Sportökonomie und Sportmanagement haben jedoch in den letzten Jahren eine rasante Entwicklung zurückgelegt und in Lehre und Forschung die Pionierphase verlassen: Sportökonomie-Kongresse und Arbeitskreise haben sich etabliert, wissenschaftliche Fachzeitschriften wurden der Thematik gewidmet, und die Ausbildung wurde der steigenden Nachfrage nach qualifizierten Sportmanagern zunehmend gerecht, indem sportökonomische Studiengänge und entsprechende Weiterbildungsangebote eingerichtet wurden. Letzteres unterstreicht insbesondere die gestiegenen Erwartungen, die die Praxis an die Entwicklung der Sportökonomie knüpft.

Mit Sportökonomie beschäftigen sich traditionell Wissenschaftler unterschiedlicher Disziplinen, um sowohl den Sportmarkt als auch Sportunternehmen zu analysieren. Sportökonomie und Sportmanagement sind nicht zuletzt deshalb spannende Lehr- und Forschungsgebiete, weil sich hier unterschiedliche Ansätze zu einem sach- und problemadäquaten Methoden-Mix vereinen. Manche sprechen sogar von einer neuen wissenschaftlichen „Subdisziplin" (Albach/Frick, 2002, S. VII) oder gar einem eigenständigen „Wissenschaftszweig" (Heinemann, 2001, S. 17).

Aber was ist Sportökonomie überhaupt? Eine auf den Punkt gebrachte Antwort auf diese zentrale Frage gibt Horch (2007, o.S.):

> *„Sportökonomie* ist eine Wissenschaft, die die ökonomischen Aspekte des Sports untersucht."

Heinemann (1995) stellt fest, dass es eine systematisch entfaltete Ökonomie des Sports nicht gibt. Aber der Entwicklungsstand von Wirtschaft und Sport macht es unerlässlich, der Wirtschaft des Sports eine besondere Bedeutung in Lehre und Forschung beizumessen. Breuer/Thiel (2005) formulieren darauf aufbauend zwei zentrale Fragen des *Sportmanagement*:

1. Wie wird Sport gemanagt?
2. Wie ist Sport zu managen?

Das Sportmanagement fokussiert dabei auf die unterschiedlichen Systemebenen einer Sportorganisation: Sportmanager müssen sich mit *Personen* auseinandersetzen (z.B. Teilnehmer einer Veranstaltung, eigene Mitarbeiter). Sie müssen sich mit der Struktur der *Organisation* beschäftigen (etwa im Rahmen der strategischen Planung oder des organisationalen Lernens). Schließlich müssen sie die *Umwelt* der Sportorganisation im Blick behalten (beispielsweise wenn es um die Produktentwicklung und -vermarktung geht).

Innerhalb des Sportmanagements ist das *Sportmarketing* momentan die am stärksten ausdifferenzierte Disziplin, d.h. im Sportmarketing ist die betriebswirtschaftliche Professionalisierung im Sport bereits am weitesten vorangeschritten (Freyer, 2003). Grundsätzlich zu unterscheiden sind hierbei folgende Perspektiven (vgl. Kapitel 12):

- Marketing *von* Sport: Vermarktung von Sportprodukten durch Sportorganisationen und sportnahe Unternehmen.
- Marketing *mit* Sport: Instrumentelle Verwendung des Sports im Rahmen des Marketing von Unternehmen, die keine Sportleistungen herstellen.

Die Sportökonomie, das Sportmanagement und das Sportmarketing haben immer die Eigenheiten des Sports und die Besonderheit von Sportorganisationen zu berücksichtigen. Dies gelingt am besten auf der Basis einer einheitlichen Perspektive. Beide Voraussetzungen hierfür, d.h. sowohl eine Unterteilung des Sportmarktes, die die unterschiedlichen Sportorganisationen systematisiert, und die daraus abgeleitete Perspektive als auch die wesentlichen Besonderheiten des Sports aus wirtschaftlicher Sicht, werden in diesem Kapitel sukzessive erarbeitet.

1.3 Systematik des Sportmarktes

Im Folgenden werden verschiedene Ansätze vorgestellt, die versuchen, den sehr heterogenen Sportmarkt zu strukturieren. Die daraus als Synthese entwickelte Systematik erlaubt es, eine bestimmte Perspektive des Wirtschaftsmarktes Sport auszuwählen, die danach in sämtlichen Kapiteln des Bandes konsequent eingehalten wird.

1.3.1 Abgrenzungen in der Literatur

Willimczik (2007) überprüfte auf der Grundlage der Vorschläge von Digel (1984) und Heinemann (1986) im Rahmen einer empirischen Untersuchung, welche *Sportmodelle* in der Alltagssprache vorhanden sind. In einer Clusteranalyse kristallisieren sich sechs Konzepte heraus, die prototypisch bestätigt werden können: der *traditionelle Sport*, der *professionelle Hochleistungssport*, die s*portnahen Hobbys*, der *Präsentationssport*, der *Erlebnissport* und der *Gesundheitssport*. Diese Sportmodelle sind durch unterschiedliche Merkmale (z.B. Bewegung, Leistung, Entspannung) charakterisiert und realisieren sich in unterschiedlichen Aktivitäten (z.B. Fußball, Angeln, Aerobic). In Abb. 1 ist die von Willimczik ermittelte Verwandtschaft der unterschiedlichen Sportmodelle zueinander veranschaulicht.

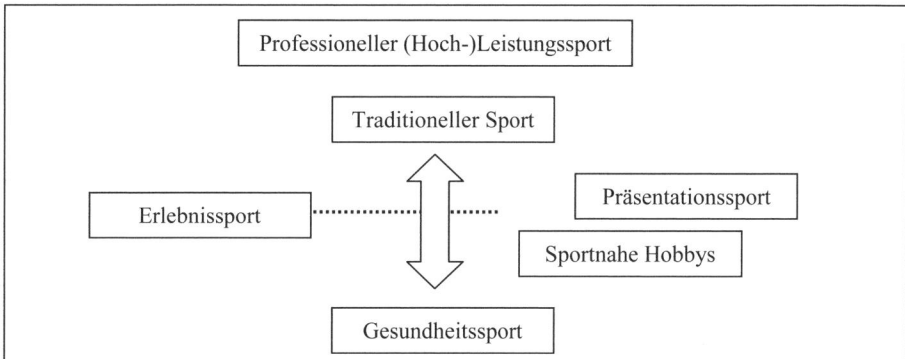

Abb. 1: Beziehungen von Sportmodellen
In Anlehnung an: Willimczik (2007), S. 29

Eine Besonderheit des Sportmarktes im Vergleich zu vielen anderen Märkten ist, dass sich die unmittelbare Nachfrage nach Sport sowohl in einem aktiven als auch in einem passiven Konsum äußern kann (Shamir/Ruskin, 1984). Der Sportmarkt lässt sich deshalb anhand der jeweiligen *Zielgruppe* zunächst in einen *Teilnehmermarkt* (Markt für aktiven Sportkonsum) und einen *Zuschauermarkt* (Markt für passiven Sportkonsum) aufteilen. Ein Tennisspieler etwa kann im Rahmen eines Tennisturniers selbstverständlich gleichzeitig als aktiver Sportler und Zuschauer auftreten, d.h. eine klare, ausschließende Zuordnung lässt sich nicht vornehmen.

Darüber hinaus bestimmt der Unternehmenszweck die *Art der Leistung*, die ein Anbieter auf dem Sportmarkt erbringt. Leistungen können grundsätzlich auf allen vertikal miteinander verbundenen Teilmärkten angeboten werden, d.h. auf dem Teilnehmermarkt wie auf dem Zuschauermarkt sowie zusätzlich auf etwaigen Folgemärkten. Hermanns/Riedmüller (2001) haben (für das Sportmarketing) versucht, die traditionellen Aufgaben verschiedener Sportanbieter innerhalb einer *Wertschöpfungskette* des Sports darzustellen (vgl. Abb. 2):

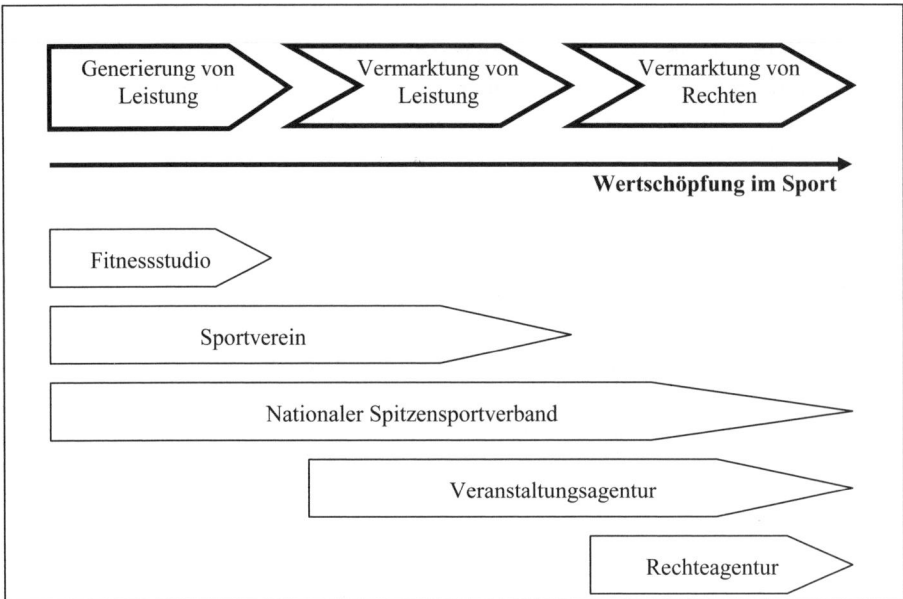

Abb. 2: Wertschöpfungskette des Sports
In Anlehnung an: Hermanns/Riedmüller (2001), S. 73

Unter den verschiedenen Anbietern innerhalb dieser Wertschöpfungskette hatte sich ursprünglich eine bestimmte Rollenverteilung entwickelt: Sportstudios konzentrierten sich beispielsweise vorwiegend auf die Betreuung ihrer Mitglieder, Sportvereine organisierten darüber hinaus Veranstaltungen für Zuschauer und Rechtevermarkter setzten ihren Schwerpunkt auf die Vermarktung von Sportrechten. Diese traditionellen Aufgaben vermischen sich jedoch zunehmend. Beispielsweise beteiligen sich Rechteagenturen inzwischen an Spitzenclubs im Fußball, um auch auf die Vermarktung der sportlichen Leistungen im Zuschauermarkt einen höheren Einfluss nehmen zu können.

Trosien (1999, 2003) führte eine Branchenanalyse des Sportmarkts in Deutschland durch. Er gelangt zu einer Unterteilung dieses Markts in folgende *Branchensektoren bzw. -segmente* (vgl. Tab. 1).

Der Sportmarkt in Deutschland	
Branchensektoren	**Branchensegmente**
1. Sportvereinigungen	▪ Sportvereine ▪ Sportverbände
2. Staatliche Sportförderung	▪ Kommunale Haushalte ▪ Länderhaushalte ▪ Bundeshaushalt
3. Medien	▪ Öffentlich-rechtliche Medien ▪ Privatrechtliche Medien
4. Wettgesellschaften	▪ Öffentlich-rechtliche Wettgesellschaften ▪ Privatrechtliche Wettgesellschaften
5. Sportwirtschaftsunternehmen	▪ Sport- und Fitness-Studios ▪ Sportfachhandel ▪ Sportindustrie ▪ Sportdienstleistungen
6. Sportsponsoring	▪ Externe Unternehmen

Tab. 1: Branchensektoren und -segmente des deutschen Sportmarkts
In Anlehnung an: Trosien (1999), S. 22

Den Jahresumsatz des gesamten deutschen Sportmarktes für 2002 beziffert Trosien mit ca. 28,5 Mrd. € und verweist hierzu auf vorliegende Daten umfangreicher repräsentativer Untersuchungen. Es kann davon ausgegangen werden, dass der Markt seither nochmals deutlich gewachsen ist.

Woratschek (1998) gibt den Anteil sportbezogener Güter und Dienstleistungen mit ca. 1,8 % der privaten Konsumausgaben in Deutschland an. Rund 1,4 % der Bruttowertschöpfung wird durch den Sport erwirtschaft. Seine *Gliederung der Sportbetriebe*, in der zum einen Sportgüterproduzenten und Sportdienstleistungen voneinander abgegrenzt werden und zum anderen die häufig anzutreffende Unterscheidung Profit- versus Non-Profit-Bereich integriert ist, wird in Abb. 3 wiedergegeben.

1.3.2 Perspektive des vorliegenden Bandes
Die vorstehenden Überlegungen und Erkenntnisse werden nun zusammengeführt und münden in einer Systematik. Auf Basis dieser Struktur wird ein einheitlicher Blickwinkel ausgewählt. Diese Perspektive ermöglicht eine stringente Diskussionsgrundlage. Sie verdeutlicht, welche Sportbetriebe im Folgenden primär zugrunde liegen, wenn auf die unterschiedlichen betriebswirtschaftlichen Disziplinen und Trends des Sportmanagement näher eingegangen wird.

```
                              ┌─────────────────────┐
                              │    Sportbetriebe    │
                              └─────────────────────┘
                  ┌───────────────────────────┴───────────────────────────┐
        ┌─────────────────────┐                         ┌─────────────────────┐
        │ Sportgüterproduzenten│                        │ Sportdienstleistungen│
        └─────────────────────┘                         └─────────────────────┘
```

Investitionsgüter-hersteller	Konsumgüter-hersteller	Dienstleistungen mit aktivem Sportkonsum	Dienstleistungen mit passivem Sportkonsum

- Sportstättenbau
- Sportgerätehersteller

- Sportartikelhersteller
- Sporternährungs-produzenten

Profit-Bereich	Non-Profit-Bereich

- Sportfachhandel
- Sporttourismus
- Sportaus- und -weiterbildung

- Sportverbände
- Sportvereine
- Betriebssport

Dienstleistungen mit passivem Sportkonsum:
- Sportunterhaltungs-betriebe (Organisation von Sportveranstaltungen)
- Sportkommunikationsbetriebe (Medien)
- Agenturen der Sportwerbung und des Sportsponsorings
- Unternehmensberatungen im Sportbereich

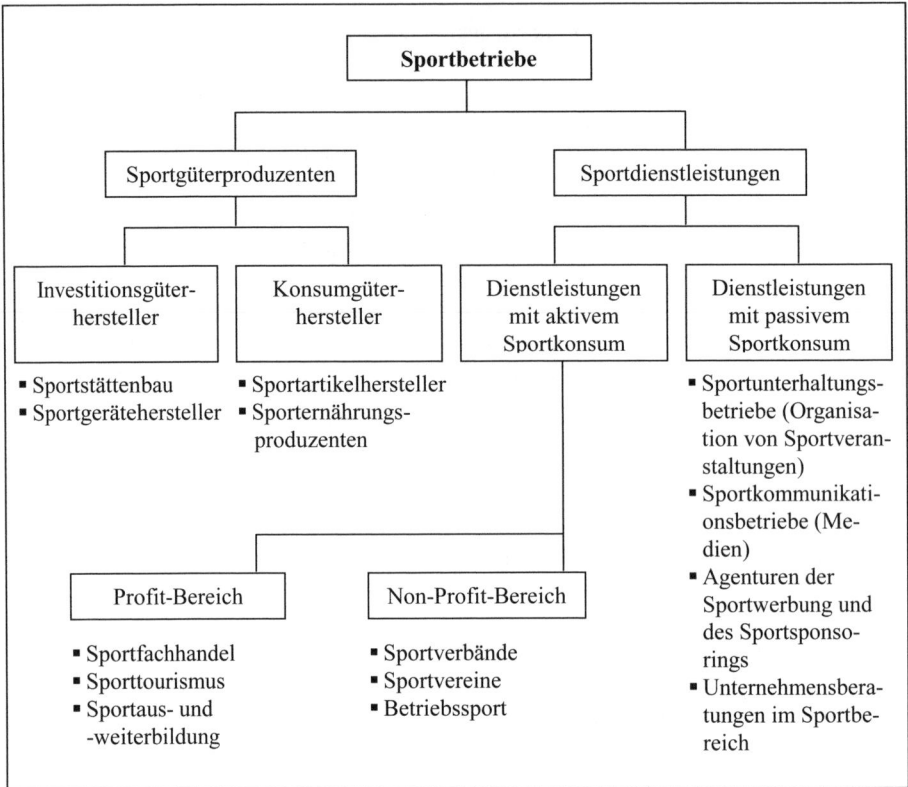

Abb. 3: Gliederung der Sportbetriebe
Quelle: Woratschek (1998), S. 348

Im in Abb. 4 grau unterlegten Fokus der Betrachtung sollen folgende Protagonisten des Sportmarktes stehen: Sportorganisationen, die sich in erster Linie an die Zielgruppe *Zuschauer* richten (in Abgrenzung zum Teilnehmermarkt und zu Folgemärkten) und bei denen das *Management von Leistungen* die dominante Wertschöpfungsstufe darstellt (v.a. Verbände und Vereine bzw. ausgegliederte Kapitalgesellschaften von Vereinen). Da hierbei Überschneidungen mit vor- und nachgelagerten Stufen möglich bzw. unumgänglich sind, soll keine ausschließliche, d.h. zu enge Einschränkung gewählt werden. Innerhalb der beschriebenen Perspektive wird das Hauptaugenmerk auf professionelle Sportbetriebe im Spitzensport gelegt, die insbesondere das Potenzial aufweisen, zukünftig (vermehrt) Bedarf nach qualifiziert ausgebildeten Absolventen der Sportökonomie zu haben.

Perspektive			
Zielgruppe/ Markt	Sportlermarkt	Zuschauermarkt	Folgemärkte
Wert- schöpfungs- kette	Generierung von Leistung	Management von Leistung	Management von Folgeleistung
Zugehörige Sport- betriebe	▪ Fitnessstudio ▪ Betriebssport ▪ Sportstättenbau ▪ Sportgerätehersteller ▪ Staatliche Sportförde- rung		
	▪ Sportartikelhersteller ▪ Sportfachhandel ▪ Sporternährungsproduzenten ▪ Sportvereinigungen (Vereine, Verbände)		
	▪ Spitzensportverein/-verband		
		▪ Sportkommunikationsbetriebe (Medien) ▪ Sportunterhaltungsbetriebe (Event-Agentur) ▪ Sportsponsoren ▪ Sportwerbetreibende Unternehmen ▪ Sporttourismus	
		▪ Rechteagentur ▪ Wettgesellschaften ▪ Agenturen (Sportwerbung/-sponsoring) ▪ Unternehmensberatungen im Sportbereich ▪ Sportaus- und -weiterbildung	

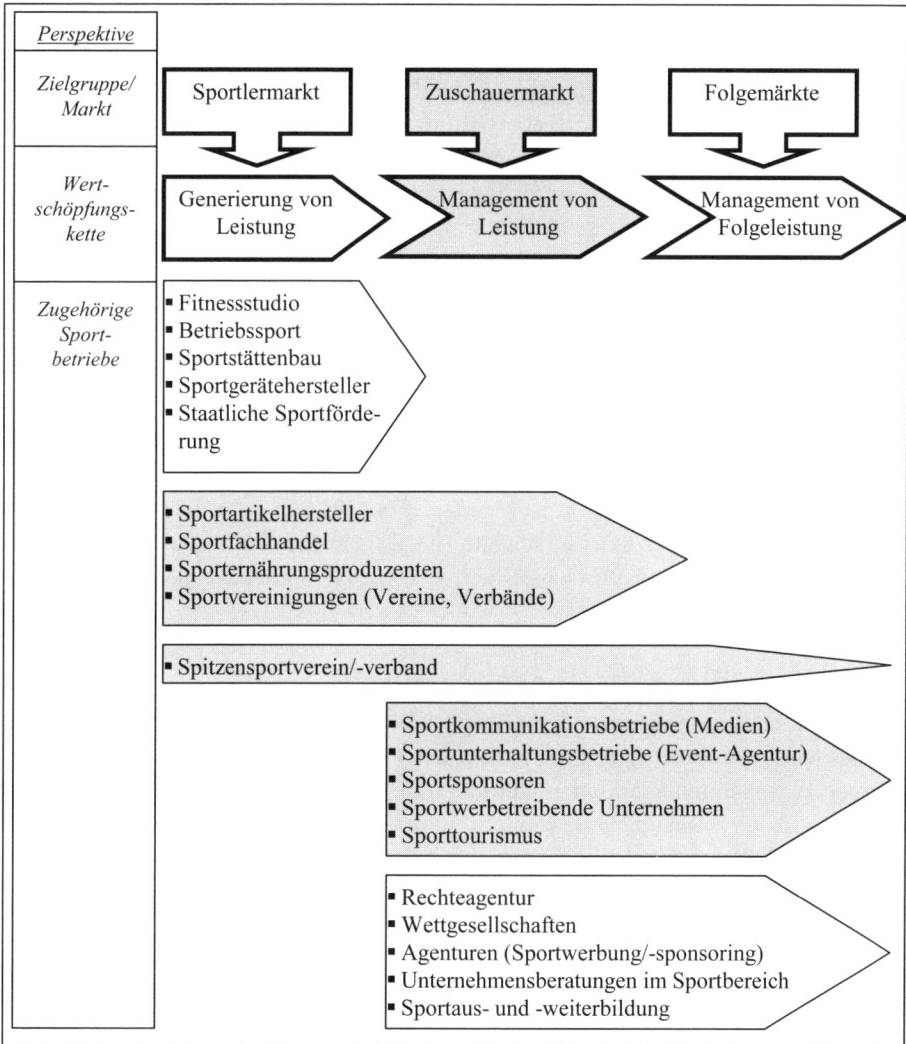

Abb. 4: Systematik des Sportmanagement

1.4 Besonderheiten des Sports aus wirtschaftlicher Sicht

Die Prinzipien der klassischen Betriebs- (und Volks-)wirtschaftslehre können nicht ohne weiteres auf den Sport übertragen werden (Nufer/Bühler, 2006). Vielmehr wird ein eigenständiger Ansatz benötigt, wenn anstelle von üblichen Produkten oder Dienstleistungen das „Produkt Sport" ins Zentrum der Betrachtung rückt. Die drei zentralen Unterscheidungsmerkmale zwischen Sportmanagement und klassischer Wirtschaftswissenschaft sollen im Folgenden diskutiert werden.

1.4.1 Der Wirtschaftsmarkt Sport

Sport wird häufig als Teil der Unterhaltungsindustrie charakterisiert. Gewisse Gemeinsamkeiten sind auch nicht von der Hand zu weisen. Menschen „konsumieren" als Zuschauer Sport bzw. Sportveranstaltungen (sowohl live vor Ort als auch vor dem Fernseher) in erster Linie, um unterhalten zu werden. Sport kann somit tatsächlich als eine Form der Unterhaltungsindustrie verstanden werden. Allerdings weist der Wirtschaftsmarkt Sport weitere Spezifika auf.

Die erste Besonderheit des Sportmarkts betrifft den *Wettbewerb*. Sportclubs messen sich in den unterschiedlichsten Wettbewerben wie beispielsweise im Ligaspielbetrieb. Diese Ligen weisen geradezu kartellähnliche Eigenschaften auf. Die jeweiligen Verbände setzen dabei die Regeln des Spiels und des Wettbewerbs fest, um ein gewisses Gleichgewicht innerhalb der Ligen zu sichern. Ehrke/Witte (2002, S. 4) bemerken hierzu:

> „Der Wettbewerb im Profisport ist (…) durch ein Maß an ‚Absprachen' – nicht in Bezug auf die Spielergebnisse, sondern die Regeln des Wettbewerbs – gekennzeichnet, das in anderen Wirtschaftsbranchen die Gerichte oder die Kartellbehörden auf den Plan rufen würde."

Die englischen Sportökonomen Szymanski/Kuypers (1999) weisen diesbezüglich darauf hin, dass es in jedem anderen Wirtschaftsmarkt als illegal angesehen werden würde, wenn die Beteiligten die Anzahl der Produzenten limitieren und die Ressourcen zwischen ihnen aufteilen würden. Im Bereich des Profisports ist diese Vorgehensweise nicht nur gängig, sondern zum Wohl des Sports und des Gleichgewichts innerhalb der Ligen sogar sinnvoll. Mag eine Monopolstellung in normalen Wirtschaftsmärkten für jedes Unternehmen ein anzustrebendes Ziel sein, so wäre eine sportliche Monopolstellung im Profisport eher schädlich für den Sport an sich.

Eine zweite spezielle Eigenschaft des Sportmarktes im Vergleich zu anderen Wirtschaftsmärkten wird gemeinhin als *„assoziative Konkurrenz"* (Heinemann, 2001) oder auch *„Kooperenz"* (Zieschang/Woratschek/Baier, 2004) bezeichnet. Damit gemeint ist die Tatsache, dass Profisportclubs auf der einen Seite miteinander konkurrieren (auf dem Spielfeld um Punkte, außerhalb um Spieler und Ressourcen), auf der anderen Seite aber auch miteinander kooperieren müssen, damit der Wettkampf und das Spiel überhaupt stattfinden können. Trotz aller Konkurrenz ist ein Mindestmaß an Kooperationsbereitschaft notwendig, damit ein vermarktungsfähiges Produkt (das Spiel selbst) entstehen kann. Aber auch darüber hinaus haben Sportclubs ein stetiges Interesse an einer engen Zusammenarbeit, beispielsweise wenn es darum geht, ihre Sportart oder ihre Liga gegenüber anderen Ligen oder Sportarten zu vermarkten.

Die dritte Eigenheit des Sportbusiness ist die Fokussierung auf den *sportlichen Erfolg*. In den meisten Branchen verfolgen Unternehmen primär ökonomische Zielsetzungen. Sportclubs hingegen möchten zuallererst Spiele, Wettbewerbe und Trophäen gewinnen. Dem sportlichen Ziel sind häufig alle anderen Ziele untergeordnet, was insbesondere in der Vergangenheit häufig dazu führte, dass Profisportorganisationen in finanzielle Schwierigkeiten gerieten. Es kann jedoch konstatiert werden, dass sich mittlerweile bei vielen Sportclubs die Erkenntnis durchgesetzt hat, dass sportliche und wirtschaftliche Erfolge auch durchaus Hand in Hand gehen.

Das vierte Unterscheidungsmerkmal des Wirtschaftsmarktes Sport im Vergleich zu anderen Wirtschaftszweigen ist in der *öffentlichen Wahrnehmung* zu sehen. Sport bewegt die Massen, popularisiert und emotionalisiert. Daher stehen viele Sportorganisationen im Blickpunkt der breiten Öffentlichkeit. Während die meisten Unternehmen unbehelligt von der Öffentlichkeit Entscheidungen treffen, werden gerade Entscheidungen von Sportorganisationen (z.B. eine Trainerentlassung) medial verbreitet und allseits kritisch beäugt. Für das Sportmanagement ergeben sich dadurch erhebliche Probleme, da man die eine oder andere kontroverse Entscheidung nicht nur intern, sondern auch vor der breiten Öffentlichkeit rechtfertigen muss.

1.4.2 Das Produkt Sport

Shank (1999, S. 16) definiert ein Sportprodukt folgendermaßen:

> „A good, a service, or any combination of the two that is designed to provide benefits to a sports spectator, participant, or sponsor."

Von Sportorganisationen angebotene Sportprodukte können in das *Kernprodukt* und in *Produkterweiterungen* unterteilt werden. Das Kernprodukt ist das eigentliche Spiel, der Wettkampf oder das Sportevent. Produkterweiterungen umfassen alle Güter und Dienstleistungen, die sich auf das Kernprodukt beziehen, respektive darauf basieren. Beispiele für Produkterweiterungen im Profisport sind Hospitality und Catering bei Sportveranstaltungen, Merchandisingprodukte oder Informationsangebote (z.B. auf Clubwebsites).

Das Kernprodukt weist darüber hinaus weitere besondere Eigenschaften auf. Wie bereits erwähnt, wird das Kernprodukt von sportlichen Konkurrenten in Gemeinschaftsproduktion (z.B. auf dem Spielfeld) produziert. So sind nicht nur die Sportteams oder individuellen Sportler an der Produktion des Gesamtproduktes beteiligt, sondern auch die teilnehmenden Zuschauer vor Ort. Die von den Fans erzeugte Atmosphäre kann einen entscheidenden Einfluss auf die Qualität des Endproduktes haben. Manch langweiliges Fußballspiel wurde erst durch die aufgeheizte Stimmung im Stadion zu einem leidenschaftlichen Kampf mit tollen Szenen und Toren. Welche Qualität das Spiel haben und wie es enden wird, steht im Voraus nie fest. Genau diese *Ungewissheit* hält zwar den Wettkampfcharakter aufrecht, ist jedoch für Sportökonomen eine nicht kalkulierbare Größe. Während Unternehmen anderer Branchen einen direkten Einfluss auf die Qualität ihrer Produkte haben und

auch gerne bereit sind, ein Qualitätsversprechen abzugeben, ist dies im Profisportbereich nur bedingt möglich.

1.4.3 Der Sportkonsument

Beim Sport lassen sich – wie bereits beschrieben – zwei wesentliche *Zielgruppen*
differenzieren: *Teilnehmer* und *Zuschauer*. Im Fall von Teilnehmersport versuchen
Sportorganisationen, so viele Menschen wie möglich für ihren Sport bzw. für ihre
Sportangebote zu begeistern und zur aktiven Teilnahme zu animieren. Beim Zuschauersport dagegen sollen möglichst viele Menschen dazu bewegt werden, die
entsprechenden Sportveranstaltungen zu besuchen oder zumindest über die Medien
zu verfolgen. Teilnehmer- und Zuschauersport basieren auch auf unterschiedlichen
Motiven der Konsumenten. Ein Teilnehmer möchte z.B. aktiv etwas für seine Gesundheit tun, ein Zuschauer dagegen möchte meistens einfach nur unterhalten werden. Obwohl die Bedeutung des Teilnehmersports in Anbetracht des aktuellen Fit-
nessbewusstseins immer stärker wächst, ist der Zuschauersport nach wie vor der
bedeutendere Teil des Wirtschaftsmarktes Sport, insbesondere wenn man bedenkt,
dass Milliarden von Menschen auf der ganzen Welt die unterschiedlichsten Sportveranstaltungen entweder live vor Ort oder vor dem Fernseher bzw. im Internet verfolgen können.

Zuschauer sind aus den unterschiedlichsten Gründen bei Sportveranstaltungen
anzutreffen: Die einen möchten ein spannendes Spiel sehen, anderen ist der Sieg
der eigenen Mannschaft am wichtigsten, und wiederum andere interessieren sich
eher für das Spektakel im Umfeld als für das eigentliche Spiel. Es ist für Sportorganisationen daher nicht einfach, diesen *unterschiedlichen Bedürfnissen* gerecht zu
werden.

1.5 Struktur des Bandes

Im Folgenden wird die grundlegende Konzeption des Sammelbandes „Management
und Marketing im Sport" vorgestellt sowie ein kurzer Überblick über die einzelnen
Kapitel gegeben.

1.5.1 Anspruch und Konzeption

Das vorliegende Buch geht von einer *interdisziplinären Managementorientierung*
aus und versucht, in systematischer Form das gesamte Spektrum des Sportmanagement und Sportmarketing vorzustellen. Die Herausgeber waren bestrebt, alle relevanten Aspekte des Sportmanagements abzudecken und die wichtigsten Trends im
Sportmarketing aufzuspüren. Ziel ist dabei ein „doppelter Brückenschlag": Einerseits zwischen *Sport und Wirtschaft,* andererseits von der *Theorie zur Praxis.*

Der Sammelband gliedert sich in insgesamt vier Teile:

- *Teil I* ist überschrieben mit *Betriebswirtschaftslehre und Sport – ein Überblick* und nähert sich den Themenfeldern Sportmanagement und Sportmarketing zunächst separat aus den beiden unterschiedlichen Perspektiven Sport und Betriebswirtschafslehre an, die im weiteren Verlauf des Buches zusammengeführt werden.
- *Teil II* widmet sich ausführlich dem Sportmanagement: *Sportmanagement – die Anwendung klassischer Disziplinen der Betriebswirtschaftslehre im Sport.* Das Management in den klassischen betriebswirtschaftlichen Betätigungsfeldern wird auf den Bereich des Sports übertragen. Dabei werden nicht nur die Prinzipien wirtschaftlichen Handelns erklärt, sondern stets auch die Besonderheiten des Wirtschaftsmarkts Sport berücksichtigt.
- *Teil III* heißt *Sportmarketing – aktuelle Entwicklungen und Trends.* Der Sportmarkt hat sich vom Verkäufer- zum Käufermarkt gewandelt, Sportorganisationen müssen aktiv um Kunden werben und dadurch kunden- bzw. marketingorientierter werden. Präsentiert werden die jüngsten Entwicklungen innerhalb des Sportmarketing, die neue spannende Betätigungsfelder für Sportmanager offerieren.
- *Teil IV Die Zukunft des Sportmanagement und Sportmarketing* beschließt den Band mit einer grenzüberschreitenden, internationalen Betrachtung, einem dezidierten Blick auf den Arbeitsmarkt für Sportmanager und Sportmanagerinnen sowie einem Ausblick in die Zukunft.

Der Band versucht grundsätzlich, das gesamte Spektrum des Sports abzubilden. Das in Deutschland herausragende Beispiel für die Professionalisierung des Sportmarktes ist zweifellos der Profi-Fußball. Zum einen liegen hierzu bereits zahlreiche Studien vor, zum anderen ist Fußball hierzulande nach wie vor die populärste Sportart. Dass Fußball deshalb im Rahmen des vorliegenden Bandes häufig das naheliegende Referenzmodell bildet und wiederkehrend Beispiele aus dem Profi-Fußball Verwendung finden, ist somit nachvollziehbar und geschieht bewusst. Nichtsdestotrotz werden in den einzelnen Kapitel auch zahlreiche Beispiele aus anderen Sportarten wie etwa Handball, Basketball, Volleyball, American Football und Eishockey aufgeführt.

1.5.2 Vorstellung der einzelnen Kapitel und Autoren

Das Buch besteht aus insgesamt 20 Kapiteln, an denen 23 Autorinnen und Autoren mitgewirkt haben.

Nach dieser *Einführung* stellen als Fortsetzung von Teil I des Bandes Christoph Breuer, Pamela Wicker und Tim Pawlowski den *Wirtschafts- und Wachstumsmarkt Sport* aus der sportwissenschaftlichen Perspektive vor. Gerd Nufer und Carsten

Rennhak präsentieren im Anschluss daran die *Grundlagen des Sportmanagements* aus der Sicht der Betriebswirtschaftslehre.

Teil II widmet sich systematisch der komplexen Thematik des Sportmanagements. Die klassischen Disziplinen der Betriebswirtschaftslehre werden im Sport angewandt. Christian Keller beschreibt in seinem Beitrag *Strategisches Management im Sport* die zentrale Aufgabe der Unternehmensführung. Frank Daumann, Mathias Langer und Markus Breuer beleuchten die *Planung im Sport* unter Berücksichtigung der Entscheidungslehre sowie der Steuerung/Kontrolle. Sebastian Kaiser und Heinz-Dieter Horch erläutern ein klassisches Kernthema des Sportmanagements, die *Organisation im Sport*. Das Thema *Personalmanagement im Sport* wird von Siegfried Nagel und Torsten Schlesinger beschrieben. Gregor Hovemann beschäftigt sich mit der *Finanzierung im Sport* und berücksichtigt dabei auch Aspekte der Investition. Christoph Jordan verdeutlicht anhand des *Controlling im Sport* die Funktionsweise des internen Rechnungswesens, während Simone Jäck und Thomas Meffert das externe Rechnungswesen im Rahmen ihres Beitrags *Rechnungslegung im Sport* veranschaulichen. Im Anschluss daran konzentriert sich Simone Jäck auf die *Ertragssteuern im Sport* als dem für das Sportmanagement wichtigstem Gebiet der Steuerlehre. Den Abschluss dieses Teils bildet der Beitrag *Marketing im Sport* von André Bühler und Gerd Nufer, der zugleich zum nächsten Teil des Bandes überleitet und damit das Bindeglied zu einer vertieften Auseinandersetzung mit dem Sportmarketing darstellt.

In Teil III wird auf aktuelle Entwicklungen und Trends im Sportmarketing näher eingegangen. Innerhalb des Sportmanagements ist das Sportmarketing die am weitesten entwickelte Teildisziplin. Michael Schilhaneck verknüpft in seinem Beitrag *Markenmanagement im Sport* leistungs- und kommunikationspolitische Aspekte des Marketing. Gerd Nufer und André Bühler setzen sich mit der umfassenden Thematik des *Veranstaltungsmarketing im Sport* auseinander. Marco Gensmüller gibt einen Überblick zum nicht minder komplexen Thema *Customer Relationship Marketing im Sport*. Helmut Digel und Marcel Fahrner knüpfen direkt an die vorigen Beiträge an und erklären das *Hospitality Marketing im Sport*. Abgerundet wird dieser Teil mit dem Beitrag *Kommunikationsmanagement im Sport*, der von Sebastian Kaiser erarbeitet wurde.

Der abschließenden Teil IV konzentriert sich auf die Zukunft des Sportmanagement und des Sportmarketing. Der englischsprachige Beitrag *Internationalisation in Sport* von Simon Chadwick hat nicht ausschließlich die britische, sondern vielmehr die globale Perspektive des Sportmanagement und Sportmarketing zum Gegenstand. Danach evaluiert Heinz-Dieter Horch kritisch den *Arbeitsmarkt für Sportmanager*, ehe André Bühler und Gerd Nufer in der *Zusammenfassung* die zentralen Erkenntnisse des Sammelbandes diskutieren und einen *Ausblick* in die Zukunft des Sportmanagement und Sportmarketing wagen.

Ein herzlicher Dank gilt sämtlichen Autoren der einzelnen Kapitel, die sich mit ihrer Mitarbeit an diesem Band parallel zu ihrem Tagesgeschäft mit Bravour einer zusätzlichen Herausforderung gestellt haben – und dies in einem so knapp bemessenen Zeitraum, der den Herausgebern eine zügige Umsetzung des Projekts ermöglichte. Die Zusammenarbeit funktionierte vorbildlich, es war für die Herausgeber wirklich ein Vergnügen, mit diesen Persönlichkeiten zusammenzuarbeiten.

1.6 Hinweise für den Leser

Jedes Kapitel des vorliegenden Bandes folgt einem *einheitlichen didaktischen Aufbau*, der in dieser Form einzigartig in der deutschsprachigen Literatur zum Sportmanagement und Sportmarketing ist:

- Zu Beginn jedes Kapitels werden dem Leser stichwortartig die *Lernziele* des jeweiligen Beitrags präsentiert. Der Leser erfährt vorab, wozu er nach der Lektüre des jeweiligen Kapitels in der Lage sein sollte.

- Es schließt sich ein kurzer *Überblick* über das Kapitel an. In kompakter Form wird dem Leser eine Inhaltsangabe zum betreffenden Kapitel gegeben.

- Der erste Gliederungspunkt jedes Beitrags ist einheitlich eine *Einführung in die Thematik*. Der Leser wird didaktisch gezielt an den Gegenstand des Kapitels herangeführt.

- Die folgenden Hauptteile der einzelnen Beiträge folgend implizit jeweils der *Struktur vom Allgemeinen zum Speziellen*: Im Sportmanagement werden die einzelnen Disziplinen typischerweise zunächst aus Sicht der Betriebswirtschaftslehre charakterisiert und darauf aufbauend die Besonderheiten bei der Anwendung des betriebswirtschaftlichen Teilgebiets im Sport herausgearbeitet. Beim Sportmarketing, wo der Sportbezug häufig bereits von Anfang an gegeben ist, werden üblicherweise zunächst die Grundlagen und Hintergründe des Themas beleuchtet und im weiteren Verlauf verstärkt auf aktuelle Entwicklungen und den besonderen Trend-Charakter eingegangen.

- Jedes Kapitel enthält eine aktuelle *Fallstudie* aus der Praxis des Sportmanagements bzw. Sportmarketing. Anhand dieser Fallstudie wird einerseits die Brücke von der Theorie zur Praxis geschlagen und andererseits die zuvor besprochene Thematik exemplarisch anhand jeweils eines konkreten Beispiels aus unterschiedlichen Sportarten, Ländern etc. leicht nachvollziehbar veranschaulicht. Zusammen genommen illustrieren die Fallstudien eindrucksvoll die Vielfalt der Anwendungsgebiete des Sportmanagement und Sportmarketing und verdeutlichen, wie professionell im Sport vereinzelt vorgegangen wird und welche Chancen sich daraus ergeben.

- Ein *Fazit und Ausblick* beschließt jedes Kapitel. Die wesentlichen Erkenntnisse werden in knapper Form zusammengefasst sowie zukünftige Herausforderungen skizziert.

- Zu jedem Kapitel sind zehn *Kontrollfragen* formuliert, die der Leser nach der Durcharbeit der jeweiligen Thematik zu beantworten im Stande ist. Es werden hierzu keine Musterlösungen bereitgestellt, sämtliche Fragen sind auf Basis der zuvor im jeweiligen Kapitel enthaltenen Informationen zu beantworten.
- Das *Literaturverzeichnis* enthält zum Nachschlagen sämtliche Quellen (Print plus ggf. Internet), auf die zuvor im Text verwiesen wurde.
- Die Rubrik *Weiterführenden Ressourcen* ist zweigeteilt und enthält einerseits zusätzliche Literaturangaben, die dem interessierten Leser eine vertiefte Auseinandersetzung mit der Thematik ermöglichen, sowie einige Links, die einen schnellen Besuch interessanter Websites, die in unmittelbarer Verbindung zur behandelten Thematik stehen, erlauben.

Die Bezeichnungen „Sportmanagement" und „Management im Sport" bzw. „Sportmarketing" und „Marketing im Sport" werden jeweils synonym verwendet. Zentrale Begriffe sind im Text – durchgängig durch alle Kapitel – *kursiv* hervorgehoben. Grundlegende Definitionen, anschauliche Illustrationen sowie sämtliche Fallstudien sind in einem *Rahmen* abgedruckt. Direkte Zitate sind stets mit der exakten Quellenangabe versehen (z.B. Nufer (2007), S. 21 f.), wohingegen bei indirekten Zitaten zur Gewährleistung des besseren Leseflusses auf Seitenangaben verzichtet wird (z.B. Bühler (2006)).

Am Ende des Buches befinden sich die Profile der Herausgeber und Autoren, anhand derer der interessierte Leser mehr über die Verfasser der einzelnen Beiträge erfahren sowie deren jeweilige Forschungsschwerpunkte ersehen kann. Die zusätzlich angegebenen Kontaktinformationen erleichtern die Kommunikation. Insbesondere die Herausgeber freuen sich über Anregungen und Rückmeldungen.

Kontrollfragen

1. Warum war die Sportwissenschaft lange Zeit von einer „Ökonomieferne" geprägt?
2. Was ist der aktuelle Stand der Sportökonomie?
3. Versuchen Sie, Sportökonomie und Sportmanagement zu definieren!
4. Erklären Sie vorhandene Abgrenzungen des Sportmarkts in der Literatur!
5. Wie sieht die Wertschöpfungskette im Sport aus?
6. Wie lässt sich die Vielfalt vorhandener Sportbetriebe sinnvoll systematisieren?
7. Charakterisieren Sie die Besonderheiten des Sports aus wirtschaftlicher Sicht!
8. Was versteht man unter „assoziativer Konkurrenz" und „Kooperenz"?
9. Was ist das Besondere am Produkt Sport?
10. Charakterisieren Sie den Sportkonsumenten!

Literaturverzeichnis

Albach, Horst / Frick, Bernd (Hrsg.) (2002): Sportökonomie, in: Zeitschrift für Betriebswirtschaft, Ergänzungsheft 4, Wiesbaden.

Breuer, Christoph / Thiel, Ansgar (2005): Sportmanagement – ein Einführung, in: Breuer, Christoph / Thiel, Ansgar (Hrsg.): Handbuch Sportmanagement, Schorndorf, S. 8-13.

Bühler, André W. (2006): Professional Football Sponsorship in the English Premier League and the German Bundesliga, Berlin.

Digel, Helmut (1984): Gesellschaftliche Entwicklung und der Auftrag des Sportvereins, in: Der Kultusminister des Landes Nordrhein-Westfalen (Hrsg.): Materialien zum Sport in Nordrhein-Westfalen, Heft 9: Sportentwicklung – Einflüsse und Rahmenbedingungen – Eine Expertenbefragung, Köln, S. 52-65.

Ehrke, Michael / Witte, Lothar (2002): Flasche Leer! Die New Economy des Europäischen Profifußballs, Bonn.

Freyer, Walter (2003): Sport-Marketing. Handbuch für marktorientiertes Management im Sport, 3. Aufl., Dresden.

Heinemann, Klaus (1986): Zum Problem der Einheit des Sports und des Verlusts seiner Autonomie, in: Deutscher Sportbund (Hrsg.): Die Zukunft des Sports. Materialien zum Kongress Menschen im Sport 2000, Schorndorf, S. 112-128.

Heinemann, Klaus (1995): Einführung in die Ökonomie des Sports. Ein Handbuch, Schorndorf.

Heinemann, Klaus (2001): Grundprobleme der Sportökonomie, in: Hermanns, Arnold / Riedmüller, Florian (Hrsg.): Management-Handbuch Sport-Marketing, München, S. 15-32.

Hermanns, Arnold / Riedmüller, Florian (2001): Standortbestimmung des Sportmarketing, in: Hermanns, Arnold / Riedmüller, Florian (Hrsg.): Management-Handbuch Sport-Marketing, München, S. 57-87.

Horch, Heinz-Dieter (2007): Was ist Sportökonomie?, http://www.sportoekonomie-dshs.de/inst_info.php4#antwort01 (Zugriff: 07.03.2007).

Nufer, Gerd (2007): Event-Marketing und -Management. Theorie und Praxis unter besonderer Berücksichtigung von Imagewirkungen, 3. Aufl., Wiesbaden.

Nufer, Gerd / Bühler, André W. (2006): Lessons from Sports: What Corporate Management can learn from Sports Management, Reutlingen Working Paper on Marketing & Management No. 2006-7, School of International Business, Reutlingen University.

Shamir, Boas / Ruskin, Hillel (1984): Sport Participations vs. Sport Spectatorship: Two Modes of Leisure Behaviour, in: Journal of Leisure Research, Heft 1, S. 9-21.

Shank, Matthew D. (1999): Sports Marketing – A Strategic Perspective, New Jersey.

Szymanski, Stefan / Kuypers, Tim (1999): Winners and Losers, London.

Trosien, Gerhard (1999): Die Sportbranche. Wachstum – Wettbewerb – Wirtschaftlichkeit, 2. Aufl., Frankfurt/Main u.a.

Trosien, Gerhard (2003): Sportökonomie. Ein Lehrbuch in 15 Lektionen, Aachen.

Willimczik, Klaus (2007): Die Vielfalt des Sports. Kognitive Konzepte der Gegenwart zur Binnendifferenzierung des Sports, in: Sportwissenschaft, Heft 1, S. 19-37.

Woratschek, Herbert (1998): Sportdienstleistungen aus ökonomischer Sicht, in: Sportwissenschaft, Heft 3-4, S. 344-357.

Zieschang, Klaus / Woratschek, Herbert / Baier, Klaus (Hrsg.) (2004): Kooperenz im Sportmanagement, Schorndorf.

Weiterführende Ressourcen

Literatur

Beech, John / Chadwick, Simon (Hrsg.) (2004): The Business of Sport Management, Harlow.

Breuer, Christoph / Thiel, Ansgar (Hrsg.) (2005): Handbuch Sportmanagement, Schorndorf.

Bühler, André W. (2005): Fans und Fanverhalten im Profifußball: Ein Vergleich zwischen England und Deutschland, in: Schewe, Gerhard / Rohlmann, Peter (Hrsg.): Sportmarketing, Schorndorf, S. 221–236.

Bühler, André W. (2006): Football as an international business – an Anglo-German comparison, in: European Journal for Sport and Society, Heft 3, S. 25-41.

Friederici, Markus R. / Horch, Heinz-Dieter / Schubert, Manfred (Hrsg.) (2002): Sport, Wirtschaft und Gesellschaft, Schorndorf.

Hermanns, Arnold / Riedmüller, Florian (Hrsg.) (2001): Management-Handbuch Sport-Marketing, München.

Hermanns, Arnold / Riedmüller, Florian (Hrsg.) (2003): Sponsoring und Events im Sport, München.

Horch, Heinz-Dieter / Heydel, Jörg / Sierau, Axel (Hrsg.) (2004): Events im Sport – Marketing, Management, Finanzierung, Köln.

Horch, Heinz-Dieter / Hovemann, Gregor / Kaiser, Sebastian / Viebahn, Kai (Hrsg.) (2005): Perspektiven des Sportmarketing. Besonderheiten, Herausforderungen, Tendenzen, Köln.

Krüger, Arnd / Dreyer, Axel (Hrsg.) (2004): Sportmanagement, München.

Nufer, Gerd (2002): Sport und Kultur – Lehren für die Strategie / Sports and Culture – Lessons for Strategy, in: Simon, Hermann (Hrsg.): Strategie International / Strategy International, zweisprachige Serie in der Frankfurter Allgemeinen Zeitung, 07.09.2002, S. 57.

Nufer, Gerd (2002): Wirkungen von Sportsponsoring. Empirische Analyse am Beispiel der Fußball-Weltmeisterschaft 1998 in Frankreich unter besonderer Berücksichtigung von Erinnerungswirkungen bei jugendlichen Rezipienten, Berlin.

Links

Bayreuther Sportökonomie-Kongress:
    http://www.sportoekonomie.uni-bayreuth.de/kongress
Deutscher Sportökonomie-Kongress, Köln:
    http://www.deutscher-sportoekonomie-kongress.de
Heidelberger Sportbusiness Forum (Kongress):
    http://www.sportbusiness.de
Horizont Sport Business (Fachzeitschrift):
    http://www.horizont-sportbusiness.de
ISPO Sportsponsoringkongress, München:
    http://www.sportsponsoringkongress.de
Sponsors (Fachzeitschrift):
    http://www.sponsors.de

Kapitel 2: Der Wirtschafts- und Wachstumsmarkt Sport

Christoph Breuer   Pamela Wicker   Tim Pawlowski

Lernziele

Nach der Durchsicht dieses Kapitels sollte der Leser in der Lage sein,

- die Akteure des professionellen Sports zu beschreiben.
- die Besonderheiten des Wirtschaftsgutes professioneller Sport zu benennen.
- Determinanten der Nachfrage nach Zuschauersport darzustellen.
- Motoren einer wachsenden Sportnachfrage aufzuzählen.
- Indikatoren zu nennen, anhand derer die ökonomischen Potenziale des Sports verdeutlicht werden.
- ökonomische Effekte von Sportveranstaltungen zu klassifizieren.
- Preiselastizitäten im Zuschauersport zu erklären.
- Kenngrößen für die Bedeutung des Sports in Deutschland darzulegen.

Überblick über das Kapitel

In diesem Kapitel findet eine Annäherung an das Thema Sportmanagement aus der Perspektive des Sports statt. Zunächst wird der professionelle Sport als besonderes Wirtschaftsgut skizziert und Motoren einer wachsenden Nachfrage nach professionellem Sport genannt. Die Darstellung der verschiedenen ökonomischen Potenziale des Sports erfolgt mit Hilfe verschiedener Indikatoren, welche verdeutlichen, dass es sich beim Sportmarkt um einen Wachstumsmarkt handelt. Die Fallstudie zu den Weltreiterspielen 2006 in Aachen soll veranschaulichen, wie auf empirischem Weg ökonomische Effekte von sportlichen Großveranstaltungen gemessen und berechnet werden können.

2.1 Einführung in die Thematik

Der Sport zeichnet sich durch eine extrem heterogene Produktpalette, verschiedene Typen von Sportorganisationen und unterschiedlich strukturierte Märkte aus (Schubert, 2005). Vor diesem Hintergrund ist es sinnvoll, zunächst die für das vorliegende Buch relevanten Produkte (Spitzen- bzw. Unterhaltungssport), Sportorganisationen (Profisport) und Märkte (Zuschauermarkt) herauszufiltern und zu beschreiben. Um als Sportmanager fundierte Empfehlungen im Bereich des professionellen Sports geben zu können, müssen zunächst die Protagonisten und Besonderheiten dieses professionellen Sports bekannt sein. Eine Kenntnis der ökonomischen Potenziale des professionellen Sports ist in diesem Zusammenhang ebenfalls unerlässlich.

2.2 Sport als besonderes Wirtschaftsgut

Im vorangegangenen Kapitel wurden bereits Besonderheiten des Sports aus wirtschaftlicher Sicht dargestellt, indem auf Besonderheiten des Sportmarktes und des Produktes Sport (Kernprodukt und Produkterweiterungen) eingegangen wurde. In diesem Zusammenhang wurde der kartellähnliche *Wettbewerb* in den Ligen, das Phänomen der *Kooperenz*, die Fokussierung auf *sportlichen Erfolg* und die starke *öffentliche Wahrnehmung* hinsichtlich der Besonderheiten des Sportmarktes genannt. Im Folgenden werden die Besonderheiten des Wirtschaftsgutes Sport dargestellt. Diese werden sowohl aus Sicht der Anbieter als auch aus Sicht der Nachfrager erarbeitet. Wie zuvor stehen im Fokus professionelle Sportorganisationen, die im Spitzensportbereich tätig und auf den Zuschauermarkt ausgerichtet sind. Es handelt sich somit um Dienstleistungen im Bereich des passiven Sports.

2.2.1 Anbietersicht

Abb. 1 illustriert das ökonomische Modell des professionellen Sports von Benner (1992). Anhand dieses Modells werden der professionelle Sport als besonderes Wirtschaftsgut aus Anbietersicht erläutert und die Besonderheiten sportbezogener Dienstleistungen herausgearbeitet.

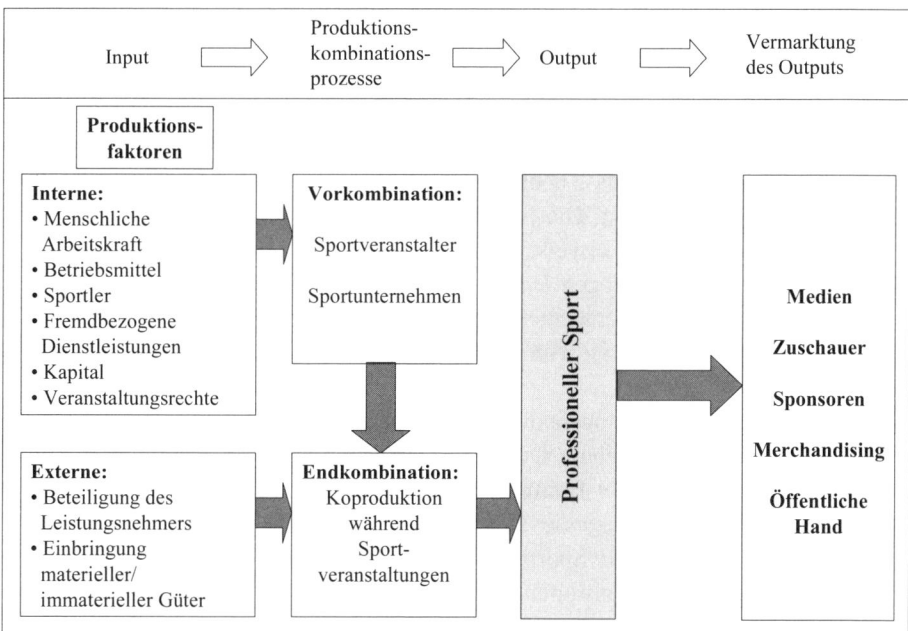

Input	Produktions-kombinations-prozesse	Output	Vermarktung des Outputs

Produktionsfaktoren

Interne:	Vorkombination:	Professioneller Sport	Medien
• Menschliche Arbeitskraft	Sportveranstalter		Zuschauer
• Betriebsmittel			
• Sportler	Sportunternehmen		Sponsoren
• Fremdbezogene Dienstleistungen			
• Kapital			Merchandising
• Veranstaltungsrechte			
Externe:	**Endkombination:**		**Öffentliche**
• Beteiligung des Leistungsnehmers	Koproduktion während Sport-veranstaltungen		**Hand**
• Einbringung materieller/ immaterieller Güter			

Abb. 1: Ökonomisches Modell des professionellen Sports (in vereinfachter und erweiterter Form) In Anlehnung an: Benner (1992), S. 30

Das ökonomische Modell des professionellen Sports deutet auf mehrere Besonderheiten hin. Erstens werden auf der Inputseite nicht nur interne, sondern auch externe Produktionsfaktoren benötigt. Zweitens teilt sich der Produktionskombinationsprozess in eine Vorkombination und eine Endkombination auf. In diesem

Zusammenhang wird von der sportspezifischen zweistufigen Leistungserstellung gesprochen. Drittens wird die Dienstleistung *professioneller Sport* an mehrere Abnehmer vermarktet. Im Folgenden wird dieses Modell am Beispiel der ersten Fußball-Bundesliga erklärt und auf aktuelle Probleme hingewiesen, die Herausforderungen für das Sportmanagement darstellen.

Charakteristisch für die Produktion des professionellen Sports ist die Tatsache, dass nicht nur interne, sondern auch externe Produktionsfaktoren benötigt werden. Zu den internen Produktionsfaktoren zählen die menschliche Arbeitskraft (z.B. Trainer, Mannschaftsarzt, Platzwart), Betriebsmittel (z.B. Sportstätte, Stadion), Sportler selbst (Spieler), fremdbezogene Dienstleistungen (z.B. Marketingagentur, Polizei), Kapital (z.B. Kalkulatorische Zinsen Fremd-/Eigenkapital, das in Betriebsmitteln eingebunden ist und nicht anderweitig zur Verfügung steht) und Veranstaltungsrechte (z.B. durch Erwerb bei der Dachorganisation). Im nordamerikanischen Profisport intervenierte der Sportveranstalter bereits bei der Gestaltung der internen Produktionsfaktoren, indem so genannte *salary caps* (Gehaltsobergrenzen) und ein *draft*-System (regulierter Zugang neuer Spielertalente in die Liga) eingeführt wurden (Kurscheidt, 2005). Der externe Produktionsfaktor im professionellen Sport ist der Zuschauer. Dieser beteiligt sich an der Produktion des professionellen Sports durch seine Anwesenheit im Stadion und durch die Einbringung materieller (z.B. Fanschals, Plakate) bzw. immaterieller (z.B. Applaus, Pfeifkonzert) Güter. Die Anzahl der Zuschauer ist jedoch durch die Kapazität des Stadions limitiert. Dabei ist zu berücksichtigen, dass heutzutage nahezu alle Großstadien über so genannte Business-Logen verfügen. Die Nutzer dieser Logen sind ebenfalls externe Produktionsfaktoren. Paradoxerweise kommen sie u.a. wegen der speziellen Atmosphäre ins Stadion, tragen jedoch eher nicht zur Gestaltung der Atmosphäre bei. Aus Sicht des Sportmanagements gilt es, einen Balanceakt zwischen der Anzahl zahlungskräftiger Nutzer von Business-Logen und „normaler" Zuschauer zu vollziehen.

Diese internen Produktionsfaktoren sind zusammen mit den Sportveranstaltern (z.B. Club der Heimmannschaft, Deutsche Fußball Liga) und den beteiligten Sportunternehmen (z.B. Clubs der Heimmannschaft und des Gegners) an einer Vorkombination des Produktionsprozesses beteiligt. Es ist zu beachten, dass der Club der Heimmannschaft sowohl als Sportveranstalter als auch als Sportunternehmen auftritt. Sowohl der Sportveranstalter als auch die Sportunternehmen versuchen, ihr Leistungspotenzial aufzubauen und erbringen eine Vorleistung. D.h. für die Sportunternehmen, dass die Fußballmannschaften trainieren müssen, und für den Sportveranstalter, dass dieser sich um die Planung und Vermarktung der Sportveranstaltung kümmern muss. Hinsichtlich der Sportunternehmen (Clubs) besteht die Vorleistung auch darin, ihre Liquidität zu dokumentieren, um vom Sportveranstalter eine Lizenzierung zu erhalten. Die Vergangenheit hat gezeigt, dass die Sicherstellung der Liquidität manchen Clubs zum Teil erhebliche Probleme bereitet hat.

Überdies werden im Rahmen dieser Vorkombination verschiedene Absprachen im Hinblick auf die Sportveranstaltung (z.B. Termine, Akzeptanz der Regeln, Uhrzeit, Vermarktung der Übertragungsrechte) zwischen den Sportunternehmen (Fußballclubs) getroffen (Stichwort *Kooperenz*). In Deutschland werden die Übertragungsrechte in der ersten Fußball-Bundesliga zentral vermarktet und die daraus resultierenden Einnahmen nach einem bestimmten Schlüssel an die beteiligten Clubs verteilt. Dabei wird angenommen, dass dadurch eine gewisse Ausgeglichenheit im Hinblick auf finanzielle Ressourcen der Clubs erreicht und in der Folge die Spannung innerhalb der Liga gesichert wird. Inwieweit dies praktisch gelingt, sei an dieser Stelle dahingestellt. Es steht jedoch fest, dass Vorstöße weniger Clubs, die Übertragungsrechte für die eigenen Spiele selbst zu vermarkten, zu einer Vergrößerung des Ungleichgewichts hinsichtlich der Verteilung finanzieller Ressourcen führen würden. Folglich könnten die Spannung der nationalen Liga und damit auch ihre Vermarktbarkeit darunter leiden. Die Clubs, die jedoch im europäischen Wettbewerb mithalten wollen, sehen sich einer Konkurrenz aus Ländern gegenüber, in denen keine Zentralvermarktung der Rechte stattfindet. Zum Beispiel nahm der FC Bayern München in der Saison 2007/08 28 Mio. € aus Übertragungsrechten ein. Im Gegensatz dazu lagen diese Einnahmen im gleichen Jahr beim FC Barcelona bei 125 Mio. € (Pfeiffer/Hovemann, 2006). Die Zentralvermarktung der Übertragungsrechte kann somit zu Wettbewerbsnachteilen auf europäischer Ebene führen *(Zwei-Ligen-Problem)*.

Der Endkombinationsprozess stellt die eigentliche Erstellung des professionellen Sports dar. Die Sportunternehmen, der Sportveranstalter und der externe Produktionsfaktor tragen dazu bei. Im Hinblick auf den Sportveranstalter und die Sportunternehmen handelt es sich um eine Koproduktion, da der Sportveranstalter (z.B. Deutsche Fußball Liga) zwei Sportunternehmen (z.B. VfB Stuttgart und FC Bayern München) gegeneinander antreten lässt. Es ist zu beachten, dass es sich um eine streng limitationale Produktionsfunktion handelt und der erstellte Output nicht teilbar ist (Kurscheidt, 2005): Eine Fußballmannschaft besteht aus elf Spielern, es spielen zwei Teams gegeneinander und ein Spiel dauert 90 Minuten.

Eine wesentliche Herausforderung bei der Endkombination stellt die Integration des externen Faktors (Zuschauer) dar. Sie ist ein Merkmal personenbezogener Dienstleitungen, bei denen der externe Faktor zum Mitproduzenten wird. Büch/Maennig/Schulke (2006) weisen in diesem Kontext darauf hin, dass der Zuschauer in der sportlichen Wertschöpfungskette verschiedene Rollen annehmen kann. Der Zuschauer kann z.B. die Rolle eines Gastes, Mitspielers oder Manipulierten annehmen. In der Rolle eines Gastes ist er lediglich ein passiver Konsument der Sportveranstaltung. Im Gegensatz dazu nimmt er die Rolle eines Mitspielers an, wenn er lautstark die eigene Mannschaft anfeuert bzw. die gegnerische Mannschaft auspfeift. Während er bei diesen beiden Rollen selbst entscheiden kann, ob er sie einnehmen möchte oder nicht, wird er in die Rolle des Manipulierten unfreiwillig gedrängt. Der Fußball-Bestechungsskandal Anfang der siebziger Jahre und der

Fußball-Wettskandal 2005 seien hier als Beispiele angeführt. Pfister (2006) weist überdies darauf hin, dass es eine Vielzahl an Motiven gibt, warum Zuschauer ins Stadion kommen, und demzufolge auch verschiedene Typen an Zuschauern. Genannt seien hier z.b. Spaß, Spannung und Entspannung. Auch differieren die Motive der Zuschauer in Abhängigkeit der Sportarten.

Das Ergebnis dieses komplexen Prozesses der Leistungserstellung ist der professionelle Sport. Dieser kann als Wirtschaftsgut bezeichnet werden, da er entsprechende Eigenschaften aufweist. Er ist Gegenstand ökonomischer Transaktionen zwischen seinen Produzenten (Sportunternehmen, Sportveranstalter) und Abnehmern (z.b. Medien, Zuschauer, Sponsoren). Der professionelle Sport kann Nutzen stiften und dient somit zur Bedürfnisbefriedigung. Überdies ist er ein knappes Gut, da nicht immer Leistungen auf höchstem sportlichem Niveau möglich sind.

Es ist überdies hervorzuheben, dass im professionellen Sport die Erstellung und der Verbrauch (Konsumption) der Leistung gleichzeitig und ortsgebunden stattfinden *(uno-actu-Prinzip)*. Der professionelle Sport als Dienstleistung kennzeichnet sich somit durch eine Nicht-Lagerbarkeit und Standortgebundenheit. Überdies besteht für alle Abnehmer der Leistung eine Qualitätsunsicherheit hinsichtlich der Spannung und der Hochklassigkeit des Fußballspiels. Dieser Aspekt ist im Hinblick auf das Management und Marketing umso bedeutender, da der Absatz der Leistung zeitlich vor der Leistungserstellung kommt. Der Sportveranstalter besitzt diesbezüglich ein geringes Maß an Kontrollierbarkeit und Gestaltbarkeit der Kernleistung (Schubert, 2005). Die Immaterialität des Wirtschaftsgutes Sport führt damit zu einer Informationsarmut. Es handelt sich somit um ein Wirtschaftsgut mit einem hohen Anteil an Erfahrungs- und Vertrauenseigenschaften (Meffert/Bruhn, 2003).

In Abhängigkeit des Abnehmers ändert sich die Art der Dienstleitung. Für die Zuschauer ist der professionelle Sport eine originäre (konsumtive) Dienstleistung, wohingegen er für Medien, Sponsoren und Merchandising-Unternehmen eine derivative (produktive) Dienstleistung darstellt.

Der Output *professioneller Sport* wird im Wesentlichen an fünf Akteure vermarktet. An die Medien werden Übertragungsrechte verkauft, an Zuschauer Eintrittsrechte, an Sponsoren Nutzungsrechte und an Merchandising-Unternehmen Lizenzen. Je nach Akzeptanz in der Bevölkerung kann die öffentliche Hand einen Imagegewinn oder -verlust erfahren, wenn z.B. der Umbau eines Stadions subventioniert wurde. Es ist hervorzuheben, dass die Medien nicht nur als Abnehmer, sondern auch als so genannter intermediärer Produktionsfaktor auftreten. Durch die Übertragung und Aufnahme der Sportveranstaltung tragen sie zur Veredelung des Outputs bei und heben teilweise die Nicht-Lagerbarkeit und Standortgebundenheit auf. Abschließend ist anzumerken, dass die Abnehmer des professionellen Sports untereinander auch in wechselseitigen Beziehungen stehen (Benner, 1992). Zum Beispiel erwerben Sponsoren Sendezeiten für Werbung bei den Medien und versuchen durch Sportsponsoring, die Aufmerksamkeit auf ihre Produkte zu lenken und diese letztendlich an Zuschauer abzusetzen.

Aus den angesprochenen Besonderheiten des Wirtschaftsgutes Sport ergeben sich Konsequenzen für das Marketing (Schubert, 2005). Aufgrund der Qualitätsunsicherheit handelt es sich beim professionellen Sport um ein sehr enttäuschungsanfälliges Wirtschaftsgut und das Angebot an Zusatzleistungen ist von besonderer Bedeutung. Das Kernprodukt Sport wird somit erweitert. Als Beispiele für derartige Produkterweiterungen kann die Gestaltung eines attraktiven Rahmenprogramms bei der Sportveranstaltung mit Gewinnspielen, Verkaufsständen und Spielgelegenheiten für Kinder genannt werden.

In Zusammenhang mit der Qualitätsunsicherheit ist auf die besondere Bedeutung kommunikationspolitischer Maßnahmen hinzuweisen. Zum Beispiel können Medienberichte im Vorfeld über die Bedeutung eines Spiels zur Reduktion von Verhaltensunsicherheiten beitragen.

Speziell in kleinen Fußballstadien gewinnen das Kapazitätsmanagement und die Nachfragesteuerung an Bedeutung und stellen eine Herausforderung an das Sportmanagement dar. Das Kapazitätsmanagement kann zum Beispiel durch Preisdifferenzierungen gemeistert werden.

Die Vielfalt der Motive, warum Zuschauer ins Stadion gehen, erfordert eine Zielgruppenorientierung und ein entsprechendes Szenemarketing. Zum Beispiel werden Kindern und Jugendlichen andere Inhalte und Werte kommuniziert als älteren Stadionbesuchern.

Seitens der Sportunternehmen (Clubs, Verbände) spielen Öffentlichkeitsarbeit und Relationship-Marketing eine entscheidende Rolle, um Gehör für ihre Anliegen zu finden. Zum Beispiel kann hinsichtlich der Umwandlung von Stadien mit Leichtathletik-Rundbahn in reine Fußballarenen, wofür öffentliche Genehmigungen und eventuell Subventionen notwendig sind, eine breit angelegte Öffentlichkeitsarbeit zum Gelingen des Vorhabens beitragen.

2.2.2 Nachfragersicht

Neben den Besonderheiten des Wirtschaftsgutes Sport aus Anbietersicht sind solche aus Nachfragersicht zu beachten, wobei es teilweise zu Überschneidungen kommen kann. In der Literatur zum professionellen Sport haben sich einige Determinanten herauskristallisiert, welche die Nachfrage nach Zuschauersport bestimmen und welche von Interesse für das Sportmanagement sind. Tab. 1 gibt eine Übersicht über die Determinanten der Nachfrage nach Zuschauersport.

Zu den ökonomischen Determinanten gehören der Ticketpreis, das Einkommen, die Anzahl bzw. der Preis der möglichen Substitute und die Marktgröße. Allen voran bestimmt der *Ticketpreis* die Nachfrage nach Zuschauersport, wobei dieser überwiegend einen negativen Einfluss auf die Nachfrage hat (z.B. Brook, 2006; Winfree/McCluskey/Mittelhammer/Fort, 2004). Diese Befunde bestätigen, dass eine idealtypische Nachfragekurve zugrunde liegt. D.h., dass mit steigendem Preis die Anzahl der Nachfrager sinkt.

Klassifikation	Determinante	Effekt
Ökonomische	Ticketpreis	−
Faktoren	Einkommen	+
	Verfügbarkeit an Substituten	
	(Anzahl)	−
	(Preis)	+
	Marktgröße	+
Soziodemografische	Anteil ethnischer Minderheiten	
Faktoren	an der Gesamtbevölkerung	−
Produktbezogene	Mannschaft (Qualität, Erfolg)	+
Faktoren	Stadion	
	(Alter)	+
	(Qualität)	−
	(Größe)	+
	Spieltermin am Wochenende	+
	Spannung	+
Nachfragebezogene Faktoren	Treue der Fans	+
Exogene Faktoren	Gutes Wetter	+

Tab. 1: Übersicht über Determinanten der Nachfrage nach professionellem Zuschauersport

Des Weiteren beeinflusst das persönliche *Einkommen* die Nachfrage nach Zuschauersport. Die überwiegende Mehrheit der Studien belegt, dass die Höhe des Einkommens sich positiv auf die Nachfrage nach Zuschauersport auswirkt (z.B. Brook, 2006; Scully, 1989; Winfree/McCluskey/Mittelhammer/Fort, 2004). Demzufolge kommen diese Studien zu dem Schluss, dass es sich beim Zuschauersport um ein *superiores* Gut handelt. Vereinzelte Studien dokumentieren jedoch einen negativen Einfluss des Einkommens auf die Nachfrage nach Zuschauersport (z.B. Bertonazzi/Maloney/McCormick, 1993; Noll, 1974). Dementsprechend gehen letztgenannte Autoren davon aus, dass es sich beim Zuschauersport um ein *inferiores* Gut handelt.

Außerdem spielt das Vorhandensein von *Substituten* eine entscheidende Rolle. Im Bereich des Zuschauersports werden sowohl die Anzahl professioneller Sportmannschaften aus anderen Sportarten im Einzugsbereich der untersuchten Sportmannschaft (Brook, 2006) als auch Preise alternativer Unterhaltungsangebote (Alexander, 2001) als mögliche Substitute angesehen. Empirische Studien belegen, dass die Anzahl möglicher Substitute in Form anderer Sportmannschaften die Nachfrage nach Zuschauersport negativ beeinflusst (z.B. Brook, 2006; Bruggink/Eaton, 1996). Die Preishöhe der alternativen Unterhaltungsangebote wirkt sich jedoch positiv aus (Alexander, 2001). Aus Sicht des Sportmanagements muss bei der Organisation einer Sportveranstaltung berücksichtigt werden, dass parallel stattfindende Veranstaltungen mit verhältnismäßig niedrigen Eintrittspreisen mögliche Substitute für den Nachfrager darstellen.

Überdies bestimmt die *Bevölkerungsgröße* (Marktgröße) des möglichen Nachfragemarkts die Nachfrage nach Zuschauersport. Empirische Analysen bezüglich des Einflusses der Bevölkerungsgröße auf die Zuschauersportnachfrage sind nicht eindeutig. Während ein Großteil der Studien einen positiven Einfluss der Bevölkerungsgröße auf die Nachfrage nach Zuschauersport dokumentiert (z.B. Brook, 2006; Bruggink/Eaton, 1996; Scully, 1989), zeigen vereinzelte Studien einen negativen Einfluss (Alexander, 2001; Schmidt/Berri, 2002) oder gar keinen signifikanten Einfluss (Fort/Quirk, 1996). Im Allgemeinen kann jedoch davon ausgegangen werden, dass mit steigender Marktgröße die Nachfrage zunimmt.

Der *Bevölkerungsanteil ethnischer Minderheiten* wird der Kategorie der demografischen Determinanten zugeordnet. Dieser Faktor findet jedoch v.a. in nordamerikanischen Studien starke Beachtung, wobei der Anteil der Farbigen im Vordergrund steht. Empirischen Studien zufolge sinkt mit steigendem Anteil ethnischer Minderheiten an der Gesamtbevölkerung die Nachfrage nach Zuschauersport (bspw. Noll, 1974; Siegfried/Eisenberg, 1980). Dabei ist jedoch zu prüfen, welchen Stellenwert die zu vermarktende Sportart in den Herkunftskulturen der zahlenmäßig dominierenden ethnischen Gruppen besitzt.

Zu den produktbezogenen Determinanten gehören die Qualität und sportliche Leistung der Mannschaft, das Stadion, der Spieltermin und die Unsicherheit des Ausgangs. Im Hinblick auf die Mannschaft ist deren Qualität und v.a. ihre *sportliche Leistung* bzw. ihr *sportlicher Erfolg* von Bedeutung. Empirischen Studien zufolge bestimmen die Qualität der Mannschaft und die daraus resultierende Qualität des Spiels die Nachfrage nach Zuschauersport positiv (Brook, 2006; Siegfried/Eisenberg, 1980; Winfree/McCluskey/Mittelhammer/Fort, 2004). Hinsichtlich der Spielleistung ist sowohl die aktuelle Spielleistung (Marcum/Greenstein, 1985) als auch die der vergangenen Saison (Fort/Quirk, 1996; Scully, 1989) ausschlaggebend. Den empirischen Befunden zufolge beeinflusst die Spielleistung, egal ob aktuelle oder vergangene, die Nachfrage nach Zuschauersport positiv.

Einen wichtigen produktbezogenen Faktor der Nachfrage nach Zuschauersport stellt das *Stadion* dar, in dem die Mannschaften spielen. In diesem Zusammenhang wird nach dem Alter, der Größe und der Qualität des Stadions differenziert. Bezogen auf das Alter des Stadions belegen empirische Studien, dass neuere Stadien die Nachfrage nach Zuschauersport steigern können (Alexander, 2001; Brook, 2006; Bruggink/Eaton, 1996; Fort/Quirk, 1996). Somit liegt ein negativer Alterseffekt vor. Als Indikatoren für die Qualität könnten die Anzahl der Luxuslogen, der sanitären Anlagen oder der überdachten Sitzplätze herangezogen werden. Überdies wird vermutet, dass alles, was zur Vermeidung langer Warteschlangen beiträgt, die Qualität erhöht. Empirischen Untersuchungen zufolge beeinflussen sowohl die Stadionqualität (Brook, 2006; Winfree/McCluskey/Mittelhammer/Fort, 2004) als auch die Stadiongröße (Coffin, 1996) die Nachfrage nach Zuschauersport positiv.

Der *Spieltermin* spielt im Hinblick auf die Nachfrage nach Zuschauersport ebenfalls eine Rolle. Generell stehen Spieltermine unter der Woche oder am Wochenende zur Verfügung. Verschiedene Studien zeigen, dass sich Spieltermine am Wochenende positiv auf die Nachfrage nach Zuschauersport auswirken (z.B. Bruggink/Eaton, 1996; Marcum/Greenstein, 1985). Dieser Effekt kann dadurch erklärt werden, dass die arbeitende Bevölkerung unter der Woche weniger Zeit hat, die Spieltermine wahrzunehmen.

Rottenberg (1956) beschäftigte sich bereits in den 50er Jahren mit dem Aspekt der *Spannung* bzw. der Unsicherheit des Spielausgangs. In diesem Zusammenhang wird in Studien häufig die so genannte *uncertainty of outcome hypothesis* einer empirischen Überprüfung unterzogen. Einigen Befunden zufolge bestimmt die Spannung die Nachfrage nach Zuschauersport positiv (bspw. Borland/Lye, 1992; Hynds/Smith, 1994), wohingegen vereinzelt kein signifikanter Effekt festgestellt wurde (Brook, 2006).

Unter den Determinanten der Nachfrage nach Zuschauersport befindet sich auch die *Treue der Fans*, die durch die Anzahl der Spielbesuche im Vorjahr operationalisiert wird. Vereinzelt wird auch die Anzahl der Jahre, in denen Spiele besucht wurden, als Indikator für die Treue der Fans herangezogen. Empirischen Befunden zufolge beeinflusst die Treue der Fans die Nachfrage nach Zuschauersport positiv (Bertonazzi/Maloney/McCormick, 1993; Winfree/McCluskey/Mittelhammer/Fort, 2004). In Zusammenhang mit der Treue der Fans steht das so genannte *Konsumkapital* der Fans. Gemäß Stigler/Becker (1977) steigt mit zunehmender Anzahl an Konsumjahren (Jahren, in denen Spiele besucht wurden) das individuelle Konsumkapital der Fans an und damit auch der Nutzen des Zielgutes *Unterhaltung*. Im Sinne der Konsumkapitaltheorie (Stigler/Becker, 1977) können Sportveranstaltungen im professionellen Sport als Markt-/Wirtschaftsgüter angesehen werden, die zusammen mit individuellen Inputfaktoren wie Zeit und Konsumkapital dazu verwendet werden, das Zielgut *Unterhaltung* herzustellen. Dabei sind soziale Netzeffekte zu berücksichtigen. Der Zuschauer kann entweder direkt durch die Sportveranstaltung unterhalten werden oder indirekt, bspw. wenn der Besuch der Sportveranstaltung als Basis für nachgelagerte Kommunikation dient, die Nutzen stiftet. Neben dem individuellen Konsumkapital spielt somit das sportspezifische Kommunikationsnetzwerk ebenfalls eine entscheidende Rolle. Aufgrund dieser sozialen Netzeffekte ist für die Sportveranstalter von Bedeutung, bereits a priori Erwartungen zu wecken und eine kritische Zuschauermasse anzulocken (Haucap, 2006).

Da es sich bei vielen Mannschaftssportarten i.d.R. um Freiluftsportarten handelt, ist der exogene Faktor *Wetter* nicht zu vernachlässigen. Operationalisiert wird der Wetterfaktor meist durch die Temperatur oder die Regenwahrscheinlichkeit an den Spieltagen. Übereinstimmend kommen empirische Studien zu dem Ergebnis, dass schlechtes Wetter (kalt, nass) sich negativ auf die Nachfrage nach Zuschauersport auswirkt (z.B. Bruggink/Eaton, 1996; Marcum/Greenstein, 1985). Es ist jedoch zu hinterfragen, inwieweit der Wetterfaktor in Zeiten ganzheitlich überdachter Stadien noch eine wichtige Rolle spielt.

Die Determinanten der Nachfrage nach TV-Übertragungen von Spielen der deutschen Fußball-Nationalmannschaft ähneln den bereits genannten Determinanten der Nachfrage nach Zuschauersport (Feddersen/Rott, 2006; vgl. Tab. 2). Auf den ersten Blick erscheint der positive Einfluss guten Wetters auf den Marktanteil fraglich. Die Ursache hierfür liegt in den unterschiedlichen Zeitpunkten des Sonnenuntergangs in Abhängigkeit der Jahreszeit.

Determinante	Operationalisierung	Effekt hinsichtlich	
		Reichweite	Marktanteil
Art des Spiels	EM-/WM-Spiele	+	+
Stars	Anzahl der Länderspiele	+	+
Qualität des Gegners	FIFA-Weltrangliste	–	–
	Top-Team	+	+
Uhrzeit	Vorabend (18.00-19.59 Uhr)	+	–
	Abend (20.00-21.59 Uhr)	+	–
Gutes Wetter	Anzahl Sonnenstunden	–	+

Tab. 2: Determinanten der Nachfrage nach TV-Übertragungen von Spielen der deutschen Fußball-Nationalmannschaft
In Anlehnung an: Feddersen/Rott (2006), S. 117

2.3 Motoren einer wachsenden Sportnachfrage

Für die wachsende Nachfrage nach Sport und somit auch für die zunehmende ökonomische Bedeutung des Sports in den letzten Jahren können verschiedene Ursachen angeführt werden.

Ein allgemeiner *sozialer Wandel* mit verschiedenen Facetten kann hierfür als erste Ursache genannt werden (Rittner, 1988). Die Wandlungen des Lebensgefühls und die Suche nach Erlebnissen tragen dazu bei, dass Sport verstärkt nachgefragt wird. Aufgrund seines *high involvement Charakters* hält der Sport ein entsprechendes Erlebnis- und Identifikationspotenzial bereit (Schubert, 2005), das durch die *Eventisierung* ausgeschöpft wird. Im Zuge der Eventisierung werden aus Sportveranstaltungen Events. Bei diesen Events ist das Zeigen und Ausleben von Emotionen erwünscht. Ein Stadionbesuch beschränkt sich demzufolge nicht mehr auf ein bloßes Informationsinteresse am Ausgang und Zustandekommen des Ergebnisses, vielmehr scheint ein entsprechendes Rahmenprogramm der Sportveranstaltung im Vordergrund zu stehen. Überdies trägt ein Wandel in den finanziellen Ressourcen zu einer wachsenden Sportnachfrage bei. Ein höheres durchschnittliches Einkommen und Bildungsniveau verändern die Präferenzen im Hinblick auf den Sportkonsum (Breuer, 2006). Hinzu kommt der Faktor Zeit. Nicht nur der aktive Sport, sondern auch der passive Sportkonsum kostet Zeit. Veränderungen in den Zeitbudgets und den Arbeitszeiten führen zu einer Veränderung der Sportnachfrage. Es ist jedoch zu beobachten, dass sich die Sportveranstaltungen an die Zeitressourcen der Konsumenten anpassen, zum Beispiel indem wichtige Spiele oder Endläufe in die Abendstunden verlegt werden.

Die *Kommerzialisierung* fungiert als Bindeglied zwischen dem sozialen Wandel und dem Sport. Sie schneidet den Sport auf die veränderten Bedingungen der Lebensführung zu und ermöglicht kurze Wege zum Genuss der Sportleistungen. Es ist eine zunehmende Kommerzialisierung in allen Bereichen des Sports zu beobachten. Als wichtigster Indikator für die Kommerzialisierung kann die Sportwerbung herangezogen werden. Die Sportwerbung hat eine fortwährende Entwicklung hinter sich. Sie hat sich in den letzten Jahren von der Schleichwerbung zum konkreten *product placement* entwickelt (Rittner, 1988).

Einher mit der Kommerzialisierung geht die Tatsache, dass Geld in zunehmendem Maße zum Steuerungsmedium für Entwicklungsprozesse im Sport wird. Zum Beispiel üben Geldgeber Einfluss auf die Uhrzeiten von Sportveranstaltungen (Endlaufzeiten), auf die Zusammensetzung von Mannschaften (Roman Abramowitsch beim FC Chelsea London) oder auch das Regelwerk von Sportarten aus (z.B. wurde im Volleyball das *Rally-Point-System* [jeder Punkt zählt anstatt wie zuvor, als nur der Aufschläger punkten konnte] eingeführt, um die Übertragungszeiten kalkulierbarer zu machen). Im Gegenzug ändern Sportarten ihr Regelwerk, um ihre Attraktivität für potenzielle Geldgeber zu erhöhen. Durch eine „Privilegierung von Siegen und Rekorden" folgen Manipulationsversuche (z.B. Doping, Bestechung) dieser Kommerzialisierung wie ein Schatten (Rittner, 1988, S. 169).

Das Resultat der Kommerzialisierung ist u.a. die Vermarktung von Spektakeln im Zuschauersport, bei denen Höchstleistungen und Rekorde angekündigt werden. Somit hat der Konsum im Zuschauersport eine neue Zeitstruktur bekommen. Es gibt ein Verlangen nach Effekten (Effekthunger) und schnellem Genuss im Zuschauersport, dem die Gestaltung der Sportevents Rechnung trägt. Auch wird das Publikum unmittelbar in die Erarbeitung von Rekorden mit einbezogen (z.B. durch rhythmisches Klatschen, Anfeuern und stehende Ovationen in der Leichtathletik).

2.4 Ökonomische Potenziale des Sports

Für die ökonomischen Potenziale können verschiedene Indikatoren herangezogen werden, auf die im Folgenden genauer eingegangen wird.

2.4.1 Ökonomische Effekte von Sportveranstaltungen

Ein erster Indikator für die ökonomischen Potenziale des Sports sind die ökonomischen Effekte von Sportveranstaltungen. Diese ökonomischen Effekte können in verschiedene Effekte unterteilt werden (Felderer/Helmenstein/Kleissner/Moser/ Schindler/Treiler, 2006; Heinemann, 1995; vgl. Abb. 2).

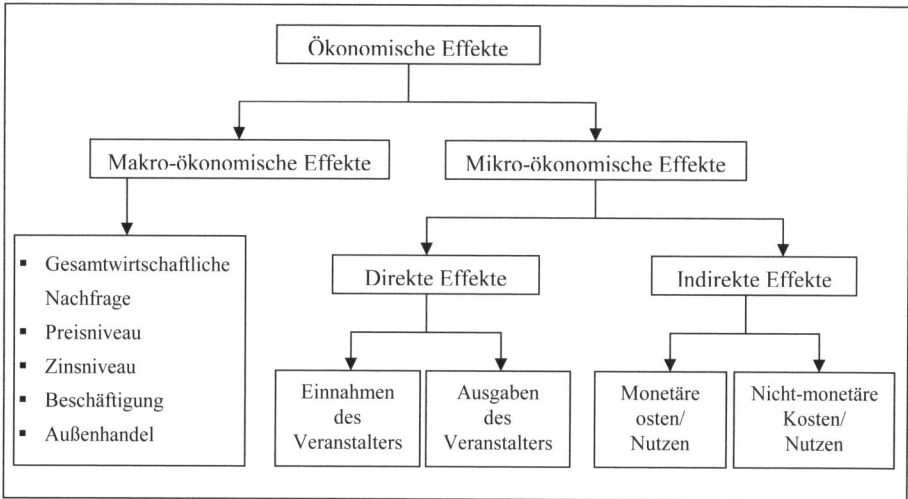

Abb. 2: Übersicht über ökonomische Effekte bei Sportveranstaltungen
In Anlehnung an: Heinemann (1995), S. 256

Makro-ökonomische Effekte beziehen sich auf die Volkswirtschaft eines Landes. Darunter fallen Änderungen der gesamtwirtschaftlichen Nachfrage, des Preis- und Zinsniveaus sowie Beschäftigungs- und Außenhandelseffekte. Zum Beispiel kann die Ausrichtung einer Sportveranstaltung zu einer (vorübergehenden) Senkung der Arbeitslosenquote beitragen.

Mikroökonomische Effekte können in direkte und indirekte Effekte unterteilt werden. *Direkte Effekte* betreffen die Einnahmen und Ausgaben des Sportveranstalters. Zum Beispiel können Einnahmen aus dem Verkauf von Eintrittskarten generiert werden und Ausgaben für die Einrichtung eines Pressezentrums anfallen. *Indirekte Effekte* betreffen nicht den Sportveranstalter, sondern Dritte (z.B. Anwohner, Gastronomie, Hotellerie, Staat). In diesem Zusammenhang wird auch von *externen Effekten* gesprochen. Es kann sich hierbei um monetäre bzw. nicht-monetäre (nicht in Geldeinheiten messbare) Kosten und Nutzen handeln. Zu *monetären Kosten* gehören bspw. staatliche Investitionen (Infrastruktur, Sportstätte, etc…), private Investitionen (Bau von Kongresszentren, Hotels, etc…), öffentliche Konsumausgaben (Sicherheit, Polizeieinsätze, etc…) und private Konsumausgaben (Ausgaben der Besucher). Letztgenannte werden jedoch aus Sicht der Gastronomie und Hotellerie zu den *monetären Nutzen* gezählt. Als weiterer monetärer Nutzen kann die so genannte *Umwegrentabilität* von Sportveranstaltungen genannt werden. Unter Umwegrentabilität ist eine indirekte Rentabilität zu verstehen, die folglich nicht durch die Sportveranstaltung selbst, sondern durch Folgewirkungen (z.B. höhere Konsumausgaben durch Touristen) entsteht und die zur Legitimation sportbezogener Staatsaktivitäten (z.B. Wirtschaftsimpulse durch öffentliche Subventionen) bemüht wird (Kurscheidt, 2005). Zu derartigen Umwegrentabilitäten können höhere Steuererlöse gezählt werden. Unter *nicht-monetäre Kosten* fallen z.B. Umweltbelastungen, erhöhtes Verkehrs- und Müllaufkommen sowie Lärmbelästigung. *Nicht-monetäre Nutzen* können in Form einer stärkeren Identifikation der Bevölkerung mit ihrer Region und einer Erhöhung ihres Erlebnis- und Freizeitwertes auftreten. Der Image- und Werbeeffekt für eine Region, der durch eine Sportveranstaltung entstehen kann, ist ebenfalls nicht zu unterschätzen. Insgesamt betrachtet können vielfältige ökonomische Effekte auftreten. Darüber hinaus müssen so genannte *multiplikative Wirkungen* (Kette wirtschaftlicher Aktivitäten) berücksichtigt werden.

Die Quantifizierung ökonomischer Effekte erfolgt anhand von Wertschöpfungs-, Beschäftigungs- und Kaufkrafteffekten. In Tab. 3 werden Beschäftigungs- und Wertschöpfungseffekte von Sportveranstaltungen dargestellt, die einen Eindruck über die ökonomischen Potenziale des Sports geben.

Sportveranstaltung	Ökonomische Effekte	
	Beschäftigung	Wertschöpfung (in Mio. €)
Olympische Sommerspiele Los Angeles 1984	73.375	1.715,8
Olympische Sommerspiele Seoul 1988	336.000	1.486
Olympische Sommerspiele Barcelona 1992	196.640	22,4
Olympische Winterspiele Lillehammer 1994	300	k.A.
Olympische Sommerspiele Atlanta 1996	77.026	3.804,6
Formel 1 Grand Prix Österreich 1997	21.000	11
Fußball-Europameisterschaft Niederlande/Belgien 2000	k.A.	92
Olympische Sommerspiele Sydney 2000	90.000	4.082
Ruder-Weltmeisterschaft Luzern 2001	87	3,75
Fußball-Europameisterschaft Portugal 2004	39.363	350
Leichtathletik-Weltmeisterschaft Helsinki 2005	1.200	140
Olympische Winterspiele Turin 2006	57.000	k.A.
Fußball-Weltmeisterschaft Deutschland 2006	40.000	10.000
Prognosen		
Fußball-Europameisterschaft Österreich/Schweiz 2008	8.600	383,8
Olympische Sommerspiele London 2012	46.000	12.240
Olympische Winterspiele Salzburg 2014	18.405	1.312,5

Tab. 3: Übersicht über ökonomische Effekte von Sportveranstaltungen in chronologischer Reihenfolge
In Anlehnung an: Felderer/Helmenstein/Kleissner/Moser/Schindler/Treiler (2006); PriceWaterhouseCoopers (2005), S 10

2.4.2 Preiselastizitäten

Ein weiterer Indikator für die ökonomischen Potenziale des Sports sind Preiselastizitäten. Preiselastizitäten sind mikroökonomische Größen, welche die Empfindlichkeit von Nachfragereaktionen auf Preisänderungen ausdrücken.

> Die *direkte Preiselastizität der Nachfrage* bezeichnet das Verhältnis der relativen Änderung der Nachfrage zur relativen Änderung des Preises eines Gutes. Ist ihr Wert größer als eins, wird von einer *elastischen* (empfindlichen) Reaktion, ist ihr Wert kleiner als eins, wird von einer *unelastischen* (unempfindlichen) Reaktion der Nachfrage gesprochen. Bei einem Wert von genau eins liegt eine *isoelastische* Nachfrage vor. Aufgrund ihres Zusammenhangs mit dem Erlös eines Gutes, werden beim Vorliegen einer elastischen Nachfrage Preissenkungen, beim Vorliegen einer unelastischen Nachfrage Preiserhöhungen empfohlen (Hardes/Schmitz/Uhly, 2002).

Im Bereich der Nachfrage nach professionellem Zuschauersport wurden zahlreiche Studien über die Preiselastizität der Ticketpreise durchgeführt. Tab. 4 zeigt einen Ausschnitt dieser Studien und soll einen Eindruck über den Forschungsstand in diesem Bereich vermitteln. Studien im deutschsprachigen Raum liegen leider nicht vor.

Land	Sportart	Zeitraum	Autor(en)	Preiselastizität
England	Fußball	1962-1991	Simmons (1996)	−0,40
		1996	Forrest/Simmons/Feehan (2002)	−0,74
		1993-1994	Baimbridge/Cameron/Dawson (1996)	1,10
	Rugby	1994-1995	Carmichael/ Millington/Simmons (1999)	−0,57
	Cricket	1984-1992	Hynds/Smith (1994)	−0,38
Schottland	Fußball	1975-1981	Jennett (1984)	−0,00
Spanien	Fußball	1992-1996	Garcia/Rodriguez (2002)	−0,30
Australien	Fußball	1981-1986	Borland/Lye (1992)	−0,50
Neuseeland	Rugby	1972-1994	Richardson (2005)	−0,22
USA	Baseball	1963-1998	Winfree/McCluskey/Mittelhammer/ Fort (2004)	−0,06
		1991-1997	Alexander (2001)	5,19
	American Football	1995-1999	Brook (2006)	−0,47
	Eishockey	1981-1983	Stewart/Ferguson/Jones (1992)	−0,99
	Basketball	1980-1986	Kahn/Sherer (1988)	−0,03

Tab. 4: Befunde zur Preiselastizität der Nachfrage nach professionellem Zuschauersport

Die in Tab. 4 dargestellten Befunde spiegeln die überwiegend unelastische Nachfrage nach professionellem Zuschauersport wieder. Eine unelastische Nachfrage deutet auf ökonomische Potenziale hin, die noch nicht ausgeschöpft sind. Grundsätzlich könnten durch eine Erhöhung der Ticketpreise die ökonomischen Potenziale besser erschlossen werden. An dieser Stelle wird die Frage aufgeworfen, warum die Zuschauersportanbieter nicht die Ticketpreise im isoelastischen Teil der Nachfragekurve ansetzen, um so ihren Gewinn zu maximieren. Als mögliche Erklärungen können angeführt werden, dass einerseits viele Dauerkarteninhaber mit günstigen Ticketpreisen gebunden werden und andererseits versucht wird, durch eine optimale Preisdifferenzierung das Stadion zu füllen. Zweitens sollen neben den Eintrittstickets Anschlussprodukte wie Fanartikel, Essen und Getränke verkauft werden. Die Zuschauer sollen mit Hilfe günstiger Ticketpreise ins Stadion *gelockt* werden und dort noch weitere Ausgaben tätigen. Der mit den Anschlussprodukten erzielte Gesamtumsatz übersteige den Umsatz, der allein durch höhere Ticketpreise erzielt werden würde (Marburger, 1997). Drittens ist die Anwesenheit der Zuschauer wichtig, da sie im Stadion für Atmosphäre sorgen. Überdies sind leere Stadien für Medien und Sponsoren uninteressant. Wie soeben erörtert, muss die Ausschöpfung dieser ökonomischen Potenziale im Einzelfall geprüft werden. Ausschlaggebend hierfür dürfte sein, welche Eintrittspreise weiterhin ein volles Stadion nach sich ziehen.

2.4.3 Konsumausgaben für Sport

Die Konsumausgaben, welche für Sportprodukte aller Art getätigt werden, stellen einen weiteren wichtigen Indikator für die ökonomischen Potenziale des Sports dar. In Deutschland werden diese Konsumausgaben für Sport im Brutto-Inlands-Produkt (BIP) miterfasst. Außerdem gibt es Studien über Sportausgaben, in denen Konsumausgaben für professionellen Sport erhoben werden.

1993 lag das sportbezogene BIP bei 22,59 Mrd. € (eigene Umrechnung der DM-Angaben im Original), was einem Anteil von 1,4 % am gesamten BIP entspricht. Der private Verbrauch stellte mit 16,96 Mrd. € den größten Anteil daran.

Für das Jahr 1998 wurde ein sportbezogenes BIP von 27,06 Mrd. € ermittelt, das rund 1,4 % des gesamten BIP ausmacht. Davon entfielen 20,75 Mrd. € auf den privaten Verbrauch (Meyer/Ahlert, 2000). Es ist zu beachten, dass unter den sportbezogenen privaten Verbrauch nicht nur Ausgaben für passiven Sportkonsum fallen, sondern auch für aktives Sporttreiben.

Um Aussagen über zukünftige ökonomische Potenziale des Sports tätigen zu können, entwickelten Meyer/Ahlert (2000) ein Prognosemodell, das Modell SPORT. Die mit diesem Modell durchgeführten Simulationsrechnungen liefern auf Basis verschiedener alternativer Annahmen (z.B. eine objektive Beschreibung alternativer ökonomischer Entwicklungspfade) Informationen über ökonomische Effekte. Der kontinuierliche Anstieg beider Größen verdeutlicht die erheblichen ökonomischen Potenziale des Sports (vgl. Tab. 5) (inwieweit diese Prognosen bis dato eingetreten sind, wurde noch nicht empirisch überprüft).

Konsumausgaben für Sport (in Mrd. €)	1999	2005	2010
Sportbezogener privater Verbrauch	17,53	21,59	25,78
Sportbezogenes BIP	23,00	28,22	33,48

Tab. 5: Prognose der Entwicklung des sportbezogenen privaten Verbrauchs und des sportbezogenen BIP von 1999 bis 2010 (in Preisen von 1991)
Quelle: Meyer/Ahlert (2000), S. 175 ff.

Bislang kaum berücksichtigt wurden die ökonomischen Potenziale des Sports im Hinblick auf dessen mediale Vermarktung durch das Internet. Theysohn (2006) untersuchte die Zahlungsbereitschaft für Fußball-Spielberichte (Live-Berichte und Zusammenfassungen) im Internet und ob sich die Spielleistung in der Liga auf die geäußerten Zahlungsbereitschaften auswirkt. Die durchschnittliche Zahlungsbereitschaft für Berichte auf nationaler Ebene lag bei 3,73 €, die auf internationaler Ebene sogar bei 6,51 €. Im Hinblick auf die Auswirkungen der Spielleistungen einer Mannschaft konnte nur eine geringe Korrelation zwischen der Zahlungsbereitschaft und dem Teamerfolg festgestellt werden. Außerdem wurden keine signifikanten Unterschiede hinsichtlich der Zahlungsbereitschaft zwischen Fans von Mannschaften aus der ersten und der zweiten Fußball-Bundesliga nachgewiesen. Die ermittelten Zahlungsbereitschaften zeigen, welches Potenzial in der Vermarktung von Spielberichten via Internet steckt. Auch Schewe/Gaede/Delonga (2003) fanden heraus, dass die Rechteinhaber an den Spielen der Fußball-Bundesliga ihr Refinanzierungspotenzial in den elektronischen Medien nicht optimal ausnutzen, da die vorhandenen Zahlungsbereitschaften der Kunden nicht vollständig ausgeschöpft werden. Abgesehen davon bedürfen die Sendeformate einer Anpassung an die Kundenwünsche.

2.4.4 Arbeitsmarkteffekte
Ein weiterer Indikator für die ökonomischen Potenziale des Sports sind Arbeitsmarkt- bzw. Beschäftigungseffekte, welche durch den Sport entstehen. Jedes Jahr wird die sportbezogene Beschäftigung ermittelt, welche durch ihren kontinuierlichen Anstieg über die Jahre die ökonomischen Potenziale des Sports verdeutlicht (vgl. Tab. 6).

Im Jahr 1993 liegt der Anteil der sportbezogenen Beschäftigung an der Gesamtbeschäftigung bei 2,3 %, im Jahr 1998 bei 2,4 % (Meyer/Ahlert, 2000).

Sportbezogene Beschäftigung	1993	1994	1995	1996	1997	1998
Sportvereine und Sportverbände	320.000	331.600	340.800	343.172	345.617	347.213
Gesamt	772.350	764.172	774.102	780.738	782.586	783.171

Tab. 6: Entwicklung der sportbezogenen Beschäftigung von 1993 bis 1998
Quelle: Meyer/Ahlert (2000), S. 155

Bezüglich der sportbezogenen Beschäftigung ist zu beachten, dass eine Unterteilung in beschäftigte Arbeitnehmer in den Sportsektoren (Sportvereine und -verbände, Sportwaren, Sportspezifische Beschäftigung der Gebietskörperschaften, erwerbswirtschaftliche Sportanbieter) und sportbezogene Beschäftigung außerhalb der Sportbranche (z.B. Herstellung von Mineralölerzeugnissen, Straßenfahrzeugen, Textilien und Nahrungsmitteln; Dienstleistungen des Groß- und Einzelhandels, des sonstigen Verkehrs, des Gastgewerbes, der Wissenschaft, Kultur und Verlage) vorliegt. Die sportbezogene Beschäftigung in Sportvereinen und Sportverbänden enthält den für dieses Buch relevanten Bereich des professionellen Zuschauersports. Es ist jedoch davon auszugehen, dass nicht alle Beschäftigten auf den Bereich des Spitzensports entfallen.

Auch hinsichtlich der sportbezogenen Beschäftigung wurden Simulationen mit Hilfe des Prognosemodells SPORT durchgeführt (vgl. Tab. 7). Diese Entwicklungsprognose lässt auf erhebliche Arbeitsmarkteffekte im Bereich des Sports schließen (inwieweit diese prognostizierten Arbeitsmarkteffekte bis dato eingetreten sind, wurde noch nicht empirisch überprüf).

Sportbezogene Beschäftigung	1999	2005	2010
Sportvereine und Sportverbände	349.589	374.480	399.632
Gesamt	496.382	898.278	992.683

Tab. 7: Prognose der Entwicklung der sportbezogenen Beschäftigung von 1999 bis 2010
Quelle: Meyer/Ahlert (2000), S. 183

2.5 Fallstudie

Die vorliegende Fallstudie setzt sich mit der Messung und Berechnung der ökonomischen Effekte der Weltreiterspiele 2006 in Aachen auseinander (Breuer/Ebbert/Haase, 2006).

Fallstudie „Weltreiterspiele 2006 in Aachen"

FEI World Equestrian Games
Aachen 2006

Vom 20.08. bis 03.09.2006 fanden die Weltreiterspiele auf dem Reitsportgelände in der Aachener Soers statt. Im Verlauf der Veranstaltungstage besuchten insgesamt 576.000 Zuschauer die Weltreiterspiele, darunter 18,5 % Ausländer sowie 56,5 % übernachtende Besucher.

Um die ökonomischen Effekte dieser Weltmeisterschaft zu messen, wurden 2.156 Personen aus 34 Ländern zu verschiedenen Aspekten mit Hilfe mehrsprachiger Fragebögen befragt. Der Großteil der befragten Zuschauer kam aus Deutschland, Belgien und den Niederlanden. 70,6 % der Befragten waren Frauen, das Durchschnittsalter der Befragten lag bei 39 Jahren. Auffällig ist das im Vergleich zum Bevölkerungsdurchschnitt relativ hohe durchschnittliche monatliche Nettoeinkommen. Anhand der Angaben der Besucher wurden Hochrechnungen im Hinblick auf Wertschöpfungs-, Steuer- und Imageeffekte getätigt.

Die Wertschöpfung im Bereich Übernachtung liegt bei rund 21,25 Mio. € (= Anzahl durchschnittliche Übernachtungen x durchschnittliche Übernachtungsausgaben pro Nacht x Anzahl übernachtende Zuschauer). Davon entfallen 12,7 Mio. € auf Deutschland, 1,6 Mio. € auf Belgien und 6,7 Mio. € auf die Niederlande. Obwohl nur 18,5 % der Zuschauer aus dem Ausland kamen, beträgt der Anteil ausländischer Besucher an der Wertschöpfung im Beherbergungsgewerbe knapp 49 % (10,4 Mio. €). Eine Differenzierung der Wertschöpfung durch Übernachtung nach der Entfernung der Übernachtungsmöglichkeit zum Reitsportgelände zeigt, dass in einem Umkreis bis zu 50 km die Wertschöpfung am höchsten ist. Die Wertschöpfung im Bereich Verkehr betrug hochgerechnet 27,55 Mio. €, wovon 11 Mio. € durch die ausländischen Besucher zustande kamen. Die größten Anteile mit jeweils 7,5 Mio. € entfielen auf die Anreise mit eigenen Fahrzeugen (PKW, Motorrad) und mit dem Flugzeug. Mietwagenfirmen und der öffentliche Personennahverkehr profitierten immerhin noch mit 2 bzw. 1,2 Mio. € von den Weltreiterspielen. Die Wertschöpfung im Bereich Nahrung, Genussmittel und Gaststätten lag insgesamt bei 33 Mio. €. Davon wurden 20 Mio. € für Essen, 12 Mio. € für Getränke und 0,5 Mio. € für Tabakwaren ausgegeben. Dabei wurde der Großteil der Ausgaben (18,2 Mio. €) außerhalb des Reitsportgeländes und durch Deutsche (24,4 Mio. €) getätigt. Im Bereich Einzelhandel wurde eine Wertschöpfung von gut 20,5 Mio. € erzielt, von der am meisten der Fachhandel für

Reitsport mit 9 Mio. € profitierte. Für allgemeine Kleidung und Schuhe wurden gut 6 Mio. €, für offizielle Fanartikel der Reit-WM 2 Mio. € und für Wellness, Parfums, Schmuck, Optik und Souvenirs jeweils 350.000 €. Zwei Drittel dieser Umsätze wurden von deutschen Besuchern generiert. Die Wertschöpfung im Bereich Kultur betrug knapp 0,5 Mio. €. Davon entfielen 196.600 € auf Besuche von Ausstellungen, 177.000 € auf Musikveranstaltungen und 112.000 € auf Theater- oder Kinobesuche.

Über alle Bereiche dürfte die gesamte Wertschöpfung der Weltreiterspiele 2006 in Aachen bei gut 100 Mio. € liegen.

Versucht man anhand der eben dargestellten Wertschöpfungen die steuerlichen Effekte der Weltreiterspiele 2006 in Aachen hochzurechnen und somit Einschätzungen über die Umwegrentabilität vorzunehmen, so dürften alleine Umsatzsteuereinnahmen in Höhe von 16 Mio. € generiert worden sein.

Dabei ist zu berücksichtigen, dass etwa die Hälfte bis zwei Drittel der Ausgaben in Deutschland getätigt wurde, was ca. 8 bis 11 Mio. € für den deutschen Fiskus bedeuten würde.

Im Hinblick auf die nicht-monetären (intangiblen) Effekte der Reit-WM schätzen 77 % der befragten Zuschauer die Imageeffekte für die Stadt Aachen als gut bis sehr gut ein. 43,15 % der Zuschauer würden der Stadt Aachen einen Wiederholungsbesuch als Tourist abstatten.

Somit hat sich die Ausrichtung der Weltreiterspiele 2006 für die Stadt Aachen samt Umgebung im Hinblick auf zentrale ökonomische Kennziffern gelohnt.

2.6 Fazit und Ausblick

Sportmanagement kann nur dann effektiv sein, wenn es die Besonderheiten des Sports als Wirtschaftsgut kennt und hinreichend berücksichtigt. Dies gilt sowohl im Hinblick auf die Anbieter- als auch die Nachfragerebene. Werden auf dieser Basis die ökonomischen Potenziale des Sports, wie sie im Rahmen des Beitrags dargestellt wurden, gezielt angesteuert, so bestehen angesichts der günstigen gesellschaftlichen Rahmenbedingungen, die als Motoren einer wachsenden Sportnachfrage wirken, gute Chancen, ökonomisch erfolgreiche Sportprodukte am Markt zu platzieren.

Um speziell im Bereich des professionellen Zuschauersports in Deutschland effektiv und effizient agieren zu können, erscheint es in Zukunft wichtig, dass verstärkt wissenschaftliche Befunde generiert werden, auf die das Sportmanagement zurückgreifen kann. Bislang kommt der Großteil der Studien aus dem nordamerikanischen Raum und die gewonnenen Erkenntnisse sind nur bedingt auf Europa und Deutschland übertragbar, da sich die Struktur und Organisation der Profiligen grundlegend unterscheiden. Somit kann festgehalten, dass zukünftig neben ökonomischen Potenzialen im Sport überdies (wissenschaftliche) Erkenntnispotenziale erschlossen werden können.

Kontrollfragen

1. Welche Besonderheiten des Wirtschaftsgutes Sport aus Anbietersicht können Sie nennen?
2. Welche Determinanten beeinflussen die Nachfrage nach Zuschauersport auf welche Weise?
3. Welche Motoren sind für eine wachsende Sportnachfrage verantwortlich?
4. Anhand welcher Indikatoren können ökonomische Potenziale des Sports festgemacht werden?
5. Wie lassen sich ökonomische Effekte von Sportveranstaltungen klassifizieren?
6. Was versteht man unter Umwegrentabilität?
7. Wie sieht die Preiselastizität der Nachfrage nach Zuschauersport aus?
8. Welches Volumen haben die Konsumausgaben für Sport in Deutschland?
9. Wie viele Personen sind im Bereich des Sports in Deutschland beschäftigt?
10. Wie wurde die Wertschöpfung der Weltreiterspiele 2006 in Aachen ermittelt?

Literaturverzeichnis

Alexander, Donald L. (2001): Major League Baseball: Monopoly pricing and profit-maximizing behaviour, in: Journal of Sports Economics, Heft 4, S. 341-355.

Baimbridge, Mark / Cameron, Samuel / Dawson, Peter (1996): Satellite television and the demand for football: a whole new ball game, in: Scottish Journal of Political Economy, Heft 3, S. 317-333.

Benner, Gerd (1992): Risk Management im professionellen Sport – auf der Grundlage von Ansätzen einer Sportbetriebslehre, Bergisch-Gladbach u.a.

Bertonazzi, Eric P. / Maloney, Michael T. / McCormick, Robert E. (1993): Some Evidence on the Alchian and Allen Theorem: The Third Law of Demand?, in: Economic Inquiry, Heft 3, S. 383-393.

Borland, Jeff / Lye, Jenny (1992): Attendance at Australian Rules Football: a panel study, in: Applied Economics, Heft 9, S. 1053-1058.

Breuer, Christoph (2006): Sportpartizipation in Deutschland – ein demo-ökonomisches Modell, in: Sportwissenschaft, Heft 3, S. 292-305.

Breuer, Christoph / Ebbert, Stephanie / Haase, Antje (2006): Ökonomische Effekte der World Equestrian Games Aachen 2006, Köln.

Brook, Stacey L. (2006): Evaluating Inelastic Ticket Pricing Models, in: International Journal of Sport Finance, Heft 3, S. 140-150.

Bruggink, Thomas H. / Eaton, James W. (1996): Rebuilding attendance in Major League Baseball: The demand for individual games, in: Fizel, John / Gustafson,

Elizabeth / Hadley, Lawrence (Hrsg.): Baseball Economics – Current Research, Westport, S. 9-31.

Büch, Martin-Peter / Maennig, Wolfgang / Schulke, Hans-Jürgen (2006): Der Sportzuschauer: Gast, Mitspieler, Manipulierter?, Köln.

Carmichael, Fiona / Millington, Janet / Simmons, Robert (1999): Elasticity of demand for Rugby League attendance and the impact of BskyB, in: Applied Economics Letters, Heft 12, S. 797-800.

Feddersen, Arne / Rott, Armin (2006): Determinanten und Prognose der Nachfrage nach TV-Übertragungen von Spielen der deutschen Fußball-Nationalmannschaft, in: Büch, Martin-Peter / Maennig, Wolfgang / Schulke, Hans-Jürgen (Hrsg.): Der Sportzuschauer als Konsument: Gast, Mitspieler, Manipulierter?, Köln, S. 99-127.

Felderer, Bernhard / Helmenstein, Christian / Kleissner, Anna / Moser, Bernhard / Schindler, Julia / Treiler, Roland (2006): Sport und Ökonomie in Europa – Ein Tour d'Horizon, Wien.

Forrest, David / Simmons, Robert / Feehan, Patrick (2002): A spatial cross-sectional analysis of the elasticity of demand for soccer, in: Scottish Journal of Political Economy, Heft 3, S. 336-355.

Fort, Rodney / Quirk, James (1996): Over-stated exploitation: monopsony versus revenue sharing in sport leagues, in: Fizel, John / Gustafson, Elizabeth / Hadley, Lawrence (Hrsg.): Baseball Economics – Current Research, Westport, S. 159-175.

Garcia, Jaume / Rodriguez, Placido (2002): The determinants of football match attendance revisited, in: Journal of Sports Economics, Heft 1, S. 18-38.

Hardes, Heinz-Dieter / Schmitz, Frieder / Uhly, Alexandra (2002): Grundzüge der Volkswirtschaftslehre, 8. Aufl., München u.a.

Haucap, Justus (2006): Warum sind einige Spielfilme erfolgreich, andere aber nicht: Einige ökonomische Überlegungen, in: MedienWirtschaft, Heft 1, S. 6-15.

Heinemann, Klaus (1995): Einführung in die Ökonomie des Sports. Ein Handbuch, Schorndorf.

Hynds, Michael / Smith, Ian (1994): The demand for test match cricket, in: Applied Economics Letters, Heft 7, S. 103-106.

Jennett, Nicholas (1984): Attendances, Uncertainty of Outcome and Policy in Scottish League Football, in: Scottish Journal of Political Economy, Heft 2, S. 176-198.

Kahn, Lawrence M. / Sherer, Peter D. (1988): Racial differences in professional basketball players' compensation, in: Journal of Labor Economics, Heft 1, S. 40-61.

Kurscheidt, Markus (2005): Finanzwissenschaftliche Analyse des Sports: Empirische Befunde und allokationstheoretische Erklärungen zur staatlichen Sportpolitik, in: Napp, Hans-Georg (Hrsg.): Finanzwissenschaft im Wandel, Frankfurt/Main u.a., S. 211-229.

Marburger, Daniel R. (1997): Optimal ticket pricing for performance goods, in: Managerial and Decision Economics, Heft 5, S. 375-381.

Marcum, John P. / Greenstein, Theodore N. (1985): Factors Affecting Attendance in Major League Baseball II: A Within-Season Analysis, in: Sociology of Sport Journal, Heft 4, S. 314-322.

Meffert, Heribert / Bruhn, Manfred (2003): Dienstleistungsmarketing, 4. Aufl., Wiesbaden.

Meyer, Bernd / Ahlert, Gerd (2000): Die ökonomischen Perspektiven des Sports, Schorndorf.

Noll, Roger G. (1974): Attendance and price setting, in: Noll, Roger G. (Hrsg.): Government and the sports business, Washington, S. 115-157.

Pfeiffer, Stefan / Hovemann, Arnd (2006): Bälle, Tore und Finanzen III, Stuttgart.

Pfister, Gertrud (2006): Was macht den Sport so spannend? Bewegungsaktivitäten und Zuschauerkulturen im historischen Wandel, in: Büch, Martin-Peter / Maennig, Wolfgang / Schulke, Hans-Jürgen (Hrsg.): Der Sportzuschauer als Konsument: Gast, Mitspieler, Manipulierter?, Köln, S. 11-27.

PriceWaterhouseCoopers (2005). Olympic Games Impact Study: Final Report, London.

Richardson, Sam (2005): Determinants of attendance and the value of consumption benefits for provincial rugby in New Zealand: the case of Wanganui 1972-1994, Palmerston Discussion Paper No. 05-06, Massey University, Palmerston North.

Rittner, Volker (1988): Sport als ökonomisches Interessenobjekt, in: Digel, Helmut (Hrsg.): Sport im Verein und Verband, Schorndorf, S. 158-187.

Schewe, Gerhard /Gaede, Nicolas / Delonga, Daniel (2003): Fußballberichterstattung in elektronischen Medien – eine empirische Analyse von Konsumgewohnheiten und Zahlungsbereitschaften, Münster Arbeitspapier Nr. 23 des Lehrstuhls für BWL, Westfälische Wilhelms-Universität Münster.

Schmidt, Martin B. / Berri, David J. (2002): Competitive balance and attendance. The case of Major League Baseball, in: Journal of Sports Economics, Heft 2, S. 145-167.

Schubert, Manfred (2005): Sport-Marketing – einige Überlegungen zu den konstitutiven Grundlagen eines neuen Forschungs- und Aufgabenfeldes, in: Breuer, Christoph / Thiel, Ansgar (Hrsg.): Handbuch Sportmanagement, Schorndorf, S. 237-257.

Scully, Gerald W. (1989): The business of Major League Baseball, Chicago.

Siegfried, John J. / Eisenberg, Jeff D. (1980): The demand for minor league baseball, in: Atlantic Economic Journal, Heft 2, S. 59-69.

Simmons, Robert (1996): The demand for English league football: a club-level analysis, in: Applied Economics, Heft 2, S. 139-155.

Stewart, Kenneth G. / Ferguson, Donald G. / Jones, J. Colin H. (1992): On violence in professional team sport as the endogenous result of profit maximization, in: American Economic Journal, Heft 4, S. 55-64.

Stigler, George J. / Becker, Gary S. (1977): De gustibus non est disputandum, in: The American Economic Review, Heft 2, S. 67-90.

Theysohn, Sven (2006): Willingness to pay for soccer reports on the internet, in: International Journal of Sports Marketing and Sponsorship, Heft 1, S. 16-33.

Winfree, Jason A. / McCluskey, Jill J. / Mittelhammer, Ron C. / Fort, Rodney (2004): Location and attendance in major league baseball, in: Applied Economics, Heft 19, S. 2117-2124.

Weiterführende Ressourcen

Literatur

Berri, David J. / Schmidt, Martin B. / Brook, Stacey L. (2004): Stars at the Gate: The Impact of Star Power on NBA Gate Revenues, in: Journal of Sports Economics, Heft 1, S. 33-50.

Breuer, Christoph / Thiel, Ansgar (Hrsg.) (2005): Handbuch Sportmanagement, Schorndorf.

Büch, Matin-Peter / Schellhaaß, Horst M. (2005): Ökonomik von Sportligen, Schorndorf.

Ernst & Young (2004): Bälle, Tore und Finanzen, Band I bis IV, Essen.

Heyne, Malte / Süssmuth, Bernd (2006): Wie viel ist den Deutschen die Ausrichtung der FIFA-WM 2006 wert und warum?, Diskussionspapier Sportökonomie aktuell Nr. 17 des Arbeitskreises Sportökonomie e.V., Bonn.

Rascher, Daniel A. / McEvoy, Chad D. / Nagel, Mark S. / Brown, Matthew T. (2007): Variable Ticket Pricing in Major League Baseball, in: Journal of Sport Management, Heft 3, S. 407-437.

Schmidt, Martin B. / Berri, David J. (2001): Competitive balance and attendance. The case of Major League Baseball, in: Journal of Sports Economics, Heft 2, S. 145-167.

Trosien, Gerhard (Hrsg.) (1994): Die Sportbranche. Wachstum – Wettbewerb – Wirtschaftlichkeit, 2. Aufl., Frankfurt/Main.

Voeth, Markus / Schumacher, Arne (2003): Ticket-Pricing für die WM 2006 – Empfehlungen auf Basis von Informationen zur Zahlungsbereitschaft der deutschen Bevölkerung. Hohenheimer Arbeits- und Projektberichte zum Marketing, Nr. 9, Stuttgart-Hohenheim.

Links

Deutscher Sportökonomie-Kongress:
    http://www.deutscher-sportoekonomie-kongress.de

European Association for Sport Management (EASM):
    http://www.easm.net

Journal of Sports Economics (Fachzeitschrift):
    http://jse.sagepub.com

Journal of Sport Management (Fachzeitschrift):
    http://www.humankinetics.com/jsm/journalAbout.cfm

Sportmanagementportal (Internetportal):
    http://www.sportmanagementportal.de/sportmanagement-news.htm

Kapitel 3: Betriebswirtschaftliche Grundlagen des Sportmanagements

Gerd Nufer   Carsten Rennhak

Lernziele

Nach der Durchsicht dieses Kapitels sollte der Leser in der Lage sein,

- verschiedene Systematisierungen in der Betriebswirtschaftslehre zu diskutieren.
- den Erfahrungs- und Erkenntnisgegenstand der Betriebswirtschaftslehre zu charakterisieren.
- Zieldimensionen und Zielbeziehungen in einem Unternehmen aufzuzeigen.
- konstitutive Unternehmensentscheidungen zu benennen.
- die Vor- und Nachteile unterschiedlicher Führungsmodelle herauszuarbeiten.
- den Erklärungsbeitrag der Nachbardisziplinen der Sportökonomie zu erläutern.
- aktuelle Entwicklungen in der Betriebswirtschaftslehre einzuordnen.

Überblick über das Kapitel

Das vorliegende Kapitel nähert sich dem Erkenntnisbereich des Sportmanagements von Seiten der Betriebswirtschaftslehre. Hierzu werden zunächst grundlegende Systematisierungsansätze in der Betriebswirtschaftslehre vorgestellt. Die unterschiedlichen Arten von Betrieben werden klassifiziert und das Ökonomische Prinzip erörtert. Danach wird auf die Zielsetzungen eines Unternehmens eingegangen, zusätzlich werden mögliche Zielbeziehungen aufgezeigt. Als die wichtigsten konstitutiven Unternehmensentscheidungen werden die Gründung, die Standortwahl, die Rechtsformwahl und Entscheidungen über Unternehmenszusammenschlüsse besprochen. Welches Führungsmodell für eine Sportorganisation am Erfolg versprechendsten ist, muss im Einzelfall entschieden werden. Ferner wird der Erklärungsbeiträgen der wichtigsten Nachbardisziplinen des Sportmanagements – der Sportsoziologie, der Sportpsychologie und des Sportrecht – untersucht, ehe aktuelle Entwicklungen innerhalb der klassischen Betriebswirtschaftslehre skizziert werden. Anhand des Beispiels der National Football League im Allgemeinen und der Football-Mannschaft Detroit Lions im Speziellen wird illustriert, wie weit die Professionalisierung des Sports aus betriebswirtschaftlicher Sicht schon vorangeschritten ist. Das Kapitel schließt mit einem Fazit und einem Ausblick auf mögliche zukünftige Aufgabenstellungen im Sportmanagement.

3.1 Einführung in die Thematik

In einem zunehmend professionellen Umfeld ist für Sportmanager ein solides betriebswirtschaftliches Grundverständnis unabdingbar. Betriebswirtschaftliche Kenntnisse sind sowohl für die Führung eines Sportbetriebes als auch für effiziente ökonomische Entscheidungen in einzelnen Funktionsbereichen unerlässlich. Der vorliegende Band trägt der Systematisierung entlang der verschiedenen funktionalen Betriebswirtschaftslehren mit der sportmanagementspezifischen Diskussion der relevanten betriebswirtschaftlichen Funktionen Rechnung. Dieser Beitrag konzentriert sich auf die allgemein-betriebswirtschaftlichen Grundlagen des Sportmanagements und bildet die Basis für die folgenden Beiträge.

Bei ihren Handlungen müssen die Akteure im Sportmanagement stets die verschiedenen Interessen sämtlicher Stakeholder berücksichtigen. Um diesen optimal Rechnung zu tragen, setzt das Sportmanagement die Methoden der modernen Betriebswirtschaftslehre ein.

3.2 Systematisierungsansätze in der Betriebswirtschaftslehre

Die beiden wichtigsten Teildisziplinen in den *Wirtschaftswissenschaften* sind die Volkswirtschaftslehre und die Betriebswirtschaftslehre. Daneben existieren Brückendisziplinen wie die Wirtschaftsgeschichte oder die Wirtschaftsgeografie, deren Erkenntnisgegenstand in verwandte Fachgebiete hineinreicht. Nachbar- und Hilfsdisziplinen der Betriebswirtschaftslehre sind beispielsweise die Psychologie, die Soziologie, das Recht und die Mathematik (Schweitzer, 2004; Wöhe/Döring, 2005).

Die *Volkswirtschaftslehre* untersucht die Allokation von knappen, d.h. beschränkt verfügbaren, Gütern und Produktionsfaktoren sowohl auf der Ebene einzelner Wirtschaftssubjekte wie z.B. Konsumenten und Unternehmungen (Mikroökonomie) als auch gesamtwirtschaftlich (Makroökonomie). Die Mikroökonomie befasst sich insbesondere mit ökonomischen Motiven menschlichen Handelns, während die Makroökonomie z.B. aus erkannten Gesetzmäßigkeiten Handlungsempfehlungen für die Wirtschaftspolitik abzuleiten sucht.

Die *Betriebswirtschaftslehre* befasst sich in ihrem Kern zunächst mit den allgemeinen planerischen, organisatorischen, steuernden und kontrollorientierten Funktionen in Betrieben. Sie ist somit grundsätzlich funktions- und branchenübergreifend ausgerichtet.

Die *„speziellen"* Betriebswirtschaftslehren konzentrieren sich auf ausgewählte Fragestellungen, die jeweils nur für Unternehmen einer bestimmten Branche (oder einer bestimmten Betriebsgröße bzw. eines bestimmten Betriebsalters) bzw. für bestimmte Funktionsbereiche innerhalb eines Unternehmens relevant sind. Dies spiegelt sich in der gängigen Unterteilung der Betriebswirtschaftslehre nach Wirtschaftsbereichen („Institutionenlehren") und Funktionsbereichen („Funktionenlehren") wider (Schweitzer, 2004).

Institutionelle Betriebswirtschaftslehren sind z.B. die Industriebetriebslehre, die Handelsbetriebslehre, die Bankbetriebslehre, die Versicherungsbetriebslehre, die Immobilienbetriebslehre, die Betriebswirtschaftslehre kleiner und mittelständischer Unternehmungen, das Konzernmanagement, das Medienmanagement, die Öffentliche Betriebswirtschaftslehre – und auch das Sportmanagement. Letzteres stellt sich als sehr facettenreich dar und reicht vom Management im Bereich des Vereins-sports über den Fitnesssektor, die Sportartikel- und -ausrüstungsindustrie, Sport-dienstleistungen, den Sportstättenbau bis hin zu den Vermarktern von Sport- und Medienrechten und Sportanschlussprodukten wie Sponsoring, Sportwetten oder Sportmedizin.

Funktionale Betriebswirtschaftslehren lassen sich entlang der Wertschöpfungs-kette eines Unternehmens systematisieren, wobei in den verschiedenen Branchen den jeweiligen Funktionen durchaus stark unterschiedliche Bedeutung zukommt. Funktionale Betriebswirtschaftslehren sind u.a. Einkauf und Beschaffung, Materi-alwirtschaft und Logistik, Produktion, Operations Research, Qualitätsmanagement, Marketing, Strategisches Management und Unternehmensführung, Human Resour-ce Management, Finanzen, Innovations- und Technologiemanagement, internes Rechnungswesen und Controlling, externes Rechnungswesen einschließlich Revi-sions- und Treuhandwesen sowie Wirtschaftsprüfung und die Steuerlehre.

Beide Systematisierungsansätze ergänzen sich: Während die funktional-orientierten Betriebswirtschaftslehren nur schwer in der Lage sind, branchenspezi-fische Probleme zu behandeln, liefern sie im Gegenzug branchenunabhängige Aus-sagen. Die institutionell-orientierten Betriebswirtschaftslehren fokussieren nur auf die für die jeweils betrachtete Branche relevanten funktionalen Aspekte, bestehen aber in weiten Teilen aus Doppelungen mit anderen institutionellen Betriebswirt-schaftslehren.

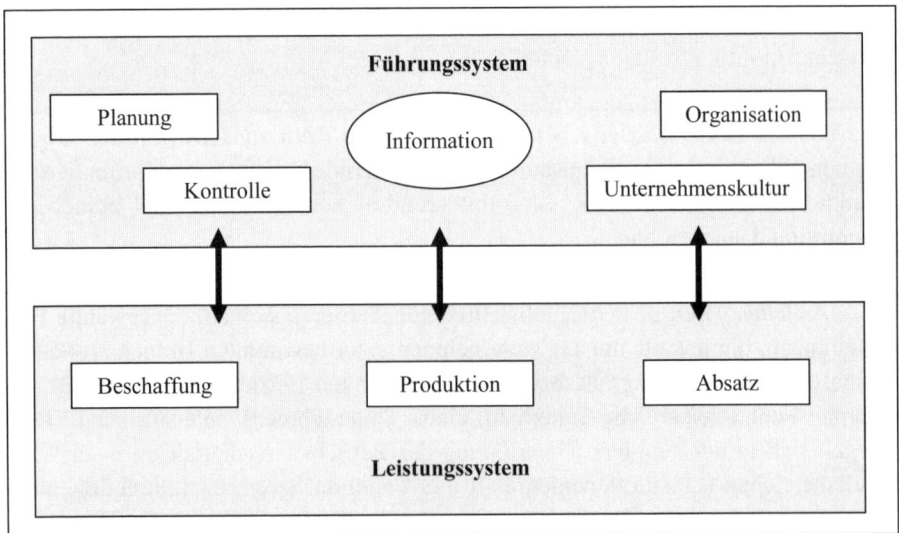

Abb. 1: Die Funktionssysteme eines Unternehmens

Abb. 1 gibt einen Überblick zu den verschiedenen Systemen in einem Unternehmen und ihren Interdependenzen. Die institutionelle Betriebswirtschaftslehre Sportma-nagement befasst sich wie die allgemeine Betriebswirtschaftslehre zunächst mit den planerischen, organisatorischen, steuernden und kontrollorientierten Funktionen im Sport (Führungssystem). Das Leistungssystem kann sich in Sportorganisationen dagegen von der klassischen Sichtweise der Betriebswirtschaftslehre unterscheiden, in der häufig die Anknüpfung an den Realgüterstrom bzw. Auftragsablauf (Dreiteilung: Beschaffung – Produktion – Absatz) dominiert.

3.3. Gegenstand der Betriebswirtschaftslehre

Die Betriebswirtschaftslehre beschäftigt sich mit dem Wirtschaften in Betrieben unter Berücksichtigung der Interdependenzen zu anderen Betrieben und den sie umgebenden Wirtschaftsbereichen (Schweitzer, 2004).

3.3.1 Erfahrungsgegenstand

Der traditionelle Erfahrungsgegenstand der Betriebswirtschaftslehre sind Betriebe:

> „Ein *Betrieb* ist eine planvoll organisierte Wirtschaftseinheit, in der Sachgüter und Dienstleistungen erstellt und abgesetzt werden" (Wöhe/Döring, 2005, S. 2).

Aus ökonomischer Sicht ist ein Betrieb zunächst eine Kombination von Inputfaktoren bzw. Ressourcen, die zu einem Output (Produkte, Dienste) verarbeitet werden, also als „Produktionsstätte" eine technisch-organisatorische Einheit. Das zentrale Merkmal zur weiteren Klassifizierung von Betrieben bildet die Art ihrer Bedarfsdeckung: Betriebe, die in erster Linie den Bedarf fremder Betriebe decken, werden *Unternehmen* genannt, während Betriebe mit überwiegender Eigenbedarfsdeckung als *Haushalte* bezeichnet werden (Schweitzer, 2004).

Anhand der Unterscheidung nach der Art der Bedarfsdeckung einerseits und der Kapitalbeteiligung andererseits kann eine Übersicht über die verschiedenen Wirtschaftseinheiten gegeben werden (vgl. Tab. 1).

Art der Bedarfsdeckung Kapital-beteiligung	Eigenbedarfsdeckung (Konsumtionswirtschaften)	Fremdbedarfsdeckung (Produktionswirtschaften)
öffentlich	Öffentliche Haushalte	Öffentliche Unternehmen und Verwaltungen
		Gemischtwirtschaftliche Unternehmen
privat	Private Haushalte	Private Unternehmen

Tab. 1: Einteilung der Wirtschaftseinheiten
Quelle: Thommen/Achleitner (2006), S. 39

Im Fokus der weiteren Ausführungen stehen Unternehmen. Konstitutive Merkmale von privaten Unternehmen – wie sie auch im professionellen Sportbereich anzutreffen sind – sind die rechtliche, wirtschaftliche und finanzielle Selbständigkeit sowie eine eigene Führung (Wöhe/Döring, 2005).

3.3.2 Erkenntnisgegenstand

Den traditionellen Erkenntnisgegenstand der Betriebswirtschaftslehre bildet das Wirtschaften:

> *„Wirtschaften* ist das Entscheiden über knappe Güter in Betrieben" (Schweitzer, 2004, S. 54).

Die menschlichen Bedürfnisse sind praktisch unbegrenzt, die zur Bedürfnisbefriedigung geeigneten Mittel stehen dagegen nicht in unbeschränkter Menge zur Verfügung. Die naturgegebene Knappheit der Güter, d.h. das Spannungsverhältnis zwischen Bedarf und Bedarfsdeckung, zwingt die Menschen zu wirtschaften: Die vorhandenen Mittel sind dabei grundsätzlich so einzusetzen, dass ein möglichst großes Maß an Bedürfnisbefriedigung erreicht wird.

Das *Ökonomische Prinzip* ist ein formaler Grundsatz, der die Art und Weise des Wirtschaftens beschreibt, jedoch keinerlei Aussagen über Ziele oder Motive des Wirtschaftens (wie z.B. Maximierung des Shareholder Value oder Maximierung des Nutzens der Konsumenten) macht. Das Ökonomische Prinzip ist entweder als *Minimumprinzip* (Minimierung des Mitteleinsatzes zur Erreichung eines vorgegebenen Ziels) oder *Maximumprinzip* (Maximierung des Ergebnisses bei vorgegebenem Mitteleinsatz) zu operationalisieren. Beide Ausprägungen implizieren das ökonomische Basiswerturteil: die Vermeidung jeder Verschwendung. In der Realität ist jedoch oft eine Entscheidung zwischen Optionen nötig, die sich sowohl im möglichen Ergebnis als auch im notwendigen Mitteleinsatz unterscheiden. Das *Optimumprinzip* besagt deshalb, dass unter mehreren Alternativen diejenige zu wählen ist, die das günstigste Verhältnis zwischen Ergebnis und Mitteleinsatz aufweist (Vahs/Schäfer-Kunz, 2007; Thommen/Achleitner, 2006).

Zwei Erfolgsgrößen, die in diesem Kontext häufig verwechselt oder fälschlicherweise synonym gebraucht werden – und auch für das Sportmanagement von zentraler Bedeutung sind –, sind Effektivität und Effizienz: *Effektivität* wird durch eine Relation aus aktuellem und erwünschtem Output erfasst. Die *Effizienz* misst dagegen das Verhältnis von aktuellem Output zu aktuellem Input. Insofern kann die Effektivität als Leitlinie für langfristiges Handeln, die Effizienz als Kriterium für das kurzfristige Handeln angesehen werden (Bea/Haas, 2005). Hofer/Schendel (1996) drücken dies anschaulich folgendermaßen aus: Effektivität heißt, die richtigen Dinge tun („to do the right things"), Effizienz heißt, die Dinge richtig tun („to do things right").

3.4 Ziele im Unternehmen

Ziele stellen ein wesentliches Element eines privaten Unternehmens im marktwirtschaftlichen System dar. Im Gegensatz zum öffentlichen Unternehmen kann sich das private Unternehmen seine Ziele selbst setzen.

3.4.1. Zieldimensionen

Im *Zielinhalt* kommt zum Ausdruck, worauf sich das Handeln des Unternehmens ausrichten soll. Bei einer systematischen Betrachtung der Zielinhalte kann grundsätzlich zwischen Sach- und Formalzielen unterschieden werden (Thommen/Achleitner, 2006).

Formalziele (Erfolgsziele) sind dadurch gekennzeichnet, dass sie sich am Erfolg der betrieblichen Tätigkeiten ausrichten, d.h. sie zeigen das Resultat des güter- und finanzwirtschaftlichen Umsatzprozesses. Sie sind deshalb den Sachzielen übergeordnet. Ausgangspunkt der Formalziele ist das Ökonomische Prinzip. Wegen ihrer großen Bedeutung für die Praxis stehen bei der Verfolgung des Ökonomischen Prinzips folgende Erfolgsziele im Vordergrund:

- Produktivität (mengenmäßiges Verhältnis zwischen Output und Input des Produktionsprozesses),
- Wirtschaftlichkeit (Wertverhältnis von Ertrag zu Aufwand),
- Gewinn (Differenz zwischen Ertrag und Aufwand),
- Rentabilität (Relation zwischen Gewinn und dem zur Erwirtschaftung des Gewinns eingesetzten Kapital).

Sachziele beziehen sich auf das konkrete Handeln bei der Ausübung der verschiedenen betrieblichen Funktionen. Geht man bei der Zielformulierung vom güter- und finanzwirtschaftlichen Umsatzprozess aus, so können vier Bereiche von Sachzielen unterschieden werden:

- Leistungsziele (im Vordergrund stehen Markt- und Produktziele, die aus den Bedürfnissen abgeleitet werden, welche das Unternehmen befriedigen will),
- Finanzziele (z.B. Kapital, Liquidität),
- Führungs- und Organisationsziele (z.B. Führungsstil, Arbeitsteilung),
- soziale und ökologische Ziele (mitarbeiterbezogene und gesellschaftsbezogene Ziele).

Für eine operationale Zielformulierung sind neben dem Zielinhalt weitere Zieldimensionen zu beachten (Nufer, 2007; Berndt, 2005):

- *Angestrebtes Ausmaß*: Es lassen sich die Extremierung von Zielgrößen (Maximierung oder Minimierung), das Anstreben eines festen Wertes (Fixierung) sowie das Ansteuern eines zufrieden stellenden Mindestwertes (Satisfizierung) unterscheiden.

- *Zeitlicher Bezug*: Hier wird zwischen kurzfristigen Zielen (Zeitraum bis zu einem Jahr), mittelfristigen Zielen (Zeitraum ein bis fünf Jahre) und langfristigen Zielen (Zeitraum über fünf Jahre) differenziert.
- *Organisatorischer Bezug*: Es sind Unternehmensziele (beziehen sich auf das Unternehmen als Ganzes, z.b. Wachstum), Bereichsziele (beziehen sich nur auf bestimmte Teilbereiche des Unternehmens, z.B. Kapazitätsauslastung in der Produktion) und Mitarbeiterziele (Ziele, die dem einzelnen Mitarbeiter vorgegeben oder gemeinsam mit ihm erarbeitet werden, z.B. Umsatzziele im Außendienst) voneinander abzugrenzen.

3.4.2 Zielbeziehungen

Die Menge gleichzeitig verfolgter Ziele bildet das Zielsystem. Schon zwischen zwei parallel verfolgten Zielen können drei verschiedene Zielbeziehungen bestehen: Komplementarität, Konkurrenz und Indifferenz (Thommen/Achleitner, 2006; Nufer/Bühler, 2006):

- Eine Zielbeziehung ist *komplementär*, wenn durch die Erreichung des einen Zieles gleichzeitig die Erfüllung des anderen Zieles gesteigert wird.
- Führt hingegen die Erfüllung des einen Ziels zu einer Minderung des Zielerreichungsgrades des zweiten Zieles, so spricht man von einer *konkurrierenden* (oder *konfliktären*) Zielbeziehung.
- Beeinflussen sich die beiden Ziele gegenseitig nicht, so liegt eine *indifferente* (oder *neutrale*) Zielbeziehung vor.

Besteht zwischen zwei Zielen eine Konkurrenz, so ist eine Gewichtung der beiden Ziele notwendig. In diese Gewichtung fließen die Wertvorstellungen und Ansprüche des Entscheidungsträgers ein. Der Entscheidungsträger schafft durch seine Präferenzen *Haupt- und Nebenziele*.

Voraussetzung für die Unterscheidung in *Ober-, Zwischen- und Unterziele* ist eine Komplementarität zwischen den Zielen. Diese Unterscheidung beruht auf einer Zielhierarchie, bei der Mittel-Zweck-Beziehungen zwischen den verschiedenen Zielen bestehen. Oft ist es so, das ein Unterziel (z.B. Lärmschutz für den Mitarbeiter) ein Mittel zum Zweck, d.h. zur Erfüllung eines Oberziels (in diesem Fall die Gesundheit der Mitarbeiter) darstellt. Die Aufteilung in Mittel-Zweck-Beziehungen hat somit eine große praktische Bedeutung, weil Oberziele häufig nicht operational sind und keine konkrete Zielvorgabe beinhalten. Daher ist es nötig, die Oberziele so lange in Zwischen- und Unterziele zu untergliedern, bis eine Zielvorgabe entsteht, an der sich der Mitarbeiter orientieren und seine Arbeit ausrichten kann.

Ein Sportanbieter hat die Aufgabe, seine unterschiedlichen Zielvorgaben zu bestimmen. Daraus kann folgen, dass seine Arbeit u.U. unterschiedlichen Rationalitäten unterworfen ist, denen er nicht gleichermaßen gerecht werden kann. Gesellschaftsorientierung und ökonomische Orientierung können sich widersprechen, v.a. wenn die ökonomische Orientierung auf Gewinnmaximierung ausgerichtet ist. Andere Zielorientierungen können sich gegenseitig unterstützen, beispielsweise wenn die Mitgliederorientierung und die Sachorientierung dieselbe Priorität besitzen (Heinemann, 1995).

3.5 Konstitutive Unternehmensentscheidungen

Konstitutive Entscheidungen sind die grundlegenden Entscheidungen im Leben einer Unternehmung, die den grundlegenden Handlungsrahmen – meist auf längere Sicht – festlegen (Bea, 2004).

Zu den wichtigsten konstitutiven Unternehmensentscheidungen – sowohl in der klassischen Betriebswirtschaftslehre als auch im Sportmanagement – gehören (Vahs/Schäfer-Kunz, 2007; Thommen/Achleitner, 2006; Bea, 2004):

- die Unternehmensgründung,
- die Standortwahl,
- die Rechtsformwahl und
- Entscheidungen über Unternehmenszusammenschlüsse.

3.5.1 Unternehmensgründung

Ein Unternehmen entsteht mit seiner *Gründung*. Der Unternehmensgründer steht dabei einer Vielzahl unbekannter Variablen gegenüber. Zu entscheiden ist über die Gesamtheit jener Maßnahmen, die im Zusammenhang mit der Errichtung des neuen Unternehmens ergriffen werden müssen. Zum eigentlichen Gründungsprozess werden auch die *Planungen im Vorfeld* (z.B. Erstellen eines Business-Plans) gezählt. Zu den *Einzelmaßnahmen* gehören die Wahl des zu adressierenden Zielmarktes (Kesting/Rennhak, 2008) und davon abhängig die Wahl des anzubietenden Produkts bzw. der anzubietenden Dienstleistung, die Ermittlung des Kapitalbedarfs und die Kapitalbeschaffung, die Wahl des Unternehmensstandorts, die Wahl der Rechtsform bis hin zur Entscheidung über das anzuwendende Führungsmodell (Witte, 2007). Erschwerend wirkt der Umstand, dass der Informationsstand bei der Gründung im Vergleich zu den anderen konstitutiven Entscheidungen i.d.R. am geringsten ist. Insbesondere die Unsicherheit bezüglich der Unternehmensentwicklung fällt hier ins Gewicht. Zudem sind die Informationsbeschaffungsmöglichkeiten bei Neugründungen – v.a. bei kleinen Unternehmen und Sportorganisationen – beschränkt und aufgrund finanzieller Restriktionen nur schwer zu erweitern.

3.5.2 Standortwahl

Der *Standort* des Unternehmens ist der geografische Ort, an dem Produktionsfaktoren eingesetzt werden, um Leistungen zu erstellen. Gerade in der Gründungsphase von Sportorganisationen wird er eher selten aufgrund betriebswirtschaftlicher, sondern häufiger aus pragmatischen Überlegungen heraus festgelegt. Betriebswirtschaftliche Überlegungen dominieren jedoch in der klassischen Betriebswirtschaftslehre, insbesondere wenn Unternehmen expandieren und auf der Suche nach zusätzlichen Standorten sind. Allgemein ist die Standortwahl von einer Reihe von *Faktoren* abhängig (vgl. Tab. 2).

1. Arbeitsbezogene Standortfaktoren:
▪ Zahl der Arbeitskräfte
▪ Kosten der Arbeitskräfte
▪ Qualifikation der Arbeitskräfte
2. Materialbezogene Standortfaktoren:
▪ Transportkosten
▪ Zuliefersicherheit
▪ Art des Produkts
3. Absatzbezogene Standortfaktoren:
▪ Kundennähe
▪ Vorhandene oder zukünftige Konkurrenz
▪ Transportfähigkeit der Produkte
▪ Potenzielle Nachfrage
▪ Frist zwischen Auftreten des Bedarfs und der angestrebten Versorgung des Kunden
4. Verkehrsbezogene Standortfaktoren:
▪ Verkehrsinfrastruktur
▪ Transportzeit
▪ Verkehrsmittel
5. Immobilienbezogene Standortfaktoren:
▪ Preise für Immobilien und Land
▪ Mietpreise
6. Umweltbezogene Standortfaktoren:
▪ Imagegründe
▪ Gesetzliche Vorschriften
7. Abgabenbezogene Standortfaktoren:
▪ National: Gewerbesteuerbelastung
▪ International: Steuersysteme
8. Clusterbildung:
▪ Zusammenspiel von Know-how-Trägern
9. Rechtliche und politische Standortfaktoren:
▪ Politische Stabilität
▪ Rechtssicherheit
▪ Wechselkursschwankungen

Tab. 2: Gliederung wesentlicher Standortfaktoren
Quelle: Thommen/Achleitner (2006) , S. 99 ff.

Die zunehmende Globalisierung reduziert die Bedeutung der räumlichen Nähe von administrativer Unternehmenszentrale, Fertigungsstandort und Absatzmarkt. Welche Bedeutung den jeweiligen Faktoren im Einzelnen zukommt, ist wiederum industriespezifisch verschieden. Dadurch werden Standortentscheidungen in der Praxis zu hochkomplexen Fragestellungen, die sich i.d.R. nicht mehr durch mathematische Optimierungsverfahren lösen lassen. Erschwerend wirkt zudem die wachsende Bedeutung qualitativer Kriterien, die nur schwer modellierbar sind. In der Unternehmenspraxis wird aus diesen Gründen die Suche nach einem optimalen Standort i.d.R. durch vereinfachende Auswahlverfahren ersetzt. So ist häufig ein stufenweises Vorgehen anzutreffen, das zunächst z.B. eine Länderauswahl, dann eine Grobplanung bis hin zu einer detaillierten Feinplanung und schließlich die Festlegung auf eine Gewerbefläche oder eine bestimmte Immobilie beinhaltet (Schneck, 2005). Die Entscheidungen auf den jeweiligen Ebenen werden häufig anhand von Scoring-Modellen vorgenommen (Nufer, 2007).

3.5.3 Rechtsformwahl

Die *Rechtsform* legt die gesetzlichen Rahmenbedingungen fest, innerhalb derer ein (Sport-)Unternehmen wirtschaftlich tätig werden kann. Sie bestimmt, ob das Unternehmen eine eigene Rechtspersönlichkeit besitzt oder seine Gesellschafter als natürliche Personen handeln. Sie hat unmittelbare Auswirkungen auf die Haftung der Gesellschafter – so muss bei Personengesellschaften mindestens ein Gesellschafter auch mit seinem Privatvermögen für die Verbindlichkeiten des Unternehmens haften, während die Haftung bei Kapitalgesellschaften i.d.R. auf die Einlage der Gesellschafter beschränkt ist – und deren Recht zur Geschäftsführung. Je nach Rechtsform bestehen zudem unterschiedliche Anforderungen bei Gründung, Betrieb und Liquidation des Unternehmens. Insbesondere existieren spezifische Regelungen in Bezug auf Grundkapital, Anzahl und Pflichten der Gesellschafterinnen und Gesellschafter sowie Publizitätspflichten.

Abb. 2 gibt einen Überblick über die wichtigsten *Rechtsformen* des *privaten und öffentlichen Rechts*.

3.5.4 Unternehmenszusammenschlüsse

Eine weitere wichtige Art konstitutiver Unternehmensentscheidungen sind die mit möglichen *Unternehmenszusammenschlüssen* verbundenen Entscheidungen.

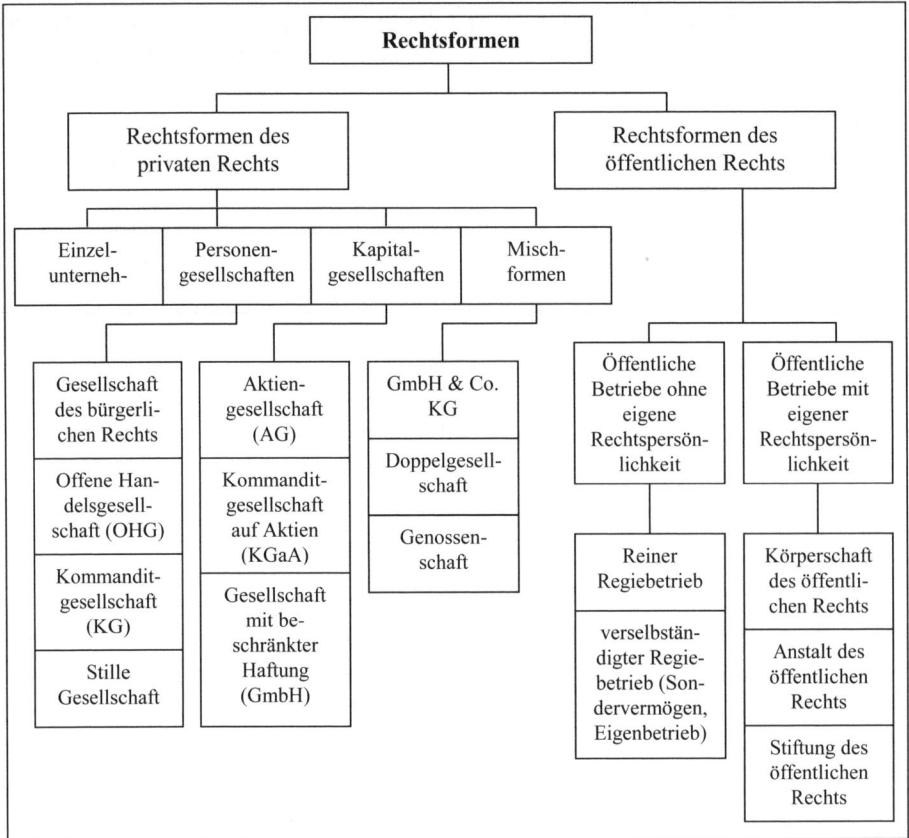

Abb. 2: Systematisierung wesentlicher Rechtsformen
In Anlehnung an: Bea (2004), S. 364

Nach dem *Grad der Bindungsintensität* ist ein Unternehmenszusammenschluss entweder eine enge Zusammenarbeit (z.B. in Form einer Kooperation oder Partnerschaft) oder eine Vereinigung (z.B. in Form einer Fusion bzw. Akquisition) mehrerer unabhängiger Unternehmen. Im Rahmen einer Zusammenarbeit bleiben die Unternehmen i.d.R. rechtlich selbständig, während sie sich bei einer Vereinigung auch rechtlich zu einer neuen Wirtschaftseinheit verbinden. Unternehmenszusammenschlüsse werden v.a. durchgeführt, weil sich die beteiligten Unternehmen hiervon ökonomische Vorteile wie z.B. erhöhte Wachstumschancen, Erhöhung der Wirtschaftlichkeit durch Synergieeffekte oder eine Minderung des Risikos erwarten. Eine Kooperation bezeichnet im Allgemeinen die mittel- bis langfristige Zusammenarbeit durch Abstimmung von Funktionen (oder deren abgestimmte Ausgliederung in gemeinschaftliche Unternehmen, z.B. in Form von Joint Ventures) zwischen rechtlich selbständig verbleibenden Unternehmen, z.B. zur Durchführung von Großprojekten oder zur Durchsetzung von gemeinsamen Interessen gegenüber

Dritten (z.B. in Form einer strategischen Allianz). Handelt es sich bei den kooperierenden Unternehmen um Wettbewerber, spricht man häufig auch von Koopetition (in diesen Fällen kommt es bisweilen zu regulatorischen Eingriffen zur Vermeidung unzulässiger Wettbewerbsbeschränkungen). In den nicht dem Kooperationsvertrag unterworfenen Bereichen bewahren die Kooperationspartner neben ihrer rechtlichen auch ihre ökonomische Selbständigkeit (Witte, 2007).

Nach der *Richtung des Zusammenschlusses* lassen sich horizontale, vertikale und konglomerate Unternehmenszusammenschlüsse unterscheiden. Bei horizontalen Zusammenschlüssen findet eine Integration auf derselben Wertschöpfungsstufe statt (z.B. zwei Sportartikelhersteller schließen sich zusammen). Bei vertikalen Zusammenschlüssen erfolgt eine Integration mit vor- oder nachgelagerten Stufen (z.B. eine Restaurantkette erwirbt einen Sporternährungsproduzenten = Rückwärtsintegration; im umgekehrten Fall liegt eine Vorwärtsintegration vor). Handelt es sich weder um einen horizontalen noch um einen vertikalen Unternehmenszusammenschluss, etwa beim Erwerb einer Sport-Event-Agentur durch eine Bank, so spricht man von einem konglomeraten (lateralen, diagonalen) Zusammenschluss (Bea, 2004; Wöhe/Döring, 2005).

3.6 Führungsmodelle

Führungsmodelle beinhalten instrumentale Aussagen über die Struktur und Funktion zielorientierter Gestaltungsprozesse und beschreiben die Führung von Unternehmen und Mitarbeitern im operativen Betrieb eines Unternehmens (Bea, 2005).

Im Folgenden sollen unterschiedliche Führungsmodelle vorgestellt werden, die in der Betriebswirtschaftslehre entwickelt wurden und auch in Sportorganisationen angewandt werden können. Während Partialmodelle nur Teilaspekte der Führung berücksichtigen, erfassen Totalmodelle alle möglichen Gestaltungsparameter der Führung (Staehle, 1999; Schneck, 2005).

Die systematische Umsetzung eines Führungsmodells soll im Unternehmen wie in Sportorganisationen ein konsistentes Führungsverhalten etablieren. Die Art der Unternehmens- und Mitarbeiterführung hat direkte Implikationen für die Produktivität einerseits und die Zufriedenheit und Motivation der Mitarbeiter andererseits. Die Wahl des optimalen Führungsmodells ist abhängig von der Größe des zu führenden Unternehmens und seiner spezifischen Situation – wie so häufig in der Betriebswirtschaftslehre ist auch hier keine allgemeingültige Pauschalaussage möglich. Jedes Führungsmodell weist spezifische Vor- und Nachteile auf, es ist also individuell für jede Sportorganisation in Bezug auf seine Entwicklungsphase, seine Historie oder die besonderen Anforderungen der jeweiligen Unternehmensumwelt zu prüfen, welches Führungsmodell anzuwenden ist.

3.6.1 Partialmodelle

(1) Management by Exception (Führung durch Eingriffe in Ausnahmefällen):
Mitarbeiter können solange selbständig entscheiden, bis vorgeschriebene Toleranz-grenzen überschritten werden oder unvorhersehbare Ereignisse eintreten. Die Füh-rungsinstanz legt Ziele und Richtlinien für die Einschätzung von Normal- und Aus-nahmefällen fest. Für Normalfälle erhält der Mitarbeiter Entscheidungskompetenz und -verantwortung.

(2) Management by Delegation (Führung durch Aufgabenübertragung):
Es erfolgt eine Delegation auf untergeordnete Hierarchieebenen. Dieses Führungs-modell erwächst beinahe zwangsläufig aus der zunehmenden Arbeitsteilung und der Größe von Unternehmen. Eine konkrete Ausgestaltung erfährt dieser Ansatz erst durch Management by Decision Rules und Management by Results.

(2a) Management by Decision Rules (Führung durch Vorgabe von Entscheidungs-regeln):
Kombiniert den Grundgedanken positiver Anreize durch Delegation mit der Vor-stellung, Mitarbeiter durch präzise Regeln steuern zu müssen. Die delegierten Auf-gaben sind nicht selbständig zu bewältigen, sondern müssen von den betroffenen Mitarbeitern im Rahmen einer genauen Regelvorgabe erfüllt werden.

(2b) Management by Results (Führung durch Ergebnisüberwachung):
Hierbei handelt es sich um eine ergebnisorientierte Unternehmensführung, die dem Mitarbeiter klare Leistungsergebnisse vorgibt. Die Vorgaben werden dabei von der Unternehmensführung festgelegt und überwacht.

3.6.2 Totalmodelle

(1) Management by Objectives (Führung durch Zielvereinbarung):
Führungsinstanz und Mitarbeiter legen gemeinsam Ziele fest. Die Ziele werden da-bei periodisch neu festgelegt, um Situationsänderungen zu berücksichtigen. Der Mitarbeiter erhält einen Ermessensspielraum bezüglich des Weges der Zielerrei-chung. Die Führungstätigkeit beschränkt sich auf die Zielvereinbarung mit den Mitarbeitern und die Kontrolle der Ziele.

(2) Harzburger Führungsmodell (Führung im Mitarbeiterverhältnis):
Basiert auf dem Grundgedanken, dass sich die Motivation der Mitarbeiterinnen und Mitarbeiter durch die Delegation von Verantwortlichkeiten und die Definition von eigenständigen Aufgabengebieten wesentlich verbessern lässt. Jeder Mitarbeiter er-hält ein festumgrenztes Aufgabengebiet, für das er die volle Verantwortung trägt; der Vorgesetzte darf in den jeweiligen Aufgabenbereich nicht eingreifen. Kernbe-

standteil dieses Ansatzes sind Kodizes in Form von Führungsregularien und
-anweisungen sowie detaillierte Stellenbeschreibungen.

(3) St. Gallener Führungsmodell (Systemansatz):
Versucht Aspekte der Führung in einem systemtheoretischen Ansatz zu integrieren.
Ein System ist eine geordnete Gesamtheit von Elementen, zwischen denen Beziehungen bestehen oder hergestellt werden können. Ein Unternehmen wird als soziotechnisches System mit Umsystemen verstanden. Das Modell leistet damit eine
Sensibilisierung für Probleme, die sich aus Veränderungen der Unternehmensumwelt ergeben.

(4) Gruppenkonzept von Likert (integrierte Gruppenentscheidungen):
Das Gruppenkonzept von Likert (1961) fokussiert auf die Doppelrolle von Managern als Vorgesetzte einerseits und Gruppenmitglieder andererseits. Abgesehen von
den Personen auf der obersten und untersten Hierarchieebene ist jeder Mitarbeiter
Mitglied zweier Gruppen („linking pin"). Netzwerke sich überlappender Gruppen
stellen kommunikativ die Integration im Unternehmen sicher. Entscheidungen werden grundsätzlich in der Gruppe getroffen und sollen soweit nach unten verlagert
werden, dass gerade noch der nötige Sachverstand in der Gruppe vorhanden ist, um
die Entscheidung treffen zu können (Prinzip der Subsidiarität).

3.7 Nachbardisziplinen des Sportmanagements
Die komplexen Strukturen in heutigen Sportorganisationen verlangen zunehmend
professionelles Engagement und den Rückgriff auf die Erkenntnisse angrenzender
Disziplinen, um eine optimale Gestaltung des Managementzyklus sicherzustellen.
Die Sportökonomik, die Sportsoziologie, die Sportpsychologie und das Sportrecht
stehen dabei in einem gleichberechtigten Verhältnis zueinander (Breuer/Thiel,
2005).

3.7.1 Sportsoziologie
Die Soziologie beschäftigt sich allgemein mit den Wechselwirkungen von Individuum und Gesellschaft. Spezieller Gegenstand der Sportsoziologie ist diese Wechselbeziehung im Bereich des Sports, d.h. Prozesse sozialer Wechselbeziehungen
und -wirkungen zwischen im Sport handelnden Menschen und Gruppen untereinander und in Bezug auf das Sozialsystem Sport. Hinzu kommen die Wechselbeziehungen und -wirkungen innerhalb der sich fortlaufend wandelnden gesamtgesellschaftlichen Rahmenbedingungen. Hier interessiert die soziale Eigenwelt des
Sports genauso wie seine Vergesellschaftung (Rigauer, 1969; Elias/Dumning,
1986).

> *„Sportsoziologie* ist die Wissenschaft, die sich mit der Erforschung sozialen Handelns im Sport sowie den sozialen Wechselwirkungen, in denen Sport relevant ist, befasst" Weiß (1999, S. 23).

Sport kann – wie die Geschichte zeigt – nicht losgelöst von seinem sozialen Hintergrund betrachtet werden. Die Sportsoziologie erklärt, inwiefern sich gesellschaftliche Veränderungen im Sport widerspiegeln: Der Sport ist dabei kein isoliertes Phänomen, sondern ist immer in einen soziokulturellen Rahmen und einen Kommunikationskontext eingebettet (Vassort, 2006). Neben dem sozialen Handeln beschäftigt sich die Sportsoziologie mit den sozialen Strukturen im Sport und untersucht die Wechselbeziehungen zwischen Sport und anderen gesellschaftlichen Handlungsfeldern.

Der Sport verfügt als soziale Institution über eine relative Eigenständigkeit, da er Strukturen aufweist, die ihn von anderen Institutionen deutlich unterscheidet. Es ist nicht zu übersehen, dass der Sport mit anderen gesellschaftlichen Bereichen in einem Verhältnis intensiver Wechselwirkungen und partieller Abhängigkeiten steht. Gesellschaftliche Institutionen wie Schule, Familie, Wirtschaft, Politik oder Recht wirken auf den Sport ein und die Institution Sport beeinflusst diese Bereiche.

3.7.2 Sportpsychologie

Die Sportpsychologie versucht, menschliches Verhalten, Handeln und Erleben von Personen im Praxisfeld Sport zu erfassen. Wichtige Teilbereiche der Sportpsychologie sind Entwicklungs-, Motivations-, Lern- und Sozialpsychologie. Zweck ist die Anwendung sportpsychologischer Methoden und Praktiken in den Praxisfeldern des Sports.

Praktiker im Bereich der Sportpsychologie vertreten häufig die Meinung, dass sich ihr Fachgebiet v.a. deshalb entwickelt hat, weil im Spitzensportbereich nach neuen Wegen der Optimierung der sportlichen Leistung gesucht wird und Sportmedizin und Trainingswissenschaften hierbei an natürliche Grenzen stoßen. Aufgabe der Sportpsychologie im engeren Sinn ist, auf der Basis von Erkenntnissen der allgemeinen Psychologie und eigener Forschung die potentielle Leistungsfähigkeit und die situative Leistungsbereitschaft der Spitzensportlerinnen und Spitzensportler optimal zu entwickeln, um im Wettkampf die maximale sportliche Leistung zu realisieren.

> Für die Zwecke des vorliegenden Bandes ist eine weiter gefasste Definition von *Sportpsychologie* zielführend. Diese zielt im Sinne des Sportmanagements auf die Berücksichtigung psychologischer Erkenntnisse in der Organisationspsychologie zur optimalen Gestaltung des Managementzyklus ab.

Die Organisationspsychologie befasst sich mit der Wechselwirkung von Individuum und Organisation und deckt die Beschreibung und Veränderung von Erleben, Verhalten und Einstellungen von Menschen in Organisationen sowie der Bedingungen, die diese Zustände und Veränderungen beeinflussen, ab (von Rosenstiel, 2003).

3.7.3 Sportrecht

Aufgrund der mannigfachen Berührungspunkte der Welt des Sports mit der des Rechts gibt es keinen eng abgrenzbaren Bereich des Sportrechts. Der Sport kann als Bündel von Verfügungsrechten betrachtet werden. Verfügungsrechte (oder „property rights") meinen alle an Sachen gebundene, sozial anerkannte Handlungsrechte (Neus, 2005). Sie legen die Nutzungs- und Verwendungsmöglichkeiten fest. Sie entstehen aufgrund von Konvention, Tradition, staatlichem Recht oder privatrechtlicher Verträge. Sie setzen sich aus Zugangs- und Nutzungsrechten (öffentliche Güter, Clubgüter, Marktgüter), Rechten auf Erträge, Rechten auf Übertragung und Partizipationsrechten zusammen. Verfügungsrechte können räumlich, zeitlich oder sachlich beschränkt werden.

I.d.R. wird der Begriff des Sportrechts in zwei Bedeutungsweisen verwendet:

- Einerseits bezeichnet er den Teil der *staatlichen Rechtsordnung*, der sportliche Sachverhalte zum Gegenstand hat und reguliert. Hier spielen verschiedene rechtliche Fachgebiete eine Rolle. Im Bereich des öffentlichen Rechts könnte man hier z.B. das Sportförderungsrecht, das Baurecht oder das (Vereins-) Steuerrecht anführen. Im Bereich des Zivilrechts sind u.a. das Vertrags- oder das Vereins- und Verbandsrecht zu nennen.
- Andererseits ist Sportrecht in Deutschland das *von den Verbänden und Vereinen autonom gesetzte Recht des Sports*. Es findet sich in Satzungen, Statuten und sonstigen Regelwerken der Sportvereine und -verbände. Hier werden die Rechte und Pflichten der Mitglieder und die vereins- bzw. verbandsmäßige Sportausübung geregelt.

Die Problematik besteht darin, dass das Verbandsrecht und die Entscheidungen von Verbandsorganen nicht außerhalb der staatlichen Rechtsordnung stehen. Vor der Ökonomisierung des Sports konnte die staatliche Rechtsordnung dem Sport eine gewisse Autonomie zugestehen: Verbandsrecht und Entscheidungen von Verbandsorganen griffen i.d.R. nicht in die Rechtspositionen der Sportlerinnen und Sportler ein. Heute hingegen sind deren Persönlichkeits- und Vermögensrechte regelmäßig von Verbandsrecht und Entscheidungen von Verbandsorganen betroffen, so dass die staatliche Rechtsordnung den Sportlerinnen und Sportlern Rechtsschutz gewähren muss.

Die staatliche Rechtsordnung muss zunehmend Besonderheiten des Sports im Allgemeinen sowie Spezifika einzelner Sportarten im Besonderen berücksichtigen. Sportler haben im Zuge der zunehmenden Professionalisierung des Sports auch ein immer stärker wirtschaftlich geprägtes Interesse daran, ihren Sport verbandsmäßig zu betreiben. Der Staat gewährt dem Sport deshalb das Recht, seine Angelegenheiten selbst zu regeln. So werden von der staatlichen Rechtsordnung z.B. typische Körperverletzungen hingenommen und führen nicht zu Schadensersatzansprüchen. Das gleiche gilt beispielsweise für (zeitweise) Sperren von Sportlern aufgrund von Verstößen gegen Verbandsregeln, was rechtlich i.d.R. auch einen Eingriff in Vermögenspositionen darstellt.

3.8 Aktuelle Entwicklungen innerhalb der Betriebswirtschaftslehre

Gegenwärtig ist die Betriebswirtschaftslehre u.a. von einer zunehmenden Mathematisierung und Betonung der empirischen Forschung geprägt (Weigand/Stadtmann, 2005, Homburg, 2000). Exemplarisch sollen in den folgenden Abschnitten zwei aktuelle Forschungsfelder innerhalb der Betriebswirtschaftslehre vorgestellt werden, die zudem interagieren: die Institutionenökonomik und die Spieltheorie. Gerade Arbeiten auf diesen Forschungsgebieten wurden in den letzten Jahren mehrfach mit Ökonomie-Nobelpreisen ausgezeichnet.

3.8.1 Institutionenökonomik

Innerhalb der Betriebswirtschaftslehre gewinnt die Sichtweise der Institutionenökonomik verstärkt an Bedeutung. Die Orientierung an einzelnen Menschen und deren Interesse an ihrem individuellen Einkommen, die Unvollkommenheit von Märkten und die asymmetrische Informationsverteilung zwischen den Akteuren sind die *konstituierenden Merkmale* der Institutionenökonomik. Abweichend von der bereits skizzierten klassischen Perspektive der Betriebswirtschaftslehre ist der Erfahrungsgegenstand in der Institutionenökonomik das einzelne *Individuum*, der Erkenntnisgegenstand dessen Bemühen um *Einkommenserzielung* (Neus, 2005; Axelrod, 2003).

Individuen sind bestrebt, ihre Bedürfnisse bestmöglich zu befriedigen, d.h. ihren Einkommensstrom zu optimieren. Eine Kooperation mit anderen Individuen ermöglicht eine Nutzensteigerung bei den Beteiligten. Allerdings entsteht durch Kooperation auch die Notwendigkeit der Koordination der Entscheidungen mehrerer Personen. Die Interessen der Beteiligten können dabei sowohl übereinstimmen (z.B. das Gelingen von gemeinsamen Projekten, Gewinnsteigerung) als auch divergieren (z.B. die Aufteilung des gemeinsam erwirtschafteten Einkommensstromes oder die Aufbringung der für den Erfolg erforderlichen Einsatzgüter). Nutzensteigerungen durch Kooperationen sind also stets von der Gefahr des Scheiterns bedroht, denn das Verfolgen eigener Interessen in einer Partnerschaft verringert häufig den möglichen Gesamterfolg. Der *Hauptgegenstand* der Institutionenökonomik ist somit die Suche nach vertraglichen, institutionellen oder auch gesetzlichen Regelungen zur Sicherung möglicher, aber gefährdeter gemeinsamer Kooperationsvorteile.

3.8.2 Spieltheorie

Die *Entscheidungstheorie* wird als Teildisziplin der angewandten Stochastik bereits in vielfältiger Weise in der Betriebswirtschaftslehre als Instrument benutzt (Bamberg/Coenenberg, 2006). Sieht sich der Entscheider einem rational handelnden Gegenspieler (beispielsweise einem Mitbewerber oder einem Verhandlungspartner) gegenüber, kommen zur Bestimmung der optimalen Handlungsoption Methoden der *Spieltheorie* zum Einsatz. Die Spieltheorie versucht, das rationale Entscheidungsverhalten in sozialen Konfliktsituationen abzuleiten. Im Unterschied zur Entscheidungstheorie beschreibt die Spieltheorie Entscheidungssituationen, in denen der Erfolg des Einzelnen nicht nur vom eigenen Handeln, sondern auch von den Aktionen anderer abhängt (Rieck, 2007). Die Ursprünge der Spieltheorie sind nicht neu (Neumann/von Morgenstern, 1944), finden gegenwärtig in der betriebswirtschaftlichen Forschung jedoch verstärkt Anwendung.

Ein bekanntes Paradoxon, das zentraler Bestandteil der Spieltheorie ist und im Folgenden exemplarisch präsentiert werden soll, ist das *Gefangenendilemma*. Es handelt sich hierbei um eine Konstellation, in der es bei Möglichkeit einer bindenden Absprache zwischen Kooperationsparteien möglich wäre, eine für alle Seiten akzeptable Lösung zu finden. Zugleich ist es für die Parteien jedoch nicht möglich, eine solche bindende Absprache zu treffen. Das Zweipersonenspiel zeigt, wie individuell rationale Entscheidungen zu kollektiv schlechteren Ergebnissen führen können (Neus, 2005).

Zwei Gefangene werden verdächtigt, gemeinsam eine Straftat begangen zu haben. Die Höchststrafe für das Verbrechen beträgt fünf Jahre. Beiden Gefangenen wird nun ein Handel angeboten, worüber auch beide informiert sind. Wenn nur einer gesteht, kommt er ohne Strafe davon – der andere, der schweigt, muss die vollen fünf Jahre absitzen. Entscheiden sich beide zu schweigen, bleiben nur Indizienbeweise, die aber ausreichen, um beide für zwei Jahre einzusperren. Gestehen aber beide die Tat, erwartet jeden eine Gefängnisstrafe von vier Jahren. Die Gefangenen werden unabhängig voneinander befragt. Weder vor noch während der Befragung haben die beiden die Möglichkeit, sich untereinander abzusprechen. Das Strafmaß eines Spielers hängt somit nicht nur von der eigenen, sondern auch von der Entscheidung des Komplizen ab.

Individuell scheint es für beide vorteilhafter zu sein, auszusagen; dies hängt nicht vom Verhalten des anderen ab, es ist anscheinend immer vorteilhafter zu gestehen. Würden beide Gefangene schweigen, müsste jeder zwei Jahre ins Gefängnis; der Verlust für beide zusammen beträgt so vier Jahre und jede andere Kombination aus Gestehen und Schweigen führt zu einem höheren Verlust.

Die Spielanlage provoziert also einen einseitigen Verrat, durch den der Verräter das für ihn individuell bessere Resultat Freispruch (falls der Mitgefangene schweigt) oder vier statt fünf Jahre (falls der Mitgefangene gesteht) zu erreichen hofft. Versuchen dies aber beide Gefangenen, so verschlimmern sie – auch individuell – ihre Lage, da sie nun je vier Jahre (wenn beide aussagen) statt je zwei Jahre (im Falle, dass beide schweigen) Gefängnis erhalten. In diesem Auseinanderfallen der möglichen Strategien besteht das Dilemma der Gefangenen. Die vermeintlich rationale, schrittweise Analyse der Situation verleitet beide Gefangenen individuell dazu zu gestehen, was zu einem schlechteren Gesamtresultat für beide führt (suboptimale Allokation).

3.9 Fallstudie

Die folgende Fallstudie zeigt am Beispiel der National Football League (NFL) und hier insbesondere in Bezug auf die Detroit Lions, eines der 32 Teams der NFL, inwieweit sich das Sportmanagement bereits der Methoden der modernen Betriebswirtschaftslehre bedient.

Fallstudie „National Football League – Detroit Lions"

American Football hat sich – obwohl als College Sportart schon lange erfolgreich – als professionelle Sportart erst relativ spät etabliert. Vorläufer der heutigen National Football League war die 1920 gegründete American Professional Football Association. Die Umbenennung in National Football League erfolgte 1922. 1933 wurde die Liga in zwei Divisionen unterteilt; nachfolgend wurde die jährliche Meisterschaft in einem Endspiel zwischen den beiden Divisionssiegern entschieden. Eine weitere wichtige Entscheidung war die Einführung des *Draft-Systems* im Jahr 1936. Der Draft ist eine Absprache zwischen den Teams, die Rekrutierung der besten Nachwuchsspieler gemeinsam in einem abgestimmten Verfahren durchzuführen. Dieses Verfahren führt zum einen dazu, dass sich die Spielstärke der Teams schrittweise nivelliert (da das schwächste Team den First Pick erhält, d.h. den besten Nachwuchsspieler aussuchen darf) und sich die Teams nicht bei den Gehaltsangeboten an die Spieler gegenseitig überbieten. Die Teams bilden aus wirtschaftswissenschaftlicher Sicht somit ein Nachfragekartell. Ähnlich kooperativ agierten die Teams auch bei der Einführung der *Salary Cap* (Gehalts-obergrenze) zur Saison 1994/1995, die für die Saison 2006/2007 je Team ca. 102 Millionen US-$ betrug. Als Gehaltsuntergrenze wurden 75% der Salary Cap fest-gelegt. Die Salary Caps werden in kollektiven Verhandlungen zwischen Spieler-gewerkschaft und Ligavertretern als Collective Bargaining Agreement ausgehan-delt. Dies führte in den vergangenen Jahren bisweilen zu Streiks und Aussperrungen (Lockouts).

Mit der Verbreitung des Fernsehens in den fünfziger Jahren wurde Profi-Football erstmalig so populär wie College-Football und Profi-Baseball, das auf-grund seiner deutlich längeren Saison und der viel kleineren Teamgröße schon deutlich früher professionalisiert werden konnte. Jetzt wurde auch ein Football-Spielbetrieb in weniger bevölkerungsreichen Städten möglich. Die zunehmende Professionalisierung führte u.a. dazu, dass mittlerweile alle Teams einem Besitzer gehören – nur ein Team wird noch als Verein geführt: die Green Bay Packers.

Die Team-Besitzer wollten jedoch keinen zusätzlichen Wettbewerb durch et-waige Neugründungen von Mannschaften zulassen. Mit Unterstützung des Fern-sehsenders ABC gründete sich daraufhin eine eigene Liga, die American Football League, die rasch zu einer ernsthaften Konkurrenz zur etablierten National Foot-ball League wurde. Der Wettbewerb um Fans, Fernsehgelder und Spieler zwang die beiden Ligen schließlich in eine Kooperation. Zur Ermittlung des jährlichen Meisters wurde – ähnlich wie bereits in den dreißiger Jahren – ein Endspiel zwi-schen den Siegern der jeweiligen Ligen vereinbart. Dieses Endspiel wurde als Super Bowl zu einem der wichtigsten Sportereignisse der Welt – die Super Bowl-Übertragung hat die höchste Einschaltquote im US-Fernsehen überhaupt.

Wirtschaftlich ist die National Football League so erfolgreich wie nie zuvor: Der jährliche Gesamtumsatz beläuft sich auf etwa sechs Milliarden US-$. Die Fernsehrechte gehören zu den teuersten der Welt – aktuell erlöst die National Football League in den USA hier pro Saison 3,7 Milliarden US-$. In der Saison 2006/07 besuchten durchschnittlich fast 70.000 Zuschauer die Spiele – bei Ti-cketpreisen von durchschnittlich etwa 60 US-$ (zum Vergleich: die Fußball-Bundesliga hatte 2006/07 einen Schnitt von rund 38.500 Zuschauern und war damit zuschauerstärkste Spielklasse des Kontinents). Das Unternehmen Electro-nic Arts veröffentlicht seit Anfang der neunziger Jahre ein Football-Spiel für PC und Spielekonsole – dieses Videospiel ist jedes Jahr das am meisten verkaufte Videospiel in Nordamerika. Bei einer Umfrage des Meinungsforschungsinstituts Harris Poll gaben 33 % der Befragten American Football als Lieblingssport an. Der urtümliche Volkssport der USA, Baseball, landete mit 14 % abgeschlagen auf Platz zwei; Basketball belegte Rang drei.

Der Hauptgrund für den wirtschaftlichen Erfolg der National Football League dürfte – neben dem Draft-System und der Salary Cap – das *Revenue Sharing-Modell* sein, bei dem alle Ligaeinkünfte, die durch Fernsehrechte oder Sponso-reneinkünfte erzielt werden, gleichmäßig auf alle Teams verteilt werden. Die –

weitgehende – wirtschaftliche Egalität erhöht die sportliche Chancengleichheit und steigert die Spannung für die Zuschauer: in den vergangenen dreizehn Jahren konnten sich 19 verschiedene Teams für die Super Bowl qualifizieren.

Die Detroit Lions existieren seit 1934 und zählen damit zu den ältesten Teams der National Football League. Nach wechselvoller Geschichte erlebte das Team seinen sportlichen Höhepunkt in den fünfziger Jahren. Nach einer Reihe von Besitzerwechseln befinden sich die Detroit Lions seit 1964 im Besitz der Familie Ford. Seit 2002 spielt das Team im Ford Field. Ein Blick auf das Organigramm der Detroit Lions zeigt, dass die *funktionale Organisation* der eines Unternehmens entspricht (vgl. Abb. 3).

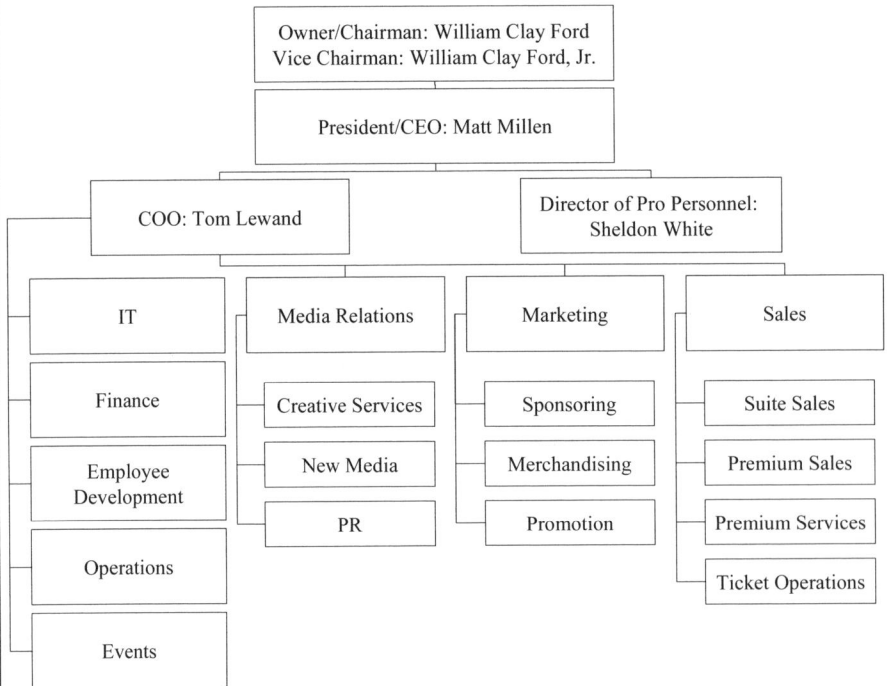

Owner/Chairman: William Clay Ford Vice Chairman: William Clay Ford, Jr.

President/CEO: Matt Millen

COO: Tom Lewand	Director of Pro Personnel: Sheldon White

IT	Media Relations	Marketing	Sales
Finance	Creative Services	Sponsoring	Suite Sales
Employee Development	New Media	Merchandising	Premium Sales
Operations	PR	Promotion	Premium Services
Events			Ticket Operations

Abb. 3: Organigramm Detroit Lions
Quelle: Detroit Lions (2008), o.S.

Darüber hinaus ergeben sich weitere Anknüpfungspunkte der Detroit Lions an die betriebswirtschaftlichen Grundlagen des Sportmanagements und angrenzender Disziplinen, beispielsweise:

- *Standortwahl*: Gerade in der National Football League erweisen sich die Teams als sehr mobil und ziehen regelmäßig um, wenn die Standortbedingungen (z.B. der lokale Fernseh- oder Werbemarkt) in einer neuen Stadt besonders viel versprechend erscheinen (so zogen z.B. die Housten Oilers nach Tennessee um und wurden über Nacht zu den Tennesee Titans – ein beispielsweise im europäischen Fußball völlig undenkbares Vorgehen). Neugründungen von Teams erfolgen gezielt in den Städten, die das höchste wirtschaftliche Potenzial versprechen. Entsprechend wurden in den vergangenen Jahren v.a. Teams im wirtschaftlich besonders prosperierenden Süden der USA gegründet.

- *Unternehmenskooperationen*: Die Teams der National Football League schließen sich im Rahmen des Draft-Systems oder bei der Durchsetzung der Salary Cap als rechtlich selbständige Einheiten zu einer Interessensgemeinschaft zusammen, um die Verhandlungsposition gegenüber den Nachwuchsspielern bzw. den Profi-Spielern zu stärken (letztere schließen sich im Gegenzug zu einer Spielergewerkschaft zusammen).

- *Sportsoziologie*: Der mit der Verbreitung des Fernsehens einhergehende Aufstieg der NFL in den fünfziger und sechziger Jahren ist ein Paradebeispiel für die möglichen Wechselbeziehungen und -wirkungen zwischen Sport und Gesellschaft innerhalb der sich fortlaufend wandelnden gesamtgesellschaftlichen Rahmenbedingungen. Es wird interessant sein zu beobachten, wie sich Trends wie Cocooning oder auch der technologische Wandel im Bereich der Online Medien auf den American Football und seine Vermarktung auswirken werden.

- *Sportpsychologie*: Die Detroit Lions sind seit ihrer Übernahme durch die Familie Ford vor über 40 Jahren sportlich wenig erfolgreich: Wurden in den fünfziger Jahren noch drei Meistertitel gewonnen, konnte seit 1964 überhaupt erst ein (!) Playoff-Spiel gewonnen werden (1991). Hierfür werden teilweise die schlechte Personalauswahl durch die Teameigentümer und die zu wenig erfolgsorientierte Organisationskultur verantwortlich gemacht.

3.10 Fazit und Ausblick

Ziel dieses Kapitels war es, einen Überblick über die wichtigsten allgemeinen betriebswirtschaftlichen Grundlagen des Sportmanagements zu geben. In den folgenden Kapiteln wird vertiefend auf die Anwendung der speziellen klassischen Disziplinen der Betriebswirtschaftslehre im Sport eingegangen. Während die betriebswirtschaftliche Professionalisierung im Bereich des Sportmarketing schon vergleichsweise weit vorangeschritten ist, bieten viele andere betriebswirtschaftliche Aufgabenfelder noch reichliches Potenzial für eine intensive Umsetzung im Sportmanagement. Zur Illustration, wie professionell punktuell im Sport schon vorgegangen wird und welche Chancen sich daraus ergeben, wurde das Beispiel der National Football League und der dort spielenden Detroit Lions vorgestellt.

Gewappnet mit dem durch den vorliegenden Band vermittelten Grundwissen in Sportmanagement und Sportmarketing werden sich Sportmanagerinnen und Sportmanager in Zukunft mit immer wieder neuen Themen- und Aufgabenfeldern auseinandersetzen, wobei eine Reihe spannender Fragestellungen auf sie wartet:

- Welche Chancen birgt die Globalisierung des Sportmanagements?
- Wie kann gleichzeitig den zunehmenden Risiken eines sportartenübergreifenden internationalen Verdrängungswettbewerbs Einhalt geboten werden?
- Wie kann es gelingen, die notwendige Innovationsfähigkeit sicherzustellen?
- Was sind die Anforderungen an Sportorganisationen in Bezug auf Total Quality Management?
- Wie kann die traditionelle Sportorganisation in eine lernende Organisation überführt werden?
- Welche Rolle wird künftig das Thema Wissensmanagement spielen?

Kontrollfragen

1. Wie lässt sich die Betriebswirtschaftslehre systematisieren?
2. Welche Arten von Betrieben kennen Sie?
3. Was ist das Ökonomische Prinzip? Welche Ausprägungen davon existieren?
4. Skizzieren Sie die Dimensionen eines Zieles! Wie könnte ein vollständig formuliertes Ziel im Sportmanagement lauten?
5. Wie lässt sich die institutionelle Betriebswirtschaftslehre Sportmanagement charakterisieren?
6. Welche Arten von Unternehmenszusammenschlüssen kennen Sie? Nennen Sie jeweils Beispiele!
7. Welches Führungsmodell empfehlen Sie dem Deutschen Fußball Bund (DFB)? Warum?
8. Charakterisieren Sie die Nachbardisziplinen des Sportmanagements!
9. Beschreiben Sie das Gefangenendilemma! Warum handelt es sich dabei um ein Dilemma?
10. Warum ist die National Football League ein gutes Beispiel um zu zeigen, inwieweit sich das Sportmanagement bereits der Methoden der modernen Betriebswirtschaftslehre bedient?

Literaturverzeichnis

Axelrod, Robert (2003): The Evolution of Cooperation, New York.

Bamberg, Günter / Coenenberg, Gerhard (2006): Betriebswirtschaftliche Entscheidungslehre, 13. Aufl., München.

Bea, Franz Xaver (2005): Führung, in: Bea, Franz Xaver / Friedl, Birgit / Schweitzer, Marcell (Hrsg.): Allgemeine Betriebswirtschaftslehre, Band 2: Führung, 9. Aufl., Stuttgart, S. 1-15.

Bea, Franz Xaver / Haas, Jürgen (2005): Strategisches Management, 4. Aufl., Stuttgart.

Bea, Franz-Xaver (2004): Entscheidungen des Unternehmens, in: Bea, Franz Xaver / Friedl, Birgit / Schweitzer, Marcell (Hrsg.): Allgemeine Betriebswirtschaftslehre, Band 1: Grundfragen, 9. Aufl., Stuttgart., S. 311-420.

Berndt, Ralph (2005): Marketingstrategie und Marketingpolitik, 4. Aufl., Berlin u.a.

Breuer, Christoph / Thiel, Ansgar (2005): Sportmanagement – eine Einführung, in: Breuer, Christoph / Thiel, Ansgar (Hrsg.): Handbuch Sportmanagement, Schorndorf, S. 8-13.

Detroit Lions (2008): Organization Chart, http://www.detroitlions.com (Zugriff: 04.01.2008).

Elias, Norbert / Dunning, Eric (1986): Quest for Excitement – Sport and Leisure in the Civilizing Process, Oxford.

Heinemann, Klaus (1995): Einführung in die Ökonomie des Sports. Ein Handbuch, Schorndorf.

Hofer, Charles W. / Schendel, Dan (1996): Strategy Formulation: Analytical Concepts, St. Paul.

Homburg, Christian (2000): Quantitative Betriebswirtschaftslehre. Entscheidungsunterstützung durch Modelle. Mit Beispielen, Übungsaufgaben und Lösungen, 3. Aufl., Wiesbaden.

Kesting, Tobias / Rennhak, Carsten (2008): Marktsegmentierung in deutschen Unternehmen, Wiesbaden.

Likert, Rensis (1961): New Patterns of Management, New York.

Neus, Werner (2005): Einführung in die Betriebswirtschaftslehre, 4. Aufl., Tübingen.

Nufer, Gerd (2007): Event-Marketing und -Management. Theorie und Praxis unter besonderer Berücksichtigung von Imagewirkungen, 3. Aufl., Wiesbaden.

Nufer, Gerd / Bühler, André W. (2006): Lessons from Sports: What Corporate Management can learn from Sports Management, Reutlingen Working Paper on Marketing & Management No. 2006-7, School of International Business, Reutlingen University.

Rigauer, Beno (1969): Sport und Arbeit, Frankfurt/Main.

Schneck, Ottmar (2005): Lexikon der Betriebswirtschaft, 6. Aufl., München.

Schweitzer, Marcell (2004): Gegenstand und Methoden der Betriebswirtschaftslehre, in: Bea, Franz Xaver / Friedl, Birgit / Schweitzer, Marcell (Hrsg.): Allgemeine Betriebswirtschaftslehre, Band 1: Grundfragen, 9. Aufl., Stuttgart, S. 23-82.

Staehle, Wolfgang H. (1999): Management, 8. Aufl., München.

Thommen, Jean-Paul / Achleitner, Ann-Christin (2006): Allgemeine Betriebswirtschaftslehre. Umfassende Einführung aus managementorientierter Sicht, 5. Aufl., Wiesbaden.

Vahs, Dietmar / Schäfer-Kunz, Jan (2007): Einführung in die Betriebswirtschaftslehre, 5. Aufl., Stuttgart.

Vassort, Patrick (2006): Football et politique – sociologie historique d'une domination, 3. Aufl., Paris u.a.

Von Neumann, John / Morgenstern, Oscar (1944): Theory of Games and Economic Behavior, Princeton.

Von Rosenstiel, Lutz (2003): Grundlagen der Organisationspsychologie, 5. Aufl., Stuttgart.

Weigand, Jürgen / Stadtmann, Georg (2005): Mit der Spieltheorie zum Nobelpreis, in: Das Wirtschaftsstudium, Heft 11, S. 1320-1322.

Weiß, Otmar (1999): Einführung in die Sportsoziologie, Stuttgart.

Witte, Hermann (2007): Allgemeine Betriebswirtschaftslehre, 2. Aufl., München.

Wöhe, Günter / Döring, Ulrich (2005): Einführung in die Allgemeine Betriebswirtschaftslehre, 22. Aufl., München.

Weiterführende Ressourcen

Literatur

Albach, Horst (2001): Allgemeine Betriebswirtschaftslehre, 3. Aufl., Wiesbaden.

Bea, Franz Xaver / Friedl, Birgit / Schweitzer, Marcell (Hrsg.) (2004): Allgemeine Betriebswirtschaftslehre, Band 1: Grundfragen, 9. Aufl., Stuttgart.

Bea, Franz Xaver / Friedl, Birgit / Schweitzer, Marcell (Hrsg.) (2005): Allgemeine Betriebswirtschaftslehre, Band 2: Führung, 9. Aufl., Stuttgart.

Beech, John / Chadwick, Simon (Hrsg.) (2004): The Business of Sport Management, Harlow.

Breuer, Christoph / Thiel, Ansgar (Hrsg.) (2005): Handbuch Sportmanagement, Schorndorf.

Brockhoff, Klaus (2002): Geschichte der Betriebswirtschaftslehre: Kommentierte Meilensteine und Originaltexte, 2. Aufl., Wiesbaden.

Dipboye, Robert L. / Smith, Carlla S. / Howell, William C. (1994): Understanding Industrial and Organizational Psychology. An Integrated Approach, Forth Worth u.a.

Domschke, Wolfgang / Scholl, Armin (2005): Grundlagen der Betriebswirtschaftslehre – eine Einführung aus entscheidungsorientierter Sicht, 3. Aufl., Berlin u.a.

Fayol, Henri (1966): Administration industrielle et générale – prévoyance organisation – commandement, coordination – contrôle, Paris.

Gutenberg, Erich (1990): Einführung in die Betriebswirtschaftslehre, unveränderter Nachdruck, Wiesbaden.

Hoffmann, Friedrich / Bühner, Rolf (1976): Organisationsgestaltung – Probleme, Konzeptmerkmale und Ergebnisse, Wiesbaden.

Horch, Heinz-Dieter / Heydel, Jörg / Sierau, Axel (Hrsg.) (2004): Events im Sport – Marketing, Management, Finanzierung, Köln.

Horch, Heinz-Dieter / Hovemann, Gregor / Kaiser, Sebastian / Viebahn, Kai (Hrsg.) (2005): Perspektiven des Sportmarketing. Besonderheiten, Herausforderungen, Tendenzen, Köln.

Horváth, Péter (2001): Controlling, 8. Aufl., München.

Kosiol, Erich (1976): Organisation der Unternehmung, 2. Aufl., Wiesbaden.

Küpper, Hans-Ulrich (2005): Controlling – Konzeption, Aufgaben, Instrumente, 4. Aufl., München.

Luhmann, Niklas (1999): Funktionen und Folgen formaler Organisation, 5. Aufl., Berlin.

Luhmann, Niklas (2000): Organisation und Entscheidung, Opladen.

March, James / Simon, Herbert (1993): Organizations, Cambridge.

Mayo, Elton (1945): Probleme industrieller Arbeitsbedingungen, Frankfurt/Main.

Mintzberg, Henry (1979): The Structuring of Organizations. A Synthesis of the Research, Englewood Cliffs.

Nufer, Gerd (2002): Sport und Kultur – Lehren für die Strategie / Sports and Culture – Lessons for Strategy, in: Simon, Hermann (Hrsg.): Strategie International / Strategy International, zweisprachige Serie in der Frankfurter Allgemeinen Zeitung, 07.09.2002, S. 57.

Nufer, Gerd (2002): Wirkungen von Sportsponsoring. Empirische Analyse am Beispiel der Fußball-Weltmeisterschaft 1998 in Frankreich unter besonderer Berücksichtigung von Erinnerungswirkungen bei jugendlichen Rezipienten, Berlin.

Peters, Thomas J. / Waterman, Robert H. (1982): Auf der Suche nach Spitzenleistungen. Was man von den bestgeführten US-Unternehmen lernen kann, 3. Aufl., München 1991 (Titel der Originalausgabe: In Search of Excellence. Lessons from America´s Best-Run Companies, übers. v. Reddman, Hartmut unter Mitwirkung von Schlichting, Gabrielle E.).

Picot, Arnold (2002): Organisation – eine ökonomische Perspektive, 3. Aufl., Stuttgart.

Rieck, Christian (2007): Spieltheorie – eine Einführung, Eschborn.

Robbins, Stephen P. / Coulter Mary / Langton Nancy (2006): Management, 8. Aufl., Upper Saddle River.

Schierenbeck, Henner (2003): Grundzüge der Betriebswirtschaftslehre, 16. Aufl., München.

Simon, Herbert (1997): Administrative Behaviour – a Study of Decision-Making Processes in Administrative Organizations, 3. Aufl., New York.

Simon, Hermann (2004): Think! Strategische Unternehmensführung statt Kurzfrist-Denke, Frankfurt/Main u.a.

Taylor, Frederick W. (2006): Shop management, Saarbrücken.

Weber, Max (1980): Wirtschaft und Gesellschaft, Tübingen.

Links

Arbeitskreis Sportökonomie e.V.:
  http://www.arbeitskreis-sportoekonomie.de
Bayreuther Sportökonomie-Kongress:
  http://www.sportoekonomie.uni-bayreuth.de/kongress
Deutscher Sportökonomie-Kongress, Köln:
  http://www.deutscher-sportoekonomie-kongress.de
Heidelberger Sportbusiness Forum (Kongress):
  http://www.sportbusiness.de
Horizont Sport Business (Fachzeitschrift):
  http://www.horizont-sportbusiness.de
Sportfive (Sportrechteagentur), Hamburg:
  http://www.sportfive.de
Sportrecht (Internet-Portal):
  http://www.sportrecht.org
Verband für Sportökonomie und Sportmanagement in Deutschland e.V.:
  http://www.vsd-online.de

Teil II:

Sportmanagement –
die Anwendung klassischer Disziplinen
der Betriebswirtschaftslehre im Sport

Kapitel 4: Strategisches Management im Sport

Christian Keller

Lernziele

Nach der Durchsicht dieses Kapitels sollte der Leser in der Lage sein,

- die Aufgaben und das Wesen des allgemeinen strategischen Managements zu erläutern.
- die verschiedenen Prozessstufen des strategischen Managements zu erklären.
- die Relevanz eines strategischen Managements im Teamsport zu verdeutlichen.
- das Zielsystem von Teamsportunternehmen zu beschreiben.
- die Stakeholder von und deren zentrale Beziehungszusammenhänge zu den Teamsportsportunternehmen zu nennen.
- das Wertschöpfungsmodell des Teamsports zu erläutern.
- typische strategische Gestaltungsaufgaben in Teamsportunternehmen darzulegen.
- die Bedeutung der strategischen Reflexion im Teamsport einzuordnen.

Überblick über das Kapitel

Im vorliegenden Kapitel werden Möglichkeiten und Werkzeuge eines strategischen Managements für Organisationen des Sports veranschaulicht. Im Fokus stehen dabei gemäß der grundlegenden Intention dieses Herausgeberbandes professionelle Sportbetriebe des Teamsports. Für letztgenannte finden im weiteren Verlauf die Bezeichnungen (Team-)Sportunternehmen und (Team-)Sportclub synonyme Verwendung. Ausgangspunkt der Analyse bildet die Vorstellung des allgemeinen Ansatzes eines strategischen Managements für Unternehmen klassischer Wirtschaftsbranchen. Auf dieser Basis kommen im Anschluss Besonderheiten und Inhalte des strategischen Managements in Teamsportunternehmen zur Sprache. Es wird sich zeigen, dass insbesondere aus dem Zielsystem der Sportclubs Spezifika resultieren, die das strategische Management im Sport maßgeblich von jenem in anderen Branchen unterscheiden. Eine Praxis-Fallstudie rundet das Kapitel ab.

4.1 Einführung in die Thematik

Die extensive Kommerzialisierung des deutschen Sportmarktes erlaubt es nicht mehr, Bundesligaclubs aus Fußball, Handball, Basketball und Eishockey ihrer ursprünglichen Intention nach, als Non-Profit-Organisationen, zu betrachten. Ehemals gemeinnützige Sportvereine haben sich zu Sportwirtschaftsunternehmen entwickelt, die in ihrer Umsatzdimension mit mittelständischen Unternehmungen klassischer Wirtschaftsbranchen vergleichbar sind. Am eindringlichsten offenbart sich dieser Sachverhalt im Profifußball: In der Saison 2005/2006 generierten die 36 Bundesligisten ein kumuliertes Umsatzvolumen von 1,52 Mrd. € (DFL, 2007). Dem dynamischen Einnahmenwachstum stand in der Vergangenheit aber häufig ein überproportionaler Anstieg der Clubausgaben gegenüber (Überinvestitionsphänomen). Verluste, steigende Verschuldungsgrade, Liquiditätskrisen sowie in Einzelfällen sogar die Einleitung der Insolvenz waren die Folge. Offensichtlich gelang es der Mehrzahl der Clubs nicht, effektiv auf die kommerzialisierungsbedingten Veränderungen in ihrer Umwelt zu reagieren. Impliziert man ferner die auch im deutschen Spitzensport immer stärker zu identifizierenden Reflexe allgemeiner Globalisierungstendenzen, bleibt der effektive Umgang mit Umweltveränderungen zentrale Voraussetzung der perspektivischen Wettbewerbsfähigkeit von Sportunternehmen. Der Einzug von Globalisierungsprozessen wird den dynamischen Wandel im Tätigkeitsfeld des Sports weiter forcieren. Bei der systematischen Gestaltung der Unternehmens-Umwelt-Beziehungen setzt die Disziplin des strategischen Managements an. Das strategische Management ermöglicht die Nachhaltigkeit der Clubentwicklung im Spannungsfeld dynamischer Veränderungen und Diskontinuitäten auf dem Wachstumsmarkt des professionellen Sports.

4.2 Grundlagen zum strategischen Management

Eines der grundlegendsten Steuerungsprobleme besteht für Unternehmen in der Prognose zukünftiger Entwicklungen auf ihren relevanten Beschaffungs- und Absatzmärkten. Aussagen zum Zukunftsverlauf erscheinen mit zunehmendem Zeithorizont spekulativ. Andererseits ist die *Prognose perspektivischer Umweltveränderungen* erfolgskritisch für eine Unternehmung (Bea/Haas, 2001). Die effektive Reaktion auf Veränderungen der Kundenanforderungen, des Verhaltens der Wettbewerber, der gesetzlichen Rahmenbedingungen etc. spielt für die Sicherung der Unternehmensexistenz eine signifikante Rolle. Dies gilt in besonderem Maße, wenn Neuerungen in Kombination auftreten. Vielfalt und Mehrdeutigkeit denkbarer Umweltveränderungen erschweren den adäquaten unternehmerischen Umgang mit dem Prognoseproblem zusätzlich. Hinzu kommt die steigende Dynamik ökonomischer Veränderungen, die realiter in nahezu allen Branchen zu beobachten ist.

Soll die Entwicklung einer Unternehmung nicht einem kontinuierlichen *„Muddling Through"* gleichen, bedarf es daher eines konzeptionellen Rasters, das hilft, potentielle Veränderungen inner- und außerhalb des Unternehmens zu erkennen, zu selektieren sowie deren Ursachen und Interdependenzen offen zu legen (Müller-Stewens/Lechner, 2005). In Konsequenz wird die Prognosekomplexität reduziert und der Weg für eine systematische Unternehmenssteuerung inmitten eines dynamischen Umweltwandels geebnet. Ein derartiges Raster stellt das Konzept des strategischen Managements dar.

4.2.1 Begriff und Wesen des strategischen Managements

Beim strategischen Management – als Synonyme finden bisweilen die Begriffe strategische Planung, strategische Unternehmensführung und Unternehmenspolitik Verwendung – handelt es sich um eine vergleichsweise junge Disziplin der Betriebswirtschaftslehre. Ihre Anfänge reichen bis in die 60er Jahre zurück. Etabliert hat sich die wissenschaftliche Diskussion zum strategischen Management aber erst ab den 80er Jahren. Ein skizzenhafter Überblick wesentlicher Entwicklungsschritte findet sich bei Bea/Haas (2001).

Trotz dieser zeitlichen Kürze war die theoretische Auseinandersetzung seither äußerst umfangreich und vielfältig. Heute existieren eine Reihe abweichender Betrachtungsweisen, theoretischer Ausgangspositionen und Fragestellungen (Müller-Stewens/Lechner, 2005). Zentral ist beispielsweise die Differenzierung in einen „Market-based View" und einen „Resource-based View" des strategischen Managements. Eine Vorstellung der unterschiedlichen Forschungsansätze scheint im vorliegenden Kontext allerdings wenig zweckmäßig. Bedeutsam ist vielmehr, dass alle bestehenden Perspektiven und Zugänge auf einem gemeinsamen Grundverständnis zum Wesen eines strategischen Managements fußen. Dessen basale Charakteristika lassen sich folgendermaßen beschreiben (Hungenberg, 2004):

- Das strategische Management befasst sich mit solchen Entscheidungen, die die grundlegende *Richtung der Unternehmensentwicklung* bestimmen oder signifikant beeinflussen. Angesichts dessen beziehen sich strategische Festlegungen auf einen langfristigen Zeithorizont. Als langfristig gilt i.d.R. eine Spanne von mehr als drei Jahren, wobei Markt- und Unternehmensspezifika den Zeithorizont strategischer Entscheidungen prinzipiell nach vorne zu öffnen vermögen.

- Im Mittelpunkt aller strategischen Entscheidungen steht das Fundamentalziel, die *Unternehmensexistenz* durch eine vorteilhafte Wettbewerbspositionierung nachhaltig zu sichern.

- Dabei kann das Fundamentalziel jedoch nicht über isolierte Positionierungsaktivitäten auf den Absatz- und Beschaffungsmärkten erreicht werden. Die *Positionierung* ist an die internen Leistungspotentiale, d.h. die *Wertschöpfung*, des Unternehmens gekoppelt.

- Bei strategischen Entscheidungen zur Positionierung und Wertschöpfung stehen aber nicht einzelne, konkrete Aktivitäten am Markt oder innerhalb des Unternehmens im Fokus. Vielmehr geben strategische Entscheidungen ein *Grundmuster* für die perspektivische unternehmerische Entwicklung vor. Die Steuerung der Einzelmaßnahmen auf tiefer gelegenen Abstraktionsebenen bis hin zum operativen Alltagshandeln basiert sodann auf dieser konzeptionellen Gesamtsicht.

- Folglich gilt es, die strategische Stoßrichtung aus einer übergreifenden Perspektive heraus festzulegen. Das strategische Management obliegt vorrangig der *Führungsspitze* des Unternehmens. Deren Entscheidungen müssen im Umkehrschluss auf einer hinreichenden Informationsbasis über die organisationalen und umweltspezifischen Faktizitäten beruhen.

Zusammenfassend strebt das strategische Management die *Gestaltung der Unternehmensentwicklung* an. Es dient vereinfacht formuliert dazu, den Zufall durch den Irrtum im Spannungsfeld von Vergangenheits-, Gegenwarts- und Zukunftsorientierung zu ersetzen. Von Relevanz sind dabei all jene Themen, die die Beziehungen des Unternehmens, nach außen zu seiner Umwelt und nach innen zu sich selbst, signifikant beeinflussen (Müller-Stewens/Lechner, 2005).

4.2.2 Prozess des strategischen Managements

Ausgehend von seinen zentralen Wesensmerkmalen lässt sich der Prozess des strategischen Managements in Form eines einfachen Phasenmodells skizzieren. Allerdings können die Teilprozesse nicht isoliert voneinander bearbeitet werden. Vor- und Rückkopplungsbeziehungen bzw. Interdependenzen zwischen den und innerhalb der einzelnen Phasen erfordern ein integriertes Zusammenwirken.

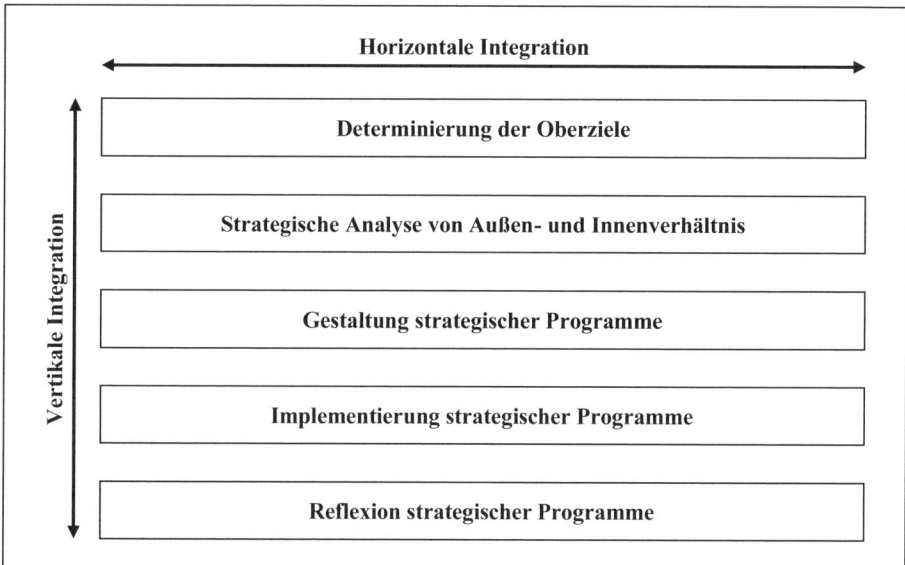

Horizontale Integration

Vertikale Integration

- Determinierung der Oberziele
- Strategische Analyse von Außen- und Innenverhältnis
- Gestaltung strategischer Programme
- Implementierung strategischer Programme
- Reflexion strategischer Programme

Abb. 1: Prozess des strategischen Managements
In Anlehnung an: Bea/Haas (2001), S. 58; Hungenberg (2004), S. 10

4.2.2.1 Determinierung der Oberziele

Zwischen unternehmerischen Zielsetzungen besteht eine asymmetrische, vertikale Ordnungsbeziehung. Sie lassen sich nach einem definitionslogischen Rangverhältnis klassifizieren. Auf das Fundamentalziel der Existenzsicherung folgen das oder die Oberziele, welche für die Unternehmung als Ganzes Gültigkeit beanspruchen. Ein Bündel mehrerer Unterziele, das seinerseits in aller Regel wiederum in Partialziele zerlegbar ist, dient zur Realisierung der Oberziele.

Strategisches Management beginnt bei der *Determinierung der Oberziele*. Als langfristige, grundlegende Richtungsvorgaben sollen die Oberziele die Basis der inhaltlichen und zeitlichen Koordination nachgelagerter Ziele und Aktivitäten, der

Auseinandersetzung mit der Unternehmensumwelt sowie der Sicherung der inneren Stabilität der Unternehmung bilden.

In der betriebswirtschaftlichen Theorie wird häufig das *Streben nach Gewinn* als Oberziel erwerbswirtschaftlich orientierter Organisationen unterstellt (Korndörfer, 1999). Dieses Vorgehen stößt jedoch genauso oft auf kontroverse Kritik. Die rein finanzielle Abbildung des Unternehmens dürfte für dessen nachhaltige Entwicklung kaum ausreichend sein (Macharzina/Wolf, 2005). Wirtschaftlicher Erfolg ist immer erst das Produkt vieler vorgelagerter Aktivitäten. Dennoch lassen sich andere Ziele monetärer (Umsatz, Wirtschaftlichkeit etc.) und nicht-monetärer Natur (Marktanteilswachstum, Produktivität, Unabhängigkeit etc.) stets in eine direkte oder indirekte Beziehung zum Gewinnmotiv setzen (Korndörfer, 1999). In Summe ist die branchenübergreifende Relevanz des Gewinnstrebens als Oberziel klassischer Wirtschaftsunternehmen daher nicht zu leugnen.

Formal wird die Festlegung der Oberziele durch die Unternehmensverfassung, inhaltlich durch die Unternehmenskultur getragen. Die *Unternehmensverfassung* steht in engem Abhängigkeitsverhältnis zur gewählten Rechtsform und legt einen generell zu respektierenden Verhaltensrahmen nach innen und nach außen fest (Bleicher, 2004). Sie ordnet Strukturen und Prozesse für die Beziehungsgestaltung zur Umwelt, v.a. aber auch für die Ausgestaltung des inneren Aufbaus der Unternehmung im Lichte der rechtlichen Möglichkeiten. Nicht minder wichtig für die Umsetzung einer intendierten Unternehmensentwicklung ist die *Unternehmenskultur*. Die in der Unternehmenskultur verankerten Normen und Werte spiegeln das Verhalten der Mitglieder eines Unternehmens wider. Mit anderen Worten prägen bestehende Normen und Werte implizit unterstützendes respektive ablehnendes Verhalten als Einfluss auf die Unternehmensentwicklung (Hungenberg, 2004).

4.2.2.2 Strategische Analyse von Außen- und Innenverhältnis

Im Zuge der strategischen Analyse ist die angestrebte zukünftige Unternehmensentwicklung auf Realisierbarkeit zu überprüfen. Aus der Positionierung des Unternehmens in seiner Umwelt sowie seiner internen Ressourcenbasis resultieren Optionen für die zielkonforme Gestaltung strategischer Programme.

Das Außenverhältnis eines Unternehmens lässt sich in Beziehungen zur *Aufgabenumwelt* (Mikroumwelt) und zur *globalen Umwelt* (Makroumwelt) gliedern. Während Unternehmen auf der Ebene ihrer Aufgabenumwelt direkt interagieren, verläuft die Beziehung zur globalen Umwelt eher mittelbar. Die direkte Aufgabenumwelt lässt sich als *System von Stakeholdern* darstellen, zu denen Beziehungen bestehen. Anspruchsgruppen reagieren auf Entscheide und Handlungen des Unternehmens und bedingen dadurch direkt oder indirekt den Grad der Zielrealisierung. Trends in der Makroumwelt sind vom Grundsatz her branchenübergreifend für alle Unternehmungen gleich. Sie können Rahmenbedingungen für das unternehmerische Handeln setzen, die in aller Regel kaum beeinflussbar sind. Gängigerweise wird die Vielzahl globaler Einflussfaktoren in ein makroökonomisches (Konjunktur, Zinsen, Arbeitslosigkeit etc.), politisch-rechtliches (Rechtsnormen, Regulation, Subventionspolitik etc.), soziokulturelles (Altersstruktur, Konsumverhalten, Arbeitseinstellung etc.) und technologisches (Produkt-, Prozessinnovationen etc.) Segment differenziert.

Die Analyse des Innenverhältnisses fokussiert die zur angestrebten Wettbewerbspositionierung erforderlichen Leistungs- bzw. Ressourcenpotentiale, deren Wirkungsweise und Zusammenspiel. Von Interesse ist die Wertschöpfung des Unternehmens, die allgemein als *„Prozess des Schaffens von Mehrwert durch Bearbeitung"* definiert werden kann (Müller-Stewens/Lechner, 2005).

4.2.2.3 Gestaltung, Implementierung und Reflexion strategischer Programme

Aufbauend auf den Erkenntnissen der strategischen Analyse sind im nächsten Schritt *strategische Programme* für die zielkonforme Gestaltung von Positionierung und Wertschöpfung zu entwickeln. In Konsequenz sollte gegenüber jedem der als relevant erachteten Stakeholder ein Konzept des Wertschöpfungsprozesses formuliert werden. Dabei gilt es, angesichts der schwierigen Prognostizierbarkeit, der Komplexität und Vielfältigkeit zukünftiger Einflüsse, mehrere Zukunftsbilder für ein solches Stakeholder Relations Managements zu zeichnen. Werden die Auswirkungen unterschiedlicher Einflüsse und Handlungsoptionen in Form alternativer strategischer Programminhalte verdeutlicht, kann ein Lernprozess für die Gestaltung zukünftiger Entscheidungen einsetzen.

Um strategische Programme zu verwirklichen, sind die intendierten Handlungen am Markt oder innerhalb des Unternehmens auszuführen. Die Implementierung strategischer Programme stellt die Schnittstelle zum operativen Management dar. Strategien werden erst dann Realität, wenn die *Menschen im Unternehmen* auch nach Maßgabe der Strategie handeln.

Umsetzung und Wirksamkeit strategischer Maßnahmen sind schließlich auf ihren Beitrag zur Zielerreichung zu reflektieren. Vor- und Rückkopplungsprozesse zwischen den einzelnen Prozessphasen machen die *strategische Reflexion* allerdings zu einem repetitiven Element, das den gesamten Prozess des strategischen Managements zu durchdringen hat. Beispielsweise sind die Oberziele, im Falle einer perspektivisch nicht zu egalisierenden Diskrepanz zwischen angestrebter Positionierung und internen Leistungspotentialen neu zu definieren.

4.3 Strategisches Management im Sport

Im Folgenden wird der Prozess des strategischen Managements nunmehr auf Teamsportunternehmen angewandt. Dabei wird zunächst evident, dass deren Zielsystem Besonderheiten aufweist, die ohne effektive Steuerung eine nachhaltige Clubentwicklung konterkarieren. Die strategische Analyse von Außen- und Innenverhältnis deckt typische Stakeholderbeziehungen und erfolgskritische Ressourcen professioneller Sportclubs auf. Hierauf basierend lassen sich clubübergreifend zu bearbeitende strategische Entscheidungskomplexe identifizieren, die für den langfristigen Erfolg systematisch zu justieren sind. Abschließend werden Möglichkeiten der strategischen Reflexion in Teamsportunternehmen aufgezeigt.

4.3.1 Determinierung der Oberziele

Bei systemisch-evolutionärem Managementverständnis ist auch für Organisationen des Sports vom Primat der Existenzerhaltung als organisatorischem Fundamentalziel auszugehen (Breuer, 2005). Sachliches Oberziel für die Sicherung der Viabilität stellt für Teamsportunternehmen das Streben nach *sportlichem Erfolg* dar. Sportliche Leistungsfähigkeit ist die Grundvoraussetzung für die Teilnahme am Wettbewerb. Mangelndes sportliches Leistungsvermögen führt durch die im deutschen Teamsport praktizierte Relegation (Aufstieg/Abstieg) letztlich zum Ausschluss aus dem Profisportsystem. Aus wertzielbezogener Sicht müssen Sportclubs das Oberziel *wirtschaftlichen Erfolg* anstreben. Mangelnde finanzwirtschaftliche Leistungsfähigkeit resultiert in finaler Konsequenz in Illiquidität und Insolvenz.

4.3.1.1 Zielbeziehungen von sportlichem und wirtschaftlichem Erfolg

Gemeinhin wird von einem komplementären Zusammenspiel der beiden zentralen Erfolgsgrößen ausgegangen. Die Wirkungskette – sportlicher Erfolg bedingt wirtschaftlichen Erfolg und umgekehrt – ist in Sportmanagementlehre und -praxis weit verbreitet. Erfolge im sportlichen Wettbewerb erhöhen die Attraktivität eines Clubs in der Wahrnehmung durch Öffentlichkeit und Medien und führen so zu Umsatzsteigerungen in den Vermarktungssegmenten Spieltag, Merchandising und Sponsoring. Je populärer ein Club, desto stärker können Sponsoren und Werbepartner i.d.R. von ihrem Engagement profitieren. Die Einnahmenquelle TV-Vermarktung ist regelmäßig direkt an das sportliche Abschneiden gekoppelt. Beispielsweise erhalten Fußballbundesligisten neben einem erfolgsunabhängigen Sockelbetrag sowohl auf nationaler (Meisterschaft, DFB-Pokal) als auch auf internationaler (Champions League, UEFA-Pokal) Ebene einen variablen Erfolgsanteil aus den von den Dachverbänden zentral vermarkteten Fernsehtöpfen.

In Summe ermöglichen die durch sportliche Siege generierten Erlösströme Investitionen in die Spielstärke der Mannschaft. Empirische Studien belegen (u.a. Ziebs, 2002; Frick, 2005; Fritz, 2006): Im Vergleich zur Konkurrenz höhere Spielstärkeinvestitionen wirken unter sonst gleichen Bedingungen statistisch signifikant positiv auf den sportlichen Erfolg eines Clubs. Die Spirale aus sportlichem und wirtschaftlichem Erfolg dreht sich im Idealfall in verstärktem Maße weiter.

Bei genauerer Betrachtung gestaltet sich die Zielharmonie zwischen den beiden Erfolgsparametern allerdings durchaus kritisch. Nach der beschriebenen Wirkungskette stellt der wirtschaftliche Erfolg eine rein umsatzbezogene Größe dar. Unter dem wirtschaftlichen Erfolgskriterium werden lediglich Steigerungen der diversen Einnahmeströme subsumiert. Die gegenüberstehenden Ausgaben zur Finanzierung der Teamsportproduktion bleiben unberücksichtigt. Wird das sportliche Leistungsziel übermäßig stark in den Vordergrund gerückt, kann die positive Korrelation von sportlichem und wirtschaftlichem Erfolg alternieren. Es besteht die Gefahr der *Überinvestition*. Sollen sportliche Erfolge durch massive Investitionen in die Spielstärke der Lizenzmannschaft erzwungen werden, genügen die ausgelösten zusätzlichen Erlösströme selbst im Falle der sportlichen Zielerreichung oftmals nicht zur Deckung der gegenüberstehenden Auszahlungen für Transfers und Spielergehälter. Hinzu kommt ein potentieller „Time Lag" zwischen sportlichen Erfolgen und positiven wirtschaftlichen Folgewirkungen. Nachfrageschübe respektive neue Vertragsabschlüsse (Sponsoring etc.) treten häufig erst mit zeitlicher Verzögerung in folgenden Spielzeiten ein. Überinvestitionen führen zu Auszahlungsüberhängen, die Liquiditätsnöte und Verluste nach sich ziehen. Anders formuliert, sind Spielstärkeinvestitionen durch abnehmende Grenzerträge gekennzeichnet und machen sportlich wie ökonomisch nur bis zu einem bestimmten Punkt Sinn (Frick, 2005).

Sportliches und wirtschaftliches Erfolgsstreben stehen folglich in einer *gemischten Interdependenzrelation* zueinander. Eine anfänglich gegebene (partielle) Zielkomplementarität kann durch Überinvestition in (partielle) Zielkonkurrenz umschlagen. Abb. 2 stellt diesen Sachverhalt graphisch dar:

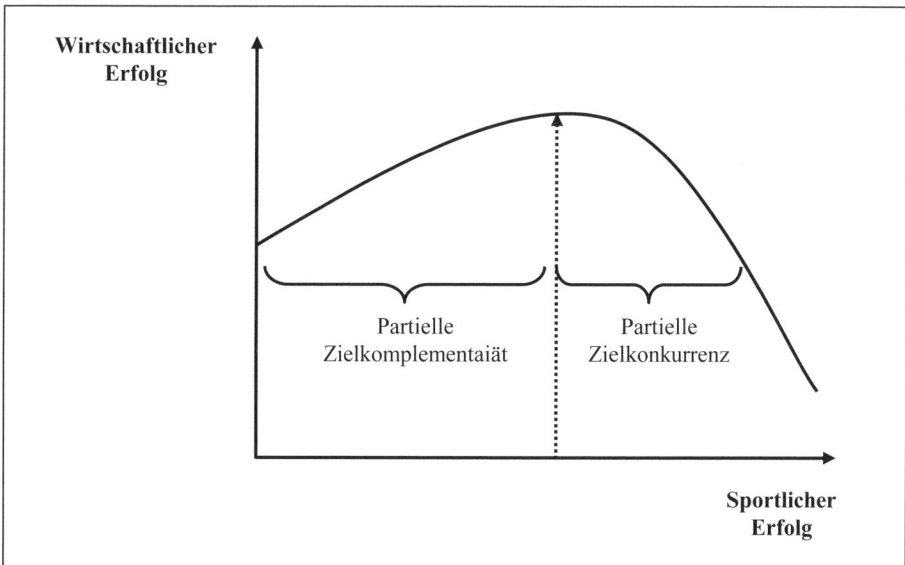

Abb. 2: Interdependenzrelation zwischen den Oberzielen von Teamsportunternehmen

Das im Teamsport realiter zu beobachtende Überinvestitionsphänomen deutet gleichzeitig auf eine kausallogisch nachvollziehbare *Präferenz für das Oberziel sportlichen Erfolgs* hin. Geschäftsgrundlage der Teamsportunternehmen ist die sportliche Leistungsdimension. Die sportlichen Ergebnisse sind der Output, der eigentliche Cashflow der Clubtätigkeit. Hinzu kommt das jahrzehntelange Dasein ohne marktwirtschaftliche Orientierung als traditionelle Non-Profit-Organisation. Vor Einzug der Kommerzialisierung galt der Fokus von Clubzielsetzungen und Clubaktivitäten v.a. sportlichen Wertparametern. Eine bisweilen in der Literatur (Erning, 2000) angeführte Präferenz für das wirtschaftliche Oberziel ist angesichts der systemimmanenten Bedeutung des Sportbereichs zu negieren. Dennoch stellt wirtschaftlicher Erfolg mehr als eine Nebenbedingung sportlichen Erfolgs dar. Finanzielle Instabilität bedroht die Existenz eines Clubs.

4.3.1.2 Relativität von sportlichem und wirtschaftlichem Erfolg

Allgemein ist die Einordnung von Erfolgszielen mit *Relativität* behaftet. Im Teamsport zeigen sich Diskrepanzen beim Erfolgsverständnis insbesondere bei der Einordnung sportlicher Ergebnisse. So messen Clubverantwortliche und Clubumfeld Prestigeduellen oder Lokalderbys häufig eine über das objektive Maß, d.h. den Spielausgang (Sieg, Unentschieden, Niederlage), hinausgehende Bedeutung zu. Auf den gesamten Saisonverlauf bezogen, wird je nach Club unter Umständen bereits das Erreichen eines Nichtabstiegsplatzes als Erfolg oder aber die verfehlte Qualifikation für einen internationalen Wettbewerb als Misserfolg erachtet.

Ursächlich für die Relativität des Erfolgsverständnisses sind v.a. die Gegebenheiten der jeweiligen *Handlungssituation*. Letztgenannte werden im Teamsport maßgeblich durch die Wettbewerbsform der *Kooperenz* determiniert. Einerseits stehen die einzelnen Clubs in sportlicher und wirtschaftlicher Konkurrenz zueinander, andererseits kooperieren sie bei der Erstellung der Teamsportproduktion sowie in bestimmten nachgelagerten ökonomischen Vermarktungsfragen. Ein Spiel sowie in noch viel umfassenderen Sinne Meisterschaft und Pokalwettbewerbe bilden Ergebnisse einer Gemeinschaftsproduktion. Im Umkehrschluss wird das sportliche und wirtschaftliche Leistungsvermögen eines Clubs nur vor dem Hintergrund seiner Positionierung im Wettbewerb evaluierbar. Erfolg in Teamwettbewerben ist ein Ergebnis relativer Stärke.

Von den einzelnen Clubs vor Saisonbeginn in den Medien veröffentlichte Erfolgserwartungen bzw. Saisonziele zeigen: Die Aggregation der über alle Ligateilnehmer hinweg angestrebten Abschlussplatzierungen fällt regelmäßig geringer aus als die Summe der tatsächlich erreichbaren Tabellenplätze. Zahlreiche Clubs streben vordere Tabellenränge an. Da selbige allerdings nur in begrenzter Zahl zur Verfügung stehen, werden einige Teams ihr sportliches Saisonziel zwangsweise nicht erreichen. Ursächlich für eine zu große sportliche Erfolgserwartung dürfte regelmäßig eine irrationale Einschätzung der clubspezifischen Handlungssituation mangels strategischer Analyse sein.

4.3.1.3 Zieldimensionen von sportlichem und wirtschaftlichem Erfolg

Um ihre entscheidungsleitende Funktion für die Gestaltung strategischer Programme zu entfalten, sind die beiden Oberziele des Teamsports nach Inhalt, Ausmaß und zeitlichem Bezug zu dimensionieren. Sportlicher und wirtschaftlicher Erfolg bilden zunächst nur *allgemeine Ausgangsziele*. Ausgangsziele stellen nach Wild (1982, S. 40) „Absichten oder Setzungen dar, die noch nicht auf ihre Realisierbarkeit geprüft und mit anderen Zielen koordiniert wurden". Sie sind im Zuge des strategischen Managementprozesses in *clubspezifische Planziele* zu transformieren. „Planziele sind Ziele, die bereits durch Planung konkretisiert, auf ihre Realisierbarkeit hinsichtlich der erforderlichen Ressourcen, Maßnahmen sowie sonstigen Voraussetzungen geprüft sind." Tab. 1 zeigt Optionen zur Dimensionierung des sportlichen Erfolgsziels:

Zielinhalt Zeitbezug	Meisterschaft	Nationaler Pokal	Internationaler Wettbewerb
Myozyklus (1 Spiel)	Sieg Unentschieden Niederlage	Sieg Niederlage	Sieg Unentschieden Niederlage
Mikrozyklus (1 Saison)	Platz x bis y	Runde	Runde / Gruppenphase
Mesozyklus (2-3 Saisons)	Aufstieg Ligaetablierung Inter. Qualifikation	Teilnahme	Teilnahme
Makrozyklus (> 3 Saisons)	Profi-Club (Mitglied des Profiteamsports) Nationaler Club (Mitglied der nationalen Spitze) Champions Club (Mitglied der europäischen Spitze) Sonstige		

Tab. 1: Dimensionierung sportlichen Erfolgs nach Inhalt, Ausmaß und Zeitbezug

Wichtigster Clubwettbewerb ist die Meisterschaft. Das Abschneiden in der Liga hat Konsequenzen für den sportlichen Auftritt eines Teamsportunternehmens in der Folgesaison. Je nach Abschlussplatzierung folgt die Qualifikation für einen internationalen Wettbewerb, der Klassenerhalt, der Ab- oder Aufstieg. Nationale Pokalwettbewerbe werden nach dem K.O.-System, internationale Konkurrenzen i.d.R. aus einem Mix aus K.O.- und Gruppenrunden ausgetragen. Da für den Ausgang einzelner Partien sowohl in Pokal- als auch in Ligaspielen unabhängig von etwaigen finanziell bedingten Spielstärkeunterschieden der aufeinander treffenden Mannschaften Ergebnisoffenheit herrscht (Quitzau, 2003), sind einzelne Spielerfolge nur bedingt planbar. Aus wirtschaftlicher Sicht müssen gerade die Einnahmen aus Pokalkonkurrenzen daher den Charakter von Zusatzerlösen besitzen, die nicht zur Deckung laufender Verpflichtungen benötigt werden. Plant ein Teamsportunternehmen hingegen ein bestimmtes Fixum an Erlösen aus den Pokalwettbewerben ein, welches das Erreichen einer höheren Wettbewerbsrunde voraussetzt, kann ein vorzeitiges Ausscheiden zu finanziellen Deckungslücken führen.

Im Ligawettbewerb relativiert die Summe der Meisterschaftsspiele die Ergebnisoffenheit der einzelnen Partien. Durch statistische Modellrechnungen, die die Interdependenz von getätigten Spielstärkeinvestitionen und sportlichem Erfolg berücksichtigen, lassen sich Häufigkeitsverteilungen für das Erreichen eines bestimmten Tabellenrangs simulieren (Dietl/Hasan/Korthals, 2005). Aufbauend sind Prognosen zum wahrscheinlichen Erfolg im Ligawettbewerb, d.h. die Formulierung eines realistischen Zielrangkorridors möglich. So könnte ein Erstligaclub nach akkurater Abwägung der Gegebenheiten im Innen- und Außenverhältnis beispielsweise den Rangkorridor 12 bis 15 als Real Case bzw. wahrscheinlichstes sportliches Verlaufsszenario determinieren und als angestrebtes Saisonziel formulieren.

Da quantitative Modelle die Realität des Profifußballs aufgrund der Komplexität sportlicher und wirtschaftlicher Einflussfaktoren aber stets nur bedingt zu erklären vermögen (Quitzau, 2003), ist auch der sportliche Worst Case – im angeführten Beispiel also der Abstieg in Liga zwei – in die Planungen zu integrieren. Seine Auswirkungen sind offen zu legen und in die (wirtschaftliche) Kalkulation aufzunehmen. Der Eintritt des sportlichen Worst Case darf ein Teamsportunternehmen nicht unvorbereitet treffen. Ansonsten ist eine nachhaltige Gefährdung der finanziellen Stabilität und damit der Bestandssicherung denkbar.

Wirtschaftlicher Erfolg lässt sich über die vier grundlegenden Bestimmungskategorien Zahlungsbereitschaft, Ertragskraft, Wirtschaftlichkeit und Finanzpotential operationalisieren. Dabei stellt die *Ertragskraft* den übergeordneten Maßstab dieser Quadratur dar. Eine geeignete Kennzahl zur Messung der Ertragskraft ist der *Free-Cashflow*. Letzterer zeigt den Einnahmenüberschuss, der einem Unternehmen am Ende einer Wertschöpfungsperiode für Zins- und Tilgungszahlungen, Gewinnausschüttungen sowie zukünftige Investitionen zur Verfügung steht. Zahlungsbereitschaft, Wirtschaftlichkeit und Finanzpotential sind Nebenbedingungen, die zur Optimierung der Ertragskraft entsprechend zu steuern sind.

Im Teamsport fokussiert sich ökonomisches Erfolgsdenken häufig auf den Nachweis der wirtschaftlichen Leistungsfähigkeit gemäß den Bedingungen der *Lizenzierung*. Allerdings ist die Lizenzierungspraxis kaum geeignet, ein fundiertes Bild des wirtschaftlichen Leistungsvermögens zu zeichnen. Lizenzierungsverfahren sind regelmäßig auf eine kurzfristige, primär liquiditätsorientierte Analyseperspektive reduziert. Daher wird nur im Falle der Lizenzverweigerung ein zweifelsfreier Rückschluss auf das wirtschaftliche Leistungsvermögen möglich. Andererseits ist ein positiver Durchlauf der Lizenzierung längst nicht gleichzusetzen mit der Sicherstellung stabiler wirtschaftlicher Verhältnisse. Auch ein Teamsportclub, der keine Einnahmen-, sondern Ausgabenüberschüsse erwirtschaftet und dadurch sein Finanzpotential substantiell schwächt, kann regelmäßig die Lizenz erhalten, wenn es ihm gelingt, mittels Kreditaufnahmen usw. seine Liquidität zu wahren.

Soll also Nachhaltigkeit bei der Clubentwicklung gewährleistet werden, darf die wirtschaftliche Erfolgsorientierung nicht primär am positiven Durchlauf des Lizenzierungsverfahrens ausgerichtet werden. Übergeordneten Stellenwert muss die Fähigkeit zur Generierung von Einnahmenüberschüssen besitzen. Der Ausweis positiver Free-Cashflows über mehrere Spielzeiten hinweg ist subsumtiv als *Steigerung des Unternehmenswertes* zu deklarieren. Verfahren zur cashflowbezogenen Berechnung des Unternehmenswertes ist die Discounted Cashflow-Methode (DCF). Für ihre Anwendung im Teamsport existieren einschlägige Untersuchungen (Korthals, 2005; Escher, 2007).

Zeitbezug	Zielinhalt	Zielausmaß	Neben-bedingungen
Myozyklus (1 Spiel)	Free-Cashflow	*Optimum:* Einnahmenüberschuss	
Mikrozyklus (1 Saison)	Free-Cashflow	*Minimum:* Deckung Kapitaldienst (Zins- & Tilgung)	Liquidität
Mesozyklus (2-3 Saisons)		*Optimum:* Deckung Kapitaldienst + Realisierung Plan-investitionen	Wirtschaftlich-keit
Makrozyklus (> 3 Saisons)	Unternehmenswert (auf Basis DCF)	*Optimum:* Realisierung sportliches Oberziel bei finanziellem Gleichgewicht	Finanzpotential

Tab. 2: Dimensionierung wirtschaftlichen Erfolgs nach Inhalt, Ausmaß und Zeitbezug

Das anzustrebende Ausmaß der Unternehmenswertsteigerung ist vor dem Hintergrund der spezifischen Gegebenheiten in Clubumwelt und -inwelt zu definieren. Die Erzielung eines Einnahmeüberschusses stellt keinen Selbstzweck, sondern Mittel zum Zweck dar: Wirtschaftliches Leistungsvermögen ist notwendige Voraussetzung für die Realisierung der präferierten sportlichen Erfolgsziele. Entsprechend gilt es, das Zielniveau des Einnahmenüberschusses nach den clubindividuellen Verwendungszwecken auszurichten. Dabei muss der Zielwert im Minimum die Leistung des Kapitaldienstes für bestehende Zins- und Tilgungsverpflichtungen abdecken. Im Falle der Unterdeckung müsste der Sportclub, um Zahlungsverzug gegenüber seinen Gläubigern zu verhindern, weiteres Fremdkapital aufnehmen und/oder

Vermögenswerte (z.B. Spieler) veräußern. Im Optimum sollte der Einnahmenüberschuss neben Zins und Tilgung geplante Investitionen in Steine (Infrastruktur) und Beine (Spielstärke) ermöglichen.

Tab. 2 fasst die im Vorfeld erläuterten Dimensionierungsvorschläge für eine adäquate wirtschaftliche Erfolgssteuerung in Teamsportclubs zusammen.

4.3.1.4 Zielkoordination von sportlichem und wirtschaftlichem Erfolg

Die bisherigen Erläuterungen haben verdeutlicht: Sportliche und wirtschaftliche Zielsetzungen können nicht losgelöst voneinander erfolgen. Trotz der Präferenz für den sportlichen Erfolg darf dessen Zielausmaß nicht als Maximierungsbedingung determiniert werden. Ein Maximierungsbestreben gewährleistet durch die fehlende Ziel-Mittel-Relation keine Kontrolle darüber, ob der Fortbestand des Teamsportunternehmens gesichert bleibt. Resultat einer Überbetonung der sportlichen Leistungsdimension ist die Überinvestitionsproblematik.

Um eine nachhaltige Clubentwicklung zu sichern, muss die Präferenzbeziehung von sportlichem zu wirtschaftlichem Oberziel vom Leitgedanken der Optimierung geprägt sein, d.h. Optimierung des sportlichen Erfolges auf der Basis langfristiger finanzieller Stabilität. Dabei meint Optimierung die wechselseitige Überprüfung auf Realisierbarkeit anhand der verfügbaren Ressourcen, erforderlichen Maßnahmen sowie sonstigen Voraussetzungen. Mit anderen Worten ist es Zweck und Aufgabe eines strategischen Managements im Teamsport, eine *langfristig effektive Koordination von sportlicher und wirtschaftlicher Erfolgsorientierung* herzustellen.

Effektivität bedeutet im Sinne Maliks (2006, S. 312) „den Unterschied zwischen Erfolg und Misserfolg, von Anstrengung und Leistung, von Arbeit und Ergebnis, von richtig und falsch".

Ob die Koordination von sportlicher und wirtschaftlicher Erfolgsorientierung effektiv ist, lässt sich angesichts der bestehenden Erfolgsrelativität nur vor dem Hintergrund der clubindividuellen Wirklichkeiten beurteilen. Unterschiede im Außen- und Innenverhältnis machen das einzelne Teamsportunternehmen zu einem *Steuerungsobjekt sui generis* sowohl im Vergleich zu Dienstleistungsunternehmen anderer Branchen, als auch im Vergleich der Teamsportunternehmen untereinander (Kupfer, 2006). Je nach Positionierung gegenüber den externen Stakeholdern einerseits, sowie den wertschöpfenden Potentialen andererseits, variiert das Niveau einer effektiven Zielkoordination. Inferiores sportliches Leistungspotential und finanzielle Stabilität schließen einander nicht aus. Die rationale strategische Analyse der eigenen Handlungssituation wird zur Prämisse einer effektiven Zielkoordination.

4.3.1.5 Zielkoordination im Lichte der Clubverfassung

Durch die Vorgabe von Verfügungsrechten, insbesondere Koordinations- und Ertragsrechten, resultieren aus der Unternehmensverfassung rechtliche Rahmenbedingungen für die unternehmerische Zielbildung. Die Unternehmensverfassung steht in engem Abhängigkeitsverhältnis zur Rechtsform. Teamsportclubs firmieren heute entweder noch im traditionellen Rechtskleid des eingetragenen Vereins oder aber als Kapitalgesellschaften.

Die Rechtsform des e.V. eröffnet im Hinblick auf die Realisierung einer effektiven Zielkoordination *opportunistische Verhaltensspielräume* für den verschwenderischen Umgang mit Ressourcen. Fehlende Ertragsanreize für Vorstand und Mitglieder sind der Sicherstellung stabiler finanzieller Verhältnisse abträglich. Der Überbetonung des sportlichen Erfolgstrebens bzw. ungezügelten Spielstärkeinvestitionen stehen keine wirksamen Verfassungsbarrieren entgegen. Hieran vermögen Anpassungsmaßnahmen in der Organstruktur der Sportclubs wenig zu ändern, da sie die grundlegende Problematik allenfalls kaschieren.

Im Unterschied zum e.V. liegen bei Kapitalgesellschaften Ertragsrechte kraft rechtlicher Norm vor und fallen den Gesellschaftern des Unternehmens zu. Aus eingetragenen Vereinen durch Ausgliederung des Lizenzspielbetriebs hervorgegangene Kapitalgesellschaften befinden sich im Teamsport jedoch zumeist mehrheitlich im Eigentum des Muttervereins. Im Fußball ist die Mehrheitsbeteiligung des Muttervereins aufgrund von Verbandsvorschriften (50 % + 1-Regel) sogar unausweichlich für den Lizenzerhalt. Teamsportkapitalgesellschaften stellen daher regelmäßig keine vollwertigen Kapitalgesellschaften im Sinne der ökonomischen Theorie dar. Ertragsanreize zur Realisierung wirtschaftlichen Erfolgs können sich in Abhängigkeit der Zielausrichtung des Muttervereins unter Umständen nicht entfalten. Dominiert im Vorstand des Muttervereins das Streben nach sportlichem Erfolg, erlaubt es die Mehrheitsbeteiligung, diese Zieldominanz auf das Handeln der Teamsportkapitalgesellschaft zu übertragen.

Die Sicherstellung einer effektiven Zielkoordination ist damit in hohem Maße an die handelnden Clubverantwortlichen gebunden. Instrumente der *Corporate Governance* helfen, diese Abhängigkeit zu reduzieren und opportunistische Verhaltensspielräume systematisch zu überwachen. Fundierte Vorschläge zur Gestaltung der Corporate Governance im Teamsport finden sich bei Lang (2007).

4.3.1.6 Zielkoordination im Lichte der Clubkultur

Anders als die Clubverfassung, die einen expliziten, formalen Rahmen absteckt, wirkt die Clubkultur implizit auf Zielkoordination und strategischen Steuerungskurs. Kognitiv entwickelte und affektiv geprägte Werte und Normen beeinflussen über bestimmte Wahrnehmungs-, Denk- und Verhaltensmuster das Entscheiden und Handeln der Organisationsmitglieder (Bea/Haas, 2001).

Für Teamsportunternehmen können (aus ihrer Vergangenheit als Non-Profit-Organisation übermittelte) *opportunistische Perzeptionen und Präferenzen* nachgewiesen werden, die die Festlegung und Umsetzung einer effektiven Zielkoordination hemmen (Keller, 2007). Vor Einzug der Kommerzialisierung zeichnete die Sportclubs ein nach innen gerichtetes, traditionsbestimmtes Normen- und Wertegefüge aus, dessen Zusammenhangskraft durch die hohe Identifikation loyaler Mitglieder, das gemeinsame Streben nach sportlichem Erfolg sowie die starke Orientierung an Verhaltensweisen der Clubführung unter Vernachlässigung wirtschaftlichen Leistungsdenkens getragen wurde. Das Erfordernis nachhaltiger wirtschaftlicher Leistungsfähigkeit als Grundlage sportlichen Erfolgs dürfte daher oft nur schwach in den Clubkulturen verwurzelt sein. Versperren tradierte kulturelle Normen und Werte aber die rationale Analyse der eigenen Situation im Spannungsfeld einer durch die Kommerzialisierung veränderten Clubumwelt, resultiert daraus eine massive Krisenanfälligkeit. Das Sportunternehmen ist dann nicht in der Lage, zukunftsweisende Strategien für eine nachhaltige Clubentwicklung zu programmieren.

Aus instrumenteller Sichtweise ergibt sich für die Clubs somit die Notwendigkeit, tradierte Normen und Werte, die eine effektive Zielkoordination verhindern, aktiv zu verlernen. Für die „Metamorphose" vom gemeinnützigen Verein zum nachhaltig agierenden Teamsportunternehmen bedarf es einer Einstellungsänderung. Grundvoraussetzung hierfür ist eine eindeutige und einheitliche Identifikation der *Clubführung* mit innovativen Normen- und Wertevorstellungen. Nur im Falle des Vorbilds und Vorlebens der Clubverantwortlichen lässt sich von den sonstigen Organisationsmitgliedern erwarten, dass sie ihre Verhaltensweisen auf ein verändertes Selbstverständnis des Teamsportunternehmens ausrichten. Ferner fördern die Implementierung von *Leitbild* und *Führungsgrundsätzen* die Entwicklung einer außen- und zukunftsorientierten Clubkultur (Keller, 2007).

4.3.2 Strategische Analyse des Außenverhältnisses
In den folgenden Abschnitten wird detailliert auf die strategische Analyse der Makroumwelt und der Aufgabenumwelt eingegangen.

4.3.2.1 Strategische Analyse der Makroumwelt
Ausgehend von der im Abschnitt 4.2.2.2 geschilderten Segmentierung der Makroumwelt sollten Teamsportclubs insbesondere Entwicklungen in der *politisch-rechtlichen Umwelt* dezidiert beobachten. Der professionelle Sport ist in den vergangenen Jahren angesichts seiner wachsenden ökonomischen Bedeutung verstärkt in den Fokus der nationalen und europäischen Gesetzgebung gerückt. Resultat sind Implikationen für das strategische Management der Teamsportunternehmen.

An erster Stelle ist das Bosman-Urteil vom Dezember 1995 zu nennen. Mit dem Bosman-Urteil erklärte der Europäische Gerichtshof unter Bezugnahme auf supranationale Bestimmungen des EU-Arbeitsrechts die bis dahin in den nationalen Sportverbänden geltenden Beschränkungen für die Beschäftigung und den Einsatz ausländischer Berufssportler (mit Herkunft aus der Europäischen Gemeinschaft) für ungültig. Zudem wurde die Geltendmachung von Transferentschädigungen beim Vereinswechsel nach Ablauf der Vertragslaufzeit untersagt. Folge der Liberalisierung des Spielermarktes war eine Umverteilung der Verfügungsrechte von den Clubs zu den Spielern, die sich empirisch durch eine Zunahme der durchschnittlichen Spielergehälter und Vertragslaufzeiten belegen lässt (Swieter, 2002).

Des Weiteren stand die Zentralvermarktung von TV-Rechten an Sportwettbewerben bereits mehrfach im Blickfeld kartellrechtlicher Prozesse, ohne das bis dato ein abschließendes Urteil über ihre Zulässigkeit gefällt wurde. Ein weiteres Thema auf der Agenda der EU-Kommission mit direkten Folgen für das Clubmanagement bzw. -sponsoring ist ein potentielles Alkoholwerbeverbot. Beispiele für sportrelevante Gesetzesdebatten auf nationaler Ebene sind die Diskussionen zur Liberalisierung des Wettmarktes oder zur Absetzbarkeit der Ausgaben für VIP-Logen.

Neben Veränderungen in der politisch-rechtlichen Umwelt können sich soziokulturelle Einflussfaktoren auf das Clubmanagement auswirken. Aspekte wie demographische Entwicklung, Gesundheitsbewusstsein, Körperbilder, Erlebnisbedürfnisse usw. sind für den Sport von hoher Relevanz. Sie wirken auf die Nachfrage nach Sportdienstleistungen (Breuer, 2005).

Technologische Entwicklungen, hier v.a. der rasante Wandel von Informations- und Kommunikationstechnologien, beeinflussen die mediale Vermarktung der Clubs. Internet, Mobilfunk, Pay-TV usw. eröffnen zukunftsträchtige, strategisch bedeutsame Einnahmepotentiale. Hingegen lebt der Teamsport ein von makroökonomischen Trends weitgehend losgelöstes Eigenleben.

4.3.2.2 Strategische Analyse der Aufgabenumwelt

Während sich die Beziehung zur Makroumwelt hauptsächlich monolateral gestaltet, d.h. i.d.R. auch langfristig nicht vom einzelnen Teamsportunternehmen zu beeinflussen ist, bestehen gegenüber der Aufgabenumwelt *wechselseitige Beziehungszusammenhänge*. Abb. 3 stellt die Aufgabenumwelt im Teamsport als System wesentlicher Stakeholder dar.

Das Wissen um die Beziehungszusammenhänge zu den Stakeholdern ist grundlegend für die strategische Positionierung. Entscheidungsträger in den Clubs müssen die fokalen Interessen ihrer Anspruchsgruppen bei der Ableitung strategischer Programme berücksichtigen, um eine effektive Koordination von sportlicher und wirtschaftlicher Erfolgsorientierung zu gewährleisten. Nachfolgend werden fokale Charakteristika der diversen Stakeholder in knapper Form vorgestellt. Sie sind vom einzelnen Club im Lichte seiner clubspezifischen Wirklichkeiten zu präzisieren.

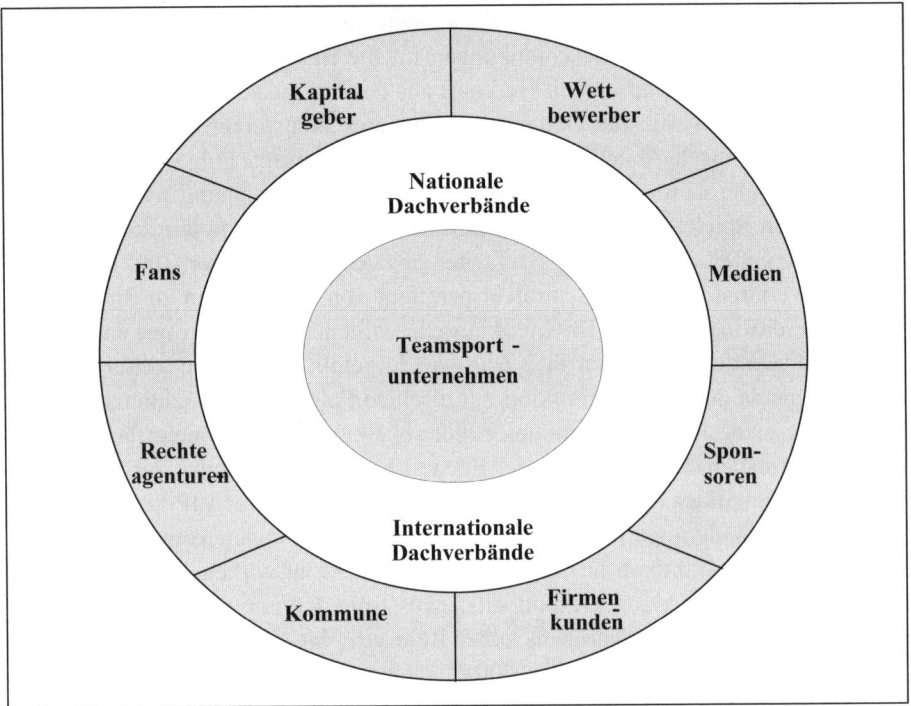

Abb. 3: Wesentliche Stakeholder von Teamsportunternehmen

Dachverbände:

Die nationalen und internationalen Dachverbände der jeweiligen Sportart geben *verbindliche Regelungen* vor, die das Entscheidungsfeld eines Teamsportunternehmens formal begrenzen und vom einzelnen Club kaum modifizierbar sind. Hierzu zählen insbesondere die Vorgabe von Spielregeln, Wettbewerbsformaten, Spielplänen, Transferrichtlinien, Lizenzierungsvorschriften und Nachwuchsförderungsauflagen, die Abstellung von Spielern für die Nationalmannschaft sowie Maßnahmen der zentralen TV-Rechtevermarktung und -einnahmenverteilung. Einfluss auf die Dachverbände kann unter Umständen durch Bündelung der Interessen mehrerer Clubs entstehen. Ein Beispiel hierfür ist die G-14, als Interessenvertretung der führenden europäischen Fußballunternehmen.

Kommune:

Als kleinste Instanz im Geflecht der öffentlichen Gebietskörperschaften kann die heimische Kommune zur Aufgabenumwelt eines Teamsportclubs gezählt werden. Zwischen Kommune und ansässigem Sportunternehmen besteht im Normalfall eine tiefe Verwurzelung. Regelmäßig übernimmt ein Proficlub die Rolle einer gesellschaftlichen Institution innerhalb seiner Heimatstadt. Dabei sind Faktoren wie die Größe und die Wirtschaftskraft der Kommune als perspektivisch unveränderliche

Rahmenbedingungen in Kauf zu nehmen, während systematische *Lobbyarbeit* die Beziehung zur Kommune im Sinne der angestrebten Clubentwicklung zu begünstigen vermag (z.B. Unterstützung beim Spielstättenneubau). Im Eishockey waren in der Vergangenheit aber auch Umzüge von Teams in andere Städte beobachtbar.

Fans:

Fans sind direkte Konsumenten der Teamsportproduktion. Sie nehmen unter emotionaler Verbundenheit mit hoher Regelmäßigkeit die angebotenen Dienstleistungen (Stadionbesuch, Merchandising) eines von ihnen loyal favorisierten Clubs in Anspruch. Allerdings wäre es strategisch fehlerhaft, die Fans ausschließlich aus ökonomischer Sicht, als Kunden zu betrachten. Die große innere Verbundenheit der Fans und deren relativ ausgeprägte Loyalitätsneigung ist das *kostbarste Gut eines Teamsportclubs* überhaupt (Bauer/Exler/Sauer, 2004). Beispiele aus dem Profifußball zeigen, dass der Fan-Faktor gerade auch in wirtschaftlichen Krisensituationen einen zentralen „Rettungsanker" darstellen kann. So brachten Fans und Gönner des FC St. Pauli im Jahr 2003 in einer bundesweiten Aktion binnen drei Monaten 2,4 Mio. € für den Fortbestand des insolvenzbedrohten Hamburger Kultclubs auf.

Medien:

Teamsportclubs weisen Beziehungszusammenhänge zu Medienunternehmen aus den Bereichen Fernsehen, Radio, Print (Zeitungen, Zeitschriften) und neue Medien (Internet, Mobilfunk) auf. Herausragende Relevanz besitzt die Beziehung zum *Leitmedium Fernsehen*. Das Interesse der Fernsehsender am Sport ist primär strategisch motiviert. Insbesondere den Programminhalt Profifußball nutzen die TV-Sender als Katalysator zur Realisierung ihrer spezifischen unternehmerischen Zielsetzungen. Fußballübertragungen erzielen hohe Zuschauerreichweiten. Hierdurch lassen sich Nachfrageverbundeffekte auf sonstige Programminhalte sowie eine gesteigerte Attraktivität als Werbeplattform generieren. Ferner stimulieren Fußballfernsehrechte die Etablierung neuer Sendeformen wie Pay-TV und Pay-per-View. Die Relevanz der anderen Teamsportarten ist aus Sicht des Fernsehens hingegen vergleichsweise inferior. Andererseits streben die Spitzenligen in Eishockey, Basketball und Handball eine Ausweitung ihrer TV-Präsenz an. Durch den Verkauf von Fernsehrechten fließen den Clubs direkte Erlösströme zu. Weiterhin dient die Fernsehpräsenz als bedeutsamer Treiber der Vermarktungsaktivitäten in den Geschäftsfeldern Sponsoring, Spieltag und Merchandising.

Sponsoren:

Sponsoring stellt eine der zentralen Einnahmesäulen des Teamsports dar. Als attraktivste Sponsoringmaßnahme gilt das Trikotsponsoring. Klassisch sind zudem Bandenwerbung und Ausrüstersponsoring. Die dynamische Verbreitung des Internets eröffnet diverse neumediale Werbeoptionen. Eine andere innovative Sponsoringmaßnahme, die sich gerade im Falle modernisierter Spielstätten wachsender

Akzeptanz erfreut, ist der Erwerb der Namensrechte an der Arena. Sponsoren sehen ihr Engagement im Sport primär vor dem Hintergrund kommunikativer Zielsetzungen. Befragungen weisen konstant die Erhöhung bzw. Stabilisierung des Bekanntheitsgrades sowie Aufbau, Veränderung oder Stabilisierung des Images als Top-Ziele der Sponsoren aus (Pilot Group, 2007). Wahrnehmungspräsenz und positive Attribute des gesponserten Sportclubs sollen auf das eigene Unternehmen transferiert werden. Direkt auf absatzpolitische Zielsetzungen ausgerichtete Sponsorships bilden hingegen eine Ausnahme, dürften zukünftig allerdings an Bedeutung gewinnen. Risiken des Sponsorings liegen in der latenten Gefahr eines *Abhängigkeitsverhältnisses*. Gerade bei kleineren, in der Vermarktung weniger breit aufgestellten Teamsportunternehmen sind in der Vergangenheit Fälle der Fremdbeeinflussung durch Sponsoren publik geworden. Clubs mit inferiorem Leistungspotential sollten ihre Sponsorenstruktur daher auf die Akquise vieler, kleiner und mittlerer Industriepartner, anstelle einzelner Großsponsoren konzentrieren.

Firmenkunden:
Charakteristisches Merkmal von Firmenkunden ist die von einer Sponsoringpartnerschaft losgelöste Nachfrage der vom Teamsportunternehmen offerierten *Hospitality-Leistungen*. Letztere beinhalten im Wesentlichen den Zugang zu Logen und Business-Seats, der am Spieltag mit besonderen Zuschauerrechten wie einer exklusiven Bewirtung und Verpflegung kombiniert wird. In der jüngeren Vergangenheit hat sich das Hospitality zu einer bedeutsamen Einnahmesäule für Sportclubs entwickelt. Ursächlich für dieses Marktwachstum sind zum einen die vielerorts durchgeführten Spielstättenmodernisierungen, die das Angebot von Logen und Business Seats überhaupt erst in nennenswertem Umfang ermöglichten. Zum zweiten scheint Hospitality ein passfähiges Produkt für die moderne Erlebnisgesellschaft zu sein, das das Grundbedürfnis der Menschen nach dem Erleben bevorzugter individueller Behandlung und Distinktion befriedigt. Firmenkunden nutzen Hospitality zur Kundenbindung und -akquise, als Plattform zum Networking, aber auch im Rahmen interner Anreizsysteme für verdiente Mitarbeiter.

Rechteagenturen:
Die Tätigkeitsfelder von Vermarktungsagenturen liegen an den Schnittstellen des Beziehungsdreiecks von Sport, Medien und Wirtschaft. Sie wirken als Intermediäre zwischen Sport und Wirtschaft, Sport und Medien sowie Medien und Wirtschaft. Relevanz für Teamsportunternehmen besitzen die beiden erstgenannten Tätigkeitsfelder. Ihre Basis ist der *Handel mit Sportrechten*. Gegen Entgelt treten die Clubs bestimmte Vermarktungsrechte für ein vertraglich fixiertes Zeitfenster (im Einzelfall bis zu 15 Jahren) an die Agenturen ab. Diese veräußern die Rechte in der Folge an die entsprechenden Nachfragergruppen (z.B. Sponsoren). Für die Agenturen als gewerbswirtschaftliche Organisationen stehen dabei ökonomische Aspekte im Vor-

dergrund. Regelmäßig befinden sie sich im Eigentum von Medienkonzernen oder institutionellen Investoren und agieren primär renditeorientiert.

Kapitalgeber:
Die Mehrzahl der Teamsportunternehmen ist neben den Vermarktungsumsätzen auf den Zufluss von externem Kapital für die Abwicklung des Geschäftsbetriebes angewiesen. Im Fokus stehen dabei Formen der Kreditfinanzierung. Teamsportkapitalgesellschaften besitzen ferner die rechtliche Zugangsoption zu Finanzierungsinstrumenten des Kapitalmarktes. Seit 2007 wird die Kreditaufnahme bei Bank- und Finanzdienstleistungsinstituten via Gesetzesvorschrift durch das so genannte *Basel II* erschwert (Keller, 2006). Basel II knüpft Kreditvergabe und -konditionen an die Fähigkeit des Kreditnehmers zur termingerechten, vollständigen Zins- und Tilgungszahlung. In Folge werden (Teamsport-)Unternehmen mit instabilem wirtschaftlichem Leistungsvermögen mit erschwerten Finanzierungskonditionen, d.h. einer erhöhten Zinsbelastung oder aber einer beeinträchtigten Kreditaufnahme an sich konfrontiert. Analog setzt die Fremd- und Eigenkapitalfinanzierung über den Kapitalmarkt eine objektive, ganzheitliche Darstellung der unternehmerischen Erfolgs- und Risikofaktoren voraus. Die Erschließung alternativer Außenfinanzierungsquellen wird nur beim *Nachweis der Kapitalmarktreife* möglich. In einer Umfrage nennen Investoren die Stabilität des sportlichen Erfolges in Verbindung mit einer nachhaltigen finanziellen Stabilität als Kernkriterien für die Erlangung der Kapitalmarktreife von Sportclubs (Metrum Managementberatung, 2004). Mit anderen Worten fundiert die Kapitalmarktreife auf einer effektiven Koordination von sportlichem und wirtschaftlichem Erfolgsstreben. Seit der Jahrtausendwende ist es einzelnen Fußballclubs gelungen, alternative Finanzierungsquellen des Kapitalmarktes, hier v.a. Kreditsubstitute (Asset Backed Securities, Fananleihe) und Mezzanine-Formen (Genussscheine), in Anspruch zu nehmen. Der bislang einzige Börsengang im deutschen Teamsport, das Going Public von Borussia Dortmund, rührt vom Oktober 2000.

Wettbewerber:
Auf die besondere Form des Wettbewerbs in Teamsport, die *Kooperenz*, wurde im Abschnitt 4.3.1.2 sowie im einführenden Kapitel des vorliegenden Handbuchs bereits hingewiesen. Bei genauerer Betrachtung stellt der sportliche Wettbewerb unter den Clubs in erster Linie einen Beschaffungs- bzw. Bieterwettbewerb um Spielstärke dar (Fritz, 2006). Die relative Spielstärke entscheidet über das Ergebnis der Teamsportproduktion, d.h. das Abschneiden in Meisterschaft und Pokalkonkurrenzen. Infolge des Bosman-Urteils können die Clubs ihre Spielstärke heute auf einem globalen Spielermarkt rekrutieren. Spielerverpflichtungen sind weitgehend losgelöst von limitierenden Vorschriften bezüglich der Nationalität der eingesetzten Akteure möglich. Bei ihren Talentinvestitionen haben sich die Clubs daher auf globale Konkurrenz einzustellen, die bereits bei der Nachwuchsförderung beginnen kann.

Der ökonomische Wettbewerb um die der Teamsportproduktion nachgelagerten Vermarktungsstufen ist ein Absatzwettbewerb. Ein Sportclub kann die Akquise von Fans, Firmenkunden und Sponsoren lokal, national oder international ausrichten. Durch ihren Standort sind Teamsportunternehmen grundsätzlich lokal verwurzelt. Die Teilnahme an der nationalen Meisterschaft und den europäischen Clubwettbewerben erlaubt jedoch eine Vermarktung über die lokalen Grenzen hinaus. Insgesamt weisen Beschaffungs- und Absatzmärkte des professionellen Teamsports lokale wie globale Elemente auf. Um innerhalb dieses Dualismus zu einer effektiven Zielkoordination zu gelangen, muss eine fundierte *Konkurrentenanalyse* im Mittelpunkt des strategischen Clubmanagements stehen. Die Überprüfung einer intendierten Clubentwicklung auf Realisierbarkeit bedingt nicht nur die Einschätzung der eigenen, sondern auch eine Beurteilung der Leistungsfähigkeit der konkurrierenden Teamsportunternehmen. Das präferierte sportliche Erfolgsziel wird erst vor dem Hintergrund der Positionierung im Wettbewerb evaluierbar. Erfolg in Teamwettbewerben ist ein Ergebnis relativer Stärke.

4.3.3 Strategische Analyse des Innenverhältnisses

Als etabliertestes Konzept zur Analyse der Wertschöpfung gilt die *Wertkette* nach Porter (2005). Sie folgt dem Grundgedanken, dass sich erfolgskritische Ressourcen bzw. Potentiale bei Betrachtung einer Organisation als Ganzes nur äußerst schwer erkennen lassen. Hierfür bedarf es einer Segmentierung des organisatorischen Handelns in zentrale Wertschöpfungsaktivitäten, die wiederum nach primären und sekundären Aktivitäten zu differenzieren sind. Primäre Aktivitäten befassen sich direkt mit der physischen Herstellung des angebotenen Produktes bzw. der offerierten Dienstleistung und dessen/deren Vertrieb. Sekundäre Aktivitäten sind für die Durchführung der primären Aktivitäten in unterstützender Funktion zuständig. Die systematische Analyse der Wertaktivitäten hilft nun, die Stärken und Schwächen einer Organisation in Relation zu ihren Wettbewerbern zu eruieren. Es wird ersichtlich, ob die internen Potentiale als dispositiver Faktor für die angestrebte strategische Positionierung genügen oder nicht.

Dem Verrichtungsprinzip des Teamsports folgend, zeigt Abb. 4 die zentralen Aktivitäten zur Bereitstellung des Leistungsangebots von Sportclubs. Insbesondere die dargestellten sekundären Wertschöpfungselemente können dabei in ihrer Gesamtheit als idealtypisch gelten. Sie sind in der Praxis kaum durchgängig anzutreffen. Beispielsweise verfügen zahlreiche Clubs bis dato weder über ein leistungsstarkes Controlling (Keller/Langner/Amann, 2006), noch über ein Customer Relationship Management, kurz CRM (Zeltinger, 2004).

Sekundäre Aktivitäten

| **Clubführung** |
| (u.a. Strategisches Management) |

| **Clubinfrastruktur** |
| (Trainingsareal, Nachwuchsleistungszentrum, Stadion, Verwaltungstrakt) |

| **Finanzierung** |
| (Kreditinstitute, Kapitalmarkt, Öffentliche Mittel) |

| **Führungsunterstützung** |
| (Rechnungswesen, Controlling, Reporting) |

| **Vermarktungsunterstützung** |
| (Clubmarke, Mitglieder/Fans, CRM) |

| **Personalbeschaffungsunterstützung** |
| (Scouting, Nachwuchsarbeit, Anreiz- & Belohnungssysteme, Ehrenamt) |

wirtschaftlicher Erfolg

Mehrwert durch Koordination

Sportlicher Erfolg

Primäre Aktivitäten

Personalbeschaffung	**Vor-Produktion**	**Vermarktung I**	**Wettkampfproduktion**	**Vermarktung II**
▪ Trainerstab ▪ Spieler ▪ Verwaltungspersonal	Herstellung des sportlichen Leistungsvermögens ▪ Training/ Trainingslager ▪ physiotherapeutische, sportmedizinische, mentale Betreuung ▪ Spielvorbereitung (Aufstellung, Taktik, Gegner, Motivation)	vor dem Spiel ▪ Ticketing (Vorverkauf, Dauerkarten) ▪ Mediale Rechte (TV) ▪ Sponsoring ▪ Hospitality ▪ Merchandising	Sportliche Leistungserstellung am Spieltag ▪ Meisterschaft ▪ Nationaler Pokal ▪ Internationale Wettbewerbe ▪ sonstige	während/ nach dem Spiel ▪ Catering ▪ mediale Rechte (neue Medien) ▪ Sponsoring ▪ Hospitality ▪ Merchandising

| Schnittstelle zur Wertkette der Konkurrenzclubs
- Teamproduktion - |

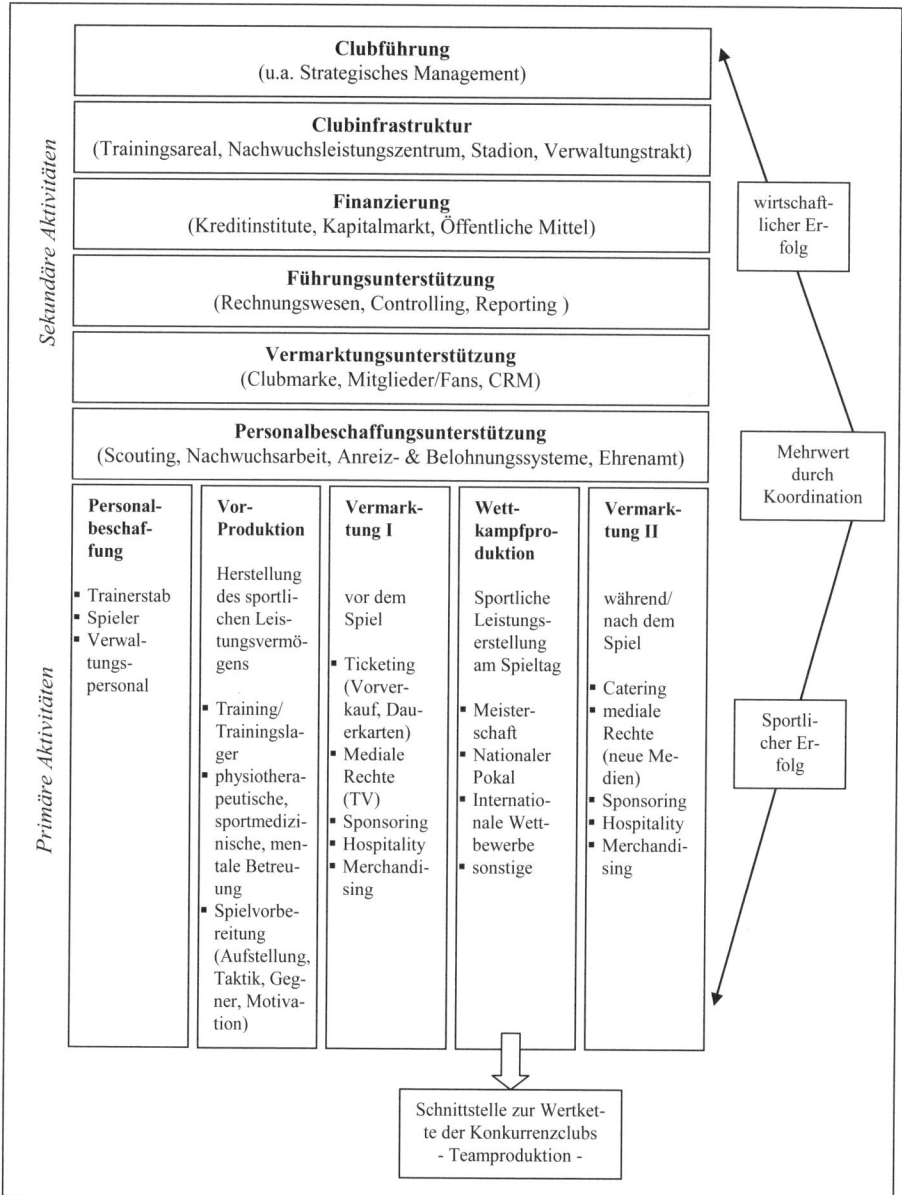

Abb. 4: Wertkette von Teamsportunternehmen

Im Fokus der primären Wertschöpfungsaktivitäten eines Teamsportunternehmens steht die *Wettkampfproduktion*, d.h. die sportliche Leistungserbringung der Mannschaft im Zuge der Teilnahme an Meisterschaft, Pokal sowie gegebenenfalls einem internationalen Wettbewerb. Natürlich zählt auch das Mitwirken an Freundschaftsspielen, -turnieren etc. zur sportlichen Leistungserbringung, ist in seiner sportlichen und monetären Relevanz den offiziellen Wettbewerbsformaten aber regelmäßig nachgeordnet. Voraussetzung der Wettkampfproduktion ist die Zusammenstellung einer leistungsfähigen Mannschaft, d.h. die Rekrutierung geeigneter Akteure am Spielermarkt. Für deren Training, Betreuung und Spielvorbereitung bedarf es eines Trainer- und Betreuerstabs. Als Dienstleistungsunternehmen muss ein Sportclub seine sportliche Leistungsbereitschaft bereits im Vorfeld der eigentlichen Wettkampfproduktion generieren (Wadsack, 2006).

Die sportliche Leistungserstellung ist conditio sine qua non für die Entstehung des Vermarktungsangebots. Sportrechte entfalten ihren ökonomischen Wert erst durch die Erstellung der sportlichen Leistung. Die Aktivitäten in den Geschäftsfeldern Spieltag (Ticketing, Catering, Hospitality), mediale Rechte, Sponsoring und Merchandising sind nicht als eigenständiger Output, sondern als Monetarisierung der Wettkampfproduktion aufzufassen. Dabei erfolgt ein Großteil des Absatzes, wie beispielsweise der Verkauf von Eintrittskarten, bereits vor der eigentlichen Wettkampfproduktion. In Konsequenz wissen die Nachfragergruppen beim Produkterwerb nicht mit Sicherheit, welche Spielqualität sie erwartet. Teamsportspiele sind Erfahrungsgüter. Allerdings können ausgehend von der abgelieferten Spielqualität Impulse positiver oder negativer Art für die zukünftige Nachfrage resultieren. Vermarktungsaktivitäten sind der Wettkampfproduktion insofern vor- und nachgelagert. Genauso wie für die sportliche Leistungserstellung bedarf es für die Vermarktung qualifizierten Personals. Die *Personalbeschaffung* gehört zu den Primäraktivitäten von Sportclubs. Der Bedarf an Verwaltungspersonal reduziert sich bei Zusammenarbeit mit einer externen Vermarktungsagentur. In Abhängigkeit des gewählten Kooperationsmodells ist die Monetarisierung der Wettkampfproduktion dann partiell oder vollständig an den Vermarktungspartner ausgelagert. Die Entscheidung Eigen- versus Fremdvermarktung gleicht folglich der Frage nach der optimalen *Wertschöpfungstiefe*, d.h. nach dem Ausmaß dessen, was an der gesamten Wertschöpfung selbst übernommen wird. Eine externe Vermarktungskooperation reduziert die Wertschöpfungstiefe. Eigenvermarktung bedeutet Wertschöpfungsautarkie: Alle wesentlichen Aufgaben zur Sicherung einer effektiven Zielkoordination liegen dann in den Händen des Teamsportunternehmens.

Die graphische Darstellung der primären Wertschöpfungsaktivitäten verdeutlicht zudem recht anschaulich das Wettbewerbscharakteristikum der Kooperenz. Über die sportliche Leistungserstellung am Spieltag ist die Wertkette eines Clubs mit jener seiner Konkurrenten verbunden.

An vorderster Front der sekundären Wertschöpfungsaktivitäten eines Sportclubs sollten die strategischen Managementvorgaben der Clubführung stehen. Die Clubverantwortlichen haben den zentralen Steuerungskurs für die Gestaltung von Wertschöpfung und Positionierung zu determinieren. Führungsunterstützend wirken Kompetenzen und entsprechend implementierte Instrumente in Rechnungswesen, Controlling und Reporting. Weiterhin muss ein Teamsportunternehmen für seine Leistungserstellung über eine adäquate *Infrastruktur* verfügen. Zur Vorbereitung der Wettkampfproduktion bedarf es eines spitzensportkonformen Trainingsgeländes, in welches im Idealfall ein Nachwuchsleistungszentrum integriert sein sollte. Die Bühne für Wettkampfproduktion und Vermarktung stellt die clubeigene oder kommunale Spielstätte dar. Ort für die Koordination der diversen Vermarktungs- und sonstiger administrativer Tätigkeiten bildet ein Verwaltungtrakt, der bei der Mehrheit der Clubs der Spielstätte angelagert oder in diese baulich integriert ist. Den Erfolg der Vermarktungsaktivitäten forciert eine univok positionierte *Clubmarke* sowie eine große Schar loyaler Mitglieder und Fans. Die Ansprache und Beziehungspflege zur Fangemeinde kann über ein CRM-System instrumentalisiert werden. Auch für die Primäraktivität Personalbeschaffung sind unterstützende Wertschöpfungsaktivitäten denkbar. Hierzu gehören das Scouting, die clubinterne Nachwuchsarbeit, die Implementierung von Anreiz- und Belohungssystemen (z.B. Siegprämien) sowie die Ausnutzung ehrenamtlicher Unterstützungspotentiale. Die Finanzierung der Wertkette ist neben der Kapitalisierung durch Vermarktung in Form der Erschließung pekuniärer Mittel bei Kreditinstituten, am Kapitalmarkt oder über die Partizipation an öffentlichen Fördertöpfen sicher zu stellen.

Ergänzend bleibt zur dargestellten Wertkette zu erwähnen, dass einige Sportclubs, v.a. aus dem Profifußball, neben ihrer wertschöpfenden Kerntätigkeit, der Herstellung und Vermarktung der Wettkampfproduktion, *Diversifizierungsmaßnahmen* eingeleitet haben. Das vorfindbare Spektrum solcher Aktivitäten gestaltet sich prinzipiell recht weitläufig. Es reicht von der Sportartikelherstellung über den Einstieg ins Tourismusgeschäft, der Beteiligung an sporttherapeutischen Rehabilitationszentren bis hin zum Angebot von Finanzdienstleistungen.

4.3.4 Gestaltung strategischer Programme

Die Analysen von Außen- und Innenverhältnis haben mit Nachdruck offenbart, wie eng Positionierung und Wertschöpfung eines Teamunternehmens beieinander liegen. Je nach Ausmaß der internen Leistungspotentiale kann die Positionierung auf den relevanten Beschaffungs- und Absatzmärkten erfolgen. Im Umkehrschluss sind Wertschöpfungsaktivitäten und Ressourcenaufbau entlang den Anforderungen der Aufgabenumwelt auszurichten. Die Beziehungspflege zu Dachverbänden, Kommune, Fans, Sponsoren, Firmenkunden, Medien, Kapitalgebern und Agenturen ist zu konzeptualisieren. Besondere Relevanz kommt in diesem Kontext dem Kooperenzverhältnis gegenüber den Konkurrenzclubs zu. Die Wertigkeit der clubindividuellen Ressourcenpotentiale wird erst in Relation zu den Leistungspotentialen der konkurrierenden Sportclubs evaluierbar. Findet zwischen Umweltpositionierung und Inweltpotentialen keine *konzeptionelle Interaktion* statt, gleicht dies einer strategischen Steuerungslücke, die zunächst zur Überbetonung des sportlichen Erfolgsziels und schließlich zu finanzieller Instabilität führt.

Durch die Gestaltung von strategischen Programmen ist die konzeptionelle und handlungsleitende Verbindung von Positionierung und Wertschöpfung oder anders formuliert, die Umsetzung einer effektiven Zielkoordination sicher zu stellen. Im Fokus hat dabei die strategische Programmierung der nachfolgend benannten, wechselseitig gekoppelten Entscheidungs- bzw. Koordinationsfelder zu stehen.

4.3.4.1 Das strategische Koordinationsfeld „Humankapital"

Das sportliche und wirtschaftliche Abschneiden eines Teamsportunternehmens ist eng mit den handelnden Personen und deren sportlichen und kaufmännischen Fähigkeiten verbunden. In letzter Konsequenz hängt die Clubentwicklung von personalstrategischen Sachverhalten ab. Die Ressourcenqualität in Profikader, Trainer- und Betreuerstab sowie im Führungs- und Verwaltungsbereich nimmt fokalen Einfluss auf die Wettbewerbsposition. Die *Clubführung* bildet die strategisch bedeutsamste Ressource eines Sportclubs überhaupt. Ihre Professionalität, Kontinuität, Solidität und Transparenz gehen einer nachhaltigen Clubentwicklung voraus.

Allgemein lässt sich konstatieren, dass die fortschreitende Kommerzialisierung eine funktionale Differenzierung der sportlichen und kaufmännischen Humanressourcen forciert. Der Einsatz wissenschaftlich qualifizierter Experten wie beispielsweise von Fitness- und Ernährungstrainern oder von Controllern und Marketingspezialisten wird zunehmend mitentscheidend für den realisierbaren Grad der Zielerreichung sein. Folglich ist der Aufbau qualifizierten Humankapitals unter restriktiver Beachtung des clubindividuellen finanziellen Handlungsrahmens sicher zu stellen. Als personenorientierte Organisation hat ein Teamsportunternehmen die strategische Steuerung seiner Humankapitalressourcen als zentrale Aufgabe für die Realisierung einer effektiven Zielkoordination zu begreifen. Aus wertschöpfungsorientierter Perspektive sollte der Fokus dabei auf den drei Teilaktivitäten strategische Personalbeschaffung, strategische Personalbeurteilung und strategische Personalentwicklung liegen (Müller-Stewens/Lechner, 2005).

4.3.4.2 Das strategische Koordinationsfeld „Marktauftritt"

Im strategischen Koordinationsfeld Marktauftritt wirken v.a. die Entscheidungen zur Positionierung der Clubmarke, zur Wertschöpfungstiefe (Eigen- versus Fremdvermarktung) sowie zur Eingrenzung des Marktareals auf die Effektivität der Zielkoordination. Markenstrategie, Arealstrategie und die Entscheidung pro oder contra Fremdvermarktung setzen Nivellierungspunkte für die Konzeptualisierung der Vermarktungsstrategien in den Geschäftsbereichen Spieltag, Sponsoring, Merchandising und mediale Rechte.

Zwischen Markenpotential und der ökonomischen Potenz eines Sportclubs besteht ein enger Zusammenhang. Die *Clubmarke* dient als Speicher von Eigenschaften, Nutzen und Einstellungen, die mit dem Teamsportunternehmen assoziiert werden (Bauer/Exler/Sauer, 2004). Aus einem überlegenen Markenpotential resultiert ein überlegenes Ertragspotential (Mohr/Merget, 2004). Teamsportunternehmen müssen ihre Clubmarke daher als zentralen Ankerpunkt der Bindung von Fans, Sponsoren, Firmenkunden und Kapitalgebern begreifen. Eine Partnerschaftsbindung über den Referenzpunkt sportlicher Erfolg ist aus strategischer Perspektive abzulehnen. Das sportliche Leistungsvermögen kann im Lauf der Zeit trotz sorgfältiger Planung Imponderabilien unterliegen. Gerade Clubs mit inferiorem sportlichem Leistungsvermögen benötigen aber ein nachhaltig wirkendes Bindungsinstrumentarium, das ihnen der sportliche Erfolg nicht in befriedigendem Ausmaß bietet. Hingegen vermag die Clubmarke ein langfristig haltbares Alleinstellungsmerkmal für die Differenzierung im Wettbewerb zu liefern.

Eine univoke Clubmarke muss mit einer stringenten *Arealstrategie* einhergehen, welche die Position des Teamsportunternehmens innerhalb des auf den Absatz- und Beschaffungsmärkten herrschenden Dualismus von Lokalität und Globalität determiniert. So dürften internationale Vermarktungsbemühungen einem Club nur dann adäquate monetäre Rückflüsse sichern, wenn er in der europäischen Leistungsspitze etabliert und infolge seiner sportlichen Auftritte in Medienberichterstattung und Öffentlichkeitsinteresse entsprechend international positioniert ist.

Als Pole des Kontinuums denkbarer *Vermarktungskonstrukte* stehen sich die vollständige Eigenvermarktung durch den Sportclub und die komplette Auslagerung der Vermarktungsaktivitäten an eine externe Agentur gegenüber. Die strategischen Implikationen der beiden kontroversen Vermarktungsextreme sind im Zuge des strategischen Managements dezidiert in ihrer Gesamtheit gegeneinander abzuwägen. Es gilt, kurzfristige Vorteile bewertend mit perspektivischen Nachteilen zu vergleichen und umgekehrt. Empirische Erkenntnisse aus dem Profifußball zeigen (Fritz, 2006): Fußballunternehmen, die keinerlei Vermarktungsaktivitäten an Agenturen ausgelagert haben, scheinen die Anforderungen der Kommerzialisierung im Vergleich zu extern vermarkteten Clubs tendenziell eher im Sinne finanzieller Stabilität zu bewältigen. Dennoch darf hieraus keine allgemein gültige Handlungsempfehlung pro Eigenvermarktung abgeleitet werden. Die Entscheidung Eigen- vs. Fremdvermarktung ist an die clubspezifische Handlungssituation gebunden.

4.3.4.3 Das strategische Koordinationsfeld „Finanzierung"

Der Finanzierung kommen beim strategischen Management eines Teamsportunternehmen zwei grundlegende Funktionen zu (Bea/Haas, 2001): Zum ersten dient sie der Absicherung des operativen Leistungsprozesses durch *Bereitstellung von Kapital*. Ein Club kann nur dann am Profiteamsport teilnehmen, wenn er die aus dem Spielbetrieb resultierenden monetären Verpflichtungen für die Beschäftigung von Mannschaft, Trainerstab und Verwaltungspersonal, die Instandhaltung bzw. Miete der Spielstätte usw. kontinuierlich erfüllt. Bleiben Verbindlichkeiten ungedeckt, droht die Verkettung von Lizenzentzug und Insolvenz. Zum zweiten besitzt die strategische Steuerung der finanziellen Ressourcen eine aktive, potentialorientierte Funktion. Einnahmeüberschüsse aus dem Leistungsprozess und die Erschließung externer Finanzierungsquellen erweitern den strategischen Gestaltungsspielraum, ermöglichen zukunftsträchtige *Investitionen* in Steine und Beine. Insbesondere im Falle des Zuflusses von Eigenkapital sorgt die Außenfinanzierung für überlegenes Finanzierungspotential.

4.3.4.4 Das strategische Koordinationsfeld „Infrastruktur"

Teamsportunternehmen sind auf zeitgemäße *Spielstätten* angewiesen. Nahezu alle Vermarktungsbereiche weisen einen mittel- bis unmittelbarem Zusammenhang zur Spielstätte auf. Die Arena ist Ort der offerierten Wettkampfproduktion und damit Bühne für die Vermarktung im Zuschauer-, Sponsoring- und Firmenkundenbereich. Über die Berichterstattung in den Medien wird das Bild der Arena an die interessierte Öffentlichkeit weitergeleitet.

Seit der Jahrtausendwende ist in allen Teamsportarten ein Drang zum Neu- oder Umbau der Stadien und Hallen beobachtbar. Grund sind die erheblichen Potentiale zur Einnahmesteigerung, die aus einer Spielstätte resultieren, die zeitgemäßen Vermarktungsanforderungen genügt. Regelmäßig verfügen Clubs mit moderner Arena über einen strategischen Vorteil im Vergleich zu Clubs, die in weniger vermarktungsadäquaten Spielstätten agieren. Zugespitzter formuliert, stehen Teamsportunternehmen mit „alter" Arena vor dem strategischen Risiko, an Wettbewerbsfähigkeit gegenüber der Konkurrenz zu verlieren.

Andererseits resultiert aus der Modernisierung der Spielstätte ein massiver Investitionsaufwand, den ein Sportclub je nach gewählter Finanzierungsform alleine, mit Unterstützung von öffentlichen Stellen (Kommune, Land) und/oder privaten Investoren zu stemmen hat. Bei den bislang abgewickelten Projekten lagen die Baukosten je nach Umfang im zwei- bis dreistelligen Millioneneurobereich. Jährlich fällt ein Kapitaldienst für Zins und Tilgung in Millionenhöhe an. Die Finanzierungsphase erstreckt sich in den meisten Fällen über einen Zeithorizont von bis zu 30 Jahren. Aus dem Um- bzw. Neubau der Spielstätte folgt somit eine langfristige Bindungswirkung mit wesentlichem Einfluss auf die zukünftige Entwicklung des Teamsportunternehmens. Das strategische Risiko der Finanzierung ist gegenüber dem Risiko des Verlustes der Wettbewerbsfähigkeit abzuwägen.

4.3.5 Implementierung und Reflexion strategischer Programme

Die strategischen Koordinationsentscheidungen sind auf *operativer Ebene* von den Teamsportunternehmen in Abhängigkeit ihrer organisatorischen Aufgaben- und Kompetenzzuweisungen umzusetzen. Regelmäßig besitzen Sportclubs eine Aufbauorganisation, die dem Prinzip der funktionalen Arbeitsteilung folgt. Es ist daher bedeutsam, ein harmonisches Zusammenwirken der einzelnen Funktionsbereiche sicher zu stellen. Weder sportliche noch vermarktungsbezogene bzw. administrative Einzelinteressen dürfen das effektive Zusammenspiel der Funktionsbereiche beeinträchtigen. Ursächlich sind die umfassend dargelegten Interdependenzen, die ausgehend von den Oberzielen in allen Steuerungssubbereichen eines Teamsportunternehmens herrschen. Beispielsweise gilt es, begrenzte finanzielle Ressourcen bei der Kaderplanung zu berücksichtigen. Das effektive, integrative Zusammenspiel bei Planung und Umsetzung strategischer Koordinationsentscheidungen bestimmt den Zielerreichungsgrad.

Letztgenannter ist durch Maßnahmen der *strategischen Reflexion* von der Clubführung fortlaufend zu überwachen. Dies bedingt den Rückgriff auf führungsunterstützende Managementsysteme. Sie projizieren durch die Aufbereitung interner und externer Unternehmensvorgänge relevante Informationen zur Reflexion von Wertschöpfung und Positionierung. Unverzichtbare Managementsysteme für die strategische Reflexion von Teamsportunternehmen sind Rechnungswesen, Controlling und Reporting. Dabei ist auch an den Einsatz einer Balanced Scorecard zu denken.

4.4 Fallstudie

Die folgende Fallstudie zeichnet am Beispiel des VfB Stuttgart ein Praxisbild strategischer Managementaktivitäten in einem ausgewählten Teamsportclub.

Fallstudie „VfB Stuttgart"

Als Gründungsmitglied der Bundesliga zählt der baden-württembergische Traditionsclub VfB Stuttgart zu den festen Größen im deutschen Profifußball. Von einem zweijährigen Intermezzo Mitte der 70er Jahre abgesehen, spielen die Schwaben stets erstklassig.

Nachdem in der Saison 1991/92 noch der vierte Meistertitel errungen wird, sieht sich der VfB in den Folgejahren jedoch einem sukzessiven sportlichen wie wirtschaftlichem Abwärtstrend ausgesetzt. Mangelnde Professionalität der Clubführung, strukturelle Defizite, Fehlinvestitionen in den Spielerkader usw. behindern die positive Fortentwicklung. Es gelingt nicht, die neuartigen ökonomischen Anforderungen des kommerzialisierten Fußballgeschäftes zu bewältigen. Am Saisonende 2000/01 kämpft der Club schließlich um seine Existenz. Erst am vorletzten Spieltag kann der überlebenswichtige Klassenerhalt in der ersten Liga gesichert werden. Beim Abstieg in Liga zwei wäre der Kapitaldienst für die angesammelte Schuldenlast in zweistelliger Millionenhöhe wegen ligabedingter Mindereinnahmen wohl kaum mehr zu erbringen gewesen. Aus der Not heraus

setzt der VfB anschließend verstärkt auf seine seit Jahren vorbildliche Jugendarbeit und integriert anstelle teurer Neuzugänge eigene Nachwuchsakteure, vorwiegend deutscher Herkunft, in die Lizenzmannschaft. Das verjüngte VfB-Team
schlägt sich beachtlich. Am Ende der Spielzeit 2002/03 stehen beinahe sensatio-
nell Vizemeisterschaft und Qualifikation zur UEFA Champions League zu Bu-
che, in der die Mannschaft in der Folgesaison Siege gegen internationale Top-
Clubs wie Manchester United feiert. Über die Grenzen des Schwabenlands hinaus
herrscht große Euphorie um die Leistungen der so genannten „Jungen Wilden".

Sportliche Erfolge und öffentliche Begeisterung nutzt das neu formierte Füh-
rungsteam mit dem ehemaligen Vorstandsvorsitzenden der IBM Deutschland
GmbH, Erwin Staudt, an der Spitze zur Neupositionierung und finanziellen Konsolidierung. Entlang ökonomischer Führungsprinzipien wird eine nachhaltig ziel-
orientierte Unternehmenspolitik zur Grundlage des Entscheidens und Handelns
beim VfB Stuttgart. Über den sportlichen Bereich hinaus werden in allen Clubbe-
reichen klare Unternehmensziele formuliert, dokumentiert und in Form von Strategien und Aktionen umgesetzt. Simulationen und Szenarioplanungen helfen, die
Zielvorgaben bzw. den mittel- bis langfristigen Verlauf der Clubentwicklung unabhängig von sportlichen Imponderabilien auf eine valide Basis zu stellen.

Instrumentalisiert wird das strategische Managementgebaren durch die Implementierung des führungsunterstützenden Managementsystems „BalPlan".
Balplan ist eine in Zusammenarbeit mit dem Beratungshaus Horváth & Partners
konstruierte Softwarelösung einer fußballspezifisch adaptierten Balanced Scorecard. Insgesamt bilden 130 Kennzahlen, von denen 30 für die oberste Führungsebene bestimmt sind, entlang von vier Betrachtungsperspektiven (Sport, Finanzen, Kunden und Mitarbeiter) steuerungsrelevante Informationen zur
angestrebten Clubentwicklung ab. Neben harten Fakten wie Umsatz, Liquidität,
Verschuldungsgrad etc. werden weiche Kennzahlen wie Anzahl Jugendspieler im
Kader, Anzahl positive und negative Pressemitteilungen usw. dargestellt. V.a.
wird auch das Verhältnis der eigenen Spielstärkeinvestitionen zu den Talentinvestitionen der Konkurrenzclubs analysiert. Basal sind in diesem Kontext die
beiden Kennzahlen absolute Personalausgaben und relative Personalausgaben in
Relation zum Umsatz. Eine Ampel-Funktion warnt vor Planabweichungen, deutet
auf Verbesserungspotentiale bzw. Korrekturmaßnahmen hin.

Zusammenfassend untermauert das Fallbeispiel des VfB Stuttgart die Relevanz des Themenfeldes Strategie für den professionellen Teamsport. Die VfB-
Führung ist in der Lage schnell und flexibel auf sich verändernde Umweltanfor-
derungen des Wachstumsmarktes Profifußball zu reagieren. Nicht zuletzt der
Gewinn der deutschen Fußballmeisterschaft im Spieljahr 2006/07 verdeutlicht,
dass sich die Schwaben mit ihrer Philosophie vom strategischen Clubmanagement auf der Überholspur befinden.

4.5 Fazit und Ausblick

Die signifikante Bedeutung des strategischen Managements zeigt sich nicht zuletzt durch seine intensive wissenschaftliche Bearbeitung. Plastisch ausgedrückt, bildet das strategische Management zugleich Fundament und Dach im Haus der betriebswirtschaftlichen Teildisziplinen. Diese Feststellung gilt analog für die ökonomischen Steuerungssubbereiche von Teamsportunternehmen wie sie im vorliegenden Herausgeberwerk zur Darstellung gelangen. Das strategische Management ermöglicht eine systematische Unternehmensentwicklung inmitten sich dynamisch verändernder Umweltverhältnisse. Gerade im Sport haben sich die Anforderungen und Rahmenbedingungen infolge dessen rapider Kommerzialisierung seit Beginn der 90er Jahre grundlegend verändert. Der Einzug von Globalisierungstendenzen und innovative Weiterentwicklungen der Kommunikations- und Informationstechnologien dürften diesen Trend zukünftig weiter forcieren. Teamsportclubs, die sich nachhaltig im Wettbewerb behaupten wollen, müssen entsprechend gewappnet sein. Jüngere Umfrageergebnisse belegen allerdings, dass ein organisiertes und koordiniertes strategisches Management nach wie vor nur in wenigen Teamsportclubs vorzufinden ist (Keller/Langner/Amann, 2006; Viemann/Filbrich/Tietje 2005). Als wesentliche Gründe für die regelmäßige Absenz nennen die Clubs die Schnelllebigkeit der Branche bzw. die Unsicherheit des sportlichen Erfolges sowie dessen Korrelation zum wirtschaftlichen Erfolg. Einer derartigen Begründung muss zwangsweise ein fehlerhaftes Verständnis des strategischen Managements zugrunde liegen. Zweifelfrei kann gerade in Bezug auf das sportliche Abschneiden eine Vielfalt an potentiellen Zukunftsbildern entworfen werden. Versteht man strategisches Management jedoch, wie im vorliegenden Beitrag dargestellt, als das Schaffen und Sichern von Erfolgspotentialen, dann ergibt sich daraus geradezu die Notwendigkeit, trotz aller Unsicherheiten im Umfeld, strategische Szenarien für die langfristige Entwicklung eines Teamsportunternehmens zu entwerfen.

Kontrollfragen

1. Was sind Aufgaben und Merkmale des strategischen Managements?
2. Welche Phasen kennt der Prozess des strategischen Managements?
3. Warum ist ein strategisches Management gerade für Teamsportunternehmen von signifikanter Relevanz?
4. Welche Spezifika kennzeichnen das Zielsystem von Teamsportunternehmen?
5. Welche Rolle spielen Clubverfassung und Clubkultur für Zielbildung und -realisierung in Teamsportunternehmen?
6. Welches sind die relevanten Stakeholder in der Aufgabenumwelt von Teamsportunternehmen und in welcher Beziehung stehen diese zu den Clubs?
7. Beschreiben Sie die Wertkette eines Teamsportunternehmens!
8. Welche strategischen Koordinationsfelder sind für die Umsetzung einer effektiven Zielkoordination systematisch zu justieren?

9. Welche Rolle spielen Interdependenzen bei der Implementierung und Reflexion strategischer Koordinationsentscheidungen?
10. Wie ist der gegenwärtige Stand eines strategischen Managements im Teamsport und wie wird sich dessen Stellenwert Ihrer Meinung nach in den nächsten Jahren verändern?

Literaturverzeichnis

Bauer, Hans / Exler, Stefanie / Sauer, Nicola (2004): Der Beitrag des Markenimage zur Fanloyalität. Eine empirische Untersuchung am Beispiel der Klubmarken der Fußball-Bundesliga, Wissenschaftliches Arbeitspapier Nr. W81, Institut für Marktorientierte Unternehmensführung, Universität Mannheim.

Bea, Franz Xaver / Haas, Jürgen (2001): Strategisches Management, 3. Aufl., Stuttgart.

Bleicher, Knut (2004): Das Konzept integriertes Management, 7. Aufl., Frankfurt/Main.

Breuer, Christoph (2005): Strategisches Management in Sportorganisationen, in: Breuer, Christoph / Thiel, Ansgar (Hrsg.): Handbuch Sportmanagement, Schorndorf, S. 148-163.

DFL (2007): Bundesliga Report 2007, Frankfurt/Main.

Dietl, Helmut / Hasan, Tariq / Korthals, Jan Peter (2005): Ein Modell zur Prognose des Erfolgs in der Fußball-Bundesliga, in: Sport und Gesellschaft, Heft 3, S. 275-295.

Erning, Johannes (2000): Professioneller Fußball in Deutschland: Eine wettbewerbspolitische und unternehmensstrategische Analyse, Essen.

Escher, Mario (2006): Unternehmensbewertung im Profifußball. Eine Untersuchung von Verfahren zur Wertermittlung, Saarbrücken.

Frick, Bernd (2005): „… und Geld schießt eben doch Tore" – Die Voraussetzungen sportlichen und wirtschaftlichen Erfolges in der Fußball-Bundesliga, in: Sportwissenschaft, Heft 3, S. 250-270.

Fritz, Thomas (2006): Fußball und Strategie. Eine effizienzorientierte Analyse der Fußballbundesliga, München u.a.

Hungenberg, Harald (2004): Strategisches Management in Unternehmen, 3. Aufl., Wiesbaden.

Keller, Christian (2006): Corporate Finance im Profifußball. Erfolgsfaktoren, Strategien und Instrumente für die Finanzierung von Fußballunternehmen, Stuttgart.

Keller, Christian (2007): Clubkultur und Erfolg im Profiteamsport, Vortrag auf dem 18. dvs-Hochschultag, 28.09.2007, Hamburg.

Keller, Christian / Langner, Volker / Amann, Tobias (2006): Controlling the Game. Status Quo des Controllingwesens im deutschen Profifußball, in: Zeitschrift für Controlling & Management, Heft 1, S. 43-49.

Korndörfer, Wolfgang (1999): Unternehmensführungslehre, 9. Aufl., Wiesbaden.

Korthals, Jan Peter (2005): Bewertung von Fußballunternehmen. Eine Untersuchung am Beispiel der deutschen Fußballbundesliga, Wiesbaden.

Kupfer, F. A. Thomas (2006): Erfolgreiches Fußballclub-Management, Göttingen.

Lang, Joachim (2007): Corporate Governance der Fußballunternehmen, Berlin.

Macharzina, Klaus / Wolf, Joachim (2005): Unternehmensführung, 5. Aufl., Wiesbaden.

Malik, Fredmund (2006): Führen, Leisten, Leben. Wirksames Management für eine neue Zeit, 13. Aufl., München.

Metrum Managementberatung (2004): Financing the Game: Die Kapitalmarktfähigkeit von Proficlubs aus Investorensicht, Marktforschungsstudie, München.

Mohr, Stefan / Merget, Jens (2004): Die Marke als Meistermacher. Strategische Markenführung im Profisport, in: Zieschang, Klaus / Klimmer, Christian (Hrsg.): Unternehmensführung im Profifußball – Symbiose aus Sport, Wirtschaft und Recht, Berlin, S. 103-120.

Müller-Stewens, Günter / Lechner, Christoph: Strategisches Management. Wie strategische Initiativen zum Wandel führen, 3. Aufl., Stuttgart.

Pilot Group (2007): Sponsor Visions 2007, Marktforschungsstudie, Hamburg.

Porter, Michael (1999): Wettbewerbsvorteile (Competitive Advantage), Deutsche Übersetzung der Originalausgabe von 1985, 5. Aufl., Frankfurt/Main.

Quitzau, Jörn (2003): Erfolgsfaktor Zufall im Profifußball: Quantifizierung mit Hilfe informationseffizienter Wettmärkte, Diskussionspapier der Fächergruppe Volkswirtschaft Nr. 20, Universität der Bundeswehr Hamburg.

Swieter, Detlef (2002): Eine ökonomische Analyse der Fußball-Bundesliga, Berlin.

Viemann, Kathryn / Filbrich, Björn / Tietje, Carsten (2005): Controlling in der Fußballbranche. Eine empirische Untersuchung zum Implementierungsstand des Controlling in den drei höchsten deutschen Fußballligen, in: Sport und Gesellschaft, Heft 3, S. 296-313.

Wadsack, Roland (2006): Krisenmanagement für Sportbetriebe. Eine betriebswirtschaftliche Einführung, in: Wadsack, Roland (Hrsg.): Krisenmanagement in Sportbetrieben, Frankfurt/Main, S. 13-70.

Wild, Jürgen (1982): Grundlagen der Unternehmungsplanung, 4. Aufl., Opladen.

Zeltinger, Julian (2004): Customer Relationship Management in Fußballunternehmen. Erfolgreiche Kundenbeziehungen gestalten, Berlin.

Ziebs, Alexander (2002): Ist Erfolg käuflich? Analysen und Überlegungen zur sozioökonomischen Realität des Berufsfußballs, München.

Weiterführende Ressourcen

Literatur

Benner, Gerd (1992): Risk Management im professionellen Sport: Auf der Grundlage von Ansätzen einer Sportbetrieblehre, Bergisch Gladbach u.a.

Cachay, Klaus / Riedl, Lars / Thiel, Ansgar / Wagner, Christian (2004): Global Player – Local Hero. Der Sportverein zwischen Spitzensport, Publikum und Vermarktung, Wissenschaftlicher Ergebnisbericht, Universität Bielefeld.

Dörnemann, Jörg (2002): Controlling von Profi-Sport-Organisationen. Dargestellt am Beispiel der Deutschen Fußballbundesliga, München.

Früh, Hans-Joachim / Mentges, Hans-Peter / Erning, Johannes (2003): Professionelle Steuerung von Fußballvereinen, in: Betriebswirtschaftliche Forschung und Praxis, Heft 5, S. 571-582.

Galli, Albert / Wagner, Marc / Beiersdorfer, Dietmar (2002): Strategische Vereinsführung und Balanced Scorecard, in: Galli, Albert / Gömmel, Rainer / Holzhäuser, Wolfgang / Straub, Wilfried (Hrsg.): Sportmanagement. Grundlagen der unternehmerischen Führung im Sport aus Betriebswirtschaftslehre, Steuern und Recht für den Sportmanager, München, S. 209-228.

Sloane, Peter J. (1984): Die Ziele des Sportvereins, in: Heinemann, Klaus (Hrsg.): Texte zur Ökonomie des Sports, Schorndorf, S. 126-137.

Teichmann, Kai (2007): Strategie und Erfolg von Fußballunternehmen, Wiesbaden.

Thiel, Ansgar (1997): Steuerung im organisierten Sport. Ansätze und Perspektiven, Stuttgart.

Wehrle, Alexander / Heinzelmann, Marcus (2004): Reporting und strategische Steuerung im Profifußball. Konzeption und Umsetzung eines Balanced Scorecard basierten Systems beim VfB Stuttgart, in: Controlling, Heft 6, 349-354.

Links

Arbeitskreis Sportökonomie e.V.:
http://www.arbeitskreis-sportoekonomie.de
Competence Site (Management-Kompetenznetzwerk):
http://www.competence-site.de
Netzathleten (Sportnetzwerk):
http://www.netzathleten.de
ViFa Sport (Virtuelle Fachbibliothek Sportwissenschaft):
http://www.vifasport.de

Kapitel 5: Planung im Sport

Frank Daumann   Mathias Langer   Markus Breuer

Lernziele

Nach der Durchsicht dieses Kapitels sollte der Leser in der Lage sein,

- den Begriff der Planung zu erläutern.
- die Bestandteile der Planung zu kennen.
- die einzelnen Stufen des Planungsprozesses zu erklären.
- die Bedeutung der Planung im Unternehmen einzuschätzen.
- die Besonderheiten der Planung im Bereich des Sports zu kennen.
- diese Besonderheiten in der Planung zu berücksichtigen.

Überblick über das Kapitel

Im folgenden Kapitel werden die Grundlagen der Planung ebenso erläutert wie ihre Bestandteile und ihre Bedeutung für das Unternehmen. Darüber hinaus werden die Schritte der Entscheidung, der Steuerung und der Kontrolle dargestellt, die untrennbar mit dem Begriff der Planung verbunden sind. Schließlich wird gezeigt, inwiefern Planung im sportspezifischen Umfeld Besonderheiten aufweist und wie diese im Rahmen der Planung des sportlichen Erfolgs zu berücksichtigen sind. Dabei liegt das Schwergewicht auf der normativen Ebene (Wie sollte Planung vonstatten gehen?) und weniger auf der deskriptiven Ebene (Wie erfolgt Planung tatsächlich?). Das Kapitel endet mit einer Fallstudie, die die Erkenntnisse am Beispiel des Basketball-Bundesligisten Science City Jena erläutert.

5.1 Einführung in die Thematik

Planung ist ein omnipräsentes Phänomen. So gibt es kaum einen Bereich, in dem nicht zumindest implizit geplant wird: Das Lesen einer Rundfunkzeitung, die den Plan der jeweiligen Sender wiedergibt und dem Zuschauer die Auswahl erleichtern soll, gehört dazu, die Vorausschau auf den nächsten Urlaub oder gar die Planung zum Bau eines Eigenheims. Pläne werden gefasst für die Freizeit ebenso wie für den Beruf, für die Gestaltung des Abends genauso wie für den Ruhestand und seine Finanzierung. Bereits dem chinesischen Philosophen Laotse wird das Zitat zugeschrieben:

> „Plane das Schwierige da, wo es noch leicht ist."

Will man seine Ziele zumindest in einem befriedigenden Ausmaß erreichen, erfordert die Komplexität der Entscheidungsumwelt planerische Maßnahmen und damit eine Abkehr von einer gänzlich spontanen Entscheidungsfindung. So ist es das Grundmuster der Planung, Entscheidungen, die in der Zukunft gefällt werden müssen, bereits in der Gegenwart so festzulegen, dass sich der Entscheidungsspielraum für die Zukunft verengt. Die Vorteile, die ein solches Vorgehen bietet, liegen auf der Hand: Durch den Prozess der Planung und das Festlegen auf eine unter mehre-

114

ren Handlungsalternativen schützt sich der Planer vor vorschnellen und unüberlegten Entscheidungen. Somit bildet Planung den Gegenpol zur Improvisation, zur Entscheidung aus dem Stehgreif.

5.2 Planung – eine begriffliche Eingrenzung

Nach Gutenberg (1957) versteht man unter betriebswirtschaftlicher Planung einen ordnenden Akt, der das betriebliche Geschehen in eine für richtig und zweckmäßig befundene Bahn drängt. Zwar grenzt Gutenberg die Kontrolle noch strikt von der Ordnungsfunktion der Planung ab, aber da Planung ohne Kontrolle keinen Nutzen generiert, soll der Teilbereich Kontrolle hier ebenfalls behandelt werden. Darüber hinaus ist die Zugehörigkeit des Akts der Entscheidung zur Planung umstritten. Im Rahmen dieses Kapitels wird analog zu Kreikebaum (1997) die Entscheidung als Bestandteil der Planung angesehen.

Unternehmerisches Handeln findet stets in einem komplexen Umfeld statt: Zum einen ist der Unternehmer aufgrund kognitiver Beschränkungen nicht in der Lage, alle wichtigen Informationen aufzunehmen und zu verarbeiten; sein Blick auf das Geschehen ist von Natur aus eingeschränkt. Zum anderen zeichnet sich die zukünftige Entwicklung durch Ungewissheit aus: Das Eintreten zukünftiger Ereignisse und deren Folgen können nur begrenzt bzw. überhaupt nicht vorhergesagt werden.

Unter diesen Bedingungen versucht der Unternehmer, seine Ziele wie etwa Gewinn- oder Umsatzmaximierung etc. zu realisieren. Hierzu setzt er das Instrument der Planung ein. Planung lässt sich dabei als zukunftsorientierter geistiger Vorgang charakterisieren, der zum einen auf Ereignisse gerichtet ist, deren Eintreten noch im Ungewissen liegt, und der zum anderen den Betriebsprozess als Ganzes und in allen seinen Teilen festlegt (Schmidt, 1982). Planung beschreibt somit das Vorwegnehmen zukünftigen Handels bzw. das Treffen von Entscheidungen (Wöhe, 2000). Neben der Zukunftsbezogenheit lassen sich nach Mag (1999) drei weitere Merkmale der Planung nennen. Demnach hat Planung die vornehmliche Aufgabe, (1) Informationen zu gewinnen, (2) ist rational, d.h. bewusst und zielgerichtet (im Gegensatz zur Improvisation), und darüber hinaus (3) gestaltend nicht nur im Sinne eines Erkennens von Problemen, sondern im Erarbeiten von Lösungen für selbige.

Wie dieser Prozess gestaltet werden sollte, welche Probleme und Chancen sich dabei bieten und in welcher Form dies für den Bereich Sport relevant ist, soll im Folgenden herausgearbeitet werden.

5.3 Planung in der Betriebswirtschaft

Die folgenden Abschnitte sollen die wichtigsten Aspekte der Planung aus der Sicht der Allgemeinen Betriebswirtschaftlehre darstellen und erläutern. Zu diesen Aspekten zählen die Teilkomplexe der Planung, die verschiedenen Planungsprinzipien, der Planungsprozess und schließlich die Kontrolle.

5.3.1 Planung und ihre Teilkomplexe

Nach Wöhe (2000) lässt sich Planung im Rahmen der strategischen Unternehmensführung in insgesamt vier Teilkomplexe einteilen. Diese sind neben der Unternehmensleitbildplanung die strategische Planung, die operative Planung und schließlich die Erfolgs- und Liquiditätsplanung. Die hier genannten Komplexe lassen sich hauptsächlich nach ihrer Aufgabenstellung unterscheiden. Zudem liegt ihnen regelmäßig ein unterschiedlicher Planungszeitraum zugrunde. Dabei ist zu beachten, dass, je länger der Planungshorizont wird, desto vager werden die zu treffenden Aussagen (Mag, 1999), da die Qualität der notwendigen Informationen mit zunehmendem Horizont abnimmt. Einige Autoren weisen neben den hier angesprochenen Ebenen zusätzlich den Bereich der taktischen Planung aus, der die Lücke zwischen strategischer und operativer Planung schließt. Angesichts der Tatsache, dass über die Fristigkeit der Begriffe jedoch keine Einigkeit besteht, wird diese Ebene in diesem Rahmen ausgelassen. Mögliche Bestandteile der taktischen Planung finden sich in der operativen oder strategischen Planung wieder.

5.3.1.1 Unternehmensleitbildplanung

Das Unternehmensleitbild stellt das oberste „handlungsorientierte Wertesystem des Managements" dar und dient dazu, „die gesellschaftliche Legitimation des unternehmerischen Handelns glaubwürdig" zu begründen (Ulrich/Fluri, 1995, S. 39). Daher erweist es sich als sinnvoll, die Planung des Unternehmensleitbildes an den *Stakeholdern*, also am sog. *Stakeholder-Ansatz* auszurichten. Gemäß diesem Ansatz gehören zu den Anspruchsgruppen einer Unternehmung nicht nur die Anteilseigner, deren Ziel in der Generierung eines möglichst großen Profits liegt (in Form des Deckungsbeitrages oder einer beliebigen Rendite), sondern darüber hinaus auch andere Gruppen wie bspw. die Mitarbeiter, die Kunden und Lieferanten oder auch die Öffentlichkeit, auf deren Interessen die Aufmerksamkeit des Managements gelenkt werden muss (Staehle, 1999). Im Rahmen der Unternehmensleitbildplanung ist es nun die Aufgabe der Führungsebene, allgemeine Aussagen zu treffen, in welcher Form sich der Betrieb gegenüber den Stakeholdern präsentieren möchte. Die Planung des Unternehmensleitbildes stellt aus dieser Perspektive den Komplex mit dem längsten Planungshorizont dar, da Leitbilder i.d.R. nur sehr selten und behutsam geändert werden sollten.

In jüngerer Zeit gehen immer mehr Unternehmen und Organisationen dazu über, statt eines impliziten Leitbildes eine explizite, ausformulierte Fassung zu erarbeiten und allen Anspruchsgruppen zugänglich zu machen. Dies bietet besonders Mitarbeitern die Möglichkeit, ihre eigene Arbeit, aber auch die ihrer Führungskräfte mit den Vorgaben zu vergleichen und ggf. anzupassen.

5.3.1.2 Strategische Unternehmensplanung

Im Rahmen der strategischen Unternehmensplanung sollen „Konzepte und Strategien entwickelt werden, mit denen die Existenz der Unternehmung dauerhaft gesichert werden kann" (Schierenbeck, 2000, S. 120); zukünftige Erfolgspotentiale sollen dabei erkannt und ausgeschöpft werden. Der Komplex der strategischen Unternehmensplanung orientiert sich daher an einem langfristigen Horizont und zeichnet sich deshalb durch große Unsicherheit in den Annahmen sowie durch unstrukturierte Problemstellungen und die Konzentration auf einzelne, wichtige Aspekte aus (Schierenbeck, 2000).

Zu den konkreten Aufgaben der strategischen Planung gehört es zum einen, sowohl das Unternehmen selbst (interne Perspektive) als auch das Umfeld bzw. die Umwelt (externe Perspektive) zu analysieren. Während die interne Perspektive darauf abzielt, Stärken und Schwächen des Unternehmens wie etwa das Vorhandensein von Kernkompetenzen oder Defizite beim Vertrieb zu ermitteln, zählt zur externen Perspektive die Ableitung von Chancen und Risiken, die sich etwa aus veränderten staatlichen Rahmenbedingungen (bspw. verschärfte Umweltauflagen) oder auch aus der Marktstruktur (Anzahl der Konkurrenten, deren Stärke etc.) ergeben können (Welge/Al-Laham, 2001). Zum anderen ist die Formulierung von Unternehmensgesamt- und Geschäftsfeldstrategien sowie Strategien für bestimmte Produkt-Markt-Kombinationen Bestandteil der strategischen Planung. Strategische Planung beantwortet somit die Frage, mit welchen Produkten eine Unternehmung auf welchen Märkten aktiv werden sollte bzw. welche Strategie (Intensivierung, Rückzug etc.) zu wählen ist (Hinterhuber, 1996).

Aus dieser Beschreibung wird bereits ersichtlich, dass dieser Bereich ebenso dem Top-Management vorbehalten ist wie die Planung des Unternehmensleitbildes.

5.3.1.3 Operative Planung

Gegenstand der operativen Planung ist die Umsetzung der strategischen Planung in einzelne betriebliche Teilpläne. So besteht die operative Planung in der Erstellung von Plänen für den Absatz, die Beschaffung, die Produktion usw. mit konkreten Zielsetzungen (Wöhe, 2000), was wiederum deren enge Abstimmung erfordert. Somit enthält die operative Planung neben den Einzelzielen eines Betriebes die zur Erreichung notwendigen Maßnahmen, Termine, Mengen und Werte (Olfert/Rahn, 2000). Ihr Planungsziel ist eher kurzfristig.

Diese Aufgabe wird in der Praxis i.d.R. vom unteren, teils auch vom mittleren Management wahrgenommen. Die einzelnen Planungsebenen stehen darüber in einer engen Wechselbeziehung: Während die Entscheidungen des Top-Managements ohne die Arbeit im operativen Bereich keinerlei Umsetzung finden, ist das operative Management seinerseits auf die koordinierenden Richtlinien der Führungsebene angewiesen.

5.3.1.4 Erfolgs- und Liquiditätsplanung

Der Erfolgs- und Liquiditätsplanung kommt in den bislang betrachteten Planungskomplexen die besondere Rolle einer Querschnittfunktion zu. Liquidität bedeutet dabei die Fähigkeit eines Unternehmens, den zwingenden Zahlungsverpflichtungen jederzeit uneingeschränkt nachkommen zu können. Ein Liquiditätsengpass entsteht dann, wenn diese Situation kurzzeitig nicht gegeben ist und stellt die Vorstufe zur Zahlungsunfähigkeit dar (Perridon/Steiner, 2002). So ist die Liquidität als notwendige, wenn auch nicht hinreichende Bedingung für den Fortbestand eines Unternehmens im Bereich der Planung zu berücksichtigen, da ein Unternehmen gezwungen ist, Insolvenz anzumelden, wenn es seinen Zahlungsverpflichtungen dauerhaft nicht nachkommen kann; in diesem Fall lässt sich der Fortbestand auch nicht durch ausgezeichnete Leistungen in den anderen Planungsbereichen sichern.

Neben die Geldsteuerung (Liquidität) tritt nun die güterwirtschaftliche Steuerung in Form des Erfolges. Dieser errechnet sich pro Periode (bspw. Monat, Quartal, Jahr) als Differenz zwischen Erträgen und Aufwendungen bzw. Leistungen und Kosten. Somit hat der Erfolg eine Vorsteuerungsfunktion für die Liquidität, ohne jedoch die Probleme der Liquiditätssteuerung selbst lösen zu können (Coenenberg, 1999). Bleiben in einem Unternehmen langfristig die entsprechenden monetären Erfolge aus, so muss aus Sicht der Kapitalgeber die Frage nach dem Sinn der Fortführung gestellt werden.

Unternehmensleitbildplanung	Erfolgs- und Liquiditätsplanung
Strategische Planung	
Operative Planung	

Tab.1: Teilkomplexe im Planungssystem
Quelle: Wöhe (2000), S. 136

Teilweise wird der hier angeführte letzte Komplex der Planung auch unter dem Begriff der operativen Planung subsumiert, was jedoch in zweifacher Hinsicht nicht gerechtfertigt scheint. Zum einen wird diese Unterordnung der Bedeutung der Liquiditätsplanung nicht gerecht, zum anderen ist es keinesfalls so, dass Entscheidungen in diesem Bereich immer kurzfristige Auswirkungen zeigen, wie sich an Hand der Ausschüttungspolitik eines Unternehmens darstellen lässt.

5.3.2 Planungsprinzip

Neben dem zeitlichen Horizont kann die Planung weiterhin nach der Stoßrichtung innerhalb der Managementebenen (Top-, Middle- und Lower-Management) des Unternehmens systematisiert werden. So unterscheidet man im Allgemeinen drei

Planungsprinzipien, deren Anwendung sich in unterschiedlichem Maße auf die Motivation der Arbeitnehmer auswirken kann (Hammer, 1998):

- Der *Top-Down-Ansatz*: Hierbei handelt es sich um ein System, das sich streng an der Hierarchie innerhalb des Unternehmens ausrichtet. Die Ziele werden durch die höchste Führungsebene festgesetzt und bekannt gegeben, während sich alle nachgelagerten Stellen für die Realisation verantwortlich zeigen.
- Der *Bottom-Up-Ansatz*: Bei diesem Ansatz ergibt sich die Gesamtstrategie "von unten nach oben". Der Rahmenplan entsteht dabei aus dem Zusammenfassen von einzelnen Teilplänen, die auf den unteren Führungsebenen nach der Maßgabe der Durchführbarkeit erstellt werden (Olfert/Rahn, 2005).
- Das *Gegenstromverfahren*: Dieser auch als „from middle both ways" bezeichnete Ansatz stellt eine Kombination der ersten beiden dar. So kommt es i.d.R. zum Aufstellen eines Rahmenplans durch die oberen Führungsebenen, der seinerseits durch die unteren Ebenen überprüft und gegebenenfalls verändert wird (Olfert/Rahn, 2000).

5.3.3 Planungsprozess

Der eigentliche Planungsprozess lässt sich in mehrere Abschnitte oder Sequenzen einteilen, die aufeinander aufbauen. In Anlehnung an Mag (1999) sollen in diesem Rahmen insgesamt fünf Phasen unterschieden werden:

- die Zielanalyse
- die Problemanalyse
- die Alternativenanalyse
- die Prognose
- die Bewertung und Entscheidung

Nach Abschluss der Entscheidung folgen in der Praxis die Durchsetzung bzw. die Realisation der gewählten Alternative, was jedoch nicht mehr dem originären Planungsprozess zuzurechnen ist. Aus diesem Grund wird darauf in diesem Rahmen nicht weiter eingegangen. Zusätzlich kann als weiterer Schritt die Kontrolle in den Kanon aufgenommen werden, da Planung – wie oben dargestellt wurde – nur im Zusammenhang mit einer abschließenden Überprüfung der Zielerreichung zu einer Verbesserung der Ergebnisse führen kann. Auf Grund der hohen Bedeutung der Kontrolle wird diese in einem gesonderten Abschnitt (5.3.4) im Anschluss an den Planungsprozess behandelt.

5.3.3.1 Zielanalyse

Im ersten Schritt muss durch das Management festgelegt werden, welche Ziele für das Unternehmen sinnvoll und erreichbar erscheinen und in welchem Zeitraum sie erreicht werden sollen. Die Ziele können dabei qualitativer Natur (bspw. Erhöhung der Mitarbeiterzufriedenheit) oder quantitativer Natur (wie bspw. Erhöhung des Marktanteils, Steigerung des Umsatzes) bzw. monetärer oder nicht-monetärer Natur sein.

Da in der Praxis i.d.R. nicht ein einzelnes Ziel, sondern vielmehr ein Bündel unterschiedlichster Ziele verfolgt wird, ist die Wirkungsbeziehung zwischen den Zielen für die Planung von maßgeblicher Bedeutung. Dabei lassen sich komplementäre, neutrale und konfligierende Zielbeziehungen unterscheiden. Während die Zielkomplementarität (Ziele ergänzen sich) oder die Zielindifferenz (Ziele sind unabhängig von einander) keine Probleme in der Planung darstellen, muss beim Zielkonflikt eine Gewichtung vorgenommen werden, da sich Einzelziele hier gegenseitig beeinträchtigen.

Im Rahmen der Zielanalyse oder Zielplanung muss weiterhin bedacht werden, dass die Überprüfbarkeit gewährleistet bleibt. Gerade im Bereich qualitativer Ziele kann dies zu Problemen führen.

5.3.3.2 Problemanalyse

In den seltensten Fällen liegen die Probleme zu Beginn eines Planungsprozesses offen; wenn dies der Fall ist, kann die Problemanalyse ausgelassen werden. I.d.R. ist es jedoch notwendig, aktuelle Defizite zu identifizieren und zu berücksichtigen. Nach Wild (1982) sind in diesem Rahmen folgende Schritte notwendig:

- *Diagnose des Ist-Zustandes*: In welcher Situation befindet sich das Unternehmen aktuell? Auf welche Ressourcen kann zurückgegriffen werden?
- *Prognose der wichtigsten Faktoren der Lageanalyse*: Wie werden sich die wichtigen (!) Faktoren, die die Entwicklung beeinflussen, in der Zukunft entwickeln? Zu diesen Faktoren können bspw. die Marktnachfrage, die Konkurrenzsituation oder auch die Rohstoffpreise gehören.
- *Gegenüberstellung von Zielen und den Ergebnissen der Lageanalyse*: Wo finden sich Abweichungen zwischen den festgelegten Zielen und dem Ist-Zustand, wo wurden die Planungsziele hingegen erreicht?
- *Auflösung der Probleme in Teilprobleme*: Da komplexe Probleme in aller Regel nur schwer zu erfassen sind und von vielen unabhängigen Variablen abhängig sein können, ist es angebracht, diese in einzelne Teilprobleme zu zerlegen, für die isolierte Lösungen gefunden werden können.
- *Strukturierung der Teilprobleme nach Abhängigkeiten*: Im Anschluss an die Zerlegung in Teilprobleme ist zu prüfen, in welcher Beziehung diese zueinander stehen. Meist greifen Teilprobleme wie Zahnränder ineinander, d.h., die Lösung des einen verändert die Ausgangssituation des anderen, so dass diese Abhängigkeiten berücksichtigt werden müssen.

5.3.3.3 Alternativenanalyse

Nach Hammer (1998) ist es das Ziel der Alternativenanalyse, alternative Lösungsansätze zu finden und inhaltlich so zu konkretisieren, dass eine Bewertung hinsichtlich des Zielerreichungsgrades möglich wird. Die eigentliche Bewertung erfolgt jedoch erst im übernächsten Schritt.

Bei der Aufstellung von Alternativen muss in der Praxis v.a. darauf geachtet werden, dass sich die genannten Alternativen gegenseitig ausschließen. Andernfalls ist keine klare Abgrenzung der Folgen und somit auch keine Bewertung möglich. Gleichzeitig sollte versucht werden, mit den bestehenden Alternativen den gesamten Entscheidungsraum abzudecken. Als notwendige Bedingung ist auch hier wieder die Finanzierbarkeit zu nennen, da ohne sie eine Alternative faktisch nicht zur Auswahl steht.

Für komplexe Alternativensysteme, die sich durch mehrstufige Entscheidungen oder Entscheidungen zu verschiedenen Zeitpunkten auszeichnen, bietet sich der sog. Alternativenbaum zur Visualisierung an. Mit seiner Hilfe können sowohl Alternativenhierarchien als auch Alternativenfolgen anschaulich dargestellt werden (Mag, 1999). Ein Alternativenbaum kann dann bspw. die folgende Form, ähnlich einem Organigramm, annehmen:

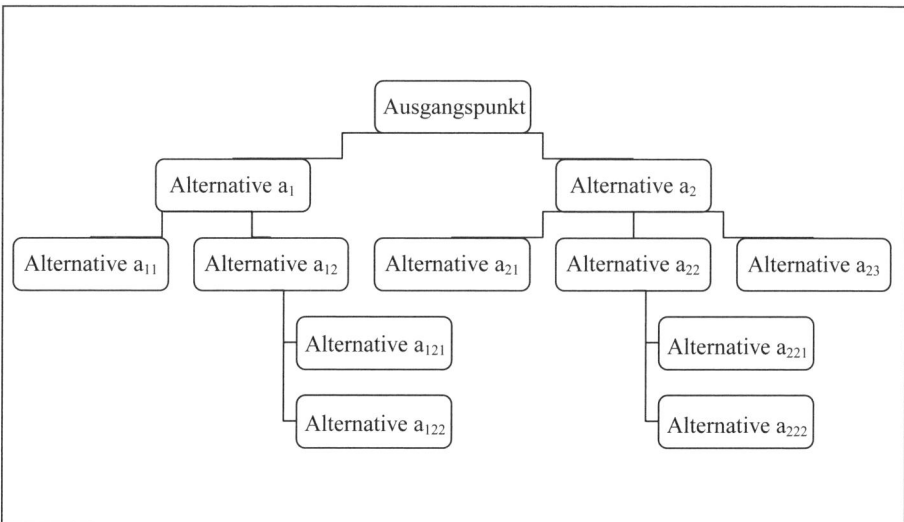

Abb.1: Alternativenbaum

5.3.3.4 Prognose

Im Rahmen der Prognose werden die ermittelten Alternativen auf ihre Auswirkungen auf die unternehmerischen Zielgrößen untersucht. Dabei soll die Frage beantwortet werden, welche Konsequenzen sich jeweils für das Unternehmen aus der Auswahl einer Alternative ergeben (Schierenbeck, 2000).

Als Methoden im Bereich der Prognose sind v.a. Befragungen der Betroffenen wie auch von Experten zu nennen. Hier empfiehlt sich ein systematisches Vorgehen, um eine optimale Informationssammlung zu gewährleisten. Neben quantitativen Prognoseverfahren wie der Trendprognose, der Portfolio-Analyse oder der Lebenszyklus-Analyse können dabei qualitative Verfahren wie die Delphi-Methode oder die Szenario-Technik zum Einsatz gelangen. All diesen Methoden ist gemein, dass sie versuchen, Ungewissheit auf der einen Seite zu reduzieren und die Prognosequalität durch die Aufnahme unterschiedlicher Perspektiven auf der anderen Seite zu erhöhen.

5.3.3.5 Bewertung und die Entscheidung

Die Schritte der Bewertung und Entscheidung bilden den Abschluss des eigentlichen Planungsprozesses. Nach Abschluss der bisherigen Phasen werden durch den oder die verantwortlichen Planer die Möglichkeiten bezüglich ihres Zielerreichungsgrades gegenübergestellt, wobei die Entscheidung zu Gunsten der Alternative ausfällt, die die höchste Übereinstimmung mit den definierten Zielen aufweist. Im Falle von Entscheidungen bei Sicherheit, also unter bekannten Umweltzuständen, stellt dies keine größeren Probleme dar. Anders gestaltet sich die Situation im Falle von unsicheren Umweltbedingungen. Der Planer bzw. Entscheider sieht sich mehreren möglichen Zuständen gegenüber, ohne zu wissen, welcher der Zustände eintreten wird. Dabei wird gewöhnlich zwischen Unsicherheit und Risiko unterschieden. Als Unsicherheit bezeichnet man eine Situation, bei der die Eintrittswahrscheinlichkeit der verschiedenen Umweltzustände dem Entscheider unbekannt ist. Bei Risiko hingegen kann der Entscheider den einzelnen Umweltzuständen Wahrscheinlichkeiten zuordnen. Um die Entscheidung unter diesen Bedingungen nachvollziehbar zu gestalten und das kurzfristige, improvisierende Element zu minimieren, empfiehlt sich die Anwendung von sog. Entscheidungsregeln.

Zunächst soll der Fall der Unsicherheit, also das Fehlen von Eintrittswahrscheinlichkeiten für die jeweiligen Umweltzustände, betrachtet werden. Die hierbei anwendbaren Regeln berücksichtigen die individuelle Sicherheitspräferenz des Entscheidungsträgers, also wie risikofreudig der Entscheider ist (Schildbach, 1999). Eine der bekanntesten Entscheidungsregeln ist die Maximin-Regel (Wald-Regel), die für risikoscheue Akteure konzipiert ist. Gegeben sei die folgende Ergebnismatrix, wobei a_1, a_2 und a_3 die denkbaren Handlungsalternativen und s_1, s_2, s_3 und s_4 die möglichen Umweltzustände darstellen:

Alternativen	Umweltzustände			
	s_1	s_2	s_3	s_4
a_1	15	20	18	**11**
a_2	14	15	**10**	17
a_3	18	12	**8**	25

Tab. 2: Ergebnismatrix bei Unsicherheit

Die Tabelle kann nun folgendermaßen gelesen werden: Für die Alternative a_1 ergibt sich im Umweltzustand s_1 eine Auszahlung in Höhe von 15 Geldeinheiten, für den Zustand s_2 eine Auszahlung von 20 Geldeinheiten usw. Gemäß der Maximin-Regel werden nun alle Zeilen*minima* gesucht und miteinander verglichen. Die Minima sind in der Tabelle jeweils fett gedruckt. Das *Max*imum dieser Minima findet sich im Beispiel in Zeile a_1, weshalb sich der Entscheidungsträger auf diese Alternative festlegt. Der Vorteil der Maximin-Regel besteht in der einfachen Anwendung. Nachteilig wirkt sich bei dieser Regel aus, dass oftmals Chancen auf hohe Auszahlungen bzw. Zielerreichungen nicht genutzt werden.

Eine Adaption dieser Regel auf risikofreudige Akteure stellt die Maximax-Regel dar. Hier wird das Maximum nicht aus den Zeilenminima gewählt, sondern aus den Zeilenmaxima. Im Beispiel stellen folgende Auszahlungen die Maxima dar: 20 Geldeinheiten für Alternative a_1, 17 Geldeinheiten für Alternative a_2 und schließlich 25 Geldeinheiten für Alternative a_3. Ein risikofreudiger Manager entscheidet sich gemäß der Maximax-Regel für a_3, da er hier die Chance auf eine möglichst hohe Auszahlung wahrt.

Weitere Entscheidungsregeln, bei denen die Risikoeinstellung des Entscheiders berücksichtigt wird, sind die Hurwicz-Regel (Pessimismus-Optimismus-Regel), die Savage-Niehans-Regel (Regel des kleinsten Bedauerns) oder die Laplace-Regel (Regel des unzureichenden Grundes) (Wöhe, 2000).

Im Falle einer Entscheidung bei Risiko – die Eintrittswahrscheinlichkeiten der Umweltzustände sind dem Entscheider bekannt – findet das Erwartungswertprinzip (Bayes-Prinzip) Anwendung. Hierbei wird allerdings davon ausgegangen, dass der Entscheider risikoneutral ist. Geht man von der oben dargestellten Ergebnismatrix aus und nimmt man zusätzlich an, dass die Zustände s_1 bis s_4 mit den folgenden Wahrscheinlichkeiten auftreten: s_1 mit 10 %, s_2 mit 30 %, s_3 mit 20 % und s_4 mit 40 %, so kann man für jede Alternative den Erwartungswert (die Summe der mit den jeweiligen Wahrscheinlichkeiten multiplizierten Auszahlungen) berechnen. Die Eintrittswahrscheinlichkeiten addieren sich dabei zu 100 % auf. Die Alternative mit dem höchsten Erwartungswert ist die Alternative der Wahl. In diesem Beispiel ergeben sich die folgenden Erwartungswerte:

$$\mu \, (a_1) = 0,1 \times 15 + 0,3 \times 20 + 0,2 \times 18 + 0,4 \times 11 = 15,5$$
$$\mu \, (a_2) = 14,7$$
$$\mu \, (a_3) = 17,0$$

Der Erwartungswert der Alternative a_3 fällt somit am größten aus. Daher würde diese Alternative ausgewählt. An die Entscheidung schließt sich nun die Umsetzung der ausgewählten Handlungsalternative an.

5.3.4 Kontrolle

Da Planung eher einen kontinuierlichen als einen abgeschlossenen Prozess darstellt, kann die Kontrolle gleichzeitig als letzter wie auch als erster Schritt der (neuen) Planung interpretiert werden. Bei der Kontrolle muss seitens des Unternehmens bestimmt werden, *wer* kontrolliert, *was* kontrolliert wird und *wie* die Kontrolle durchgeführt wird. Darüber hinaus muss explizit festgelegt werden, welche Ziele mit der Kontrolle erreicht werden sollen. Nur so lässt sich vermeiden, dass – wie in der Praxis fallweise zu beobachten – Kontrollberichte erstellt werden, deren Ergebnisse aber keine Berücksichtigung finden (Grünig, 2002). Das Kontrollverfahren als Ganzes erfüllt in einem Unternehmen dabei zwei Funktionen:

1. die Koordinationsfunktion zur Erklärung von Abweichungen zwischen Ist- und Soll-Zustand und
2. die Motivationsfunktion, die sich auf die Führung der Mitarbeiter bezieht (Olfert/Rahn, 2000).

Bei der Festlegung des Kontrolleurs stellt sich zunächst die Frage, ob das Unternehmen interne Kräfte einsetzt oder aber die Überprüfung durch externe durchführen lässt. Die erforderliche Qualifikation des Kontrolleurs, der finanzielle Aufwand, die im Unternehmen verfügbaren personellen Kapazitäten sowie die Vertraulichkeit der Daten sind Aspekte, die bei dieser Entscheidung Berücksichtigung finden sollten. Wenn sich ein Unternehmen aus einem dieser Gründe für die Kontrolle durch einen eigenen Mitarbeiter entscheidet, ist zu klären, ob ein Angestellter die Kontrolle durchführen soll, der bereits im Rahmen des bisherigen Planungsprozesses involviert war. Den Vorteil stellen in diesem Fall die umfassenden Kenntnisse dar, die bereits in den vorherigen Phasen erworben wurden. Nachteilig hingegen kann sich eine gewisse „Betriebsblindheit" oder Voreingenommenheit auswirken.

Die Kontrolle kann sich nach Mag (1999) u. a. auf die folgenden Objekte beziehen:

- Faktoren (Personal-, Material- oder Anlagenkontrollen)
- Funktionen (Beschaffungs-, Produktions- oder Absatzkontrollen)
- Phasen des Planungsprozesses (Ziel- oder Maßnahmenkontrollen)

Knappe Ressourcen erfordern die Beschränkung auf Stichproben (in der Produktion) oder aber auf Kontrollschwerpunkte. Selbst wenn die Mittel zu einer vollständigen Kontrolle zur Verfügung stünden, sollte abgewogen werden, ob diese wirtschaftlich sinnvoll erscheint.

Bei den eingesetzten Verfahren muss berücksichtigt werden, ob es sich bei den vereinbarten Zielen um quantitative oder qualitative Ziele handelt. Im Falle von quantitativen Zielen ist die Überprüfung mittels Daten aus dem betrieblichen Rechnungswesen verhältnismäßig einfach. So steht Dank der elektronischen Datenverarbeitung zeitnah eine große Menge an Informationen zur Verfügung, die einen Soll-Ist-Vergleich ermöglicht und hilft, mögliche Abweichungen zu erklären. Eine weitere Möglichkeit, erhobene Daten zu nutzen, stellen Kennzahlen wie etwa die Eigenkapitalrendite oder Kennzahlensysteme wie das ZVEI-System dar (Reichmann, 2001).

Im Falle qualitativer Ziele gestaltet sich die Kontrolle schwieriger, was an den teilweise begrenzten Möglichkeiten zur Operationalisierung der Ziele liegt. Hier sind v.a. Befragungen eine allerdings zeitintensive Möglichkeit. Einen Ansatz auch qualitative Größen in einem Kennzahlensystem zu integrieren, bieten u. a. die Balanced Scorecard oder auch der weniger bekannte Skandia Navigator (Kaplan/Norton, 1997; Edvinsson, 1997).

Eine letzte Frage im Rahmen der Kontrolle stellt sich bezüglich der Häufigkeit bzw. des Zyklus einer Kontrollmaßnahme. Hier gilt der gleiche Grundsatz wie bei der Frage nach dem Kontrollobjekt: Auf der einen Seite muss die Überprüfung häufig genug stattfinden, um ihre Wirkung nicht zu verfehlen, auf der anderen Seite muss die Wirtschaftlichkeit gewahrt bleiben.

5.4 Rahmenbedingungen der Planung im Bereich des Sports

Nach der allgemeinen Darstellung des Komplexes Planung soll dieser in den Kontext des Bereichs Sport eingeordnet werden.

Der Sportbereich ist von Rahmenbedingungen gekennzeichnet, die ihn von anderen Wirtschaftsbereichen unterscheiden. Zunächst werden dem gesamten Sportbereich ihm inhärente und ihn differenzierende Besonderheiten zugeschrieben. Wenngleich viele dieser vermeintlichen Besonderheiten auch in anderen Wirtschaftsbereichen vorliegen, beeinflussen sie im Sportbereich in besonderem Maße Entscheidungen des Managements. Um diesen Besonderheiten auch institutionell Rechnung zu tragen, wurden im Sportbereich spezifische institutionelle Arrangements getroffen (z.B. Sportligen). Darüber hinaus ist der Sportbereich derzeit besonders von dem sich ändernden gesellschaftlichen und politischen Umfeld betroffen, was insbesondere die institutionellen Anbieter vor neue Herausforderungen stellt.

Diese Rahmenbedingungen machen es erforderlich, bei der Anwendung der wirtschaftswissenschaftlichen Instrumente und dabei auch bei der Planung den Besonderheiten Rechnung zu tragen (Daumann/Langer, 2005; Freyer, 1990; Heinemann, 1998; Horch, 1994).

5.4.1 Besonderheiten

Für den Aspekt der Planung spielen die folgenden Charakteristika eine besondere Rolle:

Kennzeichnend für den Wettkampfsport ist das Phänomen der assoziativen Konkurrenz: Sportunternehmen stehen einerseits in sportlicher Konkurrenz zueinander, andererseits können sie aber nicht ohne die Kooperation mit mindestens einem weiteren Sportunternehmen einen sportlichen Wettkampf ausführen.

Die Unsicherheit über den Ausgang des sportlichen Wettkampfs bestimmt den Spannungsgrad. Dieser wiederum ist eine zentrale Determinante der Attraktivität des Zuschauersports und bildet damit ein zentrales Qualitätsmerkmal des Zuschauersports.

Zudem findet sich im Zuschauersport, wie auch bei sonstigen Dienstleistungen, die Integration des externen Faktors. In Form des Zuschauers ist er aber nicht nur in den Erstellungsprozess integriert, sondern stellt vielmehr einen Produktionsfaktor dar, der sich entscheidend auf die Produktqualität auswirkt. Er generiert die Stimmung und die Atmosphäre während des sportlichen Wettkampfs, die starken Einfluss auf die Nachfrage nimmt.

Somit zeigt sich, dass aufgrund der Integration mit den Abnehmern einerseits und der Erfordernis der Kooperation mit den Wettbewerbern andererseits die Planung der Produktqualität das Sportunternehmen vor besondere Herausforderungen gestellt ist.

5.4.2 Institutionelle Arrangements

Gerade um den Spannungsgrad des sportlichen Wettkampfs sicherzustellen, finden sich im Umfeld des sportlichen Wettkampfs zahlreiche institutionelle Arrangements, die zum einen hinsichtlich ihrer (kooperativen) Ausgestaltung selbst Gegenstand der Planung der Sportunternehmen sind, zum anderen als Rahmenfaktoren bei der Planung berücksichtigt werden müssen.

Während in anderen Wirtschaftsbereichen Unternehmen bestrebt sind, die Wettbewerbsintensität zu reduzieren und möglichst eine marktbeherrschende Stellung zu erreichen, kooperieren im Sportbereich die Unternehmen, um ausreichend Wettbewerbsintensität und damit einen hohen Spannungsgrad sicherzustellen. Hierzu gibt es Mechanismen, die auf eine Umverteilung der Erlöse (wie z.B. Einnahmen aus der Vermarktung von TV-Übertragungsrechten) abzielen oder den Input rationieren (z.B. Gehaltsobergrenzen in den US Major Leagues oder Kaderrestriktionen). Auf die Etablierung dieser Mechanismen müssen sich die beteiligten Sportunternehmen gemeinsam einigen, sie umsetzen und kontrollieren, so dass auch hier die Unternehmen in einen übergreifenden Planungsprozess gemeinsam mit ihren Wettbewerbern eingebunden sind.

Auch die Auf- und Abstiegsregeln nach sportlichen Kriterien dienen zur Erhöhung des Spannungsgrads. Sie machen eine Liga nicht nur im Hinblick auf das Erreichen des Meistertitels spannend, sondern sorgen durch den Abstiegs- und Aufstiegskampf auch für Spannung auf den unteren Rängen. Zudem zwingen sie Sportvereine, die einen Abstieg vermeiden wollen, in seine Spielstärke zu investieren und damit die Produktqualität der gesamten Liga zu erhöhen. Für die Vereine selbst stellen sie jedoch enorme Planungsrisiken dar. Im Falle eines Abstiegs sind, zumindest im kommerzialisierten Sportbereich, enorme Erlöseinbußen wirtschaftlich zu verkraften. Investieren Vereine, um den Erlöseinbußen zu entgehen, im Abstiegskampf in ihre Mannschaft und müssen dennoch absteigen, so werden sich nicht nur ihre Investitionen schwerlich amortisieren lassen, vielmehr kann der gesamte Verein in eine finanzielle Schieflage geraten. Aber auch Aufstiege stellen die Sportvereine vor schwierige Anpassungsprozesse. Dies gilt für die Planung einer ausreichend spielstarken Mannschaft ebenso wie für die Planung des erforderlichen ligaadäquaten Umfelds, das oft formal in umfangreichen Auflagen geregelt ist (z.B. Zuschauerkapazität der Sportanlage, Sicherheitsmaßnahmen, Jugendarbeit), die es zu erfüllen gilt. Die hierfür erforderlichen Investitionen muss der Verein finanzieren, wobei die für die Erlösplanung zentrale Prognose der Dauer der Zugehörigkeit aufgrund zahlreicher Unwägbarkeiten im Hinblick auf den sportlichen Erfolg nur schwer abzuschätzen ist.

5.4.3 Herausforderungen für Sportinstitutionen

Der Sportbereich ist in Deutschland traditionell gekennzeichnet von selbstverwalteten Sportanbietern. Sportvereine und -verbände organisieren sowohl das Breitensport- als auch das Spitzensportangebot. Gesellschaftliche Veränderungen führen aber auch im Sportbereich zu einem Wandel, der in der Nachfrage und dem Angebot nach Sport seinen Ausdruck findet (Langer, 2006).

Aufgrund der zunehmenden Ausdifferenzierung der Präferenzen der Sporttreibenden und einer wachsenden Individualisierung können sich neben den Vereinen oftmals kommerzielle Sportanbieter und der freie ungebundene Sport etablieren. Für Sportvereine wird es damit schwerer, Mitglieder zu halten oder gar welche hinzuzugewinnen. Vereine sind, bedenkt man zudem den demographischen Wandel mit einer zunehmenden Alterung der Bevölkerung, oftmals gezwungen, bestimmte Sparten zu schließen oder bekommen Schwierigkeiten, ihre Mannschaften in den unterklassigen Ligen ausreichend zu besetzen.

In Anbetracht der sich entwickelnden Angebotsvielfalt und der steigenden Konkurrenz gewinnt ein attraktives Angebot für Mitglieder und Kunden und eine flexible Anpassung an sich immer schneller ändernde Bedürfnisse mehr und mehr an Bedeutung. Damit einher geht die Kommerzialisierung und Professionalisierung des Sports. Sie zwingt die Vereine zu einer stärkeren Marktorientierung des Angebots. Zugleich hat sich der Zuschauersport zu einem Unterhaltungsgut entwickelt, das Gegenstand wirtschaftlicher Interessen zahlreicher Beteiligter ist.

Parallel zu den absatzseitigen Entwicklungen sind Sportvereine auch auf der Beschaffungsseite zu mehr ökonomischer Rationalität angehalten. Dies umso mehr, als die öffentliche Sportförderung zunehmend kritisch hinterfragt wird und der Erhalt, die Dauer und Höhe der Bereitstellung öffentlicher Mittel schwer kalkulierbar ist.

Die beschriebenen Entwicklungen erhöhen die Komplexität von Entscheidungen für die Institutionen des Sports. Die Umweltzustände befinden sich im Sportbereich im Vergleich zu früheren Jahren verstärkt im Fluss, verringern damit die Prognosegenauigkeit und schaffen so zusätzliche Entscheidungsunsicherheit. Umso wichtiger ist es für Sportanbieter, den Planungsprozess immer wieder zu durchlaufen, um die Situation neu zu bewerten und die ggf. erforderliche Anpassung der Zielsetzung und Neuausrichtung der Maßnahmen vorzunehmen.

5.5 Planung des sportlichen Erfolgs im Mannschaftssport

Ziel von Wirtschaftsunternehmen ist es, einen möglichst hohen Gewinn zu erwirtschaften und dabei stets liquide zu sein. Sportunternehmen indes verfolgen daneben noch ein weiteres gleichberechtigtes, wenn nicht sogar übergeordnetes Ziel: sportlicher Erfolg. Wie sich sportlicher Erfolg planen lässt, ist Gegenstand dieses Abschnitts. Um dabei dem normativen Anspruch der Abhandlung gerecht zu werden, muss jedoch die Handlungssituation näher spezifiziert werden. So wird der Aspekt der Mannschaftsplanung in den Mittelpunkt der Überlegungen gerückt, da es sich hier zum einen um ein sporttypisches Phänomen handelt und zum anderen auf umfassenden sportökonomischen Forschungsarbeiten aufgebaut werden kann.

Die Zusammenstellung einer Mannschaft verursacht Kosten und bindet – teils langfristig – finanzielle Mittel. Somit werden die Möglichkeiten der Mannschaftsplanung vom finanziellen Rahmen des Sportvereins begrenzt. Das vorliegende Budget soll als Datum vorausgesetzt werden, so dass – im Sinne des ökonomischen Maximalprinzips – die Frage nach der Verwendung des Budgets zum Erreichen des sportlichen Erfolgs über die Mannschaftsplanung zu klären ist.

Wie sich das Budget für die Mannschaftszusammenstellung als Teilbudget des gesamten Vereinsbudgets ergibt, ist Gegenstand der Budgetplanung. Diese erfolgt im Verein vergleichbar mit Wirtschaftsunternehmen und wird hier nicht näher beleuchtet. Gleiches gilt für die Generierung des Gesamtbudgets, also über welche Kanäle Erlöse generiert werden. Hierbei laufen eigene Erlösplanungsprozesse ab.

5.5.1 Sportlicher Erfolg und wirtschaftlicher Erfolg

Wie oben bereits angerissen wurde, streben Wirtschaftsunternehmen nach wirtschaftlichem Erfolg und richten daher in der Planung ihr Handeln auf Zielgrößen wie Umsatz, Marktanteil, Gewinn, Image oder Kundenzufriedenheit aus. Bei Sportunternehmen wird dieser Kanon durch das Ziel sportlicher Erfolg erweitert, das oftmals dominiert. Sportlicher Erfolg wird im Mannschaftssport anhand der relativen Positionierung einer Mannschaft gegenüber anderen Mannschaften im sportlichen Wettkampf gemessen, was in der spezifischen Produktionsstruktur des Mannschaftssports begründet liegt. So kann keine Mannschaft isoliert produzieren, sondern schon das einzelne Spiel setzt das Zusammentreffen zweier Mannschaften voraus. In Form einer Liga mit Meisterschaftsspielen oder eines Ausscheidungswettbewerbs wie Pokalspielen werden mehrere Spiele aufeinander bezogen, so dass die relative Spielstärke jeder Mannschaft innerhalb einer Gruppe von Mannschaften ermittelt werden kann. Daneben gibt es auch absolute Maßstäbe für sportlichen Erfolg, die aber insbesondere die Einzelspieler-Ebene betreffen: Anzahl erzielter Tore, verwandelter Freiwürfe, gewonnener Rebounds, gewonnener Zweikämpfe, erfolgreich gestellter Blocks etc.

Unabhängig der Entwicklung von Sportvereinen hin zu Wirtschaftsunternehmen, die sich dem sportlichen und wirtschaftlichen Ziel verpflichtet fühlen (so zumindest in Deutschland – bei den professionellen Sportteams in den US-Major-Leagues handelt es sich hingegen um reine Wirtschaftsunternehmen), ist jeder Sportverein auf eine ausreichende Ressourcenausstattung angewiesen, um überhaupt die Voraussetzungen zu schaffen, am sportlichen Wettkampfbetrieb teilnehmen und sportlichen Erfolg erzielen zu können. Somit stellt sich die Frage nach der Beziehung des sportlichen und wirtschaftlichen Ziels im Sportverein.

Grundsätzlich kann eine komplementäre Beziehung zwischen sportlichem und wirtschaftlichem Erfolg unterstellt werden. Einerseits erreichen sportlich erfolgreiche Vereine höhere Rangpositionen. Mit diesen sind i.d.R. zusätzliche Erlöse verbunden, sei es direkt in Form von höheren Erfolgsprämien oder indirekt über eine verstärkte Nachfrage nach Zuschauertickets, Merchandising-Artikeln etc. So basiert etwa der Verteilungsmodus der Einnahmen aus den Fernsehübertragungsrechten in der Fußball-Bundesliga auf dem erzielten Rangplatz: Der Erstplazierte erhält dabei doppelt soviel wie der Letztplazierte. Gleiches lässt sich bspw. auch in der Champions League beobachten: So konnte der AC Mailand als Champions League Sieger 2007 knapp 40 Mio. € einnehmen. Der in der Gruppenphase ausgeschiedene Hamburger SV hingegen erhielt nur wenig mehr als ein Drittel dieser Summe. Andererseits verfügen wirtschaftlich erfolgreiche Vereine über ein höheres Budget zur Mannschaftszusammenstellung. Somit können spielstarke Spieler verpflichtet oder sich gut entwickelnde Spieler an den Verein gebunden werden. Mit einem steigenden Leistungspotential wird sich dann ceteris paribus das sportliche Abschneiden verbessern.

Allerdings sind die aufgezeigten Zusammenhänge nicht zwingend, so dass in Teilbereichen Zielindifferenz angenommen werden muss. Zum einen gibt es Sportbereiche wie z.B. bei Sportarten wie Cross-Country-Laufen, Rudern oder Curling, die kaum kommerzialisiert sind und in denen sich auch im Falle sportlichen Erfolgs keine zusätzlichen Erlöse generieren lassen. Zum anderen ist Spielstärke kein Erfolgsgarant per se. Faktoren wie die Tagesform, Motivation, mannschaftliche Geschlossenheit, aber auch Zufallskomponenten wie Glück oder Schiedsrichterentscheidungen können die sportlichen Leistungsunterschiede kompensieren. Nicht umsonst sagt der Volksmund, der (DFB-)Pokal habe seine eigenen Gesetze.

Gerade der letzte Aspekt wird oft missachtet, wenn Sportvereine versuchen, sich sportlichen Erfolg durch die Verstärkung der Mannschaft mit Stars bzw. leistungsstarken Spielern zu „erkaufen". Sind die Erlöse von der erreichten Rangpositionen abhängig und gibt es zwischen diesen zudem große Erlössprünge, so kann das Nicht-Erreichen des gesetzten sportlichen Ziels (z.B. Qualifikation zur Teilnahme am internationalen Wettbewerb, Klassenerhalt) aufgrund der dann fehlenden Erlöse einen Sportverein schnell in eine finanzielle Schieflage bringen, wenn er für diesen Fall keine Rücklagen gebildet hat bzw. nicht flexibel auf der Kostenseite agieren kann.

Deshalb ist es bei der Planung des sportlichen Erfolgs wichtig, die Interdependenz mit dem wirtschaftlichen Erfolg zu berücksichtigen. So sollten verschiedene Szenarien des sportlichen Abschneidens analysiert und dahingehend bewertet werden, ob auch im ungünstigsten Fall zumindest die Solvenz des Sportvereins dauerhaft gesichert ist.

5.5.2 Mannschaftsplanung

Eine Mannschaft muss über ausreichend Spielstärke verfügen, um sportlich erfolgreich zu sein. Die Spielstärke ist der entscheidende Output einer Mannschaft. Sie wird fast ausschließlich von den Fähigkeiten und Fertigkeiten der Spieler bestimmt. Humankapital ist damit der zentrale, kaum subsituierbare Produktionsfaktor im Mannschaftssport. Somit ist die Generierung von Spielstärke einer Mannschaft zunächst eine Investitionsentscheidung in Bezug auf das Humankapital.

Der Output einer Mannschaft ist aber nicht nur abhängig vom Leistungsvermögen jedes einzelnen Spielers, sondern auch davon, wie gut die Spieler zusammen harmonieren. Der gemeinschaftliche Mehrwert, also der zusätzliche Output über die Summe der Einzelbeiträge der Mannschaftsmitglieder hinaus, wird zum einen durch das Einspielen und aufeinander Abstimmen der Spieler im Training und im Spielbetrieb (on-the-job) erreicht. Er stellt, bezogen auf den einzelnen Spieler, ein speziell im Team wirksames Humankapital dar. Zum anderen beeinflusst aber auch die Zusammenstellung der Mannschaft in Bezug auf bestimmte Strukturmerkmale wie Alterszusammensetzung, Nationalität etc. den Output einer Mannschaft.

Damit die Spieler dauerhaft ihr maximales Potential abrufen und sich den sportlichen (und wirtschaftlichen) Interessen des Vereins verpflichtet fühlen, müssen hierfür geeignete Anreizstrukturen geschaffen werden. Dabei handelt es sich meist um spezifische Kombinationen aus Vertragslaufzeit und Entgeltzusammensetzung. Aber auch Maßnahmen, die sich nur indirekt monetär auswirken, können leistungssteigernd gesetzt werden wie z.B. der regelmäßige Austausch von Spielern, um den teaminternen Wettbewerb um Stammplätze zu intensivieren. Gerade für letztgenannten Aspekt zeichnet der Trainer verantwortlich. Er ist es, der die Mannschaft zusammenstellt, den Aufbau individuellen und teamspezifischen Humankapitals fördert und die Leistungskontrolle der einzelnen Spieler vornimmt. Deshalb ist auch die Trainerfrage aus Sicht des Vereins im weiteren Sinne als Teil der Mannschaftsplanung aufzufassen.

Damit gilt es, im Folgenden als die Teilprobleme bei der Planung des sportlichen Erfolgs Investitionen in Humankapital, die strukturelle Zusammenstellung der Mannschaft, Anreizsysteme sowie Trainer(wechsel) zu betrachten und Handlungsalternativen für die Sportvereine aufzuzeigen.

5.5.2.1 Investition in Humankapital

Ein erster Schritt bei der Planung der Investitionen in Humankapital stellt die Bestandsanalyse dar. Vor dem Hintergrund des sportlichen Erfolgsziels geht es um die Frage, ob das vorhandene Humankapital ausreicht, dieses zu erreichen, ob es durch Fortbildung (Training) dahin entwickelt werden kann, ob zusätzliches Humankapital (neue Spieler) verpflichtet werden muss oder ob auf eigenes, neu ausgebildetes Humankapital (Nachwuchsspieler) zurückgegriffen werden kann. Die Investition in Humankapital in Form von Neuinvestitionen oder von Aus- bzw. Fortbildung der Spieler verursacht nicht nur Kosten, sondern ist mit großen Risiken behaftet, die es bei der Planung zu berücksichtigen gilt (Franck, 1995).

Der Ausbildungsprozess ist langwierig und von vielen unkontrollierbaren Faktoren beeinflusst (Talent des Spielers, Gefahr des „ewigen Talents", Einsatzwillen, Entfaltungsmöglichkeiten, Durchbruch in die aktive Mannschaft, Verweildauer im Kader, Integration etc.). Zudem ist das erworbene Humankapital im Sport extremen Gefährdungen ausgesetzt und zeitlich begrenzt. Verletzungen und Krankheiten verringern das Humankapital und führen im schlimmsten Fall zur Nichteinsatzfähigkeit des Spielers. Aber selbst wenn der Verein von diesen Gefahren, denen seine Spieler ständig ausgesetzt sind, verschont bleibt, können die Spieler Höchstleistungen nur in einem bestimmten Zeitfenster erbringen. Wann der Zeitpunkt kommt, ab dem sie körperlich nicht mehr mithalten können, variiert von Sportart zu Sportart und ist schwer abschätzbar.

Bei der Neuverpflichtung eines Spielers ist zudem ungewiss, wie sich sein Anfangskapital, das er mitbringt, entwickeln wird. Neben den bereits angeführten Faktoren ist schwer abschätzbar, was der Sportler künftig unternimmt, um sein einsatzfähiges Können zu pflegen und zu entwickeln, aber auch, um sich in die Mannschaft zu integrieren (nachvertraglicher Opportunismus). Zudem bleibt offen, wie sich sein Einsatz auf die Teamleistung auswirkt, gerade in Bezug auf das teamspezifische Humankapital, und wie sich die Kooperationsbereitschaft aller Spieler entwickelt. Aber schon zum Zeitpunkt des Vertragsschlusses läuft der Verein Gefahr, dass der neue Spieler private Informationen vorenthält, die z.B. den Gesundheitszustand, die Leistungsbereitschaft oder die körperliche Leistungsfähigkeit betreffen (vorvertraglicher Opportunismus).

Dem Verein stehen nun verschiedene Lösungsalternativen zur Verfügung, deren Vor- und Nachteile er abwägen muss, wobei er insbesondere seine langfristige strategische Planung als Bewertungsmaßstab heranziehen sollte.

Die Ausbildung von Spielern ist umso rentabler für den Verein, je größer der Anstieg der Leistungsfähigkeit des Sportlers und insgesamt seines Marktwerts ist. Je länger der Verein den Spieler an sich bindet, desto besser wird der Verein die Früchte seiner Investition ernten können. Insbesondere hat der Verein den Vorteil, dass er den Spieler lange Zeit kennt und damit Opportunismus-Problematiken weitgehend abschätzen kann. Der Verein trägt zwar die Ausbildungsrisiken, kann dafür dem Spieler aber ein geringeres Gehalt zahlen. Zudem hat der Verein die Möglichkeit, sofern er den Spieler langfristig an sich gebunden hat, sein Investment an andere Vereine zu veräußern und damit einen großen „Liquidationserlös" zu erzielen. Dabei besteht die Möglichkeit der Kooperation zwischen finanzstarken und finanzschwachen bzw. höher- und niederklassigen Vereinen in der Form, dass die finanzschwachen bzw. niederklassigen Vereine die Spieler ausbilden, ihnen die nötigen Einsatzzeiten im Wettkampfbetrieb gewähren und sie im Hinblick auf opportunistisches Verhalten kennen und einschätzen lernen, die finanzstarken bzw. höherklassigen Vereine sich hierfür an den Investitionskosten beteiligen. Die Fokussierung auf die Ausbildung von Nachwuchsspielern und das Hervorbringen neuer Talente zum Einsatz in der eigenen Mannschaft oder zum Weiterverkauf kann damit sowohl zum sportlichen wie auch wirtschaftlichen Erfolg beitragen.

Schließt der Verein einen langfristigen Vertrag mit dem Spieler, hat er nicht nur die Chance, dass der Spieler – bei guter Entwicklung seines Marktwerts – von einem anderen Verein zu einer hohen Ablösesumme aus dem Vertrag herausgekauft wird. Zudem kann der Verein einen Abschlag beim Gehalt vornehmen, übernimmt dafür aber das Risiko hinsichtlich Formschwankungen im Laufe der Zeit und der Entwicklung des Spielers. Gerade bei langfristigen Verträgen nahe des biologischen Karriereendes ist es zweifelhaft, ob der Spieler sich anstrengt, um die Investition erfolgreich zu machen, da er selbst nichts davon hat.

Im Falle eines kurzfristigen Vertrags ist davon auszugehen, dass der Spieler zur Weiterentwicklung bereit ist: Nur wenn sich das Investment für seinen Arbeitgeber als rentabel erweist bzw. er sich durch seine Leistungen für andere Vereine empfiehlt, kann der Spieler auf einen neuen Vertrag hoffen. Der Verein gewinnt zudem an Flexibilität, da er aufgrund der kurzen Vertragsbindung sein Spielerportfolio an veränderte Umweltzustände gut anpassen kann. Da nun aber das Entwicklungsrisiko beim Spieler liegt, wird er hierfür ein höheres Gehalt verlangen. Ferner läuft der Verein Gefahr, gute Spieler und die in sie gesteckten Fortbildungskosten bei einem ablösefreien Wechsel nach Vertragsablauf nicht ersetzt zu bekommen. Müssen sich immer wieder neue Spieler behaupten, kann dies den Leistungswettbewerb schüren und insbesondere zu einer schnellen Steigerung des individuellen Humankapitals führen. Ein hoher Grad an Spielerfluktuation kann sich aber auch negativ gerade auf das teamspezifische Humankapital auswirken, da immer wieder neue Spieler mit ihren ihnen eigenen Fähigkeiten und Fertigkeiten integriert, Spielzüge neu erlernt oder Taktiken angepasst werden müssen.

Bei der Neuverpflichtung eines Spielers gilt es insbesondere, sein Anfangskapital und dessen Entwicklungsmöglichkeiten richtig einzuschätzen. Zugleich müssen vor- und nachvertragliche Opportunismus-Risiken minimiert werden. Letzteres kann durch die Kombination von Vertragslaufzeit und garantiertem Einkommen erreicht werden: Sportler, die ihren Leistungshöhepunkt erreicht haben, werden langfristige Verträge präferieren, Sportler, die in naher Zukunft Leistungssteigerungen erwarten, eher kurzfristige Verträge. Ebenso werden leistungsbereite Sportler einen größeren Anteil variabler Einkommensbestandteile wählen. Über die Wahl der Vertragsalternative kann sich der Verein vom Sportler damit glaubhaft die Leistungsfähigkeit und -bereitschaft signalisieren lassen. Eine korrekte Bewertung des Anfangskapitals und Leistungspotentials erfordert das sorgfältige Zusammentragen und Auswerten sämtlicher erhältlicher öffentlicher Informationen. Neben dem Sichten des Spielers kann man Experten befragen, die in den letzten Jahren immer umfassender gewordenen Spielerstatistiken wie auch Medieninformationen auswerten, gezielt auf die Verletztenliste achten etc. Ebenso ist es ratsam, ein Probetraining wie auch eine Gesundheitsprüfung noch vor Vertragsschluss durchzuführen.

Für welche Handlungsalternative sich ein Verein letztlich entscheiden sollte, hängt von der konkreten Handlungssituation ab. Bspw. wird ein Verein, der in eine höhere Klasse aufgestiegen ist, den Erhalt in der neuen Klasse anstrebt, aber konservativ plant und auch einen Wiederabstieg mit einkalkuliert, auf eine Minimierung seines Investitionsrisikos bedacht sein. Dies gelingt ihm, wenn er flexibel seine eingesetzten Ressourcen reallozieren kann. Somit wird der Verein auf den eigenen Nachwuchs setzen, sich nur kurzfristig an neue Spieler binden und Gebrauch von den Möglichkeiten des kurzzeitigen Ausleihens von Spielern anderer Vereine machen.

5.5.2.2 Strukturelle Zusammenstellung der Mannschaft

Unter welchen strukturellen Aspekten die Mannschaft zusammenzustellen ist, und was das konkret für die Planung von Neuverpflichtungen bedeutet, soll nun als weiteres Teilproblem betrachtet werden. Bei der Darstellung der Alternativen und der Prognose der Auswirkung wird auf empirische Untersuchungen zurückgegriffen, die den Zusammenhang der strukturellen Determinanten Alter, Erfahrung, Marktwert und Nationalität auf die sportliche Leistung bei Mannschaften der Fußball-Bundesliga untersuchen (Gaede/Kleist/Schaecke, 2002).

Der Einsatz von Spielern mit geringem und hohem Alter führt zu einer höheren Leistung. Dahinter verbirgt sich die Erwartung der Vereine, dass junge und ältere Spieler aufgrund des höheren Risikos eine bessere Leistung erbringen. Zwischen der Altersstruktur und der Spielerleistung im Team lässt sich jedoch kein Zusammenhang nachweisen.

Mit zunehmender Erfahrung der Spieler steigt tendenziell die Mannschaftsleistung. Aber auch Spieler ohne Erfahrung bringen höhere Leistungen als Spieler mit ein bis zwei Jahren Bundesliga-Erfahrung. Diese Spieler sind besonders motiviert, da sie zum einen gerade den Sprung in die Mannschaft geschafft haben und sich zum anderen nun in dieser behaupten müssen. So zeigt sich auch, dass die Erfahrungsstruktur einer Mannschaft einen Einfluss auf die Spielerleistung nimmt. Heterogene Teams schneiden hier besonders erfolgreich ab. Sie können einerseits die hohe Motivation der jungen Spieler nutzen, andererseits aber auch auf die Routine der erfahrenen Spieler zurückgreifen.

Wenig überraschend ist der positive Zusammenhang des Marktwerts einer Mannschaft mit der sportlichen Leistung. Der (sportliche) Grenzertrag ist allerdings abnehmend. Hier bietet Real Madrid ein gutes Beispiel, wo der zusätzliche sportliche Effekt der Akkumulation von Stars (Raul, Figo, Zidane, Beckham etc.), anders als das mediale und wirtschaftliche Interesse am Verein, kaum auszumachen war. Auch zeigt sich, dass viele hoch bezahlte Stars auf der einen Seite und viele Geringverdiener auf der anderen Seite nicht zum Erfolg der Mannschaft beitragen. Es sind vielmehr die hinsichtlich ihres Marktwertgefüges homogenen Teams, die im sportlichen Vergleich besser abschneiden. So erspielen bzgl. des Marktwerts heterogene Mannschaften mit hohem Marktwertniveau tendenziell weniger Punkte als homogene Mannschaften mit geringem Niveau.

Mannschaften, die viele Nationalitäten vereinen, erbringen tendenziell bessere Leistungen. Hierbei kann sich gerade die unterschiedliche individuelle Ausbildung und Spielanlage positiv auswirken, während sprachliche oder kulturelle Barrieren die Leistung schmälern können. Deshalb ist besonderes Augenmerk auf die Integrationsfähigkeit dieser Spieler zu legen.

Zwar beziehen sich die beschriebenen Zusammenhänge auf die Mannschaften der Fußball-Bundesliga, dennoch scheinen die dahinter stehenden Überlegungen auch auf andere Sportarten übertragbar. Somit lassen sich hieraus Implikationen für die Planung der Neuverpflichtung von Spielern ableiten. Ausgehend vom vorhandenen Kader sollte die Erfahrungsstruktur so ergänzt werden, dass ein ausgewogenes Verhältnis von wenig und sehr erfahrenen Spielern erreicht wird. Zudem sollte der Verein bestrebt sein, langfristig das gesamte Marktwertniveau zu steigern, ohne jedoch die bestehende Marktwertstruktur zu verletzen.

5.5.2.3 Anreizsysteme

Bereits im Zusammenhang mit Investitionen in Humankapital wurde aufgezeigt, dass leistungsfähige und -willige Sportler einen Vertrag mit geringem Fixum und hohem variablen Einkommensbestandteil wählen werden. Dabei ist aber zu berücksichtigen, dass eine ausgeprägte individuelle Leistungsorientierung schnell zu egoistischem Verhalten innerhalb der Mannschaft führen kann und damit zu Lasten der für den Mannschaftserfolg unverzichtbaren Kooperationsbereitschaft eines jeden Spielers gehen kann. Deshalb ist bei der Planung der Entlohnung der Spieler darauf zu achten, dass sie zum einen die individuelle Motivation, zum anderen aber auch die Kooperation der Spieler fördert.

Leistungsanreize können neben der Höhe des variablen Anteils am Gesamteinkommen durch die Ausgestaltung der variablen Komponenten gezielt gesetzt werden. Je nach Kombination und Ausgestaltung resultieren zahlreiche Entlohnungsalternativen. Damit diese effektiv und effizient sind, sollten sie erstens an der Zielsetzung des Vereins ausgerichtet sein. Zweitens sollten sie transparent sein, also die Bemessungsgrundlage klar erkennen lassen und Diskussion vermeiden. Drittens sollten sie ohne großen Aufwand umsetzbar und damit wirtschaftlich sein. Schließlich sollten sie viertens flexibel dahingehend sein, dass sie eine einfache Nachjustierung bei veränderten Rahmenbedingungen ermöglichen.

Die gängigsten Formen von Anreizsystemen sind Punktprämien, Jahresleistungsprämien, Anlaufprämien und Torprämien oder sonstige Abschlussprämien (Schewe/Gaede/Harmann, 2002).

Die Punktprämie wird an alle Spieler und den Trainer in gleicher Höhe ausgezahlt. Dabei kann sie weiter differenziert werden nach der Spielzeit, nach Heim- oder Auswärtsspiel etc. Die Punktprämie ist an den Mannschaftserfolg gekoppelt und soll so die mannschaftsinterne Kooperationsbereitschaft während der Spiele erzeugen. Die Auszahlung der Punktprämie kann zudem an das Erreichen eines bestimmten Tabellenplatzes gekoppelt werden. Damit lässt sich ein dauerhafter Leistungsanreiz setzen.

Die Jahresleistungsprämie ist der Betrag, den ein Spieler für die Anzahl von ihm absolvierter Spiele innerhalb einer Spielzeit erhält. Sie wird individuell mit dem Spieler ausgehandelt und ist vom Erfolg unabhängig. Somit setzt sie einen dauerhaften Anreiz zur Erbringung hoher Leistungen.

Die Anlaufprämie hingegen wird für die Aufstellung bezogen auf jedes einzelne Spiel an den Spieler bezahlt. Sie zielt darauf ab, den Leistungsaspekt im Training zu verbessern und den internen Wettbewerb um die Stammplätze zu stimulieren. Sie übt also eine regelmäßig wiederkehrende Anreizfunktion aus.

Die Torprämie stellt eine Belohnung der absoluten Einzelleistung eines Sportlers während eines Spiels dar. Sie fördert zwar die individuelle Leistung, kann aber auch eine negative Wirkung auf die Kooperation mit den Mannschaftskollegen haben, wenn der Spieler bestrebt ist, zur Sicherung der Prämie unbedingt selbst ein Tor erzielen zu wollen, dabei besser positionierte Spieler nicht beachtet und somit den gesamten Mannschaftserfolg gefährdet.

So zeigen auch empirische Untersuchungen, dass Mannschaften mit einer kooperationsfördernden Entlohnung erfolgreicher sind als solche, die ausschließlich die individuelle Leistung honorieren. Bei der Wahl der Entlohnungsalternativen bedeutet dies für Vereine nun keineswegs, auf Anreize zur individuellen Leistungsförderung zu verzichten. Aber sie dürfen bei der Planung des Anreizsystems die negativen Folgen mangelnder Kooperationsbereitschaft nicht missachten, wenn sie sportlichen Erfolg anstreben.

5.5.2.4 Trainereinsatz und -wechsel

Wie schon erläutert, ist der Output der Mannschaftsproduktion mehr als die Summe der Einzelbeiträge der Spieler. Dieser Mehrwert lässt sich jedoch nur schwer verursachungsgerecht den einzelnen Spielern zuordnen. Damit einher geht die Gefahr, dass Spieler ihren Einsatz mindern. Deshalb ist es u. a. Aufgabe des Trainers, den Sportverein vor einem solchen Verhalten der Spieler zu schützen, indem er die Leistung der Spieler überwacht und sie im Falle verminderter Leistungsbereitschaft sanktioniert.

Damit der Trainer dies leisten kann, benötigt er ausreichend Kapazität, um die Spieler beobachten und bewerten zu können. Kann er eine wirksame Kontrolle ausüben, so fühlen sich auch die Spieler im Hinblick auf ihre Leistung korrekt eingeschätzt, was gerade leistungsbereite Spieler wertschätzen und anzieht.

Dies funktioniert aber nur, wenn der Trainer selbst seine volle Leistungsfähigkeit abruft. Da auch er Teil der Mannschaft ist und sein Beitrag schwer separiert werden kann, könnte auch er Einsatzwillen vermissen lassen und bedürfte selbst wieder der Kontrolle. Deshalb sollten Vereine auch den Trainer am sportlichen Erfolg beteiligen, damit er die Früchte seiner Arbeit erntet und somit einen Anreiz hat, effektiv und effizient zu arbeiten.

Im Falle von Planabweichungen beim sportlichen Erfolgsziel ist eine in der Praxis häufig beobachtete Handlungsreaktion bei Vereinen ein Trainerwechsel. Der Trainer stellt das „schwächste Glied" der Mannschaft dar und scheint leichter substituierbar zu sein als eine Mannschaft oder zumindest Teile davon. Betrachtet man jedoch die faktische Wirkung von Trainerwechseln auf den sportlichen Erfolg, so scheinen sie keine geeignete Handlungsalternative zu sein (Salomo/Teichmann, 2002).

Auch nach einem Trainerwechsel werden die anvisierten Saisonziele meist nicht erreicht, so dass der erzielte Erfolg weiterhin hinter den Erwartungen zurückbleibt. Vergleicht man Mannschaften, die den Trainer gewechselt haben mit solchen ohne Trainerwechsel, so schneiden letztere sportlich erfolgreicher ab. Auch zeigt sich, dass Mannschaften, die einen Leistungseinbruch gegenüber der Vorsaison erleiden und dann den Trainer wechseln, zwar im Anschluss wieder das Niveau der Vorsaison, aber auch kein höheres Niveau erreichen, sondern eher knapp dahinter zurückbleiben.

Gerade weil die Trainerfrage häufig sehr emotional diskutiert wird und große Anteilnahme in der Öffentlichkeit erfährt, gilt es, die Fakten nicht außer Acht zu lassen. Sie sprechen eindeutig gegen einen ad hoc durchgeführten, improvisierten Trainerwechsel und stützen die Notwendigkeit, den Planungsprozess auch für den

Vollzug eines Trainerwechsels vollständig und gewissenhaft zu durchlaufen. Dies gilt gerade auch vor dem Hintergrund der wirtschaftlichen Zielsetzung. So ist bei einem Trainerwechsel zwar keinesfalls der sportliche Erfolg garantiert, zusätzliche Kosten in Form von Abfindungen oder Entgeltfortzahlungen sind jedoch gewiss. Damit kann der Verein erheblichen finanziellen Mehrbelastungen ausgesetzt sein.

Für Vereine bieten sich deshalb insbesondere zwei Handlungsalternativen an. Sind Vereine auf Kontinuität bedacht, so scheinen die langfristige Planung mit einem Trainer und das Festhalten an diesem zielführend. Will man hingegen Flexibilität bewahren, bspw. nach einem Auf- oder Abstieg und den damit verbundenen erhöhten Schwierigkeiten bei der Prognose des sportlichen Erfolgs, so ist eine lediglich kurze Bindungszeit an den Trainer ratsam. Ungeachtet der letztlich gewählten Handlungsalternative sollte eine fortlaufende Kontrolle der Zielerreichung mit daraus abzuleitenden Maßnahmen nicht unterbleiben; diese sollte jedoch nicht unbedacht zu einem Wechsel des Trainers führen.

5.6 Fallstudie

Die folgenden Fallstudie zeigt am Beispiel der Science City Jena, die unter dem Namen POM Baskets Jena in der Saison 2006/07 in die erste Basketball-Bundesliga aufgestiegen sind, welche Schwierigkeiten mit der Planung von Sportvereinen bei Auf- oder Abstiegen bewältigt werden müssen.

Fallstudie „Science City Jena"

Die Stadt Jena kann auf eine lange Tradition im Basketball zurückblicken. So spielten die Thüringer bereits zu DDR-Zeiten in der höchsten Spielklasse. Nach der Wiedervereinigung gründete sich 1994 eine eigene Basketballabteilung des gemeinnützigen Sportvereins TuS Jena. Bereits 1995 gelang der Aufstieg in die Regionalliga, 2001 der erneute Aufstieg in die 2. Bundesliga. Die zunehmende Professionalisierung zeigt sich im Falle der Jenaer Basketballer durch die Gründung der Baskets Jena GmbH, die zu Beginn des Jahres 2005 ihre Geschäftstätigkeit aufnahm.

Im April des Jahres 2007 gelang dem Verein der sportliche Aufstieg in die höchste deutsche Spielklasse. Da der Aufstieg in den Planungen nicht hinreichend berücksichtigt worden war, musste binnen kürzester Zeit die wirtschaftli-

---

che Basis für den Erstligabetrieb geschaffen werden. Als erste Hürde erwies sich dabei der Nachweis einer größeren Halle. Die in der zweiten Liga genutzte Halle entsprach mit ca. 1.000 Plätzen nicht mehr den Mindestansprüchen. Dies führte zu einer Übergangslösung in Form eines Zeltes mit ca. 3.000 Plätzen. Der Bau einer neuen Mehrzweckhalle durch die Stadt konnte bislang jedoch nicht beschlossen werden. Diese soll 3.500 Zuschauern Platz bieten und neben der Verwendung als Sporthalle auch anderen kulturellen Ereignissen einen angemessenen Rahmen bieten. Doch selbst bei Baubeginn noch vor der ersten Spielzeit nach dem Aufstieg hätte das „Zelt" für mindestens eine Saison Heimat der Jenaer bleiben müssen.

Das zweite große Problem lag im Aufstellen eines Haushaltsplanes. So stieg das erforderliche Budget in der Saison 2007/08 von etwa 600.000 € auf ca. 1,25 Mio. € an. Die Unterdeckung belief sich dabei auf mehrere hunderttausend Euro. Verantwortlich für den Anstieg waren v.a. personelle Umstellungen. So wurden für die aus fünf Spielern bestehende Startmannschaft vier Neuzugänge verpflichtet. Einer der Hauptgründe für die finanziellen Probleme lag jedoch darin, dass der bisherige Namenssponsor – eine lokal tätige Kette von Fitnessstudios – sein Engagement nicht verlängerte. Die Suche nach einem adäquaten Ersatz sollte sich für das Management dabei als außerordentlich schwierig erweisen, so dass die Erteilung der Lizenz erst nach einer Fristverlängerung seitens der BBL (Basketballbundesliga) erfolgen konnte. Als neuer Namenssponsor konnte schließlich die Stadt Jena präsentiert werden. In Anlehnung an den Titel „Stadt der Wissenschaften", den Jena 2008 trägt, wurde das Team „Science City Jena" getauft.

Unter Berücksichtigung der hier dargestellten Ereignisse zeigt sich, inwieweit ein überraschender Aufstieg dazu führen kann, dass die gesamte Planung hinfällig wird. Wenn es dem Management nicht gelungen wäre, die Lizenzauflagen rechtzeitig zu erfüllen, wäre die Baskets Jena GmbH in große finanzielle Kalamitäten geraten. Auch wäre es dem Club nicht möglich gewesen, auf den Aufstieg zu verzichten und eine weitere Saison in der zweiten Liga zu spielen. Stattdessen wäre es zum Zwangsabstieg in die Regionalliga gekommen. Somit war das Erlangen der Lizenz nichts anderes als eine notwendige Bedingung zum sportlichen wie auch wirtschaftlichen Überleben der Mannschaft.

Um auf die veränderten Bedingungen zu reagieren, musste das Management in kürzester Zeit jede einzelne Sequenz des Planungsprozesses neu durchlaufen. Aus Sicht der Zielanalyse galt es, als Oberziel die Auflagen für den Lizenzerhalt zu erfüllen. Erst bei Erreichen dieses Primärziels konnte der Klassenerhalt als sportliche Vorgabe ausgerufen werden. Jena orientierte sich dabei an den Konkurrenten aus Ulm und Paderborn, die in den letzten Jahren nach dem Aufstieg nicht nur den Klassenerhalt schafften, sondern außerdem auf Anhieb die Play-Offs erreichen konnten. Die Situation des Vereins stellte sich besonders schwierig dar, da der Erhalt der Lizenz vor dem Engagement der Stadt keineswegs als gesichert gelten durfte. Demnach musste parallel zur Planung für die erste Liga ein „Notfallplan" für den Fall des Zwangsabstiegs in die dritte Liga erarbeitet werden. Ein weiteres, strukturelles Problem lag in der personellen Ausstattung der GmbH. So zeichneten 2007 nur drei Personen für die gesamte kaufmännische Leitung verantwortlich (Manager, Geschäftsstellenleitung, Assistenz).

Damit sind die Ziele ebenso wie die Probleme im Planungsprozess klar umrissen. Welche Alternativen boten sich dem Club? Im Falle eines Zwangsabstieges hätte man gezwungenermaßen im sportlichen wie auch im kaufmännischen Bereich Einschränkungen hinnehmen müssen. Somit dürfte die Alternative „sofortiger Wiederaufstieg in die zweite Liga" außer Reichweite stehen. Stattdessen wäre auf Grund der Prognose und der Bewertung voraussichtlich der Alternative „Konsolidierung in der Regionalliga" der Vorzug gegeben worden.

Zusammenfassend kann für die Aufstiegssaison *nach* Erteilung der Lizenz folgende Struktur gelten:

- Ziel: Klassenerhalt, schnelle wirtschaftliche Konsolidierung, Aufbau einer attraktiven und spielstarken Mannschaft, Erhöhung der Popularität.
- Probleme: In der höheren Spielklasse herrscht ein höheres Spielniveau, bei dem es mit der bestehenden Mannschaft schwer wird, die Ziele zu erreichen.
- Alternativen: (1) Leistungssteigerung der bisherigen Zweitligamannschaft; (2) Verstärkung des Teams durch neue Spieler.
- Prognose: mit der bestehenden Mannschaft ist die notwendige Leistungssteigerung unwahrscheinlich, gegen die zweite Alternative sprechen mögliche Integrationsprobleme mit den neuen Spieler und die zusätzlichen Kosten.
- Bewertung: im Rahmen der Bewertung ist das Management offensichtlich zu dem Schluss gekommen, dass der Aufbau einer neuen Mannschaft eine höhere Zielerreichung verspricht, so dass in der Folge vier Spieler neu verpflichtet wurden.

Betrachtet man die kurze Periode zwischen Erhalt der Lizenz und Aufnahme des Spielbetriebs (operative Ebene), so galt es hier, neben dem sportlichen Bereich u.a. den Vertrieb der Tickets und die Preisgestaltung zu gewährleisten sowie den Aufbau des Zeltes für die Austragung der Heimspiele zu überwachen. Auf strategischer Ebene stand neben dem Klassenerhalt auch das Suchen nach einem Namenssponsor für die Saison 2008/09 auf der Agenda, da die Stadt Jena den Titel „Stadt der Wissenschaft" nur 2008 trägt und ein weiteres Engagement demnach fraglich erscheint.

5.7 Fazit und Ausblick

„Das Schwierige da planen, wo es noch leicht ist." Der eingangs zitierte Laotse umfasst mit dieser trivialen Aussage zwar den Sinn von Planung, ist sich aber nicht über die Probleme bewusst, die sich dem Planer stellen. Auch wenn das vorliegende Kapitel nicht auf alle Aspekte der Planung eingehen konnte, sollte es doch einen Überblick über die Bedeutung von Planung und deren Durchführung gegeben haben. So lässt sich festhalten, dass der Komplex aus Zielsetzung, Entscheidungen und anschließender Kontrolle erheblich zum Erfolg einer jeden Organisation beitragen kann, wenn nicht gar als notwendige Bedingung zu gelten hat.

Dadurch, dass bereits jetzt viele Sportvereine zu mittelständischen Unternehmen angewachsen sind, ergibt sich für diese auch zunehmend die Notwendigkeit, stärker betriebswirtschaftliche Erkenntnisse – v.a. auch bei der Planung - zu berücksichtigen. In den nächsten Jahren ist zudem in vielen Bereichen des Sports mit weiterem Wachstum der Bedeutung und damit auch des Umsatzes zu rechnen. Von dieser Entwicklung werden jedoch nicht alle Akteure in gleichem Maße profitieren. Gleichzeitig wachsen jedoch auch die Ansprüche an Vereine, Verbände und Veranstalter, sei es von Seiten der Aktiven, von Seiten der Konsumenten oder sei es von Seiten der Sponsoren. Reichte es früher aus, ein Club mit einer starken regionalen Verankerung zu sein, müssen nun Leitbilder und die strategische Ausrichtung geplant werden, um langfristig erfolgreich sein und bestehen zu können. Die Bedeutung einer effizienten auf betriebswirtschaftliche Erkenntnisse basierenden Planung wird daher im Sport erheblich zunehmen.

Kontrollfragen

1. Begründen Sie, warum Planung aus wirtschaftlicher Sicht vorteilhaft ist!
2. Nennen und beschreiben Sie die einzelnen Bausteine des Planungskomplexes! Warum spricht man bei der Erfolgs- und Liquiditätsplanung von einer Querschnittsfunktion?
3. Nennen Sie einzelnen Phasen im Planungsprozess!
4. Stellen Sie das Prinzip des Alternativenbaums graphisch dar! Welche Vorteile hat diese Methode der Alternativenanalyse?
5. Unterscheiden Sie komplementäre und konfliktionäre Planungsziele voneinander!
6. Erläutern Sie die Funktion der Kontrolle! Was unterscheidet die Kontrolle von qualitativen und quantitativen Zielen?
7. Zeigen Sie auf, welche Besonderheiten des Sportbereichs bei der Planung zu berücksichtigen sind und wie sich hierdurch die Planung zum produzierenden Gewerbe unterscheidet!
8. Beschreiben Sie, wie sich das sportliche und wirtschaftliche Ziel bei Sportvereinen zueinander verhalten und berücksichtigen Sie dabei, ob es sich um einen professionellen Sportverein oder einen Breitensportverein in einer Randsportart handelt!
9. Welche Alternativen stehen einem Verein zur Verfügung, wenn er in Humankapital investieren möchte? Welche Auswirkungen hinsichtlich des sportlichen Erfolgs der Mannschaft lassen sich für die jeweiligen Alternativen prognostizieren?

10. Wenn ein Verein seine Mannschaftszusammensetzung im Hinblick auf die strukturellen Determinanten Alter, Erfahrung, Marktwert und Nationalität plant, kann er welche bekannten Zusammenhänge seiner Alternativenbewertung zugrunde legen?

Literaturverzeichnis

Coenenberg, Adolf G. (1999): Kostenrechnung und Kostenanalyse, 4. Aufl., Landsberg/Lech.

Daumann, Frank / Langer, Mathias (2005): Sportökonomie. Versuch einer Gegenstandsbestimmung, in: Wirtschaftswissenschaftliches Studium, Heft 7, S. 399-404.

Edvinsson, Leif (1997): Developing Intellectual Capital at Skandia, in: Long Range Planning, Heft 3, S. 366-373.

Franck, Egon (1995): Die ökonomischen Institutionen der Teamsportindustrie – Eine Organisationsbetrachtung, Wiesbaden.

Freyer, Walter (1990): Sport-Ökonomie oder Ökonomie des Sports? Fragmente zur Bestimmung einer neuen Wissenschaftsdisziplin, Diskussionspapier Nr. 2/1990, Forschungsinstitut für Tourismus und Sport, Berlin/Bonn.

Gaede, Nicolas / Kleist, Sebastian / Schaecke, Mirco (2002): „Elf Freunde müßt Ihr sein?“: Die strategische Entscheidung der Teamzusammensetzung, in: Schewe, Gerhard / Littkemann, Jörn (Hrsg.): Der Profifußball aus sportökonomischer Perspektive, Schorndorf, S. 213-242.

Grünig, Rudolf (2002): Planung und Kontrolle, 3. Aufl., Bern u.a.

Gutenberg, Erich (1957): Grundlagen der Betriebswirtschaftslehre, Erster Band: Die Produktion, 3. Aufl., Berlin u.a.

Hammer, Richard M. (1998): Unternehmensplanung, 7. Aufl., München u.a.

Heinemann, Klaus (1998): Was ist und wozu benötigen wir eine Ökonomie des Sports?, in: Sportwissenschaft, Heft 3-4, S. 265-282.

Hinterhuber, Hans-H. (1996): Strategische Unternehmensführung, Band 1, 6. Aufl., Berlin u.a.

Horch, Heinz-Dieter (1994): Besonderheiten einer Sport-Ökonomie: Ein neuer bedeutender Zweig der Freizeitökonomie, in: Freizeitpädagogik: Forum für Kultur, Medien und Tourismus, Heft 16, S. 3.

Kaplan, Robert S. / Norton, David P. (1997): Balanced Scorecard: Strategien erfolgreich umsetzen, Stuttgart.

Kreikebaum, Hartmut (1997): Strategische Unternehmensplanung, 6. Aufl., Stuttgart.

Langer, Mathias (2006): Öffentliche Förderung des Sports – eine ordnungspolitische Analyse, Berlin.

Mag, Wolfgang (1999): Planung und Kontrolle, in: Bitz, Michael / Domsch, Michel / Ewert, Ralf / Wagner, Franz W. (Hrsg.): Vahlens Kompendium der Betriebswirtschaftslehre, Band 2, 4. Aufl., München, S. 1-63.

Olfert, Klaus / Rahn, Horst-Joachim (2000): Lexikon der Betriebswirtschaftslehre, 3. Aufl., Ludwigshafen.

Olfert, Klaus / Rahn, Horst-Joachim (2005): Einführung in die Betriebswirtschaftslehre, 8. Aufl., Ludwigshafen.

Perridon, Louis / Steiner, Manfred (2002): Finanzwirtschaft der Unternehmung, 11. Aufl., München.

Reichmann, Thomas (2001): Controlling mit Kennzahlen und Managementberichten, 6. Aufl., München.

Salomo, Sören / Teichmann, Kai (2002): Erfolgsmessung im Sportmanagement – Trainerwechsel und Vereinserfolg, in: Schewe, Gerhard / Littkemann, Jörn. (Hrsg.): Der Profifußball aus sportökonomischer Perspektive, Schorndorf, S. 243-264.

Schewe, Gerhard / Gaede, Nicolas / Haarmann, Julia (2002): Leistungsanreize im Profifußball, in: Schewe, Gerhard / Littkemann, Jörn (Hrsg.): Der Profifußball aus sportökonomischer Perspektive, Schorndorf, S. 115-134.

Schierenbeck, Henner (2000): Grundzüge der Betriebswirtschaftslehre, 15. Aufl., München.

Schildbach, Thomas (1999): Entscheidung, in: Bitz, Michael / Domsch, Michel / Ewert, Ralf / Wagner, Franz W. (Hrsg.): Vahlens Kompendium der Betriebswirtschaftslehre, Band 2, 4. Aufl., München, S. 66-105.

Schmidt, Hans-Jürgen (1982): Betriebswirtschaftlehre für die Verwaltung, Heidelberg u.a.

Staehle, Wolfgang H. (1999): Management, 8. Aufl., München.

Ulrich, Peter / Fluri, Edgar (1995): Management. Eine konzentrierte Einführung, 7. Aufl., Stuttgart.

Welge, Martin K. / Al-Laham, Andreas (2001): Strategisches Management. Grundlagen – Prozess – Implementierung, 3. Aufl., Wiesbaden.

Wild, Jürgen (1982): Grundlagen der Unternehmensplanung, 4. Aufl., Reinbek b. Hamburg.

Wöhe, Günter (2000): Einführung in die Allgemeine Betriebswirtschaftslehre, 20. Aufl., München.

Weiterführende Ressourcen

Literatur

Daumann, Frank / Andrews, Phillip (2005): Die Stadtmarathon-Branche in Deutschland. Eine ökonomische Analyse der Marktposition der Veranstalter, in: Sport und Gesellschaft - Sport and Society, Heft 1, S. 67-91.

Hermanns, Arnold (2001): Entwicklung und Perspektiven des Sportsponsoring, in: Hermanns, Arnold /Riedmüller, Florian (Hrsg.): Management-Handbuch Sport-Marketing, München, S. 389-407.

Kohl, Thorsten (2001): Ökonomie des Profifußballs, Aachen.

Schewe, Gerhard / Littkemann, Jörn (Hrsg.) (2002): Sportmanagement, Schorndorf.

Strauß, Bernd / Kolb, Michael / Lames, Martin (Hrsg.) (2002): sport-goes-media, Schorndorf.

Trosien, Gerhard / Dinkel, Michael (Hrsg.) (2002): Sport und neue Märkte, Butz-bach-Griedel.

Links

Horizont Sport Business (Fachzeitschrift):
    http://www.sportbusiness.horizont.net/

Sport Business Magazine (Fachzeitschrift):
    http://www.sportbusiness.com/

Verband für Sportökonomie und Sportmanagement in Deutschland:
    http://www.vsd-online.de/

Zeitschrift für Planung (Fachzeitschrift):
    http://www.tu-chemnitz.de/wirtschaft/bwl3/zp/

Kapitel 6: Organisation im Sport

Sebastian Kaiser   Heinz-Dieter Horch

Lernziele

Nach der Durchsicht dieses Kapitels sollte der Leser in der Lage sein,

- die verschiedenen Perspektiven des Organisationsbegriffs zu schildern und einzuordnen.
- die Entstehung des Organisationsproblems zu erläutern und die historische Entwicklung formaler Organisationen zu beschreiben.
- zentrale Entwicklungslinien und Schulen der Organisationstheorie voneinander abzugrenzen.
- die Grundlagen der Gestaltung von Organisationssystemen sowie die zentralen Dimensionen der Organisationsstruktur darzustellen.
- Besonderheiten der Organisationsstruktur von Sportvereinen zu beschreiben und zu erklären.

Überblick über das Kapitel

Erfahrungen mit Organisationen sowie dem Organisieren sind so selbstverständlich, dass der Begriff „Organisation" im Alltagssprachgebrauch kaum reflektiert wird. Die Frage, was eine Organisation ist, wird jedoch von Organisationswissenschaftlern, je nach zu Grunde gelegter theoretischer Perspektive, unterschiedlich beantwortet. Im Rahmen des vorliegenden Kapitels wird zunächst die Vielfalt der Perspektiven des Organisationsbegriffs aufgezeigt und es wird eine kurze historisch-entwicklungsgeschichtliche Darstellung der einflussreichsten Strömungen der Organisationstheorie vorgenommen. Anschließend werden die zentralen Probleme und Aufgaben, die im Zuge der Gestaltung von Organisationssystemen zu bewältigen sind, in den Blick genommen. Einem klassischen betriebswirtschaftlichen Verständnis folgend wird Organisieren dabei als Management der Strukturen verstanden. Ausgehend von den strukturellen Voraussetzungen der Lösung des Problems der Einbindung ehrenamtlicher Mitarbeiter werden abschließend zentrale Besonderheiten der Organisationsstruktur von Sportvereinen beschrieben und erklärt.

6.1 Einführung in die Thematik

Organisationen sind zu einem zentralen Bestandteil unserer Alltagswelt geworden. Sie beeinflussen unser tägliches Erleben und Handeln grundlegend und begründen Chancen und Risiken für die Erreichung unserer individuellen Ziele (Scherm/ Pietsch, 2007). Kieser/Kubicek (1976) verdeutlichen die universelle Durchdringung moderner Gesellschaften durch Organisationen im Vorwort zur ersten Ausgabe ihres einflussreichen Organisationslehrbuchs folgendermaßen:

> „Die meisten Menschen werden in Organisationen geboren und in Organisationen ausgebildet, sie arbeiten in Organisationen, verbringen einen großen Teil ihrer Freizeit in Organisationen, und schließlich sterben sie in Organisationen und werden von Organisationen zu Grabe getragen" (Kieser/Kubicek, 1976, S. 1).

Erfahrungen mit Organisationen sowie dem Organisieren sind so selbstverständlich, dass der Begriff „Organisation" im Alltagssprachgebrauch zumeist intuitiv verwendet und kaum reflektiert wird. Die Frage, was eine Organisation ist, wird jedoch von Organisationswissenschaftlern, je nach zu Grunde gelegter theoretischer Perspektive, unterschiedlich beantwortet. Nach Picot/Dietl/Franck (1999) liegt die Wissenschaft von der Organisation, wie kaum ein anderes Teilgebiet der Betriebswirtschaftslehre, im Schnittfeld unterschiedlicher Disziplinen, wie z.B. der Betriebs- und Volkswirtschaftslehre, der Soziologie, der Psychologie, der Politologie oder den Ingenieurwissenschaften. Entsprechend umfangreich und heterogen sind die Beiträge, die die Entwicklung der Disziplin vorangetrieben haben (Picot/ Dietl/ Franck, 1999). Der Anspruch, Organisationen umfassend aus einer theoretischen Perspektive beschreiben und erklären zu wollen, wird zunehmend als unerfüllbar angesehen (Kieser/Walgenbach, 2003). In diesem Zusammenhang wird häufig eine Scheinwerfermetapher herangezogen (Kirsch/Esser/Gabele, 1979), nach der jede der vorliegenden Organisationstheorien sich in Bezug auf die Erklärung bestimmter Aspekte der Organisation als sehr hilfreich erweist, in dem sie sie gewissermaßen hell auszuleuchten in der Lage ist, wohingegen jeweils andere Aspekte im Dunkel bleiben müssen.

Die Anforderungen an moderne Organisationsgestaltung sind ebenso vielfältig und komplex. Nach Schreyögg (1999) bedarf der Horizont der Organisationsgestaltung konzeptionell einer immer weiteren Fassung, um die vorgefundenen Problemstände angemessen in den Griff bekommen zu können. Problemspezifisch, quer durch die verschiedenen organisationstheoretischen Schulen, grenzt er fünf generische Probleme der Organisationsgestaltung voneinander ab: Strukturierung von Aufgaben, Integration von Individuum und Organisation, Organisation und Umwelt, emergente Phänomene (implizite Steuerungskräfte) in Organisationen sowie Organisatorischer Wandel und Transformation.

Im Rahmen des vorliegenden Beitrags ist es nicht möglich, einen differenzierten Einblick in die vielfältigen Aspekte des Organisationsphänomens zu geben; die Beschränkung auf einige, wesentliche Aspekte ist unabdingbar. Im Anschluss an eine kurze Darstellung der wichtigsten Perspektiven der Betrachtung von Organisationen sowie der zentralen Entwicklungslinien der Organisationstheorie wird das vorliegende Kapitel daher auf den klassischen Kern einer betriebswirtschaftlichen Auseinandersetzung mit Organisationen eingehen, nämlich die *Gestaltung formaler Organisationsstrukturen*. Auf die Organisation zwischenbetrieblicher Beziehungen

147

kann dabei ebenso wenig eingegangen werden, wie auf die Einbindung in vorgelagerte Institutionen bzw. wettbewerbliche Rahmenbedingungen. Diese Beschränkung des Betrachtungsbereichs auf die Organisation des Binnenbereichs der Unternehmung entspricht einem traditionellen betriebswirtschaftlichen Organisationsverständnis, welches Mehrpersonengebilde als gegeben betrachtet und ihre Untersuchung weitgehend auf deren internes Funktionieren beschränkt.

6.2 Perspektiven des Organisationsbegriffs

Ausgangspunkt einer differenzierten Auseinandersetzung mit dem Organisationsphänomen bildet häufig die Unterscheidung zweier grundlegender Sichtweisen: der *institutionellen* und der *instrumentellen* Perspektive (vgl. Abb. 1). Während sich organisationstheoretische Betrachtungen in erster Linie auf die institutionelle Perspektive beziehen, liegt der Organisationsgestaltung v.a. ein instrumentelles Verständnis zu Grunde (Schreyögg, 1999).

Nach dem ersten Begriffverständnis werden ganze soziale Systeme mit dem Begriff der Organisation belegt, die Organisation erscheint als „regelhaft strukturierte soziale Ganzheit" (Scherm/Pietsch, 2007). Diese Regelstrukturen müssen dabei nicht unbedingt auf den kollektiven Zweck des Kooperationssystems ausgerichtet sein. Sie können sowohl funktional als auch disfunktional im Hinblick auf die Erreichung des Organisationszwecks wirken. Wir sprechen von Schulen, Kirchen, Sportvereinen etc. als Organisationen. Die institutionelle Sichtweise schreibt Organisationen einige grundlegende Merkmale zu (Scherm/Pietsch, 2007; Schreyögg, 1999; Kieser/Walgenbach, 2003):

- Organisationen sind als soziale Institutionen auf jeweils spezifische Zwecke ausgerichtet. I.d.R. wird ihre Existenz v.a. durch diese formalen – sozial akzeptierten – Zwecke begründet. Aufgrund dieser Ausrichtung erweisen sich Organisationen meist als vorsätzlich geschaffene soziale Institutionen.
- Organisationen grenzen sich über die Konstruktion der Mitgliedschaft gegenüber ihrer (sozialen) Umwelt ab. Personen werden erst Teil der Organisation, wenn sie nach jeweils formal fixierten Regeln als Organisations-„Mitglied" aufgenommen wurden. Dabei sind sie nur in ihrer Mitgliedsrolle (Partialinklusion) und keineswegs als ganze Person als ein Teil der Organisation anzusehen.
- Organisationen ergeben sich als ein Zusammenschluss einer Mehrzahl von Mitgliedern, die jeweils mehr oder weniger spezifische Beiträge zur Erfüllung des formalen Organisationszwecks leisten. Dabei müssen die Ziele der Mitglieder keinesfalls mit dem formalen Organisationszweck übereinstimmen.
- In Organisationen haben die Mitglieder grundsätzlich die Möglichkeit, ihre Mitgliedschaft aufzugeben bzw. in andere Organisationen zu wechseln; es besteht also die Möglichkeit des Ein- oder Austritts.
- Organisationen weisen ein bewusst gestaltetes formales Regelsystem (formale Organisationsstruktur) auf, das das Verhalten der Mitglieder auf den formalen

Zweck ausrichten soll. Neben dieser formalen Struktur existieren vielfältige informelle Regeln, die weitgehend spontan entstehen und nur partiell auf den formalen Organisationszweck ausgerichtet sind.

Das zweite Verständnis meint demgegenüber ein bestimmtes Merkmal sozialer Systeme. Hiernach wird etwa davon gesprochen, dass eine Agentur hervorragend organisiert sei, ein Sportverband kürzlich organisatorisch neu aufgestellt wurde usw. (*instrumentelle Sicht*). Die instrumentelle Perspektive, in der deutschen Betriebswirtschaftslehre jahrzehntelang das vorherrschende Organisationsverständnis (Schreyögg, 1999), fokussiert auf die Handlungen der organisatorischen Gestaltung bzw. des Organisierens. Organisation wird demnach als ein Instrument verstanden, das zur Steuerung des Leistungsprozesses beiträgt.

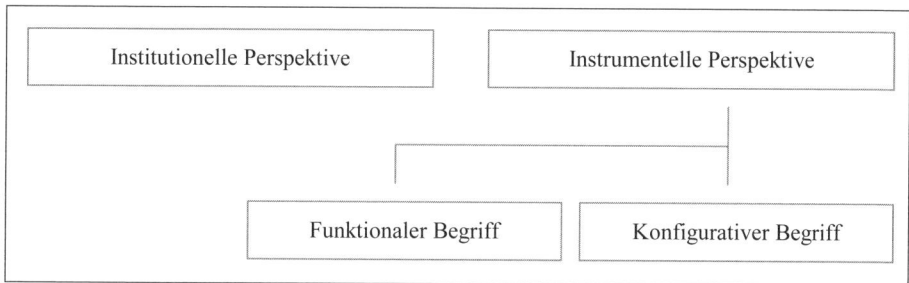

Abb. 1: Perspektiven des Organisationsbegriffs
In Anlehnung an: Schreyögg (1999)

Im Rahmen der instrumentellen Sichtweise lässt sich weiter ein *funktionaler* von einem *konfigurativen* Organisationsbegriff abgrenzen.

Der funktionale Organisationsbegriff wurde durch Gutenberg (1983) geprägt. Organisation ist hiernach in erster Linie als ein Mittel zum Vollzug der Planung zu verstehen, als eine Aufgabe, die wahrgenommen werden muss, um zur Zweckerfüllung der Unternehmung beizutragen. Während die Planung den Entwurf einer Ordnung darstellt, soll die Organisation diese Ordnung, realisieren. Diese Perspektive des Organisationsbegriffs knüpft an die übergeordnete, funktionale Sichtweise des Managements an wonach mit dem Begriff die in arbeitsteiligen sozialen Gebilden notwendigen Prozesse und Funktionen beschrieben werden (managerial functions approach; Staehle, 1999). Diesem funktionalen Organisationsbegriff zufolge ist Organisation als eine Leitungsaufgabe neben der Planung, der Personalbereitstellung und -führung sowie der Kontrolle zu verstehen. Im Rahmen der Auseinandersetzung mit der Frage, wie und von wem die anstehenden Aufgaben erfüllt werden sollen, bietet sich das Festschreiben und Autorisieren der gedachten Regeln an, die Schaffung einer formalen Organisationsstruktur. Organisatorische Regeln lassen sich als generalisierte Erwartungen an die Organisationsmitglieder verstehen. Sie bestimmen ihre Handlungsweise und machen sie vorhersagbar. Da-

149

bei gilt grundsätzlich, dass Leistungsprozesse mit steigender Anzahl festgelegter Regeln zunehmend standardisiert und Handlungsspielräume der Organisationsmitglieder eingeschränkt werden (Scherm/Pietsch, 2007). Gutenberg (1983) bezeichnet das zentrale Gestaltungsprinzip im Rahmen der Strukturierung von Aufgaben und Zuständigkeiten als „Substitutionsgesetz der Organisation". Organisieren meint hiernach die Substitution fallweiser durch generelle Regelungen. Eine generelle Regelung solcher Aufgaben, die durch eine hohe Variabilität gekennzeichnet sind, ist indessen ineffizient. Sie bietet sich dort an, wo abzusehen ist, dass sich die betreffenden Vorgänge in gleicher oder ähnlicher Weise wiederholen werden.

Die profilierteste Gegenposition im Rahmen der instrumentellen Sichtweise bildet die Organisationslehre nach Kosiol (1976). Sie versteht Organisieren als planvolle und dauerhafte Strukturierung von Arbeitsprozessen, als festes Gefüge (Konfiguration), das allen anderen Maßnahmen und Dispositionen vorgelagert ist. Das Organisationssystem wird demnach gebildet durch das integrative Strukturieren von Ganzheiten bzw. die Schaffung genereller Regelungen mit Dauercharakter.

> „Durch die Struktur erhält die Unternehmung aufgrund eines bestimmten Bauplanes ihre besondere Gestalt, im wörtlichen Sinne wird sie geprägte Form, übergreifende Einheit, organische Ganzheit" (Kosiol, 1976, S. 20).

Gegenüber dem Gutenbergschen Verständnis fällt demnach die fallweise Regelung nicht unter den Organisationsbegriff. Damit schließt das konfigurative Verständnis auch spontan entstandene Regelsysteme (informelle Strukturen, Aspekte der Organisationskultur) aus (Scherm/Pietsch, 2007).

6.2.1 Zur Entstehung des Organisationsproblems

Ausgangspunkt des Organisationsproblems ist der Tatbestand der Knappheit. Die menschlichen Bedürfnisse sind praktisch unbegrenzt, die zur Bedürfnisbefriedigung geeigneten Mittel (Güter) stehen dagegen nicht in unbeschränkter Menge zur Verfügung, sondern sind von Natur aus knapp. Aus dieser Knappheit ergibt sich die Notwendigkeit, zu wirtschaften, die vorhandenen Mittel also so einzusetzen, dass ein möglichst großes Maß an Bedürfnisbefriedigung erreicht wird (Wöhe, 1986). Nach dem Begründer der klassischen Volkswirtschaftslehre, Adam Smith, leisten (1) Arbeitsteilung und (2) Spezialisierung den größten Beitrag zur Bewältigung von Knappheit. Smith beschrieb bereits 1776 am Beispiel einer Stecknadelfabrik die Auswirkungen verschiedener Formen der Arbeitsteilung auf die Effizienz eines Unternehmens: Während der Arbeiter, der alle Tätigkeiten, die zur Fertigung einer Stecknadel notwendig sind, selber leistet, lediglich 20 Stecknadel am Tage zu produzieren in der Lage ist, können 10 Arbeiter, von denen jeder nur zwei bis drei Verrichtungen ausführen muss, pro Tag 48.000 Stecknadeln herstellen, also 4.800 pro Person (zitiert in Thommen/Achleitner, 2006).

Den enormen Produktivitätsgewinnen, die sich aus Arbeitsteilung und Speziali-sierung ergeben, stehen aber Probleme des Tausches und der Abstimmung gegenüber:

„Weil der einzelne in einer modernen Industriegesellschaft nur einen verschwin-dend geringen Bruchteil der Güter, die er zu seiner Bedürfnisbefriedigung einsetzt, selbst erzeugt, ist die Notwendigkeit zur Abstimmung und zum Leis-tungstausch mit anderen spezialisierten Akteuren dominierender Bestandteil des täglichen Lebens. Die vielfältigen Austausch- und Abstimmungsvorgänge kosten uns täglich Zeit, Mühe und Geld. Sie verbrauchen damit selbst einen Teil jener Ressourcen, die sonst direkt zur Bedürfnisbefriedigung verwendbar wären. Der Ressourcenverzehr moderner Industriegesellschaften für Tausch und Abstim-mung ist nicht unerheblich" (Picot/Dietl/Franck, 1999, S. 3).

Das Organisationsproblem lässt sich nach Picot/Dietl/Franck (1999) auch als Prob-lem der Mängelbeseitigung interpretieren. Hiernach können Strukturen der Arbeitsteilung und Spezialisierung, des Tausches und der Abstimmung dem Ziel der Knappheitsbewältigung mehr oder weniger gut dienen. Mängel treten als nicht realisierte Produktivitätspotenziale einerseits bzw. wieder verspielte Produktivitäts-gewinne andererseits zu Tage. Allgemein gilt es folglich, Strukturen zu etablieren, in denen die tatsächlich ausgeschöpften Produktivitätspotenziale die für Tausch und Abstimmung wieder verlorenen Produktivitätsgewinne in möglichst hohem Maße überkompensieren. Voraussetzung ist (1) die Versorgung der Akteure mit Informa-tionen zu ihrer jeweiligen Rolle (Koordination) sowie (2) das Schaffen von Anreizen, damit die Akteure die ihnen zugedachte Rolle tatsächlich spielen (Moti-vation).

	Produktivitätsanstieg durch
	Arbeitsteilung / Spezialisierung
./.	Ressourcenverbrauch durch
	Tausch / Abstimmung
	Nettoeffekt ⟶ Maximierung

Abb. 2: Trade-off zwischen Arbeitsteilung/Spezialisierung und Tausch/Abstimmung
Quelle: Picot/Dietl/Franck (1999), S. 6

6.2.2 Zur Entstehung formaler Organisationen

Organisationen lassen sich unter Bezugnahme auf das Organisationsproblem (vgl. Kap. 6.2.1) als Instrumente bzw. Mittel zur Umsetzung von Strategien und zur Erreichung von unternehmerischen Zielen beschreiben. Staehle (1999) spricht in diesem Zusammenhang von einer zielgerichteten Institutionalisierung genereller, formalisierter Verhaltenserwartungen. Die zu Grunde liegende praktische Annahme lautet, dass zielorientiertes Verhalten in erster Linie durch formale Strukturmerkmale (Arbeitsanweisungen, Stellenbeschreibungen, Dienstwege etc.) gesteuert und kontrolliert wird. Hiernach lassen sich Organisationen allgemein als zweckbezogene soziale Gebilde beschreiben, die auf Dauer angelegt sind und eine Organisationsstruktur aufweisen, mit deren Hilfe die Organisationsziele erreicht werden sollen (u.a. Kieser/Walgenbach, 2003).

„An organization comes into existence when explicit procedures are established to coordinate the activities of a group in the interest of achieving specified objectives" (Blau, 1972, S. 297).

Während das Organisieren von großen Projekten ein klassisches Phänomen darstellt, welches die Menschen bereits seit Jahrtausenden beschäftigt, bildeten sich (formale) Organisationen erst relativ spät heraus. Einen populären Ausgangspunkt für die Beschreibung der Entstehung von Organisationen bildet deren Charakterisierung als Ressourcenpools bzw. korporative Akteure (Coleman, 1979). Diese Darstellung erlaubt es auch, historisch, rückwärtsgewandt, Organisationen von übrigen, Vorgängerinstitutionen gewerblicher Produktion in geeigneter Weise abzugrenzen (vgl. hierzu und zum Folgenden Kieser/Walgenbach, 2003). Ressourcenpools entstehen, wenn Individuen einen Teil ihrer Ressourcen (Geld, Arbeitskraft o.ä.) zusammenlegen (Pooling), um Effizienzgewinne zu erzielen. Die zu Grunde liegende Annahme lautet demnach, dass Akteure sich durch die Zusammenlegung besser stellen können als ohne. Da sie nicht alle ihnen zur Verfügung stehenden Ressourcen einer zentralen Disposition unterstellen werden, sind Individuen i.d.R. Mitglieder mehrerer Organisationen: Mitarbeiter in einem Betrieb, Mitglied in einem Sportverein usw.

Die Basisprobleme bei der Gestaltung von Organisationen bestehen damit in der Beantwortung folgender Fragen: (1) Wie wird über den Einsatz gepoolter Ressourcen entschieden bzw. wie soll die Leitung des Ressourcenpools organisiert werden (Bestimmungs-/ Kontrollrechte)? (2) Wie wird der Ertrag auf die Organisationsmitglieder aufgeteilt (Residualeinkommen/Gewinn vs. Kontrakteinkommen/Gehalt). Zur Lösung dieser Kooperations- und Verteilungsprobleme steht ein breites Kontinuum von Gestaltungsmöglichkeiten zur Verfügung, dessen Extrempunkte die genossenschaftlich-demokratische sowie die monokratisch-hierarchische Form darstellen (zu alternativen Unternehmensverfassungen vgl. u.a. Schewe, 2005).

Wie bereits eingangs angedeutet, bildeten sich formale Organisationen erst relativ spät, nämlich im Zuge der industriellen Entwicklung, heraus. Erst sie lassen sich von früheren Institutionen der gewerblichen Produktion eindeutig abgrenzen. So waren die Hierarchien in frühzeitlichen, primitiven Gesellschaften in erster Linie durch die jeweiligen Verwandtschaftsverhältnisse bestimmt. Neben diesen gesellschaftlichen Ordnungen, an deren Spitze i.d.R. der Stammesälteste stand, existierten keine weiteren organisatorischen Strukturen. Die Angehörigen mittelalterlicher Herrenhöfe (hörige Bauern, unfreies Gesinde) brachten nicht freiwillig einige, sondern unfreiwillig alle ihre Ressourcen in die Produktion ein. Ähnliches gilt für die mittelalterlichen Zünfte. Sie vereinnahmten ihre Mitglieder vollständig, mit allen ihren Lebensbereichen (Totalinklusion; Scherm/Pietsch, 2007), ein flexibler Ein- und Austritt war nicht möglich. Sie übernahmen nicht nur ökonomische, sondern u.a. auch religiöse, politische und caritative Aufgaben (Scherm/Pietsch, 2007). Zu den ersten Organisationen gehörten nach Kieser/Walgenbach (2003) Gesellschaften von Fernhandelskaufleuten im 13. Jahrhundert. Auf diese lässt sich die Beschreibung von Organisationen als Ressourcenpools anwenden: Ihre Mitglieder konnten Ressourcen freiwillig einbringen, sie der Organisation aber auch wieder entziehen.

Die Verbreitung von Organisationen wurde durch die Industrialisierung im 18. und 19. Jahrhundert maßgeblich gefördert. Entpersonalisierte, formale Organisationen erlaubten Produktivitätszuwächse sowie weit reichende Flexibilität des Ressourceneinsatzes (Scherm/Pietsch, 2007). Der Erfolg von Organisationen lässt sich damit in erster Linie durch ihre höhere ökonomische Effizienz gegenüber ihren Vorläufer-Institutionen begründen.

6.3 Entwicklungslinien der Organisationstheorie

Die theoretischen Grundlagen der Analyse und Erklärung von Organisationssystemen sollen im Rahmen einer knappen, historisch-entwicklungsgeschichtlichen Darstellung der einflussreichsten Strömungen und Schulen der Organisationstheorie, sowie der ihnen jeweils zu Grunde liegenden Annahmen, angesprochen werden.

Erstens, da ein Einblick in die zentralen Forschungsperspektiven zu einem besseren Verständnis von Organisationen beitragen kann. Nach Schreyögg (1999) konkurrieren mehr denn je unterschiedliche Perspektiven und Theoriegebäude um *Erklärungsrelevanz* und besteht in der Organisationswissenschaft weder Konsens hinsichtlich des Gegenstandes noch hinsichtlich des methodischen Grundverständnisses. Die Deutung organisationaler Phänomene muss demnach die je spezielle Sicht des Analysegegenstandes sowie die jeweilige inhaltliche Perspektive einbeziehen (Organisation als formales Regelsystem, als Herrschaftsinstrument usw., Organisationstheorie als Lehre von der Funktionsweise von Organisationen, von der Strukturgestaltung, usw.).

Zweitens ist der Einblick in die verschiedenen theoretischen Ansätze und Perspektiven der Analyse von Organisationen von *Gestaltungsrelevanz*. Das Gestaltungsziel erweist sich bei dem Großteil der vorliegenden Theorien zwar nur als mittelbar relevant (Scherm/Pietsch, 2007). Eine Kenntnis zentraler Ursache-Wirkungs- bzw. Sinnzusammenhänge ist aber eine wichtige Voraussetzung für die Entwicklung tragfähiger Gestaltungsvorschläge im Rahmen von Prozessen der Organisationsentwicklung.

Die Organisationstheorie stellt sich als ein „Konglomerat unterschiedlichster Forschungsansätze dar" (Scherm/Pietsch, 2007, S. 11). Die einzelnen Perspektiven weichen teilweise deutlich voneinander ab und folgen zum Teil „unvereinbaren wissenschaftlichen Basisaxiomen sowie Forschungsparadigmen" (Scherm/Pietsch, 2007). Sie differieren in Abhängigkeit ihrer inhaltlichen Perspektive bzw. des jeweiligen Erkenntnisinteresses sowie vor dem Hintergrund ihrer historischen und disziplinären Einbettung. Entsprechend schwierig gestaltet sich der Versuch einer Systematisierung. Es gibt zahlreiche Konzepte der Ordnung der vorliegenden Ansätze (Schreyögg, 1999):

* historisch/entwicklungsgeschichtlich (u.a. Scott, 1961),
* methodologisch (präskriptiv, kausalanalytisch, interpretativ etc.; u.a. Burell/ Morgan, 1979),
* nach dem zu Grunde liegenden Leitbild (Maschine, Gefängnis, Kultur etc.; u.a. Morgan, 1997),
* disziplinspezifisch (ingenieurwissenschaftliche, volkswirtschaftliche, psychologische, arbeitswissenschaftliche, soziologische, betriebswirtschaftliche Ansätze etc.; u.a. Mayntz, 1963; Grochla, 1975) usw.

Die prominenteste Gliederung von Organisationstheorien ist die auf deren historischer Entwicklung basierende Klassifikation von Scott (1961, 1974). Scott unterscheidet zwischen klassischen („classical doctrine"), neoklassischen („neoclassical theory of organization") und modernen („modern organization theory") Organisationstheorien.

Die *klassischen Ansätze* gehen im Wesentlichen auf drei Wurzeln aus unterschiedlichen wissenschaftlichen Traditionen zurück: den in Deutschland entwickelten Bürokratie-Ansatz von Max Weber (1976, zuerst 1921), den US-amerikanischen Ansatz der wissenschaftlichen Betriebsführung (Frederick W. Taylor, 1911) sowie den in Frankreich entstandenen Ansatz der Administrations- und Managementlehre nach Henri Fayol (1916). Gemeinsam ist diesen Theorien die Grundannahme der Zweck-Mittel-Rationalität. Sie verstehen Organisationen als zweckgebundene und strikt rational gestaltbare soziale Systeme (Scherm/Pietsch, 2007). Zentrales Mittel zur Sicherstellung der Zielerreichung der Organisation ist die formale Organisationsstruktur sowie eine streng hierarchische Struktur.

Die *neoklassischen Ansätze* der Organisationstheorie fokussieren demgegenüber auf das tatsächliche menschliche Verhalten in Organisationen. Während im Rahmen der klassischen Analyse die „harten Fakten der Steuerung von Organisations-Maschinen" (Scherm/Pietsch, 2007, S. 11) im Vordergrund standen, geraten nun zwischenmenschliche Interaktionen, informelle Verhaltensmuster und motivationale Aspekte stärker in das Blickfeld der Forschung. Es setzt sich die Erkenntnis durch, dass sich Organisationen durch formale Organisationsstrukturen nicht friktionsfrei steuern lassen (Scherm/Pietsch, 2007). Zu den neoklassischen Organisationstheorien zählen insbesondere der Human-Relations-Ansatz (Roethlisberger/Dickson, 1939; Mayo, 1949) sowie die Anreiz-Beitrags-Theorie (Barnard, 1938).

Die seit Anfang der 50er Jahre entwickelten Ansätze werden den *modernen Organisationstheorien* zugeordnet. Es handelt sich um ein heterogenes Feld; einige der Ansätze bauen auf der klassischen Schule auf, während sich andere deutlich von ihr distanzieren. So knüpfen etwa komparative Strukturanalysen sowie der situative Ansatz (u.a. Lawrence/Lorsch, 1967) eng an die Bürokratietheorie an. Gegenüber den präskriptiv/interpretativ ausgerichteten klassischen Ansätzen verfolgen sie das Ziel, Organisationsstrukturen systematisch empirisch zu erfassen und Unterschiede in ihrer Ausgestaltung (Varianzen) zu erklären (Schreyögg, 1999). Der Human-Ressoucen-Ansatz (u.a. Argyris, 1975) stellt eine Weiterentwicklung der Human-Relations-Bewegung dar. Er sieht die Möglichkeit individueller Bedürfnisbefriedigung als wichtige Determinante organisationaler Zielerreichung. Die Grundannahme ist, dass eine traditionelle Organisationsgestaltung zu unreflektiertem Regelgehorsam führt. Sie ist ineffizient und verschwendet Human-Ressourcen da sie den natürlichen Entfaltungsbedürfnissen der Menschen im Wege steht (Schreyögg, 1999). Die verhaltenswissenschaftliche Entscheidungsprozessforschung fokussiert auf das reale Verhalten von Menschen in Organisationen. In Abgrenzung zu den (neo-) klassischen Organisationstheorien weist sie auf die kognitiven Begrenzungen des Menschen hin. Aufgrund der daraus resultierenden begrenzten Rationalität weicht das tatsächliche Entscheidungsverhalten deutlich von den normativen Annahmen der vom Weltbild des „Homo-Oeconomicus" geprägten ökonomischen Analysen ab. Die Studien dieser Schule haben zu einem realitätsnäheren Bild organisationaler Entscheidungen beigetragen (Scherm/Pietsch, 2007). Die Annahme der begrenzten Rationalität bildet auch den Ausgangspunkt der neuen Institutionenökonomik, die sich zu Beginn der 70er Jahre etablierten. Ihr werden die Property-Rights-Theorie, die Transaktionskostentheorie sowie die Principal-Agent-Theorie zugeordnet. Dieses Theoriegebäude fasst Ansätze zur Erklärung des Wirtschaftens in einer Welt zusammen „in der unvollkommene Akteure, Menschen mit begrenzter Rationalität und Moral, in ihrem ökonomischen Handeln aufeinander angewiesen sind" (Picot/Dietl/Franck, 1999, S. 54). Sie basieren auf dem Forschungskonzept des methodologischen Individualismus. Organisationsstrukturen werden demnach als das Ergebnis des Entscheidens und Handelns individueller Akteure verstanden und nicht als emergente Phänomene sozialer Systeme, wie dies soziologische Ansätze unterstellen (Picot/Dietl/Franck, 1999). Den modernen Organisationstheorien werden ferner systemtheoretische, soziologisch-neoinstitutionalistische bzw. strukturationstheoretische sowie postmoderne Anätze zugeordnet (u.a. Scherm/Pietsch, 2007).

6.4 Gestaltung von Organisationssystemen

In Anknüpfung an das Organisationsproblem (siehe Abschnitt 6.2.1) werden im Folgenden Basisaufgaben und Kernbereiche organisatorischer Gestaltung vorgestellt. Einem klassischen betriebswirtschaftlichen Verständnis folgend wird Organisieren dabei als *Management der Strukturen* verstanden. Es geht darum, innerhalb eines institutionellen Rahmens die Strukturträger zu bestimmen und deren Beziehungen untereinander dauerhaft (z.B. Linieninstanzen) oder auf Zeit (z.B. Projekt-Teams) zu regeln (Staehle, 1999). Einen sinnvollen Ausgangspunkt stellt das Konzept der Organisationsstruktur nach Kieser/Kubicek (zuerst 1976) dar. Sie stellen ihrer Auseinandersetzung mit formalen Organisationsstrukturen drei forschungsleitende Fragen voran:

1. Aus welchen Regeln setzt sich die formale Struktur einer Organisation zusammen?
2. Wie lassen sich Unterschiede in den formalen Strukturen von verschiedenen Organisationen erklären?
3. Welche Wirkungen haben formale Organisationsstrukturen auf die Organisationsmitglieder?

Diese Fragen stehen gleichermaßen im Zentrum einer populären Analyseperspektive der Organisationsforschung, die unter der Bezeichnung „situativer Ansatz" bzw. „Kontingenzansatz" firmiert (zur Einordnung der situativen Ansatzes in die Entwicklungslinien der Organisationstheorie vgl. Abschnitt 6.3). Im Vordergrund dieses Ansatzes steht die formale Organisationsstruktur. Charakteristisch ist die Annahme, dass Strukturunterschiede zwischen Organisationen zumindest teilweise auf die jeweilige Situation zurückzuführen sind, in der sich eine Organisation befindet. Der zentrale Unterschied zu den klassischen Annahmen der Bürokratietheorie besteht in der Erkenntnis der ausgesprochenen *Heterogenität von Organisationsstrukturen* in der Praxis, die dennoch gleichermaßen zum Erfolg von Organisationen beitragen können. Es lassen sich demnach keine universell effizienten Strukturen bzw. kein „one best way" des Organisierens (Scherm/Pietsch, 2007) finden. Vielmehr müssen Organisationen ihre Struktur an die vorliegenden situativen Rahmenbedingungen anpassen.

Wenngleich in der Zwischenzeit Kritik am situativen Ansatz laut geworden ist (insbesondere die Annahme weitgehend deterministischer Zusammenhänge zwischen der Organisationsstruktur, der Situation und dem Erfolg gilt als widerlegt, u.a. Scherm/Pietsch, 2007), erscheint eine Anknüpfung an die zu Grunde liegende

Forschungsperspektive dennoch in zweierlei Hinsicht funktional: Formale Organisationsstrukturen sind – gegenüber informalen Strukturen, die unbewusst aus der Interaktion der Organisationsmitglieder entstehen – geplante, meist schriftlich festgelegte, innere Ordnungen von Organisationen. Sie dienen dazu, das Handeln der Mitglieder auf die Zwecke der Organisation auszurichten (vgl. Abschnitt 6.2.1). Die Auseinandersetzung mit den relevanten Strukturdimensionen bildet insofern erstens einen sinnvollen Ausgangspunkt als sie den Blick auf die zentralen Probleme bzw. Aufgaben, die im Zuge der *Gestaltung von Organisationssystemen* zu lösen sind, lenkt. Zweitens liefert diese Betrachtung gleichermaßen einen geeigneten konzeptionellen Rahmen für die Beschreibung von Gemeinsamkeiten und Unterschieden *realer Organisationsstrukturen*, die die nachfolgende Herausarbeitung von *Besonderheiten der Organisationsstruktur von Sportvereinen* ermöglicht (vgl. Abschnitt 6.6).

Kieser/Walgenbach (2003) stellen der Herleitung der relevanten Strukturdimensionen das folgende Beispiel eines auf drei Dimensionen beruhenden Möglichkeitsraumes zur Abbildung realer Organisationsstrukturen voran. Dabei gehen sie davon aus, dass v.a. (1) Autoritätshierarchie, (2) Vorgabe von Arbeitsverfahren sowie (3) Arbeitsteilung organisatorische Regelungen darstellen, die in Zusammenhang mit der Analyse von Einflussgrößen und Wirkungen der Organisationsstruktur von Bedeutung sind und dass sich reale Organisationsstrukturen im Hinblick auf die Art oder den Umfang des Einsatzes dieser drei Regelungsarten unterscheiden lassen. Durch Einordnung in diesen Merkmalsraum lassen sich nun jeweils Gemeinsamkeiten und Unterschiede konkreter Organisationen herausstellen. Dies soll anhand der folgenden zwei Organisationen verdeutlicht werden:

Organisation A (Org$_A$) sei eine Kölner Werbeagentur mit 25 Mitarbeitern. Es herrscht eine familiäre Kultur vor, das Verhältnis der Organisationsmitglieder zueinander ist wenig autoritär. Außer dem Inhaber und Geschäftsführer der Agentur sind alle Mitarbeiter hierarchisch gleichgestellt. Sie nehmen gleichermaßen Teil an der Akquise von Neukunden und bestimmen die Art und Weise ihrer Aufgabenerfüllung weitgehend selbst.

Organisation B (Org$_B$) sei ein international operierender Sportartikelhersteller. Das Verhältnis der Mitarbeiter dieser Organisation ist streng hierarchisch gegliedert. Gemäß ihrer Stellenbeschreibung übernehmen sie je spezielle Teilaufgaben in Produktion, Marketing/Vertrieb usw. Die Arbeitsverfahren sind genau schriftlich fixiert bzw. formalisiert (vgl. Abb. 3).

Die Auswahl geeigneter Strukturdimensionen sowie deren Operationalisierung mit Hilfe der Festlegung von Merkmalsausprägungen können als zentrale Weichenstellung für Analysen und Vergleiche von Organisationsstrukturen angesehen werden. Sie sind deswegen als besonders kritisch anzusehen, da sie den Realitätsausschnitt festlegen, innerhalb dessen die Analyse stattfindet und dadurch auch bestimmen, welche Merkmale *nicht* in die Betrachtung einfließen. Damit besteht die Gefahr, dass relevante Dimensionen außen vor bleiben. Grundsätzlich besteht das folgende Dilemma: Dem Anspruch, Organisationen möglichst umfassend abzubilden, steht die, aus Gründen der Übersichtlichkeit gebotene Notwendigkeit einer sinnvollen Komplexitätsreduktion, und damit einer Begrenzung der zu betrachtenden Merkmale, gegenüber (Kieser/Walgenbach, 2003).

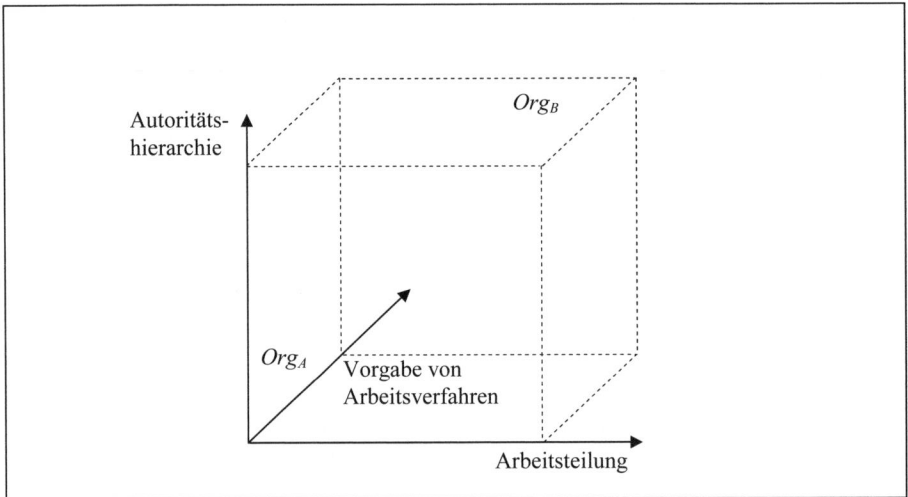

Abb. 3: Beispiel eines dreidimensionalen Möglichkeitsraumes zur Abbildung realer
      Organisationsstrukturen
In Anlehnung an: Kieser/Walgenbach (2003), S. 72

In Anknüpfung an das Bürokratiemodell von Max Weber (1976) kommen die Autoren zu *fünf Hauptdimensionen der Organisationsstruktur*, die wiederum aus mehreren Teildimensionen bestehen (vgl. Abschnitt 6.3):

1. Spezialisierung (Arbeitsteilung),
2. Koordination,
3. Konfiguration (Leitungssystem),
4. Entscheidungsdelegation (Kompetenzverteilung) sowie
5. Formalisierung.

6.4.1 Differenzierung und Integration als Grundfunktionen der Organisation
Die Notwendigkeit der Arbeitsteilung bzw. Spezialisierung stellt den Ausgangspunkt jeder organisatorischen Strukturierung dar (vgl. Abschnitt 6.2.1). Generelle Regeln zur Spezialisierung bilden den ersten Eckpfeiler von Organisationssystemen. Strukturieren bedeutet zunächst, Regelungen zu schaffen: Zur Teilung von Aufgabenvollzügen, zur Koordination, zur Bearbeitung von Vorgängen usw. Organisatorische Regeln stellen damit generalisierte (Handlungs-) Erwartungen an die

Organisationsmitglieder dar. Sie haben Ordnungsfunktion, indem sie ihren Handlungsspielraum einschränken (Schreyögg, 1999; vgl. hierzu das „Substitutionsprinzip der Organisation" nach Gutenberg in Abschnitt 6.2). Demgegenüber nimmt mit zunehmender Arbeitsteilung und Ausdifferenzierung organisatorischer Teilsysteme die Komplexität des Gesamtsystems zu. Den zweiten Eckpfeiler bildet damit die Koordinationsfunktion; Aufgaben der gezielten Zusammenführung bzw. Integration der einzelnen Teile, so dass eine geschlossene Leistungseinheit entstehen kann. Diese zwei zentralen Gestaltungsaufgaben sind ihrer Handlungslogik entsprechend latent gegenläufig:

> „Je stärker eine Organisation differenziert wird, um so problematischer wird die Integration; Intensive Integrationsbemühungen drängen auf Homogenität und verringern tendenziell die Differenzierung" (Schreyögg, 1999, S. 112).

In der Organisationsliteratur werden unterschiedliche Begriffspaare für die Erläuterung dieses generischen Problems der Organisationsgestaltung vorgeschlagen. Am häufigsten findet sich die Beschreibung von *Differenzierung* und *Integration* als Grundfunktionen der Organisation (Staehle, 1999; Schreyögg, 1999). Der u.a. von Kieser/Kubicek (1976) gewählte Koordinationsbegriff wird dahingehend kritisiert, dass er etwas unscharf sei, da er auch generell im Zusammenhang mit „Führung" verwendet werde.

Eine weitere bekannte Systematik der deutschen Organisationslehre hat Kosiol (1976) geprägt. Er unterscheidet *Analyse-* und *Syntheseprobleme* im Zuge der Gestaltung von Organisationssystemen. Im Rahmen der Aufgabenanalyse gilt es hiernach, eine systematische Durchdringung der zu organisierenden Aufgaben vorzunehmen. Die Gesamtaufgabe soll stufenweise anhand von fünf Analysedimensionen in Elementaraufgaben zerlegt werden. Das Ergebnis ist eine große Zahl an einzelnen Teilaufgaben, die dem Organisator als „Gestaltungsmasse" zur Verfügung stehen (Schreyögg, 1999). Die Analyse soll vollzogen werden

- nach den *Verrichtungen* (z.B. Sägen, Schweißen, Nieten),
- nach den *Objekten* (z.B. Aufgaben an Tischen, Stühlen, Schränken),
- nach der *Phase* (nach Planungs-, Realisierungs- und Kontrollaufgaben),
- nach dem *Rang* (nach Entscheidungs- und Ausführungsaufgaben) und
- nach der *Zweckbeziehung* (nach unmittelbar oder mittelbar auf die Erfüllung der Hauptaufgabe gerichteten Teilaufgaben).

Den zweiten Schritt, nach der Kosiolschen Gestaltungslehre der eigentliche organisatorische Akt, stellt die Aufgabensynthese dar. Es gilt, aus den zuvor analytisch ermittelten Elementarteilen sinnvolle organisatorische Einheiten zu bilden.

Probleme der Analyse und Synthese treten sowohl bei der Gestaltung von Strukturen als auch von Prozessen auf (vgl. Abb. 4). In der klassischen Organisationslehre werden traditionell zwei Gestaltungsbereiche unterschieden, die sich

gegenseitig bedingen und gemeinsam zu einer effektiven Organisationsstruktur beitragen sollen (Scherm/Pietsch, 2007; Thommen/Achleitner, 2006):

- Im Rahmen der *Aufbauorganisation* (Gebildestrukturierung) wird die Strukturierung der Gesamtorganisation in einzelne organisatorische Einheiten
vorgenommen. Sie spiegelt sich als stabiles Stellengefüge im Organigramm wider. Die Aufbauorganisation liefert den Rahmen innerhalb dessen die
erforderlichen Arbeitsprozesse zu vollziehen sind, indem sie die Verteilung von
Aufgaben und Kompetenzen auf Aufgabenträger regelt. Traditionell geht sie
der Ablauforganisation voraus.

- Die *Ablauforganisation* regelt demgegenüber die Prozesse der Aufgabenerfüllung unter Berücksichtigung von Raum, Zeit, Sachmitteln und Personal. Hierbei
sind sowohl materielle Prozesse (Fertigung) als auch informationelle Prozesse
(Büroarbeit) zu berücksichtigen.

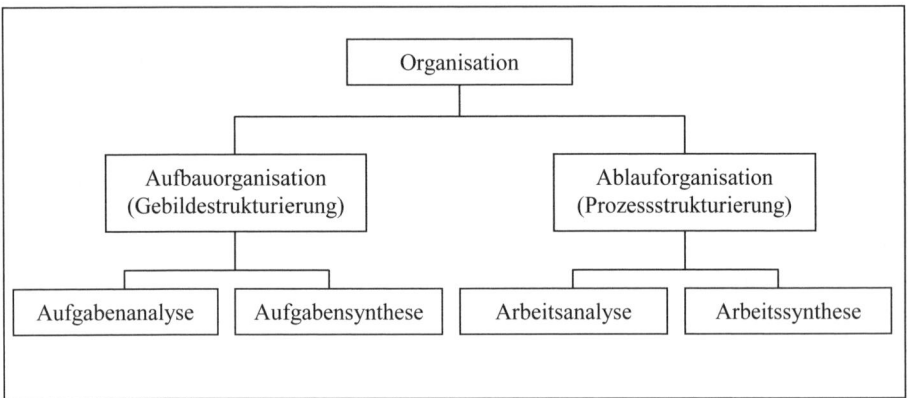

Abb. 4: Der Ansatz der klassischen Organisationslehre
Quelle: Staehle (1999), S. 672

6.4.2 Dimensionen der Organisationsstruktur

Unter Bezugnahme auf die Dimensionen des Konzepts der Organisationsstruktur
nach Kieser/Kubicek (zuerst 1976) sollen im Folgenden die zentralen Aspekte der
Gestaltung von Organisationssystemen im Überblick dargestellt werden (vgl. hierzu
und zum Folgenden Kieser/Walgenbach (2003).

6.4.2.1 Spezialisierung (Arbeitsteilung)

Generelle Regeln zur Arbeitsteilung/Spezialisierung, nach denen Teilaufgaben
mehr oder weniger ausschließlich auf verschiedene Organisationseinheiten verteilt
werden, bilden den ersten Eckpfeiler von Organisationssystemen (vgl. Abschnitt
6.4.1). Da diese Regeln die Aufgaben der Organisationsmitglieder auf Dauer festle-

gen, gehören sie zur formalen Organisationsstruktur (Kieser/Walgenbach, 2003; zu Vor- und Nachteilen der Spezialisierung vgl. ebd.). Unterschiede in der Spezialisierung lassen sich insbesondere in Bezug auf (a) deren Umfang (Anzahl der existierenden spezialisierten organisatorischen Einheiten) sowie (b) deren Art herausstellen (Spezialisierung auf Verrichtung vs. Spezialisierung auf Objekte). Idealtypisch wird dementsprechend eine *funktionale* von einer *divisionalen* Organisationsstruktur unterschieden. Von einer funktionalen Organisationsstruktur spricht man, wenn unterhalb der obersten Leitungsinstanz die Haupteinheiten der Organisation nach dem Verrichtungsprinzip, von einer divisionalen oder Spartenorganisation, wenn sie nach dem Objektprinzip gebildet werden. Im ersten Fall nennt man die Hauptorganisationseinheiten *Funktionsbereiche*, im zweiten Fall *Sparten* (Schierenbeck, 2003; vgl. Abb. 5).

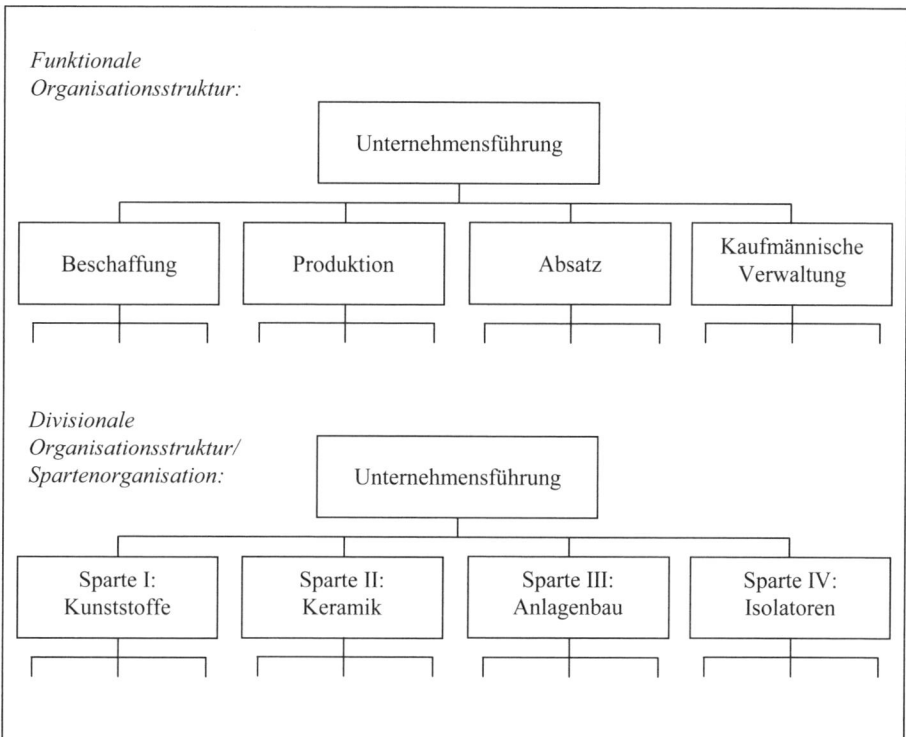

Abb. 5: Funktionale und divisionale Organisationsstruktur
In Anlehnung an: Kieser/Kubicek (1983), S. 94

6.4.2.2 Koordination

Aus der Arbeitsteilung ergibt sich die Notwendigkeit zur Koordination. Es gilt, die arbeitsteiligen Aktivitäten im Hinblick auf das Gesamtziel der Organisation abzustimmen. Hierzu bieten sich unterschiedliche organisatorische Regeln bzw. Koordinationsinstrumente an. Sie bilden den zweiten Eckpfeiler von Organisationssystemen. Der Koordinationsaufwand wird dabei allgemein durch die Ausdifferenzierung sowie Hierarchisierung der Organisationsstruktur reduziert: Erstens verringert das Zusammenfassen einzelner Stellen zu größeren Funktionseinheiten (Abteilungsbildung) die notwendigen Koordinationsbeziehungen. Die Einrichtung spezieller Instanzen, die mit Entscheidungs-, Weisungs- und Kontrollbefugnissen ausgestattet sind (Leitungsstellen), reduziert den Koordinationsaufwand zusätzlich. Die Hierarchie ist damit als eine zentrale Voraussetzung für das Funktionieren komplexer arbeitsteiliger Wirtschaftsprozesse anzusehen (Schierenbeck, 2003). Koordination kann grundsätzlich (a) als *Vorauskoordination* sowie, im Sinne einer Reaktion auf Störungen, als *Feedbackkoordination* erfolgen (Schierenbeck, 2003).

Kieser/Walgenbach (2003) unterscheiden sechs verschiedene Instrumente mit Hilfe derer die Koordination zwischen organisatorischen Einheiten zu bewerkstelligen ist:

- Koordination durch *persönliche Weisungen* (Anordnungen durch Vorgesetzte),
- Koordination durch *Selbstabstimmung* (Koordination durch die Betroffenen selbst),
- Koordination durch *Programme* (explizit formulierte Verfahrensrichtlinien sowie generelle Handlungsvorschriften, z.B. in Handbüchern/Manuals),
- Koordination durch Pläne (Sollvorgaben, Handlungsziele, Budgets),
- Koordination durch *organisationsinterne Märkte* (z.B. Profit-Center, für die ein gesonderter Erfolgsausweis vorgenommen wird, sowie Verrechnungspreise durch monetäre Bewertung von Lieferungen und Leistungen zwischen verschiedenen Bereichen einer Unternehmung) sowie
- Koordination durch *Organisationskultur* (Abstimmung durch übereinstimmende Werte und Normen, die Organisationsmitglieder verinnerlicht haben).

    Tab. 1 zeigt zentrale Vor- und Nachteile ausgewählter, alternativer Koordinationsinstrumente.

6.4.2.3 Konfiguration (Leitungssystem)

Die äußere Form des Stellengefüges, zu dem die Mechanismen der beiden vorgenannten Strukturdimensionen Spezialisierung und Koordination führen, bezeichnen Kieser/Kubicek (1976) als Konfiguration. Die Darstellung des Stellengefüges einer Organisation erfolgt dabei üblicherweise in Form von Schaubildern bzw. Organigrammen. Im Zuge der Auseinandersetzung mit der äußeren Form des Stellengefüges wird den mit Entscheidungs- und Weisungsbefugnissen sowie Aufsichtspflichten und Kontrollrechten ausgestatteten Stellen (Instanzen) besondere

Beachtung geschenkt. Daher wird diese Dimension als *Leitungssystem* bezeichnet. Zentrale Merkmale eines Leitungssystems sind dabei:

- die *Struktur* der Weisungsbeziehungen,
- die *Gliederungstiefe* des Stellengefüges sowie
- die *Gliederungsbreite* der einzelnen organisatorischen Ebenen (Leitungsspanne).

	Vorteile	Nachteile
(a) Koordination durch persönliche Weisungen	▪ ohne große organisatorische Vorkehrung leicht zu handhaben ▪ äußerst flexibel einsetzbar	▪ Überlastung der Instanzen und „Dienstwege" ▪ hohe Qualifikation des Vorgesetzten erforderlich
(b) Koordination durch Selbstabstimmung	▪ Entlastung der hierarchischen Koordination ▪ erhöhte Motivation bei den Mitarbeitern	▪ i.d.R. höherer Zeitbedarf als bei (a) ▪ setzt entsprechend qualifizierte Mitarbeiter voraus
(c) Koordination durch Programme	▪ Informationsaustausch erheblich vermindert ▪ Reduzierung von Unsicherheit für die vom Programm betroffenen Mitarbeiter	▪ nur geeignet für Routinefälle ▪ Bequemlichkeit führt leicht zur Anwendung auf eigentlich nicht programmadäquate Fälle
(d) Koordination durch Pläne	▪ Flexibler einsetzbar als (c) ▪ Vorteile von (c) ohne die Nachteile	▪ hoher Informationsbedarf in quantitativer und qualitativer Hinsicht ▪ erfordert ein ausgebautes, funktionsfähiges Planungssystem

Tab. 1: Vor- und Nachteile ausgewählter, alternativer Koordinationsinstrumente
Quelle: Schierenbeck (1987), S. 93

In Bezug auf die Struktur der Weisungsbeziehungen zwischen (a) Instanzen sowie (b) Instanzen und Ausführungsstellen lassen sich verschiedene Ausprägungen von Leitungssystemen differenzieren (u.a. Schierenbeck, 2003). Idealtypisch werden *Einlinien-* von *Mehrliniensystemen* abgegrenzt. Das Einliniensystem geht auf Henri Fayol (1916) zurück. Der Idealtyp des Einliniensystems beruht auf dem Prinzip der Einheit der Auftragserteilung. Im Rahmen der Ausübung ihrer Leitungsfunktion sind die Vorgesetzten dabei für alles zuständig, was die ihnen unterstellten Stellen betrifft. Ein zentraler Vorteil dieser Konfiguration ist die klare Zuordnung von Zuständigkeiten. Nachteilig wirkt sich die starke Beanspruchung der Instanzen durch die Notwendigkeit der Einhaltung des (hierarchischen) Dienstweges aus. Das Mehrliniensystem geht auf Frederick W. Taylor zurück und wurde in den USA zu einer Zeit entwickelt, in der es einen Mangel an qualifizierten Vorgesetzten gab (Scherm/Pietsch, 2007). Der Idealtyp des Mehrliniensystems beruht demgegenüber auf dem Prinzip der Mehrfachunterstellung. Es besteht ein funktionales Weisungsrecht der Instanzen welches die Verantwortlichkeiten der Vorgesetzten auf einzelne Sachgebiete begrenzt. Dadurch gewährleistet das Mehrliniensystem kürzere Entscheidungswege. Allerdings besteht die Gefahr, dass Funktionsüberschneidungen zu unklaren Verantwortlichkeiten bzw. zu Kompetenzstreitigkeiten führen. In der Praxis werden die Vorteile beider Konfigurationen häufig insofern kombiniert, als zwar auf eindeutige disziplinarische Unterstellungsverhältnisse geachtet wird und auch die Gesamtverantwortung nicht aufgegliedert wird, es aber zu einer zusätzlichen fachlichen oder funktionalen Unterstellung kommt (Scherm/Pietsch, 2007; vgl. Abb. 6).

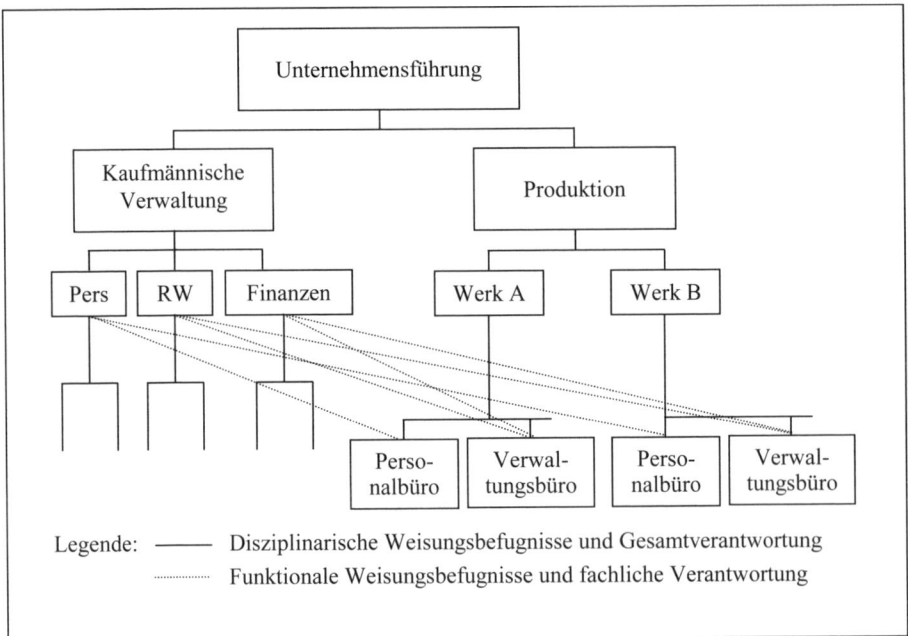

Abb. 6: Disziplinarische und funktionale Weisungsbefugnisse
Quelle: Kieser/Walgenbach (2003), S. 144

Eine weitere Veränderung erfahren Leitungssysteme durch die Einrichtung sog. *Stabsstellen* (Leitungshilfsstellen) in das Organisationssystem. Stäbe haben die Aufgabe, Instanzen bei der Erfüllung ihrer Leitungsfunktion zu unterstützen; sie sind Leistungsassistenzstellen ohne Entscheidungs- und Weisungsbefugnisse gegenüber den Linienstellen (bspw. Justiziariat, strategische Planung, EDV). Bei umfangreicheren Beratungsaufgaben, die die Kapazitäten einzelner Personen überschreitet, kann an die Stelle der Stabsstelle eine Stabsabteilung treten. In Organigrammen werden Stabsstellen von Instanzen meist dadurch unterschieden, dass sie als Kreise dargestellt werden, während Instanzen durch Rechtecke repräsentiert werden.

164

Hohe praktische Relevanz haben ferner solche Stellen, denen (zeitlich begrenzte oder unbegrenzte) Weisungsrechte/Verantwortlichkeiten für konkrete Entscheidungen übertragen werden. Sie unterscheiden sich von den Instanzen insbesondere dahingehend, dass ihre Hauptaufgabe in der Koordination einzelner Aktivitäten im Hinblick auf bestimmte Teilaufgaben bzw. Unterziele der Organisation besteht. Die Personen, die solche Stellen besetzen, nennt man *Projekt-* oder *Produktmanager* (zu unterschiedlichen Arten des Projektmanagements sowie den Besonderheiten von Produktmanagement-Stellen vgl. Kieser/Walgenbach (2003, S. 148ff.).

Im Zuge neuerer organisatorischer Konzepte wurde bewusst der Gedanke des Mehrliniensystems fortentwickelt. Ausgangspunkt ist die eingangs vorgestellte Differenzierung funktionaler und divisionaler Organisation, deren Vorteile man zu kombinieren versucht. Das Matrix-Prinzip führt zu einer zweidimensionalen Struktur, in der die üblichen vertikalen Funktionssäulen von einer horizontalen, produktorientierten Struktur überlagert werden (Schierenbeck, 2003; vgl. Abb. 7).

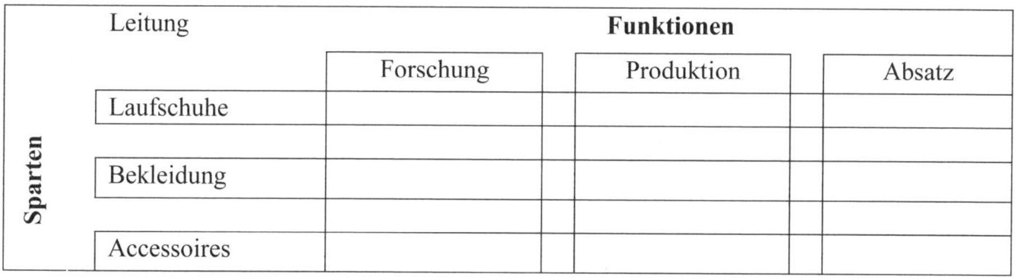

	Leitung	**Funktionen**		
		Forschung	Produktion	Absatz
Sparten	Laufschuhe			
	Bekleidung			
	Accessoires			

Abb. 7: Grundprinzip einer Matrixorganisation

Charakteristisch für die *Matrixorganisation* ist, dass die Stellenbildung auf der gleichen hierarchischen Stufe nach zwei (oder mehr) Kriterien gleichzeitig erfolgt, also z.B. nach Produktgruppen und Funktionen (Thommen/Achleitner, 2006). Die Mitarbeiter der Organisation stehen damit in unterschiedlichen Weisungsbeziehungen, indem sie sowohl den Leitern der funktionsbezogenen Abteilungen, wie auch den objektbezogenen (Produkt-) Managern unterstellt sind. Damit liegt das zentrale organisatorische Problem der Matrixorganisation in der eindeutigen Abgrenzung von Aufgaben und Kompetenzen zwischen den beiden hierarchisch gleichwertigen Leitungsebenen (Thommen/Achleitner, 2006); zu Vor- und Nachteilen der Matrixorganisation vgl. Kieser/Walgenbach, 2003).

Ein wesentliches Merkmal der Konfiguration ist schließlich die *Gliederungstiefe* des Stellengefüges sowie die *Leitungsspanne* auf den einzelnen organisatorischen Ebenen. Die Gliederungstiefe beschreibt die Anzahl der hierarchischen Ebenen. Vorteile flacher Organisationspyramiden mit wenigen hierarchischen Ebenen liegen allgemein in der Reduzierung der (vertikalen) Kommunikationswege begründet. Allerdings ist in diesem Fall (bei gleicher Organisationsgröße) die Leitungsspanne, also die Anzahl der einer Instanz direkt untergeordneten Stellen, größer (zum Zusammenhang zwischen Leitungsspanne und Gliederungstiefe sowie den Vor- und Nachteilen großer Leitungsspannen vgl. Kieser/Walgenbach, 2003).

6.4.2.4 Entscheidungsdelegation (Kompetenzverteilung)

Während im Rahmen der Abteilungsbildung Instanzen geschaffen werden, die mit Entscheidungs- und Weisungsbefugnissen ausgestattet sind, ist mit diesem Schritt der Umfang dieser Befugnisse auf den einzelnen Ebenen noch nicht berücksichtigt: die Entscheidungsdelegation. Kieser/Walgenbach (2003, S. 163) definieren Entscheidungsbefugnisse allgemein als „das Recht, zukünftige Sachverhalte für die Organisation nach innen und/oder außen verbindlich festzulegen". Es geht also um die umfangmäßige Verteilung der Entscheidungsbefugnisse in einer Hierarchie (Schierenbeck, 2003). Im Einzelnen beinhaltet eine solche Delegation (a) die Zuweisung von Aufgaben, (b) die Vorgabe von erwarteten Ergebnissen, (c) die Ausstattung mit den zur Aufgabenerfüllung notwendigen Rechten und (d) die Zuweisung von Verantwortung (Kieser/Kubicek, 1983). In diesem Zusammenhang gelte es, folgende zentrale Prinzipien zu berücksichtigen (Kieser/Kubicek, 1983; Schierenbeck, 2003)

- Das *Kongruenzprinzip*: Aufgaben, Kompetenzen und Verantwortung müssen sich decken.
- Das *Operationalitätsprinzip*: Die Entscheidungsdelegation soll so erfolgen, dass tatsächlich feststellbar ist, ob die erwarteten Ergebnisse eingetreten sind, eine Verantwortung zu tragen ist usw.
- Das *Minimal-Ebenen-Prinzip*: Die Entscheidungsdelegation soll so erfolgen, dass möglichst wenige Managementebenen zur Koordination und zur Lösung auftretender Konflikte benötigt werden.
- Das Prinzip des *„Management by Exception"*: Entscheidungen sollen von der untersten Stelle gefällt werden, die dazu über den notwendigen Überblick verfügt.

6.4.2.5 Formalisierung

Die fünfte Hauptdimension formaler Organisationssysteme lautet Formalisierung und beschreibt das Ausmaß des Einsatzes schriftlich fixierter organisatorischer Regeln, etwa in Form von Schaubildern, Handbüchern, Stellenbeschreibungen usw. Nach Schierenbeck (1987) lässt sich der Aspekt der Formalisierung grundsätzlich in drei Teildimensionen aufgliedern:

- Die *Strukturformalisierung* bezieht sich auf den Umfang, in dem organisatorische Regeln schriftlich fixiert sind.

- Die *Formalisierung des Informationsflusses* bezieht sich auf diejenigen Regelungen, die vorsehen, dass bestimmte Informationsprozesse schriftlich zu erfolgen haben und dadurch aktenmäßigen Charakter erhalten.
- Die Dimension der *Leistungsdokumentation* erfasst den Umfang der Regelungen, die ein schriftliche Erfassung und Beurteilung der Leistung der Mitarbeiter vorsehen.

6.5 Fallstudie

Fallstudie „Infront Sports & Media AG"

infront
SPORTS & MEDIA

Infront ist eine der weltweit führenden Sportmarketing-Agenturen mit Sitz im schweizerischen Zug. Die Gruppe hat sieben weitere Niederlassungen in Europa, Afrika und Asien und beschäftigt insgesamt über 400 Mitarbeiter. Unter anderem arbeitet Infront mit fünf der insgesamt sieben olympischen Wintersportverbände zusammen und ist Partner von über 80 % aller nationalen Skiverbände. Die Agentur verfügt zudem über umfassende Werberechte im Fußball. Sie ist seit vielen Jahren Vermarktungspartner des Deutschen Fußball-Bundes (DFB) und managt die TV-, Sponsoring- und Werberechte von neun Fußballverbänden und zahlreichen Clubs in Europa. Darüber hinaus hatte sie die weltweite Vermarktung der audiovisuellen Verwertungsrechte der Fußball-Weltmeisterschaften 2002 und 2006 inne.

Hauptaktionäre von Infront Sports & Media sind der frühere Adidas-Chef Robert Luis-Dreyfus und die Schweizer Beteiligungsgesellschaft Jacobs Holdings. An der Spitze von Infront steht der Schweizer Philippe Blatter, Ein Neffe von Joseph Blatter, dem Präsidenten des Weltfussball-Verbands FIFA. Er hat im Juli 2006 den langjährigen Agenturchef und -Mitgründer Oscar Frei abgelöst. Der 42-jährige Philippe Blatter war, nach 11 Jahren bei der Beratungsfirma McKinsey, seit Dezember 2005 als Vizedirektor tätig. Im Zuge der Neubesetzung der Position des Präsidenten und CEO wurde der Konzern organisatorisch umgestellt. Die Agenturstruktur ist demnach in die drei Hauptgeschäftsfelder „Summer Sports" (geleitet von Stephan Herth), „Winter Sports" (Bruno Marty) und „Asia" (John Kristick) aufgeteilt. Der Leiter des Bereichs Finanzen und Administration Wolfgang Streit sowie Günther Netzer, der Infront nach Außen repräsentiert, komplettieren das Direktorium. Im Sinne einer Matrixorganisation unterstützt ein erweitertes Managementteam die Konzernleitung in den Bereichen „Production", „Sports Services", „Media & Marketing Sales" und „New Business Develop-

---

ment" quer über alle Unternehmensbereiche. Die Unternehmensstrategie soll durch gezielte Akquisitionen und organisches Wachstum gleichermaßen gekennzeichnet sein, die neue Organisationsstruktur eine zielgerichtete Kundenbetreuung sowie eine deutlichere Zuordnung bestehender Projekte gewährleisten. Inhaltlich möchte Infront ihre Position als Full-Service-Agentur in der Wintersport-Vermarktung festigen. Im Zuge der Reorganisation wurde zudem das Angebot durch die Gründung einer Abteilung für Sport Services auf die Sponsoring-Beratung ausgeweitet. Nach dem Wegfall der nicht-asiatischen Vermarktungsrechte der FIFA – zwar wird die Infront-Tochter Host Broadcast Services 2010 die FIFA-Fussball-WM in Südafrika produzieren und übertragen, für die Vermarktung der Übertragungsrechte allerdings ist Infront nicht mehr zuständig; anders als bisher einigt sich der Fußball-Weltverband in Eigenregie und ohne Zwischenhändler direkt mit den TV-Anstalten – liegt ein zweiter Schwerpunkt in der Stärkung des Fußballgeschäfts. Durch die im Juni 2007 abgeschlossene Übernahme der in Frankfurt ansässigen DSM Sportwerbung – eine der führenden Agenturen für Stadionwerbung, die als ehemaliger Geschäftsbereich Sportwerbung aus der DSM Deutsche Städte-Medien GmbH hervorgegangen ist – konnte Infront ihr Rechteportfolio sowie ihr Serviceangebot im zentralen Geschäftsbereich Fußball ausbauen (Infront Sports & Media AG, 2007; o.V., 2006).

6.6 Besonderheiten der Organisationsstruktur von Sportvereinen

Nachdem im Abschnitt 6.4 die Hauptdimensionen formaler Organisationssysteme nach Kieser & Kubicek vorgestellt wurden (zur situativen Bedingtheit realer Organisationssysteme, zum Forschungsprogramm des situativen Ansatzes sowie zur Operationalisierung der Dimensionen formaler Organisationsstrukturen vgl. Kieser/Kubicek, 1983; Kieser/Walgenbach, 2003; zur Kritik am situativen Ansatz vgl. u.a. Kieser/Walgenbach, 2003) soll im Folgenden der Fokus auf die Charakteristika von Organisationsstrukturen im Sport und ihre Erklärung gerichtet werden. Den zentralen Bezugspunkt bilden dabei die Besonderheiten der Sportwirtschaft. Dabei handelt es sich weder um solche Aspekte, die nur im Sport vorkommen, noch betreffen sie alle Bereiche des Sports. Sie sind aber für bedeutende Bereiche des Sports jeweils typisch.

Charakteristisch für das deutsche Sportsystem ist zunächst, dass Sport zu einem bedeutenden Teil nicht erwerbswirtschaftlich sondern durch Vereine und Verbände, also Non-Profit-Organisationen (NPO) bereitgestellt wird. In Bezug auf die Gütertypen ist für den Sport die Produktion von (personenbezogenen) Dienstleistungen besonders typisch. Schließlich handelt es sich häufig um kleinbetriebliche Organisationsstrukturen. Aus diesen Tatbeständen leiten sich weitreichende Konsequenzen für die Organisationsstruktur von Sportbetrieben ab. So folgt aus der für Kleinbetriebe charakteristischen geringen Ausdifferenzierung von System und Person sowie der hohen Interaktion zwischen den Organisationsmitgliedern (Geser, 1980) allgemein ein geringes Maß an Formalisierung, Spezialisierung und Standardisierung.

Die folgenden Ausführungen nehmen aus zwei Gründen die *Strukturbesonderheiten von Sportvereinen* in den Blick. Erstens, da hier die vorgenannten Besonderheiten der Sportwirtschaft gebündelt anzutreffen sind (NPO, Dienstleistungen, Kleinbetriebe). Zweitens stellen Sportvereine aufgrund ihrer quantitativen Bedeutung die wichtigste organisatorische Basis des Sporttreibens in Deutschland dar. Aus der Fülle der relevanten Strukturmerkmale werden dazu diejenigen Aspekte herausgegriffen, die im Sinne der vorangegangenen Betrachtung von Merkmalen formaler Organisationsstruktur unmittelbar anschlussfähig sind.

Die Schwierigkeiten der Darstellung von „Strukturbesonderheiten des Sportvereins" liegen in den drei Begriffsbestandteilen des Themas begründet: Zunächst gibt es nicht „den" *Sportverein*. Diese Aussage kann angesichts der etwa 90.000 Sportvereine in der Bundesrepublik Deutschland nicht überraschen. Vielmehr existiert eine Vielzahl verschiedenartiger Sportvereine, die sich z.B. in Bezug auf ihre Größe, die Zahl ihrer Sparten, ihre regionale Lage, die angebotenen Sportarten usw. unterscheiden. Für diese unterschiedlichen Vereinstypen können nur schwer allgemeingültige Aussagen getroffen werden. *Besonderheiten* müssen im Vergleich mit anderen Organisationen, die nicht freiwillige Vereinigungen sind, herausgearbeitet werden. Funktional erscheint ferner eine Erweiterung des organisationssoziologischen *Strukturbegriffs*, nach dem Strukturen i.d.R. anhand der Elemente Norm, Position und Rolle bzw. anhand von Strukturdimensionen wie Spezialisierung, Standardisierung, Formalisierung und Zentralisierung analysiert werden (zu den gebräuchlichsten organisationssoziologischen Strukturbegriffen vgl. Horch, 1983). Ein solcher Weg ist für die Beschreibung und Erklärung der Strukturen freiwilliger Vereinigungen nur bedingt geeignet, da er den Blick auf zentrale Besonderheiten verstellt. Geeigneter erscheint ein funktionalistischer, systemtheoretischer Strukturbegriff, der unter Strukturen einen Komplex von Handlungsmustern versteht, „die im Handeln nicht expliziert, sondern vorausgesetzt werden", die den Rahmen möglicher Handlungen abstecken, „die gegenseitige Orientierung ermöglichen und den Sinn von Aktionen bestimmen" (Türk, 1978, S. 92).

Unter einem Verein soll eine Organisation verstanden werden, die durch folgende Merkmale gekennzeichnet ist: „Freiwillige Mitgliedschaft", „Orientierung and den Interessen der Mitglieder", „Unabhängigkeit von Dritten", „ehrenamtliche Mitarbeit" sowie „demokratische Entscheidungsstruktur" (zu den konstitutiven Merkmalen freiwilliger Vereinigungen vgl. Horch, 1983). Diese konstitutiven Merkmale kennzeichnen den Sportverein als freiwillige Vereinigung.

Die Struktur des jeweiligen Sportvereins – etwa als der Grad der Differenzierung und Aufgabengliederung, der Grad der Formalisierung und Regelhaftigkeit, der Grad der Professionalisierung, also der Umfang, in dem die Ausübung des

Sports zu einem Beruf für den Sportler und die Führung und Verwaltung des Vereins zu einem Beruf für den Sportfunktionär geworden sind, die spezifische Ideologie und Weltanschauung, die Loyalitäts- und Solidaritätsverpflichtungen, der Grad der Identifikation mit den Werten und Zielen der Organisation – hängt nicht allein von diesen konstitutiven Variablen ab, sie wird vielmehr durch weitere, vereinsspezifische Tatbestände geprägt. Dazu gehören zum einen der Typus des Vereins, der bestimmt wird durch die Mitgliederzahl, Art und Zahl der Sportarten, Zusammensetzung der Mitglieder, regionale Lage und Umfang der wettkampfmäßigen und leistungssportorientierten bzw. freizeit- und breitensportorientierten Sportausübung und zum anderen Umwelteinflüsse, die das Geschehen in dem jeweiligen Verein prägen. Dazu zählen der Umfang des öffentlichen Interesses an sportlichen Wettkämpfen, die finanzielle Unterstützung und die sonstigen (z.B. politischen und ideologischen) „Erhaltungsstrategien" durch den Staat oder durch kommerzielle Interessen, z.B. also das Bemühen von Wirtschaftsunternehmen, im Verein als Werbeträger und als Verkäufer für Sportartikel wirksam werden zu können. Erst das Zusammenwirken dieser einzelnen Variablen prägt den Sportverein in seinem konkreten Erscheinungsbild und in seiner Arbeits- und Funktionsweise.

Mit den konstitutiven Variablen freiwilliger Vereinigungen hängen weitere Besonderheiten der Organisationsstruktur zusammen, die diese idealtypisch von den bürokratischen Strukturen von Großbetrieben unterscheiden. Als Schlüssel zur Erklärung dieser Besonderheiten kann das *Problem der Einbindung der ehrenamtlichen Mitarbeiter* angesehen werden. Die Lösung dieses Problems verlangt besondere strukturelle Voraussetzungen. Der zu Grunde gelegte Strukturbegriff lenkt den Blick auf typische Muster der Steuerung und Koordination, die funktionale Äquivalente zu Norm, Position und Rolle sind. Die zentralen strukturellen Besonderheiten lauten:

- Interaktionsverfestigung vs. Formalisierung,
- Personalisierung vs. Spezialisierung,
- Ambivalenz vs. Standardisierung ,
- Informelle vs. formelle Kontrolle,
- Selbstabstimmung und Führung vs. Zentralisierung sowie
- Einflussnahme über persönliche Beziehungen.

6.6.1 Interaktionsverfestigung

Das Verhalten in einem Verein wird in wesentlich geringerem Ausmaß als im Betrieb und in der Verwaltung durch festgelegte, bewusst auf das Ziel ausgerichtete und rational geplante Regeln gesteuert. Ein Grund hierfür liegt in der Tatsache, dass die formalisierten Mitgliedschaftsanforderungen sehr gering sind – oft beschränken sie sich auf die Verpflichtung, die Mitgliederbeiträge zu bezahlen –, so dass Mitarbeit und Zusammenarbeit stärker durch informelle soziale Prozesse gesteuert werden. Die Zusammenarbeit im Verein ist zwar auf ein Ziel ausgerichtet, trägt aber zugleich deutlich expressive Züge. Je stärker die Übereinstimmung mit den Zielen, Werten und der Tradition des Vereins, je angenehmer die Atmosphäre bei der Vereinsarbeit, je größer die Motivation der Mitarbeiter ist, desto größer ist die Bereitschaft für eine interaktionelle Abstimmung der Handlungen, desto weniger braucht explizit geregelt zu werden. Soziale Tauschprozesse, gemeinsame Ziele, Wertorientierungen und eine Identifikation mit dem Verein dienen gleichzeitig der Einbindung wie der Verhaltenssteuerung. Regelungen ergeben sich erst aus dem offenen Zusammenspiel der Beteiligten; es stabilisieren sich die Bilder, die die Einzelnen sich von sich und den anderen machen ebenso wie die Handlungen, die sich bewährt haben. Im Laufe der Zeit verfestigen sich Handlungsmuster, so dass der Verein sein eigenes Profil unabhängig von den einzelnen Mitgliedern entwickelt: Wie was gemacht, wie was gesehen wird, über was mit welchen Begriffen gesprochen wird, verfestigt sich erst im Laufe der jeweiligen Geschichte des Vereins in je individuellen Ausprägungen. Dies gilt auch für die jeweils realisierte Ressourcenstruktur, so dass es schwer fallen wird, typische Gestaltungsformen zu identifizieren.

6.6.2. Personalisierung

Ähnlich sind auch Positionen in einem Verein wenig differenziert und ihre Aufgaben wenig standardisiert. Anstelle der Standardisierung und Spezialisierung tritt in relativ hohem Ausmaß eine Personalisierung der Verhaltenserwartung. Soziale Systeme und Personen sind vergleichsweise wenig wechselseitig ausdifferenziert. Die Mitglieder orientieren sich zu einem großen Teil an bekannten Eigenschaften der Personen und erst in zweiter Linie an abstrakten Regeln und spezifizierten Rollenerwartungen. Dadurch werden Ämter und damit die Ehrenamtlichkeit wesentlich von der Persönlichkeit des Inhabers, von seinen Fähigkeiten und Fertigkeiten, von seinem Engagement, von seinem Verständnis für die Belange des Vereins und seiner Mitglieder geprägt. In dieser Ambivalenz der Aufgabenzuweisung und der Verantwortlichkeit liegt ein Grund für die besondere Leistungsfähigkeit der Vereine (Luhmann, 1976; Geser, 1980): Die Mitarbeiter sind nicht sicher, wie weit ihre Pflichten gehen, und dank ihrer sachunspezifischen Teilnahmemotivation werden sie aufnahmebereit für verschiedenartige, unvorhersehbare Aufgaben.

6.6.3. Informelle Kontrolle

Auch explizit formalisierte Sanktionen unterhalb des Ausschlusses und der Androhung des Ausschlusses existieren i.d.R. nicht. Sie erübrigen sich auch, wenn die Mitglieder durch innere Anreize belohnt und Mitgliedschaft und Mitarbeit freiwillig sind. So haben Sanktionen meist nur informellen Charakter – etwa in Form eines Tadels, der Ironisierung, des Scherzes, durch demonstratives Schweigen, abrupten Themenwechsel, Unaufmerksamkeit. Je diffuser dabei die Beziehungen sind, desto mehr werden die Sanktionen gleichsam moralisierend auf die Gesamtpersönlichkeit zielen.

6.6.4. Selbstbestimmung und Führung

Da eine freiwillige Vereinigung i.d.R. aus Gründen der Motivation der Mitglieder weniger arbeitsteilig organisiert sein kann als z.b. ein Betrieb, besteht nur ein relativ geringer Koordinationsbedarf. Dort, wo Koordination nötig ist, kann sie nicht durch Weisung, Programmierung oder Planung erfolgen, da in Vereinen wenig Neigung besteht, Befehlen zu folgen. Außerdem fehlt jenes Maß an Formalisierung, das Planung und Programmierung erfordert. So treffen wir eher Selbstabstimmung in informellen Zusammenkünften an, im Rahmen allgemeiner Treffen oder speziell gebildeter Komitees, und wir finden als typische Koordinationsform eine Führung, die auf persönlicher Ausstrahlung und Überzeugungskraft einzelner basiert.

6.6.5. Einflussnahme über persönliche Beziehungen

Besonderheiten bestehen ferner in den Möglichkeiten der Anpassung an die äußere Umwelt. Betriebe und Verwaltungen entwickeln meist eigene Rollen oder Subsysteme, die mit effektiver Vertretungsgewalt ausgestattet sind, um auf Anforderungen der Umwelt zu reagieren und eigenen Einfluss – etwa mit ökonomischen Mitteln bzw. (bei Verwaltungen) rechtlichen Verpflichtungen – geltend machen zu können. Dieser Weg ist Vereinen i.d.R. verschlossen; Möglichkeiten rechtlicher Verpflichtungen stehen ihnen nicht zur Verfügung, die ökonomischen Mittel sind meist begrenzt. Umweltkontakte müssen stattdessen über konkrete Personen mit besonderen Beziehungen laufen. Durch die Verschiedenartigkeit der Mitglieder und über Mitgliedschaft und Mitarbeit in verschiedenen Vereinigungen kann der Verein im Einzelfall über ein Geflecht von Beziehungen verfügen, das den direkten Zugang zu vielen relevanten Institutionen und Personen ermöglicht (Stichwort: „Beziehungsressource"). Außenkontakte sind daher auch oft ein wichtiges Auswahlkriterium bei der Besetzung von Positionen (z.B. in einem Vorstand).

6.7 Fazit und Ausblick

Mit den konstitutiven Variablen freiwilliger Vereinigungen hängen Besonderheiten der Organisationsstruktur zusammen, die diese idealtypisch von den bürokratischen Strukturen von Großbetrieben unterscheiden. Als Schlüssel zur Erklärung dieser Besonderheiten kann das Problem der Einbindung der ehrenamtlichen Mitarbeiter angesehen werden. Die Lösung dieses Problems verlangt besondere strukturelle Voraussetzungen. Eine idealtypische Gegenüberstellung, wie sie im Rahmen des vorliegenden Beitrags vorgenommen wurde, ist dabei besonders gut geeignet, Besonderheiten der Organisationsstruktur von Sportvereinen herauszuarbeiten.

Andererseits gilt es jedoch zu berücksichtigen, dass es sich bei den konstitutiven Merkmalen um Attribute handelt, die in der Realität selten in reiner Form vorzufinden sind; es handelt sich vielmehr um (idealtypische) Endpunkte auf Kontinuen. So kann z.B. die Mitgliedschaft in einem Verein durch Gruppenzwang oder ökonomischen Druck bewirkt werden; sie ist oft auch Voraussetzung für soziales Ansehen und berufliches Fortkommen. Ebenso kann die Freiwilligkeit dadurch eingeschränkt sein, dass die Sportorganisation eine Monopolstellung innehat, und die Ausübung, z.B. des (Leistungs-)Sports, nur in dieser Organisation möglich ist. Finanzielle Unterstützungen durch den Staat können mit Auflagen verbunden sein. Ehrenamtlichkeit kann durch die Zunahme hauptamtlicher Funktionsträger eingeschränkt werden. Demokratische Entscheidungsmöglichkeiten können durch Mitgliederpassivität unausgeschöpft bleiben. So finden wir kontinuierliche Übergänge etwa zwischen Freiwilligkeit und Zwangsmitgliedschaft, Unabhängigkeit vom Staat und weitgehender staatlicher Einbindung, von ehrenamtlicher und hauptamtlicher Leistungserfüllung, von demokratischer und oligarchischer Herrschaftsausübung.

Vor dem Hintergrund dieser Aspekte sowie von Transformationstendenzen lässt sich die Struktur freiwilliger Vereinigungen als intermediär kennzeichnen; als nicht immer widerspruchsfreie Vermischung von Elementen aus bürokratischen Organisationen – z.B. mit den Merkmalen: ökonomische Anreize für die Mitgliedschaft, bezahlte Mitarbeit, Zugang zu den Ressourcen von Nicht-Mitgliedern, Dienstleistungsorientierung, hierarchische Strukturen – und von Kleingruppen – etwa mit den Merkmalen: hohes Mitgliederengagement, unbezahlte Arbeit, Abhängigkeit von Mitgliederressourcen und hohe Gruppenidentifikation.

Nach Wolfgang Streek (1981), Direktor des Max-Planck-Instituts für Gesellschaftsforschung in Köln (MPIfG) lassen sich die Systemprobleme freiwilliger Organisationen sämtlich auf das Problem der Integration von untereinander unverträglichen Strukturformen in ein und dieselbe soziale Einheit (z.B. Ehren- und Hauptamt, d.V.) bzw. die Erfüllung widersprüchlicher Funktionen vermittels ein und derselben Struktur zurückführen. Der amerikanische Soziologe Robert K. Merton (1976) hat deshalb die Führung freiwilliger Vereinigungen mit einem ständigen Drahtseilakt verglichen.

Kontrollfragen
1. Nennen Sie zentrale Aspekte der institutionellen Perspektive der Organisation!
2. Welche zwei Sichtweisen werden im Rahmen des instrumentellen Organisationsverständnisses voneinander abgegrenzt?
3. Was versteht man unter einer Organisation als Ressourcenpool?
4. Nennen Sie die drei zentralen Entwicklungslinien der Organisationstheorie!
5. Inwiefern lassen sich Differenzierung und Integration als Grundfunktionen der Organisation kennzeichnen?

6. Mit Hilfe welcher Instrumente lässt sich die Koordination zwischen verschiedenen organisatorischen Einheiten bewerkstelligen?
7. Was unterscheidet Einlinien- von Mehrliniensystemen?
8. Erläutern Sie das Grundprinzip einer Matrixorganisation!
9. Nennen Sie die konstitutiven Merkmale von Sportvereinen!
10. Welches sind die zentralen strukturellen Besonderheiten von Sportvereinen?

Literaturverzeichnis

Argyris, Chris (1975): Das Individuum und die Organisation, in: Türk, Klaus (Hrsg.): Organisationstheorie, Hamburg, S. 215-233.

Barnard, Chester Irwing (1938): The Functions of the Executive, Cambridge.

Blau, Peter Michael (1972): Theories of Organizations, in: International Encyclopedia of the Social Sciences, New York u.a., S. 297.

Burrell, Gibson / Morgan, Gareth. (1979): Socological paradigms and organizational analysis, London.

Coleman, James Samuel (1979): Macht und Gesellschaftsstruktur, Tübingen.

Fayol, Henry (1916): Administration industrielle et générale, Paris.

Geser, Hans (1980): Kleine Sozialsysteme, in: Kölner Zeitschrift für Soziologie und Sozialpsychologie, Heft 32, S. 205-239.

Grochla, Erwin (1975): Entwicklung und gegenwärtiger Stand der Organisationstheorie, in: Grochla, Erwin (Hrsg.): Organisationstheorie, Bd. 1, Stuttgart, S. 2-32.

Gutenberg, Erich (1983): Grundlagen der Betriebswirtschaftslehre. Band 1: Die Produktion, Berlin.

Heinemann, Klaus / Horch, Heinz-Dieter (1988): Strukturbesonderheiten des Sportvereins, in: Digel, Helmut (Hrsg.): Sport im Verein und Verband. Historische, politische und soziologische Aspekte, Schorndorf, S. 108-122.

Horch, Heinz-Dieter (1983): Strukturbesonderheiten freiwilliger Vereinigungen: Analyse und Untersuchung einer alternativen Form menschlichen Zusammenarbeitens. Frankfurt/Main u.a.

Infront Sports & Media AG (2007) Unternehmensinformation, http://www.infront-sports.com (Zugriff: 30.12.2007).

Kieser, Alfred / Kubicek, Herbert (1976): Organisation, Berlin.

Kieser, Alfred / Kubicek, Herbert (1983): Organisation, 2. Aufl., Berlin.

Kieser, Alfred / Walgenbach, Peter (2003): Organisation, Stuttgart.

Kirsch, Werner / Esser, Werner-Michael / Gabele Eduard (1979): Das Management des geplanten Wandels von Organisationen, Stuttgart.

Kosiol, Erich (1976): Organisation der Unternehmung, Wiesbaden.

Lawrence, Paul R. / Lorsch, Jay W. (1967): Differentiation and Integration in Complex Organizations, in: Administrative Science Quarterly, Heft 12, S. 1-47.

Luhmann, Niklas (1976): Funktionen und Folgen formaler Organisation, Berlin.

Mayo, Elton (1949): Probleme industrieller Arbeitsbedingungen, Frankfurt/Main.

Mayntz, Renate (1963): Soziologie der Organisation, Reinbek b. Hamburg.

Merton, Robert King (1976): Dilemmas of Voluntary Associations, in: Merton, Robert King (Hrsg.): Sociological Ambivalence and other Essays, New York, S. 105.

Morgan, Gareth (1997): Images of organization, 2. Aufl., Thousand Oaks.

O.V. (2006): Infront stellt sich neu auf, in: Sponsors, Heft 11, S. 24-26.

Picot, Arnold / Dietl, Helmut / Franck, Egon. (1999): Organisation. Eine ökonomische Perspektive, Stuttgart.

Roethlisberger, Fritz Jules / Dickson, William J. (1939): Management and the Worker, Cambridge.

Scherm, Ewald / Pietsch, Gotthard (2007): Organisation. Theorie, Gestaltung, Wandel, München.

Schewe, Gerhard (2005): Unternehmensverfassung. Corporate Governancen im Spannungsfeld von Leitung, Kontrolle und Interessenvertretung, München.

Schierenbeck, Henner (1987): Grundzüge der Betriebswirtschaftslehre, 9. Aufl., München.

Schierenbeck, Henner (2003): Grundzüge der Betriebswirtschaftslehre, 16. Aufl., München.

Schreyögg, Georg (1999): Organisation, Wiesbaden.

Scott, William G. (1961): Organization Theory: An Overview and an Appraisal, in: Academy of Management Journal, Heft 1, S. 7-26.

Scott, William G. (1974): Organization Theory: A Reassessment, in: Academy of Management Journal, Heft 2, S. 242-254.

Staehle, Wolfgang H. (1999): Management, 8. Aufl., München.

Streeck, Wolfgang (1981): Gewerkschaftliche Organisationsprobleme, Königstein.

Taylor, Frederick Winslow (1911): The principles of scientific management, New York.

Thommen, Jean-Paul / Achleitner, Ann-Kristin (2006): Allgemeine Betriebswirtschaftslehre – Umfassende Einführung aus managementorientierter Sicht, Wiesbaden.

Türk, Klaus (1978): Soziologie der Organisation. Eine Einführung, Stuttgart.

Weber, Max (1976): Wirtschaft und Gesellschaft, Tübingen.

Wöhe, Günter (1986): Einführung in die Allgemeine Betriebswirtschaftslehre, 16. Aufl., München.

Weiterführende Ressourcen

Links

Deutscher Olympischer Sportbund:
   http://www.dosb.de

Gesellschaft für Organisation e.V.:
   http://www.gfuero.org

Infront Sports & Media AG:
   http://www.infrontsports.com

Kapitel 7: Personalmanagement im Sport

Siegfried Nagel   Torsten Schlesinger

Lernziele

Nach der Durchsicht dieses Kapitels sollte der Leser in der Lage sein,

- den Begriff „Personalmanagement" zu bestimmen.
- die zentralen Aufgaben des Personalmanagements zu benennen.
- die wichtigsten Gestaltungsinstrumente des Personalmanagements zu kennen.
- die Besonderheiten des Personalmanagements im Sport herauszustellen.
- die Möglichkeiten des Personalmanagements in verschiedenen Organisationstypen des Sports zu unterscheiden.
- die ehrenamtliche Mitarbeit und ihre Spezifika in Non-Profit-Organisationen des Sports einzuschätzen.
- das Problem hauptamtlicher und ehrenamtlicher Mitarbeit in Non-Profit-Organisationen des Sports zu beurteilen.
- Aspekte des Personalmanagements in Spitzensportteams zu kennen.

Überblick über das Kapitel

Zielstellung dieses Kapitels ist es, die zentralen Probleme und Handlungsfelder des personalbezogenen Managements in Sportorganisationen unterschiedlichen Typs zu skizzieren. Einführend soll zunächst verdeutlicht werden, weshalb der Faktor Personal innerhalb des Sportmanagements zunehmend in das Blickfeld gerät. In einem zweiten Schritt sind die wichtigsten Strategien und Techniken des Personalmanagements herauszuarbeiten, wie sie in der „Allgemeinen Betriebswirtschaftslehre" diskutiert werden und demnach auch auf den kommerziellen Bereich des Sports übertragbar sind. Im Anschluss erfolgt eine Analyse der Besonderheiten des Personalmanagements in Non-Profit-Organisationen des Sports. Gesondert behandelt wird zudem der Problembereich Profisport, insbesondere der Mannschaftssport, denn dieser unterliegt besonderen Bedingungen, die sich wesentlich von anderen Mitarbeitsverhältnissen in Sportorganisationen unterscheiden. Eine Fallstudie, die die Einstellung eines hauptamtlichen Geschäftsführers beim TV Rottenburg beschreibt, schließt das Kapitel ab.

7.1 Einführung in die Thematik

Das Thema Personal gewinnt im Bereich des Sportmanagements zunehmend an Bedeutung. Die Ursachen dürften v.a. darin zu sehen sein, dass es sich bei den Angeboten bzw. Produkten des Sports i.d.R. nicht um Sachgüter handelt, sondern um personenbezogene Dienstleistungen. Die Qualität solcher Dienstleistungen, ob es sich um einen Gesundheitskurs im Fitnessstudio oder um ein Bundesligaspiel handelt, hängt dabei in hohem Maße mit den verantwortlichen Mitarbeitern wie Kursleitern, Therapeuten, Trainern, Spielern usw. zusammen. Darüber hinaus sind Dienstleistungen entscheidend von der Mitwirkung des Kunden abhangig (Integrativität). D.h., der Sporttreibende oder der Zuschauer ist selbst aktiv und emotional in den Prozess der Leistungserstellung eingebunden, wobei der verantwortliche Mitarbeiter eine zentrale Rolle im Prozess der Erstellung der sportbezogenen Dienstleistung spielt. Die Vernachlässigung des Personalmanagements würde deshalb bedeuten, den Prozess der Leistungserstellung zu gefährden.

Die zunehmende Bedeutung des Personalmanagements im Bereich des Sports hat jedoch noch eine andere wichtige Ursache. Denn die Besonderheiten von Sportorganisationen erfordern spezifische Managementkonzepte im Umgang mit Personal, die in den Standardwerken und Handbüchern der betrieblichen Personalwirtschaft nicht hinreichend erfasst werden. So ist die dominierende Organisationsform im Bereich des Sports der eingetragene Verein. Dabei kommen Spezifika sowohl in der Organisations- als auch in der Personalstruktur zum Tragen, die in gewinnorientierten Unternehmen keine Rolle spielen. Denn für Non-Profit-Organisationen des Sports ist charakteristisch, dass vorrangig ehrenamtliche Mitarbeiter tätig sind, die ihre Arbeitskraft unentgeltlich oder gegen eine geringere als die marktübliche Vergütung zur Verfügung stellen. Dies führt dazu, dass die Zuteilung bestimmter Aufgaben häufig nicht mit den aufgabenbezogenen Anforderungen übereinstimmen. Gleichzeitig ergeben sich besondere Herausforderungen hinsichtlich der Mitarbeiterrekrutierung, der Personalführung sowie der Beeinflussungsmöglichkeiten des Arbeitsverhaltens. Darüber hinaus müssen sich Vereine als Folge von Professionalisierungsprozessen auf die Kombination von entgeltlichen Beschäftigten und ehrenamtlich Tätigen einstellen. Zielstellung des entsprechenden Abschnitts soll es sein, auf die Besonderheiten des Personalmanagements in Non-Profit-Organisationen des Sports einzugehen und tragfähige Maßnahmen aufzuzeigen.

7.2 Grundlagen des Personalmanagements

Im Sinne einer möglichst umfassenden Analyse des Personalmanagements im Sport, wie sie in diesem Kapitel angestrebt wird, soll zunächst der Blick auf allgemeine betriebswirtschaftliche Erkenntnisse zum Personalmanagement in Organisationen des For-Profit Sektors gerichtet werden. Denn diese gelten auch für solche Sportorganisationen, die sich durch gewinnorientierte Strukturen (z.B. Sportmarketing-Agenturen, produzierende Unternehmen im Sportbereich, kommerzielle Fitnessanbieter) charakterisieren lassen. Dabei soll an den entsprechenden Stellen auf die Besonderheiten des Personalmanagements im Bereich sportbezogener Dienstleistungen eingegangen werden.

7.2.1 Ausgangslage: Von der Personalverwaltung zum Personalmanagement

Zunächst ist die Frage zu klären, was denn überhaupt unter Personalmanagement zu verstehen ist? Personalmanagement (auch als Human Resource Management bezeichnet) beschäftigt sich mit der Steuerung personaler Prozesse unter besonderer Berücksichtigung der wirtschaftlichen, technischen und organisatorischen Gegebenheiten innerhalb und außerhalb des Unternehmens (Oechsler, 2006). Unter Personalmanagement ist demnach der gesamte Aufgabenbereich zu verstehen, der sich mit der Ressource Personal in einem Unternehmen befasst.

Die Durchsicht der jüngeren Literatur über Personalwesen, Personalführung und Arbeitsbeziehungen in Unternehmen (z.B. Staehle, 1999; Scholz, 2000; Drumm, 2005; Jung, 2006; Oechsler, 2006) lässt dabei einen grundlegenden Perspektivwechsel erkennen: Während der Funktionsbereich Personal lange Zeit als ein betriebliches Aufgabengebiet neben anderen Funktionsbereichen (z.B. Beschaffung, Produktion, Absatz) behandelt wurde, hat in jüngerer Zeit ein Umdenken hin zu einer aktiven und integrierten Sichtweise des Faktors Personal innerhalb des gesamten betriebswirtschaftlichen Gestaltungsprozesses stattgefunden. Nicht zuletzt aufgrund der zunehmenden Knappheit hochqualifizierter Fachleute und der zentralen Bedeutung eines hochmotivierten Mitarbeiterstammes für den dauerhaften Unternehmenserfolg wird heutzutage das Personal als wertvolle Ressource angesehen, die es gezielt aufzubauen, pfleglich zu erhalten und anforderungsgerecht weiterzubilden gilt (Staehle, 1999). Der auf der Unternehmung lastende Problemdruck hinsichtlich der Ressource Personal hat somit zu einem Paradigmenwechsel von der Personalverwaltung hin zum Personalmanagement geführt. Personal wird längst nicht mehr als reiner Kostenfaktor angesehen und ein erfolgreiches Personalmanagement an der Unauffälligkeit des Personalabbaus beurteilt, sondern als ein zentraler Vermögensbestandteil (Humankapital) des Unternehmens verstanden, in den gezielt investiert werden sollte (Scholz, 2000). Damit verknüpft ist ein Wandel des konzeptionellen und methodischen Instrumentariums, dass im Bereich des personenbezogenen Managements eingesetzt wird. Denn Personalarbeit lässt sich nicht mehr nur auf die Anwendung von Personaltechniken, wie Personalplanung, -einsatz, -entwicklung, oder -entlassung reduzieren, deren Einsatz an Stabstellen wie eine Personalabteilung zu delegieren ist. Vielmehr gehört sie zu den zentralen Managementaufgaben und muss demzufolge strategisch in die Unternehmung eingebunden werden. Dies gilt insbesondere für Anbieter sportbezogener Dienstleistungen: Gutes Personal ist aufgrund hoher Integrativität der entscheidende Faktor für qualitativ hochwertige Angebote. Wegen der Immaterialität besteht zudem ein hohes Maß an Verhaltensunsicherheit, so dass bewährtes Personal bzw. der persönliche Kontakt zu den Kunden die Grundlage für eine vertrauensvolle und dauerhafte Geschäftsbeziehung darstellt.

7.2.2. Personalmanagement im Kontext der Unternehmensstrategie

Die Strategie eines Unternehmens ist als unternehmenspolitische Handlungsorientierung zu verstehen, die vorgibt, welche systematischen Entwicklungen und Veränderungen der Organisation sinnvoll sind und angesteuert werden sollten. Die Unternehmensstrategie umfasst dabei zwei wesentliche Aspekte: Sie wird abgeleitet aus den langfristigen Zielen des Unternehmens, und sie legt Maßnahmen und Wege fest, die erforderlich sind, um diese Ziele zu erreichen. Dabei stellt sich die Frage, wie das Personalmanagement in die Unternehmensstrategie eingebunden werden kann. Hierfür stehen prinzipiell vier Möglichkeiten zur Verfügung (Scholz, 2000):

1. Personalstrategie und Unternehmensstrategie sind voneinander unabhängig, d.h. inhaltlich besteht kein Zusammenhang zwischen diesen.

2. Die Personalstrategie folgt der Unternehmensstrategie, d.h. sie besitzt einen derivativen Charakter.

3. Die Unternehmensstrategie folgt der Personalstrategie, d.h. es erfolgt zu großen Teilen eine Ausrichtung der Unternehmensstrategie an den vorhandenen personellen Gegebenheiten, welche implizit die Personalstrategie widerspiegelt.

4. Die Personalstrategie stellt einen Teil der Unternehmensstrategie dar, d.h. die Unternehmensstrategie ergibt sich aus mehreren funktionalen Teilstrategien, aber auch einer Personalstrategie. Ziel ist die Vereinigung zu einem integrativen Gesamtsystem von verschiedenen Strategiekomponenten, wobei diese in gegenseitiger Abhängigkeit formuliert, implementiert und kontrolliert werden müssen.

V.a. die vierte Möglichkeit lässt es zu, Personal- und Unternehmensstrategie simultan und integrativ zu entwickeln, so dass strategische Veränderungen im Personalbereich schnell und flexibel eingeleitet werden können. Dies scheint insbesondere für die Bereiche des Sports von zentraler Bedeutung zu sein, die personenbezogene Dienstleitungen anbieten. Denn aus dieser Perspektive bekommt die Personalstrategie der Unternehmung einen Doppelcharakter: Einerseits zeigt sie die für die Unternehmensstrategie und deren Teilstrategien bestehenden Beschränkungen aus personalwirtschaftlicher Sicht und andererseits verdeutlicht sie die vorhandenen Chancen und Potentiale (Scholz, 2000).

Merkmale	Handlungshorizont		
	strategisch	taktisch	operativ
Entscheidungsobjekt	Gesamtunternehmen	Mitarbeitergruppen Unternehmensbereiche	Einzelne Mitarbeiter Mitarbeitergruppen
Organisatorische Einbindung	Obere Hierarchieebene	Mittlere Hierarchieebene	Untere Hierarchieebene
Freiheitsgrad	Hoch	Mittel	Niedrig
Zeithorizont	Langfristig	Mittelfristig	Kurzfristig

Tab. 1: Kennzeichnung der einzelnen Ebenen des Personalmanagements
In Anlehnung an: Oechsler (2006), S. 120

Sofern das Personalmanagement integrativer Bestandteil des allgemeinen Managementprozesses ist, kann eine Unterscheidung in die drei üblichen Handlungsebenen strategisch, taktisch und operativ vorgenommen werden. Allerdings sind diese mit spezifisch personalwirtschaftlichen Inhalten zu füllen (vgl. Tab. 1). Eine Unterscheidung dieser drei Handlungshorizonte bietet sich unter anderen gemäß des Entscheidungsobjektes, der Hierarchieebenen, des Freiheitsgrads und des Zeithorizonts an (Oechsler, 2006).

7.2.3 Handlungsfelder des Personalmanagements

Unter Handlungsfeldern sind die Aktivitätsbereiche zu verstehen, auf denen das Personalmanagement tätig wird und auf die es Einfluss nimmt, um das Humanpotential einer Unternehmung möglichst effizient zu gestalten. Die Auffassungen darüber, was alles diesen Handlungsfeldern zuzuordnen ist, gehen allerdings in der Literatur weit auseinander (z.B. Staehle, 1999; Scholz, 2000). Trotz unterschiedlicher Perspektiven besitzen die vorgeschlagenen Handlungsfelder grundlegende Gemeinsamkeiten: Sie betreffen einerseits die *personelle Leistungsbereitstellung* (Personalplanung) und andererseits den *personellen Leistungserhalt bzw. -förderung* innerhalb einer Unternehmung.

7.2.3.1 Personalplanung

Die Personalplanung einer Unternehmung soll in die nahe, mittlere und ferne Zukunft vorausschauend alle Maßnahmen berücksichtigen, die erforderlich sind, damit dem Unternehmen zur Erreichung seiner Ziele die dazu erforderlichen Mitarbeiter zur Verfügung stehen. Die Besonderheiten von Dienstleistungen führen dabei zu Konsequenzen hinsichtlich der Bedarfsermittlung, Beschaffung, Entwicklung sowie des Personaleinsatzes.

(1) Personalbedarf:

Den Ausgangspunkt für das personale Planungsmanagement stellt die Bedarfsanalyse dar. Die Personalbedarfsplanung legt fest, wie viele Mitarbeiter mit welchen Qualifikationen zu welchen Zeitpunkten an welchen Orten zur Realisierung des geplanten Produktions- und Leistungsprogramms erforderlich sind (Scholz, 2000). Als vorgelagerte personalwirtschaftliche Teilplanung liefert sie wichtige Informationen über notwendige Beschaffungs- und Freisetzungsmaßnahmen wie auch Kosten, die aus künftig geplanten Bedarfen resultieren. Entsprechend der Zielsetzung der Personalplanung unterscheidet man dabei in verschiedene Bedarfsarten (vgl. Tab. 2).

Im Mittelpunkt der Personalbestandsplanung stehen die Ermittlung des derzeitigen Personalbestands (Ist-Personalbestand) und die Prognose des zukünftigen Personalbestands (Soll-Personalbestand). Unabhängig von den zur Bedarfsplanung eingesetzten Instrumenten erfolgt die Berechnung des Bedarfs grundsätzlich in drei Schritten (Wimmer/Neuberger, 1998):

Bedarfsarten	Erklärung
Ersatzbedarf	Der durch ausscheidende Mitarbeiter verursachte Bedarf (Gründe sind: Tod, Invalidität, Pensionierung, Kündigung durch Arbeitnehmer oder Arbeitgeber)
Erweiterungsbedarf	Der über den augenblicklichen Personalbestand hinausgehende (zusätzliche) Personalbedarf (Gründe sind: Erhöhung der Unternehmenskapazität, gestiegene Nachfrage nach Sportangeboten)
Reservebedarf	Abrufbereites Personal („Rufbereitschaft" zusätzlich zum Stammpersonal kann in Notsituationen noch ein weiterer Personalstamm abgerufen werden)
Zusatzbedarf	Kurzfristiges zusätzliches Personal (Gründe sind: saisonale Schwankungen wie z.B. die Sommersaison eines Freibadbetreibers)
Freistellungsbedarf	Personalüberschuss, der aus verschiedenen Gründen abgebaut werden muss, z.B. bei Nachfragerückgang, bei Angebotseinschränkungen, Schließung von Filialen

Tab. 2: Bedarfsarten im Überblick
In Anlehnung an: Jung (2006), S. 116 ff.

1. Schritt: Bestimmung des Bruttobedarfs:
Ermittlung des gesamten zukünftigen Arbeitszeitbedarfs, der erforderlich ist, um die geplanten Leistungen zu realisieren. Allerdings lassen sich sportliche Angebote, die produzierenden Bereiche ausgenommen, aufgrund ihres Dienstleistungscharakters nicht auf solche konkrete Absatzmengen reduzieren. Demnach können Eingangsgrößen wie der Zeitbedarf pro Arbeitsgang (z.B. Betreuung eines Patienten) nicht einfach standardisiert werden, sondern sind konsequent an den Bedürfnissen und Verhaltensweisen der Kunden hinsichtlich Zeitpunkt, Dauer oder Umfang der Inanspruchnahme sportbezogener Dienstleistungen auszurichten.

2. Schritt: Bestimmung des zukünftigen Personalbestands:
Ist davon auszugehen, dass ein Teil der aktuellen Belegschaft auch in der Planungsperiode noch zur Verfügung steht, so muss die Entwicklung dieses Bestandes abgeschätzt werden. Dabei sind, ausgehend vom gegenwärtigen Bestand, Abgänge durch Kündigungen, Altersruhestand, Wehrdienst u.ä. ebenso zu berücksichtigen, wie eventuelle Zugänge durch Neueinstellungen oder Rückkehrer (z.B. Mutterschaftsurlaub).

3. Schritt: Ermittlung des Nettopersonalbedarfs:
In diesem letzten Schritt wird ein Abgleich von künftigen Bruttopersonalbestand und künftigen Bestand vorgenommen, der den Nettopersonalbestand ergibt. Ist der Bruttobedarf bspw. kleiner als der künftige Personalbestand, entsteht ein Überhang, also ein Freistellungsbedarf.

Zur Bedarfsplanung steht eine Reihe von Verfahren zur Verfügung, mit der Aufgabe, die im Rahmen der Beobachtung der unternehmensinternen und -externen Umwelt gesammelten Informationen in die zur Bestimmung des Nettopersonalbedarfs notwendigen Größen umzuwandeln. Unterschieden werden dabei *intuitive Verfahren* (z.B. Schätzverfahren, Stellenplan-/Arbeitsplatzmethode, Funktionendiagramm), *arbeitswissenschaftliche Verfahren* (REFA, MTM) und *mathematische Verfahren* (Trendverfahren, Simulationen/Modellbildung) (zur ausführlichen Betrachtung der einzelnen Verfahren vgl. Jung, 2006). Im Sport sind zudem *Befragungen zum Sportverhalten* (z.B. gewöhnliche Trainingszeiten, bevorzugte Sportangebote) zweckdienlich, um eventuelle Stoßzeiten der Inanspruchnahme von Sportangeboten auszuloten, die einen besonders hohen Personalbedarf erfordern. Dennoch besteht bei der Bedarfsanalyse im Dienstleistungssektor das Problem einer hohen Planungsunsicherheit.

(2) Personalbeschaffung:
Die grundsätzliche Aufgabe der Personalbeschaffung ist, das Unternehmen bedarfsgerecht und kostengünstig mit potenziellen Arbeitskräften nicht nur für einen derzeitigen Personalbedarf, sondern auch mit Blick auf zukünftige, unternehmensstrategische Entwicklungen zu versorgen. Dabei stellt die Personalbeschaffung keinen einfachen Handlungsprozess dar, sondern muss sich bezüglich ihrer Aufgabenstellung unter Berücksichtigung wettbewerbsbedingter Erfordernisse (z.B. hinreichende Abgrenzung von anderen Sportanbietern), der Arbeitsmarktsituation, des normativen Regelungsrahmens (z.B. Arbeitsrecht) und der spezifischen Arbeitnehmerinteressen sehr differenziert ausgestalten. Zudem hat der sich verschärfende Wettbewerb um qualifizierte Arbeitskräfte zur Folge, dass die Personalbeschaffung auch Strategien der Personalwerbung, Personalerhaltung bzw. Personalbindung umfassen muss. Auf die systematische Gestaltung der Attraktivität des Unternehmens für das Personal ausgerichtete Strategien werden oft auch als *Personalmarketing* bezeichnet (Staehle, 1999).

Es lassen sich *externe* und *interne Personalbeschaffung* unterscheiden. Die externe Personalbeschaffung hat den Vorteil, dass die Ausbildungskosten bei anderen Institutionen oder Unternehmen liegen und dass Bewerber Erfahrungen in anderen Organisationen sammeln konnten. Benötigtes Personal kann zudem durch gezielte Personalwerbung auf einem breiteren Spektrum angesprochen werden, allerdings stets auch mit dem Risiko der Fehleinschätzung und des Motivationsverlusts des bereits vorhandenen Personals (Oechsler, 2006). Externe Personalbeschaffung macht den Einsatz von Instrumenten der Personalwerbung erforderlich, um den externen Arbeitsmarkt zu bearbeiten. Dabei ist zwischen passiven und aktiven Beschaffungswegen zu differenzieren. Bei der passiven Personalbeschaffung weist ein Unternehmen ausschließlich auf vakante Stellen hin (z.B. Stellenausschreibungen, Anschläge an das schwarze Brett, Inserate in Medien) und wartet entsprechende Bewerbungen ab (Drumm, 2005.). Dabei bleibt oftmals unklar, ob die entsprechenden Zielgruppen auch erreicht werden. Dementsprechend greifen Unternehmen immer häufiger auf eine aktive Personalbeschaffung zurück. Hierzu zählen z.B.

Recruting-Veranstaltungen, Informationsgespräche oder das Einschalten von Arbeitsvermittlern. Als weitere – nicht zu unterschätzende – Beschaffungsalternative sollten auch Empfehlungen durch Mitarbeiter (soziale Netzwerke) gesehen werden. Dies scheint insbesondere im Bereich des Sports besonders erfolgswirksam zu sein. Denn persönliche Erfahrungen und sportspezifische Kompetenzen sind oft wichtiger als bestimmte Ausbildungszertifikate. Dies zeigt sich bspw. besonders deutlich bei der Besetzung von Trainerposten im Spitzensport.

Von zunehmender Bedeutung ist die unternehmensinterne Beschaffung (Hausbesetzung). Die interne Personalbeschaffung bietet dabei viele Vorteile: dazu gehören ein hohes Maß an Betriebsverbundenheit und Vertrautheit mit den Verhältnissen und Problemen, langfristige Beurteilungsmöglichkeiten bei der Arbeit, gezielte Fördermöglichkeiten sowie die Schaffung eines Motivationspotenzials durch innerbetriebliche Aufstiegsmöglichkeiten. Diesen Vorteilen stehen allerdings potenzielle Spannungen beim nicht berücksichtigten Personal sowie das Risiko der Betriebsblindheit und Probleme bei der Korrektur von Fehlbesetzungen gegenüber (Oechsler, 2006). V.a. im organisierten Sport (Sportvereine, -verbände) erfolgt die Besetzung hauptamtlicher Stellen vielfach intern.

(3) Personalauswahl und Personaleinsatz:
An den Prozess der Personalbeschaffung schließt sich die Auswahl geeigneter Bewerber und deren Einsatz im Leistungsprozess des Unternehmens an. Bei der Personalauswahl werden die Bewerber geprüft und ihre Fähigkeiten mit den Anforderungen der zu besetzenden Stelle verglichen. Dabei bilden Basisqualifikationen die Grundlagen, die von den Mitarbeitern für eine bestimmte Aufgabe und Position beherrscht werden müssen. Damit sind die berufsfachliche Grundausbildung, betriebswirtschaftliches Wissen sowie bestimmte Fachkompetenzen (z.B. Lizenzen, Trainerscheine) gemeint. Bei Dienstleistungen entsteht aufgrund des Zusammenfalls von Produktion und Verbrauch unter unmittelbarer Beteiligung des Kunden eine besonders hohe Sensibilität für Qualitätsmängel. Dadurch rücken bei der Personalauswahl neben fachspezifischen Kompetenzen auch fachübergreifende, interpersonelle Fähigkeiten als Bewertungsdimension stärker in den Mittelpunkt (vgl. Tab. 3). Nur wenn beispielsweise der Kursleiter gut vorbereitet ist und entsprechend auf die Teilnehmer eingeht, ist die Chance für eine qualitativ hochwertige Dienstleistung gegeben. Hinzu kommen weitere Besonderheiten bei der Personalauswahl im Sportsektor, die meist nur bedingt steuerbar sind. So trägt das äußere Erscheinungsbild (z.B. bei Fitnesstrainern) aufgrund der ästhetischen Besonderheiten und Erwartungen des Sports zur Qualität einer Dienstleistung bei. Zudem schaffen sportliche Erfahrungen der Mitarbeiter ein hohes Maß an Glaubwürdigkeit. Auch die sportlichen Erfolge eines Mitarbeiters sind für ein Unternehmen aufgrund bestehender Kontakte zu potentiellen Geschäftspartnern und Medien sowie aus Imagegründen nicht zu unterschätzen.

Fähigkeit	Beschreibung
Empathie/ Perspektivübernahme	Die Empathie/Perspektivübernahme macht es leichter, Dinge so zu formulieren, so dass sie an die Bedürfnisse des jeweiligen Individuums anschlussfähig sind. Zudem wird die Antizipation unterschiedlicher Bedürfnisse und Interessen der Kunden begünstigt.
Toleranz	Kunden zeichnen sich häufig durch unterschiedliche Verhaltenserwartungen aus. Daher ist eine gewisse Toleranz gegenüber divergierenden Interessen und Meinungen zu entwickeln.
Techniken der Gesprächsführung	Dazu gehören aufmerksames Zuhören, gezieltes Nachfragen, um die Kommunikation mit dem Kunden zu intensivieren und um Missverständnisse im Kundendialog zu vermeiden.
pädagogisch-didaktische Fähigkeiten	Hierbei geht es v.a. um Kompetenzen zur effektiven Steuerung von Lern-/Lehrprozessen sowie um Fähigkeiten zur Begeisterung/Motivation der Sporttreibenden.

Tab. 3: Überblick zu sozialen und kommunikativen Kompetenzen von Mitarbeitern im Sport
In Anlehnung an: Borggrefe/Thiel/Cachay (2006), S. 63

Beim Personaleinsatz geht es darum, dem ausgewählten Personal entsprechend seinen Fähigkeiten und dem Bedarf bestimmte Aufgaben zuzuweisen. Im Folgenden soll auf die zwei wesentlichen Elemente des Personaleinsatzes eingegangen werden, die zur Anpassung der Unternehmen im Dienstleistungsbereich an betriebliche und marktbezogene Notwendigkeiten von Bedeutung sind: Die *Flexibilisierung der Arbeitsverhältnisse* und *der Arbeitszeit*.

Das am weitesten verbreitete Instrument des flexiblen Personaleinsatzes ist der *befristete Arbeitsvertrag*, der durch Zeitablauf (z.B. Wintersaison) oder durch Zweckerreichung (z.B. Ende einer Sportveranstaltung) endet. Als weitere wesentliche Flexibilisierungsvariante können die verschiedenen Formen der Teilzeitarbeitsverhältnisse angesehen werden. Dazu gehört vor allen das *Job-Sharing-Arbeitsverhältnis* (Arbeitsplatzteilung). Aus personalwirtschaftlicher Sicht ergibt sich durch das Job Sharing gegenüber normaler Teilzeitarbeit der entscheidende Vorteil, dass der Arbeitsplatz während der gesamten betriebsüblichen Zeit besetzt ist (z.B. die Rezeption eines Gesundheits- und Wellnesszentrums) und damit keine Präsenzprobleme auftreten. Mit der Anpassung der Arbeitszeit an den Arbeitsanfall (KAPOVAZ - Kapazitätsorientierte variable Arbeitszeit) ist eine weitere Flexibilisierungsform im Rahmen von Teilzeitarbeitsverhältnissen gemeint (für einen ausführlichen Überblick vgl. z.B. Frey, 1985). Besonders sinnvoll ist diese Variante für solche Sportanbieter, bei denen ein erhöhter Arbeitsanfall zu bestimmten Stoßzeiten vorkommt (z.B. in Fitnesseinrichtungen am Abend). Nur bedingt geeignet für einen flexiblen Personaleinsatz scheinen dagegen Formen der Arbeitnehmerüberlassung (Personalleasing) zu sein. Denn Zeitarbeitsverhältnisse eignen sich v.a. zum Abdecken kurzfristiger Personalengpässe, vertrauensvolle Beziehungen zu Kunden (z.B. Patient - Therapeut) bedürfen jedoch längerfristig angelegter Arbeitsverhältnisse.

Mit flexiblen Formen der Voll- und Teilzeitarbeit ist v.a. das betriebswirtschaftliche Ziel verbunden, durch eine Entkopplung der Betriebs- und Öffnungszeiten von den individuellen Arbeitszeiten eine verbesserte Anpassung der Arbeitskräfte-nutzung an Schwankungen der Nachfrage sowie an Kundenbedürfnisse zu errei-chen (Marr, 2001). Daher kommen im Dienstleistungssektor vorrangig folgende Grundtypen der Arbeitszeitflexibilisierung zur Anwendung:

- Die Variation der Dauer bzw. des Volumens der Arbeitszeit, z.B. bei der Teil-zeitarbeit,
- Die Veränderung der Lage bzw. Verteilung eines bestimmten Arbeitszeitvolu-mens, z.B. Job Sharing,
- Die Veränderung von Dauer und Lage der Arbeitszeit, z.B. bei Gleitzeitmodel-len.

(4) Personalentwicklung:
Die Aufgabe von Personalentwicklungsmaßnahmen ist die Erweiterung bzw. Ver-tiefung bereits bestehender und/oder die Vermittlung neuer Qualifikationen, die an die Bedürfnisse des Unternehmens, besonders auch im Hinblick auf zukünftige Aufgaben, angepasst werden (Neuberger, 1994). Dabei lassen sich vielfältige Gründe anführen, die Impulse für Qualifizierungsmaßnahmen auslösen (vgl. Tab. 4)

Institutionell-unternehmerische Faktoren
• verfahrenstechnische Veränderungen (neue Sportgeräte, neue Herstellungsverfahren, Trai-ningsmethoden, neue Sportarten und Bewegungsaktivitäten), • Änderung der Marktverhältnisse (erhöhter Konkurrenzdruck, veränderte Sportnachfrage), • Veränderungen im Managementbereich (Änderung der Unternehmensgröße, der Unterneh-mensziele, personelle Veränderungen in der Geschäftsleitung).
Personell-politische Faktoren
• Veränderung im Betriebklima (Mitarbeiterfluktuation, Arbeitszufriedenheit), • bildungspolitische Entwicklungen (neue Vorschriften und Verbandsrichtlinien, veränderte Qualitätsstandards).

Tab. 4: Anlässe für Maßnahmen der Personalentwicklung
In Anlehnung an: Staehle (1999), S. 874 f.

Im Folgenden werden Konzepte erläutert, die im Rahmen der Personalentwicklung zur Anwendung kommen. Die wohl gängigste Systematisierung ist dabei die Eintei-lung in Maßnahmen, die (a) außerhalb des Arbeitsplatzes durchgeführt werden (Training off the Job) und denen, die (b) am Arbeitsplatz angewandt werden (Trai-ning on the Job). Zu berücksichtigen sind zudem Maßnahmen (c) in ummittelbarer Nähe zum Arbeitsplatz (Training near the Job).

(a) *Training off the Job* erfolgt meist in institutionalisierter Form. Es kann in in-nerbetrieblichen eigenen Einrichtungen (z.B. Ausbildungszentren), in innerbetrieb-lichen fremden Einrichtungen (z.B. Herstellerschulung), überbetrieblichen Einrich-tungen (z.B. Wirtschaftsverbänden, Innungen, Kammern) sowie außerbetrieblichen Weiterbildungsinstituten (z.B. freie Träger) erfolgen. Auch im Bereich des Sports hat sich inzwischen ein dichtes Netz an Weiterbildungseinrichtungen und Institutionen mit entsprechenden Lizenzausbildungen entwickelt. Gerade solche von Mitarbeitern extern erworbene Lizenzen stellen ein wichtiges Kompetenz- und Qualitätsmerkmal von Sportangeboten dar.

(b) Die große Beliebtheit des *Training on the Job* lässt sich v.a. mit der realitätsnahen Vermittlung notwendiger Qualifikationen erklären. Die Qualifikationsmaßnahmen finden dabei in unmittelbarem Zusammenwirken mit Vorgesetzten und weiteren Mitarbeitern sowie der täglichen Arbeitsaufgabe am Arbeitsplatz statt. Insbesondere im Dienstleistungsbereich ist die gelenkte Erfahrungsvermittlung besonders effizient, um die Mitarbeiter mit den Anforderungen und Besonderheiten neuer Stellen vertraut zu machen. Gleichzeitig wird dadurch eine einheitliche Informationsgrundlage unter den Mitarbeitern geschaffen, die von Kunden als weiteres Qualitätsmerkmal des Unternehmens empfunden wird.

(c) *Training near the Job* beschäftigt sich mit aktuellen Problemen in unmittelbarer Nähe des Arbeitsplatzes. Für die Teilnehmer ergeben sich so direkte Transfermöglichkeiten zu ihren Aufgaben. Eine bewährte Methode ist dabei der Qualitätszirkel (auch Lernwerkstatt, Problemlösegruppe genannt). Die Grundidee ist, dass die Mitarbeiter ihren Arbeitsbereich selbst am besten kennen und somit großes Problemlösungs- und Kreativitätspotenzial besitzen. Insbesondere bei der Entwicklung neuer Dienstleistungsangebote können solche Maßnahmen besonders zielführend sein.

7.2.3.2 Leistungserhalt bzw. -förderung

Weitere zentrale Handlungsfelder des Personalmanagements sind darauf ausgerichtet, den Erhalt und die Förderung der Leistungsprozesse in Kooperation mit den Mitarbeitern sicherzustellen. Der Leistungsbeitrag des Personals im Leistungsprozess wird dabei unter motivationalen Gesichtspunkten vorgenommen. Zudem kann mittels der Personalführung auf das Verhalten der Mitarbeiter im Leistungsprozess Einfluss ausgeübt werden.

(1) Motivation im Leistungsprozess:

Im Dienstleistungssektor, wo es aufgrund der Nähe zum Kunden besonders darauf ankommt, dass sich die Mitarbeiter in hohem Maße mit ihren Kompetenzen und ihrer Kreativität in den Prozess der Leistungserstellung eines Unternehmens einbringen, spielt die Mitarbeitermotivierung eine entscheidende Rolle. Der Blick auf die facettenreiche Literatur zur Mitarbeitermotivation in Unternehmen macht deutlich, dass hierbei v.a. der Faktor Zufriedenheit von zentraler Bedeutung ist. Denn diese hat einerseits positive Konsequenzen auf die Arbeitsleistung. Andererseits zeigen sich Zusammenhänge zwischen Arbeitszufriedenheit und Abwesenheitszeiten sowie Fluktuation (von Rosenstiel, 2003). Fragt man an dieser Stelle nach Gestaltungsmöglichkeiten mit denen auf die Arbeitszufriedenheit eingewirkt werden kann, so wird deutlich, dass diese sich aus unterschiedlichen Teilaspekten zusammensetzt. Arbeitsanreize, denen eine besondere Motivkraft zukommt, lassen sich in zwei Kategorien einteilen: erstens in Anreize, die sich auf die *Arbeitsinhalte* beziehen und zweitens in *materielle Anreize*, die zur Erbringung von Arbeitsleistungen beitragen (Staehle, 1999).

Die Arbeit selbst stellt einen wichtigen Motivationsfaktor dar, der zu Arbeitszufriedenheit führt (vgl. dazu das Motivationsmodell von Herzberg, 1982). Bei der Gestaltung der Arbeitsinhalte ist dabei zu unterscheiden, ob die Maßnahmen einen Bezug zur Tätigkeit des Mitarbeiters haben oder sie sich auf tätigkeitsübergreifende Aspekte der Mitarbeit beziehen. Besonders motivierende Arbeitssituationen sind v.a. dann gegeben, wenn die Tätigkeit einen hohen Grad an Autonomie (Mitbestimmung, Entscheidungsfreiheit) aufweist, über Variabilität (Anforderungswechsel) und Flexibilität (gleitende Arbeitszeiten) verfügt, Lernchancen (Qualifizierungsangebote) eröffnet und zur Selbstverwirklichung beiträgt. V.a. Tätigkeitsfelder im Bereich des Sports bieten Mitarbeitern die Möglichkeit, ihr Hobby zum Beruf zu machen. Zudem wirkt motivierend auf die Mitarbeit, wenn sich im Arbeitsalltag über die konkrete Tätigkeit hinaus, Möglichkeiten sozialer Unterstützung (z.B. durch Vorgesetzte oder Kollegen) sowie der Aufbau informeller Beziehungen und sozialer Netzwerke bieten, die als sinnvoll und transparent erlebt werden (von Rosenstiel, 2003).

Unter den materiellen Arbeitsanreizen kommt dem Arbeitsentgelt als zentraler Einkommensquelle des Arbeitnehmers, als Quelle der Anerkennung seiner Arbeitsleistung, als Symbol für Erfolg und Prestige eine überragende Bedeutung zu. Das Arbeitsentgelt bezieht sich dabei meist auf monetäre Anreize, wie die Struktur und Höhe des Gehalts, die Beteiligung am Betriebsvermögen, Leistungsprämien, Sonderzahlungen (z.B. Weihnachts- und Urlaubsgeld) oder Aufwendungen für Vorsorgeeinrichtungen (vgl. ausführlich dazu z.B. Scholz, 2000). Dabei gewinnt die Flexibilisierung von Entgelten in der Unternehmenspraxis an Bedeutung. Bezogen auf die Anreizfunktion verfolgt eine Flexibilisierung von Entgelten das Ziel, Anreize sowohl in der richtigen Höhe (Entgelthöhe) und richtigen Art (Leistungsarten), als auch in der richtigen Richtung (für welche Leistungen werden Belohnungen gewährt) setzen zu können. Das zentrale Problem besteht demnach in der Wahl geeigneter monetärer Anreizsysteme sowie der Festlegung geeigneter Ziele und Bemessungsgrundlagen für die zu belohnende Leistung.

Hinsichtlich der Gewichtung der Anreizsysteme ist zu beachten, dass die materiellen Anreize allenfalls Unzufriedenheit abbauen (Hygienefaktoren). Dagegen kann die Ausgestaltung der Arbeitsinhalte die Zufriedenheit erhöhen (Motivatoren) (Herzberg, 1982).

(2) Personalführung im Leistungsprozess:
Personalführung ist ein Prozess zielgerichteter Beeinflussung des arbeitsbezogenen Verhaltens von Personen durch eine andere Person, i.d.R. durch deren Vorgesetzte (von Rosenstiel, 2003). Die Geführten sollen dazu bewegt werden, bestimmte Ziele,

die sich vorrangig aus den Zielen des Unternehmens ableiten, zu erreichen. Dabei verfügen Vorgesetzte im Idealfall über ein Führungskonzept sowie über unterschiedliche Führungsstile, die situationsspezifisch zur Anwendung kommen sollten. Ein Führungskonzept lässt sich daher als ein (normatives) System von Handlungsempfehlungen für den Manager mit Personalverantwortung begreifen und zwar hinsichtlich seiner Personalführungsaufgaben (Staehle, 1999). Die Wahl des Führungsstils ist dabei von den Zielen, der zu bewältigenden Aufgabe, der jeweiligen Situation, der Merkmale des Vorgesetzten, der spezifischen Merkmale der Organisation und der Merkmale der Mitarbeiter abhängig (von Rosenstiel, 2003). Ein wichtiges Differenzierungskriterium von Führungsstilen stellt die Entscheidungsautorität dar, d.h. die Verteilung von Beteiligung, Mitbestimmung und Kontrolle zwischen Führendem und Geführten. Danach werden auf einem Kontinuum der autoritäre und der kooperative Führungsstil als jeweilige Extreme definiert (vgl. Abb. 1). In reiner Ausprägung kommen diese Führungsstile jedoch nur sehr selten vor. Entsprechend werden in Abhängigkeit vom Entscheidungsspielraum der Geführten über die oben genannte grobe Differenzierung hinaus verschiedene Führungsstile von autoritär bis delegativ unterschieden.

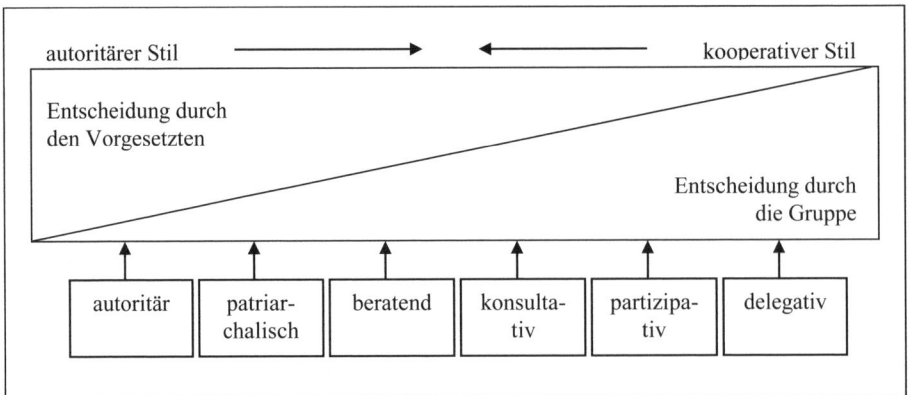

Abb. 1: Systematik von Führungsstilen
In Anlehnung an: Tannenbaum/Schmidt (1958), S. 95

Zunehmend werden in der Arbeitswelt kooperative Führungsstile favorisiert. Der Führende soll nicht nur im klassischen Sinn anleiten, sondern auch Hilfestellungen zur Aufgabenerledigung geben. Dabei ist jedoch zu berücksichtigen, dass der Vorgesetzte durch Anwendung eines geeigneten Führungsstils Anreize schaffen soll, um entsprechende (zieladäquate) Beiträge der Mitarbeiter zu erhalten. Studien zu Führungsstilen machen jedoch deutlich, dass kein spezieller Führungsstil hinsichtlich bestimmter Leistungsmaße (z.B. Qualität, Produktivität) zu präferieren ist. Es gibt nicht *den* besten Führungsstil. Mit Blick auf Einstellungsveränderungen bei

Mitarbeitern weisen jedoch kooperative Führungsstile gewisse Vorteile auf (Oechlser, 2006).

7.3 Personalmanagement in Non-Profit-Organisationen des Sports

Die Erkenntnisse zum Personalmanagement in gewinnorientierten Unternehmen lassen sich auch für die Praxis des Personalmanagements in Non-Profit-Organisationen des Sports nutzen, doch decken sie keinesfalls sämtliche Problembereiche ab. Vielmehr ist davon auszugehen, dass je stärker sich eine Sportorganisation hinsichtlich ihrer Organisations- und Personalstruktur von den Merkmalen einer For-Profit-Organisation unterscheidet, desto weniger kann auf die Managementstrategien und -instrumente der betrieblichen Personalwirtschaft zurückgegriffen werden. Man vergleiche beispielsweise einen Sportartikelhersteller auf der einen Seite mit einem Sportverein ohne hauptamtliche Mitarbeiter auf der anderen Seite. Unter Bezugnahme auf sportsoziologische Arbeiten zur Spezifik von Non-Profit-Organisationen im Sport (Sportvereine und -verbände) ist das Personalmanagement daher gesondert zu betrachten und erfordert, zumindest teilweise, eigenständige Managementkonzepte. Zwar haben sich in den letzten Jahren viele Autoren mit dem Problem der Ehrenamtlichkeit und Hauptamtlichkeit in Sportvereinen auseinandergesetzt (z.B. Winkler, 1988; Dierkes, 1989; Heinemann/ Schubert, 1992; Jütting 1998; Thiel/Meier/Cachay, 2006), auf personalwirtschaftliche Aspekte gehen hingegen nur wenige Beiträge explizit ein (z.B. Horch, 2005; Thiel/Meier, 2005; Wadsack, 1992, 2004), so dass fundierte Konzeptionen bislang weitestgehend noch ausstehen.

7.3.1 Ehrenamtliche Mitarbeit in Non-Profit-Organisationen des Sports

Befasst man sich mit dem Personalmanagement in freiwilligen Sportorganisationen, dann sollte zunächst auf die ehrenamtliche Mitarbeit und ihre Besonderheiten eingegangen werden, da diese für einen Sportverein konstitutiv ist. Eine Abgrenzung des Ehrenamtes gegenüber hauptamtlicher Tätigkeit kann anhand der folgenden strukturellen Merkmale vorgenommen werden (Heinemann, 1988):

- *Freiwilligkeit*: Es liegt kein Arbeitsvertrag zugrunde.
- *Organisatorische Anbindung*: Aktivität im Rahmen einer Vereinsmitgliedschaft.
- *Nebenberuflichkeit*: Engagement außerhalb der Hauptberuflichkeit.
- *Unentgeltlichkeit*: Einkommenserzielung ist nicht Hauptzweck der Tätigkeit.
- *Laienarbeit*: Oftmals keine fachspezifische Ausbildung der Ehrenamtlichen.
- *Fremdhilfe*: Die Arbeit kommt - zumindest teilweise - Dritten zugute.

Ehrenamtliche Mitarbeit stellt eine der wesentlichen Ressourcen des Sportvereins dar, welche die Mitglieder als unentgeltliche und freiwillige Leistung in den „Pool" ihres Sportvereins einbringen. Ehrenamtliches Engagement in Sportvereinen lässt sich dabei in unterschiedliche Bereiche unterteilen, wobei viele ehrenamtliche Mitarbeiter in mehreren Bereichen gleichzeitig tätig sind. Dazu zählen operative Tätigkeiten im Sportbereich (z.B. als Trainer und Übungsleiter, Schiedsrichter), die Wartung und Pflege von Vereinsanlagen, aber auch administrative Tätigkeiten im Bereich Führung und Verwaltung (insbesondere in Vereinsgremien).

Vielfach wird in Sportvereinen eine nachlassende Bereitschaft der Mitglieder, freiwillig und ehrenamtlich mitzuarbeiten, vermutet. Obwohl in Sportvereinen nach wie vor sehr viele Menschen ehrenamtlich tätig sind, gäbe es – so die Aussagen von vielen Vereins- und Verbandsvertretern – v.a. bei der Besetzung von Ämtern in der Vereinsführung, aber auch in anderen Bereichen Schwierigkeiten. Inwiefern existieren bei der Rekrutierung von Ehrenamtlichen tatsächlich größere Probleme und inwieweit wurden tatsächlich vermehrt bezahlte Arbeitskräfte eingestellt? Aktuelle Befunde zeigen relativ einheitlich, dass ein großer Teil der Vereinsarbeit immer noch ehrenamtlich und ohne größere finanzielle Entlohnung geleistet wird und die Engagementbereitschaft der Mitglieder nur bedingt nachgelassen hat. Nach wie vor gibt es nur relativ wenige Vereine, die bestimmte Positionen und Ämter nicht besetzen können (Emrich/Pitsch/Papathanassiou, 2001). In Anlehnung an empirische Befunde (Nagel, 2006; Schubert/Horch/Hovemann, 2007) lässt sich dabei festhalten, dass ehrenamtliches Engagement umso einfacher generiert werden kann, je kleiner der Verein ist (v.a. bei älteren Einspartenvereinen) und je homogener die Mitgliederinteressen sind. Doch auch mit zunehmender Mitgliederzahl sinkt das ehrenamtliche Engagement nur bedingt (vgl. hierzu die Diskussion um die „Krise des Ehrenamtes", Pitsch/Emrich, 1997). Dabei sind nach Schubert/Horch/Hovemann (2007) 12,7% aller Mitglieder auf Positionen der Führungs- und Verwaltungsebene und 18,8% auf Positionen der Ausführungsebene tätig. Gleichwohl wird die freiwillige Bereitschaft zur Mitarbeit immer ein „knappes" Gut für Sportvereine darstellen, das unter Umständen durch bezahlte Arbeit von Honorarkräften oder Vereinsangestellten ersetzt wird. Allerdings beschäftigt bislang lediglich ein geringer Teil der Sportvereine meist nur einige wenige hauptamtliche Mitarbeiter. Fasst man alle Formen der bezahlten Mitarbeit zusammen, so zeigt sich, dass ca. 38% der Sportvereine bezahlte Mitarbeiter haben (Horch/Hovemann/Schubert, 2007). Insgesamt gilt, dass v.a. Großvereine und Vereine mit Prestigesportarten professionalisiert sind (Nagel/Conzelmann/Gabler, 2004).

Allerdings ist zu beachten, dass ehrenamtliche Mitarbeit sich nur bedingt mit den professionellen Strukturen verträgt, weil die wichtigsten Anreize zu ehrenamtlichen Engagement aus dem besonderen Organisationscharakter freiwilliger Vereinigungen und der besonderen Art der Zusammenarbeit erwachsen (Heinemann/Horch, 1988). Je mehr Arbeiten von bezahlten Mitarbeitern ausgeführt werden, desto größer werden die Ansprüche der Mitglieder, während gleichzeitig ihre Mitarbeitsbereitschaft sinkt, weil die Notwendigkeit dazu nicht mehr gesehen wird. Umgekehrt sehen Hauptamtliche die Effektivität ihrer Arbeit beeinträchtigt, weil sie oftmals nur als „verlängerter Arm" von ehrenamtlichen Entscheidungsträgern fungieren und mit begrenzter Entscheidungsbefugnis ausgestattet sind. Zwischen ehrenamtlicher und hauptamtlicher Arbeit in Sportvereinen besteht also ein Spannungsverhältnis (Dierkes, 1989). Deshalb gilt es im Rahmen des Personalmanagements eine optimale Balance zu finden, damit in Sportvereinen ehrenamtliche und hauptamtliche Mitarbeiter gleichermaßen gut zusammenarbeiten können. Dabei zeigen aktuelle Befunde, dass dies in vielen Vereinen relativ gut funktioniert und die Mitglieder trotz professionalisierter Strukturen zu ehrenamtlicher Mitarbeit bereit sind (z.B. Nagel, 2006; Thiel/Meier/Cachay, 2006).

7.3.2 Handlungsfelder des Personalmanagements in Non-Profit-Organisationen des Sports

Im Folgenden werden die bereits bei der Betrachtung des For-Profit-Sektors zugrunde gelegten Handlungsfelder des Personalmanagements erneut aufgegriffen. Anhand dieses Analyserasters sollen sowohl Besonderheiten als auch Lösungsansätze für das personenbezogene Management diskutiert werden, die sich aus den strukturellen Besonderheiten der Sportvereine ergeben.

7.3.2.1 Personalplanung

Beleuchtet man zunächst den Prozess der Personalplanung, so geht es auch in freiwilligen Sportorganisationen vornehmlich darum, personelle Ressourcen sicherzustellen, die zur Realisierung der (satzungsmäßigen) Zwecke des Sportvereins erforderlich sind. Während bezüglich hauptamtlicher Mitarbeiter in Sportvereinen auf die Ansätze des For-Profit-Bereichs verwiesen werden kann, bedarf die ehrenamtliche Tätigkeit wegen ihrer spezifischen Qualifikations- und Aktivitätsgrade einer gesonderten Betrachtung.

(1) Personalbedarfsplanung:
Die Bedarfsanalyse ermittelt den quantitativen und qualitativen, zeitlichen und örtlichen Arbeitskräftebedarf. In Sportvereinen ist jedoch eine rationale Planung des Personalbedarfs untypisch und vielfach nur bedingt möglich. Denn erstens erfolgt die Mitarbeit unentgeltlich, so dass Kostenaspekte bei eventuellen Überkapazitäten keine Rolle spielen. Andererseits stellt sich für die meisten Sportvereine häufig nicht die Frage, wie bestimmte Stellen zu besetzen sind, sondern ob bestimmte Stellen überhaupt besetzt werden können. In vielen Sportvereinen können Aufgaben nicht oder nur unzureichend erfüllt werden, weil die vorhandenen ehrenamtlich tätigen Personen überlastet sind und neue Freiwillige sich nur äußerst schwer gewinnen lassen. Dies führt zu einer Umkehrung der Logik der Personalbedarfsplanung, so dass Positionen häufig nicht nach Bedarf, sondern jeweils erst nach dem quantitativen und qualitativen Angebot an Arbeitskräften gebildet oder ausgestaltet wer-

den (Geser, 1980). Daher kann ein Sportverein bspw. Trainingseinheiten für den Nachwuchs erst dann anbieten, wenn ein Trainer zur Verfügung steht. Bei der Personalbedarfsplanung ist zudem zu berücksichtigen, dass bei den ehrenamtlichen Mitarbeitern meist nur eine begrenzte Einsetzbarkeit vorhanden ist (Horch, 2005). So wird bspw. ein ehrenamtlich tätiger Fußballtrainer nicht ohne weiteres das Amt des Handballtrainers übernehmen. Da Ehrenamtlichkeit nur in der Freizeit ausgeübt werden kann, entstehen weiterhin Unsicherheiten hinsichtlich der zeitlichen Verfügbarkeit (z.B. Familiensituation, berufliche Entwicklung), so dass der Aktivitätsgrad eines Mitarbeiters durchaus variieren kann. Als Folge der mangelnden Planbarkeit und tendenziellen Knappheit der Ressource Ehrenamt, ist im Rahmen der Bedarfsanalyse abzuwiegen, inwieweit bestimmte Aufgabenbereiche, je nach Bedeutsamkeit für den Sportverein, besser durch nebenamtliche bzw. hauptamtliche Mitarbeiter abgedeckt werden sollten.

(2) Personalbeschaffung:
Die Rekrutierung qualifizierter und engagierter ehrenamtlicher Mitarbeiter wird als eines der größten Managementprobleme gesehen (Heinemann/Schubert, 1994). Gelingt es Sportvereinen nicht, Menschen zu ehrenamtlichen Engagement zu bewegen, geht ihnen somit ein hohes Maß ihrer Leistungsfähigkeit verloren. Dabei ist davon auszugehen, dass in vielen Vereinen das Freiwilligenpersonal immer weniger auf traditionellen Wegen – quasi wie von selbst – gewonnen werden kann.

Ein wesentliches Merkmal freiwilliger Sportorganisationen bei der Rekrutierung ehrenamtlicher Mitarbeit ist, dass diese i.d.R. innerhalb der eigenen Reihen erfolgt. Als Beschaffungspotential können daher alle bereits im Sportverein vorhandenen aktuellen und potentiellen unbezahlten Arbeitskräfte angesehen werden. Im Rahmen der internen Personalbeschaffung geht es folglich darum, bisher passive Mitglieder des Sportvereins zu aktivieren bzw. den Aktivitätsgrad von Mitarbeitern zu steigern (Wehling, 1993). Die Mitarbeiterrekrutierung erfolgt dann typischerweise durch persönliche Ansprache. Dazu sollte der Rekrutierende die entscheidenden Mitarbeitshemmnisse kennen und potentielle Mitarbeitsmotive (siehe unten) aufzeigen. Dabei sollte der Aufgabenbereich Mitarbeit strukturell einem Vorstandsmitglied zugeordnet werden, der von anderen Mitarbeitern (z.B. Abteilungsleiter) entsprechend unterstützt wird (Wadsack, 2004). Die externe Personalbeschaffung von Freiwilligen geht zunächst mit der Gewinnung neuer Mitglieder einher. Bereits bei Eintritt sollte dabei die Mitarbeitsbereitschaft inklusive bestimmter Fähigkeiten (z.B. berufliche Tätigkeit, sportfachliche Fähigkeiten usw.) in einer Mitgliederdatei erfasst werden. Anschließend sollte die Ansprache zur gelegentlichen Mitarbeit erfolgen. Insbesondere in solchen Vereinen, wo die Bereitschaft zur ehrenamtlichen Mitarbeit besonders gering ist, sollte geprüft werden, inwieweit Mitarbeit als Mitgliedschaftserwartung satzungsmäßig verankert werden kann. Allerdings könnte dies wiederum eine Eintrittsbarriere für potenzielle Interessenten darstellen.

(3) Personalauswahl und Personaleinsatz:

In Unternehmen werden vakante Stellen i.d.R. in Orientierung an Anforderungs- und Fähigkeitsprofilen an Personen mit den entsprechenden Kompetenzen vergeben. Dies ist in Sportvereinen vielfach anders, denn die Besetzung bestimmter Ämter erfolgt weder rational geplant, noch orientiert sie sich vorrangig an aufgabenbezogenen Kriterien. Denn Sportvereine schreiben offene Stellen weder aus noch sind von den Mitarbeitern bestimmte Qualifikationen nachzuweisen. Zudem müssen die ehrenamtlich tätigen Personen Mitglieder des Vereins sein, was den Kreis an potentiellen Mitarbeitern und deren Kompetenz erheblich einschränkt (Heinemann/Horch, 1988). Demzufolge können qualitative Maßstäbe v.a. bei der Ämterbesetzung auf unterer Ebene kaum angesetzt werden, zumal es oft nur einen Bewerber für ein Amt gibt und dieser eher gebeten als gewählt wird. Stehen tatsächlich mehre Bewerber für ein Amt zur Verfügung, so sind aufgrund der Strukturbesonderheiten von Sportvereinen i.d.R. nicht die fachlichen Kompetenzen für dieses Amt, sondern etwa die Bewährung in anderen Aufgaben und der Bekanntheitsgrad innerhalb des Vereins zentrale Kriterien, nach denen die Mitglieder ihre Wahl treffen (Grosskopff, 1967).

Bei der Besetzung von hauptamtlichen Stellen ist man dagegen nicht auf den Kreis der Mitglieder beschränkt. Die Besetzung erfolgt aufgrund der auf dem Arbeitsmarkt verfügbaren Qualifikationen, so dass eine größere Chance besteht, für ein spezifisches Aufgabenfeld Mitarbeiter mit entsprechender Fachkompetenz auszuwählen. Da in den Sportvereinen vielfach jedoch keine öffentliche Ausschreibung stattfindet, sondern oftmals eine interne Rekrutierung erfolgt, besteht weiterhin die Gefahr, dass fachliche Kompetenzen gegenüber Persönlichkeitseigenschaften und Vereinskarrieren in den Hintergrund rücken. Bei der Personalauswahl hauptamtlicher Mitarbeiter gibt es in den Sportvereinen somit noch erhebliches Rationalisierungspotenzial.

(4) Personalentwicklung:

Durch Personalentwicklung sollen Kenntnisse und Fähigkeiten der Mitarbeiter verbessert werden, die für die Ausführung einer Tätigkeit in der Sportorganisation erforderlich sind. In Sportvereinen kommt v.a. internen Entwicklungsmaßnahmen eine zentrale Bedeutung zu, um die Mitarbeiter sowohl mit den Anforderungen der Vereinsarbeit als auch mit den Vereinsstrukturen vertraut zu machen. Dabei vertrauen Sportvereine weniger auf konkrete Entwicklungsmaßnahmen, sondern eher auf lang andauernde Sozialisationsprozesse innerhalb der Vereinigung. Deshalb kommt es darauf an, ein in seinen quantitativen und qualitativen Anforderungen abgestuftes Programm an Mitarbeitsmöglichkeiten zu schaffen. Je mehr der einzelne schrittweise in die Vereinsarbeit hineinwächst und dabei in unterschiedlichen Tätigkeitsbereichen agiert, desto größer werden seine Fähigkeiten. Allerdings besteht dabei das Problem, dass all denjenigen qualifizierten Personen der Zugang zu höheren Vereinsämtern erschwert wird, deren berufliche Tätigkeit ein hohes Maß an Mobilität erfordert (Horch, 2005).

Vereine sind zumeist nicht in der Lage, kostspielige Qualifizierungsangebote und Fortbildungsmaßnahmen von externen Bildungsträgern für ihre Mitarbeiter zu finanzieren. Dennoch stehen die Ausbildungs- und Lizenzsysteme der Sportfachverbände als vergleichsweise kostengünstige Alternative zur Verfügung, um Mitarbeiter im sportfachlichen Bereich zu qualifizieren (Jütting, 1996). Zudem sollten die von vielen Landessportverbänden angebotenen Seminare zum Vereinsmanagement genutzt werden, um die Mitarbeiter für die komplexen Aufgaben in der Führung und Verwaltung zu qualifizieren.

7.3.2.2 Leistungserhalt bzw. -förderung

Auch wenn freiwillige Sportorganisationen nicht gewinnorientiert ausgerichtet sind, ist es das Ziel des Sportvereins, den Leistungsprozess (z.B. Trainings- und Spielbetrieb) möglichst optimal zu gestalten. Dies ist entscheidend von der ehrenamtlichen Mitarbeit abhängig. Daher sind in erster Linie Erhaltungsmaßnahmen erforderlich, die das vorhandene Personal an den Verein dauerhaft binden und Rücktrittsentscheidungen unentgeltlicher Arbeitskräfte verhindern können.

(1) Motivation ehrenamtlicher Mitarbeiter:

Aufgrund der hohen Bedeutung ehrenamtlicher Tätigkeit für Sportvereine besteht eine wesentliche Aufgabe des personalbezogenen Managements darin, die Mitglieder zu ehrenamtlichen Engagement zu motivieren und sich zum Nutzen aller für die Belange ihres Sportvereins einzusetzen. Da im Gegensatz zu For-Profit-Organisationen keine monetären Anreize zur Verfügung stehen, ist demnach von anderen Motivationsstrukturen auszugehen, was zu erheblichen Konsequenzen bei der Anreizgestaltung führt. Denn die Übernahme ehrenamtlicher Tätigkeiten ist direkt mit dem Ziel, der Struktur, bestimmten Personen oder Gruppen der Organisation oder mit dem Selbst des Handelnden verbunden (Dierkes, 1989). Dabei lassen sich unterschiedliche Motive für ehrenamtliches Engagement kennzeichnen (vgl. Tab. 5).

Diese allgemeinen Motivstrukturen machen deutlich, warum sich Personen überhaupt ehrenamtlich in Sportvereinen engagieren. Jedoch stellt sich für Sportvereine die Frage, in welchem Maße sich die Mitglieder in die Organisation einbringen. Gleichzeitig besteht stets das Problem der Aufkündigung der Mitarbeit. Um die freiwillige Mitarbeit nachhaltig sicherzustellen und den Aktivitätsgrad zu erhöhen, können jedoch nur solche motivierenden Maßnahmen herangezogen werden, die der Sportorganisation auch zur Verfügung stehen. In diesem Zusammenhang ist Kreativität gefragt, weil beispielsweise die klassischen monetären Anreizsysteme in Sportvereinen nur dann eine Rolle spielen, wenn hauptamtliche Mitarbeiter, z.B. bei der Anstellung eines Geschäftsführers, beschäftigt werden. Deshalb muss der

Verein besondere Anreize und Einbindungsmechanismen bieten, um Mitglieder zur aktiven Mitarbeit zu motivieren (Wehling, 1996). Dabei kommen zunächst solche Anreize in Frage, die sich auf die Art der übernommenen Tätigkeit (Arbeitsinhalte) und die Arbeitsbedingungen beziehen. Hierbei ist davon auszugehen, dass sämtliche Faktoren, die bereits im For-Profit Bereich erläutert wurden (Autonomie, Mitbestimmung usw.), auch Gültigkeit für die Mitarbeit in freiwilligen Sportorganisationen haben. Die Strukturen und Kultur eines Sportvereins bilden dabei den Rahmen, die eine Entfaltung solcher Anreize begünstigen oder erschweren kann. Förderlich sind daher v.a. solche Vereinsstrukturen, die nur wenig formalisiert, standardisiert und zentralisiert sind (Heinemann, 1988).

Motive	Beschreibung
Persönlicher Nutzen/ Selbstverwirklichung	den eigenen Interessen nachgehen, Anerkennung finden, soziales Ansehen erwerben,
Persönliche Wertvorstellungen	es macht Spaß sich zu engagieren, die Tätigkeit befriedigt auch ganz persönlich
Soziales Engagement	anderen Menschen helfen, die Solidarität unter den Mitgliedern ist sehr ausgeprägt
Gemeinschaftsorientierung	aktiv in das Vereinsleben einbringen, hohe emotionale Verbundenheit mit dem Verein
Gemeinsinn	etwas für das Gemeinwohl und die Allgemeinheit tun, der Bürgerpflicht nachkommen

Tab. 5: Motivstrukturen ehrenamtlichen Engagements in Sportorganisationen
In Anlehnung an: Braun (2003), S. 249

Auch wenn in Sportvereinen die klassischen monetäre Anreizsysteme (Gehälter, Prämien usw.) bei der Motivation ehrenamtlicher Mitarbeiter kaum eine Rolle spielen, können doch andere materielle Anreize herangezogen werden, die sich außerhalb von Entgeltregelungen bewegen. So sind bspw. Vergünstigungen bei der Beitragsgestaltung sowie der Nutzung von Sportstätten und Sportangeboten von Bedeutung. Attraktiv ist auch die Vergabe von Eintrittskarten für Sportveranstaltungen im Bereich des Spitzensports. Denkbar sind auch Anreize in Form von Sachgeschenken für langjährige Mitarbeit. Allerdings sind neben dem Problem der Finanzierbarkeit auch steuerrechtliche Aspekte zu beachten (Thiel/Meier, 2005). Von besonderer Bedeutung sind v.a. immaterielle Anreize. Klassische Anreize von Vereinen stellen hierbei symbolische Gratifikationen und Honorierungen, wie Ehrungen für jahrelange Mitarbeit, die i.d.R. durch Urkunden oder Ehrenmitgliedschaften dokumentiert werden (Horch, 2005). Dabei spielt auch die öffentliche Anerkennung außerhalb der Sportorganisation eine wichtige Rolle. Dies kann z.B. durch Presseberichte in lokalen Zeitungen oder Sportfachmagazinen realisiert werden. Weitere immaterielle Anreize sind im Aufstieg in der Ämterhierarchie zu sehen, wenn z.B. ein engagiertes Mitglied für eine Position im Vorstand vorgeschlagen wird. Motivierend wirkt außerdem, wenn den Mitarbeitern Gelegenheiten zur

Fortbildung eingeräumt werden, die möglicherweise auch außerhalb der Sportorganisation von Belang sein können.

(2) Personalführung:
V.a. Thiel/Meier (2005) haben sich bislang mit den Besonderheiten der Personalführung in Sportvereinen auseinandergesetzt. Während in Unternehmen Führungskräfte gezielt rekrutiert werden können, kommt in Sportvereinen nur eine eingeschränkte Auswahl von Personen für Führungspositionen in Frage, nämlich solche, die einerseits freiwillig zur Verfügung stehen und andererseits dafür geeignet sind. Dabei sind v.a. solche ehrenamtlichen Funktionsträger in Vereinsgremien mehrheitsfähig, die ihre Eignung durch langjährige Mitgliedschaft unter Beweis gestellt haben. Denn aufgrund demokratischer Entscheidungsstrukturen in Sportvereinen sind Führungspersonen (z.B. Vorstand) keinesfalls das mächtigste Entscheidungsgremium, sondern vielmehr der Mitgliederversammlung verpflichtet. Deshalb muss der Führende bei Mitgliedern und Mitarbeitern zunächst Vertrauen in die Richtigkeit seiner Entscheidungen erwerben. Dabei stellt die langjährige Mitgliedschaft und Verbundenheit die wichtigste Legitimation für Führungshandeln in Sportvereinen dar (Thiel/Meier, 2005).

Für Führungspersonen kommt es bei wichtigen Entscheidungen nicht unbedingt darauf an, eigene Vorschläge mit der Begründung der fachlichen Richtigkeit durchzusetzen, vielmehr gilt es zwischen Partikularinteressen einzelner Gruppierungen zu vermitteln oder Kompromisse auszuhandeln. Eine wesentliche Personalführungsaufgabe in Sportvereinen ist es daher, i.d.R. ohne direktes Einbeziehen der Mitgliederversammlung Entscheidungen zu treffen, ohne dass dabei die Mitgliederinteressen konterkariert werden. Dies erfordert in hohem Maße aufgabenübergreifende Kompetenzen, so genannte soziale Kompetenzen (Thiel/Meier, 2005).

Die Notwendigkeit sozial kompetenter Führungsstile wird darüber hinaus durch den Umstand verstärkt, dass sich die Mitarbeiter vorrangig unentgeltlich engagieren. Dies erfordert enorme Sensibilität beim Umgang mit den Mitarbeitern. Kritik an der Arbeitsweise ehrenamtlicher Mitarbeiter kann dagegen zu irrationalen Abwehrstrategien (z.B. dem Verweis auf das fehlende Entgelt trotz hohen Zeitaufwands), und im Extremfall zur Beendigung der Mitarbeit führen. Deshalb sollte der kompetente Einsatz von Anreizsystemen zentraler Bestandteil eines jeden Personalführungskonzepts in Sportvereinen sein. Denn sowohl Non-Profit-Organisationen des Sports als auch als auch professionelle Sportorganisationen des Spitzensports sind auf ehrenamtliche Mitarbeiter angewiesen.

7.4. Personalmanagement in Spitzensport-Teams
Profi-Sportler im bezahlten Mannschaftssport stellen eine besondere Art von Mitarbeitern dar und ihre Tätigkeit zeichnet sich durch folgende Spezifika aus: Für den sportlichen Erfolg werden von den Spielern ständig Leistungen auf absolutem Top-

niveau erwartet. Dabei ist zu beachten, dass der Mannschaftserfolg nicht nur die bloße Addition der Einzelleistungen darstellt, sondern in entscheidendem Maße von der Kooperation und Interaktion der Spieler abhängig ist, wie das Beispiel der deutschen Fußballnationalmannschaft bei der WM 2006 zeigt. Denn auf die Frage nach den Gründen für das erfolgreiche Abschneiden der deutschen Mannschaft wurde von Trainern, Spielern und Experten in Interviews immer wieder ein Faktor als erfolgsrelevant herausgestellt: der Zusammenhalt im Team. Dagegen lag das enttäuschende Abschneiden einiger Top-Favoriten für viele Fußball-Fachleute v.a. daran, dass einzelne Spieler nicht optimal motiviert waren und es Probleme hinsichtlich der mannschaftlichen Geschlossenheit gab. Aufgrund dieser Überlegungen liegt es nahe, bei der Betrachtung von Spitzensport-Teams nicht (nur) von Personalentwicklung und -führung, sondern von Teamentwicklung und Mannschaftsführung zu sprechen. Eine solche Betrachtungsweise wurde im Personalmanagement bislang allenfalls am Rande im Rahmen von Arbeiten zum Hochleistungsmanagement behandelt (z.B. Pawlowsky/Mistele, 2008). Deshalb wird im Folgenden der Blick auf die vorliegenden sportökonomischen Arbeiten gerichtet, bevor die Befunde einer eigenen Pilotstudie vorgestellt werden.

7.4.1 Teams im Spitzensport aus sportökonomischer Perspektive

Da im Spitzensport der Erfolg die entscheidende Orientierungsgröße darstellt, werden im Zusammenhang mit Fragen des Personalmanagements i.d.R. Erfolgsdeterminanten (meist im Fußball) untersucht. Der Forschungsüberblick bei Frick (2005) macht deutlich, dass die sportliche Performance von der Spielerentlohnung, dem Marktwert einer Mannschaft und dem Trainergehalt abhängt. Gaede/Kleist/Schaecke (2002) betrachten die Bedeutung strategischer Entscheidungen der Teamzusammensetzung im Fußball. Dabei weisen sie nach, dass sich ein homogenes Marktwertgefüge positiv auf den Mannschaftserfolg auswirkt, während hinsichtlich des Faktors Erfahrung heterogene Teams Vorteile haben. Dagegen haben die Alters- und die Nationalitätenstruktur keinen Einfluss auf die Team-Performance. In den vorliegenden sportökonomischen Arbeiten werden allerdings nur monetäre und soziodemographische Aspekte der Teamzusammensetzung beleuchtet, während informelle soziale Strukturen, wie die Beziehungen der Spieler untereinander und der Zusammenhalt innerhalb der gesamten Mannschaft, bislang nicht untersucht wurden.

Hierzu liegen v.a. sportpsychologische Arbeiten vor, die den Zusammenhang der Kohäsion einer Mannschaft und sportlicher Leistung beleuchten. Dabei wird zwischen aufgabenorientierter (Wie wichtig ist es mir, die Mannschaftsaufgaben und -ziele zu verwirklichen?) und sozialorientierter Kohäsion (Wie wichtig ist es mir, soziale Beziehungen innerhalb der Gruppe aufzubauen und zu pflegen?) unterschieden. Während die zentrale Bedeutung einer hohen Aufgabenkohäsion für eine hohe Mannschaftsleistung belegt ist (z.B. Wilhelm, 2001), bleibt die Rolle der sozialorientierten Kohäsion und insbesondere die Frage nach dem für Mannschaftsleistungen günstigen Ausprägungsgrad umstritten.

7.4.2 Bausteine zur Herstellung von Zusammenhalt in Spitzensport-Teams
Zur Frage, wie sich Kohäsion, sozialer Zusammenhalt und Teamgeist in einer Sportspielmannschaft entwickeln und gefördert werden können, liegen bislang keine umfassenden Arbeiten vor. Es existieren lediglich Handbücher zum erfolgreichen Team-Coaching, die mehr oder weniger fundierte Hilfestellungen zur Steuerung der Teambildung liefern (z.B. Linz, 2004; Trosse, 2003). Angesichts dieses Forschungsdefizits soll im Folgenden eine eigene aktuelle Pilotstudie zur Frage der Teamentwicklung in Sportspielmannschaften vorgestellt werden (Nagel/Schlesinger, 2008). Die Befunde der Experteninterviews lassen sich zu folgenden Bausteinen zusammenfassen, die mit Blick auf die Teamentwicklung und damit für den Mannschaftserfolg eine zentrale Rolle spielen.

(1) Sportlicher Erfolg als gemeinsames Ziel:
Zentrales Ziel jeder Mannschaft im Hochleistungssport ist der sportliche Erfolg. Dabei scheint es für den aufgabenbezogenen Teamzusammenhalt von wichtiger Bedeutung zu sein, dass die Mannschaft ein gemeinsam formuliertes sportliches Ziel anstrebt und jeder einzelne Spieler dieses auch konsequent verfolgt. Dazu ist es wiederum notwendig, dass die persönlichen Erwartungshaltungen entlang kollektiver Erwartungen und Zielvorgaben der Mannschaft ausgerichtet werden. Nur wenn alle Spieler „an einem Strang ziehen" und sich gegenseitig unterstützen und motivieren, kann die Mannschaft ihr volles Leistungspotential abrufen und erfolgreich sein. Dabei dürfte es aus der Sicht des Trainers wichtig sein, bei der Formulierung von Zielen die Mannschaft mit einzubeziehen und diese Ziele mit den individuellen Zielen der einzelnen Spieler abzustimmen.

(2) Personalisierte Beziehungen:
Neben gemeinsamen sportlichen Zielen dürften persönliche Beziehungen zwischen den Spielern einer Mannschaft von großer Bedeutung für den Teamzusammenhalt sein. Denn gerade persönliche und Sympathie getragene Beziehungsstrukturen sowie gegenseitiges Vertrauen tragen vermutlich dazu bei, sich absolut für die Mannschaft einzusetzen, Fehler zu verzeihen oder sich gegenseitig zu motivieren. Dadurch entsteht eine positive leistungsfördernde Atmosphäre, in der Mannschaften über sich hinauswachsen und andere Teams, die vermeintlich mit individuell besseren Spielern besetzt sind, besiegen können. Für die Qualität des Trainings ist es jedoch vermutlich auch wichtig, dass sich die Spieler hinsichtlich der Wettkampfsimulation in Trainingssituationen auch als Gegner betrachten können.

Um die Kooperationsbereitschaft innerhalb einer Mannschaft zu erhöhen, dürften v.a. auch gemeinsame Erlebnisse außerhalb von Training und Wettkampf wichtige, den Zusammenhalt fördernde, Elemente darstellen. Dies sind v.a. gemeinsame Freizeitaktivitäten (z.b. Grillen, Bowling). Angesichts der hohen Bedeutung von Vertrauen sind in diesem Zusammenhang zudem spezifische vertrauensbildende Maßnahmen zu nennen, wie beispielsweise simulierte Extremsituationen (Klettern im Hochseilgarten, Abenteuer- und Sportcamps), in denen sich die Akteure gegenseitig unterstützen und einander vertrauen müssen, um Aufgaben erfolgreich bewältigen zu können. Weiterhin können gruppenspezifische Rituale (z.b. Spielerkreis vor den Spielen oder „Taufen" neuer Spieler), äußerliche Symbole (z.b. einheitliche Trainings- und Spielkleidung in den Vereins- oder Landesfarben) sowie nichtformale Verhaltensregeln und Absprachen (z.b. keine öffentliche Kritik an Mannschaftskameraden) die Identifikation mit dem Team fördern und sich positiv auf den Zusammenhalt auswirken.

(3) Hierarchien und Rollenstrukturen:
Einerseits sind für die erfolgreiche Steuerung einer Mannschaft im Spitzensport formalisierte und klar geregelte Hierarchien notwendig, wobei der Trainer eine spezifische Führungsrolle einnimmt. Andererseits sind für den Erfolg auch flache und informelle Hierarchiestrukturen wichtig, da im Wettkampf, insbesondere in entscheidenden Spielsituationen, die Selbststeuerungsfähigkeit einer Mannschaft von zentraler Bedeutung ist. In diesem Zusammenhang ist die hohe Bedeutung von so genannten „Führungsspielern" zu beachten, die unter Umständen als „verlängerter Arm des Trainers" fungieren und für ein funktionierendes Mannschaftsgefüge eine wichtige Funktion übernehmen. Diese Führungsspieler verfügen auf dem Spielfeld zumeist über eine informelle Weisungsbefugnis gegenüber anderen Spielpositionen und sind mit einem hohen Maß an Verantwortung ausgestattet, wobei vom Rolleninhaber erwartet wird, in entscheidenden und riskanten Situationen des sportlichen Wettkampfes auch entsprechend zu handeln.

Weiterhin ist zu beachten, dass der Kader einer Mannschaft im Hochleistungssport i.d.R. doppelt so viele Spieler als im Regelwerk vorgeschrieben umfasst. Diese größere Zahl an Spielern dürfte einerseits für den internen Konkurrenzkampf förderlich sein, andererseits können Ersatzspieler unter Umständen auch den Prozess der Teamentwicklung behindern, da ihre Erwartung am Spiel beteiligt zu sein, nicht permanent erfüllt werden kann. Umso wichtiger scheint einerseits deren Einbindung in den Leistungsprozess der Mannschaft, andererseits bedarf es der hinreichenden Transparenz und Objektivität von Entscheidungsprozessen. Neben der Einbindung von Ersatzspielern stellt die Auswahl und Integration von neuen Spielern, die in das taktische Konzept der Mannschaft passen müssen, einen wichtigen Schritt im Rahmen der Teamentwicklung und damit der Optimierung der sportlichen Leistung dar.

(4) Monetäre Anreize:

Auch innerhalb von Sportspielmannschaften des Spitzensports dürften finanzielle Mittel ein wichtiges Medium darstellen, das Handeln von Spielern zu steuern. Monetäre Anreize beeinflussen die Akzeptanz formaler Mitgliedschaftserwartungen, z.B. die Einhaltung von Vereinbarungen, Trainingsumfängen und Trainingszeiten. Allerdings greifen monetäre Anreize hinsichtlich der Steuerung von Mannschaften wahrscheinlich vielfach zu kurz, weil sie zwar eine Verhaltenskonformität sicherstellen können, nicht notwendigerweise jedoch eine Einstellungskonformität. Gerade die Einstellungskonformität im Sinne des gemeinsamen sportlichen Ziels stellt innerhalb einer Mannschaft eine wichtige Voraussetzung für eine hohe Trainings- und Wettkampfleistung dar. Deshalb ist zu vermuten, dass Sieg- und Punktprämien zwar als zusätzlicher motivationaler Anreiz im Wettkampf dienen können, man jedoch nicht davon ausgehen kann, dass die Leistung umso besser ausfällt, je höher die Siegprämie ist. Zudem lassen sich die personalen Erwartungen der Spieler durch finanzielle Anreize nicht einfach ausblenden, im Gegenteil: sie können sogar verschoben oder verstärkt werden. Denn aufgrund des sportlichen Leistungsgefälles der Spieler innerhalb einer Mannschaft (z.B. „Superstars" und „Wasserträger") ist von Unterschieden in den Gehaltszahlungen und Erfolgsprämien auszugehen. Diese können Unzufriedenheit und Neid auslösen und damit den Zusammenhalt der Mannschaft eher negativ beeinflussen.

7.4.3 Übertragbarkeit auf andere Teams im Sport

Es stellt sich nun die Frage, inwieweit sich Faktoren des Zusammenhalts in Sportspielmannschaften des Spitzensports auch auf andere Arbeitsgruppen und Teams im Bereich des Sports (z.B. Projektteams in Sportmarketing-Agenturen) übertragen lassen. Mit Blick auf die wesentlichen Bausteine, die nachfolgend zusammengefasst werden, ist dabei festzuhalten:

(1) Zunächst ist es notwendig, dass aus den individuellen Interessen der Spieler ein *kollektives Mannschaftsziel* entwickelt wird. Hierzu ist ein gemeinsames sportliches Ziel zu formulieren, dass vielfach schriftlich fixiert wird. Hinsichtlich der Übertragbarkeit auf andere Bereiche scheint es jedoch fraglich, ob dort ähnlich klar messbare Erfolgskriterien und Sachziele formulierbar sind wie im Spitzensport.

(2) Einerseits sind für die erfolgreiche Steuerung einer Mannschaft im Spitzensport formalisierte und klar geregelte hierarchischen Strukturen notwendig, wobei der Trainer eine spezifische Führungsrolle einnimmt. Andererseits sind für den Erfolg auch *flache und informelle Hierarchien* wichtig, da im Wettkampf, insbesondere in entscheidenden Spielsituationen, die Selbststeuerungsfähigkeit einer Mannschaft zentrale Bedeutung hat. Dieser Faktor dürfte auch für Hochleistungsteams in anderen Bereichen eine wichtige Rolle spielen.

(3) Weiterhin sind *personalisierte Beziehungen zwischen den Spielern*, die mit Vertrauen, Loyalität und offener Kommunikation verbunden sind, wichtig für ein

erfolgreiches Team im Spitzensport. Auch die vielfach auf engem Körperkontakt basierenden Rituale und/oder Identität stiftender Evidenzen (z.B. einheitliche Spielkleidung) können auch in anderen Bereichen des Hochleistungsmanagements die Teamentwicklung fördern.

7.5 Fallstudie

Die folgende Fallstudie verdeutlicht am Beispiel des TV Rottenburg den Prozess der Einstellung eines hauptamtlichen Mitarbeiters (Gewinnung, Auswahl und Einsatz) in Non-Profit-Organisationen des Sports (vgl. auch Nagel, 2006).

Fallstudie „TV Rottenburg"

Einführende Bemerkungen:
Der TV Rottenburg hat etwa 2760 Mitglieder und wurde 1861 gegründet. Der Verein gliedert sich in 15 Abteilungen, die die gesamte Bandbreite sportlicher Aktivitäten abdecken, und er bietet ein umfangreiches Kursprogramm, das offen für Nicht-Mitglieder ist. Das Jahresbudget betrug zum Zeitpunkt der Befragung etwa 230.000 € im Jahr. Der jährliche Mitgliedsbeitrag für Erwachsene beträgt 75 €, Kinder und Jugendliche bezahlen 50 €, Familien 115 €. Die Stadt Rottenburg am Neckar hat etwa 42.000 Einwohner, wovon etwa 18.000 in der Kernstadt leben. Die übrige Bevölkerung verteilt sich auf 17, z.T. sehr ländlich strukturierte Stadtteile. Rottenburg liegt in unmittelbarer Nachbarschaft zur Universitätsstadt Tübingen. Nicht zuletzt durch sein auch für Nicht-Mitglieder offenes Kursprogramm, das unter dem Motto „Sport für eine ganze Stadt" steht, zeigt sich der TV Rottenburg aufgeschlossen für neue Trends und Entwicklungen. Seit 2005 existiert der vereinseigene „Sportpark 18-61", ein modernes Sport- und Bewegungszentrum. Das sportarten- und wettkampfbezogene Sportangebot und das Vereinsleben im TV Rottenburg finden v.a. in den Abteilungen statt, die z.T. sehr selbständig agieren und eigene Finanzbudgets zugewiesen bekommen. Der Vorstand des Vereins, bestehend aus dem ersten und zweiten Vorsitzenden, dem Kassenwart, dem Schriftführer sowie den technischen Leitern Wettkampfsport und Freizeitsport, bestimmt wesentlich die Politik des Hauptvereins. Wichtige Vereinsangelegenheiten und Entscheidungen werden im Ausschuss behandelt, der etwa alle zwei Monate tagt und dem neben dem Vorstand die Abteilungsleiter und – je nach Mitgliederzahl der Abteilung – weitere Vertreter der Abteilungen

---

angehören. Neben diesen ehrenamtlich besetzten Gremien hat der TV Rottenburg seit 2001 einen hauptamtlichen Geschäftsführer und im Sportbereich drei teilzeitbeschäftigte Mitarbeiter. Weiterhin gibt es im Bereich Training und Sportbetrieb etwa 50 Mitarbeiter, die stundenweise oder als geringfügig Beschäftigte bezahlt werden. Darüber hinaus sind etwa 200 Vereinsmitglieder im Sportbereich regelmäßig ehrenamtlich tätig.

Darstellung des Entscheidungsprozesses:
Ausgangspunkt für die Entscheidung, einen Geschäftsführer einzustellen, war die Klausurtagung im Jahr 2000. Im Rahmen einer Schwächenanalyse wurde als zentrales Problem die fehlende Kommunikation im Verein herausgearbeitet. Da zudem in verschiedenen Bereichen die anfallende Arbeit des Vorstands ehrenamtlich kaum noch zu bewältigen war, entstand die Idee, einen hauptamtlichen Geschäftsführer einzustellen. Dem Vorstand war zu diesem Zeitpunkt bekannt, dass N.V. als potentieller Kandidat für diesen Aufgabenbereich im Verein Interesse zeigte. N.V. war Vereinsmitglied und engagierte sich damals bereits innerhalb der Volleyballabteilung. Weiterhin wurde im Jahr 2000 mit Unterstützung des Fördervereins des TV Rottenburg eine Machbarkeitsstudie zum Sponsoring durchgeführt. Dabei ergab sich das Problem, dass im Vorstand zeitlich niemand in der Lage war, als Ansprechpartner für mögliche Sponsoren zuständig zu sein. Insbesondere diese Studie machte deutlich, dass es fast unmöglich war, den Verein weiterhin auf der Basis ehrenamtlicher Tätigkeit zu führen. Daraufhin wurde die Suche nach einem hauptamtlichen Geschäftsführer intensiviert.

Die erste Kontaktaufnahme des Vorstandes mit dem potentiellen Kandidaten fand bei einem Helferfest des TV Rottenburg im Oktober 2000 statt. Daraufhin entwickelte N.V. gemeinsam mit dem Vorstand Ziele für die Vereinsentwicklung und ein Sponsoring-Konzept. Grundlage für die spätere Einstellung war diese qualifizierte konzeptionelle Vorarbeit. Zunächst war allerdings das Problem der Finanzierung zu lösen, denn der Verein sah sich zu diesem Zeitpunkt nicht in der Lage, eine Vollzeitstelle zu schaffen. Da N.V. in einem Gespräch dem Vorstand anbot, eine Teilzeitstelle (60%) zu übernehmen, konnte die Einstellung eines Geschäftsführers in die Wege geleitet werden. Nachdem sich der Vorstand für N.V. als Geschäftsführer ausgesprochen hatte, wurde anschließend im Ausschuss dieser Entscheidung ohne Gegenstimme zugestimmt.

Weitere Entwicklung:
In der Folgezeit konnte der neue Geschäftsführer eine Reihe von Finanzquellen, Zuschussmöglichkeiten und mit Geld dotierte Preise für den Verein erschließen und somit selbst zu seiner eigenen Finanzierung beitragen. Dem TV Rottenburg wurde z.B. im Jahr 2003 im Rahmen des Innovationspreises für Turn- und Sportvereine der „Sonderpreis zum Europäischen Jahr für Behinderungen: Integrative Sportangebote" verliehen. Insgesamt zeigte sich, dass sich der Verein durch die

Einstellung eines Geschäftsführers in vielen Bereichen weiterentwickeln und kontinuierlich verbessern konnte.

Abschließende Bemerkungen:
Auslöser für die Überlegungen zur Einstellung eines hauptamtlichen Geschäftsführers bildeten verschiedene organisationsinterne Probleme, die mit modernen Managementmethoden herausgearbeitet wurden. Die mangelnde Kommunikation und die Notwendigkeit eines Sponsoring-Konzepts sowie die Überlastung der ehrenamtlichen Mitarbeiter veranlassten den Vorstand, nach einem hauptamtlichen Mitarbeiter zu suchen. Dabei wurde auf informellem Wege ein Kandidat rekrutiert, der als Vereinsmitglied dem Vorstand bekannt war und bereits vor der Einstellung seine Kompetenzen in die Vereinsarbeit einbrachte. Da durch dieses Vorgehen eine geeignete Person in Teilzeit gefunden werden konnte, wurde auf ein aufwändiges Ausschreibungsverfahren verzichtet. Damit ist die Suche nach einem Geschäftsführer als begrenzt rationales Vorgehen zu charakterisieren, bei dem die Verantwortlichen mit einer akzeptablen Lösung zufrieden waren („satisficing"). Die Entscheidung für die Einstellung wurde zwar letztlich im Vereinsausschuss getroffen; die notwendigen Gespräche und Verhandlungen wurden jedoch vom Vorstand geführt.

7.5 Fazit und Ausblick

Ziel dieses Kapitels war es, die zentralen Handlungsfelder des Personalmanagements in Sportorganisationen unterschiedlichen Typs zu beleuchten. Im Sinne des gegenseitigen Wissenstransfers soll abschließend die Frage gestellt werden, was Sportvereine und kommerzielle Sportanbieter hinsichtlich des Managements personalbezogener Prozesse voneinander lernen können?

In Sportvereinen ist das Personalmanagement weniger rational gestaltet als in Unternehmen, so dass die Anwendung etablierter Maßnahmen aus der Unternehmenspraxis nur mit Einschränkung möglich ist. Vor dem Hintergrund, dass die Mitarbeit im Sportverein ein knappes Gut darstellt, sollte in Non-Profit-Organisationen des Sports dennoch ein systematischeres Personalmanagement angestrebt werden. Dazu ist es notwendig, die Personalbedarfsplanung strategisch und strukturell in die Vereinsarbeit einzubinden, damit personelle Prozesse weniger zufällig, sondern stärker aktiv mitgestaltet werden können. Bei der Personalbeschaffung gilt es, die externe Rekrutierung von Mitarbeitern stärker in Erwägung zu ziehen, um den Sportverein mit den erforderlichen Fachkompetenzen auszustatten. Die Personalauswahl sollte dabei stärker nach fachlichen Gesichtspunkten erfolgen und nicht nur nach der langjährigen Erfahrung oder der Mehrheitsfähigkeit eines Mitarbeiters. Auch die Personalentwicklung kann durch eine gezielte Steuerung von Weiterbildungsmaßnahmen optimiert werden. Hinsichtlich der Mitarbeitermotivation sollte geprüft werden, inwieweit die Formen der Mitarbeit noch zeitgemäß, also flexibel, überschaubar und ggf. zeitlich begrenzt sind. Die Personalführung kann in Sportvereinen effizienter gestaltet werden wenn es gelingt, Aufgabenbereiche und Zuständigkeiten der Führenden eindeutig zu fixieren.

Umgekehrt stellt sich die Frage, was Unternehmen von Non-Profit-Organisationen des Sports lernen können. Unternehmen neigen bei der Personalbeschaffung oftmals dazu, jüngere Mitarbeiter extern zu rekrutieren und älteres Personal freizusetzen. Dabei zeigen Sportvereine beispielhaft – wenn auch gezwungenermaßen und weitgehend unreflektiert – welche Bedeutung langjährige Erfahrung und Vertrauen der Mitarbeiter für die Organisation haben kann. Weiterhin sind Sportvereine Experten, wenn es um die Frage geht, wie man Mitarbeiter ohne monetäre Anreize und nicht nur zum Mitarbeiten, sondern auch zum Mitdenken, motivieren kann (Horch, 2005). Sportvereine haben auch hinsichtlich der Anwendung sozial kompetenter Führungsstile durchaus Vorbildcharakter. Nicht umsonst wird der Sportverein vielfach als ein „Übungsfeld" für demokratische Menschenführung und soziale Verantwortlichkeit verstanden.

Kontrollfragen

1. Welche Entwicklungen haben sich in der Personalwirtschaft in den letzten Jahren vollzogen?
2. Welche Instrumente stehen For-Profit-Organisationen bei der Personalplanung zur Verfügung? Finden Sie konkrete Beispiele!
3. Stellen Sie sich vor, Sie sind Geschäftsführer eines neu gegründeten kommerziellen Sportanbieters. Wie wollen Sie die Leistungsbereitschaft ihrer Mitarbeiter stärken bzw. hochhalten?
4. Welche Besonderheiten charakterisiert die Freiwilligenarbeit in Non-Profit-Organisationen des Sports?
5. Welche Probleme treten bei der Rekrutierung von ehrenamtlichen Mitarbeitern in Sportvereinen auf?
6. Was sind die Besonderheiten bei der Stellenbesetzung in Sportvereinen und zu welchen Konsequenzen führt dies?
7. Durch welche Anreize lässt sich die Arbeitsmotivation in freiwilligen Sportorganisationen steigern?
8. Welchen Führungsstil würden Sie als Vorsitzender eines Sportvereins pflegen? Warum?
9. In wieweit können kommerzielle Sportanbieter mit Blick auf das Personalmanagement von Sportvereinen lernen? Inwieweit ist die Situation eher umgekehrt?
10. Von welchen Faktoren ist der Zusammenhalt in Spitzensportteams abhängig?

Literaturverzeichnis

Braun, Sebastian (2003): Zwischen Gemeinschaftsorientierung und Selbstverwirklichung, in: Baur, Jürgen / Braun, Sebastian (Hrsg.): Integrationsleistungen von Sportvereinen als Freiwilligenorganisationen, Aachen, S. 243-267.

Borggrefe, Carmen / Thiel, Ansgar / Cachay, Klaus (2006): Sozialkompetenz von Trainerinnen und Trainern im Spitzensport, Köln.

Dierkes, Ekkehard (1989): Die Mitarbeiterstruktur in den Organisationen des Sports, in: Sportwissenschaft, Heft 1, S. 9-35.

Drumm, Hans-Jürgen (2005): Personalwirtschaftslehre, 5. Aufl., Berlin u.a.

Emrich, Eike / Pitsch, Werner / Papathanassiou, Vassilios (2001): Die Sportvereine. Ein Versuch auf empirischer Grundlage, Schorndorf.

Frey, Helmut (1985): Flexible Arbeitszeit. Zeitgemäße Vertragsformen bei wechselndem betrieblichem Personalbedarf, München.

Frick, Bernd (2005): „...und Geld schießt eben doch Tore", in: Sportwissenschaft Heft 3, S. 250-270.

Gaede, Nicolas /Kleist, Sebastian / Schaecke, Mirco (2002): „Elf Freunde müsst ihr sein?": Die strategische Entscheidung der Teamzusammensetzung, in: Schewe, Gerhard / Littkemann, Jörn (Hrsg.): Sportmanagement, Schorndorf, S. 213-242.

Geser, Hans (1980): Kleine Sozialsysteme: Strukturmerkmale und Leistungskapazitäten, in: Kölner Zeitschrift für Soziologie und Sozialpsychologie, Heft 2, S. 205-239.

Grosskopff, Rudolf (1967): Wem der Verein ein Amt gibt, in: Hamburger Turnerschaft von 1816 e.V. (Hrsg.): Der Verein. Standort, Aufgabe, Funktion in Sport und Gesellschaft, Schorndorf, S. 151-167.

Heinemann, Klaus (1988): Zum Problem ehrenamtlicher und hauptamtlicher Mitarbeiter in Vereinen, in: Digel, Helmut (Hrsg.): Sport im Verein und Verband, Schorndorf, S. 123-137.

Heinemann, Klaus / Horch, Heinz-Dieter (1988): Strukturbesonderheiten des Sportvereins, in: Digel, Helmut (Hrsg.): Sport im Verein und Verband, Schorndorf, S. 108-122.

Heinemann, Klaus / Schubert, Manfred (1992): Ehrenamtlichkeit und Hauptamtlichkeit in Sportvereinen, Schorndorf.

Heinemann, Klaus / Schubert, Manfred (1994): Der Sportverein. Ergebnisse einer repräsentativen Untersuchung, Schorndorf.

Herzberg, Frederick (1982): The managerial choice: To be efficient and to be human, 2. Aufl., Salt Lake City.

Horch, Heinz-Dieter (2005): Personalwirtschaft in Sportorganisationen, in: Breuer, Christoph / Thiel, Ansgar (Hrsg.): Handbuch Sportmanagement, Schorndorf, S. 80-93.

Horch, Heinz-Dieter / Hovemann, Gregor / Schubert, Manfred (2007): Bezahlte Mitarbeit im Sportverein, in: Breuer, Christoph (Hrsg.): Sportentwicklungsbereicht 2005/2006 – Analyse zur Situation der Sportvereine in Deutschland, Köln, S. 166-194.

Jung, Hans (2006): Personalwirtschaft, München u.a.

Jütting, Dieter, H. (1996): Mitarbeitende Mitglieder und verbandliche Qualifizierungssysteme im deutschen Sportvereinswesen: Struktureigenschaften und Modernisierungserwartungen, in: Jütting, Dieter, H. / Jochinke, Michael (Hrsg.): Standpunkte und Perspektiven zur Ehrenamtlichkeit im Sport, Münster, S. 73-87.

Jütting, Dieter, H. (1998): Geben und nehmen: ehrenamtliches Engagement als sozialer Tausch, in: Strachwitz, Rupert (Hrsg.): Dritter Sektor - Dritte Kraft, Stuttgart, S. 271-290.

Linz, Lothar (2004): Erfolgreiches Teamcoaching. Ein sportpsychologisches Handbuch für Trainer, Aachen.

Marr, Rainer (2001): ‚Arbeitszeitmanagement: Die Nutzung der Ressource „Zeit" - zur Legitimation einer bisher vernachlässigten Managementaufgabe, in: Marr, Rainer (Hrsg.): Arbeitszeitmanagement: Grundlagen und Perspektiven, 3. Aufl., Berlin, S. 13-32.

Nagel, Siegfried (2006): Sportvereine im Wandel, Schondorf.

Nagel, Siegfried / Conzelmann, Achim / Gabler, Hartmut (2004): Sportvereine Auslaufmodell oder Hoffnungsträger, Tübingen.

Nagel, Siegfried / Schlesinger, Torsten (2008): Teamentwicklung in Sportspielmannschaften des Hochleistungssports, in: Pawlowsky, Peter / Mistele, Peter (Hrsg.): Hochleistungsmanagement: Entwicklung und Nutzung vorhandener Leistungspotenziale in Organisationen, Wiesbaden.

Neuberger, Oswald (1994): Personalentwicklung, 2. Aufl., Stuttgart.

Oechsler, Walter A. (2006): Personal und Arbeit. Grundlagen des Human Resource Management und der Arbeitgeber-Arbeitnehmer-Beziehungen, 8. Aufl., München u.a.

Pankoke, Eckart (1996): Ehre und Engagement im Sport. Zwischen starker Kultur und aktiver Gesellschaft, in: Jütting, Dieter, H. / Jochinke, Michael (Hrsg.): Standpunkte und Perspektiven zur Ehrenamtlichkeit im Sport, Münster, S. 109-113.

Pawlowsky, Peter / Mistele, Peter (2008): Hochleistungsmanagement: Entwicklung und Nutzung vorhandener Leistungspotenziale in Organisationen, Wiesbaden.

Pitsch, Werner / Emrich, Eike (1997): „Krise des Ehrenamts?" Eine Analyse alter Daten, in: Sportwissenschaft, Heft 4, S. 391-408.

Rosenstiel, Lutz v.(2003). Führung von Mitarbeitern. Handbuch für erfolgreiches Personalmanagement, Stuttgart.

Scholz, Christian (2000): Personalmanagement. Informationsorientierte und verhaltensorientierte Grundlagen, 5. Aufl., München.

Schubert, Manfred / Horch, Heinz-Dieter / Hovemann, Gregor (2007): Ehrenamtliches Engagement in Sportvereinen, in: Breuer, Christoph (Hrsg.): Sportentwicklungsbereicht 2005/2006 – Analyse zur Situation der Sportvereine in Deutschland, Köln, S. 196-225.

Staehle, Wolfgang H. (1999): Management. Eine verhaltenswissenschaftliche Perspektive, 8. Aufl., München.

Tannenbaum, Robert / Schmidt, Warren H. (1958): How to Choose a Leadership Pattern, in: Harvard Business Review, Heft 3, S. 95-101.

Thiel, Ansgar / Meier, Heiko (2005): Besonderheiten der Personalführung in Sportorganisationen, in: Breuer, Christoph / Thiel, Ansgar (Hrsg.): Handbuch Sportmanagement, Schorndorf, S. 15-28.

Thiel, Ansgar / Meier, Heiko / Cachay, Klaus (2006): Hauptberuflichkeit im Sportverein: Voraussetzungen und Hindernisse, Schorndorf.

Trosse, Hans-Dieter (2003): Die erfolgreiche Mannschaft: Untersuchungen und Ergebnisse aus der ersten Fußball und Handballbundesliga, Aachen.

Wadsack, Ronald (1992): Attraktives Ehrenamt. Motivation ehrenamtlicher Mitarbeiter, Witten.

Wadsack, Ronald (2004): Mitarbeitermanagement im Sport, in: Krüger, Arnd / Dreyer, Axel (Hrsg.): Sportmanagement, München u.a., S. 113-140.

Wehling, Margret (1993): Personalmanagement für unbezahlte Arbeitskräfte, Gladbach u.a.

Wehling, Margret (1996): Zum Problem der Honorierung und Gratifikation: Anmerkungen aus betriebswirtschaftlicher Sicht, in: Jütting, Dieter, H. / Jochinke, Michael (Hrsg.): Standpunkte und Perspektiven zur Ehrenamtlichkeit im Sport, Münster, S. 109-113.

Wimmer, Peter / Neuberger, Oswald (1998): Personalwesen. 2. Personalplanung, Beschäftigungssysteme, Personalkosten, Personalcontrolling, Stuttgart.

Winkler, Joachim (1988): Das Ehrenamt: Zur Soziologie ehrenamtlicher Tätigkeit dargestellt am Beispiel der deutschen Sportverbände, Schorndorf.

Wilhelm, Andreas (2001): Im Team zum Erfolg. Ein sozial-motivationales Verhaltensmodell zur Wettkampfleistung, Lengerich.

Weiterführende Ressourcen

Literatur

Badelt, Christoph (1997): Handbuch der Nonprofit Organisation, Stuttgart.

Eckardstein, Dudo v. (1997): Personalmanagement in NPOs, in: Badelt, Christoph (Hrsg.): Handbuch der Nonprofit-Organisationen. Strukturen und Management, Stuttgart, S. 257-276.

Michalik, Claudia (2002): Ehrenamtliches Engagement im Profifußball – ein Auslaufmodell? in: Schewe, Gerhard / Littkemann, Jörn (Hrsg.): Sportmanagement, Schorndorf, S. 99-114.

Radtke, Sabine (2007): Ehrenamtliche Führungskräfte im organisierten Sport, Hamburg.

Schack, Thomas / Thiel, Ansgar (2005): Gesprächsführung in Sportorganisationen, in: Breuer, Christoph / Thiel, Ansgar (Hrsg.): Handbuch Sportmanagement, Schorndorf, S. 29-46.

Thiel, Ansgar / Ribler, Angelika (2005): Mediation von Konflikteskalationen in Sportorganisationen, in: Breuer, Christoph / Thiel, Ansgar (Hrsg.): Handbuch Sportmanagement, Schorndorf, S. 47-60.

Trosien, Gerhard / Dinkel, Michael (2004): Personalentwicklung im Sportmanagement, Butzbach-Griedel.

Links

Deutsche Gesellschaft für Personalführung e.V.:
http://www1.dgfp.com/dgfp/data/index.php

Deutscher Olympischer Sportbund, Förderung Ehrenamt:
http://www.ehrenamt-im-sport.de

Internationale Fitness- und Aerobic-Akademie:
http://www.ifaa.de

Weiterbildungsangebote im Bereich Sport und Management:
http://www.ist.de/Sport-und-Management

Kapitel 8: Finanzierung im Sport

Gregor Hovemann

Lernziele

Nach der Durchsicht dieses Kapitels sollte der Leser in der Lage sein,

- die Begriffe Finanzierung und Investition zu definieren und ihren Zusammenhang zu erläutern.
- unterschiedliche Formen der Finanzierung in Sportorganisationen voneinander abzugrenzen.
- die Bedeutung der Finanzierung für das Management von Sportorganisationen allgemein und der unterschiedlichen Formen der Finanzierung im speziellen bewerten und einordnen zu können.
- Probleme der Finanzierung in Sportorganisationen identifizieren und lösen zu können.

Überblick über das Kapitel

In dem folgenden Kapitel werden grundlegende Aspekte der Finanzierung und Investition in Sportorganisationen vorgestellt und diskutiert. Hierzu werden zunächst die zentralen Begriffe definiert, um darauf aufbauend die unterschiedlichen Formen der Finanzierung zu beschreiben und in ihrer Bedeutung für Sportorganisationen zu diskutieren. Damit soll der Leser anhand zahlreicher Beispiele aus dem Sport die Logik der unterschiedlichen Formen der Finanzierung verstehen lernen. Das Kapitel schließt mit dem Beispiel von Borussia Dortmund als Fallstudie zur Finanzierung im Sport.

8.1 Einführung in die Thematik

Für die folgenden Ausführungen ist es wichtig, dass die zentralen Begrifflichkeiten in ihrer Bedeutung geklärt und v.a. auch in den differenzierten Erscheinungsformen und Unterkategorien erfasst werden. Somit erfolgt nun in zwei kurzen Abschnitten die Klärung des Begriffes „Finanzierung" und „Investition".

8.1.1 Finanzierung

Investitionen in Sportorganisationen müssen finanziert werden. Dies bedeutet, dass in einer Sportorganisation zur Beschaffung von Produktionsfaktoren geklärt sein muss, woher die Finanzmittel hierfür stammen. Dies kann einerseits aus dem innerbetrieblichen Leistungsprozess geschehen, dann spricht man von einer Innenfinanzierung, oder aber von unternehmensexternen Quellen stammen, dann spricht man von einer Außenfinanzierung. Auch sind zur Beurteilung der Finanzierung die Rechtsstellung der Kapitalgeber und die Kapitalhaftung wichtig. Hierdurch kommt man zur Unterscheidung in Eigenfinanzierung und Fremdfinanzierung. Die folgende Abbildung veranschaulicht Alternativen der Kapitalaufbringung nach diesen vier begrifflichen Zuordnungen und stellt sie in einen logischen Zusammenhang:

212

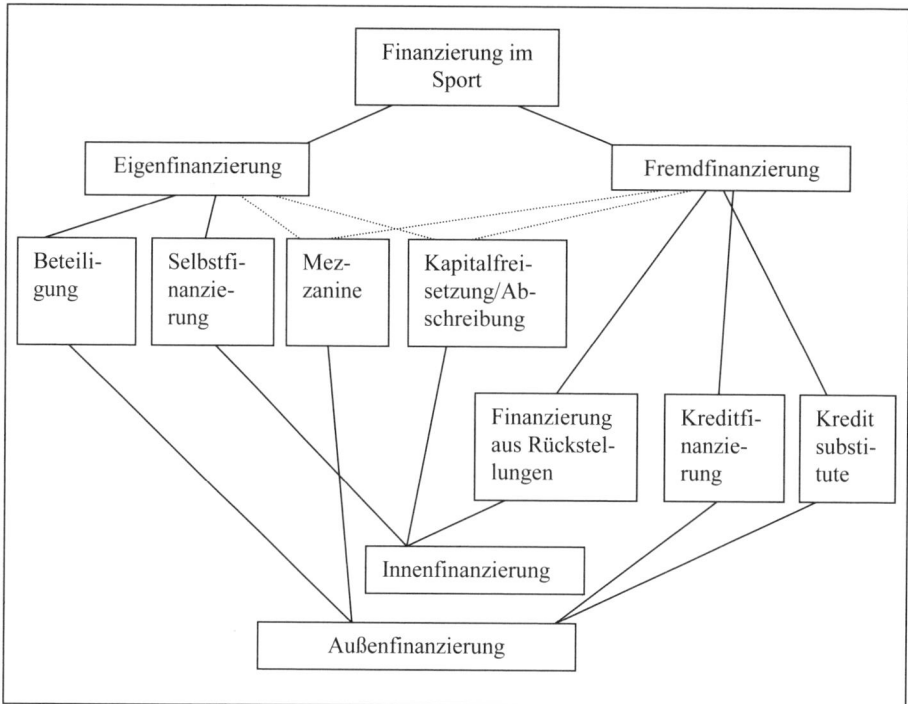

Abb. 1: Einteilungen der Finanzierung in Sportorganisationen im Gesamtüberblick

Die gestrichelten Linien sollen im Unterschied zu den durchgezogenen Linien, die eine eindeutige Zuordnung symbolisieren, anzeigen, dass beispielsweise die Kapitalfreisetzung nicht eindeutig der Eigenfinanzierung oder der Fremdfinanzierung zuzuordnen ist, sondern nur der Blick auf das konkrete Beispiel eine Zuordnung ermöglicht. Die richtige Bewertung der Finanzierung im Rahmen des Managementprozesses ermöglicht den Sportmanagern eine Sicherstellung einer stabilen und nachhaltigen Ressourcenversorgung, damit das dauerhafte Geschäft gesichert bleibt. Für einen Sportmanager, der seine Organisation erfolgreich steuern möchte, ist es also von großer Wichtigkeit, ein Gespür für die zentralen Probleme der Finanzierung zu haben, aus der er die Kompetenz zur Problemlösungsfähigkeit entwickeln kann.

Grundlage für die Überlassung von Geldmitteln und Kapital ist eine vertragliche Einigung, die so genannten Finanzierungskontrakte. Unter Finanzierungskontrakten ganz allgemein werden im Folgenden nicht nur Verträge verstanden, die eine Bereitstellung und Überlassung einer bestimmten Kapitalsumme für einen bestimmten Zeitraum unter bestimmten Bedingungen von einem Kapitalgeber an einen Kapitalnehmer zum Vertragsgegenstand haben (Bernet/Denk, 2000). Vielmehr soll in Anlehnung an die sehr weite Definition von „Finanzierung" von Swoboda (1973) die Gestaltung der Beziehung der beteiligten Finanzakteure untersucht werden. Swoboda zeigt sehr anschaulich auf, dass eine zu enge Definition des Finanzierungsbegriffs, bei dem der Zugang von liquiden Mitteln in den Vordergrund gerückt wird, nicht sinnvoll ist, da damit vielfältige Aspekte nicht berücksichtigt würden wie etwa Sacheinlagen oder auch das Leasing. Wichtige Aspekte von Finanzierungsentscheidungen haben aber „nicht nur zum Inhalt, in welchem Verhältnis Kapital von Anteilseignern und Kreditgebern beschafft werden soll, sie beziehen sich auch auf die zu gewährenden Kreditbedingungen, wie die Fristigkeit der Mittel, Sicherungen, die Zinssätze und die Informations- und Mitspracherechte der Kapitalgeber" (Swoboda, 1973, S. 9).

Demnach sollen im Folgenden, diese sechs Aspekte als Grundbausteine von Finanzierungskontrakten verstanden werden:

1. *Rechtstellung des Kapitalgebers*: Hierbei gilt es zu untersuchen, welche günstige bzw. ungünstige Situation sich aus der rechtlichen Stellung der Kapitalgeber zur Sportorganisation ergibt. Mit der Ausprägung dieser Variablen sind insbesondere Haftungsfragen, Mitbestimmung und Mitwirkungsrechte sowie Entscheidungen über die Verwendung von Residualeinkommen verbunden. In einer groben Einteilung wird in diesem Zusammenhang in der Betriebswirtschaftsehre in die Kategorien Eigenkapital, Fremdkapital und hybrides Kapital eingeteilt. Dabei steht Eigenkapital unbefristet zur Verfügung und partizipiert an eventuellen Gewinnen und Verlusten. Fremdkapital steht demgegenüber lediglich zeitlich befristet zur Verfügung, wofür ein vertraglich fixiertes Entgelt zu zahlen ist (Zins). Hybrides Kapital nimmt eine Zwischenposition zwischen diesen beiden Kapitalarten ein und ist wegen seiner Eigenschaften weder eindeutig dem Eigenkapital noch dem Fremdkapital zuzuordnen.

2. *Preiselemente:* In Finanzierungskontrakten sind die einzelnen Preiselemente zu fixieren, welche neben der Berücksichtigung der zeitlichen Überlassung des Kapitals auch die Verteilung des Risikos zum Ausdruck bringen.

3. *Fristenelemente:* Vielfach lassen sich Vor- und Nachteile bei der Finanzierung daraus ableiten – und hiermit ist v.a. die Liquiditätssituation angesprochen –, zu welchen Zeitpunkten die Ein- und Auszahlungen vertraglich fixiert werden. Typisch sind hier Unterscheidungen in starre, gestaffelte und variabilisierte Zins- und Tilgungszahlungen.

4. *Amortisationselemente:* Neben den Zahlungszeitpunkten ist in Finanzierungskontrakten auch die Höhe der Zahlungen zu vereinbaren. Dabei ist nicht nur denkbar, eine rein betragsmäßige Vereinbarung über die Zahlungen im Sinne starrer oder gestaffelter Beträge zu fixieren. Vielmehr ist auch möglich, dass Tilgungsbeträge als Funktion einer unternehmerischen Variablen definiert werden. So ist es etwa in der Fußballbundesliga üblich (Beispiel 1. FC Köln), dass die Zahlungen für die Sportstättennutzung von der Zugehörigkeit zur ersten oder zweiten Liga abhängen. Konkret zahlt der 1. FC Köln rund 6 Mio. € jährli-

cher Miete, wenn er in der ersten Fußballbundesliga angehört und nur 3 Mio. €, wenn er der zweiten Fußballbundesliga angehört (Vornholz, 2005a).

5. *Besicherungselemente:* V.a. die Risikokosten, die die Preiselemente beeinflussen, können durch Besicherungselemente beeinflusst werden. Immobilien wie Sportstätten stellen grundsätzlich einen positiven Aspekt bezüglich der Besicherungsmöglichkeit dar.

6. *Optionselemente:* Schließlich lassen sich Finanzkontrakte durch Optionselemente flexibilisieren und den individuellen Bedürfnissen der Finanzkontraktpartner anpassen. Beispiele sind Kaufoptionen im Rahmen von Leasingverträgen oder auch die Gewährung von Kreditlinien, deren Ausschöpfung optional ist.

Stellt man beispielhaft Eigenkapital und Fremdkapital anhand unterschiedlicher Bewertungskriterien gegenüber, so zeigt sich folgendes:

- *Haftung*: Der Eigenkapitalgeber haftet mindestens in Höhe seiner Einlage und hat damit eine Eigentümerstellung inne, die der Gläubigerstellung gegenüberzustellen ist. Diese hat der Fremdkapitalgeber inne und mit dieser ist keine Haftung verbunden.

- *Ertragsbeteiligung*: Während der Eigenkapitalgeber in vollem Umfang an Gewinn und Verlust partizipiert, hat der Fremdkapitalgeber normalerweise einen festen Zinsanspruch, erhält aber keinen Anteil am Residualeinkommen.

- *Finanzierungsvolumen*: Eigenkapital ist auf die Vermögenslage der Eigenkapitalgeber beschränkt, während das Fremdkapital prinzipiell unbeschränkt zur Verfügung steht, wobei die Aufnahme durch die mangelnde Bonität limitiert sein kann.

- *Fristigkeit*: Eigenkapital wird in der Regel unbefristet zur Verfügung gestellt, während die Fremdkapitaltilgung terminiert ist.

- *Mitsprache*: Eigenkapitalgeber erwerben in der Regel durch das dem Unternehmen zur Verfügung gestellten Kapital Mitspracherechte. Derartige Mitspracherechte sind normalerweise nicht mit der zur Verfügungstellung von Fremdkapital verknüpft.

Wenngleich sich noch weitere Bewertungskriterien diskutieren ließen, zeigt diese Aufstellung sehr deutlich, wie wichtig es ist, dass der Sportmanager unterschiedliche Alternativen der Kapitalaufbringung kennt und anhand verschiedenen Kriterien differenziert bewerten und einordnen kann.

8.1.2 Investition

Die Verwendung der durch die Kapitalaufbringung erlangten Mittel stellt die Investitionsentscheidung dar, die ein Sportmanager in einer Sportorganisation zu treffen hat. Investitionsarten werden häufig nach der Art der Vermögensgegenstände eingeteilt. Nach dieser Unterscheidung unterteilt man in Sach- und Finanzinvestitionen sowie immaterielle Investitionen. In Sportorganisationen stellen Sachinvestitionen beispielsweise der Erwerb von Grundstücken für die Errichtung neuer Trainingsanlagen, der Erwerb von Gebäuden wie Sporthallen, Stadien oder einem Vereinsheim oder auch der Kauf von neuen Sportgeräten dar. Finanzinvestitionen können zum Beispiel Beteiligungen an anderen Unternehmen sein, um eine Diversifikationsstrategie zu realisieren (siehe abschließendes Fallbeispiel weiter unten). Allerdings ist die Beteiligung an mehreren und zwischen Sportorganisationen innerhalb einer Liga in der Regel verboten bzw. stark eingeschränkt, um wettbewerbliche Verzerrungen zu unterbinden bzw. zumindest zu minimieren. Immaterielle Investitionen sind Ausgaben für Werbung oder auch die für die Ausbildung der Spieler eines Sportclubs. Das Besondere an immateriellen Investitionen ist, dass zwar die erforderlichen Auszahlungen direkt messbar sind, dass es aber sehr schwierig und teilweise unmöglich ist, die aus diesen Investitionen erzielten Einnahmen exakt zu quantifizieren. Wichtig für Sportmanager ist weiterhin die Unterscheidung aller Investitionsausgaben (Bruttoinvestitionen) in (1) Ersatzinvestitionen bzw. Reinvestitionen und (2) Nettoinvestitionen/Erweiterungsinvestitionen. Erstere dienen lediglich der Erhaltung der Produktionskapazität, während die Zweiten zu einer Ausweitung der Produktionskapazität führen. Allerdings sind Abgrenzungen dieser beiden Formen nicht immer trennscharf möglich. Wird beispielsweise ein altes Stadion durch ein neues mit mehr Sitzplätzen und zusätzlich Logenplätzen errichtet, handelt es sich sowohl um eine Ersatz- als auch eine Erweiterungsinvestition.

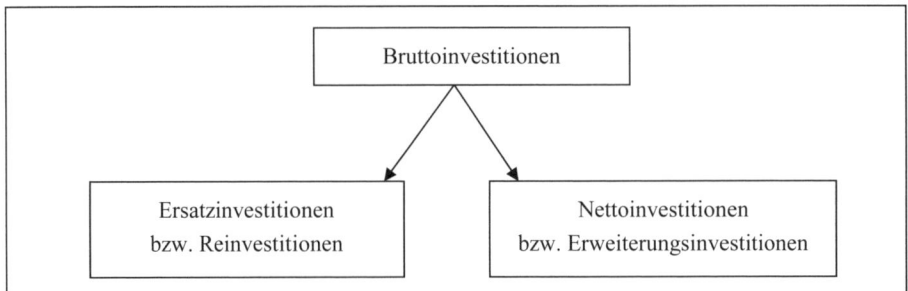

Abb. 2: Typen der Investition

Dem Begriff der Investition steht der Begriff der Desinvestition gegenüber. Dies bedeutet, dass beim Investitionsprozess Kapital gebunden wird, während beim Desinvestitionsprozess Kapital freigesetzt wird. Der Kauf einer Bewässerungsanlage für das Trainingsfreigelände stellt eine Form der Bindung von Kapital dar, während der Verkauf von Merchandisingartikeln eine Form der Kapitalfreisetzung ist.

216

8.2 Besonderheiten der Finanzierungssituation von Sportorganisationen

Die Situation von Sportorganisationen unterscheidet sich in einigen Punkten von der normaler Marktakteure. Diese Besonderheiten lassen sich durch folgende Aspekte erfassen. Werden die Rechte an Profiligen zentral vermarktet, haben Organisationen wie die Deutsche Fußball Liga eine *Monopolstellung*. Die Finanzielle Konsequenz ist die, dass sich somit wegen mangelnder Konkurrenz erhöhte Einnahmen erzielen lassen. Allerdings ist die gesamte Liga mit ihren Mitgliedern (Vereinen) nicht nur durch diese Zusammenarbeit in einem Kartell gekennzeichnet (Kooperation), sondern konkurrieren die Vereine beim Spiel um die nationale Meisterschaft auch gegeneinander (Konkurrenz). Diese Gleichzeitigkeit von Kooperation und Konkurrenz wird als *Koopetition, assoziative Konkurrenz* oder auch *Cooperenz* bezeichnet (Franck, 1995; Lehman/Weigand, 2002; Dietl/Pauli, 2002). Zum Erhalt eines möglichst spannenden Wettbewerbs unter möglichst gleichstarken Konkurrenten ist eine finanzierungsrelevante Konsequenz die Umverteilung der in der Zentralvermarktung erzielten Einnahmen. Weitere Besonderheit für Profisportorganisationen ist eine Verschiebung in der strategischen *Zielsetzung*. Dominiert in normalen erwerbswirtschaftlichen Unternehmen die Gewinnerzielungsabsicht, kann dieses Ziel in Sportorganisationen durch das Ziel des sportlichen Erfolgs dominiert werden. Die finanzierungsrelevante Konsequenz ist die, dass sich in Profisportorganisationen häufig desolate Eigenkapitalausstattungen identifizieren lassen und teilweise über mehrere Perioden keine Gewinne realisiert werden. Vielfach diskutiert ist weiterhin die Gefahr des Wohlstand zersetzenden Rüstungswettlaufs (Franck, 2000). Dieser kann den Sportvereinen bzw. Profiteams die notwendige Liquidität entziehen, die Verpflichtungen aus Finanzkontrakten einzuhalten. Bezüglich der Gefahr von Überinvestitionen zeigen Dietl/Franck/Roy (2003, S. 539) in einer modelltheoretischen Untersuchung auf, dass „die Wahrscheinlichkeit einer Überinvestition der Clubs in die Spieler ceteris paribus steigt, je größer die Preisdifferenz zwischen den Turnierrängen ist, je größer die Liga ist, je geringer die Produktivitätsunterschiede zwischen den Clubs sind und je mehr die Clubs gezwungen sind, simultan zu investieren".

8.3 Alternativen der Finanzierung im Sport

In einem ersten Überblick zeigt die folgende Abbildung aus einer Befragung der Fußballmanager der ersten beiden Fußballbundesligen, wie die Experten unterschiedliche Finanzierungsformen einschätzen (vgl. Abb. 3). Nach Meinung der Befragten wird der klassischen „Kreditfinanzierung" nach wie vor die größte Wichtigkeit beigemessen. Die Finanzierungsform des „Private Equity" hat in ihrer Bedeutung im Vergleich zu den Untersuchungsergebnissen aus dem Jahr 2004 deutlich zugenommen. Abgenommen hat demgegenüber die Bedeutung von „Asset Backed Securities" und zwar von 25 % im Jahr 2004 auf nur noch 3 % im Jahr 2007. Das Thema „Börsengang" scheint nach einer Phase der Ernüchterung zumindest bei einigen wenigen Clubs wieder an Bedeutung zu gewinnen. Spielte diese Finanzierungsform in der Befragung des Jahres 2004 bei keinem Club eine Rolle, so ist sie aktuell zumindest für 10 % der Clubs bedeutsam.

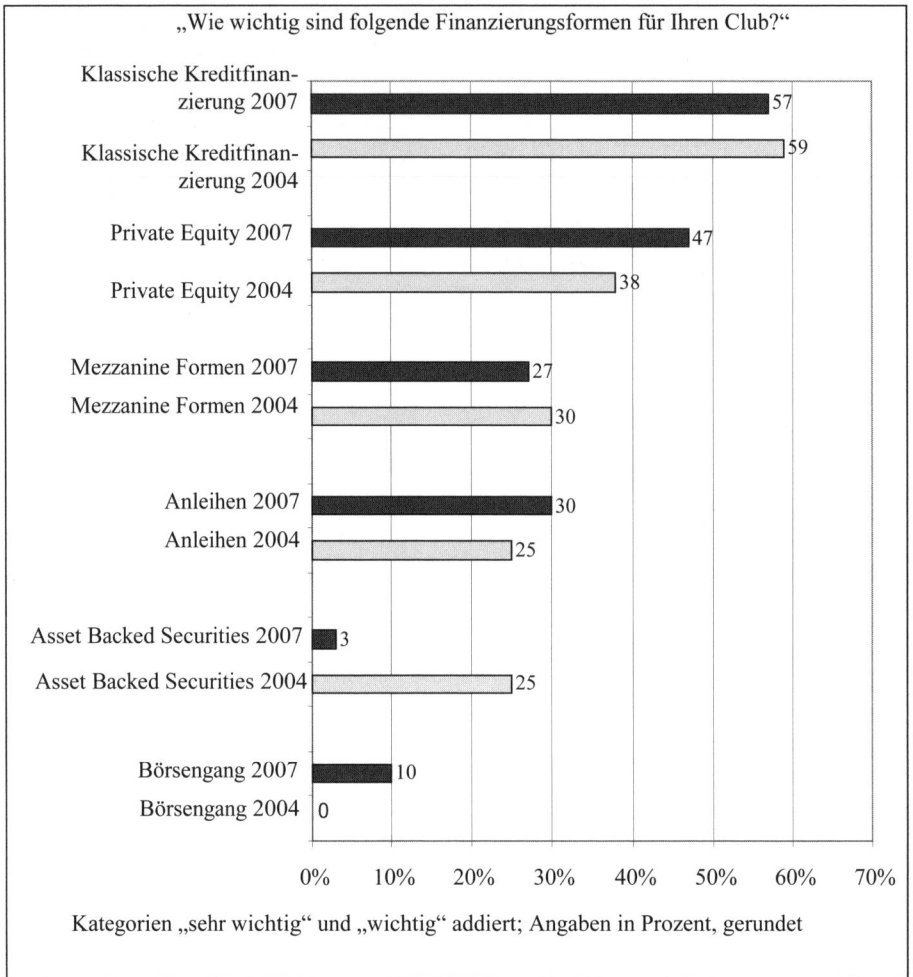

"Wie wichtig sind folgende Finanzierungsformen für Ihren Club?"

Finanzierungsform	Prozent
Klassische Kreditfinanzierung 2007	57
Klassische Kreditfinanzierung 2004	59
Private Equity 2007	47
Private Equity 2004	38
Mezzanine Formen 2007	27
Mezzanine Formen 2004	30
Anleihen 2007	30
Anleihen 2004	25
Asset Backed Securities 2007	3
Asset Backed Securities 2004	25
Börsengang 2007	10
Börsengang 2004	0

0%   10%   20%   30%   40%   50%   60%   70%

Kategorien „sehr wichtig" und „wichtig" addiert; Angaben in Prozent, gerundet

Abb. 3: Einschätzung unterschiedlicher Formen der Finanzierung seitens der Manager der ersten beiden Fußballbundesligen in Deutschland
Quelle: Ernst & Young (2007), S. 9

Um die unterschiedlichen Formen, wie eine Sportorganisation sich finanzieren kann, strukturiert und systematisch darzustellen, wird zunächst auf die Möglichkeiten der Innenfinanzierungen und dann auf die Möglichkeiten der Außenfinanzierungen eingegangen (vgl. Abb. 1).

8.3.1 Innenfinanzierungen im Sport

Innenfinanzierungen werden üblicherweise in drei Unterformen eingeteilt: Diese sind die Selbstfinanzierung, die Finanzierung über Kapitalfreisetzung und die Finanzierung aus Rückstellungen. Was diese Formen im Einzelnen konkret in Sportorganisationen bedeuten, soll im Folgenden erläutert und diskutiert werden.

8.3.1.1 Selbstfinanzierung

Selbstfinanzierung bedeutet, dass aus den Mitteln finanziert wird, die der Organisation als Gewinne im Unternehmen zurückbleiben und nicht an die Anteilseigner ausgeschüttet werden. Dabei kann der Finanzierungseffekt antizipativ auch dadurch erreicht werden, dass die Überschussverwendungsentscheidung vor der eigentlichen bilanziellen Gewinnermittlung erfolgt.

Als Beispiel kann angeführt werden, dass eine *Selbstfinanzierung einer Investition* vorliegt, wenn die Geschäftsführung einer Sportorganisation entscheidet, dass von den Gewinnen, die im letzten Geschäftsjahr erzielt wurden, ein bestimmter Betrag für den Kauf neuer Trainingsgeräte verwendet wird. Diese Form der Finanzierung hat viele Vorteile, da keine externe Interessengruppen beteiligt sind, sich auch keine Verschiebung in den Anteilseignerstruktur ergibt, kein Zinsaufwand anfällt und auch keine Tilgungszahlungen in Zukunft folgen. Allerdings muss der begrenzte Rahmen der Selbstfinanzierung auch gesehen werden, insbesondere vor dem Hintergrund, dass unter den Clubs der ersten und zweiten Fußballbundesliga in den letzten Jahre nur wenige waren, die überhaupt Gewinne erwirtschaftet haben.

8.3.1.2 Kapitalfreisetzung

Abschreibungen in Unternehmen geben an, welche Wertminderungen abnutzbarer Anlagegüter als periodenbezogener Aufwand erfolgt sind. Neben einem kalkulatorischen Effekt im Rahmen der Kostenkalkulation können Abschreibungen auch einen Finanzierungseffekt haben, denn Abschreibungen spiegeln den Desinvestitionsprozess wieder. Dazu sind allerdings zwei Voraussetzungen notwendig. So müssen in Höhe der Abschreibungen Umsatzerlöse erzielt worden sein und als Einzahlungen bei der Sportorganisation eingegangen sein.

8.3.1.3 Rückstellungen

Die Finanzierung aus Rückstellungen ist eine Form der innerbetrieblichen Fremdfinanzierung. Dabei sind Rückstellungen dadurch gekennzeichnet, dass sie Verbindlichkeiten darstellen, die noch nicht dem Grunde nach oder aber der Höhe und Fälligkeit nach feststehen. Rückstellungen sind beispielsweise für ungewisse Verbindlichkeiten wie Pensionszahlungen, drohende Verluste aus schwebenden

Geschäften oder aber Gewährleistungen ohne rechtliche Verpflichtungen, etc. zu bilden.

Betrachtet man vor diesem Hintergrund der Innenfinanzierungsmöglichkeiten als Beispiel die Umsatzerlöse der Vereine der ersten deutschen Fußballbundesliga, so waren diese in den vergangenen Jahren wie folgt strukturiert:

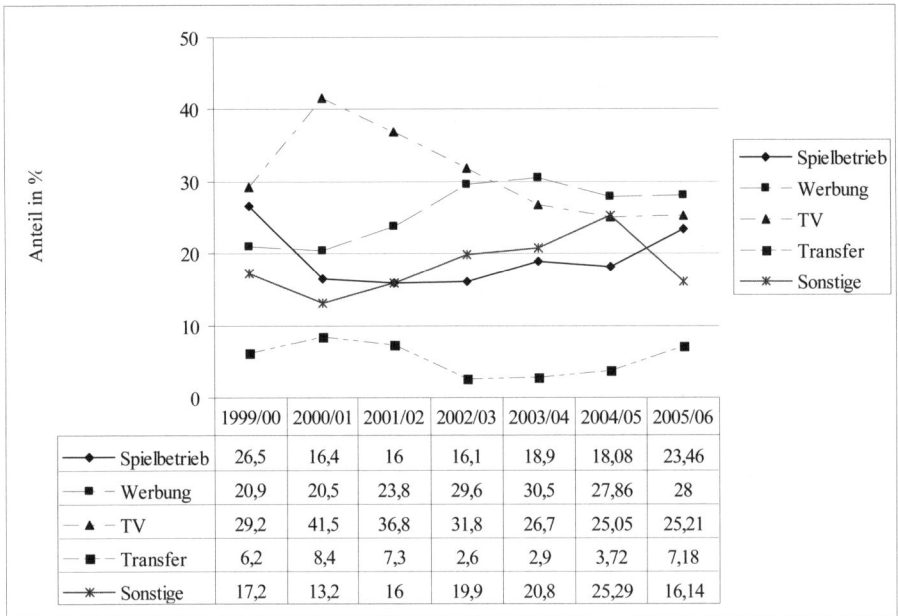

	1999/00	2000/01	2001/02	2002/03	2003/04	2004/05	2005/06
Spielbetrieb	26,5	16,4	16	16,1	18,9	18,08	23,46
Werbung	20,9	20,5	23,8	29,6	30,5	27,86	28
TV	29,2	41,5	36,8	31,8	26,7	25,05	25,21
Transfer	6,2	8,4	7,3	2,6	2,9	3,72	7,18
Sonstige	17,2	13,2	16	19,9	20,8	25,29	16,14

Abb. 4: Struktur der Umsatzerlöse der Clubs der ersten Fußball Bundesliga
Quellen: DFL (2006), S. 25 ; DFL (2007), S. 48

Es zeigt sich, dass die Einnahmen aus TV-Erlösen einen sehr hohen Anteil innehatten, der jedoch deutlich gesunken ist. Einen recht kleinen Anteil stellen die Einnahmen aus den Transfererlösen dar. Jedoch ist auch ein seit der Saison 2002/2003 anhaltender ansteigender Trend des Anteils dieser Einnahmekategorie an den Gesamterlösen erkennbar. Insgesamt zeigt sich, dass die Proficlubs sich sehr gut diversifiziert finanzieren.

8.3.2 Außenfinanzierungen im Sport

Bei der Außenfinanzierung ist die (1) Beteiligungsfinanzierung von der (2) Kreditfinanzierung abzugrenzen. Weiterhin werden einige Sonderformen der Finanzierung in dieser Kategorie genannt. Dies sind einerseits (3) Mezzanine Formen und (4) Kreditsubstitute.

8.3.2.1 Beteiligungsfinanzierung

Bei der Beteiligungsfinanzierung wird Eigenkapital durch Kapitaleinlagen der bisherigen oder neuen Anteilseigner der Sportorganisation beschafft. Damit wird klar, dass die Beteiligungsfinanzierung in ihrer konkreten Ausprägung stark von der Rechtsform der Sportorganisation abhängt. So kann sich eine GmbH & Co. KG aA durch die Ausschüttung neuer Aktien neues Kapital beschaffen (Börsengang, siehe abschließendes Beispiel der Borussia Dortmund GmbH & Co. KG aA). Im Fall einer GmbH können die Gesellschafter ihre Einlagen erhöhen oder es tritt ein neuer Gesellschafter mit seiner Einlage hinzu. Nicht erlaubt sind allerdings Mehrfachbeteiligungen von Investoren in den Führungs- und Kontrollgremien der Fußballclubs. Dies stellt gerade auf der europäischen Ebene ein Problem dar. Die UEFA untersagt ein direktes Aufeinandertreffen von Clubs in europäischen Wettbewerben, wenn ein Investor eine Kapitalbeteiligung von mehr als 10 % besitzt. Nicht verboten ist grundsätzlich allerdings das Investment der Medienunternehmen und Vermarktungsgesellschaften. Betrachtet man die häufige Präsenz bestimmter Vermarkter, so kann dies allerdings als problematisch eingestuft werden. Beispielsweise ist bekannt, dass die Beeinflussung von Anstoßzeiten ein Konfliktbereich sein kann, da Liegeninteressen und Medieninteressen divergieren. Weiterhin ist denkbar, dass die Medien aus Eigeninteresse bestimmte Vereine gezielt fördern, um so deren Siegwahrscheinlichkeit zu erhöhen. Um Konflikte unterschiedlicher Interessensgruppe auszuschließen, sind bestimmte Gruppen wie Spieler, Trainer, Manager, Schiedsrichter, Spielervermittler, Aufsichtsräte von Fußballclubs, Lizenzprüfer, etc. in den Möglichkeiten der Finanzbeziehung zu Fußballclubs stark eingeschränkt (vgl. ausführlich hierzu: Schwendowius, 2003). Für Sportmanager ist die Erkenntnis besonders wichtig, dass die Beteiligungsfinanzierung zu einer Veränderung der Entscheidungsrechtestruktur der Anteilseigner führen kann.

8.3.2.2 Kreditfinanzierung

Kreditfinanzierung bedeutet, dass eine Sportorganisation bei einem Kreditinstitut die notwendigen Finanzmittel beschafft. Im Kreditvertrag üblicherweise zu fixierende Elemente sind der Kreditbetrag, der Auszahlungskurs, die Kreditart (Annuitäten-, Raten-, Festkredit), die Tilgung (Prozentsatz, Ratenhöhe, Laufzeit, Tilgungsfreijahre), die Zinsbindung, die Zahlungstermine, der Auszahlungstermin und die Bereitstellungszinsen (Albers, 2000). Die Festlegung der Rückzahlungszeitpunkte ist grundsätzlich frei vereinbar, jedoch können die Abschreibungsdauern eine erste Orientierung sinnvoller Laufzeiten geben. Das zentrale Merkmal der Kreditfinanzierung liegt darin, dass der Sportorganisation Kapital zur Verfügung gestellt wird und die Gegenleistung in festem Zahlungsanspruch besteht, der nicht vom Erfolg bzw. erzielten Zahlungsüberschüssen abhängt (Neus, 2003). Insbesondere Mitspracherechte sind im Rahmen der Kreditfinanzierung nicht vorgesehen bzw. nur im Falle der Insolvenzgefahr bzw. Zahlungsschwierigkeiten in Form von bedingten

Mitsprache- und Mitentscheidungsrechten üblich (Neus, 2003). Die Bonität bestimmt die Kreditwürdigkeit und aus ihr lässt sich ableiten, ob ein Kredit überhaupt erteilt wird und wenn ja, zu welchen Konditionen. Um Kredite zu erhalten, sind vielfach Bürgschaften notwendig. „Durch den Bürgschaftsvertrag verpflichtet sich der Bürge gegenüber dem Gläubiger eines Dritten, für die Erfüllung der Verbindlichkeit des Dritten einzustehen" (§ 765 BGB). Bei einer Ausfallbürgschaft verpflichtet sich der Bürge nur gegenüber dem Gläubiger für Verluste einzustehen, die nachweisbar nach einer erfolgten Zwangsvollstreckung noch vorhanden sind (Perridon/Steiner, 2003).

Bei den Profisportclubs liegt ein Problem darin, dass in der Regel die gesamte Finanzsituation der Clubs durch teilweise enorme Verschuldungsgrade zu einer ungünstigen Bonität führt (Ernst & Young, 2004). Die jüngsten Entwicklungen im Bankensektor (Basel II, s.u. Exkurs) lassen befürchten, dass es durch das individuelle Rating der Kreditnehmer zu einer weiteren Verschlechterung der Kreditkonditionen der Proficlubs kommen kann. Durch das Bosmann-Urteil ist eine weitere Schwierigkeit für die Profisportclubs entstanden, bankenübliche Sicherheiten zu stellen. War es vor dem Bosmann-Urteil möglich, die nach Ablauf der Spielerverträge anfallenden Ablösesummen als Sicherheiten an die Banken im Voraus abzutreten (Wertenbruch, 1993), besteht diese Möglichkeit nun nicht mehr. Aber auch für Sachwerte wie Immobilien bestehen Probleme des Einsatzes als Gläubigersicherheiten. So sind gerade die modernen Stadien im Fußball, die selten im Vereinsbesitz sind (Wilms, 2004), reine Fußballstadien, was die Abhängigkeit des Ertragswertes von Tabellenstand und von der Ligen-Zugehörigkeit deutlich erhöht (Dietl/Pauli, 2002). Eine andere Verwendung oder ein Verkauf ist beim Abstieg eines Clubs keine attraktive Alternative. Multifunktionsarenen bieten vielmehr aus portfoliotechnischen Überlegungen als Sicherheiten Vorteile, da im Sinne der Diversifizierung Risiko gestreut wird. Als Alternative zu den normalen bankenüblichen Sicherheiten sind für Profisportclubs Ersatzsicherheiten denkbar. Dies können zum Beispiel Zahlungsansprüche sein, welche abgetreten werden oder auch Bürgschaften von Kommunen und Ländern.

Durch deutliche Veränderungen der Rahmenbedingungen in der Kreditwirtschaft werden auch die Möglichkeiten der Finanzierung im Sport beeinflusst. Deshalb sollen im Folgenden die unter dem Stichwort „Basel II" zu subsumierenden Fakten im kurzen Überblick dargestellt und in ihrer Relevanz für die Finanzierung im Sport diskutiert werden.

Exkurs Basel II:

Der Kern der Initiative des Baseler Ausschusses für Bankenaufsicht, welches ein die Zentralbanken der wichtigsten Industrieländer repräsentierendes Gremium darstellt, liegt in der Individualisierung der Vergabekriterien für Kredite (Bundesverband deutscher Banken, 2003; Grundke/Spörk, 2003; Everling, 2003). So sollen die Kapitalanforderungen für Ausleihungen an die individuelle Bonität des jeweiligen Kreditnehmers gekoppelt werden. Diesbezüglich galt für alle Kredite bisher eine einheitliche Behandlung, bei der ein Unterlegungssatz von 8 % angesetzt worden ist. Diese pauschale Gleichstellung hatte zur Folge, dass schlechte Kreditrisiken durch gute subventioniert wurden. Nun sollen in Zukunft Kredite, die an Organisationen mit einem guten Rating vergeben werden, mit weniger Eigenkapital hinterlegt werden und an Organisationen mit einem negativen Rating mit einem entsprechend höheren Anteil. Somit soll eine verursachungsgerechte Kreditbepreisung realisiert werden, was mit einer Spreizung der Zinssätze einhergeht. Ziel von Basel II „ist die Erhöhung der Stabilität und der Wettbewerbsgleichheit des internationalen Finanzsystems" (Bundesverband Deutscher Banken, 2005, S. 8). Wenn also durch Basel II erreicht wird, dass das im Kreditgeschäft durch die Banken übernommene Risiko stärker bonitätsabhängig durch Eigenkapital besichert wird, so bewirkt dies, dass die Banken Anreize haben, in Zukunft moderne Verfahren der Bonitätsbeurteilung einzusetzen (Ahrweiler/Börner, 2003). Beim individuellen Rating werden insbesondere die folgenden Komponenten berücksichtigt:

1. Tätigkeitsbereich und generelle Brancheneinschätzung
2. Marktbedingungen und Position im Wettbewerb
3. Einschätzung der Qualität des Managements
4. Finanz- und Ertragslage
5. Prognosen bezüglich Umsätzen, Erträgen und der Finanzlage
6. Kontoführung
7. Haftungsaspekte der Rechtsform

Anhand dieser Kriterien wird deutlich, dass Sportorganisationen, die noch in der Rechtsform eines eingetragenen gemeinnützigen Sportvereins geführt werden, in Zukunft Schwierigkeiten haben werden, sich positiv mittels der durchgeführten Rankings darzustellen, da v.a. die Haftungsaspekte, aber auch Ertragsaspekte zu negativen Ratings führen werden. Insbesondere rein ehrenamtlich geführte Sportvereine werden auch Schwierigkeiten haben, eine positive Bewertung der Qualität des Managements zu erreichen. Dabei scheint sich in positiver Weise langsam die Erkenntnis zu verbreiten, dass die Vorgehensweise des Ratings von Non-Profit-Organisationen spezifischer Beurteilungsverfahren bedarf, deren genaue Ausgestaltung es allerdings noch zu erforschen gilt. Bei der Analyse von Non-Profit-Organisationen sind nach Kramer (2005) tendenziell eher die Merkmale aus den Bereichen der Vermögens- und Finanzlage zu fokussieren und weniger die der Ertragslage. In § 18 des Gesetzes über das Kreditwesen sind die folgenden Grenzen festgelegt: „Ein Kreditinstitut darf einen Kredit, der insgesamt 750.000 € oder 10 vom Hundert des haftenden Eigenkapitals des Instituts überschreitet, nur gewähren, wenn es sich von dem Kreditnehmer die wirtschaftlichen Verhältnisse, insbesondere durch Vorlage der Jahresabschlüsse, offen legen lässt". Vereinen kann also nur nahe gelegt werden, dass sie wie mittelständische

> Unternehmen auch das Wahlrecht nutzen und freiwillig einen Jahresabschluss aufstellen und diesen von einem Wirtschaftsprüfer prüfen und testieren lassen.

8.3.2.3 Mezzanine Finanzierung

Für Sportvereine bzw. Abteilungen des Profibereichs (z.B. in den Sportarten Fußball, Handball, Eishockey oder auch Basketball), die ihre Rechtsform gewandelt haben (Hovemann, 2005), eröffnen sich weitere Finanzierungsformen, die nicht eindeutig der Eigen- bzw. Fremdfinanzierung zuzuordnen sind, sondern eine Art Mischform darstellen. Darunter werden Nachrangdarlehen, stille Beteiligungen, Wandelanleihen und Genussscheine subsumiert. Gerade Genussscheine stellen dabei eine Form der Finanzierung dar, die sehr gut die Besonderheiten der Finanzströme in Profisportunternehmen berücksichtigen kann. Im Unterschied zu Anleihen, die lediglich mit Zins- und Rückzahlungsansprüchen verbunden sind, sind Genussscheinrechte auch durch vermögensrechtliche Ansprüche gekennzeichnet, die typischerweise Anteilseignern wie zum Beispiel Aktionären vorbehalten sind (Harrer/Janssen/Halbig, 2005; Küting/Dürr, 2005). Eine gesetzliche Definition des Genussscheinkapitalbegriffs existiert nicht, obwohl der Begriff in verschiedenen gesetzlichen Vorschriften verwendet wird (z.B. § 221 Abs. 3 des Aktiengesetzes, vgl. Tanski, 2005). In der Bilanz wird das Genussscheinkapital nach den Eigenkapitalpositionen und vor den Sonderposten mit Rücklagenanteil positioniert. Genussscheine verbriefen keine Mitgliedschaftsrechte, sondern lediglich Gläubigerrechte. Dabei ist in der Regel neben einer Basisverzinsung ein Anteil am Reingewinn und teilweise auch am Liquidationserlös vorgesehen. Es ist üblich, dass ebenfalls eine Beteiligung an eventuell realisierten Verlusten erfolgt. Damit liegen die Vorteile für den Emittenten in dem Aufbau eines Verlustpuffers, ohne dass die Genussscheininhaber wie andere Eigenkapitalgeber mitgliedschaftlichen Einfluss erlangen, der ihnen die Mitsprache an Unternehmensentscheidungen ermöglichen würde (Perridon/Steiner 2003; Ahrweiler/Börner, 2003). Wenngleich der Einsatz von Genussscheinkapital erst sehr zögerlich Einzug in den Bereich des Sport erhält und zunächst auch nur große bzw. umsatzstarke Profisportorganisationen diese innovative Form der Finanzierung wählen, gilt auch für kleinere Sportorganisationen, die im Wettkampfsystem partizipieren, dass ihre Einnahmen (Zuschauer, Sponsoren, etc.) vom sportlichen Erfolg abhängen. Somit stellt die bedingte Auszahlung an die Genussrechteinhaber auch für diese Art der Organisationen eine Chance dar, die Möglichkeiten bzw. das Spektrum der Finanzierung auszuweiten. Im Jahr 2004 wurden 5 Mio. € vom 1. FC Köln über Genussscheine beschafft. In diesem Fall ist das Genussrechtskapital als Sonderposten des Eigenkapitals anzusetzen, da folgende Kriterien erfüllt sind: (1) Es existiert eine Beteiligung an eventuell realisierten Verlusten, (2) Das Genussrechtskapital ist gegenüber dem Fremdkapital, als Kapital von sonstigen Kreditgebern nachrangig, (3) Das Genussrechtskapital steht der GmbH & Co. KGaA dauerhaft zur Verfügung und (4) Die Vergütung für die Bereitstellung des Kapitals ist abhängig von den realisierten Gewinnen (Ernst & Young, 2005). Somit liegt durch eine geringe Basisverzinsung und andererseits einer erfolgsabhängigen Komponente eine Finanzierungsform vor, die sehr gut zur vom sportlichen Erfolg abhängigen Finanzlage von Profisportunternehmen passt.

8.3.2.4 Kreditsubstitute

Von den möglichen Formen der Finanzierung durch Kreditsubstitute soll abschließend auf das Leasing, das Contracting und die so genannten Asset Backed Securities eingegangen werden.

Leasing:

Vom Grundgedanken sind Leasingverträge „Mietverträge mit besonderen Ausgestaltungsmerkmalen" und damit sind sie von Kreditkauf-, Miet- und Mietkaufverträgen abzugrenzen (Kroll, 2003, S. 7). Hierbei mangelt es dem aus dem anglo-amerikansichen stammenden Begriff „Leasing" in Deutschland einer Legaldefinition, ist aber in den Grundelementen der Vermietung und Verpachtung gemäß §§ 535 ff. BGB sehr nahe. Leasingverträge weisen folgende Grundstruktur auf: Der Leasingnehmer least beim Leasinggeber den Leasinggegenstand wie beispielsweise eine Sportstätte, die dieser plant und baut und zahlen dafür ein Entgelt in Form der Leasingrate. Der Leasinggeber kann sich, muss aber nicht, eine Finanzierung über einen Dritten finanzieren (Bank). Am Ende der Vertragslaufzeit besteht die Möglichkeit, dass die Sportstätte optional erworben werden kann. Möglich ist, dass der Leasingnehmer die Sportstätte an weitere Beteiligte vermietet. Neben eventuellen Regelungen zur Verteilung des Risikos zwischen Leasingnehmer und Leasinggeber sind die Besonderheiten von Leasingverträgen in Vereinbarungen wie Optionselementen, Mehr- bzw. Mindererlösbeteiligungen, Abschlusszahlungen etc. zu sehen (Kroll, 2003). Eine privatwirtschaftliche Initiative zur Förderung des Neubaus und der Sanierung von Sportanlagen mit Kunstrasenfläche, welche vom Deutschen Olympischen Sportbund empfohlen wird, stellt das Angebot der Sport StadiaNet GmbH Düsseldorf dar. Dabei übernimmt Sport StadiaNet als Generalunternehmer die Erstellung der Baumaßnahme, deren Finanzierung über zehn Jahre mit monatlich gleichen Raten sowie die fachspezifische Wartung der Sportstätte und garantiert die Bespielbarkeit für die Dauer von zehn Jahren. Sicherheiten sind grundsätzlich nicht notwendig. Die Sportstätte geht sofort ins Eigentum der Sportorganisation über. Falls ein Sportorganisation Auftraggeber ist, muss allerdings eine Kommune eine Bürgschaft übernehmen. Wie die folgende Beispielrechnung von Sport StadiaNet aufzeigt, sei bei einer Investitionssumme von 400.000 € eine Verminderung der monatlichen Belastung von 994,63 € möglich (vgl. Tab. 1).

Sport StadiaNet		Kommune
400.000 €	Investitionswert (netto)	400.000 €
inkl.	Risiko der Investitionsüberschreitung (10 %)	40.000 €
entfällt	Umsatzsteuer 16 %	70.400 €
0 €	Restwert	0 €
120	Laufzeit (in Monaten)	120
inkl.	Kalkulatorischer Zinssatz	4,35 %
vorsch.	Zahlungsweise	vorsch.
inkl.	Finanzierungsrate (monatlich)	5.209,96 €
inkl.	Wartung und	
inkl.	Bespielbarkeitsgarantie 2.000 Std./p.a. (monatlich)	1.740 €
inkl.	Absicherung des Zinsrisikos	31,93 €
5.317,93 €	Zwischensumme Rate (monatlich) netto	
669,33 €	Umsatzsteuer 16 % (nicht auf Zinsen)	inkl.
5.987,26 €	Monatliche Belastung insgesamt, inkl. MwSt.	6.981,89 €
994,63 €	Preisvorteil absolut	
14,25	Preisvorteil in %	

Tab. 1. Beispielrechnung für eine Leasingbelastung einer Kommune
In Anlehnung an: Sport StadiaNet (2004), S. 12

Contractingmodelle:
Grundsätzlich versteht man unter Contracting „Betriebs- und Finanzierungsverfahren zur Bereitstellung gebäudespezifischer Energiedienstleistungen" (Umweltbundesamt, 2002, S. 8). Dabei ist ein zentrales Element die Übernahme des Bewirtschaftungsrisikos von Seiten des die Sportstätte bewirtschaftenden Dienstleisters (Kirchmann/Lanzinger, 2003). Von den grundsätzlich denkbaren Varianten des Contractings interessiert hier insbesondere das Finanzierungscontracting. Dabei übernimmt ein Investor neben der Finanzierung der Anlagen in der Regel auch deren Planung. Die Refinanzierung erfolgt über Pacht-, Miet- oder Ratenzahlung des Betreibers der Sportstätten. Schätzungen gehen davon aus, dass sich der größte Teil (90 %) von Contractingvarianten der Kategorie des Energieliefercontractings zuordnen lässt, während nur ein kleiner Marktanteil (10 %) der Kategorie des Einsparcontractings zuzuordnen ist. Die Relevanz dieser Finanzierungsalternative zeigt sich in Schätzungen, die davon ausgehen, dass in Deutschland rund 122.000 Sportstätten prinzipiell für die Anwendung von Contracting geeignet sind und Minderungen des Energieverbrauchs von 5 bis 14 % möglich sind (Umweltbundesamt, 2002). Die betriebswirtschaftliche Sinnhaftigkeit des Contractings für Sportstätten liegt darin, dass durch die Kapitalwertbetrachtung unter Ansatz realistischer Zinssätze ein positiver Beitrag erwirtschaftet werden kann (Energieagentur Nordrhein-Westfalen, o.J.).

Die Chancen des Contractings sind v.a. darin zu sehen, dass bei Liquiditätsengpässen die Finanzierung von moderneren und optimierten energietechnischen Anlagen überhaupt möglich wird bzw. eine frühere und schnellere Umsetzung von Investitionsprojekten möglich wird. Weiterhin lassen sich Kostensenkungen durch

Effizienzsteigerungen erreichen und natürliche Ressourcen werden geschont bzw. die Umwelt wird entlastet. Durch den Effekt des Outsourcings von Leistungen lassen sich auch innovative Motivationswirkungen erreichen (im Vergleich zu traditionellen Hausmeistereien) und das technische Know-how des Contractors nutzen. Schließlich liegt ein wesentlicher Vorteil darin, dass eine Risikoverlagerung der Investition auf den Contractor stattfindet.

Forderungsverkauf und Forderungsverbriefungen:
Eine besondere Variante dieser Art der Finanzierungen stellen die so genannten ,Asset Backed Securities' dar. Dabei zeigt der Blick ins Ausland, dass die Finanzierung über Asset Backed Securities (ABS) zwar in einem ersten Schritt durchaus „exotisch" klingt, mit dreizehn europäischen Fußballclubs bis Ende 2002, die diesen Weg gewählt haben, aber nicht mehr von Einzelfällen gesprochen werden kann (Kern, 2003; Kern, 2007; vgl. auch Ernst & Young, 2004). In Deutschland ist Schalke 04 als Vorreiter mit einer großvolumigen Transaktion aufgetreten. Die Grundstruktur einer ABS Konstruktion lässt sich wie folgt beschreiben: Das Recht auf die Einnahmen aus der Nutzung einer Sportstätte werden an das ,spezial purpose vehicle' abgetreten, wofür ein bestimmter Betrag gezahlt wird. Als Besicherung dient die Immobilie, die Sportstätte. Die Forderungen werden eventuell mit anderen Forderungen gesammelt und verbrieft. Schließlich erfolgt ein Verkauf über einen Arrangeur an interessierte Investoren. Durch die Verbriefung von Forderungen können ursprünglich nicht handelbare Assets marktgängig gemacht werden. Dabei werden bestehende oder zukünftige Forderungen an eine speziell gegründete Gesellschaft (spezial purpose vehicle) veräußert, welche sich wiederum durch die Ausgabe von Wertpapieren refinanziert. Damit stellt dies eine dem traditionell üblichen Factoring verwandte Finanzierungsform dar. Für den Sportbereich typisch ist die Verbriefung zukünftiger Einnahmen aus dem Spielbetrieb (Ticketing, Vermietung von Logen, Catering etc.). Dabei lassen sich folgende Kriterien als so genannte Anforderungen oder Gütekriterien an den Forderungspool nennen:
1. Der aus den verbrieften Forderungen resultierende Cash Flow sollte möglichst stabil sein.
2. Die verbrieften Forderungen müssen wirtschaftlich und rechtlich separierbar sein.
3. Sicherheiten sollten eingebunden werden (Sportimmobilie).
4. Die Bonität des Emittenten sollte möglichst gut sein.
5. Die Forderungen sollten eine möglichst starke Homogenität aufweisen.

In einer Bewertung von ABS Strukturen kommen Röder/Sonnenmann (2005) zu dem Ergebnis, dass die komplexe Struktur und Vielzahl der beteiligten Partner leicht zu einer Gefahr werden kann. Asymmetrische Informationsverteilung zwischen den Beteiligten kann der Grund für Adverse Selection oder Moral Hazard sein. Dies bedeutet im Fall der ABS-Beziehungen, dass die Qualität der ausplatzierten Forderungen für den Originator gut, für die ABS-Investoren aber nur sehr schlecht zu bewerten ist. Eine weitere zentrale Schwäche dieser Finanzierungsform liegt in der exklusiven Eignung für Großprojekte, bei denen durch die Einnahmen des Betreibers ein Refinanzierungspotential gegeben ist. So sind ABS-Emmissionen grundsätzlich erst ab relativ hohen Volumina lohnenswert. Dies ist v.a. damit verbunden, dass hohe Koordinations- und Transaktionskosten anfallen. Kern (2003) nennt in Einklang mit der einschlägigen Literatur zum Thema Asset Backed Securities eine Größenordnung von 40 Mio. € als Mindestvolumen. Teilweise findet man in Empfehlungen für den Mittelstand auch Einschätzungen der bedingten Eignung ab einem Volumen von 15 Mio. € (Venture Capital Magazin, 2003). Die erwartete Stabilität des Cash Flows wird sich im zu zahlenden Zins für eine derartige Finanzierungsform widerspiegeln. Somit sind die mit der Ligaspezifität verknüpften Besonderheiten für diese Finanzierungsform von vorrangigem Belang. Erwarteter dauerhafter sportlicher Erfolg und damit stabile Zuschauerzahlen und sonstigen Einnahmen bestimmen die Kosten und damit die Vorteilhaftigkeit dieses Finanzierungsinstrumentes. Die Stärken dieser Finanzierungsform liegen (1) in der möglichen Senkung der durchschnittlichen Finanzierungskosten, (2) dem langfristigen Charakter dieser Finanzierungsform, was mit der langen Nutzungsdauer einer Sportimmobilie korrespondiert und langfristige Planungssicherheit ermöglichst, (3) der Tatsache, das sonstige Vermögensgegenstände – anders als beim klassischen Bankkredit – frei bleiben für zusätzliche Besicherung und (4) in der Unabhängigkeit von kurz- und mittelfristigen Krediten. Weiterhin bleiben die Eigentumsverhältnisse und die Betriebsstrukturen unberührt. V.a. der zügige Liquiditätseffekt kann je nach finanzieller Situation von Vorteil sein. Schließlich stellt diese Finanzierungsform ein Risikotransferinstrument dar (Rudolph, 2005), welches je nach Situation dazu genutzt werden kann, sich des mit den verkauften Forderungen verbundenen Risikos zu entledigen.

Beispielfall Schalke 04:
Der FC Schalke 04 hat im Jahr 2002 eine Anleihe in Höhe von 85 Mio. € von amerikanischen Versicherungsunternehmen und Pensionsfonds aufgenommen. Im Gegenzug hat der Verein über die Laufzeit der Vereinbarung von 23 Jahren einen Teil seiner Einnahmen aus dem Zuschauer-Aufkommen in der Arena „Auf Schalke" bis zu maximal 9 Mio. € pro Saison abgetreten. Der FC Schalke 04 kalkulierte mit etwa 15 Mio. € aus den Zuschauer-Aufkommen, nicht eingeschlossen sind die Einnahmen aus dem Bereich der Logen und VIP-Räume. Die Anleihe gegen Verpfändung eines Teils der Ticketerlöse wollte Schalke zum Bau von einem Reha-Zentrum, Trainingsplätzen, Parkhäusern und zur Tilgung von Schulden verwenden. Dem Verein sind also neben den 85 Mio. € noch die Differenz zwischen den 15 Mio. € und den abgetretenen 9 Mio. € zugeflossen. Der Liquiditätszufluss aufgrund der ABS betrug im Jahr 2003 somit 91 Mio. €. Die „Arena auf Schalke" bietet 61.000 Zuschauern Platz und der Verein hat in den ersten Jah-

ren der Benutzung bei Heimspielen fast immer eine Vollauslastung erreicht. Im Kontext des Schalker Beispiels einer ABS-Transaktion werden v.a. die Vorteile genannt, dass nur eine geringe Eigenkapitalbindung vorliegt, neue Liquidität zu attraktiven Marktkonditionen beschafft und schließlich eine Bilanzentlastung erreicht wurde. Allerdings ist bei der Schalker ABS-Konstruktion den Investoren kein Zugriff auf das Stadion möglich, da der Verein über eine Stadion-Beteiligungs-GmbH nur eine Minderheitsbeteiligung von knapp über 30 % hält.

8.4 Fallstudie

Die folgende Fallstudie veranschaulicht am Beispiel eines Börsengangs, wie Borussia Dortmund einen bis dahin in Deutschland noch nicht beschrittenen Weg der Finanzierung gewählt hat und welche Chancen aber auch Schwierigkeiten damit verbunden waren und immer noch sind.

Fallstudie „Borussia Dortmund"

Neben den Umsatzerlösen bieten sich weitere Formen an, wie sich die Profisportgesellschaften finanzieren können. Ein viel diskutierte Musterbeispiel ist der Börsengang von Borussia Dortmund. Die Ausgabe von Aktien, also Anteilen am Unternehmen, stellt eine Form der Außenfinanzierung dar. Damit dies möglich war, musste die Lizenzspielerabteilung die Rechtsform wandeln. Borussia Dortmund wählte die Rechtsform der GmbH & Co. KG aA. Dies bietet aus der Perspektive der Finanzierung den Vorteil, dass die durch die Ligaverbandssatzung (Die Liga – Fußballverband e.V.) vorgegebene Grenze der Ausschüttung der Aktienanteile nicht begrenzt ist. Die Rahmendaten stellen sich wie folgt dar:

Die Borussia Dortmund GmbH & Co. KG aA ist eines der führenden Unternehmen im internationalen Profifußballgeschäft. Schwerpunkt der Geschäftstätigkeit ist der Profifußball und die wirtschaftliche Nutzung damit verbundener Einnahmepotenziale. In diesem Zusammenhang soll auch die Marke „Borussia Dortmund" so effektiv wie möglich genutzt werden. Neben der Lizenzspielermannschaft ist die Gesellschaft auch für die Amateurmannschaft sowie die A-Jugend verantwortlich.

Neben dem Kerngeschäft Profifußball engagiert sich Borussia Dortmund in sportnahen Geschäftsfeldern. Hier werden teilweise zusammen mit strategischen Partnern Gemeinschaftsunternehmen gebildet. Von zentraler Bedeutung ist dabei das bei nationalen Spielen 83.000 Zuschauer fassende Dortmunder Westfalensta-dion, dessen Eigentümerin die Stadion-Besitzgesellschaft BVB Stadion GmbH (ehemals Westfalenstadion Dortmund GmbH & Co. KG) ist. Ihre ehemalige 75-%-Beteiligung an dieser Gesellschaft hatte Borussia Dortmund 2002/03 bis auf 6 % reduziert; dabei war den Angaben zufolge allerdings auch der Nutzungsver-trag für das Stadion geändert worden, und zwar dahingehend, dass Borussia Dortmund „die uneingeschränkte Nutzungsbefugnis des Westfalenstadions für Veranstaltungen sämtlicher Art und aller hieraus jetzt und zukünftig resultieren-den Einnahmen zu 100 %" zuflossen – ferner bestehe nach 15 Jahren eine Rück-kaufvereinbarung für die 94 % an der Gesellschaft, so wurde erklärt. Im Rahmen der im Geschäftsjahr 2004/05 (30.06.) durchgeführten Sanierungsmaßnahmen wurde der Verkauf der Anteile an der Westfalenstadion Dortmund GmbH & Co. KG rückabgewickelt. Seit dem 1. Dezember 2005 heißt das Stadion SIGNAL IDUNA PARK.

Daneben ist Borussia Dortmund mit 100 % an der goool.de Sportswear GmbH beteiligt, die seit der Saison 2000/01 eine eigene Sporttextilmarke ver-marktet und noch bis einschließlich 2003/04 den Profifußballclub ausstattete. Die Sports & Bytes GmbH (seit Ende 2003 Anteil 100 %) entwickelt und betreibt di-gitale Marketing- und Vertriebsplattformen für Sport im Internet. Über die B.E.S.T. – Borussia Euro Lloyd Sports Travel GmbH (Anteil 51 %) werden ne-ben allgemeinen Reisebürodiensten Veranstaltungen, Tagungen und Kongresse konzipiert, geplant und durchgeführt. Zudem ist Borussia Dortmund über die Or-thomed Medizinisches Leistungs- und Rehabilitationszentrum GmbH (Anteil 33,4 %) in der medizinischen Rehabilitation und körperlichen Wiederherstellung, insbesondere im Leistungssport, engagiert. Schließlich ist das Unternehmen über seine 100-Prozent-Tochter BVB Merchandising GmbH in der Vermarktung von Merchandisingartikeln aktiv.

Im Geschäftsjahr 2005/06 begrenzten die fehlende Teilnahme an internationa-len Wettbewerben und das frühe Ausscheiden bei dem DFB-Pokal das Erlös-wachstum. Allerdings konnte trotzdem der Umsatz um 19,2 % auf 89,06 (Vor-jahr: 74,70) Mio. € erhöht werden. In diesem Geschäftsjahr bilanzierte das Unternehmen erstmals nach den internationalen Rechnungslegungsvorschriften IFRS, so dass der Vergleich mit den Vorjahren nur bedingt möglich ist. Das Vor-jahr wurde der besseren Vergleichbarkeit halber jedoch rückwirkend angepasst. Wichtigste Erlösquelle war das Sponsoring mit einem Beitrag von 27,4 (Vorjahr: 26,6) Mio. €, gefolgt von dem Ticketing (Einnahmen aus Dauer- und Tageskarten sowie der Teilnahme an Freundschaftsspielen) in Höhe von 17,2 (Vorjahr: 17,5) Mio. € und dem Merchandising/Catering/Sonstiges mit 17,2 (Vorjahr: 15,0) Mio. €. Im Bereich Transfer wurden insbesondere wegen des Verkaufs der Transfer-rechte an Tomas Rosicky an Arsenal London 12,4 (Vorjahr: 0,7) Mio. € erzielt und im Segment TV-Vermarktung 14,8 (Vorjahr: 14,9) Mio. €. Der Verlust konn-te v.a. wegen des gestiegenen Umsatzes, gesunkener Personalaufwendungen (um

6,9 Mio. auf 39,77 Mio. €), um 11,3 Mio. auf 14,23 Mio. € gesunkenen Abschreibungen auf Spielerwerte und einem um 2,43 Mio. auf 11,36 Mio. € verbesserten Finanzergebnis deutlich gesenkt werden. Die sonstigen betrieblichen Aufwendungen (insbesondere Wertberichtigungen auf Forderungen) sanken um 3,1 Mio. auf 46,3 Mio. €. Das Ergebnis vor Steuern (EBT) betrug minus 22,6 (minus 55,3) Mio. €. Unter dem Strich wurde der Jahresverlust auf 20,80 (Vorjahr: 54,52) Mio. € mehr als halbiert. Das Ergebnis je Aktie gibt der Vorstand mit minus 0,70 (minus 2,04) € an. Das Kapital wurde im Juli 2006 um 14.625.000 neue Aktien auf 43,88 Mio. € erhöht. Die dem Unternehmen zugeflossenen 29,25 Mio. € wurden zur Rückführung von Altverbindlichkeiten eingesetzt.

Mit Beschlüssen der Mitgliederversammlungen des Ballspielverein Borussia 09 e.V. Dortmund vom 28. November 1999 und 26. Februar 2000 wurde der gesamte bisherige steuerpflichtige wirtschaftliche Geschäftsbetrieb ausgegliedert und in die neu gegründete Borussia Dortmund GmbH & Co. KGaA eingebracht. Bei der gesellschaftsrechtlichen Strukturierung von Borussia Dortmund werde bewusst, so wird betont, Sorge getragen, dass eine enge personelle Verzahnung zwischen Verein und Gesellschaft gewährleistet sei. Borussia Dortmund verfolgt das sportliche Ziel, sich durch hochklassigen Fußballsport langfristig in der Spitzengruppe des nationalen und internationalen Profifußballs zu etablieren. Der sportliche Erfolg soll Umsatz, Geschäftsergebnis und Wert der Gesellschaft nachhaltig steigern. Im Oktober 2000 erfolgte der erste Börsengang eines deutschen Fußballvereins. Heute notieren die Aktien der Gesellschaft im General Standard der Frankfurter Wertpapierbörse (Deutsche Bank, 2007).

Den Kursverlauf der Dortmunder Aktie der letzten drei Jahre zeigt die folgende Abbildung (untere Linie Kursverlauf der BVB-Aktie, obere Referenzline DAX-Verlauf).

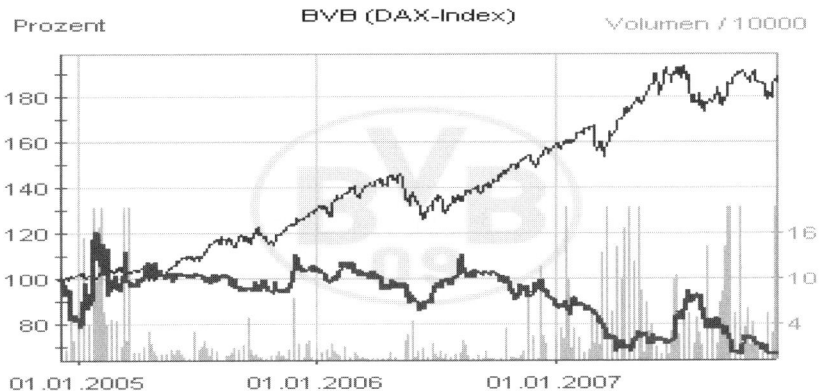

Abb. 5: Kursindex der Aktie von Borussia Dortmund (01.01.2005= 100)
Quelle: Borussia Dortmund (2007), o.S.

8.5 Fazit und Ausblick

Sportmanagern stellt sich ein breites Spektrum an Finanzierungsmöglichkeiten für die in Sportorganisation notwendigen Investitionen dar. Zur Auswahl eines optimalen Finanzierungsmix sind die unterschiedlichen Formen der Finanzierung, die in diesem Kapitel vorgestellt wurden, miteinander zu kombinieren. Die diskutierten Stärken und Schwächen der jeweiligen Finanzierungsform sind dabei achtsam abzuwägen und in Einklang mit der spezifischen Situation in der sich die Sportorganisation aktuell befindet abzugleichen. Somit gibt es keine ideale Finanzierung im Sport, sondern nur ein zu der spezifischen Situation gerade passender Mix an Finanzierungsmöglichkeiten. Deshalb wurden in diesem Kapitel die unterschiedlichen Formen vorgestellt und in den zentralen Aspekten ihrer Bewertung diskutiert, womit den Sportmanagern der Zukunft Wissen für die Optimierung des Finanzmanagement bereitgestellt ist.

Kontrollfragen

1. Was versteht man unter Finanzierung in Sportorganisationen?
2. In welcher Beziehung steht die Finanzierung zur Investition in Sportorganisationen?
3. Was versteht man unter der Innen- und Außenfinanzierung?
4. Wieso ist es schwierig, manche Finanzierungsformen eindeutig einer Analysekategorie zuzuordnen?
5. Was ist eine Genussscheinfinanzierung und was macht sie für Sportorganisationen attraktiv?
6. Welches sind die wichtigsten Quellen, aus denen sich Sportorganisationen des Profisportmarktes finanzieren?
7. Wie hat sich die Bedeutung der Finanzvolumina im Profifußball in den letzten Jahren entwickelt?
8. Wieso ist eine zu hohe Fremdfinanzierung bzw. negatives Eigenkapital für Sportorganisation problematisch?
9. Mit welchen zentralen Konsequenzen ist die Finanzierungsform des Going Public gekennzeichnet?
10. Was versteht man unter Asset Backed Securities und welchen Chancen und Risiken sind mit ihnen für Sportorganisationen verbunden.

Literaturverzeichnis

Ahrweiler, Sonja / Börner, Christoph (2003): Neue Finanzierungswege für den Mittelstand: Ausgangssituation, Notwendigkeit und Instrumente, in: Kienbaum, Jochen / Börner, Christoph J. (Hrsg.): Neue Finanzierungswege für den Mittelstand. Von der Notwendigkeit zu den Gestaltungsformen, Wiesbaden, S. 3-73.

Albers, Heinrich (Hrsg.) (2000): Finanzierung kommunaler Investitionen, 2. Aufl., Wiesbaden.

Bernet, Beat / Denk, Christoph (2000): Finanzierungsmodelle für KMU, Bank- und finanzwirtschaftliche Forschung, Bd. 314, Bern u.a.

Borussia Dortmund (2007) Borussia Investor Relations, http://www.borussia-aktie.de (Zugriff: 01.12.2007).

Bundesverband Deutscher Banken (Hrsg.) (2005): Bankinternes Rating mittelständischer Kreditnehmer im Zuge von Basel II, Berlin.

Bundesverband Deutscher Banken (Hrsg.) (2003): Mittelstandsfinanzierung vor neuen Herausforderungen, Reihe: Daten , Fakten, Argumente, Berlin.

Deutsche Bank (2007) Marktinformationen, http://www.deutsche-bank.de/pbc/marktinformationen (Zugriff: 26.04.2007).

Deutsche Fußball Liga GmbH (2005): Die Wirtschaftliche Situation im Lizenzfußball, Frankfurt/Main.

Deutsche Fußball Liga GmbH (2006): Bundesligareport, Frankfurt/Main.

Deutsche Fußball Liga GmbH (2007): Bundesligareport, Frankfurt/Main.

Deutscher Sportbund (2005a): Clearingstelle Sport und Umwelt, http://www.dsb-clearingstelle.de (Zugriff: 20.06.2005).

Dietl, Helmut / Pauli, Markus (2002): Die Finanzierung von Fußballstadien – Überlegungen am Beispiel des deutschen Profifußballs, in: Zeitschrift für Betriebswirtschaft, Ergänzungsheft Sportökonomie, S. 239-262.

Dietl, Helmut / Franck, Egon / Roy, Patrick (2003): Überinvestitionsprobleme in einer Sportliga, in: Betriebswirtschaftliche Forschung und Praxis, Heft 5, S. 528-540.

Energieagentur NRW (EA NRW) (o.J.): Sport braucht Energieeffizienz. Ein Leitfaden für Sportstättenbetreiber, Wuppertal.

Ernst & Young (2004): Bälle, Tore und Finanzen: Wege aus dem finanziellen Abseits, Essen.

Ernst &Young (2005): Bälle, Tore und Finanzen II: Aktuelle Perspektiven und Herausforderungen für den Profifußball, Essen.

Ernst & Young (2007): Bälle, Tore und Finanzen IV: Aktuelle Perspektiven und Herausforderungen für den Profifußball, Essen.

Everling, Oliver (2003): Rating für den Mittelstand, in: Kienbaum, Jochen / Börner, Christoph (Hrsg.): Neue Finanzierungswege für den Mittelstand. Von der Notwendigkeit zu den Gestaltungsformen, Wiesbaden, S. 165-187.

Franck, Egon (1995): Die ökonomischen Dimensionen der Teamsportindustrie. Eine Organisationsbetrachtung, Wiesbaden.

Franck, Egon (2000): Die Verfassungswahl bei Fußballclubs unter besonderer Beachtung der spezifischen Produktionsstruktur des Teamsports, in: Büch, Martin-Peter (Hrsg.): Märkte und Organisationen im Sport: Institutionenökonomische Ansätze, Schorndorf, S. 11-26.

Grundke, Peter / Spörk, Wolfgang (2003): Basel II – Struktur und Auswirkung auf das Kreditgeschäft, in: Kienbaum, Jochen / Börner, Christoph (Hrsg.): Neue

Finanzierungswege für den Mittelstand. Von der Notwendigkeit zu den Gestaltungsformen, Wiesbaden, S. 11-26.

Harrer, Hermann / Janssen, Uwe / Halbig, Udo (2005): Genussscheine – Eine interessante Form der Mezzanine Mittelstandsfinanzierung, in: Finanzbetrieb, Heft 1, S. 1-7.

Hovemann, Gregor (2005): Das Problem der Rechtsformwahl im Sport, in: Breuer, Christoph / Thiel, Ansgar (Hrsg.): Handbuch Sportmanagement, Schorndorf. S. 228-237.

Kern, Markus (2003): Securitization – Allheilmittel für die Fußballbundesliga, in: Die Bank, Heft 7, S. 444-449.

Kern, Markus (2007): Besonderheiten der Unternehmensfinanzierung und der Investitionseffizienz im professionellen Fußball, Hamburg.

Kirchmann, Hans-Peter / Lanzinger, Christoph (2003): Vom Konzept zur innovativen Finanzierung kommunaler Sportprojekte, in: Kommunale Sportstättenverwaltung zwischen Tradition und Privatisierung „Kommune und Sport", 18. IAKS-Kongress, Köln, 05.-07.11.2003.

Kramer, Jens (2005): Internes Rating spezieller Kundensegmente bei den Banken in Mecklenburg-Vorpommern unter besonderer Berücksichtigung von Nonprofit-Organisationen, Wismarer Diskussionspapiere, Heft 10/2005, Hochschule Wismar.

Kroll, Markus (2003): Leasing-Handbuch für die öffentliche Hand, 9 Aufl., Lichtenfels.

Küting, Karlheinz / Dürr, Ulrike (2005): Mezzanines Kapital - Finanzierungsentscheidung im Sog der Rechnungslegung, in: Der Betrieb, Heft 29, S. 1529-1534.

Lehmann, Erik / Weigand, Jürgen (2002): Mitsprache und Kontrolle im professionellen Fußball: Überlegungen zu einer Corporate Governance., in: Zeitschrift für Betriebswirtschaft, Ergänzungsheft Sportökonomie, S. 43-62.

Neus, Werner (2003): Einführung in die Betriebswirtschaftslehre aus institutionenökonomischer Sicht, 3. Aufl., Tübingen.

Perridon, Louis / Steiner, Manfred (2003): Finanzwirtschaft der Unternehmung. 12. Aufl.. München.

Röder, Kai / Sonnemann, Uwe (2005): Asset Backed Securities. Chancen ohne Risiko?, in: Wirtschaftswissenschaftliches Studium, Heft 6, S. 328-333.

Rudolph, Bernd (2004): Mezzanine Finanzierungen im Rahmen der Kapitalstrukturpolitik von Unternehmen, in: Gerke, Walter / Siegert, Thomas (Hrsg.): Aktuelle Herausforderungen des Finanzmanagements, Dokumentation des 57. Deutschen Betriebswirtschafter-Tags 2003, Stuttgart, S. 153-183.

Rudolph, Bernd (2005): Risikotransferinstrumente und Unternehmensfinanzierung, in: Zeitschrift für betriebswirtschaftliche Forschung, Heft 3, S. 176-181.

Schwendowius, Daniel (2003): Finanzierungs- und Organisationskonzepte für den deutschen Profifußball - Eine Analyse der finanzierungsrelevanten Vertragsbeziehungen von Fußballclubs unter besonderer Berücksichtigung der Spielerfinanzierung, Digitale Dissertation, http://www.diss.fu-berlin.de/2003/21/index. html (Zugriff: 12.05.2004).

Sport StadiaNet (2004). Sport StadiaNet schafft Spielräume! Der einfache und clevere Weg zu einer neuen Sportanlage. Düsseldorf: Sport StadiaNet.

Swoboda, Peter (1973): Finanzierungstheorie, Würzburg u.a.

Tanski, Frank (2005): Genussrechtskapital – Finanzierungsalternative für Genossenschaften, in: Finanzbetrieb, Heft 1, S. 8-12.

Umweltbundesamt (Hrsg.) (2002): Contracting für kommunale Sportstätten. Strategien zu Klimaschutz und Kostensenkung. Leitfaden, Berlin.

Venture Capital Magazin (2003): Sonderausgabe Mittelstandsfinanzierung, Heft 4, S. 15.

Vornholz, Günter (2005a): Rentabilität von Stadien. Können Stadien wirtschaftlich erfolgreich sein oder welchen Beitrag hat die öffentliche Hand, unveröffentlichtes Diskussionspapier.

Vornholz, Günter (2005b): Finanzierung von Sport- und Freizeitanlagen, Schorndorf.

Wertenbruch, Jürgen (1993): Der Lizenzspieler als Gläubigersicherheit im Konkurs eines Vereins der Fußball-Bundesligen, in: Zeitschrift für Privatrecht, Heft 17, S. 1292-1298.

Wilms, Werner (2004): Die regionalwirtschaftliche Bedeutung des Profifußballs am Beispiel des Vfl Bochum 1848 e.V., in: Hamman, Peter / Schmidt, Lutz / Welling, Michael (Hrsg.): Ökonomie des Fußballs, Wiesbaden, S. 61-85.

Weiterführende Ressourcen

Literatur

Born, Jürgen / Mohr, Stefan / Bohl, Markus (2004): Financing the Game – Erfolgsfaktoren, Strategien und Instrumente zur Finanzierung eines Fußballclubs, in: Zieschang, Klaus / Klimmer, Christian (Hrsg.): Unternehmensführung im Profifußball. Symbiose von Sport, Wirtschaft und Recht, Berlin, S. 199-206.

Elter, Vera Carina (2003): Verwertung medialer Rechte der Fußballunternehmen. Vermarktung und Refinanzierung im Sport, Berlin.

Hockenjos, Christian (1995): Öffentliche Sportförderung in der Bundesrepublik Deutschland: Darstellung und finanztheoretische Analyse, Frankfurt/Main.

Kern, Markus / Haas, Oliver / Dworak, Alexander (2002): Finanzierungsmöglichkeiten für die Bundesliga und andere Sportligen, in: Galli, Albert / Gömmel, Rainer / Holzhäuser, Wolfgang / Straub, Wilfried (Hrsg.): Sportmanagement. Grundlagen der unternehmerischen Führung im Sport aus Betriebswirtschaftslehre, Steuern und Recht für den Sportmanager, München, S. 395-448.

Leki, Oliver (2004): Alternative Formen der Finanzierung, in: Zieschang, Klaus / Klimmer, Christian (Hrsg.): Unternehmensführung im Profifußball. Symbiose von Sport, Wirtschaft und Recht, Berlin, S. 167-176.

Meyer, Bernd / Ahlert, Gert (2000): Die ökonomischen Perspektiven des Sports, Schorndorf.

Müller, Christian (1991): Rechtsfragen der Finanzierung im „bezahlten Sport" dargestellt am Beispiel des Bundesligafußballs, Frankfurt/Main.

Sigloch, Jochen / Schmidt, Ingo (2003): Innovative Finanzierung bei Sportveranstaltungen durch den Verkauf künftiger Leistungen – einige Grundsatzfragen, in: Sigloch, Jochen / Klimmer, Christian (Hrsg.): Rechnungslegung und Besteuerung im Sport, Bayreuth, S. 225-242.

Weber, Wolfgang / Schnieder, Claudia / Kortlüke, Norbert / Horak, Birgit (1995): Die wirtschaftliche Bedeutung des Sports, Schorndorf.

Zacharias, Erwin (1999): Going Public einer Fußball Kapitalgesellschaft, Bielefeld.

Links

Beratung Sportstättenfinanzierung:
http://www.sportstadianet.de

Borussia Dortmund:
http://www.bvb.de

Dow Jones Stoxx Football Index:
http://www.stoxx.de

FC Schalke 04:
http://www.schalke04.de

Kapitel 9: Controlling im Sport

Christoph Jordan

Lernziele

Nach der Durchsicht dieses Kapitels sollte der Leser in der Lage sein,

- die Funktionen des Controlling für die Unternehmensführung einzuordnen.
- Unterschiede zwischen strategischem und operativem Controlling darzustellen.
- die Bedeutung und die Phasen eines Risikomanagements für Sportorganisationen darzulegen.
- verschiedene Techniken der Budgeterstellung aufzuzeigen.
- das System der Balanced Scorecard allgemein zu erläutern.
- die Möglichkeiten der Balanced Scorecard für ein Controlling im Sportbereich aufzuzeigen.
- die Informationsbeschaffung für operative und strategische Controllingtätigkeiten in Sportorganisationen vorzustellen.
- die Vorteile eines systematischen Controlling für Sportorganisationen zu verdeutlichen.

Überblick über das Kapitel

In diesem Kapitel werden die Grundlagen des Controlling erläutert und auf den Bereich des Sports übertragen. Nach einer kurzen Einführung in die Thematik werden in einem ersten Schritt allgemeine Grundlagen des Controlling dargelegt, bevor auf das Controlling in Sportorganisationen eingegangen wird und hierfür notwendige Modifikationen der Systeme und Instrumente aufgezeigt werden. Im Mittelpunkt der Ausführungen steht hierbei die Beschreibung der Balanced Scorecard (BSC) als umfassendes Controllingsystem. Abgerundet wird dieses Kapitel mit einer Praxis-Fallstudie, in der die Einführung der Balanced Scorecard im Württembergischen Fußballverband beschrieben wird.

9.1 Einführung in die Thematik

Die Rahmenbedingungen für Sportorganisationen unterliegen einem permanenten Veränderungsprozess. Sportvereine sind heutzutage einem erhöhtem nationalen und internationalen Wettbewerb ausgesetzt. Weiterhin konkurrieren viele Sportvereine und -verbände vermehrt mit kommerziellen Sportanbietern um die Aufmerksamkeit von aktiven und passiven Sportkonsumenten. Vereine wie Borussia Dortmund unterliegen durch ihren Börsengang erweiterten rechtlichen Anforderungen wie z.B. dem KonTraG (Gesetz zur Kontrolle und Transparenz im Unternehmensbereich), das u.a. die Einführung und Dokumentation eines Risikomanagements verlangt. Vor diesem Hintergrund wird der Einsatz geeigneter Managementmethoden für Sportorganisationen immer entscheidender. Eine wichtige Rolle kommt hierbei v.a. dem Controlling als Planungs-, Steuerungs- und Informationssystem zu, damit die Sportorganisationen auf die veränderten Umstände reagieren können. Ein System, welches im Rahmen des Controlling eine wichtige Funktion einnehmen kann, ist die BSC. Dieses System, wie die meisten anderen betriebswirtschaftlichen Konzepte, wurde ursprünglich für Industrieunternehmen entwickelt. Sportorganisationen weisen im Vergleich zu diesen Unternehmen jedoch einige Besonderheiten auf, weshalb für die Anwendung dieser Systeme im Alltagsgeschäft Modifikationen nötig sind. Bevor auf diese Punkte eingegangen wird, ist in einem ersten Schritt zu klären, was unter Controlling generell zu verstehen ist und welche Rolle diesem Bereich zukommt.

9.2 Grundlagen des Controlling

Nach einer Begriffs- und Funktionsklärung (Abschnitt 9.2.1) werden in zwei Abschnitten die Planungs- und Kontrollaufgaben des Controlling (Abschnitt 9.2.2) und die hierfür notwendige Informationsversorgung (Abschnitt 9.2.3) thematisiert.

9.2.1 Begriff und Funktionen des Controlling

Eine allgemeingültige Definition des Begriffs Controlling existiert nicht in der Literatur. Weit verbreitet ist jedoch folgende Definition von Horváth (2003, S. 151):

> „Controlling ist – funktional gesehen – dasjenige Subsystem der Führung, das Planung und Kontrolle sowie Informationsversorgung systembildend und systemkoppelnd ergebniszielorientiert koordiniert und so die Adaption und Koordination des Gesamtsystems unterstützt."

Controlling dient demnach der Koordination in einer Unternehmung. Ursache für den Koordinationsbedarf ist die Zerteilung von Handlungsfeldern, die zu Sach- und Verhaltensinterdependenzen zwischen den Führungssystemen führt. Sinn des Controlling ist es, diese Interdependenzen durch Koordination beherrschbar zu machen (Horváth, 2003). Unterschiede liegen in der Literatur über das Ausmaß an Koordinationsaufgaben und somit bei den Kompetenzen vor. Für Müller (1974) bedeutet Controlling die Koordination von Informationserzeugung und -bereitstellung mit dem Informationsbedarf. Andere Autoren messen dem Controlling die Koordination des Führungsgesamtsystems zu (Küpper, 1988; Küpper/Weber/Zünd, 1990). Das Ausmaß an Koordinationsaufgaben und die Kompetenzen des Controlling liegen der Definition von Horváth nach zwischen den beiden zuvor genannten Ansätzen. Controlling wird demnach als Subsystem der Führung verstanden, dem die Aufgabe zukommt, die Systeme der Planung und Kontrolle sowie der Informationsversorgung zu gestalten und zu steuern.

Es sollen geeignete Strukturen geschaffen und das Management mit relevanten Informationen und Methoden versorgt werden, damit die Unternehmung ihre Ergebnis- und Sachziele erreichen und allgemein ihre Koordinations-, Reaktions- und Adaptionsfähigkeit aufrechterhalten kann. Das Hauptaugenmerk des Controlling als

Koordinationsinstrument innerhalb und zwischen Führungsteilsystemen liegt auf der Abstimmung von Planung und Kontrolle, da das Management durch das Controlling wichtige Informationen über Notwendigkeiten der Anpassung (Feedback-Funktion des Controlling) und über Innovationen (Feedforward-Funktion des Controlling) erhalten soll (Ossadnik, 2003). Somit wird auch deutlich, dass Controlling nicht der Kontrolle gleichgesetzt werden darf, sondern darunter ein zukunftsgerichteter Prozess zu verstehen ist, der das Management mit wichtigen Führungs- und Steuerungsinformationen versorgt.

Eine praxisnahe Beschreibung des Aufgabenfelds eines Controllers liefert folgende Definition der International Group of Controlling (2002):

Controller gestalten und begleiten den Management-Prozess der Zielfindung, Planung und Steuerung und tragen damit eine Mitverantwortung für die Zielerreichung. D.h.:

- Controller sorgen für Strategie-, Ergebnis-, Finanz- und Prozesstransparenz und tragen somit zu höherer Wirtschaftlichkeit bei.
- Controller koordinieren Teilziele und Teilpläne ganzheitlich und organisieren unternehmensübergreifend das zukunftsorientierte Berichtswesen.
- Controller moderieren und gestalten den Management-Prozess der Zielfindung, der Planung und der Steuerung so, dass jeder Entscheidungsträger zielorientiert handeln kann.
- Controller leisten den dazu erforderlichen Service der betriebswirtschaftlichen Daten- und Informationsversorgung.
- Controller gestalten und pflegen die Controllingsysteme.

9.2.2 Planungs- und Kontrollaufgaben des Controlling

Wild (1974, S. 13) definiert die Planung als „ein systematisches, zukunftsbezogenes Durchdenken und Festlegen von Zielen, Maßnahmen, Mitteln und Wegen zur künftigen Zielerreichung". Sie bildet mit der Kontrolle ein gemeinsames System, da die vorgegebenen Soll-Größen der Planung unzertrennlich mit den durch Kontrollen ermittelten Ist-Größen verbunden sind (Hahn, 1996).

Innerhalb des Planungs- und Kontrollsystems wird im Folgenden der Fokus auf das strategische und operative Controlling, das Risikomanagement, die Budgetierung und die BSC als umfassendes Controllinginstrument gelegt.

9.2.2.1 Strategisches und operatives Controlling

Die Aufgabe des auf qualitative Größen ausgerichteten *strategischen Controlling* besteht in der Unterstützung der Unternehmensführung bei der strategischen Planung und Kontrolle sowie deren Informationsversorgung. Es begleitet das Management bei der Durchführung von Analysen zur Positionierung und Entwicklung

240

eines Stärken- und Schwächen-Profils. Es hilft, Strategien zu entwickeln, zu über-prüfen und sie in einen logischen Zusammenhang zu bringen. Eine Erweiterung des operativen Controlling stellt es einerseits zeitlich dar, indem weiter in die Zukunft geblickt wird und andererseits inhaltlich, indem der Fokus auf die Unternehmens-umwelt erweitert wird. Durch das strategische Controlling wird der Bereich der Kontrolle um eine Feedforward-Funktion erweitert, da festgelegte Prämissen im Zeitverlauf auf ihre Aktualität und Angemessenheit hin überprüft werden und dar-über hinaus eine strategische Überwachung gewährleistet werden kann.

Das auf quantifizierbare Größen ausgerichtete *operative Controlling* hat seinen Fokus auf der Ein- oder Mehrjahresplanung und -budgetierung. Informationsquelle hierfür ist v.a. eine Kosten- und Erlösrechnung, die der kurzfristigen Planung und Kontrolle sowie der Informationsversorgung des Managements dient. Im Bereich der Kontrolle nimmt es eine vergangenheitsorientierte Feedback-Funktion ein, da festgelegte Soll-Werte zu einem fixen Überprüfungszeitpunkt tatsächlichen Ist-Werten gegenübergestellt werden (Durchführungskontrolle). Strategisches und ope-ratives Controlling sind jedoch nicht getrennt voneinander zu betrachten, sondern eine Hauptaufgabe der Unternehmung ist in der Verbindung dieser Ebenen durch geeignete Konzepte und Instrumente zu sehen. Eine strategische Ausrichtung ohne operative Umsetzung wird ebenso erfolglos bleiben wie operative Arbeit ohne den Bezug zur Strategie (Ossadnik, 2003).

9.2.2.2 Risikomanagement

Das Risikomanagement im Rahmen des Controlling ist entscheidend, um das Ma-nagement zu jeder Zeit über potentielle Chancen und Risiken zu informieren und es dabei zu unterstützen, rechtzeitig die richtigen Maßnahmen zu ergreifen. Folgende fünf Teilprozesse sind hierbei typisch (vgl. Abb. 1).

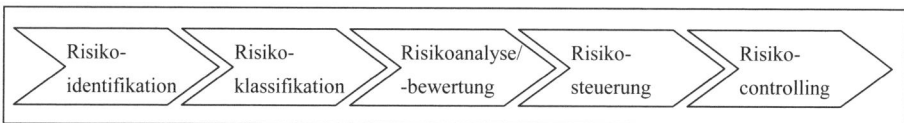

Abb. 1: Phasenmodell des Risikomanagements
In Anlehnung an: Scharpf/Lutz (2000), S. 77

Bei der *Risikoidentifikation* gilt es, in allen unternehmensrelevanten Bereichen Ri-sikofaktoren auszumachen. Die heutige Situation der Unternehmen ist von Diskon-tinuitäten geprägt, weshalb das Aufspüren von „weak signals" eine sinnvolle Me-thode darstellt (Rockart, 1979). Hierbei wird in einem ersten Schritt (Scanning) kontinuierlich nach schwachen Signalen gesucht. Ist ein solches Signal identifiziert, wird es durch das Monitoring vertiefend im Hinblick auf die Auswirkung auf das Unternehmen untersucht. Eine solche Betrachtung ist Aufgabe jeden Mitarbeiters in jedem Unternehmensbereich. Im Rahmen der *Risikoklassifikation* wird zunächst überprüft, wie schwerwiegend die Folgen der ermittelten Risiken auf den Unternehmenserfolg sind. Für Risiken, für die spontan Gegenmaßnahmen ergriffen werden können oder deren Eintritt keinen hohen finanziellen Schaden bedeutet, können die Kosten der Überwachung die des Eintritts übersteigen. Das ist der Grund, warum es ökonomisch nicht immer sinnvoll ist, jedes Risiko im weiteren Prozess des Risikomanagements zu betrachten. Für eine detaillierte *Risikoanalyse* können z.B. Checklisten eingesetzt werden. Das Portfoliomanagement stellt eine sinnvolle Methode dar, um die *Risiken zu bewerten* und auch graphisch anschaulich darzustellen. Abb. 2 kann eine Risikomatrix entnommen werden, die die identifizierten Risiken auf Verlustgefahr für das Unternehmen und die Eintrittswahrscheinlichkeit hin bewertet.

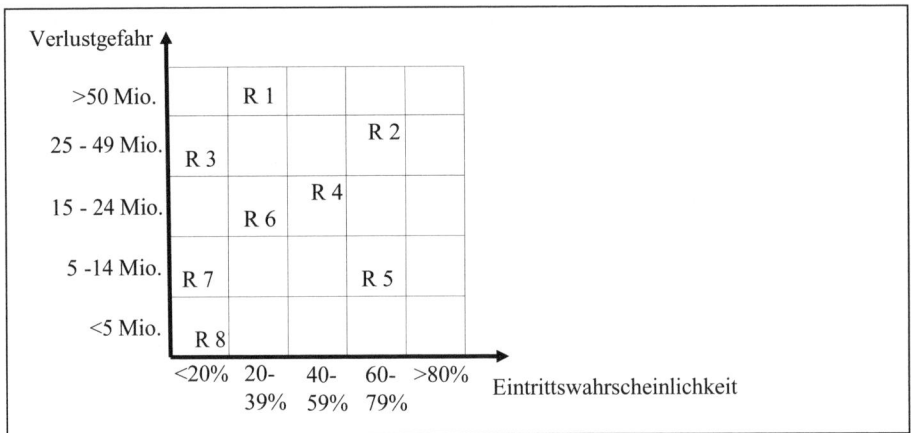

Abb.2: Risikomatrix
In Anlehnung an: Fröhling (2000), S. 96

Es wird hieraus ersichtlich, dass z.B. das Risiko 2 (R2) einen hohen finanziellen Schaden ausrichten und mit einer hohen Wahrscheinlichkeit eintreten wird, weshalb eine besondere Überwachung für dieses Risiko notwendig ist. Für die *Risikosteuerung* werden im nächsten Schritt Sollgrößen und Toleranzgrenzen definiert, bei deren Über- bzw. Unterschreiten gehandelt wird. Hierfür werden Maßnahmen für den Eintrittsfall geplant. *Risikocontrolling* ist als bereichsübergreifende Führungs- und Entscheidungshilfe zu verstehen. Der Controller liefert dem Management Informationen über bestehende und drohende Risiken und unterstützt die Kontrolle der Maßnahmen zur Risikoverminderung und Steuerung der potentiellen Risiken.

9.2.2.3 Budgetierung

Mit Hilfe der Budgetierung werden Sachziele in wertmäßige Größen überführt. Der Begriff des Budgets kann wie folgt definiert werden (Horváth, 2003, S. 231):

> „Ein Budget ist ein formalzielorientierter, in wertmäßigen Größen formulierter Plan, der einer Entscheidungseinheit für eine bestimmte Zeitperiode mit einem bestimmten Verbindlichkeitsgrad vorgegeben wird."

Budgets helfen bei der Lösung des Gemeinkostenproblems in der Unternehmung, indem diese Kosten in einzelne Teile zerlegt und Verantwortlichkeiten zugeordnet werden. Sie haben eine zentrale Koordinationsfunktion, da sie die einzelnen Teilpläne im Budgetierungsprozess aufeinander abstimmen. Weiterhin entfalten sie eine Kontrollfunktion und wirken verhaltensbeeinflussend, da durch die Vorgabe von Soll-Werten ein bestimmtes Ergebnis der Unternehmensbereiche erwartet wird (Küpper, 2005; Konetzny, 2007). Der Controller unterstützt das Management bei der Koordination und Abstimmung der Teilbudgets, der Gestaltung des Soll-/Ist-Vergleichs und der Erstellung der Abweichungsanalysen (Horváth, 2003). Folgende Techniken stehen bei der Aufstellung von Budgets zur Verfügung (Küpper, 2005).

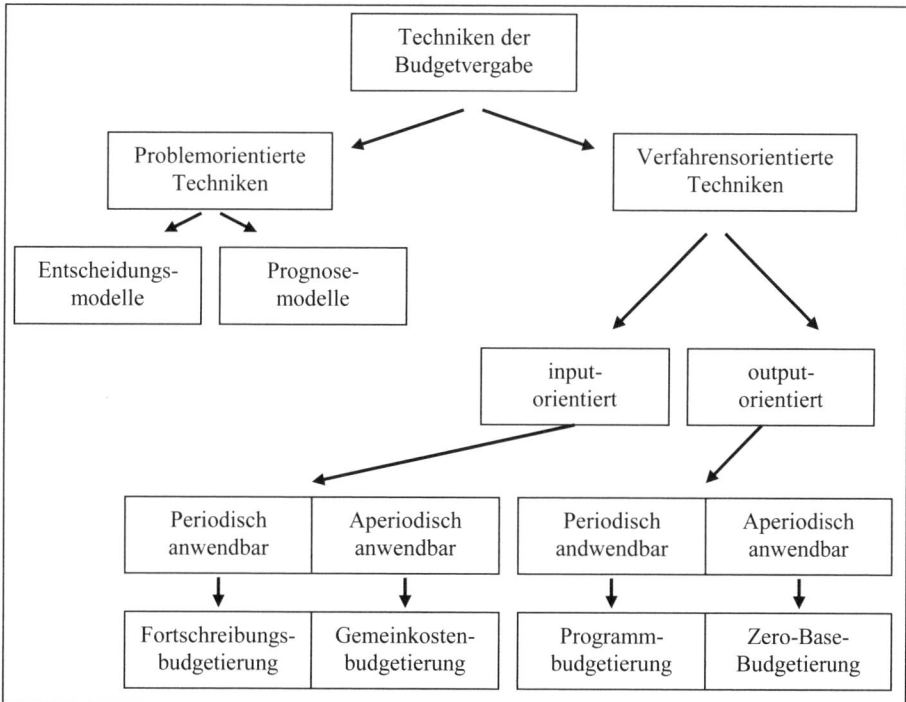

Abb. 3: Techniken der Budgetvorgabe
In Anlehnung an: Küpper (2005), S. 340

Problemorientierte Techniken werden eingesetzt, wenn genaue Input-Output-Beziehungen vorliegen und die Budgets über Entscheidungs- und Prognosemodelle errechnet werden können. Bei den inputorientierten Methoden innerhalb der verfahrensorientierten Techniken bilden der Budgetinput und seine Kosten den Ausgangspunkt der Analyse. Bei der periodisch anwendbaren Methode der *Fortschreibungsbudgetierung* orientiert sich die Budgeterstellung an Werten der Vorperiode, die i.d.R. situationsbedingt gekürzt oder erweitert werden. Bei outputorientierten Verfahren werden die Leistungen in den Mittelpunkt der Betrachtung gestellt. Es wird überprüft, inwieweit der bisherige Budgetoutput beibehalten, abgebaut oder ausgeweitet werden soll. Beim *Zero-Base-Budgeting (ZBB)* stellt die Budgeterstellung einen mehrstufigen Prozess dar, bei dem die einzelnen organisatorischen Einheiten zunächst abteilungsintern Entscheidungspakete mit unterschiedlicher Priorisierung zusammenstellen. Die einzelnen Pakete werden anschließend abteilungsübergreifend auf die Übereinstimmung mit der Unternehmensstrategie hin gemessen und priorisiert. Die Unternehmensleitung entscheidet abschließend über die Budgetverteilung und über durchzuführende Maßnahmen (zu den einzelnen Schritten vgl. auch Tab. 1).

	Zero-Base-Budgeting
Vorbereitung	1. Festlegung der Unternehmensziele, der verfügbaren Mittel und der ZBB-Bereiche
	2. Festlegung der Entscheidungseinheiten und ihrer Teilziele
Analysephase	3. Bestimmung der Leistungsniveaus
	4. Festlegung der Entscheidungspakete
	5. Abteilungsweise Rangordnung der Entscheidungspakete
	6. Abteilungsübergreifende Rangordnung
	7. Budgetschnitt
Realisierung	8. Maßnahmenplanung/Budgetvorgabe
	9. Überwachung und Abweichungsermittlung

Tab. 1: Schritte des Zero-Base-Budgeting
In Anlehnung an: Meyer-Piening (1990), S. 16

9.2.2.4 Balanced Scorecard

Die BSC kann als übergreifendes Controllingsystem bezeichnet werden, mit dem wichtige Controllingaufgaben erledigt werden können bzw. für die mit diesem System ein Handlungsrahmen bereit gestellt wird, innerhalb dessen diese Aufgaben ablaufen können. Abb. 4 verdeutlicht die Zusammenhänge zwischen den Größen der einzelnen Perspektiven.

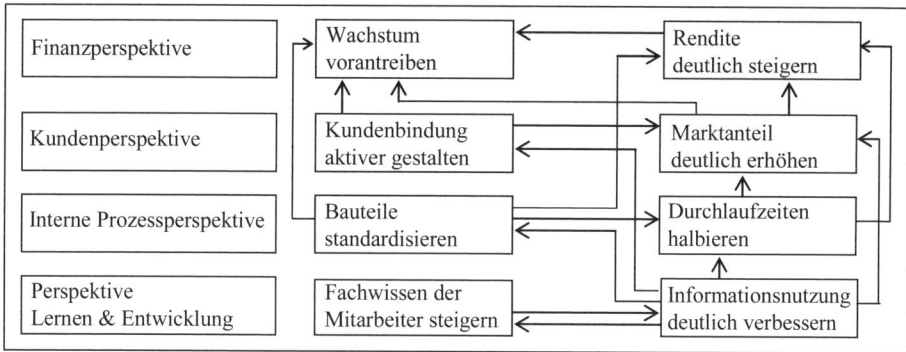

Abb. 4: BSC-Perspektiven und Ausschnitt aus der Strategy Map
In Anlehnung an: Jossé (2005), S. 73

Die Ziele der *Finanzperspektive* bilden einerseits die finanzielle Leistung ab, die von der gewählten Strategie erwartet wird und dienen andererseits als Endgrößen für Ziele und Kennzahlen anderer Perspektiven. Typische Kennzahlen für diese Perspektive sind die Kapitalrentabilität und der Cashflow. In der *Kundenperspektive* werden Ziele und Kennzahlen bezüglich den Anforderungen der Kunden abgebildet. Beispielhaft sind die Größen Marktanteil, Kundentreue und Kundenzufriedenheit zu nennen. In der *Perspektive der Internen Prozesse* werden Ziele zur Verbesserung bzw. zum Aufbau von internen Prozessen formuliert. Mögliche Kennzahlen sind die durchschnittliche Wartezeit eines Kunden oder der Anteil nachbetreuter Kunden. Die *Perspektive Lernen und Entwicklung* bildet Ziele und Kennzahlen zum Erreichen des langfristigen Überlebens der Unternehmung ab. Dies kann anhand der Kennzahlen Fluktuation von Leistungsträgern und dem Umsatzverhältnis Neu- zu Altprodukten gemessen werden.

Für jedes strategische Ziel innerhalb einer Perspektive werden Kennzahlen gebildet, Vorgaben und Maßnahmen definiert sowie die Verantwortlichkeiten für die Zielerreichung geklärt. Die BSC erlaubt, durch die Einbeziehung monetärer und nicht-monetärer Größen sowie Frühindikatoren und Ergebniskennzahlen, in den verschiedenen Perspektiven eine ausgewogene Betrachtung der Organisation. Die einzelnen Kennzahlen sind über Ursache-Wirkungsbeziehungen miteinander verknüpft, wodurch die Abhängigkeiten zwischen einzelnen Zielen deutlich werden. Hilfreich bei der Erstellung einer BSC ist die Methode der strategy maps, da sie die einzelnen Ziele und Teilstrategien mit ihren gegenseitigen Abhängigkeiten graphisch anschaulich darstellt und somit bei der Strukturierung und der Übersetzung der Strategie in Ziele, Kennzahlen, Zielwerte und Maßnahmen eine sehr gute Vorbereitung darstellt (Kaplan/Norton, 2000 sowie Abb. 4, rechts).

Der große Nutzen der BSC im Controllingkonzept einer Unternehmung zeigt sich v.a. in ihrer Variabilität und Vielseitigkeit. Mit ihr können die jeweilige Strategie und die Anforderungen aufgegriffen und in spezifische Perspektiven, Kennziffern und Vorgaben übersetzt werden. Die Vielseitigkeit zeigt sich darin, dass sie in verschiedenen Stufen des Managementprozesses ansetzen und das Management unterstützen kann, wie beispielsweise bei der Strukturierung im Rahmen der Strategiefindung bis zur Abbildung von Soll-Ist-Vergleichen bei Kontrollen. Sie bietet für die entscheidende Aufgabe der Schließung der Lücke zwischen Strategiefindung und -umsetzung weit reichende Möglichkeiten (Horváth/Gaiser, 2000).

Ein weiterer großer Vorteil besteht darin, weitere Controllingsysteme und -instrumente an die BSC zu koppeln bzw. sie damit zu steuern. Die BSC kann beispielsweise die Funktionen der in Abschnitt 9.2.2.2 besprochenen Risikosteuerung und des Risikocontrolling übernehmen, indem potentielle Risiken gezielt operationalisiert und durch die BSC kontinuierlich verfolgt werden. Besonders die Frühindikatoren der BSC sind hierbei von großer Bedeutung, da sie drohende Abweichungen mit teils deutlich zeitlichem Vorlauf anzeigen und somit Handlungsbedarf signalisieren.

Das Zusammenspiel zwischen BSC und Budgetierung wird durch die Tatsache verdeutlicht, dass beim Herunterbrechen der Organisationsziele die finanziellen Rahmenbedingungen abgesteckt werden müssen. Die Einhaltung der Budgetvorgaben kann mit der BSC verfolgt werden. Oehler (2002) sieht gerade in der Verbindung des Zero-Base-Budgeting und der nach dem Top-Down-Prinzip funktionierenden BSC die Möglichkeit, die eher operativ ausgerichtete Budgetierung mit der strategischen Ebene zu verbinden.

Durch die Fokussierung auf relevante Steuerungsgrößen, die regelmäßigen Soll-Ist-Abgleiche und die Verknüpfung von Messgrößen und Maßnahmen eignet sich die BSC auch als Standardberichtssystem und damit zur Kommunikation innerhalb der Unternehmung (Horváth & Partner, 2001). Durch die Ermittlung und das Anzeigen von Über- oder Unterschreitungen von festgelegten Toleranzwerten kann die Notwendigkeit von Maßnahmen signalisiert und kommuniziert werden.

9.2.3 Informationsversorgungssystem
Einer kurzen Darstellung grundlegender Phasen der Informationsversorgung (Abschnitt 9.2.3.1) folgt die Beschreibung der Phase der Informationsbeschaffung mit dem Schwerpunkt Unternehmensrechnung (Abschnitt 9.2.3.2).

9.2.3.1 Phasenmodell der Informationsversorgung
Das Informationsversorgungssystem hat die Aufgabe, alle für die Planung und Kontrolle relevanten Informationen zur richtigen Zeit, am richtigen Ort und mit dem notwendigen Genauigkeits- und Verdichtungsgrad bereitzustellen. Informationen werden als zweckorientiertes Wissen verstanden, das zur Lösung von Planungs- und Kontrollproblemen führt (Barth/Barth, 2004). Abb. 5 verdeutlicht die einzelnen Phasen des Informationsversorgungssystems. Im Zentrum der weiteren Ausführun-

gen steht die Phase der Informationsbeschaffung mit der Darstellung der Informationsquellen für die Controllingtätigkeiten.

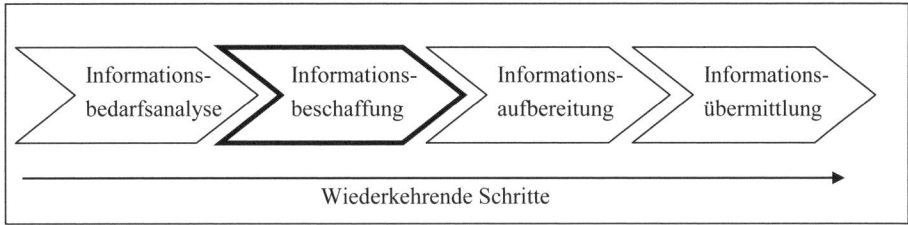

Abb. 5: Phasen des Informationsversorgungssystems

9.2.3.2 Informationsbeschaffung

Der Informationsbedarf an Einzelinformationen, Methoden und Modellen für die Planung und Kontrolle wird zum Großteil durch die Unternehmensrechnung gedeckt, deren Bestandteile in Tab. 2 dargestellt sind.

Das interne Rechnungswesen ist in diesem Zusammenhang ein wichtiges Instrument, das Informationen sowohl für die operative als auch für die strategische Planung und Kontrolle liefert. Im Zentrum des *operativ ausgerichteten Rechnungswesens* steht die Kosten- und Leistungsrechnung, bei der der gesamte Leistungserstellungsprozess und dessen Wirtschaftlichkeit abgebildet werden. Sie liefert wichtige Informationen zur Entscheidungsfindung des Managements, wie z.B. Angaben zu Preisuntergrenzen oder zur Entscheidung zwischen Eigenerstellung und Fremdbezug.

	Finanzziele	Erfolgsziele	Potentialziele	Produkt-ziele	Sozial-/ Umweltziele
Vergangen-heits-orientiert	Liqudiltäts-rechnung Finanzierungs-rechnung	Ist-Kosten- und Erlös-rechnung Ist-Bilanz-rechnung	Anlagenrech-nung Lohn- und Ge-haltsrechnung Humanvermö-gensrechnung		Sozial-bilanzen
Zukunftsorien-tiert *- kurzfristig*	Liquiditätspla-nungs- und kontrollrech-nung	Plankosten- und Erlös-rechnung			
- mittel- bis langfristig *- langfristig*	Finanzpla-nungs- und kontrollrech-nung	Investitions-rechnung			
	Chancen-/Risikofaktoren Früherkennungssysteme				

Tab. 2: Teilsysteme der Unternehmensrechnung
Quelle: Küpper (2005), S. 130

Bei der Ausgestaltung des unternehmungsspezifischen Kosten- und Leistungsrechnungssystems ist eine einheitliche Systematik wichtig, die es ermöglicht, angefallene Kosten und Erlöse eindeutig zuzuordnen und für geforderte Informationen umzuwandeln.

Folgende Unterteilung des *Kosten- und Leistungsrechnungssystems* ist typisch:

Kostenartenrechnung:	„Welche Kosten sind entstanden?"
Kostenstellenrechnung:	„Wo sind die Kosten entstanden?"
Kostenträgerrechnung:	„Wofür sind die Kosten entstanden?"

Diese einheitliche Systematik der Teilsysteme ermöglicht es dem Controller, eine Erfassung nach bestimmten Kriterien, eine Zuordnung auf bestimmte Bezugsgrößen und letztendlich eine zielgerechte Auswertung und Analyse von Kosten und Leistungen durchzuführen.

Die *Deckungsbeitragsrechnung* ist eine sehr wichtige Informationsquelle für den Controller, da durch die Gegenüberstellung von Erlösen und variablen Kosten die Erlös- und Kostenseite gleichermaßen berücksichtigt wird. Die entstehende Differenz (Deckungsbeitrag) ist derjenige Überschuss, der für die Deckung der Fixkosten zur Verfügung steht.

Im Vergleich zur einstufigen Deckungsbeitragsrechnung, bei der die fixen Kosten nicht weiter unterteilt werden, wird der Fixkostenblock bei der mehrstufigen Rechnung weiter aufgeteilt, was eine Erhöhung der Kostentransparenz zur Folge hat (vgl. Tab. 3).

Einstufige Deckungsbeitragsrechnung	Mehrstufige Deckungsbeitragsechnung
Umsatzerlöse	Umsatzerlöse
./. Variable Kosten	./. Variable Kosten
= Deckungsbeitrag	= Deckungsbeitrag I
./. Fixe Kosten	./. Produktfixe Kosten
= Ergebnis	= Deckungsbeitrag II
	./. Bereichsfixe Kosten
	= Deckungsbeitrag III
	./. Unternehmensfixe Kosten
	= Betriebsergebnis

Tab. 3: Arten der Deckungsbeitragsrechnung

Aufbauend auf der Konzeption der Deckungsbeitragsrechnung stellt die *Break-Even-Analyse* ein vielfach benutztes Instrument des Controllers in der Kommunikation mit dem Management dar. Diese Analyse zeigt die Auswirkungen von Änderungen der Größen Preis, Kosten und Menge auf das Ergebnis anschaulich auf (Horváth, 2003; Schweitzer/Troßmann, 1998).

Für den Erfolg einer Unternehmung reicht eine operativ ausgerichtete Unternehmensrechnung nicht aus. Vielmehr muss das Management künftige Entwicklungen und Störungen antizipieren und die sich daraus ergebenden Chancen und Risiken abschätzen und versuchen für sich auszunutzen. Hierbei zeigt sich noch einmal die Wichtigkeit eines geeigneten Früherkennungssystems, wie es auch im Rahmen des Risikomanagements (Abschnitt 9.2.2.2) angesprochen wurde (siehe hierzu auch Krystek/Müller-Stewens, 1999).

Ziel ist der Aufbau eines strategieorientiertes Kostenmanagements (Horváth/Brokemper, 1998), welches in allen Phasen und Ebenen des Managementprozesses eine Entscheidungsunterstützung für das Management darstellt. Eine Erweiterung der operativen Instrumente und Methoden ist erforderlich, da im strategischen Rahmen eine stärkere Betrachtung der Unternehmensumwelt nötig ist und nicht von gegebenen Kapazitäten ausgegangen wird, sondern diese als gestaltbar gelten. Langfristige Kostenbestimmungsfaktoren wie Erfahrung und Economies of Scale werden analysiert, die Vorsteuergrößen für Kostenstruktur, -verlauf und -niveau darstellen. Wichtige Instrumente des strategieorientierten Kostenmanagements sind die Lebenszykluskostenrechnung (Back-Hock, 1992) und die Erfahrungskurve (Henderson, 1984).

9.3 Controlling im Sport

Die in Abschnitt 9.2 beschriebenen Grundlagen des Controlling werden unter Berücksichtigung besonderer Aspekte des Anwendungsfelds Sport dargelegt.

9.3.1 Planungs- und Kontrollaufgaben des Controlling in Sportorganisationen

Besonderer Fokus wird auf den Einsatz der Balanced Scorecard in Sportorganisationen gelegt (Abschnitt 9.3.1.4). Davor werden die Einsatzmöglichkeiten von strategischem und operativem Controlling (Abschnitt 9.3.1.1), Risikomanagement (Abschnitt 9.3.1.2) und Budgetierung (Abschnitt 9.3.1.3) diskutiert.

9.3.1.1 Strategisches und operatives Controlling

In Sportorganisationen wird die Wichtigkeit des Controllers als Managementunterstützer und Informationsversorger sehr deutlich. Er wirkt bei der strategischen Ausrichtung der Organisation mit und hilft bei der Etablierung eines strategischen Planungssystems. Er unterstützt das Management dabei, ein breites Einverständnis in der Sportorganisation über die Ziele zu erreichen, die mit einem professionellen Controlling verfolgt werden sollen und wie ein solches System funktionieren kann (Dörnemann, 2002). Dies ist sehr entscheidend, wenn man sich das differenzierte Zielsystem mit sportlichen und wirtschaftlichen Zielen sowie dem Imageaufbau vor Augen hält (Wehrle/Heinzelmann, 2004; Haas, 2002). Bei diesem Zielfindungsprozess zeigt sich zumeist ein Zielkonflikt in der Gewichtung von sportlichen und wirtschaftlichen Zielen, da die einzelnen Personengruppen unterschiedliche Strategien verfolgen. Der Geschäftsführer eines Vereins ist auf ein sicheres eigenes Einkommen angewiesen, weshalb für ihn die finanzielle Stabilität höchste Priorität hat. Prestigeträchtige Auftritte in den Medien hingegen sind für Ehrenamtliche wie den Präsidenten sehr reizvoll, weshalb sie für die Steigerung des sportlichen Erfolgs möglicherweise bereit sind, mehr zu riskieren.

Neben der Strukturierung des Zielfindungsprozesses ist die Verknüpfung der strategischen mit der operativen Ebene durch geeignete Methoden und Instrumente entscheidend. Diese Methoden und Instrumente müssen v.a. bei Organisationen mit ehrenamtlichen Strukturen den jeweiligen Bedingungen angemessen sein, um die Akzeptanz der Mitarbeiter zu erhalten, die oftmals der Einführung neuer betriebswirtschaftlicher Methoden oder Systemen skeptisch gegenüber stehen bzw. unterschiedliche ökonomische Vorkenntnisse haben (Horak, 1993). Nur so können die entwickelten Strategien Eingang in die operative Arbeit finden.

9.3.1.2 Risikomanagement

Die Unsicherheit des sportlichen Erfolgs und die damit zusammenhängenden Auswirkungen auf den finanziellen Erfolg erfordern im Rahmen des Controlling den Einsatz eines Risikomanagements.

Für die *Identifikation der Risiken* muss die In- und Umwelt der Sportorganisation kontinuierlich und umfassend auf schwache Signale hin untersucht werden *(Scanning)* und ermittelte Risikofaktoren detaillierter betrachtet und überwacht werden *(Monitoring)*. Die in Tab. 4 aufgeführten Risikoursachen liefern erste Anhaltspunkte möglicher Gefahrenquellen.

Natur/ Höhere Gewalt	Subjektbedingte Faktoren	Objektbedingte Faktoren	Gesellschaftliche Faktoren	Ökonomische Faktoren
▪ Witterung, ▪ Klima ▪ Elementarereignisse wie Tod, Krankheit, Unfall	▪ Verhalten der Beteiligten ▪ Leistungsvermögen und -willen ▪ Risikoverhalten der Sportler ▪ Verhalten der Entscheidungsträger, Schiedsrichter, etc.	▪ Existenz und Beschaffenheit der Betriebsmittel ▪ Sportgeräte ▪ Trainingsstätten	▪ (Sport-) politische Eingriffe ▪ Rahmenbedingungen ▪ Sportartenimage ▪ Image der Profi-Sportorganisation	▪ Volks- und marktwirtschaftliche Faktoren ▪ Spielermärkte ▪ Änderung der Wettbewerbsverhältnisse ▪ Nachfrageverhalten ▪ Betriebsspezifische Faktoren ▪ sportartenspezifische Produktionsbedingungen

Tab. 4: Potentielle Gefahrenquellen
In Anlehnung an Dörnemann (2002), S. 164, Benner (1992), S. 191

Identifizierte Risiken werden einer ersten *Klassifikation* unterzogen. Die Beschaffenheit der Sportgeräte kann im Einzelfall als Risiko identifiziert worden sein, jedoch kann entschieden werden, dass eine kontinuierliche Verfolgung dieses Risikos ökonomisch nicht sinnvoll ist. Im Gegensatz hierzu haben Änderungen der Wettbewerbsverhältnisse einen großen Einfluss auf den Erfolg von Sportorganisationen und müssen kontinuierlich überwacht werden.

Für die *Analyse und Bewertung* der Risiken können unterschiedliche sportliche Szenarien (worst-case, most-likely- und best-case-Szenario) gebildet und für alle Alternativen die finanziellen Auswirkungen bestimmt werden. Die finanziell bewerteten Szenarien kombiniert mit deren subjektiv geschätzten Eintrittswahrscheinlichkeiten ergeben eine Risikokurve, die dem Management wichtige Anhaltspunkte für die Planung geben (Haas, 2002). Diese Zusammenhänge können der folgenden Matrix (Abb. 6) entnommen werden:

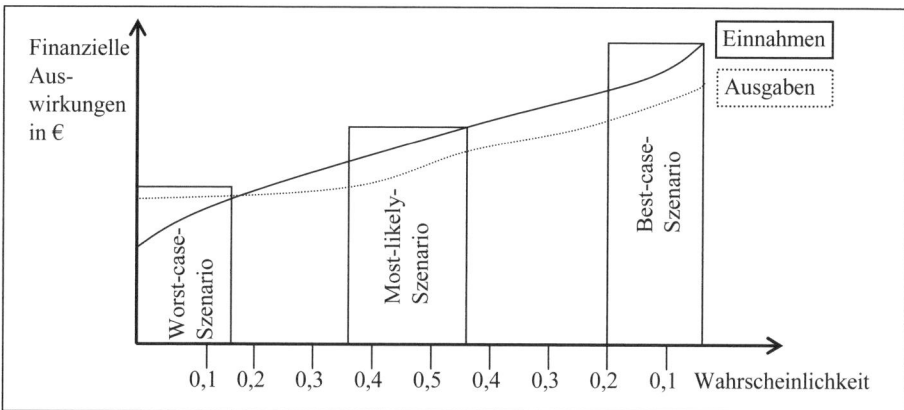

Abb. 6: Risikomatrix
In Anlehnung an: Haas (2002), S. 100

Die Steuerung und das Controlling der Risiken können z.B. mit Hilfe der BSC erfolgen. In der BSC des VfB Stuttgart wurden beispielsweise relevante Kennzahlen entsprechend zusammengefasst, so dass die Größen TV-Vergütung, Zuschauereinnahmen und Prämienausschüttung je nach sportlichem Erfolg planbar sind (Wehrle/Heinzelmann, 2004). Die notwendigen Faktoren Sollgrößen, Toleranzgrenzen und zu ergreifende Maßnahmen sind in der Systematik der BSC vorgesehen und bieten sich auch für die kontinuierliche Verfolgung von Risikofaktoren an.

9.3.1.3 Budgetierung

Ein wichtiger Schritt bei der Verknüpfung der Strategie mit der operativen Ebene stellt die Budgetierung dar. Für die geplanten Maßnahmen auf sportlicher Ebene und Verwaltungsebene müssen die jeweiligen Budgets festgelegt werden. Im Be-

251

reich des Sports ist im Vergleich zur Industrie zu beachten, dass oftmals im Vorhinein keine starren Budgets aufgrund der Wechselwirkungen zwischen sportlichem und wirtschaftlichem Erfolg errechnet werden können. Somit können nur verfahrensorientierte Methoden in Betracht gezogen werden (Haas, 2002). Die in Abschnitt 9.2.2.3 beschriebene *Fortschreibungsbudgetierung* ist in ihrer Durchführung sehr einfach. Allerdings erscheint sie nicht besonders zielführend, da die Budgetposten des Vorjahres relativ unreflektiert für die kommende Planungsperiode übernommen werden. In stark hierarchisch geprägten Sportorganisationen, in denen einzelne Abteilungen ein hohes Standing genießen, kann es dazu führen, dass die Mittel mehr nach Einfluss denn nach Leistung verteilt werden.

Die Methode des *Zero-Base-Budgeting* ist zwar in ihrer Durchführung sehr aufwendig, jedoch erscheint sie besonders im Bereich des Sports Erfolg versprechend, da bei der Budgetbestimmung alle Posten auf den Prüfstand gestellt werden. Gewohnheitsposten („Pauschalen für die erste Mannschaft"), die bisher ohne große Überlegungen weiter gewährt wurden, werden in Frage gestellt und somit versucht, Ineffizienzen in der Organisation zu beheben (Wadsack, 2004). Die einzelnen Abteilungen der Sportorganisation definieren hierbei ihre bevorzugten Maßnahmen für die kommende Planungsphase. Die Lizenzspielerabteilung kann hierbei z.B. ein Trainingslager einfordern, während die Marketingabteilung zur genaueren Zielgruppenansprache eine Zuschaueranalyse plant. Aus den unterschiedlichen Entscheidungspaketen wird anschließend ein Ranking erstellt und das Gesamtbudget vom Präsidium auf die wichtigsten Maßnahmen aufgeteilt (Haas, 2002). Das Zero-Base-Budgeting bietet durch die Bottom-Up-Vorgehensweise den Vorteil, dass die einzelnen Abteilungen einen Entscheidungsspielraum erhalten, den sie durch ihr operatives Wissen ausfüllen können. Dadurch kann erreicht werden, dass dem Einzelnen die Auswirkungen seines Handelns auf den Gesamterfolg bewusst werden.

9.3.1.4 Balanced Scorecard
Dem Controlling in Sportorganisationen kommt, wie bereits erwähnt, auch die Aufgabe zu, den Strategiefindungs- und -umsetzungsprozess zu begleiten und zu unterstützen, wofür die BSC genutzt werden kann. Als Vorbereitung hierfür können die einzelnen Teilstrategien und Ziele mit der Methode der strategy maps strukturiert werden. Die strategy maps stellen eine einfache und kommunikationsfördernde Methode dar, mit der der Controller seiner Aufgabe als Planungskoordinator beikommen und den Prozess strukturieren kann. Die relevanten Ursache-Wirkungs-Beziehungen zwischen einzelnen Zielen aus den verschiedenen Bereichen können aufgezeigt und Teilstrategien zu einem Gesamtbild zusammengefügt werden. Abb. 7 zeigt einen Ausschnitt der strategy map einer Sportorganisation.

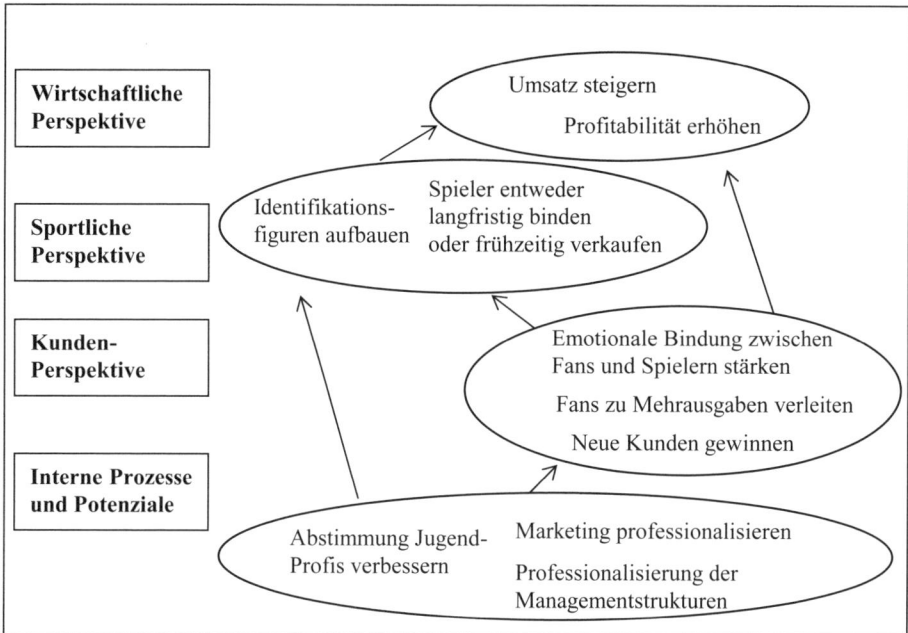

Abb. 7: Ausschnitt der strategy map einer börsennotierten Profi-Sport-Organisation
In Anlehnung an: Dörnemann (2002), S. 132

Der Vorteil an dieser Methode ist, dass die Personen gezwungen werden, ihre Strategien darzulegen und zu formulieren. Es wird verhindert, dass Strategien „in den Köpfen der Verantwortlichen" zwar oftmals vorhanden sind, jedoch nicht nach Außen getragen werden. Eine graphisch dargelegte und formulierte Strategie erleichtert auch den Schritt der Konsistenzprüfung, da man schneller beurteilen kann, ob einzelne Teilstrategien Sinn ergeben oder verworfen werden müssen. Die Überlegung, einen gestandenen Profi zur Imageförderung zu verpflichten, muss dann entschieden abgelehnt werden, wenn die Auswirkungen des Transfers auf den finanziellen Bereich deutlich werden und man sich eingestehen muss, dass die finanziellen Mittel nicht zur Verfügung stehen (Dörnemann, 2002).

Nach der Entwicklung der Strategie gilt es mit der BSC ein System aufzubauen, mit dem die Umsetzung bis in die operative Ebene gelingt. Der Controller hat mit ihr ein System zur Hand, mit dem er die sportlichen und wirtschaftlichen Ziele über Kennzahlen und Aktionen in das Alltagsgeschäft überführen kann.

Ein prominentes Beispiel für den Einsatz der BSC im Sportbereich stellt das BalPlan-System des VfB Stuttgart dar. Dass die vorher genannten Aufgaben mit der BSC v.a. auch im Sportbereich zu erreichen sind, unterstreicht die Aussage von VfB-Präsident Erwin Staudt (zitiert in: Horváth AG, 2004, o.S.):

> „BalPlan (*Balanced Scorecard Planning System*) ist sowohl ein Controlling-Instrument, mit dem wir die Analyse der eigenen Prozesse und Standortbestimmungen durchführen können, als auch eine strategische Ausrichtung des Unternehmens VfB Stuttgart."

Die BSC des Bundesligisten weist folgende Perspektiven und Messgrößen auf:

Wirtschaftliche Perspektive	Sportliche Perspektive	Kunden-Perspektive	Prozess- & Potenti-alperspektive
• Umsatz • Profitabilität • Liquidität • Verschuldungsgrad • Etateffizienz • Gehaltssumme des Profiteams • Wertsteigerung für die Aktionäre	• Tabellenplatz in der Meisterschaft • Erreichen bestimmter Runden in anderen Wettbewerben • Trainerkontinuität • Teamwert	• Stadionauslastung • Anteil Neukunden • Cateringumsatz pro Stadionbesucher • Zufriedenheit aller Zielgruppen • Loyalität der Fans	• Erfolgsquote Talent-Scouting • Anteil der aus der eigenen Jugend übernommenen Profispieler • Verfügbarkeit Telefonhotline • Managementkontinuität

Tab. 5: Perspektiven und Kennzahlen der BSC des VfB Stuttgart
Quelle: Jossé (2005), S. 281

Das Zielsystem von Sportorganisationen ist durch die Wechselwirkungen von wirtschaftlichem und sportlichem Erfolg sehr komplex und die Finanzperspektive besitzt anders als in den meisten erwerbswirtschaftlichen Unternehmen nicht das Alleinstellungsmerkmal, an dem sich alle anderen Ziele ausrichten. Diese Besonderheit kann in der BSC berücksichtigt und anschaulich abgebildet werden.

Das Beispiel VfB Stuttgart zeigt weiterhin, dass Teile eines Risikomanagements durch die BSC gesteuert werden können. Der Einsatz der BSC im Zusammenspiel mit einem Risikomanagement wird von Wurl und Mayer (2001) besonders für börsennotierte Sportorganisationen herausgestellt, die aufgrund des KonTraG zur Einführung eines Risikomanagements gezwungen sind und die BSC als zentrales Steuerungsinstrument dafür nutzen können.

9.3.2 Informationsbeschaffung in Sportorganisationen

Formen der Informationsbeschaffung in Sportorganisationen werden getrennt nach operativem (Abschnitt 9.3.2.1) und strategischem Fokus (Abschnitt 9.3.2.2) besprochen.

9.3.2.1 Informationsbeschaffung für operative Controllingaufgaben

Für operative Controllingaufgaben benötigt der Controller einer Sportorganisation als Grundlage für seine Arbeit eine effektive und gut systematisierte Kosten- und Leistungsrechnung. Innerhalb der *Kostenartenrechnung* kann zwischen Einzelkosten, wie z.b. Bälle einer genormten Größe für eine Mannschaft einer bestimmten Altersklasse und Gemeinkosten, wie die Kosten des Hausmeisters oder der Geschäftsleitung differenziert werden. Im Rahmen der *Kostenstellenrechnung* kann ein Mehrspartenverein für seine Abteilungen wie z.b. Handball, Fußball und Leichtathletik separate Kostenstellen einrichten. Die *Kostenträgerrechnung* eines Vereins kann so aufgebaut werden, dass innerhalb des Marketing im Bereich des Fanartikelverkaufs für einzelne Produkte wie Fanschals, Trikots und Wimpel Kostenträger gebildet werden. Aufbauend hierauf ermöglicht dies dem Controller z.B. Angaben über Preisuntergrenzen einzelner Fanartikel zu machen.

Eine gute Systematik ist wichtig, da der Controller laufend Informationen aus dem wirtschaftlichen und sportlichen Bereich beschaffen und diese an Empfänger aus sehr unterschiedlichen Tätigkeitsfeldern weiterreichen muss. Sowohl Spieler- und Trainererfolgsrechnungen und Erfolgsrechnungen für die Nachwuchsarbeit als auch Werbeerfolgs- und Spieltagserfolgsrechnungen gehören zum Aufgabenbereich des Controllers im Rahmen der Informationsbeschaffung (Haas, 2002).

Am Beispiel der deckungsbeitragsbezogenen Spieltagsrechnung (vgl. Tab. 6) wird eine Informationsbeschaffungsmaßnahme für das Management erläutert. Diese Rechnung informiert darüber, ob die Kernumsätze aus dem Ligabetrieb mit den dazugehörenden Nebengeschäftsfeldern die laufenden Kosten der Geschäftstätigkeit decken. Ziel ist die Erwirtschaftung eines möglichst hohen Deckungsbeitrags, um v.a. den hohen Fixkostenblock der Personalkosten zu decken.

9.3.2.2 Informationsbeschaffung für strategische Controllingaufgaben

Ein strategieorientiertes Kostenmanagement, welches nicht von einem statischen Zustand ausgeht, sondern das Management auf Optimierungspotential in den Bereichen der Kostenstruktur, des Kostenniveaus und des Kostenverlaufs aufmerksam macht, ist in Sportorganisationen sehr wichtig (Dörnemann, 2002). Im Bereich der *Kostenstruktur* wird eine Optimierung der Relation von Fix- und Gemeinkosten angestrebt. Eine Fragestellung in diesem Bereich ist die Entscheidung zwischen Eigenfertigung und Fremdbezug. Der Manager eines Vereins benötigt bei der Entscheidung, ob er das Catering für Heimspiele intern ausführen möchte oder den Auftrag extern vergeben soll, entscheidungsrelevante Daten vom Controller. Muss der Geschäftsführer hierfür eine neue Stelle schaffen, erhöht dies wiederum den Fix- und Gemeinkostenblock. Der Controller muss über Investitions- und Szenario-Rechnungen und über eine Break-Even-Rechnung ermitteln, unter welchen Umständen welche Entscheidung zu fällen ist. Die Senkung der Kostenhöhe wird bei der Untersuchung des *Kostenniveaus* angestrebt, wofür u.a. Prozessoptimierungen notwendig sind. Der Controller eines Verbandes kann aufbauend auf den Ergebnissen einer Prozessanalyse oder Benchmark-Studien mit Vorschlägen auf das Management zukommen, wie die Kosten bei der Vorbereitung und Durchführung von Trainerfortbildungen verringert werden können. Beim *Kostenverlauf* steht das Kostenverhalten in Abhängigkeit der Beschaffung im Mittelpunkt. Im professionell geführten Vereinsbereich kann das Yield Management genutzt werden. Hierbei wird ausgelotet, wie über eine Preisdifferenzierung bei Eintrittskarten eine maximale Stadion- bzw. Hallenauslastung erreicht werden kann. Der Controller muss diese Effekte quantifizieren und steuerbar machen, weshalb er hierfür historische Nachfragedaten sammelt, Nachfrageprognosen erstellt und mathematische Optimierungsmodelle anwendet.

		(Heim-) Spieltag							
	Beispielsaison	1	...	17	DFB-Pokal	Halle	International	Sonstige	Summe
	Zuschauerzahl								
./.	**Umsätze (spieltagsbezogen):** Zuschauereinnahmen Bandenwerbung Anzeigetafeln/Durchsagen usw **Variable Kosten (spieltagsbezogen):** Reisekosten/Trainingslager Stadionnutzung Kassen-/Ordnungs-/Sanitätsdienst Schiedsrichter usw								
=	**DB I**								
	DB I / Zuschauerzahl								
+ ./.	**Umsätze (zusätzl.):** TV/Hörfunk Merchandising Werbung (Haupt-/Co-Sponsoren; Ausstatter) usw Brand-Marketing *Personalkosten (Sportbetrieb) incl. Transfers*								
	DB II								
./.	**Var. Kosten (zusätzl.):** Materialkosten, Personalkosten (sonstige) Grundstücke & Gebäude -abzügl. AfA- Sonstige Kosten (Dienstleistungskosten) Kapitalkosten								
=	**(Jahres) überschuss**								

Tab. 6: System der spieltagsbezogenen Deckungsbeitragsrechnung
In Anlehnung an: Dörnemann (2002), S. 171

In vielen Sportorganisationen ist die Planung, Steuerung und Kontrolle des Personalbereichs ein wichtiges Thema, da er einen Großteil der anfallenden Kosten ausmacht. Um diesen Bereich zu steuern, können auch im Rahmen der Erstellung der BSC z.B. gezielt für den Bereich der Verwaltung personalbezogene Kennzahlen wie Fehlzeiten und Wertschöpfung pro Mitarbeiter aufgenommen und spezifische Ziele formuliert werden. Ebenfalls können über Benchmarking und qualitative Mitarbeiter- und Managementbefragungen Entwicklungen festgestellt werden, die in die Planung des Personalbereichs einfließen können. Jedoch ist zu berücksichtigen, dass diese Daten oftmals nur vage Steuerungsgrößen sind und nur Daten mittlerer Härte darstellen. Im Sportbereich ist dies besonders schwerwiegend, da der Output nicht problemlos gemessen werden und z.B. der Anteil eines Spielers am Mannschaftserfolg nicht ohne weiteres festgestellt werden kann (Haas, 2002). Bei der Vertragsgestaltung kann jedoch angesetzt und stark leistungsbezogene Vergütungsmodelle in Betracht gezogen werden. Dies erscheint sinnvoll, wenn man sich die Wechselwirkungen von sportlichem und wirtschaftlichem Erfolg vor Augen hält. Eine weitere Möglichkeit stellt die Bildung einer Kennzahl dar, die das Gehalt in Bezug zur Höhe des gesamten Etats des Spielerkaders angibt. Eine entsprechende Leistungsbewertung im sportlichen Bereich (objektivierbare Größen wie die Anzahl der Pflichtspiele, der Tore oder die subjektive Einschätzung durch die sportliche Leitung) wird der finanziellen Größe gegenübergestellt, um die leistungsgerechte Entlohnung zu ermitteln.

9.4 Fallstudie

Die folgende Fallstudie verdeutlicht am Beispiel des Württembergischen Fußballverbands (wfv), wie die BSC als umfassendes Controllingsystem in Sportorganisationen eingesetzt werden kann.

Fallstudie „Balanced Scorecard im Württembergischen Fußballverband"

Württembergischer
Fußballverband e.V.

Der wfv wurde 1954 in Ulm gegründet und hat heute seinen Sitz in Stuttgart. Gemessen an Mitgliedern ist er der viertgrößte Fußball-Landesverband im Deutschen Fußballbund. Im Rahmen eines Pilotprojekts hat er im Bereich Bildung die BSC eingeführt. Im ehrenamtlichen Umfeld ist dieser Bereich durch einen eigenen Ausschuss und im Hauptamt durch die Abteilung Bildung & Qualifizierung vertreten.

Mit der Einführung der BSC wird das Ziel verfolgt, die Inhalte der Bildungsarbeit, ausgedrückt durch die Optimierung der Ausbildungsordnung, der Qualifizierungsebenen, der modernen Lehrmethoden und der Qualitätssicherung, die in Übereinstimmung mit den Richtlinien des DOSB zur Qualifizierung entwickelt wurden, abzubilden und zu steuern. Die BSC dient als umfassendes Controllingtool, das die Verantwortlichen im Bereich Bildung bei ihren Führungsaufgaben unterstützt und mit wichtigen Informationen versorgt sowie die Kostenstruktur transparent macht. Die BSC des wfv, „Qualitätskarte" genannt, besteht aus vier Perspektiven bzw. „Karten". Die *„Zielkarte: was wollen wir?"* (Karte I) beinhaltet die strategischen Ziele bzw. Schwerpunkte und zeichnet somit die grobe Richtschnur ab, die verdeutlicht, was dem wfv als wichtig erscheint und dementsprechend verfolgt wird. In der *„Zielgruppenkarte: wen meinen wir?"* (Karte II) liegt der Fokus auf den Personen im wfv, an die diese strategischen Ziele aus Karte I gerichtet sind. In der *„Mitarbeiterkarte: wen haben bzw. brauchen wir?"* (Karte III) sind diejenigen Mitarbeiter im wfv angesprochen, die für das Erreichen eines Oberziels aus Karte I eine spezifische Aufgabe zu übernehmen haben. In der *„Ressourcenkarte: was brauchen wir?"* (Karte IV) ist das Budget abgetragen. Es ist aufgelistet, was die Verfolgung eines Oberziels kostet bzw. welche Mittel dafür bereitzustellen sind. Hierbei wird deutlich, dass die finanzielle Perspektive nicht die dominante Rolle wie in Industrieunternehmen einnimmt, sondern eher als einschränkende Bedingung für die Verwirklichung der Sachziele dient. Die Optimierung der Qualifizierungsebenen (Karte I) wird anhand der Anzahl der Kurzschulungen gemessen, die in 2006 bei 218 liegt und für 2007 und 2008 bei über 200 Schulungen liegen soll. Hierfür sollen die flächendeckenden Schulungen im Verbandsgebiet weiterhin durchgeführt werden, wofür die Verbandssportlehrer, die Jugendabteilung und der Leiter der Abteilung Bildung & Qualifizierung zuständig sind. Die Zielgruppe (Karte II) sind die Teilnehmer der Schulungen, deren Zufriedenheit als Kennzahl herangezogen wird. Die Zufriedenheitswerte liegen momentan bei „gut", was auch in den kommenden beiden Jahren erreicht werden soll. Diese Werte werden vom jeweiligen Schulungsleiter ermittelt und an die Geschäftsstelle rückgemeldet. Für die Erreichung dieses Ziels müssen vom DFB und wfv gute Materialien bereit gestellt und die DFB-Kurzschulungen in das wfv-Modell integriert werden, da bisher ein anderes Modell vorlag. In der Mitarbeiterkarte (Karte III) geht es darum, dass der zuständige Mitarbeiter die Veranstaltung gut organisiert, was an der Prozentzahl der nicht stattgefundenen, aber geplanten Kurzschulungen gemessen wird und bis 2008 auf 0% gesenkt werden soll. Ein entsprechender Organisationsablauf existiert bereits in der Geschäftsstelle des wfv, aber weiterhin wird ein Aufgabenkatalog für die Schulungsleiter vor Ort erstellt, um die Organisation dort zu verbessern. In der Ressourcenkarte (Karte IV) ist das Budget aufgelistet, welches aufgrund tendenziell zurückgehender Fördermittel zumindest aufrechterhalten werden soll. Tab. 7 zeigt einen Ausschnitt der Qualitätskarte mit den Verknüpfungen zwischen den einzelnen Perspektiven:

I: Zielkarte: Was wollen wir?

Ziel	Zielbeschreibung	Ist - Wert 2006	Zielwert		Konkrete Aktionen auf Landesverbands- ebene	verantwortlich
			2007	2008		
Optimierung der Qualifizie- rungsebenen	Anzahl der statt- gefundenen Kurz- schulungen	218	>200	>200	Flächendeckende Schulungen durch Trainerlehrstab und Instruktoren	Verbandssport- lehrer/ Abteilungslei- ter Bildung & Qualifizierung

II: Zielgruppenkarte: Wen meinen wir?

Ziel	Zielbeschreibung	Ist - Wert 2006	Zielwert		Konkrete Aktionen auf Landesverbands- ebene	verantwortlich
			2007	2008		
Teilnehmer der Kurzschulun- gen	Zufriedenheit der Teilnehmer im Bezirk mit Mate- rial (DFB) und Unterstützung des LV	Gut (Feed- back Schu- lungs- leiter)	Gut	Gut	▪ LV und DFB Materia- len ▪ Integration der DFB- Kurzschulungen in wfv-System ▪ Zufriedenheit der Schulungslei- ter/Referenten wird abgefragt	Ausschuss- Vorsitzender/ Abteilungslei- ter

III: Mitarbeiterkarte: Wen haben/brauchen wir?

Ziel	Zielbeschreibung	Ist - Wert 2006	Zielwert		Konkrete Aktionen auf Landesverbands- ebene	verantwortlich
			2007	2008		
Geschäftsstelle LW, zuständi- ger hauptamtli- cher Mitarbei- ter, Jugendbil- dungsbeauf- tragter	Rechtzeitige rei- bungslose Orga- nisation von Ver- anstaltungen; *%-Zahl der nicht stattgefundenen – aber geplanten Kurzschulungen*	2 %	1 %	0 %	▪ Läuft bereits ▪ Erstellung eines Auf- gabenkatalogs für Schulungsleiter	Ausschuss- Vorsitzender/ Abteilungslei- ter

IV: Ressourcenkarte: Was brauchen wir?

Ziel	Zielbeschreibung	Ist - Wert 2006	Zielwert		Konkrete Aktionen auf Landesverbands- ebene	verantwortlich
			2007	2008		
Kostenstruktur Kurzschulun- gen	Kosten der Schu- lungen von In- struktoren Trai- nerlehrstab		Erhal tung Etat	Erhal tung Etat	Vorhanden	Ausschuss- Vorsitzender/ Abteilungslei- ter

Tab. 7: Ausschnitt aus der BSC des wfv
In Anlehnung an: Jordan (2006), S. 74

Die BSC hat sich für die Beteiligten als sehr wirksames System erwiesen, das den Verantwortlichen bei der Planung, Kontrolle und Informationsversorgung hilft. Im Rahmen der Planung unterstützt es die handelnden Personen dabei, ihre Ziele zu konkretisieren und zu operationalisieren sowie sie in Abhängigkeit zu anderen Zielen zu sehen. Durch das Herunterbrechen in konkrete Teilziele, das Festsetzen von Soll-Werten und die Ableitung von Maßnahmen kann die Überführung in die operative Ebene gewährleistet werden. Durch regelmäßige Soll-Ist-Abgleiche wird der Fortschritt der Planung überwacht und ein kontinuierlicher Lernprozess angestoßen. Durch die Aufnahme der Kostenstruktur der Ziele kann weiterhin untersucht werden, inwiefern sich der erzielte Erfolg zu den Kosten verhält und dadurch diskutiert werden, ob sich diese Ziele rechnen und weitergeführt werden sollen. Die Ergebnisse der Kontrollen werden auf Tagungen, Sitzungen sowie informellen Gesprächen diskutiert und die Informationen an die Beteiligten kommuniziert. An die Entscheidungsgremien im wfv werden Erfahrungsberichte gesendet. Somit dient die BSC auch als effektives Kommunikations- und Berichtssystem. Da die BSC auf dem Bildungskonzept des wfv aufbaut und dieses steuert, kann es als umfassendes System angesehen werden, welches die gegebenen Strukturen berücksichtigt und somit individuell an die jeweiligen Anforderungen anpassbar ist. Auf Externe verbreitet es eine vertrauensbildende Wirkung, da der wfv aufzeigt, dass er sich systematisch mit seinem Bereich auseinandersetzt, strukturiert und somit für Transparenz sorgt.

9.5 Fazit und Ausblick

Die Ausführungen und die Fallstudie haben verdeutlicht, dass das Controlling für Sportorganisationen ein wichtiges Teilsystem darstellt, um die vielfältigen Prozesse und Systeme untereinander zu koordinieren und somit nicht zuletzt für Transparenz zu sorgen. Änderungen der Rahmenbedingungen können frühzeitig erkannt und geeignete Maßnahmen ergriffen werden. Für das Management einer Sportorganisation stellt das Controlling insgesamt eine wichtige Führungsunterstützungs- und Informationsversorgungsfunktion dar. Ein besonderer Fokus liegt bei diesen Ausführungen auf dem System der BSC, da es in der Controllingkonzeption einer Sportorganisation eine zentrale Rolle einnehmen kann. Aufgrund ihrer Flexibilität stellt sie ein geeignetes System dar, das an die jeweiligen Gegebenheiten der Organisation anpassbar ist und mit wichtigen Controllingteilsystemen wie dem Risikomanagement und der Budgetierung kombinierbar ist. Besonders das Praxisbeispiel aus der Fallstudie ist ein ermutigendes Beispiel dafür, dass die Anwendung von betriebswirtschaftlichen Systemen mit den notwendigen Modifikationen möglich ist. Sie kann jedoch nicht auf alle aufkommenden Fragestellungen Antworten geben. Für ein effektives Controllingsystem und somit eine geeignete Unterstützung für die Führung von Sportorganisationen ist die kontinuierliche Überprüfung und Verbesserung der eigenen Tätigkeit und gegebenenfalls die Implementierung weiterer geeigneter Controllingsysteme notwendig. Nur damit können die Sportorganisationen den zukünftigen Herausforderungen in adäquater Weise begegnen und ihre Umwelt aktiv steuern.

Kontrollfragen

1. Was versteht man allgemein unter Controlling und welche Funktionen erfüllt es für die Unternehmensführung?
2. Wie unterscheidet sich das operative vom strategischen Controlling?
3. Welche Teilsysteme der Unternehmensrechnung lassen sich unterscheiden?
4. Was ist unter strategieorientiertem Kostenmanagement zu verstehen und welche Zielsetzung wird damit verfolgt?
5. Warum ist ein Risikomanagement für Sportorganisationen wichtig und wie lässt es sich konzeptionell umsetzen?
6. Wie lassen sich die Techniken der Budgetierung unterscheiden und welche Konzeptionen sind für Sportorganisationen sinnvoll?
7. Welche Möglichkeiten bieten strategy maps für die Gestaltung des Planungs- und Kontrollsystems von Sportorganisationen?
8. Wie ist eine Balanced Scorecard aufgebaut und welche Funktionen kann sie im Rahmen des Controlling von Sportorganisationen erfüllen?
9. Wie lassen sich Deckungsbeitragsrechnungen im Sportbereich ausgestalten?
10. Welche Möglichkeiten stehen bereit, um den Personalbereich von Sportorganisationen zu steuern?

Literaturverzeichnis

Back-Hock, Andrea (1992): Produktlebenszyklusorientierte Ergebnisrechnung, in: Männel, Wolfgang (Hrsg.): Handbuch Kostenrechnung, Wiesbaden, S. 703-714.

Barth, Thomas / Barth, Daniela (2004): Controlling, München u.a.

Benner, Gerd (1992): Risk Management im professionellen Sport- auf der Grundlage von Ansätzen einer Sportbetriebslehre, Bergisch Gladbach u.a.

Dörnemann, Jörg (2002): Controlling für Profi-Sportorganisationen: dargestellt am Beispiel der Deutschen Fußballbundesliga, München.

Fröhling, Oliver (2000): KontraG und Controlling, München.

Haas, Oliver (2002): Controlling der Fußballunternehmen. Management und Wirtschaft in Sportvereinen, Berlin.

Hahn, Dietger (1996): PuK: Planung und Kontrolle, Planungs- und Kontrollsysteme, Planungs- und Kontrollrechnung, 5. Aufl., Wiesbaden.

Henderson, Bruce D. (1984): Die Erfahrungskurve in der Unternehmensstrategie, 2.Aufl., Frankfurt/Main u.a.

Horak, Christian (1993): Controlling in Nonprofit-Organisationen - Erfolgsfaktoren und Instrumente, Wiesbaden.

Horváth, Peter (2003): Controlling, 9.Aufl., München.

Horváth, Peter / Brokemper, Andreas (1998): Strategieorientiertes Kostenmanagement, in: Zeitschrift für Betriebswirtschaft, Heft 6, S. 581-604.

Horváth, Peter / Gaiser, Bernd (2000): Implementierungserfahrungen mit der Balanced Scorecard im deutschen Sprachraum – Anstöße zur konzeptionellen Weiterentwicklung, in: Betriebswirtschaftliche Forschung und Praxis, Heft 1, S. 17-35.

Horváth AG (2004): Managementsystem für VfB Stuttgart, http://www.content-manager.de/magazin/news_h6455_managementsystem_fuer_vfb_stuttgart.html (Zugriff: 13.06.2007).

Horváth & Partner (2001): Balanced Scorecard umsetzen, 2.Aufl, Stuttgart.

International Group of Controlling (2007): http://www.igc-controlling.org/DE/_leitbild/leitbild.php (Zugriff: 30.07.2007).

Jordan, Christoph (2006): Die Balanced Scorecard im Sportverband – konkretisiert am Beispiel der Aus-, Fort- und Weiterbildung im Württembergischen Fußballverband, unveröffentlichte Diplomarbeit, Universität Bayreuth.

Jossé, Germann (2005): Balanced Scorecard. Ziele und Strategien messbar umsetzen, München.

Kaplan, Robert S. /Norton, David P. (2000): Having Trouble with Your Strategy? Then Map it!, in: Harvard Business Review, Sept-Oct, S. 167-176.

Konetzny, Michael (2007): http://www.mkonetzny.de/aufsatz/budget.htm (Zugriff: 30.07.2007).

Krystek, Ulrich / Müller-Stewens, Günter (1999): Strategische Frühaufklärung, in: Hahn, Dietger / Taylor, Bernard (Hrsg.): Strategische Unternehmensplanung – Strategische Unternehmensführung: Stand und Entwicklungstendenzen, 8.Aufl., Heidelberg, S. 497-517.

Küpper, Hans-Ulrich (1988): Koordination und Interdependenz als Bausteine einer konzeptionellen und theoretischen Fundierung des Controlling, in: Lücke, Wolfgang (Hrsg.): Betriebswirtschaftliche Steuerungs- und Kontrollprobleme, Wiesbaden, S. 163-183.

Küpper, Hans-Ulrich (2005): Controlling: Konzeption, Aufgaben, Instrumente, 4.Aufl., Stuttgart.

Küpper, Hans-Ulrich / Weber, Jürgen / Zünd, André (1990): Zum Selbstverständnis des Controlling, in: Zeitschrift für Betriebswirtschaft, Heft 3, S. 281-293.

Meyer-Piening, Arnulf (1990): Zero Base Planning. Zukunftssicherndes Instrument der Gemeinkostenplanung, Köln.

Müller, Wolfgang (1974): Die Koordination von Informationsbedarf und Informationsbeschaffung als zentrale Aufgabe des Controlling, in: Zeitschrift für betriebswirtschaftliche Forschung, Heft 26, S. 683-693.

Oehler, Karsten (2002): Balanced Scorecard und Budgetierung - (wie) passt das zusammen?, in: Controlling, Heft 2, S. 85-92.

Ossadnik, Wolfgang (2003): Controlling, 3.Aufl., München u.a.

Rockart, John F. (1979): Chief executives define their own data needs, in: Harvard Business Review, March-April, S. 81-93.

Scharpf, Paul / Lutz, Günther (2000): Risikomanagement, Bilanzierung und Aufsicht von Finanzderivaten, 2.Aufl., Stuttgart.

Schweitzer, Marcell / Troßmann, Ernst (1998): Break-even-Analysen: Methodik und Einsatz, 2.Aufl., Berlin.

Wadsack, Ronald (2004): Budgetierung, http://www.wir-im sport.de/vibss/live/ vibssinhalte/show.php3?id=859&nodeid=39 (Zugriff: 31.07.2007).

Wehrle, Alexander / Heinzelmann, Marcus (2004): Reporting und strategische Steuerung im Profifußball, in: Controlling, Heft 6, S. 349-354.

Wild, Jürgen (1974): Grundlagen der Unternehmensplanung, Reinbek b. Hamburg.

Wurl, Hans-Jürgen / Mayer, Jörg (2001): Balanced Scorecards und industrielles Risikomanagement - Möglichkeiten der Integration, in: Klingebiel, Norbert (Hrsg.): Performance Measurement & Balanced Scorecard, München, S. 179-216.

Weiterführende Ressourcen

Literatur

Büch, Martin P. (1979): Modell und Realität der Fußball-Bundesliga - eine ökonomische Betrachtung, in: Zeitschrift für Wirtschafts- und Sozialwissenschaften, S. 447-466.

Dörnemann, Jörg / Kopp, Jens (2000): Mit Controlling an die Tabellenspitze? - Eine kritisch-konstruktive Analyse des Ausbaustandes betriebswirtschaftlicher Steuerungsinstrumente in der deutschen Fußballbundesliga, in: Controller Magazin, Heft 6, S. 484-489.

Galli, Albert (1997): Das Rechnungswesen im Berufsfußball, Düsseldorf.

Galli, Albert / Wagner, Marc (2002): Zur Anwendbarkeit einer Balanced Scorecard im Sportverein, in: Scherer, Andreas G. / Alt, Jens M. (Hrsg.): Balanced Scorecard in Verwaltung Non-Profit-Organisationen, Stuttgart, S. 265-283.

Kilger, Wolfgang (1993): Flexible Plankostenrechnung und Deckungsbeitragsrechnung, 10.Aufl., Wiesbaden.

Lehmann, Erik / Weigand, Jürgen (1999): Determinanten der Entlohnung von Profifußballspielern - Eine empirische Analyse für die deutsche Bundesliga, in: Betriebswirtschaftliche Forschung und Praxis, Heft 2, S. 124-135.

Littkemann, Jörn / Sunderdiek, Bernd (1998): Besonderheiten der Rechnungslegung von Vereinen der Fußball-Bundesliga, in: Wirtschaftswissenschaftliches Studium, Heft 5, S. 253-255.

Maenning, Wolfgang (1998): Möglichkeiten und Grenzen von Kosten-Nutzen-Analysen im Sport, in: Sportwissenschaft, Heft 3-4, S. 311-327.

Madl, Roland (1994): Der Sportverein als Unternehmen, Wiesbaden.

Reichmann, Thomas (1997): Controlling mit Kennzahlen und Managementberichten, 5. Aufl., München

Seufert, Gernot (1999): Verbandscontrolling, Wiesbaden.

Weber, Jürgen / Hamprecht, Markus (1995): Controlling in Non-Profit-Organisationen, in: Controlling, Heft 3, S. 124-131.

Woratschek, Herbert (1999): Verhaltensunsicherheit und Preispolitik - Konsequenzen für Betriebe im Bereich der Sportökonomie, in: Betriebswirtschaftliche Forschung und Praxis, Heft 2, S. 166-182.

Zischg, Kurt (1998): Controlling in Non-Profit-Organisationen. Frankfurt/Main.

Links

Controller Magazin (Fachzeitschrift):
    http://www.controllermagazin.de
Controllingportal (Fachportal):
    http://www.controllingportal.de
Controlling-Portal (Fachportal):
    http://www.controlling-portal.org
Dreamteam Solutions (Consulting-Unternehmen):
    http://www.dreamteam-solutions.de
Forum Balanced Scorecard (Fachportal):
    http://www.balancedscorecard.de
Internationaler Controllerverein (Controlling Fachverband):
    http://www.controllerverein.de
International Group of Controlling (Controlling Fachverband):
    http://www.igc-controlling.org

Kapitel 10: Rechnungslegung im Sport

Simone Jäck   Thomas Meffert

Lernziele

Nach der Durchsicht dieses Kapitels sollte der Leser in der Lage sein,

- Grundmodelle der Vermögens- und Erfolgsermittlung darzustellen.
- die Aufgaben und Instrumente handelsrechtlicher Jahresabschlüsse zu erläutern.
- die gesetzlichen Rechnungslegungspflichten für Sportvereine darzustellen.
- die bilanzielle Behandlung von Übertragungsrechten zu erläutern.
- darzustellen, in welchen Fällen Sportler in der Bilanz erfasst werden.
- sich zur bilanziellen Bewertung von Sportlern zu äußern.
- Grundidee und Umsetzung der Überprüfung der wirtschaftlichen Leistungsfähigkeit im Rahmen des Lizenzierungsverfahrens der DFL wiederzugeben.

Überblick über das Kapitel

In diesem Kapitel werden die Grundlagen des externen Rechnungswesens erläutert und zentrale Problemfelder im Bereich des Sports angesprochen. Hierzu wird zunächst grundlegendes Wissen der Rechnungslegung vermittelt, wobei der handelsrechtliche Jahresabschluss im Vordergrund steht. Anschließend erfolgt eine Übertragung dieser Grundlagen auf Sportvereine und kaufmännische Sportunternehmen. Im Folgeabschnitt widmet sich der Beitrag der bilanziellen Abbildung von Übertragungs- und Werberechten sowie der besonderen Problemstellung der Bilanzierung von Sportlern. Zuletzt wird auf Anforderungen durch Lizenzierungsverfahren am Beispiel der Deutschen Fußball Liga (DFL) eingegangen. Eine Fallstudie, die sich mit der Rechnungslegung eines imaginären Basketballbundesligisten beschäftigt, rundet das Kapitel ab.

10.1 Einführung in die Thematik

Die Begriffe Sport und Rechnungslegung werden in der Öffentlichkeit nur sehr selten miteinander in Verbindung gebracht. Dabei sind letztlich auch Sportvereine als Unternehmen anzusehen, für die ebenfalls Rechenschaftspflichten aus verschiedensten Quellen bestehen können. Für Sportunternehmen in anderen Rechtsformen gelten die gesetzlichen Vorschriften für das externe Rechnungswesen ohnehin. Auch in der Sportbranche sind deshalb Kenntnisse der komplexen Materie „Rechnungslegung" für Entscheidungsträger unabdingbar. Grundvoraussetzung für die Einarbeitung stellt ein guter Überblick über die Technik der Finanzbuchhaltung dar, um sich darauf aufbauend den allgemeinen Grundfragen der Bilanzierung nähern zu können. Unternehmen der Sportbranche müssen sich darüber hinaus mit Sonderproblemen der Rechnungslegung beschäftigen, die oftmals nicht oder nur unzureichend von den allgemeinen Bilanzierungsregelungen gelöst werden. Das vorliegende Kapitel soll daher all denjenigen, die mit sportspezifischen Fragestel-

266

lungen der Rechnungslegung konfrontiert werden, einen generellen systematischen Überblick sowie erste Lösungsansätze anbieten.

10.2 Grundlagen der Rechnungslegung

Jedes Unternehmen verfügt über ein Rechnungswesen, welches alle Daten, die das tägliche betriebliche Geschehen beschreiben, fortlaufend und lückenlos erfasst und auswertet. Dabei können aus dem Rechnungswesen verschiedene Rechenwerke entwickelt werden: neben Rechenwerken für bestimmte Sonderanlässe wird, je nach vorrangigem Adressat, traditionell in externe und interne Modelle der Unternehmensrechnung unterschieden. Während interne Rechenmodelle auf einer freiwilligen Basis erfolgen und durch das Unternehmen zu Zwecken der Unternehmenssteuerung durchgeführt werden, sind externe Rechenmodelle i.d.R. gesetzlich oder vertraglich vorgeschrieben und dienen der Erfüllung von Rechenschaftspflichten der Unternehmensverantwortlichen. Diese laufende finanzielle (externe) Rechenschaftslegung, die Sachverhalte erfasst, die für das Unternehmen unmittelbar mit Zahlungswirkungen verbunden sind, nennt man Rechnungslegung. Sie ist in den Hauptausprägungen einer einfachen Einnahmen-Ausgaben-Rechnung und bilanzbasierten Jahresabschlüssen zu finden.

Die Rechnungslegung hat dabei mehrere Funktionen gleichzeitig zu erfüllen:

- So soll mit einer sorgfältigen *Dokumentation* der Geschäftsvorfälle für beweissichere Unterlagen gesorgt und der Rechtsverkehr erleichtert werden.
- Die *Informationsfunktion* umfasst nicht nur die gesetzlich verankerte Selbstinformation zum eigenen Schutz und damit auch mittelbar zum Schutz Dritter (z.B. Hinweis auf eine bevorstehende Überschuldung oder Mindestinformationspflichten gegenüber den Gesellschaftern). Daneben soll die Fremdinformation sicherstellen, dass alle nicht an der Unternehmensleitung beteiligen Teilnehmer sowie interessierte Außenstehende (z.B. potentielle Kapitalanleger) über den Stand der Vermögens-, Finanz- und Ertragslage des Unternehmens informiert werden.
- Zudem soll (insb. durch den Jahresabschluss nach deutschem Handelsrecht) die *Zahlungsbemessungsfunktion* erfüllt werden. So greift das Gesellschaftsrecht zur Zahlungsbemessung für die Residualanspruchsberechtigten (z.B. Anteilseigner) auf den Jahresabschluss zurück und bildet regelmäßig die Grundlage für die Ableitung der erfolgsabhängigen Steuerzahlungen an den Fiskus. Dabei kann nur der ermittelte Gewinn auch einer Gewinnverwendungsentscheidung unterworfen werden.

10.2.1 Vermögens- und Erfolgsermittlung

Das betriebliche Rechnungswesen unterscheidet in seinen unterschiedlichen Rechenmodellen verschiedene Kategorien von Rechengrößen. Für die Rechnungslegung kommt es dabei auf die Begriffspaare Ein-/Auszahlung, Einnahme/Ausgabe sowie Ertrag/Aufwand an:

1. Unter *Ein-/Auszahlung* wird die Erhöhung/Verminderung des Zahlungsmittelbestands verstanden. Diese Rechenkategorie hat insbesondere im Bereich der Investitionsrechnung eine größere Bedeutung.

2. Die *Einnahme/Ausgabe* beinhaltet über die Zahlungsmittel hinaus noch den Bereich der Forderungen und Schulden – dies wird auch als Geldvermögen bezeichnet.

3. Die Kategorie *Ertrag/Aufwand* stellt auf das bilanzielle Reinvermögen ab, erweitert also das Geldvermögen noch um das Sachvermögen.

Während sich ein betrieblicher Totalerfolg (also die Summe des Erfolgs über die Totalperiode hinweg) unabhängig vom gewählten Modell der Periodenerfolgsermittlung darstellt, ist für die Ermittlung von Periodenerfolgen eine Entscheidung für ein bestimmtes Modell der Periodenerfolgsermittlung – und damit eines der obigen Begriffspaare – notwendig. Das Spektrum denkbarer Konzepte reicht hierbei von der umfassenden und hochkomplexen Unternehmenswertrechnung (= Gesamtvermögensvergleich) über variantenreiche Zwischenformen bis hin zu einer einfachen, reinen Zahlungsrechnung – korrespondierend gilt dasselbe auch für das Modell der Vermögensermittlung. Abb. 1 zeigt das mögliche Spektrum verkürzt auf:

Ein *Gesamtvermögensvergleich* interpretiert das Vermögen im Sinne zukünftiger Ein-/Auszahlungserwartungen. Das periodische Einkommen ergibt sich somit aus der Differenz der Barwerte am Ende und zu Beginn einer Periode. Eine Vermögensänderung (und damit auch Erfolgsänderung) ergibt sich somit bereits bei der Erkennbarkeit einer künftigen Ein-/Auszahlung.

Der *Einzelvermögensvergleich* hingegen beschränkt das Vermögen auf (bilanzierungsfähige) Vermögens- bzw. Schuldpositionen. Hierbei ist durch Konvention festzulegen,

1. was konkret eine Vermögens- bzw. Schuldposition ist (Frage des *Bilanzansatzes*),

2. und wie dieses Vermögen zu bewerten ist (Frage der *Bilanzbewertung*).

```
                    Ermittlung von Periodenerfolgen

        ┌───────────────────────┼───────────────────────┐

Aktivierung/Passivierung                          Aktivierung/Passivierung
auf der Basis abgezinster    Aktivierung/Passivierung   (ggf.) auf der Basis
künftiger Zahlungen          auf der Basis          erfolgter Zahlungen

                    ┌──────────┼──────────┐
                  künftiger   fiktiver   erfolgter
                  Zahlungen  Tageswerte  Zahlungen

                  Einzel-      Tages-    Anschaffungs-
                  ertragswert- wert-     wert-
                  bilanz       bilanz    bilanz

Gesamtvermögens-        Einzelvermögensvergleich        Kassenvermögens-
vergleich              (kaufmännische Mischversion)      vergleich
```

| Umfassende Information, aber nur schwer überprüfbar | ⟷ | Eingeschränkte Information, jedoch leicht überprüfbar |

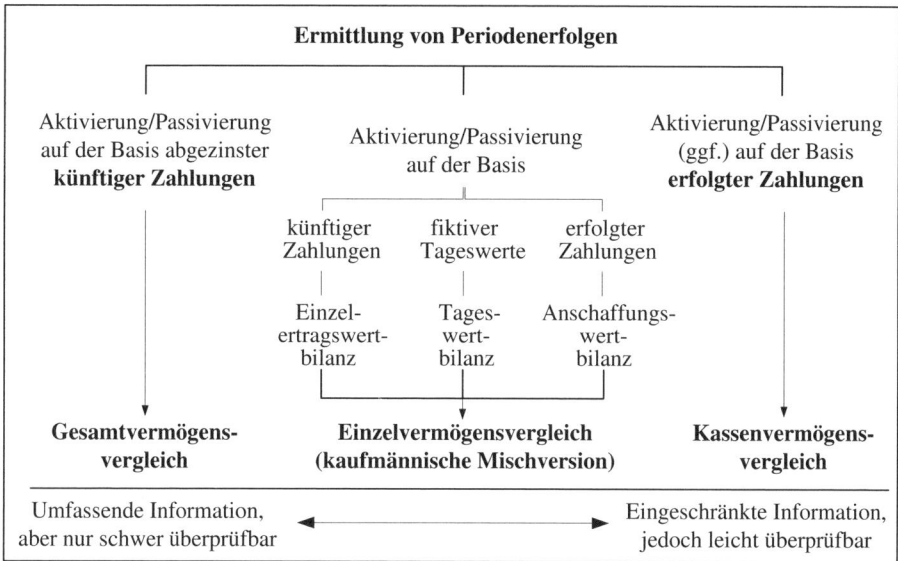

Abb. 1: Modelle der Periodenerfolgsermittlung
In Anlehnung an: Sigloch (2007), S. 32

Der Zeitpunkt und die Höhe der Ertragsrealisation sowie der Vermögenssituation hängen ganz zentral von der Antwort auf diese beiden Grundfragen der Rechnungslegung ab. Derzeit basieren alle relevanten Rechnungslegungsmodelle auf dem Einzelvermögensvergleich, unterscheiden sich aber in der Festlegung von Bilanzinhalt und -bewertung teilweise erheblich. Nicht zu übersehen ist jedoch ein Trend hin zu einer möglichst umfassenden und vollständigen Information und damit zu einem Gesamtvermögensvergleich.

Das andere Extrem des *Kassenvermögensvergleichs* beschränkt das Vermögen auf das reine Kassenvermögen (eventuell erweitert um Forderungen/Verbindlichkeiten). Die Erfolgsrealisation fällt in diesem Fall mit den Zahlungszeitpunkten zusammen.

Es leuchtet unmittelbar ein, dass zwischen den beiden Extremen nicht unerhebliche Zielkonflikte bestehen: während ein Kassenvermögensvergleich zwar leicht überprüfbar aber sehr unvollständig ist, liefert ein Gesamtvermögensvergleich eine sehr umfassende Abbildung, die aber nur sehr schwer objektivierbar ist.

10.2.2 Aussage und Instrumente des Jahresabschluss

Der deutsche handelsrechtliche Jahresabschluss verfolgt als Leitbild die Erfüllung aller drei Funktionen der Dokumentation, Information und insbesondere Zahlungsbemessung. Da ein Einzelvermögensvergleich aufgrund der Zukunftsbezogenheit der Bilanzbewertung Schätzungen enthält, ist im Rahmen der Zahlungsbemessungsfunktion – und damit bei der Ermittlung der ausschüttbaren Gewinne –

Vorsicht geboten, damit nicht überhöhte Gewinne für die Ausschüttung zur Verfügung stehen, deren Rückholung aus rechtlichen oder faktischen Gründen nicht möglich ist. Mit dieser Tatsache wird in Deutschland die Notwendigkeit einer vorsichtigen Gewinnermittlung v.a. bei Kapitalgesellschaften gerechtfertigt (im Sinne einer Ausschüttungssperre durch Nichtermittlung von Gewinnen) (Schneider, 1994). Dies bedeutet jedoch nicht, dass die Vermögens- und Finanzlage „wider besseren Wissens" als ungünstig darzustellen ist, sondern lediglich dass sich der Kaufmann „im Zweifel" eher ungünstiger als günstig darstellt (*Vorsichtsprinzip*) (Schneider, 1997).

Stark beeinflusst wird der deutsche Jahresabschluss zudem durch die enge Bindung der Steuerbilanz an die Handelsbilanz (*Maßgeblichkeit*). So bildet nach dem Steuergesetz das nach den handelsrechtlichen Grundsätzen ordnungsmäßiger Buchführung ermittelte Betriebsvermögen am Ende eines Wirtschaftsjahres den Ausgangspunkt für die Ermittlung des steuerlichen Gewinns. Dies bedeutet derzeit jedoch keine zwingende Identität von Handels- und Steuerbilanz, vielmehr existieren abweichende Sonderregelungen im Steuerrecht, die für die steuerliche Gewinnermittlung zu berücksichtigen sind (Sigloch, 2007).

Die handelsrechtliche Rechnungslegung legt zunächst für alle Kaufleute eine liberale Grundsatzregelung der Bewertung und des Umfangs des Jahresabschlusses fest. Für Kapitalgesellschaften sowie bestimmte Personengesellschaften (die keine natürlichen Personen als persönlich haftende Gesellschafter haben) gelten dann – abhängig von bestimmten Größenklassen – ergänzende Vorschriften (*Dualismus* der handelsrechtlichen Rechnungslegung). Während Personengesellschaften nur zur Aufstellung einer (einfachen) Bilanz und Gewinn- und Verlustrechnung verpflichtet sind, haben Kapitalgesellschaften zusätzlich in Abhängigkeit der Größenklasse in einem (detaillierteren) Anhang weitere Informationen zu unterbreiten.

Darüber hinaus besteht in Deutschland abhängig von Rechtsform und Größe eine Pflicht zur Prüfung und Offenlegung (Publizität) des Jahresabschlusses. Diese Regelung folgt der – umstrittenen und ökonomisch in keiner Weise überzeugenden – Ausgangswertung, dass der „Preis der Haftungsbeschränkung die Offenlegung" sei. So sind alle Kapitalgesellschaften zur Offenlegung ihres Jahresabschlusses verpflichtet, während Personenunternehmen unabhängig von Ihrer Größe (!) keinerlei Offenlegungspflichten unterliegen. Auch hinsichtlich der Prüfungspflicht durch einen Wirtschaftsprüfer bestehen rechtsformabhängige Unterschiede: So sind Personenunternehmen und „kleine" Kapitalgesellschaften (aus Kostengründen) von der Prüfungspflicht befreit (Sigloch, 2007).

10.2.3 Internationalisierung der Rechnungslegung

Neben nationalen Regelungen zur Rechnungslegung wurde in den vergangenen Jahrzehnten die Entwicklung einheitlicher internationaler Rechnungslegungsvorschriften voran getrieben. So wurden durch das International Accounting Standards

Board (IASB, ehemals International Accounting Standards Committee) nach und nach die so genannten International Financial Reporting Standards (IFRS) entwickelt (ältere Standards werden dabei mit International Accounting Standards (IAS) bezeichnet) (Coenenberg, 2005). Ziel des IASB ist dabei die Entwicklung und Verbreitung international einheitlicher Rechnungslegungsgrundsätze zum Zweck der Verbesserung und Harmonisierung weltweiter Rechnungslegungsbestimmungen.

Spätestens mit der Umsetzung der IAS-Verordnung der Europäischen Union in deutsches Recht im Jahr 2002 wurden diese internationalen Vorschriften ab dem 01.01.2005 für deutsche Unternehmen relevant. Bereits seit 1998 war eine freiwillige Anwendung auf Konzernebene für deutsche Unternehmen möglich. Mittlerweile müssen deutsche kapitalmarktorientierte Unternehmen ihren Konzernabschluss nach den IAS/IFRS aufstellen – darüber hinaus gilt im Einzelabschluss ein Wahlrecht die IAS/IFRS zusätzlich anzuwenden sowie im Konzernabschluss für nicht kapitalmarktorientierte Unternehmen ein Wahlrecht sie befreiend (an Stelle eines handelsrechtlichen Jahresabschlusses) anzuwenden.

Dabei entstammen die Rechnungslegungskonzeptionen des HGB und IAS/IFRS verschiedenen „Bilanzierungswelten". Da der Abschluss nach IAS/IFRS (noch) keine Relevanz für die Steuer- und Zahlungsbemessung besitzt und die Zielsetzung hauptsächlich auf die Informationsfunktion ausgerichtet ist, zeichnet er sich in der Festlegung des Bilanzinhalts durch einen weiteren Vermögens- und engeren Schuldbegriff aus. Zudem orientieren sich die IAS/IFRS in der Frage der Bewertung stärker an einem so genannten „Fair Value", der eine Bewertung nach zukunftsorientierten Tageswerten ermöglicht (im Unterschied zu den handelsrechtlichen Regelungen, die tendenziell zu historischen Kosten „eher vorsichtig" bewerten).

10.3 Rechnungslegungspflichten von Sportorganisationen

Traditionell wird der institutionell organisierte Sport in Deutschland innerhalb von Vereinen und Verbänden betrieben. Die Sportvereine haben dabei regelmäßig den steuerlichen Status eines gemeinnützigen Vereins inne (vgl. dazu Abschnitt 10.3.2), was auch auf das externe Rechnungswesen Auswirkungen hat.

10.3.1 Gemeinnützige Sportvereine

Die Verpflichtung zur Rechnungslegung von Vereinen kann aus verschiedenen gesetzlichen Grundlagen erwachsen. Rechnungslegungspflichten können sich aus dem Zivilrecht (Bürgerliches Gesetzbuch oder Handelsgesetzbuch) oder aus dem Steuerrecht ergeben. Das Steuerrecht stützt sich – wenn möglich – auf die zivilrechtlichen Vorgaben, ordnet beim Fehlen handelsrechtlicher Pflichten aber gegebenenfalls auch eine eigenständige Rechnungslegung an.

10.3.1.1 Bürgerliches Recht

Der Vereinsvorstand hat nach bürgerlichem Recht spätestens nach Ablauf seiner Amtszeit eine Rechenschaftspflicht gegenüber den Mitgliedern. Das Bürgerliche Gesetzbuch (BGB) enthält zwar keine expliziten Normen zur externen Rechnungslegung, sieht jedoch Benachrichtigungs-, Auskunfts- und Rechenschaftspflicht des Vereinsvorstands vor. Dieser Pflicht ist jedoch bereits mit einer ordentlichen Aufzeichnung aller Einnahmen und Ausgaben, der Aufbewahrung entsprechender Belege und einem Verzeichnis über das Vereinsvermögen genüge getan.

10.3.1.2 Handelsrecht

Die handelsrechtliche Pflicht zur Rechnungslegung ist von der Eigenschaft als Kaufmann abhängig. Ob nach geltendem Recht ein gemeinnütziger Sportverein als Kaufmann anzusehen ist, wird kontrovers diskutiert. Im Wesentlichen existieren die folgenden drei Ansichten (mit weiteren Nachweisen: Sigloch, 2005):

- Gemeinnützige Sportvereine können auf keinen Fall als Kaufmänner eingestuft werden.
- Die Kaufmannseigenschaft wäre zwar grundsätzlich denkbar, ist aber bei gemeinnützigen Sportvereinen i.d.R. zu verneinen.
- Ein gemeinnütziger Sportverein ist zwingend als Kaufmann zu behandeln, wenn er über einen wirtschaftlichen Geschäftsbetrieb verfügt, der nach Art und Umfang in kaufmännischer Weise eingerichtet ist.

In der gängigen Praxis erfolgt in Deutschland bisher keine Einstufung von Vereinen als kaufmännische Organisationen, so dass Vereine grundsätzlich keiner handelsrechtlichen Rechnungslegungspflicht unterliegen. Auch Vorschriften zur Prüfung oder Publizität des Jahresabschlusses bestehen nicht. Vorschläge zur Einführung einer gesetzlichen Rechnungslegungspflicht für Vereine sind jedoch durchaus vorhanden. So empfiehlt Sigloch (2005a) die Anwendung der allgemeinen handelsrechtlichen Bilanzierungsvorschriften mit bestimmten Vereinfachungen für kleinere Vereine. Ein derartiger Weg wurde beispielsweise mit der Reform des österreichischen Vereinsgesetzes im Jahr 2002 beschritten, mit der die vereinsrechtliche Rechnungslegung in Österreich mit den zwei Grundprinzipien der Festsetzung eines Mindestumfangs für die Rechnungslegung sowie der Einführung einer zwingenden Rechnungsprüfung erweitert wurde (Lansky/Matznetter/Pätzold/Steinwandtner/Thunshirn, 2006).

Da jedoch zahlreiche Vereine freiwillig oder auf Grund satzungs- oder verbandsrechtlicher Vorgaben einer Rechnungslegungspflicht nachkommen und ihre Jahresabschlüsse auch von Wirtschaftsprüfern testieren lassen, hat inzwischen auch das Institut der Wirtschaftsprüfer (IDW) eine Stellungnahme zur Rechnungslegung von Vereinen verabschiedet, um die Lücke fehlender Rechnungslegungsvorschriften zu schließen. In der Stellungnahme wird unabhängig von anderen Verpflichtungen grundsätzlich eine freiwillige Rechnungslegung in Form einer kaufmännischen Bilanz empfohlen – hierbei orientiert sich das IDW an den allgemeinen Vorschriften für Kapitalgesellschaften (auch in Hinblick auf die Offenlegungsvorschriften).

10.3.1.3 Steuerrecht

Aus steuerlicher Sicht dient die Rechnungslegung insbesondere der Ermittlung des Gewinns als Bemessungsgrundlage für die Ertragsteuern. Zwar sind gemeinnützige Sportvereine grundsätzlich steuerbefreit, allerdings ist diese Befreiung für wirtschaftliche Aktivitäten durchbrochen. Deshalb hat auch ein Sportverein unter Umständen im Rahmen eines wirtschaftlichen Geschäftsbetriebs den steuerlichen Gewinn zu ermitteln.

Das deutsche Steuerrecht greift dabei gegebenenfalls auf bestehende handelsrechtliche Vorschriften zurück und regelt nur im Ausnahmefall eigene Rechnungslegungspflichten.

- Organisationen, die nach anderen als den Steuergesetzen Bücher führen und regelmäßig Abschlüsse tätigen müssen, legen das Ergebnis dieser Rechnungslegung auch der Besteuerung zu Grunde (derivative steuerliche Rechnungslegungspflicht).

- Bei gewerblicher Tätigkeit und fehlender derivativer Rechnungslegungspflicht, ergibt sich eine originäre steuerliche Pflicht, wenn entweder der Umsatz eines Kalenderjahres 350.000 € oder der Gewinn 30.000 € überschreitet.

Da Vereine auf Grund der fehlenden Kaufmannseigenschaft keiner handelsrechtlichen Rechnungslegungspflicht unterliegen, kommt für diese höchstens die originäre steuerliche Rechnungslegungspflicht in Frage. Sind die Größengrenzen nicht überschritten, wird der steuerliche Gewinn nicht durch Bilanzierung, sondern durch Einnahmen-Ausgaben-Rechnung ermittelt.

Im Rahmen des Gemeinnützigkeitsrechts kommt der Rechnungslegung neben der Gewinnermittlung eine weitere Funktion zu, da für den Nachweis der Erfüllung der gemeinnützigkeitsrechtlichen Vorgaben ebenfalls ein Rechenwerk notwendig ist. Gemeinnützige Vereine sind deshalb unabhängig von der Notwendigkeit der Ermittlung eines Gewinns verpflichtet, Aufzeichnungen über Einnahmen und Ausgaben zu führen. Dies dient zur Überprüfung, ob die tatsächliche Geschäftsführung des Vereins auf die ausschließliche, unmittelbare und selbstlose Erfüllung ihrer steuerbegünstigten Zwecke gerichtet ist. Eine bestimmte Form ist dabei nicht vorgeschrieben, so dass es als ausreichend angesehen wird, einfache Aufzeichnungen über die Art und die Höhe der Einnahmen und Ausgaben zu machen, aus denen sich die Finanzbehörden einen Überblick verschaffen können, ob die Voraussetzungen für die Steuerbegünstigungen auch tatsächlich erfüllt wurden.

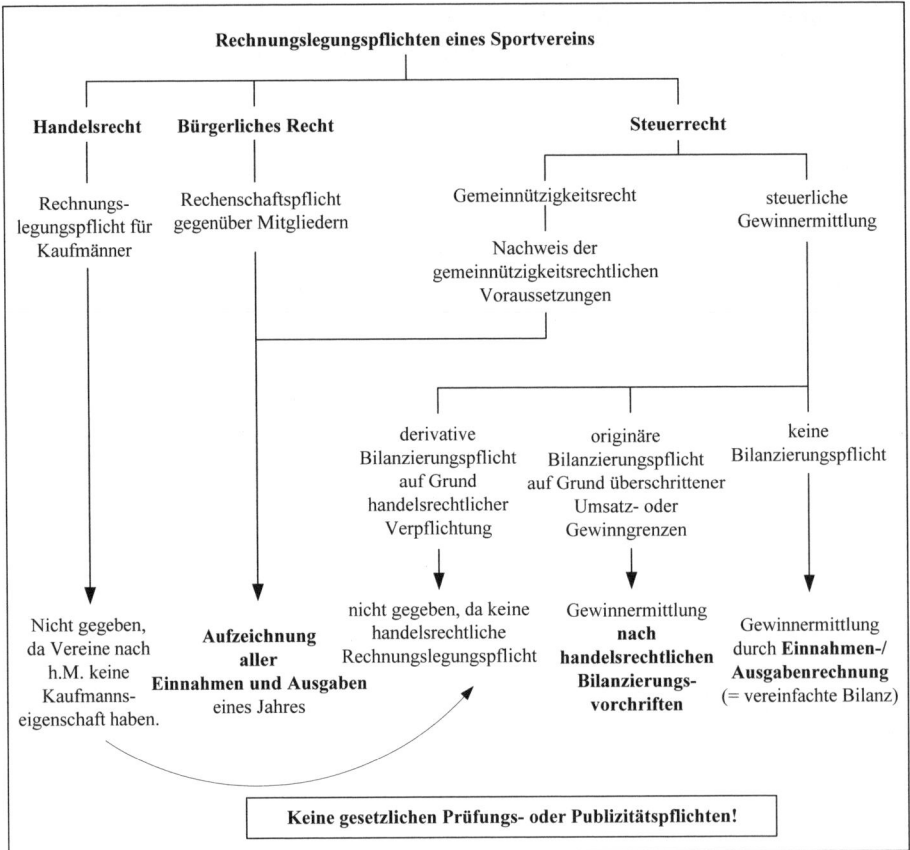

Abb. 2: Rechnungslegungspflichten von Vereinen

10.3.2 Kaufmännische Sportunternehmen

Sport wird heute nicht mehr nur in der traditionellen Rechtsform des Vereins betrieben. Insbesondere im Bereich des Profisports erlangen kaufmännische Rechtsformen eine immer stärkere Bedeutung. Sportorganisationen, die in der Rechtsform einer Kapitalgesellschaft (z.B. GmbH) oder Personengesellschaft (z.B. GmbH & Co. KG) geführt werden, unterliegen auf Grund ihrer Kaufmannseigenschaft den handelsrechtlichen Pflichten. Daneben sind in zunehmendem Maße auch die internationalen Vorschriften der IAS/IFRS zu berücksichtigen. Die handelrechtliche Rechnungslegung ist auch für die steuerliche Gewinnermittlung „maßgeblich". Im Ergebnis bedeutet dies, dass sich Sportunternehmen, die nicht in der Rechtsform des Vereins organisiert sind, bezüglich der gesetzlichen Rechnungslegungs-, Prüfungs- und Offenlegungspflichten nicht von anderen Unternehmen unterscheiden. Besonderheiten können sich jedoch auf Grund verbandsrechtlicher Vorgaben ergeben (vgl. Abschnitt 10.5).

10.4 Besonderheiten der Rechnungslegung im Sport

Sind Sportorganisationen zur Erstellung eines Jahresabschlusses verpflichtet, gelten für sie die allgemeinen Regelungen. Besonderheiten für die Sportbranche sind nicht vorgesehen – allerdings zeichnet sich der professionelle Sport durch Geschäftsmodelle aus, die in anderen Branchen so nicht zu finden sind. Zu nennen sind hierbei v.a. der Verkauf von Übertragungs- und Werberechten sowie der entgeltliche Transfer von Fußballspielern, auf die im Folgenden eingegangen wird.

10.4.1 Bilanzielle Behandlung von Übertragungs- und Werberechten

Der Verkauf von *Übertragungsrechten* an Sportveranstaltungen stellt für Sportorganisationen als Veranstalter und Rechteinhaber regelmäßig eine der wichtigsten Einnahmequellen dar. Gegenstand des Verkaufs ist dabei immer das Recht eines Fernsehsenders, über eine Veranstaltung zu berichten – dabei bestehen grundsätzlich drei Möglichkeiten der Verwertung eines solchen Rechtes:

1. Verwertung als Direktübertragung („Live"),
2. als zeitversetzte Ausstrahlung,
3. oder als zusammenfassende Berichterstattung.

Bilanziell stellen die Übertragungsrechte aufgrund der fehlenden „Körperlichkeit" so genannte *immaterielle Vermögenswerte* dar, deren konkrete bilanzielle Behandlung von der jeweiligen Sichtweise (Käufer oder Verkäufer), der Art der Verwertung sowie verschiedenen anderen Faktoren abhängig ist. Im Folgenden soll die häufigste Form des Verkaufs eines Übertragungsrechtes von einem kaufmännischen Sportunternehmen an einen TV-Sender betrachtet werden.

Genau wie die Übertragungsrechte sind auch die *Werberechte* eine wichtige Finanzierungsquelle für Sportorganisationen – die bilanzielle Behandlung erfolgt wie bei den Übertragungsrechten und wird daher in den folgenden Abschnitten nicht explizit erwähnt.

Immaterielle Vermögenswerte zeichnen sich besonders durch die bereits angesprochene fehlende Körperlichkeit sowie eine erschwerte Bewertbarkeit aus. Dabei können sie in einzelne identifizierbare Rechte oder wirtschaftliche Werte (wie z.B. Patente oder Geheimrezepte) und den so genannten Geschäfts-/Firmenwert („Goodwill") unterschieden werden. Eine weitere Unterscheidung ist in selbstgeschaffen („originär") und entgeltlich erworben („derivativ") zu treffen.

Nach allgemein anerkannten handelsrechtlichen Grundsätzen müssen immaterielle Vermögensgegenstände die folgenden Kriterien erfüllen („abstrakte Bilanzierungsfähigkeit"), bevor überprüft werden kann, ob sie in eine Bilanzposition aufgenommen werden können („konkrete Bilanzierungsfähigkeit"):

1. Es muss sich um einen inventarfähigen Vorteil über den Bilanzstichtag hinaus handeln,
2. der Vermögensgegenstand muss selbstständig bewertbar
3. und einzeln verwertbar (z.B. durch einen Verkauf) sein.

Nur wenn ein immaterieller Vermögensgegenstand all diese Kriterien erfüllt, kann im nächsten Schritt geprüft werden, ob eine Erfassung in der Bilanz möglich ist. Das nachfolgende Schema gibt die Regelungen wieder:

		Erfassung in der Bilanz
Immaterielle Werte des Anlagevermögens	selbst geschaffen (originär)	**Verbot** der Erfassung in der Bilanz (§ 248 Abs. 2 HGB)
	entgeltlich erworben (derivativ)	**Pflicht** zur Erfassung in der Bilanz Behandlung in den Folgeperioden: – *planmäßige Abschreibungen,* – *ggf. auch außerplanmäßige Abschreibungen*
Immaterielle Werte des Umlaufvermögens	selbst geschaffen (originär)	**Pflicht** zur Erfassung in der Bilanz Behandlung in den Folgeperioden: – *keine planmäßigen Abschreibungen,* – *ggf. außerplanmäßige Abschreibungen*
	entgeltlich erworben (derivativ)	

Tab. 1: Bilanzierung immaterieller Einzelwerte
In Anlehnung an: Sigloch (2007), S. 267

Auch nach IAS/IFRS kommt es auf das Erfüllen bestimmter Kriterien an, die im Vergleich zu den handelsrechtlichen Kriterien tendenziell weiter gefasst sind und teilweise auch eine Erfassung selbst geschaffener immaterieller Einzelwerte bereits im Anlagevermögen ermöglichen (z.B. bei originärer selbstgenutzter Software). Eine ähnliche Entwicklung zeichnet sich für das deutsche Handelsrecht durch das neue Bilanzrechtsmodernisierungsgesetz (BilMoG) ab, das die deutsche Rechnungslegung der internationalen annähern soll (Fülbier/Gassen, 2007).

10.4.1.1 Bilanzierung beim Verkäufer

Übertragungsrechte stellen beim Verkäufer unzweifelhaft einen selbsterstellten immateriellen Vermögensgegenstand dar. Wie die bilanzielle Behandlung erfolgt (vgl. Tab. 1), ist abhängig von der – theoretisch noch nicht eindeutig geklärten – Klassifizierung von Übertragungsrechten als Gegenstände des Anlage- oder Umlaufvermögens. Falls eine Einordnung ins Anlagevermögen erfolgt, besteht derzeit ein Verbot der Erfassung in der Bilanz. Dieser Einordnung kann dann gefolgt werden, falls die Vermögensgegenstände (also das Übertragungsrecht) dauerhaft dem Unternehmen dienen sollen. Betrachtet man die Rechte hingegen als Vermögenswerte, die der Weiterveräußerung oder dem sofortigen Verbrauch dienen sollen, sind sie als Umlaufvermögen zu klassifizieren – im Umlaufvermögen besteht eine Aktivierungspflicht. Nicht zu vernachlässigen ist dabei jedoch das notwendige Kriterium der selbstständigen Bewertbarkeit des immateriellen Vermögensgegenstandes. Die dazu notwendige Ermittlung und Zuordnung der Aufwendungen des Sportunternehmens für die „Erstellung" der Übertragungsrechte wird nur in den seltensten Fällen möglich sein, so dass auch im Umlaufvermögen oftmals ein Erfassen nicht möglich sein wird.

10.4.1.2 Bilanzierung beim Käufer

Beim Käufer stellen Übertragungsrechte zweifelsfrei derivative immaterielle Vermögensgegenstände dar, die grundsätzlich in Höhe der Anschaffungskosten in der Bilanz erfasst werden müssen. Allerdings besteht bei den Übertragungsrechten die Besonderheit, dass es sich nach herrschender Meinung zunächst um ein so genanntes schwebendes Geschäft handelt: Schwebende Geschäfte bezeichnen Transaktionen, bei denen der zur Leistung Verpflichtete (also das Sportunternehmen) seine Leistung noch nicht vollständig erbracht hat (für das Übertragungsrecht besteht die Leistung in der Erlaubnis der Übertragung, und diese kann erst am Veranstaltungstag erbracht werden). In der deutschen Rechnungslegung, wie auch der Rechnungslegung nach IAS/IFRS werden schwebende Geschäfte grundsätzlich so lange nicht erfasst, bis die Hauptleistung erbracht wurde (also am Tag der Veranstaltung). Nach herrschender Meinung sind daher Übertragungsrechte beim Käufer vor dem Zeitpunkt der Veranstaltung bilanziell nicht zu erfassen.

Nur im Falle der zeitversetzten Ausstrahlung und zusammenfassenden Berichterstattung wird insofern am Tag der Veranstaltung ein immaterieller Vermögensgegenstand („Senderecht") erfasst, der am Tag der Ausstrahlung erfolgswirksam ausgebucht wird. Bei Direktübertragungen hingegen erfolgt im Zeitpunkt der Veranstaltung (= Zeitpunkt der Ausstrahlung) die sofortige erfolgswirksame Verbuchung.

Es ist jedoch zu beachten, dass der Kaufpreis des Übertragungsrechts regelmäßig *vor* dem Zeitpunkt der Veranstaltung (zumindest in Teilen) bezahlt wird – in diesen Fällen stellt sich die Frage nach dessen Erfassung, denn die aufwandswirksame Erfassung des Kaufpreises darf erst in der Periode der Veranstaltung und nicht bereits im Zahlungszeitpunkt erfolgen. Eine sofortige aufwandswirksame Erfassung der Zahlung ist nur zulässig, sofern Kaufpreiszahlung und Veranstaltung in derselben Periode stattfinden. Im anderen Fall (Zahlung des Kaufpreises in einer früheren Periode) kann eine Erfassung des Kaufpreises als immaterielles Recht aufgrund des Schwebezustandes nicht erfolgen. Es verbleibt nur die – nicht ganz unumstrittene – Möglichkeit der Erfassung als aktiver Rechnungsabgrenzungsposten. Im Zeitpunkt der Veranstaltung erfolgt bei Direktübertragungen die aufwandswirksame Auflösung des aktiven Rechnungsabgrenzungspostens, im Falle der zeitversetzten Übertragung und zusammenfassenden Berichterstattung wird – wie bereits ausgeführt – zunächst ein „Senderecht" erfasst und der Rechnungsabgrenzungsposten dadurch ersetzt.

Die nachfolgende Abbildung soll die Behandlung des Übertragungsrechts in der Bilanz des Käufers noch einmal verdeutlichen:

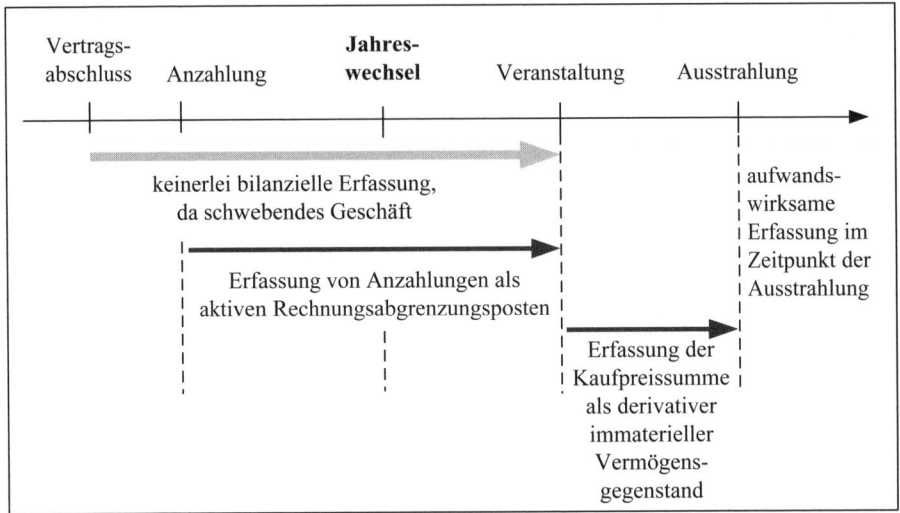

Abb. 3: Behandlung von Übertragungsrechten in der Bilanz des Käufers bei zeitversetzter Ausstrahlung

Besondere Probleme ergeben sich, falls die Veranstaltung zwischen Vertragsabschluss und Veranstaltungszeitpunkt an Attraktivität verliert – beispielsweise da die Sportart auf Grund von Doping-Fällen für negative Presse gesorgt hat und der Fernsehsender geringere Einschaltquoten befürchtet. In diesem Fall wären die bereits geleisteten Kaufpreiszahlungen bzw. die noch zu leistenden (vertraglich fest vereinbarten) Zahlungen bereits zum Zeitpunkt des Bekanntwerdens des Wertverlustes aufwandswirksam zu berücksichtigen. Handelsrechtlich würde dies durch die Bildung einer Rückstellung für drohende Verluste aus schwebenden Geschäften erfolgen – diese Lösung ist jedoch in Hinblick auf das Steuerrecht aufgrund der steuerlichen Nichtanerkennung derartiger Rückstellungen unmöglich.

10.4.2 Bilanzierung von Sportlern

Sportler gehören zum so genannten Humankapital eines Profisportunternehmens. Humankapital wird grundsätzlich nicht in der Bilanz ausgewiesen, lediglich die laufenden Gehaltszahlungen werden in der Gewinn- und Verlustrechnung als Aufwand erfasst und mindern den Jahresüberschuss.

Im professionellen Mannschaftssport (v.a. Fußball) existiert jedoch die Besonderheit, dass beim Vereinswechsel von Sportlern regelmäßig Transferentschädigungen und/oder Handgelder bezahlt werden, denen auf Grund ihrer Höhe große wirtschaftliche Bedeutung zukommt. Da die Entschädigungen in den allermeisten Fällen für eine Verpflichtung über mehrere Jahre geleistet werden, wird die aufwandswirksame Erfassung des Aufwands im Jahr der Zahlung regelmäßig als nicht sachgerecht angesehen, weshalb Sportler ausnahmsweise in den Bilanzen von Sportunternehmen auftauchen. Auf diese Weise kann erreicht werden, dass die Zahlung nicht nur einer Periode, sondern der gesamten Vertragslaufzeit zugeordnet wird und es jeweils nur zu einer anteiligen Minderung des Gewinns kommt.

10.4.2.1 Aktivierung von Transferentschädigungen

In der Bilanz eines Sportunternehmens tauchen nicht die Sportler selbst auf, vielmehr werden die so genannten Transferentschädigungen aktiviert. Solche Transferentschädigungen sind im Profisport bei einem Clubwechsel eines Spielers üblich, um den Ursprungsclub für Aufwendungen zu entschädigen, die in Zusammenhang mit dem Spieler angefallen sind und in Zukunft dem aufnehmenden Club zu Gute kommen werden. (z.B. Ausbildung, Training oder medizinische Betreuung). Im deutschen Profifußball waren solche Entschädigungen bis Mitte der 1990er Jahre verpflichtend zu entrichten, da sonst keine Spielerlaubnis des Spielers für die Bundesligen erteilt wurde. Diese Verpflichtung zur Bezahlung von Transferentschädigungen besteht heute nicht mehr, so dass ein Club nur dann eine Entschädigung zu bezahlen hat, wenn ein bestehender Vertrag mit dem alten Club ohne reguläre Kündigungsmöglichkeit vor Ablauf der Vertragsdauer aufgelöst werden soll.

Als die Praxis von Transferentschädigungszahlungen in Deutschland aufkam, wurde zunächst von einem Bilanzierungswahlrecht ausgegangen. Den Sportunternehmen stand es frei, die Zahlung im ersten Jahr als Aufwand zu verbuchen oder eine Aktivierung und die damit verbundene Verteilung des Aufwands auf mehrere Jahre vorzunehmen. Auf Grund des verhältnismäßig hohen Gewichts der aktivierten Transferentschädigungen in den Bilanzen einiger Sportunternehmen und einer vergleichsweise geringen Eigenkapitalausstattung spricht die Abwendung der Gefahr einer bilanziellen Überschuldung und die Sicherung der Spiellizenz für eine Aktivierung. Steuerlich hat die sofortige Aufwandsverrechnung dagegen den Vorteil erst späterer Steuerzahlungen.

Aus steuerlicher Sicht besteht genau aus diesem Grund seit 1992 die Pflicht zur Aktivierung der Transferentschädigungen, da die hohe Gewinnminderung im Jahr der Zahlung als ungerechtfertigte Steuerstundung angesehen wurde. Die Transferentschädigung wurde vom Bundesfinanzhof (BFH) als Anschaffungskosten für einen immateriellen Vermögensgegenstand „Spielerlaubnis eines Spielers" interpretiert, da zu dieser Zeit die Bezahlung von Transferentschädigungen noch verbandsrechtlich vorgeschrieben war. Die Spielerlaubnis stellt nach dieser Sichtweise einen entgeltlich erworbenen immateriellen Vermögenswert dar, der zwingend in die Bilanz aufzunehmen ist. Nach herrschender Meinung blieb aus handelsrechtlicher Sicht das frühere Wahlrecht jedoch erhalten.

Die von Anfang an kritisierte steuerliche Klassifizierung ist seit dem Wegfall der verbandsrechtlichen Verpflichtung zur Bezahlung der Transferentschädigungen in höchstem Maße umstritten, da die auf Grund vertraglicher Bindungen bezahlten Entschädigungen in keinem Zusammenhang mehr zur Spielerlaubnis stehen und damit die Bilanzierungsmöglichkeit als immaterieller Vermögenswert „Spielerlaubnis" eigentlich unmöglich geworden ist (Jansen, 2007).

In der Praxis des deutschen Profifußballs wurde die bisherige Handhabung jedoch beibehalten, wobei es durchaus auch Bundesligateilnehmer gibt, die Transfersummen zumindest in der Handelsbilanz als Sofortaufwand verbuchen (Müller, 2003b). Von Seiten des Fiskus dürfte diese Praxis jedoch auf Grund des Urteils von 1992 nicht akzeptiert werden (kritisch zur Verwaltungspraxis Jansen, 2007). Die praktische Handhabung im Rahmen der Handelsbilanz hängt nicht zuletzt mit den geltenden Bestimmungen des Lizenzierungsverfahrens zusammen, das eine Aktivierung geleisteter Transferentschädigungen explizit vorsieht. Dies wird durch die Erweiterung der Gliederungsvorschriften des HGB um einen fußballspezifischen Posten „Spielerwerte" deutlich.

Im Schrifttum wird die Aktivierungsfähigkeit von Transferentschädigungen in einer v.a. von formalrechtlichen Argumenten getragenen Diskussion sowohl aus handelsrechtlicher als auch aus steuerrechtlicher Sicht weitestgehend abgelehnt (Kaiser, 2004; Littkemann, 2003; Reiter, 2004; Steiner/Bross, 2005). Der Ansicht, dass formalrechtlich aus der Bezahlung der Transferentschädigung kein Vermögenswert resultiert, ist hier zu folgen. Allerdings kann die von der Praxis durchgeführte Aktivierung als angemessen angesehen werden, wenn die Bilanzierung *wie* ein immaterieller Vermögenswert eingestuft wird. Die durch die Aktivierung vollzogene Verteilung der Transferentschädigungszahlung über die Vertragslaufzeit als Zeitraum, in dem der verpflichtete Spieler dem Verein durch seine potentiellen Einsätze in der Mannschaft entsprechenden Nutzen stiftet (z.B. durch finanzielle Rückflüsse in Form von Vermarktungseinnahmen oder Erhöhung des sportlichen Erfolgs), ist ökonomisch sinnvoll (Sigloch, 2005b).

Nicht zu den Transfersummen werden die Handgelder gezählt, die häufig bei Vertragsschluss oder Vertragsverlängerung an den Sportler bezahlt werden. Die Aktivierung eines an den Spieler gezahlten Handgeldes oder einer Wechselprämie wird nicht nur theoretisch durch die h.M. abgelehnt, sondern auch in der Praxis nicht vorgenommen. Allerdings kann es sich bei den zum Teil beträchtlichen Handgeldern wirtschaftlich betrachtet, und ohne Anspruch auf formalrechtliche Fundierung, durchaus um amortisationsfähige Aufwendungen für die Verpflichtung eines Spielers über mehrere Jahre handeln. Schließlich soll der Spieler auch das in ihn investierte Kapital über die Vertragslaufzeit im Rahmen seines Beitrags zum sportlichen und somit finanziellen Erfolg der Mannschaft wieder einspielen. Konsequenterweise müsste deshalb überlegt werden, ob nicht auch Handgelder analog zu den Transferentschädigungen wie ein immaterieller Vermögensgegenstand bilanziert werden müssen oder beim Erwerb eines Spielers durch Bezahlung einer Ablösesumme als Anschaffungsnebenkosten behandelt werden.

Selbst wenn man die Handgelder lediglich als Lohnvorauszahlung ansieht, dürfte keine sofortige aufwandswirksame Verbuchung erfolgen. Vielmehr müsste das Handgeld bei einer mehr als einjährigen Vertragslaufzeit mittels eines Rechnungsabgrenzungspostens auf die Laufzeit verteilt werden.

Kosten für die Ausbildung von Spielern aus der eigenen Jugend können dagegen nicht aktiviert werden. Hierbei würde es sich höchstens um einen selbsterstellten immateriellen Vermögenswert des Anlagevermögens handeln, für den derzeit ein bilanzielles Ansatzverbot gilt.

Nach internationalen Rechnungslegungsvorschriften ergibt sich – trotz tendenziell großzügigeren Ansatzmöglichkeiten – eine ähnlich Problematik bei der Frage nach der Aktivierung von Spielerwerten. Insbesondere wird auch hier die Aktivierung selbst ausgebildeter Sportler im Ergebnis nicht möglich sein, da die notwendigen Voraussetzungen nicht erfüllt werden können. Jedoch gilt auch hier die ökonomische Forderung der Verteilung der Transferentschädigung auf die Laufzeit des Vertrags.

10.4.2.2 Bewertung der bilanzierten Spielerwerte

Sollen die Transferentschädigungen wie ein immaterieller Vermögensgegenstand in die Bilanz aufgenommen werden, müssen die in der handelsrechtlichen Bilanzkonzeption festgelegten Bewertungsmaßstäbe angewendet werden. Die Spielerwerte sind deshalb zunächst mit den Anschaffungskosten zu bewerten (primäre Wertart). Dazu gehören die Transferentschädigung einschließlich eventueller nachträglicher Zahlungen aus rückwirkenden Erhöhungen sowie weitere Anschaffungsnebenkosten (z.B. Spielervermittlungsgebühren, Kosten der Beantragung der Spielerlaubnis für den Spieler).

In der Folge ist der Spielerwert als abnutzbarer immaterieller Vermögenswert über die Nutzungsdauer planmäßig abzuschreiben. Nutzungsdauer dürfte dabei regelmäßig die Vertragslaufzeit des entsprechenden Spielers sein, wobei eventuelle Verlängerungsoptionen, die verbandsrechtlichen Höchstlaufzeiten und Kündigungsmöglichkeiten sowie ein möglicher „Wiederverkaufspreis" kurz vor Ende der Laufzeit zu berücksichtigen sind.

Neben der planmäßigen Abschreibung kommen außerplanmäßige Abschreibungen in Frage, wenn der tatsächliche Wert am Bilanzstichtag niedriger als die fortgeführten Anschaffungskosten ist (sekundäre Wertart). Eine Zuschreibung auf einen höheren Wert ist dagegen wegen des Vorsichtsprinzips regelmäßig nicht möglich. Eine außerplanmäßige Abschreibung auf den niedrigeren Stichtagswert ist nur dann vorzunehmen, wenn die festgestellte Wertminderung von Dauer ist. Bei dauernder Spielunfähigkeit (z.B. Invalidität) kann eine dauerhafte Wertminderung auf 0 zweifelsfrei angenommen werden. Bei bloßen Verletzungen stellt sich die Qualifizierung als dauerhafte Wertminderung und die Feststellung des verminderten Werts deutlich schwieriger dar.

Entfallen in einem späteren Geschäftsjahr die Gründe, die zu einer außerplanmäßigen Abschreibung geführt haben ganz oder teilweise, ist eine Zuschreibung bis maximal zu den (gedanklich) fortgeführten Anschaffungskosten möglich.

Die in der Bilanz aktivierten Spielerwerte sind dabei nicht dazu geeignet, eine verwertbare Aussage über den Wert des Spielervermögens zu geben, da es sich lediglich um die Abbildung historischer Anschaffungskosten handelt. Dazu wäre eine Bewertung der Spieler mit einer Methode der Unternehmensbewertung notwendig.

10.5 Lizenzierungsverfahren der Deutschen Fußball Liga

Der Deutsche Fußball-Bund (DFB) hat bereits in den 1960er Jahren Anforderungen an Rechnungslegung und Prüfung im Rahmen eines jährlichen Lizenzierungsverfahrens kodifiziert. Diesen Vorgaben kommt noch heute sowohl für andere Ligasportarten in Deutschland als auch für den europäischen Fußball eine Vorbildfunktion zu, so dass im Folgenden beispielhaft für die Überprüfung der wirtschaftlichen Leistungsfähigkeit dieses Verfahren dargestellt werden soll. Ähnliche Verfahren finden sich jedoch auch in den anderen deutschen Ligasportarten (z.B. Basketball) oder werden auf europäischer Ebene (z.B. UEFA) umgesetzt (zum Verfahren der UEFA siehe Galli, 2002).

10.5.1 Grundproblematik und Lizenzierungsverfahren als Lösung

In einigen Ligasportarten sind die teilnehmenden Clubs bezüglich Größe und Umsatz durchaus mit mittelständischen Unternehmen zu vergleichen. Trotzdem ist die vorherrschende Rechtsform nach wie vor die des eingetragenen Vereins, so dass sich für diese grundsätzlich keine zwingende handelsrechtliche Pflicht zur externen Rechenschaftslegung ergibt (vgl. Abschnitt 10.3.1). Gleichzeitig basiert die Vereinsführung traditionell auf ehrenamtlichen Strukturen, so dass in vielen Fällen kaum funktionierende interne Kontrollsysteme vorhanden sind. Diese beiden Punkte bergen vor dem Hintergrund steigender wirtschaftlicher Aktivitäten und den hohen Kosten der Verfolgung sportlicher Ziele die Gefahr, dass die teilnehmenden Clubs – unbemerkt von Ligaverwaltung und Öffentlichkeit – an den Rand der Insolvenz gedrängt werden. In Sportarten, die in einem Ligasystem organisiert sind, ist die Insolvenz einzelner Teilnehmer als besonders problematisch anzusehen, da sich aus dem Wegfall eines Teilnehmers während einer laufenden Runde auch negative Konsequenzen für die anderen Teilnehmer ergeben können. Die Insolvenz einzelner Teilnehmer soll deshalb vermieden werden, indem mangelnde gesetzliche Vorschriften zur Rechenschaftslegung und das etwaige Fehlen interner Kontrollsysteme durch ein ligainternes Regelwerk ausgeglichen werden. An den Ligawettbewerben dürfen nur solche Vereine teilnehmen, die im Rahmen des Lizenzierungsverfahrens eine ausreichende wirtschaftliche Leistungsfähigkeit zum Bestehen mindestens einer Spielzeit nachweisen können.

10.5.2 Zielsetzung

Voraussetzung für die Teilnahme an den drei höchsten Fußball-Ligen in Deutschland ist es, dass im Rahmen des Lizenzierungsverfahrens unter anderem die notwendige wirtschaftliche Leistungsfähigkeit für das wirtschaftliche Überleben mindestens einer Spielzeit nachgewiesen werden kann. Die Verantwortung dafür liegt seit dem Jahr 2000 nicht mehr beim DFB selbst, sondern beim „DFL Deutsche Fußball Liga e.V." bzw. der die operativen Geschäfte führenden „DFL Deutsche Fußball Liga GmbH". Die entsprechenden Vorschriften sind in einer so genannten Lizenzierungsordnung (LO) und ihren Anhängen (insb. VII und IX) niedergelegt (Deutsche Fußball Liga, 2007).

Ausgangspunkt für die Überprüfung der wirtschaftlichen Leistungsfähigkeit in Sportarten mit Ligasystemen ist das (finanzielle) Risiko aller interagierenden Gruppen im Falle eines insolvenzbedingten Ausscheidens eines Teilnehmers, da in dann der Spielplan nicht mehr durchführbar wäre. Mit den Vorgaben des Lizenzierungsverfahrens soll daher insbesondere die Insolvenz einzelner Teilnehmer vermieden werden, damit der Spielbetrieb während einer gesamten Spielzeit aufrecht erhalten werden kann. Dazu ist Zahlungsunfähigkeit und Überschuldung der Teilnehmer möglichst auszuschließen. So kann Stabilität, Integrität und Kontinuität der Wettbewerbe gewährleistet und gleichzeitig das Markenkapital der Liga geschützt werden. Außerdem soll das Lizenzierungsverfahren zur Erhöhung der Transparenz und Glaubwürdigkeit, zu verbessertem Gläubigerschutz und zu verbesserter wirtschaftlicher und finanzieller Leistungsfähigkeit der teilnehmenden Mannschaften führen. Zusätzlich soll die Überprüfung der wirtschaftlichen Leistungsfähigkeit gewährleisten, dass alle Teilnehmer eines Ligawettbewerbs unter gleichen Bedingungen starten und nicht einzelne Mannschaften sich Vorteile in einer Saison „erkaufen", indem sie ihren finanziellen Rahmen überschreiten.

Durch die Lizenzierung wird allen Teilnehmern eine strikte Planung auferlegt, die sie zwingt, nicht mehr Geld auszugeben als sie einnehmen oder durch fest zugesagte Kredite aufbringen können. Nur Mittel, die unzweifelhaft zur Verfügung stehen, dürfen als Ausgaben eingeplant werden.

Ziele der Überprüfung der wirtschaftlichen Leistungsfähigkeit

Hauptziel **Nebenziele**

Vermeidung des insolvenzbedingten   Gläubiger-   Transparenz   Gleichheit
Ausscheidens während einer Spielzeit   schutz   im sportlichen
  Wettbewerb

Sicherstellung,   Vermeidung einer
dass alle finanziellen   **Überschuldung**
Verpflichtungen rechtzeitig erfüllt
werden können
(= Sicherung der **Liquidität**)

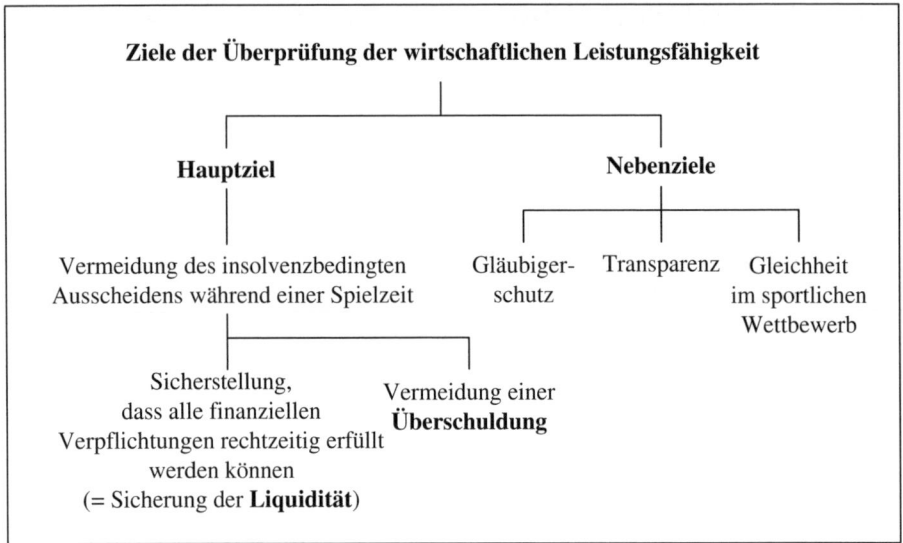

Abb. 4: Ziele der Überprüfung der wirtschaftlichen Leistungsfähigkeit

10.5.3 Einzureichende Unterlagen

I.d.R. kann eine externe Bilanzanalyse wie sie von der DFL im Rahmen der Lizenzierung durchgeführt wird, nur auf Grundlage publizitätspflichtiger Bestandteile des Jahresabschlusses erfolgen. Wegen der fehlenden Rechnungslegungs- und Publizitätspflichten der teilnehmenden Vereine müssen die benötigten Unterlagen jedoch im Rahmen einer vertraglichen Regelung zwischen Ligaorganisation und Ligateilnehmern angefordert werden. Die Vorgaben der DFL übersteigen die gesetzlichen Vorgaben des HGB dabei bezüglich Umfang und Ausführlichkeit der Unterlagen bei Weitem, so dass im Grunde eine sehr detaillierte Analyse der wirtschaftlichen Situation der teilnehmenden Clubs möglich wird.

Die DFL greift dabei auf die handelsrechtlichen Vorschriften zurück und verlangt auch von den teilnehmenden Vereinen Jahresabschlüsse nach den handelsrechtlichen Regelungen für Kapitalgesellschaften, die von Wirtschaftsprüfern zu testieren sind. Auf diesem Weg erlangen auch die Verlautbarungen des IDW hinsichtlich der Rechnungslegung von Vereinen (vgl. Abschnitt 10.3.1) Bedeutung. Diese Jahresabschlüsse sind dann im Übrigen auch für die steuerliche Gewinnermittlung grundlegend. Auch für Kapitalgesellschaften ergibt sich eine Erweiterung der gesetzlichen Pflichten, da die DFL von ihren potentiellen Teilnehmern Unterlagen fordert, die andere Unternehmen so nicht erstellen und weitergeben müssen. Im Wesentlichen sind dabei folgende Unterlagen einzureichen:

- Testierter Jahresabschluss (Bilanz, Gewinn- und Verlustrechnung, Anhang und Lagebericht) einschließlich Bericht eines Wirtschaftprüfers für die letzte Spielzeit und die erste Hälfte der laufenden Spielzeit (bei Lizenzierung für 2009/2010: 01.07.2007-30.06.2008 und 01.07.2008-31.12.2008)

- Testierte Planjahresabschlüsse für die zweite Hälfte der laufenden Spielzeit und für das Jahr der Lizenzierung (bei Lizenzierung für 2009/2010: 01.01.2009-30.06.2009 und 01.07.2009-30.06.2010) mit Bericht des Wirtschaftsprüfers.
- Weitere Unterlagen z.B. über wesentliche Verträge im Rahmen von Vermarktung und Sponsoring, gesellschaftsrechtliche Strukturen, Transferverpflichtungen.

10.5.4 Beurteilung der wirtschaftlichen Leistungsfähigkeit und Konsequenzen

Nachdem die einzureichenden Unterlagen bereits von einem externen Wirtschaftsprüfer geprüft wurden (1. Stufe), folgt die verbandsinterne Überprüfung durch die DFL (2. Stufe) insbesondere vor dem Hintergrund der Insolvenzvermeidung. Basierend auf den vom Lizenzbewerber bereitgestellten Unterlagen und Rechenwerke, urteilt der Ligaverband über die wirtschaftliche Leistungsfähigkeit des Fußballunternehmens.

Erstes Kriterium für die Beurteilung der wirtschaftlichen Leistungsfähigkeit ist die *Liquidität*. Es muss gewährleistet sein, dass der Lizenzbewerber während der kommenden Spielzeit jederzeit in der Lage ist, allen Zahlungsverpflichtungen nachzukommen. Die Operationalisierung erfolgt durch eine Liquiditätsberechnung. Ausgangspunkt sind der Bestand an liquiden Mitteln zu Beginn der laufenden Spielzeit und alle zahlungswirksamen Vorgänge, die sich aus den (Plan-)Gewinn- und Verlustrechnungen ergeben. Der Bestand wird um die Zahlungsabflüsse vermindert und um Zuflüsse erhöht. Ergibt sich auf diese Weise ein negativer Betrag, sind entsprechende zusätzliche Einnahmen oder eine Bürgschaft/Bankgarantie nachzuweisen. Ist dies nicht möglich, wird die Lizenzerteilung an die Erfüllung von Bedingungen geknüpft.

Zweites Kriterium für die Überprüfung der wirtschaftlichen Leistungsfähigkeit ist die *Vermögenslage* der Teilnehmer. In diesem Zusammenhang geht es insbesondere darum, zu vermeiden, dass die Vereine über ein negatives Eigenkapital verfügen. Dies ist immer dann der Fall, wenn das Eigenkapital durch Verluste vollständig aufgebraucht wurde und kein weiterer Verlustausgleich mehr möglich ist. Man spricht hierbei zunächst von Überschuldung im externen Rechnungswesen. Wenn gleichzeitig auch eine insolvenzrechtliche Überschuldung vorliegt, gilt das betroffene Unternehmen als insolvent. Ob auch insolvenzrechtlich Überschuldung vorliegt, wird mit einer so genannten Überschuldungsbilanz festgestellt, die dem internen Rechnungswesen zuzuordnen ist und in der auch Vermögenswerte berücksichtigt werden, die im handelsrechtlichen Jahresabschluss entweder gar nicht oder nur in geringerer Höhe angesetzt werden dürfen. Die Überprüfung der DFL setzt an den eingereichten handelsrechtlichen Jahresüberschüssen an und überprüft, ob noch

Eigenkapital vorhanden ist. Weist dies einen negativen Bestand auf, ist die Ligateilnahme höchstens unter Auflagen möglich.

Das abschließende Urteil zur wirtschaftlichen Leistungsfähigkeit stellt gleichzeitig auf beide Kriterien ab. Wird eines der beiden Kriterien nicht erfüllt, kann eine Lizenz unter Auflagen oder Bedingungen erteilt werden. Bei Nichterfüllung beider Kriterien, ist eine Teilnahme i.d.R. ausgeschlossen.

11.6 Fallstudie
Folgender Fall soll einige sportspezifische Aspekte des externen Rechnungswesens beispielhaft verdeutlichen.

Fallstudie „Waldsee Warriors"

(1) Sachverhalt:
Gernot Genau ist neuer Leiter des Rechnungswesens des Basketballbundesligisten „Waldsee Warriors", der aus einem gemeinnützigen eingetragenen Verein und der ausgegliederten Lizenzspielabteilung in der Rechtsform einer GmbH besteht. Die Vereinssatzung sieht keine besonderen Rechnungslegungspflichten vor. Für den amerikanischen Basketballstar M. J., der für den Zeitraum vom 01.01.2008-31.12.2010 verpflichtet werden konnte, hat die GmbH am 01.01.2008 eine Ablösesumme/ Transferentschädigung in Höhe von 3 Mio. € bezahlt. Am Tag seines Arbeitsbeginns (01.01.2008) macht sich G. Genau zunächst einige Gedanken, welche Aufgaben und Probleme wohl in Zukunft auf ihn zukommen werden.

(2) Externes Rechnungswesen der Waldsee Warriors:
Gesetzliche Rechnungslegungspflichten des Vereins:
- Keine handelsrechtliche Rechnungslegungspflicht, da Kaufmannseigenschaft verneint wird. Da die GmbH und nicht der Verein als Ligateilnehmer gilt, treffen ihn auch keine verbandsrechtlichen Rechnungslegungspflichten. Die Satzung sieht ebenfalls keine besonderen Pflichten vor. Eine freiwillige Rechnungslegung nach handelsrechtlichen Vorschriften wäre dagegen jederzeit möglich. Es bestehen keine Prüfungs- oder Publizitätspflichten.
- Nach dem BGB hat der Vereinsvorstand eine Rechenschaftspflicht gegenüber den Vereinsmitgliedern. Dazu muss G. Genau zumindest alle Einnahmen und Ausgaben des Vereins aufzeichnen.
- Zum Nachweis einer gemeinnützigen Geschäftsführung ist aus steuerlicher Sicht eine Aufzeichnung aller Einnahmen und Ausgaben notwendig.
- Falls der Verein einen steuerpflichtigen wirtschaftlichen Geschäftsbetrieb (z.B. durch Sponsoring) unterhält, ist der steuerliche Gewinn zu ermitteln. Da kein Rückgriff auf die handelsrechtliche Rechnungslegung möglich ist (außer

es wurde auf freiwilliger Basis ein handelsrechtlicher Jahresabschluss erstellt), ergeben sich steuerliche Bilanzierungspflichten nur, wenn die Gewinn- oder Umsatzgrenzen überschritten sind. Ansonsten ist zur steuerlichen Gewinnermittlung lediglich eine Einnahmen-Ausgaben-Rechnung anzufertigen.

Gesetzliche Rechnungslegungspflichten der GmbH:

- Die GmbH unterliegt als Formkaufmann zwingend den handelsrechtlichen Rechnungslegungspflichten. Je nach Größe der GmbH kommen Prüfungs- und Publizitätspflichten hinzu. Da sich die Wirtschaftsjahre der Ligateilnehmer regelmäßig an der Spielzeit orientieren, wird die GmbH ein Wirtschaftsjahr vom 01.07.-30.06. haben, so dass G. Genau zum 30.06.2008 seinen ersten handelsrechtlichen Jahresabschluss aufstellen muss.

- Für die zwingend notwendige steuerliche Gewinnermittlung ist der handelsrechtliche Jahresabschluss maßgeblich.

Pflichten der GmbH gemäß dem BBL-Lizenzstatut:

Zum Nachweis der wirtschaftlichen Leistungsfähigkeit für die Teilnahme an der Basketballbundesliga hat G. Genau im Frühjahr 2008 einen handelsrechtlichen Jahresabschluss für das Wirtschaftsjahr 01.07.2006-30.06.2007 und einen Zwischenabschluss auf den 31.12.2007 einzureichen. Außerdem sind Planrechnungen für die kommende Saison zu erstellen. Alle Unterlagen müssen von einem Wirtschaftsprüfer testiert werden. Vor der Lizenzerteilung für die Saison 2008/2009 wird die BBL auf dieser Grundlage überprüfen, ob die wirtschaftliche Leistungsfähigkeit der Waldsee Warriors ausreicht, um die gesamte Spielzeit seinen finanziellen Verpflichtungen nachkommen zu können.

Bilanzielle Behandlung der Transferentschädigung:

Aus ökonomischen Gesichtspunkten ist die Transferentschädigung nicht bei Zahlung am 01.01.2008 als Aufwand zu verbuchen, da sie für die Verpflichtung von M. J. für drei Jahre und nicht nur für das Wirtschaftsjahr 2007/2008 bezahlt wurde. In der Bilanz ist die Entschädigung deshalb mit den Anschaffungskosten von 3 Mio. € erfolgsneutral zu aktivieren. G. Genau hat jedoch zu beachten, dass M. J. am Bilanzstichtag (30.06.2008) bereits seit einem halben Jahr (von insgesamt drei Jahren) für die Waldsee Warriors spielt. Es hat deshalb eine planmäßige Abschreibung für ein halbes Jahr zu erfolgen:

	Anschaffungskosten 1.1.2008	*3.000.000 €*
./.	*Abschreibung bis 30.06. 2008*	*500.000 €*
=	***Bilanzansatz zum 30.06.2008***	***2.500.000 €***

Sollte sich M. J. verletzen und sein Wert deshalb dauerhaft unter den fortgeführten Anschaffungskosten liegen, wäre gegebenenfalls eine außerplanmäßige Abschreibung vorzunehmen.

11.7 Fazit und Ausblick

Im professionalisierten Sport zeigt sich in den letzten Jahren eine deutliche Tendenz der Gründung kaufmännischer Rechtsformen anstelle der traditionellen Idealvereine. Damit gehen umfangreiche handelsrechtliche Rechnungslegungspflichten einher, die auch für die steuerliche Gewinnermittlung Bedeutung erlangen. Doch auch gemeinnützige Sportvereine ohne Kaufmannseigenschaft und handelsrechtliche Pflichten kommen nicht ganz ohne Rechenwerke aus, da das Bürgerliche Recht, das Gemeinnützigkeitsrecht und das Ertragsteuerrecht ebenfalls bestimmte Pflichten vorsehen. In diesem Fall kann jedoch anstatt der Bilanzierung die einfachere Einnahmen-Ausgaben-Rechnung ausreichend sein. Schließlich taucht bei Sportarten mit Ligasystem noch die Besonderheit auf, dass neben den gesetzlichen Pflichten verbandsrechtliche Vorgaben mit dem Ziel des Nachweises der wirtschaftlichen Leistungsfähigkeit zu erfüllen sind. Diese Vorgaben gehen dabei teilweise über die gesetzlichen Verpflichtungen hinaus und stellen für Vereine unter Umständen die einzige Verpflichtung zur handelsrechtlichen Rechnungslegung dar.

Für die Verantwortlichen in den Sportorganisationen ist jedoch nicht nur eine genaue Kenntnis aller gesetzlichen und gegebenenfalls verbandsrechtlichen Rechnungslegungspflichten unumgänglich. Vielmehr müssen auch die besonderen bilanziellen Problemfelder des Sports (z.B. Bilanzierung von Werberechten oder Spielerwerten) bekannt sein.

Kontrollfragen

1. Welches Grundmodell der Vermögens-/Erfolgsermittlung kommt in der Rechnungslegung typischerweise zur Anwendung und wodurch ist es charakterisiert?
2. Wodurch zeichnet sich die Rechnungslegung nach deutschem Handelsrecht aus?
3. Welche Unterschiede gibt es zu der Rechnungslegung nach IAS/IFRS?
4. Wann kommen die internationalen Normen zur Anwendung?
5. Welche gesetzlichen Rechnungslegungspflichten haben Sportvereine unter welchen Voraussetzungen zu erfüllen?
6. Wie sind Übertragungsrechte beim Sportunternehmen als Veranstalter zu bilanzieren?
7. Unter welchen Umständen stellt ein Übertragungsrecht einen immateriellen Vermögensgegenstand beim Käufer dar?
8. Wie ist die Transferentschädigung eines Sportlers beim kaufenden Verein zu erfassen?
9. Welches Ergebnis ergibt sich hinsichtlich der Bilanzbewertung falls der Sportler dauerhaft invalide wird?
10. Warum und wie überprüft die DFL die wirtschaftliche Leistungsfähigkeit der potentiellen Teilnehmer der Fußball-Bundesliga?

Literaturverzeichnis

BFH-Urteil v. 26.08.1992 (ergangen zu Transferentschädigungen des Deutschen Fußballbundes), BStBl. II 1992, S. 977.

Coenenberg, Adolf (2005): Jahresabschluss und Jahresabschlussanalyse, 20. Aufl., Stuttgart.

Galli, Albert (2002): Das Lizenzierungsverfahren der Union des Associations Européennes de Football (UEFA): Anforderungen an die Rechnungslegung und Prüfung, in: Galli, Albert / Gömmel, Rainer / Holzhäuser, Wolfgang / Straub, Wilfried (Hrsg.): Sportmanagement. Grundlagen der unternehmerischen Führung im Sport aus Betriebswirtschaftslehre, Steuern und Recht für den Sportmanager, München, S. 97-128.

Jansen, Rudolf (2007): Sind die Voraussetzungen für eine Aktivierung nach § 5 Abs. 2 EStG erfüllt, wenn beim Vereinswechsel eines Spielers der Fußball-Bundesliga der aufnehmende Verein an den abgebenden Verein eine Abfindung zahlt?, in: Finanz-Rundschau, Heft 17, S. 837-838.

Fülbier, Rolf Uwe/ Gassen, Joachim (2007): Das Bilanzrechtsmodernisierungsgesetz (BilMoG): Handelsrechtliche GoB vor der Neuinterpretation, in: Der Betrieb, Heft 48, S. 2605-2612.

IDW Stellungnahme zur Rechnungslegung von Vereinen (IDW RS HFA 14) (2006), in: Die Wirtschaftsprüfung, Heft 10, S. 646-651.

Kaiser, Thomas (2004): Die Behandlung von Spielerwerten in der Handelsbilanz und im Überschuldungsstatus im Profifußball, in: Der Betrieb, Heft 21, S. 1109-1112.

Lansky, Gabriel / Matznetter, Christoph / Pätzold, Dörk / Steinwandtner, Marlis / Thunshirn (2006): Rechnungslegung der Vereine. Praxisleitfaden. Vereinsrecht, Gebarung und Prüfung, 2. Aufl., Wien.

Littkemann, Jörn (2003): Ökonomische Probleme der bilanziellen Behandlung von Transferentschädigungen in der Fußball-Bundesliga, in: Dietl, Helmut (Hrsg.): Globalisierung des wirtschaftlichen Wettbewerbs im Sport, Schorndorf, S. 141-166.

Müller, Christian (2003b): Die Praxis der bilanziellen Behandlung von Transferentschädigungen in der Bundesliga, in: Dietl, Helmut (Hrsg.): Globalisierung des wirtschaftlichen Wettbewerbs im Sport, Schorndorf, S. 191-204.

Reiter, Gregor (2004), Zur Frage der Bilanzierbarkeit einer „Spielererlaubnis" im Lizenzfußball, in: Sport und Recht, Heft 2, S. 55-59.

Schneider, Dieter (1994): Betriebswirtschaftslehre. Band 2: Rechnungswesen, München.

Schneider, Dieter (1997): Betriebswirtschaftslehre. Band 2: Rechnungswesen, 2. Aufl., München.

Sigloch, Jochen (2005b): Fußballspieler in der Bilanz – Chimäre oder Notwendigkeit?, in: Brehm, Walter / Heermann, Peter / Woratschek, Herbert (Hrsg.):

Sportökonomie – Das Bayreuther Konzept in zehn exemplarischen Lektionen, Festschrift für Prof. Dr. Klaus Zieschang, Bayreuth, S. 51-69.

Sigloch, Jochen (2007): Rechnungslegung, 5. Aufl., Bayreuth.

Steiner, Eberhard / Bross, Beatrix (2005): Die Bilanzierung von Spielerwerten im Berufsfußball nach HGB und IFRS, in: Steuern und Bilanzen, Heft 12, S. 531-536.

Weiterführende Ressourcen

Literatur

Baetge, Jörg / Kirsch, Hans-Jürgen / Thiele, Stefan (2005): Bilanzen, 8. Aufl., Düsseldorf.

Deutsche Fußball Liga (2007): Ligastatut Deutsche Fußball Liga, http://www.bundesliga.de/de/dfl/interna/index.php (Zugriff: 15.12.2007).

Galli, Albert (1997): Das Rechnungswesen im Berufsfußball. Eine Analyse des Verbandsrechts des Deutschen Fußball-Bundes unter Berücksichtigung der Regelungen in England, Italien und Spanien, Düsseldorf.

Galli, Albert / Dehesselles, Thomas (2002): Rechnungslegung im Verein, in: Galli, Albert / Gömmel, Rainer / Holzhäuser, Wolfgang / Straub, Wilfried (Hrsg.): Sportmanagement. Grundlagen der unternehmerischen Führung im Sport aus Betriebswirtschaftslehre, Steuern und Recht für den Sportmanager, München, S. 45-73.

Herzig, Norbert (1998): Bilanzierung von Fernseh- und Sportübertragungsrechten bei werbefinanzierten Privatsendern, in: Matschke, Manfred / Schildbach, Thomas (Hrsg.): Unternehmensberatung und Wirtschaftsprüfung. Festschrift für Professor Dr. Günter Sieben zum 65. Geburtstag, Stuttgart, S. 223-241.

Homberg, Andreas / Elter, Vera-Carina / Rothenburger, Manuel (2004): Bilanzierung von Humankapital nach IFRS am Beispiel des Spielervermögens im Profisport, in: Kapitalmarktorientierte Rechnungslegung, Heft 6, S. 249-263.

Karsten, Klaus (2006): Der Geschäftsbericht nach § 63 AO, in: BetriebsBerater, Heft 34, S. 1830-1832.

Lehmann, Manfred (2006): Bilanzielle Behandlung von Zuwendungen (Spenden) an gemeinnützige Einrichtungen, in: Der Betrieb, Heft 24, S. 1281-1285.

Lehmann, Manfred (2007): Aktuelle Aspekte der bilanziellen Behandlung von Zuwendungen (Spenden) an gemeinnützige Organisationen, in: Der Betrieb, Heft 12, S. 641-645.

Littkemann, Jörn / Brast, Christoph / Stübinger, Tim (2003): Neuregelung der Prüfungsvorschriften für die Fußball-Bundesliga, in: Steuern und Bilanzen, Heft 14, S. 635-642.

Littkemann, Jörn / Schulte, Klaus / Schaarschmidt, Peter (2005): Außerplanmäßige Abschreibungen auf Spielerwerte im Profifußball. Theorie und Praxis, in: Steuern und Bilanzen, Heft 15, S. 660-666.

Lüdenbach, Norbert / Hoffman, Wolf-Dieter (2004): „Der Ball bleibt Rund" – Der Profifußball als Anwendungsfeld der IFRS-Rechnungslegung, in: Der Betrieb, Heft 27/28, S. 1442-1447.

Müller, Christian (2003a): Das Lizenzierungsverfahren für die Fußball-Bundesliga, in: Betriebswirtschaftliche Forschung und Praxis, Heft 5, S. 556-570.

Parensen, Andreas (2003): Transferentschädigungen im Kontext von HGB und IAS, in: Dietl, Helmut (Hrsg.): Globalisierung des wirtschaftlichen Wettbewerbs im Sport, Schorndorf, S. 167-189.

Rodewald, Jörg (1995): Die Bilanzierung von Rechten zur Berichterstattung und Übertragung von Sportereignissen im Fernsehen, in: BetriebsBerater, Heft 41, S. 2103-2108.

Schmeisser, Wilhelm (2007): Zur Ansatz- und Bewertungsproblematik von Humankapital nach IFRS, in: Betriebswirtschaftliche Forschung und Praxis, Heft 1, S. 1-19.

Segna, Ulrich (2006): Rechnungslegung und Prüfung von Vereinen – Reformbedarf im deutschen Recht, in: Deutsches Steuerrecht, Heft 35, S. 1568-1573.

Sigloch, Jochen (1987): Das Rechnungswesen im Sportverein, in: Heinemann, Klaus (Hrsg.): Betriebswirtschaftliche Grundlagen des Sportvereins, Schorndorf, S. 86-100.

Sigloch, Jochen (2005a): Rechnungslegung, in: Breuer, Christoph / Thiel, Ansgar: Handbuch Sportmanagement, Schorndorf, S. 195-215.

Straub, Wilfried / Holzhäuser, Wolfgang / Gömmel, Rainer / Galli, Albert (2002): Das Lizenzierungsverfahren des Ligaverbandes „Die Liga Fußball-Verband e.V.": Anforderungen an die Rechnungslegung und Prüfung, in: Galli, Albert / Gömmel, Rainer / Holzhäuser, Wolfgang / Straub, Wilfried (Hrsg.): Sportmanagement. Grundlagen der unternehmerischen Führung im Sport aus Betriebswirtschaftslehre, Steuern und Recht für den Sportmanager, München, S. 75-95.

Thyll, Alfred (2004): Jahresabschluss und Prüfung nach der Lizenzierungsordnung: Grundlagen und Gegenüberstellung mit den handelsrechtlichen Vorschriften, in: Hammann, Peter / Schmidt, Lars / Welling, Michael (Hrsg.): Ökonomie des Fußballs, Wiesbaden, S. 163-192.

Vogelbusch, Friedrich (2006): Primat des Handelsrechts in der Rechnungslegung von Vereinen? – Eine kritische Kommentierung von IDW RS HFA 14, in: Der Betrieb, Heft 37, S. 1967-1969.

Wehrheim, Michael (2004): Bilanzierung von Aufhebungszahlungen im Lizenzfußball, in: BetriebsBerater, Heft 8, S. 433-435.

Links

Deutsche Fußball Liga (Lizenzierungsverfahren):
  http://www.bundesliga.de
Literatur und Unterlagen zum Sportrecht:
  http://www.sportrecht.org

Kapitel 11: Ertragsteuern im Sport

Simone Jäck

Lernziele

Nach der Durchsicht dieses Kapitels sollte der Leser in der Lage sein,

- die Grundstruktur der deutschen Ertragsbesteuerung zu erläutern.
- die verschiedenen Ertragsteuerarten darzustellen.
- die Voraussetzungen für die Erlangung des Gemeinnützigkeitsstatus zu nennen.
- die ertragsteuerlichen Begünstigungen der Gemeinnützigkeit aufzuzeigen.
- sich zur Besteuerung von national und international tätigen Sportlern zu äußern.
- Problemfelder in Zusammenhang mit Sponsoring zu erkennen.
- die Anmietung einer VIP-Loge aus steuerlicher Sicht zu beurteilen.

Überblick über das Kapitel

In diesem Kapitel werden die Grundlagen der deutschen Ertragsbesteuerung erläutert und zentrale Problemfelder im Bereich des Sports angesprochen. Nachdem zunächst grundlegendes steuerliches Wissen vermittelt wird, erfolgt eine Vertiefung von sportspezifischen Aspekten. Dabei steht zunächst das für traditionelle Sportvereine wichtige Thema der Gemeinnützigkeit im Mittelpunkt. Anschließend widmet sich der Beitrag den steuerlichen Rahmenbedingungen für Berufssportler. Die Ausführungen schließen mit ausgewählten Problemen des Sponsorings. Eine Fallstudie, Kontrollfragen sowie Literaturhinweise runden das Kapitel ab.

11.1 Einführung in die Thematik

Steuern begleiten unseren Alltag, da die meisten unserer Handlungen steuerliche Wirkungen nach sich ziehen. Dies gilt insbesondere auch für die Ertragsteuern, die auf das Einkommen erhoben werden. Trotz dieser Allgegenwart der Ertragsbesteuerung handelt es sich dabei um ein komplexes Feld, das für den Laien kaum zu durchschauen ist, was das oftmals sehr medienwirksam inszenierte Verlangen nach Steuervereinfachung eindrucksvoll belegt. Auf den ersten Blick scheint die Ertragsbesteuerung kaum Überschneidungen zum Sport aufzuweisen. Jedoch bewegt sich auch die Sportbranche nicht im rechtsfreien Raum, so dass sich selbst der traditionell in gemeinnützigen Vereinen organisierte Freizeitsport entsprechenden Regelungen der Besteuerung unterwerfen muss. Gleiches gilt selbstverständlich in verstärktem Maße für den immer stärker kommerzialisierten Profisport. Dabei ist die Sportbranche nicht nur von den allgemeinen Regelungen betroffen, sondern es tauchen zahlreiche Sonderprobleme auf, die über einen außergewöhnlich hohen Komplexitätsgrad verfügen und vertiefte Kenntnisse erfordern. Für all diejenigen, die im Bereich des Sports Entscheidungen treffen sollen, ist es deshalb unabdingbar, einen Überblick über die grundsätzlichen Problemfelder der Besteuerung zu haben, um steuerliche Fallstricke frühzeitig erkennen zu können. Diesen Überblick soll das folgende Kapitel verschaffen.

11.2 Grundlagen der Ertragsbesteuerung in Deutschland

Die Ertragsbesteuerung in Deutschland – insbesondere die Besteuerung von Unternehmen – erfuhr durch das Unternehmensteuerreformgesetz 2008 gravierende Änderungen, die ab 2008 bzw. 2009 zur Anwendung kommen werden. Im Folgenden sind ausschließlich diese neuen Regelungen dargestellt.

11.2.1 Begriffsabgrenzung und Überblick

Das deutsche Steuersystem besteht aus einer Vielzahl verschiedener Steuern, die an ganz unterschiedlichen Tatbeständen anknüpfen (Schneider, 1994). Neben der Umsatzsteuer, die den Endverbrauch von Gütern und Dienstleistungen besteuert, kommt den Ertragsteuern eine zentrale Rolle zu. Diese setzen grundsätzlich an der Einkommenserzielung an und sollen das Einkommen eines Steuersubjekts besteuern, wobei in Deutschland verschiedene Ertragsteuerarten bestehen. Neben der Frage, wer überhaupt verpflichtet ist, die jeweilige Ertragsteuer zu entrichten, spielt dabei die Ermittlung der Steuerlast eine zentrale Rolle. Diese errechnet sich aus dem Produkt von Bemessungsgrundlage (Schneider, 1997) und Steuersatz, wobei vor allem die Abgrenzung des zu besteuernden Einkommens als Bemessungsgrundlage zahlreiche Fragen und Probleme aufwirft.

11.2.2 Ertragsteuerarten

Die verschiedenen Ertragsteuerarten in Deutschland unterscheiden sich grundsätzlich danach, wessen Ertrag besteuert wird. So besteuern Einkommen- und Körperschaft den Ertrag von natürlichen Personen bzw. Körperschaften. Dagegen knüpft die Gewerbesteuer am Gewerbeertrag des inländischen Gewerbebetriebs an. Dabei sind die verschiedenen Arten nicht gleich ausgestaltet, so dass eine getrennte Betrachtung notwendig ist.

11.2.2.1 Einkommensteuer

Der Einkommensteuer unterliegen grundsätzlich alle natürlichen Personen, die einen Wohnsitz oder ihren ständigen Aufenthaltsort in Deutschland haben (unbeschränkte Steuerpflicht) oder zumindest in Deutschland Einkommen erzielen (beschränkte Steuerpflicht). Besteuert wird das *zu versteuernde Einkommen* eines Jahres der natürlichen Person. Zur Ermittlung der *Steuerlast* ist diese Bemessungsgrundlage mit dem individuellen *Einkommensteuersatz* zu multiplizieren, wobei ein progressiver Tarif zur Anwendung kommt. Bei einem progressiven Tarif steigt der anzuwendende Steuersatz mit dem zu versteuernden Einkommen an. In Deutschland unterliegen Einkommen unter dem Grundfreibetrag (7.664 €) keiner Besteuerung. Danach steigt der Steuersatz von 15 % bis auf 45 % an. Auf Beträge, die 52.152 € übersteigen, werden 42 % erhoben (Spitzensteuersatz). Ist das Einkommen einer Person höher als 250.000 €, kommt auf den übersteigenden Betrag ein Steuersatz von 45 % zur Anwendung (so genannte „Reichensteuer"). Für verheiratete Personen besteht mit der Möglichkeit des Ehegatten-Splittings eine Sonderregelung.

Schwierigkeiten bei der Ermittlung der Steuerlast bereitet insbesondere die Frage, was zum zu versteuernden Einkommen gehört und in welcher Höhe dieses festzusetzen ist. Im Rahmen der Ertragsbesteuerung ist dabei im ersten Schritt zwischen der Erzielung von Einkommen (betriebliche oder berufliche Sphäre) und der Verwendung dieses Einkommens (private Sphäre) zu unterscheiden, da die Ertragsteuern nur die Erzielung von Einkommen erfassen sollen.

Für die Abgrenzung des erzielten Einkommens existieren in der Theorie zahlreiche verschiedene Konzepte. In Deutschland wird Einkommen dann besteuert, wenn es einer der sieben Einkunftsarten des deutschen Einkommensteuergesetzes zugeordnet werden kann:

1. Einkünfte aus Land- und Forstwirtschaft
2. Einkünfte aus Gewerbebetrieb
3. Einkünfte aus selbständiger Arbeit (z.B. Ärzte, Rechtsanwälte, Künstler)
4. Einkünfte aus nichtselbständiger Arbeit
5. Einkünfte aus Kapitalvermögen (z.B. Zinsen und Dividenden)
6. Einkünfte aus Vermietung und Verpachtung (z.B. Wohnungen, Gebäude)
7. Sonstige Einkünfte (kein allgemeiner Auffangtatbestand, sondern nur die im Gesetz genannten Einkünfte)

Da die Trennlinien zischen den Einkunftsarten oftmals unscharf sind und sich Überschneidungen ergeben können, gilt die Regel, dass Einkünfte vorrangig den Nummern 1-4 zuzuordnen sind. Werden beispielsweise Aktien im Rahmen eines Gewerbebetriebs als Zwischenanlage flüssiger Mittel erworben, stellen die Dividenden Einkünfte aus Gewerbebetrieb dar. Sind die Aktien dagegen als private Geldanlage dem Privatvermögen zuzuordnen, realisiert der Steuerpflichtige Einkünfte aus Kapitalvermögen.

Innerhalb einer Einkunftsart ist gemäß dem objektiven Nettoprinzip der Unterschied zwischen Einnahmen und dazugehörigen Ausgaben zu ermitteln, da nur Nettoerträge der Steuer unterworfen werden sollen. Die Ermittlung kann nach unterschiedlichen Konzepten erfolgen, wobei das deutsche Einkommensteuerrecht traditionell nicht einheitlich vorgeht, sondern sowohl auf den Gewinn als Unterschied zwischen Ertrag und Aufwand (Einkunftsarten 1-3) als auch auf den Überschuss der Einnahmen über die Ausgaben (Einkunftsarten 4-7) zurückgreift, was je nach Einkunftsart völlig unterschiedliche Ergebnisse nach sich ziehen kann. Einen Sonderfall stellen die Einkünfte aus Kapitalvermögen dar, die ohne die Berücksichtigung von angefallenen Ausgaben mit einer pauschalen Abgeltungssteuer von 25 % belastet werden.

Alle innerhalb eines Jahres erzielten Einkünfte werden zusammengefasst. Von dieser Summe dürfen zur Ermittlung des zu versteuernden Einkommens verschiedene Ausgaben zum Abzug gebracht werden, die eigentlich der privaten Verwendung zuzurechnen sind (subjektives Nettoprinzip), wie beispielsweise bestimmte außergewöhnliche Belastungen oder Spenden an gemeinnützige Vereine (Tipke/Lang, 2005).

11.2.2.2 Körperschaftsteuer

Der Körperschaftsteuer unterliegen im Gegensatz zur Einkommensteuer nicht natürliche Personen, sondern alle juristischen Personen und diesen gleichgestellte Organisationen (z.b. nicht eingetragene Vereine und Stiftungen). Auch hier wird zwischen unbeschränkter Steuerpflicht bei Sitz oder Geschäftsleitung in Deutschland oder beschränkter Steuerpflicht bei inländischen Einkünften ohne Sitz oder Geschäftsleitung unterschieden.

Besteuert wird ebenfalls das *zu versteuernde Einkommen*, welches nach den Vorschriften des Einkommensteuergesetzes ergänzt um verschiedene Sonderregelung des Körperschaftsteuergesetzes ermittelt wird. Besonderheit ist, dass bei Kapitalgesellschaften grundsätzlich alle Einkünfte als Einkünfte aus Gewerbebetrieb behandelt werden. Bei Vereinen oder Stiftungen sind dagegen grundsätzlich alle Einkunftsarten denkbar, außerdem steht ihnen ein Freibetrag von 3.835 € zu. Auch im Körperschaftsteuerrecht ist der Abzug von Spenden an gemeinnützige Organisationen vorgesehen.

Der *Körperschaftsteuersatz* beträgt unabhängig von der Höhe des Einkommens 15 %. In Zusammenhang mit der daraus resultierenden – vermeintlich sehr geringen – Steuerlast ist jedoch zu beachten, dass das Einkommen einer Körperschaft noch nicht zur Verwendung durch die beteiligten natürlichen Personen zur Verfügung steht. Es muss zunächst eine Einkommensverteilung erfolgen, die eine zusätzliche Einkommensteuerlast nach sich zieht (Tipke/Lang, 2005).

11.2.2.3 Gewerbesteuer

Die Gewerbesteuer wird parallel zu Einkommen- und Körperschaftsteuer erhoben und soll nicht natürliche oder juristische Personen, sondern das Objekt „inländischer Gewerbebetrieb" erfassen. Trotzdem ist sie als Ertragsteuer ausgestaltet, da grundsätzlich der Gewinn aus dem Gewerbebetrieb als Ausgangspunkt für die Ermittlung der Bemessungsgrundlage dient. Um dem Objektsteuercharakter Rechnung zu tragen, sind zur Ermittlung des *Gewerbeertrags* jedoch verschiedene Modifikationen in Form von Hinzurechnungen und Kürzungen vorzunehmen. Einzelunternehmen und Personengesellschaften steht ein Freibetrag in Höhe von 24.500 € zu. Der *Gewerbesteuersatz* setzt sich aus der so genannten Messzahl in Höhe von 3,5 % und dem Hebesatz zusammen. Da die Gewerbesteuer den Gemeinden zusteht, dürfen diese selbst über die endgültige Höhe der Gewerbesteuer in ihrer Gemeinde entscheiden, indem sie einen Hebesatz von mindestens 200 % selbst festlegen. Bei einem Hebesatz von 400 % ergibt sich so beispielsweise ein Steuersatz in Höhe von 3,5 % x 400 % = 14 %.

Die Gewerbesteuer wird zusätzlich zur Einkommen- oder Körperschaftsteuer erhoben, wenn gewerbliche Einkünfte erzielt werden, so dass diese eine Zusatzbelastung darstellt. Diese Zusatzbelastung wird für Einzelunternehmer und Personengesellschaften insofern vermieden bzw. vermindert, als die Gewerbesteuer pauschal auf die Einkommensteuer angerechnet werden darf. Dazu wird das 3,8-fache des Produkts aus Gewerbeertrag und Messzahl von der Einkommensteuerlast abgezogen. Ob die Gewerbesteuer dadurch vollständig eliminiert wird oder eine Restbelastung verbleibt, hängt auf Grund der pauschalen Anrechnung vom jeweiligen gemeindlichen Hebesatz ab.

11.2.3 Besteuerungssysteme

Grundsätzlich zielt die Ertragsbesteuerung auf die Belastung des Einkommens natürlicher Personen ab, das diesen zur Verwendung in der privaten Sphäre zur Verfügung steht. Zur Erzielung dieses Einkommens werden natürliche Personen jedoch nicht nur alleine tätig, sondern organisieren sich oftmals rechtsförmlich (z.b. als Personengesellschaften, Kapitalgesellschaften oder Vereine), so dass die Einkommenserzielung mittels mehr oder weniger verselbständigten Organisationen verfolgt wird. Letztendlich können allerdings nur natürliche Personen und nicht Organisationseinheiten Einkommen für private Zwecke nutzen (Schneider, 1994). Die Ertragsteuern sollen deshalb insgesamt das, einer natürlichen Person jeweils zur Verfügung stehende Einkommen, genau einmal belasten. Wird das Einkommen dabei durch einen Personenzusammenschluss erzielt, stellt sich die Frage, wie dieses Ziel zu erreichen ist. In Deutschland kommen dabei in Abhängigkeit der rechtsförmlichen Organisation verschiedene Varianten zur Anwendung.

11.2.3.1 Natürliche Personen, Einzelunternehmen und Personengesellschaften

Natürliche Personen, die in keiner Weise rechtsförmlich organisiert sind, unterliegen selbst und unmittelbar der Einkommensteuer. Dies gilt steuerlich auch für natürliche Personen, die mit der Gründung eines Einzelunternehmens zumindest eine gewisse Verselbständigung ihrer Einkommenserzielung erreicht haben. Zwischen Unternehmer und Unternehmen herrscht vollständige Transparenz. Das erzielte Einkommen wird auf Ebene der natürlichen Person von der Einkommensteuer erfasst. Werden Einkünfte aus Gewerbebetrieb erzielt, tritt eine zusätzliche Belastung durch die Gewerbesteuer hinzu, die durch die Anrechnungsmöglichkeit auf die Einkommensteuer jedoch wieder abgemildert wird.

Auch Personengesellschaften unterliegen dem Transparenzprinzip (Tipke/Lang, 2005). Obwohl diese über eigenes Vermögen verfügen und zivilrechtlich selbst Verträge abschließen können, werden sie für Zwecke der Einkommensbesteuerung nicht als eigenes Steuersubjekt behandelt. Die Steuerpflicht entsteht trotz rechtsförmlicher Organisation auf Ebene der beteiligten Gesellschafter. Dazu wird das Einkommen der Personengesellschaft zwar einheitlich ermittelt, anschließend aber den Gesellschaftern anteilig zugerechnet, die es gemäß ihrer jeweiligen persönlichen Merkmale der Besteuerung zu unterwerfen haben. Die Personengesellschaft selbst ist nicht Subjekt der Einkommensteuer (Brönner, 2007). Ist die Personengesellschaft gewerblich tätig, kommt es zur Gewerbesteuerpflicht, die direkt auf Ebene der Personengesellschaft erhoben wird, dann allerdings wiederum auf die Einkommensteuer der Gesellschafter angerechnet werden kann.

Damit stellt sich bei Einzelunternehmen oder Personengesellschaften aus steuerlicher Sicht grundsätzlich nicht die Frage, ob Einkommen für private Zwecke verwendet oder im Unternehmen belassen wird. Ausnahmsweise kann jedoch ein niedrigerer Steuersatz von 28,25 % beantragt werden, wenn nachgewiesen wird, dass erzieltes Einkommen nicht entnommen wird. Bei einer späteren Entnahme kommt es zur Nachversteuerung mit einem Steuersatz von 25 %. Der Steuerpflichtige hat ein Wahlrecht zwischen Sofortversteuerung oder ermäßigter Besteuerung mit eventueller Nachversteuerung (Blumenberg/Benz, 2007).

natürliche Person	Einkommensteuer	*Beispiel: Einkünfte aus Gewerbebetrieb*	
		zu versteuerndes Einkommen	*100*
		- Gewerbesteuer (3,5 %, 400 %)	*- 14*
Einzelunternehmen	Gewerbesteuer (bei gewerblicher Tätigkeit)	*Gewinn nach Gewerbesteuer*	*86*
		Variante I: Entnahme	
		- Einkommensteuer (z. B. 40 %)	*- 40,0*
natürliche Person	Einkommensteuer	*+ pauschale Anrechnung Gewerbesteuer (100 x 3,5 % x 3,8)*	*+ 13,3*
		= Gewinn nach Steuern I	*59,3*
Personengesellschaft	Gewerbesteuer (bei gewerblicher Tätigkeit)	*Variante II: Einbehaltung*	*„oder"*
		- Einkommensteuer	*- 30,0*
		+ pauschale Anrechnung Gewerbesteuer (100 x 3,5 % x 3,8)	*+ 13,3*
natürliche Person	Einkommensteuer	*= vorläufiger Gewinn nach Steuern II*	*69,3*
		- Nachversteuerung bei Entnahme	*- 17,3*
		= Gewinn nach Entnahme II	*52,0*

Abb. 1: Einkommensbesteuerung natürlicher Personen mit Beispiel

11.2.3.2 Kapitalgesellschaften und andere Körperschaften

Kapitalgesellschaften und andere Körperschaften wie z.B. Vereine oder Stiftungen sind i.d.R. als juristische Personen in vollem Umfang rechtsfähig und zivilrechtlich völlig eigenständig. Dieser Sichtweise schließt sich auch die deutsche Ertragsbesteuerung an, so dass an Stelle des Transparenzprinzips das Trennprinzip zur Anwendung kommt (Tipke/Lang, 2005). Demnach ist die Gesellschaft neben ihren Gesellschaftern selbständiges Besteuerungssubjekt der Körperschaftsteuer. Diese strikte Trennung könnte dazu führen, dass durch die Belastung der Gesellschaft und später durch die Ausschüttung an die Gesellschafter dasselbe Einkommen doppelt erfasst wird (Schneider, 1994). Um dies zu vermeiden, könnte entweder nur die Gesellschaft oder aber nur die Gesellschafter (ähnlich der Personengesellschaft) belastet werden. Neben diesen beiden Extremformen sind zahlreiche Mischvarianten denkbar, wie sie auch Eingang in das deutsche Besteuerungssystem gefunden haben. Auf Ebene der Gesellschaft wird Körperschaftsteuer in moderater Höhe und regelmäßig auch Gewerbesteuer erhoben. Kommt es zur Verteilung des Einkommens an die Gesellschafter, wird dort zusätzlich (ebenfalls in verminderter Höhe) Einkommensteuer erhoben:

1. Wird die Gewinnausschüttung im Rahmen einer betrieblichen Tätigkeit (insbesondere als Einkünfte aus Gewerbebetrieb) erzielt, geht die Ausschüttung gemäß dem so genannten Teileinkünfteverfahren nur in Höhe von 60 % in die Bemessungsgrundlage ein, wo sie mit dem individuellen Einkommensteuersatz belastet wird. Ist der Steuerpflichtige mit weniger als 15 % an der Kapitalgesellschaft beteiligt, fällt nochmals Gewerbesteuer an.

2. Wird die Dividende dagegen im Rahmen der Einkünfte aus Kapitalvermögen erzielt, wird unabhängig von der Höhe eine pauschale Abgeltungssteuer von 25 % erhoben. Im Privatvermögen fällt keine Gewerbesteuer an.

		Beispiel: Kapitalgesellschaft	
Körperschaft	Körperschaftsteuer und Gewerbesteuer	*zu versteuerndes Einkommen*	*100*
		- Gewerbesteuer (3,5 %, 400 %)	*- 14*
		- Körperschaftsteuer (15 %)	*- 15*
		= Gewinn nach Steuern	*71*
natürliche Person	Einkommensteuer (nur bei Gewinnausschüttung)	*Variante I: Teileinkünfteverfahren*	
		Ausschüttung	*71*
		Bemessungsgrundlage (60 % von 71)	*(42,6)*
		- Einkommensteuer (z. B. 40 %)	*- 17*
Variante I: Einkünfte aus Gewerbebetrieb	Teileinkünfteverfahren	*= Ausschüttung nach Steuern*	*54*
		Variante II: Abgeltungssteuer	
Variante II: Einkünfte aus Kapitalvermögen	Abgeltungssteuer	*Ausschüttung*	*71*
		- Einkommensteuer (pauschal 25 %)	*- 18*
		= Ausschüttung nach Steuern	*53*

Abb. 2: Besteuerung von Körperschaften mit Beispiel

11.3 Besteuerung von Sportorganisationen

Grundsätzlich steht dem im Bereich des Sports tätigen Unternehmen jede Rechtsform offen, wobei heute neben der traditionellen Rechtsform des Vereins insbesondere im professionellen Mannschaftssport die Form der Kapitalgesellschaft vorherrschend ist. Aus steuerlicher Sicht gelten für den Sport dabei keine besonderen Regelungen, so dass sich die Sportunternehmen den allgemeinen Besteuerungsvorschriften zu unterwerfen haben.

Jedoch existiert im deutschen Steuerrecht ein Steuerbegünstigungstatbestand, der unter anderem auch im Bereich des Sports eine zentrale Stellung einnimmt. Es handelt sich um den Gemeinnützigkeitsstatus, den im institutionell organisierten Sport in Deutschland vor allem die traditionellen Sportvereine inne haben.

11.3.1 Gemeinnützigkeit im deutschen Sport

Das so genannte Gemeinnützigkeitsrecht bezieht sich nicht nur auf eine einzelne Steuerart, sondern ist bei zahlreichen Steuerarten als Begünstigungstatbestand zu finden. Deshalb sind die Voraussetzungen zur Erlangung dieses Status in der Abgabenordnung als Rahmengesetz des deutschen Steuersystems geregelt. Die verschiedensten Steuererleichterungen, die daran anknüpfen, finden sich dann im jeweiligen Einzelsteuergesetz.

Die Anerkennung als gemeinnützige Organisation stellt hohe Anforderungen an die steuerlichen Kenntnisse der Vereinsführung, da dieser Bereich des Gemeinnützigkeitsrechts über eine außerordentliche Komplexität verfügt. Besonders die zahlreichen Ausnahmen erschweren eine einfache Anwendbarkeit der Regelungen. Andererseits ermöglichen es gerade die Ausnahmen, dass trotz Gemeinnützigkeitsstatus im Ergebnis doch eine große Handlungsfreiheit besteht, die von Sportvereinen genutzt werden kann.

11.3.2 Voraussetzungen für die Gemeinnützigkeit

Grundvoraussetzung für die Erlangung des Gemeinnützigkeitsstatus ist die Verfolgung eines als gemeinnützig anerkannten Zwecks. Die Förderung der Sportausübung gilt explizit als gemeinnütziger Zweck, so dass jeder Verein und jede Kapitalgesellschaft, deren Tätigkeit auf die Ausübung von Sport ausgerichtet ist, gemeinnützig sein kann. Selbst die im Profisport engagierten Vereine besitzen regelmäßig diesen Status. Neben der gemeinnützigen Zweckverfolgung ist jedoch auch die Art der Zweckverfolgung von entscheidender Bedeutung, die ganz bestimmten Anforderungen genügen muss.

Wichtige Voraussetzung ist, dass die begünstigten Zwecke selbstlos – also uneigennützig – verfolgt werden. Selbstlosigkeit ist gegeben, wenn die Sportorganisation nicht in erster Linie eigenwirtschaftliche Zwecke (z.B. Erwerbszwecke der Mitglieder, Mehrung des Organisationsvermögens) verfolgt. Vielmehr dürfen nur

Aktivitäten zur Förderung des Sports wie beispielsweise die Organisation von Training und Wettkampf oder Bau und Unterhalt von Sportanlagen verfolgt werden. Dabei ist es nicht vollständig untersagt, bestimmte wirtschaftliche Zwecke zu verfolgen, sofern diese nicht Hauptzweck darstellen. Diese großzügige Auslegung ist insbesondere im Sport von großer Bedeutung, da so die Möglichkeit eröffnet wird, notwendige Mittel nicht nur durch Spenden und Mitgliederbeiträge, sondern auch durch wirtschaftliche Aktivitäten wie beispielsweise Sponsoring aufzubringen oder neben der Förderung des Amateur- oder Jugendsports auch professionellen Sport zu betreiben, sofern auch Jugend- und Amateurmannschaften unterhalten werden.

Die Selbstlosigkeit verlangt darüber hinaus, dass sämtliche der Körperschaft zufließenden Mittel für deren Satzungszwecke verwendet werden. So sind Gewinnausschüttungen oder die Hingabe anderer materieller Begünstigungen an Mitglieder oder Gesellschafter untersagt. Vorhandene Mittel dürfen außerdem nur unter bestimmten Voraussetzungen angespart werden und müssen i.d.R. spätestens in dem auf den Zufluss folgendem Kalenderjahr für gemeinnützige Zwecke verwendet werden. Bei Auflösung der Körperschaft oder bei Verlust des Gemeinnützigkeitsstatus sind alle vorhandenen Mittel für steuerbegünstigte Zwecke zu verwenden – beispielsweise indem die Mittel in diesem Fall einer anderen ebenfalls gemeinnützigen Organisation zufließen.

Abb. 3: Voraussetzungen für die Steuerbegünstigungen
In Anlehnung an: Jäck (2006), S. 76

Neben der Selbstlosigkeit sind Ausschließlichkeit und Unmittelbarkeit zu wahren. Ausschließlichkeit verbietet die Verfolgung von Zwecken außerhalb der gemeinnützigen Zielsetzung. Die Unmittelbarkeit erfordert grundsätzliche eine Verwirklichung des gemeinnützigen Satzungszwecks durch die Körperschaft selbst, d.h. durch eigenes Tätigwerden. Im Bereich des Sports erlangt diese Voraussetzung jedoch nur in Ausnahmefällen Bedeutung.

11.3.3 Ertragsteuerliche Folgen

Dem Aufwand stehen jedoch zahlreiche steuerliche, aber auch außersteuerliche Vorteile gegenüber. Im Bereich der Ertragsteuern liegen die Vorteile dabei hauptsächlich in der Steuerbefreiung des Vereins, der grundsätzlich der Körperschaft- und gegebenenfalls Gewerbesteuer unterliegen würde (direkte Begünstigung) und in der Begünstigung von Spendern und ehrenamtlichen Mitarbeitern (indirekte Begünstigung).

Die *direkte Begünstigung* besteht in der Befreiung von Körperschaft- und Gewerbesteuer, die jedoch nicht einheitlich für die gesamte Organisation gilt. Der gemeinnützige Verein ist deshalb in vier Sphären einzuteilen. Alle Einnahmen und Ausgaben des Vereins sind einer dieser Sphäre zuzuordnen, wodurch die jeweilige ertragsteuerliche Behandlung determiniert wird.

Grundsätzlich stellt die *ideelle Sphäre* der begünstigten Organisation den Hauptbereich der Organisation dar, sie ist von der Körperschaft- und Gewerbesteuersteuerpflicht befreit. Ihr werden alle Einnahmen und Ausgaben zugeordnet, die direkt die Sportausübung betreffen. Auf Grund der Mittelbindung an die satzungsmäßigen Zwecke, findet die Verwendung aller Mittel i.d.R. in diesem Bereich statt. Der ideellen Sphäre sind insbesondere alle Einnahmen zuzuordnen, die der Organisation ohne Gegenleistung zur Verfügung gestellt werden. Dies sind Spenden und Zuschüsse sowie i.d.R. Mitgliederbeiträge. Alle anderen Formen der Mittelaufbringung gehören in einen anderen Organisationsbereich.

Ebenfalls nicht steuerpflichtig sind Überschüsse, die im Rahmen der *Vermögensverwaltung* erzielt werden. Vermögensverwaltung liegt vor, wenn Vermögen lediglich unter Substanzerhaltung zur Fruchtziehung genutzt wird, also beispielsweise Kapitalvermögen angelegt oder unbewegliches Vermögen vermietet oder verpachtet wird. Steht dagegen die Vermögensumschichtung im Mittelpunkt oder werden weitere Leistungen von nicht untergeordneter Bedeutung erbracht, wird die Grenze der Vermögensverwaltung überschritten.

Überschreitet die Mittelaufbringung durch selbständige und nachhaltige Tätigkeit der Organisation die Grenzen der Vermögensverwaltung, liegt ein *wirtschaftlicher Geschäftsbetrieb* vor, der im Gegensatz zu den anderen Bereichen der begünstigten Organisation nicht steuerbefreit ist (Schauhoff, 2005). Um gemeinnützige Organisationen, die ihre Zwecke nicht ohne einen wirtschaftlichen Geschäftsbetrieb verfolgen können (z.B. Altenheime) nicht zu benachteiligen, sind solche wirtschaftlichen Geschäftsbetriebe, die für die gemeinnützige Zweckverfolgung unmittelbar und zwingend notwendig sind und nicht in vermeidbaren Wettbewerb zu kommerziellen Anbietern treten, ebenfalls steuerbefreit. Dem Zweckbetrieb kommt im Sport eine nur sehr untergeordnete Bedeutung zu, insbesondere können so genannte Mittelbeschaffungsbetriebe (v.a. Sponsoring) nie einen Zweckbetrieb darstellen. Einzig Sportveranstaltungen eines Vereins (Wettkämpfe, Schauveranstaltungen, Übungsstunden) können als Zweckbetrieb und damit als steuerfrei eingestuft werden, wenn alle Einnahmen aus Veranstaltungen eines Jahres (Eintritt, Teilnahmegebühren, *nicht* Sponsoring/Bewirtung) die Grenze von 35.000 € nicht überschreiten. Alternativ kann der Verein dafür optieren, dass alle Veranstaltungen Zweckbetriebe darstellen, an denen keine bezahlten Sportler teilnehmen und damit die Grenze von 35.000 € nicht zur Anwendung kommt.

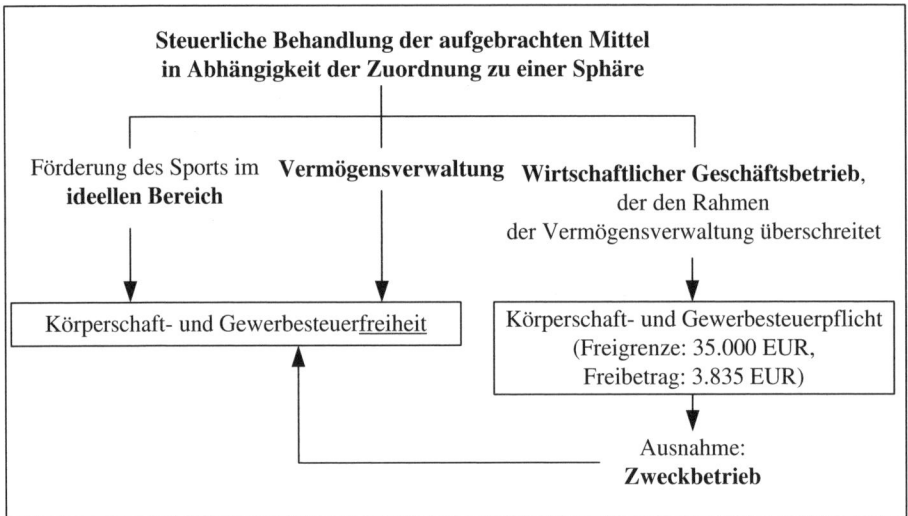

Abb. 4: Sphären des gemeinnützigen Vereins
In Anlehnung an: Jäck (2006), S. 113

Die Ausgaben sind ebenfalls je nach Verursachung zuzuordnen, wobei zu beachten ist, dass Ausgaben nur denn dem steuerpflichtigen Gewinn eines wirtschaftlichen Geschäftsbetriebs mindern dürfen, wenn diese ausschließlich durch die Tätigkeit dieser Sphäre veranlasst wurden.

Die Aufteilung der Vereinsaktivitäten in die vier genannten Geschäftsbereiche führt zu zahlreichen Abgrenzungsproblemen, wobei es im Interesse des Steuerpflichtigen liegen wird, Einnahmen möglichst einem der steuerbefreiten Bereiche zuzuordnen und Ausgaben zur Minderung der steuerlichen Bemessungsgrundlage im wirtschaftlichen Geschäftsbetrieb zu erfassen.

Ideelle Sphäre	Vermögens-verwaltung	Zweckbetrieb (Sport-veranstaltungen)	Wirtschaftlicher Ge-schäftsbetrieb
Einnahmen: ▪ Aufnahmegebühren ▪ Mitgliederbeiträge ▪ Spenden ▪ Zuschüssen	**Einnahmen:** ▪ langfristige Vermie-tungen/Verpacht-ungen (z.B. Vereins-gaststätte) ▪ Dividenden, Zinsen	**Einnahmen:** ▪ Eintritt ▪ Teilnahmegebühren ▪ Startgelder	**Einnahmen:** ▪ Sponsoring ▪ Fernsehrechte ▪ Verkauf von Essen und Getränken
Ausgaben: ▪ Sportanlagen ▪ Ausrüstung ▪ Übungsleiter, Trainer ▪ Verwaltung	**Ausgaben:** ▪ Ausgaben für ver-mietete/verpachtete Güter ▪ Bankgebühren	**Ausgaben:** ▪ Kosten der Veran-staltung	**Ausgaben:** ▪ nur direkt zurechen-bare Kosten (z.B. Einkauf Essen und Getränke, Aufbau von Banden)

Tab. 1: Typische Einnahmen und Ausgaben in den verschiedenen Sphären

Im Gegensatz zu anderen gemeinnützigen Bereichen kommt im Sport der *indirekten Begünstigung* durch die Möglichkeit des *Spendenabzugs* beim Spender nur geringe Bedeutung zu. So finanziert sich der deutsche Sport kaum durch Spenden. Mitgliederbeiträge an Sportvereine, denen eine größere Bedeutung zukommt, sind von der Abzugsfähigkeit dagegen ausgeschlossen. Grundsätzlich dürfen Spender unentgeltliche Zuwendungen an Sportvereine von ihrer Bemessungsgrundlage abziehen, wenn bestimmt Höchstbeträge (i.d.R. 20 % des zu versteuernden Einkommens des Spenders) nicht überschritten sind (Troll/ Wallenhorst/ Halaczinsky, 2005; Hüttemann, 2007). Daraus resultiert ein zusätzlicher Anreiz, der das Spendenaufkommen erhöhen kann.

Erhebliche Bedeutung kommt dagegen dem so genannten *Übungsleiterfreibetrag* für die Sportvereine zu. Nebenberuflich tätigen Übungsleitern eines als gemeinnützig anerkannten Sportvereins steht für ihre Betreuungs- und Trainertätigkeit ein jährlicher Freibetrag von 2.100 € zu. Ehrenamtlichen Helfern in anderen Bereichen (z.B. Verwaltung) steht ein Freibetrag von 500 € zu, der jedoch nicht mit dem Übungsleiterfreibetrag kombiniert werden kann (Schauhoff/Kirchhain, 2007).

11.4 Besteuerung von Sportlern

Erreicht ein Sportler ein Niveau, das es ihm in seiner jeweiligen Sportart erlaubt, Einkommen zu erzielen, sind auch Überlegungen in steuerlicher Hinsicht anzustellen.

11.4.1 National tätige Sportler

Einnahmen aus Sponsoring- oder Werbeverträgen, Anstellungsverträgen bei Sportunternehmen und Preis- oder Antrittsgeldern stehen Ausgaben für Ausrüstung,

Training und Reisen gegenüber. Wird Sport als Freizeitbeschäftigung betrieben, übersteigen diese Ausgaben regelmäßig die Einnahmen bei weitem. Ein daraus resultierender „Verlust" ist der privaten Lebensführung zuzuordnen und entfaltet keine ertragsteuerliche Wirkung. Anders bei Profisportlern, die ihren Lebensunterhalt mit Sport verdienen: hier werden hohe Überschüsse erzielt, die entsprechende steuerliche Konsequenzen nach sich ziehen. Ein solcher Profisportler darf – insbesondere zu Beginn der Karriere oder in Schwächephasen – durchaus auch Verluste erwirtschaften, die dann steuerlich anerkannt sind. Deshalb taucht insbesondere im Übergangsbereich zwischen Amateur- und Profisport oder in Randsportarten, in denen nur geringe Einnahmen realisiert werden können, die Frage auf, ob Ausgabenüberhänge eines Sportlers steuerlich relevant sind oder es sich lediglich um Ausgaben der privaten Lebensführung handelt (Tipke/Lang, 2005).

Ist festgestellt, dass der sportlichen Betätigung eine klare Einkünfteerzielungsabsicht zu Grunde liegt, hat für den Sportler, der als natürliche Person der Einkommensteuer und gegebenenfalls auch der Gewerbesteuer unterliegt, eine Einordnung der Einkünfte in die sieben Einkunftsarten nach den allgemeinen Grundsätzen zu erfolgen.

Land- und Forstwirtschaft	Keine sportspezifische Bedeutung.
Gewerbebetrieb	▪ Preis- und Antrittsgelder ▪ Sponsoring und Werbung (einschließlich Übertragung des Rechts an Bild und Namen) sofern nicht im Rahmen nichtselbständiger Arbeit bezahlt
Selbständige Arbeit	▪ Sportler gelten grundsätzlich nicht als Künstler, so dass aus sportlicher Tätigkeit an sich keine Einkünfte aus selbständiger Arbeit realisiert werden können ▪ Schriftstellerische Tätigkeit (Autobiographie, Erfahrungsberichte, Trainingsliteratur)
Nichtselbständige Arbeit	Sportler als Arbeitnehmer eines ▪ Sportvereins ▪ Sponsors
Kapitalvermögen	▪ Zinsen ▪ Dividenden aus Kapitalanlagen. Keine sportspezifische Bedeutung.
Vermietung und Verpachtung	▪ Grundsätzlich keine sportspezifische Bedeutung ▪ Diskutiert für die Überlassung von Rechten am eigenen Bild/ Namen, i.d.R. handelt es sich dabei jedoch um gewerbliche Einkünfte
Sonstige Einkünfte	▪ Zahlungen der deutschen Sporthilfe

Tab. 2: Einkunftsarten bei Sportlern
In Anlehnung an: Klimmer (2004), S. 104

11.4.2 International tätige Sportler

Sportler, die international tätig sind und ihr Einkommen durch Aktivitäten in vielen verschiedenen Ländern erzielen, unterliegen sehr viel komplexeren Besteuerungsproblemen als Sportler, die nur in ihrem Heimatland tätig werden. Dabei dürfte der international tätige Sportler jedoch eher die Regel als die Ausnahme sein, so dass die damit verbundenen steuerlichen Probleme nicht vernachlässigt werden können.

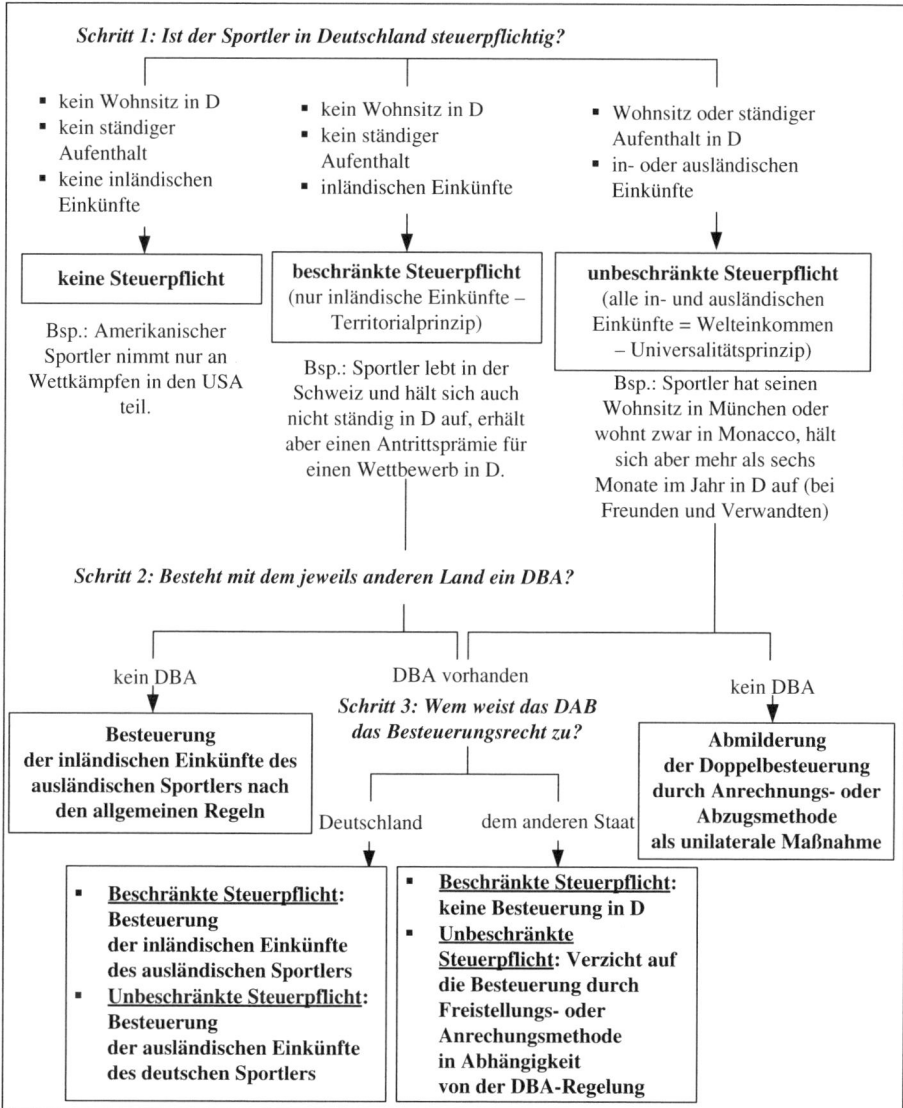

Schritt 1: Ist der Sportler in Deutschland steuerpflichtig?

- kein Wohnsitz in D
- kein ständiger Aufenthalt
- keine inländischen Einkünfte

- kein Wohnsitz in D
- kein ständiger Aufenthalt
- inländischen Einkünfte

- Wohnsitz oder ständiger Aufenthalt in D
- in- oder ausländischen Einkünfte

keine Steuerpflicht

Bsp.: Amerikanischer Sportler nimmt nur an Wettkämpfen in den USA teil.

beschränkte Steuerpflicht (nur inländische Einkünfte – Territorialprinzip)

Bsp.: Sportler lebt in der Schweiz und hält sich auch nicht ständig in D auf, erhält aber einen Antrittsprämie für einen Wettbewerb in D.

unbeschränkte Steuerpflicht (alle in- und ausländischen Einkünfte = Welteinkommen – Universalitätsprinzip)

Bsp.: Sportler hat seinen Wohnsitz in München oder wohnt zwar in Monacco, hält sich aber mehr als sechs Monate im Jahr in D auf (bei Freunden und Verwandten)

Schritt 2: Besteht mit dem jeweils anderen Land ein DBA?

kein DBA

DBA vorhanden
Schritt 3: Wem weist das DAB das Besteuerungsrecht zu?

kein DBA

Besteuerung der inländischen Einkünfte des ausländischen Sportlers nach den allgemeinen Regeln

Deutschland

dem anderen Staat

Abmilderung der Doppelbesteuerung durch Anrechnungs- oder Abzugsmethode als unilaterale Maßnahme

- **Beschränkte Steuerpflicht:** Besteuerung der inländischen Einkünfte des ausländischen Sportlers
- **Unbeschränkte Steuerpflicht:** Besteuerung der ausländischen Einkünfte des deutschen Sportlers

- **Beschränkte Steuerpflicht:** keine Besteuerung in D
- **Unbeschränkte Steuerpflicht:** Verzicht auf die Besteuerung durch Freistellungs- oder Anrechnungsmethode in Abhängigkeit von der DBA-Regelung

Abb. 5: Besteuerung international tätiger Sportler aus deutscher Sicht

Es ist international üblich, dass der Staat, in dem eine natürliche Person ihren Wohnsitz oder ständigen Aufenthalt hat, nicht nur das in diesem Staat erzielte Einkommen besteuert, sondern ihr gesamtes Welteinkommen (unbeschränkte Steuerpflicht). Andererseits sehen die meisten Staaten aber auch eine Besteuerung vor, wenn eine Person ohne Wohnsitz oder ständigen Aufenthalt in diesem Staat Einkünfte erzielt (beschränkte Steuerpflicht). Diese Situation kann eine Doppelbesteuerung verursachen, die im Extremfall sogar dazu führt, dass die Steuerlast über den erzielten Einnahmen liegt. Eine solche ungemilderte Doppelbesteuerung würde internationale Aktivitäten in allen Bereichen hemmen und auch im Bereich des Sports ein großes Hindernis darstellen. Es ist deshalb allgemein anerkannt, dass diese Doppelbesteuerung zu vermeiden oder zumindest abzumildern ist (Schmidt/ Sigloch/Henselmann, 2005). Dies kann grundsätzlich auf zwei Wegen erfolgen:

- Der Wohnsitzstaat verzichtet unilateral auf eine Besteuerung.
- Die beiden betroffenen Staaten einigen sich in einem bilateralen Vertrag (Doppelbesteuerungsabkommen/DBA), wem das Besteuerungsrecht für welche Einkünfte zukommt und auf welche Weise der Verzicht des jeweils anderen Staates erfolgen soll.

In Deutschland sind beide Varianten in Gebrauch. Erstere findet jedoch nur in Zusammenhang mit Einkünften aus Staaten Anwendung, mit denen kein DBA abgeschlossen wurde.

11.4.2.1 Deutsche Sportler im Ausland

Ein in Deutschland ansässiger Sportler ist in Deutschland unbeschränkt steuerpflichtig, er muss seine gesamten Einkünfte unabhängig vom Tätigkeitsland in Deutschland besteuern. Parallel sehen jedoch viele Länder – so beispielsweise auch Deutschland selbst (siehe dazu unter 11.4.2.2) – vor, dass Einnahmen aus sportlicher Betätigung in ihrem Land unabhängig von Wohnsitz und ständigem Aufenthalt besteuert werden. Damit droht für den deutschen Sportler eine Doppelbesteuerung seiner im Ausland erzielten Einkünfte. Da diese regelmäßig vermieden oder abgemildert werden soll, ist zu prüfen, welchem Staat ein etwaiges DBA das Besteuerungsrecht zuweist und mittels welcher Methode gegebenenfalls auf die Besteuerung verzichtet werden muss.

Hat der Sportler in einem Land Einkünfte erzielt, mit dem Deutschland kein DBA abgeschlossen hat, verzichtet Deutschland einseitig auf eine Besteuerung. Dabei handelt es sich jedoch nicht um eine gänzliche Befreiung der ausländischen Einkünfte von der Besteuerung, sondern nur um eine Abmilderung. Bei Sportlern wird in aller Regel die so genannte Abzugsmethode zur Anwendung kommen, die es dem Sportler erlaubt, die im Ausland bezahlte Steuer wie Betriebsausgaben oder Werbungskosten von der Bemessungsgrundlage für die deutsche Steuer abzuziehen. Die für den Steuerpflichtigen etwas günstigere Anrechnungsmethode, bei der die im Ausland bezahlte Steuer von der deutschen Steuerlast abgezogen wird, ist nur unter bestimmten Voraussetzungen, die von Sportlern regelmäßig nicht erfüllt werden, anwendbar.

Ist ein DBA vorhanden, ist die Zuordnung des Besteuerungsrechts zu überprüfen. Die meisten DBA, die Deutschland abgeschlossen hat, enthalten dabei eine Spezialnorm für Sportler, die festlegt, dass Einkünfte, die in engem Zusammenhang mit sportlicher Betätigung erzielt werden (z.B. Antrittsgelder, Preisgelder, Werbeprämien), nur in dem Land besteuert werden, in dem die sportliche Tätigkeit ausgeübt wurde. Einkünfte, die ein Sportler aus sportlichen Aktivitäten im Ausland erzielt, werden damit nicht vom deutschen Fiskus erfasst. Grundgedanke dieser Regelung ist, dass viele Profisportler ihren Sport – sei es auf Grund von Training oder Wettkämpfen – regelmäßig auf der ganzen Welt ausüben und ihren Wohnsitz deshalb nahezu beliebig wählen können. Die Steuereinnahmen sollen deshalb auf die Länder verteilt werden, in denen die Sportveranstaltungen ausgerichtet werden. Der Verzicht auf die Besteuerung erfolgt in Deutschland entweder durch eine vollständige Freistellung der Einkünfte (Freistellungsmethode) oder durch eine Anrechnung der ausländischen Steuer auf die zu bezahlende deutsche Steuer (Anrechnungsmethode). Welche Methode zur Anwendung kommt, ist im jeweiligen Abkommen festgelegt. I.d.R. kommt jedoch die Freistellungsmethode mit Progressionsvorbehalt zur Anwendung, wodurch die ausländischen Einkünfte zwar nicht der deutschen Steuer unterliegen, jedoch trotzdem einen Einfluss auf die Höhe des progressiven Einkommensteuersatzes haben.

Erzielt der deutsche Sportler im Ausland Einkünfte, die in keinem direkten Zusammenhang mit einer sportlichen Tätigkeit stehen (z.B. Werbeauftritte) kommen die allgemeinen Regelungen des DBA zur Anwendung.

11.4.2.2 Ausländische Sportler in Deutschland

Ein ausländischer Sportler, der in Deutschland weder Wohnsitz noch ständigen Aufenthalt hat, wird in Deutschland nur steuerpflichtig, wenn er ganz bestimmte Einkünfte mit einem besonderen Inlandsbezug erzielt. Man spricht in diesem Fall von einer beschränkten Steuerpflicht. Grundsätzlich sind auch hier die sieben Einkunftsarten relevant. Allerdings müssen diese bei ausländischen Steuerpflichtigen einen besonderen Inlandsbezug, wie beispielsweise eine Betriebsstätte in Deutschland oder einen längeren Aufenthalt des Steuerpflichtigen aufweisen. Dies dürfte bei ausländischen Sportlern regelmäßig vermeidbar sein, jedoch sieht das deutsche Steuerrecht speziell für Sportler eine Sonderregelung vor: so werden Inlandsbezug und damit beschränkte Steuerpflicht in Deutschland bereits dann angenommen, wenn ein ausländischer Sportler in Deutschland Einkünfte aus sportlicher Betätigung erzielt.

Auch bei den ausländischen Sportlern stellt sich auf Grund der deutschen Steuerpflicht die Frage der Doppelbesteuerung. Da Deutschland in diesem Fall Tätigkeitsland und nicht Wohnsitzland ist, sind keine unilateralen Maßnahmen vorgesehen. Allerdings muss auch hier in den meisten Fällen auf das vorhandene DBA zurückgegriffen werden, welches in aller Regel Einkünfte aus sportlicher Tätigkeit Deutschland als Tätigkeitsland zuordnet, so dass kein Verzicht notwendig ist. Die Verpflichtung zur Abmilderung der Doppelbesteuerung trifft in diesem Fall den Wohnsitzstaat.

Schwierigkeiten bereitet jedoch die Frage, auf welche Weise die Steuer von beschränkt steuerpflichtigen Sportlern, die sich regelmäßig nur für eine wenige Tage in Deutschland aufhalten und danach für die deutschen Finanzbehörden nicht mehr greifbar sind, erhoben werden soll (Schmidt/Sigloch/Henselmann, 2005). Anders als bei unbeschränkt Steuerpflichtigen, deren Steuerlast normalerweise im Rahmen eines Veranlagungsverfahrens nach Ablauf des Kalenderjahres ermittelt wird, erfolgt die Steuererhebung bei ausländischen Sportlern im Rahmen eines Abzugsverfahrens mit Abgeltungswirkung. Beim Abzugsverfahren behält derjenige, der eine Zahlung leistet, die Steuer ein und führt diese für den Steuerschuldner an den Fiskus ab (z.b. Lohnsteuer). Unbeschränkt Steuerpflichtige haben dabei regelmäßig die Möglichkeit, im Rahmen einer Veranlagung die tatsächliche Steuerlast ermitteln zu lassen und eine etwaige Erstattung zu viel abgezogener Steuer zu verlangen (Abzugsverfahren *ohne* Abgeltungswirkung). Beim Abzugsverfahren *mit* Abgeltungswirkung ist eine solche Korrektur nicht vorgesehen. Da deshalb Ausgaben des Steuerpflichtigen nicht beachtet werden können, kommt es zu einer Bruttobesteuerung, die teils erhebliche Nachteile für den Steuerpflichtigen haben kann. Für beschränkt steuerpflichtige Sportler sieht das deutsche Einkommensteuergesetz eine solche Abzugsbesteuerung in Höhe von 20 % der Bruttoeinnahmen vor. Für einen deutschen Sportveranstalter oder Sponsor bedeutet dies, dass Zahlungen an ausländische Sportler nur in Höhe von 80 % ausbezahlt werden dürfen. 20 % müssen direkt an den deutschen Fiskus abgeführt werden. Wird dies versäumt, kommt es zur Haftung für eventuell ausgefallene Steuern. Da diese Vorgehensweise die ausländischen Sportler in Abhängigkeit ihrer Ausgaben stark benachteiligen kann, ist unter bestimmten Umständen eine Erstattung der Steuer möglich. Auf Grund massiven Drucks der EU, die eine Besserstellung inländischer Steuerpflichtiger im Vergleich zu anderen EU-Bürgern verbietet (vgl. Schoen, 2006), ist das Erstattungsverfahren in den letzten Jahren vereinfacht worden, steht jedoch nach wie vor unter kritischer Beobachtung (Fuhrmann, 2003, jüngste Äußerung der Rechtsprechung vom FG Berlin-Brandenburg: Beschluss vom 29.08.2007, vgl. dazu die Anmerkungen von Kühnen, 2007).

11.5 Ertragsteuerliche Problemfelder des Sponsoring

Im Bereich des Sponsoring ergeben sich völlig unterschiedliche steuerliche Fragestellungen je nachdem, ob der Sponsor oder der Gesponserte betrachtet wird. Im Folgenden sollen deshalb die beiden Seiten eines Sponsorship getrennt voneinander betrachtet werden.

11.5.1 Besteuerung der Sponsoringeinnahmen beim Gesponserten
Wird eine natürliche Person gesponsert, stellt sich die Frage, ob und gegebenenfalls welche steuerpflichtigen Einkünfte erzielt werden. Bei Individualsportlern handelt es sich i.d.R. um Einkünfte aus Gewerbebetrieb. Mannschaftssportler erhalten einen Anteil an Sponsoringeinnahmen oftmals auch in Form von Arbeitslohn und realisieren damit Einkünfte aus nichtselbständiger Arbeit. Werden körperschaftsteuerpflichtige Sportunternehmen (z.B. Fußballkapitalgesellschaften) gesponsert, stellen die Zahlungen Betriebseinnahmen dar und unterliegen der regulären Besteuerung.

Besonderheiten bezüglich der Einordnung von Sponsoringleistungen ergeben sich deshalb insbesondere dann, wenn ein gemeinnütziger Verein Empfänger von Sponsoringleistungen ist. Hier ist entscheidend, welcher Sphäre die Sponsoringleistung zuzuordnen ist (vgl. auch Abschnitt 11.3.2.2). Sponsoringleistungen sind nur dann als Spende der steuerbefreiten ideellen Sphäre zuzuordnen, sofern der Gesponserte keine Werbetätigkeit für den Sponsor entfaltet oder diesem das Recht einräumt, mit seinem Namen und Logo zu werben. Mithin dürfte dies bei einem ernsthaft ausgestalteten Sponsoringengagement kaum mehr der Fall sein. Auch die Einordnung in die steuerbefreite Vermögensverwaltung stellt in Zusammenhang mit Sponsoring einen Ausnahmefall dar. Eine vermögensverwaltende Tätigkeit könnte höchstens dann angenommen werden, wenn beispielsweise alle Werbeflächen auf einem Sportgelände in einem einmaligen Akt langfristig an einen Vermarkter vermietet werden, der diese einzeln und für kürzere Perioden weitervermietet. Wird der Verein selbst aktiv und vermietet einzelne Flächen selbständig an verschiedene Personen oder erbringt er sogar noch weitere Zusatzleistungen, kommt Vermögensverwaltung nicht mehr in Frage. Im Regelfall dürften die Sponsoringeinnahmen dem wirtschaftlichen Geschäftsbetrieb zuzuordnen sein, der immer dann vorliegt, wenn der Gesponserte aktiv tätig ist und entsprechende Gegenleistungen erbringt. Diese Tätigkeiten dienen lediglich der Mittelbeschaffung und sind körperschaft- und gewerbesteuerpflichtig. Eine Zuordnung zum steuerfreien Zweckbetrieb ist bei Sponsoringeinnahmen generell nicht möglich.

Bei gemeinnützigen Organisationen ist in diesem Zusammenhang problematisch, dass Ausgaben, die dem Gesponserten im Rahmen des ideellen Bereichs entstehen, nicht zum Abzug gebracht werden dürfen, obwohl diese gleichzeitig auch in Zusammenhang mit den Sponsoringeinnahmen stehen. Dazu gehören beispielsweise die Ausgaben für die Wettkampfmannschaft oder die Sportstätte. Die Sponsoringeinnahmen unterliegen in diesem Fall nahezu ungeschmälert der Besteuerung. Um dies und die damit verbundene Schlechterstellung gegenüber nicht gemeinnützigen Sportorganisationen, die alle Ausgaben abziehen können, zu vermeiden, sieht das deutsche Gemeinnützigkeitsrecht eine Pauschalierung vor. Dabei werden 15 % des Umsatzes aus Sponsoring als Gewinn angenommen und der Besteuerung unterworfen, ohne dass der Steuerpflichtige Betriebsausgaben nachweisen muss. Alle tatsächlichen Aufwendungen sind damit abgegolten.

11.5.2 Steuerliche Abzugsfähigkeit der Sponsoringausgaben beim Sponsor
Steuerrechtlich stellt sich die grundsätzliche Frage, ob die Ausgaben für das Sponsoring in Hinblick auf die mit den Sponsoringmaßnahmen verfolgten unternehmerischen Ziele wie die klassischen Formen der Werbung und der Reklame als Betriebsausgaben angesehen werden können, und ob sie in Hinblick auf ihre Förderungswirkung beim Gesponserten als Spenden eingestuft werden müssen oder ob sie nicht abziehbare Kosten der Lebensführung darstellen. Dazu muss geklärt werden, ob die Sponsoringaufwendungen betrieblich oder privat veranlasst sind.

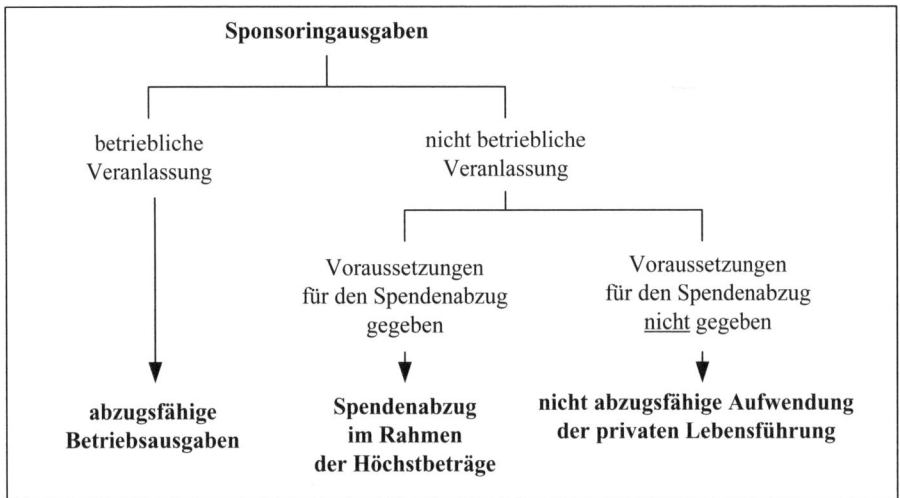

Abb. 6: Einordnung von Sponsoringausgaben

Die betriebliche Veranlassung und damit das Vorliegen von *Betriebsausgaben* setzt voraus, dass die Ausgaben
- objektiv mit dem Betrieb zusammenhängen und
- subjektiv die Einnahmenerzielung fördern sollen.

Ausreichend ist es, wenn die Ausgaben zur Verbesserung der betrieblichen Rahmenbedingungen beitragen. Üblichkeit oder Zweckmäßigkeit der Ausgaben spielen dagegen keine Rolle, sofern die Zahlungen nicht in der wirtschaftlichen oder gesellschaftlichen Stellung des Steuerpflichtigen begründet liegen und einen engen Bezug zur privaten Lebensführung aufweisen.

Ausgaben des Sponsors sind Betriebsausgaben, wenn sie zur Erzielung von Einnahmen getätigt werden, der Sponsor also wirtschaftliche Vorteile für sein Unternehmen generieren will. Als wirtschaftliche Vorteile gelten beispielsweise die Erhöhung des Ansehens des Unternehmens oder Werbeeffekte für einzelne Produkte, die Absatzchancen verbessern sollen. Indiz für das Vorliegen eines wirtschaftlichen Vorteils ist dabei, dass der Gesponserte eine Gegenleistung wie aktive

Werbung für den Sponsor oder die Gestattung der Verwendung von Logo und Namen erbringt. Sponsoringausgaben können jedoch auch dann Betriebsausgaben darstellen, wenn das Sponsoring ohne Gegenleistung des Gesponserten erfolgt, und wenn der Sponsor das Sponsorship entsprechend in die eigene Öffentlichkeitsarbeit einbindet. Beim Sponsoring im professionellen Sport dürften der Nachweis der betrieblichen Veranlassung und damit der Betriebsausgabenabzug kein Problem darstellen.

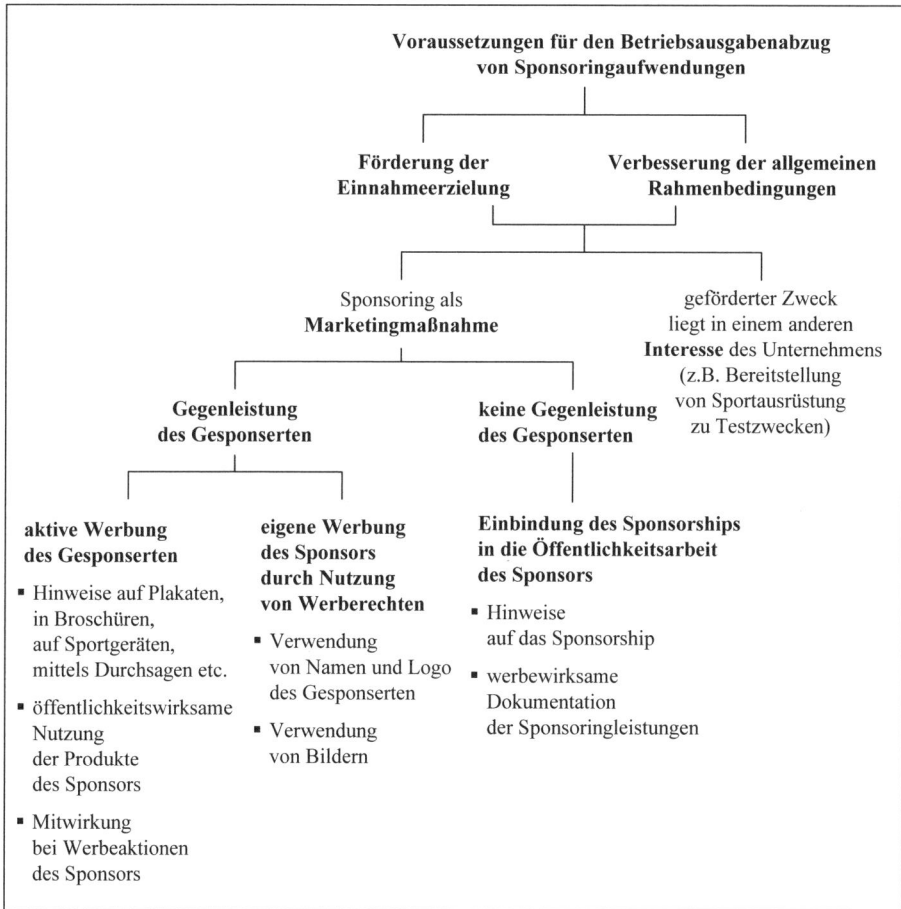

Abb. 7: Betriebsausgabenabzug von Sponsoringaufwendungen

Eine betriebliche Veranlassung ist dagegen immer dann zweifelhaft, wenn das Sponsorship ein persönliches Anliegen eines Unternehmers darstellt, beispielsweise wenn ein Sportverein gesponsert wird, in dem der Unternehmer selbst oder dessen Familie aktiv ist. Der Eindruck der privaten Veranlassung wird immer dann unterstützt, wenn Leistung und Gegenleistung in einem krassen Missverhältnis stehen.

313

Ist der Betriebsausgabenabzug auf Grund privater Veranlassung ausgeschlossen und wird die Leistung freiwillig und unentgeltlich für bestimmte förderungswürdige Zwecke geleistet, liegt eine Spende vor. Steuerbegünstigt sind die Spenden nur dann, wenn sie zur Förderung gemeinnütziger Zecke hingegeben werden. Die Spende ist im Vergleich zur Betriebsausgabe insofern nachteilig, als ein Abzug nur bis zur Höhe eines bestimmten Bruchteils (20 %) des zu versteuernden Einkommens des Spenders möglich ist. Ist dieser überschritten, ist die Spende i.d.R. steuerlich „verloren".

11.5.3 Steuerlicher „Problemfall" VIP-Logen

Bei Sportveranstaltungen werden in den Sportstätten nicht mehr nur einzelne Sitzplätze, sondern in zunehmendem Umfang auch so genannte „Logenpakete" angeboten. Diese werden weniger von Privatpersonen, sondern i.d.R. Unternehmen angemietet. Damit einhergehend ändert sich der Hintergrund für den Besuch der Sportveranstaltung. Während der Besuch einer Sportveranstaltung typischerweise von privatem Unterhaltungsinteresse geprägt ist, werden nunmehr auch geschäftliche Interessen verfolgt. Die unter Umständen vollkommen unterschiedliche Motivation zum Besuch von Sportveranstaltungen kann aus steuerlicher Sicht von entscheidender Bedeutung sein. Während Ausgaben, die in den Bereich der privaten Lebensführung gehören, steuerlich nicht berücksichtigungsfähig sind, kann das geschäftliche Interesse an der Anmietung einer Loge zu einer Abzugsfähigkeit der Kosten als Betriebsausgaben führen. Für Werbemaßnahmen in Sportstadien wird diese Abzugsfähigkeit i.d.R. bejaht (vgl. auch Abschnitt 11.5.2). Aus diesem Grund sind viele Unternehmen lange davon ausgegangen, dass dies für die gesamte VIP-Logen-Miete gilt. Die Logenkosten zeichnen sich jedoch dadurch aus, dass neben herkömmlichen Werbemaßnahmen auch die Bewirtung der Gäste und Eintrittskarten, die an Geschäftspartner und Mitarbeiter weitergegeben werden können, im Gesamtpreis enthalten sind. Für die Bewirtung von Geschäftspartnern und Geschenke greifen jedoch – trotz einer grundsätzlichen betrieblichen Veranlassung – steuerliche Abzugsbeschränkungen. Trotz erheblicher Proteste der Sportbranche wendet die Finanzverwaltung diese allgemeinen Abzugsbeschränkungen auf die VIP-Logen an, kommt der Branche jedoch mit großzügigen Pauschalierungsmöglichkeiten entgegen.

11.5.3.1 Abzugsbeschränkungen beim Logenmieter

Die Abzugsbeschränkungen erlangen nur dann Bedeutung, wenn die Mietzahlungen grundsätzlich betrieblich veranlasst sind. Privat veranlasste Anmietungen (z.B. für Geburtstagsfeiern oder Besuche mit Freunden und Familien) schließen die steuerliche Anerkennung ohnehin aus. Doch auch Betriebsausgaben sind nicht in jedem Fall abzugsfähig. So sind Geschenke an Geschäftspartner vom Abzug ausgeschlossen, wenn eine Freigrenze von 35 € pro Person und Jahr überschritten wird. Eine Einladung in eine VIP-Loge (Eintrittskarte und anteilige Miete), die mangels konkreter Gegenleistung nahezu in allen Fällen ein Geschenk darstellen wird, dürfte diesen Betrag regelmäßig übersteigen, so dass die Abzugsfähigkeit ausgeschlossen ist. Dies gilt nicht für die Einladung von Mitarbeitern.

Der auf die Bewirtung entfallende Anteil ist wie bei jedem Geschäftsessen nur in Höhe von 70 % abzugsfähig. Dies gilt auch für Mitarbeiter, sofern diese an einem Geschäftsessen teilnehmen und nicht nur Mitarbeiter bewirtet werden.

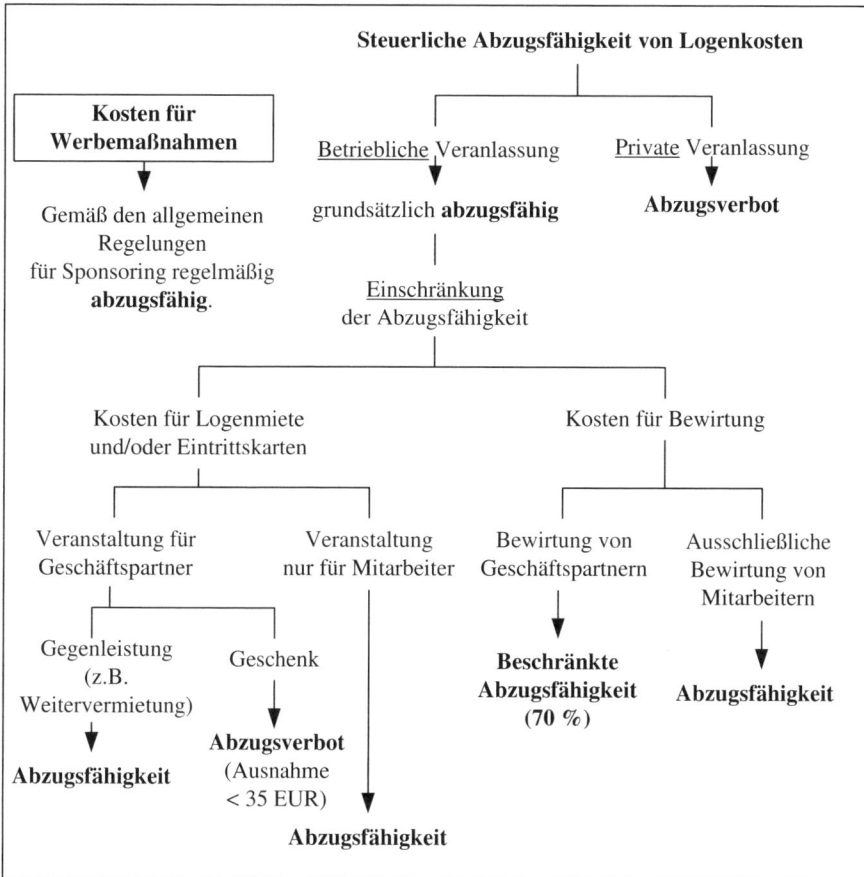

Abb. 8: Abzugsfähigkeit und Abzugsbeschränkungen von Logenkosten

Konsequenz dieser unterschiedlichen Behandlung ist nun, dass das Gesamtentgelt für die Anmietung einer Loge auf die Bereiche vorgenommen werden muss, wobei ein Ausweis in der Rechnung oder im Vertrag nur dann anerkannt wird, wenn die Aufteilung marktgerecht ist. Für den Steuerpflichtigen wäre eine möglichst starke Gewichtung der voll abzugsfähigen Werbemaßnahmen wünschenswert, was jedoch häufig nicht den tatsächlichen Verhältnissen entsprechen dürfte. Zur Vereinfachung akzeptiert die Finanzverwaltung grundsätzlich die nachfolgend abgebildete – für den Steuerpflichtigen wohl sehr günstige – pauschale Aufteilung der Kosten. Der Nachweis einer anderen Aufteilung ist jederzeit möglich.

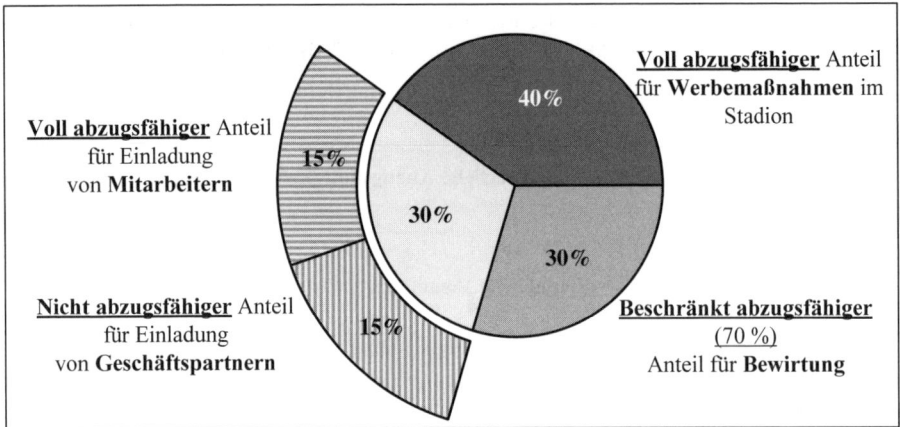

Abb. 9: Pauschale Aufteilung des Gesamtentgelts für ein Logen-Paket

11.5.3.2 Steuerliche Folgen für den Logengast

Auch für den Logengast kann die Einladung steuerliche Folgen nach sich ziehen. Bei Mitarbeitern ist zu unterscheiden, ob die Einladung im Interesse des Mitarbeiters (z.B. in Form eines Incentives) oder in betrieblichem Interesse erfolgt (z.B. Besprechungen, Betreuung von Geschäftspartnern). Dabei kann bei einer Einladung während einer Sportveranstaltung nur von betrieblichem Interesse ausgegangen werden, wenn dem Mitarbeiter eine ausreichende Anzahl von Geschäftspartnern gegenübersteht, die von ihm zu betreuen sind. Steuerliche Folgen in Form eines einkommensteuerpflichtigen Lohnbestandteils (Sachbezug) sind dabei immer dann anzunehmen, wenn die Einladung im Interesse des Mitarbeiters erfolgt.

Ungeachtet der unter Umständen fehlenden Abzugsfähigkeit beim Gastgeber kann der aus dem Besuch der Loge resultierende Vorteil bei Geschäftspartnern zu einer Betriebseinnahme – im Falle eines Unternehmers – oder zu einem Arbeitslohn von dritter Seite im Sinne eines geldwerten Vorteils – im Falle eines Arbeitnehmers eines anderen Unternehmens – führen.

Die Tatsache, dass auf die Gäste eines Logenmieters steuerliche Forderungen zukommen, ist für den Gastgeber unangenehm, da das Geschenk „Logeneinladung" am Ende doch mit Kosten in Form einer höheren Steuerlast für den Gast verbunden ist. Der Gesetzgeber hat darauf insofern reagiert, als der Gastgeber die Sachzuwendung in Form der Logeneinladung pauschal mit einem Steuersatz von 30 % mit befreiender Wirkung für den Gast besteuern kann. Auch dies kann als Begünstigung angesehen werden, bedeutet der Pauschalsteuersatz doch eine effektive Belastung mit nur ca. 23 %.

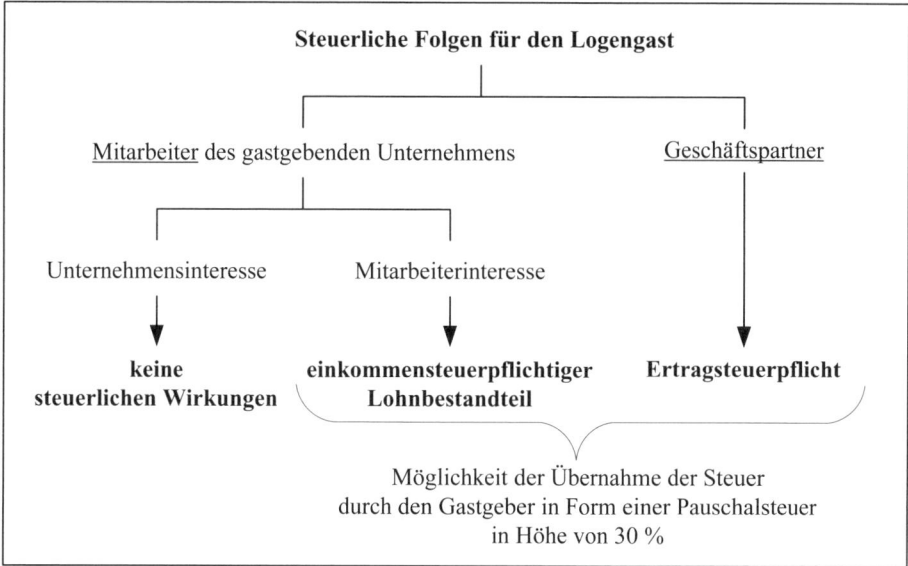

Abb. 10: Steuerliche Folgen für den Logengast

11.6 Fallstudie

Folgender Fall soll einige sportspezifische Aspekte der Ertragsbesteuerung beispielhaft verdeutlichen.

Fallstudie „Speedy e.V."

(1) Sachverhalt:

Der eingetragene und als gemeinnützig anerkannte Laufsportverein „Speedy e.V." Satzungszweck: Organisation und Durchführung von Training und Wettbewerben im Bereich des Laufsports) realisiert im Jahr 2008 folgende Einnahmen und Ausgaben:

- 1.000 x 20 € echte Mitgliederbeiträge.
- Zuwendung in Höhe von 10.000 € von einem Gönner, der gerne ungenannt bleiben möchte.
- Zahlung der Powerstar AG (Hersteller für Sportgetränke) für Werbung auf den Lauftrikots in Höhe von 20.000 €.
- Einnahme von 1.000 x 40 € Startgeld aus der Organisation eines großen Volkslaufes, an dem keine bezahlten Sportler teilnehmen.
- Organisation eines hochkarätig besetzten Laufwettkampfs über 10.000 m, bei

---

317

dem unter anderem dem mexikanische Läufer S. Gonzales eine Antrittsprämie von 5.000 € bezahlt wurde. Außerdem fielen Kosten in Höhe von 15.000 € an, wovon 1.000 € auf die Herstellung und Installation geeigneter Werbebanden entfallen. Die Powerstar AG bezahlte für Banden an der Laufstrecke nochmals 5.000 €.

- Langfristige Verpachtung der Gaststätte auf dem vereinseigenen Sportplatz für monatlich 1.500 €.

- Überschüsse aus dem Verkauf von Speisen und Getränken bei diversen Sportveranstaltungen in Höhe von 5.000 € (Umsatz 20.000 €).

- Für Training, Wettbewerbe und Unterhalt des Sportplatzes sind Ausgaben in Höhe von 40.000 € angefallen. Davon entfallen 2.500 € auf die Entlohnung eines selbständig und nebenberuflich tätigen Übungsleiters und 400 € auf die Entschädigung einer ehrenamtlichen Bürohilfe.

(2) Steuerliche Auswirkungen:

Ideelle Sphäre:

Die Mitgliederbeiträge in Höhe von 20.000 € und die unentgeltliche Zuwendung des anonymen Gönners (10.000 €) sind dem steuerfreien ideellen Bereich zuzuordnen, da die Mittel für den ideellen Zweck gewährt wurden und ihnen keine Gegenleistung gegenübersteht. Insbesondere erhält der Sponsor keine entsprechenden Werbeleistungen. Den Einnahmen stehen alle Ausgaben gegenüber, die auf Grund des Satzungszwecks angefallen sind. Mithin die allgemeinen Ausgaben in Höhe von 40.000 € und die Kosten für die Laufwettbewerbe in Höhe von 14.000 € (Die 1.000 € für die Bande und die Bezahlung des Sportlers in Höhe von 5000 € sind dem wirtschaftlichen Geschäftsbetrieb zuzurechnen). Im Ergebnis ergibt sich damit in der ideellen Sphäre ein Verlust in Höhe von 30.000 €, der den Gemeinnützigkeitsstatus nicht gefährdet, das steuerpflichtige Einkommen aber auch nicht mindert.

(- 24.000 €)

Vermögensverwaltung:

Die Pachteinnahmen sind der Vermögensverwaltung zuzuordnen, da der Verein lediglich vorhandenes Vermögen durch die langfristige Verpachtung nutzt. Die Einnahmen bleiben daher steuerfrei. *(+ 18.000 €)*

Wirtschaftlicher Geschäftsbetrieb:

Dieser Sphäre sind alle Tätigkeiten zuzuordnen, die der Verein selbständig, nachhaltig und mit der Absicht, Einnahmen zu erzielen, verfolgt und die weder Vermögensverwaltung noch Zweckbetrieb darstellen. Dazu gehören zweifelsfrei alle Zahlungen des Sponsors (25.000 €) und die Überschüsse aus dem Verkauf von Speisen und Getränken (5.000 €). Grundsätzlich stellt auch die Organisation von Sportveranstaltungen ein wirtschaftlicher Geschäftsbetrieb dar. Da jedoch der Wettkampf über 10.000 m nicht zu Einnahmen führt und der Volkslauf einen Zweckbetrieb (s. u.) darstellt, sind diese (abgesehen von der Bezahlung des Mexikaners) hier nicht weiter zu beachten. Im wirtschaftlichen Geschäftsbetrieb tritt im Übrigen nur Steuerpflicht ein, wenn die Umsätze (!) die Freigrenze von 35.000 € überschreiten. Dies ist hier der Fall (25.000 € aus Sponsoring, 20.000 € aus Verkauf von Speisen und Getränken = 45.000 €). Damit ist der entstehende Gewinn der Körperschaft- und Gewerbsteuer zu unterwerfen. Besonders gravierend wirkt sich dies auf die Sponsoringumsätze aus, da von diesen keine Ausgaben für die Durchführung des Trainings oder des Wettbewerbs abgezogen werden können. Die Ausgaben wären ohne den wirtschaftlichen Geschäftsbetrieb Sponsoring in gleicher Höhe angefallen und sind deshalb der ideellen Sphäre zuzurechnen. Als Ausgleich sind dafür jedoch nur 15 % der Einnahmen zu besteuern, was mittels eines pauschalen Abzug von 85 % erreicht wird: Die direkt zurechenbaren Ausgaben bleiben dann jedoch außer Betracht:

Einnahmen aus Bewirtung	*20.000 €*
abzgl. Ausgaben 15.000 €	*- 15.000 €*
Sponsoringeinnahmen	*+ 25.000 €*
abzgl. Kostenpauschale (85 % von 25.000 €)	*- 21.250 €*
zu versteuerndes Einkommen	***8.750 €***
abzgl. Freibetrag	*- 3.835 €*
	4.915 €
Gewerbesteuer (Hebesatz 400 %)	
(4.915 x 3,5 % x 400 %)	*688 €*
Körperschaftsteuer (15 %)	*737 €*

Zweckbetrieb:

Als Zweckbetrieb kommen nur die Sportveranstaltungen in Betracht. Der Verein wird die Möglichkeit nutzen, dass alle Veranstaltungen, an denen nur unbezahlte Sportler teilnehmen, als Zweckbetrieb klassifiziert werden, da die Einnahmen in Höhe von 40.000 € (1.000 x 40 €) die Umsatzgrenze überschreiten und es sich ohne die Wahlalternative um einen wirtschaftlichen Geschäftsbetrieb handelt. Da an dem großen Volkslauf keine bezahlten Sportler teilnehmen handelt es sich um einen steuerfreien Zweckbetrieb: *(40.000 €)*

Anmerkungen:

- Die Gesamttätigkeit des Vereins gefährdet den Status der Gemeinnützigkeit nicht.
- Wird dem anonymen Gönner eine ordnungsgemäße Spendenquittung ausgestellt, kann dieser die Spende in Höhe von bis zu 20 % seines zu versteuernden Einkommens zum Abzug bringen und so seine individuelle Steuerlast mindern.
- Für die Powerstar AG stellen die Sponsoringausgaben Betriebsausgaben dar

und mindern deshalb deren körperschaft- und gewerbesteuerpflichtiges Einkommen.

- Da S. Gonzales keinen Wohnsitz und keinen ständigen Aufenthalt in Deutschland hat, ist er nur beschränkt steuerpflichtig. Die Antrittsprämie wird aus sportlicher Betätigung in Deutschland erzielt, so dass sie grundsätzlich der deutschen Besteuerung unterliegt. Auch das DBA zwischen Deutschland und Mexiko steht dem nicht entgegen, da es das Besteuerungsrecht für die Antrittsprämie ebenfalls Deutschland zuweist. Der Verein hatte 20 % des Antrittsgeldes einzubehalten und an das Finanzamt abzuführen. An S. Gonzales durften nur 4.000 € ausbezahlt werden. Wurde dies versäumt, haftet der Verein für die Steuer in Höhe von 1.000 €. Falls dem mexikanischen Läufer Betriebsausgaben entstanden sind und seine effektive Steuerlast deshalb die eines Inländers übersteigt, kann er eine Erstattung beantragen.

- Der Übungsleiter muss wegen des Freibetrags in Höhe von 2.100 € nur 400 € der Besteuerung unterwerfen. Die Entschädigung der Bürokraft bleibt vollständig steuerfrei, da der Freibetrag von 500 € nicht überschritten ist.

11.7 Fazit und Ausblick

Die immer rascher voranschreitende Professionalisierung des Sportsektors, die verstärkte Teilnahme von Sportlern und Sportorganisationen am allgemeinen Wirtschaftsverkehr und nicht zuletzt das gestiegene finanzielle Volumen dieser Branche haben dazu geführt, dass sich auch die ehemals private Freizeitbeschäftigung des Sporttreibens in vielen Bereichen mit steuerlichen Fragestellungen auseinandersetzen muss. Einen zentralen Punkt stellt dabei die Ertragsbesteuerung von Sportlern und Sportorganisationen dar, die einen hohen Komplexitätsgrad aufweist. Fehlplanungen in diesem Bereich können dabei schnell zu einer empfindlichen Steigerung der Steuerlast der Beteiligten führen. Andererseits kann durch umsichtige Steuerplanung eine günstigere Besteuerung erreicht werden. Führungskräfte im Bereich des Sports müssen deshalb über ein Mindestmaß an steuerlichem Verständnis verfügen, um Problemfelder erkennen zu können, damit gegebenenfalls entsprechender Rat eingeholt werden kann. Aber auch jede andere betriebswirtschaftliche Tätigkeit im Sport erfordert steuerliche Grundkenntnisse, da im Dialog zwischen Sportorganisation, Sportveranstalter, Sportler und Sponsoren die Problematik der steuerlichen Auswirkungen immer öfter zur Sprache kommen wird und in vielen Fällen auch entscheidungserheblich sein wird.

Kontrollfragen

1. Welche Besteuerungssysteme kommen bei der Ertragsbesteuerung von Personen- und Kapitalgesellschaften zur Anwendung?
2. Welche Ertragsteuerarten gibt es in Deutschland und wie sind diese ausgestaltet?
3. Welche Voraussetzungen muss ein Sportverein erfüllen, um den Gemeinnützigkeitsstatus zu erlangen?
4. Welche ertragsteuerlichen Folgen hat die Anerkennung als gemeinnütziger Sportverein?
5. Unter welchen Umständen stellt eine Sportveranstaltung einen steuerfreien Zweckbetrieb dar?
6. Wie sind Spenden und Sponsoringleistungen beim gemeinnützigen Verein zu behandeln?
7. Welche Einkunftsarten sind bei einem Profisportler denkbar?
8. Welche ertragsteuerlichen Folgen ergeben sich aus einem bezahlten Antritt eines ausländischen Sportlers bei einem inländischen Wettkampf für Sportler und Veranstalter?
9. Welche Voraussetzungen müssen erfüllt sein, damit Sponsoringausgaben die ertragsteuerliche Bemessungsgrundlage mindern?
10. Welche ertragsteuerlichen Probleme ergeben sich aus der Anmietung einer VIP-Loge?

Literaturverzeichnis

Blumenberg, Jens / Benz, Sebastian (2007): Die Unternehmensteuerreform 2008. Erläuterungen und Gestaltungshinweise, Köln.

Brönner, Herbert (2007): Die Besteuerung der Gesellschaften, 19. Aufl., Stuttgart.

Fuhrmann, Claas (2003): Einkommensbesteuerung ausländischer Künstler und Sportler, in: Kölner Steuer-Dialog, Heft 9, S. 13880-13888.

Hüttemann, Rainer (2007): Gesetz zur weiteren Stärkung des bürgschaftlichen Engagements und seine Auswirkungen auf des Gemeinnützigkeits- und Spendenrecht, in: Der Betrieb, Heft 38, S. 2053-2059.

Jäck, Simone (2006): Gemeinnützige Organisationen im Ertragsteuerrecht. Kritische Bestandsaufnahme der geltenden Regelungen für Mittelerwerb und Mittelverwendung in Deutschland, Schweiz und USA und Reformüberlegungen, Aachen.

Klimmer, Christian (2004): Besteuerung international tätiger Sportler in der Bundesrepublik Deutschland. Unbeschränkte und beschränkte Steuerpflicht, Zwischenschaltung von Gesellschaften, Berlin.

Schauhoff, Stephan (2005): Handbuch der Gemeinnützigkeit. Verein, Stiftung, GmbH, Recht, Steuern, Personal, 2. Aufl., München.

Schauhoff, Stephan / Kirchhain, Christian (2007): Das Gesetz zur weiteren Stärkung des bürgerschaftlichen Engagements, in: Deutsches Steuerrecht, Heft 45, S. 1985-1992.

Schmidt, Lutz / Sigloch, Jochen / Henselmann, Klaus (2005): Internationale Steuerlehre. Steuerplanung bei grenzüberschreitenden Transaktionen, Wiesbaden.

Schneider, Dieter (1997): Betriebswirtschaftslehre. Band 3: Theorie der Unternehmung, München, S. 590-698.

Schneider, Dieter (1994): Grundzüge der Unternehmensbesteuerung, 6. Aufl., Wiesbaden.

Schoen, Oliver (2006): Steuerabzug nach § 50a EStG von den Bruttoeinnahmen EU-rechtswidrig!, in: Neue Wirtschaftsbriefe, S. 3723-3732.

Tipke, Klaus / Lang, Joachim (2005): Steuerrecht, 18. Aufl., Köln.

Troll, Max / Wallenhorst, Rolf / Halaczinsky, Raymond (2004): Die Besteuerung gemeinnütziger Vereine, Stiftungen und der juristischen Personen des öffentlichen Rechts, 5. Aufl., München.

Weiterführende Ressourcen

Literatur

Becker, Joachim (2002): Betriebsausgabenabzug von Sponsoringaufwendungen?, in: Deutsche Steuer-Zeitung, Heft 19, S. 663-668.

Binz, Hans-Bert (2007): Unternehmenssteuerreform 2008: Rechtsformspezifische Steuerwirkungen im Überblick, in: Deutsches Steuerrecht, Heft 38, S. 1692-1695.

Birk, Dieter (2006): Steuerrecht, 9. Aufl., Heidelberg.

Dehesselles, Thomas (2002): Vereinsführung: Rechtliche und steuerliche Grundlagen, in: Galli, Albert / Gömmel, Rainer / Holzhäuser, Wolfgang / Straub, Wilfried (Hrsg.): Sportmanagement. Grundlagen der unternehmerischen Führung im Sport aus Betriebswirtschaftslehre, Steuern und Recht für den Sportmanager, München, S. 5-43.

Dehesselles, Thomas / Siebold, Michael (2002): Sponsoring: Rechtliche und steuerliche Grundlagen, in: Galli, Albert / Gömmel, Rainer / Holzhäuser, Wolfgang / Straub, Wilfried (Hrsg.): Sportmanagement. Grundlagen der unternehmerischen Führung im Sport aus Betriebswirtschaftslehre, Steuern und Recht für den Sportmanager, München, S. 355-372.

Egner, Thomas / Jäck, Simone (2006): Steuerminderung durch VIP-Logen – Wunsch oder Wirklichkeit?, in: Sport und Recht, Heft 3, S. 90-96.

Graf, Helmut / Bisle, Michael (2006): Besteuerung beschränkt steuerpflichtiger Sportler, in: Internationales Steuerrecht, Heft 2, S.44-49.

Henselmann, Klaus / Schmidt, Lutz (1999): Besteuerung ausländischer Berufssportler, in: Steuer und Studium, Heft 10, S. 449-459.

Homburg, Stefan (2007): Allgemeine Steuerlehre, 5. Aufl., München.

Kasper, Andreas (2005): Sponsoring im Steuerrecht, in: Deutsche Steuer-Zeitung, Heft 12, S. 397-403.

Kühnen, Sabine (2007): Anmerkung zum Beschluss des FG Berlin-Brandenburg v. 29.08.2007, in: Entscheidungen der Finanzgerichte, Heft 23, S. 1882-1884.

Kußmaul, Heinz (2005): Betriebswirtschaftliche Steuerlehre, 4. Aufl., München.

Melchior, Jürgen (2007): Unternehmenssteuerreform 2008 und Abgeltungsteuer, in: Deutsches Steuerrecht, Heft 29, S. 1230-1237.

Merker, Christian (2007): Unternehmenssteuerreformgesetz 2008. Teil I und II, in: Steuer und Studium, Heft 9, S. 431-437 und S. 500-505.

Ortmann-Babl, Martina / Zipfel, Lars (2007): Unternehmenssteuerreform 2008. Teil I: Gewerbesteuerliche Änderungen und Besteuerung von Kapitalgesellschaften und deren Anteilseigner und Teil II: Besteuerung von Personengesellschaften insbesondere nach der Einführung der Thesaurierungsbegünstigung, in: BetriebsBerater, Heft 35 und 41, S. 1869-1882 und S. 2205-2217.

Paus, Bernhard (1993): Kultur- und Sportsponsoring aus steuerlicher Sicht, in: Information über Steuer und Wirtschaft, Heft 14, S. 320-322.

Rose, Gerd (2004): Betrieb und Steuer. Grundlagen zur Betriebswirtschaftlichen Steuerlehre. Erstes Buch: Die Ertragsteuern, 18. Aufl., Wiesbaden.

Scheffler, Wolfram (2004): Besteuerung von Unternehmen. I und II Kombipaket, 3. Aufl., Heidelberg.

Schmidt, Ludwig (2007): Kommentar zum Einkommensteuergesetz (EStG), 26. Aufl., München.

Seifert, Michael (2005): VIP-Logenaufwendungen: Anmerkungen und Praxishinweise zum BMF-Schreiben vom 22.08.2005, in: Steuern und Bilanzen, Heft 24, S. 1037-1040.

Thiel, Jochen (1998): Sponsoring im Steuerrecht, in: Der Betrieb, Heft 17, S. 842-848.

Watermeyer, Heinrich (2007): Die Unternehmenssteuerreform 2008. Überblick über die wesentlichen Änderungen, in: Der GmbH-Steuer-Berater, Heft 7, S. 207-212.

Watrin, Christoph / Wittkowski, Ansas / Strohm, Christiane (2007): Auswirkungen der Unternehmenssteuerreform 2008 auf die Besteuerung von Kapital-gesellschaften, in: GmbHRundschau, Heft 15, S. 785-793.

Zenthöfer, Wolfgang / Schulze zur Wiesche, Dieter (2007): Einkommensteuer, 9. Aufl., Stuttgart.

Verlautbarungen der Finanzverwaltung (BMF-Schreiben)

23.01.1996: Steuerabzug bei künstlerischen, sportlichen, artistischen oder ähnlichen Darbietungen gemäß § 50a Abs. 4 EStG, BStBl. I 1996, S. 89.

18.02.1998: Ertragsteuerliche Behandlung des Sponsoring, BStBl. I 1998, S. 212.

03.11.2003: Vereinfachtes Steuererstattungsverfahren gemäß § 50 Abs. 5 Satz 2 Nr. 3 EStG bei beschränkt Steuerpflichtigen mit Einkünften, die dem Steuerabzug nach § 50a Abs. 4 EStG unterliegen, Umsetzung des EuGH-Urteils vom 12.06.2003 – C-234/01 (Gerritse), BStBl. I 2003, S. 553.

22.08.2005: Ertragsteuerliche Behandlung von Aufwendungen für VIP-Logen in Sportstätten, BStBl. I 2005, S. 845.

30.03.2006: Ertragsteuerliche Behandlung von Aufwendungen für VIP-Logen in Sportstätten; Hospitality-Leistungen im Rahmen der Fußballweltmeisterschaft, BStBl. I 2006, S. 307.

05.04.2007: Steuerabzug bei beschränkt Steuerpflichtigen aus EU/EWR-Staaten mit Einkünften im Sinne des § 50a Abs. 4 EStG, BStBl. I 2007, S. 449.

Links

Aktuelle Dokumente zum Steuerrecht:
 http://www.taxlinks.de
Allgemeine Informationen zu Steuerrecht und Steuerberatung:
 http://www.steuermonitor.de
Bundesministerium der Finanzen:
 http://www.bundesfinanzministerium.de
Datenbank zu den Steuern in den europäischen Ländern:
 http://ec.europa.eu/taxation_customs/taxation/gen_info/info_docs/tax_ inventory/index_de.htm

Kapitel 12: Marketing im Sport

André Bühler   Gerd Nufer

Lernziele

Nach der Durchsicht dieses Kapitels sollte der Leser in der Lage sein,

- die Aufgaben des Marketing zu erläutern.
- die verschiedenen Stufen einer Marketingkonzeption zu erklären.
- die wichtigsten Marketinginstrumente zu kennen.
- den Begriff Sportmarketing zu definieren.
- Sportmarketing vom allgemeinen Marketing zu unterscheiden.
- die zwei wichtigsten Formen des Sportmarketing zu erläutern.
- die Bedeutung des Sports für werbetreibende Unternehmen einzuschätzen.
- die Bedeutung des Marketing für Sportorganisation zu beurteilen.

Überblick über das Kapitel

In diesem Kapitel werden die Grundlagen des Marketing erläutert und auf den Bereich des Sports übertragen. Nach einer kurzen Einführung in die Thematik werden in einem allgemeinen Teil die Grundlagen des Marketing beschrieben. Anschließend wird näher auf den Bereich des Sportmarketing eingegangen und aufgezeigt, inwiefern sich Sportmarketing vom allgemeinen Marketing unterscheidet. In den folgenden Abschnitten wird an realen Beispielen ausführlich erläutert, wie Sportorganisationen ihre Sportart und sich selbst vermarkten können. Abschließend wird vorgestellt, wie Unternehmen Marketing mit Hilfe des Sport betreiben können. Abgerundet wird dieses Kapitel mit einer Fallstudie, die sich mit Marketing beim Fußball-Zweitligisten FC St. Pauli beschäftigt.

12.1 Einführung in die Thematik

Das Sportmarketing boomt. Werbetreibende Unternehmen haben im Jahr 2007 geschätzte 2,5 Mrd. € für Sportsponsoring ausgegeben (Pilot Group, 2007). Im Jahr zuvor nahmen die 18 Vereine der Fußballbundesliga über 100 Mio. € aus dem Merchandisinggeschäft ein (PR Marketing, 2006). Jedes Wochenende konkurrieren Tausende von großen und kleinen Sportclubs um die Gunst der Zuschauer. All diese Beispiele werden gemeinhin unter Sportmarketing subsumiert, ohne weiter zu differenzieren. Sportmarketing hat viele verschiedene Facetten, aber nur die Wenigsten wissen wirklich mit diesem Begriff etwas anzufangen. Was ist Sportmarketing und was ist es nicht? Warum wächst die Bedeutung von Marketing im Sport und welche Rolle wird das Marketing mit Sport in der Zukunft spielen? Die Antworten soll dieses Kapitel liefern. Um Sportmarketing verstehen zu können, muss zunächst abgegrenzt werden, was Marketing allgemein überhaupt ist.

12.2 Grundlagen des Marketing

In diesem Abschnitt werden die grundlegenden Marketingbegriffe definiert und erläutert. Darüber hinaus werden die einzelnen Stufen des Marketingmanagement-Prozess im Detail beschrieben.

12.2.1 Begriffsabgrenzung zum Marketing

Der Begriff des Marketing findet seinen Ursprung in den USA. Von dort stammen auch die gängigsten Definitionen, wie etwa die folgende von Kotler (1994, S. 5):

> „Marketing is a social and managerial process by which individuals and groups obtain what they need and want through creating and exchanging products and value with others."

Marketing wird also als Prozess verstanden, der den Austausch von Produkten und Werten zwischen Anbietern und Nachfragern zum Ziel hat. Die American Marketing Association geht in ihrer Definition (zitiert in Kotler, 1997, S. 15) nicht nur auf eben jenen Austauschprozess sondern auch auf die unterschiedlichen Produkte und Marketinginstrumente ein:

> „Marketing (Management) is the process of planning and executing the conception, pricing, promotion, and distribution of ideas, goods, and services to create exchanges that satisfy individual and organizational goals."

Abb. 1 stellt die obige Definition grafisch dar.

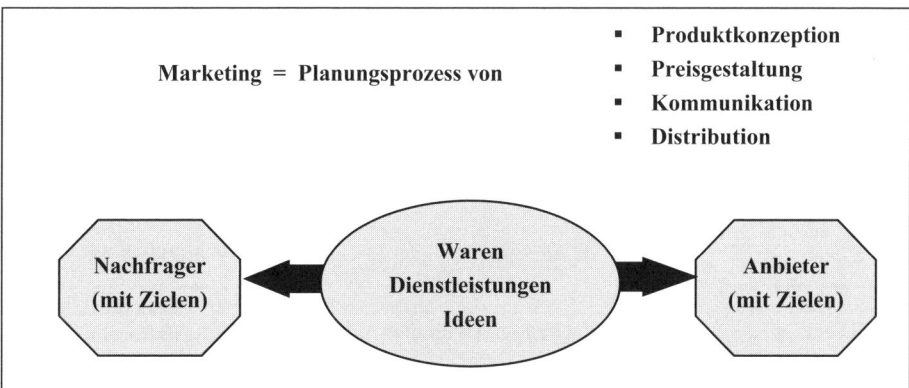

Abb. 1: Grafische Darstellung des Marketingbegriffs
In Anlehnung an: Ramme (2004), S. 2

327

In Deutschland wurde der Begriff Marketing lange gemieden und stattdessen von *Absatzwirtschaft* (und Handelsfunktionen) gesprochen. Erst im Laufe der siebziger Jahre setzte sich Marketing als Begriff auch in den deutschsprachigen Ländern durch. Ramme (2004) sieht den Grund hierfür v.a. in der Wandlung der Märkte. Dominierten in Deutschland bis in die fünfziger Jahre noch Verkäufermärkte (in denen die Nachfrage das Angebot übersteigt und die Bedingungen somit vom Verkäufer diktiert werden), so entwickelten sich die Absatzmärkte immer mehr zu Käufermärkten (in denen das Angebot die Nachfrage übersteigt und somit den Käufer in eine bessere Verhandlungsposition bringt). Dadurch ergab sich die Notwendigkeit der *marktorientierten Unternehmensführung*. Diese kennzeichnet die Ausrichtung aller Unternehmensaktivitäten auf den Markt respektive den Kunden.

Bruhn (2004, S. 14) verdeutlicht die zentrale Philosophie des Marketing durch folgende Definition:

> „Marketing ist eine unternehmerische Denkhaltung. Sie konkretisiert sich in der Analyse, Planung, Umsetzung und Kontrolle sämtlicher interner und externer Unternehmensaktivitäten, die durch eine Ausrichtung der Unternehmensleistungen am Kundennutzen im Sinne einer konsequenten Kundenorientierung darauf abzielen, absatzmarktorientierte Unternehmensziele zu erreichen."

12.2.2 Marketing-Managementprozess

Unter einer Marketingkonzeption versteht man im Allgemeinen einen ganzheitlichen Fahrplan, der aus drei Konzeptionsebenen besteht, die wiederum auf verschiedenen konzeptionellen Grundfragen basieren (vgl. Abb. 2). Die Marketingkonzeption kann aber auch als eine sequentielle Abfolge von verschiedenen Phasen verstanden werden.

Abb. 2: Ebenen der Marketingkonzeption
In Anlehnung an: Becker (2001), S.4

Abb. 3 illustriert den Prozess der Marketingkonzeption, deren einzelne Phasen auf den folgenden Seiten im Detail erläutert werden.

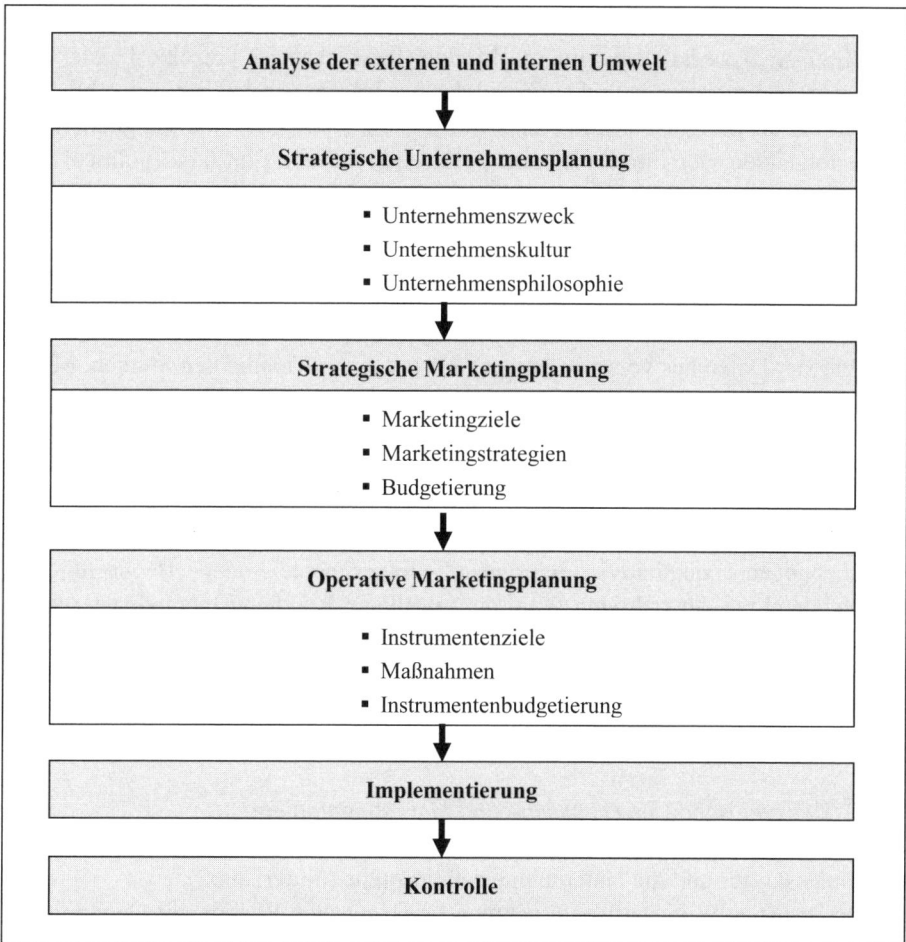

Abb. 3: Darstellung der Marketingkonzeption als Prozess
In Anlehnung an: Meffert/Bruhn (1997), S. 116

12.2.2.1 Analyse der externen und internen Umwelt

Jede Marketingkonzeption sollte auf einer detaillierten Analyse der externen und internen Umwelt aufbauen. Eine der bekanntesten und beliebtesten Analyseinstrumente in der Wirtschaft ist die *SWOT-Analyse*, die die internen Stärken (strengths) und Schwächen (weaknesses) eines Unternehmens sowie die Chancen (opportunities) und Risiken (threats) des gesamten Marktes untersuchen soll. Hilfreich ist es häufig, diese Analyse mit einer Benchmarkanalyse zu verknüpfen, um so die Stärken und Schwächen des eigenen Unternehmens in Bezug zum besten Mitbewerber zu erkennen.

Ein weiteres Instrument zur Analyse der externen Umwelt ist die *PEST-Analyse*, die v.a. für international agierende Unternehmen von Bedeutung ist. Ziel der PEST-Analyse ist es, bestimmte Märkte (beispielsweise einzelne Länder oder Regionen) zu untersuchen und aufgrund der Analyse zu vergleichen, um schließlich den am besten geeigneten Markt zu identifizieren. Die PEST-Analyse gliedert sich in die folgenden vier Einzelanalysen: politisch-rechtliche Einflüsse (political-legal factors), ökonomische Einflüsse (economic factors), sozio-kulturelle Einflüsse (sociocultural factors) und technologische Einflüsse (technological factors).

Grundsätzlich ist im Rahmen der *Marktforschung* zwischen Sekundär- und Primärdaten zu unterscheiden. Sekundärforschung (desk research) bedient sich bereits vorhandener Daten aus verschiedenen Quellen wie veröffentlichten Studien, Marktforschungsberichten oder Statistiken sowie eigenen Daten aus bestehenden unternehmensinternen Datenbanken. Sollten Sekundärdaten nicht zur Verfügung stehen (weil es keine Daten gibt oder man keinen Zugang zu bestehenden Daten hat), müssen Primärdaten erhoben werden. Unternehmen stehen dabei eine Vielzahl an Datenerhebungsmethoden zur Verfügung, die gängigsten sind quantitative Fragebogenerhebungen, qualitative Interviews, Experimente oder Beobachtungen. Entscheidend bei der richtigen Wahl der jeweiligen Erhebungsmethode ist zum einen die Eignung (werden dadurch die benötigten Daten auch wirklich generiert?) und zum anderen der finanzielle und zeitliche Rahmen (können wir uns die Datenerhebung finanziell und zeitlich leisten?).

12.2.2.2 Strategische Unternehmens- und Marketingplanung

Die *strategische Unternehmensplanung* definiert den Unternehmenszweck, die Unternehmenskultur und die Unternehmensphilosophie (Nufer, 2007).

Die meisten Wirtschaftsunternehmen verfolgen das Prinzip der Gewinnmaximierung. Im Laufe der Jahre haben sich des Weiteren andere *Unternehmenszwecke* entwickelt, zum Beispiel ökologische, soziale und gesellschaftspolitische Zwecke, die aber letztlich nur verfolgt werden, wenn sie sich für das Unternehmen auch in finanzieller Hinsicht bezahlt machen.

Die *Unternehmenskultur* basiert auf gewachsenen Werten, Normen, Symbolen und Ritualen und wird in vielen Fällen von der Unternehmensleitung geprägt und vorgelebt. Eine starke, einheitliche Unternehmenskultur sorgt für inneren Zusammenhalt und Motivation für die Unternehmensmitglieder.

Die *Unternehmensphilosophie* ergibt sich aus dem Unternehmenszweck und der Unternehmenskultur und spiegelt grundlegende Überzeugungen, Verhaltensrichtlinien und Leitprinzipien wider. Die Unternehmensphilosophie hat somit einen direkten Einfluss auf das Verhalten der Unternehmensmitglieder und daher nicht zuletzt auch einen erheblichen Einfluss auf das gesamte Marketing. Die Unternehmensphilosophie gibt den Rahmen vor, in dem marketingpolitische Entscheidungen getätigt werden.

Die strategische Unternehmensplanung basiert auf präzisen und realistischen Unternehmenszielen, die in langfristigen Unternehmensplänen resultieren. Die übergeordneten Unternehmensziele werden auf die einzelnen Unternehmensbereiche heruntergebrochen, die zur allgemeinen Unternehmenszielerreichung beitragen sollen.

Die *strategische Marketingplanung* orientiert sich an den übergeordneten Unternehmenszielen und den sich daraus ableitenden Vorgaben. Allerdings kann bei einer markt- und kundenorientierten Unternehmensführung nicht immer eindeutig zwischen strategischen Unternehmenszielen und strategischen Marketingzielen unterschieden werden, da die Grenzen fließend sind. Ziel der strategischen Marketingplanung ist es, strategische Marketingziele zu definieren, daraus Marketingstrategien zu entwickeln und eine strategische Budgetierung festzulegen.

Bei den *strategischen Marketingzielen* kann man zwischen quantitativen/ökonomischen Zielen (z.B. Marktanteil in den nächsten fünf Jahren auf 30 % steigern) und qualitativen/außerökonomischen Zielen (z.B. das Image von „altmodisch" in „modern" umwandeln) unterscheiden. Hermanns/Riedmüller (2001) unterscheiden außerdem zwischen *Marktzielen* (z.B. Erweiterung der Absatzmärkte), *Ertragszielen* (z.B. Steigerung des Gewinns) und *Leistungszielen* (z.B. Steigerung der Mitgliederzufriedenheit). Wichtig ist in diesem Zusammenhang die ständige Überprüfung der strategischen Marketingziele auf ihre Gültigkeit und Bedeutung und gegebenenfalls die Anpassung der Marketingziele an veränderte Marktbedingungen und aktuelle Trends.

Es gibt eine Vielzahl von unterschiedlichen *Marketingstrategien*. Die in der Praxis am häufigsten verfolgten sollen kurz vorgestellt werden (Becker, 2001; Ramme, 2004):

- *Marktfeldstrategien*: Als Kriterium gilt die Neuartigkeit von Produkt und Markt, was zu vier unterschiedlichen Strategien führt. Bei der *Marktdurchdringungsstrategie* wird das bisherige Produkt auf dem angestammten Markt verkauft. Die *Marktentwicklungsstrategie* zielt auf die Erschließung von neuen Märkten unter Beibehaltung des bisherigen Produktes ab. Bei der *Produktentwicklungs-/Innovationsstrategie* werden ständig Verbesserungen des Produktes realisiert oder sogar neue Produkte entwickelt, um den Abnehmern auf angestammten Märkten etwas Neues zu bieten. Mit der *Diversifikationsstrategie* werden neue Marktsegmente mit neuen Produkten erschlossen.

- *Marktstimulierungsstrategien*: Als Kriterium gilt die Art und Weise der Marktbeeinflussung. Der Markt soll entweder durch Qualitätsprodukte (*Präferenzstrategie*) oder durch niedrige Preise (*Preis-Mengen-Strategie*) stimuliert werden.

- *Marktparzellierungsstrategien*: Als Kriterium gilt der Differenzierungsgrad der Marktbearbeitung. Entweder wird ein Massenmarkt mit einem undifferenzierte Marketingmix bedient (*Massenmarktstrategie*), oder es erfolgt eine Segmentierung des Marktes (*Marktsegmentierungsstrategie*) mit Abstimmung der Marketinginstrumente auf die einzelnen Segmente.

- *Wettbewerbsstrategien*: Als Kriterium dient die relative Position zum Wettbewerb. Bei der *Marktführerstrategie* will das Unternehmen seine Marktführerschaft verteidigen bzw. ausbauen. Die *Herausfordererstrategie* wird von Unternehmen verfolgt, die um den ersten Platz im Markt kämpfen und den Marktführer angreifen. Die *Mitläuferstrategie* ahmt den Marktführer nach, ohne ihm den ersten Platz streitig zu machen. Die *Nischenbesetzungsstrategie* wird meistens von kleineren Unternehmen verfolgt, die sich auf eine Marktnische spezialisiert haben, die von anderen Anbietern bisher vernachlässigt wurde.

12.2.2.3 Operative Marketingplanung

Ziel der operativen Marketingplanung ist die Umsetzung der strategischen Marketingziele durch den Einsatz diverser *Marketinginstrumente*. Üblicherweise werden vier verschiedene Marketinginstrumente unterschieden: die Produktpolitik, die Preispolitik, die Kommunikationspolitik und die Distributionspolitik. In Anlehnung an die Anfangsbuchstaben der englischen Begriffe (product, price, promotion, place) spricht man auch von den 4 P's. Die von einem Unternehmen zu einem bestimmten Zeitpunkt eingesetzte Kombination von marketingpolitischen Instrumenten wird auch als Marketingmix verstanden (Weis, 2004). Eine ausgewogene und optimale Kombination der Marketinginstrumente ist wichtig, um die vorgegebenen strategischen Marketingziele zu erreichen. Im Folgenden sollen die vier marketingpolitischen Instrumente, deren Aufgaben und Handhabung näher erläutert werden.

Die *Produktpolitik* wird oft als „das Herz des Marketing" bezeichnet, da das Produkt in aller Regel im Fokus des Marketing steht und die übrigen Instrumente auf den produktpolitischen Entscheidungen aufbauen.

Die Produktpolitik umfasst im Wesentlichen zwei Aufgaben: Zum einen sollen Entscheidungen über das Produkt selbst (z.B. die Gestaltung der Produktbeschaffenheit, die Gestaltung der Produktverpackung sowie Entscheidungen über die Markenbildung) getroffen werden. Die *Produktqualität* bezieht sich auf den *Produktkern* (technisch-konstruktive Eigenschaften), die *Produktfunktion* (Zuverlässigkeit, Wirtschaftlichkeit) und die *Produktform* (Verpackung, Design, Farbe).

Zum anderen geht es um Entscheidungen hinsichtlich des *Produktmix* (d.h. die Gesamtheit der verschiedenen Produkte, die ein Unternehmen anbietet) und in diesem Zusammenhang um die Handlungsalternativen *Produktinnovationen* (Entwicklung neuer Produkte), *Produktmodifikationen* (Weiterentwicklung von Produkten),

Produktdiversifikation (Aufnahme neuer Produktlinien) und *Produktelimination* (Einstellen des Angebots eines Produktes).

Besonderer Bedeutung in der Produktpolitik kommt der *Markierung* (im Englischen: *Branding*) zu. Als Markierung bezeichnet man die Strategie der Heterogenisierung homogener Produkte. Eine *Marke* dient im Wesentlichen der Differenzierung gegenüber der Konkurrenz. Damit soll erreicht werden, dass ein Konsument eine bestimmte Marke eines Anbieters kauft und nicht etwa ein ähnliches Produkt eines Wettbewerbers. Deshalb werden an sich gleiche Produkte (*me-too-Produkte*) durch besondere Produktgestaltung, Verpackung, Namensgebung und Werbung zu Produkten, die vom Konsumenten als unterschiedlich wahrgenommen werden (Ramme, 2004).

Mit Hilfe der *Preispolitik* versuchen Unternehmen, direkten Einfluss auf die Preise der eigenen Produkte zu nehmen und diese durchzusetzen. Die Produktpolitik umfasst im Wesentlichen die folgenden Aufgaben:

- Festlegung der *Preislage* (untere, mittlere, obere), in der ein Unternehmen operieren will,
- *Preisbestimmung* für neu in das Sortiment aufzunehmende Produkte,
- *Preisänderung* von Produkten und Produktgruppen des bestehenden Sortiments,
- *Preisdifferenzierung* bei Produkten, d.h. Festlegung unterschiedlicher Preise für das gleiche Produkt in verschiedenen Marktsegmenten,
- *Preisfestlegung* der Preise für die einzelnen Stufen des Distributionsprozesses,
- *Preisvergleich* mit den Konkurrenzpreisen.

Zur *Preisbildung* stehen dem Unternehmen verschiedene Preisbildungsverfahren zur Verfügung, z.B. die *kostenorientierte Preisbildung* (unter Berücksichtigung der eigenen Kosten, um Produkte zumindest kostendeckend anzubieten), die *nachfrageorientierte Preisbildung* (unter Berücksichtigung der Zahlungsbereitschaft potentieller Nachfrager), die *konkurrenzorientierte Preisbildung* (unter Berücksichtigung der Preise der Wettbewerberprodukte) und die *nutzenorientierte Preisbildung* (auf der Basis von Leistungsmerkmalen oder ökonomischer Größen). In der Praxis wird häufig eine Kombination dieser vier Verfahren angewandt, um eine *Preisuntergrenze*, eine *Preisobergrenze* und einen *marktgerechten Preis* zu definieren (Weis, 2004; Ramme, 2004).

Die *Kommunikationspolitik* hat zur Aufgabe, den Konsumenten über das Produkt zu informieren und ihn zum Kauf zu motivieren. Dafür stehen dem Unternehmen verschiedene Kommunikationsinstrumente zur Verfügung, die in Kombination den *Kommunikationsmix* ergeben. Ganz allgemein kann man zwischen *klassischer Kommunikation* (*above-the-line-Aktivitäten*) und *innovativen, nicht-klassischen Kommunikationsinstrumenten* (*below-the-line-Aktivitäten*) unterscheiden. Abb. 4 veranschaulicht diese Unterscheidung.

KOMMUNIKATIONSMIX	
Klassische Kommunikationsinstrumente *(Above the line)*	**Nicht-klassische Kommunikations-instrumente** *(Below the line)*
Werbung Printwerbung TV-Werbung Radio-Werbung Außenwerbung	Corporate Identity Policy
	Öffentlichkeitsarbeit
	Verkaufsförderung
	Sponsoring
	Event-Marketing
	Messen/Ausstellungen
	Product Placement
	Direktmarketing

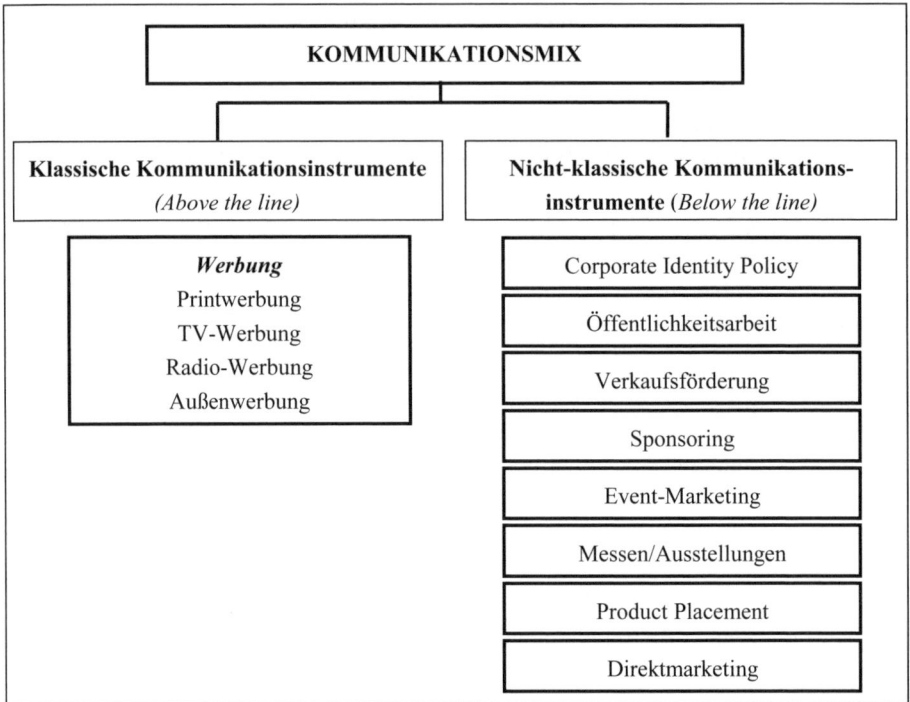

Abb. 4: Übersicht über die Kommunikationsinstrumente

Die in Abb. 4 vorgestellten *Kommunikationsinstrumente* sollen im Folgenden näher charakterisiert werden (Bühler, 2006a; Nufer, 2007):

- *Corporate Identity Policy:* Stellt das strategische Dach für alle anderen Kommunikationsinstrumente dar und kann damit als übergeordnetes, integriertes Konzept der unternehmensbezogenen Kommunikationspolitik bezeichnet werden.

- *Werbung*: Werbliche Maßnahmen wie Printwerbung in Zeitungen, Zeitschriften oder Magazinen, TV- und Radio-Werbung, oder Außenwerbung auf Litfasssäulen oder Transportmitteln sollen bei Konsumenten einen Einfluss auf die Kaufentscheidung zugunsten des werbenden Unternehmens ausüben. Die klassische Werbung ist zwar nach wie vor das meistgenutzte Kommunikationsinstrument, allerdings ist die Werbewirkung von Massenwerbung aufgrund der Werbeüberfrachtung (advertising clutter) häufig als eher gering einzuschätzen. Unternehmen versuchen daher zunehmend, mit humorvoller, skurriler oder teils auch schockierender Werbung auf sich aufmerksam zu machen.

- *Öffentlichkeitsarbeit (Public Relations):* Unternehmen versuchen, mit Hilfe der PR eine langfristige Beziehung zu verschiedenen Gruppen (z.B. Kunden, Journalisten, Aktionäre, Arbeitnehmer) zu etablieren, um dadurch Vertrauen und Verständnis aufzubauen. Die Öffentlichkeitsarbeit bedient sich hierbei verschiedener Instrumente wie Pressekonferenzen, PR-Anzeigen, PR-Veranstaltungen (Ausstellungen, Tag der offenen Tür), Spenden für wohltätige Zwecke, Gründung von eigenen Stiftungen oder auch redaktionelle Beiträge in Zeitungen oder Fachzeitschriften.

- *Verkaufsförderung (Sales Promotions)*: Um den Abverkauf von Produkten und Dienstleistungen zu fördern, setzen Unternehmen gezielte Verkaufsförderungsmaßnahmen ein, wie z.B. Preisausschreiben, Gutscheine, Preisnachlässe, Verkaufspromotions oder Displays bzw. Sonderplatzierungen am Ort des Verkaufs (point of sale).

- *Sponsoring*: Hierunter lassen sich sämtliche Aktivitäten subsumieren, die mit der Bereitstellung von Geld, Sachmitteln, Dienstleistungen oder Know-how durch Unternehmen zur Förderung von Personen, Organisationen oder Events verbunden sind, um damit Ziele der Unternehmenskommunikation (insbesondere die Steigerung des Bekanntheitsgrades oder die Verbesserung des eigenen Images) zu erreichen. Die älteste und am weitesten verbreitete Form des Sponsoring ist das Sportsponsoring. Im Laufe der vergangenen Jahre haben sich jedoch auch andere Sponsoringformen wie Kultursponsoring, Sozialsponsoring, Ökosponsoring oder Wissenschaftssponsoring etabliert.

- *Event-Marketing*: Hierbei handelt es sich um ein interaktives sowie erlebnisorientiertes Kommunikationsinstrument, das der zielgerichteten, zielgruppen- bzw. szenenbezogenen Inszenierung von eigens initiierten und inszenierten Veranstaltungen dient.

- *Messen/Ausstellungen*: Messen und Ausstellungen dienen nicht nur der Anbahnung von Geschäften und der Pflege von Geschäftskontakten, sondern auch der Anpreisung von Produkten bzw. Dienstleistungen.

- *Product Placement*: Die werbewirksame Integration von Produkten in Kinofilme oder Fernsehprogramme ist ein besonders effektives Kommunikationsinstrument, da sich der Konsument dieser Art der Werbebotschaftenübermittlung nicht so leicht entziehen kann.

- *Direktmarketing*: Im Gegensatz zur klassischen Werbung, die eine breite Masse anonym anspricht, versucht die Direktwerbung (oder auch Dialogmarketing), dem individuellen Konsumenten die Werbebotschaft direkt und mit persönlicher Adressierung zu übermitteln. Die beliebtesten Direktwerbeformen sind das Direktmailing (personalisierter Werbebrief) und das Telefonmarketing.

Da sich die Kommunikationsbotschaft eines Unternehmens im täglichen Werbedschungel gegen eine Vielzahl anderer Botschaften durchsetzen muss, versuchen Unternehmen, ihr Kommunikationsbudget so effektiv wie möglich zu nutzen, indem die verschiedenen Kommunikationsinstrumente miteinander vernetzt werden.

Im Rahmen der *Distributionspolitik* sind alle betrieblichen Aktivitäten festzulegen, die darauf gerichtet sind, eine Leistung vom Ort ihrer Entstehung – unter Überbrückung von Raum und Zeit – in den Verfügungsbereich der Nachfrager zu überbringen. Die Distributionspolitik kann untergliedert werden in die Vertriebspolitik und die Verkaufspolitik (Berndt, 2005, S. 201 ff.).

Die *Vertriebspolitik* umfasst Entscheidungen zur Standortwahl eines Unternehmens, zur Wahl der Absatzwege und Absatzmittler sowie zur physischen Distribution. Bei der *Standortwahl* sind v.a. Beschaffungs-, Produktions- und Absatzmöglichkeiten zu berücksichtigen. Bei den *Absatzwegen* ist grundsätzlich zwischen direktem Absatz (z.b. durch Handelsvertreter, eigene Filialen, Telefon- und Internetverkauf) und indirektem Absatz (z.b. durch zwischengeschaltete Groß- und Einzelhändler, Vertragshändler oder Franchisingunternehmen) zu unterscheiden. Als *Absatzmittler*, d.h. als Verkauforgane, können grundsätzlich Reisende oder Handelsvertreter eingesetzt werden. Bei der *physischen Distribution* der Produkte geht es um die Wahl der Transportmittel, des Auslieferungszeitpunktes und der vordefinierten Lieferzeiten.

Gegenstand der *Verkaufspolitik* sind alle betrieblichen Aktivitäten im Zusammenhang mit dem persönlichen Verkauf durch Mitarbeiter eines Unternehmens an die Nachfrager. Während bei der Medienwerbung i.d.R. eine unpersönliche, einseitige Kommunikation erfolgt, ist mit dem persönlichen Kauf eine wechselseitige und unmittelbare Kommunikation verbunden.

12.2.2.4 Implementierung und Kontrolle

Nachdem die strategische und operative Marketingplanung abgeschlossen ist, gilt es, die Pläne in die Tat umzusetzen. Etwaige Probleme in der *Realisierungsphase* sollten schon in der Planungsphase so gut wie möglich antizipiert werden. Wichtig ist, dass die Marketingkonzepte realistisch und den eigenen Möglichkeiten angemessen sein müssen. Risiko kann durch die Aufstellung von Zeit-, Organisations- und Finanzplänen für die jeweiligen Marketingprojekte minimiert werden. In dieser Phase sind auch Krisenmanagementfähigkeiten gefragt, um auftretenden Probleme schnellstmöglich zu lösen.

Um rechtzeitig auf veränderte Marktbedingungen reagieren zu können, ist außerdem eine ständige Kontrolle der geplanten und/oder realisierten Marketingprojekte erforderlich. Im Rahmen der *Marketing-Kontrolle (marketing controlling)* kann zwischen prozessorientierter Parallel-Kontrolle und ergebnisorientierter Ex-Post-Kontrolle unterschieden werden. Die *prozessorientierte Parallel-Kontrolle* (auch *Marketing-Audit* genannt) beinhaltet eine ständige, systematische Prüfung und Überwachung der einzelnen Phasen der Marketingkonzeption und betrachtet die Arbeitsweise des Marketing-Managements. So können eventuelle Fehlentwicklungen in einem frühen Stadium identifiziert und korrigiert werden. Bei der *ergebnisorientierten Ex-Post-Kontrolle* werden hauptsächlich die Endresultate des abgeschlossenen Marketingprojekts mit den zugrunde liegenden Zielen verglichen, um so den Erfolg oder Misserfolg eines Marketingprojekts anhand von vordefinierten Kennzahlen zu evaluieren. Mit Hilfe des Marketing-Controllings kann man somit zum einen auf das aktuelle Marketingprojekt regulierend einwirken, zum anderen werden durch die Evaluierung wichtige Hinweise auf zukünftige Marketingprojekte geliefert.

12.3 Grundlagen des Sportmarketing

Was ist Sportmarketing? Lediglich eine leicht abgewandelte Form von allgemeinem Marketing oder ein völlig selbstständiges Phänomen? Im folgenden Abschnitt werden der Begriff des Sportmarketing erläutert, die besonderen Charakteristika herausgearbeitet und ein Modell präsentiert, das das Prinzip des Sportmarketing näher erklären soll.

12.3.1 Begriffsabgrenzung zum Sportmarketing

Ein Problem des Sportmarketing ist es, dass keine einheitliche Begriffsdefinition existiert, aber gleichzeitig viele unterschiedliche Auffassungen kursieren, was unter Sportmarketing zu verstehen sei.

Vergleicht man die gängigen Sportmarketing-Definitionen, so erkennt man zwei verschiedene Lager. Auf der einen Seite diejenigen Ansätze, für die Sportmarketing die Vermarktung von Produkten mit Hilfe des Sports darstellen. Diesem Ansatz zufolge ist der Sport Mittel zum Zweck, wobei die vermarktungsfähigen Produkte nicht unbedingt etwas mit Sport zu tun haben müssen. Kaser/Oelkers (2005, S. 9) sind prominente Vertreter dieser Auffassung:

> „Sport marketing means using sports to market products."

Auf der anderen Seite stehen diejenigen Definitionsansätze, die Sportmarketing aus Sicht der Sportanbieter betrachten. Für sie stellt der Sport das Produkt selbst dar, das mit Hilfe von allgemeinen Marketinginstrumenten vermarktet werden soll. Die davon ausgehenden Sportmarketingdefinitionen sind im Kern lediglich modifizierte Definitionen des allgemeinen Marketing. So haben Shilbury/Quick/Westerbeck (1998, S. 13) beispielsweise die in diesem Kapitel bereits erwähnte Definition von Kotler in Nuancen verändert:

> „Sport marketing is a social and managerial process by which the sport manager seeks to obtain what sporting organisations need and want through creating and exchanging products and value with others."

Van Heerden (2001, S. 93) führt in seiner Definition die Ansichten beider Lager zusammen:

> „Sport marketing is the specific application of theoretical marketing principles and processes to sport products and services; the marketing of non-sport and sport-related products and services through an association – such as a sponsorship – with sport; and the marketing of sport bodies and codes, their personalities, their events, their activities, their actions, their strategies and their image."

Diese Definition vereint die zwei Perspektiven von Sportmarketing: Marketing *von* Sport und Marketing *mit* Sport. Beide Formen des modernen Sportmarketing werden im Verlauf dieses Kapitels noch näher erläutert. Darüber hinaus impliziert van Heerden's Definition, dass Sportmarketing einerseits auf den Grundlagen des allgemeinen Marketing basiert, andererseits aber auch eine spezielle Adaption notwendig ist, damit Sportmarketing funktioniert. Inwiefern und durch welche Charakteristika sich Sportmarketing von allgemeinem Marketing unterscheidet, wird im folgenden Abschnitt näher behandelt.

12.3.2 Charakteristika des Sportmarketing

Der amerikanische Sportmarketingexperte Bernard J. Mullin bemerkte, dass ein völlig neuer Marketingansatz benötigt wird, wenn es sich bei dem zu vermarktenden Produkt um Sport handelt. In der Tat ergeben sich drei wesentliche Unterschiede beim Vergleich zwischen Sportmarketing und allgemeinem Marketing.

Erstens unterscheidet sich der Sportmarkt von den üblichen Wirtschaftsmärkten, in denen Marketing betrieben wird. Beispielsweise ist trotz aller Konkurrenz ein Mindestmaß an Kooperationsbereitschaft nötig, damit ein vermarktungsfähiges Produkt (das Spiel selbst) entstehen kann. Aber auch darüber hinaus haben Sportclubs ein Interesse an einer engen Zusammenarbeit, wenn es beispielsweise darum geht, ihre Sportart oder ihre Liga gegenüber anderen Ligen oder Sportarten zu vermarkten.

Zweitens gibt es Unterschiede beim vermarktungsfähigen Produkt selbst. So sind nicht nur die Sportteams oder individuellen Sportler an der Produktion des Gesamtproduktes beteiligt, sondern auch die teilnehmenden Zuschauer vor Ort. Die von den Fans erzeugte Atmosphäre kann einen entscheidenden Einfluss auf die Qualität des Endproduktes haben. Manch langweiliges Fußballspiel wurde erst durch die aufgeheizte Stimmung im Stadion zu einem leidenschaftlichen Kampf mit tollen Szenen und Toren. Welche Qualität das Spiel haben und wie es enden wird, ist im Voraus nie zu sagen. Genau diese Ungewissheit hält zwar den Wettkampfcharakter aufrecht, ist jedoch für Marketingfachleute eine nicht kalkulierbare Größe. Während Unternehmen anderer Branchen einen direkten Einfluss auf die Qualität ihrer Produkte haben und auch gerne bereit sind, ein Qualitätsversprechen abzugeben, ist dies im Profisportbereich nur bedingt möglich.

Drittens gibt es einen signifikanten Unterschied in Bezug auf den Konsumenten respektive die Zielgruppe. Zuschauer nehmen aus den verschiedensten Gründen an

Sportveranstaltungen teil. Die einen wollen ein spannendes Spiel sehen, anderen ist der Sieg der eigenen Mannschaft wichtiger und wiederum andere interessieren sich primär für das Spektakel im Umfeld als für das eigentliche Spiel. Es ist für Sportorganisationen daher nicht einfach, die verschiedenen Motive der unterschiedlichen Zielgruppen unter einen Hut zu bringen. Darüber hinaus unterscheiden sich Sportkonsumenten von Konsumenten anderer Wirtschaftszweige in einer Vielzahl von Punkten. Diese Unterscheidung soll im Folgenden anhand von traditionellen Fußballfans dargestellt werden.

Echte Fußballfans empfinden für ihren speziellen Fußballclub in aller Regel mehr Leidenschaft als für ihre präferierte Waschmittelmarke und offenbaren darüber hinaus auch ein höheres Maß an Loyalität. Die britischen Autoren Dempsey/Reilly (1998) erklären sich diese Loyalität mit der Tatsache, dass Fans im Fußball etwas finden, das sie sonst nirgendwo finden. Daraus resultiert eine innige Verbundenheit mit dem Lieblingsverein. Leidenschaft und Loyalität führt zu einem weiteren Unterscheidungsmerkmal: Fußballfans legen im Allgemeinen ein höchst irrationales Konsumentenverhalten an den Tag. Kaufentscheidungen basieren oftmals nicht auf kommerziellen Gründen. Cashmore (2003) bemerkte diesbezüglich, dass Fans alles kaufen, was mit ihrer Leidenschaft zu tun hat – unabhängig vom Preis und der Qualität des Produktes. Infolgedessen haben Fans gar keine echte Wahl, wenn es um Kaufentscheidungen geht. Auch wenn normale Verbraucher vielleicht die eine oder andere Markenpräferenz haben, so können und werden sie doch zwischen verschiedenen Produkten wählen. Echte Fußballfans hingegen würden niemals auf die Idee kommen, zum gegnerischen Club zu wechseln, nur weil dort die Eintrittskarten billiger sind oder ein breiteres Merchandisingsortiment angeboten wird (Bühler, 2005; Bühler, 2006b). Aufgrund dieses Phänomens wird ein Fußballfan in der englischsprachigen Literatur als „captive consumer" (Pierpoint, 2000; Banks 2002) in einem „captive market" (Morrow, 1999; Conn, 2001) bezeichnet. Gemeint sind Konsumenten, die – wenn überhaupt – nur eine begrenzte Auswahl an Produkten haben bzw. keine andere Alternative, als Waren und Dienstleistungen von einer einzigen Quelle zu beziehen.

12.3.3 Modell des Sportmarketing
Aufgrund der vorangegangenen Erläuterungen zu den Besonderheiten des Sports ist es sinnvoll, Sportmarketing nicht lediglich als Modifikation von allgemeinem Marketing, sondern als eine sehr spezielle – fast eigenständige – Form des Marketing zu betrachten. Sportmarketing kombiniert demzufolge die einzigartigen Charakteristika des Sportmarktes mit den allgemeinen Marketinggrundlagen.

339

Protagonisten	**SPORTORGANISATIONEN** **(Verbände, Clubs, Individuen)**	**UNTERNEHMEN**

Produkte	**Sportprodukt** (Waren und Dienstleistungen)	**Sportfremde und sportver-** **wandte Produkte**

Teilnehmer

Kernprodukt
(Spiel, Veranstaltung, Wettkampf)

Zuschauer

Produkterweiterungen
(Hospitality, Merchandising, Rechte)

Sportmarketingart

MARKETING MIT SPORT

MARKETING VON SPORT

Werbung
(genereller Sport als Instrument zur Produktpromotion)

Sportsponsoring
Assoziation mit bestimmten Sportorganisationen zur Erreichung kommerzieller Ziele

Zielgruppe	**Teilnehmer**	**Zuschauer**	**Konsumenten**	**Unternehmen**

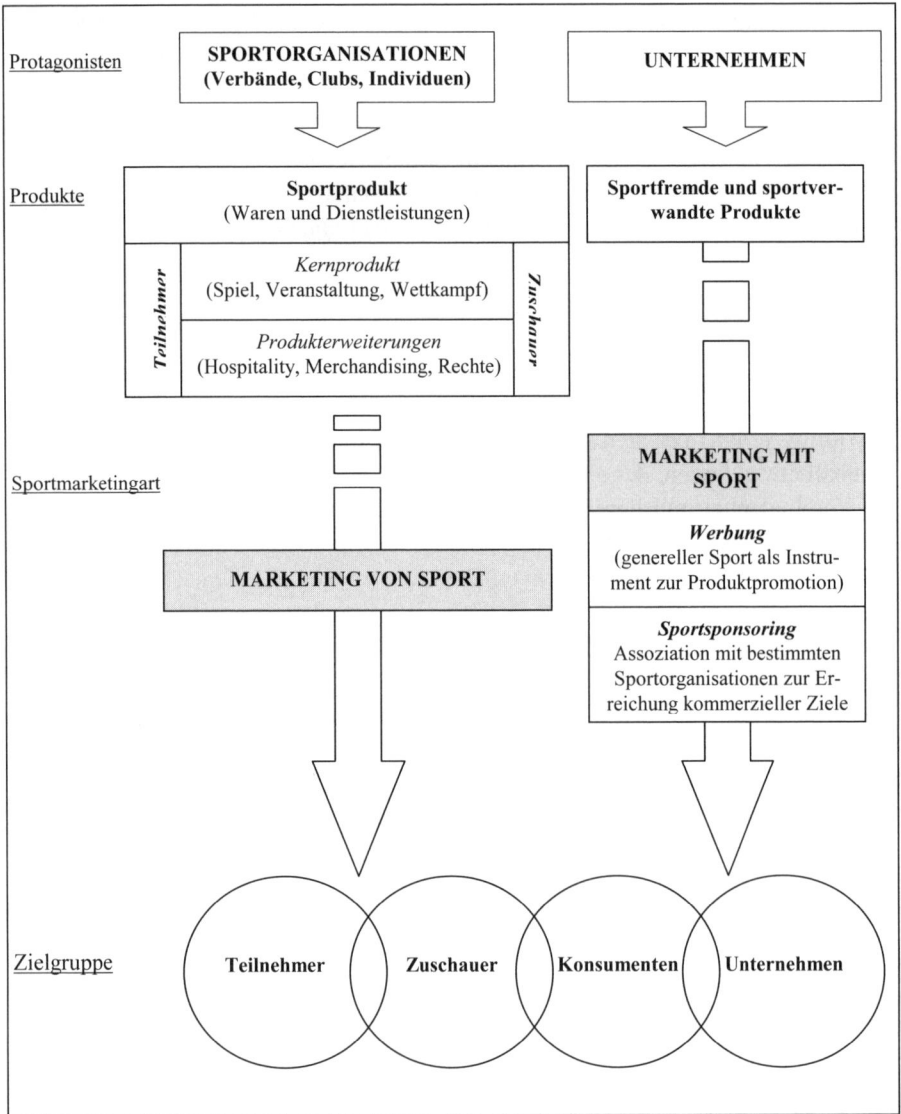

Abb. 5: Sportmarketing-Modell

Abb. 5 präsentiert ein Sportmarketingmodell, das die Protagonisten, die zu vermarktenden Produkte und die Zielgruppen des Sportmarketingmarktes sowie die beiden Hauptformen des Sportmarketing vorstellt: *Marketing von Sport* und *Marketing mit Sport*. Beide Sportmarketingformen sollen in den folgenden Abschnitten näher erläutert werden.

12.4 Marketing von Sport

Der Wettbewerb im Sportmarkt hat sich in den letzten Jahren drastisch verschärft. Sportorganisationen und insbesondere Sportclubs sehen sich zahlreichen Konkurrenten ausgesetzt: Ein professioneller Handballverein muss sich beispielsweise gegen direkte Ligarivalen, gegen Handballclubs anderer nationaler und internationaler Ligen, gegen andere Zuschauersportarten und schließlich auch gegen alternative Freizeitmöglichkeiten (wie Kino, Theater oder Konzerte) durchsetzen, um Zuschauer, Sponsoren, Medien und zukünftige Mitarbeiter für sich zu gewinnen. Darüber hinaus arbeiten Sportorganisationen mehr und mehr mit professionellen Partnern (z.B. Sponsoren, Agenturen, Rechtevermarktern) zusammen, die eine zunehmende Professionalisierung als Grundlage einer langfristigen Geschäftsbeziehung fordern. Dies führt dazu, dass Sportorganisationen in verstärktem Maße ihre Sportart und v.a. sich selbst vermarkten müssen. Inwiefern sie sich dabei den Grundlagen des Marketing bedienen und diese Marketinggrundlagen auf den Sportbereich anwenden können, wird im Folgenden gezeigt.

12.4.1 Analysephase im Sportmarketing

Wie bereits erwähnt, sollte jede Marketingkonzeption auf einer systematischen und profunden Analyse der internen und externen Umwelt basieren. Sportorganisationen können sich diesbezüglich einer Vielzahl von grundlegenden Analysemethoden aus dem allgemeinen Marketing bedienen. Wie eine SWOT-Analyse für einen deutschen Fußballbundesligisten in verkürzter Form aussehen könnte, illustriert Abb. 6.

Um die Umfeldbedingungen zu analysieren, bietet sich die PEST-Analyse zum einen für Sportorganisationen, die im internationalen Wettbewerb stehen und neue Märkte anstreben, und zum anderen für Sportorganisationen, die auf dem heimischen Markt wachsen wollen, an. Mit Hilfe dieser Analyse werden systematisch die politisch-rechtlichen Einflüsse (z.B. die Vergabe von staatlichen Zuschüssen und Subventionen im Sport, die Besteuerung von Sportsponsoringzuwendungen), die ökonomischen Einflüsse (z.B. Einkommensverhältnisse der sportinteressierten Bevölkerung), soziokulturelle Einflüsse (z.B. die Altersstruktur der sportbegeisterten Bevölkerung, Trends im Sportmarkt) und technologische Entwicklungen (z.B. Innovationen im Sportmarkt) identifiziert und bewertet.

Darüber hinaus sollten Sportorganisation in verstärktem Maße Zielgruppenanalysen sowie Wettbewerbs- und Wettbewerberanalysen durchführen, um sich selbst und den jeweiligen Sportmarkt genauer beurteilen zu können. Des Weiteren müssen sie bereit sein, diese Analysen und Befragungen von Marktforschungsexperten durchführen zu lassen (entweder inhouse oder durch ein Marktforschungsinstitut), damit die Validität der Ergebnisse auch gewährleistet ist. Eine Marketingstrategie, die auf falschen oder falsch interpretierten Daten basiert, ist schon im Voraus zum Scheitern verurteilt.

Im Laufe der Jahre haben sich im Sportbusiness einige sehr gute Marktfor-schungsberichte von Agenturen, Unternehmensberatungen oder Marktforschungs-unternehmen etabliert, die wichtige Erkenntnisse über Entwicklungen, Trends und demografische Strukturen im Wirtschaftsmarkt Sport liefern. Exemplarisch seien hier die Unternehmensberatungen *Deloitte* („Annual Review of Football Finance") und *Ernst & Young* („Bälle, Tore und Finanzen"), der Sportrechtevermarkter *Sport-five* („Fußballstudie" und „Affinitäten") sowie das Marktforschungsinstitut *Sport + Markt* („Jersey Report") genannt. Sollten Sekundärdaten dieser oder anderer Art nicht vorliegen, so müssen durch eigene Datenerhebungen (z.b. durch Befragun-gen) Primärdaten erhoben werden, die ggf. mit Hilfe von Spezialsoftware ausge-wertet werden können.

Interne Stärken	Interne Schwächen
▪ Konstanter sportlicher Erfolg in den letz-ten 5 Jahren (ständige Teilnahme am in-ternationalen Wettbewerb) ▪ Loyales Stammpublikum und gewachsene Fankultur ▪ Auslastungskapazität Stadion bei 95 % ▪ Steigender Professionalisierungsgrad durch hauptamtlichen Manager und neu gegründete Marketingabteilung mit 5 Mitarbeitern	▪ Gelegentliche Finanzierungs- und Liqui-ditätslücken ▪ Durchschnittsalter des Stammpublikums bei 56 Jahren, Anteil des jungen Publi-kums zu gering ▪ Stadionkapazität bei Spitzenspielen zu gering ▪ Ausbau der Marke dümpelt seit Jahren vor sich hin
Externe Chancen	**Externe Risiken**
▪ Gesteigertes Interesse an der Fußballbun-desliga durch die WM 2006 bei Zuschau-ern und werbenden Unternehmen ▪ Verstärkte Fußballbegeisterung in Asien und Nordamerika und dadurch neue Wachstumsmärkte ▪ Fußballbundesliga als finanzielles und wirtschaftliches Vorzeigemodell	▪ Konkurrenz durch andere Sportarten und Freizeitaktivitäten verschärft sich ▪ Gehälter der Spitzenspieler steigen an ▪ Englische und spanische Clubs mit höhe-ren Einnahmen aus TV-Vermarktung ▪ Schlechte Quote im internationalen Ver-gleich und Gefahr des Verlusts von Start-plätzen in den europäischen Wettbewer-ben

Abb. 6: Fiktive SWOT-Analyse eines deutschen Fußballbundesligisten (in verkürzter Form)

12.4.2 Strategische Unternehmens- und Marketingplanung im Sport

Wichtig für die Gestaltung der strategischen Marketingplanung und die Aufstellung von spezifischen Marketingzielen ist die strategische Unternehmensplanung der je-weiligen Sportorganisation. Ein professioneller Basketballverein in Deutschland kann sich beispielsweise zum Ziel setzen, in den nächsten zehn Jahren zum wirt-schaftlich und sportlich erfolgreichsten Basketballclub Europas zu werden. Der Un-ternehmenszweck besteht also darin, den Zuschauern permanent hochklassigen Spitzensport zu bieten, nationale und internationale Titel zu gewinnen und darüber hinaus finanziellen Gewinn anzustreben. Aus dieser Zielstellung leiten sich dann die Unternehmenskultur, die Unternehmensphilosophie sowie die weiteren Ziele ab. Um das gemeinsame Ziel zu erreichen, ist eine Unternehmenskultur vonnöten, die auf Identifikation und Zusammenhalt basiert. Die Unternehmensphilosophie ist von einer Siegermentalität geprägt, die aber gleichzeitig auch maßvoll sein sollte, um das wirtschaftliche Risiko zu minimieren. Aus dem übergeordneten Unternehmensziel ergeben sich abgeleitete Unterziele, die für die jeweiligen Abteilungen gelten. So könnte die Controllingabteilung das Ziel haben, die Balanced Score Card als Kontrollinstrument einzuführen. Die Personalabteilung könnte zum Ziel haben, Experten für die jeweiligen Unternehmensbereiche zu rekrutieren oder die bisherigen Mitarbeiter durch Schulungen und Weiterbildungsangebote für die zukünftigen Aufgaben vorzubereiten. Für den sportlichen Bereich würde sich wiederum das Ziel ergeben, Topspieler zu verpflichten, sie zu einem Team zu formen und eine Spielkultur zu entwickeln, die zukünftigen Erfolg möglich macht. Für die Marketingabteilung würde sich schließlich eine Vielzahl an Zielen ergeben, z.B. Aufbau und Etablierung der Clubmarke oder Aufbau von langfristigen Sponsoren- und Kundenbeziehungen.

In der Phase der strategischen Marketingplanung steht die Sportorganisation vor der Aufgabe, die sich aus der strategischen Unternehmensplanung ergebenden Zielvorgaben auf den Bereich des Marketing zu übertragen, die Vorgaben und Maßstäbe in strategische Marketingziele abzuleiten und schließlich Richtungsanweisungen für die operative Marketingplanung und somit für den Einsatz der Marketinginstrumente zu geben.

Die Sportorganisation kann quantitative Marketingziele (z.B. Steigerung des Marktanteils um 10 % innerhalb der nächsten drei Jahre) oder qualitative Marketingziele (z.B. Steigerung der Kundenzufriedenheit bei Heimspielen) definieren. Wichtig bei allen Zielvorgaben ist die Operationalisierung der Ziele, d.h. Ziele müssen so definiert sein, dass man in der Evaluierungsphase eindeutig bestimmen kann, ob ein vorgegebenes Ziel erreicht wurde oder nicht. In aller Regel definieren professionelle Sportorganisationen eine ganze Reihe von strategischen Marketingzielen, die permanent auf ihre Gültigkeit und auf veränderte Marktbedingungen hin überprüft werden.

Wie bereits beschrieben, stehen verschiedene Marketingstrategien zur Verfügung, die zum einen von den spezifischen Marketingzielen der Sportorganisation und zum anderen vom jeweiligen Umfeld und der Situation abhängen. In Bezug auf die Wettbewerbsstrategien wird der FC Bayern München innerhalb der Fußballbundesliga eine andere Marketingstrategie anwenden, um die Marktführerschaft im deutschen Profifußball zu verteidigen, als der FSV Mainz 05, der eher eine Nischenbesetzungsstrategie verfolgen wird, um sich als „der etwas andere Club" zu positionieren. Im internationalen Vergleich wird der FC Bayern hingegen eher die Herausfordererstrategie anwenden, um die eigene Wettbewerbssituation im europäischen Profifußball auszubauen und den größeren Clubs (wie Manchester United, Real Madrid, AC Mailand) Paroli bieten zu können.

Im Laufe der Jahre hat sich die Zusammensetzung der Stadionbesucher in der Fußballbundesliga erheblich verändert. War früher der Großteil der Zuschauer männlich, zwischen 20 und 50 Jahre alt und der unteren bis mittleren Einkommensschicht zugehörig, so findet man heutzutage Männer und Frauen aller sozialen Klassen und Altersschichten, Familien und Kinder fast gleichermaßen im Stadion vor. Diese Entwicklung hat zur Folge, dass der Zuschauermarkt nicht mehr mit einer Massenmarktstrategie bearbeitet werden kann, sondern eine Marktsegmentierungsstrategie angebracht ist.

Was die Marktstimulierungsstrategie betrifft, so unterscheiden sich sicherlich die Ansätze zwischen den jeweiligen Ligen. In der Ersten Fußballbundesliga sollen Zuschauer durch die Qualität ins Stadion gelockt werden, wohingegen in den unteren Ligen eher niedrige Preise als Stimulierung verwendet werden.

In Bezug auf Marktfeldstrategien kann man ebenfalls im Fußball einige Beispiele für die unterschiedlichen Strategieausprägungen vorfinden. Die Fußballbundesligisten versuchen, durch die Deutsche Fußball Liga (DFL) ihre Sportart und ihre Liga gegenüber anderen Sportarten und Ligen auf dem deutschen Markt zu positionieren und somit Zuschauer-, Sponsoren- und Mediengelder für sich zu gewinnen. Einige Fußballbundesligisten verfolgen darüber hinaus die Marktentwicklungsstrategie, indem sie mit ihrer Marke und ihrem Angebot andere Märkte erschließen möchten (z.b. der FC Bayern München in Japan und China, der VfB Stuttgart in Mexiko). Um das Produkt Fußball attraktiver zu gestalten (Innovationsstrategie), wurden im Laufe der Jahre andere Fußball-Formen entwickelt, wie zum Beispiel beach soccer oder indoor soccer. Damit wollen sich Fußballverbände von anderen Sportarten abgrenzen und mit alternativen Freizeitangeboten konkurrieren. Als Beispiel für eine Diversifikationsstrategie dient Borussia Dortmund, die Anfang des 21. Jahrhunderts nicht nur auf das Kernprodukt Fußball setzten, sondern andere Geschäftsfelder in ihr Produktportfolio aufnahmen. So wurden beispielsweise ein Hotel, ein Sportstudio, ein Reisebüro und eine eigene Ausrüsterfirma gegründet, allerdings mit nur mittelmäßigem Erfolg.

12.4.3 Operative Marketingplanung im Sport
Im Anschluss an die strategische Marketingplanung erfolgt die operative Marketingplanung, die die strategischen Marketingziele durch den Einsatz von diversen Marketinginstrumenten zu erreichen versucht. Im Folgenden wird gezeigt, wie professionelle Sportorganisationen den Marketingmix zur Zielerreichung gestalten können.

12.4.3.1 Produktpolitik im Sport

Die Besonderheiten des Sportproduktes haben einen direkten Einfluss auf die Produktpolitik von Sportorganisationen. Letztere müssen sich die Frage stellen, ob ihr Kernprodukt (die Sportart, das Spiel, der Wettkampf, das Event) attraktiv genug ist, um die strategischen Marketingziele zu erreichen, oder ob eine Produktentwicklung vonnöten ist. Das Kernprodukt selbst kann nicht so leicht modifiziert werden (was im Bereich des Fußballs sehr anschaulich ist, da jede kleine Änderung durch einen jahrelangen Bewertungsprozess seitens des Weltfußballverbandes FIFA begleitet wird und auch dann noch auf einigen Widerstand verschiedener Gruppen trifft). Daraus folgt, dass Sportorganisationen eher Modifikationen im Umfeld anstreben können. Ein Eishockeyclub kann nicht dafür garantieren, dass das individuelle Eishockeymatch ein spannendes und tolles Spiel wird oder dass die eigene Mannschaft gewinnt, aber er kann alles daran setzen, dass sich die Zuschauer auf den Rängen und in den VIP-Logen wohlfühlen und amüsieren, die Merchandisingartikel von höchster Qualität sind und Sponsoren die Werberechte zielgerichtet für ihr Unternehmen einsetzen können.

Besonderer Bedeutung im Kontext der Produktpolitik kommt dem Branding, der Markenführung, zu. Die meisten professionellen Sportclubs behaupten zwar von sich selbst, dass sie Marken seien, aber nur die wenigsten werden auch wie Marken geführt. Auch hier heißt das Schlüsselwort Marktforschung, denn erst durch Analysen und Befragungen kann in Erfahrung gebracht werden, wofür der Club in der Öffentlichkeit tatsächlich steht und welche Attribute mit ihm assoziiert werden. Die wenigen Sportorganisationen, die eine stringente Markenpolitik verfolgen, wissen hierüber genau Bescheid. Ein effektives Instrument zur Markenbildung und -pflege stellt das Merchandising dar. Merchandisingartikel transportieren den Namen und das Logo des Clubs und erhöhen somit auch den Wiedererkennungswert der Marke.

12.4.3.2 Preispolitik im Sport

Sportorganisationen tun sich traditionell schwer, den richtigen Preis für ihre Produkte zu finden. Viele Unternehmen kombinieren die vier Formen der Preisbildung. Um etwa den Preis für eine Dauerkarte in der Eishockeybundesliga zu definieren, wäre es ratsam, die Zahlungsbereitschaft der Zuschauer (nachfrageorientierte Preisbildung) und die Dauerkartenpreise der anderen Eishockeyclubs zu analysieren (konkurrenzorientierte Preisbildung) sowie Preis-Leistungs-Verhältnisse kritisch zu prüfen (nutzenorientierte Preisbildung). Sportökonomische Probleme treten bei der kostenorientierten Preisbildung auf, da die Einnahmen aus Eintrittsgeldern in den meisten Fällen nur zu einem Bruchteil die tatsächlichen Kosten des Spielbetriebs decken. Würde man also ausschließlich die kostenorientierte Preisbildung anwenden, so würde sich der Preis einer Eintritts- oder Dauerkarte um ein vielfaches erhöhen, was vermutlich einen starken Nachfragerückgang zur Folge hätte. Fans mögen zwar loyal sein, aber auch ihre finanziellen Ressourcen sind endlich. Welche Preisstrategie zu wählen ist, hängt hauptsächlich von den strategischen Marketingzielen ab. So sollte ein Sportanbieter, der sich als Premiummarke positionieren möchte, auch eine Hochpreisstrategie wählen, um konsistent zu sein. Auf der anderen Seite macht sich ein Sportclub, der sich selbst als bodenständig und volksnah sieht, unglaubwürdig, wenn die Eintrittspreise so hoch angesetzt sind, dass die mittleren und unteren Einkommensgruppen faktisch ausgegrenzt werden. Professionelle Sportorganisationen wenden zunehmend die gängigen preispolitischen Instrumente wie Preisdifferenzierung (z.b. Kinder- und Seniorenkarten, Gruppentarife) oder Rabatte respektive Boni (z.b. alle acht Spiele der Rückrunde zum Preis von sieben) an. Doch nicht nur für Eintrittskarten müssen Preise festgelegt werden, sondern auch für die anderen Produkte professioneller Sportorganisationen wie z.b. Entgelte für Merchandisingprodukte, Mitgliedsbeiträge oder Werberechte.

12.4.3.3 Kommunikationspolitik im Sport

Die kommunikationspolitischen Instrumente sollen Sportorganisationen helfen, ihre Produkte und Dienstleistungen zu bewerben, bekannt zu machen und gegenüber Produkten und Dienstleistungen der Konkurrenz abzuheben.

Zunächst geht es darum, die jeweilige Sportart ins Rampenlicht der Öffentlichkeit zu führen. Sportarten wie Fußball oder Leichtathletik haben es diesbezüglich leichter als Sportarten, die eher ein Schattendasein führen, wie z.b. Synchronschwimmen oder Faustball. Von entscheidender Bedeutung ist in diesem Zusammenhang das Zusammenspiel der Sportorganisationen mit den Medien. Durch dauerhafte mediale Präsenz ist es gelungen, auch einstige Randsportarten zu einem medialen Volkssport zu machen, wie das Beispiel von Skispringen und RTL zeigt.

Wichtig ist auch eine klare strategische Positionierung unter Berücksichtigung der Wettbewerbssituation. So kämpfen seit Jahren Handball, Basketball, Volleyball um den Titel der „zweitwichtigsten Ballsportart nach Fußball". Parallel dazu versuchen sich die jeweiligen Clubs, innerhalb der Sportarten zu positionieren.

Auch hier sind Medienkooperationen und Öffentlichkeitsarbeit wichtige Bestandteile einer systematischen Kommunikationspolitik. Nach dem Motto „Tue Gutes und sprich darüber" unterstützen einige Sportorganisationen soziale Projekte, die dann wiederum medial aufbereitet werden. Außerdem kooperieren immer mehr professionelle Sportorganisationen mit Schulen und Hochschulen, in denen Vereinsvertreter Unterricht bzw. Vorlesungen halten und somit für ihre Sportorganisation werben.

Darüber hinaus stehen Wirtschaftsunternehmen eine ganze Reihe anderer Kommunikationsinstrumente zur Verfügung. Diese finden auch mehr und mehr im Wirtschaftsmarkt Sport Verwendung. Professionelle Sportorganisationen haben die Möglichkeit, sich selbst durch klassische Werbemaßnahmen ins Gespräch zu bringen. Ein gutes Beispiel stellt der Fußballbundesligist VfB Stuttgart dar, der nicht

nur seine Heimspiele mit kreativen Slogans auf großflächigen Werbeanzeigen an-
kündigt (vgl. Abb. 7), sondern auch einen Imagefilm erstellt hat, der in den Kinos
der Stuttgarter Region im Rahmen des normalen Kinobetriebs gezeigt wurde.

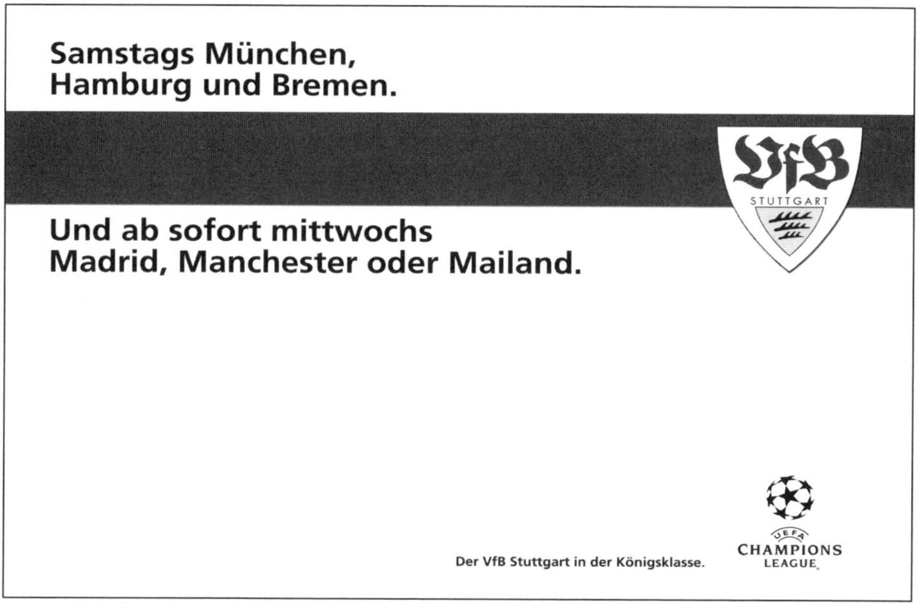

**Samstags München,
Hamburg und Bremen.**

**Und ab sofort mittwochs
Madrid, Manchester oder Mailand.**

Der VfB Stuttgart in der Königsklasse.

CHAMPIONS LEAGUE

Abb. 7: Beispiel einer Werbeanzeige des VfB Stuttgart zur Bewerbung eines Heimspiels
Quelle: VfB Stuttgart Marketing GmbH (2007), o.S.

Um die Stadien und Arenen zu füllen, setzen Sportclubs verstärkt auf Verkaufsförderungsmaßnahmen wie Gewinnspiele oder Gruppentarife. Außerdem werden immer mehr Elemente der Direktwerbung eingesetzt (z.B. Direktmailings an die Ver-
eins- oder Fanclubmitglieder, in denen für bestimmte Aktionen des Sportclubs
geworben werden).

Das in der Wirtschaft beliebte Kommunikationsinstrument Sponsoring hat für
professionelle Sportorganisationen eher den Charakter eines Beschaffungsinstru-
ments, da sie diejenigen sind, die Geld für die Überlassung werblicher Rechte erhalten. Dass Sponsoring aber auch als PR-Instrument genutzt werden kann, zeigt
das Beispiel des FC Barcelona. Seit der Saison 2006/2007 ziert erstmals in der über
hundertjährigen Vereinsgeschichte ein Logo die Brust der Katalanen. Auf den blau-
rot gestreiften Trikots ist jedoch nicht etwa das Logo einer der vielen multinationa-
len Unternehmen (die für dieses Trikotsponsoring bereit wären, Mio. von Euro zu
bezahlen) zu sehen, sondern der Schriftzug des Kinderhilfswerks der Vereinten Na-
tionen UNICEF. Das eigentlich ungewöhnliche daran ist die Tatsache, dass nicht
der Trikotsponsor die Sportorganisation für das Sponsorship bezahlt, sondern in
diesem Fall der FC Barcelona jährlich 1,5 Mio. € dem Kinderhilfswerk zur Verfü-

gung stellt. Dadurch entsteht für beide Seiten eine win-win-Situation, da UNICEF und Barcelona durch diesen Deal gegenseitig an Image und Bekanntheit gewinnen.

Für Wirtschaftsunternehmen und professionelle Sportorganisationen gilt gleichermaßen, dass die Wirkung der Kommunikation multipliziert wird, wenn die Kommunikationsinstrumente aufeinander abgestimmt und vernetzt werden.

12.4.3.4 Distributionspolitik im Sport

Die Distributionspolitik im Bereich des Sports bezieht sich sowohl auf die Standortwahl (wo soll das neue Stadion gebaut werden? In welches Land bzw. welche Stadt wird das nächste sportliche Großereignis vergeben?), die Absatzwege (werden Eintrittskarten nur an der Kasse oder auch im Internet oder über Absatzmittler wie etwa professionelle Ticketagenturen verkauft?) als auch die physische Distribution der Produkte (werden Tickets verschickt oder müssen sie abgeholt werden?). Auch hier gilt es, den effektivsten und für den Kunden bequemsten Weg zu finden.

12.4.4 Implementierung und Marketingcontrolling im Sport

Um die strategischen und operativen Marketingziele zu erreichen, ist es v.a. wichtig, die Implementierung respektive Realisierung der einzelnen marketingpolitischen Instrumente professionell zu begleiten. Dies kann zum einen durch die Aufstellung von detaillierten Aktionsplänen bewerkstelligt werden, zum anderen auch durch die Zusammenarbeit mit externen Agenturen, die sich auf die jeweiligen Instrumente spezialisiert haben.

Um die Wirksamkeit aller Instrumente des Marketingmix beurteilen zu können, ist auch im Wirtschaftsmarkt Sport eine ständige Kontrolle der Marketingaktivitäten sowie eine Ex-Post-Kontrolle nötig.

Marketing von Sport hat sich durch einen verschärften Wettbewerb um die freie Zeit der Konsumenten zu einer Notwendigkeit entwickelt, der sich keine professionelle Sportorganisation mehr entziehen kann. Sportverbände und -clubs sind gut beraten, sich dem Thema in verstärkter Form anzunehmen und dabei die allgemeinen Marketinggrundsätze auf die Besonderheiten des Wirtschaftsmarkts Sport anzuwenden.

12.5 Marketing mit Sport

Wie in Abb. 5 ersichtlich, ist der Bereich Marketing mit Sport zweigeteilt: Zum einen verwenden Unternehmen den Sport als Werbemittel, beispielsweise als thematischen Bezugspunkt in der Werbung. Während der Fußball-WM 2006 gab es kaum einen Werbespot oder eine Zeitungsanzeige in Deutschland, die sich nicht auf das runde Leder bezog (wobei nicht alle der mit der WM werbenden Unternehmen auch offizielle Sponsoren des FIFA World Cup 2006 waren). Sponsoring ist die zweite – und vermeintlich wichtigere – Möglichkeit, wenn es um Marketing mit Sport geht. In Anbetracht der Tatsache, dass Sportorganisationen direkt von Sportsponsoring profitieren, soll diese Form des Marketing mit Sport aus drei verschiedenen Perspektiven betrachtet werden: aus Sicht der Sponsoren, aus Sicht der Gesponserten und aus einer gemeinsamen Sicht (Bühler, 2006a; Nufer, 2002).

12.5.1 Sportsponsoring aus Sicht der Sponsoren

Unternehmen haben schon frühzeitig erkannt, dass die Assoziation mit einem bestimmten Sportclub/-team oder einer bestimmten Sportveranstaltung einen werblichen Vorteil gegenüber der Konkurrenz verspricht. Was Anfangs noch eine Form des Gönnertums war (das lokale Unternehmen sponserte den lokalen Club eher aus persönlichen Gründen, denn aus kommerziellen), entwickelte sich im Laufe der Jahre zu einem wichtigen und ausdifferenzierten Marketinginstrument. Einer der sichersten Wege, um heutzutage als neues Unternehmen oder neue Marke den Bekanntheitsgrad innerhalb kürzester Zeit auf ein akzeptables Niveau zu heben, ist das Platzieren des Markenlogos auf der Brust eines Fußballbundesligisten (Bühler, 2006a). Allerdings ist dabei zu beachten, dass das Sponsorship seine volle Wirkung erst entfalten kann, wenn es durch flankierende Maßnahmen unterstützt wird. Neueste Studien (Pilot Group, 2006) haben ergeben, dass die großen deutschen Sportsponsoren für jeden Euro, den sie in ein Sponsorship investieren, mindestens genauso viel für vernetzende Kommunikationsmaßnahmen (z.B. Werbespots, Printanzeigen, Public Relations) ausgeben. Sportsponsoring ist heutzutage nicht nur ein populäres Mittel zur Bekanntheitssteigerung und Imageverbesserung, sondern auch ein effektives Instrument zur Kundengewinnung respektive Kundenbindung sowie zur Umsatzsteigerung. So können speziell an die Fans des gesponserten Clubs gerichtete Produkte und Aktionen zu einem gewinnbringenden Abverkauf führen. Nicht zu unterschätzen ist Sportsponsoring darüber hinaus als Instrument zur Netzwerkbildung. In den Sponsorenpools einiger Sportorganisationen finden sich häufig Unternehmen verschiedener Branchen, die durch das gemeinsame Sponsorship Kontakte knüpfen und lukrative Geschäfte abschließen. In diesem Fall dient das Sportsponsoring als Plattform für Geschäftskontakte und Folgegeschäfte.

12.5.2 Sportsponsoring aus Sicht der Gesponserten

Sponsoring war schon immer eine wichtige Einnahmequelle für Sportorganisationen, die im Laufe der Jahre essentielle Bedeutung erlangte. Spitzensport ist heutzutage ohne die finanzielle Unterstützung der Sponsoren nicht mehr möglich. Infolgedessen fand auch ein Umdenken bei den Sportorganisationen statt. Früher wurden Sponsoren als selbstverständliche Geldgeber angesehen, denen als Gegenleistung ein paar werbliche Zugeständnisse (z.B. eine Bande am Spielfeldrand oder eine Autogrammstunde mit einem Spieler) gemacht wurden. Heute haben viele Sportorganisationen verstanden, dass Unternehmen mit ihren Sponsorships klar definierte Kommunikationsziele verfolgen und daher eine entsprechende Gegenleistung erwarten. Auch im Sportsponsoring haben inzwischen die ökonomischen Prinzipien Einzug gehalten. Allein daraus ergibt sich für Sportorganisationen die Notwendigkeit der Professionalisierung. Konkret heißt das, dass sich um die Angelegenheiten der Sponsoren nicht mehr ausschließlich marketingbegeisterte Ex-Sportler, sondern verstärkt sportbegeisterte Marketingfachleute bzw. Sportökonomen kümmern sollten. Clubs, Verbände und Ausrichter von Sportveranstaltungen sollten Sportsponsoring nicht nur als Einkommensquelle betrachten, sondern auch als eine gute Gelegenheit zur eigenen Markenpositionierung. Viele große Unternehmen können mit ihrer Strahlkraft und ihrem Marketing-Knowhow den Sportorganisationen zu einer besseren Marktstellung verhelfen.

12.5.1 Sportsponsoring aus gemeinsamer Sicht

Sportsponsoring ist nicht nur eine wichtige Einkommensquelle für Sportorganisationen oder ein wichtiges Marketinginstrument für Unternehmen, sondern stellt v.a. auch eine reziproke Geschäftsbeziehung zwischen Sponsor und Gesponserten dar. Wie in jeder Geschäftsbeziehung hängt auch in dieser der Erfolg des Geschäfts von der Beziehungsqualität zwischen den Geschäftspartnern ab. Dies gilt um so mehr für langfristige Sponsoringbeziehungen, wie sie im Sport immer mehr zum Tragen kommen. Neueste Studien (z.B. Bühler, 2006a; Bühler, 2006b) belegen, dass erfolgreiche Sponsoringbeziehungen sich v.a. durch gegenseitiges Vertrauen auszeichnen. Andere Erfolgsfaktoren können Kommunikation, Kooperation und gegenseitiges Verständnis sein. Sponsoren und Gesponserte sind daher gut beraten, sich für die Ziele des anderen zu interessieren und sich gemeinsam für die Erreichung dieser Ziele einzusetzen.

12.6 Fallstudie

Die folgende Fallstudie verdeutlicht am Beispiel des Fußballclubs und Traditionsvereins FC St. Pauli, wie Sportorganisationen Marketing betreiben.

Fallstudie „FC St. Pauli"

Seit Jahren fristet der FC St. Pauli ein eher trauriges sportliches Dasein. Dennoch hat es der ehemalige Bundesligist geschafft, sich als eine der wenigen echten Marken im deutschen Fußball zu etablieren und durch kreatives Marketing dringend benötigte Gelder zu akquirieren.

Die vergangenen Jahre waren beim FC St. Pauli durch einen finanziellen und sportlichen Überlebenskampf geprägt. Daher standen strategische Marketingziele auf der Prioritätenliste zunächst eher unten, was sich nicht zuletzt in der Tatsache bemerkbar machte, dass (wie bei so vielen anderen Sportorganisationen) sämtliche finanziellen Mittel entweder in die Schuldentilgung oder in den sportlichen Bereich investiert wurden. Dementsprechend bescheiden fällt auch das Marketingbudget der Kiezkicker aus. Trotzdem wird in der fünfköpfigen Marketingabteilung des FC St. Pauli systematisch und professionell gearbeitet. So wurde beispielsweise ein schriftliches Strategiekonzept erstellt, in dem die Marke definiert, das Corporate Design beschrieben und der Markenwert erläutert wird. Die Marke des FC St. Pauli basiert v.a. auf der Vereinsphilosophie „Non Established since 1910" und kommt in den Attributen „nicht etabliert", „anders", „selbstironisch" und „rebellisch" zum Ausdruck. Diese Andersartigkeit wird nicht nur von allen Vereinsangestellten sowie den Partnern und Fans des Vereins gelebt, sondern auch in kreativen Ideen umgesetzt. Um trotz der finanziellen Engpässe die strategischen Marketingziele zu erreichen, wird in den meisten Bereichen systematisch mit Partnern zusammengearbeitet.

Die *Analyse der internen und externen Umwelt* beschränkt sich bei St. Pauli hauptsächlich auf eine Wettbewerberanalyse. In unmittelbarer Konkurrenz zum FC St. Pauli stehen der Fußballbundesligist Hamburger SV, der Eishockey-Club Hamburg Freezers, der Herrenhandball-Bundesligist HSV Handball sowie der Damenhandball-Bundesligist Buxtehuder SV. Doch auch andere Anbieter (Kinocenter, Theater, Musicals oder sonstige Kulturangebote) konkurrieren um die Freizeit der Hamburger Bevölkerung. Um das eigene Angebot einschätzen und gegebenenfalls verbessern zu können, werden Vergleichsstudien und Fanbefragungen (z.B. per Stadionheft oder Internet) durchgeführt.

Die *Produktpolitik* konzentriert sich beim FC St. Pauli auf zwei Bereiche. Im Bereich Sponsoring werden den jeweiligen Sponsoren individuelle Kombinationen diverser Werberechte (z.B. TV-Banden, Hospitality, Gewinnspiele, Anzeigen im Stadionheft) angeboten. Des Weiteren wird versucht, mit gemeinsamen Aktionen einen möglichst hohen Return on Investment für den Sponsoringpartner zu erzielen und die Marken der Sponsoren mit der Clubmarke zusammenzuführen. Die Andersartigkeit des gesamten Clubumfelds kommt beispielsweise in kreativen Botschaften zum Ausdruck, die aufgrund der Markenattribute nur auf St. Pauli funktionieren (z.B. die selbstironische Bandenwerbung von Toyota „FC St. Pauli – Deutscher Meister 2010" und Peugeot „Der ganze Kiez steht auf Französisch", oder die Anpreisung einer Sprecherkabine inklusive eines Kasten Bier als „die kleinste VIP-Lounge der Welt"). Der zweite Aspekt der Produktpolitik bezieht sich auf das Thema Merchandising. Um eine weitere Einkommensquelle zu erschließen, wurde im Merchandisingbereich diversifiziert und mit der Kollektion „20359" (die Postleitzahl des Hamburger Stadtteils St. Pauli) ein fußballfremdes Modelabel ins Leben gerufen. Die 20359-Kleidungsstücke werden in ganz normalen Bekleidungsgeschäften verkauft, was unterstreicht, dass der FC St. Pauli nicht nur für Fußball, sondern auch für ein Lebensgefühl steht.

Bei der *Preisbildung* für Eintrittskarten und Dauerkarten orientiert man sich zum einen am Markt (d.h. an den Preisen der ortsansässigen Sportclubs) und zum anderen am Einkommensniveau der St. Pauli-Fans (konkurrenz- bzw. nachfrageorientierte Preisbildung). Bei den Kartenpreisen werden verschiedene Instrumente der Preisdifferenzierung angewandt. So zahlen Studenten, Rentner und Arbeitslose beispielsweise nur zwei Drittel des regulären Ticketpreises.

Durch das geringe Marketingbudget stehen dem FC St. Pauli nur eingeschränkte *Kommunikationsmaßnahmen* zur Verfügung, um Botschaften zu kommunizieren und die Marke zu entwickeln. Durch kreative Ideen und enge Kooperationen mit Sponsoren wird aber auch mit bescheidenen Mitteln vergleichsweise viel erreicht. So wird zum Beispiel jede Saison unter ein bestimmtes Motto gestellt. Das Motto der Saison 2006/07 „Rock'n'Roll – wir rocken die Liga" wird durch den eigenen Internetauftritt, den Fanartikelkatalog und das punkrockige Spielertrikot ausgedrückt. Des Weiteren werden in Eigenregie kreative und selbstironische Spielankündigungsplakate in Hamburgs Geschäften und Kneipen ausgehängt sowie durch Medien- und Sponsorenpartnerschaften großflächige Anzeigen im Outdoor- und Zeitungsbereich geschaltet. Durch das Alleinstellungsmerkmal „Andersartigkeit" wird darüber hinaus versucht, Aufmerksamkeit zu erlangen. Eine Weihnachtskarte zeigte einen nackten Weihnachtsmann mit St.-Pauli-Tattoo auf dem Allerwertesten unter der Dusche, was prompt die Bild-Zeitung zu einem ganzseitigen Artikel veranlasste. Kreative Kampagnen wie diese führen immer wieder zu einer verstärkten Berichterstattung in den Medien, wodurch die Botschaft multipliziert und die Kontaktzahl erhöht wird, was wiederum der Marke St. Pauli zugute kommt und bei Sponsorengesprächen ein wichtiges Verkaufsargument darstellt.

Um die Effektivität diverser Marketingaktivitäten zu evaluieren, werden vereinzelt Instrumente des *Marketingcontrolling* eingesetzt. So wird der Erfolg einer

Mailingaktion beispielsweise anhand der Rücklaufquote gemessen. Auch im Marketingcontrolling arbeitet man mit Sponsoren zusammen, um durch deren Marktforschungsstudien den Bekanntheits- und Imagegrad des FC St. Pauli zu messen.

Insgesamt ist es beeindruckend, wie professionell im Marketingbereich des FC St. Pauli mit begrenzten Ressourcen gearbeitet wird. Fehlende Finanzmittel werden durch kreative Ideen und sinnvolle Kooperationen mit Partnern und Sponsoren des Vereins ausgeglichen. Die St.-Pauli-spezifischen Attribute spielen in den Marketingaktiviäten eine herausragende Rolle und werden immer in den Vordergrund gestellt. Dadurch wird nicht nur die Marke FC St. Pauli gepflegt und gefördert, sondern es werden auch Aktionen ermöglicht, die in dieser Art und Weise nur auf St. Pauli funktionieren. Der FC St. Pauli ist somit ein hervorragendes Beispiel dafür, wie professionelle Sportorganisationen mit geringem Budget systematisch und erfolgreich Marketing betreiben können.

12.7 Fazit und Ausblick

Das Sportmarketing hat sich in den letzten Jahren nicht nur zu einem bedeutenden Wirtschaftssektor, sondern auch zu einer eigenständigen Wissenschaftsdisziplin entwickelt. Die Etablierung von akademischen Journals im Bereich Sportmarketing (z.B. International Journal of Sport Marketing and Sponsorship; Sport Marketing Quaterly; Sport Marketing Europe), die regelmäßige Durchführung diverser Sportmarketing-Kongresse (z.B. der Deutsche Sportökonomiekongress in Köln; der ISPO-Sportsponsoringkongress in München; das Sportbusiness-Forum in Heidelberg) als auch die Gründung diverser Sportmarketingorganisationen (z.B. die Sports Interest Group der Academy of Marketing, The European Network of Sports Marketing Academics) führen zu einem stetigen Wissenstransfer zwischen Theorie und Praxis. Immer mehr professionelle Sportorganisationen beschäftigen Marketingfachleute, was wiederum zu einer zunehmenden Professionalisierung im Sportmarketing führt. Betrachtet man die verschiedenen betriebswirtschaftlichen Disziplinen, so nimmt das Sportmarketing innerhalb der Sportökonomie eine Vorreiter-Rolle ein und ist bereits mit am weitesten ausdifferenziert. Allerdings bleibt festzuhalten, dass es immer noch genügend professionelle Sportorganisationen (Clubs wie Verbände) gibt, die amateurhaftes Marketing betreiben und sich der Bedeutung und der Möglichkeiten des modernen Sportmarketing nicht bewusst sind. Trotz aller positiven Signale gibt es also noch genügend Verbesserungspotential. Sportmarketing wird in den nächsten Jahren v.a. aus zweierlei Gründen noch weiter an Bedeutung gewinnen: Zum einen wird sich der Wettbewerb auf dem Freizeit- und Vergnügungsmarkt noch weiter verschärfen und somit professionelle Sportorganisationen geradezu dazu zwingen, ihre Produkte, ihre Angebote und sich selbst besser zu vermarkten. Zum anderen wird der Sport weiterhin Menschen begeistern und somit ein attraktives Umfeld für werbetreibende Unternehmen darstellen. Der zu-künftige Erfolg des Sportmarketing hängt von der Kreativität der Protagonisten und deren Fähigkeiten, neue Vermarktungspotentiale zu entwickeln, ab. Bei allen Innovationen und Wachstumsbestrebungen darf die Glaubwürdigkeit des Sports dabei allerdings niemals aufs Spiel gesetzt werden.

Kontrollfragen

1. Welche Aufgaben hat das Marketing?
2. Durch welche Phasen zeichnet sich eine systematische Marketingkonzeption aus?
3. Welche Instrumente stehen Unternehmen in der operativen Marketingplanung zur Verfügung?
4. In welchen Punkten unterscheidet sich Sportmarketing von allgemeinem Marketing?
5. Warum kann Sportmarketing als eine eigenständige Marketingform betrachtet werden?
6. Warum ist eine profunde Analyse der internen und externen Umwelt so wichtig für professionelle Sportorganisationen?
7. Welche Möglichkeiten haben professionelle Sportorganisationen, um ihre strategischen Marketingziele zu erreichen?
8. Welche kommunikationspolitischen Instrumente können professionelle Sportorganisationen nutzen, um ihre Produkte und sich selbst zu vermarkten?
9. Warum ist ein systematisches Marketingcontrolling so wichtig für professionelle Sportorganisationen?
10. Wie ist der gegenwärtige Stand des Sportmarketing und wie wird sich Sportmarketing Ihrer Meinung nach in den nächsten Jahren entwickeln?

Literaturverzeichnis

Banks, Simon (2002): Going Down – Football in Crisis, Edinburgh.

Becker, Jochen (2001): Marketing-Konzeption. Grundlagen des ziel-strategischen und operativen Marketing-Managements, 7. Aufl., München.

Berekoven, Ludwig / Eckert, Werner / Ellenrieder, Peter (2004): Marktforschung. Methodische Grundlagen und praktische Anwendung, 10. Aufl., Wiesbaden.

Berndt, Ralph (2004): Marketingstrategie und Marketingpolitik, 4. Aufl., Berlin u.a.

Bruhn, Manfred (2004): Marketing, 7. Aufl., Wiesbaden.

Bühler, André W. (2005): Fans und Fanverhalten im Profifußball: Ein Vergleich zwischen England und Deutschland, in: Schewe, Gerhard / Rohlmann, Peter (Hrsg.): Sportmarketing, Schorndorf, S. 221–236.

Bühler, André W. (2006a): Professional Football Sponsorship in the English Premier League and the German Bundesliga, Dissertation, Berlin.

Bühler, André W. (2006b): Football as an international business – an Anglo-German comparison, in: European Journal for Sport and Society, Heft 3, S. 25-41.

Bühler, André W. / Nufer, Gerd (2006): The Nature of Sports Marketing, Reutlingen Working Paper on Marketing & Management No. 2006-6, School of International Business, Reutlingen University.

Cashmore, Ellis (2003): The marketing Midas with a golden boot, in: The Times Higher, London, 26.09.2003, S. 22-23.

Conn, David (2001): The Football Business, 5. Aufl., Edinburgh.

Dempsey, Paul / Reilly, Kevan (1998): Big money, beautiful game – saving soccer from itself, London.

Fantapié Altobelli, Claudia (2006): Marktforschung. Methoden - Anwendungen - Praxisbeispiele, Stuttgart.

Hermanns, Arnold / Riedmüller, Florian (2001): Standortbestimmung des Sportmarketing, in: Hermanns, Arnold / Riedmüller, Florian (Hrsg.): Management-Handbuch Sport-Marketing, München, S. 57-87.

Kaser, Ken / Oelkers, Dotty B. (2005): Sports and Entertainment Marketing, Mason.

Kotler, Philip (1994): Marketing Management, London.

Kotler, Philip (1997): Marketing Management, 9. Aufl., Upper Saddle River.

Kotler, Philip / Armstrong, Gary / Saunders, John / Wong, Veronica (2007): Grundlagen des Marketing, 4. Aufl., München.

Meffert, Heribert (2000): Marketing. Grundlagen marktorientierter Unternehmensführung, 9. Aufl., Wiesbaden.

Meffert, Heribert / Bruhn, Manfred (1997): Dienstleistungsmarketing, Wiesbaden.

Morrow, Stephen (1999): The New Business of Football – Accountability and Finance in Football, London.

Nufer, Gerd (2002): Wirkungen von Sportsponsoring. Empirische Analyse am Beispiel der Fußball-Weltmeisterschaft 1998 in Frankreich unter besonderer Berücksichtigung von Erinnerungswirkungen bei jugendlichen Rezipienten, Berlin.

Nufer, Gerd (2007): Event-Marketing und -Management. Theorie und Praxis unter besonderer Berücksichtigung von Imagewirkungen, 3. Aufl., Wiesbaden.

Pierpoint, Barrie (2000): Heads above Water: Business Strategies for a New Football Economy, in: Garland, Jon / Rowe, Michael / Malcolm, Dominic (Hrsg.): The Future of Football – Challenges for the Twenty-First Century, London, S. 29-38.

Pilot Group (2006): Sponsors Vision 2006, Hamburg.

Pilot Group (2007): Sponsors Vision 2007, Hamburg.

PR Marketing (2006): 9. Fanartikel-Barometer, Herne.

Ramme, Iris (2004): Marketing. Einführung mit Fallbeispielen, Aufgaben und Lösungen, 2. Aufl., Stuttgart.

Sander, Matthias (2004): Marketing-Management. Märkte, Marktinformationen und Marktbearbeitung, Stuttgart.

Shilbury, David / Quick, Shayne / Westerbeek, Hans (1998): Strategic Sport Marketing, Crow Nest.

Van Heerden, Cornelius H. (2001): Factors affecting decision-making in South African sport sponsorships, Doctoral Thesis, University of Pretoria.

VfB Stuttgart Marketing GmbH (2007): Werbeanzeige für den VfB Stuttgart, Stuttgart.

Weis, Hans C. (2004): Marketing, 13. Aufl., Ludwigshafen.

Weiterführende Ressourcen

Literatur

Beech, John / Chadwick, Simon (Hrsg.) (2004): The Business of Sport Management, Harlow.

Breuer, Christoph / Thiel, Ansgar (Hrsg.) (2005): Handbuch Sportmanagement, Schorndorf.

Bruhn, Manfred (2003): Sponsoring. Systematische Planung und integrativer Einsatz, 4. Aufl., Wiesbaden.

Bruhn, Manfred (2005): Unternehmens- und Marketingkommunikation. Handbuch für ein integriertes Kommunikationsmanagement, München.

Freyer, Walter (2003): Sport-Marketing. Handbuch für marktorientiertes Management im Sport, 3. Aufl., Dresden.

Hermanns, Arnold (1997): Sponsoring. Grundlagen, Wirkungen, Management, Perspektiven, 2. Aufl., München 1997.

Horch, Heinz-Dieter / Heydel, Jörg / Sierau, Axel (Hrsg.) (2004): Events im Sport - Marketing, Management, Finanzierung, Köln.

Horch, Heinz-Dieter / Hovemann, Gregor / Kaiser, Sebastian / Viebahn, Kai (Hrsg.) (2005): Perspektiven des Sportmarketing. Besonderheiten, Herausforderungen, Tendenzen, Köln.

Krüger, Arnd / Dreyer, Axel (Hrsg.) (2004): Sportmanagement, München.

Nufer, Gerd (2005): Ambush Marketing - Angriff aus dem Hinterhalt oder eine Alternative zum Sportsponsoring? in: Horch, Heinz-Dieter / Hovemann, Gregor / Kaiser, Sebastian / Viebahn, Kai (Hrsg.): Perspektiven des Sportmarketing. Besonderheiten, Herausforderungen, Tendenzen, Köln, S. 209-227.

Nufer, Gerd (2006): Wirkungsvolles WM-Sponsoring, in: Absatzwirtschaft, Heft 11, S. 65.

Nufer, Gerd / Bühler, André W. (2006): Lessons from Sports: What Corporate Management can learn from Sports Management, Reutlingen Working Paper on Marketing & Management No. 2006-7, School of International Business, Reutlingen University.

Rennhak, Carsten (2006): Herausforderung Kundenbindung, Wiesbaden.

Trosien, Gerhard (2003): Sportökonomie. Ein Lehrbuch in 15 Lektionen, Aachen.

Walliser, Björn (1995): Sponsoring. Bedeutung, Wirkung und Kontrollmöglichkeiten, Wiesbaden.

Woratschek, Herbert (1998): Sportdienstleistungen aus ökonomischer Sicht, in: Sportwissenschaft, Heft 3-4, S. 344-357.

Zieschang, Klaus / Woratschek, Herbert / Baier, Klaus (Hrsg.) (2004): Kooperenz im Sportmanagement, Schorndorf.

Links

Bayreuther Sportökonomie-Kongress:
http://www.sportoekonomie.uni-bayreuth.de/kongress

Deutscher Sportökonomie-Kongress, Köln:
http://www.deutscher-sportoekonomie-kongress.de

Heidelberger Sportbusiness Forum (Kongress):
http://www.sportbusiness.de

Horizont Sport Business (Fachzeitschrift):
http://www.horizont-sportbusiness.de

International Journal of Sports Marketing and Sponsorship (Fachzeitschrift):
http://www.imrpublications.com/JSMS

ISPO Sportsponsoringkongress, München:
http://www.sportsponsoringkongress.de

Sponsors (Fachzeitschrift):
http://www.sponsors.de

Sport + Markt (Marktforschungsunternehmen), Köln:
http://www.sportundmarkt.com

Sport Marketing Europe (Fachzeitschrift):
http://www.sportmarketingeurope.com

Sport Marketing Quaterly (Fachzeitschrift):
http://www.fitinfotech.com/smq/smq.tpl

Sportfive (Sportrechteagentur), Hamburg:
http://www.sportfive.de

Teil III:

Sportmarketing –

aktuelle Entwicklungen und Trends

Kapitel 13: Markenmanagement im Sport

Michael Schilhaneck

Lernziele

Nach der Durchsicht dieses Kapitels sollte der Leser in der Lage sein,

- die Begriffe (Unternehmens-)Marke und Markenmanagement zu definieren.
- die Konstrukte des Markenwerts und der Markenstärke zu erläutern.
- die Markenfunktionen aus Nachfrager- und Anbietersicht zu beschreiben.
- die ökonomischen Branchenbesonderheiten des professionellen Teamsports benennen sowie kurz umschreiben zu können.
- die strategischen Basisentscheidungen des Clubmarkenmanagementprozesses zu erklären.
- die wichtigsten Kernwerte von Clubmarken aufzählen zu können.
- die zentralen Instrumente des Clubmarkenmanagements benennen sowie deren Zusammenwirken erklären zu können.
- determinierende Rahmenfaktoren des Clubmarkenmanagements zu skizzieren.

Überblick über das Kapitel

Das vorliegende Kapitel setzt sich mit dem Markenmanagement von Proficlubs auseinander. Ausgehend von einer kurzen Einführung in die Thematik werden zunächst die Grundlagen des Markenmanagements ausgeführt (begriffliche Grundlagen, Konstrukte Markenwert und Markenstärke, Markenfunktionen, branchenunspezifischer Markenführungsansatz). Daraufhin werden ökonomische Besonderheiten der Branche des professionellen Teamsports sowie sich daraus ergebende Probleme für das Markenmanagement von Proficlubs erläutert. Weiterführend wird ein spezifisches Markenmanagementmodell für Proficlubs vorgestellt und dessen Komponenten näher erläutert. Anhand eines Fallbeispiels aus der nordamerikanischen National Hockey League (NHL) werden die Inhalte des Modells abschließend veranschaulicht.

13.1 Einführung in die Thematik

Die wirtschaftliche Bedeutung der Clubmarke wird insbesondere durch die empirischen Untersuchungen von Gladden/Milne (1999) bzw. Bauer/Sauer/Schmitt (2004) belegt. In beiden Studien konnte ein signifikanter Einfluss der Clubmarke auf den ökonomischen Erfolg der Profisportorganisationen nachgewiesen werden. Gleichzeitig deuten Marktforschungsergebnisse regelmäßig und unmissverständlich auf Defizite im Markenmanagement von Proficlubs hin. So zeigen beispielsweise Umfrageresultate, dass die deutschen Fußballprofiiclubs zwar einen relativ hohen nationalen Bekanntheitsgrad erzielen, das mit den Clubmarken verbundene Vorstellungsbild in den meisten Fällen jedoch sehr unscharf und diffus ausfällt. Eigenständige und prägnante Clubmarkenpositionierungen werden nur selten erreicht (UFA Sports, 1998, 2000; Sportfive, 2002, 2004).

Der Frage, der dieses Kapitel nachgeht, lautet deshalb wie folgt: Welche Komponenten und Kombinationsprozesse sind für ein erfolgreiches Markenmanagement von Proficlubs relevant? Der Beitrag hat das Ziel, dem Leser die Grundlagen des Markenmanagements zu vermitteln, die sich aus den ökonomischen Branchenbesonderheiten des professionellen Teamsports ergebenden Probleme des Markenmanagements von Proficlubs zu verdeutlichen sowie Managementlösungen dazu aufzuzeigen. Darüber hinaus soll dem Leser ein idealtypisches Markenmanagementprozessmodell für Proficlubs vorgestellt werden.

13.2 Grundlagen des Markenmanagements

Nachfolgend werden die begrifflichen Grundlagen sowie die Konstrukte des Markenwerts und der Markenstärke erläutert. Weiterführend werden die Funktionen der Marke aus Nachfrager- und Anbieterperspektive beschrieben sowie der identitätsorientierte Markenführungsansatz nach Meffert/Burmann (2002) vorgestellt.

13.2.1 Begriffliche Grundlagen

Nach Meffert/Burmann/Koers (2002, S. 6) sind Marken als ein „in der Psyche des Konsumenten und sonstiger Bezugsgruppen der Marke fest verankertes, unverwechselbares Vorstellungsbild von einem Produkt oder einer Dienstleistung" zu verstehen.

Dieses geistige Bild repräsentiert die affektiven (gefühlsmäßige Einschätzungen), kognitiven (subjektives Wissen) sowie konativen (Verhaltensabsichten, Kaufbereitschaft) Einstellungskomponenten gegenüber der Marke. Voraussetzung dazu ist, dass die markierte Leistung sowohl langfristig, in gleichartigem Auftritt als auch in gleich bleibender oder verbesserter Qualität angeboten wird.

Die Marke als Vorstellungsbild resultiert aus einer Vielzahl über einen längeren Zeitraum durchgeführter Marketingmaßnahmen und der sich daraus ergebenden direkten und indirekten Erfahrungen der Marktteilnehmer. Die Planung, Koordinierung und Kontrolle dieser Maßnahmen wird als Markenmanagement bezeichnet (Esch, 2003; Meffert/Burmann/Koers, 2002).

13.2.2 Die Konstrukte des Markenwerts und der Markenstärke

Im Folgenden werden die Konstrukte des Markenwerts und der Markenstärke vorgestellt und deren Zusammenhang erklärt.

13.2.2.1 Markenwert

Zur Erfassung des Markenwerts ist zwischen einer konsumerbezogenen und einer unternehmensbezogenen Sichtweise zu unterscheiden.

Betrachtet man zunächst die *Konsumerperspektive*, kommt dem Markenwert ein verhaltenssteuernder Charakter zu. So beeinflusst die Marke als Vorstellungsbild im Gedächtnis der Marktteilnehmer nur dann das Kaufverhalten positiv, wenn mit ihr ein Mehrwert bzw. Zusatznutzen verbunden wird. Dieser Mehrwert basiert auf einem von dem Nachfrager vollzogenen Vergleich zwischen einer markierten sowie einer unmarkierten Leistung mit den jeweils gleichen Leistungsmerkmalen (z.B. T-Shirt weiß: 20 €; identisches T-Shirt mit Club-Logo-Bestickung: 30 €). Der wahrgenommene Zusatznutzen der Marke (z.B. Imageübertrag, Prestigeerfüllung, Identitätskonstruktion durch „Markennutzung") repräsentiert den Markenwert aus Konsumentensicht und schlägt sich im Kaufverhalten nieder (Kauf oder Nicht-Kauf).

Im Rahmen der *Unternehmensperspektive* ist der Markenwert hingegen ökonomisch zu interpretieren. Der ökonomische Markenwert basiert auf dem von den Konsumenten wahrgenommenen Zusatznutzen der Marke und wird als Preisprämie operationalisiert, die der Nachfrager für ein mit einer Marke versehenes Produkt gegenüber dem identischen, unmarkierten Produkt zu zahlen bereit ist. Hochgerechnet ist der ökonomische Markenwert demnach als jener Teil des Gewinns zu verstehen, der auf die Leistungsmarkierung zurückzuführen ist (Biel, 2001; Esch, 2003; Meffert/Burmann/Koers, 2002).

13.2.2.2 Markenstärke

Grundlage des zuvor umschriebenen ökonomischen Markenwerts ist die Markenstärke. Diese definiert sich anhand der tatsächlichen Kaufverhaltensrelevanz der im Gedächtnis der Konsumenten abgespeicherten Vorstellungen (Bruhn/Hennig-Thurau/Hadwich, 2004; Meffert/Burman/Koers, 2002).

Die Markenstärke wird über drei interdependente Dimensionen bestimmt:
a) Markenbekanntheit,
b) Markenassoziationen,
c) Markentreue.

Die *Markenbekanntheit* beschreibt die Fähigkeit des Konsumenten, sich an eine Marke unter verschiedenen Umständen zu erinnern bzw. diese zu identifizieren. Markenbekanntheit bedeutet, einer Leistung eine Grundidentität zu geben, indem die Markierungselemente wie Name und Logo mit einer bestimmten Leistungs- und Nutzenkategorie verbunden werden (best-case-scenario: Konsumenten denken an die betreffende Marke, wenn sie von der jeweiligen Leistungs- oder Nutzenkategorie bzw. Branchenart hören). Die Bedeutung der Markenbekanntheit für die Markenstärke beruht v.a. auf folgenden beiden Aspekten:

- Markenbekanntheit muss gegeben sein, damit eine Marke für eine Kaufentscheidung überhaupt berücksichtigt werden kann.
- Nur wenn Markenbekanntheit vorhanden ist, kann der Konsument weitere Assoziationen bilden und speichern.

Jedoch zeigen Untersuchungen, dass die Markenbekanntheit als isolierte Größe nur eine gering positive Korrelation zu nachgelagerten, erfolgskritischen Größen wie der Kaufwahrscheinlichkeit oder der zusätzlichen Zahlungsbereitschaft aufweist. Dies bedeutet folglich, dass die Markenbekanntheit zwar eine notwendige, jedoch nicht hinreichende Bedingung für die Markenstärke ist (Aaker, 1991; Bruhn/Hennig-Thurau/Hadwich, 2004; Esch, 2003; Meffert/Burman/Koers, 2002; Keller, 1993; Keller, 1998).

Markenassoziationen sind all das, was Kunden mit einer Marke in Verbindung bringen. Sie reflektieren direkte Charakteristika der Marke sowie Merkmale, welche die Bedeutung der Marke für den Kunden widerspiegeln. Markenassoziationen entstehen in komplexen Prozessen im Kopf von Individuen, wobei diese Vorgänge durch direkte sowie indirekte Erfahrungen mit der Marke beeinflusst und gesteuert werden. Je nach Qualität und Quantität der Markeninformationen und Markenerfahrungen erreichen die Markenassoziationen ein bestimmtes Ausprägungs- bzw. Stärkeniveau. Die Summe der wahrgenommenen und im Gedächtnis gespeicherten Assoziationen bildet das Markenimage. Insgesamt gilt: Je lebendiger, klarer, angenehmer und eigenständiger die Markenassoziationen in den Köpfen der Rezipienten leben, desto größer ist ihr Einfluss auf das menschliche Verhalten. In Anknüpfung an die Formulierung zur Markenbekanntheit sind die Markenassoziationen als die hinreichende Größe der Markenstärke zu kennzeichnen (Aaker, 1991; Esch, 2003; Keller, 1998). Markenassoziationsformen von Proficlubs sind beispielsweise bildliche Vorstellungen von den Markenproduzenten (Spieler, Trainer, Management), den Markenkonsumenten (Fans, VIPs) oder dem Umfeld, in dem die Marke genutzt wird (Stadion), leistungsbezogene Attribute (technisch, ästhetisch, kampfbetont usw.), mit der Clubmarke verbundene Gestaltungsparameter (Vereinsfarben, Logo etc.) aber auch emotionale Ausdrucksformen wie die Clubsympathie.

Starke Marken zeichnen sich insbesondere durch eine hohe *Markentreue* aus. Von Markentreue bzw. Markenloyalität wird dann gesprochen, wenn der Marktpartner eine positive Einstellung gegenüber der Marke besitzt und diese wiederholt nachfragt. Neben der charakteristischen Wiederabnahme der Leistung zeichnen sich markentreue Kunden des Weiteren durch folgende absatzrelevante Eigenschaften aus: Sie verfügen über eine hohe Kaufbereitschaft gegenüber anderen Leistungen des Markeneigners, weisen eine geringe Aufgeschlossenheit und Wechselbereitschaft gegenüber Konkurrenzangeboten auf, besitzen eine hohe Preistoleranz und sind als wichtige Mund-zu-Mund-Kommunikatoren (Weiterempfehlungen) der Marke zu sehen. Im Gegensatz zu den beiden zuvor erläuterten Dimensionen setzt die Markentreue einen Leistungskonsum und somit eine Gebrauchserfahrung voraus. Markenloyalität stellt die finale Konsequenz des Aufbaus von starken Marken dar (Aaker, 1991; Aaker, 1996; Aaker/Joachimsthaler, 2001; Bruhn/Hennig-Thurau/Hadwich, 2004; Esch, 2003; Meffert/Burman/Koers, 2002).

Fazit: Die beschriebenen Dimensionen der Markenstärke (Markenbekanntheit, Markenassoziationen, Markentreue) sind als managementnahe Markenbezugsgrößen zu verstehen. An diesen hat das Clubmarkenmanagement anzusetzen. Gleichzeitig geben Veränderungen in jenen Dimensionen Aufschluss über den Erfolg der ausgeführten Marketingmaßnahmen.

13.2.3 Funktionen der Marke aus Nachfrager- und Anbietersicht

Die vorausgehenden Ausführungen deuten bereits an, dass die Marke sowohl für das Unternehmen als auch die Konsumenten unterschiedliche Funktionen erfüllt. Im Folgenden werden diese beiden Perspektiven näher erläutert.

13.2.3.1 Funktion von Marken aus Nachfragersicht

Marken übernehmen für die Konsumenten folgende Funktionen (Biel, 2001; Esch, 2003; Meffert/Burmann/Koers, 2002):

- *Orientierungsfunktion/Entlastungsfunktion*: Das Wiedererkennen einer Marke erleichtert die Orientierung in der Vielfalt der Angebote (Leistungsidentifizierungshilfe). Die Orientierungsfunktion der Marke kommt somit dem Bequemlichkeitsstreben der Nachfrager entgegen (Entlastung durch Reduktion von Such- und Informationsaufwand).

- *Vertrauensfunktion/Qualitätsfunktion*: Starke Marken signalisieren eine bestimmte Leistungsqualität. Das der Marke dadurch entgegengebrachte Vertrauen reduziert bestehendes Kaufrisiko und erleichtert die Kaufentscheidung.

- *Prestigefunktion*: Die Nutzung exklusiver Marken kann für den Nachfrager zu einer Prestigeerfüllung im sozialen Umfeld beitragen (z.B. Rolex, Jaguar, Hugo Boss).

- *Identifikationsfunktion/Identitätsfunktion*: Marken kommen verschiedene identitätsstiftende Wirkungen zu. Einerseits überträgt der Konsument bestimmte Attribute der Marke, mit der er sich identifiziert, durch deren Nutzung auf sich selbst und formt dadurch sein Eigenbild. Weitere Beiträge zur Identitäts- bzw. Selbstkonzeptkonstruktion erfährt der Nachfrager dadurch, dass Marken sowohl soziale Gruppenzugehörigkeit als auch bestimmte Wertvorstellungen sowie Einstellungen ausdrücken.

Je nach Branche kommt den ausgeführten Markenfunktionen eine unterschiedliche Bedeutung zu. So entfallen bei Versicherungsunternehmen beispielsweise die Prestige- sowie die Identifikationsfunktion, vielmehr spielt die Orientierungs- und Entlastungsfunktion sowie die Qualitäts- und Vertrauensfunktion eine entscheidende

Rolle. Bei Lebensmitteln des täglichen Bedarfs sind wiederum Orientierungs-, Entlastungs- und Qualitätsfunktion als kennzeichnende Markenfunktionen herauszustellen, während in der Automobilindustrie die Qualitäts- und Vertrauensfunktion, die Prestigefunktion sowie die Identifikationsfunktion der Automarke von primärer Kaufrelevanz sind. Auch für Proficlubs sind einige der ausgeführten Markenfunktionen hervorzuheben: So ist für die Fans v.a. die Identifikationsfunktion der Clubmarke bestimmend (Übertrag von Clubmarkenassoziationen zur Eigenidentitätskonstruktion, Zugehörigkeitsausdruck zur Fangemeinschaft). Im Fall von Hospitalitykunden ist neben der Identifikationsfunktion v.a. die Prestigefunktion der Markennutzung hervorzuheben. Die Qualitäts- und Vertrauensfunktion von Clubmarken ist demgegenüber wiederum bei finanzintensiven Sponsoringengagements verhaltensentscheidend (z.B. FC Bayern München).

Vor dem Hintergrund dieser Ausführungen kommt einer Leistung/einem Produkt/einem Unternehmen/einer Organisation dann ein *Markenstatus* zu, wenn die branchenrelevanten, nachfragerseitigen Markenfunktionen erfüllt werden.

13.2.3.2 Funktion von Marken aus Anbietersicht

Für Unternehmen erfüllen starke Marken ebenfalls eine Vielzahl an Funktionen (Biel, 2001; Esch, 2003; Meffert/Burmann/Koers, 2002):

- *Differenzierungsfunktion*: Eine starke Unternehmensmarke dient dem Anbieter zur Differenzierung bzw. Profilierung des eigenen Angebots gegenüber dem der Konkurrenz (Markenimage als Differenzierungsinstrument).
- *Präferenzbildungsfunktion*: Kaufentscheidung zugunsten des Anbieters aufgrund positiver Markenassoziationen (Markenimage als Präferenzbildungsinstrument).
- *Kundenbindungsfunktion*: Starke Marken realisieren eine höhere Markentreue als schwache Marken (Planungssicherheit durch Kundenbindungseffekte starker Marken).
- *Stabilisationsfunktion*: Starke Marken schützen die unternehmenseigenen Produkte/Leistungen vor Krisen (Fehlertoleranz, starke Marken erhalten eine zweite Chance). Sie stärken die Wettbewerbsposition und schaffen Wettbewerbsbarrieren.
- *Erweiterungsfunktion*: Starke Marken bieten eine Plattform für neue Produkte/Leistungen bzw. können für Lizenzierungen genutzt werden.
- *Preispolitischer Spielraum*: Je besser es Unternehmen gelingt, ihre Marke im Vergleich zur Konkurrenz als „einzigartig" zu positionieren, desto höher fällt der preispolitische Spielraum aus.

Fasst man die Ausführungen zu den Markenfunktionen aus Anbietersicht zusammen, so ist festzuhalten, dass diese jeweils einen Beitrag zur Wertsteigerung des Unternehmens liefern.

13.2.4 Der identitätsorientierte Markenführungsansatz nach Meffert/Burmann
Aufgrund der ständig wechselnden Veränderungen der Markt- und Umweltbedingungen hat das Markenmanagement im Laufe der Zeit zahlreiche Neuausrichtungen durchlaufen. Die letzte Entwicklungsstufe ist durch eine starke Identitätsorientierung gekennzeichnet (identitätsorientierte Markenführung). Zurückzuführen ist dies auf die sozialwissenschaftliche Interpretation des Markenkonstrukts, im Rahmen dessen die Kaufverhaltensrelevanz einer Marke insbesondere durch die Ausprägung der Markenidentität erklärt wird. Das Modell von Meffert/Burmann (2002) stellt einen anerkannten Ansatz der identitätsorientierten Markenführung dar und wird nachfolgend genauer vorgestellt.

Meffert/Burmann (2002) zufolge resultiert die Markenidentität aus der Wechselwirkung zwischen marktbezogenen Handlungen des Markeneigners und der Wahrnehmung dieser Aktivitäten durch die Marktpartner. Sie differenzieren in ihrem Modell demnach zwischen dem *Selbstbild* der Marke aus organisationsinterner Perspektive (= Aussagenkonzept) und dem *Fremdbild* der Marke aus Sicht der externen Anspruchsgruppen (= Akzeptanzkonzept). Das Markenselbstbild wird durch die Markenphilosophie als Kernkomponente sowie die vier Dimensionen „Marke als Produkt“, „Marke als Symbol“, „Marke als Organisation“ und „Marke als Person“ bestimmt. Jede der Markendimensionen ist wiederum in weitere Subkomponenten unterteilt. Durch die spezifische Ausprägung dieser Merkmale wird die Identität der Marke bestimmt und für den Kunden wahrnehmbar bzw. erlebbar. Jedoch kann die Bedeutung der verschiedenen Subkomponenten für die Entwicklung einer starken Markenidentität nicht pauschal festgelegt werden, vielmehr sind diese branchen- bzw. situationsspezifisch zu bewerten. Das Fremdbild der Markenidentität ist demgegenüber das Ergebnis der subjektiven Wahrnehmung, Dekodierung und Akzeptanz der von der Marke ausgehenden Impulse.

Abb. 1 zeigt den Ansatz der identitätsorientierten Markenführung nach Meffert/Burmann (2002) im Überblick.

13.3 Ökonomische Besonderheiten im professionellen Teamsport und daraus resultierende Probleme für das Clubmarkenmanagement

Wie in Abschnitt 13.1.1 ausgeführt, handelt es sich bei der Marke um ein subjektives, leistungsbezogenes Gedankenkonstrukt, dessen externe „Steuerung“ grundsätzlich problembehaftet ist. Neben dieser Schwierigkeit der Markenführung ist der professionelle Teamsport darüber hinaus durch einige ökonomische Besonderheiten gekennzeichnet, welche zusätzliche Problembereiche für das Clubmarkenmanagement darstellen. Folgende Aspekte sind in diesem Zusammenhang anzuführen:
- Hohe Kundengruppenheterogenität der Proficlubs.
- Kennzeichnende Dienstleistungsspezifika (Immaterialität, notwendige Einbringung eines externen Faktors, Erfahrungsgutcharakter).
- Besonderheiten in der Leistungserstellung (Koproduktion).

Nachfolgend werden diese Punkte näher ausgeführt und Anforderungen an das Markenmanagement von Proficlubs abgeleitet.

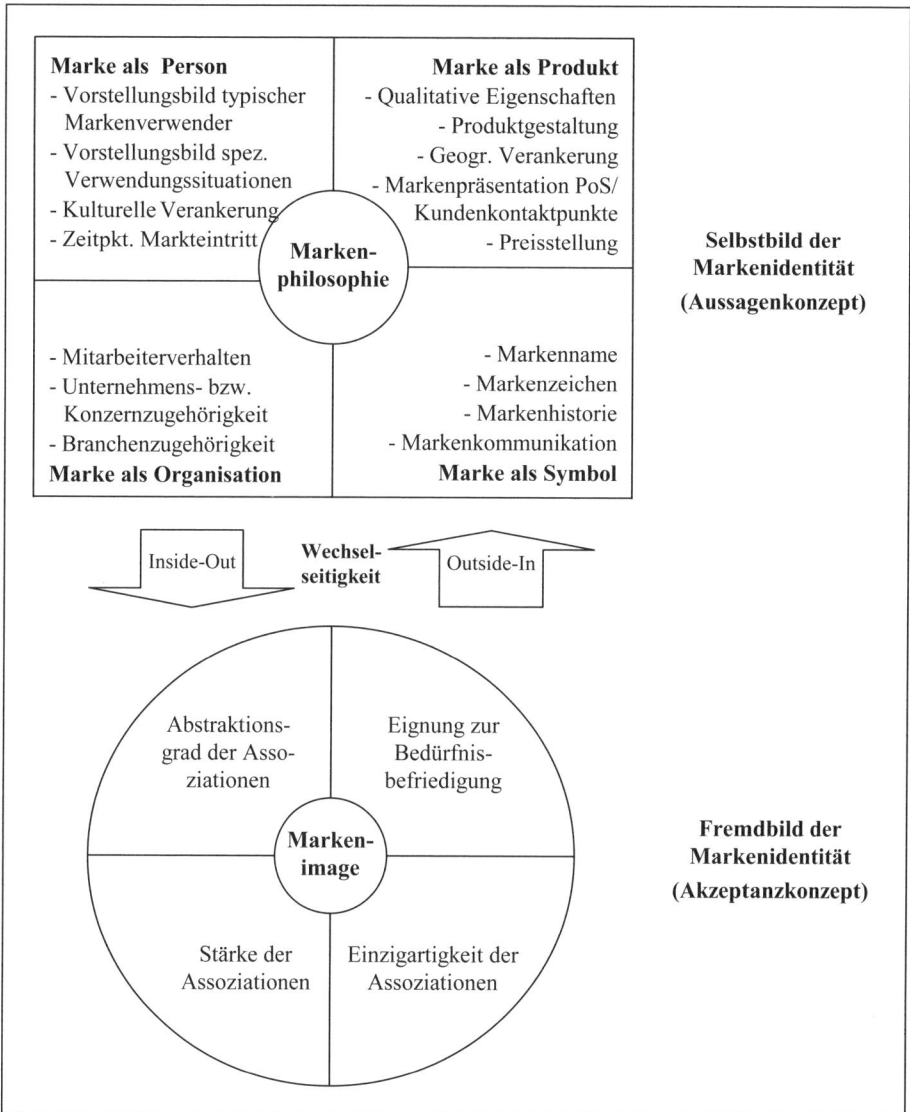

Marke als Person
- Vorstellungsbild typischer Markenverwender
- Vorstellungsbild spez. Verwendungssituationen
- Kulturelle Verankerung
- Zeitpkt. Markteintritt

Marke als Produkt
- Qualitative Eigenschaften
- Produktgestaltung
- Geogr. Verankerung
- Markenpräsentation PoS/ Kundenkontaktpunkte
- Preisstellung

Marken-philosophie

- Mitarbeiterverhalten
- Unternehmens- bzw. Konzernzugehörigkeit
- Branchenzugehörigkeit

Marke als Organisation

- Markenname
- Markenzeichen
- Markenhistorie
- Markenkommunikation

Marke als Symbol

Selbstbild der Markenidentität

(Aussagenkonzept)

Inside-Out

Wechsel-seitigkeit

Outside-In

Abstraktions-grad der Asso-ziationen

Eignung zur Bedürfnis-befriedigung

Marken-image

Stärke der Assoziationen

Einzigartigkeit der Assoziationen

Fremdbild der Markenidentität

(Akzeptanzkonzept)

Abb. 1: Identitätsorientierter Markenführungsansatz
In Anlehnung an: Meffert/Burmann (2002), S. 51

13.3.1 Besonderheit 1: Kundengruppenheterogenität

Proficlubs verfügen über folgende zentrale, jedoch äußerst heterogene Kunden-gruppen: direkte Zuschauer (Zuschauer vor Ort: Fans, Hospitalitykunden und Tagesbesucher wie Familien/Kinder), indirekte Zuschauer (TV-Publikum), Sponsoren, Lizenznehmer, Agenturen sowie Medien. Für das Clubmanagement leitet sich aus diesem Spannungsfeld unterschiedlicher zielgruppenspezifischer Wahrnehmungen ab, eine weitreichende Markenintegration in allen genannten Nachfragegruppen zu realisieren. Integration bedeutet dabei, möglichst viele konsensuelle Bereiche zwischen den verschiedenen Rezipienten zu schaffen und sie gleichermaßen an der Marke zu beteiligen, um ihnen ein gleichgerichtetes, „integriertes" Vorstellungsbild zu ermöglichen (corporate branding). Hier deutet sich bereits die Notwendigkeit eines umfassenden und verzahnten Einsatzes an geeigneten Marketingmix-Instrumenten an (Gladden/Irvin/Sutton, 2001; Meffert/Bierwirth, 2005).

13.3.2 Besonderheit 2: Dienstleistungsspezifika

Ein offensichtliches markentechnisches Problem resultiert daraus, dass die Immaterialität der von den Proficlubs angebotenen Dienstleistungen eine direkte Markierung nicht zulässt. Aufgrund dieses Visualisierungsproblems müssen alternative Markierungswege gefunden werden, die für eine Kennzeichnung im physischen Sinne zur Verfügung stehen. In diesem Zusammenhang erhalten alle internen sowie externen Kontaktsubjekte bzw. Kontaktobjekte eine zentrale markenpolitische Bedeutung (Bruhn, 2004; Benkenstein/Spiegel, 2004; Fassnacht, 2004; Schleuser 2002). Im Kontext von Proficlubs sind darunter beispielsweise Aspekte wie Dresscodes der Mitarbeiter, Markierung von Bezugsobjekten (Eintrittskarten, Merchandising, Plakatierungen, Drucksorten, Fuhrpark, Sitzplätze) sowie die Infrastrukturgestaltung (Stadion, Geschäftsstelle, Trainingsgelände, Fanshops, Vorverkaufsstellen, Clubheim) anzuführen.

Da sich die von Proficlubs angebotenen Dienstleistungen vorwiegend durch Erfahrungs- und Vertrauenseigenschaften auszeichnen, ist es aufgrund der damit verbundenen schweren Beurteilung des Leistungsergebnisses vor Leistungsinanspruchnahme sinnvoll, im Rahmen der Markenpolitik auch den Aufbau von Reputation anzustreben. Dies kann jedoch nur durch mehrmaliges Signaling verbunden mit positiven Erfahrungen der Nachfrager über die Eigenschaften, Aktivitäten und Verhaltensweisen der Anbieter erreicht werden (Bruhn/Hennig-Thurau/Hadwich, 2004; Fassnacht, 2004; Schleuser, 2002; Woratschek/Roth, 2004). Für Proficlubs ist der Reputationsgrad insbesondere im Bereich der Managementkompetenzen von Bedeutung. Betrachtet man beispielsweise das Erlösmodell des Sponsorings, so kann die Clubführung durch aufgebaute und signalisierte Managementreputation vorherrschende Unsicherheiten auf der Seite der werbetreibenden Unternehmen über mögliches opportunistisches Clubverhalten nach Vertragsabschluss bereinigen (z.B. geringe Service- und Kooperationsbereitschaft).

13.3.3 Besonderheit 3: Leistungserstellung

Die gleich bleibende Qualität wurde in Abschnitt 13.1.1 als ein zentrales Merkmal von Marken angeführt. Nun sind Dienstleistungsunternehmen im Allgemeinen bereits dem Problem ausgesetzt, dass das Leistungsergebnis aufgrund der konstitutiven Kundenbeteiligung schwer konstant zu halten ist (Bruhn, 2004; Benkenstein/Spiegel, 2004). Da sich der Leistungserstellungsprozess im professionellen Teamsport zudem durch die Besonderheit auszeichnet, dass mindestens zwei Organisationen zur Austragung eines sportlichen Wettkampfes beteiligt sein müssen (Koproduktion), stellt die Aufrechterhaltung eines gleich bleibenden Qualitätsniveaus insgesamt eine besondere Herausforderung an das Clubmarkenmanagement dar. Zur Problemlösung sollten Proficlubs deshalb ihr Leistungsspektrum, welches das sportliche Geschehen umrahmt, weitestgehend standardisieren, da auf diese Weise Substitutbezugspunkte für eine gleich bleibende Qualitätswahrnehmung geschaffen werden. Für Leistungsstandardisierungen bieten sich folgende Ansatzpunkte an:

- Standardisierung materieller bzw. immaterieller Inputfaktoren (z.B. Erlebnismarketing für Stadionbesucher, angebotene Servicequantität und -qualität, Homepage Content).

- Standardisierung personeller Inputfaktoren (einheitlich gutes Ausbildungs- und Erfahrungsniveau der Mitarbeiter, Erscheinungsbild der Mitarbeiter, Verhaltensregeln Kundenkontakt, hohe Anzahl an Stadionpersonal).

- Standardisierung ausgewählter Leistungsprozesse bzw. Leistungsteilergebnisse (z.B. Sponsoringumsetzung, Sponsorenbetreuung, Fixierung von Wartezeiten in Bereichen wie Ticketing, Einlass, Catering, Parkplätze).

Insbesondere tragen auch alle infrastrukturellen Gegebenheiten im Stadionbereich (Gestaltung Hospitalitybereich, Großbildleinwände, Kindererlebnispark, Überdachung, Parkplätze, Verkehrsanbindung, Situation öffentliche Verkehrsmittel etc.) sowie die Fangemeinde als Produzent der Stadionatmosphäre zu einer einheitlichen Qualitätswahrnehmung bei.

13.4 Ein Markenmanagementmodell für die Clubs des professionellen Teamsports

Die aus den ökonomischen Besonderheiten des professionellen Teamsports abgeleiteten Markenführungsanforderungen verdeutlichen, dass branchenübergreifende Markenführungsansätze den Spezifika des Profisports lediglich eingeschränkt gerecht werden (so sind beispielsweise nur wenige der in Abschnitt 13.3 ausgeführten Markenmanagementanforderungen an Proficlubs in dem branchenunspezifischen Markenführungsansatz von Meffert/Burmann enthalten). Nachfolgend wird deshalb ein spezifisches Markenmanagementmodell für Proficlubs vorgestellt, das den skizzierten Besonderheiten Rechnung trägt (zur Modellbegründung vgl. Schilhaneck,

371

2006; Schilhaneck, 2007). Anspruch des Modells ist es, diejenigen Komponenten und Kombinationsprozesse abzubilden, die für ein erfolgreiches Clubmarkenmanagement von Relevanz sind.

Abb. 2 zeigt den Modellansatz zunächst im Überblick. Im Weiteren wird der Ansatz über die drei unterschiedenen Ebenen näher erläutert.

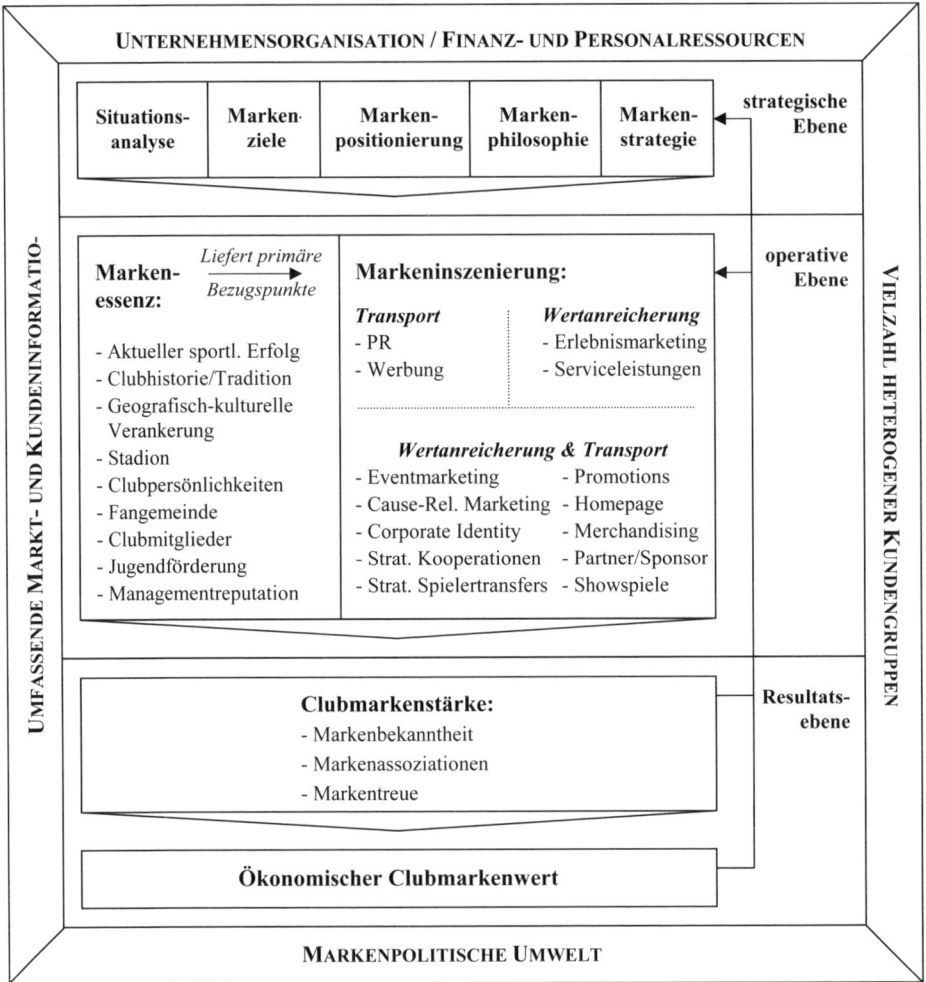

UNTERNEHMENSORGANISATION / FINANZ- UND PERSONALRESSOURCEN					
Situations-analyse	Marken-ziele	Marken-positionierung	Marken-philosophie	Marken-strategie	strategische Ebene

Marken-essenz: *Liefert primäre → Bezugspunkte*

- Aktueller sportl. Erfolg
- Clubhistorie/Tradition
- Geografisch-kulturelle Verankerung
- Stadion
- Clubpersönlichkeiten
- Fangemeinde
- Clubmitglieder
- Jugendförderung
- Managementreputation

Markeninszenierung: operative Ebene

Transport   *Wertanreicherung*
- PR   - Erlebnismarketing
- Werbung   - Serviceleistungen

Wertanreicherung & Transport
- Eventmarketing   - Promotions
- Cause-Rel. Marketing - Homepage
- Corporate Identity   - Merchandising
- Strat. Kooperationen - Partner/Sponsor
- Strat. Spielertransfers - Showspiele

Clubmarkenstärke: Resultats-ebene
- Markenbekanntheit
- Markenassoziationen
- Markentreue

Ökonomischer Clubmarkenwert

MARKENPOLITISCHE UMWELT

UMFASSENDE MARKT- UND KUNDENINFORMATIO-

VIELZAHL HETEROGENER KUNDENGRUPPEN

Abb. 2: Ein Markenmanagementmodell für Proficlubs

13.4.1 Strategische Ebene

Die strategische Ebene des Modellansatzes setzt sich aus den Elementen Situationsanalyse, Markenziele, Markenpositionierung, Markenphilosophie und Markenstrategie zusammen.

Gegenstand der Situationsanalyse sollte eine Erfassung von Eigen- und Fremd-verständnis der Clubmarke sowie eine Wettbewerberbetrachtung sein. Ausgehend von den Analyseergebnissen sind sodann die Markenziele zu formulieren (psycho-graphische Ziele: Markenbekanntheit, Markenassoziationen, Markentreue; ökono-mische Ziele: Markenumsatz, Marktanteil). Mit der Fixierung der erwünschten Markenassoziationen wird gleichermaßen die Markenpositionierung festgelegt (= angestrebte Stellung der Marke in den Köpfen der Konsumenten i.S.e. Definition von Kernassoziationen, welche von den Zielgruppen entwickelt werden sollen). Die Anforderung an die Markenpositionierungsmerkmale muss dabei sein, eine mög-lichst trennscharfe und dauerhafte Abgrenzung gegenüber den Konkurrenzmarken zu realisieren, um entsprechende Differentialrenten abschöpfen zu können (Unique Selling Proposition). Die Abgrenzung beruht auf der Eigenständigkeit, Unverwech-selbarkeit, Authentizität sowie Bedürfnisrelevanz der definierten Clubmarkenasso-ziationen. Insgesamt gibt die Markenpositionierung mit ihrer Aufgabe, die Stellung der Marke im Markt festzulegen, eine erste Richtungsweisung für die qualitative und quantitative Ausgestaltung der markenpolitisch-relevanten Marketingmix-Instrumente vor, da fortan geeignete Programme geschaffen werden müssen, wel-che eine zukünftige Verbindung jener Assoziationen mit der Clubmarke gewähr-leisten. Die daraufhin zu formulierende Markenphilosophie ist als unterstützendes Instrument zur Umsetzung der Markenpositionierung zu sehen, welches die zentra-len Positionierungsmerkmale zusammenfasst. An die Entscheidung der Markenpo-sitionierung schließt sich letztlich die Festlegung der Markenstrategie an (= lang-fristiger Verhaltensplan zur Erreichung der Markenziele; *Frage:* Welche Maßnahmen sind wann, wie und mit welcher Intensität auszuführen?), welche den Zusammenhang zwischen der Marke und den Leistungen weiter konkretisiert (*Grundstrategien:* regionale Markenstrategie, z.B. SC Freiburg, „Inselclub" im Breisgau, 3-Länder-Pokal; nationale Markenstrategie, z.B. FC Schalke 04, deutsch-landweites Fanturnier zum 100-jährigen Clubjubiläum; internationale Markenstra-tegie, z.B. FC Bayern München, jährliche internationale Turnier- und Freund-schaftsspielreisen) (Aaker/Joachimsthaler, 2001; Bruhn, 2004; Bruhn/Hennig-Thurau/Hadwich, 2004; Esch, 2003; Fassnacht, 2004).

13.4.2 Operative Ebene

Auch wenn die Clubmarke im Kopf der Rezipienten entsteht, so bringt der Profi-club das entsprechende „Rohmaterial" ein, aus dem sich letztlich das Markenbild zusammensetzt. In diesem Zusammenhang sind zwei Komponenten von Bedeu-tung: die Markenessenz sowie der Instrumenteneinsatz.

Markenessenz:

Die Markenessenz beinhaltet alle Werte, für die eine Marke primär steht (Aa-ker/Joachimsthaler, 2001). Sie ist als das Fundament des „Markenproduktionsprogramms" zu verstehen und liefert die zentralen inhaltlichen Bezugspunkte für alle Markenmanagementmaßnahmen.

Als kennzeichnende Elemente der Clubmarkenessenz sind der aktuelle sportliche Erfolg (z.B. FC Bayern München), die Clubhistorie (z.B. „Arbeiterclub" FC Schalke 04), die geographisch-kulturelle Clubverankerung („Karnevalclubs" 1. FC Köln und 1. FSV Mainz 05, „Kietzclub" 1. FC St. Pauli), das Stadion (z.B. farbig leuchtende Allianzarena) sowie die mit dem Club in Verbindung gebrachten Persönlichkeiten (v.a. Spieler, Trainer, Manager, Altstars) zu kennzeichnen. Ergänzende potentielle Markenessenzwerte stellen die Fangemeinde bzw. die Clubmitglieder (z.B. „alternatives" Gesellschaftsmilieu im Fall des FC St. Pauli), die Jugendförderung (z.B. VfB Stuttgart, SC Freiburg) sowie die Managementreputation dar (z.B. FC Bayern München) dar. Jene Sachverhalte liefern die zentralen Kernwerte, auf welche Proficlubs bei entsprechender Ausprägung bzw. Differenzierung im Rahmen der Markenführung in erster Linie zurückgreifen sollten (so genannte „key brand associations").

Instrumenteneinsatz:
Eine ausreichend attraktive Markenessenz stellt jedoch nur eine Grundvoraussetzung für ein erfolgreiches Markenmanagement dar. Zudem bedarf es der systematischen Anreicherung der Markenessenz um Zusatzwerte sowie der umfassenden Kommunikation all jener Werte an die Anspruchsgruppen (Aaker, 1996; Meffert/Burmann, 2002).

Transport- bzw. Kommunikationsfunktion übernehmen v.a. die Public Relations sowie Werbemaßnahmen. Als ergänzende, wertstiftende Instrumente sind das Erlebnismarketing (z.B. Rahmenprogramm, Arena-TV) sowie die zur Beziehungspflege durchgeführten Serviceleistungen (z.B. Fanworkshops, Kundengeschenke) anzuführen. Sowohl wertanreichernde als auch kommunikative Maßnahmen sind hingegen das Eventmarketing (z.B. Fanfestival), Promotions (z.B. Fanmobileinsatz, Free-Give-Aways), Cause-Related Marketingmaßnahmen (= Leistungsvermarktung mittels sozialer Ansätze, z.B. Unterstützung karitativer Einrichtungen), die Clubhomepage (z.B. interaktive/multimediale Angebote wie Chat-Room, Fan-Forum, Audio- und Videodownloads), die Corporate Identity (z.B. einheitlicher Corporate Design-Ansatz), kreative Merchandising-Kollektionen (z.B. Pillendreher/Werkself-Kollektion Bayer 04 Leverkusen), strategische Clubkooperationen (z.B. Manchester United und New York Yankees, FC Bayern München und Urawa Red Diamonds), strategische Partner/Sponsoren (z.B. VW und VfL Wolfsburg, adidas und FC Bayern München), strategische Spielertransfers (z.B. Real Madrid und die Verpflichtung von David Beckham) sowie die Durchführung von Showspielen (z.B. jährliche USA- und Asienreisen von Clubs wie Manchester United, Real Madrid oder dem FC Bayern München) zu sehen.

Angesichts der begrenzten Ressourcen der Proficlubs stellt sich nach dieser um Wertanreicherungs- bzw. Werttransporteigenschaften systematisierten Instrumentenauflistung die Frage nach einer Bedeutungsordnung. Eine allgemeingültige Hierarchisierung ist aufgrund der äußerst inhomogenen Clubsituationen nur schwer vorzunehmen, jedoch lassen sich folgende Grundstrategieansätze festhalten: Instrumenteneinsatz Markenaufbau vs. Instrumenteneinsatz Markenpflege.

Wie in Abschnitt 13.1.2 ausgeführt, sind die kaufverhaltensrelevanten Markenassoziationen nachweislich eng mit der Markenbekanntheit verknüpft, wobei eine ausreichend hohe Markenbekanntheit die Grundvoraussetzung für scharfe Gedächtnisprojektionen darstellt. Aus dieser zeitlichen Wirkungsdifferenz ist folglich die Notwendigkeit abzuleiten, dass Clubs in der Phase des Markenaufbaus („New Player") zunächst die Markenbekanntheit sowie erste prägnante Clubmarkenassoziationen (basierend auf den kennzeichnenden Clubmarkenessenzwerten) ausreichend zu fördern haben. Der Aufbau von Clubmarkenbekanntheit bedeutet, die Marke zu thematisieren und „ins Gespräch zu bringen", idealerweise sollte sie im Einzugsgebiet nach ausreichendem Zeitraum hohe aktive Markenbekanntheitswerte erzielen. Für den Aufbau von Markenbekanntheit sowie der Festigung erster klarer Clubmarkenassoziationen bedarf es eines umfassenden Einsatzes von Massenkommunikationsmaßnahmen, da sowohl zur Bekanntmachung der Marke als auch zur Vermittlung und Festigung erster Markeninhalte eine Vielzahl an Kontakten bzw. zahlreiche Wiederholungen erforderlich sind. Als zentral sind dabei die Public Relations (v.a. Pressearbeit) sowie die Werbung zu sehen, die flächendeckend sowie mit hoher Kontaktfrequenz anzusetzen sind. Ergänzend sind zudem erste (erlebnisvermittelnde) Sonderkommunikationsmaßnahmen wie z.B. Events in Betracht zu ziehen. Die damit erzielten direkten Kontakte wirken i.d.R. stärker als mediale Kontakte, wodurch ein schnellerer Aufbau von Markenbekanntheit erfolgt, allerdings ist der Rezipientenkreis eingeschränkt.

Demgegenüber liegt die Aufgabe für Proficlubs mit etablierten Marken (z.B. konsolidierte Fußballbundesligisten) v.a. in der Festigung bestehender bzw. der gezielten Anreicherung ergänzender Markenassoziationen. Für die Massenkommunikationsbereiche (PR, Werbung) ist daraus neben der Aufrechterhaltung von Reichweite und Kontaktfrequenz eine zusätzliche qualitative Anforderungskomponente ableitbar, indem z.B. über „nostalgische" PR- und Werbekampagnen oder regelmäßige Personality-Berichte „künstliche" Zusatzassoziationen inszeniert und verbreitet werden. An dieser Stelle setzt schließlich auch der umfassende Einsatz wertanreichernder Instrumente und die Verzahnung dieser mit kommunikativen Maßnahmen an, in dem z.B. über Cause-Related Marketingprogramme, Erlebnis- und Eventmarketingmaßnahmen, attraktive Promotionprogramme oder einer Servicestrategie zusätzliche Markenbilder bzw. Markenzugänge erzeugt und konsequent über die Kommunikationsmaßnahmen verbreitet werden.

13.4.3 Resultatsebene

Die Resultatsebene umfasst die Ergebnisse der zuvor skizzierten Markenmanagementprozesse. So äußert sich das Zusammenwirken der strategisch-konzeptionellen Vorarbeiten, der Markenessenz sowie der Maßnahmen zur Wertanreicherung und des Transports letztlich in der Clubmarkenstärke (Bestimmungsgrößen: Markenbekanntheit, Markenassoziationen, Markentreue) bzw. dem daraus folgenden ökonomischen Clubmarkenwert (vgl. Abschnitt 13.1.2). Allerdings darf der bis zu diesem Punkt erläuterte Prozess der Clubmarkenführung nicht als statisch verstanden werden. So bedarf es eines regelmäßigen Abgleichs der erreichten Ergebnisse mit den gesetzten Zielen (z.B. regelmäßige Analyse der Clubmarkenbekanntheit; Abgleich der definierten Soll-Clubmarkenassoziationen mit den tatsächlich erzielten Ist-Clubmarkenassoziationen; Untersuchung von Indikatoren der Markentreue wie Dauerkartenabsatz-, Vereinsmitgliedschafts- oder Fanclubmitgliedschaftsentwicklung). In Abhängigkeit von den Kontrollresultaten ist der Clubmarkenmanagementzyklus daraufhin entweder gänzlich neu zu durchlaufen (in diesem Fall sind grundlegende strategische Veränderungen wie Ziel- bzw. Positionierungsanpassungen, Veränderung des Grundstrategieansatzes, Veränderung des Zielgruppenfokus mit entsprechenden Anpassungen der operativen Maßnahmen vorzunehmen) oder es ist lediglich auf der operativen Ebene anzusetzen (reaktive Anpassungen wie z.B. verstärkte PR- und Werbeaktivitäten, Ausbau des Erlebnismarketings etc.).

13.4.4 Rahmenfaktoren

Anzumerken verbleibt, dass die markenpolitischen Gestaltungsoptionen der Proficlubs von folgenden Rahmenfaktoren bestimmt werden:

- Es bedarf einer angepassten Unternehmensorganisation (klare Verantwortlichkeitsverteilungen) sowie ausreichender Personal- und Finanzressourcen.
- Generell hängt die Effizienz der markenpolitischen Entscheidungen von der Qualität und Quantität der vorliegenden Markt- und Kundeninformationen ab.
- Erschwerend wirkt sich die für Proficlubs charakteristische Vielzahl an heterogenen Kundengruppen mit jeweils unterschiedlichen Bedürfnissen aus.
- Letztlich bedingen auch die fortlaufenden gesellschaftlichen und ökonomischen Umweltveränderungen Neuausrichtungen im Rahmen des Markenmanagements der Proficlubs.

13.5 Fallstudie

Nachfolgend wird das Markenmanagement von Proficlubs anhand des Fallbeispiels der Washington Capital (NHL) veranschaulicht. Die Darstellungen beziehen sich auf eine Studie aus der Saison 2002/2003 (Schilhaneck, 2004; Schilhaneck, 2005).

Fallstudie „Washington Capitals"

Strukturangaben und ökonomische Kennziffern der Washington Capitals:
Die Aufbauorganisation des NHL-Franchises gestaltet sich wie folgt: Ausgehend von der Besitzergruppe Lincoln Holdings LLC unterteilt sich der Club in einen kaufmännischen Bereich („Business Operations") sowie einen sportlichen Bereich („Hockey Operations") mit insgesamt 60 Mitarbeiter. Der kaufmännische Bereich setzt sich aus den Abteilungen „Marketing", „Communications", „Ticket Sales" und „Finance" zusammen. Der sportliche Bereich untergliedert sich in die Abteilungen „Team", „Pro Scouting", „Amateur Scouting", „Medical Staff", „Team Services" sowie „Player Development". Die Vermarktung der Hospitality- und Marketingrechte wird von dem externen Vermarktungsunternehmen WSLEP durchgeführt. Der Umsatz der Washington Capitals betrug in der Saison 2003/04 85 Mio. US-$. In jenem Spieljahr gewann der Club den „Southeast Division"-Titel, in den Play-Offs schieden die Washington Capitals jedoch bereits in der ersten Runde aus.

Nachfolgend werden die Umsetzungsformen einiger ausgesuchter Elemente der strategischen und operativen Ebene des Markenmanagementmodells für Proficlubs (vgl. dazu Abb. 2) am Beispiel der Washington Capitals skizziert.

Folgende *Markenziele* sind im strategischen Businessplan des NHL-Franchises festgehalten:
- Kontinuierliche Wertsteigerung der Marke „Washington Capitals".
- Förderung des Bekanntheitsgrades der Marke „Washington Capitals" in der Öffentlichkeit.
- Förderung des Bekanntheitsgrades der Marke „Washington Capitals" in den Zielmärkten und den Zielgruppen.
- Steigerung des Identifizierungsgrades der Jugend mit der Marke.
- Image eines sozial engagierten Unternehmens kreieren.
- Steigerung des Wiedererkennungswertes der Marke.
- Gewährleistung einer starken lokalen Medienvertretung.
- Gewährleistung einer starken Medienvertretung in den nationalen Zielmärkten Los Angeles, Chicago, Toronto und New York.
- Verstärkte Medienvertretung in den benachbarten Regionen Baltimore, Annapolis und Richmond.

Zur *Situationsanalyse* führt der NHL-Club jede Saison verschiedene Befragungen durch (Zuschauerbefragungen an Spieltagen, Brief-/Email-/Homepage-Umfragen, Fokusgruppen-Interviews mit Vertretern der Hauptkundengruppen des Clubs). In diesen werden u.a. auch markenbezogene Aspekte thematisiert (z.B. gestützte/ungestützte Abfrage von Kernclubassoziationen, Wirkungsüberprüfung PR-/Werbekampagnen).

Im Rahmen der *Public Relations* tragen v.a. folgende Maßnahmen zur Pflege der Clubmarke bei:

- Erstellung von mindestens zwei Presseberichten über den Club pro Woche und Versendung dieser an die komplette Medien-Liste.
- Erstellung eines monatlichen Presseberichts nur speziell mit Informationen über die Spieler, die Trainer, die Besitzergruppe etc. und Versendung des Berichts an die komplette Medien-Liste.
- Clubinformationsübermittlung an die Medien der gegnerischen Mannschaft drei Tage vor Spielbeginn (unabhängig, ob Heim- oder Auswärtsspiel).
- Wöchentlicher Kontaktpflegeanruf bei den verschiedenen Medienvertretern.
- Organisation von zwei Events für die Medienvertreter zur Kontaktpflege.

Auch das Kommunikationsinstrument der *Werbung* wird von den Washington Capitals umfassend genutzt. So wird für die drei Hauptwerbephasen jeder Saison (September, Dezember und Februar) je eine neue Werbekampagne für das gesamte Media-Mix (TV, Radio, Printmedien, Anzeigen, Postwerbung) konzipiert.

Die *Serviceleistungen* des NHL-Clubs für die beiden Kundengruppen „Saisondauerkartenbesitzer" sowie „VIP-Kunden" umfassen folgende Punkte:

- Reservierte Play-Off Karte.
- Ticketbestellmöglichkeit für Extra Play-Off Karten vor öffentlichem Verkauf.
- Ticketaustauschprogramm an drei Spieltagen.
- 4 Private Skating Parties im MCI Center.
- 2 Appreciation Parties (Draft Day Party, Meet the Team Party).
- Spezielles Kundengeschenk.
- Möglichkeit der monatlichen Ratenzahlung.
- Washington Capitals Media Guide.
- Stadionzeitschrift.

Der Ansatz des *Erlebnismarketings* für die Stadionbesucher gestaltet sich bei den Washington Capitals wie folgt:

- Jeweils ein neues Video-Intro für die Saison und die Play-Offs.
- Jeweils eine neue Art der Spielervorstellung für die Saison und die Play-Offs (Audio, Video, Licht).
- Heimspiele: Verpflichtung eines lokal bekannten Künstlers für die Nationalhymne.
- Verbesserung des Pausenentertainments (Einführung von 10 neuen Pausen-

events pro Saison). Veranstaltungen von 10 Eiskunstlaufzeremonien als Sonderpausenprogramm.

Das *Eventmarketing* stellt einen wichtigen Bestandteil des Markenmanagements des Clubs dar. Folgende Events werden im Laufe einer Saison durchgeführt:

- Organisation von „Theme Nights" (= Motto-Parties) zu folgenden Anlässen: Halloween, Thanks Giving, Weihnachten, Ostern, St. Patricks, Vatertag.
- Organisation eines Fan Festivals während des Training-Camps in der Saisonvorbereitung.
- Organisation eines Fan Festivals bei dem Saisoneröffnungsspiel.
- Organisation eines Fan Festivals bei dem Saisonabschlussspiel.
- Organisation eines Fan Festivals bei jedem Play-Off Heimspiel.
- Organisation des jährlichen „Alumni Golf Turniers".

Promotions sind im Rahmen des Markenmanagementansatzes des NHL-Franchises als ein ergänzendes Instrument zu sehen. Im einzelnen setzt der Club folgende Arten von Promotions um:

- Organisation verschiedener Sonderticketaktionen: für Familien (10 Termine), für Kinder (4 Termine), für Schüler/Studenten (4 Termine).
- Organisation von gesponserten „Free Give-Away" Aktionen (jedes vierte Heimspiel).
- 25 Fanmobileinsätze („Caps Caravan") bei Großevents in der Region um Washington DC.

Zum Ausdruck von Sozial- und Gesellschaftsverantwortung und somit als einen weiteren Ansatz zur Profilschärfung der Clubmarke führen die Washington Capitals zudem zahlreiche *Cause-Related Marketingprogramme* aus:

- Organisation der NHL Street Hockey-Eventserie in Kooperation mit Schulen (25 Veranstaltungen).
- Organisation des Schulprogramms „Reading is Cool" (Besuch von Schulen).
- Organisation eines Hockey-Camps für Kinder.
- Organisation eines Wohltätigkeits-Karnevals mit Beteilung aller Spieler (Erlöse gehen sozialen Einrichtung zu).
- Sammelaktion spezieller Sachmittel an drei Heimspielen für soziale Einrichtungen (Spielzeug, Schulmaterial, Winterkleidung).
- "The Annual Ollie Kölzig Children Hospital Golf Classic".
- "The Annual Ollie Kölzig Children Hospital Tennis Classic".
- Kooperation mit den Programmen "Great Guys for a Great Cause" (Krebshilfe) und "Special Hockey Washington" (Behindertensportprogramm).

Die Ausführungen zum Fallbeispiel „Washington Capitals" veranschaulichen zum einen die Maßnahmenintensität bzw. den damit verbundenen Ressourceneinsatz, den das NHL-Franchise zur Pflege seiner Marke aufwendet. Zum anderen wird die Verknüpfung zwischen strategischer und operativer Markenführung ersichtlich. So führt der NHL-Club ausgehend von formulierten Markenzielen zahlreiche auf die verschiedenen Zielparameter ausgerichtete Maßnahmen durch. Insgesamt ist das Markenmanagement der Washington Capitals somit als umfassend und stringent zu bewerten und stellt eine wertvolle Orientierungshilfe für die Managementpraxis dar.

13.6 Fazit und Ausblick

Zentraler Gegenstand des Kapitels war die Vorstellung eines Markenmanagementmodells für Proficlubs, welches Abfolge und Zusammenwirken der relevanten Markenmanagementkomponenten abbildet. Das Modell veranschaulicht den komplexen Clubmarkenbildungsprozess, ausgehend von den strategischen Basisentscheidungen über die operativen Umsetzungsmöglichkeiten bis hin zu den damit zu beeinflussenden Markendimensionen (Markenbekanntheit, Markenassoziationen, Markentreue).

Vor dem Hintergrund der in Abschnitt 13.1 skizzierten Defizite des Clubmarkenmanagements verdeutlicht der Modellansatz, dass den Proficlubs zahlreiche Ansatzpunkte zur gezielten Markenführung zur Verfügung stehen. Insbesondere die operative Modellebene (Markenessenzwerte, Instrumentenset) stellt einen pragmatischen Bezugspunkt zur Ableitung von praxisrelevanten Managementimplikationen dar.

Zukünftige Forschungsarbeit sollte sich zum einen auf die Untersuchung des Einflusses der verschiedenen Instrumente der operativen Modellebene auf die Clubmarkenstärke richten. Derartige Erkenntnisse würden wesentlich zur aufgetretenen Fragestellung der Hierarchisierung des clubmarkenpolitisch relevanten Instrumentariums beitragen und somit wichtige praxisrelevante Hilfestellungen leisten (*wann sind welche Instrumente mit welcher Intensität und in welcher Kombination einzusetzen?*). Zum anderen gilt es, weiterführende Strategieansätze für das Clubmarkenmanagement zu erarbeiten. Dabei muss insbesondere den unterschiedlichen Clubtypen (Schwellenclubs vs. etablierte Clubs vs. Top-Clubs) Rechnung getragen werden.

Kontrollfragen

1. Was verstehen Sie unter einer (Unternehmens-)Marke bzw. dem Markenmanagement?
2. Was ist der Unterschied zwischen der konsumerbezogenen und der unternehmensbezogenen Sichtweise des Markenwerts?
3. Durch welche Dimensionen wird die Markenstärke operationalisiert? Bitte erklären Sie diese genauer!

4. Welche nachfrager- bzw. anbieterbezogenen Markenfunktionen gibt es? Bitte erklären Sie diese genauer! Welche der nachfragerbezogenen Markenfunktionen sind für Proficlubs besonders bedeutend?

5. Welche Komponenten stehen hinter dem Aussagenkonzept bzw. dem Akzeptanzkonzept des Markenführungsansatzes von Meffert/Burmann? Erklären Sie die Wechselseitigkeit zwischen Aussagenkonzept und Akzeptanzkonzept im Markenführungsansatz von Meffert/Burmann!

6. Durch welche ökonomischen Branchenbesonderheiten ist der professionelle Teamsport gekennzeichnet? Welche Probleme für das Clubmarkenmanagement ergeben sich daraus und was sind mögliche Managementlösungen?

7. Was sind strategische Basisentscheidungsbereiche für das Markenmanagement von Proficlubs? Was ist im Rahmen dieser vorzunehmen?

8. Was sind die zentralen Kernwerte von Clubmarken? Was sind sinnvolle Instrumente für das Clubmarkenmanagement? Wie wirken diese Instrumente bei geeignetem Einsatz zusammen?

9. Welche Unterschiede ergeben sich hinsichtlich des Instrumenteneinsatzes von Clubs mit weniger etablierten Clubmarken gegenüber Clubs mit bereits etablierten Clubmarken?

10. Was sind Ansatzpunkte zur Überprüfung der Wirkung ausgeführter Markenmanagementmaßnahmen?

Literaturverzeichnis

Aaker, David (1991): Managing Brand Equity, New York.

Aaker, David (1996): Building Strong Brands, New York.

Aaker, David / Joachimsthaler, Erich (2001): Brand Leadership, München.

Bauer, Hans / Sauer, Nicola / Schmitt, Philipp (2004): Die Erfolgsrelevanz der Markenstärke in der 1. Fußball-Bundesliga, Wissenschaftliches Arbeitspapier Nr. W75, Institut für Marktorientierte Unternehmensführung, Universität Mannheim.

Benkenstein, Martin / Spiegel, Thomas (2004): Entwickelungstendenzen der Markenführung aus Dienstleistungsperspektive, in: Bruhn, Manfred (Hrsg.): Handbuch Markenführung, Wiesbaden, S. 2747-2763.

Biel, Alexander (2001): Grundlagen zum Markenaufbau, in: Esch, Franz-Rudolf (Hrsg.): Moderne Markenführung, Wiesbaden, S. 63-90.

Bruhn, Manfred (2004): Markenführung für Nonprofit-Organisationen, in: Bruhn, Manfred (Hrsg.): Handbuch Markenführung, Wiesbaden, S. 2297-2330.

Bruhn, Manfred / Hennig-Thurau, Thorsten / Hadwich, Karsten (2004): Markenführung und Relationship Management, in: Bruhn, Manfred (Hrsg.): Handbuch Markenführung, Wiesbaden, S. 392-420.

Esch, Franz-Rudolf (2003): Strategie und Technik der Markenführung, München.

Fassnacht, Martin (2004): Markenführung für Dienstleistungen, in: Bruhn, Manfred (Hrsg.): Handbuch Markenführung, Wiesbaden, S. 2161-2181.

Gladden, James / Irwin, Richard / Sutton, William (2001): Managing North American Major Professional Sport Teams in the New Millenium: A Focus on Building Brand Equity, in: Journal of Sport Management, Heft 4, S. 297-317.

Gladden, James / Milne, George (1999): Examining the importance of brand equity in professional sports, in: Sport Marketing Quarterly, Heft 1, S. 21-29.

Keller, Kevin (1993): Conceptualizing, Measuring, and Managing Customer Based Brand Equity, in: Journal of Marketing, Heft 1, S. 1-22.

Keller, Kevin (1998): Strategic Brand Management. Building, Measuring and Managing Brand Equity, Upper Saddle River.

Meffert, Heribert / Bierwirth, Andreas (2005): Corporate Branding - Führung der Unternehmensmarke im Spannungsfeld unterschiedlicher Zielgruppen, in: Meffert, Heribert / Burmann, Christoph / Koers, Martin (Hrsg.): Markenmanagement, 2. Aufl., Wiesbaden, S. 143-162.

Meffert, Heribert / Burmann, Christoph (2002): Managementkonzept der identitätsorientierten Markenführung, in: Meffert, Heribert / Burmann, Christoph / Koers, Martin (Hrsg.): Markenmanagement, 2. Aufl., Wiesbaden, S. 73-99.

Meffert, Heribert / Burmann, Christoph / Koers, Martin (2002): Stellenwert und Gegenstand des Markenmanagements, in: Meffert, Heribert / Burmann, Christoph / Koers, Martin (Hrsg.): Markenmanagement, 2. Aufl., Wiesbaden, S. 3-16.

Schilhaneck, Michael (2004): Wirtschaftliche Erfolgsfaktoren in Profivereinen, Bayreuth.

Schilhaneck, Michael (2005): Managementleitlinien für Proficlubs. Die Umsetzung wirtschaftlicher Erfolgsfaktoren in Profivereinen veranschaulicht am Beispiel eines US-Profiklubs, in: Spectrum der Sportwissenschaften, Heft 1, S. 62-78.

Schilhaneck, Michael (2006): Markenmanagement im professionellen Teamsport, in: Sport und Gesellschaft, Heft 3, S. 283-305.

Schilhaneck, Michael (2007): Zielorientiertes Management von Fußballunternehmen - Konzepte und Begründungen für ein erfolgreiches Marken- und Kundenbindungsmanagement, Inaugural-Dissertation, Institut für Sportwissenschaft, Universität Bayreuth.

Schleuser, Michael (2002): Identitätsorientierte Markenführung bei Dienstleistungen, in: Meffert, Heribert / Burmann, Christoph / Koers, Martin (Hrsg.): Markenmanagement, 2. Aufl., Wiesbaden, S. 263-289.

Sportfive (2002): Fußballstudie/European Football, Hamburg.

Sportfive (2004): Fußballstudie/European Football, Hamburg.

Woratschek, Herbert / Roth, Stefan (2004): Informationsökonomischer Erklärungsansatz der Markenführung, in: Bruhn, Manfred (Hrsg.): Handbuch Markenführung, Wiesbaden, S. 347-370.

UFA Sports (1998): UFA Fußballstudie, Hamburg.

UFA Sports (2000): UFA Fußballstudie, Hamburg.

Weiterführende Ressourcen

Literatur

Bauer, Hans / Exler, Stefanie / Sauer, Nicola (2004): Der Beitrag des Marken-images zur Fanloyalität, Wissenschaftliches Arbeitspapier Nr. W81, Institut für Marktorientierte Unternehmensführung, Universität Mannheim.

Bauer, Hans / Exler, Stefanie / Sauer, Nicola (2005): Brand Communities im professionellen Teamsport, in: Thexis, Heft 3, S. 11-15.

Couvelaere, Vincent / Richelieu, André (2005). Brand Strategy in Professional Sports: The Case of French Soccer Teams, in: European Sport Management Quarterly, Heft 5, S. 23-46.

Gladden, James / Funk, Daniel (2001): Understanding Brand Loyalty in Professional Sport: The Link Between Brand Associations and Brand Loyalty, in: International Journal of Sports Marketing and Sponsorship, Heft 2, S. 67-91.

Gladden, James / Funk, Daniel (2002): Developing an Understanding of Brand Associations in Team Sport: Empirical Evidence from Consumers of Professional Sport, in: Journal of Sport Management, Heft 3, S. 54-81.

Gladden, James / Milne, George / Sutton, William (1998): A Conceptual Framework for Assesing Brand Equity in Division I College Athletics, in: Journal of Sport Management, Heft 1, S. 1-19.

Mohr, Stefan (2001): Neue Regeln für ein neues Spiel, München.

Mohr, Stefan / Merget, Jens (2004): Die Marke als Meistermacher - Strategische Markenführung im Sport, in: Zieschang, Klaus / Klimmer, Christian (Hrsg.): Unternehmensführung im Profifußball, Berlin, S. 103-122.

Ross, Stephen (2006): A Conceptual Framework for Understanding Spectator-Based Brand Equity, in: Journal of Sport Management, Heft 1, S. 22-38.

Welling, Michael (2004): Die (Fußball-)Vereinsmarke – Konzeptionelle Grundlagen und ausgewählte Besonderheiten der Markenführung von Fußballvereinen, in: Hammann, Peter / Schmidt, Lars / Welling, Michael (Hrsg.): Ökonomie des Fußballs, Wiesbaden, S. 391-418.

Welling, Michael (2005): Markenführung im professionellen Ligasport, in Meffert, Heribert / Burmann, Christoph / Koers, Martin (Hrsg.): Markenmanagement, 2. Aufl., Wiesbaden, S. 496-522.

Links

Washington Capitals:

http://www.washcaps.com

Kapitel 14: Veranstaltungsmarketing im Sport

Gerd Nufer   André Bühler

Lernziele

Nach der Durchsicht dieses Kapitels sollte der Leser in der Lage sein,

▪ die unterschiedlichen Instrumente des Veranstaltungsmarketing zu definieren und voneinander zu differenzieren.

▪ die grundlegenden Ziele im Veranstaltungsmarketing zu benennen.

▪ die unterschiedlichen Erscheinungsformen von Event-Sponsoring, Event-Marketing und Ambush Marketing aufzuzeigen.

▪ zahlreiche Beispiele aus dem Veranstaltungsmarketing im Sport zu beschreiben.

▪ die jeweiligen Vor- und Nachteile der einzelnen Instrumente des Veranstaltungsmarketing zu erörtern.

▪ die Kommunikationsinstrumente Event-Sponsoring, Event-Marketing und Ambush Marketing anhand des Beispiels Fußball-Weltmeisterschaft 2006 zu kennzeichnen.

Überblick über das Kapitel

In diesem Kapitel werden die verschiedenen Möglichkeiten, bei und mit Sport-Events Kommunikationspolitik zu betreiben, vorgestellt und voneinander abgegrenzt. Die jeweiligen Besonderheiten der unterschiedlichen Instrumente des Veranstaltungsmarketing *(Event-)Sponsoring*, *Event-Marketing* und *Ambush Marketing* werden nacheinander präsentiert, wobei jeweils die Vorgehensweise vom Allgemeinen zum Besonderen eingehalten wird. D.h. jeder Ansatz wird zunächst allgemein definiert und anhand seiner konstitutiven Merkmale gekennzeichnet. Danach werden die jeweiligen Ziele beschrieben sowie die möglichen grundsätzlichen Erscheinungsformen systematisiert. Es schließt sich eine spezielle Betrachtung ausgewählter Beispiele aus dem Sport an. Abschließend wird jedes Instrument individuell kritisch gewürdigt. Abgerundet wird dieses Kapitel mit einer Praxis-Fallstudie zur Fußball-Weltmeisterschaft 2006, einem Fazit inklusive Zukunftssausblick, Kontrollfragen sowie der Angabe weiterführender Ressourcen zum Thema Veranstaltungsmarketing im Sport.

14.1 Einführung in die Thematik

„Consumers love events, corporations love consumers ... this is a match made in heaven" (D´Alessandro, 1993, S. 507). Unter Beachtung dieser „Zauberformel" gehen insbesondere international agierende Unternehmen zunehmend auf die Suche nach attraktiven Veranstaltungen, die auf die Öffentlichkeit eine große Anziehungskraft ausüben. Es ist nicht verwunderlich, dass v.a. internationale Sportgroßereignisse von zahlreichen Unternehmen genutzt werden, um ihre kommunikative Zielgruppenansprache in ein attraktives Umfeld einzubetten.

Es gibt zahlreiche Aspekte, die das Veranstaltungsmarketing für Unternehmen so interessant machen (Bruhn, 2003; Berndt, 2005): Angestrebt wird ein positiver

Imagetransfer vom Event auf die Marke bzw. das Unternehmen. Die kommunikative Ansprache erfolgt in einem attraktiven sportlichen Umfeld. Es lassen sich hohe (internationale) Reichweiten und damit vergleichsweise günstige Tausenderkontaktpreise realisieren. Der Multiplikatoreffekt der Massenmedien kann voll ausgenutzt werden.

14.2 Grundlagen des Veranstaltungsmarketing

„*Veranstaltungen* (i.e.S.) sind personendominant erstellte Dienstleistungs-Angebote mit begrenzter zeitlicher Nutzenstiftung, die unter raumzeitlicher Integration mehrerer Nachfrager abgegeben werden" (Wochnowski, 1996, S. 17).

Im Rahmen des Veranstaltungsmarketing können zwei unterschiedliche *Perspektiven* voneinander abgegrenzt werden (Nufer, 2007):

▪ Marketing *bei* Veranstaltungen:
Bereits bestehende Veranstaltungen werden von Unternehmen als Werbeträger für Botschaften verwendet. Die kommunikative Ansprache findet somit innerhalb eines fremdorganisierten Rahmens statt, d.h. die Initiative geht auf professionelle Veranstalter und nicht auf die Sponsoren zurück. Letztere nutzen eine existierende Veranstaltung als attraktive Plattform für ihre Kommunikationspolitik.

▪ Marketing *mit* Veranstaltungen:
Für Produkte oder Marken werden von Unternehmen eigens Veranstaltungen inszeniert und als Kommunikationsplattform genutzt. Die Veranstaltung wird dabei vom Unternehmen selbst initiiert. Die inszenierte Markenwelt soll für den Rezipienten erlebbar werden und zu einer emotionalen Bindung des Rezipienten an die Marke führen.

Das Marketing *bei* Sportveranstaltungen (z.B. Olympische Spiele oder Fußball-Weltmeisterschaften) ist somit dem Kommunikationsinstrument Sponsoring zuzuordnen, etabliert hat sich für diese Sponsoringform der Begriff *Event-Sponsoring*. Beim Marketing *mit* Veranstaltungen handelt es sich dagegen um *Event-Marketing*. Event-Marketing ist enger gefasst und anhand seiner konstitutiven Merkmale deutlich vom Sponsoring abzugrenzen (vgl. Abb. 1).

Innerhalb der Perspektive „Marketing *bei* Veranstaltungen" ist weiter zu differenzieren: Insbesondere für international agierende Unternehmen ist der Rahmen einer sportlichen Großveranstaltung wie beispielsweise eine Fußball-Weltmeisterschaft die ideale Plattform, sich vor einem weltweiten Publikum werbekommunikativ in Szene zu setzen. Event-Veranstalter verkaufen deshalb privilegierte Vermarktungsrechte ihres Events an Sponsoren. *Offizielle Sponsoren* erwerben damit exklusive Rechte, mit und im Rahmen des Events werben zu dürfen. *Ambush Marketing* dagegen kennzeichnet die Vorgehensweise von Unternehmen, die keine legalisierten Vermarktungsrechte an einer Veranstaltung besitzen, aber dennoch dem Publikum durch ihre Kommunikationsmaßnahmen eine Verbindung zu diesem Event signalisieren. Ziel des Ambush Marketing ist es, von den Erfolgen des Sportsponsoring zu profitieren, ohne die Pflichten eines offiziellen Sponsors einzugehen.

Art der Durchführung \ Art der Kommunikation		einseitig ←→ interaktiv informativ ←→ erlebnisorientiert	
fremdorganisiert	in bestehenden, vom Unternehmen unabhängigen Rahmen eingeordnet	**(Event-)Sponsoring** *(z.B. einer Fußball-Weltmeisterschaft)*	**Messen** *(z.B. Messebeteiligung bei der ISPO)*
eigeninitiiert	eigens vom Unternehmen inszeniert	**Sales Promotions** *(z.B. Verteilen von Give-aways)*	**Event-Marketing** *(z.B. Ausrichtung von Streetball-Turnieren)*

Tab. 1: Abgrenzung des Event-Marketing vom (Event-)Sponsoring
Quelle: Nufer (2007), S. 30

Insgesamt existieren somit drei völlig unterschiedliche Möglichkeiten, eine Sportveranstaltung werblich im Rahmen der Unternehmenskommunikation zu nutzen:

- *Event-Sponsoring*,
- *Event-Marketing* und
- *Ambush Marketing*.

Diese drei Kommunikationsinstrumente sollen in den folgenden Abschnitten detailliert vorgestellt und kritisch gewürdigt werden.

14.3 (Event-)Sponsoring

Sponsoring zählt zu den nicht-klassischen Formen der Marketing-Kommunikationspolitik und spricht Menschen in nicht-kommerziellen Situationen an. Auf diese Weise können Zielgruppen erreicht werden, die z.B. Werbung gegenüber negativ eingestellt oder durch klassische Kommunikationsinstrumente nicht erreichbar sind. Auch wird ein Sponsoringengagement i.d.R. eher akzeptiert als klassische Werbung, da dem Sponsoring per se eine gewisse Förderabsicht zugrunde liegt (Bayerl/Rennhak, 2006).

Das Sponsoring ist heute ein etabliertes Kommunikationsinstrument, das in den Marketingplänen von Unternehmen ebenso seinen Platz gefunden hat wie in der Fachliteratur zur Unternehmenskommunikation. Diese Akzeptanz ist dem Sponsoring vergleichsweise schnell gelungen, denn noch Mitte der 80er-Jahre war dieses Kommunikationsinstrument weder weit verbreitet, noch theoretisch aufgearbeitet (Drees, 2003).

14.3.1 Definition und Merkmale

> „*Sponsoring* bedeutet die:
> - Analyse, Planung, Durchführung und Kontrolle sämtlicher Aktivitäten,
> - die mit der Bereitstellung von Geld, Sachmitteln, Dienstleistungen oder Know-how durch Unternehmen und Institutionen
> - zur Förderung von Personen und/oder Organisationen in den Bereichen Sport, Kultur, Soziales, Umwelt … verbunden sind,
> - um damit gleichzeitig die angestrebten kommunikativen Ziele des Unternehmens zu erreichen" (Bruhn, 2005, S. 811).

Gegenüber allen anderen Erscheinungsformen nimmt das *Sportsponsoring* eine dominante Stellung ein. Begründet ist dies im hohen Sportinteresse der Konsumenten und der breiten gesellschaftlichen Akzeptanz von entsprechenden Sponsoringmaßnahmen: Nach wie vor wird der Sport mit Tugenden wie Fairness, Teamgeist, Leistungsorientierung oder Leidenschaft, Attraktivität und Emotionen assoziiert. Die zunehmende Verbreitung und Akzeptanz des Sportsponsoring folgt auch der generellen Tendenz, verstärkt Freizeitinteressen der Bevölkerung für Zwecke der Unternehmenskommunikation zu nutzen (Hermanns, 1997; Deimel, 1992; Drees, 1992).

Bei Sponsoren setzt sich zunehmend die Erkenntnis durch, dass klassisches Sponsoring (von Einzelpersonen oder Teams) sehr riskant sein kann, da im Falle eines Imageeinbruchs seitens der Gesponserten (beispielsweise hervorgerufen durch Skandale oder Niederlagenserien) auch das Ansehen des Sponsors in Mitleidenschaft gezogen werden kann. Insbesondere internationale Unternehmen agieren deshalb immer häufiger als Sponsoren attraktiver Großveranstaltungen, die auf die Öffentlichkeit eine enorme Anziehungskraft ausüben und bei denen sie dieses Risiko nicht fürchten müssen. Man spricht in diesem Zusammenhang vom *Event-Sponsoring* (Nufer, 2002).

Die zielbezogene Zusammenarbeit zwischen einem Sponsor und einem Gesponserten basiert auf zumeist vertraglich vereinbarten Leistungen und Gegenleistungen (Berndt, 2005). Von einem Sponsorship wird gesprochen, wenn sich Sponsor und Gesponserter geeinigt haben, ein konkretes Projekt in einem festgelegten Zeitraum unter bestimmten Bedingungen gemeinsam durchzuführen (Bruhn, 2003). Bruhn (2005) hebt sechs konstitutive *Merkmale* des Sponsoring hervor, die ungeachtet der unterschiedlichen Vorgehensweisen sämtlichen Sponsoringaktivitäten gemeinsam sind:

- Sponsoring basiert auf dem Prinzip von *Leistung und Gegenleistung*: Der Sponsor stellt seine Fördermittel in der Erwartung zur Verfügung, vom Gesponserten eine bestimmte Gegenleistung zu erhalten.

- Beim Sponsoring kommt der *Fördergedanke gegenüber dem Gesponserten* zum Ausdruck: Sponsoring entspricht nicht dem reinen Verkauf von Werbefläche gegen Entgelt, vielmehr identifiziert sich der Sponsor inhaltlich mit seinen Aufgaben.

- Sponsoring erfüllt *kommunikative Funktionen*: Diese werden vom Gesponserten erbracht, durch Medien transportiert oder können auch vom Sponsor selbst geschaffen werden.

- Sponsoring verlangt einen *systematischen Planungs- und Entscheidungsprozess*: Die Maßnahmen sind auf Basis einer Situationsanalyse und Zielformulierung im Einzelnen zu planen, durchzuführen und kontrollieren.

- Im Rahmen des Sponsoring lassen sich bei der Imagebeeinflussung *Botschaft und Medium nicht trennen*: Das Objekt eines Sponsoringengagements (z.B. ein Sport-Event) verkörpert sowohl die Botschaft als auch das Medium an sich.

- Sponsoring ist aus Unternehmenssicht ein Baustein zur *Integrierten Kommunikation*: Es ist nicht isoliert, sondern und im Verbund mit anderen Kommunikationsinstrumenten einzusetzen.

14.3.2 Ziele und Erscheinungsformen

Das Spektrum der *Kommunikationsziele*, die sich durch Sportsponsoring erreichen lassen, ist breit (Berndt, 2005; Drees, 2003):

- Bekanntheitsgradziele (Erhöhung bzw. Stabilisierung der Unternehmens- bzw. Markenbekanntheit),
- Imageziele (Aufbau bzw. Veränderung bestimmter Imagedimensionen),
- Kontaktpflege mit geladenen Gästen (Hospitality),
- Leistungsdemonstration von Produkt und Unternehmen,
- Schaffung von Goodwill und Demonstration gesellschaftlicher Verantwortung,
- Motivationsförderung bei den eigenen Mitarbeitern.

In Verbindung mit gesponserten Sportveranstaltungen lassen sich – völlig unabhängig vom Ausgang des sportlichen Wettkampfs – z.B. durch den Aufbau einer emotionalen Erlebniswelt kommunikative Wettbewerbsvorteile erzielen, womit eine Differenzierung von Werbemaßnahmen der Konkurrenz erreichen werden kann.

Die *Erscheinungsformen* des Sportsponsoring sind vielfältig. Wie ein Sponsoring-Engagement gegenüber der Zielgruppe in Erscheinung tritt, ist von vielfältigen Ent-

scheidungen des Sponsors abhängig. Insbesondere drei Entscheidungsfelder determinieren die konkrete Ausgestaltung des Sponsoring (Drees, 2003):
(1) Die Wahl des Sponsoring Objektes,
(2) die Spezifikation der Maßnahmen und
(3) eine Festlegung hinsichtlich des Umfangs des Sponsoringengagements.

(1) Formen nach dem Sportsponsoring-Objekt:
Folgende Dimensionen legen ein Sportsponsoring-Objekt in seinem Ausmaß fest:
- Sportart (z.B. Fußball, Formel 1, Radsport, Skispringen usw.),
- Leistungsebene (Spitzen- bzw. Leistungssport, Breitensport, Nachwuchssport),
- Organisatorische Einheit (sportartenübergreifende Sportorganisationen, Verbände, Vereine, Teams, Einzelsportler, Events).

(2) Formen nach der Nutzung und Umsetzung des Sportsponsoring:
Grundsätzlich lassen sich folgende Kernmaßnahmen unterscheiden, die sich in unterschiedlichem Umfang und jeweils spezifischen Ausprägungen bei den verschiedenen Objekten realisieren lassen:
- Markierung von Ausrüstungsgegenständen (z.B. Trikotwerbung),
- Präsenz im Vorfeld von Sportveranstaltungen (z.B. Presseinfomationen),
- Präsenz im Umfeld von Sportveranstaltungen (z.B. Bandenwerbung),
- Nutzung von Prädikaten (z.B. „offizieller Ausrüster von…"),
- Benennung eines Sponsoring-Objekts nach dem Sponsor (z.B. Titelsponsoring),
- Markierung von Drucksachen des Gesponserten (z.B. Autorgrammkarten),
- Einsatz von Sportlerpersönlichkeiten (als Testimonials),
- Ausrichtung sportiver Veranstaltungen (z.B. Volksläufe).

(3) Formen nach dem Umfang des Sportsponsoringengagements:
- Full-Sponsoring (alleiniges kommunikatives Nutzungsrecht),
- Hauptsponsoring (Dominanz gegenüber Co-Sponsoren),
- Co-Sponsoring (keine exklusiven Rechte).

Event-Sponsoring bildet somit einen Spezialfall im Rahmen der Formen nach der Nutzung und Umsetzung des Sportsponsoring: Das Engagement ist in aller Regel nicht auf einen längeren Zeitraum, sondern nur auf die Dauer der Veranstaltung angelegt. Sportgroßveranstaltungen haben sich zu fest stehenden Begriffen für Spannung, Unterhaltung und sportliche Höchstleistungen entwickelt. Sport-Events besitzen bei der sportinteressierten Bevölkerung einen hohen Bekanntheitsgrad und üben eine riesige Faszination aus (vgl. Abb. 1). Die Reichweite solcher Sportereignisse liegt bereits vor Ort bei zigtausend Zuschauern und kann mittels medialer Multiplikatoren wie TV, Hörfunk, Print oder Internet ein internationales Publikum in Milliardenhöhe erreichen.

391

	Faszination	Bekanntheit
Fußball-WM	75%	100%
Olympische Spiele	70%	99%
Formel 1	67%	100%
Fußball-EM	63%	99%
Champions League	52%	97%
Wimbledon	47%	99%
Tour de France	45%	98%
Vierschanzentournee	37%	95%
ATP World Championship	31%	86%

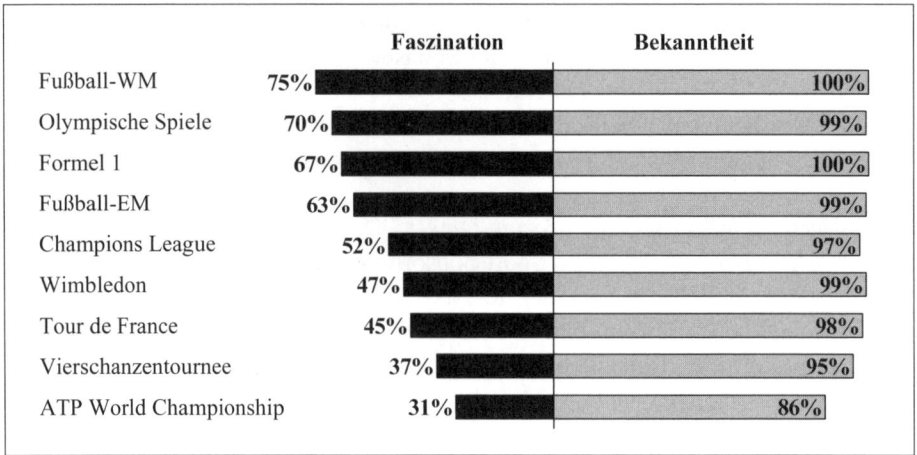

Abb. 1: Faszination und Bekanntheit ausgewählter Sportereignisse
In Anlehnung an: Hermanns/Riedmüller (2001), S. 6

14.3.3 Ausgewählte Beispiele aus dem Sport

Beim Event-Sponsoring werden nationale und internationale Sportereignisse finanziell unterstützt mit dem Ziel, die Veranstaltung für das Unternehmen werblich zu nutzen. Werbemöglichkeiten ergeben sich beispielsweise in Form der Bandenwerbung, des Titelsponsoring, der Einrichtung von VIP-Lounges zur Bewirtung von Ehrengästen, der Werbung an Gebäuden, in Programmheften, auf Eintrittskarten u.a.m. Häufig werden dabei Einzelmaßnahmen nicht isoliert genutzt, sondern vom Veranstalter Sponsorenpakete zusammengestellt, um Sponsoren ein attraktives Bündel werblicher Maßnahmen anzubieten (Bruhn, 2005).

Eine große Abhängigkeit von Sponsorengeldern besteht mittlerweile v.a. bei großen, internationalen Sportveranstaltungen des Hochleistungssports. Internationale Fußballturniere sind heute zu einem großen Teil auf zahlungskräftige Sponsoren angewiesen. Die Anteile der Einnahmen durch Werbung und Fernsehgelder beliefen sich bei früheren Fußball-Weltmeisterschaften sogar auf rund zwei Drittel. Die Entscheidung, sich bei einer Sportveranstaltung als Sponsor zu engagieren, hängt auf Unternehmensseite fast ausschließlich vom indirekten Publikum ab, wobei dem Fernsehen hierbei die absolute Schlüsselrolle zukommt (Walliser, 1995; Bruhn, 2005).

Bei der *Fußball-Weltmeisterschaft 2006 in Deutschland* waren 21 Unternehmen in zwei unterschiedlichen Sponsoring-Kategorien als offizielle Sponsoren mit von der Partie (vgl. Abb. 2). Zu den autorisierten Unternehmen gehörten 15 offizielle Hauptsponsoren. Zusätzlich erlaubte die FIFA dem deutschen Organisationskomitee, diesen Kreis um sechs nationale Partner zu erweitern. Die Sponsorshipkosten beliefen sich auf ca. 45 Mio. € pro offiziellem Hauptsponsor und ca. 13 Mio. € pro nationalem Förderer. Diesem Kreis von Unternehmen war es vorbehalten, die offiziellen Logos und Maskottchen, die in ihrer Mehrzahl eigens für diese WM kreiert wurden, in ihrer Kommunikationspolitik zu nutzen (Schröder, 2006; Nufer, 2006).

Abb. 2: Die offiziellen Sponsoren der Fußball-Weltmeisterschaft 2006 in Deutschland

Zum Vergleich: Acht Jahre zuvor, bei der *Fußball-Weltmeisterschaft 1998 in Frankreich*, durften sich noch insgesamt 45 Unternehmen offizielle Sponsoren nennen. Neben den zwölf offiziellen Hauptsponsoren (Sponsoring-Kategorie I, Kosten: ca. 30 Mio. US-$) agierten 33 weitere Unternehmen in den zusätzlichen Sponsoring-Kategorien II (8 offizielle Lieferanten, jeweils ca. 10 Mio. US-$), III (9 offizielle Produkt- und Serviceunternehmen, jeweils ca. 5 Mio. US-$) und IV (16 offizielle Ausstattungs- und Gerätelieferanten, individuelle Verträge). Hinzu kamen auf der untersten Vermarktungsebene noch zahlreiche Lizenznehmer mit ebenfalls individuellen Verträgen (Nufer, 2002).

14.3.4 Kritische Würdigung

Die wichtigsten *Vorteile* des Event-Sponsoring, die dieses Kommunikationsinstrument für zahlreiche Unternehmen so attraktiv machen, sind (Bruhn, 2003; Berndt, 2005; Nufer, 2007):

- Die kommunikative Ansprache erfolgt in einem attraktiven sportlichen Umfeld.
- Es lassen sich hohe (internationale) Reichweiten und damit vergleichsweise günstige Tausenderkontaktpreise realisieren.
- Der Multiplikatoreffekt der Massenmedien kann voll ausgenutzt werden.
- Angestrebt wird ein positiver Imagetransfer vom Event auf die Marke bzw. das Unternehmen (anders als beim Sponsoring von Einzelsportlern oder Teams ist beim Event-Sponsoring keine Gefahr eines negativen Imagetransfers zu befürchten, beispielsweise hervorgerufen durch Skandale um Einzelsportler oder Niederlagenserien von Mannschaften).

Nachteilig stehen dem insbesondere hohe Kosten und eine begrenzte Zahl in Frage kommender (Mega-)Events gegenüber.

14.4 Event-Marketing

Mit dem Event-Marketing hat sich ein innovatives nicht-klassisches Kommunikationsinstrument etabliert, das – sofern man die gesamte Bandbreite der sich damit ergebenden Möglichkeiten nutzt – eine moderne Ergänzung des bestehenden Kommunikationsmix darstellt. Die vielfältigen Einsatzmöglichkeiten und Potenziale des Event-Marketing ermöglichen es, entsprechend dem momentanen Zeitgeist relevante Zielgruppen zu erreichen, markenrelevante Wirklichkeiten und Erlebniswelten zu generieren, Emotionen und Sympathiewerte zu erzeugen und auf diese Weise insbesondere durch den Einsatz im Sport eine Bindung zwischen Marke bzw. Unternehmen und Rezipienten herzustellen (Nufer, 2007).

14.4.1 Definition und Merkmale

Marketing-Events zeichnen sich dadurch aus, dass sie aus einer Veranstaltung etwas Besonderes oder sogar Einmaliges generieren, sie ermöglichen ein Erleben von Marken bzw. Unternehmen. Durch produkt-, unternehmens- oder dienstleistungsbezogene Ereignisse sollen kognitive, emotionale und physische Reize dargeboten, Aktivierungsprozesse ausgelöst sowie unternehmensgesteuerte Botschaften, Informationen und Assoziationen kommuniziert werden, die zum Aufbau von Unternehmens- und Markenwerten einen positiven Beitrag leisten. Marketing-Events sind also im Auftrag inszenierte Ereignisse, die das zentrale Ziel haben, den Teilnehmern Erlebnisse zu vermitteln. Events sind ein Kommunikationsmittel und können prinzipiell auch im Rahmen anderer Kommunikationsinstrumente eingesetzt werden (Nufer, 2007).

Daran anknüpfend ist unter Event-Marketing das zielgerichtete Gestalten eines solchen Ereignisses im Rahmen eines Planungs- und Steuerungsprozesses zu verstehen:

> *„Event-Marketing* ist ein interaktives sowie erlebnisorientiertes Kommunikationsinstrument, das der zielgerichteten, zielgruppen- bzw. szenenbezogenen Inszenierung von eigens initiierten Veranstaltungen sowie deren Planung, Realisation und Kontrolle im Rahmen einer Integrierten Unternehmenskommunikation dient" (Nufer, 2007, S. 21).

Event-Marketing beinhaltet die systematische Planung, Organisation, Durchführung und Kontrolle von Events sowie die sinnvolle Einbindung in die Integrierte Unternehmenskommunikation. Beim Event-Marketing handelt es sich also um ein eigenständiges Kommunikationsinstrument.

Anhand seiner *konstitutiven Merkmale* lässt sich Event-Marketing insbesondere vom (Event-)Sponsoring klar abgrenzen (vgl. Tab. 1): Ein wesentliches Kommunikationsmerkmal des Event-Marketing ist seine *Interaktionsorientierung* im Rahmen einer *Erlebnisstrategie.* Auf der einen Seite ermöglicht die Dialogfähigkeit einen unmittelbaren, persönlichen Kontakt mit der Zielgruppe, wodurch Streuverluste relativ gering gehalten werden können. Auf der anderen Seite werden die Anwesenden im Unterschied zum Sponsoring oder zu Sales Promotions emotional angesprochen und über die Verhaltensebene aktiv in die Veranstaltung miteinbezogen. Ein weiteres Charakteristikum des Event-Marketing ist die eigenverantwortliche Durchführung. Die Veranstaltung wird vom Unternehmen selbst *initiiert;* es wird nicht wie beispielsweise beim Sponsoring oder auf Messen ein fremdgeschaffener Rahmen als Präsentationsplattform genutzt. Die eigens *inszenierte* Markenwelt soll für den Rezipienten erlebbar werden und zu einer emotionalen Bindung des Konsumenten an die Marke führen (Nufer, 2007).

14.4.2 Ziele und Erscheinungsformen

Event-Marketing wird in erster Linie zur Erreichung des Oberzieles „Emotionalisierung der Zielgruppe" durchgeführt. Psychologische *Kommunikationsziele* stehen deshalb beim Event-Marketing als Detailziele im Vordergrund. Es kann dabei zunächst differenziert werden zwischen affektiv-orientierten und kognitiv-orientierten Kommunikationszielen. Die jeweilige Gewichtung erfolgt dabei in Abhängigkeit von Anlass und Zielgruppe. Diese doppelte Dichotomisierung erlaubt eine Einteilung der psychologischen Kommunikationsziele des Event-Marketing in vier Gruppen, die in Tab. 2 zusammengefasst und illustriert sind:

Affektiv-orientierte externe Ziele	Kognitiv-orientierte externe Ziele
• emotionales Erleben von Unternehmen und Produkten bzw. Marken • Aufbau, Pflege oder Modifikation des Unternehmens- bzw. Markenimages • emotionale Markenpositionierung • Integration der Marke und ihrer Inhalte in die Erlebniswelt des Rezipienten • Aktivierung der Wahrnehmung • Aufbau und Pflege einer Beziehung zwischen Unternehmen und Kunden auf der Basis eines kollektiven Erlebnisses • Erreichen von Sympathie und Glaubwürdigkeit • Einstellungsänderung bei der Zielgruppe	• Bekanntmachung insbesondere neuer Produkte • Vermittlung von Schlüsselinformationen über Produkte • aktive Auseinandersetzung der Teilnehmer mit der Thematik • Kontaktpflege mit ausgewählten Kunden, Meinungsführern und Medienvertretern
Affektiv-orientierte interne Ziele	**Kognitiv-orientierte interne Ziele**
• Motivation der Mitarbeiter • Identifikation der Mitarbeiter mit dem Unternehmen • Integration der Mitarbeiter • Schaffung eines Zugehörigkeitsgefühls	• Fachwissen • Weiterbildung • Persönliche Fähigkeiten • Kundenbewusstsein

Tab. 2: Katalog psychologischer Kommunikationsziele des Event-Marketing
Quelle: Nufer (2007), S. 59

In Theorie und Praxis wird inzwischen eine Vielzahl von *Erscheinungsformen* als Realisierungen von Event-Marketing-Konzepten aufgeführt. Zur Systematisierung werden oftmals Kriterien in Form von Merkmalspaaren herangezogen (Zanger/Sistenich, 1996; Bruhn, 2005; Nufer, 2007).

(1) Interne Events, externe Events und Mischformen:
Dieses Kriterium fokussiert auf einer Systematisierung der Zielgruppen. Während unternehmensinterne Events (z.B. Kongresse und Fortbildungsveranstaltungen) primär der Mitarbeiteridentifikation und -motivation dienen, haben Events, die sich an externe Zielgruppen richten (z.B. Sport- und Kulturveranstaltungen), vordergründig die Kundenakquisition und -bindung zum Gegenstand. Mischformen (wie beispielsweise Kick-Off-Events oder Jubiläen) sind ebenfalls denkbar.

(2) Arbeitsorientierte, freizeitorientierte und Infotainment-Events:
Je nach Veranstaltungsart und -zielen kann die Inszenierung des Event-Erlebnisses einen stärker bzw. schwächer informierenden oder unterhaltenden Charakter aufweisen, so dass eine Polarisierung in arbeitsorientierte (z.B. Produktschulungen) und freizeitorientierte Aktivitäten (z.B. Incentive-Reisen) vorgenommen werden kann, wobei Infotainment-Events die dazwischen liegende Mischform darstellen

(ein Beispiel hierfür ist die Vorstellung eines neuen Produktes im Rahmen einer multimedialen Präsentation mit Showelementen).

(3) Anlassorientierte, markenorientierte sowie anlass- und markenorientierte Events:
In diesem Kontinuum beziehen sich die Abgrenzungsmerkmale auf das zugrunde liegende Event-Marketing-Konzept. Anlassorientiertes Event-Marketing zielt auf die Darstellung des Unternehmens im Rahmen der Feier historischer (z.B. Jubiläen) oder geschaffener Anlässe (z.B. Grundsteinlegung für ein neues Werk). Markenorientiertes Event-Marketing soll eine emotionale Positionierung der Marke sowie deren dauerhafte Verankerung in der Erlebniswelt des Rezipienten erreichen (bei derartigen Unternehmensveranstaltungen werden häufig Mottos eingesetzt, die die Aspekte des angestrebten Erlebnisprofils konkretisieren). Zugleich anlass- und markenorientiertes Event-Marketing bezieht sich auf einen zeitlich festgelegten Anlass, wird aber zusätzlich zur Vermittlung produkt- bzw. markenbezogener Botschaften eingesetzt.

An allen drei aufgeführten Merkmalsskalen kann kritisiert werden, dass sie lediglich einzelne Ansatzpunkte für eine Systematisierung offerieren, aber kein in sich geschlossenes Kategorisierungssystem darstellen. Im Folgenden soll deshalb der Versuch unternommen werden, Elemente aus allen drei Kategorisierungsansätzen zu einem *integrierenden Gesamtkonzept* zu fusionieren (Nufer, 2007). Eine Typologie der Event-Marketing-Formen kann mittels einer dreidimensionalen Grafik dargestellt werden (vgl. Abb. 3), die einen Kompromiss aus der Steigerung des Allgemeinheitsgrades und der Reduktion des Bestimmtheitsgrades bildet. Der resultierende „Event-Marketing-Würfel" besteht dabei aus folgenden drei *Dimensionen:*

- Die erste Dimension fokussiert die in der Literatur zum Event-Marketing am häufigsten anzutreffende Systematisierung nach den *Zielgruppen*: Es werden unternehmensinterne und unternehmensexterne Adressaten voneinander getrennt, wobei Mischformen dazwischen stehen können.
- Die zweite Dimension baut auf einer Kategorisierung der Events auf: Nach der Art ihrer *Inszenierung* wird auf die Unterscheidung in freizeitorientierte und arbeitsorientierte Events zurückgegriffen, dazwischen werden die Infotainment-Veranstaltungen platziert.
- Die dritte Dimension bezieht sich auf das zugrunde liegende *Konzept* des Event-Marketing: Es wird der Frage nachgegangen, ob der Einsatz des Event-Marketing eher markenorientiert, anlassorientiert oder anlass- und markenorientiert erfolgt.

Der gesamte Würfel kann demzufolge in 27 Teilwürfel aufgeteilt werden. Jeder dieser Teilwürfel repräsentiert somit einen von 27 möglichen Event-Typen.

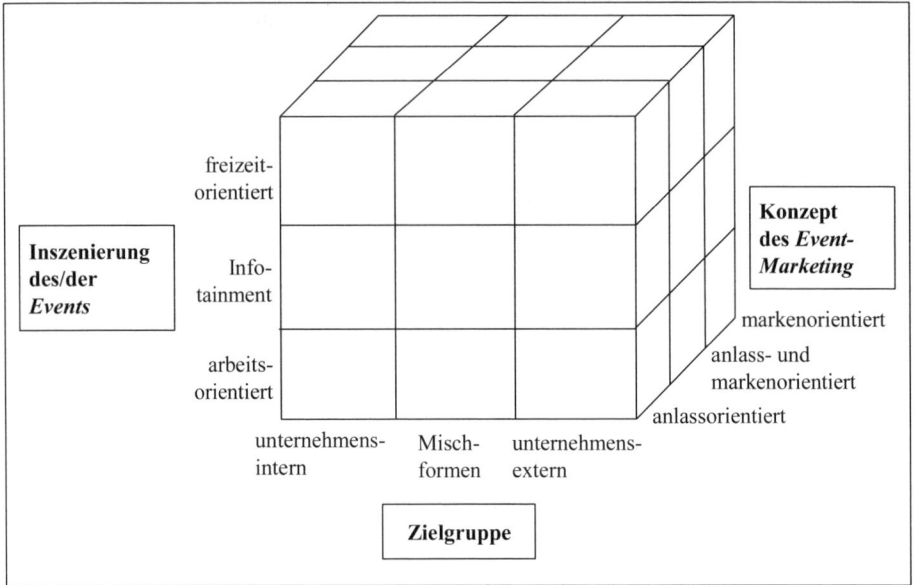

Abb. 3: Dreidimensionale Typologie der Event-Marketing-Formen
Quelle: Nufer (2007), S. 42

14.4.3 Ausgewählte Beispiele aus dem Sport

Aufgrund seines Event-Marketing-Engagements gilt *adidas* bis heute als der Event-Marketing-Pionier in Deutschland, weshalb im Folgenden erfolgreiches Sport-Event-Marketing anhand des Beispiels adidas illustriert werden soll (Nufer, 2007; Runau, 2007).

Das Ergebnis einer Anfang der neunziger Jahre durchgeführten Marktforschungsstudie brachte es auf den Punkt: Die Marke adidas wurde bei Jugendlichen als konservativ, verstaubt, altmodisch und nicht trendy angesehen. V.a. junge amerikanische Sportmarken hatten adidas den Rang abgelaufen. Vor diesem Hintergrund musste adidas für die Ansprache von Jugendlichen neue Wege finden. Kern der neuen Marketing-Strategie war es, die Jugendlichen mit markenspezifischen Events zur Interaktion zu motivieren und künstliche Erlebniswelten der Werbung durch zielgruppenspezifische Realerlebnisse zu ersetzen: „adidas goes street". „Coole", sportbezogene Events sollten die Kompetenz von adidas ins rechte Licht rücken. Adidas betrachtete dabei die mit den Events angesprochenen trendsensiblen Zielgruppen nicht als Absatzmarkt, sondern versucht vielmehr, mit den Trendsettern und Opinion Leadern eine Partnerschaft aufzubauen. Sie sollten Botschaft und soziales Prestige an die Basis weitertragen und multiplizieren.

Neben den „Originals" (wiederaufgelegte Schuhmodelle und Textilien aus den siebziger Jahren) verhalfen die folgenden Event-Marketing-Serien der Marke adidas ab 1992 zum Comeback:

- *adidas Streetball Challenge:*
  Adidas brachte die Idee der vereinfachten Basketball-Hinterhof-Variante, die ihren Ursprung in den USA hat, nach Europa. Adidas hat den Begriff „Streetball" nicht nur hierzulande lanciert, sondern ihn zudem auch weltweit urheberrechtlich schützen lassen.

- *adidas Adventure Challenge:*
  Bei diesem Event bewältigen Abenteurer in einem sportlichen Wettbewerb Herausforderungen wie Mountainbiking, Trailrunning oder Hydro Speed.

- *Predator-Cup:*
  1994, im Jahr der Fußball-Weltmeisterschaft in den USA, fanden in Deutschland die ersten von adidas organisierten Fußball-Nachwuchsturniere statt, die die verkrusteten Strukturen des organisierten Vereinsfußballs aufbrechen sollten, um der Jugend mehr Spaß in Verbindung mit Fußball zu vermitteln.

- *DFB-adidas-Cup:*
  Ab 1995 wurde der Predator-Cup unter dem Namen DFB-adidas-Cup mit umfangreicherer Inszenierung fortgeführt.

Abb. 4: Impressionen von der adidas Streetball Challenge und vom DFB-adidas-Cup

V.a. die strategisch geplanten „Grass-Root"-Events im sportlichen Umfeld verhalfen der Marke adidas binnen kurzer Zeit zu einer erfolgreichen Renaissance inklusive der gewünschten Imagekorrektur in Richtung jugendlich, cool, lifestyle- und erlebnisorientiert. Insbesondere die adidas Streetball Challenge wird in der wissenschaftlichen Literatur seither immer wieder als Paradebeispiel für die erfolgreiche Konzeption und Realisation internationaler Marketing-Events aufgeführt (Plewe, 1996; Zanger/Sistenich, 1996; Bruhn, 2005).

14.4.4 Kritische Würdigung

Da die Entwicklungen, die maßgeblich zur Entstehung des Event-Marketing beigetragen haben – wie beispielsweise die sinkende Effizienz klassischer Kommunikationsinstrumente oder das Erlebnisbedürfnis von Konsumenten –, noch lange nicht abgeschlossen sind, ist davon auszugehen, dass die *Bedeutung* des Event-Marketing innerhalb der Unternehmenskommunikation weiterhin zunehmen wird.

Event-Marketing ist insbesondere hinsichtlich der Zielsetzung „Emotionalisierung der Zielgruppe" dem Event-Sponsoring tendenziell überlegen: Hohe Emotionen sind beim Sportsponsoring oftmals eher hinderlich, da hier die Aufmerksamkeit in erster Linie auf das sportliche Geschehen und nicht auf die kommunikationspolitische Ansprache fokusiert ist. Beim Event-Marketing dagegen können Emotionen positiv genutzt werden, da eigene positive Markenerlebnisse zum Aufbau langfristiger Gedächtnisinhalte beitragen (Nufer, 2007).

Neben aller Euphorie, die mit diesem Kommunikationsinstrument – zurecht – verbunden werden kann, sind von Unternehmen aber auch *Risiken* des Event-Marketing-Einsatzes zu antizipieren: Der verstärkte Einsatz des Event-Marketing kann mittelfristig zu Reaktanzen und einer abnehmenden Effektivität dieses Kommunikationsinstrumentes führen, da bei den Zielgruppen Sättigungserscheinungen („wear-out-Effekte") in Bezug auf häufig eingesetzte Eventtypen und Inszenierungsinhalte auftreten könnten.

Durch die kaum mehr zu überblickende Vielfalt an Freizeitangeboten steigt der Wettbewerb der einzelnen Angebote untereinander, die allesamt um die Freizeitbudgets und die Zeit der Zielgruppen konkurrieren. Hinzu kommt das „Variety Seeking", insbesondere im Sport- und Freizeitbereich: Zielgruppen suchen immer wieder nach Abwechslung und neuen Herausforderungen, so dass es schwieriger wird, sie an die Events eines bestimmten Unternehmens zu binden (Bruhn, 2005).

14.5 Ambush Marketing

Die steigende Wettbewerbsintensität auf dem Sponsoringmarkt führt zu einer Explosion der Preise für Sponsorships und hat zur Folge, dass nicht alle am Ereignis interessierten Unternehmen sich ein offizielles Sponsoringengagement leisten können oder wollen. Zusätzlich nimmt die Gestaltung der Sponsoring-Regelungen bei Mega-Events selbst (z.B. die Gewährleistung von Branchenexklusivität für offizielle

Sponsoren) oftmals Konkurrenten jegliche Chance, „legitim" im Rahmen des Events mit der Zielgruppe in Kontakt zu treten und bildet somit geradezu eine Provokation zur Durchführung von Ambush-Aktivitäten.

14.5.1 Definition und Merkmale

„Ambush" bedeutet wörtlich übersetzt Hinterhalt, „to ambush" soviel wie aus dem Hinterhalt überfallen. Ambush Marketing kennzeichnet demzufolge einen Marketing-Überfall aus dem Hinterhalt. In der eher populärwissenschaftlichen Literatur wird Ambush Marketing häufig synonym verwendet zu Begriffen wie „Trittbrettfahren", „parasitäres Marketing" und „Schmarotzer-Marketing" (o.V., 2004). Deutlich wird, dass der Begriff Ambush Marketing zunächst negativ besetzt ist. Der Grat zwischen kreativer Kommunikationspolitik und der Verletzung von Sponsorenrechten ist oft sehr schmal: Offizielle Sponsoren bezeichnen diesen Überfall aus dem Hinterhalt auf teuer gekaufte Werberechte als „Diebstahl" und betonen die illegalen Aspekte des Ambush Marketing (Payne, 1998; Townley/Harrington/Couchman, 1998). Es gibt jedoch auch Vertreter einer Gegenposition. Sie sehen Ambush Marketing als eine „legitime Kraft", die dem Sponsoringmarkt zu mehr Effizienz verhilft: „... all this talk about unethical ambushing is ... intellectual rubbish and postured by people who are sloppy marketers" (Welsh, 2002, o.S.). Das Phänomen Ambush Marketing ist insgesamt keineswegs neu, hat jedoch in den letzten Jahren deutlich an Professionalität hinzugewonnen. Obwohl die Thematik zunächst fast ausschließlich von angloamerikanischen Autoren aufgegriffen wurde, handelt es sich längst nicht mehr um ein amerikanisches Phänomen. Die zunehmende Aggressivität in den Kommunikations- und Sponsoringmärkten hat dazu geführt, dass Ambush Marketing heute weltweit beobachtet werden kann und immer stärker zunimmt.

Eine frühe wissenschaftliche Definition zum Ambush Marketing geht zurück auf Meenaghan (1994). Er umschreibt Ambush Marketing als „the practice whereby another company, often a competitor, intrudes upon public attention surrounding the event, thereby deflecting attention toward themselves and away from the sponsor" (Meenaghan, 1994, S. 79). Von Bortoluzzi Dubach/Frey (2002) stammt eine der bislang wenigen deutschsprachigen wissenschaftlichen Auseinandersetzungen mit der Thematik. Sie charakterisieren Ambush Marketing als „unerlaubtes Trittbrettfahren, bei dem ein Außenseiter von einem Anlass profitiert, ohne selbst Sponsor zu sein." (Bortoluzzi Dubach/Frey, 2002, S. 149). Für die nachfolgende Betrachtung soll folgende Arbeitsdefinition verwendet werden:

> „*Ambush Marketing* ist die Vorgehensweise von Unternehmen, dem direkten und indirekten Publikum durch eigene Kommunikationsmaßnahmen eine autorisierte Verbindung zu einem Event zu signalisieren, obwohl das Unternehmen keine le-

galisierten oder lediglich unterprivilegierte Vermarktungsrechte an dieser (von Dritten gesponserten) Veranstaltung besitzt" (Nufer, 2005, S. 211).

Die wesentlichen *Merkmale* des Ambush Marketing können somit folgendermaßen zusammengefasst werden (Bruhn/Ahlers, 2003; Nufer, 2007; Nufer, 2005).

- Es handelt sich um einen bewussten bzw. geplanten Versuch eines Unternehmens, die Wirkung der Aktivitäten eines offiziellen Sponsors zu schwächen.
- Ambush Marketing wird insbesondere von direkten Branchenkonkurrenten autorisierter Sponsoren praktiziert und dient hauptsächlich als Alternative zum Event-Sponsoring.
- Es erfolgt eine Täuschung der Zielgruppe im Hinblick auf die Verbindung zwischen Sponsoringanlass und Sponsor bzw. Ambusher; die Aufmerksamkeit wird durch Ambush Marketing weg vom offiziellen Sponsor, hin zum Ambusher verschoben.
- Angestrebt wird eine Assoziation mit einem speziellen Event oder einem Projekt zu vergleichsweise geringen Kosten; Ambush Marketing lässt den finanziellen Beitrag von Sponsoren gewissermaßen unnötig erscheinen.

14.5.2 Ziele und Erscheinungsformen

Die Idee des Ambush Marketing ist es, von den Erfolgen des Event-Sponsoring zu profitieren, ohne die Pflichten eines offiziellen Sponsors einzugehen. Damit sind die *Ziele* von Ambush Marketing weitgehend deckungsgleich mit den Zielen des (Event-)Sponsoring, sollen jedoch mit reduziertem finanziellen Aufwand erreicht werden. Im Vordergrund steht das Erreichen psychologischer bzw. kommunikativer Zielsetzungen (Nufer, 2005):

- Aufmerksamkeit,
- Aufbau bzw. Verbesserung bestimmter Imagedimensionen,
- Stabilisierung bzw. Erhöhung der Marken-/Unternehmensbekanntheit,
- Schaffung von Goodwill und Demonstration gesellschaftlicher Verantwortung.

Als *Erscheinungsformen* können folgende Strategien des Ambush Marketing unterschieden werden (Pechtl, 2007; Crow/Hoek, 2003; Bruhn/Ahlers, 2003; Nufer, 2002):

(1) Programmsponsoring der Medienberichterstattung eines Sport-Großereignisses:
Die Übernahme eines Programmsponsorings ist grundsätzlich völlig legitim, kann jedoch als Ambush Marketing interpretiert werden, wenn der Programmsponsor Konkurrent eines offiziellen Sponsors ist.

(2) Engagement als offizieller Sponsor einer preiswerteren untergeordneten Sponsoring-Kategorie:
Auch diese zunächst einwandfreie Vorgehensweise wird zu Ambush Marketing, sofern sie mit einer „Überinterpretation" der eingeräumten Rechte der untergeordneten Sponsoren-Kategorie einhergeht und/oder einem direkten Branchenkonkurrenten in der ersten Sponsoren-Reihe das Werbefeld nicht alleine überlassen werden soll.

(3) Sponsoring bzw. Ausstattung der Teilnehmer einer Veranstaltung:
Verträge mit einzelnen Mannschaften oder Individualsportlern bescheren zahlreichen Unternehmen sowohl die Präsenz bei und im Umfeld einer Veranstaltung als auch in der Medienberichterstattung – ohne die Notwendigkeit, offizieller Sponsor der Veranstaltung zu sein.

(4) Außenwerbung zeitgleich mit einem Event:
Ambush-Aktivitäten können sowohl auf dem Veranstaltungsgelände als auch im Umfeld der Veranstaltung zum Einsatz kommen; eine weitere Möglichkeit stellt beispielsweise der Luftraum dar (z.B. Flugzeuge mit Werbebannern).

(5) Klassische Werbekampagnen (TV, Print), die ein Event zeitlich überlagern:
Unternehmen greifen das Thema/Motto einer Veranstaltung direkt auf oder erzeugen durch Andeutungen eine Assoziation mit dem Event; dasselbe Ziel lässt sich durch Schalten von TV-Werbung in den Werbepausen eines Sport-Events erreichen; nicht zuletzt durch die Möglichkeit der vergleichenden Werbung eröffnen sich insbesondere für Wettbewerber offizieller Sponsoren zusätzliche Ambush-Möglichkeiten.

(6) Bewusstes Verdecken der Logos der offiziellen Sponsoren durch Sportler zugunsten eines Ambushers:
Ambusher können die Markenzeichen und Werbeflächen offizieller Sponsoren blockieren (lassen), indem sie deren Logos verdecken und ggf. stattdessen ihr eigenes Logo zeigen.

(7) Entwicklung weiterer kreativer Ansätze:
Ein Unternehmen erweckt den Eindruck, eine bestimmte Lizenz zu halten; es erfindet fantasievolle eigene Logos, kopiert den Werbeauftritt eines Mitbewerbers oder kooperiert mit einem offiziellen Sponsor als Trittbrettfahrer usw. – wie die Praxis zeigt, sind der Kreativität keine Grenzen gesetzt.

(8) „Fun Ambushing":
Im Sommer 1999 versah der Mars-Konzern jede Packung seiner Marke „m&m's" mit dem scherzhaften Prädikat „Unofficial Sponsors of the New Millenium". Diese

besondere, „softe" Form von Ambushing lässt sich am trefflichsten mit „Fun Ambushing" charakterisieren.

14.5.3 Ausgewählte Beispiele aus dem Sport

Die Grenzen zwischen Erlaubtem und Verbotenem bzw. zwischen fairem und unfairem Wettbewerb sind beim Ambush Marketing häufig nur sehr schwer zu ziehen. Die folgende Liste enthält ausgewählte innovative und interessante *Beispiele* für Ambush Marketing (Nufer, 2007; Nufer, 2005):

- Einer der ersten Fälle dessen, was heute als Ambush Marketing bezeichnet werden würde, ereignete sich im Rahmen der Olympischen Sommerspiele 1984 in Los Angeles: Fuji-Film war offizieller Sponsor der Spiele, Kodak wurde davon unbeeindruckt Programmsponsor im US-Fernsehen und „offizieller Film" (heutzutage wird Vergleichbares i.d.R. durch die Vergabe von Exklusivrechten verhindert).

- Olympische Winterspiele 1994 in Lillehammer: American Express warb zeitgleich zum Event mit dem griffigen Slogan: „If you´re travelling to Norway this winter, you´ll need a passport – but you don´t need a visa" (Konkurrent Visa ist offizieller Olympia-Sponsor).

- Fußball-Weltmeisterschaft 1994 in den USA: McDonald´s setzte sich als „inoffizieller Nahrungslieferant der deutschen Fußball-Fans" in Szene, ohne auch nur einen Pfennig an Lizenzgebühren bezahlt zu haben (was unter „softem Ambush Marketing" subsumiert werden kann, zumal McDonald´s seit 1998 zum Kreis der offiziellen Hauptsponsoren von Fußball-Weltmeisterschaften zählt).

- Fußball-Weltmeisterschaft 1994 in den USA: Während der amerikanische Sportartikelhersteller Nike die Fußball-WM im eigenen Land zunächst weitgehend ungenutzt vorüber ziehen ließ, meldete sich die Marke rechtzeitig zum Finale Brasilien – Italien in Los Angeles mit einem Paukenschlag. Vor und im Stadion wurden 70.000 Baseball-Caps in den brasilianischen Landesfarben und mit dem Nike-Swoosh verschenkt, obwohl zum damaligen Zeitpunkt noch der Konkurrent Umbro Ausrüster der Brasilianer war. Dadurch glich das Stadion einem Nike-Meer.

- Der 100m-Sprinter Linford Christie erhielt 1996 angeblich 1 Million Pfund vom Sportartikelhersteller Puma allein dafür, dass er in Pressekonferenzen mit Kontaktlinsen auftrat, die unübersehbar das Puma-Logo zeigten.

- Olympische Winterspiele 1998 in Nagano: Hier sponserte Nike einen zwar sportlich hoffnungslos unterlegenen schwarzafrikanischen Ski-Langläufer, dem aber als vermeintlichem „Exoten" in dieser Sportart die Medienaufmerksamkeit gewiss war, was dem Ausstatter Nike zahlreiche Fernseh-Einblendungen bescherte.

- Der australische Schwimm-Star Ian Thorpe (der persönlich von adidas gesponsert wird) verdeckte bei einer Medaillen-Verleihung mit einem Handtuch das

Logo auf seiner Kleidung (Nike ist offizieller Ausrüster des australischen Teams).

- Ein ähnlicher Vorfall ereignete sich 1992 im Rahmen der Olympischen Sommerspiele in Barcelona: Charles Barkley und Michael Jordan aus dem siegreichen US-Basketball-Dream-Team hüllten sich während der Medaillen-Zeremonie in US-Flaggen ein. Wie sie hinterher eingestanden, hatten sie dabei weniger patriotische Beweggründe, sondern verfolgten vielmehr das Ziel, zugunsten ihres persönlichen Sponsors Nike den Schriftzug des Team-Sponsors Reebok auf ihren Trikots zu verdecken.

- Auch bei den Olympischen Sommerspielen 2004 in Athen konnte Ambushing beobachtet werden: Eine griechische Telefongesellschaft (deren Konkurrent nationaler Olympia-Sponsor war), warb großflächig auf sieben Fähren, die im Hafen von Piräus ankerten – und nur schwer zu übersehen waren.

Abb. 5 gibt exemplarisch *Anzeigen-Motive* wieder, die zeitgleich zu sportlichen Mega-Events geschaltet wurden:

- Fußball-Weltmeisterschaft 1998 in Frankreich: Canon wirbt als offizieller Hauptsponsor ganz legal in seiner Anzeige mit dem Logo France ´98 und rückt das Thema Fußball in das Zentrum der Anzeige.

- Die Brauerei Warsteiner, die nicht zum Kreis der offiziellen Sponsoren gehört, steht dem kaum nach: Auch in dieser Anzeige regiert „König Fußball", und es wird mehrfach auf die WM Bezug genommen.

- Genauso beliebt ist es, Reisen und Tickets von Events zu verlosen, um damit eine Assoziation zwischen Unternehmen und Veranstaltung herzustellen, die per se nicht gegeben ist. Die beste Wirkung wird erzielt, indem zusätzlich die Elemente (hier die WM-Trophäe) und Farben des Veranstalters abgebildet bzw. imitiert werden.

- Auch vor dem Aufgreifen olympischer Motive in Werbekampagnen machen gewiefte Werber keinen Halt. Im abgedruckten Beispiel gelingt es sogar, die gewünschte Assoziation herzustellen, ohne dass Logos, Markenzeichen, Farben oder geschützte Ausdrücke missbraucht werden.

14.5.4 Kritische Würdigung

Gegner des Ambush Marketing verdammen Ambushing als „illegalen Diebstahl" teuer erkaufter Werberechte: „... ambush marketing is not a game ...; ambush marketers are thieves knowingly stealing something that does not belong to them" (Payne, 1998, S. 232 ff.). Contra Ambush Marketing können ferner folgende Argumente vorgebracht werden:

- Die Effektivität der Aktivitäten der offiziellen Sponsoren wird geschmälert: allein Unternehmen, die Sponsoringbeiträge entrichten, sollten auch vom Event profitieren dürfen,

- Irreführung der Konsumenten,
- Schaden für Event-Veranstalter,
- Unsicherheit bei Medien.

Diese Argumente lassen sich in folgendem Szenario verdichten: Was wäre, wenn alle Unternehmen Ambushing dem Engagement als offizieller Sponsor vorziehen würden?

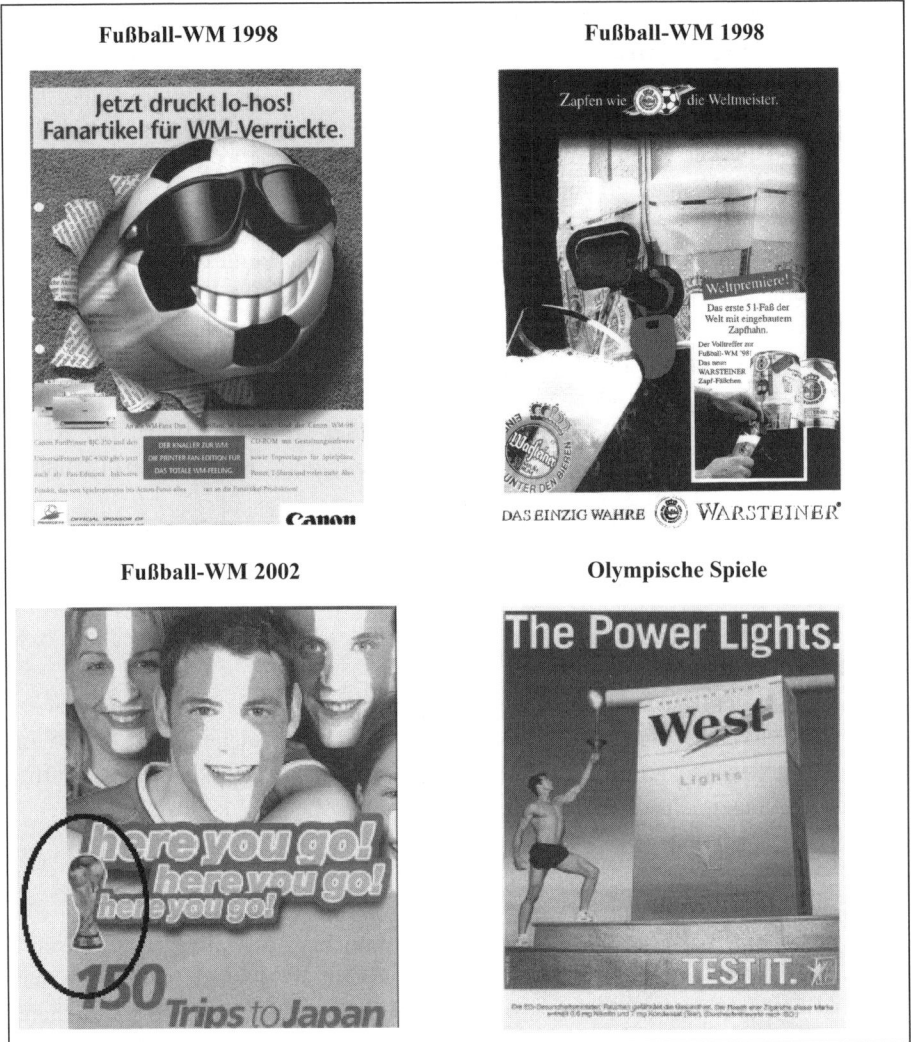

Abb. 5: Exemplarische Print-Anzeigen
Quelle: Nufer (2005), S. 217

Wie bereits skizziert, existiert jedoch auch eine Gegenposition, die sich *für Ambush Marketing* ausspricht und Ambushing als „legitime Kraft" bezeichnet, die dem Sponsoringmarkt zu mehr Effizienz verhilft: „When you own and license Kermit you have only given the rights you own to one specific frog, and maybe not even to all green ones" (Welsh, 2002, o.S.). Pro Ambush Marketing lässt sich also vorbringen:

- Offizielle Sponsoren kaufen zwar Werberechte an einem Event, nicht aber das gesamte thematische Umfeld,
- Ambush Marketing ist die natürliche Konsequenz eines gesunden Wettbewerbs und der aktuellen Entwicklungen im Sponsoringmarkt,
- erfolgreiches Ambush Marketing ist das Ergebnis hervorragender Marketingaktivitäten und hoher Kreativität,
- Ambush Marketing ist nur dann möglich/effizient, wenn die offiziellen Sponsoren ihre Aktivitäten nicht genügend abschirmen bzw. ihr Potenzial nicht vollständig ausschöpfen.

Ambush Marketing ist demnach in der Summe ein neues, innovatives Instrument im Marketing-Mix.

14.6 Fallstudie

Im Rahmen der folgenden Fallstudie soll aufgezeigt werden, welche *Kommunikationswirkungen* durch die unterschiedlichen Instrumente des Veranstaltungsmarketing erzielt werden können. Im Fokus der Studie stehen Erinnerungsleistungen, die auf das Engagement werbetreibender Unternehmen im Rahmen der Fußball-Weltmeisterschaft 2006 in Deutschland zurückzuführen sind (eine Übersicht der offiziellen Sponsoren der WM 2006 ist Abb. 2 zu entnehmen). Im Zuge einer empirischen Untersuchung wurden über 2.000 jugendliche Fernsehzuschauer zwischen 13 und 18 Jahren in Deutschland befragt (Nufer, 2006).

Fallstudie „Das Mega-Sport-Event Fußball-Weltmeisterschaft 2006"

Die grundlegende Voraussetzung für den Erfolg von Kommunikationsmaßnahmen ist deren Wahrnehmung. Im Rahmen eines *ungestützten Erinnerungstests (Unaided Recall)* wurden die Versuchspersonen gebeten, ohne Erinnerungshilfen alle Marken- oder Unternehmensnamen wiederzugeben, die sie für die offiziellen

Sponsoren des Events hielten. Die Ergebnisse dieser Untersuchung sind in Tab. 3 auszugsweise wiedergegeben (die offiziellen Sponsoren sind grau hinterlegt):

Platz	Marke bzw. Unternehmen	Unaided Recall (%)
1.	McDonald's	59,5
2.	adidas	51,9
3.	Coca-Cola	46,6
4.	Deutsche Telekom	28,8
5.	Nike	20,2
6.	nutella	18,8
7.	Puma	17,8
8.	Hyundai	16,9
9.	OBI	14,2
10.	MasterCard	13,6
11.	Yahoo	10,6
12.	Vodafone	9,4
13.	Bitburger	8,9
14.	Philips	6,3
	Toshiba	6,3
16.	Media-Markt	5,5
17.	Postbank	5,3
18.	Gilette	3,8
19.	Emirates	3,1
20.	Continental	3,0
	Reebok	3,0
...		
23.	Fuji-Film	2,7
...		
28.	Budweiser	2,2
...		
33.	Avaya	1,9

Tab. 3: Ergebnisse des Unaided Recall bei der Fußball-Weltmeisterschaft 2006
Quelle: Nufer (2006), S. 65

Mit ihren Resultaten zufrieden sein dürften insbesondere die drei Erstplatzierten McDonald's, adidas und Coca-Cola, die jeweils von rund der Hälfte der Befragten ungestützt genannt wurden. Drei der *offiziellen Hauptsponsoren* schaffen dagegen den Sprung in die Top 20 nicht (Fuji-Film, Budweiser, Avaya). Der durchschnittliche Unaided-Recall-Wert der 15 Hauptsponsoren beträgt 17,1%. Jeder Proband konnte durchschnittlich 2,57 der 15 Hauptsponsoren erinnern.

Adidas flankierte sein Sponsoringengagement im Rahmen der WM 2006 erneut durch eine internationale *Event-Marketing-Serie*, der „adidas +Challenge". Hierbei handelt es sich um eine Serie von Fußball-Nachwuchsturnieren mit aufwändig inszeniertem Rahmenprogramm, die im Frühjahr/Sommer 2006 in verschiedenen Großstädten ausgetragen wurden und bei denen die jugendlichen Teilnehmer die Möglichkeit hatten, ihr fußballerisches Können unter Beweis zu stellen. Zusätzlich baute adidas in Berlin direkt neben dem Reichstagsgebäude das Berliner Olympiastadion im Kleinformat nach: In der „adidas World of Football" fanden 8.000 Zuschauer Platz und konnten als Gäste von adidas auf einer Großleinwand sämtliche WM-Spiele verfolgen.

Was die ungestützten Erinnerungswerte anbelangt, können sich einige *Nicht-Sponsoren und Ambush Marketer* scheinbar mühelos in die Phalanx der offiziellen Sponsoren einreihen: Nike und Puma waren als Sportartikelausrüsterfirmen zahlreicher beteiligter Teams tätig; sie waren damit zwar nicht auf den Banden vertreten, wohl aber auf dem Spielfeld präsent (z.B. Trikots und Schuhe der Spieler). Nutella warb im Untersuchungszeitraum in TV-Werbespots mit verschiedenen deutschen Nationalspielern. Vodafone fungiert seit Jahren als Sponsor der Champions League. Media-Markt setzte bei seiner Marketing-Kommunikation im Jahr 2006 auf die Thematik „Wir werden Weltmeister". Es wird deutlich, dass diese Marken bzw. Unternehmen sehr eng mit den Themen Fußball und WM verbunden sind, was offensichtlich zu Verwechslungen bei den Probanden führte. Weitere Falschnennungen entstehen, wenn der Proband sich womöglich zwar an die Branche eines Sponsors erinnern kann, sich aber beim Namen des Unternehmens irrt; Angaben von Nike, Puma, Reebok, Vodafone und Bitburger lassen sich beispielsweise so erklären.

Diese auszugsweise wiedergegebenen Ergebnisse der Unaided-Recall-Befragung im Rahmen der Fußball-Weltmeisterschaft 2006 können selbstverständlich eine umfassende Wirkungsuntersuchung nicht ersetzen, vermitteln jedoch einen ersten vergleichenden Einblick in die durch die unterschiedlichen Instrumente des Veranstaltungsmarketing – Event-Sponsoring, Event-Marketing und Ambush Marketing – erzielten Wirkungen.

14.7 Fazit und Ausblick

Sponsoring hat in den letzten 20 Jahren so stark wie kaum ein anderes Kommunikationsinstrument an Bedeutung gewonnen und ist heute aus dem Kommunikationsmix nicht mehr wegzudenken. Zurückzuführen ist diese Entwicklung v.a. auf die spezifischen Vorteile des Sponsoring gegenüber anderen Kommunikationsinstrumenten in einem reizüberfluteten Kommunikationsmarkt und gegenüber „werbemüden" Konsumenten (Bruhn, 2005). Die entscheidende Stärke des *Event-Sponsoring*, die diese Sponsoring-Form von allen anderen im Rahmen des Sportsponsoring abhebt, ist, dass keine negativen Implikationen, hervorgerufen durch einen Imageeinbruch seitens der Gesponserten, befürchtet werden müssen.

„Events haben sich inzwischen vom Spielzeug zum Werkzeug der Markenführung entwickelt" (Nickel, 2002, S. 79). Zanger (2007) kommt anhand einer Umfrage unter Event-Praktikern zu der Schlussfolgerung, dass das Kommunikationsinstrument *Event-Marketing* am Ende seiner Wachstumsphase angekommen ist, d.h.

sich derzeit im Übergang zur Reifephase befindet. Die Zahl der Event-veranstaltenden Unternehmen weist ihrer Untersuchung zu Folge keinen wesentlichen Anstieg mehr aus, während die Zahl der durch diese Firmen veranstalteten Events stetig weiter zunimmt. Ein Drittel der in der Studie befragten Unternehmen wollen ihre Eventbudgets zukünftig steigern, während nur 11 % an Einschränkungen denken.

Ambush Marketing ist und bleibt umstritten. Insbesondere Ambush Marketing und Event-Sponsoring werden sich auch in Zukunft als konkurrierende Kommunikationsinstrumente insbesondere bei sportlichen Großereignissen gegenüberstehen, da die Anzahl offizieller Sponsoren beschränkt ist und sich nicht jedes Unternehmen ein Sponsoringengagement leisten kann. Ambusher werden es aufgrund zunehmender Sponsoren-Schutz-Programme seitens der Event-Veranstalter zukünftig jedoch immer schwerer haben, ohne offizielle Rechte eine Event-Plattform intensiv kommunikativ zu nutzen. Bei der Diskussion von Ambush Marketing sollte man den Blick in Richtung eines pro-aktiven Vorgehens zur Prävention von direktem, „illegalem" Ambush Marketing lenken, anstelle über mögliche nachträgliche Strafen für identifizierte Ambusher nachzudenken (Nufer, 2007).

Kontrollfragen
1. Welche Perspektiven können im Rahmen des Veranstaltungsmarketing grundsätzlich unterschieden werden?
2. Grenzen Sie die Kommunikationsinstrumente (Event-)Sponsoring, Event-Marketing und Ambush Marketing voneinander ab!
3. Welche Ziele stehen beim Sportsponsoring im Mittelpunkt?
4. Was ist der grundlegende Vorteil des Event-Sponsoring im Vergleich zu allen anderen Formen des Sponsoring?
5. Charakterisieren Sie die konstitutiven Merkmale des Event-Marketing!
6. Wie lassen sich die möglichen Erscheinungsformen des Event-Marketing systematisieren?
7. Welche Strategien des Ambush Marketing kennen Sie?
8. Beschreiben Sie innovative Beispiele für Ambush Marketing im Sport!
9. Nehmen Sie eine kritische Würdigung des Ambush Marketing vor! Welche Position nehmen Sie ein? Begründen Sie Ihre Antwort!
10. Wer waren die Gewinner der Fußball-Weltmeisterschaft 2006 in Deutschland, wenn man die erzielten ungestützten Erinnerungswirkungen der Unternehmenskommunikation als Maßstab heranzieht?

Literaturverzeichnis

Bayerl, Simone / Rennhak Carsten: Entwicklungslinien Sponsoring, in: Rennhak Carsten (Hrsg.): Unternehmenskommunikation 2.0 – Neue Wege im Marketing, Ibidem, Hannover, S. 123-137.

Berndt, Ralph (2005): Marketingstrategie und Marketingpolitik, 4. Aufl., Berlin u.a.

Bortoluzzi Dubach, Elisa / Frey, Hansrudolf (2002): Sponsoring. Der Leitfaden für die Praxis, 3. Aufl., Bern u.a.

Bruhn, Manfred (2003): Sponsoring. Systematische Planung und integrativer Einsatz, 4. Aufl., Wiesbaden.

Bruhn, Manfred (2005): Unternehmens- und Marketingkommunikation. Handbuch für ein integriertes Kommunikationsmanagement, München.

Bruhn, Manfred / Ahlers, Grit Mareike (2003): Ambush Marketing – „Angriff aus dem Hinterhalt" oder intelligentes Marketing?, in: GfK-Jahrbuch der Absatz- und Verbrauchsforschung, Heft 3, S. 271-294.

Crow, Dean / Hoek, Janet (2003): Ambush Marketing: A Critical Review and Some Practical Advice, in: Marketing Bulletin, No. 14, Article 1, http://www.marketing-bulletin.massey.ac.nz (Zugriff: 20.10.2004).

D'Alessandro, David F. (1993): Event Marketing: The Good, the Bad & the Ugly, in: Vital Speeches of the Day, Heft 16, 1993, S. 503-507.

Deimel, Klaus (1992): Wirkungen der Sportwerbung. Eine verhaltenswissenschaftliche Analyse, Frankfurt/Main.

Drees, Norbert (1992): Sportsponsoring, 3. Aufl., Wiesbaden.

Drees, Norbert (2003): Bedeutung und Erscheinungsformen des Sportsponsoring, in: Hermanns, Arnold / Riedmüller, Florian (Hrsg.): Sponsoring und Events im Sport, München, S. 47-66.

Hermanns, Arnold (1997): Sponsoring. Grundlagen, Wirkungen, Management, Perspektiven, 2. Aufl., München.

Hermanns, Arnold / Riedmüller, Florian (2001): Neuorientierung des Sportmarketing, in: Hermanns, Arnold / Riedmüller, Florian (Hrsg.): Management-Handbuch Sport-Marketing, München, S. 3-13.

Meenaghan, Tony (1994): Point of View: Ambush Marketing: Immoral or Imaginative Practice?, in: Journal of Advertising Research, September/October, S. 77-88.

Nickel, Oliver (2002): Hürden erfolgreicher Marketingevents – Eine Betrachtung aus Sicht der strategischen Markenführung, in: Hosang, Michael (Hrsg.): Event & Marketing. Konzepte – Beispiele – Trends, Frankfurt/Main, S. 59-80.

Nufer, Gerd (2002): Wirkungen von Sportsponsoring. Empirische Analyse am Beispiel der Fußball-Weltmeisterschaft 1998 in Frankreich unter besonderer Berücksichtigung von Erinnerungswirkungen bei jugendlichen Rezipienten, Berlin.

Nufer, Gerd (2005): Ambush Marketing – Angriff aus dem Hinterhalt oder eine Alternative zum Sportsponsoring? in: Horch, Heinz-Dieter / Hovemann, Gregor / Kaiser, Sebastian / Viebahn, Kai (Hrsg.): Perspektiven des Sportmarketing. Besonderheiten, Herausforderungen, Tendenzen, Köln, S. 209-227.

Nufer, Gerd (2006): Wirkungsvolles WM-Sponsoring, in: Absatzwirtschaft, Heft 11, S. 65.

Nufer, Gerd (2007): Event-Marketing und -Management. Theorie und Praxis unter besonderer Berücksichtigung von Imagewirkungen, 3. Aufl., Wiesbaden.

O.V. (2004): Kreativität schützt vor Ambush Marketing, in: Guerilla Marketing Fachportal, http://www.guerilla-marketing-portal.de/body.cfm?id=224 (Zugriff: 20.10.2004).

Payne, Michael (1998): Ambush Marketing – The Undeserved Advantage, in: Psychology & Marketing, Heft 4, S. 323-331.

Pechtl, Hans (2007): Trittbrettfahren bei Sportevents: das Ambush Marketing, Wirtschaftswissenschaftliches Diskussionspapier 01/07, Rechts- und Staatswissenschaftliche Fakultät, Ernst-Moritz-Arndt-Universität Greifswald.

Plewe, Heidrun (1996): Event-Marketing. Zum größeren Ruhm des Veranstalters, in: Absatzwirtschaft, Heft 7, S. 77-85.

Runau, Jan (2007): Adidas: Events als Ausgangspunkt einer Markenverjüngung, in: Nickel, Oliver (Hrsg.): Event-Marketing. Grundlagen und Erfolgsbeispiele, 2. Aufl., München, S. 3-16.

Schröder, Andreas (2006): Der verzweifelte Kampf gegen die „Trittbrettfahrer", in: Stuttgarter Zeitung, 03.05.2006, S. 13.

Townley, Stephen / Harrington, Dan / Couchman, Nicholas (1998): The Legal and Practical Prevention of Ambush Marketing in Sports, in: Psychology & Marketing, Heft 4, S. 333-348.

Walliser, Björn (1995): Sponsoring. Bedeutung, Wirkung und Kontrollmöglichkeiten, Wiesbaden.

Welsh, Jerry (2002): Ambush Marketing. What it is and What it isn´t, in: Pool Online, No. 19, http://www.poolonline.com/archive/issue19/iss19fea5.html (Zugriff: 17.08.2004).

Wochnowski, Holger (1996): Veranstaltungsmarketing. Grundlagen und Gestaltungsempfehlungen zur Vermarktung von Veranstaltungen, Frankfurt/Main u.a.

Zanger, Cornelia (2007): Eventmarketing als Kommunikationsinstrument – Entwicklungsstand in Wissenschaft und Praxis, in: Nickel, Oliver (Hrsg.): Event-Marketing. Grundlagen und Erfolgsbeispiele, 2. Aufl., München, S. 3-16.

Zanger, Cornelia / Sistenich, Frank (1996): Eventmarketing. Bestandsaufnahme, Standortbestimmung und ausgewählte theoretische Ansätze zur Erklärung eines innovativen Kommunikationsinstruments, in: Marketing ZFP, Heft 4, S. 233-242.

Weiterführende Ressourcen

Literatur

Ahlert, Dieter / Woisetschläger, David / Vogel, Verena (Hrsg.) (2007): Exzellentes Sponsoring. Innovative Ansätze und Best Practices für das Markenmanagement, 2. Aufl., Wiesbaden.

Beech, John / Chadwick, Simon (Hrsg.) (2004): The Business of Sport Management, Harlow.

Bühler, André W. (2006): Professional Football Sponsorship in the English Premier League and the German Bundesliga, Berlin.

Bühler, André W. / Nufer, Gerd (2006): The Nature of Sports Marketing, Reutlingen Working Paper on Marketing & Management No. 2006-6, School of International Business, Reutlingen University.

Erdtmann, Stefan L. (1989): Sponsoring und emotionale Erlebniswerte. Wirkungen auf den Konsumenten, Wiesbaden 1989.

Freyer, Walter (2003): Sport-Marketing. Handbuch für marktorientiertes Management im Sport, 3. Aufl., Dresden.

Glogger, Anton (1999): Imagetransfer im Sponsoring. Entwicklung eines Erklärungsmodells, Frankfurt/Main u.a.

Hermanns, Arnold / Riedmüller, Florian (Hrsg.) (2001): Management-Handbuch Sport-Marketing, München.

Hermanns, Arnold / Riedmüller, Florian (Hrsg.) (2003): Sponsoring und Events im Sport, München.

Horch, Heinz-Dieter / Heydel, Jörg / Sierau, Axel (Hrsg.) (2004): Events im Sport – Marketing, Management, Finanzierung, Köln.

Horch, Heinz-Dieter / Hovemann, Gregor / Kaiser, Sebastian / Viebahn, Kai (Hrsg.) (2005): Perspektiven des Sportmarketing. Besonderheiten, Herausforderungen, Tendenzen, Köln.

Nickel, Oliver (Hrsg.) (2007): Event-Marketing. Grundlagen und Erfolgsbeispiele, 2. Aufl., München.

Nufer, Gerd (1998): Event-Sponsoring am Beispiel der Fußball-Weltmeisterschaft 1998 in Frankreich – Kritik und Implikationen für die Praxis, Tübinger Diskussionsbeitrag Nr. 151, Wirtschaftswissenschaftliche Fakultät der Eberhard Karls Universität Tübingen.

Nufer, Gerd (2002): Bestimmung und Analyse der Erfolgsfaktoren von Marketing-Events anhand des Beispiels DFB-adidas-Cup, Tübinger Diskussionsbeitrag Nr. 229, Wirtschaftswissenschaftliche Fakultät der Eberhard Karls Universität Tübingen.

Nufer, Gerd (2002): Erinnerungsleistungen an Sponsoren der Fußball-Weltmeisterschaft 1998 – Ergebnisse einer empirischen Untersuchung, in: GfK-Jahrbuch der Absatz- und Verbrauchsforschung, Heft 2, S. 149-171.

Nufer, Gerd (2002): Sport und Kultur – Lehren für die Strategie / Sports and Culture – Lessons for Strategy, in: Simon, Hermann (Hrsg.): Strategie International /

Strategy International, zweisprachige Serie in der Frankfurter Allgemeinen Zeitung, 07.09.2002, S. 57.

Nufer, Gerd (2003): Der Imagetransfer im Event-Marketing, in: GfK-Jahrbuch der Absatz- und Verbrauchsforschung, Heft 4, S. 385-406.

Nufer, Gerd (2004): Wirkungen von Event-Sponsoring – Ergebnisse empirischer Analysen zur Fußball-Weltmeisterschaft 1998, in: Horch, Heinz-Dieter / Heydel, Jörg / Sierau, Axel (Hrsg.): Events im Sport – Marketing, Management, Finanzierung, Köln, S. 239-255.

Nufer, Gerd (2006): Die Wirkung klassischer Bandenwerbung, in: Bank und Markt – Zeitschrift für Retailbanking, Heft 7, S. 33-35.

Nufer, Gerd (2006): Sportsponsoring bei Fußball-Weltmeisterschaften: Wirkungsvergleich WM 2006 versus WM 1998, Reutlinger Diskussionsbeitrag zu Marketing & Management Nr. 2006-5, School of International Business, Reutlingen University.

Nufer, Gerd / Bühler, André W. (2006): Lessons from Sports: What Corporate Management can learn from Sports Management, Reutlingen Working Paper on Marketing & Management No. 2006-7, School of International Business, Reutlingen University.

Nufer, Gerd / Perkovic, Marc (1998): Event-Marketing – Positionierung und Implementierung, in: Brockes, Hans-Willy (Hrsg.): Leitfaden Sponsoring & Event-Marketing. Für Unternehmen, Sponsoring-Nehmer & Agenturen, Düsseldorf, B 4.3, S. 1-16.

Sander, Matthias (2004): Wirkungen von Drehbanden als innovative Form der Bandenwerbung, in: Marketing ZFP, Heft 3, S. 199-213.

Voeth, Markus / Herbst, Uta / Sandulescu, Stefan (2006): Vermarktungspotenziale bei der „FIFA WM 2006". Eine Untersuchung im Rahmen der empirischen Langzeitstudie „Akzeptanz und Einstellungen der Bevölkerung", Hohenheimer Arbeits- und Projektberichte zum Marketing Nr. 13, Förderverein für Marketing e.V. an der Universität Hohenheim.

Walliser, Björn (1997): Über den Zusammenhang zwischen Markenbekanntheit und Wiedererkennung bei der Bandenwerbung, in: Marketing ZFP, Heft 1, S. 43-52.

Zanger, Cornelia / Drengner, Jan (2005): Eventreport 2004. Die Wirkungen von Ambush Marketing bei sportlichen Großevents, Chemnitz.

Links

Bayreuther Sportökonomie-Kongress:
　http://www.sportoekonomie.uni-bayreuth.de/kongress
Deutscher Sportökonomie-Kongress, Köln:
　http://www.deutscher-sportoekonomie-kongress.de
Heidelberger Sportbusiness Forum (Kongress):
　http://www.sportbusiness.de

Horizont Sport Business (Fachzeitschrift):
http://www.horizont-sportbusiness.de
ISPO Sportsponsoringkongress, München:
http://www.sportsponsoringkongress.de
Sponsors (Fachzeitschrift):
http://www.sponsors.de
Sport + Markt (Marktforschungsunternehmen), Köln:
http://www.sportundmarkt.com
Sportfive (Sportrechteagentur), Hamburg:
http://www.sportfive.de

Kapitel 15: Customer Relationship Marketing im Sport

Marco Gensmüller

Lernziele

Nach der Durchsicht dieses Kapitels sollte der Leser in der Lage sein,

- die Ziele des Customer Relationship Marketing wiedergeben zu können.
- die Kundenbindung sowohl aus Kunden- als auch Unternehmenssicht zu erklären.
- die wichtigsten Kundenbindungsinstrumente zu kennen.
- zwischen Ver- und Gebundenheit zu unterscheiden.
- die Besonderheiten des Customer Relationship Marketing im Sport zu erklären.
- zwischen den einzelnen Einsatzmöglichkeiten des Customer Relationship Marketing in Profisport-Unternehmen zu unterscheiden.

Überblick über das Kapitel

Das Thema Customer Relationship Marketing (CRM) wurde in den letzten Jahren sowohl bei Unternehmen in der Praxis als auch in der Wissenschaft intensiv diskutiert. Das vorliegende Kapitel widmet sich, nach der theoretischen Würdigung und konzeptionellen Einbettung des Beziehungsmarketing, zum einen der Kundenbindung aus Sicht der Unternehmen und zum anderen aus Sicht der Kunden. Daran anknüpfend werden mögliche Ansatzpunkte und Implikationen eines Customer Relationship Marketing für den Sport abgeleitet. Wie ist der Status Quo? Welche Anwendungsmöglichkeiten gibt es im Sport? Auf diese Fragen sollen Antworten gegeben werden. Abgerundet wird dieses Kapitel mit einer Praxis-Fallstudie, die die Konzeption und Implementierung von Customer Relationship Marketing beim Fußballbundesligisten Bayer 04 Leverkusen beschreibt.

15.1 Einführung in die Thematik

Einhergehend mit der raschen Verbreitung des Konzeptes der Kundenbindung in der Marketingforschung wurde in der wissenschaftlichen Marketingliteratur schon vor einiger Zeit von einem Teil der Autoren ein Wechsel vom Transaction Marketing zum – die Entwicklung dauerhafter Kundenbeziehungen anstrebenden – Customer Relationship Marketing beschrieben (z.B. Kotler, 1989; Grönroos, 1993). Dem gegenüber gingen andere Marketing-Wissenschaftler davon aus, dass es sich bei den Ansätzen des Customer Relationship Marketing weniger um eine Neuorientierung, als vielmehr um eine „Rückbesinnung des Marketing auf das zentrale Konzept der marktbezogenen Austauschprozesse zwischen Anspruchsgruppen" (Bruhn/Bunge, 1994, S. 42) handelt.

Als maßgebliche Triebfedern für die Hinwendung zur Pflege der Kundenbeziehung bei einer Vielzahl von Unternehmen lassen sich insbesondere die Ausschöpfung der Ertragspotenziale vorhandener Kunden in gesättigten Märkten, die steigende Abhängigkeit von Großkunden durch Konzentrationsprozesse sowie wachsende Dienstleistungsanteile im Leistungsspektrum der Unternehmen anführen. Hinzu kommt ein sich verschärfender Qualitätswettbewerb, aus dem Kundennähe und Kundenzufriedenheit als wichtige Kriterien für den Markterfolg hervorgehen.

Dieses Kapitel soll einen Überblick zum Thema Customer Relationship Marketing mit seinen einzelnen Ausprägungen und Anwendungsmöglichkeiten geben. Darüber hinaus werden die Besonderheiten der Sportbranche und die daraus resultierenden Implikationen für ein CRM-Konzept im Sport herausgearbeitet.

15.2 Grundlagen des Customer Relationship Marketing

Zunächst wird auf die begrifflichen Grundlagen sowie die Entstehung des Customer Relationship Marketing eingegangen, ehe die Kundenbindung sowohl aus der Unternehmens- als auch der Kundensicht beleuchtet wird.

15.2.1 Terminologische Klärung

Sowohl in der aktuellen wissenschaftlichen als auch in der praxisbezogenen Diskussion finden sich für den vermeintlichen Wandel in der marketingspezifischen Betrachtungsperspektive zahlreiche Terminologisierungen. Vom „Beziehungsmarketing" und „Beziehungsmanagement" über „Relationship Marketing" und „One-to-One-Marketing" (Peppers/Roggers, 1999), bis hin zum „Handshake-Marketing" (Lammoth, 1997), existiert eine Vielzahl an Begriffsbestimmungen, die den zugrunde liegenden Sachverhalt jedoch bis auf Nuancen unter dem gleichen Blickwinkel betrachten.

> Customer Relationship Marketing lässt sich definieren als „strategisches Konzept des Marketing [...], bei dem der Marketingerfolg durch systematisches Management individueller Kundenbeziehungen im Hinblick auf die Pflege und Etablierung von kooperativen, d.h. auf langfristigen gegenseitigen Nutzen ausgerichteten, Geschäftsbeziehungen gesucht wird" (Diller, 2001, S. 163 f.).

Das Konzept sieht somit die Gewinnung neuer Kunden „lediglich" als Zwischenstufe im gesamten Marketingprozess an, und versucht darauf aufbauend, in gesättigten Märkten bereits bestehende Kunden zu loyalen Geschäftspartnern zu machen und somit dauerhafte Kundenbeziehungen zu etablieren. Die „Chemie" zwischen den Geschäftspartnern entscheidet immer häufiger über den Erfolg einer Geschäftsbeziehung. Das Beziehungsmarketing visiert auf der menschlich-emotionalen Ebene eine Geschäftsatmosphäre an, die durch gegenseitige Anerkennung und Sympathie der Beziehungspartner gekennzeichnet ist (Belz, 1998).

Wilson/Kothandaraman (1998, S. 23) betonen in diesem Zusammenhang nachdrücklich die Bedeutung der menschlich-emotionalen Ebene, welche gerade im Anfangsstadium einer Geschäftsbeziehung zukommt: „In the early stages of a relationship, success or failure is determined by the individuals involved since in the early stages the relationship is more vulnerable to the human factors".

Damit Unternehmen in unserer globalisierten Geschäftswelt von heute gegenüber der Konkurrenz bestehen können, rückt der Kunde mit seinen Wünschen und Ansprüchen immer mehr in den Mittelpunkt bei der Entscheidungsfindung. Mittlerweile ist die Betrachtung und Bewertung einer Kundenbeziehung aus ökonomischer Sicht für viele Manager zu einem wichtigen Entscheidungskriterium geworden. Raab (2005, S. 13) verdeutlicht diese entscheidende Zielsetzung durch den folgenden Leitspruch:

> „Kenne deine Kunden und du weißt, was sie kaufen."

Customer Relationship Marketing stellt eine Managementphilosophie dar, die eine komplette Ausrichtung des Unternehmens auf vorhandene bzw. potenzielle Kundenbeziehungen vorzieht. Der Kunde steht bei allen unternehmerischen Entscheidungen im Mittelpunkt. Ziel ist der Aufbau und die Pflege dauerhafter und profitabler Kundenbeziehungen.

Insgesamt beschäftigt sich Customer Relationship Marketing mit dem Management von Kundenbeziehungen. Nach Bruhn (2002, S. 133) umfasst es „sämtliche Maßnahmen der Analyse, Planung, Durchführung und Kontrolle, die der Initiierung, Stabilisierung, Intensivierung und der Wiederaufnahme von Geschäftsbeziehungen zu den Anspruchgruppen – insbesondere zu den Kunden – des Unternehmens mit dem Ziel des gegenseitigen Nutzens dienen."

15.2.2 Vom Transaction Marketing zum Relationship Marketing

Einen großen Einfluss auf die Entstehung und Weiterentwicklung des Customer Relationship Marketing ist auf einen Trend in der Wissenschaftsdisziplin Marketing zurück zu führen. Dabei handelt es sich um die Entwicklung vom Transaktionsmarketing hin zum Beziehungsmarketing. In Zeiten zunehmender Austauschbarkeit von einzelnen Leistungen der Unternehmen ist es sehr wichtig, einzelne Kundengruppen differenziert zu bearbeiten.

Für den überwiegenden Teil der Wissenschaftler handelt es sich beim Konzept des Customer Relationship Marketing um kein vollkommen neuartiges Konzept, sondern um eine Akzentuierung einzelner Marketingaspekte und damit letztendlich um die konsequente Weiterentwicklung des verhaltenswissenschaftlichen Marketingansatzes (Meffert, 1994; Bruhn/Bunge, 1994).

Wurden im klassischen Marketing Massen durch Segmente ersetzt und dann Segmente durch Zielgruppen, so stehen heute in vielen Unternehmen Beziehungen zu einzelnen Personen im Mittelpunkt des Interesses. Customer Relationship Marketing ist deshalb nicht etwa die neuste Entwicklung, sondern letzter Stand eines seit Jahren beobachtbaren Prozesses, der den veränderten Gegebenheiten auf den

Märkten Rechnung trägt. Das Customer Relationship Marketing stellt eine nachhaltige Möglichkeit zur Generierung von Konkurrenzvorteilen im Umfeld eines sich zuspitzenden Verdrängungswettbewerbs in stagnierenden Märkten dar.

Demnach ist Customer Relationship Marketing vorteilhaft, wenn die Relevanz eines einzelnen Kunden für einen Anbieter sehr hoch ist und Bindungspotenziale vorhanden sind. Geht die Bedeutung eines Kunden dagegen im anonymen Massenmarkt verloren, ist eine Abwägung der Erfolgswahrscheinlichkeit der betreffenden Einzeltransaktionen sinnvoller (vgl. Abb. 1).

Während das Beziehungsmarketing bspw. im Dienstleistungs- und Investitionsgüterbereich aufgrund der vorliegenden Marktstrukturen bereits seit geraumer Zeit praktiziert wird, verkörpert es für die Konsumgüterbranchen (Industrie wie Handel), in denen die Vermarktung immer größtenteils als Massengeschäft interpretiert wurde, in vielen Bereichen Neuland. Reinecke/Sausen (2002, S. 2) fokussieren weniger auf den Neuheitsgrad, sondern betonen „dass [...] es vielmehr um eine effiziente Nutzung der Chancen des Customer Relationship Marketing geht".

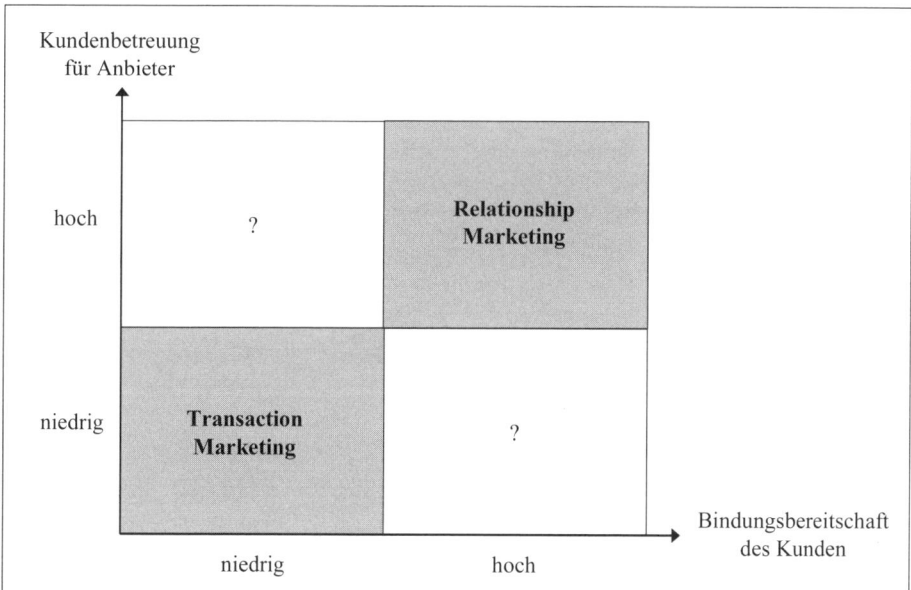

Abb. 1: Matrix der Einsatzmöglichkeiten von Customer Relationship und Transaction Marketing

Beim Customer Relationship Marketing handelt es sich um einen ganzheitlichen Ansatz. Nur wenn Customer Relationship Marketing vom Topmanagement verinnerlicht, von den Mitarbeitern verstanden und in der Struktur des Unternehmens verankert wird, lassen sich die Potenziale dieses Ansatzes sinnvoll nutzen. Als integriertes Gesamtkonzept ist Customer Relationship Marketing ein entscheidender Faktor zur Steigerung des Unternehmenserfolges. Je höher die Kenntnisse eines

Unternehmens über die Wünsche der Nachfrager sind, desto größer ist die Chance, die Zufriedenheit der Kunden langfristig zu steigern und deren Loyalität bzw. Bindungsbereitschaft an das Unternehmen zu erhöhen (Raab, 2005).

Die technologische Komponente spielt eine große Rolle bei der Einführung eines CRM-Konzeptes in einem Unternehmen. Nur mit einer technischen Infrastruktur ist es möglich, Daten über bestehende und potenzielle Kunden zu sammeln bzw. zu speichern, um damit auf die entsprechenden Kundenbedürfnisse adäquat reagieren zu können. Bei aller Relevanz des technologischen Aspektes ist jedoch die in Unternehmen häufig zu beobachtende Annahme, Kundenorientierung sei v.a. durch den Einsatz moderner CRM-Technologien umzusetzen und damit primär ein IT-Projekt, als Irrtum anzusehen (Bruhn, 2002). Erste Ziele des Customer Relationship Marketing lassen sich mit qualifizierten und motivierten Mitarbeitern und einer entsprechenden Organisationsstruktur häufig auch ohne größere Investitionen in neue Technologien erreichen.

Nach Homburg/Sieben (2000) umfasst eine CRM-Konzeption sechs elementare Komponenten.

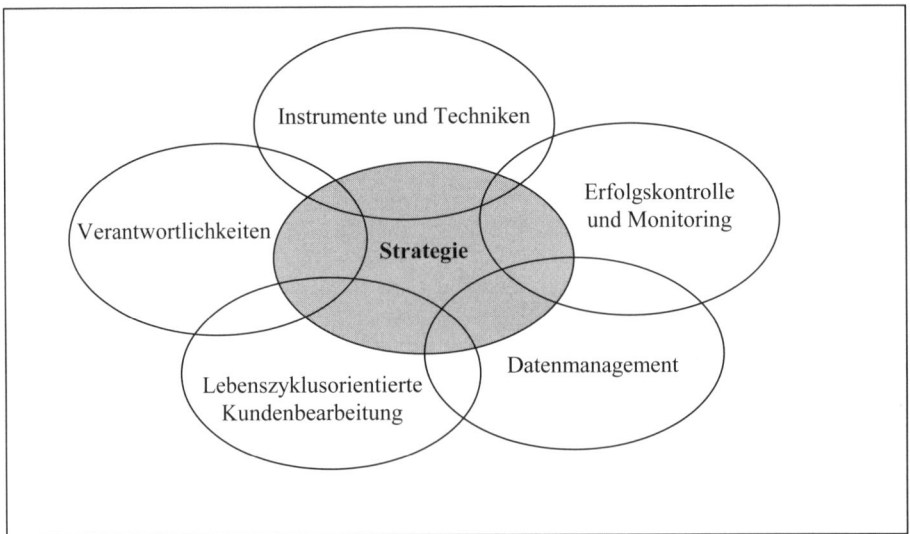

Abb. 2: Elementare Komponenten eines CRM-Systems
In Anlehnung an: Homburg/Sieben (2000), S. 486

Am Anfang sollte eine spezifische Strategie bestimmt werden, welche sich auf die zentralen Zielgedanken besinnt. Als zweites Element sind die bereits erwähnten Instrumente und Techniken zu nennen, ohne die ein effizientes CRM-Konzept nicht durchzusetzen ist. Das dritte Element ist die Abbildung einer lebenszyklusorientierten Kundenbearbeitung. Hier wird festgelegt, welche Kundensegmente zu welchem Zeitpunkt kontaktiert und betreut werden sollten. Neben der Festlegung von Verantwortlichkeiten, nimmt das Datenmanagement als weiteres Element eine wichtige Rolle ein. Hierbei geht es verstärkt um die Erfassung, Verwaltung und Nutzung von spezifischen Kundendaten unter dem Blickwinkel der Kundenzufriedenheit.

Als letztes Element ist die Erfolgskontrolle und das Monitoring zu nennen, um die einzelnen Maßnahmen des CRM-Konzeptes unter dem Blickwinkel des Erfolges zu beurteilen. Als Maßstab des Erfolges kann hierbei die Kundenzufriedenheit bzw. die Kundenbindung herangezogen werden.

15.2.3 Kundenbindung aus Unternehmenssicht

Im Customer Relationship Marketing kann man bezüglich der Kundenbindung zwischen einer nachfrager- und einer anbieterbezogenen Perspektive unterscheiden. Bis dato standen jedoch vorwiegend einseitig anbieterlastige Betrachtungsweisen im Vordergrund. So definieren bspw. Bruhn/Homburg (2003, S. 8) Kundenbindung als „sämtliche Maßnahmen eines Unternehmens, die darauf abzielen, sowohl die bisherigen Verhaltensweisen als auch die zukünftigen Verhaltensabsichten eines Kunden gegenüber einem Anbieter oder dessen Leistungen positiv zu gestalten, um die Beziehung zu diesem Kunden für die Zukunft zu stabilisieren bzw. auszuweiten".

Untersuchungen haben gezeigt, dass es je nach Einsatz der Mittel bis zu 600 % teurer ist, neue Kunden durch Marketingmaßnahmen zu gewinnen, als vorhandene Kunden zu halten (McGovern/Panaro, 2004). Da Kunden einen sehr wichtigen Vermögenswert für ein Unternehmen darstellen, sollte im jeweiligen Management die oberste Priorität auf die Kundenbeziehungen gelegt werden.

Nicht alle Kunden-Unternehmens-Beziehungen können und müssen gleich intensiv gepflegt werden. Dies resultiert aus der Tatsache unterschiedlicher Kundenwertigkeiten bzw. Kundenverlustrisiken durch Wettbewerbsaktivitäten auf der einen, und begrenzten Unternehmens- und Kommunikationsressourcen auf der anderen Seite. Eine grundlegende Aufgabe des Customer Relationship Marketing ist demnach darin zu sehen, diejenigen Kundengruppen zu identifizieren, für die sich der Aufbau von langfristigen Geschäftsbeziehungen lohnt.

Der Analyseschritt einer qualitativ-quantitativen *Kundenbewertung* und *Kundensegmentierung* bildet dementsprechend das Fundament eines erfolgreichen CRM-Prozesses. Entlang der identifizierten Unterschiede in der Kundenwertigkeit variiert somit die Intensität der Beziehungsgestaltung (Kotler, 1989).

Neben der Differenzierung variierender Kundenwertigkeiten kommt hinzu, dass eine Geschäftsbeziehung unterschiedliche Phasen durchläuft, die, analog zum Produkt-Lebenszyklus-Konzept, jeweils spezifische strategische Entscheidungen und Marketingmaßnahmen erfordern (Tillmanns, 2000). Die zunehmende Bedeutung der Kundenbindung beruht in diesem Kontext nicht zuletzt auf der Erkenntnis, dass die Profitabilität einer Kundenbeziehung mit fortschreitender Dauer zunimmt. Fünf

Prozent weniger Kundenabwanderung können den Gewinn von Unternehmen um bis zu 85 % erhöhen (Reichheld/Sasser, 1990).

15.2.3.1 Ziele des Customer Relationship Marketing

Nach Raab (2005) gibt es eine Vielzahl ökonomischer Gründe, die für den Aufbau und die Umsetzung von Customer Relationship Marketing sprechen:

- Jeder zufriedene Kunde bringt mindestens drei weitere Kunden.
- Ein unzufriedener Kunde erzählt sein Negativerlebnis zehn weiteren potenziellen Kunden.
- Die Wiederkaufrate steigt, je vertrauter und zufriedener Kunden mit den Leistungen ihres Lieferanten sind.
- Stammkunden weisen eine geringere Preisempfindlichkeit als Neukunden auf.
- Kundenorientierte Unternehmen können sogar höhere Preise verlangen als der Wettbewerb.
- Marketing- und Vertriebskosten zur Erhaltung der Kundenbeziehung sinken.

Primäres Ziel ist es, potenzielle Kunden zum Erstkauf zu bewegen. Neben den klassischen Marketingbemühungen kann jedoch auch das Customer Relationship Marketing im Kontext der Neukundengewinnung akquisitorischen Charakter entfalten, wenn es gelingt, in die sozialen Netzwerke der Altkunden vorzudringen und dort bei Dritten Empfehlungsgeschäfte zu stimulieren (Fuchs, 1998). Im Gegensatz zum klassischen Marketing liegen die Bestrebungen im Beziehungsmarketing hierbei jedoch nicht darin, mit einer einheitlichen, unpersonalisierten Werbebotschaft eine möglichst große Zielgruppe zu erreichen. Es geht vielmehr darum, auf Kundenseite soziale Netzwerke Gleichgesinnter zu identifizieren und in ihnen langfristige Geschäftsbeziehungen aufzubauen. Dabei kann es sich um Personen völlig heterogener demografischer Gruppen handeln, die mit der klassischen Marketingtechnik nicht mehr zu fassen sind, jedoch eine Einheit bilden, weil sie sich in einer ähnlichen Situation befinden. Die Relevanz des Aufspürens und Nutzbarmachens solcher Netzwerke unterhalb der demografischen Oberfläche verdeutlicht unter anderem eine Untersuchung der 800 größten Unternehmen in den USA, wonach rund 90 % der dort vertretenen Vorstandsmitglieder in irgendeiner Form miteinander vernetzt sind. Im Rahmen solcher Netzwerke von Entscheidern der Wirtschaft werden häufig nicht nur hochkarätige Führungskräfte an andere Unternehmen vermittelt, sondern auch und insbesondere umfangreiche Geschäfte eingefädelt (Fuchs, 1998). Ausgehend von empirischen Erhebungen, die belegen, dass Investitionen in die Bindung bestehender Kunden im Vergleich zu identischen Investitionen in Maßnahmen der Neukundengewinnung relativ gesehen profitabler sind, kommt der Kundenbindung(-sphase) als strategischer Managementaufgabe im Marketing eine steigende Relevanz zu.

Dies bedeutet, das gesamte unternehmerische Handeln auf den Kunden mit seinen vorhandenen und potenziellen Bedürfnissen, Wünschen und Problemen auszurichten. Vorteilhaft ist es z.b., die Bedürfnisse der Kunden vom Entwurfsstadium an konsequent in die Produkte einzubauen. Statt Kunden für Produkte zu finden, sollte die Unternehmensmaxime „Produkte für unsere Kunden finden" heißen. Die Aufgabe eines Unternehmens sollte darin bestehen, dem Kunden genau die Leistungen anzubieten, die seinen Bedürfnissen entsprechen und für die er bereit ist, einen entsprechenden Preis zu zahlen (Raab, 2005).

15.2.3.2 Kundenbindungsinstrumente
Bruhn/Homburg (2003) gehen davon aus, dass sich die Instrumente des Kundenbindungsmanagements anhand produkt-, preis-, kommunikations- sowie distributionspolitischer Maßnahmen unterscheiden lassen.

PRODUKTPOLITIK
- Verbesserung des Leistungsprogramms:
  - gemeinsame Produktentwicklung
  - individualisierte Produktangebote
  - besonderes Produktdesign
- Serviceprofilierung/-optimierung:
  - kernleistungsbezogene Zusatzleistungen (value-added services)
  - Einführung besonderer Qualitätstandards
  - Leistungsgarantien

PREISPOLITIK
- Einwirken auf die Wechselkosten der Kunden
- Schaffen monetärer Anreize:
  - Einsatz attraktiver Rabatt- und Bonussysteme
  - Preisgarantien
  - Preisdifferenzierung
  - Kundenkarten (Rabattgewährung)

Relationship

Marketing

Mix

DISTRIBUTIONSPOLITIK
- Product Sampling
- Internet/Gewinnspiele
- Online-Bestellung
- Abonnements
- Katalogverkauf
- Direktlieferung

KOMMUNIKATIONSPOLITIK
- Kontinuierlicher Dialog mit dem Kunden (proaktive Kundenkontakte)
- Intensivierung der direkten Kundenansprache
  - Events   - Beschwerdemanagement
  - Kundenforen   - Kundenzeitschriften
  - Kundenclubs   - Online-basierte Kundenberatung
  - Direct Mailings - persönliche Kommunikation
  - Aufbau kundenspezifischer Kommunikationskanäle

Abb. 3: Customer Relationship Marketing-Mix
In Anlehnung an: Bruhn/Homburg (2003), S. 140

Anhand der in Abb. 3 exemplarisch angeführten Instrumente eines *Beziehungsmarketing-Mix* wird deutlich, dass es im Customer Relationship Marketing nicht um den Einsatz neuer, sondern um die am Kundenbedarf ausgerichtete Ausgestaltung herkömmlicher Instrumente geht.

Die vorgenommene Aufzählung verschiedener Instrumente der Kundenbindung ist weder erschöpfend, noch sollte der Eindruck entstehen, dass der Einsatz eines dieser Instrumente das Ziel der Kundenbindung alleine bewirken kann. Vielmehr ist es notwendig einen, aufeinander abgestimmten kombinierten Einsatz von mehreren Maßnahmen vorzunehmen (Integriertes Kundenbindungsmanagement).

Im Kontext des Customer Relationship Marketing liegt der Fokus der Produktpolitik neben Bemühungen um die Verbesserung des Leistungsprogramms v.a. auf Zusatzleistungen, den *„value added services"*, welche die Zufriedenheit des Kunden und damit letzten Endes die Kundenbindung steigern sollen. Sie beinhaltet die Entscheidungstatbestände, die sich auf die kundenorientierte Gestaltung aller vom Unternehmen angebotenen Leistungen beziehen. Zudem kann eine Bindung der Kunden über das Produkt in einer gemeinsamen Produktentwicklung des Kunden und des Anbieters erfolgen. Durch die Integration des Kunden in den Entwicklungsprozess kann sichergestellt werden, dass die Erwartungshaltung der Nachfrager getroffen wird.

Als preispolitische Kundenbindungsinstrumente stehen Rabatt- und Bonussysteme, zufriedenheitsabhängige Preisgestaltungen, die Gewährung von Preisgarantien und darüber hinausgehende Zahlungs- und Kreditierungsbedingungen zur Verfügung. Sie sind kurzfristig und flexibel einsetzbar und besitzen eine hohe Wirkungsstärke. So könnte das Unternehmen einem Nachfrager z.B. mit zunehmender Dauer der Geschäftsbeziehung oder einer größeren Abnahmemenge günstigere Konditionen anbieten. Der Kunde würde bei dieser flexiblen Preisgestaltung länger überlegen, den Anbieter zu wechseln.

Die partnerschaftliche Beziehungsgestaltung in Form eines kontinuierlichen Dialogs mit dem Kunden steht im Mittelpunkt kommunikationspolitischer Maßnahmen des Beziehungsmarketing. Die Intensivierung der direkten Kundenansprache lässt sich unter anderem durch Maßnahmen des Event-Marketing, der Kundenforen und -clubs, des aktiven Beschwerdemanagements und nicht zuletzt der persönlichen Kommunikation realisieren. Der Kommunikationskanal „Online" über Internet, E-Mail, Homepage, Blog, etc. wird in der Zukunft von Unternehmen immer stärker genutzt werden. Neue, online-basierte Bestelloptionen eröffnen nicht nur in der Kommunikationspolitik, sondern gerade auch im Bereich der beziehungsbasierten Distribution verschiedenste Möglichkeiten, Kunden langfristig zu binden.

Die Aufgabe eines Kundenbindungsmanagements ist es, die Bindungsarten im Rahmen einer geeigneten Kundenbindungsstrategie zu beeinflussen. In Abhängigkeit von der Strategie werden dann die oben angesprochenen Kundenbindungsinstrumente festgelegt, die je nach Ausrichtung einen emotionalen Mehrwert oder ökonomische Wechselbarrieren erzeugen (vgl. Abschnitt 15.2.4). Die Zielsetzung eines effektiven Kundenbindungsmanagements sollte dabei in der Erhöhung einer freiwilligen und nicht auf Zwängen beruhenden Bindung liegen. Mithilfe von Kundenbindungsinstrumenten soll die Zufriedenheit zielgerichtet gesteuert werden, so dass eine emotionale Bindung entsteht, bei der ein Wechsel des Kunden aufgrund persönlicher Präferenzen unterbleibt.

15.2.4 Kundenbindung aus Kundensicht

Kundenbindung kann zwischen zwei Bindungszuständen der Kunden – Verbundenheit und Gebundenheit – unterscheiden, und stellt so betrachtet die Sicht der Kunden in den Mittelpunkt. Unternehmen haben jedoch gerade bei der Analyse, Planung, Durchführung und Kontrolle von Maßnahmen des Beziehungsmarketings häufig Schwierigkeiten, die „Kundenbrille aufzusetzen und die Kundenperspektive einzunehmen" (Reinecke/Köhler/Roos, 2002, S.61 ff.).

Übergeordnet lassen sich mit Meyer/Oevermann (1995) fünf generische Ursachen der Kundenbindung unterscheiden:

1. situative Bindungsursachen
2. vertragliche Bindungsursachen
3. ökonomische Bindungsursachen
4. technisch-funktionale Bindungsursachen
5. psychologische Bindungsursachen

Unter *situativen* Ursachen der Kundenbindung sind äußere Faktoren zu verstehen, wie bspw. Marktbeschaffenheit oder der Standortvorteil eines Anbieters. So dürfte z.B. der Fußball-Bundesligist Hertha BSC Berlin alleine aufgrund des vorliegenden Wirtschaftsraumes und einer regionalen Vormachtstellung gewisse situative Bindungsvorteile vorfinden, die bspw. Vereinen im Ruhrgebiet und Westfalen mit einer hohen Anbieterdichte (Borussia Dortmund, Schalke 04, VfL Bochum, Arminia Bielefeld, MSV Duisburg) zunächst verwehrt bleiben.

Beim Vorliegen einer *vertraglichen* Bindungsursache ist der Kunde durch eine Vereinbarung an einen Anbieter gebunden. Der Kunde wird somit primär über die Vertragsgestaltung gehalten.

Eine *ökonomische* Bindungsursache liegt bei einer Geschäftsbeziehung vor, in der die Geschäftspartner aufgrund der zu hoch wahrgenommenen finanziellen Wechselkosten die Geschäftsbeziehung fortführen. So entstehen bei der Fortsetzung einer Geschäftsbeziehung u.a. beiderseitige Transaktionskostenvorteile, welche beim Eingehen einer neuen Verbindung verloren gingen.

In *technisch-funktionaler* Hinsicht vorliegende Bindungsursachen resultieren, insbesondere im Computer- und Softwarebereich, aus der Tatsache, dass mit der Implementierung spezieller Betriebssysteme (z.B. SAP-Software) die Notwendigkeit eines regelmäßigen Updates entsteht.

Im Customer Relationship Marketing sind die *psychologischen* Bindungsursachen von hoher Bedeutung, die aus Kundenzufriedenheit, persönlichen Beziehungen und Gewohnheiten der Kunden resultieren können. Ein zufriedener Kunde muss jedoch nicht automatisch einen hohen Bindungsgrad zum Anbieter aufweisen (Bruhn/Homburg, 2003). Basierend auf diesem Sachverhalt unterscheidet man die bereits erwähnten Zustände Verbundenheit und Gebundenheit, die nun anschließend näher beleuchtet werden.

15.2.4.1 Strategie der Verbundenheit

Mit der Verbundenheitsstrategie sollen sich Kunden mit dem Anbieter und dessen Leistungen verbunden fühlen. Sie sollen ihren Anbieter im Konkurrenzvergleich bevorzugen und nach einer Fortführung der Austauschbeziehung streben. Aus Anbietersicht sind dazu der Aufbau und die Förderung von Kundenzufriedenheit wichtige Schritte, um loyale Kunden zu gewinnen.

Empirische Studien und zahlreiche wissenschaftliche Abhandlungen belegen, dass zwischen Kundenzufriedenheit und Kundenbindung in Form der Verbundenheit oftmals nur eine geringe Korrelation besteht. Kundenzufriedenheit alleine reicht somit zur Schaffung von Kundenbindung nicht aus (Bruhn/Homburg, 2003), da sie ausschließlich auf einem vergangenheitsbezogenen Abgleich des erfahrenen Nettonutzens mit den diesbezüglichen Erwartungen des Kunden resultiert. Die emotionale und zukunftsgerichtete Ergänzung der Kundenzufriedenheit wird über das Konstrukt des Kundenvertrauens erreicht.

„Relationship marketing is built on the foundation of trust, as accumulating research demonstrates. Trust is a willingness to rely on an exchange partner in whom one has confidence" (Berry, 1995, S. 242).

Kundenvertrauen ist die Einstellung des Kunden gegenüber dem Anbieter und dessen Produkt- und Dienstleistungspalette. Im Sinne des vorangegangenen Zitats lässt sich der gedankliche Rahmen der Verbundenheitsstrategie zusammenfassend somit als ein „Nicht-Wechseln-Wollen" der Kunden charakterisieren. Kundenbindung in Form von Verbundenheit geht demnach „vom Interesse der Kunden aus und (entspricht) ihrem Willen" (Bliemel/Eggert, 1998, S. 41).

15.2.4.2 Strategie der Gebundenheit

Bei der Gebundenheitsstrategie wird die Bindung der Kunden an einen Anbieter über den Aufbau von Wechselbarrieren (z.B. über lange Vertragslaufzeiten, Abnahmeverpflichtungen, Exklusivitätsvereinbarungen etc.) erzielt. Der Anbieter versucht auf diesem Wege Kundenverluste bei zukünftig eintretenden Wettbewerbs-schwächen oder Leistungsdefiziten zu vermeiden.

Die Einwilligung von Kunden in eine Geschäftsbeziehung, welche Wechselbar-rieren inkludiert, wird nur dann erfolgen, wenn letztere im Gesamtangebot durch andere Vorteile überkompensiert werden (Bliemel/Eggert, 1998). Ein Anbieter-wechsel ist für die Kunden mit hohen Wechselkosten verbunden. So soll eine Ab-wanderung verhindert werden.

15.3 Customer Relationship Marketing im Sport

Im vorherigen Abschnitt wurde gezeigt, dass Customer Relationship Marketing da-zu dienen kann, in enger werdenden Märkten mit einer zunehmenden Konkurrenz-situation Kundenbeziehungen aufzubauen, um sich dadurch einen Wettbewerbsvor-teil zu verschaffen.

Der Sport bzw. die Profivereine der größeren deutschen Ligen haben in der Vergangenheit wenig bis gar keine Kundenorientierung an den Tag gelegt.

Aufgrund der bisweilen hohen Neukundenquote und einer daraus häufig resultie-renden schlechten Betreuungs- und Serviceleistung wurden Kunden in diesem Kon-text lange Zeit regelrecht „verheizt", weil z.B. auf Maßnahmen des Beschwerde-managements und der Kundenrückgewinnung in weiten Teilen verzichtet wurde. Die insbesondere z.B. bei Fußball-Bundesligisten diesbezüglich häufig innewoh-nende „Anbieterarroganz" könnte langfristig Wettbewerbsnachteile gegenüber kon-kurrierenden Branchen mit sich bringen (u.a. Unterhaltungsindustrie, Werbewirt-schaft etc.).

Die fehlende Kundenorientierung scheint in der Historie und den Strukturen ei-nes Vereins zu liegen. So konzentrieren sich die meisten Vereinsverantwortlichen auf die direkten Haupteinnahmequellen ihres Vereins, die meist aus dem Verkauf der TV-Rechte und den Werbeeinnahmen resultieren. Im Vergleich dazu fallen die Einnahmen aus dem Verkauf von Eintrittskarten zumindest im Fußball oftmals eher geringer aus. Dies ist jedoch nur sehr kurzfristig gedacht, da der Zuschauer den Ur-sprung jeder Einnahmequelle darstellt. Durch ihn werden erst die Voraussetzungen für weitere Quellen geschaffen. So würde sich z.B. kein Sponsor dafür interessie-ren, bei einem Handball-Bundesligisten Trikotwerbung zu betreiben, wenn er keine Fans bzw. Zuschauer hat. Und auch die TV-Sender würden keine hohen Summen für TV-Rechte bezahlen, wenn kein Fernsehzuschauer an der Übertragung interes-siert ist.

15.3.1 Eignung von Customer Relationship Marketing im Sport
Oberstes Ziel eines jeden Profivereins sollte es sein, den einzelnen Anspruchsgrup-pen (z.B. Fans, Mitglieder, Mitarbeiter, etc.) einen besonders guten Service in allen Bereichen zu garantieren. Je erfolgreicher ein Profiverein in seiner entsprechenden

Sportart ist, desto attraktiver erscheint er für die einzelnen Kunden. Bei der Kundenzufriedenheit spielt daher die sportliche Komponente eine wesentliche Rolle.

Dies ist auch der Grund, warum dem Customer Relationship Marketing gerade im Sport eine so enorme Bedeutung zugewiesen werden kann. Sportlicher Erfolg ist nämlich nicht planbar. Gerade dies macht den besonderen Reiz des Sports aus. Immer wieder gelingt es vermeintlich hoffnungslos unterlegenen Mannschaften in den verschiedensten Sportarten, die „großen" Vereine zu „ärgern" oder gar zu besiegen. Wer kennt nicht den Ausruf „Der Pokal hat seine eigene Gesetze", der jedes Jahr aufs Neue bei den ersten beiden DFB-Pokalrunden im Profifußball in Deutschland bestätigt wird. Dann nämlich, wenn sich der Erstligist mit einem vielfach höheren Etat bei einem Dritt- oder sogar Viert-Ligisten aus dem Pokal-Wettbewerb verabschiedet. Auch in anderen Sportarten ist diese Unvorhersehbarkeit des sportlichen Erfolges zu beobachten (z.B. der erste Wimbledon-Sieg von Boris Becker als 17-Jähriger).

Der ungewisse Ausgang stellt jedoch auch für die einzelnen Vereine eine Gefahr dar. Viele Einnahmequellen von Profivereinen sind direkt an deren sportlichen Erfolg gekoppelt. Wen dieser ausbleibt, muss mit geringeren Einnahmen gerechnet werden. Daher ist es sehr wichtig, dass in allen anderen Bereichen den Kunden von Seiten des Vereins ein außerordentlicher Service geboten wird. Nur dadurch kann der Verein den wirtschaftlichen vom sportlichen Erfolg ein wenig abkoppeln. Denn läuft es im sportlichen Bereich einmal weniger erfolgreich, haben viele Profivereine Probleme, die Umsätze zu steigern bzw. die Stadien/Hallen zu füllen (Picarille, 2003).

Das Mitglied oder der Fan sollte nicht nur mit den Leistungen des Vereins zufrieden gestellt werden, sondern im Idealfall einen gewissen Stolz verspüren, ein Teil „seines" Vereins zu sein. Neben dem treuen Fan oder Mitglied sollte hierbei auch versucht werden, die Kundengruppe „Gelegentliche Zuschauer" zu identifizieren und mit ihnen eine langfristige Kundenbeziehung aufzubauen.

Im Vergleich zu „normalen Kunden" von Unternehmen unterscheidet sich der Kunde/Fan eines Profivereins v.a. durch die Emotionen, die er seiner Mannschaft entgegen bringt, denn „teilweise werden extreme Gefühle, vergleichbar mit Liebe und Hass, dem Verein gegenüber empfunden und auch zum Ausdruck gebracht" (Greuel, 2007, S. 69). Dies kann sich bei einem sportlichen Erfolg (z.B. Meisterschaft oder Pokalerfolg) durch große Sympathiebekundungen seitens der Fans äußern, aber genauso gut bei schlechten Mannschaftsleistungen in wüsten Beschimpfungen enden (z.B. Belagerung des Mannschaftsbusses durch aufgebrachte Fans nach einem verlorenen Meisterschaftsspiel). Diese Emotionen gilt es, von Seiten der Managementverantwortlichen der Vereine einzukalkulieren. Das wirtschaftliche Überleben eines Profivereins ist, wie bereits erwähnt, nur sichergestellt, wenn die Fans und Mitglieder mit ihren Anliegen ernst genommen werden.

Um alle Fans mit entsprechenden Maßnahmen zielgruppengenau ansprechen zu können, empfiehlt es sich eine Aufteilung in einzelne Anspruchsgruppen vorzunehmen. Hunt/Bristal/Bashaw (1999) schlagen eine Segmentierung von Sportfans in fünf Gruppen vor. Ausgehend von der Motivationslage des Fans, warum er einen Profiverein unterstützt, wird zwischen dem „temporary fan", „local fan", „devoted fan", „fanatacil fan" und „dysfunctional fan" unterschieden.

Der *„temporary fan"* unterliegt einer zeitlichen Begrenzung. Er ist Fan nur für einen bestimmten Zeitraum, der zwischen einigen Stunden oder weniger Jahre liegen kann. Im Gegensatz dazu unterliegt der *„local fan"* einer geografischen Begrenzung. Dies kann z.B. dann der Fall sein, wenn eine Person jahrlang Fan des örtlichen Basketballvereins war, nach dem beruflichen Umzug in eine andere Stadt aber kaum noch Interesse für den damaligen Heimatverein zeigt.

Die anderen drei Fansegmente sind hingegen immer Fans; unabhängig von Raum und Zeit. Der *„devoted fan"* war i.d.R. zunächst ein „temporary" oder „local fan". Die Beziehung zum Profiverein ist aber im Laufe der Zeit so tief verwurzelt, dass zeitliche oder örtliche Begrenzungen keine Rolle mehr spielen. So würde der Basketballfan seinem Verein als „devoted fan" auch treu bleiben, wenn er in eine andere Stadt zieht. Der *„fanatical fan"* geht schon eine sehr intensive Beziehung zu seinem Verein ein. Die Profimannschaft stellt jedoch nur einen Teil seiner Selbstidentifikation dar. Daneben gibt es noch weitere Aspekte wie der Job, die Familie oder Freunde. Der *„dysfunctional fan"* hingegen identifiziert sich ausschließlich über sein Fandasein. Er identifiziert sich so stark mit seiner Rolle als Fan, dass es ihm im Gegensatz zum *„fanatical fan"* nicht mehr möglich ist, eine normale Rolle im gewöhnlichen Familien- und Arbeitsleben einzunehmen (Hunt/Bristal/Bashow, 1999).

Wenn ein Profiverein seine Fans in diese unterschiedliche Anspruchsgruppen aufteilt, ist es ihm möglich dadurch auch eine zielgruppengenaue Ansprache bzw. auf die jeweilige Zielgruppe abgestimmte Kundenbindungsmaßnahmen durchzuführen. Diese Methode ist viel versprechender als die gesamte „Masse" der Fans mit den gleichen Methoden an den Verein binden zu wollen.

15.3.2 CRM-Instrumente im Sport

Im Abschnitt 15.2.3 wurden bereits unterschiedliche Kundenbindungsinstrumente vorgestellt. Von zentraler Bedeutung sowohl für ein Unternehmen als auch für einen Profiverein ist es, Kenntnis darüber zu haben, ob die Kunden/Fans mit den angebotenen Produkten und Leistungen zufrieden sind. Eine effiziente Kundenbegeisterung und eine daraus resultierende Kundenbindung erfordert einen „langen Atem" und ist nur durch den gezielten und kombinierten Einsatz von einzelnen Kundenbindungsinstrumenten erreichbar, die auf einzelne Kundensegmente zugeschnitten sind.

In diesem Abschnitt sollen ausgewählte Kundenbindungsinstrumente für Profivereine vorgestellt werden, die sowohl über Massenkunden (Fans/Mitglieder), als auch über Geschäftskunden (Sponsoren, Logenbesitzer) verfügen. Das Hauptaugenmerk soll in diesem Beitrag jedoch auf die Privatkunden gelegt werden. Der in Abb. 2 aufgezeigte CRM-Marketing-Mix hat schon verdeutlicht, welche unzähligen Möglichkeiten für ein Unternehmen bestehen, sein Handeln an den Bedürfnissen des Kunden auszurichten. In Anlehnung an die bestehenden Elemente des Marketing-Mix können auch im Sport entsprechende CRM-Maßnahmen realisiert werden.

Das Kernprodukt im Rahmen der *Produktpolitik* eines Profivereins ist die eigentliche sportliche Leistung, für die keine Qualitätsgarantie übernommen werden kann. So sind z.B. die Managementverantwortlichen eines Volleyball-Bundesligisten machtlos, wenn die Spieler beim Meisterschaftsspiel nicht ihr volles Leistungsvermögen abrufen. Sie haben lediglich die Möglichkeit, mit den gegebenen Mitteln die passenden Rahmenbedingungen zu schaffen. Der Zuschauer/Fan besucht die Heimspiele seiner Mannschaft jedoch noch aus weiteren Gründen. Hier spielt der Erlebnisfaktor eine große Rolle. Durch neue moderne multifunktionale Sportstätten kann der Erlebniswert für den Zuschauer erhöht werden. Ziel eines Profivereins sollte es sein, alle Nebenleistungen des Kernproduktes, deren Qualität man aktiv beeinflussen kann (hierzu zählen z.B. Gastronomie im Stadion, Fanartikel, Tag der offenen Tür, etc.), auf die Kundenwünsche auszurichten.

Im Bereich der *Preispolitik* ist bei den Profivereinen v.a. auf die Preisdifferenzierung bei Mitgliedschaften, Eintrittskarten oder Merchandisingartikel Wert zu legen, um entsprechenden Kundenbedürfnissen entgegen zu kommen.

So differenziert der Verein bei den Plätzen im Stadion die Eintrittspreise nach räumlichen Kriterien. Der Stehplatz hinter dem Tor kostet weniger als der Sitzplatz in Höhe der Mittellinie. Natürlich sollte auch eine Preisdifferenzierung nach abnehmerorientierten Kriterien stattfinden. Besondere Anspruchsgruppen wie Studenten, Rentner oder Hartz IV-Empfänger mit geringeren Einkommen sollten entsprechende Reduzierungen erhalten. Eine zeitliche Differenzierung ist bei einem Dienstleistungsprodukt – wie es ein sportlicher Wettkampf darstellt – aufgrund der Nichtlagerfähigkeit des Produktes nur schwer möglich. So kann ein Profiverein jedoch z.B. einen Frühbucherrabatt für Tickets einführen oder bei Außensportarten aufgrund der Jahreszeit (z.B. Fußballspiel im Dezember) Eintrittspreise senken.

Eine quantitative Preisdifferenzierung im ursprünglichen Sinne einer Gruppenermäßigung ist bei Profivereinen nur selten anzutreffen. Jedoch sind Dauerkarten, die für alle Meisterschaftsspiele Gültigkeit haben, preislich wesentlich attraktiver als wenn Tickets für alle Heimspiele einzeln gebucht werden.

Im Bereich der *Distributionspolitik* sind bei Profivereinen v.a. der Vertrieb von Fanartikeln und das Ticketing zu beachten. Im Bereich des Ticketing sollte ein Verein die Bestellwege für den Kunden so einfach wie möglich gestalten. War früher zumeist der persönliche Verkauf bei der Geschäftsstelle die einzige Bestellmöglichkeit, bietet sich heute neben Telefon, Fax und Internet auch die komplette Auslagerung des Ticketverkaufs an eine darauf spezialisierte Ticketagentur an. Auch im Merchandisinggeschäft sollte es das Ziel eines jeden Profivereins sein, dem Kunden seine Produktpalette leicht zugänglich zu machen. Neben einem Fanshop an der Geschäftsstelle würde sich je nach Einzugsgebiet des Vereins auch ein Fanshop in zentraler Innenstadtlage anbieten. Kooperationsformen mit anderen Unternehmen, insbesondere aus dem eigenen Sponsorenkreis bieten sich an, um Trikots, Schals und andere Fanartikel zu vertreiben (Greuel, 2007).

Fast alle Instrumente, die ein Profiverein im Rahmen der *Kommunikationspolitik* einsetzt, dienen auch der Zufriedenheit des Kunden und damit der Kundenbindung. In diesem speziellen Kontext ist v.a. auf die Instrumente Wert zu legen, die eine direkte Kommunikation mit dem Fan/Zuschauer herstellen. Hierzu können z.B. die Bereiche Verkaufsförderung, Public Relation oder Direktmarketing gezählt werden. Auch Kundenclubs oder -magazine sind für Profivereine ein hilfreiches Instrumentarium, um mit den Fans bzw. Mitgliedern zu interagieren.

Das besondere Konstrukt „Kundenclub" als ein Bestandteil der zahlreichen CRM-Instrumente zur Kundenbindung soll nun exemplarisch näher beleuchtet werden.

15.3.3 Kundenbindung durch Kundenclubs

Sämtliche Profivereine bieten allen Interessenten die Möglichkeit, Mitglied im Verein zu werden. Zumeist bekommen diese Mitglieder ein Vorkaufsrecht auf Eintrittskarten (und dies auch noch zu einem vergünstigten Preis), Rabatte auf Fanartikel und eine Kunden-/Mitgliederzeitschrift zugesendet. Eine Vielzahl von Fans, Sympathisanten oder Interessenten werden jedoch kein Mitglied und sind trotzdem eine sehr interessante Zielgruppe für die Vereine. Der überwiegende Teil z.B. der Stadionbesucher ist beim Verein nicht registriert und kann somit auch nicht mit entsprechenden Kundenbindungsinstrumenten angesprochen werden. Diese Zielgruppen sind somit außerhalb des Stadions für den Verein nicht ansprechbar, da namentlich nicht bekannt. Dieser Personenkreis, den man eher den „local" oder „temporary fans" (vgl. Abschnitt 15.3.1) zurechnen kann, besitzt zudem eine hohe Wechselbereitschaft. Als Profiverein mit seinen Meisterschaftsspielen konkurriert man nicht nur mit anderen Vereinen bzw. Sportarten, sondern auch mit der zunehmenden Anzahl an Entertainment-Veranstaltungen (z.B. Spaßbäder, Kinobesuche, Stadtfeste, etc.).

Mit Loyalitätsprogrammen versuchen z.B. einige Fußball-Bundesligisten diese bisher noch nicht registrierten Kundengruppen anzusprechen bzw. für den Verein (durch Adressgenerierung) ansprechbar zu machen. Hierzu zählen neben den bereits angesprochenen Vereinsmitgliedschaften auch Clubmagazine, die eine direkte Kommunikation mit dem Kunden ermöglichen. Der FC Schalke 04 war mit der „Knappenkarte" Vorreiter für ein elektronisches Bezahlsystem. Es wurden somit die Voraussetzungen für die Generierung sowohl von Daten über das Kaufverhalten, als auch von Adressen neuer Kunden gelegt. Diese Karte fungiert gleichzeitig als Ausweis- und Zahlungsmittel (Zeltinger, 2004).

Nach Bruhn (1999) vereint ein Kundenclub mehrere Kundenbindungsinstrumente wie Kundenkarte, Kundenzeitschrift und Clubveranstaltungen in einem Gesamtkonzept. Durch den Dialog mit verschiedenen Anspruchsgruppen (außerhalb der Vereinsmitglieder) kann es dem Profiverein gelingen, neben der Generierung neuer Adressen ein Gespür dafür zu bekommen, welche Service-Leistungen vom Verein erwartet werden. Tomczak/Dittrich (2000) haben festgestellt, dass durch Kundenclubs kundenbezogene Daten gewonnen werden können, die in einer umfassenden Datenbank gespeichert werden sollten. Diese Datenbank bietet dem Verein bei der individuellen Betreuung einzelner Kunden eine große Hilfe.

Greuel (2007) hat die Vorteile eines Kundenclubs wie folgt zusammengefasst:
- Verbesserung der Wettbewerbssituation durch Zusatzleistungen
- Aufbau eines emotionalen, persönlichen Verhältnisses zum Kunden
- Steigerung der Zielorientierung der Kommunikation
- Steigerung der Kundenbindung durch Erhöhung der Wechselkosten
- Verkaufsfördernde Wirkung und Möglichkeit der Neukundengewinnung bei Clubaktivitäten
- Beobachtung der Kundenzufriedenheit
- Möglichkeit der Kundenbefragung und Datenermittlung
- Grundlage für Database-Marketing und weiterführende Aktionen
- Umwandlung von Kunden zu Unterstützer

15.4 Fallstudie

Die folgende Fallstudie zeigt am Beispiel des Fußball-Bundesligisten Bayer 04 Leverkusen die Einführung und Etablierung eines CRM-Konzeptes.

Fallstudie „Bayer 04 Leverkusen"

Der Fußball-Bundesligist Bayer 04 Leverkusen war einer der ersten Profisport-vereine, der ein ganzheitliches CRM-Konzept eingeführt hat. Das Customer Relationship Marketing steht bei Bayer 04 Leverkusen für eine kundenorientierte strategische Ausrichtung des gesamten Unternehmens und eine damit verbundene Neuorientierung sämtlicher Geschäftsprozesse und Verantwortlichkeiten am Kunden.

Seit Ende der 90er-Jahre wurde in der Geschäftsstelle von Bayer 04 Leverkusen (damals noch unsystematisch) begonnen, alle möglichen Adressdaten von Kunden oder Interessenten zu sammeln. Als einziger Fußball-Bundesligist werden in Leverkusen seit Jahren alle Eintrittskarten nur personalisiert (sprich: der Käufer muss seine komplette Adresse beim Kauf angeben) verkauft. Dies ist sicherlich aufgrund der recht überschaubaren Größe der BayArena (22.500 Zuschauer) eher realisierbar als bei Vereinen wie Dortmund, Schalke oder Bayern München. Die erhobenen Adressdaten waren jedoch teilweise unvollständig, fehlerhaft und wurden in keiner Weise systematisch genutzt.

Geschäftsführer Wolfgang Holzhäuser gab 2003 den Anstoß für die Weiterentwicklung zu einem ganzheitlichen CRM-Konzept. Er hatte erkannt, welch immensen Stellenwert die *Kundenorientierung* für die Entwicklung eines Profisportvereins haben kann. So wurde das CRM-Konzept als Unternehmensstrategie von der Geschäftsführung eingesetzt, mit dem Ziel, dass alle Ebenen des Unternehmens die Philosophie der Kundenorientierung unterstützen. Mittels eines professionellen Customer Relationship Marketing kann eingeschätzt werden, durch welche gezielten Maßnahmen ein Mehrwert sowohl für die Kunden als auch den Verein entstehen kann. Ein effektives Customer Relationship Marketing führt zur größeren Kundenzufriedenheit. Zufriedene Kunden wiederum liefern eine höhere Widerkaufrate und tragen somit zu einem höheren Umsatz bei.

Nach Etablierung der Idee des CRM-Konzeptes in die Unternehmensstrategie wurde eine neue Stelle im Verein geschaffen, die mit der Einführung des Konzeptes betraut wurde. Im Jahr 2004 wurde dann ein Projektteam gegründet, um die Vorgehensweise, die einzuleitenden notwendigen Arbeitsschritte und den konkreten Handlungsbedarf zu diskutieren und festzulegen. Es wurde zum damaligen Zeitpunkt beschlossen, dass Bayer 04 Leverkusen eine Software benötigt, die alle Mitarbeiter bei ihren Kontakten mit Kunden- und Geschäftspartner unterstützt. Geschäftsprozesse sollen erleichtert und Vorgänge so dokumentiert werden, dass ein effizienter Informationsaustausch gewährleistet ist. Hierzu existierte im Hause Bayer 04 bereits ein Adresssystem namens „*Navision*", welches Anfang 2005 um ein CRM-Tool erweitert wurde.

In den Jahren 2005 und 2006 war das Projektteam, dem auch ein IT-Mitarbeiter für die technische Entwicklung angehörte, mit den Vorarbeiten beschäftigt, um durch das CRM-Konzept ökonomisch messbare Erfolge für den Verein zu realisieren. In einem ersten Schritt wurden die bereits erfassten Adressen bereinigt. Hierzu wurden zunächst Kunden, deren letzter Einkauf mehr als 2,5 Jahre bzw. Interessenten, deren letzte Kontaktaufnahme mehr als 1,5 Jahre zurück lag in der Kundendatei auf „Inaktiv" gestellt. Zudem wurde alle Adressen gelöscht, die unvollständig (Mindestanforderung sind: Vorname, Name, Straße, Hausnummer, Postleitzahl und Ort) waren. Neben dem „Bereinigen" der alten Adressen wurden einheitliche Standards wie die Pflege und Neuanlage von Adressen von der Geschäftsführung für die Mitarbeiter vorgegeben. So wurden alle Mitarbeiter dazu verpflichtet, regelmäßig Adressen zu überprüfen bzw. zu vervollständigen und auf eine ordnungsgemäße und pflichtbewusste Eingabe von Kundendaten zu achten. Mit dem CRM-Tool „Navision" arbeiten bei Bayer 04 Leverkusen nicht nur die Mitarbeiter im Verkauf oder Service, sondern auch das Marketing verwaltet hierüber die Sponsoren und VIP-Kunden oder das Finanzwesen verbucht Rechnungen gegenüber einzelnen Debitoren. In einem nächsten Schritt wurde ein Dublettenabgleich gefahren, um somit doppelt erfasste Adressdaten zu eliminieren.

Eine weitere wichtige Aufgabe des Projektteams war die Koordination der Wünsche der einzelnen Abteilungen an das Adresssystem. Kundenorientierte Aktionen sollen effizient und auf der Basis einer qualitativ hochwertigen Kundendatenbank möglich sein. Hierzu wurden von dem Projektteam alle möglichen Geschäftsabläufe, bei denen ein Kundenkontakt stattfindet, beschrieben und abgebildet. Zudem wurde festgehalten, welche Informationen bei dem jeweiligen Prozess vom Kunden aufgenommen werden bzw. welche Dinge der Mitarbeiter beim Kundenkontakt beachten soll. Das CRM-Konzept kann nur ein Erfolg werden, wenn es von den Mitarbeitern bei den alltäglichen Arbeitsschritten auch gelebt wird. So musste das Projektteam alle Mitarbeiter von Bayer 04 Leverkusen für Customer Relationship Marketing sensibilisieren und so schulen, dass sie die Funktionen von „Navision" optimal nutzen können. Hierzu wurde in jeder Abteilung ein „*Key-User*" bestimmt, der primärer Ansprechpartner des Teams bei Fragen, Problemen, Anregungen zum CRM-System ist. Die Key-User wurden besonders intensiv nach und nach auf alle CRM-Funktionen des Navisionsystems geschult und geben ihre erworbenen Kenntnisse an die Teammitglieder weiter. Zudem werden Sie bei der Weiterentwicklung des CRM-System mit einbezogen. Ende 2006/Anfang 2007 waren die zuvor geschilderten Vorarbeiten für die Einführung des CRM-Konzeptes bei Bayer 04 Leverkusen abgeschlossen und das System eingeführt. Seitdem wird das CRM-Tool Navision von den einzelnen Abteilungen intensiv in der täglichen Arbeit genutzt.

An folgendem „Geschäftsfall" soll die Möglichkeiten eines funktionierenden CRM-Systems aufgezeigt werden:

Der Bayer-04-Leverkusen-Fan Herr Pillendreher will im Fanshop für sein Patenkind zum Geburtstag ein Heimtrikot kaufen. Als er an der Kasse steht, wird er nach seinem Namen gefragt. Der Mitarbeiter des Fanshops kann nach Eingabe des Namens die komplette „Historie" des Kunden einsehen. So weiß er, dass Herr Pillendreher in der laufenden Saison bei den Heimspielen gegen Schalke 04 und VfB Stuttgart im Stadion war und dabei jeweils im Block F3 auf der Westtribüne gesessen hat. Des Weiteren sieht er die Einkäufe im Fanshop (in jeder Saison das neue Trikot, zudem mehrere Sätze Autogrammkarten und weitere Fanutensilien für sein Patenkind) und das er schon mehrere Male bei der Hotline nach den aktuellen Anstoßzeiten der Heimspiele nachgefragt hat. Auch ist die Fanreise zum Champions-League-Spiel nach England eingetragen. Der Verkäufer kann mit diesen Informationen viel individueller mit dem Kunden kommunizieren. So kann er z.B. fragen, ob das neue Trikot für sein Patenkind bestimmt ist, auf den wöchentlichen Internet-Newsletter hinweisen, in dem u.a. immer die aktuellen Anstoßzeiten von Bayer 04 Leverkusen mitgeteilt werden, oder sich nach den Eindrücken der Auswärtsfahrt nach England erkundigen. Herr Pillendreher wird ob des Hintergrundwissens des Verkäufers sicherlich überrascht sein und aufgrund so intensiver Kundenorientierung von Seiten des Vereins zufrieden den Fanshop verlassen.

Damit sind die Einsatzmöglichkeiten eines funktionierenden CRM-Systems jedoch noch lange nicht erschöpft. Über verschiedenen Filtereinstellungen können Informationen oder Werbemailings zielgerichtet an bestimmte Nutzergruppen adressiert werden. Hierzu ein weiteres Beispiel:

Vor der neuen Saison mit einem neuen Trikot stellt der Fanshopleiter nach der Inventur fest, dass er noch einen großen Bestand an Hosen und Stutzen passend zum alten Heimtrikot auf Lager hat. Er möchte nun ein Werbemailing an alle Kunden senden, die in der letzten Saison das alte Heimtrikot, jedoch keine passende Hose und Stutzen erworben haben. Mit einem Knopfdruck kann er diese Zielgruppe (zu er auch Herr Pillendreher gehört) selektieren und die Hosen/Stutzen zu einem Sonderpreis anbieten.

Diese Selektionen und Filtereinstellung im Navisionsystem haben einen weiteren Vorteil, wie das folgende Beispiel zeigt:

In früheren Zeiten wurden die neuen Merchandisingkataloge im Vorfeld der Saison an den kompletten Kundenstamm gesendet. Seit Einführung des CRM-Tools werden nur noch solche Kunden beliefert, die in den letzten zwei Jahren einen Einkauf im Fanshop getätigt haben, nachdem sie den Katalog zugesendet bekommen haben. Die Dauerkartenbesitzer werden beim Versand komplett außen vorgelassen, da diese die Möglichkeit haben, die Kataloge direkt am Spieltag im

Fanshop vor Ort mitzunehmen. Durch diese Selektion ist die insgesamt versandte Menge an Fankatalogen stark zurück gegangen, der entsprechende Pro-Kopf-Umsatz pro versandten Katalog jedoch um ein Vielfaches gestiegen. An diesem Beispiel lässt sich erkennen, dass der Einführung eines CRM-Tools neben der Steigerung der Kundenzufriedenheit auch direkte ökonomisch messbare Erfolge zugewiesen werden können.

Nach der vollständigen Einführung des CRM-Systems ist die Arbeit des Projekt-teams noch lange nicht beendet. Vielmehr gilt es, das bestehende System weiter zu modifizieren und die Anregungen, Wünsche und Feedbacks der Mitarbeiter an das System zu analysieren und entsprechend zu steuern. V.a. neue Entwicklungen in der Zukunft, wie der geplante Ausbau der Bayarena oder die Einführung eines elektronischen Paymentsystems, bieten zahlreiche Chancen für das CRM-System.

15.5 Fazit und Ausblick

Profivereine haben gegenüber anderen Unternehmen aus der freien Wirtschaft noch einen enormen Nachholbedarf im Bereich Kundenorientierung. Schlüssige CRM-Konzepte sind im Sportbereich nur rudimentär vorhanden. Vorreiter in Deutschland – wie in so vielen Bereichen in der Sportbranche – sind die Vereine aus der ersten und zweiten Fußball-Bundesliga (vgl. „Fallstudie Bayer Leverkusen"). Dies liegt sicherlich auch daran, dass in der Fußball-Branche die professionellsten Rahmen-bedingungen in der Sportbranche vorherrschen. Eine gewisse Organisationsstruktur muss gegeben sein, um ein erfolgversprechendes CRM-Konzept etablieren zu kön-nen.

In der Zukunft wird sich der Kampf um einzelne Kunden sowohl zwischen den Profivereinen als auch mit anderen Marktbeteiligten aus der Freizeit- und Vergnü-gungsbranche verschärfen. Dadurch wird es für den einzelnen Verein immer wich-tiger werden, einen möglichst großen und treuen Kundenstamm aufgebaut zu ha-ben. Es geht hier nicht um die „fanatical" oder „dysfunctional fans, die ihrem Verein so große Emotionen entgegen bringen, dass es fast egal ist, was passiert. Es gibt jedoch viele weitere Anspruchsgruppen, deren „Fanverhalten" weniger intensiv ist. Diese Kunden gilt es, mit einem funktionierenden und auf die spezielle Situati-on des Vereins abgestimmten CRM-Konzept anzusprechen und mit entsprechenden Maßnahmen an den Verein zu binden. Natürlich sind dies im ersten Schritt Kosten, die dem Verein bei der Etablierung der CRM-Maßnahmen entstehen. Diesen Kos-ten stehen aber nach der Einführung und Etablierung des Konzeptes auch steigende Umsätze durch Zusatzverkäufe an zufriedene Kunden gegenüber. Will ein Verein in der Zukunft gegenüber der wachsenden Konkurrenz bestehen, wird er nur schwer am Thema „Customer Relationship Marketing im Sport" vorbeikommen. Die aktu-ellen Entwicklungen bei den Vereinen in der Fußball-Bundesliga sind nur die Vor-boten einer generellen Stärkung des Themas „Kundenorientierung" im professionellen Vereinssport.

Kontrollfragen

1. Welche unterschiedlichen Definitionen von Customer Relationship Marketing kennen Sie?
2. Was versteht man unter der Entwicklung des Transaction Marketing zum Relationship-Marketing?
3. Was bedeutet ein „ganzheitlicher Ansatz" beim Thema Customer Relationship Marketing?
4. Welche elementaren Elemente sollte eine CRM-Konzeption enthalten?
5. Warum ist es wichtig, zwischen verschiedenen Kundenwertigkeiten zu unterscheiden?
6. Welche ökonomischen Gründe sprechen für die Etablierung eines CRM-Konzeptes?
7. Welchen Unterschied gibt es zwischen der „Verbundenheit" und der „Gebundenheit" eines Kunden?
8. Welche Gründe gibt es für die bisher zu beobachtende fehlende Kundenorientierung von Profivereinen?
9. Warum eignet sich ein CRM-Konzept für Profivereine?
10. Welche Vorteile können durch das Einrichten eines Kundenclubs von einem Profiverein generiert werden?

Literaturverzeichnis

Belz, Christian (Hrsg.) (1998): Management von Geschäftsbeziehungen: Konzepte – Integrierte Ansätze – Anwendungen in der Praxis, St. Gallen.

Berry, Leonard L. (1995): Relationship Marketing of Services. Growing Interest, Emerging Perspectives, in: Journal of the Academy of Marketing Science, Heft 4, S. 236-245.

Bliemel, Friedhelm / Eggert, Andreas (1998): Kundenbindung – die neue Sollstrategie?, in: Marketing ZFP, Heft 1, S. 37-46.

Bruhn, Manfred (1999): Kundenorientierung – Bausteine eines exzellenten Unternehmens, München.

Bruhn, Manfred (2002): Integrierte Kundenorientierung – Implementierung einer kundenorientierten Unternehmensführung, Wiesbaden.

Bruhn, Manfred / Bunge, Bettina (1994): Beziehungsmarketing – Neuorientierung für Marketingwissenschaft und -praxis, in: Bruhn, Manfred / Meffert, Heribert / Wehrle, Friedrich (Hrsg.): Marktorientierte Unternehmensführung im Umbruch: Effizienz und Flexibilität als Herausforderungen des Marketing, Stuttgart, S. 41-84.

Bruhn, Manfred / Homburg, Christian (Hrsg.) (2003): Handbuch Kundenbindungs-management, Wiesbaden.

Diller, Hermann (Hrsg.) (2001): Vahlens Großes Marketinglexikon, München.

Fuchs, Hans-Joachim (1998): Netzwerke und Szenen: Wie man in Kundennetzwer-ken Empfehlungsgeschäfte stimuliert, in: Belz, Christian (Hrsg.): Management von Geschäftsbeziehungen: Konzepte – Integrierte Ansätze – Anwendungen in der Praxis, St. Gallen, S. 135-142.

Homburg Christian / Sieben, Frank (2000). Customer Relationship Management (CRM) – Strategische Ausrichtung statt IT-getriebenem Aktionismus, in: Bruhn, Manfred / Homburg, Christian (Hrsg.): Handbuch Kundenbindungsma-nagement – Grundlagen – Konzepte – Erfahrungen, 3. Aufl., Wiesbaden, S. 473-504.

Hunt, Kenneth / Bristol, Terry / Bashaw, Edward (1999): A conceptual approach to classifying sport fans, in: Journal of Services Marketing, Heft 6, S. 439-465.

Greuel, Wanja (2007): CRM im Sport – Wie der Club mit dem Kunden gewinnt, Saarbrücken.

Grönroos, Christian (1993): From Marketing Mix to Relationship Marketing. Working Paper No. 263 of the Swedish School of Economics and Business Administration, Helsingfors.

Kotler, Philip (1989): Marketing-Management. Analyse, Planung, Kontrolle, Stutt-gart.

Lammoth, Frank (1997): Handshake-Marketing und Customer Value: Die neuen Aktiva des Wandels, Ettlingen.

McGovern, Todd / Panaro, Joseph (2004): The Human Side of Customer Relation-ship Management, in: Benefits Quartely, Heft 3, S. 26-34.

Meffert, Heribert (1994): Marketing-Management. Analyse, Strategie, Implementie-rung, Wiesbaden.

Meyer, Anton / Oevermann, Dirk (1995): Kundenbindung, in: Tietz, Bruno / Köhler, Richard / Zentes, Joachim (Hrsg.): Handwörterbuch des Marketing, Stuttgart, S. 1340-1351.

Peppers, Don / Rogers, Martha (1999): Enterprise one-to-one: tools for building un-breakable customer relationships in the interactive age, London.

Picarille, Lisa (2003): CRM Scores With Sports Fans – It's About The Fan Experi-ence, in: CRM Magazine, Heft 8, S. 42-45.

Raab, Gerhard (2006): Customer Relationship Management: Aufbau dauerhafter und profitabler Kundenbeziehungen, Frankfurt/Main.

Reichheld, Frederick F. / Sasser, Earl W. (1990): Zero Defections – Quality Comes to Service, in: Harvard Business Review, Heft 5, S. 255-271.

Reinecke, Sven / Köhler, Sven / Roos, Udo (2002): Kundenmanagement bei Dienst-leistungsunternehmen – Ergebnisse einer CRM-Benchmarking-Studie, in: The-xis, Heft 1, S. 59-63.

Reinecke, Sven / Sausen, Karsten (2002): CRM als Chance für das Marketing, in: Thexis, Heft 1, S. 2-5.

Tillmanns, Ulrich (2000): Erfolgsfaktor Client Loyality. Kunden-Agentur-Beziehungen erfolgreich gestalten, Frankfurt/Main.

Tomczak, Torsten / Dittrich, Sven (2000): Kundenbindung durch Kundenclubs, in: Bruhn, Manfred / Homburg, Christian (Hrsg.): Handbuch Kundenbindungsmanagement – Grundlagen – Konzepte – Erfahrungen, 3. Aufl., Wiesbaden, S. 251-268.

Wilson, David / Kothandaraman, Prabakar (1998): Relationship Maintenance, in: Thexis, Heft 4, S. 22-24.

Zeltinger, Julian (2004): Customer Relationship Management in Fußballunternehmen – Erfolgreiche Kundenbeziehungen gestalten, Berlin.

Weiterführende Ressourcen

Literatur

Bruhn, Manfred / Meffert, Heribert / Wehrle, Friedrich (Hrsg.) (1994): Marktorientierte Unternehmensführung im Umbruch: Effizienz und Flexibilität als Herausforderungen des Marketing, Stuttgart.

Eggert, Andreas (1999): Kundenbindung aus Kundensicht: Konzeptualisierung, Operationalisierung, Verhaltenswirksamkeit, Wiesbaden.

Meffert, Heribert (2000): Marketing: Grundlagen marktorientierter Unternehmensführung. Konzepte – Instrumente – Praxisbeispiele, Wiesbaden.

Sportfive GmbH (2004): Fußballstudie 2004, Hamburg.

Links

Bayer 04 Leverkusen:
http://www.bayer04.de
FC Schalke 04:
http://www.schalke04.de
Sponsors (Fachzeitschrift):
http://www.sponsors.de
Sport + Markt (Marktforschungsunternehmen):
http://www.sportundmarkt.com
Sportfive (Sportrechteagentur):
http://www.sportfive.de

Kapitel 16: Hospitality Marketing im Sport

Helmut Digel   Marcel Fahrner

Lernziele

Nach der Durchsicht dieses Kapitels sollte der Leser in der Lage sein,

- Sport Hospitality als spezifisches Produkt im Kontext von Sport-Events zu beschreiben.

- die mit Hospitality als Instrument betrieblicher Kommunikationspolitik verbundenen Zielsetzungen nachzuvollziehen.

- gängige Leistungsbestandteile und Preisrelationen ausgewählter Sport Hospitality-Produkte zu beschreiben.

- Idealtypen von Sport Hospitality-Konsumformen wiederzugeben.

- Trends zukünftiger Entwicklung von Hospitality zu kennzeichnen.

Überblick über das Kapitel

In diesem Kapitel werden Grundlagen des Hospitality Marketing erläutert und an Beispielen aus dem Sport illustriert. Dabei gilt es zunächst, Hospitality als eigenständiges Produkt zu kennzeichnen und diesbezüglich grundlegende Marketing-Entscheidungen aufzuzeigen. Dann wird Hospitality als Instrument betrieblicher Kommunikationspolitik beschrieben und Ziele der beteiligten Markt-Akteure am Beispiel ausgewählter Sport-Events verdeutlicht. Typisierung von Hospitality-Konsumformen und Überlegungen zu Trends weiterer Entwicklung von Sport Hospitality folgen, bevor eine Fallstudie, die sich mit dem Hospitality-Programm der Fußball WM 2006 beschäftigt, das Kapitel beschließt.

16.1 Einführung in die Thematik

„Hospitality" ist heute wichtiger Bestandteil von Veranstaltungen in Kunst, Kultur, Musik oder Sport und hat nicht nur unter Marketing-Gesichtspunkten relevante ökonomische Bedeutung. Wird Hospitality als eigenständiges Produkt auf einem Markt angeboten, können dabei beträchtliche Gewinne erzielt werden. V.a. in der Welt des Sports und hier vorrangig in medienattraktiven Sportarten, wie z.B. Fußball, Golf, Tennis und Formel 1, sind besondere räumliche Arrangements mit einer entsprechenden Ausgestaltung zu einer Selbstverständlichkeit geworden. Hier definiert und trifft man sich als „besondere Personen", wobei die Zugehörigkeit zu einem ausgewählten Personenkreis unter anderem über Armbänder, besondere Eintrittskarten oder Namensschilder dokumentiert wird.

Anforderungen an strategische Planung, operative Umsetzung und Erfolgs-Kontrolle von Hospitality führen dabei mitunter zu erheblichen Management-Aufgaben. Folgt man dabei lediglich persönlichen Intuitionen, können die mit Hospitality verknüpften Erwartungen allerdings nur selten erfüllt werden; zudem sind die von beteiligten Akteuren eingegangenen Risiken teilweise beträchtlich. Eine solche Situationsbeschreibung überrascht allerdings kaum, denn ein Blick in Marketing-Lehrbücher zeigt, dass man sich in Bezug auf Hospitality Marketing bislang auf einem weitgehend unbekannten Feld befindet. Fundierte wissenschaftliche Reflexionen über das Phänomen des Hospitality Marketing existieren derzeit so gut wie nicht, Hospitality wird allenfalls als Randnotiz bearbeitet. Experten des Hospitality Marketing, die über jahrelange Erfahrungen in diesem Tätigkeitsfeld verfügen, haben im Wesentlichen Lernprozesse nach dem Prinzip des „trial and error" durchlaufen. Ihr erfahrungsbasiertes Wissen wurde dabei bis heute kaum systematisiert zusammengetragen.

In einem von der Fédération Internationale de Football Association (FIFA) in Auftrag gegebenen Forschungsprojekt wurden Hospitality-Marktdaten ausgewählter Sport-Events sowie aktuelle Entwicklungen und Trends im Sport Hospitality Marketing beleuchtet (Digel/Fahrner, 2007). Mit der hier vorgenommenen Einführung in Hospitality Marketing wird das Phänomen genauer gekennzeichnet und am Beispiel von Sport Hospitality werden relevante Wissensbestände bereitgestellt, um zukünftige Investitionen in diesem attraktiven Markt planen und absichern zu können. Dabei kommen ausgewählte Daten des genannten Forschungsprojekts zur Darstellung.

16.2 Grundlagen des Hospitality Marketing

Bei gesellschaftlichen, kulturellen und sportlichen Anlässen zählte ein Teil der Zuschauer schon immer zur besonderen Gruppe „wichtiger Gäste", heute als „Very Important Persons" (VIP) bezeichnet.

> Bei Ritterwettkämpfen oder Pferderennen wurde Angehörigen oberer Gesellschaftsschichten meist besondere, „standesgemäße" Betreuung und Bewirtung zuteil. Zugehörigkeit zur „besseren" Gesellschaft ließ sich auf diese Weise ebenso dokumentieren, wie persönlicher Luxus darstellen und konsumieren. In ähnlicher Weise gilt dies heute für Ehrenlogen und Hospitality-Bereiche. Auch hier stehen Prachtentfaltung und Machtdemonstration in besonderer Weise im Vordergrund (Veblen, 1899/2007).

Insbesondere der Blick auf gesellschaftliche Entwicklung und Veränderung hilft, das Phänomen „Hospitality" im gesellschaftlichen Kontext einzuordnen und zu erklären. Gesellschaftliche Entwicklung ist dabei v.a. durch zunehmende Differenzierung gekennzeichnet, also durch den Wandel vormals gleichartig einfach strukturierter Gesellschaften hin zu komplexen Gesellschaften. Vor dem Hintergrund gesellschaftlichen Wandels ändern sich die Lebensumstände der Gesellschafts-Mitglieder, die über spezifische Leistungsrollen in gesellschaftliche Teilsysteme eingebunden sind. Gesellschaftliche Ausdifferenzierung wird dabei in vielen Fällen von einer allgemeinen Erhöhung des Lebensstandards begleitet: einer Ausweitung von Freizeit steht weniger körperliche Arbeit gegenüber. Die Lebensorientierung der Menschen ist weniger auf Bewältigung äußerer Lebensumstände gerichtet, sondern verstärkt der Erreichung innerer Zustände gewidmet. Zunehmende Konsum- und Erlebnisorientierung in der Freizeitgestaltung ist eine wesentliche Folge dieser Entwicklung (Schulze, 1993; Digel, 1990). Dies erklärt, warum „Events" im weitesten Sinne gesellschaftliche und ökonomische Relevanz erlangt haben (Nufer, 2007) – und warum diese unter anderem für Hospitality attraktive Plattformen darstellen.

Gesellschaftliche Entwicklung geht außerdem mit Individualisierungsprozessen einher, die Personen vielfältige Optionen der Lebensgestaltung eröffnen (Beck/ Beck-Gernsheim, 1994). Mittels bewusster Entscheidungen zur Lebensführung strebt folglich jeder Einzelne vor dem Hintergrund eigener Wertmaßstäbe und verfügbarer Ressourcen danach, sich von anderen abzugrenzen und dabei auch eigenen Wohlstand zur Darstellung zu bringen. Der Wunsch nach Distinktion ist allenthalben zu beobachten (Bourdieu, 1979). Gesellschaftliche Entwicklung führt unter anderem auch zur Veränderung individueller Wertmuster. Ein solcher Wertewandel hin zur positiven Bewertung post-materialistischer Werte wie Selbstverwirklichung, Ungebundenheit, Hedonismus, Transparenz, Gesundheit, Spannung und Geselligkeit macht insbesondere jene Formen der Lebensführung attraktiv, die solchen Werten entsprechen (Digel, 1986; Digel, 1995).

16.2.1 Hospitality Marketing-Mix

Eine erste Annäherung an die Bedeutung des Begriffs „Hospitality" macht deutlich, dass dieser äußerst unscharf ist und in der Marketing-Praxis von Beteiligten verschieden definiert wird. Im englischsprachigen Raum beispielsweise wird unter anderem das gesamte Hotelgewerbe unter „Hospitality" gefasst. Basis aller erkennbaren Semantiken ist dabei der Begriff „Gastfreundschaft". Hiervon ausgehend steht „Hospitality" zunächst für Interaktionen von Einzelpersonen, die durch besondere zwischenmenschliche Atmosphäre charakterisiert und nach Möglichkeit an exklusive und einzigartige Erlebnisse gebunden sind (Masterman/Wood, 2003). Hospitality als „vermarktete Gastfreundschaft" im Rahmen gesellschaftlich relevanter Events ist als eigenständiges Produkt dabei auch Gegenstand expliziter Marketing-Aktivitäten von Wirtschaftsunternehmen (vgl. Abb. 1).

Marketing als Geschäftsphilosophie stellt Kunden in den Mittelpunkt betrieblicher Aufmerksamkeit. Es kann dabei als Set von Marketing-Instrumenten gekennzeichnet werden, um Kunden-Bedürfnisse besser zu verstehen und diesbezüglich adäquate Produkte und Leistungen zu entwickeln. Im Hospitality Marketing bedarf es dabei Entscheidungen zu Produkt, Preis, Kommunikation und Vertrieb im Sinne eines integrierten Marketing-Konzepts. Einzelne Marketing-Instrumente sollten nicht unabhängig voneinander konzipiert und eingesetzt, sondern zu einem stringenten Marketing-Mix kombiniert werden (Bruhn, 2002; Berndt, 2004; Kuß/Tomczak, 2004; Homburg/Krohmer, 2003).

Mit Blick auf Hospitality-Märkte ist zu beachten, dass potenzielle Kunden über vielfältige Optionen verfügen. Sie können aus Events unterschiedlicher gesellschaftlicher Lebensbereiche auswählen. Fokussiert man sich jedoch auf Top-Veranstaltungen, so gibt es nur wenige Events, die über vergleichbare gesellschaftliche Bedeutung und Prestige verfügen, wie die größten Events aus dem Bereich des Sports, z.B. Olympische Spiele oder Fußball-Weltmeisterschaften.

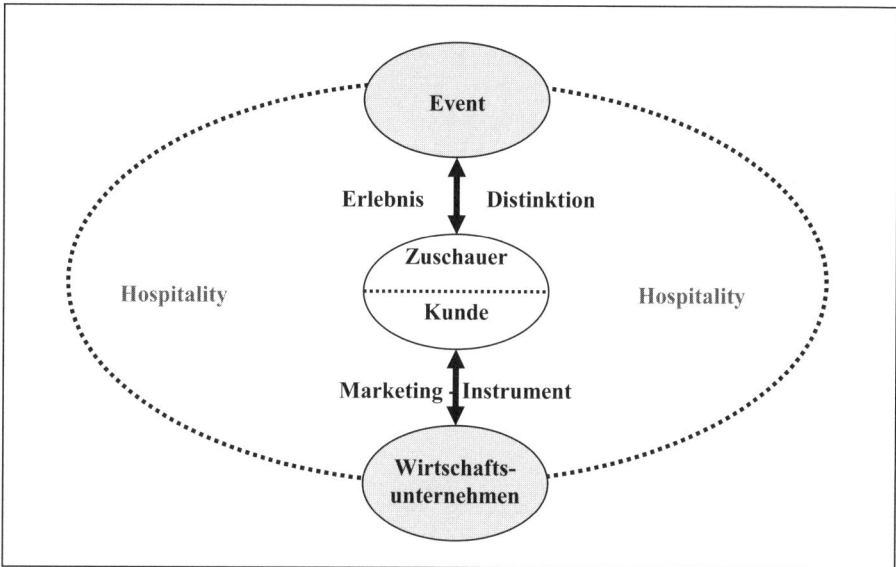

Abb. 1: Beziehungsgefüge des Hospitality Marketing

16.2.1.1 Hospitality-Produkte

Hospitality-Produkte werden schon seit längerer Zeit in Verbindung mit vielfältigen Leistungen offeriert, wobei der privilegierte Zugang zu einem Event und Catering zentrale Bestandteile darstellen. Betrachtet man hochwertige Sport-Hospitality-Produkte, lassen sich weitere grundlegende Leistungsbestandteile kennzeichnen (vgl. Abb. 2):

- Reservierte Parkplätze in Relation zur Anzahl der Gäste (1:2, 1:4 oder 1:10),
- Event-Information mittels Event-Zeitung oder TV,
- Unterhaltung durch prominente Gäste, Conférenciers, Musik/Bands oder Schauspieler/Künstler,
- Geschäftsräume, Internet-Zugang,
- Service-Teams (Hostessen),
- Branding reservierter Tische, Hinweise am Eingang zu Hospitality-Bereichen,
- Souvenirs in Form von Geschenken oder Merchandising-Artikeln, z.T. mit Branding-Optionen (Digel/Fahrner, 2007).

Die Möglichkeiten der Produktgestaltung werden unter anderem dadurch bestimmt, ob Veranstaltungs-Orte über fest eingerichtete Hospitality-Infrastrukturen verfügen oder ob diese z.B. in Form von Zelten temporär aufgebaut werden müssen. Die Qualität der Infrastrukturen wirken sich dabei sehr direkt auf Prestige und Image von Hospitality-Produkten und auf damit verbundene Investitionen aus. Außerdem legen sie den Zugang zum Event selbst sowie Möglichkeiten sozialer Interaktion der Gäste fest.

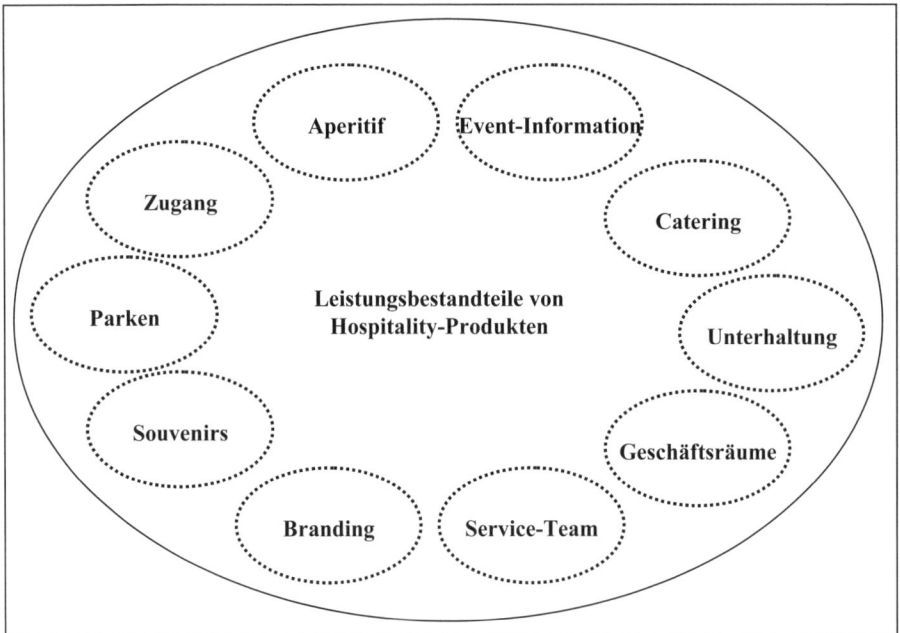

Abb. 2: Bestandteile von Hospitality-Produkten

Die Qualität von Hospitality-Produkten hängt meist auch vom Personal ab, mit dem die Serviceleistungen gewährleistet werden. Hohe Servicequalität verlangt v.a. Kompetenz, Zuverlässigkeit, Einfühlungsvermögen, Verantwortung und Vertrauen, weshalb Ausbildung und Training des Service-Personals eine entscheidende Rolle spielen (Bowie/Buttle, 2004; Kotler, 2003; Homburg/Krohmer, 2003; Kotler/Armstrong/Saunders/Wong, 2003).

Im Rahmen der Produktgestaltung sind ferner Entscheidungen in Bezug auf Standardisierung und Individualisierung zu treffen. Werden standardisierte Produkte angeboten, sind Änderungen gemäß Kundenwünschen nicht möglich. Allerdings können über die Zeit gleich bleibende und verlässliche Produkte angeboten werden, wobei die Anbieter von einer reduzierten Management-Komplexität profitieren können. Individualisierte Produkte zielen hingegen direkt auf Kundenwünsche. Sie sind aber i.d.R. auch mit höheren Kosten verbunden.

Bei Produktentscheidungen im Sport Hospitality gilt es außerdem zu beachten, dass sich jede Sportart durch historisch bedingte spezifische Wettbewerbe auszeichnet. Diese haben sich in Abhängigkeit von je spezifischen ökonomischen Rahmenbedingungen zu einem globalen Wettkampfsystem weiter entwickelt. Zu beachten sind dabei v.a. die Anzahl wichtiger Wettbewerbe, deren globale Verteilung im Jahreskalender, die jeweilige zeitliche Dauer sowie die grundsätzlich erforderlichen Rahmenbedingungen vor Ort (z.B. Wettkampfstätten). Darüber hinaus verfügen Sportarten und Sport-Events über je spezifisches Image und Prestige, so dass sich differenzierte Hierarchien zwischen Wettkampf-Veranstaltungen und „offiziellen" Meisterschaften (inter)nationaler Sport-Verbände entwickelt haben. Auch in der Konkurrenz zwischen verschiedenen Kulturbereichen lassen sich solche Differenzierungen erkennen.

16.2.1.2 Preise von Hospitality-Produkten

Beim Verkauf von Hospitality-Produkten lassen sich verschiedene Preisstrategien beobachten, die Nachfrage und damit mögliche Umsatzvolumina von Hospitality beeinflussen. Diese Strategien tragen auch zum Produkt-Image bei, denn Preise determinieren Kunden-Erwartungen und erzeugen gleichzeitig auch Produkt-Relevanz Kotler, 2003; Bowie/Buttle, 2004). Veränderungen im Preisniveau führen gerade bei prestigeträchtigen, gesellschaftlich bedeutsamen Events nur selten zu Veränderungen der Hospitality-Nachfrage. Auch auf stabilen Märkten und bei großer Zuversicht in gesamtwirtschaftliche Entwicklungen ist i.d.R. die Preissensitivität von Hospitality-Kunden gering. Die Nachfrage nach Hospitality hängt zudem von lokalen Gegebenheiten (z.B. Wohlstandsniveau, Wirtschaftskraft) ab.

16.2.2 Ziele von Hospitality Marketing

Hospitality-Märkte sind grundsätzlich durch drei Akteure gekennzeichnet, die in einer reziproken Beziehung zueinander stehen: (1) Hospitality-Rechteinhaber, die auch Organisation und Marketing der Events verantworten; (2) Hospitality-Kunden, die Hospitality-Produkte kaufen und z.T. unter Ergänzung zusätzlicher Leistungen an eigene Klienten weiter vermarkten; (3) Hospitality-Gäste, die von Hospitality-Kunden zu Events eingeladen und damit zu direkten Leistungs-Empfängern werden.

Geben Organisatoren von Events ihre Hospitality-Rechte an Dritte ab, treten spezialisierte Hospitality-Agenturen am Markt auf, die Leistungen bezüglich Organisation und Vermarktung von Hospitality-Produkten anbieten und gleichzeitig als Anbieter und Nachfrager agieren. Ihre Position zwischen Rechteinhabern und potentiellen Kunden machen sie zu Zwischenhändlern. In Folge von Differenzierungsprozessen agieren auf Hospitality-Märkten außerdem vermehrt Agenturen als „operative Dienstleister". Auf Anbieter-Seite sorgen sie z.B. für Catering, Sicher-

449

heit, Popularität und Image der Events sowie künstlerisches Rahmenprogramm. Darüber hinaus agieren zunehmend auch Reiseveranstalter und Ticketanbieter auf dem Markt. Auf der Nachfrage-Seite wird die operative Verantwortung häufig an Dritte abgegeben, z.B. offerieren Agenturen potenziellen Hospitality-Kunden vollständige „Paket-Leistungen", die unter anderem das Einladungsverfahren, die Dekoration der Räumlichkeiten, den Transfer der Gäste sowie unterstützende Leistungen und die abschließende Evaluation umfassen (vgl. Abb. 3).

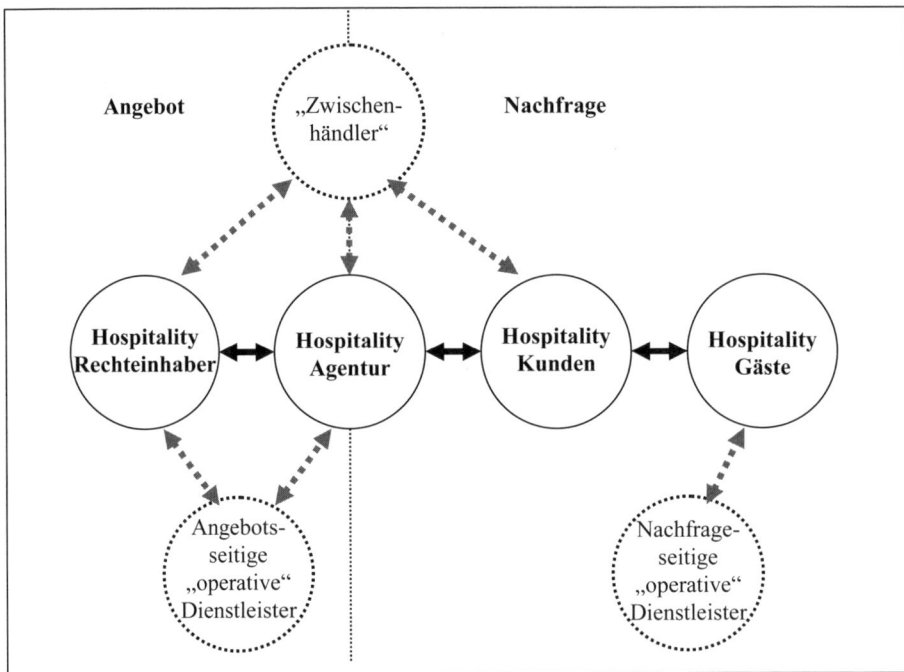

Abb. 3: Komplexität von Hospitality-Märkten

Die genannten Akteure verbinden mit ihren Markt-Aktivitäten jeweils spezifische Zielsetzungen, die im Folgenden skizziert werden.

16.2.2.1 Ziele von Hospitality-Rechteinhabern

Zur Vermarktung gesellschaftlich relevanter Events verfügen Hospitality-Rechteinhaber grundsätzlich über drei Möglichkeiten: Sie können ihre Rechte selbst nutzen und eigene Gäste einladen, sie können Rechte an Sponsoren weitergeben oder Rechte kommerziell vermarkten.

(1) Eigennutzung von Hospitality-Rechten durch Rechteinhaber
Originäre Hospitality-Rechteinhaber können selbst Gäste einladen, wobei es sich dabei entweder um Personen handelt, die sich um das Zustandekommen des Events besonders verdient gemacht haben – oder von denen man sich zukünftig Unterstützung erhofft (z.B. Politiker und Repräsentanten von Medien und Wirtschaft). Auch Personen des öffentlichen Lebens, z.B. TV-Stars, Persönlichkeiten aus Sport, Wissenschaft, Musik werden häufig eingeladen, da ihre Anwesenheit den öffentlichen Fokus auf das Event lenkt und damit indirekt positive Beiträge zu dessen Reputation leistet.

(2) Nutzung von Hospitality-Rechten durch Sponsoren
Hospitality-Rechteinhaber können aber auch Sponsoren ihres Events Hospitality-Rechte zur Verfügung stellen, so dass diese exklusive Möglichkeiten erhalten, eigene Gäste einzuladen und zu betreuen. Hospitality-Rechte sind mittlerweile häufig grundlegender Bestandteil von Sponsoring-Vereinbarungen bei (Sport-)Events. Der Zugriff von Sponsoren auf Hospitality-Rechte ist dabei Teil klar definierter Leistungs- und Gegenleistungs-Beziehungen, meist in Form garantierter Erstkaufrechte.

(3) Kommerzielle Vermarktung von Hospitality-Rechten
Bei einer entsprechenden Größe und gesellschaftlichen Relevanz eines Events ist es möglich, eine kommerzielle Vermarktung von Hospitality-Rechten auf einem freien Markt anzustreben, was Veranstaltern lukrative Finanzierungsmöglichkeiten eröffnet. Der ökonomische Erfolg von Hospitality Marketing ist dabei vor dem Hintergrund einer Gesellschaft zu sehen, in welcher immer mehr Personen über finanzielle Ressourcen verfügen, um persönliche Luxus- und Erlebnisbedürfnisse zu befriedigen.

16.2.2.2 Ziele von Hospitality-Kunden und -Gästen
Individuelle, bevorzugte Behandlung ist für viele Menschen heutiger Gesellschaften zum zentralen Bedürfnis geworden. Rundumversorgung in emotionaler Atmosphäre, ausgerichtet auf Einzigartigkeit und verbunden mit erinnerungswürdigen Erlebnissen ermöglicht gezielte persönliche Hervorhebung. Die Ziele gelten für Privatpersonen als Käufer von Hospitality-Produkten gleichermaßen wie für Unternehmen als Kunden der Hospitality-Märkte.

(1) Kundenbindung und Kundenakquise – Hospitality als Marketing-Instrument externer Beziehungen:
Der Bedeutungszuwachs von Hospitality Marketing ist vor dem Hintergrund gesättigter Märkte, austauschbarer Produkte und Informationsüberflutung zu erklären. Kunden stehen immer mehr im Fokus betrieblicher Interessen und klassische Pro-

dukt-Wettbewerbe werden durch „Kommunikations-Wettbewerbe" ergänzt. V.a. Aufbau und Pflege von Beziehungen zu Kunden und Meinungsbildnern gewinnen somit an Bedeutung. Hospitality-Einladungen intensivieren Beziehungen, emotionalisieren Bindungen und schaffen ökonomisch relevante Präferenzen auf zwischenmenschlicher Ebene durch gemeinsames Erleben. Es geht darum, „wertvolle Zeit" mit Geschäftspartnern zu verbringen; sie auf persönlicher Ebene besser kennen zu lernen und in angenehmer Atmosphäre Gespräche (auch) über geschäftlich relevante Themen zu führen. Aus dem Erlebnis heraus soll Vertrauen entstehen, das als dauerhafte Basis für geschäftliche Verbindungen dienen kann (Katalysator-Funktion). Einzigartige Rahmenbedingungen von Hospitality ermöglichen eine gezielte persönliche Ansprache von Zielgruppen. Hospitality kann also für B2B- und B2C-Kommunikationen bedeutsam und damit relevanter Bestandteil eines Customer Relationship Management (CRM) sein.

(2) Imagepflege:
Hospitality Marketing mittels Sport erweist sich insofern als vorteilhaft, als Sport aufgrund seiner gesellschaftlichen Position in vielen Situationen emotional hochwertigen Gesprächsstoff liefert. *„Sports talk"* kann komplizierte Kommunikation auflockern und im Rahmen geschäftlicher Kontakte willkommene Abwechslung ermöglichen. Darüber hinaus bietet Hospitality die Möglichkeit von Transfereffekten bezüglich Unternehmens- oder Marken-Images. Gerade im Sport geteilte Werte wie Leistungsoptimierung, bedingungslose Hingabe für individuellen oder kollektiven Erfolg und Streben nach Perfektion verbunden mit Strategie und Taktik bieten hierfür in ihrer Verbindung mit hoher Emotionalität optimale Bedingungen.

(3) Incentives – Sport Hospitality als Marketing-Instrument interner Beziehungen:
Hospitality eröffnet außerdem die Möglichkeit, Hospitality-Einladungen im Rahmen betrieblicher *Incentives* einzusetzen. Auf diese Weise können Mitarbeiter für Fleiß und Treue belohnt oder für zukünftige Leistungen motiviert werden. So kann das betriebliche Zugehörigkeitsgefühl erhöht und als Unternehmenskultur kommuniziert werden. Dabei bietet Hospitality eigenen Mitarbeitern die Möglichkeit unvergesslicher gemeinsamer Erlebnisse, wodurch auch Loyalität gesteigert werden kann. Außerdem offerieren Einladungen größerer Mitarbeiter-Gruppen im Rahmen von *Incentives* Gelegenheiten, im Sinne des *Team Buildings* Bindungen, Zusammenhalt und Leistungsbereitschaft der Gruppen zu stärken.

(4) „Networking":
Anlässlich von Hospitality ist ferner auch Öffentlichkeitsarbeit gegenüber potenziell interessanten Geschäftspartnern möglich, mit denen in legerer Atmosphäre Gespräche geführt und Beziehungen aufgebaut werden können. Hospitality-Bereiche fördern somit B2B-Kommunikation, so dass ökonomisch relevante Netzwerke entstehen und gepflegt werden können.

(5) Befriedigung persönlicher Interessen:
Hospitality-Produkte sind schließlich auch deshalb interessant, weil Entscheidungsträger von Unternehmen selbst begeisterte Anhänger bestimmter kultureller Events
sind. Sie zielen somit im Zusammenhang mit betrieblichen Marketing-Aktivitäten
auch auf die Befriedigung ihrer persönlichen Interessen.

Mit Ausnahme der Motive „Kundenbindung/akquise" und „Imagepflege" gelten
die genannten Ziele in ähnlicher Weise auch für potenzielle Hospitality-Gäste. Mit
der Annahme von Hospitality-Einladungen geht der Hospitality-Gast in gewisser
Weise Verpflichtungen gegenüber seinem Gastgeber ein, ihm zukünftig „gewogen"
zu sein, sich möglicherweise erkenntlich zu zeigen oder auch zu revanchieren.
Hospitality bei Sport-Events ermöglicht außerdem gesellschaftlichen „Eliten", sich
„volksnah" zu zeigen, dabei aber gleichzeitig gegenüber „normalen" Zuschauern
deutlich abgegrenzt zu bleiben und das Event in hochexklusivem Rahmen zu verfolgen.

16.2.2.3 Ziele von Hospitality-„Dritten"

16.2.2.3 Ziele von Hospitality-„Dritten"
Das Motiv aller „Dritten", seien es Agenturen, Zwischenhändler und „operative
Dienstleister", ist die Aufrechterhaltung ihrer Branche und damit die Sicherung von
Geschäftsgrundlagen zur Erwirtschaftung ökonomischen Gewinns.

16.3 Hospitality-Produkte und -Preise ausgewählter Sport-Events

Betrachtet man ausgewählte Sport-Events professioneller Sportarten, stellt man
fest, dass deren Hospitality-Produkte vergleichbare Service-Leistungen enthalten,
gleichzeitig aber teils große Unterschiede in ihren Preisstrukturen aufweisen. So
reichen in 2007 die Preise von 355 €/Person und Tag für die Business Lounge beim
Weltfinale der Leichtathletik in Stuttgart bis zu 4.000 €/Person und Tag für den
Keith Prowse Gatsby Club beim Finaltag in Wimbledon (vgl. Abb. 4). Dies ist v.a.
mit der unterschiedlichen Wertigkeit der Sport-Events und ihres Prestiges zu erklären. Solche Unterschiede lassen sich auch im Verhältnis von Events der gleichen
Sportart beobachten.

Im Folgenden werden beispielhaft Hospitality-Produkte und -Preise ausgewählter
Rugby- und Golf-Events dargestellt mit dem Ziel, die bisher erfolgte Kennzeichnung des Phänomens zu belegen und zu illustrieren (Digel/Fahrner, 2007).

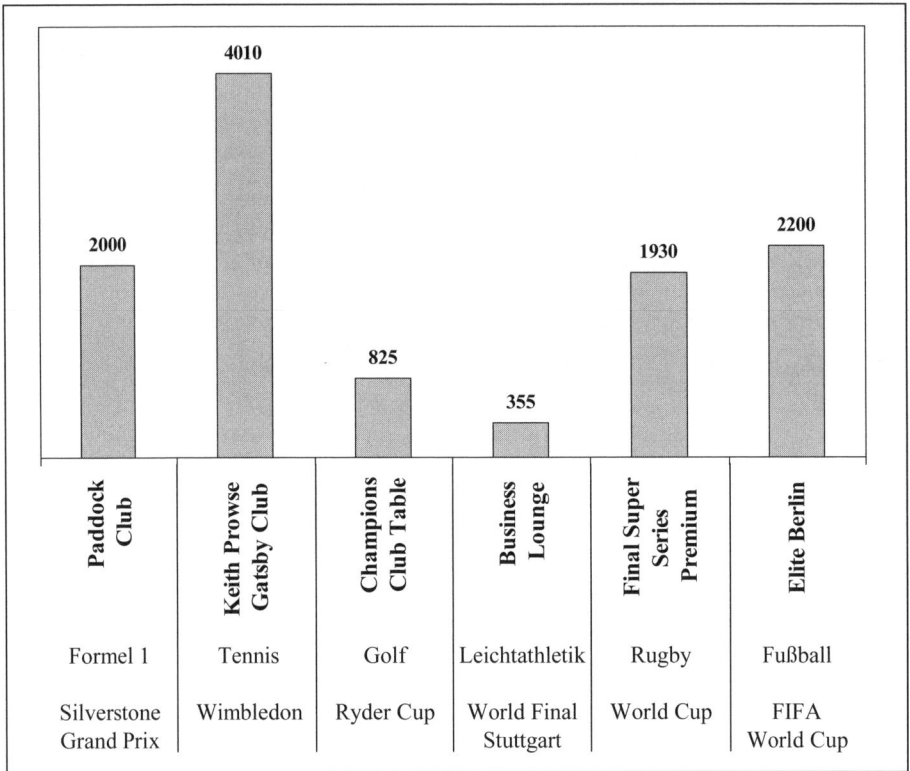

Abb. 4: Hospitality-Preise ausgewählter Sport-Events 2007 (pro Person/Tag in €)

16.3.1 Hospitality-Produkte und -Preise bei Rugby-Events

Die Sportart Rugby hat in Großbritannien und den Ländern des Commonwealth eine lange Tradition, deren weltweite Dachorganisation das International Rugby Board (IRB) ist. Zu den international bedeutsamsten Turnieren zählen die Weltmeisterschaft (mit 15 Spielern), die während fünf Wochen 48 Spiele zwischen 20 Mannschaften umfassen. Das IRB 6 Nationen-Turnier ist das weltweit älteste Rugby-Event. An ihm nehmen jedes Jahr während sechs Wochen die Nationalmannschaften von England, Wales, Schottland, Irland, Frankreich und Italien teil, wobei die Spiele an verschiedenen Wochenendtagen erfolgen und jede Mannschaft mindestens zwei Heimspiele austrägt. Die teuersten Hospitality-Produkte im Rahmen des IRB 6 Nations-Turniers kosten 2007 bis 1.320 €/Person und Tag. Deutlich teurer ist Hospitality im Rahmen von Halbfinale und Finale der Rugby-Weltmeisterschaft (vgl. Abb. 5).

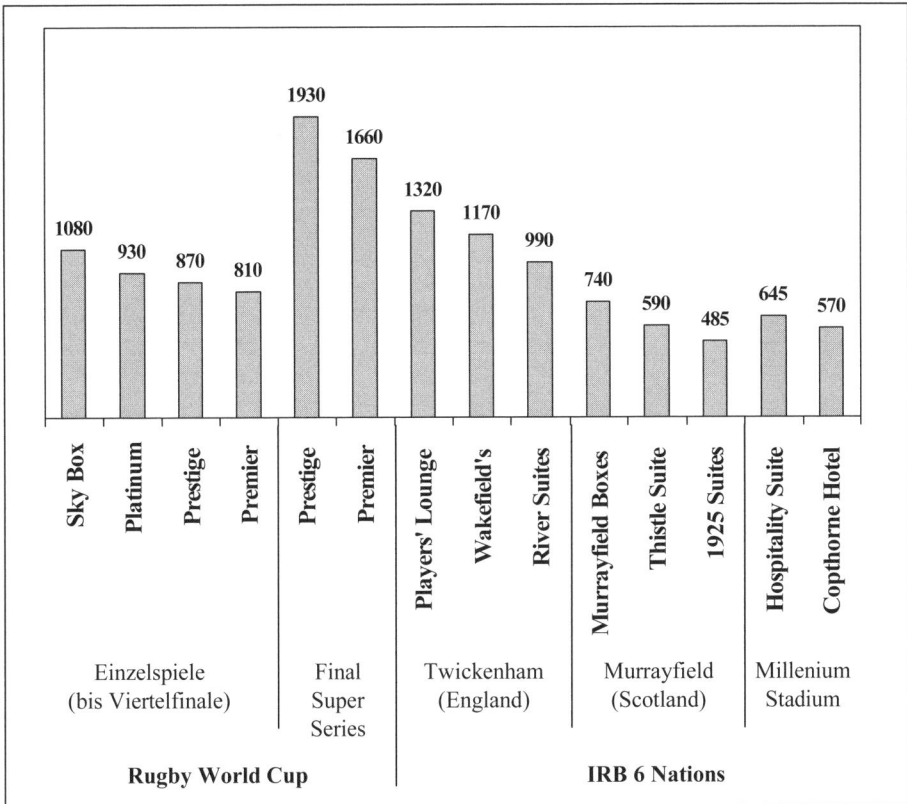

Abb. 5: Hospitality-Preise ausgewählter Rugby-Events 2007 (pro Person/Tag in €)

Die Spiele der Final Super Series werden im Stade de France in Paris ausgetragen. Hier umfassen „Prestige"-Produkte folgende Leistungen: Akkreditierung für den Hospitality-Bereich, Tickets für Plätze der gehobenen Kategorie, exklusive Veranstaltungsinformationen (Programm und Lagepläne), Champagner-Empfang, prominente Gastredner und Conférenciers, TV-Bildschirme, Markierung reservierter Tische (à zehn Personen) mit Unternehmens-Logos (*Branding*), Betreuung durch erfahrene Service-Teams, 3-Gänge Menü mit Weinauswahl, warme Snacks nach Spielende, reservierte Parkplätze (einer für je vier Personen), Erinnerungs-Geschenk.

16.3.2 Hospitality-Produkte und -Preise bei Golf-Events

Das traditionsreichste und prestigeträchtigste Golf-Event ist der Ryder Cup, bei dem sich alle zwei Jahre während einer sechstägigen Wettkampfwoche zwölf der besten Spieler von PGA Tour und PGA European Tour gegenüber stehen. „The Open Championship" wiederum ist das einzige europäische von vier „Major"-

Turnieren, die mit ihren jeweils vier Turniertagen zwar nicht die höchsten Preisgelder aufweisen, aber dennoch die hochkarätigsten Teilnehmerfelder anziehen. Weitere Turniere der PGA European Tour mit mindestens drei Mio. US-$ Preisgeld sind die ebenfalls in Abb. 6 genannten Turniere. Deren Hospitality-Produkte kosten 2007 zwischen 520 € und 825 €/Person und Tag.

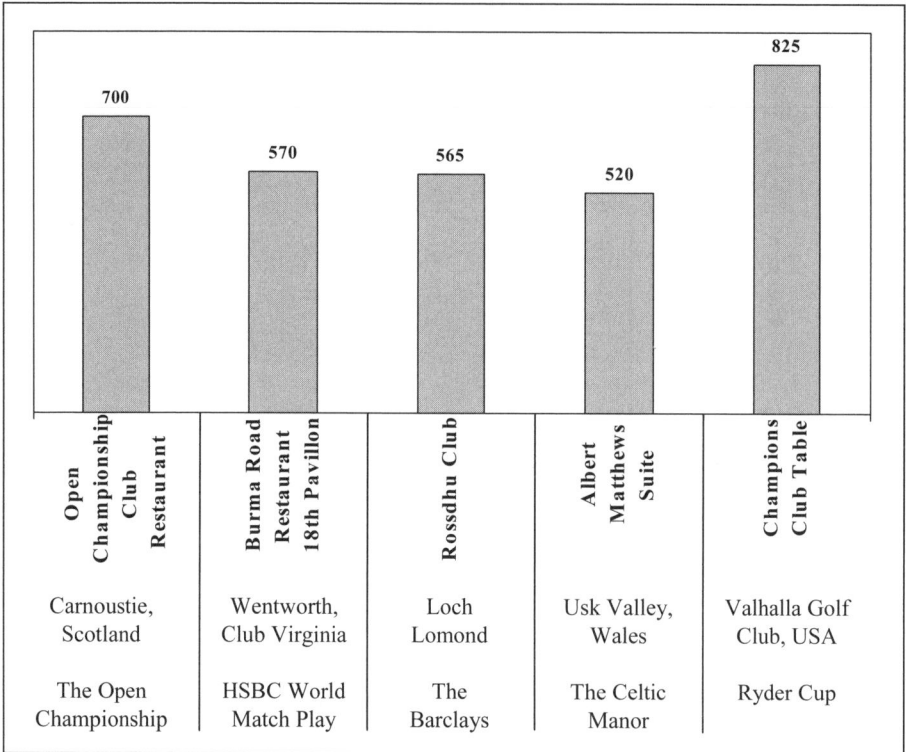

Abb. 6: Hospitality-Preise ausgewählter Golf-Events 2007 (pro Person/Tag in €)

Das Hospitality-Produkt des Ryder Cup umfasst dabei folgende Leistungen: Champions Club Ticket mit Zugang zum Fairway, Offizielles Ryder Cup Journal, Ryder Cup pairing sheets, computergestütztes Scoring Informationssystem, Premium Bar, TV im Champion Club, Unternehmenszeichen (*Branding*) am Eingang zum Hospitality-Bereich und an reservierten Tischen (à zehn Personen), Möglichkeit zur Nutzung des Ryder Cup Logos für eigene Hospitality-Einladungen, continental breakfast, Mittagsbuffet, Snacks am Nachmittag, reservierte Parkplätze in der Nähe des Ryder Cup-Geländes, Business Area, Telefon- und Faxservice, Möglichkeit zur Übernachtung in reservierten Hotels, Möglichkeit zum Kauf doppelt gebrandeter Merchandising-Artikel (Ryder Cup *und* Hospitality-Kunde/Unternehmen).

16.4 Hospitality-Konsumformen

Hospitality-Märkte sind mittlerweile ausdifferenziert und angebotene Produkte richten sich auf spezifische Bedürfnisse. Im Folgenden wird deshalb eine Typisierung von Hospitality-Konsumformen vorgenommen, die ungeachtet divergierender Ziele und Interessen von Markt-Teilnehmern und unterschiedlichen Hospitality-Anlässen/Events erkennbare Gemeinsamkeiten aufzeigen kann. Dabei liegt es zunächst nahe, sich in einem ersten Schritt mit Sportart-bezogenen Konsumformen zu befassen. In einem zweiten Schritt werden dann Zweck-Orientierungen des Hospitality-Konsums als Merkmale herangezogen.

16.4.1 Sportart-bezogene Typisierung von Hospitality-Konsumformen

Gerade im Rahmen von Golf-Events zeigt sich eine besondere Form gesitteten Umgangs. Auf Basis seiner historischen Entwicklung zeichnet sich der Golfsport durch distinktive Etikette und Umgangsformen britisch-aristokratischer Tradition aus – was nicht zuletzt auch im Golf-Hospitality erkennbar ist. Hinzu kommen v.a. Charakteristika wie Naturbezug, Nähe zu Spielern sowie luxuriöse Gastronomie und elitäre Atmosphäre. Außerdem ermöglicht die Wettkampfform von Golf – im Rahmen mehrtägiger Veranstaltungen werden jeweils mehrere „Löcher" pro Tag gespielt – zeitlich flexiblen Hospitality-Konsum. Rugby als körperbetontes, maskulines Spiel spiegelt sich hingegen auch im Hospitality wider, wobei Tradition und Geschichte der Sportart in besonderer Weise kultiviert werden. Formel 1 legt wiederum andere Formen des Hospitality nahe. Die „Boliden" der verschiedenen Teams und ihre Piloten spielen dabei eine zentrale Rolle.

16.4.2 Zweck-orientierte Typisierung von Hospitality-Konsumformen

Blickt man auf das Phänomen „Sport-Hospitality" aus einer Perspektive, bei der die dominanten Zwecke im Mittelpunkt stehen, lässt sich eine weitere Form der Typisierung finden. Beobachtbare Konsumformen werden dabei idealtypisch rekonstruiert. Dass dabei Idealtypen formuliert werden, die in solcher Eindeutigkeit in der Praxis nicht existieren, ist einschränkend anzumerken. Anlässlich eines Sport-Events können nämlich mehrere Hospitality-Typen gleichzeitig anzutreffen sein, die jeweils auf eine spezifische Klientel ausgerichtet sind.

(1) Hospitality-Typ „Sport pur":

Im Zentrum dieses Typs steht das Sport-Event selbst, das Match, der sportliche Wettbewerb. Insofern kann man in gewisser Weise von einer Ticket-Orientierung sprechen. Wichtig ist, dass man „live" am Event teilhaben kann, weshalb es insbesondere nach dem Sportereignis zu Ausgelassenheit, Siegesfreude oder Frust kommt. Bei Hospitality dieses Typs ist oftmals Freizeit-orientierte Kleidung vorherrschend, z.T. dominieren Sport-/Mannschafts-Trikots. Essen ist dabei weniger wichtig, insbesondere spielt dessen Qualität keine besondere Rolle. Hingegen ist der Konsum von Alkohol (je nach Sportart) bedeutsam. In Abhängigkeit der Sportart wird dieser Hospitality-Typus v.a. von Männern nachgefragt (z.B. Fußball, Eishockey, Rugby). Erzählungen von Helden-Geschichten, Erinnerungen an vergangene Siege und Niederlagen bestimmen die Kommunikation; z.T. wird dies durch ehemalige Stars der Sportart unterstützt, die aktuelles Sportgeschehen kommentieren oder moderieren.

Eine Variante dieses Hospitality-Typs ergibt sich, wenn v.a. Tickets, also der Zugang zum „Erlebnis Sport-Event" im Mittelpunkt steht und die Preise von vielen Konsumenten bezahlt werden können. Dann wird aus dem Typus „Sport pur" schnell eine „Großgaststätte" mit touristischem Charakter, da Personen Zugang erhalten, die das Sportevent als Anlass für Familienausflüge oder ähnliches nutzen – für die ein solches Umfeld eine besondere Ausnahme darstellt. Oftmals gewinnen dann Essen und Trinken an Bedeutung, denn „es kostet nichts" oder man „hat es ja bereits vorab bezahlt". Hier wird dann weniger Qualität nachgefragt, hauptsächlich geht es darum, möglichst viel für sich persönlich mitzunehmen.

(2) Hospitality-Typ „Sehen und gesehen werden":
Eine andere Form von Hospitality stellt der „Sehen und gesehen werden"-Typ dar. Hier steht die erkennbare Anwesenheit bei Anlässen mit hoher gesellschaftlicher Relevanz im Zentrum. Bereits der Zugang zu dieser Form von Hospitality gilt als Status-Symbol, weshalb sich unter den Gästen überwiegend Prominenz aus Wirtschaft, Politik, Kultur und Medien findet. Die Exklusivität dieser Anlässe wird dabei oftmals medial transportiert und in einschlägigen TV- und Print-Magazinen der Öffentlichkeit präsentiert.

Kommunikation in solchen Hospitality-Bereichen zeichnet sich eher durch „Small talk" aus. „Dabei sein" ist (fast) alles. Es gilt, Kontakte zur „High Society" und zu Entscheidungsträgern aus Politik und Wirtschaft zu knüpfen und zu pflegen. Kleidung dokumentiert dabei in hohem Maße Zugehörigkeit und Besonderheit/Relevanz des Anlasses (z.B. Smoking, Abendkleid). Häufig werden diesbezüglich auch besondere Normierungen (z.B. Kleiderordnungen) festgelegt, um „gesittetes Auftreten" bewusst zu steuern.

(3) Hospitality-Typ „Fünf Sterne Küche/Luxus":
Im Rahmen dieses Typs Hospitality geht es v.a. darum, es sich anlässlich eines Sport-Events einmal „richtig gut gehen", sich verwöhnen und belohnen zu lassen – und zwar auf Kosten eines Dritten, meist eines geschäftlichen Gastgebers. Insofern steht genussvoller Konsum hochwertiger Speisen und Getränke im Zentrum; Qualität und Exklusivität, z.B. Champagner und Kaviar, sind relevante Kriterien. Außerdem soll persönlicher Service freundlicher Hostessen ein „Wohlfühl-Ambiente" schaffen.

(4) Hospitality-Typ „Business-Orientierung":
Im Zentrum dieses Hospitality-Typus steht das Auffrischen und Vertiefen geschäftlicher Kontakte zu aktuellen wie potenziell zukünftigen Geschäftspartnern und/oder
Kunden. Networking im Sinne einer B2B-Kommunikation wird dabei vordergründig angestrebt, das Event selbst wird lediglich als Anlass genutzt, um geschäftliche
Interessen zu verfolgen. Teilweise werden dabei spezielle Business-Bereiche offeriert, um sich mit Geschäftspartnern zurückziehen, geschäftliche Transaktionen
vorbereiten oder diese sogar direkt vor Ort abschließen zu können.

(5) Hospitality-Typ „Einmaliges Erlebnis":
Hospitality dieses Typs stellt ein hochexklusives Angebot dar, in dessen Zentrum
unmittelbares Erleben des Events, z.B. des Sportanlasses steht. Es geht dabei um
größtmögliche Nähe zum Geschehen, weshalb das Angebot stark begrenzt und sehr
teuer ist. Einzigartige Erlebnisse mit Sportbezug, die man sich selbst nicht ermöglichen oder kaufen kann, fungieren als exklusives Angebot für ganz besondere Per-
sonenkreise. Eine Variante ist beispielsweise der Blick hinter die Kulissen („back-
stage"), möglicherweise unter Führung/Moderation eines Experten/Heroes der
Sportart. Gesteigert wird dies durch verschiedene Varianten des Mitmachens, indem die sportliche Aktivität unter Anleitung von Experten nachvollzogen wird, z.B.
Radfahren auf einer Tour-Etappe in den Bergen, Mitfahren in einem Motorsport-
Wagen, Mitsegeln beim Americas Cup, Tennis spielen gegen (aktuelle) Tennis-
Stars. Begünstigt werden solche Erlebnisse durch außergewöhnliche (Sport-) Akti-
vitäten mit Naturbezug.

16.5 Trends und weitere Entwicklung von Sport-Hospitality

Grundsätzlich kann von einer positiven Entwicklung des Hospitality Marketing ausgegangen werden, die auch Marktwachstum bedeutet. Insgesamt wird das gesellschaftliche und unternehmerische Bedürfnis, sich in einem besonderen Umfeld als
VIP zu treffen, bestehen bleiben oder sogar zunehmen. Insbesondere im Rahmen
globalisierter Wirtschaft werden gesellschaftlich relevante Events als Marketing-
Instrumente an Bedeutung gewinnen und die bestehenden Hospitality-Märkte vermutlich weiter wachsen. V.a. auch im Rahmen von B2B/B2C-Kommunikation wird
Hospitality zunehmende Bedeutung erlangen, da zukünftig persönliche Beziehungen noch relevanter sein werden. Dabei gewinnt Customer Relationship Management für immer mehr Branchen an Bedeutung, weshalb zukünftig Unternehmen unterschiedlichster Branchen Investitionen in (Sport) Hospitality tätigen werden, allen
voran der Finanzsektor mit Banken und Versicherungen, die Automobil- und Com-
puter-Industrie sowie der Energie- und Beratungssektor.

Allerdings darf das Marktwachstum der letzten Jahre (Masterman/Wood, 2003)
nicht vorbehaltlos fortgeschrieben werden, die Hospitality-Märkte müssen nicht
notwendigerweise wachsen. Die weitere Entwicklung von Sport Hospitality-

Märkten dürfte vielmehr durch weitere Ausdifferenzierung und eine fortschreitende Professionalisierung der Hospitality-Anbieter geprägt sein. Dabei werden sich die Hospitality-Produkte in naher Zukunft nicht dramatisch verändern, sondern auch zukünftig die in Abb. 2 aufgeführten Elemente umfassen. Regionale Märkte werden dabei ihre Besonderheiten aufweisen, z.B. hinsichtlich Sicherheit oder Catering. Bezogen auf Sport-Events, in deren Rahmen Hospitality stattfindet, wird auch zukünftig das Prestige entscheidend die Attraktivität dieser Produkte bestimmen. Attraktivität und Exklusivität wird man möglicherweise auch vermehrt in „künstlichen", explizit für Hospitality-Anlässe konstruierten Sport-Events herzustellen versuchen. Neben dem Sport-Event als Anlass werden Catering und Service insgesamt zunehmend bedeutsam.

Auch zukünftig wird der Preis von Sport Hospitality nicht das entscheidende Options-Kriterium für die Kunden sein. Vielmehr wird die Transparenz von Leistung und Gegenleistung an Bedeutung gewinnen, wobei Qualität zum entscheidenden Faktor wird. Es wird dabei nicht mehr in erster Linie darum gehen, *was* angeboten wird. Die Frage nach dem *„wie"* und insbesondere die Betreuung der Gäste wird hingegen zum entscheidenden Qualitätskriterium.

Außerdem werden zukünftig auch „added values" an Bedeutung gewinnen, z.B. prominente Gäste/Moderatoren (aktuelle Spieler oder ehemalige Heros), technologische Unterstützung (Monitore, Teamfunk, Computersimulationen), Zugang zur „Hinterbühne" (Fahrerlager, Boxengasse, Umkleideräume) oder Zusatzveranstaltungen (Gala Dinners). Im Servicebereich werden außerdem auch vermehrt neuere technische Entwicklungen zum Tragen kommen, denn Hospitality-Gäste sind in allen Bereichen kurzweiliger zu unterhalten. Sie wollen nicht zu lange an einem festen Platz verweilen, und v.a. nicht davon abhängig sein, dass ihr Nebensitzer darüber bestimmt, ob es ein schöner oder schlechter Abend ist.

Technische Entwicklungen werden auch Innovation ermöglichen, die v.a. darauf gerichtet sein wird, Prinzipien wie Exklusivität und individuelle Beachtung gewährleisten zu können. „Gewöhnliche" Sport Hospitality vermittelt bereits heute kaum noch das Gefühl von Exklusivität. Die rasante Entwicklung der letzten Jahre hat dazu geführt, dass ein Neuigkeitswert für Hospitality-Angebote nicht mehr gegeben ist. Beinahe jede Führungskraft war bereits einmal Hospitality-Gast, Top-Entscheider werden nicht selten mehrfach zum gleichen Event eingeladen. Deshalb werden die angebotenen Produkte kreativ zu verändern sein, will man auch zukünftig seinen Kunden etwas ganz Besonderes bieten. So deutet sich bereits an, dass mittels Zusatzleistungen zum eigentlichen Hospitality-Produkt zukünftig „hybride" Hospitality-Produkte entstehen werden, z.B. wenn Reisen mit Sport-Hospitality-Elementen kombiniert werden.

Den insgesamt sehr positiven Entwicklungschancen des Hospitality Marketing stehen einige Restriktionen entgegen, die zu beachten sind. So müssen die z.T. sehr hohen Hospitality-Investitionen mehr und mehr gegenüber unternehmensinternem Controlling gerechtfertigt werden. Von Unternehmen wird vermehrt gefordert, den

Nutzen von Hospitality-Investitionen transparent zu machen. Auch können restriktive Corporate Governance Regelungen und staatliche Steuerregeln weiteres Wachstum von Sport-Hospitality behindern. Außerdem könnte eine zu umfassende Vermarktung von Hospitality Produkten zu Beeinträchtigungen im Sponsoring-Bereich führen, insbesondere wenn Hospitality-Kunden umfassende Rechte bezüglich des Branding angeboten werden.

Die noch immer wachsende Zahl der Events und das allgemeine Wachstum des Hospitality-Markts im Sport und auch in anderen Kulturbereichen erhöht zudem den Wettbewerbsdruck in der Branche insgesamt. Zwar wird die Nachfrage nach Hospitality bei Großveranstaltungen wie Olympischen Spielen oder Fußball-Weltmeisterschaften weiter zunehmen; jedoch könnten Events, die nicht der Spitzenklasse angehören, in die Defensive geraten.

16.6 Fallstudie

Die folgende Fallstudie verdeutlicht, welche Überlegungen anzustellen und welche Entscheidungen zu treffen sind, wenn Hospitality als Instrument betrieblicher Kommunikationspolitik eingesetzt werden soll.

Fallstudie „Hospitality Marketing bei der Fußball-WM 2006"

Der Verkauf von Hospitality-Produkten anlässlich der Fußball-Weltmeisterschaft 2006 in Deutschland hat sich aus Sicht der FIFA und des DFB als besonders erfolgreich erwiesen. Der große Hospitality-Erfolg anlässlich der Fußball-WM 2006 basierte insbesondere darauf, dass die Stadien ausverkauft waren und die Möglichkeit zur Partizipation an den Spielen live vor Ort bereits einen hohen Wert an sich darstellte.

In allen zwölf WM-Stadien und bei allen 64 WM-Spielen wurde ein umfangreiches Hospitality-Angebot offeriert. Den insgesamt mehr als 300.000 Hospitality-Gästen standen vor Ort beispielsweise Pavillons und Terrassen zur Verfügung. Neben diesen temporären mobilen Bauten wurden auch bestehende Hospitality-Infrastrukturen der Stadien genutzt.

Im Anschluss an eine öffentliche Ausschreibung 2003 erhielt die iSe-Hospitality AG von der FIFA die weltweit exklusiven Rechte zur Vermarktung des gewerblichen Hospitality-Programms der Fußball-Weltmeisterschaft 2006.

An der operativen Umsetzung der Hospitality waren weitere Vertragspartner zur Sicherung von Qualität, Service und Exklusivität der Hospitality-Produkte beteiligt (z.b. Catering, Hostessen-Service, Sicherheitsfirmen), so dass ein komplexer Markt entstand. Insgesamt waren 28 Unternehmen an der Umsetzung der Hospitality-Programme beteiligt, die pro Spiel rund 4.000 Arbeitskräfte im Einsatz hatten.

Herausfordernd war für die Hospitality-Verantwortlichen v.a. die Aufgabe, einer so großen Gästezahl aus aller Welt ein exklusives Angebot zu unterbreiten, das unterschiedlichsten Erwartungen entsprach. Das FIFA-Hospitality-Programm der Fußball-Weltmeisterschaft 2006 unterschied drei grundsätzliche Produkt-Gruppen: (1) exklusive Hospitality für die Sponsoren und Geschäftspartner der FIFA, (2) exklusive Hospitality für Gäste der FIFA und des lokalen Organisationskomitees, (3) gewerbliche Hospitality-Produkte für das allgemeine Publikum. Man verfolgte also eine differenzierte Produktpolitik zur gezielten Bedürfnisbefriedigung unterschiedlicher Zielgruppen.

Die gewerblichen Hospitality-Produkte für das allgemeine Publikum waren wiederum in drei Kategorien differenziert, sie waren als „Prestige", „Elite", „Skybox" bezeichnet und umfassten jeweils die besten Sitzplätze im Stadion. Außerdem waren sie kombiniert mit reservierten Parkplätzen, gesondertem Zugang zum Stadion, herausragender Gastronomie sowie persönlicher Betreuung und Entertainment. „Prestige"-Hospitality kombinierte beispielsweise Einzelsitze mit Zugang zum Hospitality-Village in unmittelbarer Nähe des Stadions. „Elite"-Hospitality umfasste Einzelsitze und größere Logen sowie Restaurants, die mit anderen Gästen geteilt wurden. „Skybox"-Hospitality schließlich offerierte exklusive Privatatmosphäre in Stadion-Logen.

16.7 Fazit und Ausblick

Hospitality Marketing im Rahmen gesellschaftlicher Anlässe hat sich zu einem allgegenwärtigen Phänomen entwickelt. Für Veranstalter von Events bietet Hospitality Marketing günstige Finanzierungs-Chancen. Gleichzeitig eröffnet es Möglichkeiten, Image und Prestige von Veranstaltung und Veranstalter aufzuwerten. Hospitality als Marketing-Instrument und das Wachstum des Hospitality-Markts insgesamt haben dabei die ökonomischen Chancen dieser Branche erhöht. Dieses Wachstum geht jedoch einher mit einer zunehmenden Öffnung der Hospitality-Bereiche für „Jedermann" – so dass die Grundidee von Hospitality zurückgenommen wird. Denn es geht auch zukünftig vorrangig darum, den Kunden als „Auserwählten" zu betrachten, der in exklusiver Atmosphäre an einem Event teilhaben darf. Hinzu kommt, dass die Vielzahl angebotener Hospitality-Produkte inzwischen zu einer harten Konkurrenz um Kunden geführt hat. Diese Konkurrenz besteht dabei sowohl zwischen Sport-Events als auch zwischen diesen und Events anderer Kultur- und Unterhaltungsbereiche.

Für Anbieter von Hospitality-Produkten gilt es deshalb mehr denn je, stimmige Gesamtkonzepte zu erarbeiten und diese individuell in Events einzupassen. Grenzen bestehen dabei im Sport v.a. hinsichtlich der Wettkampfstrukturen und Rahmenbedingungen der verschiedenen Sportarten. Diese definieren neben zeitlichen (z.B. Spieldauer, globale Verteilung der Events) v.a. auch räumliche Bedingungen (z.B. Wettkampfstätte und vorhandene Hospitality-Infrastruktur) für Hospitality. Ferner beeinflussen sowohl die Infrastruktur (z.B. Anbindung an internationalen Flugverkehr, Verkehrsnetz, logistische Möglichkeiten und Hotelwesen) als auch die nationalen kulturellen und gesellschaftlichen Aspekte des Events die jeweils sehr unterschiedlichen Hospitality-Möglichkeiten.

Vor diesem Hintergrund sind Entscheidungen zur Produkt- und Preisgestaltung zu treffen. Will man dabei den Bedürfnissen der jeweiligen Zielgruppen gerecht werden, sollten systematische Analysen der Kunden und Gäste den notwendigen Entscheidungen zugrunde gelegt werden. Prestige, Image und Tradition der Sport-Events tragen dabei ein hohes Nachfragepotential in sich. Darüber hinaus gilt es in Zukunft, vermehrt die Qualität der operativen Umsetzung von Hospitality zu beachten. Auf diese Weise lässt sich unter anderem eine exklusive Preispolitik legitimieren. V.a. das Service-Personal stellt diesbezüglich eine wichtige Herausforderung dar. Hochwertiger und souveräner Umgang mit Hospitality-Gästen bedarf dabei einer spezifischen Ausbildung sowie hinreichender Erfahrung.

Hospitality hat als Marketing-Instrument mittlerweile für Unternehmen fast aller Branchen an Bedeutung gewonnen. Mit seiner Etablierung hat dieses Instrument allerdings auch seinen Charakter des „Neuen" verloren. Aus diesem Grund wird eine kreative, innovative und systematische Planung und eine qualitativ hochwertige operative Umsetzung wichtiger. Die potenziell möglichen Hospitality-Gäste stellen dabei den entscheidenden Bezugspunkt dar, da sie mit ihren Erwartungen und Bedürfnissen im Zentrum des Interesses der Anbieter stehen. Prestige und Tradition von Sportarten und Events sowie deren spezifische Hospitality-„Kultur" sind weitere wichtige Entscheidungsgrößen, die mit den Unternehmenszielen und Gästeinteressen in Einklang zu bringen sind.

Kontrollfragen

1. Worin liegen die Ursprünge des Phänomens, das heute als „Hospitality" bezeichnet wird?
2. Wie lässt sich der Begriff „Hospitality" kennzeichnen?
3. Welche Rolle spielt gesellschaftlicher Wandel für den Bedeutungszuwachs von Sport-Hospitality?
4. Welche grundsätzlichen Leistungsbestandteile umfassen Hospitality-Produkte?
5. Welche Akteure sind für Hospitality-Märkte grundsätzlich kennzeichnend?
6. Welche Ziele verbinden Hospitality-Rechteinhaber mit Hospitality Marketing?

7. Welche Ziele verbinden Hospitality-Kunden und -Gäste mit Hospitality-Marketing?
8. Welche typischen Konsumformen von Sport-Hospitality können unterschieden werden?
9. Wie könnte die weitere Entwicklung von Sport-Hospitality aussehen?
10. Welchen Herausforderungen hat sich Sport-Hospitality zu stellen?

Literaturverzeichnis

Beck, Ulrich / Beck-Gernsheim, Elisabeth (1994): Individualisierung in modernen Gesellschaften – Perspektiven und Kontroversen einer subjektorientierten Soziologie, in: Beck, Ulrich / Beck-Gernsheim, Elisabeth (1994): Riskante Freiheiten, Frankfurt/Main, S. 10-39.

Berndt, Ralph (2004): Marketingstrategie und Marketingpolitik, 4. Aufl., Berlin u.a.

Bourdieu, Pierre (1979): Die feinen Unterschiede. Kritik der gesellschaftlichen Urteilskraft, Frankfurt/Main.

Bowie, David / Buttle, Francis (2004): Hospitality Marketing. An Introduction, Amsterdam u.a.

Bruhn, Manfred (2002): Marketing. Grundlagen für Studium und Beruf, 6. Aufl., Wiesbaden.

Digel, Helmut (1986): Über den Wandel der Werte in Gesellschaft, Freizeit und Sport, in: Deutscher Sportbund (Hrsg.): Materialien zum Kongreß „Menschen im Sport 2000", Schorndorf, S. 14-43.

Digel, Helmut (1990): Die Versportlichung unserer Kultur und deren Folgen für den Sport – ein Beitrag zur Uneinheitlichkeit des Sports, in: Gabler, Hartmut / Göhner, Ulrich (Hrsg.): Für einen besseren Sport… Themen, Entwicklungen und Perspektiven aus Sport und Sportwissenschaft, Schorndorf, S. 73-96.

Digel, Helmut (1995): Wertorientierung und Wertewandel im Sport, in: Stierlin, Max (Hrsg.): Sport in unserer Kultur, Magglingen, S. 93-109.

Digel, Helmut / Fahrner, Marcel (2007): The International Sports Hospitality Market, unveröffentlichter Forschungsbericht, Tübingen.

Homburg, Christian / Krohmer, Harley (2003): Marketingmanagement. Strategie – Instrumente – Umsetzung – Unternehmensführung, Wiesbaden.

Kotler, Philip (2003): Marketing Management, 11. Aufl., New Jersey.

Kotler, Philip / Armstrong, Gary / Saunders, John / Wong, Veronica (2003): Grundlagen des Marketing, 3. Aufl., München.

Kuß, Alfred / Tomczak, Torsten (2004): Marketingplanung, 4. Aufl., Wiesbaden.

Masterman, Guy / Wood Emma H. (2006): Innovative Marketing Communications. Strategies for the Events Industry, Amsterdam u.a.

Nufer, Gerd (2007): Event-Marketing und -Management. Theorie und Praxis unter besonderer Berücksichtigung von Imagewirkungen, 3. Aufl., Wiesbaden.

Schulze, Gerhard (1993): Die Erlebnisgesellschaft. Kultursoziologie der Gegenwart, Frankfurt/Main.

Veblen, Thorstein (1899/2007): Theorie der feinen Leute. Eine ökonomische Untersuchung der Institutionen, Frankfurt/Main.

Weiterführende Ressourcen

Links

Fédération Internationale de Football Association (FIFA):
http://www.fifa.com

Fußball-Weltmeisterschaft Deutschland 2006:
http://www.wm2006.deutschland.de

Kapitel 17: Kommunikationsmanagement im Sport

Sebastian Kaiser

Lernziele

Nach der Durchsicht dieses Kapitels sollte der Leser in der Lage sein,

- Veränderungen im Umfeld von Organisationen und ihre Auswirkungen auf deren Kommunikationshandeln darstellen zu können.

- die Relevanz einer Auseinandersetzung mit dem Kommunikationsmanagement national und international operierender Sportorganisationen zu diskutieren.

- beispielhaft besondere Herausforderungen an das Kommunikationsmanagement von Sportbetrieben zu nennen und adäquate Problemlösungen vorschlagen zu können.

Überblick über das Kapitel

„Man kann nicht nicht kommunizieren". Dieses berühmte Zitat des kürzlich verstorbenen amerikanischen Sozialpsychologen und Kommunikationswissenschaftlers Paul Watzlawick verweist auf die besondere Bedeutung der Planung und Steuerung von Kommunikation, der Wahrnehmung also von Funktionen des Kommunikationsmanagements (KM). Professionelle Kommunikation ist auch für Sportorganisationen/Sportbetriebe von hoher und steigender Bedeutung. Die Begriffe „Sportorganisation" und „Sportbetrieb" werden im Folgenden synonym verwendet. Sie sind geeignet, die Vielfalt der Institutionen abzubilden, in denen in unserer Gesellschaft Sportprodukte hergestellt werden und die sich mit Fragen der Planung und Steuerung von Kommunikation auseinandersetzen müssen. Von der Betrachtung ausgeschlossen sind private Haushalte. Von „(Sport-) Unternehmen" wird nur dann gesprochen, wenn es speziell um (Sport-) Betriebe mit erwerbswirtschaftlicher Zielsetzung geht.

Die bloße Übertragung allgemeiner Methoden und Instrumente des Kommunikationsmanagements auf den Sport ist allerdings nicht angemessen, um den vielfältigen Besonderheiten der Sportwirtschaft gerecht zu werden. Vor welchen besonderen Herausforderungen steht das Kommunikationsmanagement von Sportorganisationen und woraus ergeben sich diese? Welche konkreten Lösungsmöglichkeiten bieten sich für spezifische Problemlagen an? Das sind die zentralen Fragen, mit denen sich das vorliegende Kapitel beschäftigt.

Zunächst werden allgemeine begriffliche Abgrenzungen getroffen und es werden zentrale Veränderungen im Umfeld von Organisationen beschrieben, die deren kommunikative Situation beeinflussen. Im Anschluss an einige Hinweise, die Relevanz einer Auseinandersetzung mit dem Kommunikationsmanagement von Sportbetrieben betreffend, werden zentrale Besonderheiten der Sportwirtschaft dargestellt. Auf Basis dieser wird schließlich beispielhaft aufgezeigt, welche besonderen Herausforderungen sich für das Kommunikationsmanagement von Sportbetrieben ergeben und welche konkreten Lösungsmöglichkeiten sich jeweils anbieten.

17.1 Einführung in die Thematik

Organisationen befinden sich heute in einer komplexen und schwierigen Kommunikationssituation. Die steigende Bedeutung einer Auseinandersetzung mit dem Management von Kommunikation ergibt sich dabei in erster Linie aus Veränderungen im Umfeld von Organisationen, welche die bisherigen kommunikativen Aktivitäten einschränken oder in Frage stellen. Im Wesentlichen wird die kommunikative Situation von Organisationen von Entwicklungen in drei Bereichen beeinflusst (Unger/Fuchs, 1999):

1. Veränderungen im wirtschaftlichen Umfeld,
2. Veränderungen im sozial-gesellschaftlichen Bereich und
3. Veränderungen im kommunikativen Bereich.

Diese Veränderungen haben auch vielfältige Auswirkungen auf die Kommunikation von Sportorganisationen. Einige Beispiele:

Ein zentraler Aspekt im Rahmen von Veränderungen im *wirtschaftlichen Umfeld* ist die zunehmende Internationalisierung der Wirtschaft, Stichwort: Globalisierung. Auch große Sportorganisationen agieren zunehmend international. Der FC Bayern München etwa kommuniziert über seine Homepage mit seinen Fans in deutscher, englischer, spanischer, japanischer und chinesischer Sprache. Er hat 163 offiziell eingetragene internationale Fanclubs mit über 10.000 Mitgliedern.

Im *sozial-gesellschaftlichen Bereich* werden eine zunehmend kritische Öffentlichkeit sowie steigende Ansprüche konstatiert. Allgemein wächst die Bedeutung der Kommunikation einer Organisation, je stärker das gesellschaftliche und politische Umfeld in die Überlegungen mit einbezogen werden müssen. Auch Sportbetriebe müssen ihr Handeln zunehmend gegenüber der Öffentlichkeit legitimieren. Verschärfend kommt hinzu, dass an Sportbetriebe eine Vielzahl unterschiedlicher Anforderungen von einer Vielzahl unterschiedlicher Institutionen gestellt werden. Zu denken ist hier etwa an die Instrumentalisierung des Sports für wohlfahrtsstaatliche Zielsetzungen (Gesundheit, Bildung, Integration etc.).

Die Veränderungen im *kommunikativen Bereich* haben sicherlich besonders starke und nachhaltige Wirkungen auf den Sport wie auch das Kommunikationshandeln von Sportorganisationen. Nicht zuletzt haben die unterschiedlichen Kommunikationssysteme die Sportentwicklung vorangetrieben, indem sie längst Grundlagen der Sport-Finanzierung bilden. Der Leistungssport ist schon lange aus dem mitgliederfinanzierten Beitragssystem entwachsen und hat, neben den Zuschauerentgelten, zwei wesentliche Finanzierungsquellen: Zum einen das Sponsoring und zum anderen den Verkauf von Übertragungsrechten an die Medien.

Die genannten Veränderungen sind zwar teilweise besonders kritisch für Sportorganisationen. Dennoch gelten sie zunächst einmal für alle Organisationen gleichermaßen. Um die besonderen Anforderungen an ein Kommunikationsmanagement für

Sportbetriebe herauszuarbeiten, sind stets die Besonderheiten der Sportwirtschaft als zentraler Bezugspunkt zu berücksichtigen.

17.2 Kommunikationsmanagement: eine begriffliche Abgrenzung

Für das weitere Verständnis ist zunächst eine terminologische Abgrenzung des Begriffs „Kommunikationsmanagement" vorzunehmen. Dabei erscheint eine möglichst umfassende Definition von Kommunikationsmanagement funktional. Das komplexe Beziehungsgeflecht, in dem Organisationen heute agieren, wird von verschiedenen Anspruchsgruppen (Kommunen, Unternehmen, Mitarbeiter, Mitglieder, Konsumenten u.v.a.m.) mit jeweils unterschiedlichen Interessenslagen geknüpft. Kommunikationsprozesse dienen dabei einer fortlaufenden Abstimmung der Interessen. Entstehen solche Kommunikationsprozesse nicht zufällig sondern werden sie systematisch geplant und gesteuert spricht man von Kommunikationsmanagement (Zerfaß, 2006). Von einem solchen, weiten Begriffsverständnis werden alle internen und externen Kommunikationsaktivitäten erfasst, „die von professionellen Kommunikationsexperten und -abteilungen ausgeführt oder vorstrukturiert werden. Das Spektrum reicht von der Gestaltung der Mitarbeiterbeziehungen über die Marketing- und Finanzkommunikation bis hin zur kommunikativen Auseinandersetzung mit Anwohnern, Gemeinden und Behörden; außen vor bleibt nur die ungeplante, ‚naturwüchsige' Kommunikation" (Zerfaß, 2006).

„Bei einem ganzheitlichen Kommunikationsmanagement beziehen sich die Managementfunktionen Planung, Organisation, Führung, Durchführung und Kontrolle auf alle kommunikativen Instrumente und Maßnahmen eines Unternehmens, die zielorientiert das Unternehmen und seine Leistungen bei den relevanten Kommunikations-Zielgruppen darstellen" (Unger/Fuchs, 1999, S. 18).

Wie in der allgemeinen betriebswirtschaftlichen und Managementliteratur so wird der Begriff „Kommunikationsmanagement" auch in der sportbezogenen Literatur bislang nicht einheitlich verwendet. Im Sportmanagement-Handbuch von Breuer/Thiel (2005) etwa werden unter der Überschrift „Kommunikationsmanagement" in erster Linie Beiträge zu Themen wie Mediation und Gesprächsführung, also interner Kommunikation behandelt. Abzugrenzen ist insbesondere *interne* Kommunikation von Kommunikation *nach Außen* sowie *individuelle* von *Massenkommunikation*. Im Folgenden wird in erster Linie auf das Management der Kommunikation nach Außen bzw. Aspekte der Marktkommunikation eingegangen.

470

17.3 Relevanz einer Auseinandersetzung mit dem Kommunikations-management von Sportbetrieben

Insbesondere sechs Aspekte lassen sich als Belege für die Bedeutung einer Auseinandersetzung mit Problemen des Kommunikationsmanagements von Sportbetrieben heranziehen:

(1) Zunächst hat die empirische Management-Verhaltensforschung gezeigt, dass der Informationsverarbeitung eine Schlüsselrolle im Rahmen der täglichen Arbeit von Managern zukommt. Die Manager, die Mintzberg (u.a. 1973) in seiner Studie über die wahre Natur des Arbeitsverhaltens von Managern untersuchte, verbrachten 40 % ihrer Arbeitszeit mit Aktivitäten, die ausschließlich der Übertragung von Informationen gewidmet waren.

(2) Das gilt auch für Sportmanager: Das Sammeln und Verteilen von Informationen, Gesprächsführung sowie Aufbau und Pflege von Kontakten sind für Sportmanager von besonderer Bedeutung (u.a. Hovemann/Kaiser/Schütte, 2003; Horch/Niessen/Schütte, 2003; Kaiser, 2004, 2006).

(3) Demgegenüber hat eine Auseinandersetzung mit dem Kommunikationsmanagement von Sportbetrieben bislang kaum stattgefunden. In der Sportwissenschaft wird das Thema Kommunikation in erster Linie in der Sportpädagogik bzw., aus publizistischer Perspektive, im Rahmen der Kommunikation von sportlichen Großereignissen behandelt. Im Sportmanagement wird Kommunikation/Kommunikationspolitik als ein Instrument des Marketings behandelt. Inhaltlich geht es dabei v.a. um die Bedingungen der Nutzung des Sports als Medium für Werbebotschaften. Das Sport-Marketing beschäftigt sich also ganz überwiegend mit Fragen der Vermarktung *mit* Sport aus der Perspektive der werbetreibenden Wirtschaft, aber kaum mit der Vermarktung *von* Sport durch Sportorganisationen.

(4) Die steigende Bedeutung des Handlungsfeldes Kommunikation zeigt sich auch in einer zunehmenden Ausdifferenzierung von Aufgabenbereichen, etwa der Spezialisierung des Journalismus nach Medienformaten, Medienressorts und unterschiedlichen Fachkompetenzen.

(5) Außerhalb des Sports wird der hohen und steigenden Bedeutung des Themas durch die Einrichtung neuer, spezieller Studiengänge (siehe u.a. der Leipziger Master-Studiengang „Communication Management" oder der B.A. Studiengang „Kommunikationsmanagement" der University of Management and Communication/UMC FH Potsdam) Rechnung getragen. Die Deutsche Sporthochschule Köln trägt der besonderen Relevanz des Themas für die Ausbildung von Sportmanagern mit der Einrichtung des neuen B.A. Studiengangs „Sportmanagement und Kommunikation" Rechnung.

(6) Schließlich kann man sicher einerseits von den genannten Bildungsangeboten, wie auch der allgemeinen Marketing-Literatur, vieles lernen. Die bloße Übertragung allgemeiner Methoden und Instrumente auf den Sport ist andererseits nicht angemessen, um den vielfältigen Besonderheiten des Sports gerecht zu werden.

17.4 Besondere Herausforderungen an das Kommunikationsmanagement von Sportbetrieben

Als zentralen Bezugspunkt für die Herausarbeitung von besonderen Anforderungen an das Kommunikationsmanagement für Sportbetriebe gilt es, die Besonderheiten der Sportwirtschaft zu betrachten. Hierbei ist es wichtig, darauf hinzuweisen, dass es um Aspekte geht, die erstens nicht überall im Sport und zweitens nicht nur im Sport vorkommen. Es handelt sich aber um Aspekte, die in zentralen Bereichen des Sports und hier häufig gebündelt auftreten (Horch, 1994). Die besondere Relevanz ihrer systematischen Berücksichtigung ergibt sich nicht zuletzt daraus, dass sie in der traditionellen, auf Sachgüterproduktion für Märkte in großen erwerbswirtschaftlichen Betrieben konzentrierten, Ökonomie nicht im Zentrum der Aufmerksamkeit gestanden haben.

Als heuristisches Hilfsmittel zur Entdeckung der relevanten Besonderheiten, die besondere Anforderungen an das Kommunikationsmanagement von Sportbetrieben begründen, dient folgende Matrix (vgl. Tab. 1). Auf der Abszisse sind als Funktionen des Kommunikationsmanagements vereinfachend strategische und operative Planung sowie Durchführung aufgetragen (Unger/Fuchs, 1999), denen auf der Ordinate die zentralen Besonderheiten der Sportwirtschaft gegenübergestellt werden.

Besondere Herausforderungen an das KM	Strategische Kommunikationsplanung	Operative Kommunikationsplanung	Durchführung
Besonderheiten der Sportwirtschaft			
Anbieter			
Güter			
Personenbezogene Dienstleistung			
Öffentliches Gut			
Nachfrage			
Märkte			
Ziele			
Besondere Beziehung zu den Medien			
Rahmenbedingungen und aktuelle Problemfelder des Sports			

Tab.1: Funktionen des Kommunikationsmanagements und Besonderheiten der Sportwirtschaft

Neben den Besonderheiten der Sportwirtschaft können weiterhin Rahmenbedingungen und aktuelle Problemfelder des Sports besondere Herausforderungen an ein Kommunikationsmanagement für Sportbetriebe begründen, etwa die hohe Substitutionskonkurrenz aufgrund der Zunahme an Angeboten alternativer Zeitverwendungen.

Auf der *Anbieterseite* ist das Hauptcharakteristikum die Vielfalt unterschiedlicher ökonomischer Institutionen, in denen Sport produziert wird. Dies gilt nicht nur für die Organisation des Sports in Deutschland sondern auch im internationalen Vergleich. So sind etwa in den USA Kommunen, Colleges und Universitäten sowie Vereine (Young Mens Christian Association, YMCA etc.) wichtige Sportanbieter. Besonders typisch für das deutsche Sportsystem ist, dass Sport zu einem bedeutenden Teil nicht erwerbswirtschaftlich, sondern staatlich und durch Vereine und Verbände, also Non-Profit-Organisationen bereitgestellt wird.

In Bezug auf die *Güter* ist als besonders typisch der Produktmix herauszustellen: Sportgüter weisen ein Vielzahl von Besonderheiten auf, die sich unter Bezugnahme auf die konstitutiven Merkmale des Sports herausarbeiten lassen. So ist ein Grund für die besondere Attraktivität des Sports die Spannung und die Unvorhersagbarkeit, also die Tatsache, dass das Ergebnis eines sportlichen Wettkampfes nicht im Vorfeld zu bestimmen ist. Damit können Sportanbieter aber den Kern ihres Produktes nicht bzw. nur mittelbar kontrollieren. Besonders typisch ist ferner, dass im Sport, einzigartig für moderne Gesellschaften, Personen/Sportler wie Produkte gehandelt werden. Schließlich handelt es sich bei vielen Sportprodukten um Rechte (Übertragungs- und Werberechte etc., vgl. u.a. Horch, 1994).

Viele Sportprodukte haben ferner den Charakter von öffentlichen Gütern, Clubgütern, meritorischen Gütern und personenbezogenen Dienstleistungen.

Öffentliche Güter (Samuelson, 1954) sind dadurch gekennzeichnet, dass a) niemand von ihrer Nutzung ausgeschlossen werden kann und dass b) keine Rivalität im Konsum besteht, dass also, wenn eine Person das Gut nutzt, andere in ihrem Konsum nicht beeinträchtigt werden. Typische Beispiele für öffentliche Güter im Sport sind der (sportinduzierte) volkswirtschaftliche Nutzen der öffentlichen Gesundheit oder die Freude über einen Sieg der Fußballnationalmannschaft.

Bei *Clubgütern* bzw. nicht reinen öffentlichen Gütern (Buchanan, 1965) funktioniert das Prinzip des Ausschlusses, sie weisen aber nur bis zum Erreichen einer Überfüllungsgrenze keine Rivalität im Konsum auf.

Meritorische Güter (Musgrave, 1969) können, gegenüber öffentlichen Gütern, die wegen der typischen Trittbrettfahrerproblematik (man kann auch ohne für sie zu zahlen in ihren Genuss kommen) in erster Linie durch Zwangsbeiträge/Steuern finanziert werden müssen, am Markt angeboten werden. Sie werden aber aufgrund von verzerrten Präferenzen aus gesellschaftspolitischer Sicht nicht in ausreichendem Maße nachgefragt. Ein typisches Beispiel ist der Nutzen des Sporttreibens für die individuelle Gesundheit.

Besonders weit reichende und für den Sport charakteristische Besonderheiten ergeben sich aus den Merkmalen *personenbezogener Dienstleistungen* (u.a. Herder-Dorneich/Kötz, 1972). Gegenüber Sachgütern sind Dienstleistungen immaterieller Art. Personenbezogene Dienstleistungen werden, im Unterschied zu sachbezogenen Dienstleistungen (Reparaturleistungen, Installation etc.) an Personen erbracht. Dienstleistungen sind allgemein durch eine ausgeprägte Potenzialorientierung gekennzeichnet und müssen unabhängig von ihrer Nutzung bereitgestellt werden. Sie sind nicht transport- und lagerfähig und können, bei (bilateral) personenbezogenen Dienstleistungen, nur in engem räumlichen und zeitlichen Kontakt zum Kunden erbracht werden („Uno Actu-Prinzip"). Die Konsumenten sind beteiligt an der Produktion, der Produzent ist Teil der Leistung. Aus dieser engen sozialen Beziehung ergibt sich eine Reihe von Problemen, auf die mit den rationalen Kalkülen der Sachgüterproduktion nicht adäquat reagiert werden kann (Horch, 1994). Die Besonderheiten von Sportdienstleistungen sind aus ökonomischer Sicht insbesondere auf die Notwendigkeit der Koproduktion von Anbieter und Nachfrager sowie die gegenseitigen Unsicherheiten bezüglich des Leistungswillens und der Leistungsfähigkeit der Marktpartner zurück zu führen (Woratschek, 2002).

In Bezug auf die *Nachfrage* sind u.a. das Sporttreiben als sozialer Konsum, die mangelnde Rationalität des Entscheidungsprozesses, etwa im Zuge des Nachfrageversagens bei meritorischen Gütern, sowie die Tatsache, dass es eine Reihe von Ausnahmen vom Nachfragegesetz gibt (z.B. steigender Grenznutzen sportlicher Aktivität) zu nennen. Allgemein basiert die Nachfrage nach Sport auf Entscheidungen über a) die Verwendung von Zeit (Sporttreiben sowie die Vorbereitung des Sporttreibens konkurrieren mit anderen Möglichkeiten der Zeitverwendung) und b) Konsumausgaben (Ausgaben für Sport stellen nur eine mögliche vieler alternativer Mittelverwendungen dar). Bei dem Wunsch, Sport zu treiben, ist der Einzelne Zeit- und Ausgabenrestriktionen unterworfen (Heinemann, 1995). Als Determinanten dieser Entscheidungen sind u.a. folgende Faktoren zu betrachten (Heinemann, 1995):

- die Präferenzen der Sportinteressierten,
- die Höhe der Preise der nachgefragten Güter und Dienste,
- Art, Qualität, Technologie und räumliche Verteilung der angebotenen Güter und Dienste,
- die Informationen der Sportinteressierten über die vorhandenen Möglichkeiten, Sport zu treiben,
- Umfang und Lage der zur Verfügung stehenden, disponiblen Zeit,
- die Höhe des Einkommens und des vorhandenen Vermögens.

Einerseits kann man, in Anknüpfung an die ökonomische Theorie des Konsums, untersuchen, wie die Sportnachfrage auf Preis- und Einkommensveränderungen reagiert (Heinemann, 1995; Woll, 2007). Will man die Besonderheiten der Nachfrage nach Sport herausarbeiten, reicht es aber nicht aus, sich auf die Ableitungen der allgemeinen ökonomischen Theorie zu beziehen, da sie keine Aussagen über die Entstehung und Ausgestaltung von Präferenzen ermöglicht und den Faktor Zeit sowie weitere wichtige Rahmenbedingungen entsprechender Entscheidungen unberücksichtigt lässt (Heinemann, 1995; Woll, 2007). So erfolgt Sporttreiben etwa häufig als sozialer Konsum, mit bzw. in Auseinandersetzung mit Anderen, und ist häufig Teil eines breiteren Unterhaltungsprogramms. Zudem sind Entscheidungen über Sporttreiben häufig „make or buy-" Entscheidungen, im Rahmen derer zwischen Kauf und Eigenproduktion abgewogen werden muss (Horch, 1994). Sportler kaufen Güter und Dienste, die sie für ihr Sportengagement benötigen, um damit bestimmte Nutzenerwartungen zu erfüllen (Gesundheit, Fitness, Körperformung, Freude, Geselligkeit, Prestige, soziale Akzeptanz u.ä.). Aus diesen Nutzenerwartungen leiten sich Präferenzen ab, die die kaufkräftige Nachfrage bestimmen. Die erwünschten Nutzen können also nicht direkt mit dem Kauf erworben werden. Die Produktion erfordert zusätzlichen Einsatz von Energie, Zeit und Kompetenz. Das bedeutet auch, dass im Vorfeld (strukturelle) Unsicherheit darüber besteht, ob mit der Sportaktivität der jeweils gewünschte Nutzen erreicht wird oder nicht. Nutzenerwartungen können daher auch unerfüllte Hoffnungen bleiben (Heinemann, 1995).

> „Das substantielle, nachgefragte und gekaufte Gut ist nicht gleichbedeutend mit dem Nutzen, den der einzelne daraus zieht. Man erwirbt mit dem Kauf z.B. eines Sportgeräts bzw. mit einer Mitgliedschaft in einem Verein lediglich globale Nutzungspotenziale. Ein Nutzen lässt sich aus solchen Gütern und Diensten nicht durch passiven Konsum, als Lust oder Unlusteffekt einer äußeren Situation erreichen. Vielmehr sind weiter Zeit und Anstrengung nötig, um künftig in vielen Einzelsituationen den erhofften Nutzen zu produzieren. Ein Kauf wäre sinnlos und bliebe ohne Wert, wenn das Erworbene nicht für die Verwirklichung solcher Ziele genutzt würde" (Heinemann, 1995, S. 100 f.).

Schließlich weisen diese Nutzenerwartungen ihrerseits eine Vielzahl von Besonderheiten auf, die für Nachfrage von Relevanz sind. Typischerweise gibt es im Sport keine natürlichen Sättigungsgrenzen. So lässt sich die Nachfrage nach einzelnen, sportbezogenen Effekten immer wieder anregen (z.B. ist Gesundheit nie sicher, es müssen fortlaufend Anstrengungen unternommen werden, um gesund zu bleiben). Zudem ist die Bewertung des Nutzens sportbezogener Güter und Dienste im höchsten Maße subjektiv:

> „Was von den einen in besonderem Maß goutiert wird, ist für andere abstoßend. Dies wird zum einen deutlich am Beispiel der Vereinsmitgliedschaft: Partizipation etwa bedeutet für den einen Chance aktiver Gestaltung, für den anderen Vereinsmeierei; Leistungssport ist für den einen schlimme Schinderei, für den anderen ein besonderes Erlebnis der eigenen Grenzen" (Heinemann, 1995, S. 105).

In Bezug auf die *Märkte* ist beispielsweise für den Zuschauersport als typisch herauszustellen, dass er durch, in der Wettkampflogik des Sports begründeten, Konkurrenz und Kooperation der Anbieter gleichermaßen geprägt ist. Die Fertigung im professionellen Mannschaftssport ist durch die Notwendigkeit der Koproduktion mindestens zweier Partner gekennzeichnet. Mit dieser Besonderheit lässt sich auch das hohe Ausmaß an Regulierungen begründen. So sind zentrale ökonomische Größen (Menge und Zeit des Angebots, Anzahl der Anbieter etc.) festgelegt. Charakteristisch sind ferner Anbieter-Monopole, wie Verbände und Ligen (Horch, 1994).

Besonderheiten lassen sich weiterhin in Bezug auf die Ziele herausstellen: Typisch sind heterogene Zielsysteme. Neben ökonomischen Formalzielen sind u.a. Sachziele, wie die Verwirklichung der Interessen der Mitglieder, gesellschaftliche wie auch individuelle Ziele der beteiligten Personen von Bedeutung.

Schließlich ist die besondere Beziehung zu den *Medien* hervorzuheben, die im Wesentlichen dadurch gekennzeichnet, dass es (im Spitzensport) im Gegensatz zu anderen Bereichen, in denen Organisationen ihre Informationen aktiv in die Medien bringen müssen, im Gegenteil eine besondere Nachfrage von Seiten der Medien gibt, die fortlaufend befriedigt werden muss.

Die vorgenannten Besonderheiten begründen jeweils besondere Herausforderungen an das Kommunikationsmanagement von Sportbetrieben. Im Folgenden wird auf drei dieser Aspekte genauer eingegangen und es werden die besonderen Herausforderungen, die sich aus diesen jeweils charakteristischen Eigenschaften ergeben, diskutiert sowie Beispiele dafür angeführt, wie man ihnen adäquat begegnen kann. Aus den Güterbesonderheiten werden (1) die Besonderheiten (bilateral) personenbezogener Dienstleistungen sowie (2) die besonderen Eigenschaften des Sports als öffentliches Gut ausgewählt. Schließlich wird (3) die besondere Beziehung national und international tätiger Sportorganisationen zu den Medien thematisiert, die im Wesentlichen dadurch gekennzeichnet ist, dass es (typischerweise im Spitzensport) im Gegensatz zu anderen Bereichen, in denen Organisationen ihre Informationen aktiv in die Medien bringen müssen, eine besondere Nachfrage von Seiten der Medien gibt, die fortlaufend befriedigt werden muss („Nachfragesog").

17.4.1 Besonderheiten personenbezogener Dienstleistungen

Informationsökonomisch sind Dienstleistungen keine Suchgüter, deren Qualität man vor dem Kauf beurteilen kann, sondern zunächst bloße Leistungsversprechen (Erfahrungs-, Vertrauensgüter). Der Konsument ist Mitproduzent, er ist als externer Faktor in den Prozess der Leistungserstellung eingebunden. Mit der Bereitstellung von Dienstleistungen sind Unsicherheiten für Nachfrager und Anbieter verbunden, und das gilt noch einmal verstärkt für bilateral personenbezogene Dienstleistungen, wie sie für den Sport besonders typisch sind (also Dienstleistungen von Personen an

Personen). Diese Unsicherheiten müssen kommunikativ verarbeitet werden. Es ergibt sich

- *Verhaltensunsicherheit* darüber, wie sich Anbieter und Nachfrager in einer Kundenkontaktsituation verhalten und

- *Ergebnisunsicherheit*, da das Ergebnis vorher nicht beurteilt werden kann. Es gibt keine Garantie für Befriedigung von Nutzenerwartungen, Sport ist typischerweise durch eine hohe Enttäuschungsanfälligkeit gekennzeichnet.

Die besondere Herausforderung für das Kommunikationsmanagement ist demnach, dass es zum Abbau von Informationsasymmetrien beitragen muss bzw. dazu, durch besondere kommunikationspolitische Maßnahmen diese Unsicherheiten zu reduzieren. Eine mögliche Lösung liegt in Kooperationsdesigns. Diese können in folgenden Konstrukten zum Ausdruck kommen (Woratschek, 2002):

- *Signaling/Aussenden von Qualitätssignalen*: Von besonderer Bedeutung sind dabei Instrumente, mit deren Hilfe Teile des Leistungspotenzials, des Leistungsprozesses und Leistungsergebnisses materialisiert und visualisiert werden können und die Qualität symbolisieren (Zertifikate, Fotos, Ausstattungs- und Einrichtungskomfort und Erscheinungsbild einer Sportstätte, Probetraining etc.).

- *Signaling in Form von Informationssurrogaten*: Eines der wichtigsten Informationssurrogate ist die Marke. Die Wirkung der Marke als Informationssurrogat ergibt sich daraus, dass sie für den Abnehmer ein glaubwürdiges Qualitätssignal darstellt. In diesem Zusammenhang ist also die Investition in Markenpolitik geboten.

- *Reputation*: Das zentrale Ziel besteht in diesem Zusammenhang darin, durch wiederholtes, dauerhaftes Signaling die Organisation als vertrauenswürdig zu profilieren. Die Schwerpunktsetzung bei der Auswahl der Kommunikationsinstrumente liegt dabei auf dialogorientierter Kommunikation. Gegenüber anonymisierter Mittel der Massenkommunikation ist sie in besonderem Maße zur Vertrauensbildung geeignet.

17.4.2 Sport als Öffentliches Gut/Produktion von Externalitäten

Ein zentraler Aspekt, der besondere Herausforderungen an das Kommunikationsmanagement von Sportbetrieben begründet, aber auch Chancen eröffnet, ist die Tatsache, dass im Sport vielfältige positive externe Effekte erzeugt werden, die den Charakter öffentlicher Güter haben. Für den organisierten Sport ergibt sich angesichts eines zunehmenden Finanzdrucks der öffentlichen Haushalte ein hoher und steigender Legitimationsdruck, dem er durch den Verweis auf seine Funktionen begegnen muss. Es bedarf also überzeugender Argumente, will man die Subventionen auch in Zukunft sichern. Die dazugehörige Argumentationskette lautet, dass a) der Sport vielfältige positive externe Effekte erzeugt, dass b) mit der Bereitstellung dieser Güter der Markt versagt und dass c), würde es den Sport in Vereinen organisiert nicht geben, der Staat diese Leistungen anders organisiert u.U. teuer bereitstellen müsste (Horch, 1994).

Die besondere Herausforderung, die sich daraus ergibt, besteht demnach in der Notwendigkeit der Kommunikation der positiven Wirkungen bzw. externen Effekte des Sports in Zeiten zunehmender Infragestellung öffentlicher Zuschüsse. Traditionell haben die Sportorganisationen in Deutschland diese Subventionierung auf dem Weg persönlicher/politischer Netzwerke eingefordert bzw. sichergestellt. Lobbyismus und personelle Verflechtung spielen im Rahmen der Kommunikation in den politischen Raum typischerweise eine wichtige Rolle. Anders formuliert geht es also nicht nur darum, positive externe Effekte zu produzieren, sondern diese auch zu dokumentieren und zu kommunizieren bzw. zu belegen, dass weder Staat noch Markt in der Lage sind, diese Leistungen in gleichem Umfang und gleicher Qualität zur Verfügung zu stellen. Dabei ist in Bezug auf die Inhalte wichtig, dass nicht nur die Dienstleistung bzw. deren Ergebnis selbst, sondern in erster Linie der Dienstleistungsprozess, also die Art, wie sie erstellt wird, einen sozialen Nutzen hat und damit kommuniziert werden muss.

Eine zentrale Planungsgrundlage für das Kommunikationsmanagement besteht demnach in der Ermittlung geeigneter Indikatoren als Kommunikationsinhalte. So kann eine Mitgliederstrukturanalyse etwa dazu dienen, die besonderen Integrationsleistungen einer Sportorganisation oder ihren Beitrag zur Jugendförderung offen zu legen. Eine zentrale Rolle spielen solche Maßnahmen die geeignet sind, den gesellschaftlichen Bezug einer Sportorganisation herauszustellen. Auf der operativen Ebene sind dabei v.a. die veranstaltungsbezogene Öffentlichkeitsarbeit sowie die Bildung strategischer Allianzen zu nennen.

Beispiel „Handballvereine – Partner der Schulen":

Unter diesem Motto haben das Ministerium für Schule und Weiterbildung (MSW) NRW, der Deutsche Handballbund (DHB) und der Westdeutsche Handball-Verband (WHV) am 26.3.2007 eine enge Kooperation vereinbart. Der jüngste Erfolg der deutschen Handballer sowie die Aufmerksamkeit im Nachgang zur Handball Weltmeisterschaft soll dazu genutzt werden, um in Schulen Kinder für die (vereinsgebundene) Ausübung dieser Sportart zu gewinnen. Im Kern geht es um die zeitnahe Umsetzung von fünf Teilprojekten: (1) Entwicklung eines Leitfadens für die Intensivierung der Zusammenarbeit von Schulen und Handballsport treibenden Vereinen, (2) Entwicklung einer Materialhilfe „Spielen mit Hand und Ball – Handreichung für die Schulen der Primarstufe", (3) Entwicklung einer Materialhilfe „Handball – Handreichung für die Schulen der Sekundarstufe I", (4) Entwicklung eines Binnenportals „Handball spielen in der Schule" im Bildungsportal NRW/ Schulsportportal NRW und (5) Entwicklung zielgruppenspezifischer und zeitgemäßer und Fortbildungskonzepte zum Handballspielen in der Schule.

17.4.3 Besondere Anforderungen, die sich aus der besonderen Beziehung zu den Medien ergeben

Besondere Anforderungen an das Kommunikationsmanagement national und international operierender Sportorganisationen werden ferner durch die besondere, teilweise symbiotische, Beziehung des Sports zu den Medien begründet. Eine differenzierte Betrachtung ist insbesondere aufgrund der typischerweise ungleichen Verteilung des Medieninteresses geboten.

> „Most sport organizations are blessed with so much mass appeal that media organizations are compelled to cover these entities on a regular basis. This popularity creates a 'pull' from the media, whereas most other industries have to 'push' their information to the media and hope to receive publicity for their efforts. In other words, it is highly unlikely that the local company has someone from the local newspaper showing up every day needing to fill a number of inches in the paper. And most media outlets, esp. newspapers, turn the public's insatiable desire to know all they can about their favourite team and players into dollars by selling more papers and advertising to increase their own profits" (McGowan/Bouris, 2005, S. 342).

Aus der besonderen Beziehung von Sportorganisationen zu den Medien ergeben sich vielfältige Konsequenzen, die in Abhängigkeit der Nachfrage von Seiten der Medien zu betrachten sind. In diesem Zusammenhang sind generell zwei Fälle zu unterscheiden:

1. Bei *hoher Nachfrage von Seiten der Medien* gilt es einerseits, deren Informationsinteresse zu befriedigen. Andererseits besteht die besondere Herausforderung darin, sicherzustellen, dass sich die Kommunikationsinhalte nicht dem eigenen Einfluss entziehen. Sportorganisationen können dieser Gefahr z.B. dadurch entgegen wirken, dass sie als professioneller Anbieter von Mediencontent in Erscheinung treten. Die kann etwa durch gezielte Aufbereitung von Beiträgen für Journalisten erfolgen und bis zum Aufbau einer eigenen Redaktion führen, die in den vier relevanten Mediensäulen: Hörfunk, Fernsehen, Print und Online tätig ist. Die besondere Chance dieses Vorgehens besteht nicht zuletzt in der Perspektive einer gezielten Steuerung, nicht nur dessen, was publiziert wird, sondern auch der Inhalte, die nicht veröffentlicht werden sollen (Stichworte: „Maulkorb", „Stallregie"). Wenngleich sich diese Möglichkeit nur wenigen, großen national und international operierenden Sportorganisationen eröffnet, erlaubt es die Produktion eines eigenen TV-Signals in besonderem Maße, Herr über die Berichterstattung zu bleiben (siehe Fallstudie 17.5). In diesem Zusammenhang spielt auch der Versuch der Erschließung eigener Distributionswege eine wichtige Rolle (siehe Stadion-TV oder die Eigenproduktionen großer Fußballclubs, etwa FCB.tv).

2. Im Falle *geringer Mediennachfrage* – typischerweise bei kleineren Sportorganisationen sowie sog. „Randsportarten" – besteht umgekehrt die besondere Herausforderung darin, das Interesse der Medien zu wecken.

> „In einer Gesellschaft, in der die Menschen ihre Welt v.a. über die Medien wahrnehmen, gewinnt der Sport als bevorzugtes Medienereignis eine vorher unerreichbare Prominenz und Geltung. Dies gilt allerdings nur für eine begrenzte Zahl von Sportarten. Solche, die mit dem Blick auf Publikum – von außen oft nicht nachvollziehbar – als wenig attraktiv eingeschätzt werden, geraten zu ‚Randsportarten'. […] Im Ungleichheitssystem des Sports geht es […] so ungerecht zu, wie in der gesellschaftlichen Vermögensverteilung generell: Auch die Vorteile der Medialisierung des Sports konzentrieren sich massenhaft auf wenige Beteiligte: in Deutschland v.a. auf Fußball, dann auch Skisport, bislang ebenso Formel 1 und zumindest zeitweilig Radsport" (Neidhardt, 2007, S. 4).

Hier gilt es, anhand eines geeigneten Kommunikationsmanagements, die Distribution der gewünschten Kommunikationsinhalte gezielt zu befördern. Dabei ist zunächst eine geeignete kommunikative Positionierung anzustreben. Die Genaue Kenntnis der Zielgruppen (Mitglieder, Sponsoren, Medien) sowie des eigenen Produktes bzw. der eigenen Dienstleistung sind hierfür wichtige Voraussetzungen. In diesem Zusammenhang ist ferner eine genaue Kenntnis des Mediensystems, etwa der medienspezifischen Berichterstattung im Wochenverlauf/Jahresverlauf (u.a. montags: Ereignis- und Ergebnisberichterstattung, „Saure-Gurken-Zeit") von zentraler Bedeutung. In Bezug auf die operative Planung im Bereich der Printmedien ist, bei hoher Konkurrenz mit dem Spitzensport in den Sportteilen, die Hinwendung zu anderen Ressorts ein geeigneter Weg (z.B. Lokales, Politik, Feuilleton, Wirtschaft). Darüber hinaus ist in diesem Zusammenhang die Kontinuität der Informationsbereitstellung wichtig. Informationsdichte und -quantität sollten im Sinne einer Dramaturgie gesteuert werden. Im Sinne eines effizienten Einsatzes von Kommunikationsinstrumenten bietet sich die Integration der neuen Medien an (z.B. digitale Pressemappe). Das Eingehen strategischer Allianzen, etwa durch die Anbindung an eine Nachrichtenagentur (bspw. „Vereins-Informations-Dienst" des SID), ist ein weiteres probates Mittel, um im Bereich des operativen Kommunikationsmanagements zu einer Optimierung beizutragen.

Zur Steigerung der TV-Präsenz einzelner, bislang weniger im Zentrum medialer Aufmerksamkeit stehenden, Sportarten werden, neben dem traditionellen Mittel des Übertragungskostenzuschusses, Kooperations- und Beteiligungsmodelle sowie der Aufbau eigener Fernsehkanäle diskutiert und praktiziert. Beispielhaft ist hier „sportdigital.tv" zu nennen. Die Plattform, die der Sportrechtevermarkter SPORT-FIVE gemeinsam mit der Handball Bundesliga (HBL) und der Basketballbundesliga (BBL) ins Leben gerufen hat, war zunächst mit dem Angebot, alle Spiele der Handball WM zu empfangen, gestartet. Ab Oktober 2007 ist der Bezahlsender über

Satellit zu empfangen. Pro Saison und Liga bezahlen die Sportfans 49,99 € bzw. 54,99 € für die populärere Handball-Liga, und können so (fast) alle Ligaspiele der Handball-, Basketball- und Volleyball-Liga, live sehen.

17.5 Fallstudie

Die nachfolgende Fallstudie beinhaltet ein aktuelles Beispiel zum Thema Eigenproduktion: Die Kölner SPORTCAST GmbH produziert als 100 %-ige Tochtergesellschaft der DFL Deutsche Fußball Liga GmbH die Fernsehbilder ihrer Spiele über ihr Tochterunternehmen selbst und leitet diese an Abnehmer wie Premiere oder die ARD weiter. Im Zuge dessen werden in jüngster Zeit die Bedingungen und Folgen der Etablierung eines eigenen Fernsehkanals der Liga kontrovers diskutiert. Unter anderem wird argumentiert, die DFL könne durch das drohende Szenario einer vollständigen Produktion und Distribution in Eigenregie ihre Verhandlungsposition gegenüber den klassischen Fernsehanstalten stärken. Aus kommunikationspolitischer Sicht ist in diesem Zusammenhang v.a. die Perspektive interessant, die Kontrolle über das Produkt sowie dessen Präsentation, einschließlich Dramaturgie und Inszenierung zu behalten.

Fallstudie „Eigenproduktion"

Die im Frühjahr 2006 gegründete Produktionsgesellschaft SPORTCAST GmbH mit Sitz in Köln produziert als 100 %-ige Tochtergesellschaft der DFL Deutsche Fußball Liga GmbH seit der Saison 2006/07 das TV-Basissignal der Fernsehbilder von den Spielen der Bundesliga und 2. Bundesliga für die Medien-Partner. Sie versteht sich als Kompetenzzentrum für Sport-TV-Produktionen und will darüber hinaus sowohl Sendern als auch Dienstleistern, Verbänden und Vereinen in allen Fragen rund um die Produktionsrealisierung beratend zur Seite stehen. Das Portfolio der SPORTCAST GmbH setzt sich aus den vier Geschäftsfeldern Live Produktion, Produktion redaktioneller Formate, Signalkontribution und -distribution sowie ARENA Consulting zusammen.

Der Bereich Signalerstellung besteht in erster Linie aus der Produktion des Basis-TV-Signals aller 612 Spiele der Bundesliga und der 2. Bundesliga. In diesem Zusammenhang verfolgt SPORTCAST das Ziel, die Präsentationsqualität der Spiele unter anderem durch erhöhte Kamera-Standards weiter zu optimieren. Demnach gilt für alle Bundesliga-Spiele ab der kommenden Saison mindestens

---

die Regel „8+1". D.h., es werden acht Kameras plus eine Super-Slowmotion-Kamera eingesetzt. Zusätzlich wird das Top-Spiel des Samstags im Standard „10+1" und in HD-Qualität im Format 16:9 produziert. Auch die 2. Bundesliga, von der alle Spiele live und in voller Länge ausgestrahlt werden, soll von den erhöhten Kamera-Standards profitieren. Sechs Kameras und eine Slowmotion-Kamera zeichnen die Spiele auf. Im Bereich „Redaktionelle Formate" wird z.B. zu jedem Spieltag eine Highlightshow produziert, die, wie auch die Live-Spiele, in spanischer und englischer Sprache produziert und international distribuiert wird. Im Geschäftsfeld „ARENA Consulting" schließlich berät SPORTCAST im Zuge des Neubaus, Ausbaus oder Umbaus von Stadien und Arenen mit dem zentralen Ziel, optimale Produktionsumgebung für die Medien zu erzielen.

Im Zuge der Vergabe der Vermarktungsrechte der Fußball-Bundesliga durch die DFL an den einstigen Medienmogul Leo Kirch, dessen Agentur Sirius damit ab dem Jahr 2009 für eine Dauer von zunächst sechs Jahren die Inlandsvermarktung der kommenden Ausschreibungen übernehmen wird, wurde auch bekannt gegeben, dass die DFL ab der Saison 2009/10 im entgeltpflichtigen Live-Bereich nicht mehr nur die Ausstrahlungsrechte vergeben, sondern vielmehr ein fertig produziertes Produkt vertreiben möchte.

17.6 Fazit und Ausblick

Die vielfältigen Besonderheiten der Sportwirtschaft bedingen eine Reihe besonderer Herausforderungen an das Kommunikationsmanagement von national und international agierenden Sportorganisationen, die sowohl Aspekte der strategischen wie auch der operativen Planung als auch Durchführung von Kommunikationsmaßnahmen betreffen. Dies wurde beispielhaft anhand der Besonderheiten personenbezogener Dienstleistungen, den besonderen Eigenschaften des Sports als öffentliches Gut sowie der besonderen Beziehung von Sportorganisationen zu den Medien gezeigt. Eine unreflektierte Übernahme von allgemeinen Methoden des Kommunikationsmanagements auf den Sport ist nicht adäquat, um den besonderen Anforderungen gerecht zu werden. Auch hier gilt, dass die Erkenntnisse und Modelle der allgemeinen Ökonomie daraufhin geprüft werden müssen, inwieweit sie sinnvoll auf die vielfältigen Besonderheiten von Sportbetrieben übertragen werden können.

Kritisch bleibt auf die Gefahr hinzuweisen, die Kosten und potenziellen Dysfunktionen bzw. negative Folgewirkungen von Kommunikationsmanagement aus dem Auge zu verlieren. Gerade für das Kommunikationsmanagement kleinerer Sportbetriebe bedeutet das, dass eine Professionalisierung von Tätigkeiten in diesem Bereich vielfach kaum, oder nur zu prohibitiv hohen Kosten bzw. unter nicht zu rechtfertigendem Ressourceneinsatz möglich ist. Hier gilt es umso mehr, geeignete Kommunikationsinstrumente zu identifizieren und strategische Allianzen ins Auge zu fassen.

Kontrollfragen

1. Nennen Sie zentrale Veränderungen im Umfeld von Organisationen mit Auswirkung auf deren kommunikative Situation!
2. Begründen Sie die besondere Relevanz einer Auseinandersetzung mit dem Kommunikationsmanagement von Sportbetrieben!
3. Welches sind die zentralen Determinanten der Sportnachfrage?
4. Was sind öffentliche Güter?
5. Nennen Sie zentrale Charakteristika personenbezogener Dienstleistungen!
6. Nehmen Sie Stellung zu folgender Aussage: „Typischerweise gibt es im Sport keine natürlichen Sättigungsgrenzen"!
7. Nennen Sie besondere Herausforderungen an das Kommunikationsmanagement von Sportbetrieben, die sich aus den Besonderheiten personenbezogener Dienstleistungen ergeben! Wie kann man ihnen adäquat begegnen?
8. Was versteht man unter „Kooperationsdesigns"?
9. Der Einsatz welcher Kommunikationsinstrumente bietet sich für große, im Zentrum medialer Aufmerksamkeit stehende, Sportorganisationen an. Was können sie tun, um Herr über die Kommunikationsinhalte zu bleiben?
10. Über welche Tatbestände sollten sich kleine, nicht im Zentrum medialer Aufmerksamkeit stehende, Sportorganisationen im Rahmen der strategischen Kommunikationsplanung informieren?

Literaturverzeichnis

Breuer, Christoph / Thiel, Ansgar (2005): Handbuch Sportmanagement, Schorndorf.

Buchanan, James M. (1965): An Economic Theory of Clubs, in: Economica, New Series, February, S. 1-14.

Heinemann, Klaus (1995): Einführung in die Ökonomie des Sports, Schorndorf.

Horch, Heinz-Dieter (1994): Besonderheiten einer Sport-Ökonomie, in: Freizeitpädagogik, Heft 3, S. 243-257.

Horch, Heinz-Dieter / Niessen, Christoph / Schütte, Norbert (2003): Sportmanager in Verbänden und Vereinen, Köln.

Hovemann, Gregor / Kaiser, Sebastian / Schütte, Norbert (2003): Der Sporteventmanager, Düsseldorf.

Kaiser, Sebastian (2004): Competence Research in Sport Management – The German Case, in: Papanikos, Gregory T. (Hrsg.): The Economics and Management of Mega Athletic Events: Olympic Games, Professional Sports, and Other Essays, Athens, S. 253-265.

Kaiser, Sebastian (2006): Das Sportstudiomanagement, Saarbrücken.

McGowan, Andrew / Bouris, Gregory (2005): Sport Communications, in: Masteralexis, Lisa Pike / Barr, Carol A. / Hums, Mary A. (Hrsg.): Principles and Practice of Sport Management, Sudbury, S. 340-359.

Mintzberg, Henry (1973): The nature of managerial work, New York.

Musgrave, Richard (1969): Finanztheorie, Tübingen.

Neidhardt, Friedhelm (2007): Sport und Medien. Rede anlässlich der Verleihung der Honorarprofessur an Dr. Georg Anders am 18. November 2006 an der Deutschen Sporthochschule Köln, Deutsche Sporthochschule Köln, Universitätsreden 13, S. 1-18.

Samuelson, Paul Anthony (1954): The Pure Theory of Public Expenditure, in: Review of Economics and Statistics, Heft 4, S. 387-390.

Schauerte, Thorsten / Schwier, Jürgen (2004): Die Telegenisierung von Sportereignissen – Anpassung von Sportarten und Regelwerk an mediale Bedingungen, in: Schierl, Thomas (Hrsg): Die Visualisierung des Sports in den Medien, Köln, S. 164-186.

Unger, Fritz / Fuchs, Wolfgang (1999): Management der Marketing-Kommunikation, Heidelberg.

Woll, Artur (2007): Allgemeine Volkswirtschaftslehre, München.

Woratschek, Herbert (2002): Theoretische Elemente einer ökonomischen Betrachtung von Sportdienstleistungen, in: Zeitschrift für Betriebswirtschaft, Ergänzungsheft 4, S. 1-19.

Zerfaß, Ansgar (2006): Unternehmensführung und Öffentlichkeitsarbeit. Grundlegung einer Theorie der Unternehmenskommunikation und Public Relations, Wiesbaden.

Weiterführende Ressourcen

Literatur

Benner, Gerd (1992): Risk Management im professionellen Sport, Bergisch-Gladbach u.a.

Franck, Egon (1995): Die ökonomischen Dimensionen der Teamsportindustrie. Eine Organisationsbetrachtung, Wiesbaden.

Heinemann, Klaus (1984): Probleme der Ökonomie des Sports, in: Heinemann, K. (Hrsg.): Texte zur Ökonomie des Sports, Schorndorf, S. 17-51.

Herder-Dorneich, Philipp / Kötz, Werner (1972): Zur Dienstleistungsökonomie, Berlin.

Maleri, Rudolf (1973): Grundlagen der Dienstleistungsproduktion, Berlin.

Links

Deutsche Fußball Bundesliga:
  http://www.bundesliga.de

Sportcast (Produktionsfirma), Köln:
  http://www.sportcast.de

Sportdigital TV (Digital-Fernsehsender), Hamburg:
  http://www.sportdigital.tv

Teil IV:

Die Zukunft
des Sportmanagement und Sportmarketing

Kapitel 18: Internationalisation in Sport

Simon Chadwick

Learning outcomes

Upon completion of this chapter the reader should be able to

- summarise how sport is internationalising.
- provide a definition of internationalisation.
- highlight factors that have resulted in the internationalisation of sport.
- present a range of theories that explain internationalisation.
- identify the implications of internationalisation for sport managers.

Overview of the chapter

In recent years, there has been a dramatic growth in the internationalisation of sport. This chapter therefore begins by identifying where internationalisation is taking place in sport and provides some initial insights into the reasons why sport has internationalised. Respective theoretical contributions to understanding internationalisation will then be addressed, with the implications of each perspective being indicated. Thereafter, definitions of internationalisation will be presented and the characteristics of the phenomenon identified. Towards the end of the chapter, the implications of internationalisation for sport managers will be discussed, and the chapter concludes with a case study of FC Barcelona.

18.1 Introduction

Across the world, many sports have developed as socio-culturally embedded activities, first played as part of local ceremonies, rituals or leisure pursuits. Some sports have remained largely domestic, for instance kabaddi in India; other sports have spread to more countries alongside colonisation and the development of trade routes, for instance cricket; and some sports have developed in a truly international way, such as football and motor racing. In this sense, one can therefore say that even today different sports are at various stages of internationalisation.

At this stage, it is worthwhile considering who and what has been subject to the phenomenon of internationalisation. Given the central premise of sport, a contest between two parties with the intention of their being a winner, there has always been an inevitability that sports people will naturally seek out new, different and more challenging opponents against whom to compete. At the same time, there has also been a long held view that sport is an important way of promoting and facilitating peace, of strengthening bonds between nations, and of encouraging a healthy, active lifestyle. This would explain therefore why events such as the modern day Olympics and the FIFA football World Cup were introduced. Clubs and teams have also internationalised for numerous reasons including the support of an expatriate community, the broadcasting of games overseas, and legal or regulatory change leading to the signing of foreign players or the setting up of overseas scouting networks. What has been most stark over the last five to ten years however, is the way in which the internationalisation of sports personalities and fans has taken place. In notable cases, this has resulted in people such as David Beckham and Anna Kournikova becoming global icons, and organisations such as the National Basketball Association (NBA) creating an extensive overseas fan base via the creation of an international network of operations.

Motivated more by the quest for commercial gain and market share, internationalisation has sometimes subjugated the sporting dimension of competitive international contests. Alongside these changes, the broadcasting and media coverage of sport as well as the development of markets for sport merchandise has paradoxically motivated, but also emerged as an outcome of, such changes. Indeed, it is now commonplace for the leading organisations, clubs and teams in some sports to produce and sell a variety of merchandise, sell multimedia broadcasting rights and to target product offerings at specific consumer groups across the world. In so doing, this has led to the emergence of a new sporting model to which a number of leading international sports now adhere. Rather than being characterised by sport for sport's sake, off-field performance has become at least as important as on-field performance in some cases. Moreover, instead of focusing on the short-term consideration of winning games, tournaments and events, it is now commonplace in internationalised sport to think in strategic terms, to talk of long-term value generation and to think of returns on investment.

18.2 Theories of internationalisation

There is no clear agreement concerning how internationalisation comes about or what drives the phenomenon. What appears below is a brief commentary on the most commonly cited theoretical perspectives. For a more detailed insight into each of these perspectives, it is recommended that readers take a look at one or more of the following: Lam/White (1998), Andersson (2000), Whitelock (2002) and Chetty/Campbell-Hunt (2003).

18.2.1 Industrial network theory

At the heart of network theories is the 'Uppsala Model' which states that organisations are part of a network of other interrelated organisations, although individual firms and groups nevertheless decide which international markets they will enter and why. As such, network theories explain that an organisation's commitment to *internationalisation progresses through four stages*:

1. No exporting
2. Adhoc exporting
3. Establishment of subsidiary operations
4. Full commitment to overseas production

In moving from one stage to another, the decision to engage in international operations will be influenced by the culture, language and education of another country.
Internationalisation will be more likely to take place where there is a smaller psychic distance between the host country and the overseas country or market.

Implications of this theoretical perspective for sport: A sport organisation such
as the football club Ajax Amsterdam is part of a large network of inter-related organisations. This network will include sponsors, sportswear manufacturers, media
corporations, players, fans and commercial partners. The recent internationalisation
of organisations such as Ajax has seen them move from simply being domestic
football clubs, in this case, a Dutch club, to being international business organisations. The most tangible evidence of this in Ajax's case has been the formation of a
franchise in South Africa – Ajax Cape Town. One reason the club pursued such a
strategy was the relatively small psychic distance between the Netherlands and
South Africa, a result of the colonial links between the two countries.

18.2.2 Business strategy theory

Business strategy theories are based on the pragmatic view that internationalisation
is only one choice from a range of expansion strategies that are open to an organisation. The decision to pursue such a strategy will ultimately be guided by nature of
market opportunity, the nature and extent of an organisation's resources and the
philosophy characterising management within an organisation. These in turn will be
influenced by market attractiveness, psychic distance between the company and the
market, market accessibility and the existence of informal barriers.

Implications of this theoretical perspective for sport: If one is to compare Madrid's two leading football clubs – Real and Atletico – one would find two very different entities: Despite their common characteristics, the former has pursued a strategy characterised more by international development whereas the latter has adopted
a stronger domestic focus in its operations. Hence, one can contrast the pragmatism
of the two as Real, the economically and politically more powerful organisation,
has pursued a more overtly international strategy characterised by overseas growth.
In Atletico's case, although its strategy is not exclusively domestic, there has been a
much stronger emphasis on targeting domestic and local fans. This has been based
on two key factors: (1) the established view that Atletico are the underdog's team
and therefore represent, for example, the working classes (organisation philosophy);
and (2) an entrepreneurial and innovative approach to marketing communications,
that have resulted in series Atletico television advertisements winning creativity
awards (organisation resources – management competence).

18.2.3 Innovation-related theory

This perspective holds that innovation is the basis for internationalisation. Organisations are thought to innovate in response to the influence of two factors: (1) the influence of *change agents* such as key decision makers; and/or (2) the influence of *external stimuli* such as overseas customers. The response of organisations to either of these two factors will be to move from marketing products domestically to a pre-export phase then through to an experimental and subsequently an active and committed phase of international operation and marketing.

Implications of this theoretical perspective for sport: In 2003, FC Barcelona members elected a progressive young reformer, Joan Laporta, as President of the club. Alongside people such as the Finance Director (Ferran Sorriano) and the Director of Marketing (Marc Ingla), Laporta set about introducing a new business model into the club. These change agents were acting in response to developments in the football industry, including a growth in the importance of sponsorship and the emergence of potentially valuable new market places. In response, the club has been innovative and experimental in the way it has, for instance, embraced sponsorship and targeted new customers. In relation to the former, the club was amongst the last in the world to place a sponsors logo on team shirts – an international charity: UNICEF. Regarding the latter, one example of the club's innovativeness is the establishment of a series of soccer camps in US states such as New Mexico where large Hispanic communities can be found.

18.2.4 Adaptive choice theory

According to Adaptive Choice theorists, organisations are open, natural, living systems. As such, they are influenced by external events and changes meaning that, in some respects, organisations are in a constant state of flux. They must therefore respond to the world around them and to their changing environments in order to survive.

Implications of this theoretical perspective for sport: If one considers the recent history of English Premier League football clubs, many of them appear to be living organisms that are heavily influenced by external events. A decade ago, numerous clubs were heavily affected by the tendency of clubs to publicly float on the London Stock Exchange. At the same time, the 'dot.com' boom resulted in a large-scale rush to construct elaborate web sites. More recently, at the turn of the 21st century, clubs began to target markets in the Far East, especially China. Currently, the trend is for new owners to become involved in football, with many American entrepreneurs having bought majority shareholdings in English clubs. The openness and adapativeness of these clubs is just as suitably illustrated when one considers what has happened after each of the developments noted above. Stock Exchange listings have been followed by many de-listings as financial returns have failed to reach expected levels; web site developments have become much less elaborate and in many cases are contracted out to specialist companies, largely due to the costs that such developments imposed on clubs; and the rush for market share in places such as China has subsided, due to the competitive nature of the market, the costs associated with targeting it and the unsatisfactory financial returns the market has delivered.

18.2.4 Transaction cost view

From the transaction cost perspective, all decisions to internationalise are seen as rational economic ones. That is, the costs of taking a particular course of action will be the principle driver for international decision makers. The socio-cultural context and connections of managers and organisations, evident in network theories, are therefore unimportant for transaction cost theorists, unless they have a direct implication on the costliness of a particular decision.

Implications of this theoretical perspective for sport: Over the last decade, transfer fees and salaries have risen dramatically in English football, fuelled by the revenue from large television deals, changes in the transfer regulations and a diminishing domestic pool of skilled labour. In the years since 2000, the English domestic transfer record has consistently been broken with spending on players such as Wayne Rooney, Rio Ferdinand, Juan Sebastian Veron and Fernando Torres. In addition, annual salary inflation has often run at double figure levels, and it has not been unknown for some clubs to operate at salary levels that have been as much as 150% of club turnover. In attempts to address the financial implications of a challenging labour market, clubs have therefore increasingly sought to acquire players from overseas markets in which cost levels are lower. In the case of a club like Arsenal, a club that has traditionally taken the view that cost control is important, this has meant signing players from countries including Ukraine, Liberia, the Ivory Coast, Denmark, Switzerland, Nigeria and Greece. Indeed, such has been the effectiveness of this cost minimisation strategy that Arsenal has at times fielded a starting eleven in the Premier League that consists solely of overseas players.

18.3 The nature of internationalisation in sport

There is no commonly held definition of internationalisation and so one can generally say that internationalisation has taken place when the operations of an organisation have ceased to be exclusively domestic. Dictionary definitions indicate that internationalisation takes place when entities become international in scope or character. They alternatively state that internationalisation involves placing or bringing entities under international control. In the business literature, the following definitions have been postulated:

"The process of increasing involvement in international operations"

(Welch/Luostarinen, 1988, p. 35)

"The process of adapting firms' operations (strategy, structure, resources, etc.) to international environments"

(Calof/Beamish, 1995, p. 117)

In essence, the implications of these definitions for sport have been twofold:

1. Sports organisations have sought to internationally acquire and retain *resources* e.g. in the case of labour, football clubs have increasingly bought in playing talent from overseas (for instance, football club Beveren, playing in the Jupiler League in Belgium, fielded a team of eleven players from the Ivory Coast). Regarding capital, changing ownership patterns and the need for capital project funding has resulted in flows across boundaries (for instance, a large proportion of the funding used to cover the cost of constructing the new Wembley Stadium in London – England's national football stadium – was secured from the Westdeutsche Landesbank, a German bank). In addition, land has been purchased by foreign nationals (Mohammed al-Fayed, an Egyptian, now owns Craven Cottage – the home of Fulham Football Club – prime real estate in West London), and even sporting entrepreneurship has become internationalised (for instance, Jefferson Slack, an American, was recruited by Internazionale of Milan to head up their marketing operations).

2. Sport organisations have sought to internationally acquire and retain *customers* e.g. television, and latterly media corporations. For instance, the English Football Association has historically sold the rights to televised football in more than 70 countries. This continues to be the case, one argument being that media corporations are driving internationalisation in sport. Consider Formula 1 motor racing: it is thought that an average of up to 100 million people worldwide watch each F1 race on television. Otherwise, international customers have become increasingly important, with sport organisations becoming more and more reliant on people from overseas buying merchandise, buying tickets to games, subscribing to electronic services and, in a more intangible way, having an affiliation with the organisation.

18.4 Factors contributing to the internationalisation of sport

If one were to consider the origins of a sport such as football, you would find that numerous activities and games similar to the modern day version of the game have long been played around the world. Yet it was not until the 19th century, when the English codified the game in a way that forms the basis for football today, that football really began to emerge as an international sport. With its vast colonial empire, the English were able to export the game worldwide, although ironically people in the British colonies were actually more receptive to cricket. Instead, the industrial revolution and the development of international trade routes and flows had a much greater impact on the growth of football around the world. Hence, in places such as Spain, Italy, Argentina and South Africa, the sport developed as the result of an influx of overseas workers and industrialists. In this sense, the internationalisation of sport is not a new phenomenon. Indeed, just as other industrial sectors have increasingly operated across international boundaries in recent decades, so too has football and most other sports. Such is the international dimension of sport that we find football clubs such as Manchester United attributed as having more than 1 million fans worldwide, events such as the Olympics being watched by 4 billion people and Formula 1 motor racing events taking place in countries as diverse as China, Bahrain and Brazil. It seems a long way from foreign railway engineers in Argentina organising football matches against local people to the now oft-used term that football is 'the global game'. At the same time, a sport such as French cycling has gone from being an egalitarian mode of transport to a way of promoting national newspapers (the Tour de France) through to what is now a major international sporting event.

In accounting for the internationalisation of sport therefore, eight factors have had a varying impact on different sports as explained in the following.

18.4.1 Competition and competition formats
In the pursuit of new competitors, sports people and the bodies representing them have always sought out new rivals. As has already been illustrated, colonial powers and industrially developed nations have long been the source of sports being introduced into countries with little or no history of previously staging them. Alongside the global proliferation of some sports, new creation of new competition formats has helped to perpetuate the international development and popularity of some sports. Tournaments such as golf's Ryder Cup are an example of this, and recent series like the A1 Grand Prix motor racing championship are heightening the sense of international competition.

18.4.2 Socio-cultural shifts
Throughout many parts of the world, there have been major socio-cultural shifts that have fuelled both the consumption of sport and the way in which it is consumed. Growing disposable incomes and a reduction in working hours in some countries have created opportunities for people to watch, travel to or participate in sport, and such changes have gained momentum due to factors such as the development of low cost airlines which have made it easier for fans to follow a team or series throughout the year. When Liverpool appeared in the 2007 UEFA Champions

League Final, as many as 40,000 people travelled to Athens, even though only 17,000 people were thought to have tickets. At the same time, many countries have also witnessed the development of a celebrity culture in which sporting icons have played a major part. Despite never having won a Grand Slam tennis tournament, Anna Kournikova nevertheless became a major global personality, appearing in advertisements and promotions across the world.

18.4.3 Regulatory change

Following World War II, there has been a major trend towards the liberalisation of free global trade. This has resulted in the removal of barriers to trade flows across the world, although this may not immediately appear to have had a major impact on sport. Yet free trade philosophy has had an immense effect, most notably in relation to the broadcasting of sport. In countries where the state is likely to have once controlled the televising of sporting events, the United Kingdom being a prime example, private corporations are now allowed to bid for, and routinely win, the rights to televise games, leagues, events and tournaments. These corporations are often non-indigenous, the market being dominated by organisations such as Time-Warner and News International, which operate on a global, boundary-spanning basis. At the same time, such is the commercial orientation of the corporations involved that the maximum financial return can only be achieved through the international sale of the broadcast content they produce. Alongside global trade liberalisation, the emergence of trading blocs such as the European Union (EU) has also helped create conditions that have fostered sporting internationalisation. Based upon the principle of 'freedom of movement', the most obvious sporting manifestation of this was the 1995 Bosman Ruling. Having established the right of a player to move unimpeded across international boundaries within the EU, the principles of 'Bosman' were subsequently applied to movements into the EU by players from other European countries (the Kolpak Ruling) and from outside Europe into the EU (the Cotonou Ruling). Free movement as a central tenant of EU philosophy has also been evident in, for instance, the application of competition law. In the case of the English Premier League, the EU Competition Commissioner – Massimo Monti – has long railed against the domestic, collective sale of broadcasting rights, preferring a more open, liberal and international approach.

18.4.4 Industrial change

Most sports are likely to have started as a matter of ceremony, thereafter developing according to local custom and practice. With the onset of industrialisation, the role of sport changed somewhat, taking on a more clearly defined role as a form of leisure activity. As teams and clubs organised themselves to compete against one another, an amateur ethos developed whereby formal rules and regulations were encouraged but payments and financial returns were not. In the 20th century, the sporting model changed again with the onset of professionalism and payments for players. We are arguably now in the fourth age of sport, one where the exploitation of commercial rights and properties has transcended the professionalisation of sport. Increasingly, for commercial partners involved in sport and, indeed, for some sports clubs themselves, the pursuit of profit has become the most important aspect of sport, superseding even the central spectacle of a sporting contest with an uncertain outcome. This fourth age is characterised by its emphasis revenue generation, cost control and competitive advantage, each of which can be achieved by pursuing international strategies. Hence, whether sports organisations are seeking to enter potentially lucrative new overseas markets in order to sell their products or they have established scouting networks across the world to sport new talent, internationalisation has become an inevitable dimension of a new sporting age.

18.4.5 Resource acquisition

Given the commercial pressures that many sports organisations now face, the need to access, and possibly control, resources has been a major feature of sport. For teams and clubs seeking to acquire the best playing talent, non-traditional markets have become an important source of players. In the case of Ajax, one of the Netherlands' leading football clubs, this entailed attempts to set up a franchise network, of which the Ajax Cape Town club is one part. For a football club like Arsenal, an alternative strategy has been to establish an integrated global scouting network which, in this particular case, links the Ivory Coast with Belgium and the UK. In addition, the naturally converging interests of teams and sportswear suppliers, sponsors and other commercial partners have alternatively created opportunities for collaborative, cross border relationships to develop. Hence, sportswear manufacturers such as Nike and Adidas have attempted to colonise the world's leading sports even though they are essentially based in only two countries, the United States and Germany respectively. In tandem with this, clubs and teams have been able to benefit from such competition by selecting from the most commercially lucrative kit deals that often extend beyond domestic boundaries. The recent contest between Adidas, the incumbent, and Nike, the predator, to supply the German national football team is a good example of just how competitive internationalised sport has become.

18.4.6 Emergence of new technology

Sporting contests may have been the basis for social relationships between colonialists and locals or the imposition of alien norms and values on indigenous communities by invading nations. In either case, 200 years ago, such contests will have been talked or written about rather than seen or heard. With the advent of, first, radio and then television, international sport for the first time was transmitted either live or in the form of edited highlights. The growth in satellite technology resulted in the further proliferation of televised sport, introducing different sports to new market places in an array of formats. Digital television is set to result in the even more sophisticated, some might say complex, delivery of sport into international markets. In particular, 'on-demand' facilities, where consumers can decide what and when they want to watch or listen, and in what format. Alongside the new ways of watching sport, there are also new ways of consuming information about it and of buying sport products. The internet, a truly global phenomenon – even if it has developed in equitably across the world – is now a boundary-spanning tool that enables fans and others to consume their sport in a way that was not possible, even as late as the early 1990's. Mobile telephones, especially the 3rd generation of phones, have also enhanced the immediacy of sport's availability, with texting, the internet and downloads now all available to people. A further extension of this is the 'pod' phenomenon, a growing number of 'podcasts' now being available.

18.4.7 Market maturity

The sports organisations that have deliberately, aggressively and/or successfully internationalised are commonly those from North America and Western Europe. In one sense this is unsurprising given the economic and political power of these regions. However, the nature of domestic markets in countries like the UK and Germany is such that the pressure for sport organisations to internationalise is immense. Proliferating purchase alternatives, particularly in the leisure sector, allied to the maturity of markets, means opportunities for successfully developing new revenue streams are limited. Organisations have therefore sought to sell more products overseas and to enter new international markets. At the same time, markets such as China have developed rapidly, the changes spurred on by rapid economic growth and the emergence of a consumer culture.

18.4.8 Mass transportation

Mass transportation – when football in England was formally codified more than 130 years ago, it was simply a domestic pursuit that ultimately came to be played for a while on a regional basis. As the train network grew, so did the number of people travelling to away games. In turn, as car ownership has grown, road travel became the primary means of travelling to away games. Now, fans are frequently using aeroplanes to get to overseas games. Indeed, with the advent of low-cost airlines, many English fans will routinely travel to the European mainland, not only to watch their team but also simply just to watch a sporting contest. The importance of cheap, widely available transport should not be underestimated. Although the 2007 UEFA Champions League, staged in Athens, was a relatively short trip across the

Adriatic for the fans of AC Milan, Liverpool (Milan's opponents) were thought to have five times as many fans as Milan in Athens, with most of the English fans having travelled to Greece on low cost airlines.

18.5 Implications for sport managers

There is no clear agreement concerning how internationalisation comes about or what drives the phenomenon. What appears below is a brief commentary on the most commonly cited theoretical perspectives. Within each of the above theoretical perspectives, it is implicit that there are clear, identifiable and tangible benefits associated with a strategy of internationalisation. In addition to the benefits mentioned above, further *benefits* might include:

- Facilitating access to new markets e.g. Formula 1 staging a race in China.
- Facilitating access to new sources of labour e.g. Arsenal and Beveren agreeing to share players.
- Facilitating access to new sources of finance e.g. the English FA securing a German loan in order to fund the construction of Wembley Stadium.
- Enabling diversification and growth e.g. Manchester United opening up new retail outlets in Asia.
- Promoting market development and growth e.g. the NBA has been working in Africa both to promote the brand and to help create new market opportunities.
- Providing opportunities for collaboration and alliances e.g. Ajax Amsterdam worked with Cape Town Spurs and Seven Stars to create a new sporting franchise – Ajax Cape Town.
- Stimulating learning amongst organisations and managers e.g. in an attempt to understand and respond to new market opportunities, football clubs including Everton and FC Barcelona have recruited Asian members of staff to build knowledge of overseas markets.
- Enabling organisations and managers to build competence and capability e.g. Chelsea has variously recruited staff from Portugal, the Netherlands, Spain, Denmark and Israel in an effort to improve the quality of its management team.

Although internationalisation can bring benefits for sports and sport organisations, it also poses a series of management challenges. Amongst these are the following points. However, the points below are not intended to be a definitive list of the challenges facing managers. Rather, it is intended to be illustrative, providing an insight into some of the issues that international sport managers have to contend with.

18.5.1 Marketing Management

At the 1998 World Cup Final in Paris, the football world was sent into uproar when it was announced that Ronaldo would not be playing. The player nevertheless appeared on the pitch but seemed to struggle throughout the game. Afterwards, theories abound that Ronaldo and the Brazilian football authorities had been pressured by Nike to make sure the player took part in the game thereby fulfilling his contractual obligations to the company. More recently, reports have suggested that tennis' Williams sisters have struggled to maintain their form due to contractual demands of some of their corporate partners. Some reports have even suggested that the sisters have been required to play in exhibitions when injured. Whatever the true story in both cases, the two illustrate some of the challenges sport managers can face when trying to marketing personalities. Using a celebrity to promote a product, a brand or a sport is a rewarding proposition for corporations and the sportsman or woman involved. However, there is also the issue of how to manage the nature and the extent of this activity because too much promotional work may ultimately detract from the very qualities that make the celebrity such a valuable individual in the first place. Indeed, when people such as David Beckham are global icons, this presents particular problems as there may well be extensive travelling involved, which may cause problems for the individual, the team and/or the commercial partner.

18.5.2 Organisation Management

Despite spending millions of Euros on their respective returns to Formula 1 motor racing, Toyota and Honda have won only one race between them. For strategic marketing purposes, each team's involvement in F1 is very important, as is their success in the sport. However, one has to say that the return on their respective investments has thus far been poor. It has been suggested that one reason for Toyota and Honda's respective performances has been the way in which the Japanese companies organise their operations. Such is the geographic distance between the racing team and team headquarters in Japan, that problem diagnosis, decision making and effective communication have been major problems. As such, readers should think about how these types of problems should be addressed when sports organisations are involved in international operations.

18.5.3 Human Resource Management

Take a look at any leading European football team, for example Real Madrid, AC Milan, Bayern Munich, Lyon or Manchester United. What you will invariably find is that each team's squad consists of a rich mix of players from different countries. Immediately the problems of internationalisation should become apparent – how do the players and club officials communicate with each other when they all speak different languages. In the case of, say, Real Madrid, one should recall that during the 2006/2007 season, the club's leading centre forward was Dutch, their star midfielder was English, one of their best defenders was Brazilian and the team manager was Italian. It is also worth mentioning that in Spain, Real are nicknamed 'The Vikings' because of the club's history of signing players from Northern Europe. The mix creates challenges other than language; for instance, integrating players and managing multi-cultural teams is a major issue, especially when one considers the differences in attitudes and behaviour between people from Anglo-Saxon, Northern European cultures and Latin, Mediterranean, Southern European cultures. While such issues may not always been acknowledged or managed effectively, they are paramount if organisational performance is to be optimised.

18.5.4 Supply Chain Management

Despite the lack of English playing success at the annual Wimbledon tennis championship, the tournament nevertheless remains one of the most important events on both the playing and social calendars. More than half a million spectators from around the world will normally attend the event and part of the overall experience for many of them is eating strawberries and cream – an established Wimbledon tradition. On average, 27,000 kilos of strawberries and 7,000 litres of cream will be consumed at the tournament during Wimbledon fortnight. Given that the strawberries and cream and the tennis are synonymous, this poses some interesting challenges for supply-chain managers. Ensuring that international fans get what they expect is the overall challenge they face; but ensuring the correct quantity and quality of strawberry is sourced is equally as important. When one factors in the vagaries of the English weather, the managerial challenge is heightened. Although it might seem almost incidental to sport, strawberries and cream are part of the overall sporting experience and the task for managers therefore is to ensure that the expected experience is delivered to customers.

18.5.5 Risk Management

In 2003, there was a major outbreak of the SARS virus in China, which had a major impact on sport in the country. At the time, numerous sporting events were either cancelled or postponed. At the time, China was emerging as an important market for European football teams and many club tours to the country were abandoned. This required some very careful thinking as clubs sought to address the potential risks of touring and of not touring. In the latter case, this meant losing out on an important revenue stream and on the opportunity to establish and build fan affiliation. But the risks of players contracting the virus, allied to the likelihood that stadiums would be cancelled and matches would not take place any way, ultimately led clubs to cancel their tours.

18.6 Case study

The following case study describes the internationalisation process of FC Barcelona, a truly international and multicultural club in the world of football and the business of sport.

Case Study "FC Barcelona – an international football club in Catalonia"

FC Barcelona was founded in 1899 by a group of Swiss, British, Spanish and Catalonian footballers. One could therefore say that from the outset the club was an international one. Whereas football clubs in countries such as England and Italy have traditionally been owned by local business people or industrial families FC Barcelona was founded as a membership club. This is still the case, with the club achieving a total worldwide membership of 145,000 in 2006. These members are referred to as socios or culés and many of them are members of penés or supporter's clubs, of which there are almost 1800 worldwide.

Historically, Barca has held something of a stranglehold on Spanish football, along with their closest and bitterest rivals Real Madrid. This rivalry became one of the most passionate in world football following the Spanish Civil War, during which Franco's Madrid based government fought a vicious and bloody campaign against Catalan separatists. FC Barcelona became a symbol of Catalan identity and defiance and, in the minds of many football fans and Catalans alike, has helped to cement the club as 'més que un club' – more than a club. Importantly, many Catalonians, afraid of the Madrid regime, emigrated to places such as Mexico and Argentina, countries that are now important international market places for Barca.

Since 1957, FC Barcelona has played at their iconic home – the Nou Camp Stadium. With a capacity of almost 99,000, it is Europe's biggest football stadium and home games are often complete sell-outs. Many of those who attend games are from overseas but more startling is the fact that the Nou Camp is one of the most popular tourist attractions in Barcelona, drawing as many as 1.2 million visitors each year.

Arguably the most successful period of Barca's history was that when Johan Cruyff was playing for the club between 1973 and 1978. Cruyff is often thought to have been one of the world's greatest ever players and his impact on FC Barcelona has been profound. Most notably, it appears to have created a Dutch heritage that resulted in Cruyff's return to the club as manager in 1988. More recently, the

---

club has appointed Dutch managers such as Frank Rijkaard, Ronald Koeman and Loius van Gaal, as well as a stream of Dutch players such as Ronald Koeman, Marc Overmars, Winston Bogarde, Giovanni van Bronkhorst, Edgar Davids, Boudwijn Zenden, Philip Cocu, Patrick Kluivert and Michael Reiziger.

In 2003, FC Barcelona members elected a progressive young reformer, Joan Laporta, as President of the club. This signalled major changes at the club, including a newly established focus on targeting international markets. Having commercially fallen behind rivals like Manchester United and Real Madrid, Barca have set up soccer camps in the United States, notably in those areas that have large Hispanic communities, targeted fans in Japan and signed a commercial deal with Tiger Beer in Singapore.

For many years, Barcelona had been one of the last major professional football clubs in the world not to have a shirt sponsor. In 2006 this changed, when the club announced a not-for-profit deal with UNICEF. At one level, this reinforced Barca's international credentials, committing the club to make a series of financial contributions to development projects across the world. At another level however, it simply added to the activities of Fundacio FC Barcelona, a charitable organisation promoting social/solidarity, institutional/cultural and education/care programmes across the world.

18.7 Conclusion and outlook

In some respects, one might argue that sport has always been international. A review of historical literature shows that in many countries games have always been played and that these have often been exported to other countries. As a result, sport has often been a universal phenomenon that has transcended language, culture and geography. However, it is only in recent decades that the international nature of sport has increasingly been recognised as a focus for business managers. There are a number of reasons for this, including regulatory changes and the challenges of acquiring scarce, valuable resources. In this context, various theoretical approaches have been employed in an attempt to explain why internationalisation has become so important in the business world. At this point, however, understanding international sport has received rather less attention. There is therefore still some way to go before we can fully understand why, for instance, there are 100 million Manchester United fans worldwide or why Formula 1 motor racing holds events in China, Bahrain, Turkey and Malaysia when there aren't any drivers or teams involved in F1 from these countries. Clearly some of the reasons why sport has internationalised have been identified in this chapter, although there may be more. The challenge remains for readers to think how the framework of ideas presented in this chapter can be applied to a range of sports, both those that have a strongly specific domestic basis and those that are more clearly 'international'. Above all, as we enter a new age of internationalisation, with new player supply routes opening up, overseas markets forming the basis for increasingly overt commercial strategies and technological developments fuelling media proliferation, managing the process and consequences of internationalisation are key challenges for sport managers. Precedents have already been set in the management of other industrial sectors where internationalisation has taken hold. However, such is the socio-cultural embeddedness of sport, as well as the nature of the product on offer (a contest that has an uncertain outcome) that sport is unique in many respects and therefore requires specific attention in the literature and in practice. Hopefully this chapter goes some way to addressing this distinctiveness in an international context.

Discussion questions

1. Using existing definitions of internationalisation, how might they be applied to a sport such as football, car rallying, handball or volleyball?
2. For a sport of your choice, identify how it has 'internationalised', indicating the most important factors that have influenced this process!
3. Is the internationalisation of all sports inevitable?
4. Compare and contrast how the US National Basketball Association (NBA) and English Premier League football clubs have internationalised! What lessons can sport managers learn from both cases?
5. If you had to advise a major sport organisation about its internationalisation strategy, what would you tell them?
6. Is the internationalisation of sport a good thing or a bad thing?
7. Using the theories of internationalisation presented in the chapter, explain how different theorists might account for the growth and development of mega events such as the Olympic Games or the FIFA World Cup!
8. Select a number of cases in which a sport or a sport organisation has internationalised. Of the factors that have contributed to internationalisation in sport, which do you think have been the most powerful in the cases you have selected?
9. Compare and contrast the internationalisation of FC Barcelona and that of Real Madrid!
10. For a sport organisation of your choice, develop a plan for the internationalisation of the organisation!

References

Andersson, Svante (2000): The Internationalisation of the Firm from an Entrepreneurial Perspective, in: International Studies of Management and Organisation, No. 1, pp. 63-92.

Bridgewater, Susan (2006): International Sport Marketing and Globalisation, in: Beech, John / Chadwick, Simon (eds.): The Marketing of Sport, Harlow, pp. 446-464.

Calof, Jonathan / Beamish, Paul (1995): Adapting to foreign markets: explaining internationalisation, in: International Business Review, No. 2, pp. 115-131.

Chadwick, Simon / Arthur, Dave (2007): Mes que un club (More than a club). The commercial development of FC Barcelona, in: Chadwick, Simon / Arthur, Dave (eds.): International Cases in the Business of Sport, Oxford, pp. 8-15.

Camuffo, Arnaldo / Furlan, Andrea / Romano, Pietro. / Vinelli, Andrea. (2006): The process of supply network internationalisation, in: Journal of Purchasing and Supply Management, No.3, pp. 135-147.

Chetty, Sylvie / Campbell-Hunt, Colin (2003): Paths to internationalisation among small- to medium-sized firms, in: European Journal of Marketing, No. 5/6, pp. 796-820.

Desbordes, Michel (ed.) (2006): Marketing and Football: An International Perspective, Oxford.

Hutchinson, Karise / Quinn, Barry / Alexander, Nicholas (2005): The Internationalisation of Small to Medium-Sized Retail Companies: Towards a Conceptual Framework, in: Journal of Marketing Management, No. 1-2, pp. 149-179.

Lam, Long W. / White, Lawrence P. (1999): An adaptive choice model of the internationalisation process, in: The International Journal of Organisational Analysis, No. 2, pp. 105-134.

Welch, Lawrence S. / Luostarinen, Reijo (1988): Internationalisation: evolution of a concept, in: Journal of General Management, No. 2, pp. 34-55.

Whitelock, Jeryl (2002): Theories of internationalisation and their impact on market entry, in: International Marketing Review, No. 4, pp. 342-347.

Yakhlef, Ali / Maubourguet, Francois (2004): The Lexus and the Olive Tree: a rising mode of internationalisation, in: International Journal of Entrepreneurial Behaviour and Research, No. 3, pp. 192-205.

Guided Reading

Although there are very few studies that provide detailed definitions of internationalisation, the reader is directed to Welch/Luostarinen (1988) and Calof/Beamish (1995) for citations presented in this chapter. Elsewhere, Lam/White (1998), Andersson (2000), Whitelock (2002) and Chetty/Campbell-Hunt (2003) provide an overview of the different theoretical perspectives that have attempted to account for internationalisation. The underpinning forces and benefits of internationalisation are highlighted by Hutchinson/Quinn/Alexander (2005). Yakhlef/Maubourguet (2004) and Camuffo/Furlan/Romano/Vinelli (2006) explore the process of internationalisation, indicating how firms move from domestic to international operations. For an overview of internationalisation and sport, it is recommended that the reader take a look at Bridgewater (2006). A more specific analysis of an individual sport and internationalisation can be found in Desbordes' (2006) text on football. Chadwick/Arthur (2007) provide a more detailed insight into the case presented in this chapter – FC Barcelona.

The following links are recommended:
Asian Football Dynamics:
    http://footballdynamicsasia.blogspot.com
Institute for International Sport:
    http://www.internationalsport.com
Sport and the EU:
    http://www.jiscmail.ac.uk/lists/SPORTANDEU.html
Sport Business:
    http://www.sportbusiness.com

Kapitel 19: Der Arbeitsmarkt für Sportmanager

Heinz-Dieter Horch

Lernziele

Nach der Durchsicht dieses Kapitels sollte der Leser in der Lage sein,

- die einfachen allgemeinen Gesetzmäßigkeiten und Einflussfaktoren des Arbeitsmarktes, der Arbeitsnachfrage und des Arbeitsangebotes aufzuzeigen.
- die sportspezifisch interessanten Besonderheiten zu erkennen.
- Verberuflichung und Professionalisierung unterscheiden und die Entwicklung des Sportmanagements in Deutschland danach beurteilen zu können.
- zu verstehen, was es bedeutet, dass der Arbeitsmarkt für Sportmanager jung, offen und unreguliert ist.
- die Fragestellungen der Arbeitsmarkt- und Berufsforschung sowie die Vorgehensweise und Schwierigkeiten bei der Erstellung einer Prognose der Entwicklung der Arbeitskräftenachfrage nach Sportmanagern zu kennen.
- das Berufsfeld für Sportmanager systematisch beschreiben zu können.
- die Bedeutung der Managementfunktionen und Managerrollen zur Beschreibung der Tätigkeit von Sportmanagern zu kennen.
- die Bedeutung des Sportbezuges für Tätigkeit, Kompetenzen und Rekrutierung von Sportmanagern ermessen zu können.
- Gemeinsamkeiten und Unterschiede der Tätigkeitsschwerpunkte und Kompetenzanforderungen verschiedener Sportmanagementbereiche zu bezeichnen.
- Quantität und Qualität der Nachfrage nach Managern in Profisportclubs und -ligen beurteilen zu können.

Überblick über das Kapitel

In diesem Kapitel werden die Grundlagen der Theorie des Arbeitsmarktes sowie der Arbeitsmarkt- und Berufsforschung vorgestellt und auf den Arbeitsmarkt für Sportmanager angewandt. Nach einer kurzen Einführung werden die einfachen allgemeinen Grundlagen beschrieben, und es wird auf Spezifika eingegangen, die für den Sport von Bedeutung sind. Anschließend geht es speziell um den Arbeitsmarkt für Sportmanager. Betrachtet werden die Marktform, Quantität und Qualität, Homogenität bzw. Heterogenität der Nachfrage sowie des Angebots. Abschließend wird der Sonderfall „Fußballmanager" behandelt und Links zu Jobbörsen aufgeführt.

19.1 Einführung in die Thematik

In den letzten Jahrzehnten hat sich mehr und mehr die Erkenntnis durchgesetzt, dass Sport nicht nur professionelle Sportler und Trainer, sondern auch professionelle Manager braucht. Seit Mitte der achtziger Jahre wurden von immer mehr Universitäten und Fachhochschulen entsprechend spezielle Ausbildungsangebote konzipiert, die auf eine sehr hohe Bildungsnachfrage treffen. Aber entsprechen diese quantitativ und qualitativ dem, was die Praxis braucht? Um diese Frage beantworten zu können, braucht man ein Verständnis der theoretischen Zusammenhänge eines Arbeitsmarktes für Akademiker und entsprechende empirische Forschung. Ein Grundproblem dabei ist, dass das Feld der Sportprodukte und Sportorganisationen in sich sehr heterogen ist. Deshalb sind im Folgenden drei Fragen von besonderem Interesse:

- Gibt es Sportbesonderheiten, unterscheiden sich Sportmanager von Managern in anderen Branchen?
- Existiert überhaupt ein einheitlicher Markt, oder führt die Vielfalt der Produkt- und Organisationstypen zu einer Ausdifferenzierung?
- Wie weit ist der Verberuflichungs- bzw. Professionalisierungsprozess vorangeschritten?

19.2 Grundlagen

Die grundlegenden Konzepte zur Beantwortung der Fragestellungen, Arbeitsmarkt, Managerkompetenzen und Professionalisierung, stammen aus der Volkswirtschafts- sowie der Managementlehre und der Berufssoziologie.

19.2.1 Arbeitsmarkt

Arbeitsmarkt heißt der Markt, auf dem Angebot von und Nachfrage nach Arbeit aufeinander treffen und im Gleichgewicht die Menge an Arbeitsstunden und ihr Preis, der Lohn, sowie die übrigen Beschäftigungsbedingungen bestimmt werden (vgl. zum Folgenden z.B. Ulbrich/Warner, 1990). Da die Arbeit von Selbständigen nicht auf einem Markt angeboten wird, werden diese nicht in die Betrachtung einbezogen. Generell gelten auf dem Arbeitsmarkt die allgemeinen Aussagen der Ökonomie zur Erklärung von Angebot und Nachfrage sowie des Marktgleichgewichts. Aufgrund der zentralen Rolle menschlicher Arbeitskraft für den Produktionsprozess hat der Arbeitsmarkt eine besondere Bedeutung für die meisten Branchen der Wirtschaft. Der Markt ist häufig *zweistufig* organisiert. Auf der Endstufe trifft die individuelle betriebliche Nachfrage auf das individuelle Haushaltsangebot. Auf dieser Stufe hat der Markt meist die Form eines beiderseitigen – mehr oder weniger vollständigen – Wettbewerbs. Von besonderer Bedeutung sind jedoch branchenspezifische Abweichungen davon, u.a. in Form eines *Monopsons* (Nachfragemonopols). So manifestierte sich z.B. die Konkurrenzlosigkeit der amerikanischen Profiligen auf dem Arbeitsmarkt bis in die siebziger Jahre in der „reserve clause", d.h. einem Verbot des Wechsels von Spielern ohne Zustimmung des alten Clubs. Auf einer vorgelagerten Stufe können Wirtschaftsverbände und Gewerkschaften in Form eines *bilateralen Monopols* Rahmenbedingungen in einem Tarifvertrag festlegen, wie dies seit einigen Jahrzehnten Profiligen und Spielergewerkschaften in den USA tun. Speziell für den Sport relevant sind auch die Ökonomie von *Tournaments* (Turnier zur Ermittlung von Rangplätzen; Lazear, 1998) und Superstars. Falls die absolute Produktivität von Arbeitern schwer zu bestimmen ist und/oder geringe Produktivitätsunterschiede große Einnahmeunterschiede verursachen, kann sich die Belohnung an der relativen Produktivität orientieren. Durch eine deutliche Belohnungsdifferenzierung kann versucht werden, die Wettkampfteilnehmer zu Höchstleistungen anzuspornen. Dies kann eine der Erklärungen für die hohen Gehälter der *Superstars* sein, eine andere ist Knappheit an Talenten in Relation zu hoher über Medien multiplizierter Nachfrage. So ein Wettlauf um sehr ungleich verteilte Belohnungen kann zu *Hyperaktivität* (Akerlof, 1976), zu einer „Rüstungsspirale" führen, weil jede relative Verbesserung eines Wettkämpfers zu entsprechend relativen Verschlechterungen aller anderen führt, sind diese gezwungen nachzuziehen. Dies ist volkswirtschaftlich ineffizient, weil der Output, die Leistung nicht in dem Maße gesteigert wird wie der Input. Sind z.B. Fußballspiele heute um so viel attraktiver als vor 40 Jahren wie die Spielergehälter in dieser Zeit gestiegen sind? Je höher die Gehaltsdifferenzen sind, desto höher wird auch der Anreiz zum Betrug, z.B. durch Doping.

Bei der *Arbeitsnachfrage* der Betriebe handelt es sich um eine *abgeleitete Nachfrage*, die von der Nachfrage auf dem entsprechenden Produktmarkt, in unserem Fall dem jeweiligen Sportmarkt, abhängt. Die Nachfrage wird mit Hilfe des Gesetzes des sinkenden Grenzertrages und der *Grenz(-wert)produktivitätstheorie* erklärt. Demnach wird ein profitorientierter Betrieb – entsprechend der allgemeinen Maximierungsbedingung „Grenzkosten = Grenzertrag" – so lange Arbeit nachfragen, bis der Outputzuwachs der letzten Einheit seinem individuellen Lohn, bzw. im Fall eines vollkommenen Wettbewerbs, dem Marktlohn entspricht. Falls die Annahme der Profitorientierung nicht stimmt, gilt auch die Schlussfolgerung nicht. Dies ist z.B. der Fall bei Proficlubs, die sportliche Siege maximieren wollen. Hier wird so lange Personal eingestellt, bis vereinfacht gilt „Gesamtkosten = Gesamteinnahmen" (Kesenne, 1996). Falls – wie für den Sport nicht untypisch – Mäzenatentum im Spiel ist, werden sogar Verluste in Kauf genommen. Der Output des Personals ist abhängig von der Arbeitsproduktivität. Ein neuer Zweig der Ökonomie, die *Personalökonomik,* beschäftigt sich mit dem Zusammenhang von Lohn und Produktivität, z.B. den Fragen, wie Vertragslaufzeiten, der Anteil von Leistungsprämien am Einkommen von Spielern, oder die Verteilung der Einkommen in einer Fußballmannschaft die sportliche Leistung beeinflussen (Frick/Prinz, 2005).

Die Quantität des *Arbeitsangebots* erklären Ökonomen mit Hilfe der *Freizeitökonomie.* Sie geht davon aus, dass Individuen die Wahl zwischen dem Nutzen der Freizeit und der Arbeit (Einkommen) haben. Realistischerweise muss bei Sportmanagern, wie bei vielen Berufen, diese vereinfachende Annahme modifiziert werden. Da Betriebe Manager wünschen, die sich mit vollem Einsatz engagieren, dürfte man kaum Angebote für stundenweises oder Teilzeit-Managen finden (Ausnahme Projektmanager). Demnach können Manager nur entscheiden, ob sie Wochenarbeitszeiten in den üblichen großen Blöcken wählen oder nicht. Diese Arbeitszeit dürfte meistens über der gewünschten liegen. Viele Manager haben daher den Traum, ihre Lebensarbeitszeit entsprechend zu verkürzen, d.h. nur bis zu einem bestimmten Alter zu arbeiten. Bei steigendem Lohn wirken zwei gegenläufige Effekte: ein Substitutions- und ein Einkommenseffekt. Der Substitutionseffekt führt wegen der steigenden Opportunitätskosten zu sinkender Nachfrage nach Freizeit, also steigendem Arbeitsangebot. Der durch den gestiegenen Lohn ausgelöste Einkommenseffekt bewirkt jedoch eine steigende Nachfrage nach dem (normalen oder superioren) Gut Freizeit. Wegen der Gegenläufigkeit dieser Wirkungen kann der Nettoeffekt letztlich nur empirisch geklärt werden. Nach dem zweiten Weltkrieg gab es hier offenbar unterschiedliche Präferenzen in den USA und Großbritannien einerseits und Kontinentaleuropa andererseits. Während sich in den angelsächsischen Ländern der Wohlfahrtszuwachs v.a. in Form von Einkommenssteigerungen niederschlug (Schor, 1991), wurde in Kontinentaleuropa die Freizeit stark ausgeweitet. Die in manchen Sportmarketinglehrbüchern als Mega-Trend bezeichnete Entwicklung zu immer mehr Freizeit muss also sowohl örtlich als auch zeitlich differenziert betrachtet werden. Eine besondere Problematik ergibt sich aus der Bindung der Arbeitskraft an *menschliche Träger*. Für diese hat die Arbeit eine zentrale Bedeutung für ihre Lebensqualität, und das nicht nur indirekt über das erzielte monetäre Einkommen. Hieraus resultieren eine große Heterogenität und auch räumliche Immobilität des Angebots und anomale Reaktionen dergestalt, dass das Angebot bei sinkendem Lohn nicht gesenkt, sondern erhöht wird, falls das Ziel nicht Nutzenmaximierung, sondern Einkommensstabilisierung ist. Die Qualität des Arbeitsangebots wird mit Hilfe der *Humankapitaltheorie* erklärt (Becker, 1964). Demnach investieren Individuen in Ausbildung, beginnen z.B. ein Studium, insoweit sie in der Zukunft entsprechende Einkommenszuwächse und eine geringere Konkurrenz auf dem Arbeitsmarkt erwarten. Dem Arbeitsangebot vorgelagert ist der *Bildungsmarkt*, auf dem entsprechende Ausbildungen nachgefragt und angeboten werden. Betriebe werden nur in die Ausbildung ihrer Mitarbeiter investieren, insoweit es sich nicht um *generelles*, sondern um *spezifisches* Humankapital handelt, das nur in ihrem Betrieb genutzt werden kann, oder bereits während der Ausbildung ein Überschuss geschaffen wird. Beides ist z.B. bei Fußballspielern überwiegend nicht der Fall. Die positiven *externen Effekte* eines hohen Ausbildungsniveaus für die Gesellschaft können durch staatliche Subventionen oder Verpflichtungen wie (Hoch-)Schulgeldfreiheit und Schulpflicht gesichert werden. Branchenspezifische, positive externe Effekte können auch durch kollektive Regelungen, wie im Falle der Transfergeldzahlung lange Zeit im deutschen Fußball geschehen, internalisiert werden (Büch/Schellhaaß, 1984).

19.2.2 Arbeitsmarkt- und Berufsforschung

In der Arbeitsmarkt- und Berufsforschung geht es u.a. darum, die Art des Marktes (Regulierungen) sowie Quantität, Qualität und Differenzierung der Arbeitskräftenachfrage und des Arbeitskräfteangebots zu klären und gegenüberzustellen sowie Ausmaß und Art der Zu- (Substitution) und Abwanderung (Mobilität) auf diesem

Markt zu bestimmen (vgl. Abb. 1). Qualitativ werden Berufe v.a. anhand der spezifischen Tätigkeiten und Kompetenzen beschrieben. *Kompetenzen* heißen die Fähigkeiten, Fertigkeiten, Kenntnisse und Einstellungen, die man braucht, um die beruflichen Tätigkeiten ausüben zu können (Staehle, 1991). Neben den funktionalen, d.h. fachgebundenen Qualifikationen haben aufgrund der zunehmend geforderten Mobilität der Arbeitskräfte extrafunktionale berufsübergreifende, so genannte Schlüsselqualifikationen, an Bedeutung gewonnen.

In der Managementlehre wurden entsprechende Studien zur Tätigkeit und Qualifikation von Managern durchgeführt. *Manager* heißen – im weiten englischsprachigen Verständnis – alle Personen, die die Tätigkeiten anderer Personen leiten, d.h. die Entscheidungs- und Anordnungskompetenzen haben (dispositiv), im Unterschied zu Arbeitskräften ohne Führungsaufgaben, die nur mit ausführenden Tätigkeiten (operativ) betraut sind (Robbins/DeCenzo, 1997). Die Tätigkeit von Managern wird traditionell mit den auf Fayol (1929) zurückgehenden *Management-Funktionen*: Planung, Organisation, Führung und Kontrolle beschrieben. Die empirische Managementforschung wendet sich gegen diese rein analytische (logische, prozessorientierte) Beschreibung. Sie versucht dagegen, empirisch herauszufinden, was wirklich die wichtigsten Tätigkeiten von Managern sind (work-activity research) und welche Kompetenzen (function-based research) sie brauchen. Als wegweisend gilt eine Untersuchung von Mintzberg (1973). Er fasste das Ergebnis seiner Studie zu zehn *Manager-Rollen* in drei Gruppen zusammen: interpersonelle, informationelle und Entscheidungsrollen. Die Manager-Rollen verdeutlichen, wie sehr die Tätigkeit von Managern nicht nur innen-, sondern auch außenorientiert ist, und dass Manager nicht nur technische Kompetenz brauchen, sondern auch konzeptionelle und soziale (Katz, 1974). Andere Kernergebnisse der Work-Activity-Forschung sind, dass die Arbeit von Managern stark fragmentiert ist und verbale Kommunikation dabei einen zentralen Stellenwert einnimmt. Sie ist weniger geordnet und geplant, beruht mehr auf Spekulationen als auf Analysen, ist informeller und konfliktbeladener, als das funktionale Konzept vermuten lässt (Schirmer, 1992).

Aufgrund der ursprünglich amateurmäßigen und ehrenamtlichen Form der Arbeit in zentralen Sportbereichen ist es für das Thema von Bedeutung zu klären, inwieweit sich in den letzten Jahrzehnten Verberuflichungs- bzw. Professionalisierungstendenzen durchgesetzt haben. Erst damit konnten im engeren Sinne Arbeitsmärkte entstehen, auf denen Arbeit gegen Geld getauscht wird.

„Beruf" wird nach Weber (1972, S. 80) definiert als „jene Spezifizierung, Spezialisierung und Kombination von Leistungen einer Person [...], welche für sie die Grundlage einer kontinuierlichen Versorgungs- oder Erwerbschance ist".

Unter *Verberuflichung* kann man demnach den Ersatz freiwilliger, unbezahlter durch bezahlte und nebenberuflich-gelegentlicher Freizeitarbeit durch hauptberuflich-kontinuierliche Arbeit verstehen. Die weitere Konsolidierung der Berufsbilder im engeren Verständnis von *Professionalisierung* umfasst weitere Aspekte, wie sie in unserer Gesellschaft in letzter Konsequenz z.B. bei Medizinern oder Juristen anzutreffen sind. Dazu gehören eine lange, formalisierte (wissenschaftliche) Ausbildung, Qualifikations- und Zulassungskontrollen und festgelegte Karrieremuster, Organisation in einem Berufsverband, ein besonderes Berufsethos und hohes Prestige und Einkommen.

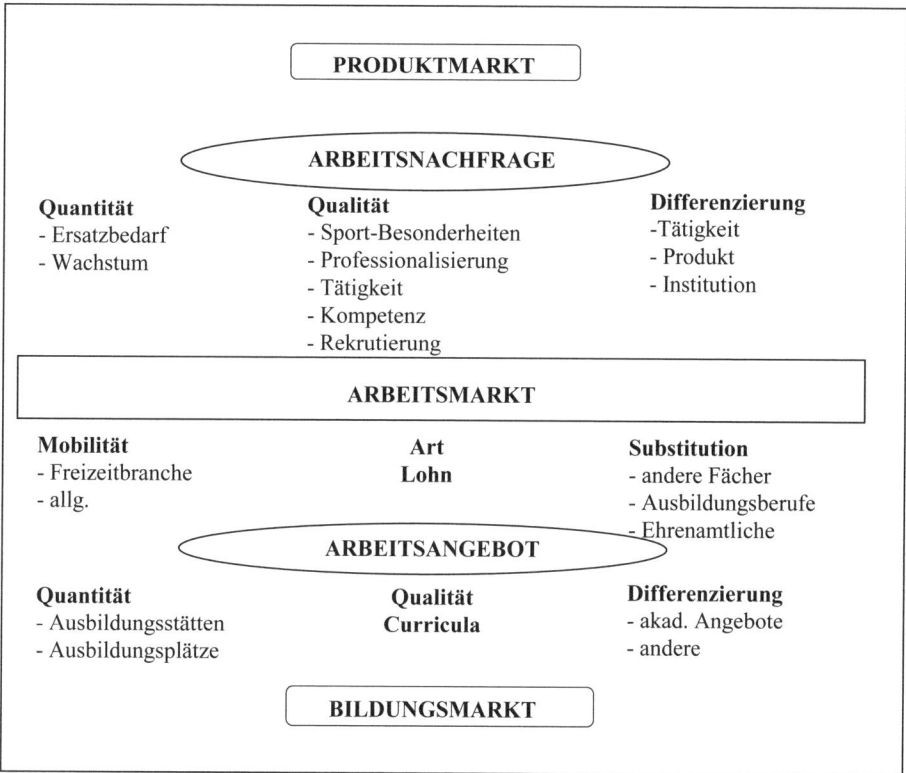

Abb. 1: Der Arbeitsmarkt für Sportmanager

19.3 Arbeitsmarkt für Sportmanager

Der *Arbeitsmarkt für Profisportler* ist eines der zentralen Themen, mit denen sich die Sportökonomik beschäftigt (Rottenberg, 1956). Dies liegt einerseits darin begründet, dass es hier viele Besonderheiten und Regulierungen gab bzw. gibt, wie ein Monopson der Liga, Reservierungsklauseln, Transferzahlungen bzw. Draft-Systeme, Gehaltsbeschränkungen (salary caps), und die Clubs nicht nur Profit-, sondern auch Siegmaximierer sein können (Kesenne, 1996), d.h. sportliche und nicht wirtschaftliche Ziele im Fordergrund stehen. Andererseits interessieren sich

Ökonomen für Profisport, weil hier – anders als in anderen Branchen der Wirtschaft – sowohl Daten über die unabhängige (Leistung) als auch die abhängige Variable (Lohn) der Personalökonomik in großem Umfang öffentlich zugänglich sind. Im Folgenden soll dies aber nicht das Thema sein, sondern der Arbeitsmarkt für Sportmanager.

Sportmanager heißen alle Manager, die in Organisationen oder Abteilungen arbeiten, die Sportgüter oder -dienstleistungen anbieten (DeSensi/Kelley/Blanton/ Beitel, 1990). Im Folgenden soll geklärt werden, welcher Art der Arbeitsmarkt für Sportmanager ist, wie groß die Substitution und die Mobilität sind, und wie Nachfrage und Angebot nach Qualität, Differenzierung und Quantität aussehen (vgl. Abb. 1). Dabei sind drei Fragen von besonderem Interesse:

- Gibt es Sportbesonderheiten, unterscheiden sich Sportmanager von Managern in anderen Branchen?
- Existiert überhaupt ein einheitlicher Markt, oder führt die Vielfalt der Produkt- und Organisationstypen zu einer Ausdifferenzierung?
- Wie weit ist der Verberuflichungs- bzw. Professionalisierungsprozess vorangeschritten?

19.3.1 Forschungsstand

Im Folgenden soll kurz der Forschungsstand geschildert werden. Auf inhaltliche Ergebnisse wird dabei erst in den weiteren Abschnitten eingegangen.

Zur *quantitativen Bedeutung* des Arbeitsmarktes Sportmanager in Deutschland gibt es nicht viele Informationen. Einzig Weber (1996) hat im Anschluss an seine Studie zur Ermittlung der ökonomischen Bedeutung des Sports eine entsprechende Prognose gewagt. Einige Informationen können aus dem Verbleib der Absolventen entsprechender Studiengänge (Bayreuth: Buchmeier/Zieschang, 1992; Köln: Ecke, 2004; Hartmann-Tews/Mrazek, 2006) abgeleitet werden. Mehr Daten stehen speziell über die Arbeitsplätze für Sportmanager in Vereinen und Verbänden (Cachay/Thiel/Meier, 2001; Horch/Hovemann/Schubert, 2006) sowie den Profisportclubs (Lohmar, 2007) zur Verfügung. Informationen über die Bedeutung und Entwicklung der angrenzenden Produkt- und Bildungsmärkte finden sich z.B. bei Breuer/Wicker/Pawlowski (Kapitel 2 des vorliegenden Bandes) und bei Hovemann (2003).

Deutlich besser sieht die Datenlage aus, was die *qualitativen Aspekte* anbetrifft, also die Fragen nach Rekrutierung, Tätigkeit und Kompetenzen. Hier kann man v.a. auf die Studien des Instituts für Sportökonomie und Sportmanagement der Deutschen Sporthochschule Köln zurückgreifen (vgl. Abschnitt 19.3.4). Ähnliche Studien wurden ca. ein Jahrzehnt früher in den USA durchgeführt. Diese firmierten unter dem Etikett „competency based approach to curriculum development". Einen zusammenfassenden Überblick der Ergebnisse bieten z.B. Lambrecht (1991) und DeSensi/Kelley/Blanton/Beitel (1990). Relevanz für das Thema haben darüber hinaus die Analysen jener allgemeineren Berufsfelder, die sich beim Sportmanager überschneiden: das außerschulische Berufsfeld von Sportlehrern (z.B. Heinemann/Dietrich/Schubert, 1990; Cachay/Thiel, 1999) und das von Betriebswirten (z.B. Heinzel, 1997).

19.3.2 Markt

Der Arbeitsmarkt für Sportmanager ist – ähnlich wie der außerschulische Arbeitsmarkt für Sportlehrer (Schubert, 1991) – *jung, offen und unreguliert*. Die letzten beiden Punkte dürften in etwas abgeschwächter Form jedoch auch für den Arbeitsmarkt für Manager generell gelten. Es ist auch unwahrscheinlich, dass in Zukunft Berufsverbände bzw. der Staat hier regulierend eingreifen können bzw. wollen. Akademisch ausgebildete Sportmanager können u.a. durch andere Professionen (nicht nur Betriebswirte), durch Ausbildungsberufe (Sportkaufmann), Absolventen von Ausbildungskursen, wie die des IST-Studieninstituts in Düsseldorf, ehemalige Profisportler oder sogar unbezahlte ehrenamtliche Kräfte *substituiert* werden. Umgekehrt zeigen die Verbleibsstudien von Absolventen jedoch, dass diese zu einem merklichen Anteil (Buchmeier/Zieschang, 1996: 14 % außerhalb des Sports; Ecke 2004: 21 % in der Kategorie „Sonstiges") auch außerhalb des Sports Arbeit finden. Ob diese hohe *Mobilität* aus der Not geboren ist oder die Multifunktionalität der Ausbildung beweist, kann anhand dieser Daten nicht beurteilt werden.

Für den Arbeitsmarkt von Sportmanagern sind – wie für Arbeitsmärkte von Akademikern aufgrund der langen Ausbildungszeit generell – so genannte Schweinezyklen typisch. Als *Schweinezyklus* werden in der Ökonomie zeitliche Verzögerungen der Anpassung des Angebots an die Nachfrage bezeichnet. In Zeiten eines Unterangebots und entsprechend hoher Löhne beginnen viele ein Studium, so dass nach einigen Jahren ein Überangebot erzeugt wird und die Löhne sinken. Daraufhin gehen die Studierendenzahlen zurück, so dass wieder ein Unterangebot entsteht usw.

Es steht zu vermuten, dass viele Stellen nicht auf einem Markt, d.h. öffentlich, ausgeschrieben werden. Bei den Sportvereinen und -verbänden waren dies z.B. ca. 40 %, dabei hatte die *Ausschreibung* oft auch nur formalen Charakter (Horch/Niessen/Schütte, 2003). Aufgrund des Überangebots an Arbeitskräften in den letzten Jahren waren die Betriebe in der Lage, Kosten und Risiken zu minimieren, indem sie auf bekannte und erprobte Kräfte zurückgriffen (Stichwort „Generation Praktikum"). Von zunehmender Bedeutung sind allerdings Internet-Jobbörsen (vgl. Auswahl bei den „weiterführenden Ressourcen").

Nach den Informationen der Absolventenstudien lag der *Lohn* für Berufsanfänger Ende der achtziger Jahre typischerweise bei 2.300 € brutto (Buchmeier/Zieschang, 1996), und Anfang des neuen Jahrtausends durchschnittlich bei 1.700 € netto (Hartmann-Tews/Mrazek, 2006). Ecke (2004) ermittelte eine zweigipflige Verteilung mit 1.000 € brutto für die Hälfte, die sich vielleicht noch in einer Art

„Trainee-Programm" befand, und 3.000 € brutto für die andere Hälfte. Man kann vermuten, dass viele Sportmanager ihr Interesse am Arbeitsfeld Sport mit einem entsprechenden Gehaltsabschlag bezahlen, nicht zu reden von den häufig typischen Arbeitszeiten am Abend und an Wochenenden. Dies kann als Hinweis darauf gewertet werden, dass die vereinfachenden Annahmen der Ökonomie in solchen Fällen, wo mit der Art der Arbeit – wie analog auch des Studiums – direkt Anreize verbunden sind, modifiziert werden müssen. Hier wird nicht nur Arbeitsleid durch monetäres Einkommen kompensiert, sondern die Arbeit verschafft durch die emotionale Verbindung mit dem Sport auch einen direkten Nutzen (Arbeitsfreud).

19.3.3 Quantität der Nachfrage

Die vorgelagerten *Produktmärkte* sind in den vergangenen Jahrzehnten gewachsen, und dies wird allgemein auch für die Zukunft erwartet. Hinzu kommen qualitative Veränderungen des Sports und der Gesellschaft, die in Richtung einer zunehmenden Kommerzialisierung und – daraus abgeleitet – Verberuflichung auch des Sport-Managements wirken. Die *Produktnachfrage* wird durch die demographische Entwicklung sowie durch die Entwicklung und Verteilung der Präferenzen und der Geld- und Zeit-Ressourcen der Nachfrager bestimmt und ist von allgemeinen gesellschaftlichen, wirtschaftlichen und politischen Rahmenbedingungen abhängig. Die *letzten Jahrzehnte* brachten bekannterweise einen enormen Anstieg der Nachfrage nach aktivem und passivem Sport. Getragen wurde das Wachstum durch eine zunehmende Instrumentalisierung des Sportreibens für andere Zwecke, wie Gesundheit, Geselligkeit oder Schönheit. Völlig neue Konsumentengruppen, wie v.a. die Frauen, wurden erfasst. Das Wachstum der notwendigen beiden Ressourcen Einkommen und Freizeit ermöglichte eine Zunahme kommerzieller Angebote. *Für die Zukunft* nahmen z.B. Meyer/Ahlert (2000) ein jährliches Wachstum der Ausgaben der privaten Haushalte für Sport von 2 % an. Einschränkend wirken könnten das Schrumpfen und die Überalterung der Bevölkerung (Breuer, 2007) sowie Wirtschaftskrisen, die – wie im letzten Jahrzehnt – für große Bevölkerungsteile zu sinkendem Einkommen und steigender Arbeitszeit geführt haben. Von zentraler Bedeutung ist die Art der Institution, in der das *Angebot* produziert wird. Wenn, wie in Deutschland, große Teile des Sportangebots in freiwilligen Vereinigungen ehrenamtlich erstellt werden, wird natürlich die Nachfrage nach bezahlten Arbeitskräften entsprechend geringer sein.

Einzig Weber (1996) hat eine *Prognose der Entwicklung des Arbeitsmarktes* Sport erstellt. Er ging dabei wie folgt vor: Ausgehend vom sportinduzierten Einkommen privater Haushalte, dem Sportanteil am Gesamtoutput einer Branche sowie anhand der Analyse von Sekundärstatistiken wurde in einem ersten Schritt die Zahl der zum Untersuchungszeitpunkt abhängig Beschäftigten ermittelt. Im Folgenden konzentrierte er sich auf die Arbeitsplätze, die einen sportbezogenen Expertenstatus, d.h. ein Sportstudium, verlangen. Unter der Annahme einer durchschnittlichen

Verweildauer der Absolventen und Absolventinnen im Beruf von ca. 30 Jahren wurde dann der jährliche Ersatzbedarf errechnet. Für die Bereiche der Vereine und Verbände, der kommerziellen Anbieter und der sonstigen Unternehmen (also ohne die Arbeitsplätze beim Staat, z.B. die Sportlehrer) kam er so auf einen Bedarf von 1.300 bis 1.400 Arbeitsplätze pro Jahr nach Arbeitskräften mit einer sportwissenschaftlichen Qualifizierung, darunter jedoch nur 100 bis 150 speziell für Sportökonomen, d.h. Sportmanager mit entsprechender akademischer Ausbildung (Horch/Kreiß/Laflör, 1996). Die Entwicklung seitdem hat gezeigt, dass diese Prognose viel zu konservativ war, weil sie nur vom Ersatzbedarf ausging und das Wachstum dieses Arbeitsmarktes nicht berücksichtigte. Dafür sprechen alleine die Verbleibsstudien der Kölner Absolventen. Denn von diesen – bereits mehr als 200 Absolventen pro Jahr – sind nur 3-5 % arbeitslos (Ecke, 2004; Hartmann-Tews/Mrazek, 2006). Da allerdings diese neu geschaffenen Positionen erst vor kurzem erstmalig besetzt wurden, muss man davon ausgehen, dass sie nicht kontinuierlich, sondern erst in ca. dreißig Jahren wieder besetzt werden. Prognosen bleiben weiterhin schwierig, weil bereits die Ausgangszahl der derzeit beschäftigten Sportmanager nicht bekannt ist. Eine Ausnahme sind die Sportvereine. Horch/Hovemann/Schubert (2007) kommen im Rahmen des Sportentwicklungsberichtes für 2005 nach einer sehr vorsichtigen Schätzung auf z.B. 3.500 Geschäftsführer im Vergleich zu den 1.800, von denen Weber für 1991 ausging. Das entspräche immerhin einem Wachstum von ca. 100 % in diesen 14 Jahren, allerdings ausgehend von einem sehr niedrigen Niveau.

19.3.4 Qualität und Differenzierung der Nachfrage

Wenn man die *Kompetenzanforderungen* eines neuen Berufes beschreiben möchte, sollte man dann einfach von der Logik der Aufgabenstellung ausgehen oder sollte man dazu die bereits bestehende, vielleicht nur rudimentäre Praxis untersuchen? Einerseits kann man ohne Zweifel, wenn es um Wirtschaften und Managen geht, eine Menge aus der allgemeinen Betriebswirtschaftslehre lernen, besonders wenn es sich um Organisationen wie Sportvereine handelt, in denen bisher eher traditional als rational gehandelt wurde. Andererseits kann man vom Schreibtisch aus, wie die Work-Activity-School der Managementforschung gezeigt hat, auch Mythen über Managen zum Opfer fallen, die nicht viel mit den tatsächlichen Tätigkeiten eines Managers gemein haben. Dies droht vermutlich umso mehr, je mehr es sich, wie bei Sport, um Produkte und Organisationen handelt, mit denen sich die Betriebswirtschaftslehre nur am Rande beschäftigt hat. Deshalb ist es unverzichtbar, das Wissen der Personen zu Rate zu ziehen, die zurzeit diese Tätigkeit ausüben. Bei der Interpretation der Antworten der Praktiker muss man allerdings berücksichtigen, dass es sich um subjektive Perzeptionen handelt, die durch den eigenen Wissensstand, den eigenen Lebens- und Berufsweg sowie durch aktuelle praktische Probleme und Trends beeinflusst werden.

Analytisch kann man das *Berufsfeld für Sportmanager* nach drei Dimensionen differenzieren: dem Schwerpunkt der Tätigkeit, dem Produktfeld und der Art der Institution (vgl. Abb. 2). Tätigkeitsschwerpunkte können sein: wirtschaften (Umgang mit knappen Ressourcen), managen, kommunizieren, „verkaufen" (marktorientiertes Handeln) und finanzieren/kalkulieren. Nach Art des Sportbezugs und nach der Nähe zum Sport kann man vier Produktbereiche unterscheiden: die Güter und Dienstleistungen des aktiven Sports, des Zuschauersports, das Feld der kommunikativen sportbezogenen Dienstleistungen sowie Produkte anderer sportnaher Felder, wie Freizeit, Tourismus und Gesundheit. Sportgüter bzw. -dienstleistungen werden in drei Institutionentypen produziert bzw. bereitgestellt, die Manager beschäftigen: erwerbswirtschaftliche Betriebe, Nonprofit-Organisationen und staatliche Organisationen.

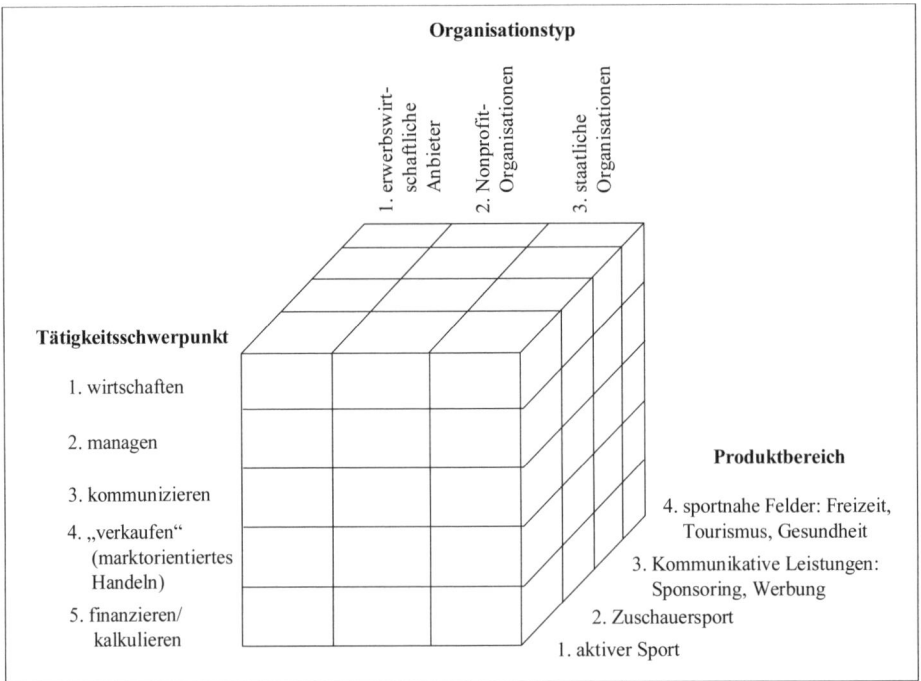

Abb. 2: Das Berufsfeld der Sportmanager

Konkret wurden u.a. folgende Berufsfelder vom Institut für Sportökonomie und Sportmanagement untersucht: *Verbände und Vereine* (Horch/Niessen/Schütte, 2003), *Sportartikelindustrie und -handel* (Hettlich, 1998), *kommunale Sportverwaltungen* (Horch/Schütte, 2003), *Sportmarketingagenturen* (Lohmar, 2002), *Eventagenturen* (Hovemann/Kaiser/Schütte, 2003), *Fitnessstudios* (Kaiser, 2006), *Profisportclubs* (Lohmar, 2007), *Spielervermittler* (Raab, 2007). Vergleichbar mit diesen Untersuchungen ist einzig die von Nichelmann (1999). Er befragte Sportmanager aus verschiedenen Organisationstypen (Vereine, Verbände, Verwaltungen, kommerzielle Anbieter, Marketing-Agenturen). Damit sind – wie Vergleiche mit den Beschäftigungsbereichen von Absolventen zeigen – die wichtigsten Berufsfelder erfasst worden (Ecke, 2004; ähnlich Buchmeier/Zieschang, 1996) (vgl. Abb. 3): Agenturen, Sportartikelindustrie und -handel, Vereine und Verbände und kommerzielle Sportanbieter. Überwiegend wurden die Untersuchungen mit Hilfe schriftlicher standardisierter Fragebögen durchgeführt. Befragt wurden neben den Praktikern auch Arbeitgeber, Absolventen, Studenten und Wissenschaftler. Gefragt wurde überwiegend nach den Tätigkeiten, den Kompetenzen und Ausbildungsinhalten, aber auch nach Rekrutierungskriterien und dem notwendigen Niveau des Abschlusses.

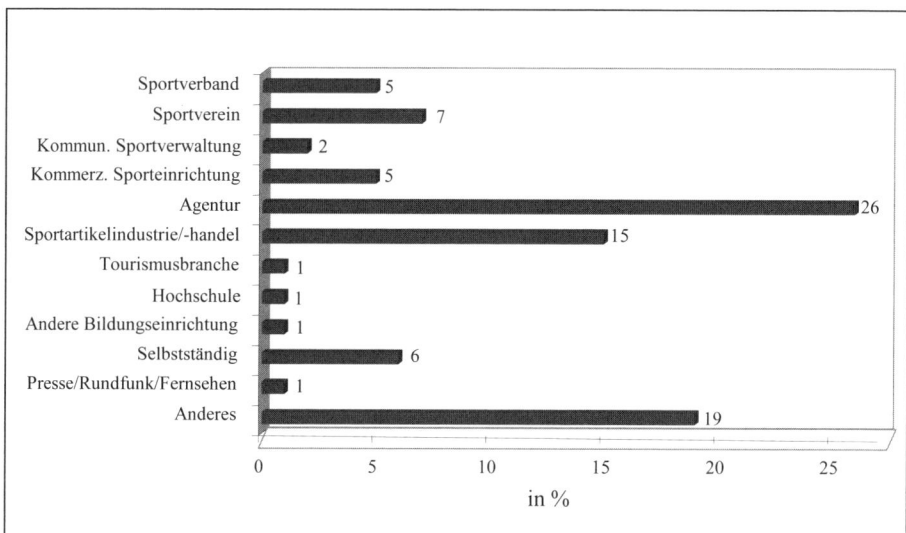

Abb. 3: Berufsfelder der Absolventen
Quelle: Ecke (2004), S. 118

Was sind die Schwerpunkte der *Tätigkeit* von Sportmanagern?
1. Sind es die klassischen rationalen Management-Funktionen oder die von Mintzberg empirisch ermittelten Management-Rollen?
2. Welche Rolle spielen sportpädagogische Tätigkeiten?

Über die verschiedenen Sektoren hinweg zeigen sich große Gemeinsamkeiten (vgl. Abb. 4).

Zu 1.: Auch zur Beschreibung der tatsächlichen Tätigkeit von Sportmanager reichen die rationalen Managementfunktionen nicht aus. Interpersonelle Kommunikation, Informationsaufgaben und Außendarstellung sowie soziale Aufgaben, also

Elemente der Mintzbergschen Managementrollen, sind zentrale Bestandteile ihrer Tätigkeit.

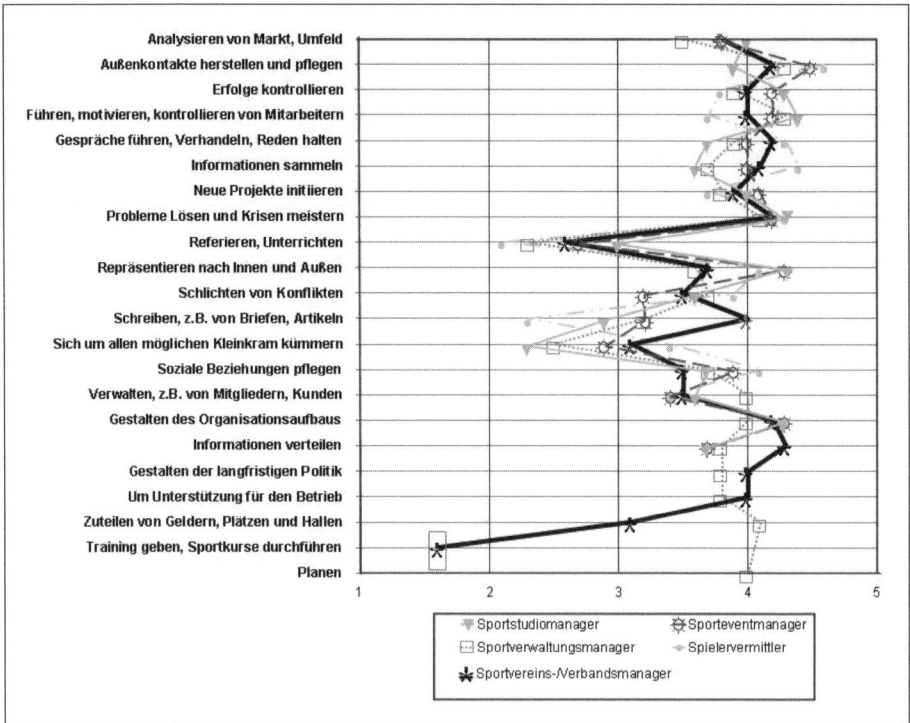

Abb. 4: Die Bedeutung unterschiedlicher Tätigkeitsfelder
(1 = „sehr unwichtig", 5 = „sehr wichtig"; kein Markierungspunkt = keine Messung)

Zu 2.: Sportmanager erfüllen v.a. Führungs- und Verwaltungsaufgaben, weniger sportpädagogische, wie „Referieren und Unterrichten" und „Training geben und Sportkurse durchführen". Letzteres gilt selbst für den Bereich der Sportvereine und -verbände. Die Tätigkeit des Managers hat sich demnach weitgehend von der des Trainers ausdifferenziert. Die einzige Ausnahme bilden in dieser Hinsicht die Fitnessstudios, in denen „Referieren und Unterrichten" noch die relativ größte Rolle spielen. Größere *Unterschiede* zeigen sich noch zwischen den Sportstudiomanagern und den Vereins- und Verbandsmanagern bezogen auf die Tätigkeiten „Schreiben" und „Gespräche führen und Reden halten" sowie „Informationen sammeln" und „Informationen verteilen", die im Verein und Verband – vermutlich im Hinblick auf die Entlastung und Information der vielen Ehrenamtlichen – eine relativ größere Rolle spielen. Während „Außenkontakt herstellen und pflegen" im Eventagenturbereich relativ am wichtigsten ist, weil es kontinuierlich darum geht, Kunden zu akquirieren. Die Spielervermittler kommunizieren am relativ wenigsten schriftlich und müssen sich ähnlich wie die Sportvereinsmanager „um allen möglichen Kleinkram kümmern". Unabhängig von den drei angesprochenen Sektoren: Nonprofit, For-Profit und staatlich konnten Kaiser/Schütte (2004a) anhand von Clusteranalysen drei *Typen von Sportmanagern* identifizieren, die sie als Generalisten (kleine Organisation, alle Tätigkeiten überdurchschnittlich wichtig), Verwalter (kleine Organisation, fast alle Tätigkeiten unterdurchschnittlich wichtig), und Delegierer (große Organisation und von daher vermutlich mehrere Manager, einige Tätigkeiten unterdurchschnittlich wichtig) bezeichnen.

Die Leitfragen zur Ermittlung der zentralen *Kompetenzen* von zukünftigen (!) Sportmanagern waren folgende:
1. Brauchen Sportmanager nur Managementkompetenzen oder auch sportwissenschaftliche Kenntnisse?
2. Benötigen sie nur rein ökonomische, wie sie die klassische deutsche Betriebswirtschaftslehre vermittelt, oder auch interdisziplinäre sozialwissenschaftliche, wie die amerikanische Managementlehre betont?
3. Wird eine allgemeine betriebswirtschaftliche Ausbildung oder eine sportspezifische verlangt, und welches Niveau soll die Ausbildung haben?

Auch hier zeigen sich wieder große Gemeinsamkeiten über die verschiedenen Sektoren hinweg (vgl. Abb. 5).

Zu 1.: Ein Sportmanager muss zwar über Grundwissen über die Sportarten, mit denen er zu tun hat, verfügen, darüber hinausgehendes sportwissenschaftliches Spezialwissen, wie in Sportmedizin oder Trainingswissenschaft, wird aber im Durchschnitt nicht gebraucht.

Zu 2.: Wie in den amerikanischen Untersuchungen zeigt sich, dass Kommunikationsqualifikationen im Bereich PR und Werbung von zentraler Bedeutung sind. Aus dem Kanon der Betriebswirtschaftslehre haben Kenntnisse über Finanzierung, speziell auch Sponsoring und Budgeterstellung den höchsten Stellenwert.

Zu 3.: Die überwiegende Mehrzahl (84 %) der befragten bezahlten Manager in Vereinen und Verbänden waren der Meinung, dass in Zukunft Fachleute gebraucht werden, die sowohl etwas von allgemeiner Betriebswirtschaft als auch von den Spezifika der Sportwirtschaft verstehen. Auch in den anderen Sektoren werden Sportökonomen (akademisch ausgebildeten speziellen Sportmanagern) mindestens ebenso gute Chancen eingeräumt, eingestellt zu werden, wie anderen Betriebswirten. Ihre Tätigkeitsfelder dürften vermutlich jedoch eher in den weichen (Marketing, Management, Kommunikation) als in den harten Feldern der Betriebswirtschaftslehre (Finanzierung, Kostenrechnung) liegen. Für die zukünftige Generation von Sportmanagern wird überwiegend (z.B. zu 62 % von den Vereins- und Verbandsmanagern) eine akademische Ausbildung verlangt.

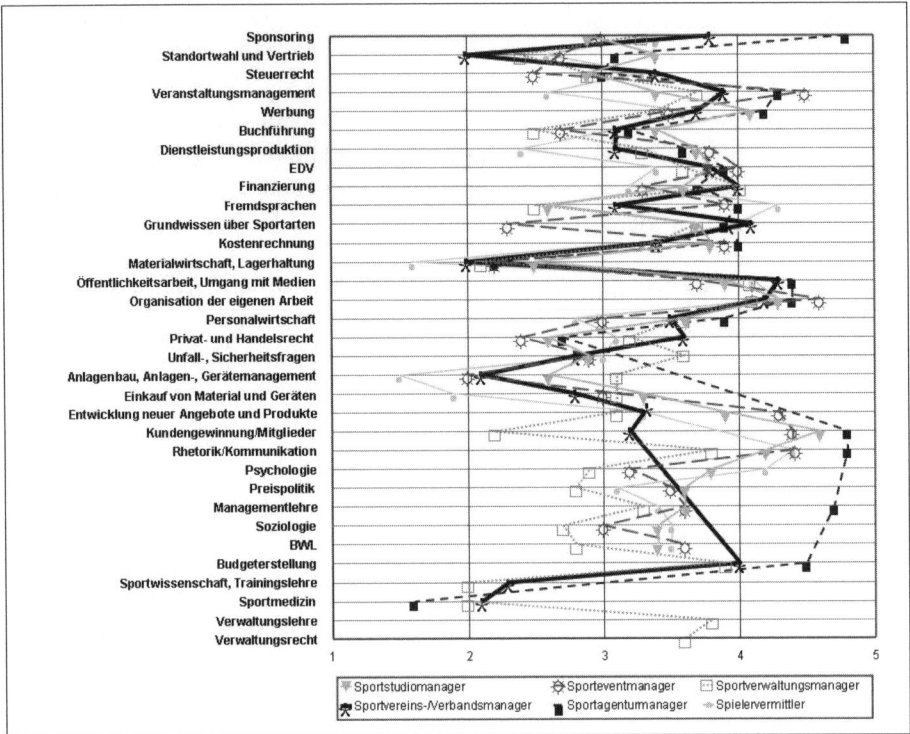

Abb. 5: Erforderliche Kompetenzen
(1 = „sehr unwichtig", 5 = „sehr wichtig"; kein Markierungspunkt = keine Messung)

Wie groß ist die *Heterogenität* der Berufsanforderungen? Zwischen den verschiedenen Sektoren zeigen sich zwar Unterschiede, insgesamt jedoch – wie bereits angeführt – überraschend wenige. Im Vergleich zu Vereinen und Verbänden sind dies v.a. folgende: Bei den Sportmanagern in *Marketingagenturen* wird vergleichsweise mehr Gewicht auf „Entwicklung neuer Angebote und Produkte", „Kundengewinnung" und „Kostenrechung" gelegt, was sich durch die stärkere Markt- und For-Profit-Orientierung erklären lässt. Von Sportmanagern in der *kommunalen Sportverwaltung* werden – nicht überraschend – Kompetenzen im Bereich der Verwaltungslehre und des Verwaltungsrechts erwartet. Bei Sportmanagern in *Eventagenturen* wird vergleichsweise weniger Gewicht auf „Grundwissen über Sportarten", „Anlagen und Geräte", und mehr Gewicht auf „Veranstaltungsmanagement", „Entwicklung neuer Angebote und Produkte" sowie „Kundengewinnung" gelegt. Letzteres ist wiederum durch die stärkere Markt- und For-Profit-Orientierung zu erklären, während der im Vergleich zu den anderen Sektoren niedrigste Sportbezug vermutlich damit zusammen hängt, dass es in den Eventagenturen häufig auch um die Organisation von Nicht-Sportevents geht. Von Sportmanagern in *Fitnessstudios* erwartet man vergleichsweise mehr Kompetenzen in den Feldern „Kundengewinnung", „Preispolitik" und „Buchführung". Auch die „Standortwahl" hat von der

Natur des Angebots her hier eine relativ große Bedeutung. *Spielervermittler* müssen von der Sache her keine Veranstaltungen organisieren, verstehen aber offensichtlich nicht, dass das, was sie machen, eine Dienstleistung ist. Fremdsprachenkenntnisse sind hier noch etwas wichtiger als bei den Agenturen. Diese Ergebnisse zu den sektoralen Differenzen werden durch Nichelmann (1999) bestätigt, der auch nur die analogen, eher doch geringen Unterschiede zwischen For-Profit- und Nonprofit-Organisationen feststellte.

Die große *Bedeutung des Sportbezuges* für Sportmanager wird noch einmal deutlich, wenn man sich den überwiegend starken Sportbezug der befragten Manager ansieht. Viele von ihnen waren oder sind Leistungssportler, ehrenamtliche Vorstandsmitglieder, bezahlte oder ehrenamtliche Trainer oder Breitensportler. Aus dem Rahmen fallen hier wiederum nur die Eventagenturen. Zusammenfassend können wir festhalten: Der Sport verfügt über eine starke, ausschließende Kultur. Betriebswirte ohne Sportbezug haben hier nur geringe Chancen. Das mag sich im Zuge einer fortschreitenden Verberuflichung in den nächsten Jahrzehnten ändern.

Häufig kritisiert werden in diesem Zusammenhang die *Rekrutierungspraktiken* von Sportorganisationen, die – so der Vorwurf – Sportbezug vor fachlicher Qualifikation stellen. Dieser Vorwurf kann anhand vorliegender Daten (Kaiser/Schütte, 2004b) jedoch nicht bestätigt werden. Zumindest nach der Selbsteinschätzung der befragten Sportmanager standen fachliche Gründe wie Erfahrung und Ausbildung bei ihrer Einstellung im Vordergrund. Die Richtigkeit dieser subjektiven Einschätzung wird durch ihre mehrheitlich akademischen Abschlüsse bestätigt. Sportbezug mag ein notwendiges Kriterium für eine Beschäftigung sein, aber kein hinreichendes. Als wichtig eingeschätzt wird jedoch auch die gegenseitige Bekanntheit von Person und Organisation. Offensichtlich muss Qualifikation zusammentreffen mit Erfahrung und gegenseitiger Bekanntheit (Funktion von Praktika), die über eine Beziehung zur Sache, d.h. einen starken Sportbezug, vermittelt wird.

Entsteht im Sportmanagement ein neues ausdifferenziertes Berufsfeld? Wie weit ist der Verberuflichungs- bzw. Professionalisierungsprozess (vgl. obige Definitionen) vorangeschritten? Anzeichen für eine *Verberuflichung* sind deutlich zu erkennen. Ausbildung und Tätigkeit sind zwar nur gering standardisiert, es zeigt sich aber empirisch eine deutliche Homogenität sowohl der Tätigkeiten als der Kompetenzen (vgl. Abb. 4 und 5). Hinzu kommt, dass sich die Tätigkeit von der des Trainers ausdifferenziert hat. V.a. aber ist die Qualität (Arbeitsplatzsicherheit, Gehalt) der Stellen – zumindest verglichen mit anderen außerschulischen Sportberufen – relativ hoch. Die Zahl der bezahlten Managementpositionen im selbstverwalteten Sport ist zwar immer noch relativ zu den ehrenamtlichen sehr klein, aber in den letzten Jahrzehnten deutlich gestiegen. Von einer *Professionalisierung* i.e.S. kann man jedoch nicht sprechen. Zwar ist die Zahl der akademischen Ausbildungsangebote gestiegen, es gibt aber keinerlei Zulassungskontrollen. Es existiert kein einheitlicher Berufsverband, in dem eine erhebliche Zahl von Sportmanagern zusammengefasst ist. Ein Versuch dazu bildet der VSD (Verband für Sportökonomie und Sportmanagement in Deutschland e.V.). Die Etablierung eines besonderen Berufsethos wird in Deutschland bisher noch nicht einmal thematisiert. Dabei muss jedoch berücksichtigt werden, dass es auch grundsätzlich sehr fraglich ist, ob Professionalisierung überhaupt ein angemessener Maßstab ist. Denn selbst was das Management in anderen Bereichen der Wirtschaft anbetrifft, kann man nur sehr eingeschränkt von Professionalisierung sprechen.

19.3.5 Angebot

Wie sieht das Arbeitsangebot nach Quantität, Qualität und Differenzierung aus? Dies hängt einmal von den Zuflüssen aus dem *Bildungsmarkt*, zum zweiten von dem bereits oben angesprochenen Ausmaß von Substitution und Mobilität auf dem Arbeitsmarkt ab. *Quantitativ* hat die Zahl spezieller Ausbildungsstätten und damit auch -plätze in den letzten Jahrzehnten ständig zugenommen. Es existiert leider keine vollständige Liste aller Angebote, noch nicht einmal für den akademischen Bereich. Es sind ungefähr je zehn Universitäten und Fachhochschulen, die solche Programme anbieten. Von den Universitäten verfügt aber z.B. nur die Hälfte über entsprechende Professuren, diese sind zudem häufig fachlich kombiniert mit Sportsoziologie. Mit dem Wachstum der Ausbildungsplätze reagiert der Bildungsmarkt auf eine entsprechend hohe Nachfrage. Auf die 90 Plätze des Bachelors „Sportmanagement und Sportkommunikation" an der Deutschen Sporthochschule bewarben sich z.B. 2007 ca. 500 Kandidaten und Kandidatinnen. Bezogen auf die Aufnahmekraft des Arbeitsmarktes ist allerdings eher zu befürchten, dass ein Überangebot erzeugt wird. Nach dem *Niveau der Ausbildung* kann man akademische Ausbildungen (neuerdings weiter differenziert nach Bachelor und Master), Ausbildungsberufe und Ausbildungskurse unterscheiden. Die *Inhalte der Ausbildung* können aus vier Teilen bestehen, die unterschiedlich gewichtet werden: allgemeine Betriebs- und Volkswirtschaftslehre, Sportökonomie/Sportmanagement, Sportpraxis und allgemeine Sportwissenschaft (Hovemann, 2003). An den Universitäten sind es fast ausnahmslos die sportwissenschaftlichen und nicht die betriebswirtschaftlichen Institute, die solche Ausbildungen anbieten. Das gilt selbst für die USA, obwohl man hier bereits auf eine mindestens vierzigjährige Tradition zurückblicken kann. Für die Betriebswirtschaftslehre an den Universitäten ist offensichtlich diese Arbeitsmarktnische zu klein, während die Sportwissenschaft – wenn auch widerstrebend – hier ein außerschulisches Arbeitsfeld für Sportwissenschaftler erkannt hat und im zunehmenden Wettbewerb der Hochschulen auf die hohe Bildungsnachfrage reagieren muss.

19.4 Fallstudie

Fallstudie „Traumberuf Fußballmanager"

„Die Bundesliga als Jobmaschine" – unter dieser Überschrift konnte man in der Welt am Sonntag vom 29.07.2007 u.a. Folgendes lesen (Flohr, 2007):

„Der deutsche Profifußball erlebt derzeit einen Aufschwung, der den bundesweiten Fortschritt noch in den Schatten stellt. […] Seit Jahren wächst die Zahl der Arbeitsplätze rasant an. In der Saison 2005/06 arbeiten laut Deutscher Fußball Liga (DFL) in der Bundesliga und Zweiten Liga 3.419 Festangestellte (gemeint sind Vollzeit-Angestellte, hinzu kommen 778 Teilzeit-Angestellte – H.-D.H.), im Schnitt also 95 pro Club. Das waren 569 mehr als im Vorjahr und (sic) entspricht damit einer Steigerung von fast 20 Prozent. […] Der sportliche Bereich spielt dabei lediglich eine untergeordnete Rolle. Die Zahl der Profispieler in den Kadern ist kaum gestiegen, neue Arbeitsplätze finden sich eher noch im Scouting und Trainerstab […] Das Gros der Stellen wird aber abseits des Platzes geschaffen – in den Geschäftsstellen, Fanshops und Stadien. […] Allerdings gab es auch einen sehr großen Nachholbedarf, viele Clubs waren bis vor kurzem ja noch Drei-Mann-Unternehmen'" (Zitat von Oliver Koppel, Fußballexperte des Deutschen Instituts für Wirtschaft Köln – H.-D. H.).

Rückt damit der Traum vieler Sportmanagement-Studierender, Fußball-Manager zu werden, einer Verwirklichung näher? Was wissen wir über die Quantität und Qualität dieser begehrten Arbeitsplätze speziell im Fußball und im Profisport generell?

Ohne Zweifel gibt es in Profisportclubs und -ligen heute mehr Arbeitsplätze im Managementbereich als früher. Dennoch darf man nicht übersehen, dass die Zahl solcher Stellen verglichen mit der Anzahl der Studierenden weiterhin verschwindend gering ist. Grundsätzlich muss man dazu erst einmal zur Kenntnis nehmen, dass wirtschaftlich gesehen der Zuschauersport und seine Produkte eine wesentlich geringere Rolle spielen als der aktive Sport. Bezogen auf das Bruttoinlandsprodukt können z.B. von den von Meek (1997) für die USA errechneten 152 Mrd. US-$ Sportprodukt höchsten 20-30 Mrd. dem Zuschauersport zugerechnet werden. Speziell bezogen auf die Ausgaben privater Haushalte waren es bei Weber/Schnieder/Kortlücke/Horak (1995) für Deutschland 1991 nur ca. 2 von 32 Mrd. DM, die allerdings nur speziell auf Eintrittsgelder entfielen. Bei aller Unklarheit der Zurechnungen von z.B. Reisekosten u.ä. und unter Berücksichtigung von staatlichen und unternehmerischen Ausgaben in den Bereichen Investitionen, Medien, Sponsoring usw., dürfte trotzdem Fakt bleiben, dass die wirtschaftliche Bedeutung des aktiven Sports ein Vielfaches der des passiven Sports ausmacht. Unsere Wahrnehmung ist hier verzerrt, weil der Zuschauersport nicht nur in den Medien, sondern bisher auch in der Wissenschaft die höhere Aufmerksamkeit erfährt. Daraus folgt, dass auch die Arbeitsfelder für Sportökonomen –

selbst wenn man den höheren Kommerzialisierungsgrad des Zuschauersports ein-kalkuliert – mehr in diesen Feldern liegen (vgl. Absolventenstudien, z.B. Ecke, 2004). Verglichen mit den USA ist jedoch der Grad der Professionalisierung des Managements im Profisportbereich in Deutschland immer noch sehr gering, so dass ein weiteres Wachstum möglich wäre. Im Management- und Verwaltungsbe-reich der Profi-Fußballvereine sind im Durchschnitt 29 Personen beschäftigt, im Handball sind es 6, im Eishockey 9, im Basketball 7 (Lohmar, 2007). Dagegen hatten die Miami Heat, ein Team in der NBA z.b. 1993 40 fest Angestellte in Management und Verwaltung beschäftigt, die Philadelphia Sixers 2004 bereits 132 (Masteralexis, 2004). Während in der DFL zurzeit ca. 50 Hauptamtliche be-schäftigt sind, waren es in der NBA z.B. 1993 148. Allerdings muss man bei dem Vergleich dieser Zahlen berücksichtigen, dass ein großer Teil des Managements im deutschen Fußball an Marketingagenturen outgesourct wurde, deren Personal und Beschäftigungschancen man also entsprechend einbeziehen müsste.

Was die Qualität der Arbeit angeht, verfügen wir über eine Schilderung des be-kanntesten deutschen Fußballmanagers Uli Hoeneß (1991, S. 8-16):
„Ich bin in erster Linie nicht fürs Geldausgeben, sondern in erster Linie fürs Geldeinnehmen zuständig. [...] Aber ich glaube, meine Stärke ist, daß ich gut de-legieren kann. [...] Alles was bei uns passiert, bis die Mannschaft den Trainings-bzw. Fußballplatz betritt, hat irgendwo mit meiner Person zu tun. Ob wir einen Spieler nach München holen, diese Entscheidung trifft sportlich einzig und allein Jupp Heynckes. [...] Dann prüfe ich die wirtschaftliche Situation, Vertragssitua-tion und Ablösesituation, gehe zum Präsidium und stelle unsere Vorschläge dar. [...] Und ich glaube, eine große Stärke von uns ist, daß wir gemeinsam richtige und gemeinsam falsche Entscheidungen treffen. [...] Dann bin ich zuständig für den gesamten PR-Bereich. [...] Das heißt, ich bin jeden Tag ein bis zwei Stunden mit der Presse beschäftigt. [...] Ich bin zuständig für den Anzeigenteil unserer Stadionzeitung, [...] für den gesamten Lizenzbereich (Merchandising – H.-D. H.) des FC Bayern. [...] Jedenfalls, Sie sehen, das sind alles Dinge, die ich auch ma-che. In der Zeitung stehe ich nur, wenn ich mal wieder für drei Millionen Spieler zu teuer gekauft habe."
In wie weit ist Uli Hoeneß' Schilderung repräsentativ für Profisportmanager? In der Vereins- und Verbandsstudie von Horch/Niessen/Schütte (2003) wurden auch Manager sowie Präsidenten und Trainer aus Profisportclubs des Fußballs, Handballs und Eishockeys befragt. Wenn man speziell die Antworten der fünf-zehn Profisport-Manager mit den oben geschilderten aller Vereins- und Ver-bandsmanager vergleicht, zeigen sich wiederum kaum Unterschiede. Ihre wich-tigsten Tätigkeiten sind auf einer Skala von 1 „sehr unwichtig" bis 5 „sehr wichtig": „Außenkontakte herstellen und pflegen" (Mittelwert 4,4 auf einer Skala von 1 bis 5), „Gespräche führen, Verhandeln, Reden halten" (4,4), „Erfolge kon-trollieren" (4,4), „Gestalten der langfristigen Vereinspolitik" (4,3) und „Führen,

Motivieren, Kontrollieren von Mitarbeitern" (4,3). Bei den gewünschten Kompetenzen wird Hoeneß in dem Sinne bestätigt, dass Finanzierungsaspekte etwas mehr im Vordergrund stehen als im Durchschnitt. Auf Rang eins liegt „Sponsoring" (4,6) noch vor „PR" und „Werbung" (je 4,3). „Budgeterstellung" (4,1) und „Finanzierung" (3,9) liegen gleichauf mit „Grundwissen über die Sportart" (4,1) sowie „Veranstaltungsmanagement" (3,9) und „Organisation der eigenen Arbeit" (3,9). Auch die Profisportmanager waren überwiegend der Meinung, dass in Zukunft ein spezifisch sportökonomisches (60 %) Studium (67 %), die beste Voraussetzung zur Erfüllung ihrer Aufgaben bieten würde. Aus dem, was aus der Presse bekannt ist, kann man vermuten, dass, um im Profisportbereich Fuß zu fassen, Beziehungen noch wichtiger sind als in anderen Sportmanagementbereichen. Gefragt danach, was sie glauben, warum sie ihre Stelle bekommen haben, kreuzen auch 72 % an, weil man sie bereits kannte. Qualifikation (79 %) und Berufserfahrung (72 %) werden aber auch hier als wesentlich wichtiger eingestuft als die eigene Sportkarriere (29 %). Diese Einschätzung wird einerseits unterstützt durch die Tatsache, dass 53 % ein Studium und zwar überwiegend ein wirtschaftswissenschaftliches (53 %) im Vergleich zu einem sportwissenschaftlichen (27 %) absolviert haben. Andererseits ist jedoch auch hier nicht zu übersehen, dass die Profisportmanager einen starken Sportbezug aufweisen. 53 % waren Leistungssportler, 33 % Trainer. Seit 1991, der Schilderung von Hoeneß, bzw. seit 1996, der Erhebung unserer Daten, ist der Verberuflichungsprozess jedoch gerade im Profisport weiter vorangekommen, so dass die wirtschaftliche Kompetenz an Bedeutung zu- und die sportliche Kompetenz an Bedeutung abgenommen haben dürfte.

Der Sport-Bezug dürfte jedoch – wie ein Blick in die USA zeigt – weiterhin für viele Positionen im Profisportmanagement von großer Bedeutung bleiben. Mit wachsender Anzahl von Managern je Organisation dürfte sich zudem das Aufgabenspektrum verengt, d.h. die Tätigkeit weiter spezialisiert haben.

19.5 Fazit und Ausblick

Arbeitsmärkte unterscheiden sich in wesentlichen Punkten sowohl von Produkt- als von anderen Faktormärkten. Sie sind – aufgrund gewerkschaftlicher und verbandsmäßiger Zusammenschlüsse – häufig zweistufig organisiert. Nachfrage und Angebot sind abgeleitet von Produkt- bzw. Bildungsmärkten. Die Bindung an menschliche Träger und die zentrale Bedeutung der Arbeit für die Lebensqualität führt teilweise zu anomalen Reaktionen. Speziell der Arbeitsmarkt für Profisportler weist darüber hinaus viele Besonderheiten auf, wie ein Monopson der Liga, Draft-Systeme oder Gehaltsbeschränkungen bzw. Superstargehälter. Zudem stehen in vielen Fällen nicht nur erwerbswirtschaftliche Ziele im Fordergrund, sondern auch sportliche, was zur Folge hat, dass die üblichen ökonomischen Lehrbuch-Gesetzmäßigkeiten entsprechend nur eingeschränkt gelten.

In der Arbeitsmarkt- und Berufsforschung geht es darum, die Art des Marktes sowie Quantität, Qualität und Differenzierung der Arbeitskräftenachfrage und des Arbeitskräfteangebots empirisch zu ermitteln und gegenüberzustellen sowie Ausmaß und Art der Zu- und Abwanderung auf diesem Markt zu bestimmen. Der Arbeitsmarkt für Sportmanager ist jung, offen und unreguliert. Über seine quantitative Bedeutung und zukünftige Entwicklung gibt es nur wenige Informationen. Ohne Zweifel ist jedoch seine Bedeutung in den letzten Jahrzehnten gewachsen. Ausgehend von den sport-typischen ehrenamtlichen, amateurhaften Tätigkeiten zeigt sich eine deutliche Verberuflichung. Eine professionelle Schließung des Arbeitsmarktes ist jedoch nicht zu erwarten. Sportmanager kann im Prinzip jeder werden. Qualitativ sind die Anforderungen an die Kompetenzen zukünftiger Sportmanager gut untersucht. Verlangt werden v.a. kommunikative Fähigkeiten und finanzwirtschaftliche Kenntnisse. Dabei zeigen sich zwar Unterschiede zwischen verschiedenen Sportbranchen z.B. dem For-Profit und dem Nonprofit-Bereich, die jedoch erstaunlich gering sind. Typisch und wichtig für dieses Berufsfeld ist der Sportbezug. Zwar werden keine sportwissenschaftlichen Spezialkenntnisse gebraucht, verlangt werden aber Grundkenntnisse der Sportart, deren Produkte die jeweilige Organisation vertreibt. Der Sport verfügt in Deutschland über eine starke, ausschließende Kultur. Betriebswirte ohne Sportbezug haben hier nur geringe Chancen. Das Interesse an einer sportbezogenen Beschäftigung wird mit entsprechenden Gehaltseinbußen bezahlt. Beides – Sportbezug und Lohnhöhe – mag sich im Zuge einer fortschreitenden Verberuflichung in den nächsten Jahrzehnten ändern. Daher bedürfen Arbeitsmarkt und Berufsfeld einer kontinuierlichen Erforschung. Die Entwicklung in den USA, in denen es entsprechende akademische Ausbildungen bereits seit den sechziger Jahren gibt, zeigt u.a., dass die Nachfrage auf dem Bildungsmarkt ungebrochen hoch ist und weiterhin fast ausnahmslos durch sport-, nicht durch wirtschaftswissenschaftliche Fakultäten abgedeckt wird.

Kontrollfragen

1. Wie erklären Ökonomen Nachfrage und Angebot auf Arbeitsmärkten?
2. Welche Spezifika des Arbeitsmarktes, des Arbeitsangebotes und der Arbeitsnachfrage gelten für Profisportler bzw. Sportmanager?
3. Was versteht man unter Verberuflichung und Professionalisierung, und wie würden Sie die Entwicklung des Sportmanagements in Deutschland anhand dieser Kriterien beurteilen?
4. Was bedeutet die Aussage, dass der Arbeitsmarkt für Sportmanager jung, offen und unreguliert ist?
5. Benennen Sie die Fragestellungen der Arbeitsmarkt- und Berufsforschung und erläutern Sie die Vorgehensweise und Schwierigkeit bei der Erstellung einer Prognose der Entwicklung der Arbeitskräftenachfrage nach Sportmanagern?
6. Wie könnte man das Berufsfeld für Sportmanager systematisch beschreiben?

7. Welche Bedeutung haben die Managementfunktionen bzw. Managerrollen zur Beschreibung der Tätigkeit von Sportmanagern?
8. Wie wichtig ist der Sportbezug für Tätigkeit, Kompetenz und Rekrutierung von Sportmanagern?
9. Was sind die Gemeinsamkeiten und Unterschiede der Tätigkeitsschwerpunkte und Kompetenzanforderungen verschiedener Sportmanagementbereiche?
10. Wie sieht die Quantität und Qualität der Nachfrage nach Managern in Profisportclubs und -ligen aus?

Literaturverzeichnis

Akerlof, Georg A. (1976): The Economics of Caste and of the Rat Race and Other Woeful Tales, in: The Quarterly Journal of Economics, Heft 4, S. 599-617.

Becker, Gary S. (1964): Human Capital, New York.

Breuer, Christoph / Thiel, Ansgar (Hrsg.) (2005): Handbuch Sportmanagement, Schorndorf.

Büch, Martin-Peter / Schellhaaß, Horst-Manfred (1984): Ökonomische Aspekte der Transferentschädigung im bezahlten Mannschaftssport, in: Heinemann, Klaus (Hrsg.): Texte zur Ökonomie des Sports, Schorndorf, S. 215-236.

Buchmeier, Wilfried / Zieschang, Klaus (1992): Sportökonomen in Beruf und Studium. Bericht über eine Untersuchung im Auftrag des Bundesministeriums für Bildung und Wissenschaft, Schorndorf.

Buchmeier, Wilfried / Zieschang, Klaus (1996): Zur beruflichen Situation ehemaliger Studentinnen und Studenten des Diplomstudiengangs Sportökonomie in Bayreuth, in: Horch, Heinz-Dieter / Kreiß, Friedhelm / Laflör, Sylvia (Red.): Arbeitsmarkt Sport, Ministerium für Stadtentwicklung, Kultur und Sport des Landes Nordrhein-Westfalen, Düsseldorf, S. 62-72.

Cachay, Klaus / Thiel, Ansgar (1999): Ausbildung ins Ungewisse?, Aachen.

Cachay, Klaus / Thiel, Ansgar / Meier, Heiko (2001): Der organisierte Sport als Arbeitsmarkt. Eine Studie zu Erwerbsarbeitspotenzialen in Sportvereinen und Sportverbänden, Schorndorf.

DeSensi, Joy T./ Kelley, Dennie R. / Blanton Mary Dale / Beitel, Patricia A. (1990): Sport Management and Curricular Evaluation and Needs Assessment, in: Journal of Sport Management, Heft 1, S. 31-58.

Ecke, Marion (2004): Der Übergang vom Bildungs- in das Beschäftigungssystem. Eine empirische Studie zur Berufseinmündungsphase von Diplomsportwissenschaftlern mit dem Schwerpunkt Ökonomie und Management und Diplomsportökonomen, Diplomarbeit, Deutsche Sporthochschule Köln.

Fayol, Henry (1929): Allgemeine und industrielle Verwaltung, München u.a.

Flohr, Sven (2007): Die Bundesliga als Jobmaschine, http://www.welt.de/wams_print/article1062888/Die_Bundesliga_als_Jobmaschine.htlm (Zugriff: 20.09.2007).

Frick, Bernd / Prinz, Joachim (2005): Spielerallokation und Spielerentlohnung im professionellen Team-Sport. Betriebswirtschaftliche Analyse und Empfehlungen für das Vereinsmanagement, Köln.

Hartmann-Tews, Ilse / Mrazek, Joachim (2006): Was kommt nach dem Studium? Kurier. Informationen der Deutschen Sporthochschule Köln, Ausgabe 2, Beilage.

Heinemann, Klaus / Dietrich, Knut / Schubert, Manfred: (1990): Akademikerarbeitslosigkeit und neue Formen des Erwerbsverhaltens. Dargestellt am Beispiel arbeitsloser Sportlehrer, Weinheim.

Heinzel, Matthias (1997): Anforderungen deutscher Unternehmen an betriebswirtschaftliche Hochschulabsolventen, Wiesbaden.

Hettlich, Lambert (1998): Die Funktion des Verkaufsrepräsentanten bei großen Sportartikelherstellern, Diplomarbeit, Deutsche Sporthochschule Köln.

Hoeneß, Uli (1991): Einblicke in die praktische Arbeit eines Fußballmanagers, in: Württembergischer Fußballverband (Hrsg.): Wirtschaftliche und rechtliche Aspekte zu Problemen des Berufsfußballs, Stuttgart, S. 7-18.

Horch, Heinz-Dieter / Hovemann, Gregor / Schubert, Manfred (2007): Bezahlte Mitarbeit im Sportverein, in: Breuer, Christoph (Hrsg.): Sportentwicklungsbericht (2005/2006). Analyse zur Situation der Sportvereine in Deutschland, Köln, S. 166-195.

Horch, Heinz-Dieter / Kreiß, Friedhelm / Laflör, Sylvia (Red.) (1996): Arbeitsmarkt Sport, Ministerium für Stadtentwicklung, Kultur und Sport des Landes Nordrhein-Westfalen, Düsseldorf.

Horch, Heinz-Dieter / Niessen, Christoph / Schütte, Norbert (2003): Sportmanager in Vereinen und Verbänden, Köln.

Horch, Heinz-Dieter / Schütte, Norbert (2003): Kommunale Sportverwaltung. Analysen zur Verwaltungsreform und zum Berufsfeld, Köln.

Hovemann, Gregor (2003): Der Markt für Sportmanagement-Ausbildungen. Bedingungen und Perspektiven der international erfolgreichen Positionierung von Bildungsdienstleistungen im Sport, Köln.

Hovemann, Gregor / Kaiser, Sebastian / Schütte, Norbert (2003): Der Sporteventmanager. Ergebnisse einer Berufsfeldanalyse, Düsseldorf.

Kaiser, Sebastian (2006): Das Sportstudiomanagement. Anforderungen, Rekrutierung, Professionalisierung, Saarbrücken.

Kaiser, Sebastian / Schütte, Norbert (2004a): Performance Patterns of Sport Managers. Further Implications for adequate educational design. Presentation at the International Conference on Leisure, Tourism and Sport, Köln.

Kaiser, Sebastian / Schütte, Norbert (2004b): Recruitment Pattern of Sport Managers, Unpublished Manuscript, Köln.

Katz, Robert L. (1974): Skills of an effective administrator, in: Harvard Business Review, Heft 5, S. 90-112.

Kesenne, Stefan L.J. (1996): League Management in professional team sports with win maximizing clubs, in: European Journal for Sport Management, Heft 2, S. 14-22.

Lambrecht, Keith W. (1991): Research, theory, and practice, in: Parkhouse, Bonnie L. (Hrsg.): The Management of Sport, St. Louis, S. 27-40.

Lazear, Edward P. (1998): Personnel Economics for Managers, New York.

Lohmar, Oliver (2002): Berufsfeldanalyse von Sportmanagern. Ein Vergleich der Qualifikationen mit Managern der kommunalen Sportverwaltung und Managern in Sportvereinen/-verbänden, Diplomarbeit, Deutsche Sporthochschule Köln.

Lohmar, Oliver (2007): Personalmanagement im Profisport, Dissertation, Deutsche Sporthochschule Köln.

Masteralexis, Lisa. P. (2005): Professional Sports, in: Masteralexis, Lisa. P. / Barr, Carol A. / Hums, Mary A. (Hrsg.): Principles and Practice of Sport Management, Gaitherburg, S. 195-220.

Meek, Alfie (1997): An Estimate of the Size and Supported Economic Activity of the Sports Industry in the United States, in: Sport Marketing Quarterly, Heft 4, S. 15-21.

Meyer, Bernd / Ahlert, Gert (2000): Die ökonomischen Perspektiven des Sports. Eine empirische Analyse für die Bundesrepublik Deutschland, Schorndorf.

Mintzberg, Henry (1973): The nature of managerial work, New York u.a.

Nichelmann, Carsten (1999): Sportmanager heute - Eine empirische Analyse theoretischer und prakischer Anforderungen des Tätigkeitsfeldes, in: Horch, Heinz-Dieter / Heydel, Jörg / Sierau, Axel (Hrsg.): Professionalisierung im Sportmanagement, Aachen, S. 287-307.

Raab, Florian (2007). Eine Berufsfeldanalyse von Spielervermittlern im deutschen Fußball, Diplomarbeit, Deutsche Sporthochschule Köln.

Robbins, Stephen P. / DeCenzo, David A. (1998): Fundamentals of Management. Essential Concepts and Applications. Upper Saddle River.

Rottenberg, Simon (1956): The Baseball Players' Labor Market, in: The Journal of Political Economy, Heft 3, S. 242-258.

Schirmer, Frank (1992): Arbeitsverhalten von Managern. Bestandsaufnahme, Kritik und Weiterentwicklung der Aktivitätsforschung, Wiesbaden.

Schor, Juliet B. (1991): The Overworked American. The Unexpected Decline of Leisure, New York.

Schubert, Manfred (1991): Neue Handlungsstrategien von Akademikern im Übergang von der Hochschule in den Beruf. Eine empirische Untersuchung zu Formen und Problemen des Einstiegs und Verbleibs von Sportlehrern in außerschulischen Tätigkeitsfeldern, Hamburg.

Staehle, Wolfgang H. (1991): Management. Eine verhaltenswissenschaftliche Perspektive, München.

Ulbrich, Holley H. / Warner, Mellie L. (1990): Managerial Economics, New York.

Weber, Max (1972): Wirtschaft und Gesellschaft, Tübingen.

Weber, Wolfgang (1996): Sportnachfrage und Arbeitsmarktnachfrage, in: Horch, Heinz-Dieter / Kreiß, Friedhelm / Laflör, Sylvia (Red.) (1996): Arbeitsmarkt Sport, Ministerium für Stadtentwicklung, Kultur und Sport des Landes Nordrhein-Westfalen, Düsseldorf, S. 6-16.

Weber, Wolfgang / Schnieder, Claudia / Kortlücke, Norbert / Horak, Birgit (1995): Die wirtschaftliche Bedeutung des Sports, Schorndorf.

Weiterführende Ressourcen

Links

Arbeitgeberverband Deutscher Fitness und Gesundheitsanlagen:
   http://www.dssv.de

Europäische Sponsoring-Börse:
   http://www.esb-online.com

Internationale Leitmesse für Fitness und Wellness:
   http://www.fibo-messe.com

Joborama (Jobbörse):
   http://www.joborama.de

Monster (Jobbörse):
   http://www.monster.de

Sportartikel Zeitung (Fachzeitschrift):
   http://www.saz.de

Sportbusiness Network (Internetportal):
   http://www.sportbusiness.com

Sportcareers (Jobbörse):
   http://www.sportcareers.com

Sportjob (Jobbörse):
   http://www.sportjob.de

Kapitel 20: Zusammenfassung und Ausblick

André Bühler   Gerd Nufer

Lernziele

Nach der Durchsicht dieses Kapitels sollte der Leser in der Lage sein,

- eine Zusammenfassung zu den in diesem Sammelband behandelten Themen zu geben.
- zu erklären, wie die zukünftige Entwicklung auf dem Wirtschaftsmarkt Sport aussehen könnten.
- zukünftige Erfolgsfaktoren im Sportmanagement zu nennen.
- die potenzielle zukünftige Entwicklung im Sportmarketing zu beschreiben.

Überblick über das Kapitel

In diesem abschließenden Kapitel erfolgt zunächst eine zusammenfassende Diskussion der verschiedenen Teilbereiche des vorliegenden Bandes und der einzelnen Kapitel. Dabei wird auf die Hauptaussagen der jeweiligen Kapitel eingegangen sowie ein Fazit zu jedem Teil gezogen. Daran anknüpfend setzen sich die Herausgeber des Bandes mit der Zukunft des Sportmanagements im Allgemeinen bzw. der des Sportmarketing im Besonderen auseinander und ziehen ein abschließendes Gesamtfazit.

20.1 Zusammenfassung und Diskussion

In den folgenden Abschnitten werden die Erkenntnisse der vier Teile des Sammelbandes sowie der jeweiligen Kapitel zusammengefasst und besprochen.

20.1.1 Betriebswirtschaftslehre und Sport (Teil I, Kapitel 1-3)

Im ersten Teil des Sammelbandes wurde unter der Überschrift *Betriebswirtschaftslehre und Sport – ein Überblick* das moderne Sportmanagement zum einen aus betriebswirtschaftlicher und zum anderen aus sportwissenschaftlicher Sicht beschrieben.

Im einleitenden Kapitel *Sportmanagement und Sportmarketing: Einführung und Perspektive* skizzierten die Herausgeber dieses Buches zunächst die Entwicklung der Sportökonomie und beschrieben den aktuellen Stand des Sportmanagement. Dabei wurde deutlich, dass viele Sportorganisationen heutzutage aufgrund ihrer Umsatzzahlen und Mitarbeiterstärke zwar mit mittelständischen Unternehmen vergleichbar sind, dass aber zahlreiche Sportclubs und -verbände immer noch ehrenamtlich und eher unprofessionell geführt werden. Als Problem wurde der Mangel an betriebswirtschaftlichem Wissen sowie fehlendes Verständnis für ökonomische Managementansätze in Sportbetrieben identifiziert. Die fachlichen Fähigkeiten und ein allgemeines Verständnis für betriebswirtschaftliche Themen sind allerdings unverzichtbar, um solides Wirtschaften sicherzustellen. Daraus ergibt sich die Forderung an Sportorganisationen, spezifisch ausgebildete Sportmanager anzustellen, die zum einen das betriebswirtschaftliche Know-how mitbringen und zum anderen um die Besonderheiten des Sports wissen – Besonderheiten, die das Sportbusiness an sich, aber auch das Sportprodukt und v.a. den Sportkonsumenten betreffen. Moderne Sportbetriebe müssen somit betriebswirtschaftlich geführt werden, man kann jedoch Sportclubs- und verbände nicht wie jedes andere Wirtschaftsunternehmen führen und managen. Vor diesem Hintergrund wurde der vorliegende Sammelband verfasst. Um eine einheitliche Sichtweise im gesamten Sammelband zu gewährleisten, wurde der Fokus auf professionelle Sportbetriebe im Spitzensport festgelegt.

In Kapitel 2 stellten Christoph Breuer, Pamela Wicker und Tim Pawlowski den *Wirtschafts- und Wachstumsmarkt Sport* aus der sportwissenschaftlichen Perspektive vor. Im Detail wurde die Anbieter- als auch die Nachfragerseite beschrieben und dabei auf die Besonderheiten des Sports eingegangen. Die Autoren betonten, dass Sportmanagement nur dann effektiv sein kann, wenn es die Spezifika des Sports als Wirtschaftsgut kennt und hinreichend berücksichtigt. Eine wichtige Kernaussage des Beitrages bezieht sich auf das Verhältnis zwischen Praxis und Theorie: Um speziell im Bereich des professionellen Zuschauersports in Deutschland effektiv und effizient agieren zu können, sollten zukünftig verstärkt wissenschaftliche Befunde generiert werden, auf die das Sportmanagement zurückgreifen kann. Die Autoren wiesen allerdings auch darauf hin, dass der Großteil der Studien bisher aus dem nordamerikanischen Raum stammt und die gewonnenen Erkenntnisse aufgrund der unterschiedlichen Organisation und Systemstruktur nur bedingt auf Europa und Deutschland übertragbar sind. Im europäischen – v.a. aber auch im deutschen – Raum ist eine verstärkte wissenschaftliche Auseinandersetzung mit sportökonomischen Themen nötig. Wichtig ist in diesem Zusammenhang auch die Praxisorientierung der sportökonomischen Forschung sowie die Umsetzungsmöglichkeiten in der Praxis.

Im dritten Kapitel präsentierten Gerd Nufer und Carsten Rennhak die *betriebswirtschaftlichen Grundlagen des Sportmanagements* – aus der Sicht der Betriebswirtschaftslehre. Mit der institutionellen und der funktionellen Betriebswirtschaftslehre wurden zwei grundlegende Systematisierungsansätze der BWL vorgestellt. Außerdem wurden die unterschiedlichen Arten von Betrieben klassifiziert, die verschiedenen Zielsetzungen eines Unternehmens erläutert und das Ökonomische Prinzip erörtert. Die Gründung des Unternehmens, die Standortwahl, die Rechtsformwahl und Entscheidungen über Unternehmenszusammenschlüsse wurden als die wichtigsten konstitutiven Unternehmensentscheidungen identifiziert. Ein weiteres zentrales Thema der allgemeinen Betriebswirtschaftslehre sind die unterschiedlichen Führungsmodelle, die einem Unternehmen und seinen Führungskräften zur Verfügung stehen. In den einzelnen Abschnitten wurde dabei kontinuierlich die Brücke zum Sport und zum Sportmanagement geschlagen. Dieses dritte Kapitel zeigte zum einen die Vielfalt der Betriebswirtschaftslehre auf und zum anderen wurde deutlich, wie wichtig ein grundlegendes betriebswirtschaftliches Verständnis für moderne Sportmanager ist.

535

Der erste Teil des Sammelbandes hatte die Funktion, den aktuellen Stand der Sportökonomie darzulegen und einen Rahmen für die weiteren Beiträge des Buches vorzugeben. Das Sportmanagement wurde sowohl aus Sicht des Sports als auch aus Sicht der Betriebswirtschaftslehre betrachtet. Als Kernaussage dieses ersten Teils kann festgehalten werden, dass sich Sportclubs und -verbände heutzutage verstärkt mit den Prinzipien des modernen Sportmanagement auseinandersetzen müssen. Das moderne Sportmanagement kombiniert dabei die betriebswirtschaftlichen Grundlagen und Ansätze mit den Besonderheiten des Sports.

20.1.2 Sportmanagement (Teil II, Kapitel 4-12)

Der zweite Teil des Sammelbandes befasste sich unter dem Titel *Sportmanagement – die Anwendung klassischer Disziplinen der Betriebswirtschaftslehre im Sport* ausführlich mit dem Sportmanagement. Dabei wurde das Management in den klassischen betriebswirtschaftlichen Betätigungsfeldern konsequent auf den Bereich des Sports übertragen.

In Kapitel 4 erläuterte Christian Keller in seinem Beitrag *Strategisches Management im Sport* die zentrale Aufgabe der Unternehmensführung. Zunächst wurden allgemeine Ansätze eines strategischen Managements für Unternehmen klassischer Wirtschaftsbranchen vorgestellt. Darauf aufbauend wurden die Besonderheiten und Inhalte des strategischen Managements in Teamsportunternehmen erläutert und die grundsätzlichen Möglichkeiten und Werkzeuge eines strategischen Managements für Sportbetriebe dargestellt. Der Autor zeigte, dass das strategische Management eine systematische Unternehmensentwicklung inmitten sich dynamisch verändernder Umweltverhältnisse ermöglicht. Da sich gerade im Sport die Anforderungen und Rahmenbedingungen in den letzten Jahren grundlegend verändert haben, müssen Sportorganisationen, die sich nachhaltig im Wettbewerb behaupten möchten, entsprechend gewappnet sein. Aktuelle Studien belegen, dass nur wenige Sportclubs ein organisiertes und koordiniertes strategisches Management implementiert haben. Christian Keller fordert daher eine intensivere Beschäftigung mit dem Thema seitens der Sportorganisationen, die aufgrund der Unsicherheiten im sportlichen Umfeld und der Besonderheiten im Wirtschaftsmarkt Sport verstärkt strategische Szenarien für die langfristige Entwicklung der eigenen Organisation entwerfen müssen.

Frank Daumann, Mathias Langer und Markus Breuer beleuchteten im fünften Kapitel die *Planung im Sport*. Berücksichtigung findet dabei auch die Entscheidungslehre sowie die Kontrolle. Die Autoren veranschaulichten, dass eine strukturierte Planung erheblich zum Erfolg einer jeden Sportorganisation beitragen kann. Der Planungsprozess mit seinen Phasen Zielsetzung, Problemanalyse, Alternativensuche, Prognose sowie Bewertung und Entscheidung wurde im Detail erläutert. Die Autoren erklärten die besonderen Rahmenbedingungen und daraus resultierenden Herausforderungen für Sportorganisationen bezüglich der Planung. Im Zuge der

Kommerzialisierung und Professionalisierung des Sports ergeben sich für Sport-clubs und -verbände die Notwendigkeit, Leitbilder zu erstellen und die strategische Ausrichtung zu planen. Die Planung des sportlichen Erfolgs geht dabei mit der Pla-nung des wirtschaftlichen Erfolgs Hand in Hand, da sich beide gegenseitig bedin-gen.

In Kapitel 6 behandelten Sebastian Kaiser und Heinz-Dieter Horch mit der *Organisation im Sport* ein klassisches Kernthema des Sportmanagements. Zunächst wurde die Vielfalt der Perspektiven des Organisationsbegriffs dargelegt und an-schließend auf die zentralen Probleme und Aufgaben, die im Zuge der Gestaltung von Organisationssystemen zu bewältigen sind, fokussiert. Einem klassischen be-triebswirtschaftlichen Verständnis folgend wurde Organisieren dabei als Manage-ment der Strukturen verstanden. Abschließend wurden zentrale Besonderheiten der Organisationsstruktur von Sportvereinen beschrieben. Eines der Hauptprobleme vieler Sportclubs und -verbände ist die Einbindung ehrenamtlicher Mitarbeiter in die Arbeit der Organisation. Die Lösung dieses Problems verlangt besondere struk-turelle Voraussetzungen, die im weiteren Verlauf des Kapitels beschrieben wurden.

Das Thema *Personalmanagement im Sport* wurde von Siegfried Nagel und Torsten Schlesinger in Kapitel 7 bearbeitet. Dabei wurden die zentralen Probleme und Handlungsfelder des personalbezogenen Managements in Sportorganisationen unterschiedlichen Typs skizziert. Der Faktor Personal wird im Kontext des Sport-management immer wichtiger, da es sich bei Sportprodukten größtenteils um per-sonenbezogene Dienstleistungen handelt. Im Zuge der Professionalisierung des Sports ergeben sich für Sportorganisationen besondere Herausforderungen hinsicht-lich der Mitarbeiterrekrutierung, der Personalführung sowie der Beeinflussungs-möglichkeiten des Arbeitsverhaltens. Eine Besonderheit vieler Sportclubs- und ver-bände ist dabei die Kombination von entgeltlichen Beschäftigten und ehrenamtlich Tätigen, die wiederum besondere Personalmanagementfähigkeiten erfordert. Diese Fähigkeiten wurden von den Autoren thematisiert. Abschließend wurden die unter-schiedlichen personalbezogenen Prozesse von Sportvereinen und kommerziellen Sportanbietern gegenübergestellt. Dabei wurde deutlich, dass beide Organisations-formen voneinander lernen können.

In Kapitel 8 beschäftigte sich Gregor Hovemann mit der *Finanzierung im Sport* und berücksichtigte dabei auch Aspekte der Investitionsrechnung. Aufbauend auf der Definition der zentralen Begriffe wurden die unterschiedlichen Formen der In-nen- und Außenfinanzierung beschrieben und in ihrer Bedeutung für Sportorganisa-tionen diskutiert. Sportmanagern stellt sich generell ein breites Spektrum an Finan-zierungsmöglichkeiten für die in Sportorganisation notwendigen Investitionen dar. Von entscheidender Bedeutung ist dabei die richtige Kombination der Finanzie-rungsinstrumente. Die zuvor im Kapitel diskutierten Stärken und Schwächen der jeweiligen Finanzierungsformen müssen dabei sorgfältig abgewogen werden. Ab-schließend wurde betont, dass es eine ideale Finanzierung im Sport nicht gibt, wohl aber eine zu der spezifischen Situation der Sportorganisation gerade passender Mix an Finanzierungsmöglichkeiten.

Christoph Jordan verdeutlichte in Kapitel 9 anhand des *Controlling im Sport* die Funktionsweise des internen Rechnungswesens. Nach einer detaillierten Einführung in die allgemeinen Grundlagen des Controlling, wurde auf das Controlling in Sportorganisationen eingegangen. Wie in den anderen Disziplinen des Sportmanagement, spielen auch im Controlling die Besonderheiten des Sports eine wichtige Rolle. Die Systeme und Instrumente, wie sie in normalen Unternehmen angewandt werden, müssen im Bereich des Sports erst modifiziert und an die Besonderheiten des Sports angepasst werden. Diese Modifikationen wurden anhand der Balanced Scorecard näher erläutert. Der Autor unterstrich, dass das Controlling für Sportorganisationen ein wichtiges Teilsystem darstellt, um die vielfältigen Prozesse und Systeme untereinander zu koordinieren und somit nicht zuletzt für Transparenz zu sorgen. Für das Sportmanagement stellt das Controlling im Allgemeinen und die Balanced Scorecard im Besonderen eine wichtige Führungsunterstützungs- und Informationsversorgungsfunktion dar.

In Kapitel 10 veranschaulichten Simone Jäck und Thomas Meffert das externe Rechnungswesen im Rahmen ihres Beitrags *Rechnungslegung im Sport*. Zunächst wurden grundlegende Kenntnisse der Rechnungslegung vermittelt und dabei besonders auf den handelsrechtlichen Jahresabschluss eingegangen. In Bezug zum Sport stellten die Autoren dabei eine deutliche Tendenz der Gründung kaufmännischer Rechtsformen anstelle der traditionellen Idealvereine fest. Dadurch ergeben sich für Sportbetriebe umfangreiche handelsrechtliche Rechnungslegungspflichten, die auch für die steuerliche Gewinnermittlung Bedeutung erlangen. Darüber hinaus müssen Sportclubs, die in einem Ligasystem aktiv sind, neben den gesetzlichen Pflichten auch verbandsrechtliche Vorgaben mit dem Ziel des Nachweises der wirtschaftlichen Leistungsfähigkeit erfüllen. Als Beispiel wurde das Lizenzierungsverfahren der Deutschen Fußball Liga im Detail erläutert und sich daraus ergebende Anforderungen an die Clubs beschrieben. Die Autoren machten deutlich, dass sich die Verantwortlichen in den Sportorganisationen zum einen mit allen gesetzlichen und gegebenenfalls verbandsrechtlichen Rechnungslegungspflichten auseinandersetzen müssen, und zum anderen auch mit den besonderen bilanziellen Problemfeldern des Sports vertraut sein sollten.

Simone Jäck erläuterte in Kapitel 11 – *Ertragssteuern im Sport* – die Grundlagen der deutschen Ertragsbesteuerung und verwies dabei auf die zentralen Problemfelder im Bereich des Sports, wie zum Beispiel das für traditionelle Sportvereine wichtige Thema der Gemeinnützigkeit. Die steuerlichen Rahmenbedingungen für Berufssportler und ausgewählte Probleme des Sponsorings wurden ebenfalls thematisiert. Das Kapitel verdeutlichte, dass sich Sportclubs und -verbände mit unterschiedlichsten steuerlichen Fragestellungen auseinandersetzen müssen. Die Autorin unterstrich, dass Führungskräfte im Bereich des Sports über ein Mindestmaß an steuerlichem Verständnis verfügen müssen, um steuerrelevante Problemfelder erkennen zu können. Werden diese Problemfelder nicht erkannt, kann dies zu erheblichen finanziellen Einbussen führen. Aber auch in der Vermarktung und dem Verkauf von Werberechten sind steuerliche Grundkenntnisse von essentieller Bedeutung.

In Kapitel 12 behandelten André Bühler und Gerd Nufer das Thema *Marketing im Sport*. Zunächst wurden die Grundlagen des Marketing, so wie sie in jedem Unternehmen zur Anwendung kommen, präsentiert. Im zweiten Teil des Kapitels wurde explizit auf das Marketing im Sport eingegangen. Dabei wurden zum einen die Besonderheiten des Sportmarketing erläutert und zum anderen ein Sportmarketing-Modell präsentiert. Anschließend beschrieben die Autoren wie Sportorganisationen sich selbst vermarkten können und was im Rahmen der Produkt-, Preis-, Distributions- und Kommunikationspolitik zu beachten ist. Als wichtiges Element des Sportmarketing wurde im weiteren Verlauf des Kapitels das Sportsponsoring thematisiert und sowohl aus Sicht der Sportclubs und -verbände als auch aus Sicht der Sponsoren beschrieben. Dieser Beitrag stellte nicht nur das abschließende Kapitel des zweiten Teiles dar, sondern bildete auch das Bindeglied zu einer vertieften Auseinandersetzung mit dem Sportmarketing in Teil III dieses Sammelbandes.

Der zweite Teil dieses Werkes präsentierte detailliert die klassischen Disziplinen der Betriebswirtschaftslehre und wendete sie konsequent auf den Sport an. In den einzelnen Kapiteln wurden nicht nur die jeweiligen betriebswirtschaftlichen Themenfelder grundlegend erläutert, sondern durchgängig die Besonderheiten des Sports als roter Faden berücksichtigt.

20.1.3 Sportmarketing (Teil III, Kapitel 13-17)

Im dritten Teil fand unter dem Titel *Sportmarketing – aktuelle Entwicklungen und Trends* eine tiefergehende Auseinandersetzung mit dem vielleicht wichtigsten Bereich des modernen Sportmanagements statt. Im Fokus des Kapitels standen v.a. die jüngsten Entwicklungen innerhalb des Sportmarketing.

Michael Schilhaneck kombinierte in Kapitel 13 *Markenmanagement im Sport* die leistungs- und kommunikationspolitische Aspekte des Sportmarketing. Zunächst wurden die Grundlagen des Markenmanagements erläutert und dabei auf die Markenfunktionen sowie auf Markenwert und Markenstärke eingegangen. Im Rahmen des hergestellten Bezugs zum Sport wurde deutlich, dass die Clubmarke zwar einen erheblichen Einfluss auf den ökonomischen Erfolg der Profisportorganisation hat, dass aber nur wenige Sportclubs und -verbände derzeit ein systematisches und erfolgreiches Markenmanagement praktizieren. Der Autor präsentierte ein Markenmanagementmodell, welches den komplexen Sportmarkenbildungsprozess abbildet. Daraus ergeben sich für Sportorganisationen eine Vielzahl von Ansatzpunkten zur gezielten Markenführung. Dass es sich beim Markenmanagement im Sport um einen aktuellen Trend handelt, wird in der verstärkten Auseinandersetzung der Wissenschaft mit diesem Phänomen deutlich. Nichtsdestotrotz gibt es noch einige offene Fragen, die durch zukünftige Forschungsarbeiten beantwortet werden müssen.

In Kapitel 14 widmeten sich Gerd Nufer und André Bühler dem Thema *Veranstaltungsmarketing im Sport*. In diesem Kapitel wurden die verschiedenen Möglichkeiten, bei und mit Sport-Events Kommunikationspolitik zu betreiben, vorgestellt und voneinander abgegrenzt. Die drei Instrumente des Veranstaltungsmarketing, das (Event-)Sponsoring, das Event-Marketing und das Ambush-Marketing, wurden nacheinander im Sportkontext vorgestellt. Sportveranstalter und Sponsoren stehen immer mehr vor dem Problem, ihre Rechte gegenüber Trittbrettfahrern zu schützen. Das Wissen um die Möglichkeiten, die sich diesbezüglich ergeben, wird zunehmend wichtiger für Sportmanager. Gespannt sein darf man deshalb insbesondere auf die zukünftige Entwicklung des Ambush Marketing, das in direkter Konkurrenz zum Event-Sponsoring steht.

Marco Gensmüller erläuterte in Kapitel 15 die Möglichkeiten des *Customer Relationship Marketing im Sport*. Nach der konzeptionellen Einbettung des Beziehungsmarketing, wurde die Kundenbindung sowohl aus Sicht der Unternehmen als auch aus Sicht der Kunden beschrieben. Daran anknüpfend wurden mögliche Ansatzpunkte und Implikationen von Customer Relationship Marketing für den Sport abgeleitet. Es wurde ersichtlich, dass viele Sportclubs und -verbände gegenüber anderen Unternehmen aus der freien Wirtschaft einen Nachholbedarf im Bereich Kundenorientierung haben. Schlüssige CRM-Konzepte sind im Sportbereich nur vereinzelt vorhanden und meist nicht ausgereift. Kundenbindung wird im professionellen Sport jedoch immer wichtiger. Die Forderung an Sportorganisationen und Sportmanager kann daher nur lauten, sich verstärkt mit Customer Relationship Management auseinanderzusetzen und CRM-Konzepte zu implementieren.

In Kapitel 16 erklärten Helmut Digel und Marcel Fahrner das *Hospitality Marketing im Sport*. Hospitality Marketing hat sich im Rahmen gesellschaftlicher Anlässe zu einem allgegenwärtigen Phänomen entwickelt. Die Vielzahl angebotener Hospitality-Produkte hat inzwischen allerdings zu einer harten Konkurrenz um Kunden geführt. Diese Konkurrenz besteht dabei sowohl zwischen Sport-Events als auch Events anderer Kultur- und Unterhaltungsbereiche. Sportanbieter müssen daher v.a. stimmige Gesamtkonzepte erarbeiten, was aufgrund der Rahmenbedingungen und Besonderheiten des Sportmarktes keine leichte Aufgabe darstellt. Die Autoren wiesen in ihrem Beitrag auf verschiedene Fallstricke hin, zeigten aber auch zahlreiche Lösungsmöglichkeiten auf.

Sebastian Kaiser widmete sich in Kapitel 17 dem *Kommunikationsmanagement im Sport*. Sportmanager stehen vor einer Reihe von Herausforderungen, die sich für die strategische und operative Planung sowie der Durchführung von Kommunikationsmaßnahmen ergeben. Der Autor betonte, dass eine unreflektierte Übernahme von allgemeinen Methoden des Kommunikationsmanagements auf den Sport nicht angemessen ist, um den besonderen Anforderungen der Sportorganisationen gerecht zu werden. Vielmehr müssen die Erkenntnisse und Modelle der allgemeinen Öko-nomie und des Kommunikationsmanagement daraufhin geprüft werden, inwieweit sie sinnvoll auf die vielfältigen Besonderheiten von Sportbetrieben übertragen wer-den können. Diese Sichtweise stellt gleichzeitig eine generelle Leitlinie im Sport-marketing dar.

Dieser dritte Teil veranschaulichte detailliert und praxisnah die gegenwärtigen Trends im Sportmarketing. Die einzelnen Kapitel machten aber auch deutlich, dass viele deutsche Sportclubs und -verbände der Entwicklung im Sportmarketing mo-mentan eher noch hinterherhinken. In Anbetracht der nationalen und internationalen Konkurrenz können es sich professionelle Sportorganisationen jedoch nicht mehr leisten, ihre Kunden (seien es Fans, Sponsoren oder die Medien) wie Bittsteller zu behandeln. Eine neue, kundenorientierte Sichtweise ist nötig. Die Kapitel im dritten Teil dieses Sammelbandes enthielten zahlreiche Ideen und Lösungsansätze, derer man sich nur noch bedienen muss.

20.1.4 Internationalisierung und Arbeitsmarkt (Teil IV, Kapitel 18-20)

In diesem vierten und letzten Teil des Sammelbandes geht es um die Zukunft des Sportmanagement und Sportmarketing.

In Kapitel 18 beschrieb Simon Chadwick in englischer Sprache den Prozess der *Internationalisation in Sport*. Zahlreiche Beispiele dienten dabei als Beleg der zu-nehmenden Internationalisierung im Sport. Daraus ergeben sich eine Reihe von Herausforderungen für den modernen Sportmanager, so beispielsweise die tieferge-hende Auseinandersetzung mit anderen Ländern und Kulturen, um mit internationa-len Fans, Sponsoren und Spielern erfolgreich kommunizieren zu können. Der Autor wies diesbezüglich darauf hin, dass Sportclubs und -verbände durchaus von Unter-nehmen anderer Wirtschaftszweige lernen können, da die meisten Industriesektoren bereits erfolgreich den Prozess der Internationalisierung und die sich daraus erge-benden Herausforderungen gemeistert haben. Die Internationalisierung des Sports wird weiter vorangetrieben und ist daher Herausforderung und Chance zugleich für Sportorganisationen.

Heinz-Dieter Horch skizzierte in Kapitel 19 den *Arbeitsmarkt für Sportmana-ger*. Betrachtet wurden dabei die Theorie des Arbeitsmarktes sowie der Arbeits-markt- und Berufsforschung. Im Rahmen der Betrachtung des Arbeitsmarkts für Sportmanager wurden die Marktform, die Quantität und Qualität sowie die Homo-genität bzw. Heterogenität der Arbeitsnachfrage und des Arbeitsangebots erörtert. Der derzeitige Arbeitsmarkt für Sportmanager kann zusammenfassend als jung, of-fen und unreguliert charakterisiert werden. Obwohl keine gesicherten Zukunftser-wartungen postuliert werden können, ist mit einer ungebrochenen Nachfrage nach hervorragend ausgebildeten Sportmanagern zu rechnen.

Im Rahmen dieses abschließenden zwanzigsten Kapitels *Zusammenfassung und Ausblick* beschäftigen sich die Herausgeber im Folgenden mit der Zukunft des Sportmanagement und des Sportmarketing und geben dabei auch einen Ausblick auf die Zukunft des Sportbusiness insgesamt.

20.2 Ausblick

In den vorangegangenen Kapiteln wurde der gegenwärtige, aktuelle Stand des jeweils behandelten Themas wiedergegeben. In diesem Abschnitt soll ein Blick in die Zukunft gewagt werden. Da auch Akademiker keine Glaskugel besitzen, die ihnen die Zukunft aufzeigt, handelt es sich bei den folgenden Ausführungen teilweise um fundierte Einschätzungen (basierend auf Fakten und Erfahrungen), teilweise um Plausibilitätsüberlegungen, z.T. jedoch auch um reine Gedankenspiele. Das Bild, das im Folgenden von der Zukunft des Sportbusiness, des Sportmanagement und des Sportmarketing gemalt wird, könnte die zukünftige Realität abbilden – muss es deshalb aber selbstverständlich nicht zwangsläufig.

20.2.1 Die Zukunft des Sportbusiness

Das Sportbusiness hat eine rasante Entwicklung hinter sich. Während sich früher ehrenamtlich geführte Sportvereine über Zuschauereinnahmen finanziert und vereinzelt mit Spielerberatern verhandelt haben, setzen sich heutzutage die meist professionell geführten Wirtschaftsunternehmen im Sport mit einer Vielzahl unterschiedlicher Interessensgruppen auseinander und finanzieren sich durch zahlreiche verschiedene Einkommensquellen.

Das professionelle Sportbusiness der heutigen Zeit ist v.a. ein milliardenschweres Geschäft, das durch *gegenseitige Abhängigkeiten* gekennzeichnet ist. Als Beispiel sei hier die Beziehung zwischen Sport und Medien genannt: Der Sport braucht die Medien, um sich medial vermarkten zu können. Nur wer in den Medien vertreten ist, kann eine große Anzahl Fans und damit potentielle Kunden erreichen. Dadurch wird nicht nur die eigene Markenbekanntheit gesteigert, sondern auch die Attraktivität für Sponsoren. Sportclubs und -verbände, die mit ihren Spielen bzw. Wettbewerben regelmäßig ein großes Publikum ansprechen, sind für Sponsoren wiederum interessanter als diejenigen, die ständig vor einer kleinen Kulisse agieren und medial nicht oder nur geringfügig stattfinden. Präsenz in den Medien bedeutet für Sportorganisationen daher wichtige Einnahmen, ohne die sie nicht oder nur sehr schwer überleben können. Auf der anderen Seite brauchen die Medien den Sport, um eine möglichst hohe Zahl von Rezipienten anzusprechen. Der Sport liefert tagtäglich interessante Geschichten, die sich sehr gut verkaufen lassen. Sport als Content wird ebenfalls immer wichtiger. Ein TV-Sender kann es sich heutzutage kaum mehr leisten, keine Sportübertragung im Programm zu haben. Sport ködert die Rezipienten und eine große Anzahl von Rezipienten ködert die werbetreibende Industrie. Der Verkauf von Werberechten an Unternehmen bzw. der Verkauf von Abos an Fans bedeutet für die Medien essentielle Einnahmen. Vor diesem Hintergrund würde es nicht überraschen, wenn diese gegenseitigen Abhängigkeiten in Zukunft sogar noch größer werden.

Nun tummeln sich im Wirtschaftsmarkt Sport aber nicht nur Sportanbieter und Medien sondern eine Vielzahl weiterer Interessensgruppen, wie zum Beispiel Sponsoren, Rechte- und Vermarktungsagenturen, Investoren und die Politik. Und jeder möchte von dem zu verteilenden Kuchen ein Stückchen abhaben. Dies führt heute schon zu *Verteilungskämpfen und Interessenskonflikten,* die in Zukunft noch zunehmen werden. Das Sportbusiness wird in verstärktem Maße Gewinner und Verlierer produzieren. Als Sieger werden auf der einen Seite die ganz großen, globalen Player hervorgehen, weil sie über die nötigen Ressourcen (finanzieller und personeller Art) verfügen, um die kleineren Konkurrenten vom Markt zu drängen. Auf der anderen Seite haben aber auch die vermeintlich kleinen Player eine Chance im Sportbusiness, erfolgreich zu sein, wenn sie die Marktnischen besetzen, die von den Großen vernachlässigt werden. Der Verlierer des zunehmenden Wettbewerbs wird die Mitte, d.h. die mittleren Player, sein, die weder die nötigen Ressourcen der Großen noch die notwendige Flexibilität der Kleinen haben. Das Sportbusiness könnte daher in Zukunft eine Übernahmewelle erfahren, die die Großen noch größer und die Kleinen noch flexibler macht.

In Zukunft werden sich auch die *Machtverhältnisse* zwischen den einzelnen Sportbusinessmärkten verändern. Immer wieder drängen neue Sportarten auf den Wirtschaftsmarkt Sport (wie zum Beispiel BMX-Rennen als neue olympische Disziplin) und versuchen, die etablierten Sportarten anzugreifen und deren Einfluss im Sportbusinessmarkt zu verringern. Die neuen Medien spielen dabei den kleineren Sportarten in die Karten. V.a. das Internet bietet den Randsportarten die Möglichkeit, medial präsent zu sein – und das weltweit. Dadurch ergeben sich erhebliche Vermarktungsmöglichkeiten und Einnahmezuwächse. Neben *neuen Sportarten* werden auch immer *mehr geografische Sportmärkte* auf der Weltkarte des Sportbusiness zu finden sein. Experten gehen beispielsweise davon aus, dass *China* in zehn bis fünfzehn Jahren der Sportbusinessmarkt Nummer eins sein wird und bis dahin mit zweistelligen Wachstumsraten aufwartet (Weilguny/Rehm, 2008). Darüber hinaus wird *Afrika* nicht nur weltpolitisch, sondern auch im Wirtschaftsmarkt Sport zukünftig eine gewichtige Rolle spielen. Die Fußball-Weltmeisterschaft 2010 wird dabei nicht nur die Aufmerksamkeit der globalen Sportfans auf sich ziehen, sondern auch der Türöffner für internationale Investoren sein.

In welche Richtung sich das Sportbusiness zukünftig entwickelt, hängt entscheidend von der Qualität und Professionalität des Sportmanagements ab.

20.2.2 Die Zukunft des Sportmanagement

Ein professionelles und effektives Sportmanagement ist bereits heutzutage ein wichtiger Erfolgsfaktor für Sportbetriebe, wird mit der zunehmenden Kommerzialisierung des Sports aber zu jenem entscheidenden Kriterium, von dem das Wohl und Wehe einer Sportorganisation abhängt.

Das moderne Sportmanagement muss strategisch ausgerichtet sein, Nachhaltigkeit sicherstellen und flexibel operieren können. Entscheidend für ein modernes und professionelles Sportmanagement ist dabei v.a. die *Personalpolitik* der jeweiligen Sportorganisation. Heutzutage werden immer noch zu viele Sportmanager nach der Anzahl ihrer absolvierten Länderspiele oder errungenen Medaillen ausgewählt und weniger nach ihrem Können bzw. der Qualität ihrer Ausbildung. Um aber erfolgreich im Sportmanagement arbeiten zu können, braucht man neben dem Einblick in die Besonderheiten des Sports auch qualitativ hochwertige betriebswirtschaftliche Kenntnisse. Ein großer Name öffnet zwar die ein oder andere Tür, kann sie aber auch schnell wieder schließen, wenn Management-Fehler offensichtlich werden. So haben beispielsweise Sponsoren, die Millionenbeträge in Sportorganisationen investieren, ein Recht auf eine professionelle Zusammenarbeit. Um eine stetige Professionalisierung zu gewährleisten, müssen nicht nur Sportorganisationen ihre Personalpolitik optimieren, sondern auch der Bildungsmarkt hierzu seinen Beitrag leisten. Wenn man Sportorganisationen auffordert, hervorragend ausgebildete Sportmanager einzustellen, dann müssen diese auch in entsprechender Qualität und Quantität vorhanden sein. Bisweilen ist es häufig noch so, dass es zwar genügend Absolventen diverser Sportmanagement-Kurse gibt, die aber leider nicht immer den Anforderungen der Sportbusinessbranche gerecht werden können. Bildungseinrichtungen, die eine auf die Bedürfnisse des Marktes ausgerichtete Sportmanagement-Ausbildung anbieten, werden in Zukunft einen Wettbewerbsvorteil gegenüber denjenigen Anbietern haben, die am Markt vorbei „produzieren".

Die Einstellung von professionellen Sportmanagement-Experten führt wiederum zu professionellen und seriösen Strukturen. *Seriosität und Professionalität* werden in Zukunft – neben dem sportlichen Erfolg – ein elementarer Faktor für den wirtschaftlichen Erfolg einer Sportorganisation sein. Die klassische Betriebswirtschaftslehre bietet schon heute die dafür notwendigen Instrumente an. So wird die Balanced Scorecard als wichtiges Controllinginstrument gegenwärtig in immer mehr Sportorganisationen integriert. Dieses Beispiel zeigt eindrucksvoll, wie aus einem betriebswirtschaftlichen Instrument für die Industrie auch ein Instrument für das Sportmanagement werden kann. Akademiker und Praktiker haben sich der Balanced Scorecard angenommen und sie soweit modifiziert und maßgeschneidert, dass auch Sportorganisationen sie nutzen können. In Zukunft werden weitere betriebswirtschaftliche Instrumente für den Wirtschaftsmarkt Sport adaptiert und somit nutzbar gemacht werden.

Abschließend ist festzustellen, dass der Erfolg einer Sportorganisation immer stärker von den Fähigkeiten und Kenntnissen des Managements abhängt. Allerdings ist modernes Sportmanagement nur ein Erfolgsfaktor. Der andere entscheidende Faktor, der über Gedeih und Verderb von Sportbetrieben entscheidet, ist der sportliche Erfolg. Beides – *betriebswirtschaftlicher Erfolg und sportlicher Erfolg* – bedingen und unterstützen sich gegenseitig. Die Aufgabe des modernen Sportmanagements ist daher nicht nur die Erfüllung der betriebswirtschaftlichen Aufgaben, sondern auch die Weichenstellung für den bestmöglichen sportlichen Erfolg.

20.2.3 Die Zukunft des Sportmarketing

Das Sportmarketing ist innerhalb des Sportmanagement zweifellos die Disziplin, die sich bereits am weitesten ausdifferenziert und entwickelt hat.

Es werden immer mehr Marketinginstrumente und -techniken im Sport adaptiert, die schon Jahrzehnte zuvor in anderen Branchen erfolgreich angewandt wurden. Marken im Sport gab es schon immer, nur heutzutage werden Clubmarken zunehmend strategisch ausgerichtet und dementsprechend gepflegt. Im Zuge der Kommerzialisierung wird das Sportmarketing sowohl auf Sportanbieterseite als auch auf Seiten der Sponsoren und Investoren immer professioneller. Beide Seiten befruchten sich dabei gegenseitig: Sportorganisationen erfahren, wie Marketing funktioniert und die werbetreibenden Unternehmen lernen, wie das Geschäft mit dem Sport zum Erfolg führt. Daraus entstehen echte *Partnerschaften*, die für alle Beteiligten gewinnbringend sind. Die *Zusammenarbeit* zwischen Sportorganisationen und deren Sponsoren wird in Zukunft noch enger werden. Strategische Allianzen und Joint Ventures, wie sie in anderen Wirtschaftsmärkten längst üblich sind, werden auch im Sportsponsoring verstärkt zu finden sein.

Da es im modernen Sportmarketing hauptsächlich um spezifische Vermarktungs- und Werberechte geht, wird die korrekte Handhabung dieser *Rechte* immer wichtiger werden. Von besonderer Bedeutung ist hierbei der Schutz der Rechte. Ein Unternehmen, das Millionenbeträge für die Verwendung exklusiver Werberechte eines Sportclubs bezahlt, muss vor Trittbrettfahrern geschützt werden. In der Tat ist es heute schon so, dass Verstöße gegen das Markenrecht teilweise empfindlich bestraft werden. Diese Entwicklung wird sich in Zukunft noch verstärken, so dass zumindest „plumpes" Ambush Marketing als Marketinginstrument im Rahmen von Sportveranstaltungen an Effektivität verlieren wird (Nufer, 2007). Mit dem Rechte-Schutz allein ist es allerdings nicht getan, wenn es darum geht, ein Sponsorship erfolgreich zu gestalten. Diesbezüglich ist eine stärkere *Proaktivität und Kreativität* seitens der Sportanbieter wünschenswert. Zu häufig ist der Sponsor heutzutage alleine dafür verantwortlich, das Sponsorship mit Leben zu erfüllen und entsprechende unterstützende Maßnahmen auf den Weg zu bringen. In Zukunft werden diejenigen Sportclubs und -verbände einen Wettbewerbsvorteil im Kampf um Sponsorengelder haben, die neben den eigentlichen Werberechten auch gleich Umsetzungskonzepte mitliefern (Bühler, 2006). Dazu sind Kreativität und *konzeptionelles Denken* notwendig, also Fähigkeiten, die man in vielen deutschen Sportorganisationen häufig noch zu selten antrifft. Diese Fähigkeiten müssen in Zukunft eingekauft werden, entweder durch die Einstellung von Marketingfachleuten oder durch die Zusammenarbeit mit Werbe- und Sponsoringagenturen. Auch hier sind strategische Kooperationen hilfreich.

Die im dritten Teil dieses Bandes vorgestellten Sportmarketing-Trends werden in Zukunft noch bedeutender werden. Sportorganisationen, die *markt- und kundenorientiert* arbeiten (entweder weil sie sich dazu entschieden haben oder weil sie es aufgrund des zunehmenden Wettbewerbsdrucks müssen), brauchen ein effektives Kommunikationsmanagement, um mit den Kunden in Kontakt zu treten. Die Implementierung eines Customer Relationship Marketing ist wichtig, um eine Beziehung mit dem Kunden aufzubauen und diese zu pflegen. Gleichermaßen wichtig sind innovative und auf Kundenbedürfnisse abgestimmte Hospitality-Angebote, die das Sportevent zu einem exklusiven Ereignis machen. Auch im Bereich Veranstaltungsmarketing ist noch Potenzial, um alle Möglichkeiten, die Sport-Events bieten, zum Wohle des Kunden auszuschöpfen. Dem Aufbau der Marke und der konsequenten Markenpflege kommt eine besondere Bedeutung zu. In Zukunft werden v.a. diejenigen Sportclubs und -verbände Erfolg im Markt haben, die sich als echte Marke positionieren. Um all diese Trends und Entwicklungen zu nutzen brauchen Sportorganisationen das nötige Know-how, das Sportmarketing-Experten einbringen.

Neben den in diesem Sammelband vorgestellten Entwicklungen im Sportmarketing sind schon jetzt neue Trends zu erahnen: So wird beispielsweise das Thema *„Social Marketing"* für Unternehmen anderer Branchen immer wichtiger. Sportorganisationen als elementarer Teil der Gesellschaft können sich dieser Marketingform in Zukunft nicht verschließen. Social Marketing ließe sich beispielsweise mit dem Sportsponsoring verbinden. Dies könnte so aussehen, dass Sportclubs im Rahmen einer Social Marketing Kampagne, die von einem Sponsor finanziell unterstützt wird, Eintrittskarten an sozial benachteiligte Familien vergeben. So gewinnen – im Sinne modernen Sportsponsorings – alle Beteiligten: Die sozial benachteiligten Familien können eine hochwertige Sportveranstaltung besuchen, der Sponsor wird publikumswirksam als sozialorientiert dargestellt und die Sportorganisation hat sich ohne finanzielle Einbußen der gesellschaftlichen Verantwortung gestellt und damit Werbung in eigener Sache betrieben.

Wie auch im Sportmanagement ist für ein effektives und erfolgreiches Sportmarketing entsprechendes *Know-how* nötig. Die notwendigen Kenntnisse und Fertigkeiten bringen Experten mit, die entsprechend ausgebildet sind und sich seit Jahren intensiv mit der Materie Sportmarketing beschäftigen. Die Investition in einen Sportmarketer wäre manchmal sinnvoller als etwa die Verpflichtung des zehnten Ersatzspielers für den sportlichen Bereich. Allerdings – und das ist wichtig zu betonen – muss die sportliche Seite stimmen. Ohne entsprechenden sportlichen Erfolg wird sich auch der beste Sportmarketing-Experte schwer tun, das Sport-Produkt erfolgreich zu vermarkten.

20.3 Fazit

Professionelles Sportmanagement und innovatives Sportmarketing werden in Zukunft eine noch wichtigere Rolle spielen als bisher. Professionelle Strukturen und ein seriöses Geschäftsgebaren werden zukünftig essentielle Erfolgsfaktoren für jede Sportorganisation sein. Durch neue Sportarten und Sportmärkte sowie einer ständig wachsenden Anzahl an alternativen Freizeitmöglichen wird der Wettbewerbsdruck für Sportbetriebe in den kommen Jahren noch weiter verschärft. Der Kampf um Kunden (Fans, Sponsoren, Medien) wird dabei stetig zunehmen. In Anbetracht dieser Entwicklung bleibt professionellen Sportclubs und -verbänden nichts anderes übrig, als markt- und kundenorientiert aufzutreten. Die in vielen deutschen Sportorganisationen immer noch vorherrschende Denkhaltung, Fans und Sponsoren als Bittsteller zu betrachten, muss einem modernen Sportmanagement- und Sportmarketing-Ansatz weichen. Modernes Sportmanagement und Sportmarketing integrieren dabei gängige Managementtechniken und Marketinginstrumente.

Die Einführung und Anwendung all dieser Maßnahmen sowie die Schaffung professioneller Strukturen hängt entscheidend von der Qualifikation der zuständigen Entscheidungsträger und Mitarbeiter in den Sportorganisationen ab. Nur Sportmanager, die die nötige betriebswirtschaftlichen Kenntnisse mit den Besonderheiten des Sports kombinieren können, werden in der Lage sein, professionelle Strukturen zu schaffen und den Anforderungen an ein modernes Sportmanagement gerecht zu werden. Dieser Sammelband diente dabei als Leitfaden, das hierfür notwendige Wissen zu vermitteln und Anregungen für die praktische Umsetzung zu geben.

Kontrollfragen

1. Durch welche Charakteristika ist modernes Sportmanagement gekennzeichnet?
2. Warum ist eine tiefergehende Auseinandersetzung mit den betriebswirtschaftlichen Themengebiete für Sportbetriebe unabdingbar?
3. Welche betriebswirtschaftlichen Kernfelder erachten Sie als die wichtigsten für professionelle Sportclubs und -verbände? Begründen Sie Ihre Antwort!
4. Welche Rolle spielt der sportliche Bereich im modernen Sportmanagement?
5. Warum ist die Personalpolitik einer Sportorganisation so wichtig?
6. Wie wird sich Ihrer Meinung nach das nationale und internationale Sportbusiness entwickeln?
7. Welche Faktoren werden in Zukunft für das Sportmanagement noch wichtiger werden?
8. Wie sieht Ihrer Meinung nach die Zukunft des Sportmarketing aus?
9. Welche neuen Sportmarketing-Trends prognostizieren Sie?
10. Wie würden Sie die Kernaussagen dieses Sammelbandes zusammenfassen?

Literaturverzeichnis

Bühler, André W. (2006): Professional Football Sponsorship in the English Premier League and the German Bundesliga, Berlin.

Nufer, Gerd (2007): Event-Marketing und -Management. Theorie und Praxis unter besonderer Berücksichtigung von Imagewirkungen, 3. Aufl., Wiesbaden.

Weilguny, Michael / Rehm, Holger (2008): Wachstumsmarkt China – Sportbusiness im Reich der Mitte, in Sponsors, Heft 1, S. 18-24.

Weiterführende Ressourcen

Literatur

Beech, John / Chadwick, Simon (Hrsg.) (2004): The Business of Sport Management, Harlow.

Breuer, Christoph / Thiel, Ansgar (Hrsg.) (2005): Handbuch Sportmanagement, Schorndorf.

Bühler, André W. / Nufer, Gerd (2006): The Nature of Sports Marketing, Reutlingen Working Paper on Marketing & Management No. 2006-6, School of International Business, Reutlingen University.

Heinemann, Klaus (1995): Einführung in die Ökonomie des Sports. Ein Handbuch, Schorndorf.

Horch, Heinz-Dieter / Hovemann, Gregor / Kaiser, Sebastian / Viebahn, Kai (Hrsg.) (2005): Perspektiven des Sportmarketing. Besonderheiten, Herausforderungen, Tendenzen, Köln.

Nufer, Gerd (2002): Wirkungen von Sportsponsoring. Empirische Analyse am Beispiel der Fußball-Weltmeisterschaft 1998 in Frankreich unter besonderer Berücksichtigung von Erinnerungswirkungen bei jugendlichen Rezipienten, Berlin.

Nufer, Gerd / Bühler, André W. (2006): Lessons from Sports: What Corporate Management can learn from Sports Management, Reutlingen Working Paper on Marketing & Management No. 2006-7, School of International Business, Reutlingen University.

Links

Horizont Sport Business (Fachzeitschrift):
    http://www.horizont-sportbusiness.de
Sponsors (Fachzeitschrift):
    http://www.sponsors.de

Profile der Herausgeber und Autoren

Herausgeber

Nufer, Gerd

Prof. Dr. Gerd Nufer (Jahrgang 1970) ist Professor für Allgemeine Betriebswirtschaftslehre mit dem Schwerpunkt Marketing an der Hochschule Reutlingen. Er studierte BWL an der Universität Tübingen und an der State University of New York at Stony Brook. Seine Doktorarbeit entstand an der Universität Tübingen in Kooperation mit adidas und einem Stipendium an der San Diego State University. Danach arbeitete er zunächst als Consultant/Projektleiter bei der Unternehmensberatung Simon-Kucher & Partners in Bonn und später als Marketing Consultant/Key Account Manager in der Marktforschung bei der Information Resources GfK in Nürnberg. Seine Forschungs- und Beratungsschwerpunkte sind Event-Marketing und -Management, Sponsoring, Ambush Marketing sowie Sportmarketing und -management. Zusätzlich nimmt er Lehraufträge an verschiedenen staatlichen und privaten Bildungseinrichtungen wahr.
Kontakt: gerd.nufer@reutlingen-university.de

Bühler, André

Dr. André Bühler (Jahrgang 1975) ist Dozent für Management & Marketing sowie Research & Scholarship Consultant an der Heidelberg International Business Academy. Er studierte BWL an der Hochschule Nürtingen mit speziellem Fokus auf Wirtschaftspsychologie und Marketing. Anschließend lebte er dreieinhalb Jahre in Großbritannien und hat dort an der englischen University of Plymouth im Bereich Sportmarketing promoviert. Seine Dissertation beschäftigte sich mit den relationalen Aspekten des Sportsponsoring im deutsch-englischen Profifußball. Seine Forschungsschwerpunkte sind Sportmanagement und Sportmarketing mit besonderem Fokus auf Sportsponsoring sowie Beziehungsmarketing im Sport. Er ist u.a. Mitglied des Arbeitskreises Sportökonomie e.V., des Verbandes für Sportökonomie und Sportmanagement in Deutschland e.V., der UK Higher Education Academy, der European Association of Sport Management sowie dem European Network of Sports Marketing Academics. Neben zahlreichen wissenschaftlichen Beiträgen in internationalen Fachpublikationen ist André Bühler außerdem mit einer regelmäßigen Kolumne in einem renommierten deutschen Fachmagazin für Sportbusiness vertreten.
Kontakt: andre@football-and-business.com

Autoren

Breuer, Christoph

Prof. Dr. Christoph Breuer (Jahrgang 1971) ist Universitätsprofessor für Sportmanagement an der Deutschen Sporthochschule Köln. Er studierte Sportwissenschaft, Volkswirtschaftslehre und Pädagogik an der TU Darmstadt und promovierte und habilitierte sich an der Deutschen Sporthochschule Köln. Seit 2005 ist er zugleich Forschungsprofessor am Deutschen Institut für Wirtschaftsforschung in Berlin. Seine Forschungsschwerpunkte liegen im Bereich Theorie und Empirie von Sportangebot und Sportnachfrage, Sportanlagenmanagement sowie Entwicklung von Sportvereinen.
Kontakt: breuer@dshs-koeln.de

Breuer, Markus

Dipl.-Volkswirt Markus Breuer (Jahrgang 1981) ist wissenschaftlicher Mitarbeiter im Fachbereich Sportökonomie (Institut für Sportwissenschaft) der Friedrich-Schiller-Universität in Jena. Nach seiner Ausbildung zum Bankkaufmann und einem berufsbegleitenden Studium der Betriebswirtschaftslehre an der Welfenakademie in Braunschweig studierte er Volkswirtschaftslehre an der TU Chemnitz.
Kontakt: Markus.Breuer@uni-jena.de

Chadwick, Simon

Prof. Dr. Simon Chadwick (Jahrgang 1964) ist Professor für Sport Business Strategy and Marketing an der britischen Coventry University, wo er außerdem die Ambushing, Sponsorship and Sport Marketing Group leitet. Er fungiert des Weiteren als Direktor des Birkbeck Sport Business Centre der University of London und als Herausgeber einer Reihe von wissenschaftlichen Publikationen, darunter das International Journal of Sports Marketing & Sponsorship, die Sportmarketingserie des britischen Verlags Elsevier sowie die Henry Stewart Sports Marketing Talk Series. Simon Chadwick ist Autor zahlreicher Bücher zum Thema Sportmanagement und Sportmarketing.
Kontakt: Simon.Chadwick@coventry.ac.uk

Daumann, Frank

Prof. Dr. Frank Daumann (Jahrgang 1964) ist Universitätsprofessor für Sportökonomie am Institut für Sportwissenschaft der Friedrich-Schiller-Universität in Jena. Er hat nach einem Studium der Betriebswirtschaftslehre und einer Promotion in Volkswirtschaftslehre im Jahre 1998 mit der Arbeit „Interessenverbände im politischen Prozeß. Eine Analyse aus Sicht der Neuen Politischen Ökonomie" an der Rechts- und Wirtschaftswissenschaftlichen Fakultät der Universität Bayreuth habilitiert. Seine bevorzugten Forschungsgebiete sind die Sportökonomie, die Gesundheitsökonomie sowie Problemstellungen der Wettbewerbs-, Institutionen- und Ordnungsökonomie. Im Bereich der Sportökonomie hat sich Frank Daumann insbesondere mit der Analyse von einzelnen Sportmärkten sowie mit den Themengebieten Doping, Sportförderung, Vermarktung im Sport und Sportverbände auseinandergesetzt. Frank Daumann ist u.a. Mitglied des Arbeitskreises Sportökonomie e.V., des Vereins für Socialpolitik (Wirtschaftspolitischer Ausschuss, Gesundheitsökonomischer Ausschuss), der American Economic Association und des Walter Eucken Instituts e.V.

Kontakt: Frank.Daumann@uni-jena.de

Digel, Helmut

Prof. Dr. Helmut Digel (Jahrgang 1944) ist Direktor des Instituts für Sportwissenschaft der Universität Tübingen. Er studierte an der Universität Tübingen Germanistik, Sportwissenschaft und Erziehungswissenschaft. Seit vielen Jahren setzt er sich mit gesellschaftlichen Wandlungsprozessen und deren Wirkung auf die Sportentwicklung auseinander. In mehreren Vereins- und Verbandsstudien wurden von ihm insbesondere Führungs- und Organisationsprobleme deutscher Sportvereine und -verbände beschrieben. In jüngerer Zeit thematisierte er in verschiedenen Untersuchungen unter anderem Visionen der Sportpolitik, also die Frage, wohin sich der Sport zukünftig vor dem Hintergrund gesellschaftlicher Veränderungsprozesse entwickeln will und kann.

Kontakt: helmut.digel@uni-tuebingen.de

Fahrner, Marcel

Dr. Marcel Fahrner M. A. (Jahrgang 1974) ist seit 2004 wissenschaftlicher Mitarbeiter am Institut für Sportwissenschaft der Universität Tübingen (Lehrstuhl Prof. Digel). Er studierte an der Technischen Hochschule Darmstadt und der Universität Tübingen Sportwissenschaft mit den Nebenfächern Betriebswirtschaftslehre und Zivilrecht. Fragen der Organisation und der Ökonomie des Sports interessieren ihn in besonderer Weise. Seine im November 2007 abgeschlossene Doktorarbeit beschäftigte sich mit der Veränderung von Sportverbänden, insbesondere mit Blick auf die Spannungsfelder zwischen Veränderungsnotwendigkeiten und strukturellen Veränderungsbedingungen.

Kontakt: marcel.fahrner@uni-tuebingen.de

Gensmüller, Marco

Dipl.-Betriebswirt Marco Gensmüller (Jahrgang 1977) ist Mitarbeiter im Fachbereich Sport & Management des nebenberuflichen Weiterbildungsträgers IST-Studieninstitut. Er studierte Sportmanagement am RheinAhrCampus in Remagen. Seine Diplomarbeit entstand in Kooperation mit Sportfive über die Chancen und Erfolgsaussichten neuer Hospitality-Räumlichkeiten für den 1. FC Nürnberg. Neben der Agenturseite war er während des Studiums innerhalb einzelner Projektarbeiten auch auf Vereinsseite beim 1. FC Köln tätig. Nach seinem Studium arbeitete

er zunächst in der Sponsoringabteilung des britischen Mobilfunkanbieters Vodafone bevor er später zum IST Studieninstitut kam. Seine Arbeitsschwerpunkte liegen in der fachlichen Beratung von Studenten und Interessenten aus den einzelnen Studiengängen und der konzeptionellen Entwicklung neuer Bildungsangebote m Bereich Sport und Management.
Kontakt: mgensmueller@ist.de

Horch, Heinz-Dieter
Prof. Dr. Heinz-Dieter Horch (Jahrgang 1947) ist Universitätsprofessor und Leiter des Instituts für Sportökonomie und Sportmanagement der deutschen Sporthochschule Köln. Er studierte Volkswirtschaftslehre, Soziologie und Statistik an der Universität zu Köln. Er promovierte an der Universität Trier zum Dr. rer. pol. und habilitierte an der Universität Hamburg. 1995 wurde er zum ersten Professor für Sportökonomie in Deutschland ernannt. Seine Forschungsschwerpunkte liegen in den Bereichen der Organisationstheorie von Non-Profit-Organisationen, des Wandels von Sportorganisationen und der Arbeitsmarkt- und Berufsforschung im Bereich Sportmanagement. Er ist stellvertretender Vorsitzender des Arbeitskreises Sportökonomie, Veranstalter des Deutschen Sportökonomiekongresses Köln und war Herausgeber des European Journal for Sport Management.
Kontakt: Horch@dshs-koeln.de

Hovemann, Gregor
Dr. Gregor Hovemann (Jahrgang 1971) ist Wissenschaftlicher Assistent am Institut für Sportökonomie und Sportmanagement der Deutschen Sporthochschule Köln. Er studierte Betriebswirtschaftslehre und Sport an der Universität zu Köln und der Deutschen Sporthochschule Köln. Weiterhin erwarb er durch sein Studium in Köln und Paris (HEC) den Master in International Management. 2006/2007 vertrat der die Professur für Sportanlagen/Sportevents an der FH Koblenz/Standort Remagen. In Forschung und Lehre beschäftigt er sich schwerpunktmäßig mit aktuellen Problemen der Finanzierung im Sport.
Kontakt: hovemann@dshs-koeln.de

Jäck, Simone
Dr. Simone Jäck (Jahrgang 1978) ist als Steuerberaterin bei der ATG Allgäuer Treuhand GmbH in Kempten (Allgäu) tätig. Schwerpunkt ihrer Tätigkeit ist die gestalterische Steuerberatung insbesondere im Rahmen von Investitionsentscheidungen, Rechtsformwahl, Unternehmensstrukturänderungen, Nachfolgeentscheidungen und internationalen Transaktionen. Sie studierte Sportökonomie an der Universität Bayreuth und arbeitete anschließend als wissenschaftliche Mitarbeiterin am Lehrstuhl für Betriebswirtschaftliche Steuerlehre und Wirtschaftsprüfung von Prof. Dr. Jochen Sigloch. Während dieser Zeit entstand ihre Dissertation, die sich mit der

steuerlichen Gemeinnützigkeit in Deutschland, der Schweiz und den USA beschäftigte.
Kontakt: s.jaeck@atg.de

Jordan, Christoph
Dipl.-Sportökonom Christoph Jordan (Jahrgang 1980) ist Consultant bei der CPC Unternehmensmanagement AG in Frankfurt am Main. Sein Aufgabengebiet umfasst Projektmanagement, Prozessgestaltung und Personalentwicklung. Er studierte Sportökonomie (Diplom) an der Universität Bayreuth. Seine Diplomarbeit verfasste er über den Einsatz der Balanced Scorecard im Bereich der Aus-, Fort- und Weiterbildung im Deutschen Fußball Bund.
Kontakt: christoph.jordan@gmx.de

Kaiser, Sebastian
Dr. Sebastian Kaiser (Jahrgang 1974) studierte Sportwissenschaften, Wirtschaftswissenschaften/BWL und Sportökonomie an der Deutschen Sporthochschule Köln (DSHS) und der FernUniversität Gesamthochschule Hagen. Er ist Habilitand am Institut für Sportökonomie und Sportmanagement der DSHS und nimmt Lehraufträge an der Carl von Ossietzky Universität Oldenburg sowie der Bergischen Universität Wuppertal wahr. In Forschung und Lehre beschäftigt er sich schwerpunktmäßig mit Aspekten der Struktur und Kultur von Sportorganisationen.
Kontakt: s.kaiser@dshs-koeln.de

Keller, Christian
Dipl.-Betriebswirt Christian Keller, MBA (Jahrgang 1978) ist Doktorand am Institut für Sportwissenschaft der Universität Tübingen. Seine Tätigkeit wird durch ein Graduiertenstipendium des Landes Baden-Württemberg gefördert. Die Dissertation beschäftigt sich mit der Konzeption eines integralen Steuerungsmodells, das Teamsportunternehmen eine effektive Koordination von sportlicher und wirtschaftlicher Erfolgsorientierung ermöglicht. Vor seiner Promotion studierte Keller im Diplomstudiengang Außenwirtschaft an der School of International Business der Hochschule Reutlingen. An derselben Institution erlangte er anschließend noch den Grad eines Master of Business Administration. Seine Forschungsschwerpunkte sind Sportökonomie und Sportmanagement mit besonderem Fokus auf dem professionellen Teamsport.
Kontakt: christian.keller@gmx.eu

Langer, Mathias
Dr. Mathias Langer (Jahrgang 1975) studierte Betriebswirtschaftslehre an den Universitäten Bayreuth, Dublin City University (IRL) und Massey University Palmerston North (NZ). Nach dem Abschluss als Diplom-Kaufmann im Jahr 2000 arbeitete er als Unternehmensberater bei Network MCE und beriet Dienstleistungs-

553

unternehmen bei Aufgaben marktorientierter Unternehmensführung in Marketing und Vertrieb. 2002 wechselte er an die Universität Jena, wo er als wissenschaftlicher Mitarbeiter im Fachbereich Sportökonomie am Institut für Sportwissenschaft arbeitete. Promoviert wurde er 2005 mit einer Dissertation zur öffentlichen Sportförderung. Seit 2006 ist Mathias Langer Manager Marketing und Vertrieb im strategischen Bereich des EnBW-Konzerns. Daneben hat er einen Lehrauftrag für Sportökonomie an der Universität Jena.
Kontakt: m.langer@enbw.com

Meffert, Thomas
Dipl.-Kfm. Thomas Meffert (Jahrgang 1980) ist seit Mai 2007 als wissenschaftlicher Mitarbeiter am Lehrstuhl für Betriebswirtschaftliche Steuerlehre und Wirtschaftsprüfung von Prof. Dr. Jochen Sigloch an der Universität Bayreuth tätig. Dort betreut er insbesondere die Studenten der Sportökonomie mit ihrer möglichen Spezialisierung auf Unternehmensrechnung und Steuern im Sport. Er studierte BWL an der Universität Bayreuth und promoviert zum Thema der Ertragsrealisation in der Rechnungslegung. Einen weiteren Forschungsschwerpunkt bildet für ihn die Rechnungslegung im Sport.
Kontakt: thomas.meffert@uni-bayreuth.de

Nagel, Siegfried
Prof. Dr. Siegfried Nagel (Jahrgang 1968) ist seit 2006 Universitätsprofessor für Sportwissenschaft mit den Schwerpunkten Sportsoziologie und Sportökonomie an der Technischen Universität Chemnitz. Er studierte Sportwissenschaft und Mathematik in München und Tübingen sowie Wirtschaftswissenschaften an der Fernuniversität Hagen. 2005 hat er an der Universität Tübingen seine Habilitation zur Thematik „Sportvereine im Wandel" abgeschlossen. Neben der Sportvereinsforschung befassen sich seine Arbeiten vor allem mit Fragen der Sportentwicklung, der sportbezogenen Sozialisations- und Lebensverlaufsforschung sowie des Managements und Marketing im Sport. Siegfried Nagel ist Mitglied im Arbeitskreis Sportökonomie e.V. und in der Deutschen Vereinigung für Sportwissenschaft.
Kontakt: siegfried.nagel@phil.tu-chemnitz.de

Pawlowski, Tim
Dipl. Volksw., Dipl. Sportwiss. Tim Pawlowski (Jahrgang 1980) ist seit April 2007 wissenschaftlicher Mitarbeiter und Promotionsstudent am Institut für Sportökonomie und Sportmanagement an der Deutschen Sporthochschule (DSHS) Köln. Er studierte Volkswirtschaftlehre mit Schwerpunkten (u.a.) in Medienökonomie, Institutionsökonomik und Marktforschung an der Universität zu Köln und Sportwissenschaften mit Schwerpunkt Ökonomie und Management sowie Europäische Sportstudien an der DSHS Köln (TOYOTA-Förderpreisträger 2006). Seine Forschungs- und Projektschwerpunkte liegen in den Bereichen der ökonometrischen Sportnach-

554

frageanalyse (Nachfragesystemschätzung) sowie des Marketingmanagements in Fußballvereinen (Amateur- und Profibereich).
Kontakt: pawlowski@dshs-koeln.de

Rennhak, Carsten
Prof. Dr. Carsten Rennhak (Jahrgang 1971) ist Professor für Allgemeine Betriebswirtschaftslehre mit dem Schwerpunkt Marketing an der Hochschule Reutlingen. Nach dem Studium der BWL an der Universität Augsburg sowie der VWL an der Wayne State University, Detroit, und seiner Promotion an der Ludwig-Maximilians Universität in München war er mehrere Jahre als Unternehmensberater und Projektleiter bei Booz Allen Hamilton in den Bereichen Telekommunikation, Medien, High Tech und Utilities sowie als Hochschullehrer an der Munich Business School tätig. Seine Forschungsinteressen liegen vor allem in den Bereichen Kundenbindung, Marketingkommunikation und Strategie.
Kontakt: carsten.rennhak@reutlingen-university.de

Schilhaneck, Michael
Dr. Michael Schilhaneck (Jahrgang 1977) ist Dozent an der Universität Bayreuth und der Berufsakademie Stuttgart. Er studierte Sportökonomie an der Universität Bayreuth (inklusive einem Auslandssemester an der Université Claude Bernard Lyon I und studienbegleitende Praktika im Organisationskomitee der Olympischen Spiele Sydney 2000 sowie in der Marketingabteilung des NHL-Klubs Washington Capitals). Nach dem Studium arbeitete er bei dem Deutschen Skiverband DSV sowie der Schweizer Sportmarketingagentur International Sports Agency ISA. Anschließend promovierte Michael Schilhaneck an der Universität Bayreuth mit einem Promotionsstipendium der Konrad-Adenauer-Stiftung. Forschungsschwerpunkte: Markenmanagement und Kundenbindungsmanagement im professionellen Teamsport.
Kontakt: michael.schilhaneck@uni-bayreuth.de

Schlesinger, Torsten
Torsten Schlesinger, M.A. (Jahrgang 1976) ist wissenschaftlicher Mitarbeiter am Institut für Sportwissenschaft der Technischen Universität Chemnitz im Arbeitsbereich Sportsoziologie & Sportökonomie. Nach einer Ausbildung zum Bankkaufmann studierte er an der TU Chemnitz den Magisterstudiengang Sportökonomie mit den Schwerpunkten Marketing und Finanzen. Derzeit promoviert er zum Thema „Emotionen im Kontext sportbezogener Marketing-Events". Seine Forschungsschwerpunkte sind Eventmarketing, Sportstättenmanagement sowie Aspekte der Teamentwicklung im Spitzensport. Torsten Schlesinger ist Mitglied in der Deutschen Vereinigung für Sportwissenschaft.
Kontakt: torsten.schlesinger@phil.tu-chemnitz.de

Wicker, Pamela

Dipl. Sportwiss. Pamela Wicker (Jahrgang 1979) ist wissenschaftliche Mitarbeiterin am Institut für Sportökonomie und Sportmanagement an der Deutschen Sporthochschule (DSHS) Köln. Sie studierte Sportwissenschaften mit Schwerpunkt Ökonomie und Management an der DSHS Köln, wobei sie zunächst am Psychologischen Institut arbeitete. Seit 2005 gehört sie dem Institut für Sportökonomie und Sportmanagement an und promoviert im Bereich Beitragselastizität in Sportvereinen. Ihre Forschungsschwerpunkte sind Preiselastizität und Zahlungsbereitschaft in der Sportnachfrage, Sportvereinsforschung sowie kommunale Sportentwicklungsplanung.

Kontakt: wicker@dshs-koeln.de

Stichwortverzeichnis

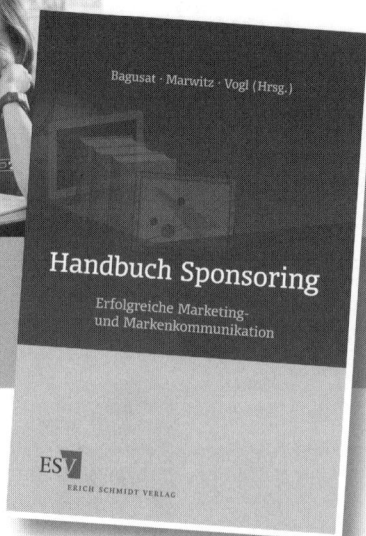